THE WEST POINT ATLAS
OF AMERICAN WARS

Volume II

1900-1953

Compiled by

**THE DEPARTMENT OF MILITARY ART
AND ENGINEERING
THE UNITED STATES MILITARY ACADEMY**

WEST POINT, NEW YORK

Chief Editor

**BRIGADIER GENERAL
VINCENT J. ESPOSITO,** USA (RET.)

FORMER PROFESSOR AND HEAD OF THE DEPARTMENT
OF MILITARY ART AND ENGINEERING
THE UNITED STATES MILITARY ACADEMY

With an introductory letter by DWIGHT D. EISENHOWER

FREDERICK A. PRAEGER, PUBLISHERS • NEW YORK • WASHINGTON • LONDON

FREDERICK A. PRAEGER, PUBLISHERS
111 Fourth Avenue, New York, N.Y. 10003, U.S.A.
77-79 Charlotte Street, London W.1, England

First published in the United States of America in 1959
by Frederick A. Praeger, Inc., Publishers

Fourth Printing, 1967

© 1959 by Frederick A. Praeger, Inc.

Library of Congress Catalog Card Number: 59-7452

Printed in the United States of America

A detailed contents page appears at the beginning of each section.

SECTION 1   •   WORLD WAR I

1914	WESTERN FRONT	EASTERN FRONT	SERBIAN AND SALONIKAN FRONTS	ITALIAN FRONT	TURKISH FRONTS		
					DARDANELLES	MESOPOTAMIA	PALESTINE
AUG.	Battle of the Frontiers	Tannenberg / Galician Battles	1st Invasion of Serbia				
SEPT.	Battle of the Marne / First Battle of the Aisne	1st Masuria / German Operations in S.W. Poland	2d Invasion of Serbia				
OCT.	Race to the Sea / First Battle of Ypres						Defense Behind the Suez Canal
NOV.		Battle of Lodz	3d Invasion of Serbia		Initial Naval Bombardment	Landing and Establishment of Bridgehead	
DEC.							
1915 JAN.							1st Turkish Attack on the Canal
FEB.	Stabilized Front with Limited Attacks on Noyon Salient in Champagne and Artois	Winter Battle of Masuria			Naval Attack		
MAR.						First British Advance	
APR.							
MAY		Gorlice-Tarnow Breakthrough			1st Landing Helles		
JUNE							Defense Just East of the Canal and Minor Raids
JULY		Russian Withdrawal		1st Isonzo			
AUG.				2d Isonzo	2d Landing Suvla Bay		
SEPT.						First Battle of Kut	
OCT.			Final Invasion / Serbia Eliminated / Salonikan Front Established	3d Isonzo			
NOV.				4th Isonzo		Battle of Ctesiphon	
DEC.					Evacuation Begun	Siege of Kut	

1916	WESTERN FRONT	EASTERN FRONT	SALONIKAN FRONT	ITALIAN FRONT	TURKISH FRONTS		
					DARDANELLES	MESOPOTAMIA	PALESTINE
JAN.					Evacuation Completed		
FEB.						Siege of Kut	
MAR.		Lake Narotch Operations		5th Isonzo			
APR.						Fall of Kut	
MAY	Battle of Jutland			Asiago Offensive			British Advance and Clearing of the Sinai Desert
JUNE							
JULY	Battle of Verdun	Brusilov Offensive					
AUG.				6th Isonzo			
SEPT.	Battle of the Somme	Rumanian Offensive		7th Isonzo			
OCT.				8th Isonzo			
NOV.		Rumania Eliminated	Fall of Monastir	9th Isonzo		Second British Advance	
DEC.							
1917 JAN							British Arrive at Turkish Border
FEB.	German Withdrawal to the Hindenburg Line					2d Battle of Kut	
MAR.	U.S. Declares War	Russian Revolution				Capture of Baghdad	1st Battle of Gaza
APR.	Allied Offensives (Arras and 2d Aisne)		Limited Operations and Advance to the Greek Frontier				2d Battle of Gaza
MAY				10th Isonzo			
JUNE	Battle of Messines						
JULY		Kerensky (2d Brusilov) Offensive					
AUG.				11th Isonzo			
SEPT.	Third Battle of Ypres	Riga Operation					
OCT.							3d Battle of Gaza
NOV.	Battle of Cambrai			Battle of Caporetto			Battles of Junction Station and Jerusalem
DEC.		Russian Armistice					

1918	WESTERN FRONT	SALONIKAN FRONT	ITALIAN FRONT	TURKISH FRONTS	
				MESOPOTAMIA	PALESTINE
JAN.					
FEB.					
MAR.	**THE GERMAN DRIVES** Somme Offensive (1st German Drive)				
APR.	Lys Offensive (2d German Drive)	Defensive Operations			
MAY	Aisne Offensive (3d German Drive)				
JUNE	Noyon-Montdidier Offensive (4th German Drive)		Battle of the Piave		
JULY	Champagne-Marne Offensive (5th German Drive) **THE REDUCTION OF THE SALIENTS** Aisne-Marne Offensive				
AUG.	Reduction of the Amiens Salient The Lys Salient Evacuated				
SEPT.	St. Mihiel Offensive **THE FINAL OFFENSIVE**	Allied Offensive Bulgarian Armistice			Battle of Megiddo Pursuit
OCT.	French and British Offensives Meuse-Argonne Offensive		Battle of Vittorio-Veneto	Advance on Mosul	Armistice
NOV.	Armistice				

BASIC SYMBOLS:

Regiment	III	Infantry	⊠
Brigade	x	Cavalry	⊘
Division	xx	Cavalry covering force	
Corps	xxx	Trains	
Army	xxxx	Artillery	
Army Group	xxxxx		

Examples of Combinations of Basic Symbols:

Small infantry detachment

Third Reserve Division

Mackensen's XVII Corps

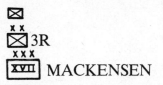

Fifth Cavalry Corps with other units attached

French Sixth Army

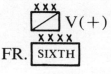

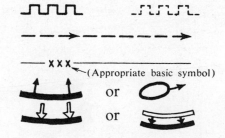

OTHER SYMBOLS:

	Actual location	Prior location
Troops on the march		
Troops in position		
Troops in bivouac or reserve		
	Occupied	Unoccupied
Field works		

Strong prepared defenses

Route of march

Boundary between units ——— xxx ——— (Appropriate basic symbol)

Troops displacing and direction   or

Troops in position under attack   or

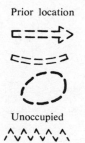

As a result of the Franco-Prussian War, the German Empire became the dominant nation on the continent of Europe. The technical advances of the Industrial Revolution, fully exploited by the hard-working Germans, made possible an enormous increase in industry and trade. This expansion led to a desire for colonies which could serve as markets and sources of raw materials. The acquisition of a colonial empire, in turn, made a strong navy necessary. Consequently, in the 1890's, Germany began the construction of a fleet. England, hitherto on good terms with Germany, considered this a direct challenge. Naval superiority was vital to England's existence as a great power—indeed, as a guarantee to feed her people.

France, suffering under the stigma of her defeat in 1870 and the attendant loss of her valuable provinces of Alsace and Lorraine, meditated a war of revenge. Her recovery was rapid; by the early 1900's, she was second only to Germany on the Continent.

In eastern Europe, there was a constant clash of Russian and Austro-Hungarian ambitions. Compounding this situation were the ferocious national aspirations of the smaller Balkan states. The most aggressive of these was Serbia, which had claims to several provinces ruled by Austria-Hungary (hereafter referred to simply as Austria). Russia, anxious to free her "little Slavic sisters" from all foreign domination except her own, supported Serbia. Russia longed to dismember Turkey and gain control of the Dardanelles. Turkey seethed with hatred of Russia—and of the Balkan states, which had driven her out of most of her European provinces in 1913.

These antagonisms, ambitions, and conflicts of interest kept the nations of Europe under the shadow of an impending general war. Seeking some measure of collective security, they therefore grouped themselves into alliances. By 1914, Germany, Austria, and Italy—the last irritated over French expansion in North Africa—had formed the Triple Alliance; England, France, and Russia, the Triple Entente. In each alliance, the members pledged that if one were attacked, the others would come to her assistance.

These powers set about diligently preparing themselves for war. Plans for general mobilization and initial operations were kept up to date. The impact of general mobilization on the national life and economy obviously would be so profound that it became universally accepted that general mobilization meant war. It was equally apparent that, if one nation mobilized, its neighbors must do likewise or risk being caught unprepared.

By 1914, tensions had tightened to the point where the slightest overt act would plunge all Europe into war. The bloody deed which actually did this was the murder of the Austrian Archduke Franz Ferdinand and his wife by a Serbian terrorist on 28 June.

Austria, having long wanted an excuse to suppress her troublesome little neighbor, confronted Serbia with a harsh ultimatum. Hoping to frighten the Austrians, Russia began partial mobilization. Austria, however, had secured promises of German backing and, when Serbia did not submit, declared war. Russia thereupon ordered general mobilization. Germany gave Russia twelve hours to halt this; when the Russians ignored the demand, the Germans declared war on them and—knowing that France intended to honor its alliance with Russia—on France as well. Great Britain was pledged, along with other European nations, to protect Belgian neutrality. When the Germans entered Belgium on 3 August, Great Britain declared war.

Thus, by 4 August, Germany and Austria were at war with Belgium, Britain, France, Russia, and Serbia. The first two were soon termed the Central Powers; the latter group, the Allies. Italy, announcing that the Triple Alliance was valid only if her allies were *attacked,* remained neutral. As the war continued, other nations entered it. Turkey and Bulgaria joined the Central Powers. Many countries took the part of the Allies; of these, only Greece, Italy, Japan, Montenegro, Portugal, Rumania, and the United States participated actively.

ARCTIC OCEAN

ICELAND

MURMANSK

WHITE SEA

FAROE ISLANDS

LAKE ONEGA

SHETLAND ISLANDS

ORKNEY ISLANDS

LAKE LADOGA

CHRISTIANIA

ST. PETERSBURG (PETROGRAD)

ATLANTIC

STOCKHOLM

GULF OF BOTHNIA

GULF OF FINLAND

ESTONIA

LAKE PEIPUS

SKAGGERAK

LIVONIA

NORTH SEA

COURLAND

KATTEGATT

IRELAND

IRISH SEA

DENMARK

COPENHAGEN

BALTIC SEA

LITHUANIA

R U S S I A

ORSHA

HELIGOLAND

KIEL

ENGLAND

LONDON

GERMANY

BERLIN

WARSAW

GOMEL

The HAGUE

NETH.

DOVER

POLAND

U K R A I N E

ENGLISH CHANNEL

BRUSSELS BEL.

PARIS

LORRAINE

ROSTOV

OCEAN

ALSACE

VIENNA

CASPIAN SEA

BAY OF BISCAY

FRANCE

BERN SWITZ.

AUSTRIA- HUNGARY

SEA OF AZOV

POLA

RUMANIA

BUCHAREST

BLACK SEA

PORTUGAL

SPAIN

ITALY

ADRIATIC SEA

BELGRADE

SARAJEVO

MONTE NEGRO

SERBIA

BULGARIA

LISBON

MADRID

CORSICA

ROME

SOPHIA

ADRIANOPLE

CONSTANTINOPLE

ALBANIA

SARDINIA

TYRRHENIAN SEA

SALONIKA

DARDANELLES

T U R K E Y

MEDITERRANEAN

SICILY

IONIAN SEA

GREECE

AEGEAN SEA

CYPRUS

ATHENS

MOROCCO

ALGERIA

SEA

CRETE

MALTA

GENERAL MAP

EUROPE IN 1914

0   100   200   300

SCALE OF MILES

Germany's master war plan was the Schlieffen Plan of 1905, the final work of Count Alfred von Schlieffen, Chief of the German General Staff, before his retirement. In the West, its purpose was to crush France before Russia could mobilize completely.

Schlieffen felt that rough terrain and French fortifications would check an attack against France's eastern frontier. An envelopment through Switzerland seemed impossible. He therefore decided to make his main effort in the north.

For this offensive, Schlieffen proposed to concentrate the German ground forces, grouped into seven armies, on the Western front. The right wing would consist of five armies (thirty-five corps), the left wing of two armies (five corps)—giving the right wing a preponderance of seven to one. The two northernmost armies were to be especially strong. Six "ersatz corps," formed from untrained reservists of military age, would follow those two armies, protect their communications, and besiege bypassed strongholds. Only local defense forces would defend eastern Germany against Russia. After the defeat of France, Schlieffen expected to move overwhelming forces to the East.

The left wing, though strategically on the defensive, was to attack immediately to lure the French into a major offensive in Alsace-Lorraine (*lower right*). Meanwhile, the right wing, pivoting on the Metz-Thionville fortress area (*center, right*), would move without warning and in overwhelming force across neutral Belgium and Holland. It would break into France as shown, the First Army swinging west and south of Paris, and strike the rear of the main French armies, by then engaged with the German left. The plan was subtle: the harder the French pushed against the left wing, the more thoroughly they would entangle themselves in Alsace-Lorraine, and the more rapid and decisive would be the German right wing's drive.

It must be noted, however, that the German Reichstag never authorized all the forces that Schlieffen considered essential. Nevertheless, his plan is outstanding in its attainment of maximum concentration of combat power in the decisive right wing through economy of force elsewhere.

Schlieffen's successor, General Helmuth von Moltke, faced a changing balance of international power. Russia, France, and England improved their armies. Italy's adherence to the Triple Alliance weakened. The Saar coal mines and the Rhineland industrial area became essential to Germany, and the five corps allotted by Schlieffen for their protection seemed inadequate.

Moltke accordingly attempted to modify the Schlieffen Plan. He decided not to violate Dutch neutrality, hoping that England would not fight for Belgium if Holland were spared. However, this decision would make it necessary to crowd the First and Second Armies through Liége (*upper right*).

Moltke also increased the forces on the Eastern Front by taking troops from the right wing. When new units were authorized, he assigned them to the left wing. Finally, he took the ersatz corps from the northernmost armies. These changes reduced the ratio of troops between the right and left wings to a bare three to one. This was largely due to Moltke's desire to be strong everywhere; but, in part, it was probably also a dim reflection of Schlieffen's advocacy of the double envelopment as the most decisive form of warfare. (In 1912, Schlieffen had recommended similar modifications to his original plan, *provided that* the army were greatly strengthened.) In the end, it was not so much Moltke's modifications of the plan as the faulty execution of it that caused its failure.

The French Plan XVII, by contrast with the Schlieffen Plan, was a general statement of intention to concentrate and attack. It was expected that this offensive would dislocate all German plans and give the French the initiative. Two attacks were planned: one north of the Metz-Thionville area, the other south of it. The possibility of a German advance through Belgium was admitted; the alternate plan, in case this occurred, is given in the note on the map. Unfortunately, the French underestimated the strength of the fully mobilized German Army and, therefore, believed that any attack through Belgium would be too weak to advance west of the Meuse River (*upper center*).

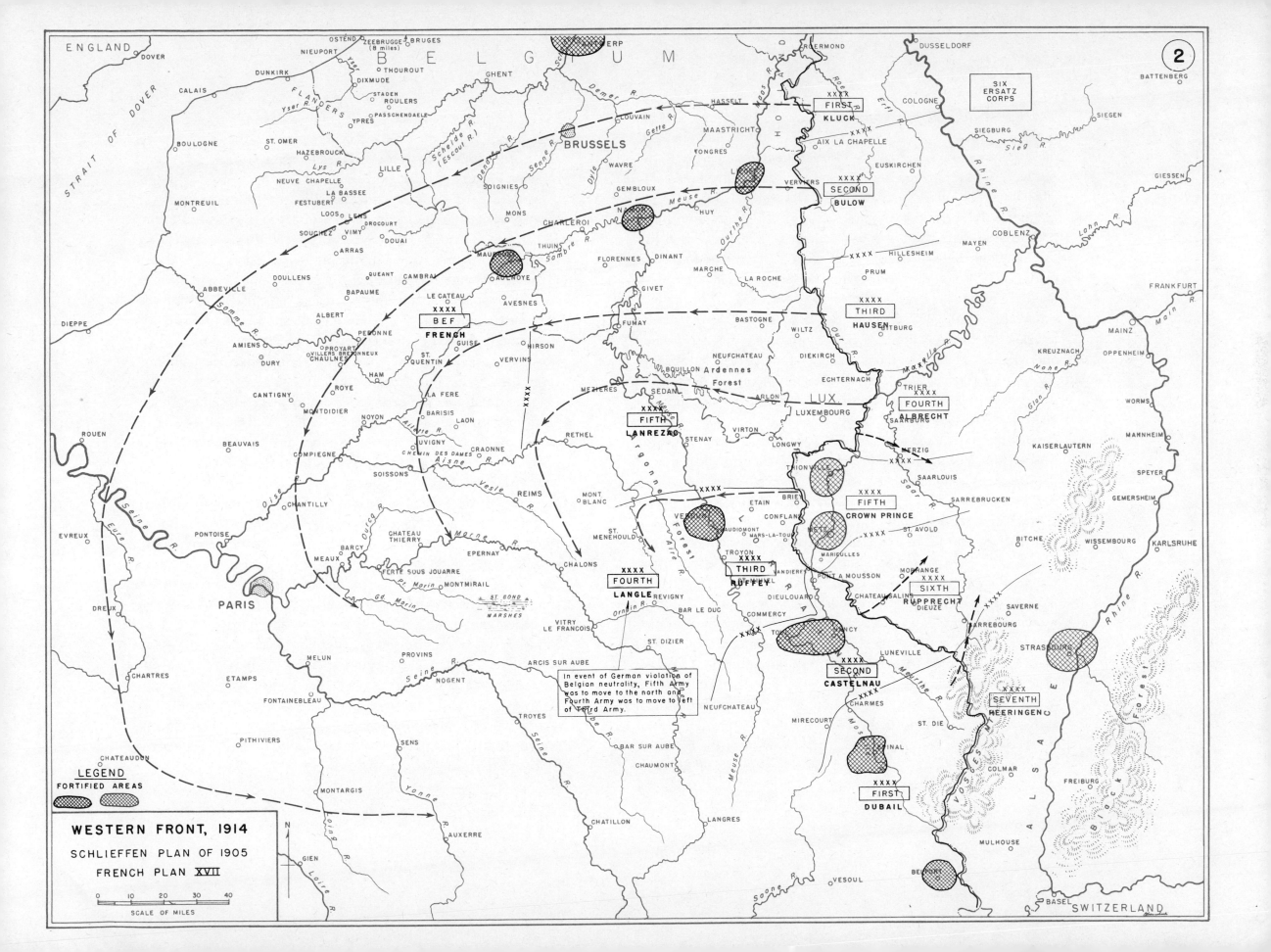

WESTERN FRONT, 1914

SCHLIEFFEN PLAN OF 1905

FRENCH PLAN XVII

The strategy on the Eastern Front and the attendant army concentration areas were largely dictated by terrain features. The most dominant of these was the Polish salient—the part of Russia outlined in blue surrounding Warsaw and its vicinity (*sketch* a). This area—230 miles long and 210 miles wide—led directly into Germany. Its western extremity was only 180 miles from Berlin and abutted the rich mining and industrial areas of Silesia. Furthermore, no natural defensive barriers separated it from Germany. The broad, sluggish Vistula River traversed the salient; located thereon was the fortress city of Warsaw. Here the Russians had established a huge base, fed by six railroads from the interior of Russia. This base had considerable defensive value, and was also a fine point from which to launch a drive into Silesia.

But the Polish salient also posed problems for Russia. Its flanks were weak. If the Germans (in East Prussia) and the Austrians (in Galicia) launched converging attacks across the base of the salient against Brest Litovsk (*center*), Russian forces west of the Vistula could be isolated. To prevent such attacks, the Russians established a system of fortresses (useful also as bases for offensives) along the Niemen and Narew Rivers (*upper center*) and around Lublin and Kholm (*center*). Furthermore, the territory to the west of this fortress system was kept devoid of railroads, roads, and built-up areas, and no Russian forces were stationed west of the Vistula.

But if East Prussia threatened the Polish salient, the former was also vulnerable to attack from Warsaw. Hence the Germans had established fortified cities along the Vistula and made it their main line of defense. A forward line ran through the lake system near Lötzen (*upper center*). The other flank, in Galicia, was traversed by the Carpathian Mountains, running from Cracow to Rumania, which afforded Austria a defensive barrier. On the northern slopes, the Austrians likewise had fortified cities—Cracow, Przemysl, and Lemberg (*center*)—which could support an offensive into Russia.

East of the Polish salient, Russia was divided by the Pripet Marshes, a region of primeval bog, forests, and few roads. To the north, south, and east stretched vast spaces which could swallow entire armies (*sketch* b).

As we have seen, the Schlieffen Plan of 1905 accepted war on two fronts, but allotted minimum forces to the Eastern Front. Reliance was placed upon the fortress system to slow any enemy advance. Anticipating a slow Russian mobilization and a speedy German conquest of France, Schlieffen planned to create a strong force in East Prussia only after the defeat of France. But Moltke's plan took cognizance of Russian revitalization, and provided for mobilization of the Eighth Army in East Prussia (*sketch* a). It was given a defensive mission, and was authorized to withdraw behind the Vistula, if necessary.

Austria and Russia each had two war plans, depending upon how hostilities developed. Austria's Plan B assumed war with Serbia alone and its invasion by three armies, while the other three armies watched Russia from Galicia. Her Plan R assumed war with both Serbia and Russia, and called for offensives on both fronts, but here the Second Army would operate against Russia instead of Serbia. Russia's Plan G assumed that Germany would make her main effort in the East, and therefore was defensive. In this plan, the Fourth Army was to be on the north flank, and both army groups would retire eastward until strength for a counteroffensive could be marshaled. Plan A was offensive in concept (envisaging the main German effort directed against France); it provided for simultaneous advances into East Prussia and Galicia, designed to clear the flanks of the Polish salient preparatory to an advance into Silesia. In this plan, the Fourth Army was to be in the south. As will be evident later, Plan A was developed under French pressure. Fearing a German onslaught in the West, the French urged an early Russian offensive to divert German forces to the East.

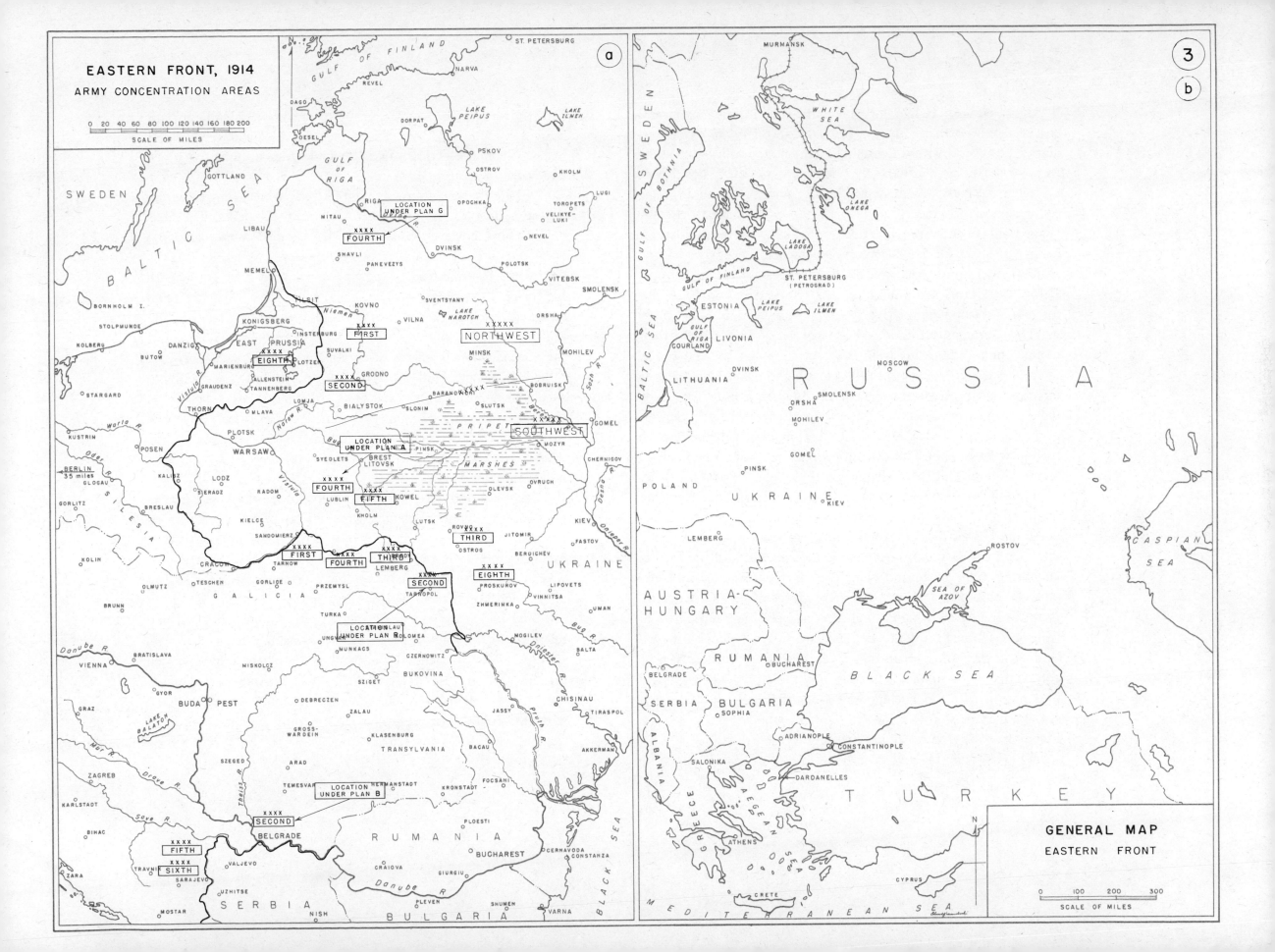

Most of southern Belgium is flat and open, forming a natural corridor into northern France. Entrance to this plain from Germany, however—without violating Dutch neutrality—must be through the Liége "bottleneck" (*right center*). Liége lies astride the Meuse River. A few miles to the north is Limbourg, the southernmost province of Holland; just south of Liége rise the rugged hills of the Ardennes Forest (*not shown*), a considerable barrier to rapid, large-scale troop movements. Liége, with its ring of forts, was considered one of the strongest places in Europe. Before the German First and Second Armies could advance, this fortress had to be captured.

The Germans required about two weeks to complete their mobilization. While this went on, they intended to take Liége. A special task force, kept at full strength and trained for this one mission, had been stationed near the Belgian border for years. On 3 August, its cavalry crossed the frontier; on the 4th, the rest of the force followed; the next day, its commander demanded the surrender of Liége. The commander of the garrison, General Gerard Leman, refused, whereupon the attack began.

Belgium's strict interpretation of her neutrality had kept her from making plans for military cooperation with friendly neighbors, and her armed forces had been neglected. King Albert had intended to assemble his army along the west bank of the Meuse, anchoring it on Liége and Namur, and attempting to hold that position until French and British reinforcements reached him. It was a bold plan which might have stopped the German right wing in its tracks; but the Belgian Army was incapable of executing it, the influx of untrained reservists having destroyed its cohesion and discipline. The Belgians therefore decided to reorganize their troops behind the Gette River (*upper center*), sending one division to reinforce Leman's 40,000 fortress troops. Leman was ordered to "hold to the end."

The German tactical plan (*not shown*) was to penetrate between the Liége forts, capture the city with its important bridges, isolate the forts, then reduce them individually. Meanwhile, German cavalry would cross the Meuse north of Liége and move to encircle that city.

Despite long planning, the first German attack failed, Leman having connected the forts with hasty entrenchments. The German cavalry, however, crossed the Meuse, and Leman—knowing he would soon be cut off—sent his infantry division back to the field army the night of 6 August, choosing to fight it out with his fortress troops alone. That same night, the Germans again attacked, but still made no appreciable headway. Their leading units were disorganized and near panic when the chief of staff of the Second Army, General Erich von Ludendorff, went forward, rallied them, and bluffed the Belgian troops in Liége itself into surrendering. Leman and his forts still held out; it took three German corps and 420-mm. siege artillery to destroy them one by one, the last fort falling on 16 August. Leman's gallant defense delayed the German right wing two or three days, at a time when hours were precious.

The First and Second Armies then poured through Liége in an effort to cut the Belgian Army off from Antwerp. Albert, however, withdrew in time. By 20 August, the Belgian Army—except one division which had reinforced the Namur garrison—was in Antwerp on the flank of the German advance. General Alexander von Kluck had to detach one corps to watch it. (Moltke had just given the ersatz troops, which Schlieffen had intended for such missions, to the left wing.)

By 7 August, General Charles L. M. Lanrezac had warned General Joseph J. C. Joffre, the French commander in chief, that the Germans were moving into Belgium in unexpected strength. Initially unconcerned, Joffre, on 15 August, ordered the French Fifth Army northward.

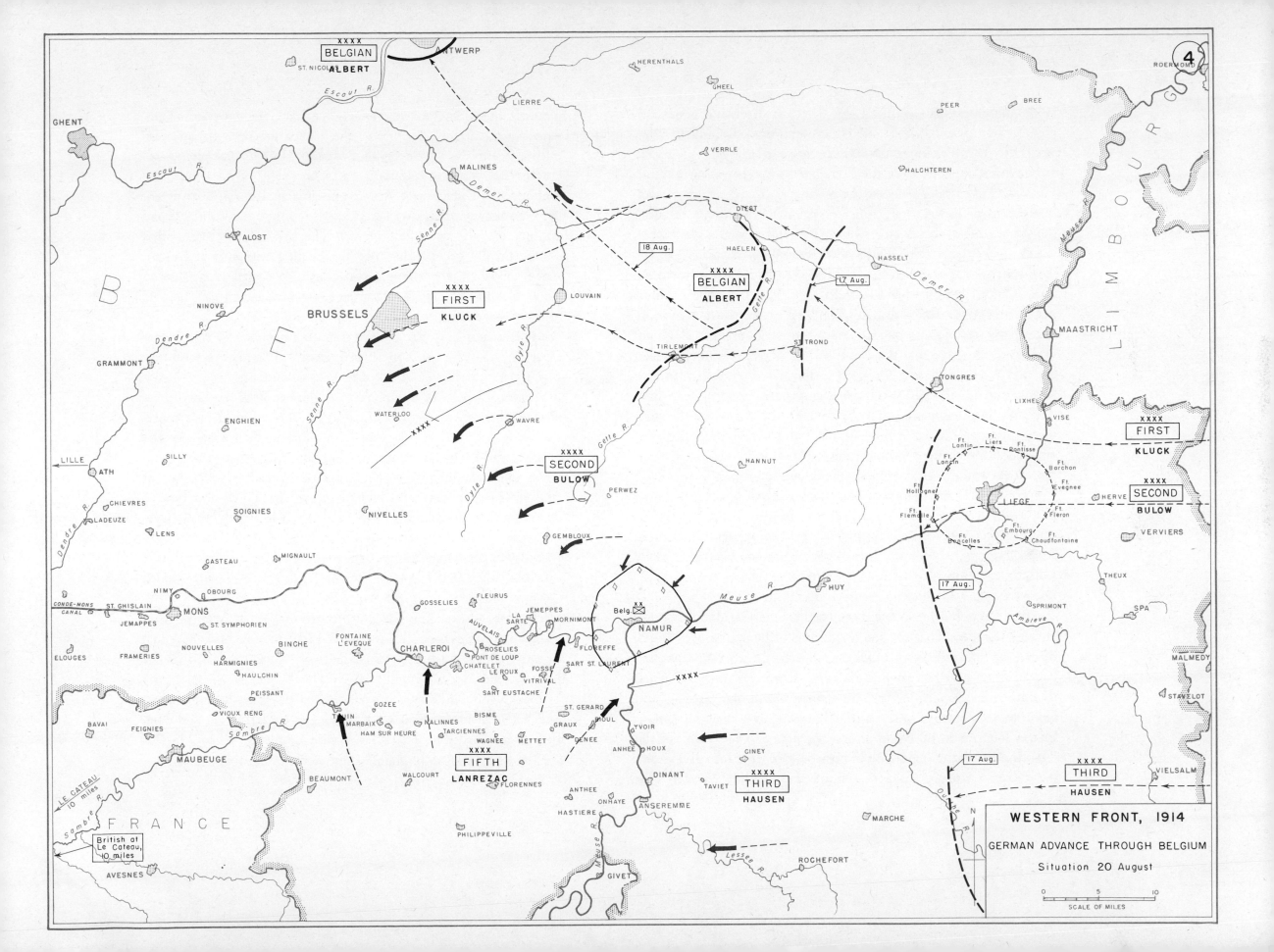

WESTERN FRONT, 1914

GERMAN ADVANCE THROUGH BELGIUM

Situation 20 August

SCALE OF MILES
0   5   10

While the Germans took the Liége forts, the French armies completed their mobilization and concentration according to Plan XVII. In a minor operation (*not shown*), designed to inspire public morale, elements of the French First Army took Mulhouse (*bottom right*) on 7 August; on 9 August, the Germans retook it. Because of this reverse, Joffre reorganized his forces, creating the Army of Alsace to cover his right flank.

On 8 August, Joffre issued his "General Instructions No. 1": the French First and Second Armies were to advance northeast into Alsace-Lorraine on 14 August, with Sarrebourg as their initial objective. Joffre and his staff were undisturbed by continuing reports of masses of German troops moving into Belgium. They were positive that the Germans did not have sufficient men on the Western Front for such extensive operations. In this assessment, they overlooked two important possibilities: first, that the Germans would gamble on the slowness of the Russian mobilization, and leave only a skeleton force in East Prussia; and second, that the German reservists would be so well trained that they could be employed immediately as first-line troops. Consequently, the Germans were able to mass approximately 2,000,000 men in the West, against 1,300,000 French, plus the small British and Belgian contingents. Had even part of the forces Joffre launched so blindly into Alsace-Lorraine been rushed by railroad to reinforce the Belgians along the Meuse (*center*), the history of the war might have been different.

This French offensive was opposed by the German Sixth and Seventh Armies. To unify the operations of his left wing, Moltke placed the Seventh Army under the control of the Sixth. Schlieffen had planned a fighting withdrawal in Alsace-Lorraine, designed to draw the French deeper into his trap. But the efficient and ambitious General Krafft von Dellmensingen—chief of staff to Prince Rupprecht of Bavaria, and the actual commander of the left wing in everything but title, browbeat Moltke into giving him the six ersatz corps for a counteroffensive. The Germans now planned first to fight a delaying action back to the line Morhange–Sarrebourg–Vosges Mountains; then, once the French had committed themselves to an attack against this line, they would launch a converging counterattack. The operation went much as planned, the French advancing to the line shown. On 20 August, the Germans struck. After a hard day's fighting, the French broke contact by a forced night march. The First Army maintained comparatively good order, but the Second was almost routed, being saved largely by the "Iron Corps" of General Ferdinand Foch. During the 21st and 22d, the French fell back to the heights around Nancy and behind the Meurthe River.

In the north, Joffre's plans for an offensive by his Third, Fourth, and Fifth Armies—based, as noted, on the assumption that the Germans would not advance west of the Meuse—were overtaken by events. Lanrezac had insisted that he should be allowed to move his entire army north into Belgium. Joffre finally (15 August) ordered him north into the angle formed by the Sambre and Meuse Rivers, replacing him in line with the Fourth Army. He also activated the Army of Lorraine, consisting of reserve units, to cover the right flank of the Third and Fourth Armies. The Third and Fourth he ordered forward through the Ardennes Forest against Arlon and Neufchâteau, respectively. The Ardennes would hamper their advance, but Joffre was certain that they could get through it before meeting any major German units.

He was wrong. The German Fourth and Fifth Armies, regulating their march by that of their First and Second, had just begun their advance. On the 22d, they struck the flank of the French offensive, crushing it.

Meanwhile, the British Expeditionary Force had disembarked and had concentrated at Le Cateau (*upper left*). On the 21st, Joffre requested that it cooperate with Lanrezac; Field Marshal Sir John French, its commander, moved it to the line shown.

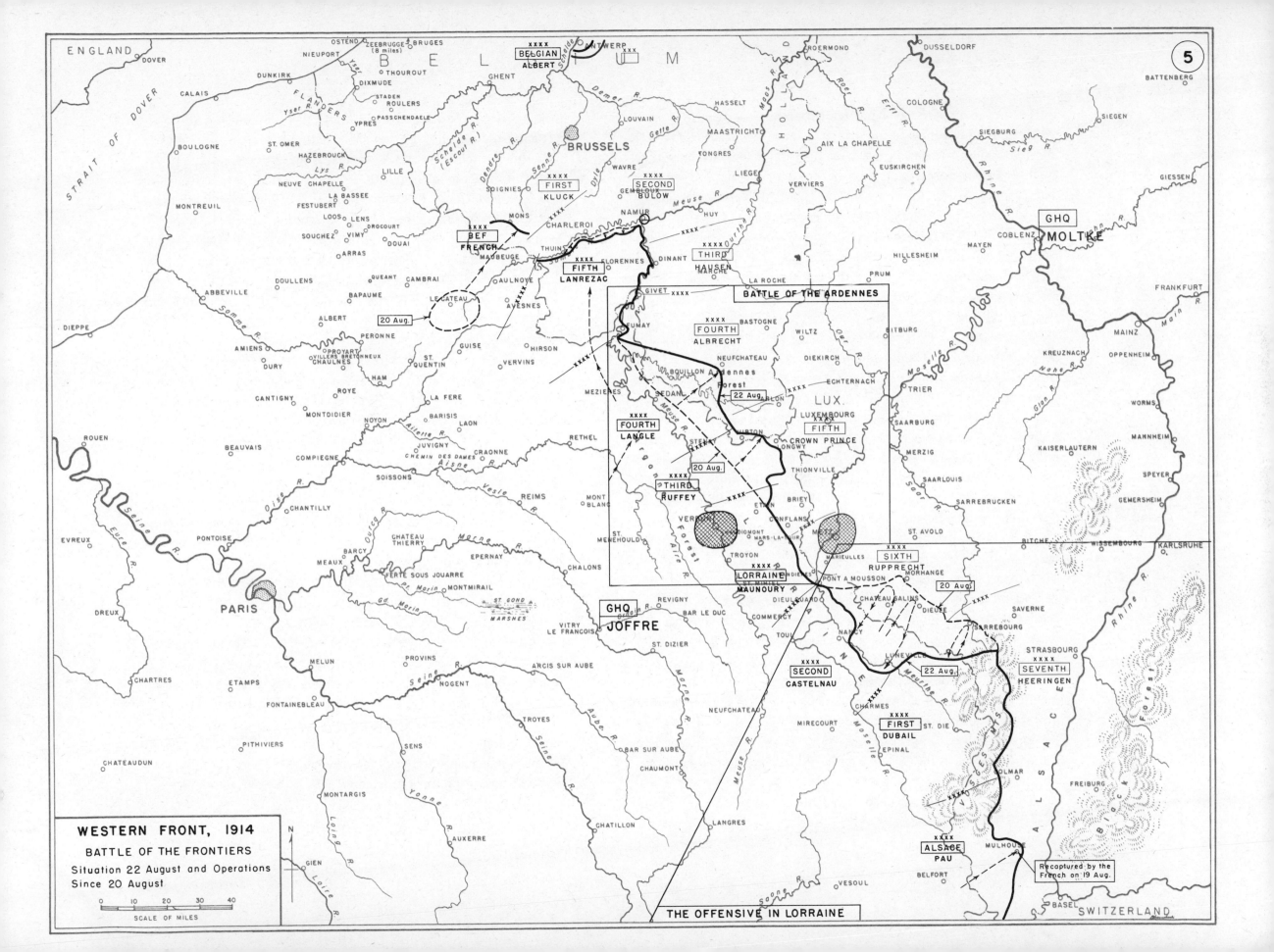

ENGLAND

B E L G I U M

STRAIT OF DOVER

OSTEND ZEEBRUGGE BRUGES
NIEUPORT
DOVER
DUNKIRK THOUROUT GHENT
CALAIS STADEN ROULERS DIXMUDE
YPRES PASSCHENDAELE
FLANDERS
ST. OMER HAZEBROUCK
NEUVE CHAPELLE
BOULOGNE LILLE
LA BASSEE
MONTREUIL FESTUBERT LOOS LENS
SOUCHEZ VIMY DROCOURT DOUAI
ARRAS

XXXX BELGIAN ALBERT ANTWERP XXX

BRUSSELS WAVRE LOUVAIN
SOIGNIES GEMBLOUX
XXXX FIRST KLUCK **XXXX SECOND BULOW**
MONS CHARLEROI NAMUR

HASSELT
MAASTRICHT TONGRES LIEGE VERVIERS
HUY

HOLLAND ROERMOND

DUSSELDORF
AIX LA CHAPELLE EUSKIRCHEN
COLOGNE SIEGBURG SIEGEN
GHQ MOLTKE COBLENZ

XXXX BEF FRENCH MAUBEUGE THUIN
XXXX FIFTH LANREZAC FLORENNES DINANT
XXXX THIRD HAUSEN MARCHE LA ROCHE

MAYEN HILLESHEIM PRUM BITBURG

FRANKFURT MAINZ

DOULLENS ABBEVILLE
DIEPPE
AMIENS DURY
QUEANT CAMBRAI
BAPAUME AVESNES
LE CATEAU
20 Aug.
HIRSON
GUISE VERVINS
ST. QUENTIN
LA FERE

GIVET XXXX
BATTLE OF THE ARDENNES
FUMAY
XXXX FOURTH ALBRECHT BASTOGNE WILTZ
NEUFCHATEAU DIEKIRCH
BOUILLON Ardennes Forest ECHTERNACH
MEZIERES SEDAM **22 Aug.** ARLON LUX. LUXEMBOURG
XXXX FOURTH LANGLE STENAY BURTON **XXXX FIFTH CROWN PRINCE**
20 Aug. LONGWY THIONVILLE

OUR R. TRIER SAARBURG MERZIG SAARLOUIS

WORMS OPPENHEIM MANNHEIM KAISERLAUTERN SPEYER GERMERSHEIM

ROUEN BEAUVAIS COMPIEGNE SOISSONS
CHANTILLY
RETHEL JUVIGNY LAON BARISIS
CHEMIN DES DAMES CRAONNE
REIMS

XXXX THIRD RUFFEY ETAIN BRIEY
VERDUN CONFLANS
XXXX SIXTH RUPPRECHT

ST. AVOLD SARREBRUCKEN

BITCHE WISSEMBOURG KARLSRUHE

PARIS
CHATEAU THIERRY
EPERNAY
CHALONS
GHQ JOFFRE
BAR LE DUC COMMERCY TOUL

PONT A MOUSSON MARIEULLES
20 Aug. MORHANGE DIEUZE
CHATEAU SALINS
XXXX SECOND CASTELNAU NANCY LUNEVILLE
22 Aug. SARREBOURG
XXXX SEVENTH HEERINGEN SAVERNE STRASBOURG

LORRAINE MAUNOURY ST. MIHIEL

XXXX FIRST DUBAIL CHARMES ST. DIE EPINAL MIRECOURT

COLMAR FREIBURG

WESTERN FRONT, 1914

BATTLE OF THE FRONTIERS

Situation 22 August and Operations
Since 20 August

N

SCALE OF MILES
0 10 20 30 40

XXXX ALSACE PAU MULHOUSE BELFORT

Recaptured by the
French on 19 Aug.

THE OFFENSIVE IN LORRAINE

SWITZERLAND BASEL

5

BLACK FOREST

ALSACE VOSGES MTS.

Joffre's order of 15 August had sent Lanrezac's Fifth Army into the angle between the Sambre and the Meuse (*right inset sketch*). On 18 August, Lanrezac received instructions to attack either north or east—depending upon the direction of their advance—against the northern German armies. His cavalry, however, could not penetrate the German cavalry screen to locate the advancing German infantry. By the 21st, Joffre realized that the Germans were west of the Meuse in Belgium in considerable strength; he then ordered an attack when Lanrezac thought the "opportune" moment had arrived, and arranged for the British Expeditionary Force to join in this offensive.

Moltke, in an effort to coordinate the actions of his First and Second Armies, had subordinated Kluck to General Karl von Bülow. This was a mistake. Kluck was an aggressive and capable commander, while Bülow—like Moltke himself—had few qualifications beyond his family name. In addition, he was a selfish individual, able to see only those matters that benefited his Second Army. General Freiherr von Hausen's Third Army was approaching from the east; Bülow decided that it should join him in his attack on Lanrezac. Hausen, subservient to nobility, agreed to a joint attack on the 22d. At the same time, Bülow ordered Kluck to change the First Army's direction of march from southwest to south (*left inset sketch*).

On the 21st, though ordered to attack, Lanrezac decided to defend his position south of the Sambre. However, he failed to establish strong bridgeheads on the north bank to protect the vital bridges over that river. The German advance guards, finding the bridges weakly defended, attacked on their own initiative and won a foothold on the south bank (*dashed blue line*). Next morning, the French corps commanders—also on their own initiative—counterattacked to drive the Germans back across the Sambre, but were unsuccessful. About noon, Bülow decided to attack Lanrezac without waiting for Hausen and gained considerable ground (*dotted blue line*).

During the 22d, Lanrezac withdrew most of the I Corps from the line along the Meuse, planning to use it to envelop Bülow's left flank the next day. He also tried, without success, to persuade Sir John French to turn east against Bülow's right flank. On the 23d, Bülow again attacked; the French resisted vigorously. General Louis F. M. F. Franchet d'Esperey's I Corps was about to attack Bülow's flank, when Hausen's advance guards crossed the Meuse. Realizing the danger to the Fifth Army, Franchet d'Esperey countermarched. Part of his corps returned to the right of the French line; the remainder checked Hausen's advance across the Meuse, but could not wipe out the German bridgeheads.

That night, Lanrezac made the decision—extremely difficult in the offensive-minded French Army—to withdraw. The Belgian division in Namur had retreated into his lines; obviously, the fortress would fall soon, releasing more German troops. His right flank was turned; the English, on his left, were under heavy pressure. Joffre concurred in his decision.

On the German side, Bülow planned a converging attack for the 24th: Hausen was asked to attack straight west; Bülow would continue south; Kluck now was ordered to turn southeast against the French left.

Kluck knew only that British troops had been reported some thirty miles northwest of Mons. Actually, Sir John French had occupied a defensive position at Mons (*left inset sketch, dashed blue line*) by the 22d. His airplanes reported masses of Germans moving to his front; consequently, he refused Lanrezac's request to turn eastward against Bülow's flank. At 0930, 23 August, Kluck struck the British. After several bloody repulses, he finally drove them back to the position shown (*solid blue line*). If Bülow had not ordered him to change his direction of march on 21 August, Kluck would have enveloped the British left flank. Sir John French organized his new position that night and prepared to fight again on the 24th. British morale was high. But, learning that Lanrezac was withdrawing, Sir John French—now highly distrustful of his French colleague—decided to do likewise.

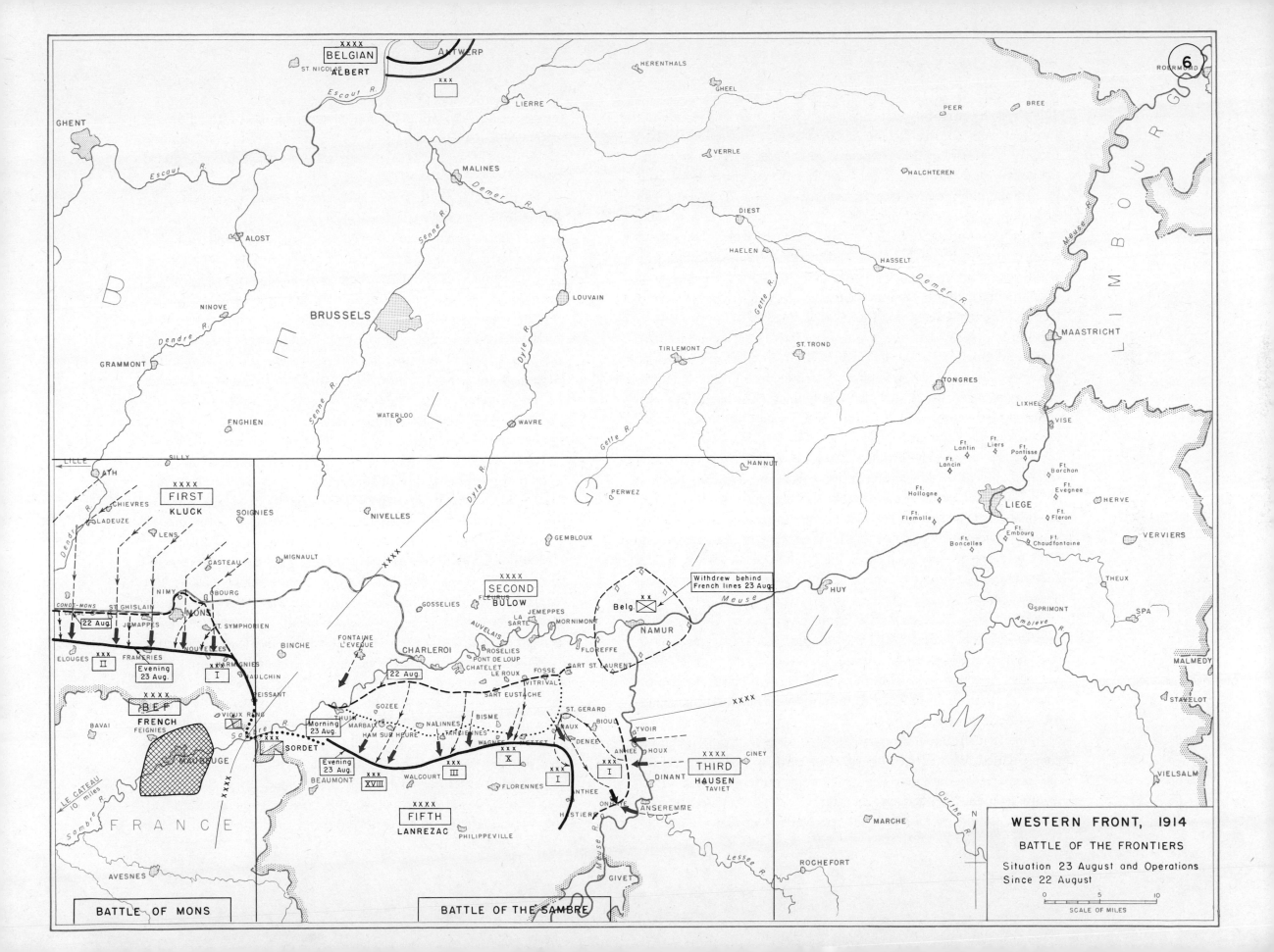

WESTERN FRONT, 1914

BATTLE OF THE FRONTIERS

Situation 23 August and Operations
Since 22 August

BATTLE OF MONS

BATTLE OF THE SAMBRE

The over-all situation on the Western Front, as shown, looked extremely unfavorable for the Allies. Joffre's grand offensive had collapsed, with over 300,000 casualties. Moltke's version of the Schlieffen Plan was driving forward; but the inherent flaws, both in his plan and in Moltke himself, were already sapping the strength of the German offensive.

In the south, the French First and Second Armies had rallied along a natural defensive line, and in three days had made the position extremely strong. On the German side, Dellmensingen was convinced that his counteroffensive of the 20th had shattered the two French armies. He therefore cajoled Moltke into allowing him to attack their new position, promising he would destroy them and turn the right flank of Joffre's line. Moltke's assent abruptly converted the Schlieffen Plan into an attempted double envelopment. It also killed the last chance that his right wing could expect reinforcements, and placed a double drain on the German supply system.

Farther north, the French Third and Fourth Armies had suffered a great defeat in the confused Ardennes fighting, but not so bad a defeat as the Germans believed. Though retreating, their organization was still intact. During the 26th, the Army of Lorraine was dissolved. Two of its divisions went to Amiens (*upper left*) to serve as the nucleus of the French Sixth Army, which Joffre planned to activate there; the rest were transferred to the Third Army.

On the French Fifth Army's front, Lanrezac had begun withdrawing before daylight of the 24th. Bülow's converging attack that morning therefore struck thin air—especially since Hausen had advanced due west from Dinant. If Hausen had followed his original intention and moved to the southwest, he might have cut off Lanrezac's retreat.

The British Expeditionary Force, however, faced the iron-willed Kluck, who carried his men forward in a driving pursuit. Sir John French had a momentary temptation to throw his weary troops into the fortified city of Maubeuge, but resisted it. The roads by which he had to withdraw were clogged with civilian refugees and wandering French cavalry. On the early morning of the 26th, General Sir Horace L. Smith-Dorrien, commanding the British II Corps, was preparing to fight a desperate rear-guard action.

On the Allied left, Joffre had hastily improvised the Group d'Amade. (These French Territorial troops were second-line reserve troops—men from thirty-seven to forty-eight—similar to the German Landwehr.)

The French Army, as a whole, was unbeaten, though tired, but many senior officers were demoralized by the complete failure of their cherished offensive. Joffre was far from a military genius, but he remained calm. Though the German plan was now obvious, the Fifth Army and the British alone could not halt the German right wing; the Allied left wing had to be strengthened. On 25 August, Joffre issued his "General Instructions No. 2." The First and Second Armies were to hold in place. The Third, Fourth, and Fifth Armies and the British were assigned zones of withdrawal to the general line Somme River–Verdun; they were to be prepared to counterattack upon reaching this line. Meanwhile, Joffre would draw troops from his right wing to form the French Sixth Army near Amiens for an eventual major counteroffensive against the tip of the German right flank.

While Joffre dealt realistically with hard facts, Moltke inhabited a fool's paradise. His headquarters remained far to the rear and his communications with his troops were extremely limited, yet neither he nor the senior members of his staff made any effort to visit the front. Instead, misled by fragmentary and overly optimistic reports of victory, he persuaded himself that the French Army was already practically destroyed. News from the Russian front being bad, he decided he could spare two corps from the West to reinforce it—and, for some unknowable reason, took them from his Second and Third Armies. These armies had already been weakened by detachments left to besiege bypassed towns. Moltke's three right-wing armies had entered Belgium with a total of sixteen corps; at this critical moment, they had only eleven left in contact with the retreating Allies.

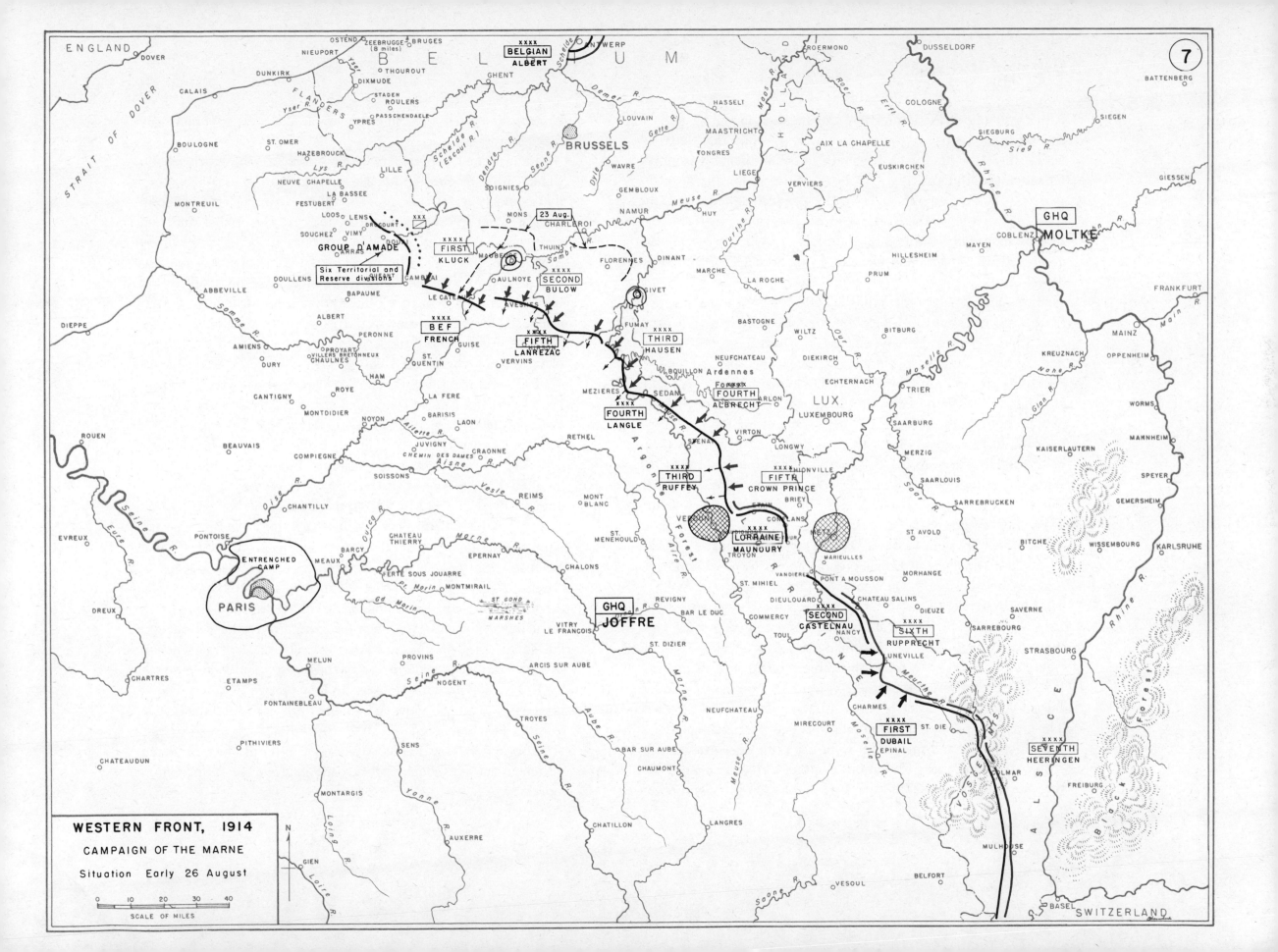

WESTERN FRONT, 1914

CAMPAIGN OF THE MARNE

Situation Early 26 August

Kluck was under the impression that the British were based on the Channel ports (*off map, northwest*). After the Battle of Mons, therefore, he directed his pursuit to cut them off from the Channel. Smith-Dorrien's II Corps, which bore the heaviest pressure, finally, on the night of 25 August, halted along the line shown (*upper sketch*). Its men were worn out by three days of marching and fighting, and the roads behind it were still encumbered by refugees and General C. C. Sordet's French horsemen.

Sir John French's orders for the 26th called for a continuation of the retreat southward. General Sir Douglas Haig's I Corps, which had been less heavily engaged at Mons than the II Corps and had been under less pressure since, was able to comply. Smith-Dorrien, who received this order sometime after midnight, felt that he could not. He would have to start before daylight to avoid a fight with the Germans, and his men were too tired to go on without rest; some of his units, in fact, had just reached his position. He therefore decided to stand his ground through the 26th, and withdraw that night. Sir John French was so informed, but his reaction was equivocal—he did not flatly order Smith-Dorrien to continue the withdrawal, and he did order the independent 4th Division to cover the II Corps' left flank. However, he made no changes in Haig's orders. The I Corps withdrew, as planned, leaving Smith-Dorrien's right flank open.

Kluck attacked as soon as he reached the British position at Le Cateau. The British held firmly in their center, but the Germans overlapped them on both flanks. By 1400, Smith-Dorrien's right-flank division was forced to retreat, losing most of its artillery. Somewhat later, the 4th Division was outflanked, but, in the nick of time, Sordet brought his worn-out cavalry forward. The Germans paused to reconnoiter this unexpected threat, darkness intervened, and the retreat went on. Both sides lost heavily, British casualties being 7,800 out of 40,000 troops engaged. By the morning of the 27th, the British had completely broken

contact, and Kluck was in considerable doubt as to which way they had retired.

Exaggerated reports concerning the British defeat at Le Cateau soon reached Joffre. He realized that he must do something quickly to take the pressure off the British, if they were to remain intact as an effective combat force. He needed time and secure east-west railroad communications in order to redeploy troops from his right wing to his left for his planned counter-offensive. Only by maintaining a cohesive, if elastic, front before the German right wing could he do this. If the British were overwhelmed, the whole front would collapse. Accordingly, on the 27th, he ordered the Fifth Army to attack westward against the flank of the German First Army.

Lanrezac was shaken by this development. He was withdrawing, and Bülow was following him closely; consequently, his new orders would be difficult to execute. He would have to turn his whole Fifth Army ninety degrees to the west and attack, thus exposing his own right flank to Bülow. Unwillingly, he prepared his plan. On 29 August, before his attack to the west could get under way, Bülow's Second Army came onto the field (*lower sketch*). After several hours of hard fighting, the French right flank was driven in, while the left flank fell back without becoming seriously engaged. At 1300, Lanrezac ordered his I Corps to attack to the north. Franchet d'Esperey, its commander, took the time to prepare a coordinated attack. Delivered at sundown, it was highly successful, though the Germans managed to hold a line south of the Oise. Lanrezac now wisely requested permission to withdraw, since his army was exposed to a converging attack by Kluck, Bülow, and Hausen. Joffre approved. Bülow halted for a day and a half, allowing both the Fifth Army and the British to withdraw unmolested.

This action—the Battle of Guise—can hardly be considered a French victory, though it did greatly improve the Fifth Army's morale.

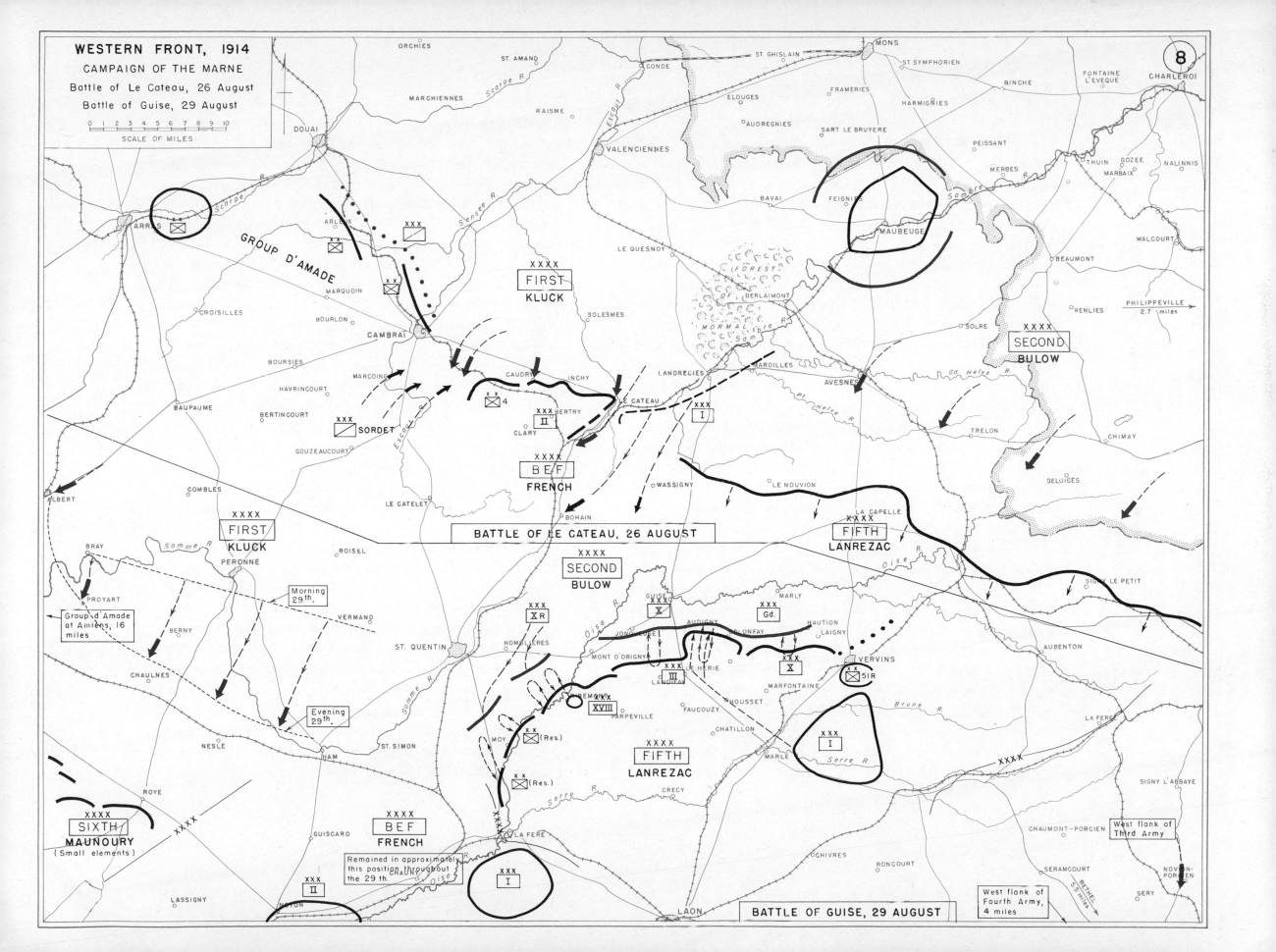

On 27 August, at Coblenz (*upper right*), 200 miles behind the battle, Moltke—ignorant of the actual course of events—concluded that the French were trying to gain time and engage as much German strength as possible, in order to aid the Russian offensive in East Prussia. He now ordered a rapid advance on Paris, designed to destroy the French Army.

The First Army was to advance down the west bank of the Oise toward the lower Seine, protect the right flank of the German offensive, be ready to aid the Second Army, and prevent the formation of new Allied 'units within its zone of advance. The Second Army was to move on Paris; the Third Army, on Château Thierry (*center, left*); the Fourth Army, through Reims on Epernay (*center, left*). The Fifth Army had a multiple mission: to invest Verdun, protect the left flank of the German right wing, and march toward the line Châlons–Vitry le François. The mission of the left wing, now unsuccessfully attacking the new French line, was considered basically defensive, but the Sixth Army could advance if the French retired. Moltke stipulated one major, overall reservation: if the Allies resisted stubbornly along the Aisne and the Marne, the direction of the right wing's advance might have to be changed from southwest to due south.

This change of direction came sooner than Moltke had anticipated. Kluck had renewed his advance on the morning of 27 August. That day, and the next two, he fought a series of successful actions against British rear guards, the Group d'Amade, and elements of the assembling French Sixth Army. These troops were driven westward or dispersed, and Kluck considered his mission of preventing the formation of new French units substantially accomplished. Apparently believing that the British were retreating toward the Channel ports, he now turned his thoughts to finding the French flank, enveloping it, and forcing the French armies eastward away from Paris. In fact, he had urged Bülow (to whom he was no longer subordinated) to join him in turning more directly south.

Now, on 30 August, he received a message from Bülow announcing a "decisive victory" at Guise and asking that Kluck help exploit this success by turning eastward toward the line La Fere–Laon. This request placed Kluck in a quandary. He could not both advance to the lower Seine, as ordered, and still support Bülow. It would be useless to ask Moltke for instructions —communications with his headquarters were atrocious, and it might take several days to get through. Kluck decided—under the circumstances, probably correctly—to help Bülow, but instead of turning east he moved southeast on the 31st, toward Compiègne and Noyon, hoping to intercept the Allied retreat. Bülow, however, remained in position during the 31st.

By Joffre's order, the French Fifth, Fourth, and Third Armies continued to fall back. The German Fourth Army forced the crossings of the Meuse and swung south. Moltke and his army commanders became increasingly convinced that the Allies were beaten. Moltke therefore issued an order on 30 August directing the center armies to pursue the French to their front rapidly, giving them no chance to rally. (Later, he approved Kluck's change of direction.) In a general sense, this order told the right-wing armies to close in and guide on the Third Army. Moltke, however, did not mention to Bülow and Kluck the important news of large troop concentrations around Paris.

Unlike Moltke, Joffre had kept in intimate touch with the situation, visiting all critical sectors of the front. He was shifting troops from his right to build up the French Sixth Army and the Foch Detachment, and had turned Paris into a huge entrenched camp. However, he now knew that it would be impossible to counterattack, as planned, from the Somme River–Verdun line, for his troops were not ready. Finally, the German right wing appeared to be changing the direction of its advance, thus altering the whole strategic problem. Accordingly, he designated a new limit of retreat (*dashed blue line*).

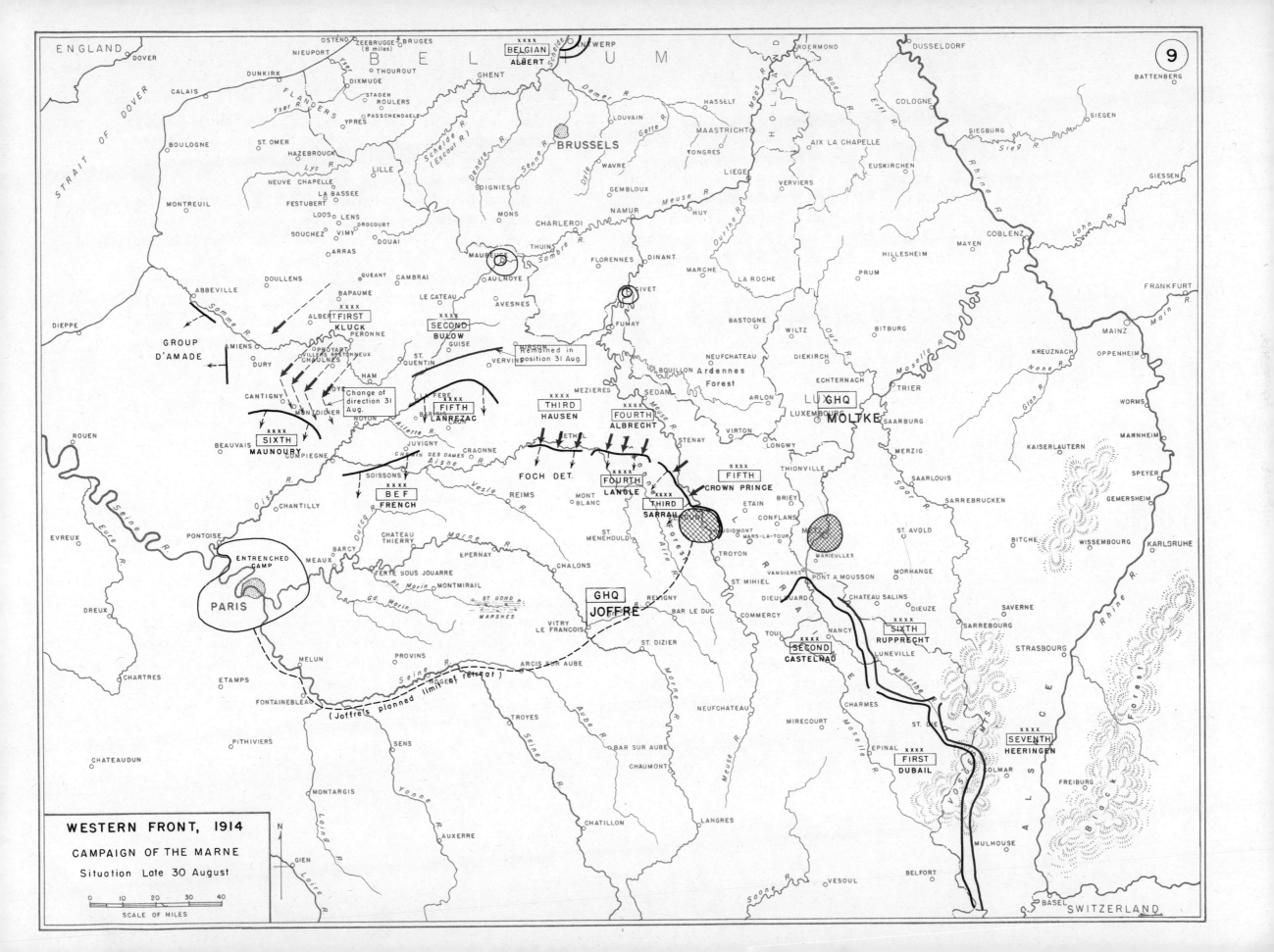

On 31 August and 1 and 2 September, Kluck drove southeast with all possible speed, determined to fix and destroy the left flank of the French Fifth Army, which he believed to be the left-flank unit of the entire French front. As previously noted, he had lost track of the British after Le Cateau, and Moltke had not told him of the growing French strength in and around Paris. However, had Kluck not been so intent on his pursuit, he might have reconnoitered and discovered for himself the true situation at Paris.

Bülow, because of his halt after the Battle of Guise, was at least a good day's march behind Kluck. Their converging advances promised to trap the French Fifth Army, thereby accomplishing the decisive envelopment planned by Schlieffen. On the evening of 2 September, Kluck's left-flank corps reached the Marne River at Château Thierry. Farther east, the German Third, Fourth, and Fifth Armies continued to gain ground.

That night, Kluck received a radiogram from Moltke, changing the entire German plan of operations. The German Second, Third, Fourth, and Fifth Armies were to shift their advance from southwest to directly south; the Sixth Army was to penetrate the line of French forts (*not shown*) on its front and cross the Moselle between Toul and Epinal. The First Army was to follow in echelon behind the Second Army, with the mission of protecting the German right flank. Thus, the spearhead of the Schlieffen Plan was to be merely a security detachment!

This order was based on Moltke's sudden grasp of the fact that his right-wing armies were too weak to swing west of Paris without becoming dangerously overextended. Therefore, he would content himself with enveloping the left flank of the French field armies, the mass of which appeared to be between Paris and Verdun (*center*). If his Sixth Army were successful, a double envelopment would complete the task. Moltke realized that the French forces around Paris had become formidable, but apparently did not know that they included the new Sixth Army. Consequently, he seems to have concluded that the troops concentrating there were merely reinforcements for the Paris garrison, and that, at any rate, Kluck should be able to deal with them until the French field armies were destroyed. But, having given Kluck this mission, he still failed to provide him with any information concerning the French forces around Paris.

Joffre still prepared for his counterattack, but there were two problems that he could not immediately solve. Kluck might once more change the direction of his advance, attempting to pass to the west of Paris, or even to advance directly against it from the north. Also, it was not yet certain that Sir John French would be able—or willing—to take part in the counterattack. Consequently, Joffre's orders of 1 and 2 September were somewhat vague. The Sixth Army was to assemble within the entrenched camp of Paris. The retirement would continue until the Fifth Army was out of immediate danger of envelopment from the west. Then the Third, Fourth, and Fifth Armies would counterattack—joined, depending on the situation at that time, by the Sixth Army and the British. The Third Army was to be reinforced by two corps drawn from the First and Second Armies, even if this meant abandoning the high ground along the Meuse south of Verdun—and the possible isolation of that fortress city. All available cavalry was to be massed on the Allied left, near Melun (*lower left*). Every effort was to be made to replace casualties.

Joffre's ideas appear to have been roughly as follows: if Kluck passed west of Paris, the British could move around Paris and meet him frontally, while the Sixth Army attacked west against his left flank; if he continued to the southeast, the Sixth Army could strike eastward against his right flank.

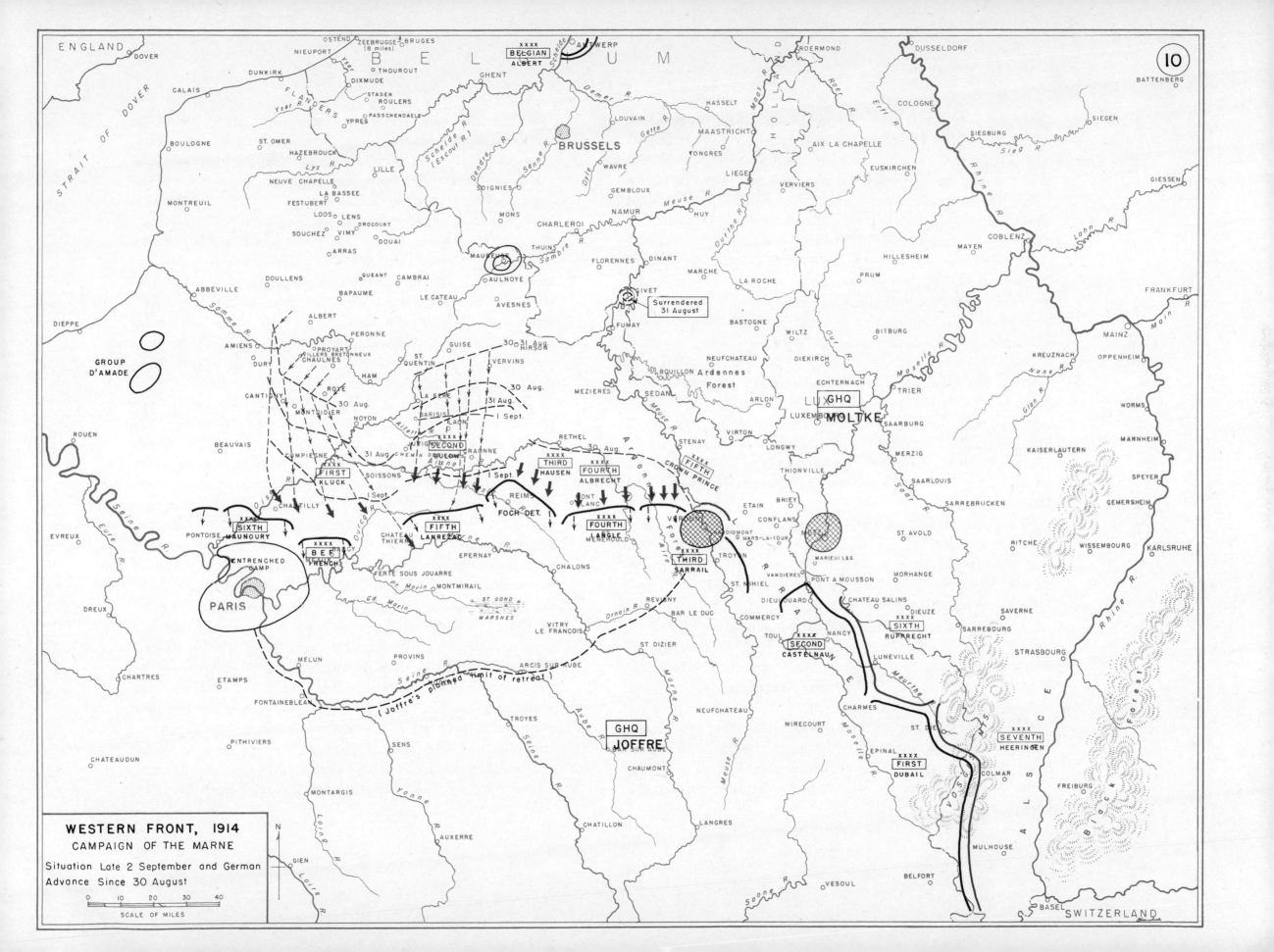

WESTERN FRONT, 1914
CAMPAIGN OF THE MARNE

Situation Late 2 September and German
Advance Since 30 August

Early on 3 September, while studying Moltke's latest order, Kluck received word that his troops had seized the Marne River bridges at Château Thierry. This news deepened Kluck's quandary; it appeared that he now had two conflicting missions. To follow Bülow "in echelon" meant that he must halt for two days, to allow Bülow to catch up; meanwhile, the French forces he was pursuing would escape or rally. On the other hand, Moltke also wanted the French driven away to the southeast of Paris. Whereas Bülow was lagging behind, Kluck—as he saw it—was ideally situated to envelop the Allied left flank. His communications with Moltke were still poor; he must make his own decision. Kluck elected to continue across the Marne.

One of Joffre's major problems was the attitude of Sir John French, who—thoroughly disillusioned with his French colleagues—was continuing his withdrawal and showing no inclination toward further combined operations. Here, however, Joffre had the complete support of Lord Kitchener, the British secretary of state for war. Alarmed by French's reports, Kitchener visited his discouraged subordinate. Thereafter, French cooperated with Joffre.

That problem solved, Joffre turned to his own armies. Their retreat had brought them nearer their depots. Troop transfers from the Lorraine front had given him numerical superiority on his left flank. Finally, Joffre had mercilessly weeded out all generals whom he considered unfit.

The large-scale troop movements required to set up Joffre's counteroffensive could not be concealed. Even Moltke recognized their implications. On 4 September, he therefore issued a new order. The German First and Second Armies were to face west and oppose any Allied attack from the Paris area. The First Army would establish a front between the Oise and Marne Rivers; the Second, between the Marne and the Seine. The Third Army would attack south toward Troyes; the Fourth and Fifth would continue driving the French forces opposing them to the southeast; the Sixth and Seventh were to attack westward "as soon as possible." Moltke had finally wrecked the Schlieffen Plan; the troops needed by his right wing were on the Lorraine front, where smaller French forces, aided by rough terrain and fortifications, could easily contain them.

In issuing this order, Moltke again included no information as to the French concentration at Paris. Kluck, insubordinately dismissing it as based on erroneous information, continued his advance. But, late on the 5th, an officer from Moltke's staff reached Kluck and explained the situation. Kluck immediately realized that he had led his army into a trap; he began planning a move back across the Marne, where he had left only his weak IV Reserve Corps (*map symbol*: IV R) under General von Gronau to cover his right flank.

Meanwhile, also on 4 September, Joffre had issued orders for his counteroffensive. It was to begin on 6 September. The French Sixth Army would attack eastward across the Ourcq River toward Château Thierry; the British would advance northeast on Montmirail; the French Fifth Army would stand ready to join this advance. Foch's new Ninth Army would cover the right flank of the Fifth, holding the line of the St. Gond Marshes; the Fourth Army would halt its withdrawal and hold in position, ready to join in the offensive; and the Third Army would attack westward. The Second and First Armies would stand fast. Joffre thus planned a double envelopment of the German right wing.

On 5 September, the French Sixth Army moved eastward into its assembly areas. Simultaneously, Gronau's IV Reserve Corps was moving south as shown across the Sixth Army's front. His cavalry reported increasing French activity to the west, but a line of wooded hills and strong French patrols blocked their efforts to obtain further information. Convinced that something important was developing on his right, Gronau made a prompt and soldierly decision. Facing his entire corps westward, he attacked, surprising and defeating the leading French divisions.

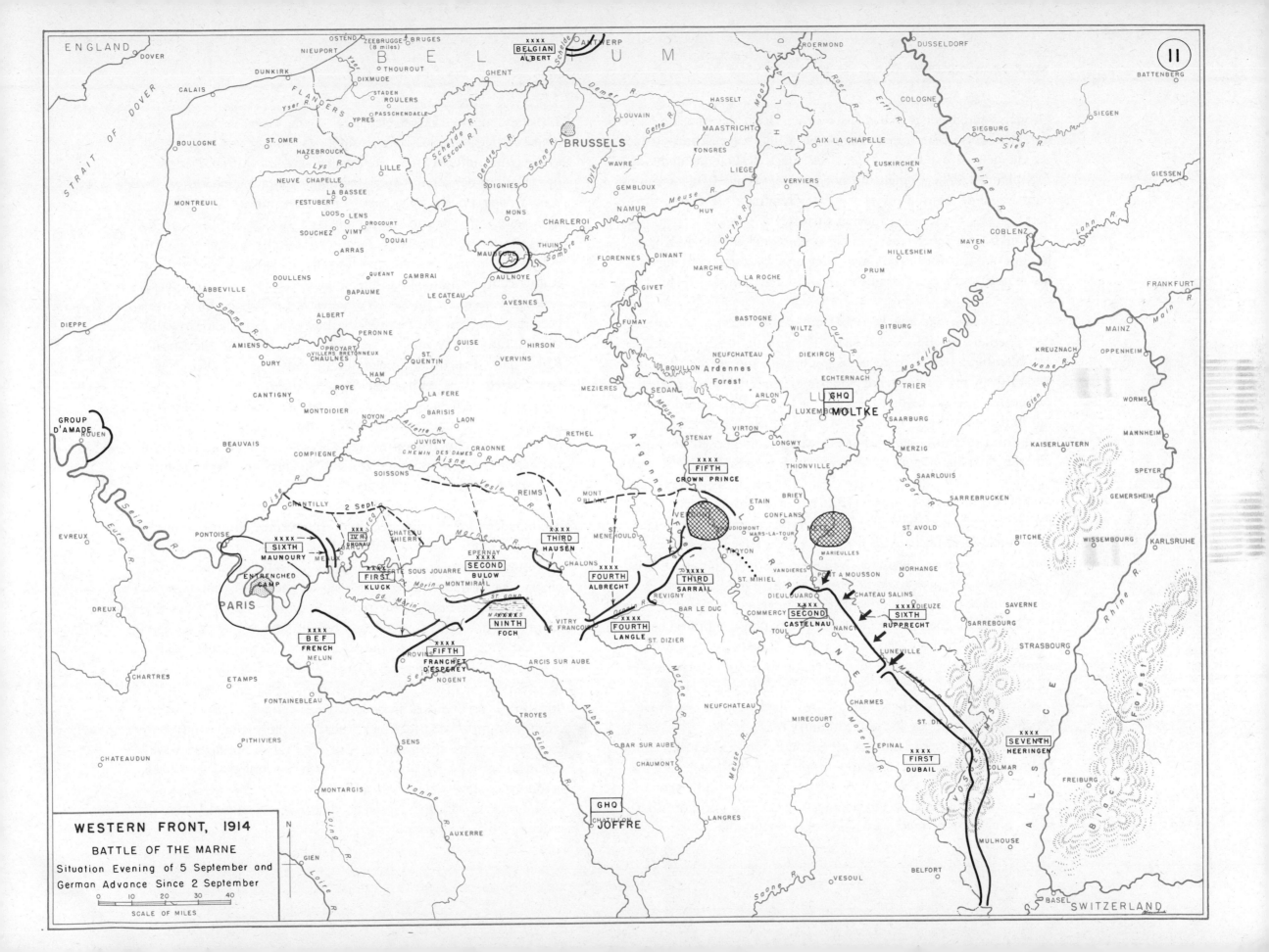

ENGLAND

BELGIUM

HOLLAND

BELGIAN
ALBERT

BRUSSELS

GROUP
D'AMADE

GHQ
MOLTKE

FIFTH
CROWN PRINCE

SIXTH
MAUNOURY

IV R.
GRONAU

THIRD
HAUSEN

SECOND
BULOW

FIRST
KLUCK

FOURTH
ALBRECHT

THIRD
SARRAIL

ENTRENCHED
CAMP

PARIS

NINTH
FOCH

FOURTH
LANGLE

SECOND
CASTELNAU

SIXTH
RUPPRECHT

BEF
FRENCH

FIFTH
FRANCHET
D'ESPEREY

SEVENTH
HEERINGEN

FIRST
DUBAIL

GHQ
JOFFRE

SWITZERLAND

WESTERN FRONT, 1914

BATTLE OF THE MARNE

Situation Evening of 5 September and
German Advance Since 2 September

0 10 20 30 40

SCALE OF MILES

Gronau's judgment matched his courage. Realizing that he had defeated only an advance guard, he withdrew eastward to a strong defensive position (*solid red line*) during the night of 5 September. The French did not pursue. About 0100, 6 September, Kluck started his II Corps to reinforce Gronau; Joffre had lost any chance of achieving surprise.

On 6 September, the French Sixth Army attacked. Kluck, hoping that this was merely a spoiling attack, designed to impede his march south, reinforced the II and IV R Corps with his IV Corps.

The British and the French Fifth Army likewise advanced on 6 September. Both—especially the British—had to make a considerable advance to regain contact with the enemy. Part of the Fifth Army encountered Kluck's III and IX Corps, which promptly attacked, halting the superior French forces until nightfall and then retiring behind the Grand Morin River. The right flank of the Fifth, meanwhile, advanced unopposed through Charleville (*lower center*), but was suddenly driven in by the German Second Army, which was attempting to carry out Moltke's order to face westward between the Marne and Seine Rivers. Bülow, however, now grew nervous about his own right flank and ordered it back of the Petit Morin River. Farther eastward, Foch—despite the defensive mission assigned him by Joffre—had moved aggressively north of the St. Gond Marshes. A skillful attack by Bülow's left wing threw him back.

On 7 September, Moltke warned Kluck that a captured copy of Joffre's orders indicated that the French Sixth Army was the major threat. Kluck thereupon ordered his III and IX Corps north of the Marne, and turned savagely on the Sixth Army. This created a gap between Kluck and Bülow, filled only by two weak German cavalry corps and some infantry rear guards.

The British were still out of contact; Moltke, Kluck, and Bülow alike considered them too crippled to constitute a serious threat. The French Fifth Army advanced slowly and overcautiously. It failed to maintain contact with Bülow's withdrawing right wing; furthermore, Foch's predicament—he was barely

withstanding attacks by elements of the German Second and Third Armies—pulled it increasingly eastward.

Having suffered from French artillery fire during 7 September, Hausen delivered a large-scale night attack at 0300 on the 8th, driving Foch's right back some three miles. But Hausen's men were too exhausted to exploit their success, and he had no reserves, having sent large forces to aid the German Fourth Army (*off map, east*). Nevertheless, Foch's position was critical. Bülow continued attacking; the counterattacks Foch continually ordered were feeble, at best. To the west, the French Fifth Army battered vainly at the Petit Morin line. The British, delayed by the skillfully led German cavalry, were still south of the Marne. Kluck had stopped the French Sixth Army, and was preparing a coordinated attack on its north flank for the 9th.

On the night of 8 September, Franchet d'Esperey launched a surprise night attack across the Petit Morin, capturing Marchais-en-Brie. Bülow thereupon pulled back his right flank, widening the gap between himself and Kluck. This probably was *the* turning point of the battle.

During 6-8 September, Moltke issued no orders; his army commanders largely ignored him. Intercepted radio messages finally gave him an inkling of the dangerous gap between Kluck and Bülow. He rose to the emergency by sending a junior staff officer, Lt. Col. Richard Hentsch, to the right-wing armies. Hentsch's exact instructions remain unknown; he did have authority—if one army were already retreating—to issue the necessary orders to coordinate the withdrawal of the others. After sending back favorable reports from the Fifth, Fourth, and Third Armies, Hentsch found Bülow personally defeated. Early on the 9th, Bülow ordered his Second Army to retreat. Hentsch acquiesced, and proceeded to Kluck's headquarters. Kluck's enveloping attack against the north flank of the French Sixth Army was advancing rapidly, but his left flank was being forced to draw back before the slow British advance across the Marne. Bülow's retreat having left the German First Army isolated, Hentsch ordered Kluck to withdraw.

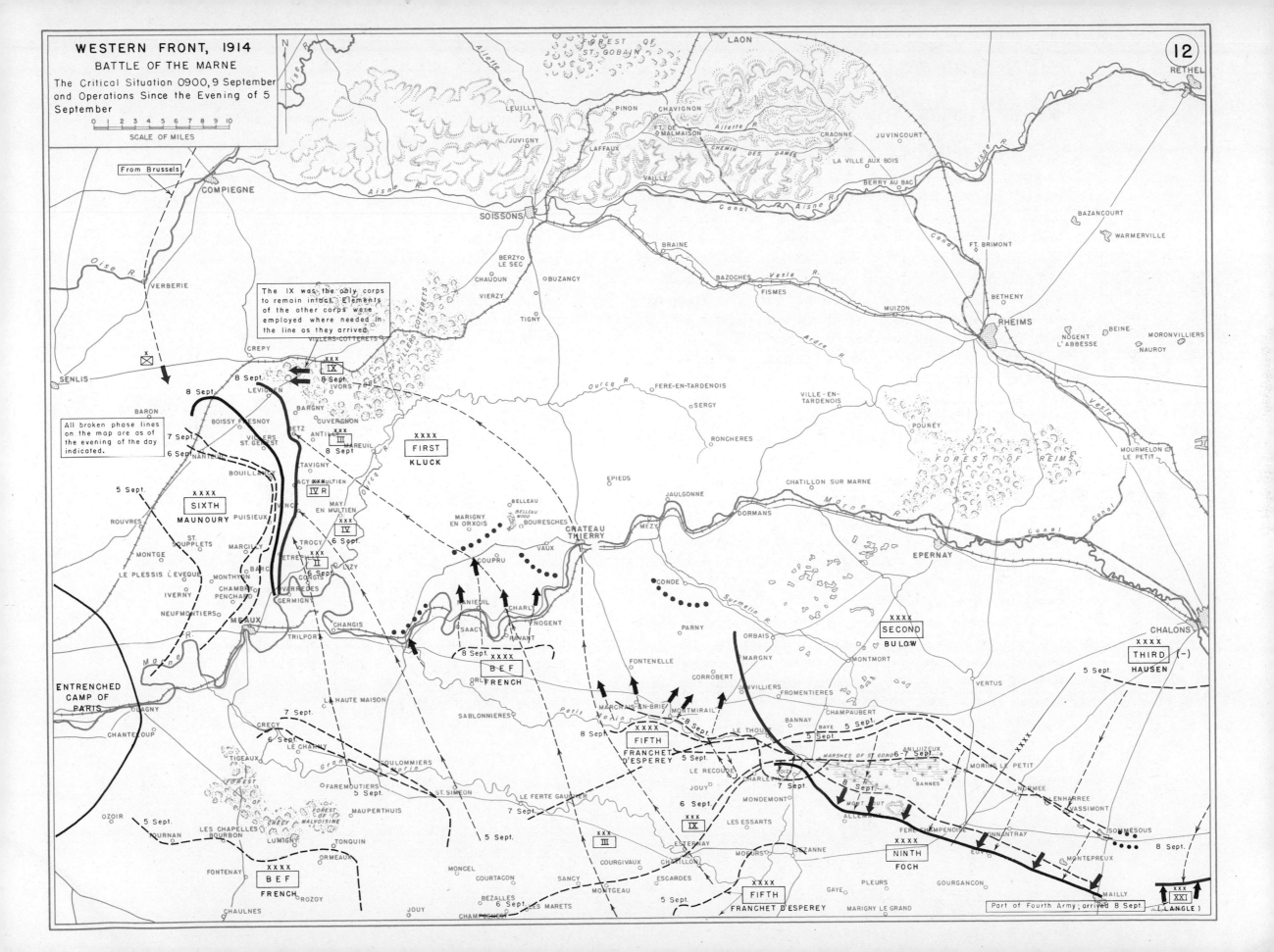

WESTERN FRONT, 1914
BATTLE OF THE MARNE
The Critical Situation 0900, 9 September
and Operations Since the Evening of 5
September

0 1 2 3 4 5 6 7 8 9 10
SCALE OF MILES

The IX was the only corps
to remain intact. Elements
of the other corps were
employed where needed in
the line as they arrived.

All broken phase lines
on the map are as of
the evening of the day
indicated.

From Brussels

COMPIEGNE

SENLIS

SOISSONS

RHEIMS

XXXX
FIRST
KLUCK

XXXX
SIXTH
MAUNOURY

XXXX
SECOND
BULOW

XXXX
THIRD (-)
HAUSEN

ENTRENCHED
CAMP OF
PARIS

MEAUX

CHATEAU
THIERRY

EPERNAY

CHALONS

XXXX
BEF
FRENCH

XXXX
FIFTH
FRANCHET
D'ESPEREY

XXXX
NINTH
FOCH

XXXX
BEF
FRENCH

XXXX
FIFTH
FRANCHET D'ESPEREY

Part of Fourth Army; arrived 8 Sept.

XXX
XXI
(LANGLE)

While the Allied armies on the left launched their highly successful counterattack at the Marne, the others turned back the German attacks on their fronts—but not without violent fighting. Hausen's Third Army had Foch's superior Ninth Army at the breaking point on 9 September (*lower center, dashed lines*), but, despite poor French tactics, Foch's fighting spirit prevented a disastrous German breakthrough. Several attacks on Verdun (*center*) by the Crown Prince failed, though the last (on 24 September) created a troublesome salient around St. Mihiel, from which German artillery could shell the main Paris-Nancy railroad. In the south, two offensives by the German Sixth and Seventh Armies failed against strong French positions—as Schlieffen had always predicted they would. Moltke then shifted the Seventh Army to the right flank.

When Hentsch returned on the afternoon of the 10th, Moltke gained his first true picture of the situation of his First and Second Armies. He ordered these—and the Third—to withdraw; the others were to hold in place. On the 11th, he made his first visit to the armies at the front. His impressions being unfavorable, he ordered a general retreat to the line Noyon-Verdun. This line was to be fortified and defended. The withdrawal was conducted with little interference from the slow and poorly directed Allied advance. By 14 September, the Germans were organizing their new positions; that same day, the Kaiser replaced Moltke with General Erich von Falkenhayn.

The German position, along the crest of the plateau about two miles north of the Aisne (*center, left*), was very strong; a series of spurs running from this high ground to the Aisne allowed them to enfilade its banks. The Allies began crossing the Aisne without serious opposition on the 13th, and on the 14th started a general advance. The main effort was made by the British in the general direction of Laon, supported by an attack of the French Fifth Army on the Craonne plateau to its front. Allied attacks continued from the 14th to the 18th, but the German

combination of field fortifications, coordinated modern firepower, and counterattacks turned back these assaults with heavy losses. It was a grim preview of the coming warfare in the West.

On the 18th, Joffre admitted a stalemate along the Aisne, and moved to envelop the German right. Falkenhayn attempted to do likewise on the Allied left. Repeated attempts (*small dated arrows*) by both the Germans and the Allies to envelop each other's north flank—known as the "Race to the Sea"—were bloody and indecisive. Eventually, the front became roughly stabilized as shown. During this maneuvering, the British were shifted from the Aisne to Flanders in the north.

Meanwhile, recognizing the Belgian Army at Antwerp (*top center*) as a possible threat to his communications, Falkenhayn had ordered the reduction of that city. Fearing that his army would be bottled up in Antwerp, King Albert withdrew westward on 6 October, accompanied by the British Naval Division which had reached Antwerp. Two other British divisions destined for Antwerp landed at Ostend and Zeebrugge (*top left*), but only in time to join the retreating Belgians. Antwerp fell on 9 October. Albert took over the Allied line north of Ypres; the British, the line from Ypres south to La Bassée.

Falkenhayn realized that any victory in the West would require a prompt attack before the Allied positions were fully organized. With the flanks on the sea, a penetration was the only recourse. The German Fourth and Sixth Armies moved north and struck the Allies on the front from the Lys River to the sea. From 12 to 20 October, the British held, but the Belgians could halt the Germans only by flooding the area from Dixmude to the sea. The Allies counterattacked from 20 to 28 October, but suffered frightfully and gained little. Falkenhayn, after careful preparations, renewed his attack on the Ypres front on the 29th, and pressed it until 11 November. At one point, he actually broke through, but was halted by the last available Allied reserves. Winter weather now set in and ended the First Battle of Ypres.

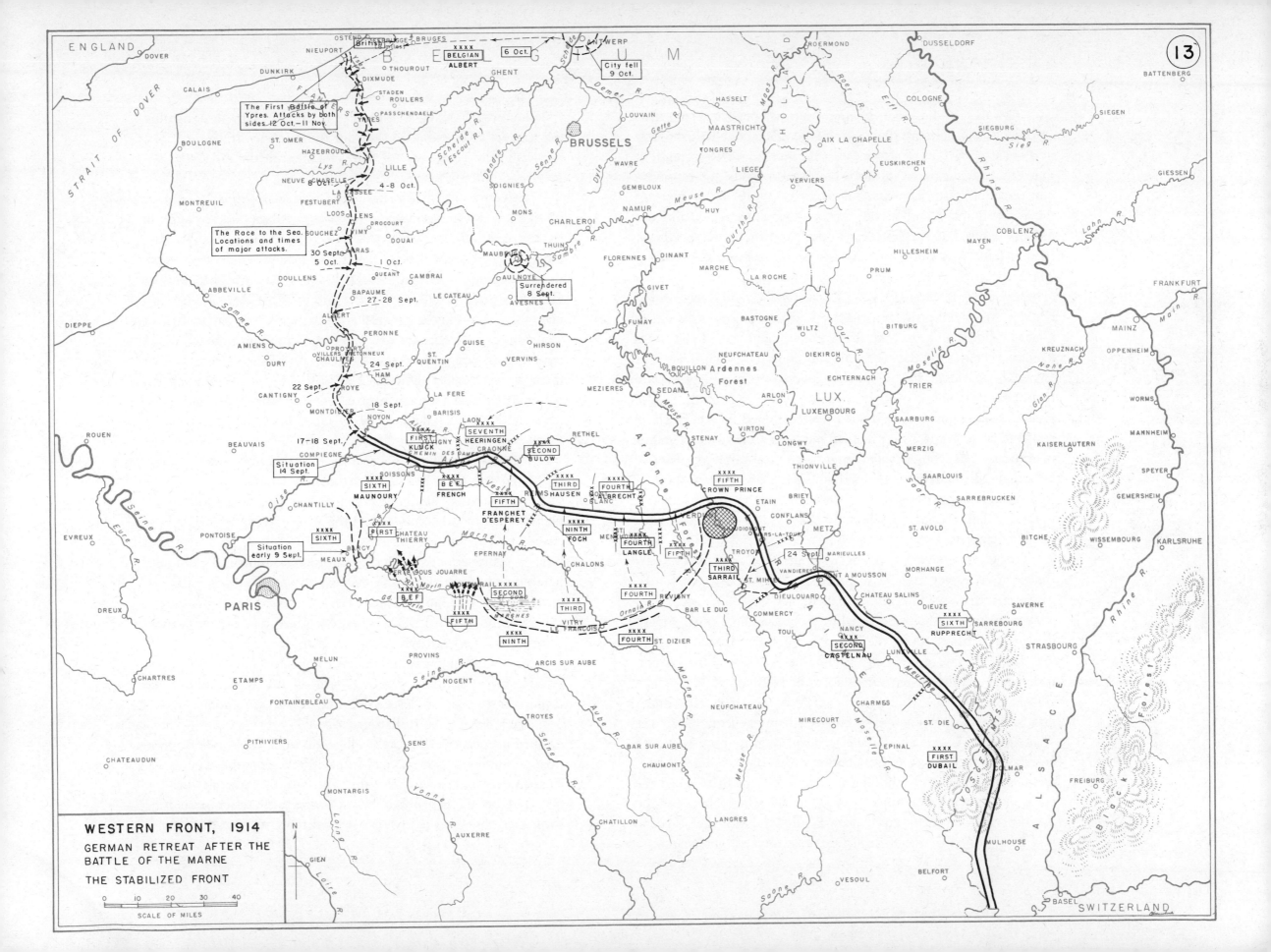

By contrast to the land fighting, naval operations in 1914 amounted to little more than cautious sparring. The British Navy in 1914 was by far the strongest in the world. Naval strength at that time was reckoned in terms of "dreadnaughts" (a relatively new type of battleship carrying eight or more heavy guns of the same caliber) and battle cruisers (warships armed like the dreadnaughts, but carrying less armor, and therefore speedier). Britain had twenty-nine of these ships to Germany's seventeen. The submarine was still an unproven weapon.

British naval strategy was simple: the Grand Fleet would be kept in the North Sea (center), where it could blockade German ports and prevent the German High Sea Fleet from leaving its bases. If the Germans did come out, they would be engaged, provided that conditions made victory nearly certain for the British. This conservative strategy was based on the simple fact that, as long as the Grand Fleet remained intact, England controlled the seas for all practical purposes, regardless of minor operations. But, should some English admiral allow the fleet to be caught divided or at a disadvantage, a good proportion of its big ships might be lost, and Germany might gain control of the seas. This would, in Churchill's words, "lose the war in a single afternoon."

The German Navy was strong, but its commanders knew that it was, as yet, unable to meet the English in open battle. Their strategy was to remain at their bases, making occasional sudden sorties in the hope of whittling away the British superiority. These bases, along the German seacoast between Holland and Denmark, were covered by mine fields, shoals, coastal batteries, and the heavily fortified island of Heligoland. The whole complex, called the "Wet Triangle," was too strong for direct attack. The Germans derived a further advantage from the Kaiser Wilhelm Ship Canal (now the Kiel Canal), through which they could shift their largest ships between the Baltic (not labeled; southeast of Sweden) and the North Sea. The British, on the other hand, were not able to get into the Baltic because the narrow channels between Denmark and Norway and Sweden had been mined by the neutral Danes as soon as war began.

The French Navy was chiefly concerned with safeguarding the transfer of colonial troops from North Africa to France. The Austrian Navy, unready for war, remained in the Adriatic (not labeled; south of Austria).

Ten German warships were caught at sea by the declaration of war. In the Mediterranean, the battle cruiser Goeben and the light cruiser Breslau escaped into the Dardanelles; Turkey, though neutral, gave them sanctuary. Besides these two ships, there were five German cruisers (under Admiral Maximilian Graf von Spee) in the Far East, one off East Africa, and two near the West Indies. These fast ships were a threat to British commerce and troop convoys from the dominions, but—in the days before long-range aircraft—the problem of intercepting them was extremely difficult. The British began by sending expeditions against German overseas naval bases in Africa. Australia and New Zealand occupied German-ruled islands in the Pacific.

When Japan entered the war in August and captured Tsingtao (right center), the German base in China, Admiral Spee sailed for South America. Detaching the Emden en route, and being joined by one cruiser from the West Indies, he reached the coast of Chile in September. On 1 November, he defeated a weaker British squadron. Receiving orders to return to Germany, he rounded Cape Horn and decided to raid the minor British base on the Falkland Islands. Here, he was intercepted by a stronger and faster British squadron. Only one of his cruisers escaped—to be destroyed later, in March, 1915.

Of the remaining cruisers, one was blockaded in an East African river, and one was destroyed off the West Indies. The Emden carried out a destructive raid across the Indian Ocean, until sunk by an Australian cruiser.

In European waters, each belligerent undertook minor operations, including two hit-and-run German bombardments of English seacoast towns. Possibly the most significant incident occurred on 22 September, when a single German submarine torpedoed three old British cruisers off the Dutch coast.

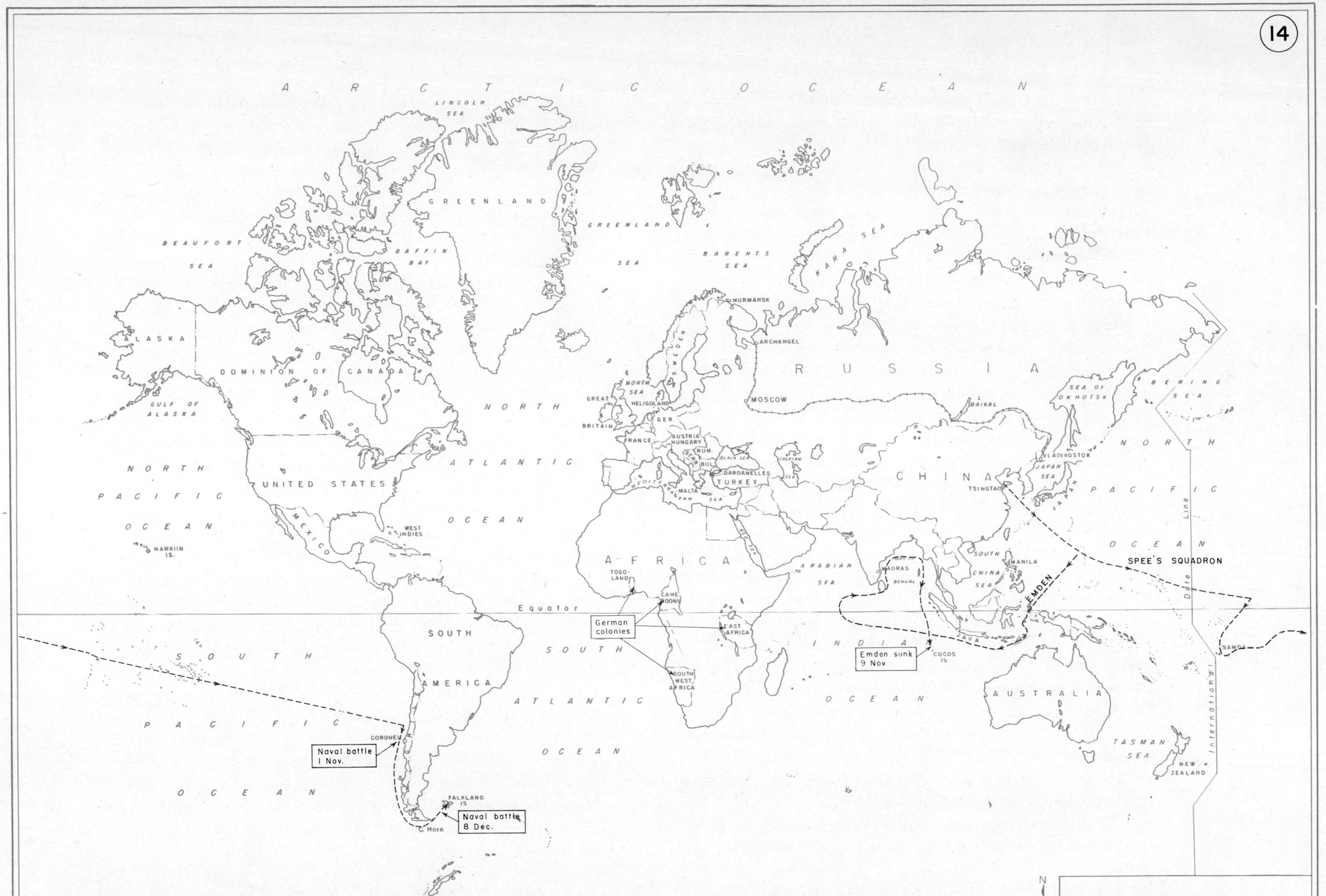

ARCTIC OCEAN

LINCOLN SEA

GREENLAND

GREENLAND

BEAUFORT SEA

BAFFIN BAY

BARENTS SEA

KARA SEA

ALASKA

DOMINION OF CANADA

GULF OF ALASKA

MURMANSK

ARCHANGEL

RUSSIA

MOSCOW

L. BAIKAL

SEA OF OKHOTSK

BERING SEA

NORTH ATLANTIC OCEAN

NORTH PACIFIC OCEAN

UNITED STATES

NORTH SEA

GREAT BRITAIN

HELIGOLAND

GER.

SWEDEN

FRANCE

AUSTRIA HUNGARY

RUM.

BLACK SEA

BUL.

MEDITERRANEAN SEA

MALTA

JAPAN

TURKEY

DARDANELLES

CASPIAN

CHINA

VLADIVOSTOK

JAPAN SEA

NORTH PACIFIC OCEAN

MEXICO

WEST INDIES

HAWAIIN IS.

AFRICA

TOGO-LAND

CAMEROONS

ARABIAN SEA

MADRAS

SOUTH CHINA SEA

MANILA

TSINGTAO

SPEE'S SQUADRON

EMDEN

Equator

German colonies

EAST AFRICA

BAY OF BENGAL

Emden sunk 9 Nov.

COCOS IS.

JAVA

International Date Line

SOUTH AMERICA

SOUTH ATLANTIC OCEAN

SOUTH WEST AFRICA

INDIAN OCEAN

AUSTRALIA

SAMOA

SOUTH PACIFIC OCEAN

CORONEL

Naval battle 1 Nov.

TASMAN SEA

NEW ZEALAND

FALKLAND IS.

Naval battle 8 Dec.

Horn

N

NAVAL OPERATIONS IN 1914

(Before studying the Tannenberg campaign, the reader should review the belligerents' war plans and the geographical considerations discussed in the text of map 3.)

By 1914, the Germans had developed an excellent system of railroads in East Prussia; the road net had also been given comparable attention. Thus, troop movements both into and within East Prussia could be made very quickly—a capability upon which German strategy in the East was largely based. On the other hand, the Russians had purposely left their communications systems near the border in an underdeveloped condition to handicap an invader. Now, this neglect was to prove a distinct disadvantage to them in their offensive operations.

Though East Prussia could be assailed from the east and the south, it held certain advantages for a defending army. The fifty-mile-long chain of lakes (the Masurian Lakes) extending from Angerburg to Johannisburg (*upper center*) formed an excellent barrier; the only major gap in the chain—at Lötzen—had been sealed by the construction of Fort Boyen. The lakes had steep, soggy, heavily wooded banks, and were patrolled by armed steamboats. From Johannisburg west, the country was thickly forested and studded with many small lakes, a condition that existed to a lesser degree as far west as Strasbourg (*lower left*). Thus, lateral communications and maneuver room for a force advancing north into the area would be severely restricted. Between Angerburg and Insterburg (*upper center*), the terrain was flat and generally open. This area, called the Insterburg Gap, afforded the best approach into East Prussia. However, the Angerapp River, which traversed its width, though fordable, could be organized into a suitable defensive position. To the west, the fortresses of Thorn (*lower left*), Graudenz, and Danzig guarded the Vistula. In the north was the fortress of Königsberg, protected further by an extensive fortified area.

The Russian preference in initial operations was to follow the general outline of their defensive Plan G—to defend, and retire if necessary, until sufficient strength for a counteroffensive could be marshaled. However, since 1910, the French had been exerting pressure on their ally to take the offensive against Germany immediately upon the outbreak of war. The Russians finally succumbed to this insistence—much to their regret. Now, the French pleaded for an attack in the direction of Posen (*off map, southwest*). General Januschkevitch, the Russian chief of staff, planned to make this attack with a new army to be formed at Warsaw. But General Jilinsky, commander of the Northwest Army Group (First and Second Armies), convinced him of Russian inability to mobilize and supply this army quickly enough. He suggested instead, that his group launch a converging attack on East Prussia from the east and southeast. Both commanders were aware that only one-third of the total Russian forces would be mobilized by 14 August, and that the logistical support necessary for the advance was not available. Nevertheless, so strong was the pressure from France that the advance was ordered on the 13th. By the 17th, it had progressed as shown.

German General Max von Prittwitz arrived at his headquarters near Allenstein (*center*) on 8 August, and ordered his four corps disposed as shown (*four large red circles*). He had authority to withdraw to the Vistula, if necessary, but he also knew that his superiors expected him to make use of the terrain and railroads to mass his strength against first one and then the other of the anticipated Russian advances. Prittwitz was well informed as to Jilinsky's movements, through spies and intercepted radio messages. He decided, on the 14th, to leave the XX Corps at Allenstein, to protect the south flank, while he moved to defeat the Russian First Army; then he would turn south to oppose the Second. However, he did not know that his fiery I Corps commander, General Hermann K. von Francois, had exceeded his orders and moved forward to Stallupönen (*upper right*), where he was about to plunge the army into battle earlier than expected.

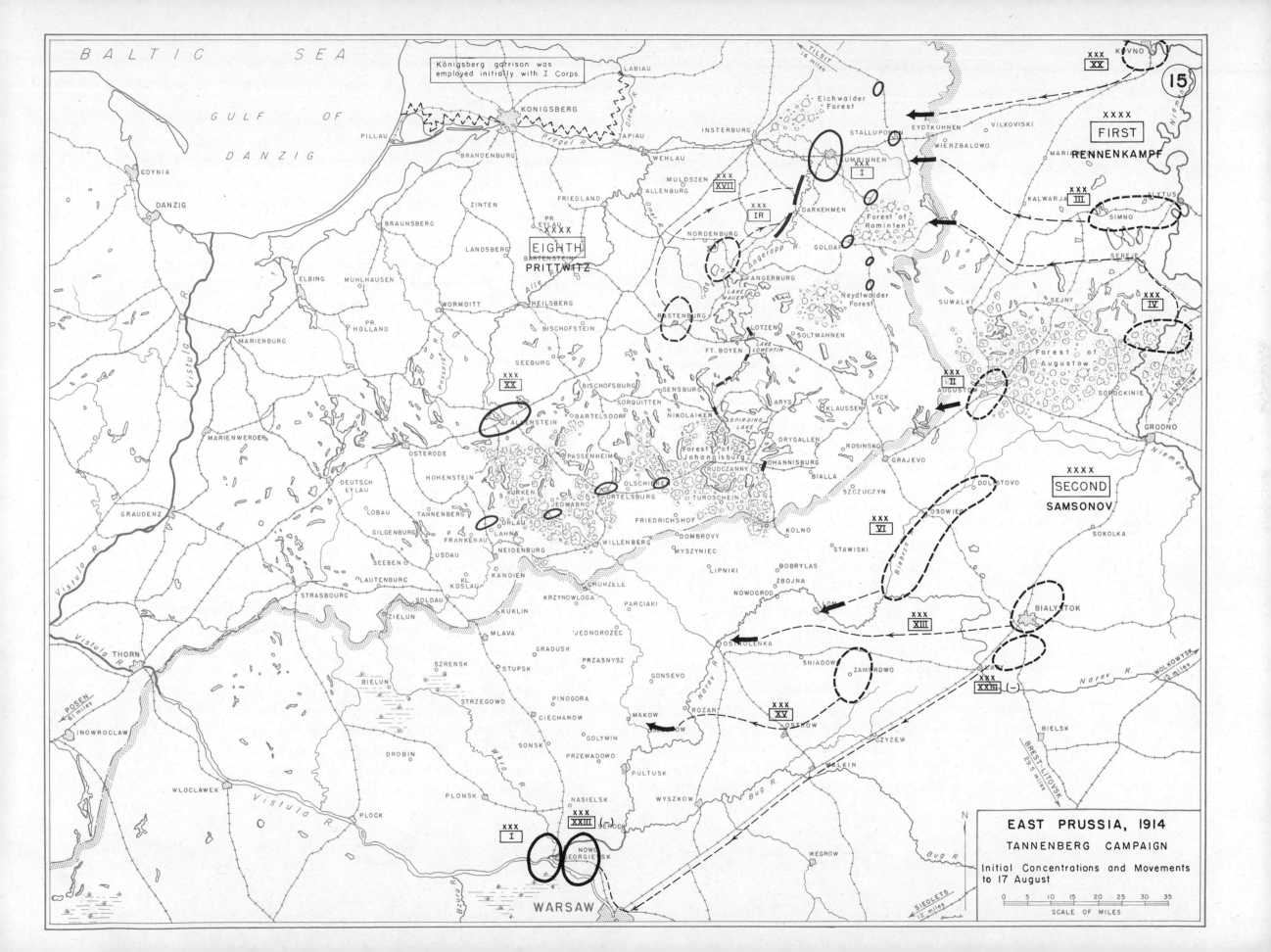

EAST PRUSSIA, 1914

TANNENBERG CAMPAIGN

Initial Concentrations and Movements
to 17 August

General Paul V. Rennenkampf's First Army crossed the East Prussian border on 17 August (*sketch* a). There was a notable lack of liaison between the various columns, no cavalry screen to the front, and—worst of all—a sizable gap between the III and IV Corps. Furthermore, Rennenkampf, completely uninformed as to German dispositions, had not weighted his north flank in compliance with his orders to drive Prittwitz away from Königsberg (*off map, west*). Plainly, he did not expect much opposition until the army reached the Angerapp River (*left center*). He knew that his army was several days in advance of the Second Army and that if trouble developed, General Alexander V. Samsonov could probably not provide assistance before the 22d. Jilinsky, too, had been aware of this fact, but had still ordered the advance. He expected the First Army to entice the Germans eastward while Samsonov got astride their rear.

On the German side, the headstrong Francois—unable to condone Russian violation of Prussia's "sacred soil"—had insubordinately disposed his I Corps well to the east of Gumbinnen (*left center*). His tactical dispositions were good—each of his forward elements was a balanced force, in constant communication with Francois' headquarters in Gumbinnen. But his aggressive intentions were in direct disobedience of Prittwitz's orders. Prittwitz intended to fight to the west (at the Angerapp River); Francois clearly planned to fight at the border. Thus, when the Russian III Corps struck his detachment at Goritten, he immediately reinforced it and launched a counterstroke. Then the detachment commander at Tollmingkehmen moved the bulk of his force north and took the enemy III Corps in the rear. The Russian force suffered 3,000 casualties, became disorganized, and withdrew to the frontier. That night, 17 August, Francois withdrew his corps to Gumbinnen. His impetuous attack was tactically commendable but strategically deplorable, for he had upset the finely balanced German strategy. Time was important to Prittwitz: he had only about five days to dispose of Rennen-

kampf before it would be necessary to move south to face Samsonov. By his action, Francois had retarded the Russian advance to the contemplated battlefield at the Angerapp. It now appeared that the Eighth Army might be forced to advance eastward in order to fight the decisive action.

But Rennenkampf rectified the German error by continuing his advance the next two days—still without an adequate screen to his front—believing that his enemy's main force was well to the west. The dispositions of the opposing forces on the night of 19 August were as shown (*sketch* b, *dashed lines*). Francois continued to urge his chief to attack Rennenkampf to the east of the Angerapp. German cavalry successes on the 18th and 19th, and Rennenkampf's order to halt on the 20th—sent by radio in the clear and intercepted by the Germans—reinforced his argument. Prittwitz finally succumbed and—in spite of the protests of his capable operations officer, Lt. Col. Max Hoffman—ordered an attack for 20 August. Hoffman did not oppose the idea of an attack; his concern was to allow time for the I R and XVII Corps to move forward so that a coordinated attack, in full strength, could be made.

Hoffman's fears were realized. The German attack on the 20th was made piecemeal and was successful only in the north. There, the I Corps attacked at 0400, achieved surprise, and forced the Russian XX Corps back five miles. This was followed by a cavalry attack which created panic among the Russian transport at Schwirgallen (*top right*). But the XVII and I R Corps, having marched all night, arrived tired and disorganized. At 0800, the XVII Corps attacked frontally, piecemeal, and without an artillery preparation; it encountered an entrenched foe and was driven back in complete disorder. The attack of the I R Corps at noon was also repulsed. The battle might be called a draw, but Prittwitz's immediate need was for a decisive victory. He was now faced with a major decision: should he renew the attack or withdraw?

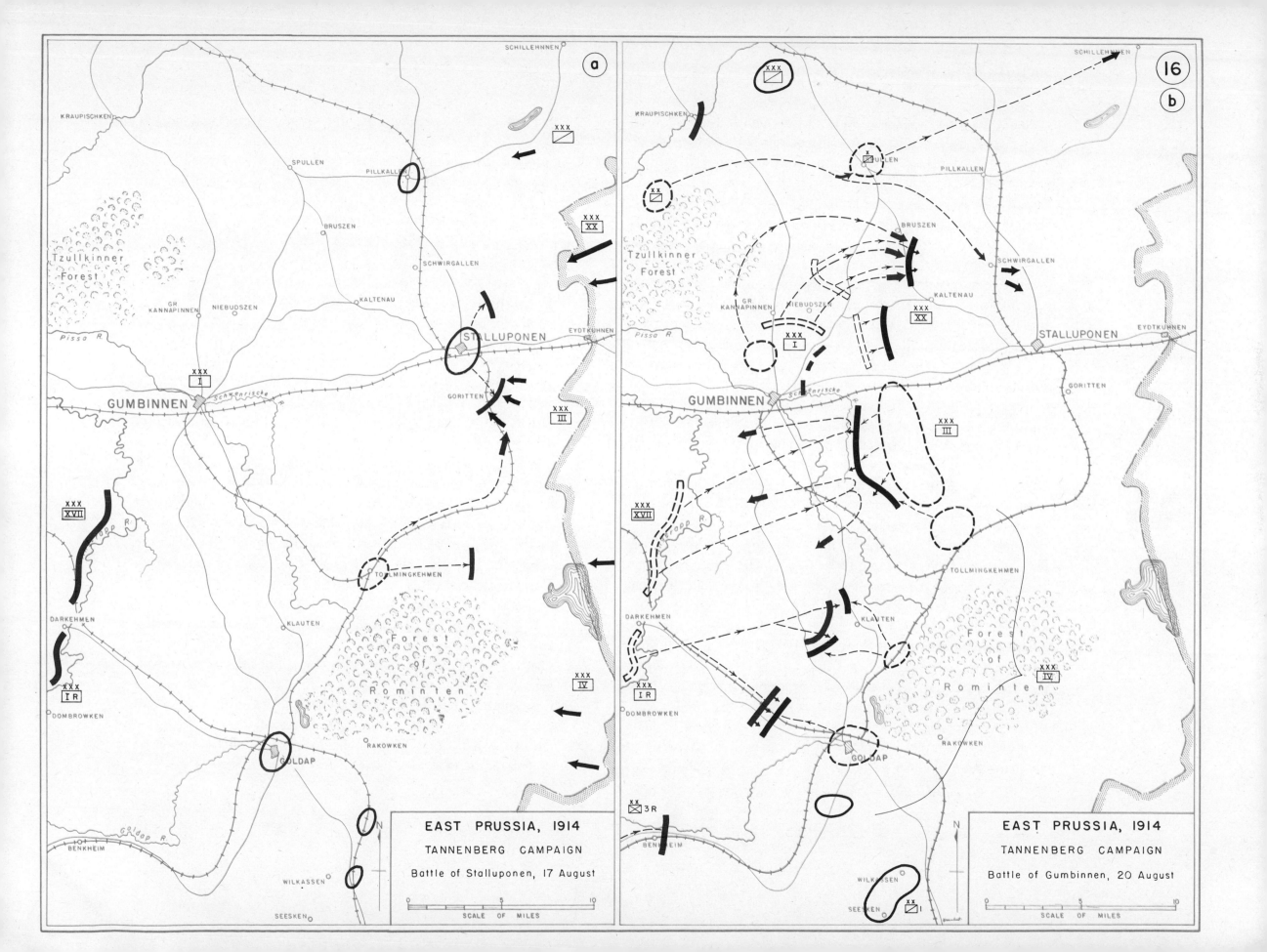

EAST PRUSSIA, 1914

TANNENBERG CAMPAIGN

Battle of Stalluponen, 17 August

EAST PRUSSIA, 1914

TANNENBERG CAMPAIGN

Battle of Gumbinnen, 20 August

SCALE OF MILES

SCALE OF MILES

Prittwitz, at his headquarters some seventy miles west of Gumbinnen, had no firsthand knowledge of the battle fought there. The rout of General August von Mackensen's XVII Corps weighed heavily on his mind, and served to confirm his apprehension that he had extended his left too far. At 1730, 20 August, he received news that Samsonov's Second Army had crossed the border that day. It seemed that all his fears were being realized. Despair and panic now seized the Eighth Army commander. Without consulting his staff, he telephoned Moltke at Coblenz and informed him that the Eighth Army would retreat to the Vistula and that he doubted his ability to hold even that river line unless reinforced.

Moltke's reaction was immediate. The weak-willed Prittwitz was relieved, and General Paul von Hindenburg (called from retirement) was placed in command. General Erich von Ludendorff, the hero of Liége, was appointed his chief of staff. By 1400, 23 August, they had arrived at Marienburg (*upper left*) to be met and briefed on events by the Eighth Army staff.

In the meantime, Hoffman was aghast when Prittwitz informed him of the planned withdrawal. He pointed out that Samsonov was already eighty miles closer to the Vistula than the bulk of the Eighth Army. Unable to convince Prittwitz, he did sway the Eighth Army chief of staff, who finally obtained Prittwitz's approval for a shift of the army to the south to fight Samsonov. No one informed Moltke of this new offensive concept. He fully expected the Eighth Army to withdraw to the Vistula, but hoped Hindenburg could breathe new life into it. Also, under the mistaken belief that affairs were going well on the Western Front, he decided to withdraw some troops from there to bolster the Eastern Front.

At Marienburg, on 23 August, Hoffman explained his plan to Hindenburg and Ludendorff; they approved it. Actually, it had been put into effect during the night of the 20th. The I Corps and 3 R Division were now en route by rail to reinforce the XX Corps. The XVII and I R Corps were moving westward, and were to turn south if Rennenkampf showed no inclination to press the advance. Only the 1st Cavalry Division and the garrison brigade assigned to the lake region remained to delay Rennenkampf. The Russian commander had not moved for sixty hours, and only now, on the 23d, did he resume his dawdling advance.

To the south, Samsonov had not moved much farther from 20 to 23 August. The inadequate railroad and road nets had begun to break down, and his hastily improvised system of logistical support had failed completely. He had been ordered by Jilinsky to move north to the line Passenheim-Rudczanny (*center*), but had decided that an advance to the northwest would be more likely to intercept the Germans. He had ordered that the line Soldau-Ortelsburg (*center, line of blue arrowheads*) be reached by the 23d, and his orders, uncoded and broadcast in the clear, had been heard by the Germans. There now followed a controversy between Jilinsky and Samsonov as to the direction of advance of the Second Army. The latter finally compromised and ordered seizure of the line Hohenstein-Sorquitten (*center*) by the 25th, while the I Corps remained at Soldau to protect the left flank. This line was in the general direction of Samsonov's movement, but farther to the east.

Samsonov advanced his army—as Rennenkampf had—without cavalry to the front. On 24 August, his XV Corps ran directly into the entrenched German XX Corps. It was somewhat of a surprise, for the Germans were presumed to be fleeing westward. The XV Corps moved clumsily to the attack; severe fighting raged all day, but the XX Corps could not be dislodged. Meanwhile, Samsonov made no effort to bring adjacent corps to the aid of the XV Corps. That night, his radio publicly announced that the 25th would be a day of rest for his troops.

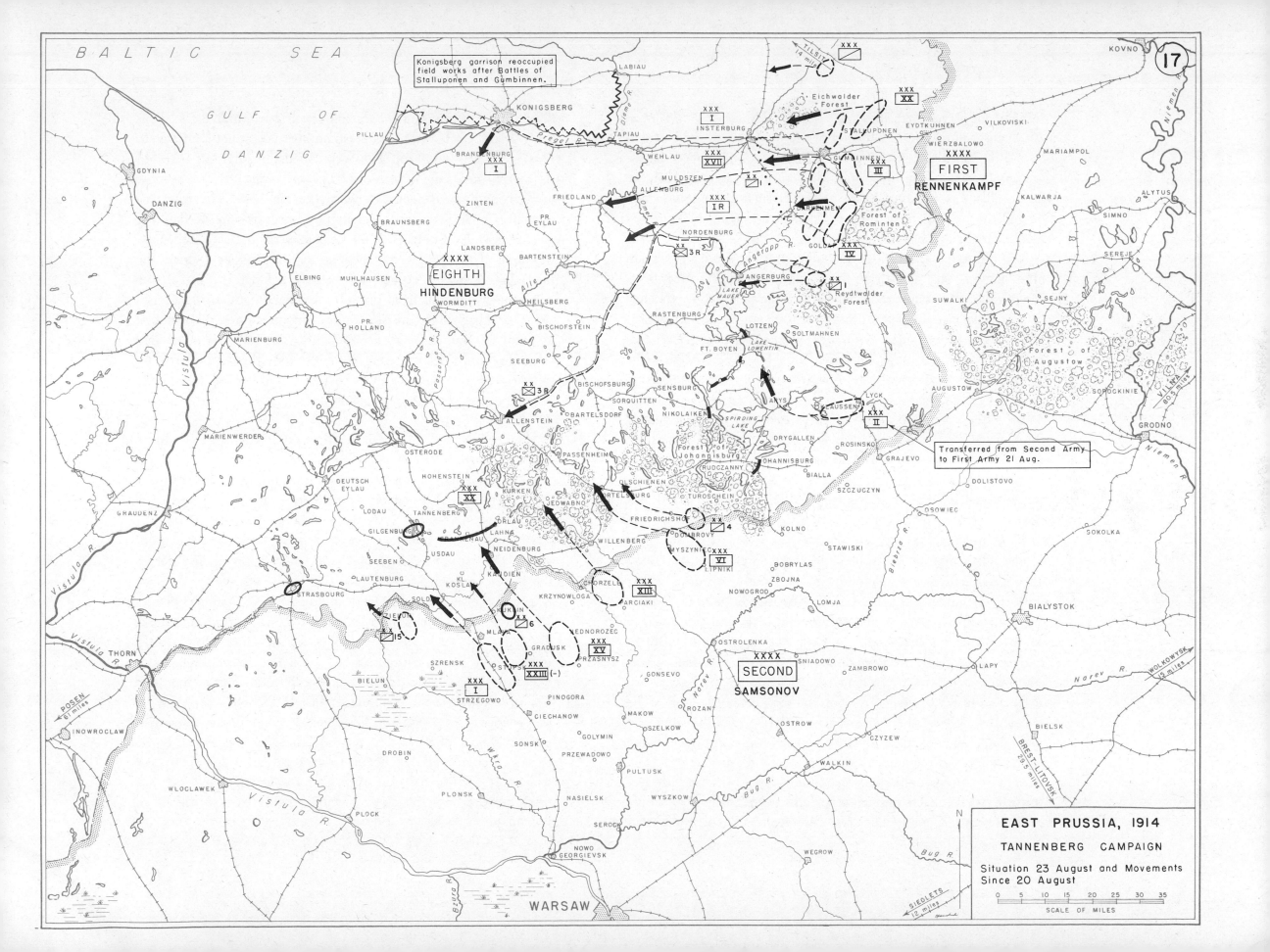

EAST PRUSSIA, 1914

TANNENBERG CAMPAIGN

Situation 23 August and Movements
Since 20 August

Rennenkampf reached the line shown (*dashed blue line*) on 25 August, all the while unaware of the weakness of the German opposition on his front. That day, his radio announced his intention to reach a line through Allenburg by the night of the 26th. This was welcome news to the Germans, for it now appeared they would have time to concentrate against Samsonov before Rennenkampf could interfere.

To the south, the XX Corps had withdrawn from Frankenau after the fight on the 24th, to the position shown at Tannenberg. Meanwhile, Samsonov received permission to move to the line Osterode-Allenstein, but Jilinsky insisted that the VI Corps and a cavalry division move to the Bischofsburg-Sensburg area (*center*) to protect the right flank. Thus, by late 25 August, the Second Army was spread along a seventy-mile arc from Zielun (*lower left*) to Sensburg, with a corps isolated on each flank. Samsonov's orders had also been broadcast, so that, on the 25th, the Germans knew the future plans of both Russian armies.

While the Russians blundered along the road to catastrophe, Ludendorff was busily making plans. On 23 August, the I Corps was ordered to detrain at Deutsch Eylau (*lower left*) and take position on the right of the XX Corps; the 3 R Division was ordered to move to the left of the XX Corps. On the night of the 24th—before learning of Rennenkampf's proposed slow advance—Hindenburg made the momentous decision to leave only the 1st Cavalry Division and a garrison brigade in front of the Russian First Army, and to move the I R and XVII Corps south to attack the Russian VI Corps at Bischofsburg. But he had no assurance that Rennenkampf would not suddenly veer southward against the German rear. (Actually, there was little to fear. Jilinsky, instead of coordinating the operations of his two armies against the German Eighth Army, would order Rennenkampf, on the 26th, to move directly west with half of his army, while the remainder laid siege to Königsberg.)

On 26 August, one division of the Russian VI Corps moved toward Allenstein, while the other advanced north of Bischofsburg. The 4th Cavalry Division was fifteen miles to the east at Sensburg. The division advancing north encountered Mackensen's XVII Corps and, underestimating its strength, attacked. It was severely repulsed. The second Russian division reversed its march and sought to assist. The German I R Corps now arrived, and the Russian VI Corps fled in rout. The way was open for a German envelopment of Samsonov's north flank.

Meanwhile, Francois' I Corps had arrived near Seeben by the night of the 25th. Ordered to attack the Russian I Corps the next day, Francois argued vehemently against the attack because he would not have his full complement of artillery until the 27th. Hindenburg insisted, and Francois launched the attack as planned—but not very energetically. The advance succeeded in taking only Seeben. On the 26th, too, the XX Corps repulsed strong attacks by the XV Corps, and even forced the XXIII Corps to withdraw somewhat.

Two matters require clarification: the Russian radio difficulties and the German command system.

The explanation for the Russian radio broadcasts in the clear seems to lie in a lack of properly trained code and communications personnel. Since the Russians advanced before they were ready, only sufficient telephone wire for communications within the corps was available—and this was frequently cut by the East Prussians almost as soon as it was installed.

Above, we say: "Ludendorff was busily making plans." Hindenburg, the commander, might have been expected to make the plans. However, since the days of the elder Von Moltke (1870), the German practice had been for the commander to make the broad basic decision, the staff to develop a plan, and the subordinate field commanders to then fight the battle in accordance with the plan. The over-all commander frequently exercised no battlefield direction. As the war progresses, it will be seen that Ludendorff begins to exercise more and more control on the battlefield; but even he leans heavily on a detailed plan prepared by the staff, which is held to as firmly as is practicable.

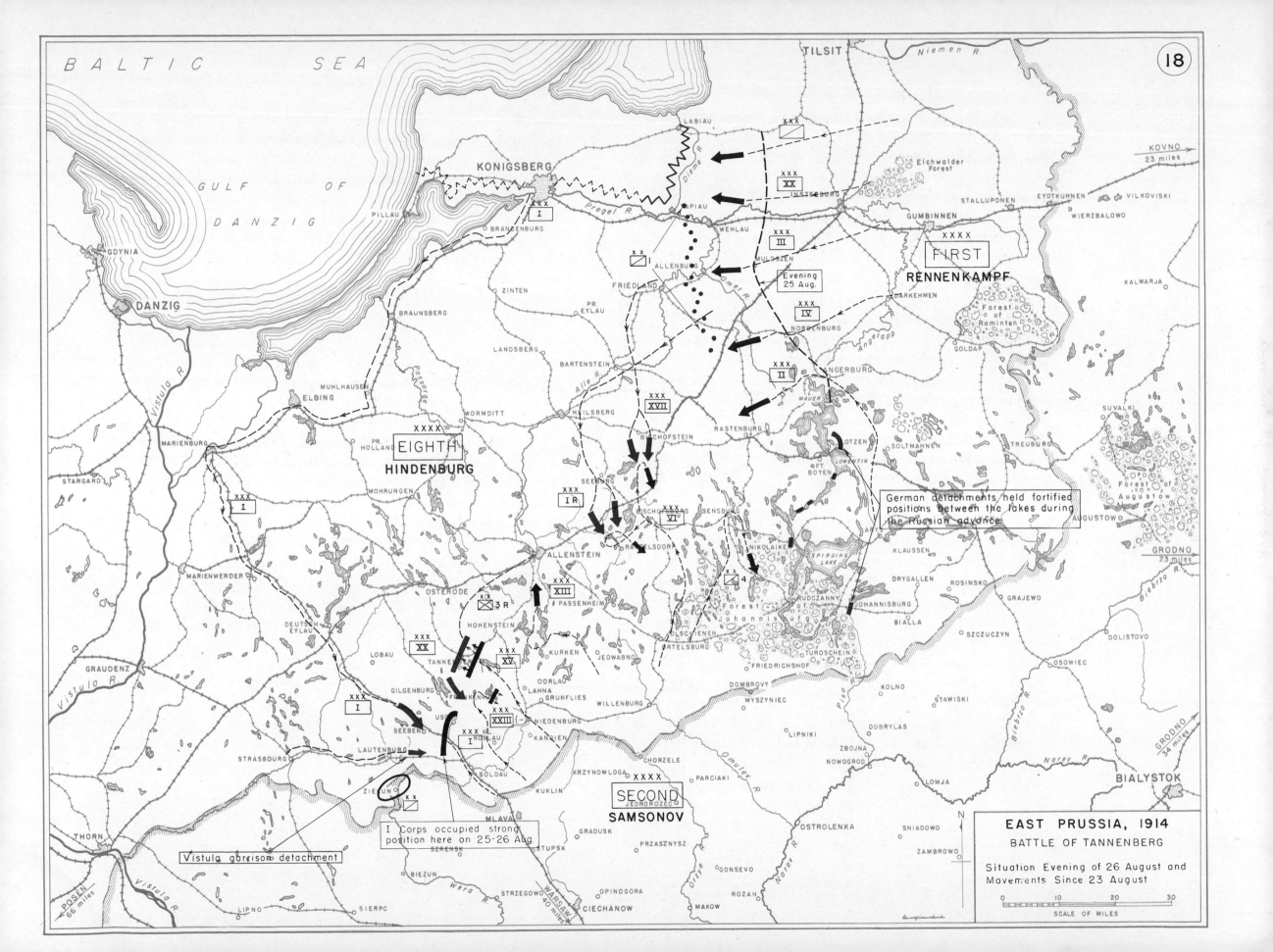

BALTIC SEA

TILSIT

Niemen R.

KOVNO
23 miles

GULF OF DANZIG

KONIGSBERG

LABIAU

XXX

XXX
XX
INSTERBURG

STALLUPONEN

GUMBINNEN

EYDTKUHNEN

VILKOVISKI

WIERZBALOWO

Eichwalder Forest

PILLAU

BRANDENBURG

Pregel R.

WEHLAU

XXX
III

MULDSZEN

XXXX
FIRST
RENNENKAMPF

KALWARJA

DANZIG

BRAUNSBERG

ZINTEN

PR. EYLAU

FRIEDLAND

ALLENBURG

Evening
25 Aug.

DARKEHMEN

Forest
of
Rominten

GDYNIA

XXX
IV

NORDENBURG

GOLDAP

STARGARD

MUHLHAUSEN
ELBING

Passarge R.

LANDSBERG

BARTENSTEIN

Alle R.

HEILSBERG

XXX
XVII

ANGERBURG

Angerapp R.

RASTENBURG

MAUER

SUVALKI

Forest
of
Augustow

MARIENBURG

Vistula R.

PR. HOLLAND

XXXX
EIGHTH
HINDENBURG

WORMDITT

BISCHOFSTEIN

MAUER

FT. BOYEN

LOWENTIN

SOLTMAHNEN

TREUBURG

AUGUSTOW

German detachments held fortified
positions between the lakes during
the Russian advance

GRODNO
23 miles

MOHRUNGEN

SEEBURG

XXX
I R

BISCHOFSBURG

XXX
VI

SENSBURG

NIKOLAIKEN

SPIRDING
LAKE

KLAUSSEN

DRYGALLEN

ROSINSKO

GRAJEWO

DOLISTOVO

MARIENWERDER

ALLENSTEIN

XXX
XIII

XX
4

Forest
of
Johannisburg

RUDCZANNY

JOHANNISBURG

GRAUDENZ

Vistula R.

OSTERODE

XX
3 R

PASSENHEIM

OLSCHIENEN

ORTELSBURG

FRIEDRICHSHOF

TUROSCHEIN

BIALLA

SZCZUCZYN

OSOWIEC

DEUTSCH
EYLAU

HOHENSTEIN

XXX
XX

TANNEN...

XXX
XV

KURKEN

JEDWABNO

DOMBROVY

MYSZYNIEC

KOLNO

STAWISKI

Biebrza R.

LOBAU

GILGENBURG

FRANKENAU

OORLAU

LAHNA

GRUNFLIES

WILLENBURG

Piso R.

LIPNIKI

ZBOJNA

DOBRYLAS

GRODNO
34 miles

Narev R.

BIALYSTOK

XXX
I

SEEBEN

USD...

XXX
XXIII (-)

NIEDENBURG

XXX KL
KOSLAU

XXX
I

KANDIEN

CHORZELE

KRZYNOWLOGA

PARCIAKI

NOWOGROD

LOMJA

ZAMBROWO

STRASBOURG

LAUTENBURG

Vistula garrison detachment

ZIELUNG

XX

SOLDAU

KUKLIN

XXXX
SECOND
JEDNOROZEC
SAMSONOV

Omulev R.

Orzye R.

Narev R.

PRZASNYSZ

SNIADOWO

OSTROLENKA

MAKOW

ROZAN

THORN

I Corps occupied strong
position here on 25-26 Aug.

MLAVA

SZRENSK

STUPSK

BIEZUN

GRADUSK

OPINOGORA

CIECHANOW

GONSEVO

OSTROLENKA

N

EAST PRUSSIA, 1914
BATTLE OF TANNENBERG

Situation Evening of 26 August and
Movements Since 23 August

POSEN
66 miles

Vistula R.

LIPNO

SIERPC

Wkra R.

STRZEGOWO

WARSAW
40 miles

0   10   20   30
SCALE OF MILES

The remnants of the fleeing Russian VI Corps (*dashed blue oval*) arrived south of Ortelsburg by nightfall, 27 August; the next day, they withdrew across the border. Had Ludendorff permitted the XVII and I R Corps to pursue, it is likely that none of the VI Corps could have escaped destruction or capture. But the chief of staff was worried about Rennenkampf, and ordered the victorious corps to move toward Allenstein (*center*) on the 27th, in order to protect the left flank of the XX Corps. On the 28th, he regained his confidence and directed Mackensen to march his XVII Corps to Jedwabno.

If Francois lacked enthusiasm in his attack on the 26th, he was in deadly earnest on the 27th. Reinforced by troops and heavy artillery from the Thorn fortress (*bottom left*), he delivered a devastating artillery bombardment on the poorly prepared enemy trenches. The Russian I Corps suffered heavy casualties, broke under the weight of the artillery fire alone, and fled. That night, thoroughly disorganized and beaten, it retired south through Soldau, thus exposing the left flank of the Russian center.

About noon on the 27th, Samsonov had finally learned of the disastrous defeat of his VI Corps, and the following morning he was informed of the withdrawal of his I Corps. But he apparently failed to appreciate the great peril now facing his center, for he ordered a continuation of the attack on the 28th. Fatalistically accepting the earlier reverses, he rode forward to the XV Corps area, expecting the tide to turn. The XIII Corps had reached Allenstein on the 27th, but before it could return to join the XV Corps in the attack, the German XX Corps—reinforced by the 3 R Division and a fortress division from the Vistula—launched an attack on the XV Corps that forced it to withdraw. By the morning of the 29th, the withdrawal had become general. During the day, confusion set in, and the retreat became disorganized as the Germans forced the three Russian corps into an ever-shrinking pocket.

Meanwhile, to the south, the advance elements of Francois' I Corps had reached Niedenburg on 28 August. There, he re-ceived orders from Ludendorff directing him to turn north to aid the XX Corps. Seeing that Russian resistance was collapsing, the intractable Francois ignored the order and drove eastward. By nightfall, he had formed a thin line of pickets—twenty-five battalions stretched over thirty-seven miles—blocking the Russian southern escape route. Had he moved north from Niedenburg, as Ludendorff had directed, the result would have been a shallow envelopment and the likely escape of large bodies of enemy troops.

On the 30th and 31st, the now thoroughly confused Russians strove to break through Francois' line, but were turned back in every instance. The Russian I Corps launched a relieving attack and succeeded in taking Niedenburg on 30 August, but Francois' countermeasures forced evacuation of the town the following day. (Fortunately for Francois, his independent exploits had all turned out well.) On the 31st, the Russians succumbed to the inevitable. The Germans captured 125,000 men and 500 guns; their own losses were between 10,000 and 15,000 for the entire campaign. Accurate figures on Russians killed and wounded are not available. The despondent Samsonov took his own life, deep in the forest.

Not until the 27th had Jilinsky ordered Rennenkampf to come to the aid of the Second Army. But by then it was too late, for, on the 30th, having reached the positions shown, Rennenkampf learned of Samsonov's defeat and turned back.

The Tannenberg campaign had ended in a dazzling German triumph, but since Rennenkampf's army was still intact, it was not decisive. A well-led German force, making excellent use of a central position, had defeated a greatly superior but poorly led Russian force. The resolute and bold handling of the German troops was the chief factor in the ultimate victory. Lack of intelligence, violations of communications security, slowness, indecision at high levels, and inadequate logistical support had all contributed to the Russian debacle.

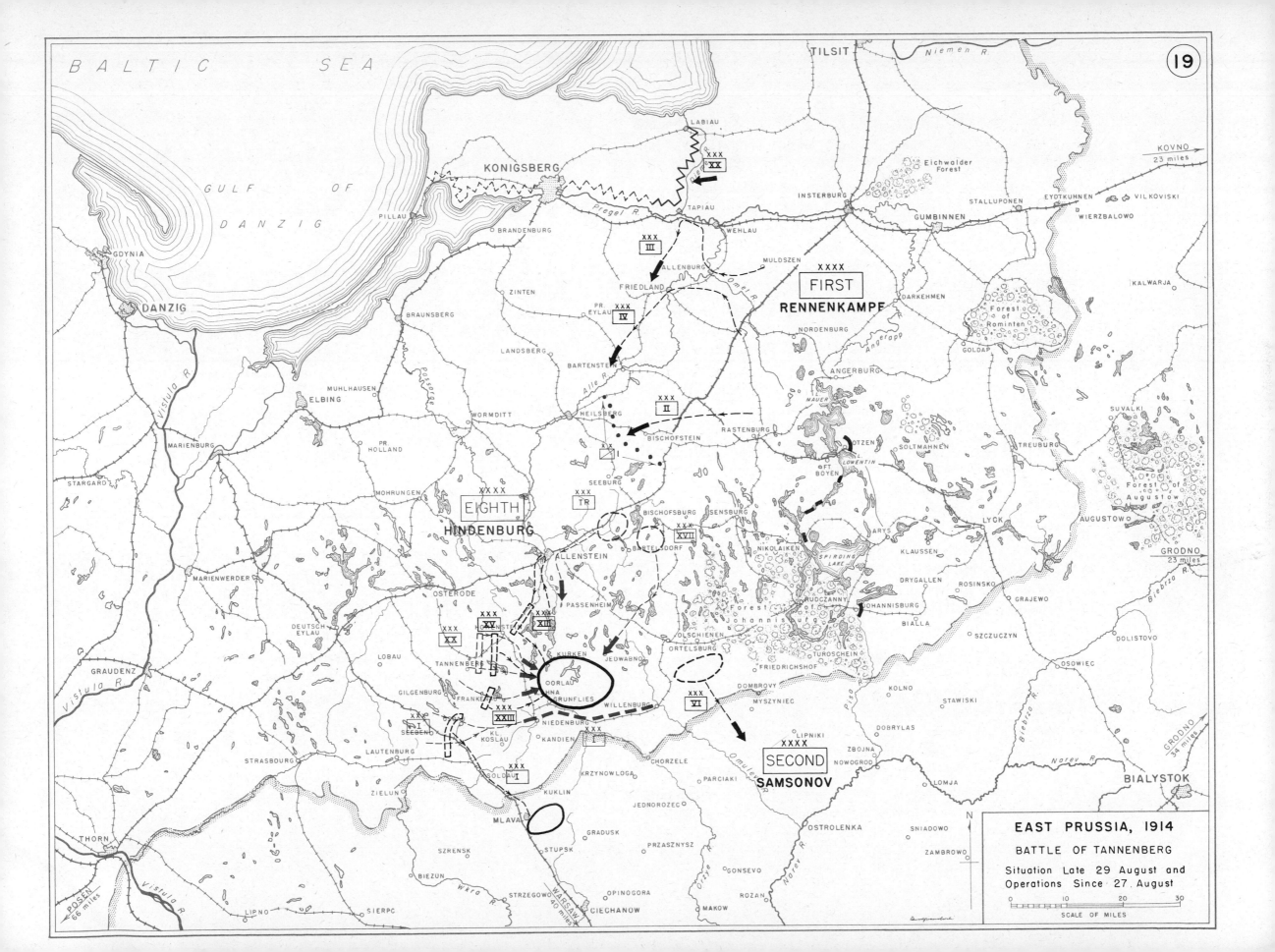

Having eliminated Samsonov's Second Army, the Hindenburg-Ludendorff team immediately and earnestly went about the task of disposing of Rennenkampf's First Army. For this endeavor, the Eighth Army was stronger than heretofore, having been reinforced on 2 September by the XI and Guard Reserve Corps and the 8th Cavalry Division from the Western Front. It was noted earlier that these units—and a third corps, later withheld—had been designated for movement eastward when Moltke received Prittwitz's call for aid on 20 August. On the 27th, Ludendorff had informed the German GHQ that the reinforcements were not essential; nevertheless, they were dispatched. Thus, considering the critical situation in France from 1 to 10 September, it has been claimed by some authors that the outcome of the Battle of the Marne might have been different had Moltke accepted Ludendorff's recommendation. It is doubtful, however, that two corps could have ensured victory for Germany in the West. (It should be remembered that Hindenburg and Ludendorff acted as one, so that when the text states that Ludendorff made a decision, Hindenburg's concurrence is implied.)

On 30 August, Jilinsky informed Rennenkampf of Samsonov's defeat and cautioned him to protect his southern flank. Rennenkampf decided to withdraw to the line shown, with his right flank on the sea and his left on the lakes. Mindful of the Lötzen Gap, he stationed most of the II Corps to block that route around his flank. The partially formed XXII Corps—part of the Russian Tenth Army—occupied key localities to the south of Lötzen. The Russian First Army troops formed in line, with only two divisions in reserve, thus taking up almost a cordon defense. Rennenkampf placed no cavalry covering force to the front to develop the situation, but he did see that the position was well entrenched.

Jilinsky expected that, while the First Army held its position, he would rebuild the Second Army, complete the forming of the Tenth, and then resume the offensive. But when General Rudiger Count von der Goltz—commanding three divisions of garrison troops from the Vistula fortress line—seized Mlava (*lower center*) on 4 September, Jilinsky jumped to the conclusion that the Germans were about to initiate a drive on Warsaw. Anxious to forestall such a move, he planned to launch an offensive on 14 September, using all three armies. Indeed, the Austrians—in trouble in Galicia—were pleading with the Germans to launch an attack on Warsaw, but Ludendorff was determined to dispose of Rennenkampf first.

Hindenburg finished regrouping by 4 September, and on the following day his advance began. The German plan envisioned an envelopment of the Russian south flank by the I and XVII Corps, the 3 R Division, and the two cavalry divisions (*not shown*)—while the other four corps executed the secondary attack against the main part of Rennenkampf's position to hold him in place. At first glance, it might appear that the secondary attack was too strong. However, Ludendorff was fearful of a Russian attack toward Friedland (*upper center*), and knew that his enveloping force would be beyond supporting distance. Furthermore, maneuver room in the south restricted the number of troops that could be used there. Von der Goltz's force was to prevent any interference by the Russian Second Army.

On 7 September, the 3 R Division seized Bialla (*lower right*), and the following day the capable Francois occupied Arys. On the 9th and 10th, the 3 R Division fought a spirited battle for Lyck, finally driving the Russians toward Augustow (*right center*) and securing the German south flank. Meanwhile, on 8 September, the German XVII Corps, attempting to break out of the Lötzen Gap, was repulsed by the Russian II Corps. In this battle, Rennenkampf committed his entire reserve of two divisions. In the north, the secondary attack was launched against the Russian line on 9 September, but was unable to achieve any gain. This same day, however, Francois' I Corps struck the Russian II Corps a savage blow in flank and rear, causing it to retire in disorder. The way was open now for the enveloping force to strike for Gumbinnen (*upper right*). Rennenkampf, having no reserves, realized the gravity of the situation and ordered a general withdrawal.

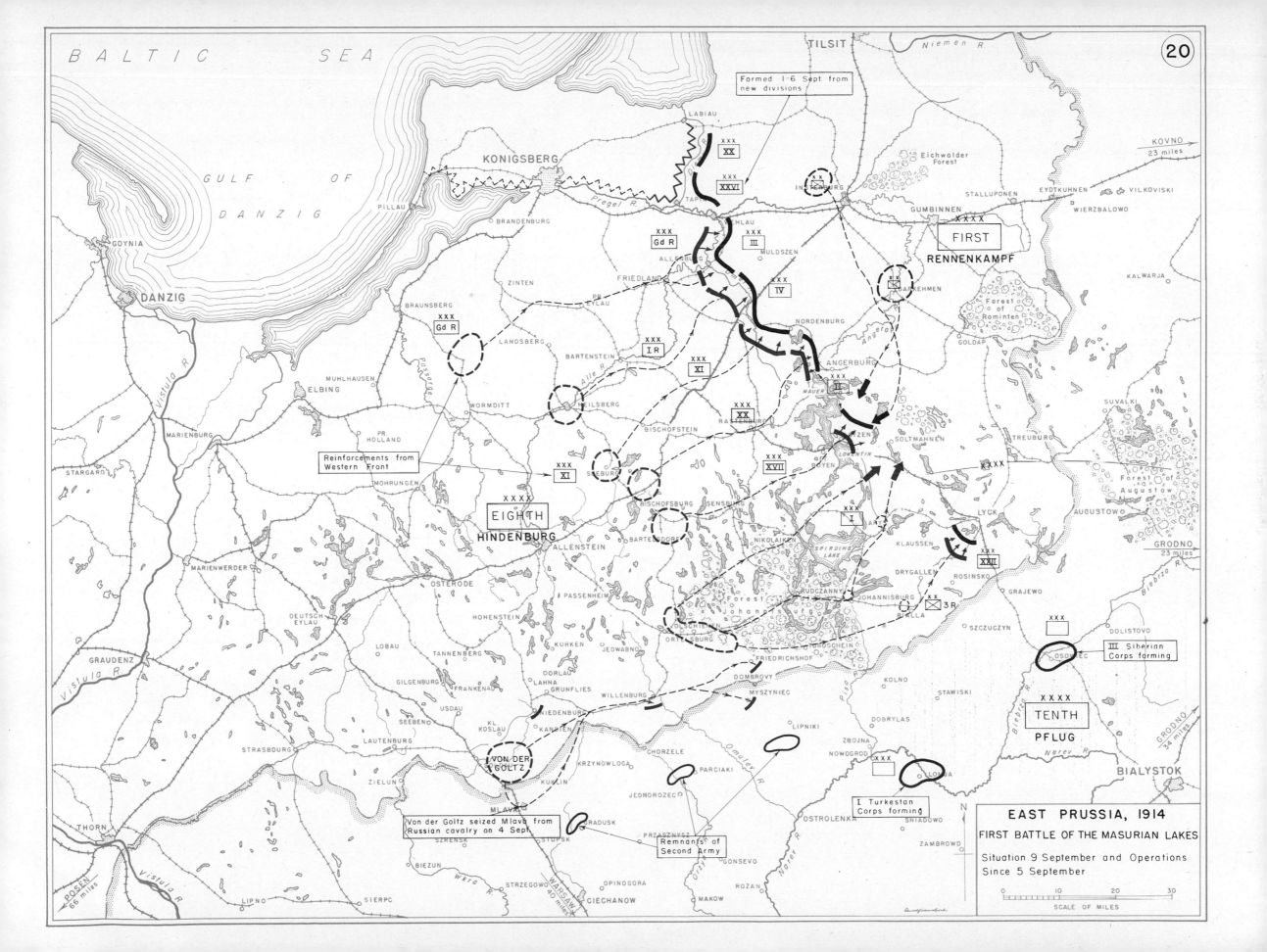

EAST PRUSSIA, 1914

FIRST BATTLE OF THE MASURIAN LAKES

Situation 9 September and Operations
Since 5 September

Rennenkampf's decision to withdraw his army reflected the desperation of his situation late on 9 September. His left-flank corps, battered and disorganized, was unable to stem the victorious march of the German I and XVII Corps. Francois' troops had covered seventy-seven miles in four days, deploying and fighting on two of them; but, driven and inspired by their fiery leader, they were still capable of exploiting their success. It was his acceptance of the certainty that Francois and Mackensen—marching upon Stallupönen (*upper right*)—could block his retreat and reenact another Tannenberg that caused Rennenkampf to react with a celerity not previously displayed. With the issuance of his orders late on the night of 9 September, the general withdrawal began. Desperately, the Russians moved to the east, divisions marching parallel on either side of a single road, which itself was clogged with the endless columns of transport. Onward they surged, marching all that night, the following day, and the next night; still, they were not out of danger, so eastward they wearily stumbled.

But not all the Russians moved east early on 10 September. Appreciating the necessity for a diversion to gain time, Rennenkampf had ordered a two-division counterattack for the 10th between Nordenburg and Angerburg. The German XX Corps, standing in the path of this attack, reeled backward with heavy losses; by the end of the day, it had been stunned into a state of apathy that persisted for forty-eight hours. Ludendorff became concerned over this German setback, and feared for the exposed right flank of the inexperienced XI Corps: the Russians at Tannenberg had not hesitated to attack, even when hopelessly surrounded; here, with a much better opportunity for success, they might well continue their counterattack. So, sacrificing the likely strategic gain to ensure a tactical success, Ludendorff limited the advance of the I and XVII Corps on 10 September; the following day, expecting a fight near Darkehmen (*upper right*), he directed

them to continue moving north, but by a route *west* of the Forest of Rominten. Thus, because a shallow envelopment had been substituted for the planned deeper one aimed at Vilkoviski (*upper right*), Rennenkampf was able to extricate much of his army from the trap. In spite of the supreme marching effort (in one fifty-hour period, his troops covered fifty-five miles across country and along roads jammed with traffic), it is doubtful that Rennenkampf could have escaped had Ludendorff not temporarily lost his nerve.

By late on 12 September, Ludendorff appreciated the true state of events, but the opportunity to block the Russian retreat had vanished. There was some rear-guard fighting as late as the 17th, but the German pursuit slackened on the 13th. The last fighting was at Vilkoviski, where Rennenkampf abandoned his rear guard to gain a few more precious hours.

The Russian First Army had escaped, but not without frightful casualties and tremendous loss of morale. In twenty-eight days in East Prussia, Rennenkampf had lost 145,000 men—all but 20,000 of them in this last battle. German losses have been estimated as low as 10,000.

In three weeks, the Hindenburg-Ludendorff team had cleared East Prussia of a superior enemy. With this brilliant triumph in the East, the competent duo had marked themselves for greater responsibilities. Eventually, they were to reach the top of the German command ladder.

Their less fortunate counterpart, Jilinsky, had continued to issue orders to Rennenkampf as late as the 15th, but that general, having broken contact, never received them. The Germans did, but had no need for them. Jilinsky poured forth his wrath over his subordinate's deficiencies in wires to supreme headquarters; the reply was notification that General Ruzski—who had been successful in the Galician theater—would take over Jilinsky's command on the 17th.

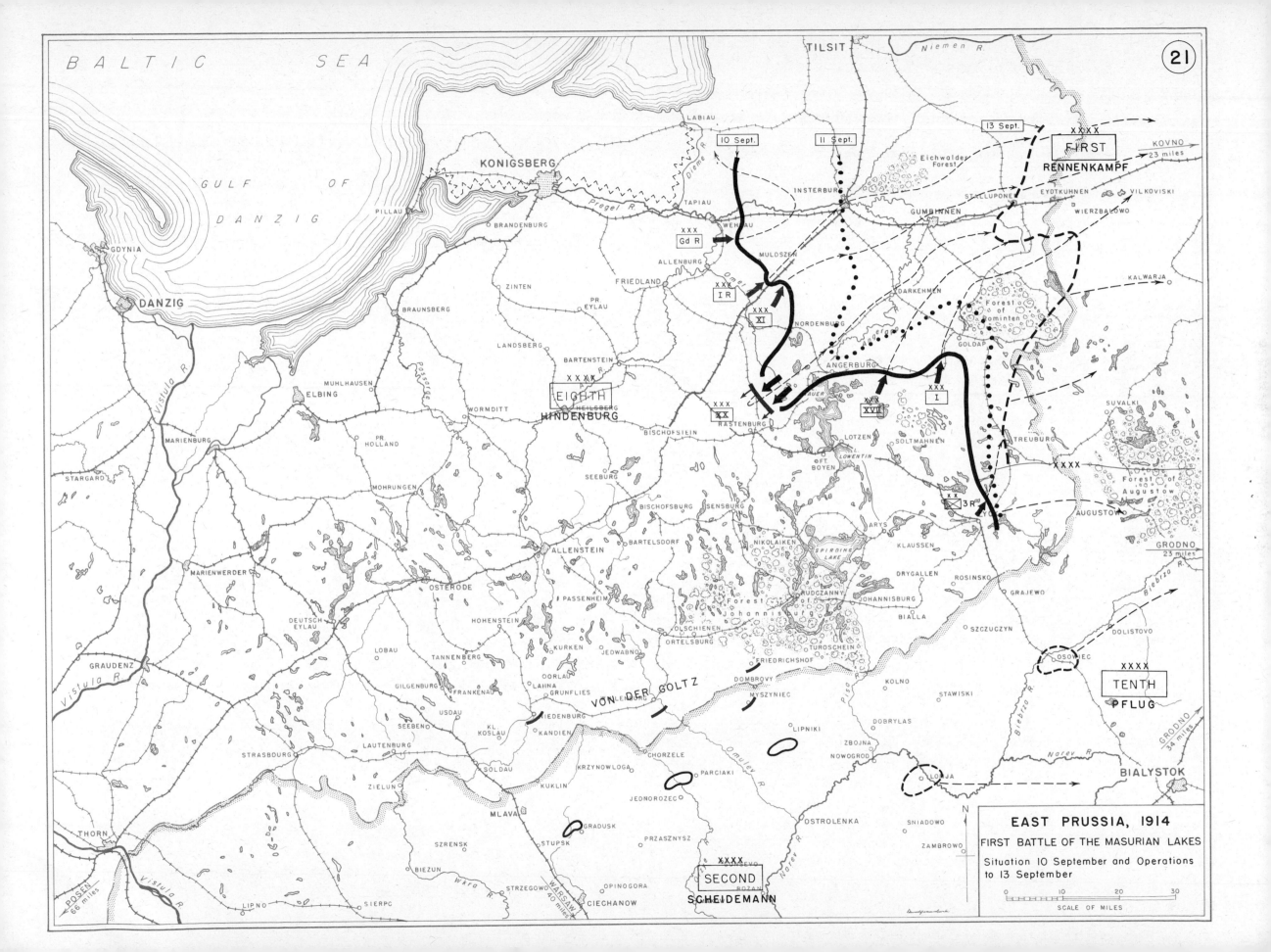

BALTIC SEA

TILSIT

Niemen R.

21

GULF OF DANZIG

KONIGSBERG

10 Sept.

11 Sept.

13 Sept.

XXXX
FIRST
RENNENKAMPF

KOVNO
23 miles

Eichwalder Forest

Pregel R.

TAPIAU

WEHLAU

INSTERBURG

GUMBINNEN

STALLUPONE

EYDTKUHNEN

VILKOVISKI

WIERZBALOWO

PILLAU

BRANDENBURG

XXX
Gd R

MULDSZEN

DARKEHMEN

KALWARJA

GDYNIA

ALLENBURG

FRIEDLAND

XXX
IR

NORDENBURG

Forest of Rominten

GOLDAP

DANZIG

BRAUNSBERG

ZINTEN

PR. EYLAU

XXX
XI

Omet R.

ANGERBURG

XXX
I

TREUBURG

LANDSBERG

BARTENSTEIN

Passarge R.

XXXX
EIGHTH
HINDENBURG

XXX
XX

RASTENBURG

XXX
XVII

SUVALKI

MUHLHAUSEN

ELBING

HEILSBERG

LOTZEN

L. LOWENTIN

SOLTMAHNEN

Forest of Augustow

MARIENBURG

BISCHOFSTEIN

ÖFT. BOYEN

XX
3 R

XXXX

PR. HOLLAND

SEEBURG

AUGUSTOW

STARGARD

MOHRUNGEN

BISCHOFSBURG

SENSBURG

ARYS

KLAUSSEN

GRODNO
23 miles

MARIENWERDER

BARTELSDORF

SPIRDING LAKE

DRYGALLEN

ROSINSKO

Biebrza R.

ALLENSTEIN

NIKOLAIKEN

JOHANNISBURG

GRAJEWO

DEUTSCH EYLAU

OSTERODE

PASSENHEIM

Forest of Johannisburg

RUDCZANNY

BIALLA

SZCZUCZYN

GRAUDENZ

LOBAU

TANNENBERG

KURKEN

JEDWABNO

ORTELSBURG

TUROSCHEIN

FRIEDRICHSHOF

KOLNO

STAWISKI

OSOWIEC

DOLISTOVO

XXXX
TENTH
PFLUG

Vistula R.

OORLAU

LAHNA

GRUNFLIES

LENDEN

DOMBROVY

MYSZYNIEC

ZBOJNA

NOWOGROD

DOBRYLAS

GRODNO
34 miles

GILGENBURG

FRANKENAU

VON DER GOLTZ

LIPNIKI

STRASBOURG

USDAU

SEEBEN

LAUTENBURG

RIEDENBURG

KL. KOSLAU

KANDIEN

CHORZELE

PARCIAKI

LOMJA

BIALYSTOK

Narev R.

GRADUSK

JEDNOROZEC

Omulev R.

KRZYNOWLOGA

KUKLIN

STUPSK

PRZASZNYSZ

SNIADOWO

OSTROLENKA

N

ZIELUN

MLAVA

SZRENSK

BIEZUN

Wkra R.

STRZEGOWO

BOZAN

OPINOGORA

CIECHANOW

ZAMBROWO

EAST PRUSSIA, 1914

FIRST BATTLE OF THE MASURIAN LAKES

Situation 10 September and Operations
to 13 September

POSEN
66 miles

THORN

Vistula R.

LIPNO

SIERPC

XXXX
SECOND
SCHEIDEMANN

WARSAW
40 miles

0   10   20   30

SCALE OF MILES

While Jilinsky's armies were suffering disastrous defeat in East Prussia, the main Russian forces were engaged with the Austrians in a massive struggle along a 200-mile front in Galicia. (In this series of maps, the situation in East Prussia is repeated, so that the reader can view the Eastern Front as a whole.)

It will be recalled that Austria had two war plans (*see text, map 3*) which differed only in one respect: in Plan B the Second Army would operate against Serbia, whereas in Plan R it would operate against Russia. On 25 July, General Conrad von Hotzendorff, the Austrian chief of staff, placed Plan B into effect; a week later, when Russia declared war, he suddenly shifted to Plan R. The Second Army, moving south to Serbia under Plan B, had to complete the movement and then reverse its course. As a result, it entered the first Galician Battles too late to play a significant role—and then only in part—for unexpected events in Serbia had forced Conrad to leave half of the army on that front.

Conrad had been urged by the Germans into immediate offensive action against the Russians to keep them occupied until a German victory could be achieved in France. He was further spurred to this line of action because his Serbian venture (*see map 46*) had been a failure, the Germans in East Prussia were retreating (at that time), the Balkan states were restive, and Russia was building up strength. His plan was based on the incorrect assumption that the main Russian forces would concentrate in the Lublin-Kholm area (*this map; center, right*). His First and Fourth Armies would advance in that direction, while the Third would remain on the defensive from Lemberg (*lower right*) south. Meanwhile, Woyrsch's German detachment and the Austrian Kummer and Kovess Groups would protect the flanks.

Oddly enough, the Russian plan was based on a similar misconception. General Ivanov expected the Austrians to make their major drive eastward from the Lemberg area; he therefore directed his main attack (Third and Eighth Armies) against that front, while the Fourth and Fifth Armies were to come down from the north across the Austrian communications.

The Russian cavalry was used to fill the gaps between their armies; Conrad dissipated his in a futile reconnaissance of the entire frontier. Consequently, the meetings of the opposing forces were more in the nature of collisions than planned engagements. The first encounter occurred on 23 August, when the Austrian First and Russian Fourth Armies ran into each other at Krasnik. After three days of fighting, the Russians—outnumbered three to two, and enveloped on their right flank—were forced back seven miles. Ivanov relieved General Salza for mismanaging the battle, and replaced him with General Ewarth. Still unaware that the Austrian main attack was in the north, Ivanov ordered the Ninth Army (then forming) to reinforce the Fourth with a corps, and directed his Fifth Army to wheel to the right and strike the Austrian First Army in flank.

On the 26th, two entirely new battles began. Conrad, elated over the success at Krasnik, urged his Fourth Army forward, reinforcing it with a corps from the Third. Then, completely unaware of the Russian main advance toward Lemberg, he authorized his Third Army to strike offensively to the east. The Third soon stumbled into the Russian main attack beyond the Gnila Lipa River (*lower right*). Outnumbered three to one, it was driven back in confusion. By 1 September, it had retreated to the line shown; the following day, the Lemberg fortress fell, and the Austrians were forced back another twenty miles. Meanwhile, the Austrian Fourth Army collided with the Russian Fifth at Komarov while the Fifth was executing its wheel. Four days of confused fighting ensued. The Austrians began to achieve success in enveloping both Russian flanks, while General Plehve persisted stolidly in his right turn. On the 30th, perceiving his danger, Plehve decided to withdraw. On the 31st, just as a stunning Austrian victory was in sight, the two enveloping Austrian corps halted—because of rumors of danger to their flanks—and the Russians escaped.

Note: On the map, upper right, Jilinski *should be* Jilinsky.

EASTERN FRONT, 1914-1915

GALICIAN BATTLES

Situation 1 September 1914 and
Opening Movements of the Opposing
Forces

SCALE OF MILES
0 10 20 30 40 50 60 70 80 90 100

On 1 September, Conrad was confronted with a momentous decision. True, his armies in the north had defeated the Russian Fourth and Fifth Armies, but they had not destroyed either of them. In the south, his weak Third Army had been routed, and the strong Russian Third and Eighth Armies were even now beginning to veer to the northwest—actually, to support Plehve, but, in Conrad's mind, to cut off his First and Fourth Armies. In view of the troop dispositions and the Russian preponderance of force, a general withdrawal and consolidation were indicated; but Conrad boldly, if not desperately or rashly, decided to renew the offensive—this time, in the Lemberg area. Believing Plehve's Fifth Army to be disorganized and now an insignificant threat, he directed his Fourth Army to discontinue the pursuit, turn 180 degrees, and advance so as to strike the right flank of the Russian Third Army. His Second Army was to envelop the Russian Eighth Army's south flank.

The Russians, meanwhile, had revived the plan they had originally wanted to adopt—to advance from the north across the Austrian communications. Their Ninth Army had been advancing south along the Vistula and was coming abreast of the Fourth at Krasnik. The Fifth Army had escaped encirclement, but it seemed to need help. Accordingly, the westward drive of the Third and Eighth Armies had been turned northwest to aid Plehve. Thus, for the second time, the plans of the opposing forces tended to be similar, but now with the main efforts reversed.

The Austrian Fourth and Russian Third Armies collided on 3 September as they moved to execute their new plans. Both commanders were confused, but eventually the Austrian Fourth wheeled into line as shown. In so doing, it opened a forty-mile gap which offered Plehve clear passage to the Austrian rear. Meanwhile, the Austrian Second Army, tired and disorganized by many days of entraining and detraining, had made little progress in the attempted envelopment of the Russian south flank. Such was the situation on 8 September.

On the 9th, the forces in the Lemberg area were locked in bitter struggle. To the north, the Austrian First Army began to give ground before the combined strength of the Russian Ninth and Fourth. Plehve moved forward into the yawning gap, pushing before him the small Fourth Army rear guard. Conrad remained undaunted and ordered another attack on the 10th against the Russian Third and Eighth Armies; but Austrian strength had been sapped, and his orders were ignored. On the 11th, intercepted Russian radio messages announced Plehve's destination for that date to be a small town some twenty miles west of Rava Russka (*lower right*). Conrad now ordered a general withdrawal which soon got out of hand and continued for 100 miles (*dashed red line, dated 26 September*).

Thus, by 11 September, the Russians had gained a stupendous victory in Galicia. In East Prussia, however, they were in mass flight—and, significantly, by this same date the Germans had suffered defeat at the Marne. The Galician Battles cost the Austrians 350,000 casualties—over two-thirds of their Galician front forces. The number of Russian casualties is not accurately known, but they certainly were not light. Most important, however, the battle took a terrific toll of the Teutonic cadre, the backbone of the heterogeneous Austrian Army. Conrad would now need German troop support—a drain Germany could ill afford.

In view of the disastrous Austrian defeat and the consequent opening of a clear road to Silesia (*lower left*) for the Russians, Germany was compelled to rush troops to bolster the Austrian defenses. Falkenhayn refused to transfer troops from the West, so Hindenburg formed the Ninth Army from four of the six corps in East Prussia. This army, led by Hindenburg and Ludendorff, began its journey from East Prussia by rail on 17 September. After a remarkable eleven-day movement, involving 750 trains, it was concentrated in the area shown, ready to engage the southern Russian armies.

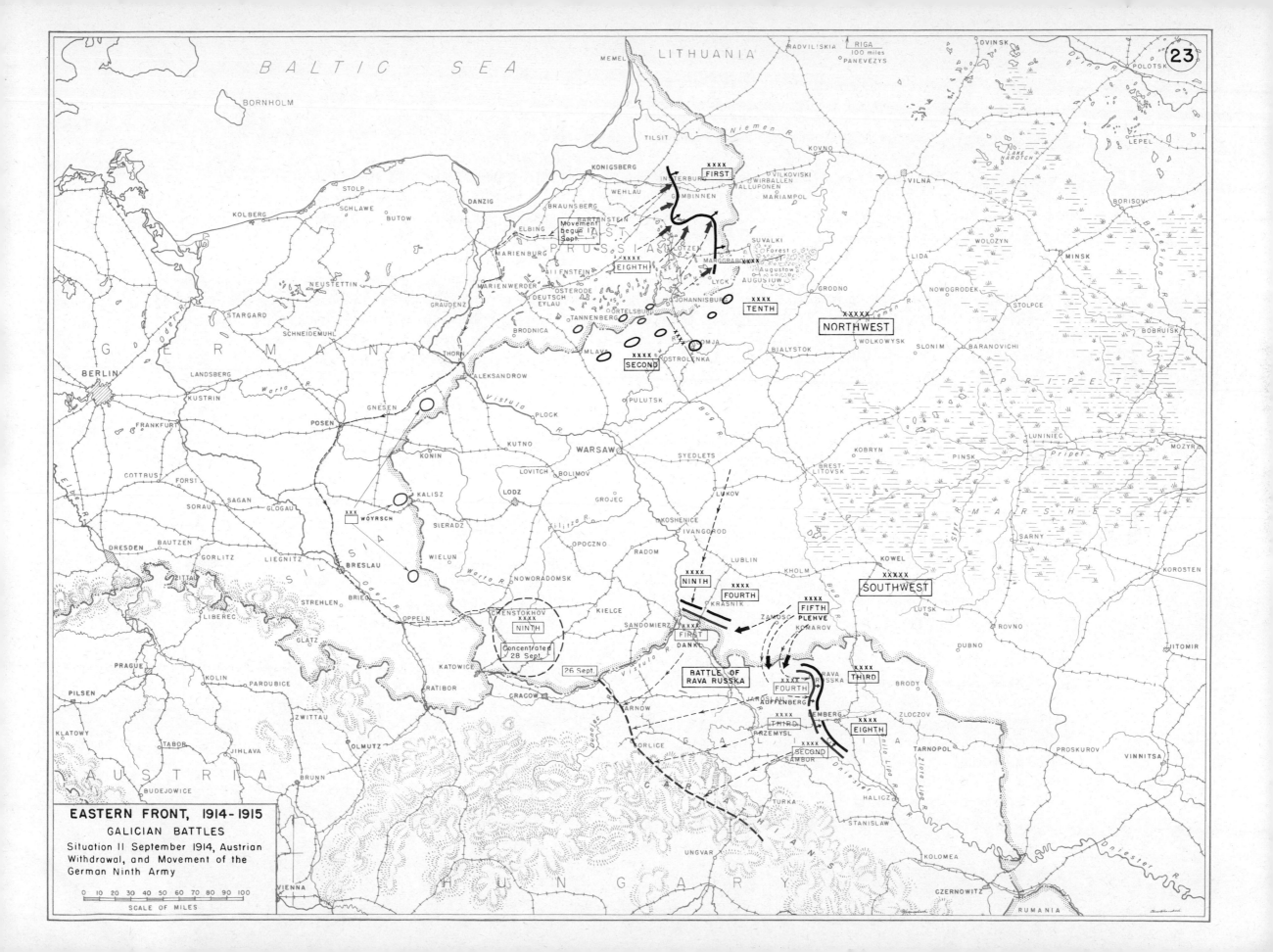

EASTERN FRONT, 1914-1915
GALICIAN BATTLES
Situation II September 1914, Austrian
Withdrawal, and Movement of the
German Ninth Army

SCALE OF MILES
0 10 20 30 40 50 60 70 80 90 100

By 28 September, Hindenburg had the newly formed Ninth Army in position on the Austrian north flank. The critical situation of the Austrians and the Russian threat to Cracow (*lower center*), one of the gateways to Silesia, dictated immediate offensive action. The German Ninth and Austrian First Armies were to close to the Vistula (*center*), seize crossings, and then advance on Warsaw. The three southern Austrian armies were to close to the San River (*center*) and raise the siege of Przemysl, which had not surrendered during the Russian advance. The weakened German Eighth Army was to defend the East Prussian border.

Meanwhile, in mid-September, the French again besought the Russians to invade Silesia via the Warsaw-Posen route. This entreaty—coupled with the worsening logistical situation in Galicia and Russian fear of a German advance from East Prussia against the ever-extending flank in Galicia—led the Stavka (Russian supreme headquarters) to order a regroupment of the Russian armies. The Fifth, Fourth, and Ninth Armies were to move north on 23 September to a line along the Vistula from Warsaw south to Sandomierz (*dashed blue line*). (On 23 September, the Russians were located just east of the dashed red line, dated 26 September, on map 23.) Thereafter, the Northwest Army Group (four armies—the Tenth, First, Second, and Fifth) would defend along the Vistula-Narew River line (*center*) to protect against invasion from East Prussia, while the Southwest Army Group moved into Silesia. This massive defense against invasion from East Prussia clearly indicates that the Russians were unaware of the southward movement of the German Ninth Army and of the actual weakness of the East Prussian defenses.

On 28 September—while the Russian Fifth, Fourth, and Ninth Armies were moving northward—Hindenburg struck. His advance was slow and deliberate; excellent communications were constructed, and key defiles prepared for demolition, in the event that a swift withdrawal became necessary. By the 30th, the Russians at last became aware of the presence of the German Ninth Army. Now, as they delayed the German-Austrian advance, the Russians prepared a trap. The First and Second Armies were to concentrate at Warsaw, prepared to execute a massive envelopment of the German north flank once it reached the Vistula.

By 9 October, the Ninth Army had reached the Vistula. Here, a captured Russian order, added to information gained from the babbling Russian radio, gave Hindenburg a clear picture of his danger and of the great odds he faced. Nevertheless, the Germans pressed on and, by the 12th, were only twelve miles from Warsaw. But Russian pressure on the north flank became increasingly grave, while Austrian cooperation degenerated. On 17 October, Hindenburg began a general withdrawal from the line then held (*dashed red line*); by 1 November, the Germans and Austrians were back to their starting line (*solid red line*). The Russians promptly followed and—though delayed by German demolitions and other measures of an efficiently executed retrograde movement—reached the line shown by 1 November.

Now the Russians planned to drive straight west into Silesia with the Second, Fifth, Fourth, and Ninth Armies, while the First Army protected the north flank. Silesia's mineral resources and industrial facilities were vital to the German war effort. The Russian offensive must be stopped; the only large force available was the Ninth Army. With knowledge of Russian movements gained from intercepted radio dispatches, and being familiar with the characteristic slow rate of Russian advance, the Germans calculated that they could move the Ninth Army over the excellent rail net to the Posen-Thorn area (*inset sketch*) in time to attack the Russian First and Second Armies. Conrad would launch a secondary attack in the south.

On 4 November, the Ninth Army began its movement north in complete secrecy; by the 10th, it had filled the gap previously occupied only by border troops, and was in position to attack. Meanwhile, it had been reinforced with additional troops from East Prussia. Elements of the Austrian Second Army and fortress troops were moved into the void left by the Ninth Army's movement.

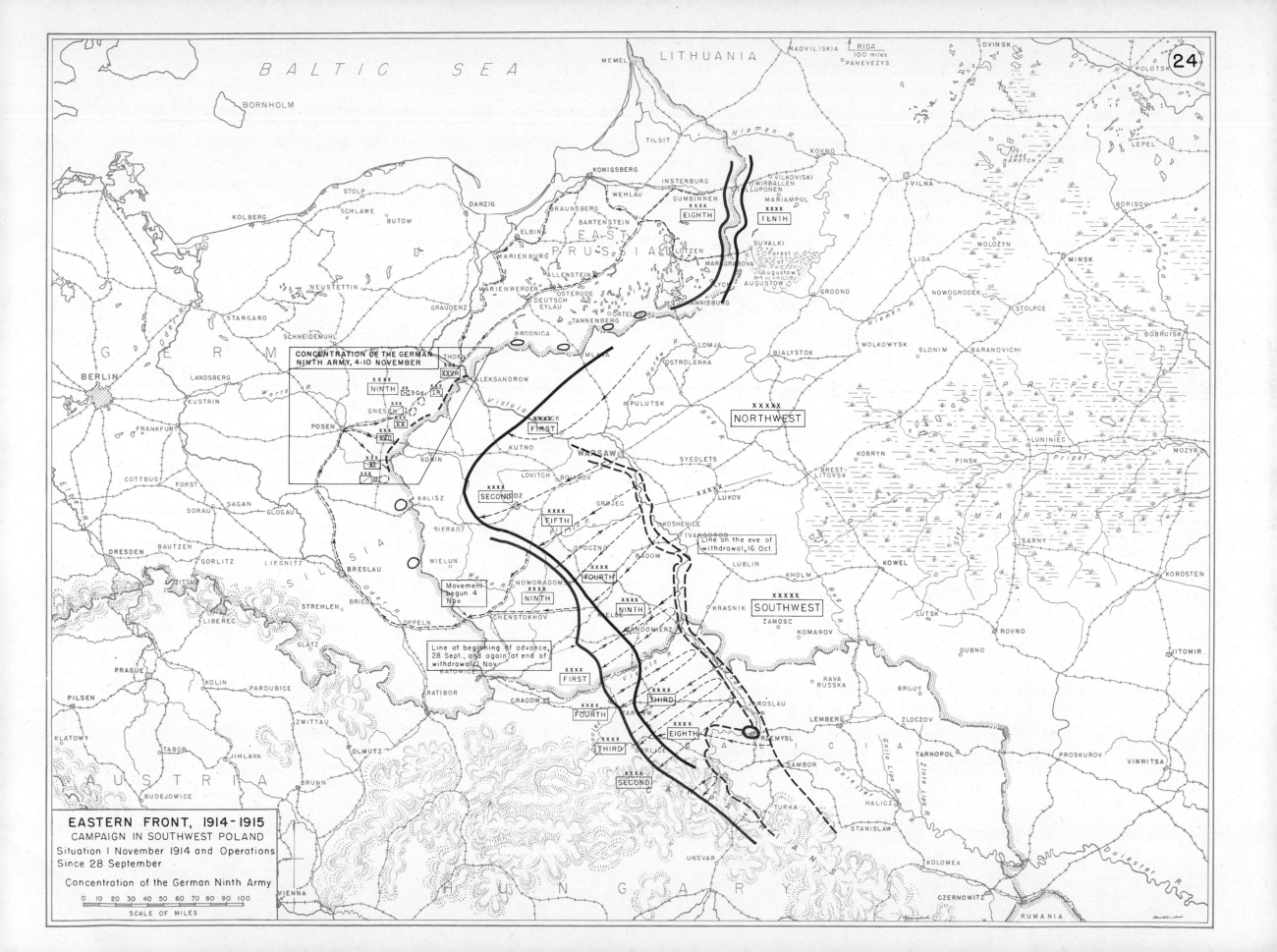

EASTERN FRONT, 1914-1915
CAMPAIGN IN SOUTHWEST POLAND
Situation 1 November 1914 and Operations
Since 28 September

Concentration of the German Ninth Army

0 10 20 30 40 50 60 70 80 90 100
SCALE OF MILES

CONCENTRATION OF THE GERMAN
NINTH ARMY, 4-10 NOVEMBER

Movement
begun 4
Nov.

Line at beginning of advance,
28 Sept., and again at end of
withdrawal, 1 Nov.

Line on the eve of
withdrawal, 16 Oct.

On 10 November, the German Ninth Army—now under Mackensen, Hindenburg-Ludendorff having been elevated to the command of all German forces in the East—prepared to attack the next day. On the same day, Falkenhayn, anticipating early victory over the British at Ypres in the West, promised to send four corps to the East in about ten days. This posed a problem for Hindenburg: should the Ninth Army attack on the 11th, as planned, or should the attack be delayed until the four corps arrived? The temptation to postpone the offensive was great, but Hindenburg was convinced that the Russians would advance into Silesia by the 22d, and was fully cognizant of the uncertainties of war. He decided to attack on the 11th. His decision was correct, for the four promised corps arrived late and piecemeal.

The initial advance of the Ninth Army achieved great success (*sketch* a). Rennenkampf, still commanding the First Army and performing as lackadaisically as he had in East Prussia, had two corps widely dispersed between the Vistula and the Bzura (*center, dashed blue symbols*). The advanced V Siberian Corps (*map symbol*: V S) was defeated and forced back as shown on 12 November. The II Corps met a like fate two days later and withdrew to Kutno (*center*). In four days, the Germans had advanced fifty miles over poor roads. Mackensen maintained pressure on the II Corps and, by the 16th, had routed and sent it fleeing eastward. Meanwhile, the German XI Corps had overwhelmed the Russian XXIII Corps of the Second Army. The Russian II S and IV Corps moved north, but were turned back. By the night of the 16th, Mackensen had achieved his initial goal—a penetration between the First and Second Armies.

The Russian drive into Silesia had started on 14 November, as planned. It was not until the 16th that the plight of the two northern armies became clear to the Stavka. Then the Silesian offensive was halted, the Fifth Army ordered north to aid the Second, and a counterattack force ordered concentrated at Lovitch (*right center*) for movement southwest against the German flank.

Mackensen proceeded to exploit the penetration and encircle the Second Army. The XXV R Corps—with the 3d Guards Division attached—and the I Cavalry Corps were to move southeast to Lódz (*lower right*), then swing westward; simultaneously, the III Cavalry Corps and the Posen and Breslau "Corps" (three Landwehr brigades each) were to attack eastward. The XI, XVII, and XX Corps would continue their attacks to pin down Second Army units, while the I R Corps blocked any relief attempt by the First Army.

The German plan was not to succeed, for the Russian reaction was surprisingly quick (*sketch* b). The Russian Fifth Army moved north—two of its corps marching seventy miles in forty-eight hours—and stopped Mackensen's right on the 19th, actually pushing it back somewhat. General Scheffer's XXV R Corps got around the Russian right, but the V Corps assailed it from the south while the Lovitch Force, after forcing the XX Corps to pull back its flank, moved down on Scheffer's rear. The predicament of the XXV R Corps was indeed perilous, and the confident Russians had already ordered trains from Warsaw to carry prisoners. But the indomitable Scheffer—calm, fearless, and inspiring—kept his troops in hand and withdrew in the bitter cold to Karpin (*lower right*). Turning north, he collided with the crack 6th Siberian Division of the Lovitch Force along the Koluszki-Lódz railroad late on the 23d. That night, the heroic 3d Guards Division pushed through to Brzeziny, the corps' objective, and the next day the XXV R Corps attacked and practically destroyed the 6th Siberian Division. The Lovitch Force, threatened from two sides, withdrew; the XXV R Corps and the cavalry moved into position between the I R and XX Corps. Scheffer, in his remarkable exploit, had brought back 16,000 prisoners and 64 guns, and had suffered only 4,300 casualties.

The battle completely stopped the Russian invasion of Silesia. On 6 December, the Russians evacuated Lódz and rearranged their line south of Warsaw (*see map 26*). The Germans, now reinforced, closed up to the new line. Tactically, Hindenburg-Ludendorff had failed, but strategically, they had been highly successful.

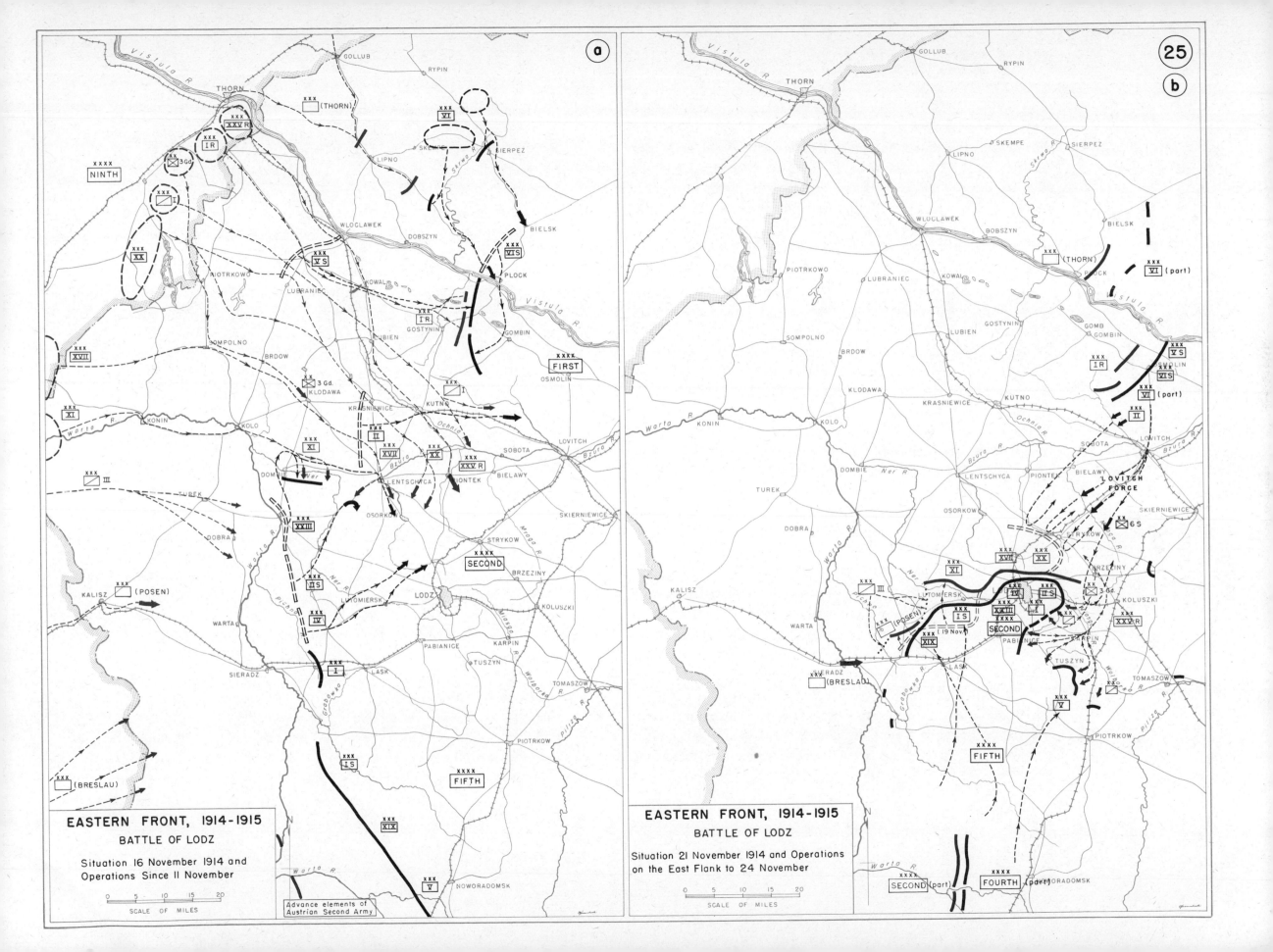

EASTERN FRONT, 1914-1915

BATTLE OF LODZ

Situation 16 November 1914 and
Operations Since 11 November

SCALE OF MILES
0   5   10   15   20

Advance elements of
Austrian Second Army

EASTERN FRONT, 1914-1915

BATTLE OF LODZ

Situation 21 November 1914 and Operations
on the East Flank to 24 November

SCALE OF MILES
0   5   10   15   20

(a)

(b)

25

Most of January, 1915, was spent by the German high command in evolving a new strategy. In the West, modern weapons, coupled with field fortifications, had given the defensive ascendancy over the offensive, and a stalemate had developed. In the East, Russian offensive designs had been frustrated, but—given time—another attack could be expected. Falkenhayn maintained that the war could not be won in the East, that Britain was the prime enemy, and that four new corps raised in Germany should go to France. Hindenburg-Ludendorff, supported by Conrad, professed an ability to seriously cripple, perhaps eliminate, Russia. Furthermore, they argued, some of the Balkan states—and Italy—might join the Allies unless a decisive success were gained in the East. Both Austria and Turkey (a recent addition to the Central Powers) were shaky and needed moral support. Thus the argument raged, with the Kaiser finally siding with Hindenburg-Ludendorff. On 8 January, he agreed to a Carpathian offensive by the Austrians, who were to be stiffened with German troops (*not shown*). Falkenhayn exacted a measure of revenge by sending Ludendorff to the Austrian front. But his victory was short-lived, for Hindenburg—indignant and exerting his great prestige —pressed for a concurrent East Prussian offensive and the restoration of Ludendorff as his chief of staff. By mid-January, he had won his points—and the four new corps as well. Falkenhayn, bitter over the Kaiser's second rebuff, sulked in Berlin, secure in his belief that the gigantic double envelopment—from the Carpathians and East Prussia—would be a failure.

The Russians were under no illusions as to their offensive capabilities. Many of their troops were without rifles, and there was a shortage of ammunition and artillery. The Stavka was content with plans for limited spring offensives on the flanks. The Twelfth Army was being formed to participate in a drive to sever East Prussia from Germany. It was hoped that a limited attack in the Carpathians would secure Rumania's allegiance and weaken Austria's position.

The Austrian offensive was a dismal failure. Even though stiffened with German troops, Conrad's forces—lacking inspiration and the desire to fight—achieved no success. In March, the starved-out Przemysl fortress surrendered. There, Conrad lost 100,000 men and 1,000 guns—and another Russian army was freed for active operations.

Hindenburg-Ludendorff, however, had expected that the decisive victory would have to be won in East Prussia. The enemy Tenth Army was their immediate objective, but severance of the Warsaw-Vilna line of communications (*center to upper right*) was the ultimate goal. The plan envisioned a double envelopment of the Russian Tenth Army by the Eighth Army and the newly formed German Tenth Army, with the last-named making the main attack. To protect the Eighth Army's flank, Mackensen moved the XX Corps to Mlava, and covered the movement with a diversionary attack at Bolimov (*center*) on 31 January—remarkable chiefly for the first (and unsuccessful) use of tear-gas shells in quantity (18,000). On 7 February, in a blinding snowstorm, the Eighth Army attacked. The Russians were unaware of the existence of the German Tenth Army; nor did they expect an attack in such miserable weather. The Eighth Army drive drew their attention southward. As a result, when the Tenth Army moved forward on 8 February, its attack was immediately successful. The map shows the progress of the offensive in which the Russians, fighting bitterly, were gradually forced back to the Forest of Augustow. Here, the heroic resistance of the Russian XX Corps enabled the other three Russian corps to escape encirclement. Exhausted and decimated, the XX Corps surrendered on 21 February.

In this battle, Russia suffered 200,000 casualties, half of them prisoners. German combat losses were light, but some units had 30 per cent of their personnel disabled by exposure. Again, the Germans had achieved a great tactical victory, but strategic gains were meager. Falkenhayn's prediction had come true.

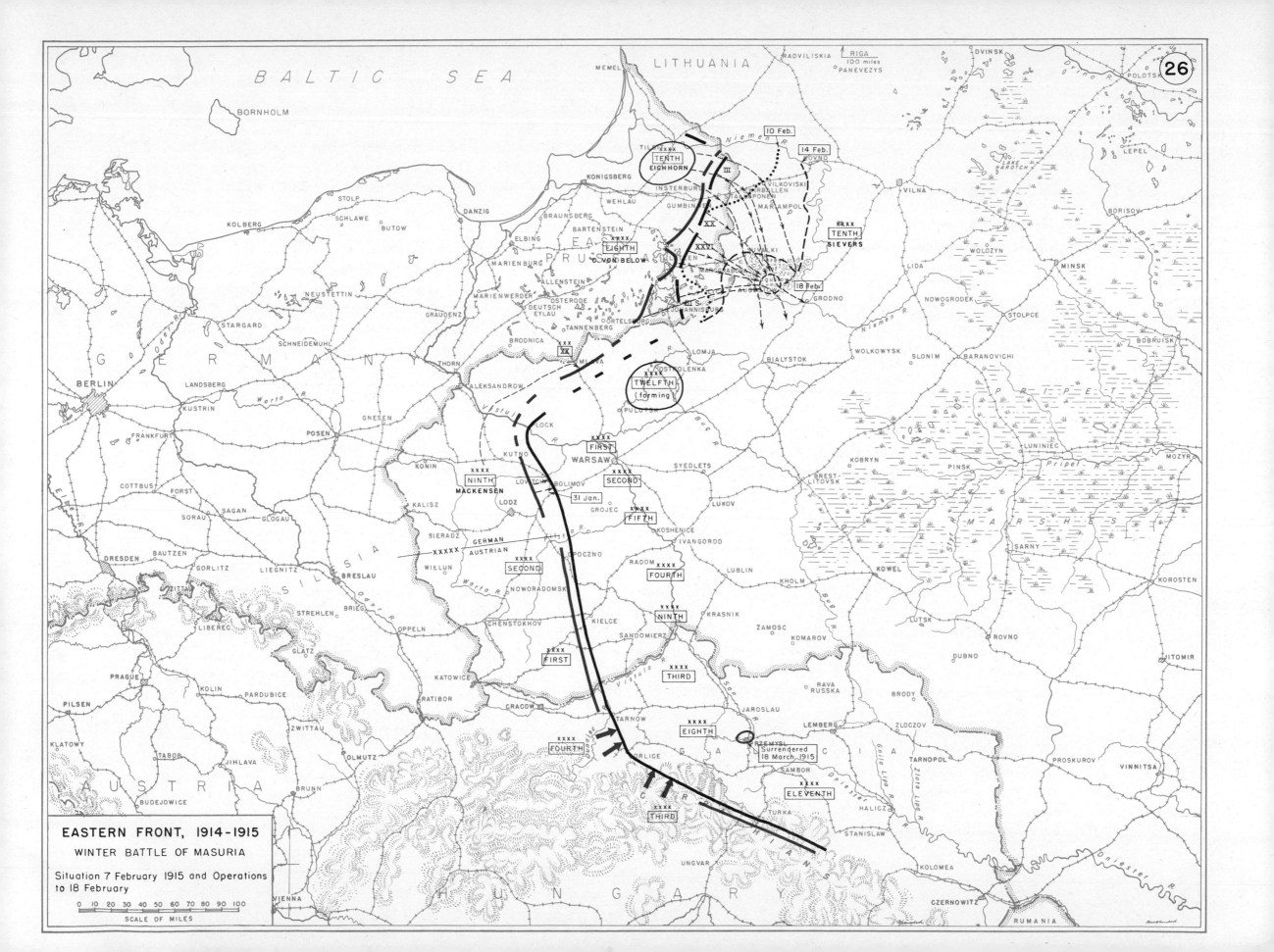

EASTERN FRONT, 1914-1915

WINTER BATTLE OF MASURIA

Situation 7 February 1915 and Operations to 18 February

0 10 20 30 40 50 60 70 80 90 100

SCALE OF MILES

By March, 1915, the equipment, training, and logistical support of the Russian armies had still not improved enough to allow a major offensive. The idea of an attack on East Prussia was given up, but preparations were made for a limited offensive in the Carpathians. In late March, the Eighth Army and part of the Third pushed forward (*action not shown*) in an attempt to reach the Hungarian plains. The fighting was severe, and gains were slight; on 18 April, the attack was stopped to await replacements and ammunition. It was never renewed, for on 2 May, Mackensen delivered a pulverizing blow at Gorlice-Tarnow (*lower center*).

Before tracing the course of the fighting in the next five months, the strategy of the Central Powers should be examined. In April, Germany had formed a new army (the Eleventh) by withdrawing infantry and artillery units from existing divisions on the Western Front. Falkenhayn proposed to use it in France, but he realized the precarious position of the Austrians (the Russians seemed capable of driving into Hungary in the summer), the need for subduing Serbia, and the importance of opening communications with Turkey. The decision, then, was to employ the army in the East—but where? Falkenhayn preferred Serbia; Hindenburg—commanding the front north of the Austrian First Army—advocated a penetration near Kovno (*upper center*) in the north, followed by an envelopment southward; Conrad—commanding the front to the south—wanted a penetration near Tarnow (*lower center*). Falkenhayn—in over-all command—eventually agreed with Conrad.

To divert Russian attention from the south, Hindenburg mounted a small attack (*not shown*) in Lithuania (*top center*) at the end of April, successfully luring considerable Russian strength north, but eventually using so many troops that they were later organized into the Niemen Army. To cover the transfer of the Eleventh Army to the East, Germany launched an attack at Ypres (*see map 32*) on 22 April. In the Gorlice-Tarnow sector (*this map*), every precaution was taken to maintain secrecy while the Germans built up a tremendous logistical base and massed 950 artillery pieces.

At 0600, 2 May, Mackensen struck behind a terrific artillery preparation. The Russian Third Army was completely surprised: there had been some reports of the German concentration, but these had been ignored. Russian troops, crazed and panic-stricken, fled blindly to the rear. The German juggernaut—well organized and controlled to perfection—rolled on, achieving a complete breakthrough by 4 May. The Russian Third Army had ceased to exist; Mackensen's advancing armies had captured 120,000 prisoners. The Russians now withdrew on the southern front. On 3 June, a strategy council was convened by Falkenhayn. Italy had entered the war on 24 May, and Conrad recommended the transfer of Austrian troops to that front; Falkenhayn, worried over Allied attacks in the West, considered sending some German troops there; Hindenburg wanted to execute a gigantic double envelopment of the entire Eastern Front. But the failure, so far, to seriously cripple Russia, and fear of Conrad's inability to stabilize the front if Germans were withdrawn, dictated a continuance of the current offensive.

Mackensen, reinforced with the newly created German Bug Army and the Austrian Third, continued his drive, taking Lemberg on 22 June. An inviting salient, with Warsaw in the center, now existed; Falkenhayn resolved to attack it concurrently from north and south. Mackensen turned north, aiming for Brest-Litovsk (*center, right*), and the German Twelfth Army attacked toward Warsaw on 13 July. To the credit of the Stavka, there were no large-scale encirclements of Russians as the retreat was accelerated. The salient was eliminated by 15 August, and two weeks later Mackensen took Brest-Litovsk. By 30 September, the Russians had fallen back to the line shown. Most of the fighting during this month was on the flanks: Hindenburg tried unsuccessfully to take Riga and Dvinsk (*top right*), and Conrad failed to take Rovno (*lower right*).

The campaign cost Russia upward of 2,000,000 casualties, half of them prisoners. Grand Duke Nicholas, a fine soldier, was relieved, and the Czar himself assumed command—a boon to the Germans.

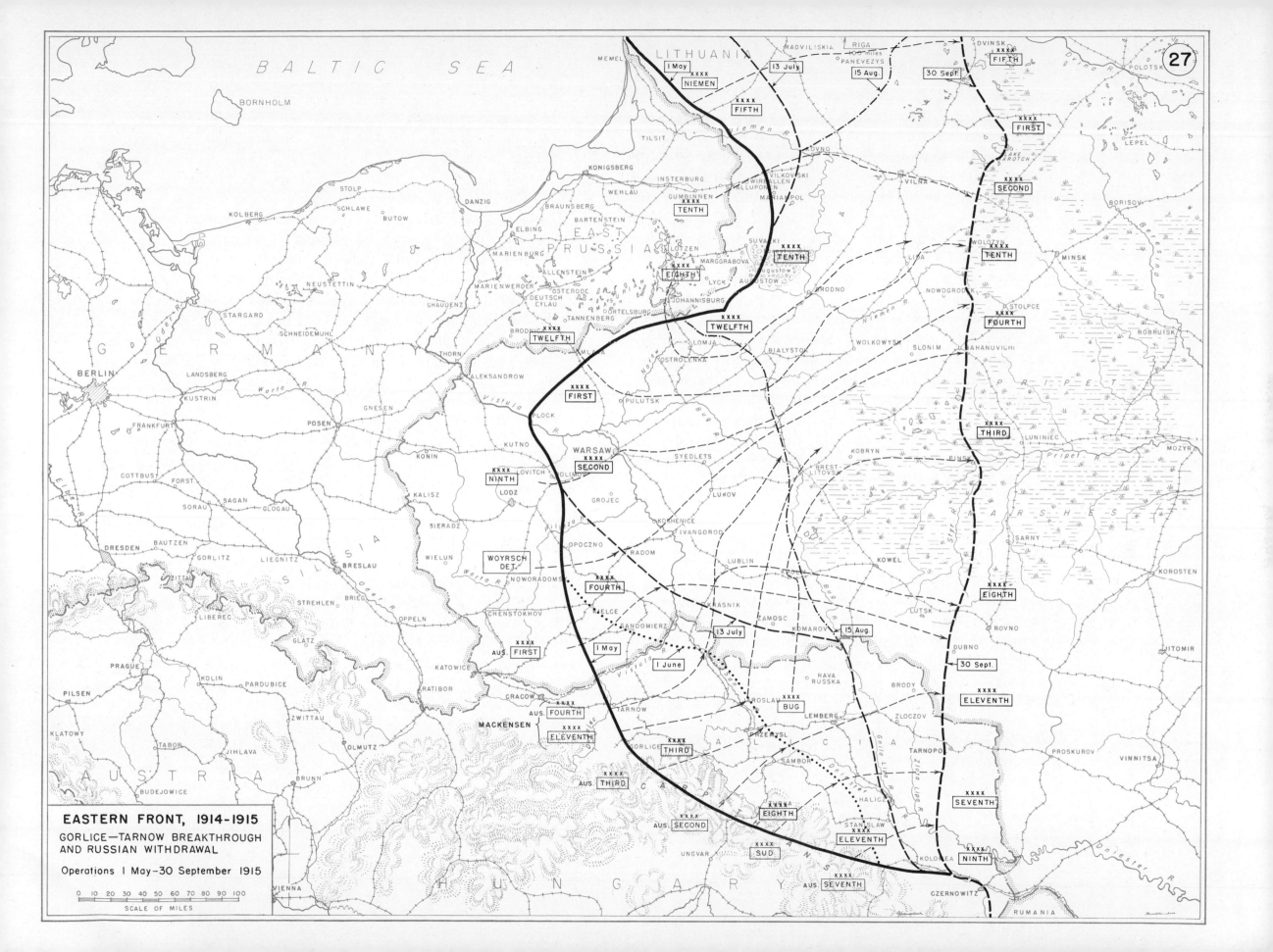

EASTERN FRONT, 1914-1915

GORLICE—TARNOW BREAKTHROUGH
AND RUSSIAN WITHDRAWAL

Operations 1 May–30 September 1915

0 10 20 30 40 50 60 70 80 90 100
SCALE OF MILES

At the outbreak of war, Turkey, though clearly under German influence, remained neutral. For many years following the Crimean War she had leaned heavily upon England, but gradually —from 1905 onward—Germany had usurped Britain's place. The Balkan Wars (1912-13), which humbled Turkey and severely reduced her territory in Europe, served to solidify the control of the "Young Turk" regime. The British, lacking their usual political astuteness, had little confidence in the young revolutionary government and refused a proposal for an Anglo-Turkish alliance.

In December, 1913, General Liman von Sanders brought a German mission to Turkey to reorganize and train her army. Prussian efficiency soon impressed the Turks, who—though not appreciative of the arrogant attitude of some of the visitors— expected a German victory should war break out.

On 2 August, 1914, the Turks finally signed a secret pact with Germany, directed primarily at Russia. The next day, the British took over two battleships being built in England for Turkey, causing great resentment among the Turks and playing into the hands of German propagandists, who now offered Turkey two German ships. On 8 August, the German warships *Goeben* and *Breslau*, being hunted by the British, took refuge in the Dardanelles (*lower center*). Britain protested, but the Turks suavely replied that the two ships had been purchased to replace those seized by the British. Germans soon began reorganizing the Turkish Navy, and continued to man the two "Turkish" warships. Then, on 26 September, when the Royal Navy refused to allow a Turkish torpedo boat—manned by Germans—to leave the Dardanelles, the German officer commanding the Gallipoli fortifications closed the straits to all traffic. Repercussions were serious, for the move cut Russia's lifeline; but the Allies, gripped in life-and-death struggles on land with Germany, took no military action.

By October, the German defeat on the Marne and the Austrian reverses in Galicia had convinced Turkey that the Central Powers were not invincible. If they lost the war, Turkey would be menaced by her old enemy, Russia, more powerful than ever. On 30 October, a Turkish fleet, under German command, shelled Odessa, on the Black Sea. This overt act propelled Turkey into the war.

This map shows the situation on the various fronts as of 1 January, 1915. In the West, the Allies had suffered nearly 1,000,000 casualties since the outbreak of war; the front was stabilized, and one British school of thought was advocating enveloping this line—perhaps via Turkey and the Balkans. In the East, Hindenburg had temporarily stalled the Russians in the campaign that ended with the Lódz battle. Conrad had still been unable to make headway against recalcitrant Serbia. The Turks opposed the British at Suez (*bottom center*) and in Mesopotamia (*lower right*), where the British had landed a force from the Persian Gulf on 6 November to secure vital oil fields. On the Turko-Russian border, two armies watched each other.

Sanders had improved the Turkish Army immeasurably in a remarkably short time. It now had forty divisions (with an average rifle strength of about 9,000 each), grouped into four armies as shown. But Turkey's lack of roads and railroads hampered supply and troop movements. The lack of adequate munitions-manufacturing facilities meant dependence upon German supply; thus, the attitude of the Balkan states between Turkey and Germany was important.

The genesis of the Dardanelles campaign lay in a Russian request in early January for a British diversion against Turkey. On 4 January, the headstrong Enver Pasha, despite Sanders' advice to the contrary, launched the Turkish Third Army in an abortive attack in the Caucasus (*right center*). Only 10 per cent of the 90,000 Turks survived the battle, the cold, and starvation. But the Stavka had feared eventual collapse of the front when it made the plea for a British attack. The British—some of whom had, for months, been anxious to reopen the supply line to Russia—replied that an early effort would be made. The British War Council began to explore possibilities in an atmosphere tainted by an unrealistic appraisal of military capabilities.

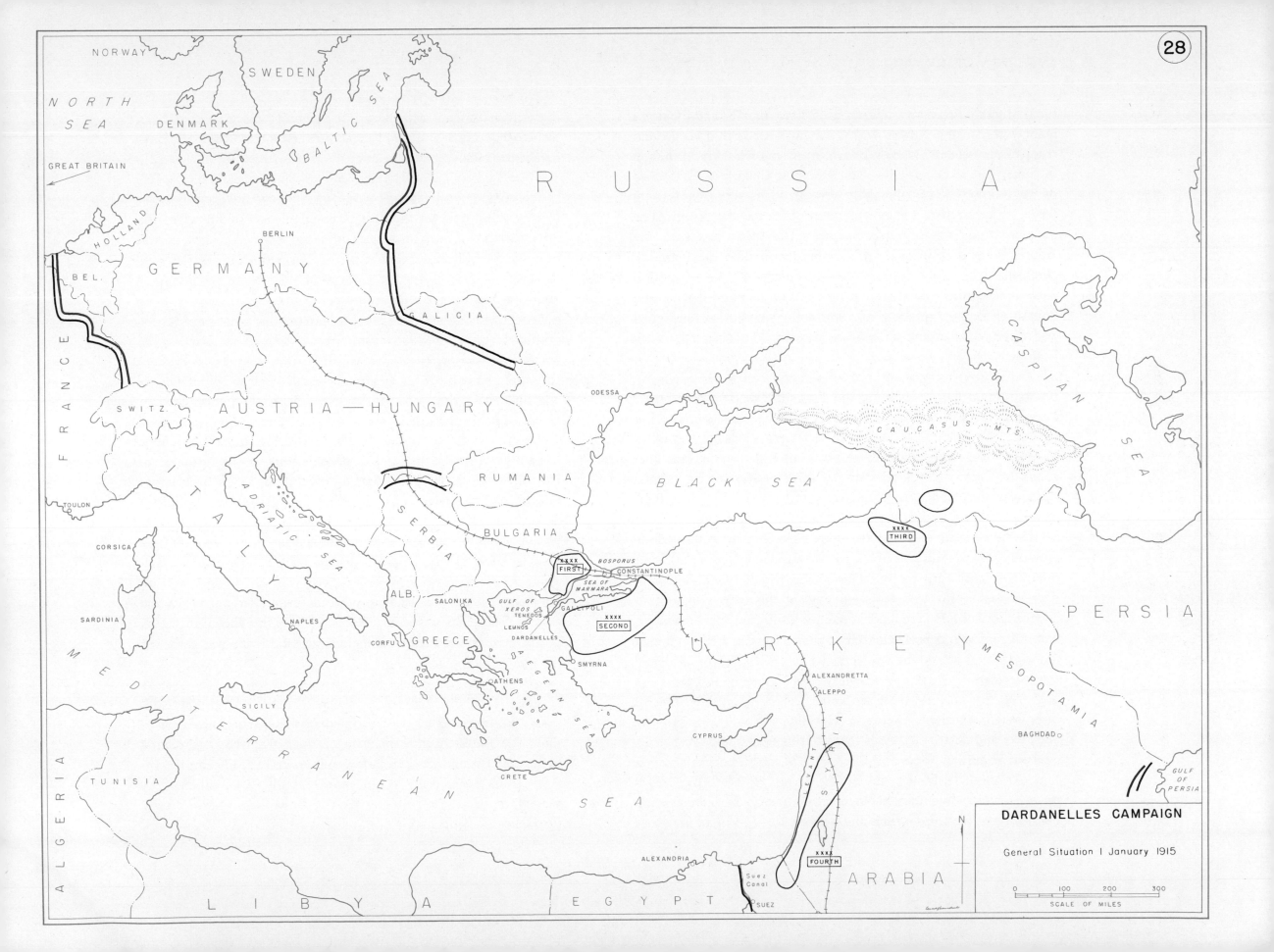

28

NORWAY

SWEDEN

*NORTH
SEA*

DENMARK

BALTIC SEA

GREAT BRITAIN

R U S S I A

HOLLAND

BEL.

GERMANY

BERLIN

GALICIA

FRANCE

SWITZ.

AUSTRIA — HUNGARY

ODESSA

CAUCASUS MTS.

CASPIAN SEA

TOULON

ADRIATIC SEA

RUMANIA

BLACK SEA

XXXX
THIRD

CORSICA

I T A L Y

SERBIA

BULGARIA

BOSPORUS

XXXX
FIRST

CONSTANTINOPLE

SARDINIA

ALB.

SALONIKA

SEA OF MARMARA

GULF OF XEROS

TENEDOS

GALLIPOLI

LEMNOS

XXXX
SECOND

P E R S I A

NAPLES

CORFU

GREECE

DARDANELLES

T U R K E Y

MESOPOTAMIA

SICILY

AEGEAN SEA

SMYRNA

ATHENS

ALEXANDRETTA

ALEPPO

BAGHDAD

TUNISIA

CRETE

CYPRUS

S Y R I A

GULF OF PERSIA

ALGERIA

M E D I T E R R A N E A N   S E A

ALEXANDRIA

Suez Canal

XXXX
FOURTH

DARDANELLES CAMPAIGN

General Situation 1 January 1915

N

SUEZ

A R A B I A

L I B Y A

E G Y P T

0   100   200   300

SCALE OF MILES

Field Marshal Kitchener, Secretary of State for War and the dominant voice on the British War Council, insisted that all ground troops were needed on the Western Front and would not sanction their use in the Dardanelles. Mr. Winston Churchill, First Lord of the Admiralty, together with several of his subordinates, believed that the Royal Navy alone could force the straits. The magnetic and forceful Churchill pressed his point and won; the Admiralty was instructed "to bombard and take the Gallipoli peninsula with Constantinople as its objective." Vice Admiral Sackville Carden, commander of the Dardanelles Blockading Squadron and a supporter of Churchill's views, was reinforced and directed to attack as soon as possible. This he did on 19 February, 1915.

Earlier—in November, 1914—a short, useless British naval bombardment had revealed to the Turks the weaknesses of their Dardanelles defenses; by now, these had been substantially improved. The defenses of the Dardanelles (sketch a) consisted of the outer forts at Cape Helles and Kum Kale, an intermediate group of forts on both sides of the strait at Kephez Point, and the inner defenses—the strongest—at the Narrows. Ten belts of mines and an antisubmarine net blocked the channel.

Carden quickly reduced the outer forts, but the intermediate defenses proved more troublesome. Mine sweeping was difficult under the guns of the forts and mobile field artillery. On 8 March, Carden went into the straits to engage the forts; some were silenced, but the British were forced to withdraw. By 17 March, enough mines had been cleared to make Carden believe that a determined effort might succeed: while smaller ships attacked the intermediate forts and trawlers swept more mines, the forts at the Narrows would be taken under long-range bombardment, after which Carden's twelve dreadnaughts would close to the Narrows and destroy the forts there. At this point, however, Carden was invalided home; Admiral John M. de Robeck succeeded him. At 1000, 18 March, the attack began; by 1400, the dreadnaughts had closed to the Narrows. However, in maneuvering for position, five ships struck mines (Belt No. 11) in an area that

the British thought was clear. De Robeck, believing the Turks to be using floating mines, became unnerved and withdrew, having lost two ships to the mines.

The Turkish defenses had been badly battered. In retrospect, a determined naval assault would very likely have cleared the Narrows and enabled the fleet to enter the Sea of Marmara for an attack on Constantinople (off map, east). In view of the brave and stubborn resistance of the Turks throughout the war, however, it is unlikely that Constantinople would have capitulated because of naval bombardment alone.

Meanwhile, there was some apprehension over the lack of ground forces in the operations. Greece offered three divisions, but Russia—suspicious of Greece's territorial ambitions—vetoed the offer. Finally, Kitchener made available the 29th Division and also the Anzac (Australian–New Zealand) Corps, then in Egypt. The French provided a division, and the Royal Naval Division joined the force. General Ian Hamilton was placed in command on 12 March and preceded his troops to the area. He joined De Robeck in time to witness the 18 March naval failure, and reported to London that the Navy alone could not do the job. De Robeck concurred. Churchill pressed for continuation of the naval attack, but to no avail.

The 29th Division, hastily loaded, left England in no condition to move directly into operations. Hamilton assembled all his troops at Alexandria, Egypt, and formulated plans for the assault. The parts to be played by his forces are shown in sketch b. The French division, after its feint at Kum Kale, was to follow the main landing.

Meanwhile, the Turks had put to good use the four weeks of grace following the naval attack. The Fifth Army, 60,000 troops under Sanders, was disposed in the Dardanelles area as shown. No attempt was made to garrison the widely separated beaches in strength; instead, most units were held in central positions from which they could move rapidly when and where needed.

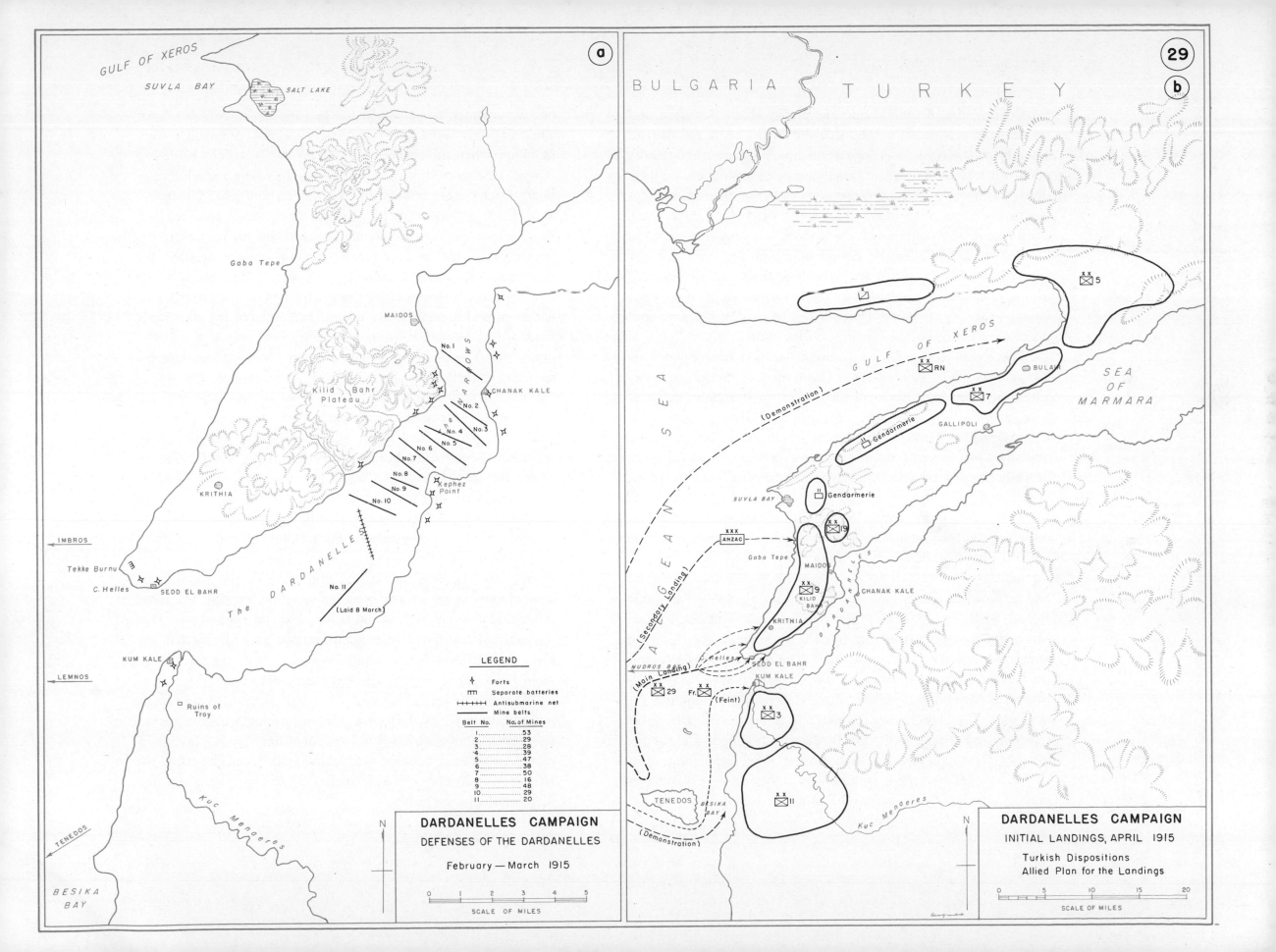

Map (a) — Left Panel

GULF OF XEROS

SUVLA BAY

SALT LAKE

Gaba Tepe

MAIDOS

No.1

THE NARROWS

CHANAK KALE

Kilid Bahr Plateau

No.2

No.3

No.4

No.5

No.6

No.7

No.8

No.9

Kephez Point

KRITHIA

No.10

IMBROS

Tekke Burnu

C. Helles

SEDD EL BAHR

The DARDANELLES

No.11

(Laid 8 March)

LEMNOS

KUM KALE

Ruins of Troy

Kuc Menderes

TENEDOS

BESIKA BAY

LEGEND

⚓ Forts
ᒣᒣᒣ Separate batteries
┼┼┼┼┼ Antisubmarine net
▬▬ Mine belts

Belt No.	No. of Mines
1	53
2	29
3	28
4	39
5	47
6	38
7	50
8	16
9	48
10	29
11	20

DARDANELLES CAMPAIGN

DEFENSES OF THE DARDANELLES

February — March 1915

N

0 1 2 3 4 5
SCALE OF MILES

Map (b) — Right Panel

a

29

b

BULGARIA   TURKEY

XX 5

GULF OF XEROS

XX RN

BULAIR

SEA OF MARMARA

XX 7

(Demonstration)

AEGEAN SEA

Gendarmerie

GALLIPOLI

SUVLA BAY

II Gendarmerie

XX 19

XXX ANZAC

Gaba Tepe

MAIDOS

THE DARDANELLES

CHANAK KALE

(Secondary Landing)

XX 9
KILID BAHR

KRITHIA

Helles

MUDROS BAY

(Main Landing)

SEDD EL BAHR

KUM KALE

XX 29   Fr. XX   (Feint)

XX 3

TENEDOS   BESIKA BAY

(Demonstration)

Kuc Menderes

XX 11

DARDANELLES CAMPAIGN

INITIAL LANDINGS, APRIL 1915

Turkish Dispositions
Allied Plan for the Landings

N

0 5 10 15 20
SCALE OF MILES

Considering the difficult conditions under which Hamilton and his staff labored, it is amazing that the British managed to land as early as 25 April. His logistician had no experience factors upon which to base his plans, intelligence concerning enemy positions was meager, weapons were in short supply, maps were practically nonexistent, there was a shortage of ships and landing craft, and joint planning with De Robeck was only introduced in the final stages. The entire period in Egypt was one of hectic improvisation. But, somehow, Hamilton managed to have his troops loaded and assembled in seventy-seven ships at Lemnos Island, fifty miles from the Dardanelles, by 21 April. There, final plans were made for the landings on the 25th.

The Royal Naval Division's demonstration near Bulair was highly successful (*see map* 29b). The division spent the entire day afloat there, covered by naval shelling of the beaches, and simulated preparations for landing. Sanders himself rode to the area and ordered the Turkish 7th Division to move up reinforcements. Similarly, the French feint at Kum Kale, where a regiment spent thirty hours ashore, was instrumental in holding Turkish troops in position.

The Anzac Corps landed at dawn but, because of an unexpected current, came ashore against negligible resistance, a mile north of the planned beach (*this map, sketch* a). There was considerable confusion, but, by 0930, General Sir William Birdwood had advance elements moving toward his objective—Sari Bahr Ridge (*upper right*). About this time, Turkey's most able soldier, Mustapha Kemal, arrived and hurried a regiment from his 19th Division forward to halt the advance. The fighting was fierce, but the Turks, though outnumbered three to one, halted Birdwood's troops. Birdwood became discouraged and asked Hamilton for authority to reembark his troops. The answer was "Dig yourselves in and stick it out," and Birdwood complied. The following day, Mustapha Kemal moved the rest of his division into line.

Meanwhile, the main landing was achieving no greater success. A covering force of seven and a half battalions, all under one commander, landed at the five beaches as shown (*sketch* b). The battalions of the main body, under another commander, were to follow when the beaches were secured. The troops landed in "tows," most consisting of four lifeboats drawn by a small motorboat, which cut them loose near the shore (*sketch* c). The troops at Y Beach (*sketch* b) met only slight resistance and had reached Krithia by nightfall; then counterattacks drove them back to the beach, and—due to a command mix-up—they evacuated the area next morning. The landings at S and X Beaches also met only sporadic opposition. By noon, Hill 114 at the latter beach had been seized, and the two reserve battalions of the main body landed. But Turkish resistance at Beaches W and V was better organized. The assault troops encountered wire, mines, and entrenchments relatively undamaged by naval gunfire. The Turks withheld their fire until the boats grounded, and then inflicted severe losses. Casualties were particularly heavy at V Beach, where the British, seeking to place maximum strength ashore quickly, attempted to beach the collier *River Clyde*. Caught under fire as they emerged from holes cut in the boat's sides, the troops were literally massacred. Late in the day, the rest of the main body, destined for V Beach, was rerouted to W.

All troops were now ashore, but lacking vigorous leadership, they made no attempt to push forward. The covering-force commander had become a casualty, and none of the subordinate commanders displayed the initiative so vitally needed. Hamilton influenced the action only through occasional suggestions. Had the desirable flexibility of communications existed, and had the success at Y Beach been exploited vigorously with the main body, Achi Baba (*upper right*) might well have been captured.

The British inched forward the next few days, but Sanders, initially deceived by the Bulair demonstration, promptly moved in reserves and established a formidable line. By 8 May, stalemate had set in at both the Anzac and Helles beachheads. If the British were to open the Dardanelles, reinforcements and a new plan would be necessary.

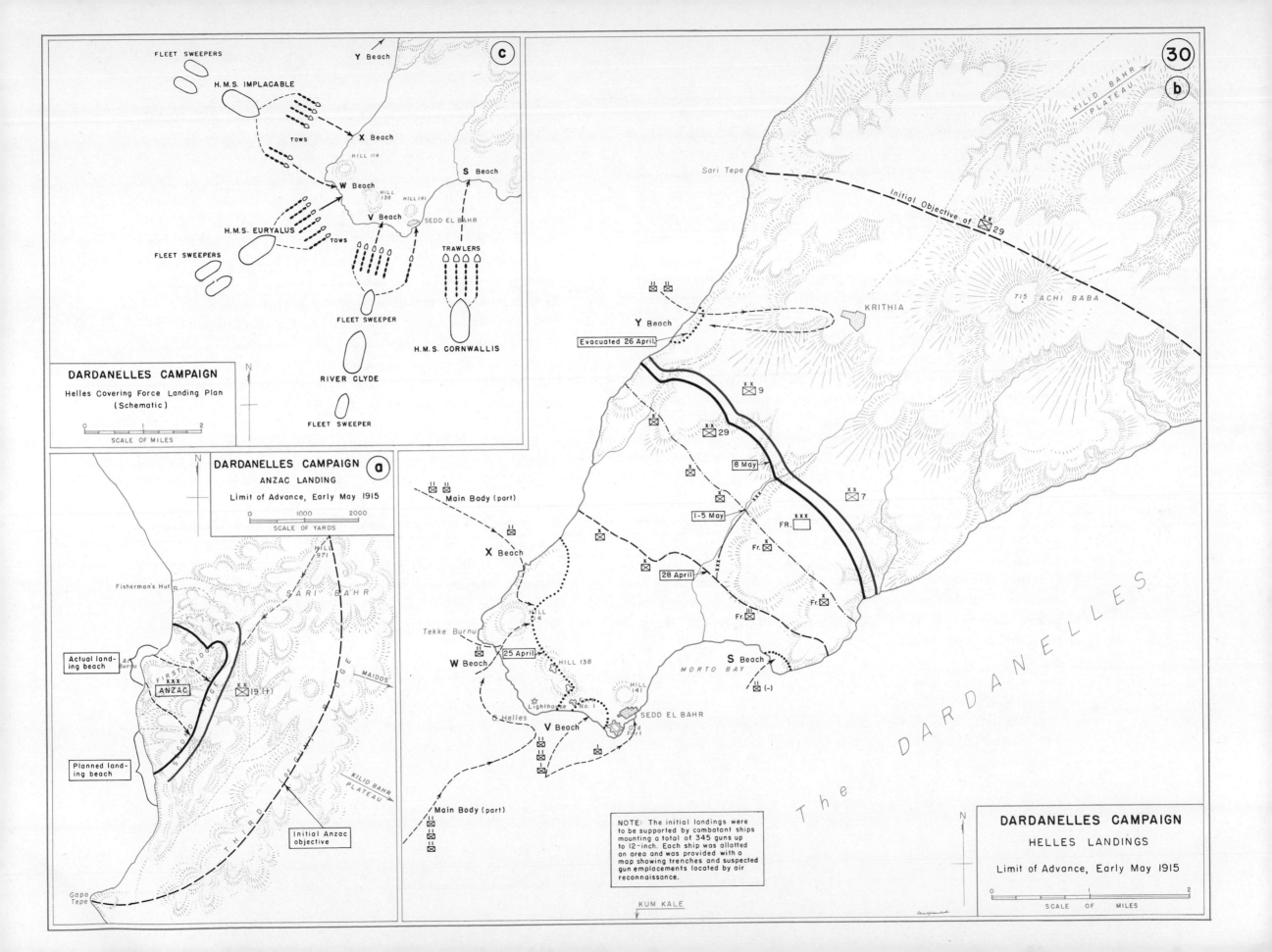

DARDANELLES CAMPAIGN

Helles Covering Force Landing Plan
(Schematic)

SCALE OF MILES
0   1   2

FLEET SWEEPERS

Y Beach

H.M.S. IMPLACABLE

TOWS

X Beach

HILL 114

W Beach

HILL 138

HILL 141

S Beach

H.M.S. EURYALUS

TOWS

V Beach

SEDD EL BAHR

TRAWLERS

FLEET SWEEPERS

FLEET SWEEPER

River Clyde

H.M.S. CORNWALLIS

FLEET SWEEPER

c

DARDANELLES CAMPAIGN

ANZAC LANDING

Limit of Advance, Early May 1915

SCALE OF YARDS
0   1000   2000

a

HILL 971

Fisherman's Hut

SARI BAHR

Actual landing beach

Ari Burnu

ANZAC

19 (†)

MAIDOS

Planned landing beach

KILID BAHR PLATEAU

Initial Anzac objective

THIRD RIDGE

Gaba Tepe

30

b

KILID BAHR PLATEAU

Sari Tepe

Initial Objective of 29

715 ACHI BABA

KRITHIA

Y Beach

Evacuated 26 April

XX 9

XX 29

8 May

1-5 May

FR.

Fr.

XX 7

28 April

Fr.

Fr.

Main Body (part)

X Beach

25 April

HILL 114

Tekke Burnu

HILL 138

W Beach

HILL 141

MORTO BAY

S Beach

Lighthouse No. 1

C. Helles

SEDD EL BAHR

V Beach

Old Fort

Main Body (part)

The DARDANELLES

NOTE: The initial landings were to be supported by combatant ships mounting a total of 345 guns up to 12-inch. Each ship was allotted an area and was provided with a map showing trenches and suspected gun emplacements located by air reconnaissance.

KUM KALE

DARDANELLES CAMPAIGN

HELLES LANDINGS

Limit of Advance, Early May 1915

SCALE OF MILES
0   1   2

After the failure of the May attacks at Helles, Hamilton lost hope of making progress without sizable reinforcements. That assault had gained little ground at great cost—by 8 May, his casualties had reached 20,000, a third of the Allied force engaged. At Anzac, conditions were no better. Though Mustapha Kemal finally accepted his inability to drive the Allies into the sea, the latter were not able to dislodge him from his commanding position. So, while the heat, unsuitable diet, flies, and crowded conditions bred disease and sickness—further crippling the British—Hamilton continued sporadic attacks through June. None were successful. Back in London, reactions to the dismal failure were serious.

April brought the slaughter at Ypres and the sensational disclosure of German use of poison gas. The Russian reverses brought no comfort either. Meanwhile, Hamilton's timid requests for reinforcements were largely ignored by Kitchener. In mid-May, a dispatch from De Robeck created a controversy. Desirous of aiding the despondent Hamilton, the navy had decided to try to force the straits again—provided that London approved. De Robeck's message completely upset the Admiralty, which was actually planning to reduce his fleet strength. Kitchener fumed, and there were political repercussions. Admiral Lord Fisher, First Sea Lord, resigned in a huff; the Asquith government tottered, but remained in power by accepting a coalition and jettisoning Churchill, upon whom the stigma of failure was placed. De Robeck's suggestion was flatly disapproved. But now, in June, Kitchener at last began to provide the supplies and men Hamilton so desperately needed. By the end of July, Hamilton had fourteen divisions; Sanders now had sixteen divisions.

Hamilton's plan for his second offensive is shown in sketch a. The Helles secondary attack was designed to hold and draw Turkish forces southward. The IX Corps, at Suvla Bay, was to seize quickly the dominating heights around the bay and then capture Anafarta Gap (*upper center*), which, in British hands, would compromise the enemy position commanding the Anzac area. The main attack sought the capture of Sari Bahr Ridge.

The Helles attack, launched at 0530, 6 August, and continuing through the 8th, made only minor gains, but did hold the Turkish troops in position. The main attack involved a major effort against Hill 971 and Chunuk Bahr, and secondary attacks against Lone Pine Ridge and The Nek (*sketch* b). The Lone Pine operation (1530, 6 August) successfully attracted the local Turkish reserves, plus two regiments from Kilid Bahr. The main effort, however, hoping to achieve surprise, attempted a difficult night march over unfamiliar terrain. Men straggled, units became lost. Consequently, though its assault on the morning of the 7th surprised the thinly spread Turks, it was too feeble to break their line—especially after the two regiments from Kilid Bahr quickly reinforced it. The attack at The Nek was a complete fiasco. Thus, Hamilton's main attack ended in unqualified failure.

But at Suvla Bay, a great opportunity to retrieve the campaign arose. The IX Corps, commanded by Gen. Sir Frederick Stopford, landed against negligible resistance. But confusion reigned on the beaches, and there was a pitiful lack of leadership at corps and division level. Sanders at once ordered two divisions to move by forced march from Bulair. Stopford spent two days dawdling on the beach and unloading supplies. Finally, late on 8 August, Hamilton exercised some direction and ordered Stopford to seize the heights. By the time the attack was made on the 9th, it was too late, for Sanders had his reinforcements in position.

On this sorry note, the campaign virtually ended. Hamilton, his stature fallen to that of Churchill, was relieved. Kitchener journeyed to the area and ultimately decided upon evacuation. All Allied troops—but little equipment—were evacuated without the loss of a single life. This humiliating operation, performed to perfection, was the most laudatory part of the entire Allied campaign. In the nine months of fighting, casualties for each side totaled about 250,000.

Note: The Allied IX Corps (Map a, upper left) had two divisions, instead of three.

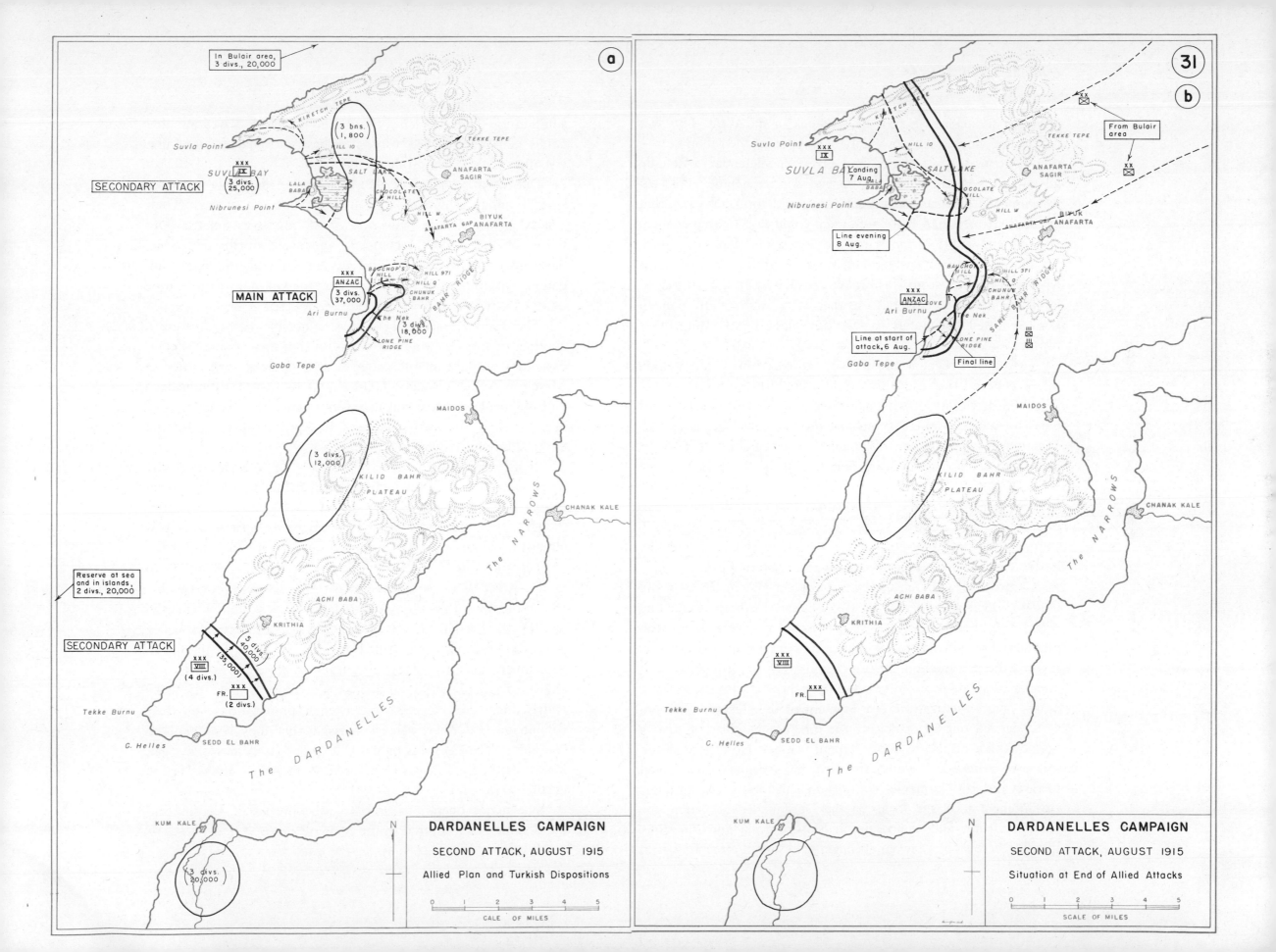

a

In Bulair area, 3 divs., 20,000

KIRETCH TEPE

(3 bns. 1,800)

HILL 10

TEKKE TEPE

Suvla Point

SECONDARY ATTACK

SUVLA BAY

XXX IX

(3 divs. 25,000)

LALA BABA

SALT LAKE

ANAFARTA SAGIR

Nibrunesi Point

CHOCOLATE HILL

HILL W

BIYUK ANAFARTA

ANAFARTA GAP

BAUCHOP'S HILL

XXX ANZAC

(3 divs. 37,000)

MAIN ATTACK

HILL 971

HILL Q

CHUNUK BAHR

SARI BAHR RIDGE

Ari Burnu

The Nek

(3 divs. 18,000)

LONE PINE RIDGE

Gaba Tepe

MAIDOS

(3 divs. 12,000)

KILID BAHR PLATEAU

The NARROWS

CHANAK KALE

Reserve at sea and in islands, 2 divs., 20,000

ACHI BABA

KRITHIA

(35,000)

5 divs. 40,000

SECONDARY ATTACK

XXX VIII

(4 divs.)

FR. XXX

(2 divs.)

Tekke Burnu

The DARDANELLES

G. Helles

SEDD EL BAHR

KUM KALE

(3 divs. 20,000)

DARDANELLES CAMPAIGN

SECOND ATTACK, AUGUST 1915

Allied Plan and Turkish Dispositions

0 1 2 3 4 5
SCALE OF MILES

b

31

XX

From Bulair area

KIRETCH TEPE

HILL 10

TEKKE TEPE

Suvla Point

XXX IX

SUVLA BAY

Landing 7 Aug.

LALA BABA

SALT LAKE

ANAFARTA SAGIR

XX

Nibrunesi Point

CHOCOLATE HILL

HILL W

BIYUK ANAFARTA

ANAFARTA GAP

Line evening 8 Aug.

BAUCHOP'S HILL

HILL 971

XXX ANZAC

HILL Q

CHUNUK BAHR

SARI BAHR RIDGE

Ari Burnu

The Nek

Line at start of attack, 6 Aug.

LONE PINE RIDGE

Final line

III

III

Gaba Tepe

MAIDOS

KILID BAHR PLATEAU

The NARROWS

CHANAK KALE

ACHI BABA

KRITHIA

XXX VIII

FR. XXX

Tekke Burnu

The DARDANELLES

G. Helles

SEDD EL BAHR

KUM KALE

DARDANELLES CAMPAIGN

SECOND ATTACK, AUGUST 1915

Situation at End of Allied Attacks

0 1 2 3 4 5
SCALE OF MILES

Nineteen fifteen was a year of deadlock in the West. This was due to the simple fact—probably less apparent then than now—that contemporary weapons had given the defender a definite advantage over the attacker. Barbed wire, machine guns, entrenchments, and supporting artillery could form a barrier that massed bayonets and human courage could not breach. Maneuver was impossible in the West; the opponents' flanks rested on the sea and neutral Switzerland. Even on those rare occasions when the enemy's front was broken—usually through surprise—large exploiting forces could neither be moved rapidly enough nor supported adequately to take advantage of the momentary rupture.

Falkenhayn recognized this fact and based his strategy upon it. He believed that a decisive victory could be won only in the West, but a variety of reasons—Hindenburg's and Ludendorff's pleas for a strong offensive against the Russians, the dangerous situation on the Austrian front, and his own failure at Ypres—made him decide to go on the defensive in the West for the time being. Realizing that the war would be a long one, he expanded the German military rail net to permit rapid movement of reinforcements and supplies, stepped up German industrial mobilization, and trained his troops for trench warfare. Meanwhile, he increased the German forces on the Eastern Front.

Confronted with the German defensive system, French and British leaders considered the two obvious methods of dealing with it: to break through, or to go around it. The French, who provided most of the troops on the Western Front, instinctively favored the first method. British opinion was divided: most commanders, like Sir John French and Haig, agreed with the French; others favored a strategic envelopment of the German position, to be carried out by exploiting the inherent mobility of British sea power for attacks against Germany's allies. No clear decision was ever reached. Usually, the British government attempted to carry out both strategies with insufficient forces. The strategic envelopment took the forms of the Dardanelles campaign, the Salonika front, and campaigns in Mesopotamia and Palestine. Finally, there were a few Englishmen who sought a technological solution to their problem: the development of a weapon that could penetrate barbed wire, trenches, and machine-gun fire. Eventually, this idea produced the tank.

During the winter of 1914-15, the Allies had launched several minor offensives with uniform lack of success. Their general scheme of maneuver involved offensives against both flanks of the great German-held salient in northern France, designed to break through and cut the German rail communications within the salient, thus forcing the Germans to withdraw or risk entrapment.

The 1915 French attacks in Champagne (*center*) were a continuation of the winter offensive in that area. Some 240,000 casualties brought minute gains. A small-scale British attack in March at Neuve Chapelle (*upper left*) was carefully rehearsed and obtained complete surprise. Communications failures, however, halted it after early successes. In April, the French suffered another bloody failure at St. Mihiel.

Shortly thereafter, the Germans made a limited attack in the Ypres area to straighten their line and to divert attention from troops moving to the Eastern Front. Apparently as an afterthought, they used poison gas experimentally. (Both sides had already used tear gas in various forms.) A panic among the French troops first engulfed by the gas cloud left a four-mile gap in the Allied line, but the Germans had no reserves available to exploit this success. Eventually, the Allies withdrew slightly. In May, the French and British failed in a joint attack at Souchez and Festubert. The final Allied offensive of 1915, beginning in September, consisted of a main attack by the French in Champagne and of French and British secondary attacks at Vimy Ridge and Loos, respectively. French preparations for their Champagne offensive were so massive that they could not be concealed. The Germans prepared a secondary defensive system, before which the offensive collapsed. Both Allied attacks in the north also failed.

The major operations in 1916—the Battles of Verdun and the Somme—are covered in the texts of maps 33 and 34.

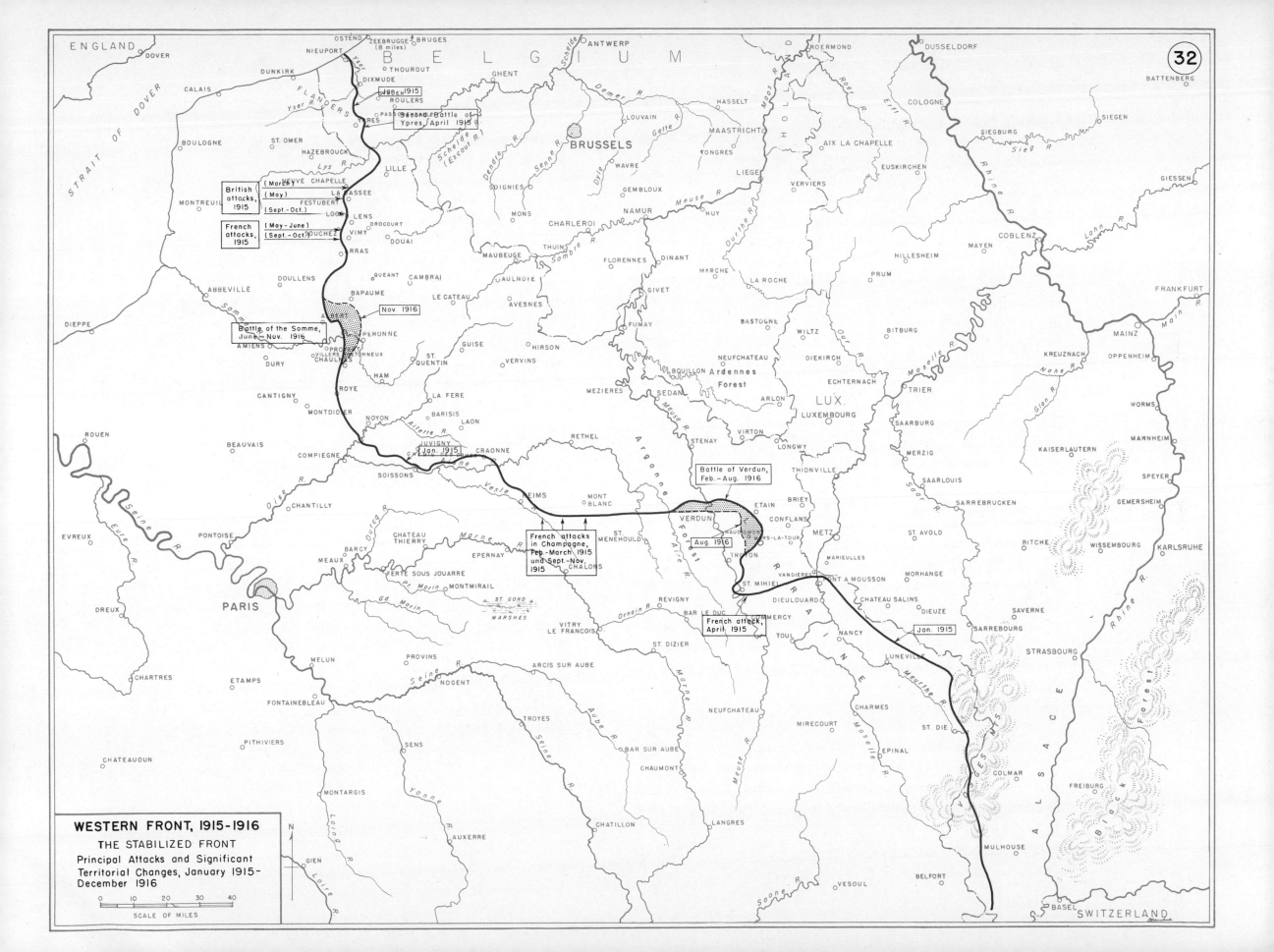

WESTERN FRONT, 1915-1916

THE STABILIZED FRONT

Principal Attacks and Significant
Territorial Changes, January 1915–
December 1916

0 10 20 30 40
SCALE OF MILES

Joffre now apparently decided that the war would have to be won by attrition. An Allied conference at Chantilly in December, 1915, planned a coordinated offensive against the Central Powers on the Western, Eastern, and Italian Fronts. The effort in the West was to be an attack astride the Somme River.

Falkenhayn anticipated the Allies. He felt that the best course of action would be an attack in Flanders, to drive the British into the sea and the French below the Somme. Unfortunately, this operation would require more troops than were available, and he consequently decided on an attack on a narrow front against either Verdun or Belfort. Signs of war-weariness, prompted by German propaganda, were appearing in France; the fall of either of these historic fortress cities would shake French morale and possibly force an early peace. Knowing this, Joffre would thrust every available French soldier into the battle, thus enabling the Germans—regardless of whether they took their objective—to bleed the French Army white. Verdun was finally chosen as the objective, largely because it threatened German railroad communications.

At the beginning of the war, Verdun had been a powerful fortress. The fall of Liége and Maubeuge, however, had left Joffre dubious as to the value of permanent fortifications; the French Army's need for heavy artillery led him to strip the Verdun forts of most of their guns. Afterward, he treated this vital sector with incomprehensible neglect.

In spite of precautions, the German build-up could not be concealed; on 8 February, a deserter warned the French. The Crown Prince (commanding the Fifth Army) was ready to attack on 12 February, but storms delayed him until the 21st. Meanwhile, French reinforcements arrived.

A twelve-hour bombardment opened the methodical German assault. French defenses were first wrecked by massed artillery fire, then occupied by infantry. German air support was aggressive. By 24 February, the two French trench lines north of Verdun had been breached, and French commanders prepared to withdraw to the west bank of the Meuse River. Imperturbable,

Joffre offered to court-martial any general who retreated. General Henri P. Pétain took command of the defense; the French improvised a new line around the dismantled forts on the dominating heights just east of the Meuse. On the 25th, the Germans seized Fort Douaumont (center), but French resistance stiffened; by the 29th, exhaustion halted the attack.

Meanwhile, French reinforcements poured in. Verdun's rail communications were limited (one standard-gauge and one narrow-gauge railroad), but this logistical problem was solved by operating an endless chain of trucks along the highway from Bar-le-Duc (off map, bottom right).

On 6 March, the Germans shifted their attack to the west bank of the Meuse. Pétain's strongpoints here were two commanding hills—Hill 304 and Le Mort Homme. German progress was slow. Renewed assaults east of the Meuse took Vaux (center) on 31 March, but a major assault on both sides of the river on 9 April failed. Falkenhayn now wished to halt the offensive, but the Crown Prince demanded that it be continued and expanded. Falkenhayn finally agreed to continue the operation, but refused to enlarge it.

The fighting west of the Meuse dwindled after 29 May. East of it, the Germans attacked on 1 June, clearing Fort Vaux and Thiaumont Farm on the 9th. On 23 June, they drove for the ridge line Fort Froide Terre–Fleury–Fort Souville, which commanded Verdun and the Meuse bridges. In one day they reached Fort Froide Terre. Pétain requested authority to withdraw; Joffre, knowing that the British were about to attack on the Somme, refused. The French hung on, though a final attack on 11 July almost broke their line.

Falkenhayn was relieved as chief of staff. Hindenburg-Ludendorff, who replaced him, suspended the Verdun offensive, since the Somme demanded priority. The French then launched a series of skillful counterattacks, regaining the area shown (dashed red line). Losses at Verdun numbered approximately 542,000 French and 434,000 Germans.

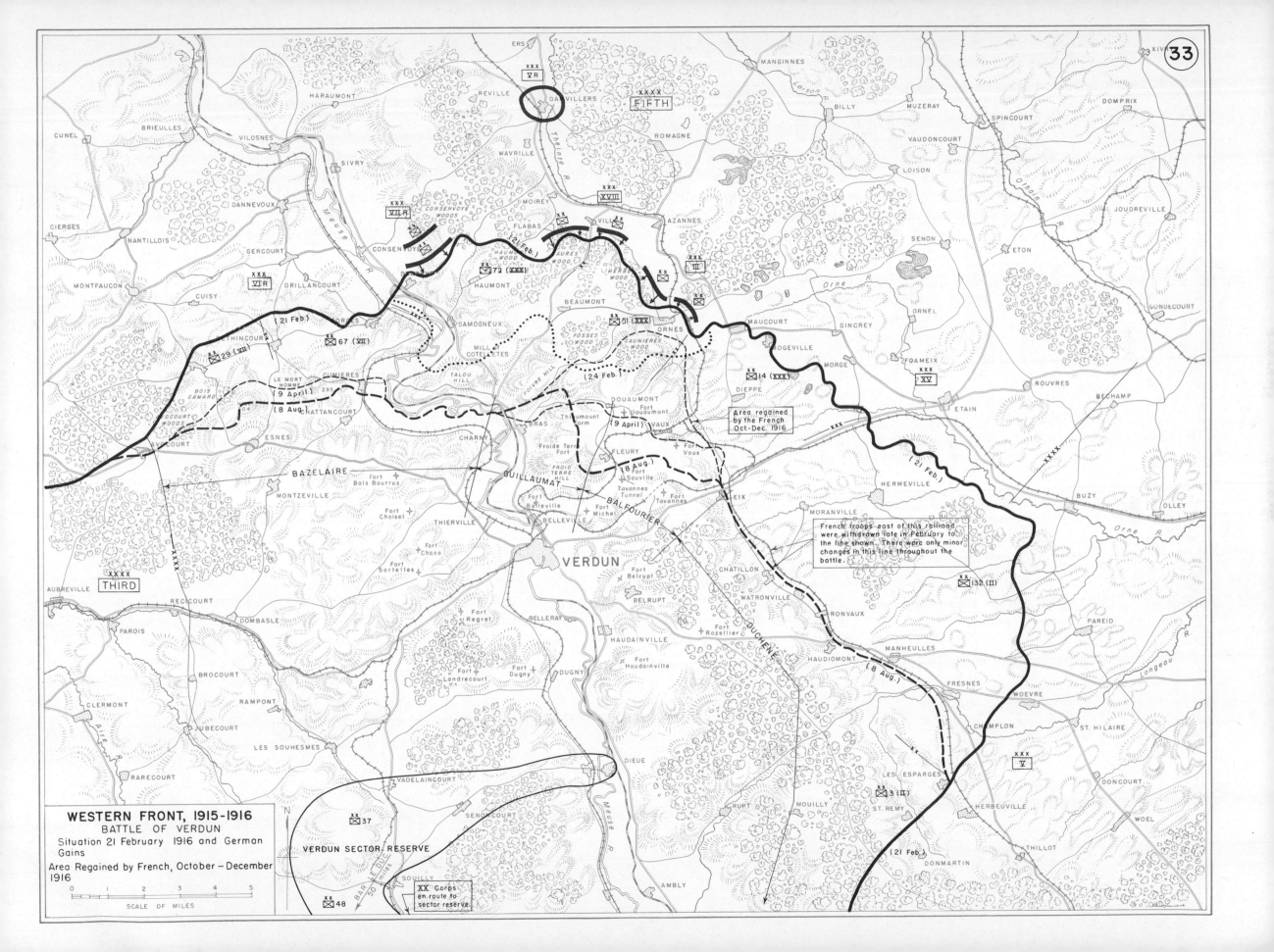

WESTERN FRONT, 1915-1916
BATTLE OF VERDUN
Situation 21 February 1916 and German
Gains

Area Regained by French, October – December
1916

SCALE OF MILES

0   1   2   3   4   5

Area regained
by the French
Oct.-Dec. 1916

French troops east of this railroad
were withdrawn late in February to
the line shown. There were only minor
changes in this line throughout the
battle.

VERDUN SECTOR RESERVE

XX Corps
en route to
sector reserve.

Joffre's selection of the Somme area for the 1916 offensive did him no credit. It had no strategic importance and had seen no fighting for two years, during which time the Germans had developed a defensive system of enormous depth and strength.

Originally, Joffre had planned to launch his main attack south of the Somme with forty French divisions, while the British made a secondary effort to the north. However, Verdun used up so many French divisions that the roles were reversed, the French making only a limited secondary attack.

According to the final plan, the French, with one corps north of the Somme, would attack generally east; the British Third Army would make a diversionary attack on the Gommecourt salient. The British Fourth Army, making the main effort, would penetrate the German lines between Maricourt and Fricourt, and seize the ridge from Montauban (*center*) to Serre (*upper left*). This gap would be widened by an advance to the high ground Ginchy (*center*)–Bapaume (*upper center*), along which a defensive line would be established. Its right flank thus protected, the British main attack would turn north, aided by a secondary attack between Fricourt and Thiepval. The final blow was to be an exploitation by the British Reserve Army—including all available cavalry—toward Douai (*off map, top right*) and Cambrai (*top right*).

The British established air superiority and massed 1,500 guns on an eighteen-mile front; the French had, proportionally, even heavier artillery support. Activity on this scale could not be hidden, but, by carrying out elaborate deceptive measures along the entire British front, Haig led Falkenhayn to believe that the Allied attack would be farther north. Falkenhayn also assumed that Verdun had so exhausted the French that they would not be able to attack on the Somme.

The artillery preparation began on 24 June. The assault was scheduled for the 29th, but bad weather delayed it until 1 July. British infantry-artillery cooperation immediately proved to be insufficiently developed. The advance of the XIII Corps was covered by a creeping barrage, but the artillery of the other corps lifted directly from one German trench line to the next, giving the German machine-gunners time to emerge from their dugouts and get into action before British infantrymen could reach them. From Fricourt north, the British were stopped with shattering losses. The XIII Corps carried Montauban, while the French made deep gains from Hardecourt south.

Lacking forces to renew his attack on the whole front, Haig reinforced his successful right flank. Falkenhayn poured in reinforcements, ordering that, if a foot of ground were lost, "put in the last man to recover it." As at Verdun, these tactics hurt the defenders worse than the attackers. After twelve days of fighting, in which Fricourt was taken, a major assault at 0325 on 14 July cracked the German second line between Bazentin-le-Petit Wood and Delville Wood. For a moment, victory seemed at hand. Cavalry got through, High Wood was cleared, but reinforcements came forward too slowly. A German counterattack restored the line.

On 15 September, after two months of costly small actions, Haig delivered his third major attack—employing tanks for the first time—against the German position between Morval and Le Sars. The tanks were effective, but mechanically unreliable; considerable gains were made, but no breakthrough. The attack was renewed on the 25th, the French helping by attacking due north against Bouchavesnes. By the end of October, the Germans had been driven off the main ridge and were fighting from a last, improvised line. The weather had grown steadily worse, but Joffre insisted on continuing a battle of attrition. A short period of better weather on 13 November allowed a successful surprise attack at Beaumont-Hamel (*upper left*) and Beaucourt in the north before Haig halted the fighting. The French had lost 195,000 men; the British, 420,000; the Germans, approximately 650,000, including most of their prewar officers and noncommissioned officers.

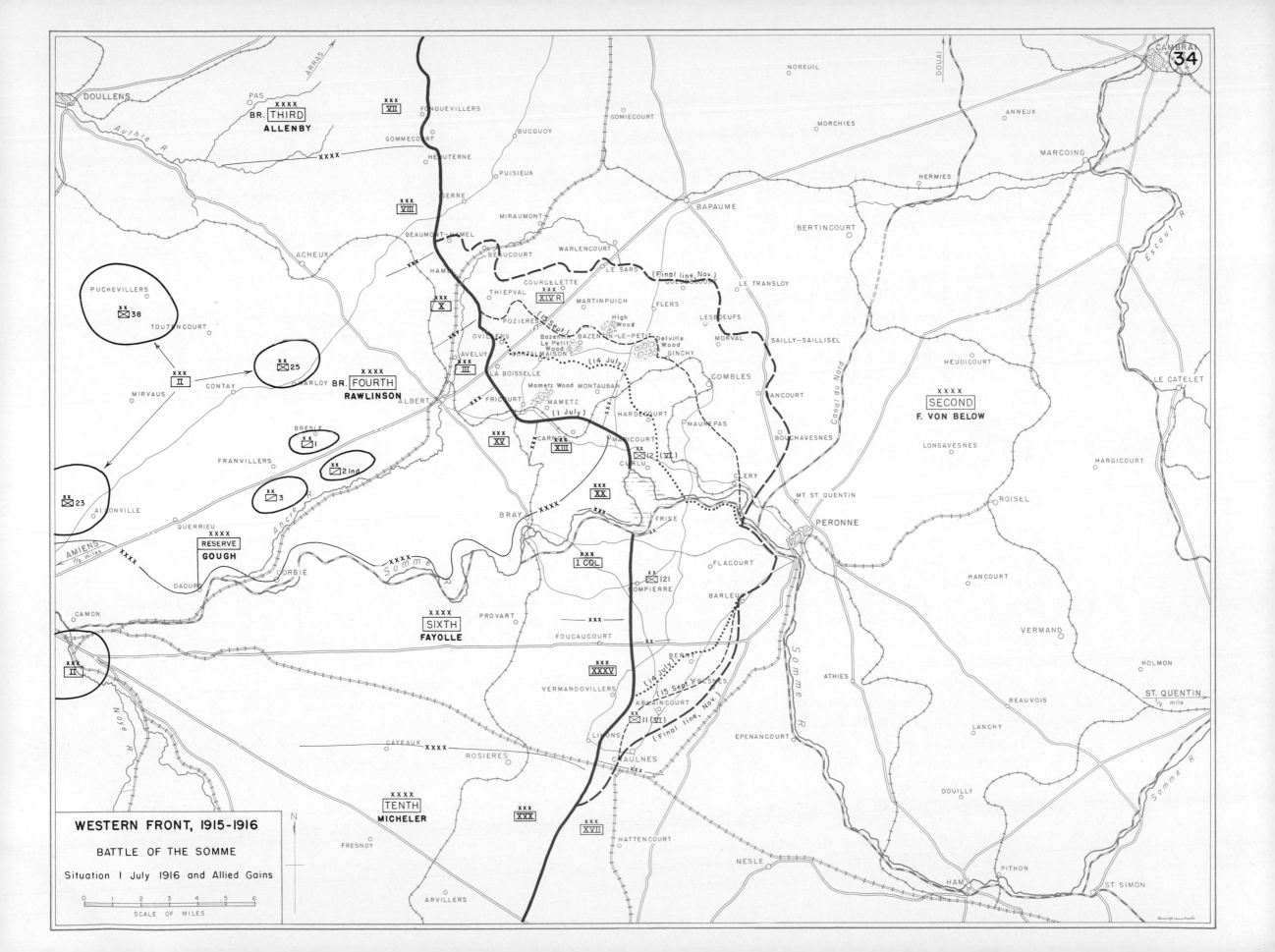

WESTERN FRONT, 1915-1916

BATTLE OF THE SOMME

Situation 1 July 1916 and Allied Gains

SCALE OF MILES
0   1   2   3   4   5   6

The British Grand Fleet (Admiral Sir John R. Jellicoe) had thirty-seven battleships and battle cruisers, eight armored cruisers, twenty-six light cruisers, and eighty destroyers. It was divided into the Battle Cruiser Fleet (Admiral Sir David Beatty)—which included four fast, new battleships (under Admiral Evan-Thomas)—and the Battle Fleet (under Jellicoe himself). The German High Sea Fleet (Admiral Reinhard von Scheer) had twenty-seven battleships and battle cruisers, eleven light cruisers, and sixty-three destroyers. It was divided into the Scouting Forces (Vice Admiral Franz von Hipper) and the Main Fleet (Scheer).

(In this map's schematic depiction, battle cruiser movements are indicated by dashed lines; battleship movements, by solid lines. Each arrow represents several such major ships. Light cruisers and destroyers are not shown. The numbers enclosed in circles match those used in this text to identify significant locations and actions; in sketches *b* and *c*, they also show the relative positions of the opposing forces at particular times.)

Sketch a. Admiral Scheer, commander of the German Fleet, was naturally aggressive; he was also under public pressure to break the throttling British blockade. He therefore launched a series of raids against the English east coast, seeking to force the dispersion of the British Grand Fleet to protect the various seaports. Apparently believing he had accomplished this, he planned a cruiser raid against Sunderland (1), to draw British warships in that vicinity toward his High Sea Fleet, which would be lurking south of Dogger Bank. Meanwhile, German submarines (2) would cruise off the British coast and mine ports used by the British Navy.

Unfavorable weather having prevented air reconnaissance, and his submarines having begun to exhaust their supplies (none participated in the ensuing battle), Scheer abandoned his original plan. Instead, he sent Hipper (3) out on 31 May as a decoy, following with his Main Fleet. British intelligence, however, had discovered his intentions, and Jellicoe (4) and Beatty (5) had put to sea on 30 May. At 1400, 31 May, these four naval forces were at positions (6).

Sketch b. (1) 1531: Beatty (six battle cruisers) sighted Hipper (five battle cruisers), who had already sighted Beatty and was turning back toward Scheer. (2) 1548: Both forces opened fire; Beatty attempted to get between Hipper and his base; Evan-Thomas was unable to catch up. (3) 1606: The British battle cruiser *Indefatigable* was sunk; Beatty shifted westward, increasing the range, but later closed it; Evan-Thomas opened fire at 1619; the British battle cruiser *Queen Mary* was sunk at 1626. (4) 1642: Beatty sighted Scheer's Main Fleet and turned north to lure it toward Jellicoe (*off map, upper left*). (5) 1647: Hipper had just turned north; Evan-Thomas now turned, heavily pounded by Hipper and Scheer. (6) 1730: The Germans pursued Beatty northward.

Sketch c. (7) 1740: Beatty turned east in search of Jellicoe; Hipper turned to close in on Scheer. (8) 1816: Jellicoe approached with his Battle Fleet in six columns, and began to form line of battle; Evan-Thomas took position behind him; the British battle cruiser *Invincible* was sunk at 1834, but Jellicoe's battleships were opening fire and the Germans were beginning to suffer. (9) 1835: Scheer turned west under cover of a heavy smoke screen and destroyer attacks; at 1850, Jellicoe turned south. (10) 1855: Scheer, possibly thinking that Jellicoe had divided the Grand Fleet, headed back toward Jellicoe, but found he was facing the massed fire of the British line of battle. (11) 1917: Scheer again turned west, covering his retreat by a smoke screen, destroyer torpedo attacks, and a "charge" by Hipper's battle cruisers; Jellicoe turned left to avoid the torpedoes; Hipper was badly battered, but got away. (12) 2020: Beatty had a last, brief clash with Scheer; at 2030, Jellicoe turned southwest. (13) 2100: Jellicoe turned south for the night. At 2106, Scheer closed up his formation; after dark, he cut behind the Grand Fleet (*action not shown*), fought his way through the British light craft covering its rear, and regained his bases. En route, he lost the old battleship *Pommern*, and had to sink the crippled battle cruiser *Lützow*. In addition to the major ships already mentioned as sunk, the British lost three armored cruisers and eight destroyers; the Germans, four light cruisers and five destroyers.

The jubilant Germans immediately claimed a victory; the British were correspondingly discouraged. Jellicoe, with some reason, was condemned as overly cautious. The Germans, however, never sought another open battle.

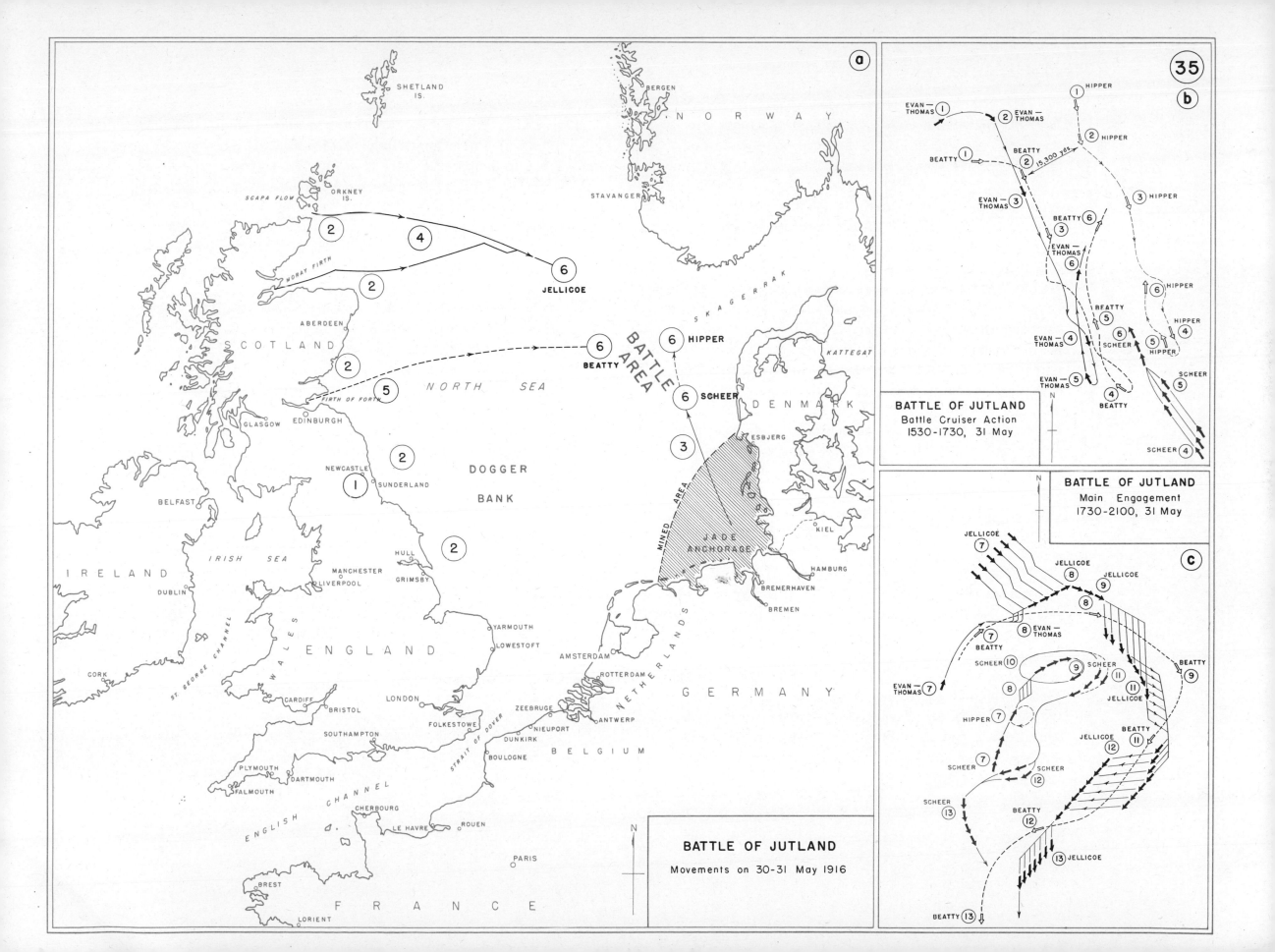

BATTLE OF JUTLAND

Movements on 30-31 May 1916

BATTLE OF JUTLAND

Battle Cruiser Action
1530-1730, 31 May

BATTLE OF JUTLAND

Main Engagement
1730-2100, 31 May

As 1915 drew to a close, the battle fronts were everywhere stabilized (*sketch* a). The 1915 Allied and German offensives in the West (*see map 32*) had made insignificant gains and had cost both sides heavily. The Russians, driven 180 miles east of Warsaw in the Gorlice-Tarnow disaster (*see map 27*), had desperately sought to rebuild their armies for the coming summer. Falkenhayn, convinced that Russian power was broken for some time, had turned to the West and moved troops to the Verdun area for his heralded battle of attrition (*see map 33*). But first he had to rid the Balkans of a nuisance—Serbia. In a whirlwind campaign in late 1915 (*see map 48*), Serbia had been overrun, and the front advanced to the Greek border. The Serbs retreated into Albania, and the Allies sent an expedition to Salonika. In Italy, the first four battles of the Isonzo had been fought (*see map 42*), and the Italians had little to show for 250,000 casualties. On the minor fronts (*none shown*), the tide of battle had turned against the Allies. The Dardanelles venture (*see map 31*) had been reluctantly abandoned; in Egypt, Turks and Britons watched each other across the Suez Canal; in Mesopotamia, General Sir Charles V. F. Townshend's force was under siege at Kut (*see map 52*); and in German East Africa, a British expeditionary force had been trounced.

At Chantilly in December, 1915, the Allies finally agreed on a combined offensive for the summer of 1916. We have seen that this plan was initially frustrated by Falkenhayn's Verdun offensive. When this began, the French appealed to the Russians for assistance. In quick response, the Russians launched a two-pronged drive (*this map, action not shown*) in the vicinity of Lake Narotch (*sketch* a, *right center*) on 18 March, 1916. During the winter, the Czar's armies had recovered somewhat, but they were still no match for the efficient Germans. By the 26th, the costly offensive had bogged down in the seas of mud resulting from the spring thaw.

Quiet returned to the Eastern Front; Russia resumed planning for the July offensive which was to be spearheaded by the West Army Group, making the main effort toward Vilna (*right center*). Again, an enemy offensive disrupted plans—this time by Austria, attacking in Italy on 14 May, 1916 (*see map 42*). When Italy appealed to the Czar for help, he promised a diversion. The intent was to move the July offensive up, but—except for General Alexei A. Brusilov—the army group commanders lacked enthusiasm. Hence, the courageous Brusilov volunteered to attack alone on 4 June. The Stavka expected the main attack to follow ten days later. Brusilov had studied German tactics and judged that concentration of combat power could be sacrificed if surprise were gained. Thus he planned to attack with all his armies (*this map, sketch* b) and forgo pronounced massing of troops. Every effort was made to preserve secrecy, enemy positions were studied in detail, artillery ammunition was accumulated, and divisions were thoroughly briefed. As a result, the attack was the greatest Russian success of the war. By 10 June, the Austrian line had been breached in two places. By late June, the important transportation center of Kowel (*upper left*) was in danger, and Germany again had to aid Austria. General Alexander von Linsingen was ordered to stop the critical northern drive. The battle seesawed, and Brusilov was slowed but not halted. Since West and North Army Groups produced no effective diversions, the Czar elected to reinforce Brusilov and let him continue attacking. Thus it became a race between the excellent German-Austrian lateral communications and the inferior Russian railroads. The Germans won. Though Brusilov's attacks continued in desperation during August and September, they gained little and resulted in tremendous losses. By 20 September, the offensive collapsed of sheer exhaustion.

Brusilov's offensive, in conjunction with reverses in France, had far-reaching strategic consequences: Conrad's Italian and Falkenhayn's Verdun attacks were weakened; Falkenhayn's position as chief of staff was undermined; Rumania joined the Allies; and battered Austria accepted German direction of the war. The Russians, however, had lost more than 1,000,000 men and were crippled and depressed. The stage was set for Lenin's return and the Revolution.

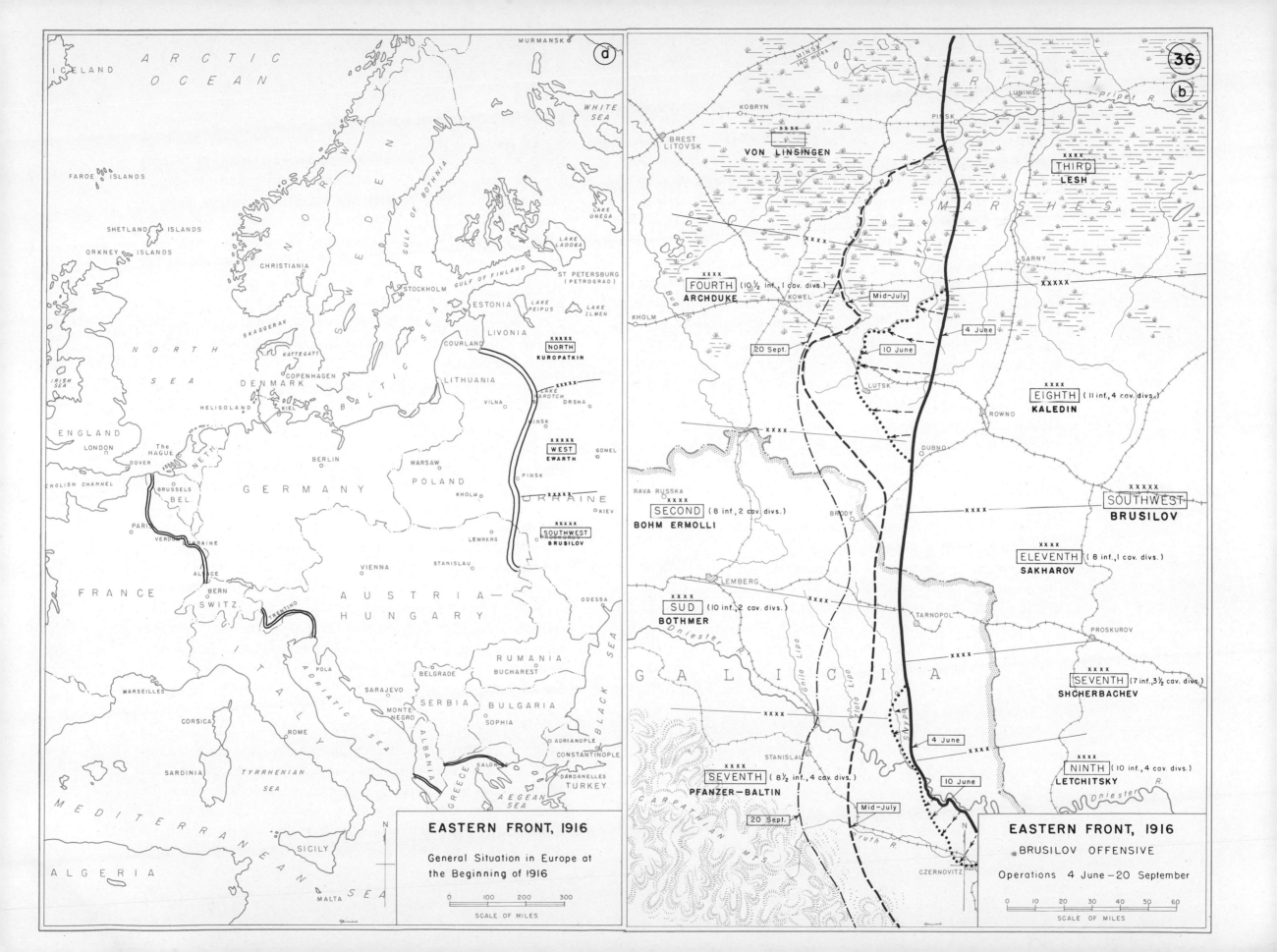

a — EASTERN FRONT, 1916

General Situation in Europe at the Beginning of 1916

SCALE OF MILES
0   100   200   300

36

b — EASTERN FRONT, 1916

BRUSILOV OFFENSIVE

Operations 4 June – 20 September

SCALE OF MILES
0 10 20 30 40 50 60

On 27 August, 1916, Rumania declared war on the Central Powers. For two years, she had watched the progress of the great struggle and contemplated joining the higher bidder. Her sympathies, it is true, had lain with the Allies (the country's Western orientation may have been a dominant factor), but by late 1915, fear of the Central Powers, surrounding her on three sides as they did, undoubtedly had a profound influence. So her scheming and vacillating government carefully eyed the unfolding drama and anxiously calculated the most opportune time to intervene. Then, as the news in the East seemed to indicate an Austrian disaster— Brusilov's offensive being the cause—Rumania bargained with the Western Allies, establishing an imposing list of territorial demands as her price for driving the last nail into the Austrian coffin. France and Britain, disconsolate over events in the West, eagerly sought her aid and were quite willing to meet almost any demand. But Russia, suspicious of her neighbor because of her pre-1914 Austrian ties, and disdainful of her military capabilities, was not at all happy about developments. (The Russians well knew that Rumania coveted Bessarabia [upper right; territory between Pruth and Dniester Rivers]: in 1877, a Russo-Rumanian war with Turkey had wrested this province from Turkey, and Russia had claimed it, giving to her ally the barren Dobruja [lower right].) So, after almost two months of bickering, Rumania joined the Allies; in exchange for four military commitments, she had forfeited her most precious advantage—time. In June, while Brusilov hammered the Galician front, a Rumanian offensive might have succeeded; but by August the Russians had been contained, and German troops were now available to test Rumania's mettle. Furthermore, Falkenhayn, watching the fence-straddling act carefully, had foreseen Rumania's likely entry into the war and prepared accordingly. Consequently, Mackensen was in Bulgaria organizing the Danube Army, and offensive plans were prepared for implementation by 30 September, the earliest date anticipated for the Rumanian entry into the war.

The map illustrates Rumania's weak strategic position. The length of her borders was out of proportion to the country's depth—Bucharest was only thirty miles from Bulgaria. The rugged Transylvanian Alps served as a barrier against Austria, as did the Danube against Bulgaria in the south. There were several passes through the mountains, the most important being those traversed by the railroads shown. The only permanent Danube bridge was at Cernavoda on the railroad to the seaport of Constanza. This latter city was important to Rumania for it was the best link to outside help—the railroads leading into Moldavia had been purposely neglected by Russia before the war when Rumania and Austria were friendly. Contrasted to the excellent railroad net in Transylvania, Rumania's system was poor and afforded little capability for rapid lateral movement. Using Austrian railroads, the distance between Predeal and Red Tower Passes (center) was 80 miles; via the Rumanian system, it was 270 miles.

Nor was the Rumanian Army very efficient. By 1916, it had twenty-three divisions, but was short of artillery, communications equipment, aircraft, rifles, and machine guns. Its senior leaders were inexperienced and none too well qualified; staff work and the state of training were notoriously poor. Lacking manufacturing facilities, the country had to rely upon Allied support.

Rumania's war plan was based upon Allied promises to: attack northward from Salonika (off map, bottom) to divert Bulgaria; attack Austria in the Bukovina (top center); send three Russian divisions to Dobruja; and supply munitions. She considered two plans: Plan A—to defend against Austria, while launching a major drive into Bulgaria to link up with the Salonika offensive; and Plan B—to launch the major attack into Transylvania, defending elsewhere. Swayed by political aims, and against Allied advice, Rumania chose Plan B. She disposed her troops as shown and prepared to attack, the initial objective being the line of the Maros River.

The plan of the Central Powers envisaged holding attacks by the First Army, while the Ninth Army, making the main effort, moved through the mountains on Bucharest. Meanwhile, Mackensen would subjugate Dobruja and eventually cross the Danube to support the Ninth Army. As chief of the general staff, Falkenhayn approved the plan, little suspecting that, upon his relief, it would be his lot to execute it.

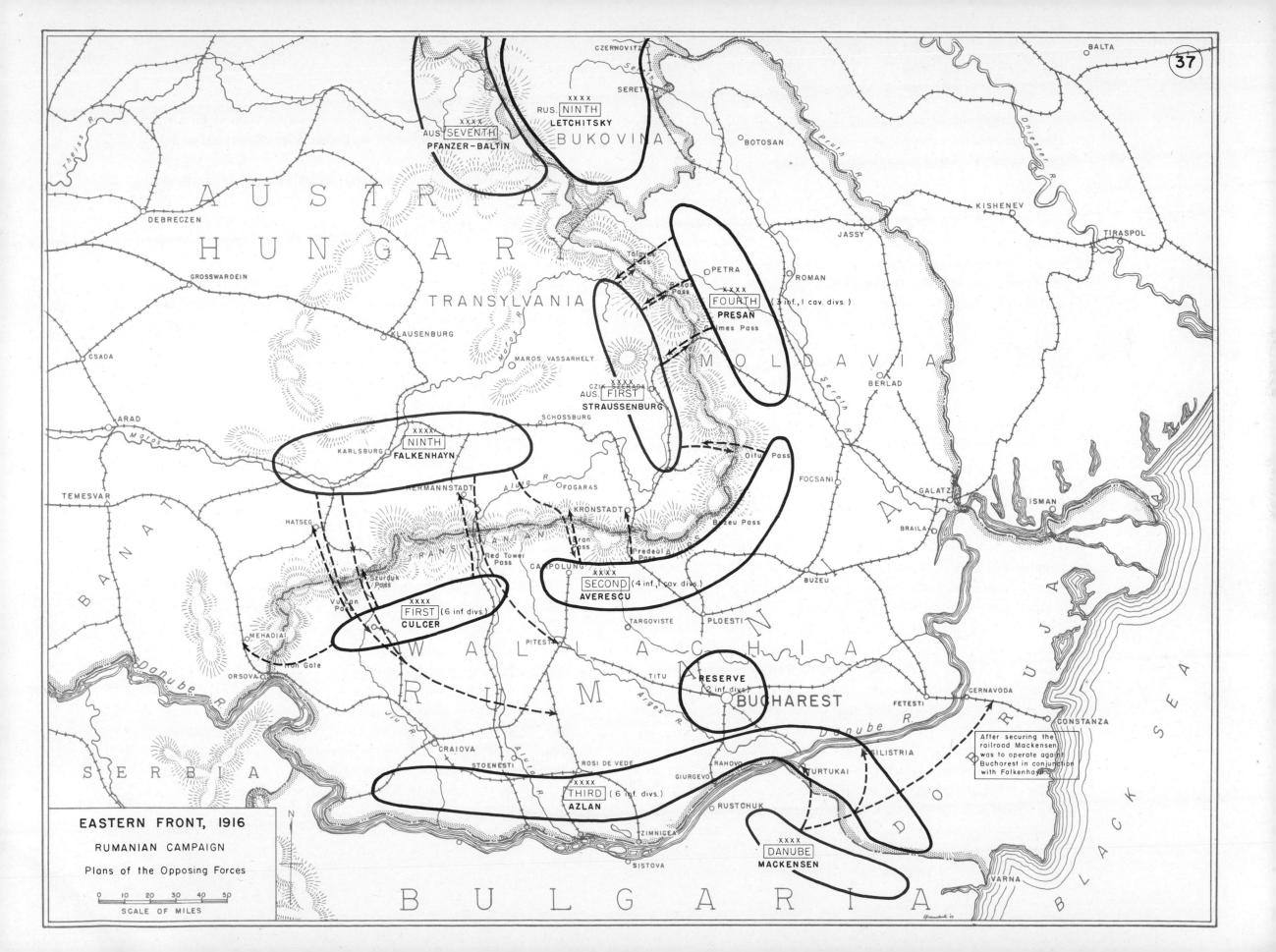

EASTERN FRONT, 1916

RUMANIAN CAMPAIGN

Plans of the Opposing Forces

0 10 20 30 40 50
SCALE OF MILES

On the night of 27-28 August, the First, Second, and Fourth Rumanian Armies began their advance into Transylvania. Ill-equipped and poorly trained for mountain warfare, hindered by lack of lateral communications, and obstructed by the dearth of roads, the Rumanians moved slowly. Austrian resistance was not spirited, their units being understrength and for the most part recuperating from the mauling administered by Brusilov. In two weeks, the Second Army had made gains of fifty miles, but, by 18 September, the Rumanian armies had been stopped on the line shown. Austrian resistance had stiffened as the defenders fell back to a shorter front, and as German troops continued to arrive to fill up the Ninth Army. To the Rumanians, now striving to improve their logistical situation, the outlook on the northern front seemed promising. Already through the worst of the mountains, they anticipated breaking out into the Hungarian plain very shortly.

But from the Dobruja (*lower right*), ominous news was trickling in to Bucharest, and in the Hermannstadt-Hatseg area (*center, left*) Falkenhayn's Ninth Army was almost ready to launch a counterattack designed to isolate the northern Rumanian armies.

Outside Rumania, the Allies were belatedly carrying out their promised diversionary operations. The attack against the Bulgars on the Salonikan front (*see map 49*) was launched on 10 September, after a month's delay occasioned by a Bulgarian spoiling attack. (The offensive continued until November, with only meager gains and without influence on the campaign in Rumania.) Russia, the most reluctant ally, was exerting pressure—if only token—on the common enemy in Bukovina (*this map, top center*) and had dispatched the three promised divisions to Dobruja.

South of the Danube, Field Marshal von Mackensen had not tarried in implementing his part of the Austro-German plan. On 1 September, his conglomerate army—made up of Bulgars, Turks, and a few Germans—crossed the border into Dobruja. Two of his Bulgarian divisions brushed aside covering forces and reached Turtukai the next day. Meanwhile, his right columns advanced north, parallel to the sea, and heavy artillery moved up from Rustchuk. The fortified city of Turtukai (25,000 men and 100 guns) surrendered on the 6th, after four days of heavy fighting and the failure of a relief column from Silistria to break through Mackensen's lines. The Danube Army continued its advance, occupying Silistria on the 9th. On the 16th, however, it came up against the remnants of the Rumanian Third Army—reinforced by a Russian corps and a division of Serbian volunteers—in a strong defensive position (*dashed blue line*) just south of the Cernavoda-Constanza railroad. The Russian General Zaionchovsky commanded this mixed force of nine divisions. Mackensen, who had left minimum security forces along the Danube, had about the same number of troops as his foe, but his artillery was superior. Appreciating the vital importance of Constanza to Rumania, he decided to attack.

Meanwhile, consternation reigned in Bucharest. There, under unopposed air attack and unnerved by Mackensen's success, the Rumanian strategists became panicky. Three divisions were ordered to Dobruja from Transylvania, thus slowing the drive on the northern front.

Mackensen's attack made no progress in four days of violent fighting. The Allies had hoped that the Bulgars would be reluctant to attack the Russians (traditionally their protectors), but Zaionchovsky made the mistake of sending his Serbs (their blood enemies) against Mackensen's Bulgars. Zaionchovsky, now reinforced with the three divisions from Transylvania, launched a counterattack. In three days, Mackensen was driven back ten miles. Here, the line temporarily stabilized as both sides, in an exhausted state, looked to their logistical problems. Up to this date, Rumania had been receiving only thirty tons of ammunition per day—one-tenth of that promised by her allies. Supplies could reach Rumania only by way of Russia, and large backlogs had developed at all Russian ports.

In the northwest, Falkenhayn had opened his counteroffensive on the 18th; and in Bucharest, Rumanian high councils were brewing a new strategy.

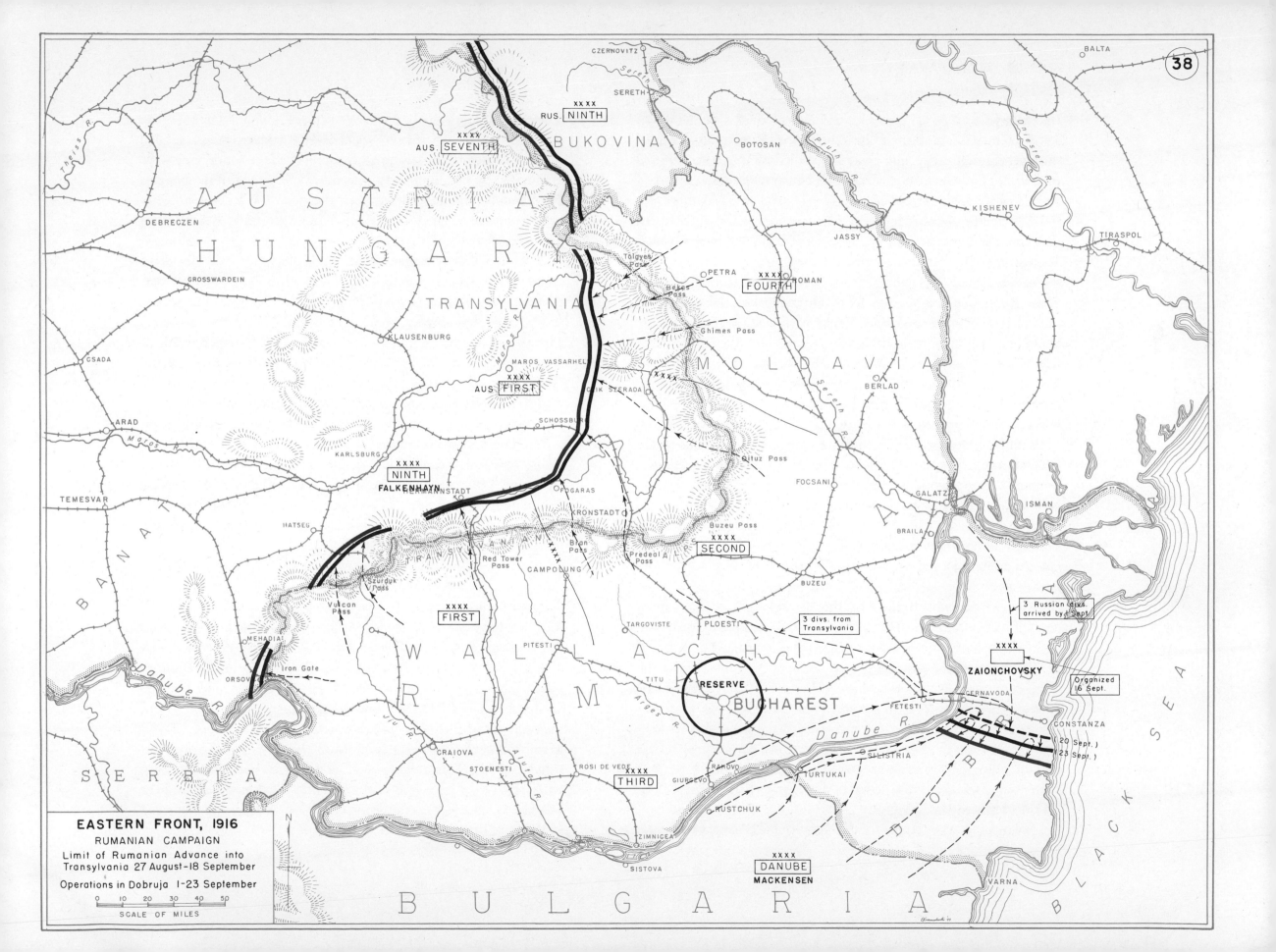

EASTERN FRONT, 1916
RUMANIAN CAMPAIGN
Limit of Rumanian Advance into
Transylvania 27 August-18 September
Operations in Dobruja 1-23 September

Falkenhayn arrived to assume command of the Ninth Army on 18 September. As previously noted, the Rumanian advance through the mountains had generally stalled by that date (*dashed blue line*). The German general's first concern was the Rumanian First Army's drive toward Hatseg (*lower left*) and the important railroad to the north. Here, on 18 September, he launched his first counterattack, seeking to force the Rumanians back through Vulcan Pass. The attack stopped the First Army advance but did not achieve its ultimate aim. On 26 September, Falkenhayn struck at the Rumanian column moving on Hermannstadt. Elite German Alpine troops enveloped both flanks of the column and barely missed cutting it off from its escape routes. The Rumanians were forced back across the border, and the Germans seized Red Tower Pass. Meanwhile, the Rumanian Second and Fourth Armies, in an attempt to remove pressure from the First Army, had advanced toward Schossburg and Maros Vassarhely by the 29th. On 4 October, the Germans attacked the left flank of the Second Army, forcing it to fall back on Kronstadt. By 10 October, the bulk of the Second Army, like the First Army, had been compelled to retreat within the Rumanian border. To the north, the Fourth Army—less from Austrian pressure than from fear of isolation when its southern neighbor withdrew—fell back on the eastern mountain passes. Now the Rumanians were on the defensive everywhere.

Meanwhile, what had been the decision of the Rumanian council of war sitting at Bucharest in late September? Concerned with Mackensen's unexpected thrust into Dobruja, but still primarily motivated by the desire to subjugate Transylvania, the high command had compromised. General Averescu's Third Army (*not shown, but then south of Bucharest*) was given the reserve divisions at Bucharest and ordered to strike Mackensen's rear by crossing the Danube at Rahovo while Zaionchovsky held him in place near Constanza with a secondary attack. At the same time, on the Transylvanian front, the Rumanian armies would continue the advance.

We have seen the repulse of the advance into Austria-Hungary.

The same fate awaited Averescu's attack. About 1 October, the crossing (*action not shown*) was begun at Rahovo, but a sudden flood disrupted it; the few units which reached the south bank were eliminated by Danube Army detachments. By then, Falkenhayn's Hermannstadt attack had created the need for Rumanian reinforcements in Transylvania; most of Averescu's troops were promptly dispatched there.

On the Transylvanian front, Falkenhayn pushed his drive through the passes. Campolung (*center*) fell on 14 October. Predeal Pass was in German hands by 25 October, but winter snows and stiffening resistance combined to halt the advance. Meanwhile, to the west, Delmensingen's troops pushed south of Red Tower Pass. In the north, the Fourth Army gave ground slowly. By 25 October, the German advance had reached the position shown (*dotted blue line*). In early November, the Russians assumed responsibility for part of the Fourth Army front.

In Dobruja, Mackensen, reinforced with two Turkish divisions, renewed the offensive on 20 October. Three days later, Constanza fell, followed by Cernavoda on the 25th. Having eliminated the vital sea and rail link to Russia, Mackensen now moved part of his army to Sistova (*bottom center*) in preparation for an attack toward Bucharest.

Since the approaching winter would soon make the mountains almost impassable, Falkenhayn had to move quickly. Though he preferred a movement through the northern passes—thus isolating more Rumanian troops—he elected to attack in the Vulcan Pass area (*lower left*), where the defenses were weaker. Reinforced by four German divisions from the Western Front, this attack jumped off on 10 November and reached Craiova by the 21st. Only one Rumanian division was cut off, the rest of the First Army withdrawing east of the Aluta River. Meanwhile, Delmensingen and Morgen were pushing forward slowly, as the Rumanians, their defenses turned on their left, withdrew (*solid blue lines*). In the south, Mackensen crossed the Danube against feeble opposition on 23 November, and advanced in the next three days to the line shown.

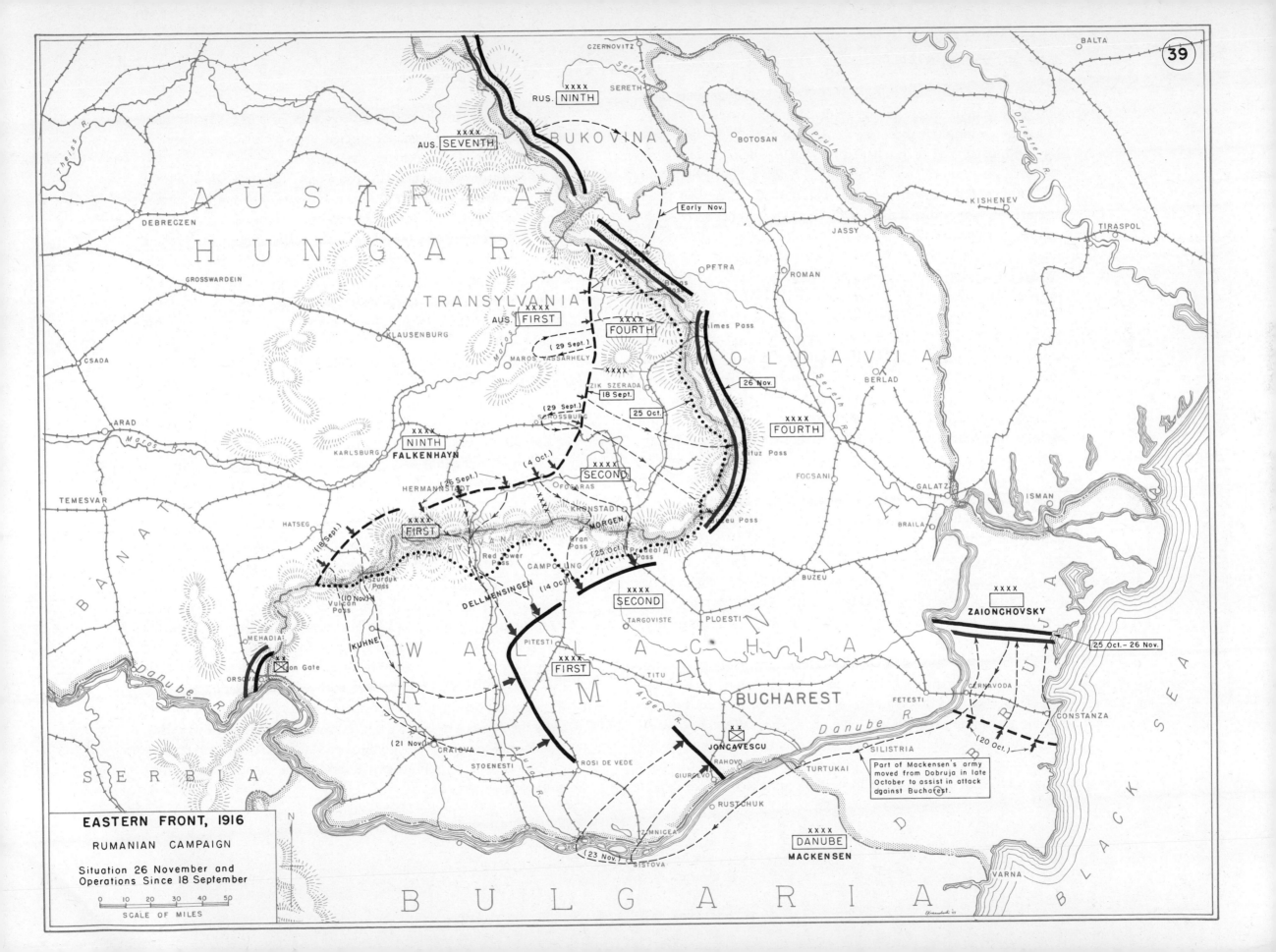

39

RUS. NINTH

AUS. SEVENTH

A U S T R I A - H U N G A R Y

TRANSYLVANIA

Early Nov.

AUS. FIRST

FOURTH

(29 Sept.)

26 Nov.

FOURTH

18 Sept.

25 Oct.

NINTH
FALKENHAYN

SECOND

(4 Oct.)

(26 Sept.)

FIRST

MORGEN

(18 Sept.)

DELLMENSINGEN

(14 Oct.)

(10 Nov.)
Vulcan Pass

ZAIONCHOVSKY

25 Oct. - 26 Nov.

SECOND

W A L L A C H I A

MEHADIA

KUHNE

FIRST

(20 Oct.)

(21 Nov.)

BUCHAREST

JONCAVESCU

Part of Mackensen's army
moved from Dobruja in late
October to assist in attack
against Bucharest.

(23 Nov.)

DANUBE
MACKENSEN

B U L G A R I A

B L A C K   S E A

EASTERN FRONT, 1916

RUMANIAN CAMPAIGN

Situation 26 November and
Operations Since 18 September

0 10 20 30 40 50
SCALE OF MILES

On 26 November, the situation of the Rumanian Army (reduced to seventeen infantry and three cavalry divisions) was desperate. Its line bulged west of Bucharest in a huge salient which invited a converging attack on the capital. Under these conditions, Falkenhayn did not anticipate a determined Rumanian stand against his twenty divisions. But there was a gap between Mackensen's army and Falkenhayn's right which served to expose the former to attack before he could be supported by the Ninth Army. Averescu, now supreme commander, agreed to the plan proposed by General Presan (commanding the forces concentrating at Bucharest), whereby Mackensen would be struck a blow while the First and Second Armies held off Falkenhayn. Under the circumstances, the Rumanians are to be admired for the boldness of their concept. Defeat was certainly not to be prevented by remaining passively on the defensive everywhere. There appeared to be little chance of success against the Ninth Army while Mackensen was on the Rumanian rear. But if Mackensen could be driven against the Danube, enough time might be gained to allow for the arrival of expected Russian reinforcements.

Presan's plan provided that three Rumanian infantry divisions—their right flank screened by two cavalry divisions which would push into the gap between Mackensen and Falkenhayn—would emerge from the Bucharest area and envelop Mackensen's left flank. Simultaneously, three Russian divisions would strike his right, while the force already in contact with him would fix him in position by frontal attacks. Two divisions were to be held in reserve.

The attack commenced on 1 December, but without the support of the Russians, who disagreed with the plan. It achieved initial success, cutting off part of Mackensen's force, but the reserve was committed too late to be of decisive value. The cavalry flank guard—its inferiority in strength was the weak link in the plan—was brushed aside by a superior force dispatched by Falkenhayn on 2 December. This force then attacked Presan's right

and rear and drove the Rumanians back in panic. At the same time, Ninth Army elements applied pressure all along the line, particularly in Delmensingen's sector.

The dispirited Rumanian troops now fell back all along the line, abandoning Bucharest, which Falkenhayn's patrols entered on 6 December. The exhausted condition of the German troops, heavy rainfall, and the resultant poor roads slowed the pursuit. By 7 January, 1917, when the campaign ended, the opposing forces were on the line shown. The last days of campaigning had seen several battles between Germans and Russians, the latter having been reinforced heavily in fear of a German advance into southern Russia.

Thus, Germany solved another Balkan problem. The Rumanians did not formally capitulate, but the bulk of the country—including the grain- and oil-producing areas—was in German hands. The Rumanian Army was no longer a threat, having been reduced to a state of impotency. (In January, it was considered capable of defending only a twenty-mile front.) The campaign cost Germany about 60,000 combat casualties (and about the same number sick); estimates of Rumanian losses vary between 300,000 and 400,000.

In retrospect, the Rumanian government obviously committed a serious error in the timing of its declaration of war, selfishly concerned as it was with postwar acquisitions. Militarily, Rumania's strategy could not have been worse. In choosing Transylvania as the initial objective, she ignored the threat to her rear. When the advance through the mountains failed, the high command refused to economize forces on that front to allow the creation of a mobile reserve, with which Falkenhayn's later thrust could be countered. Nowhere did the Rumanians properly mass their forces to achieve concentration of combat power. But, in the final analysis, the pronounced Austro-German superiority in leadership and training probably had the most decisive effect on the campaign.

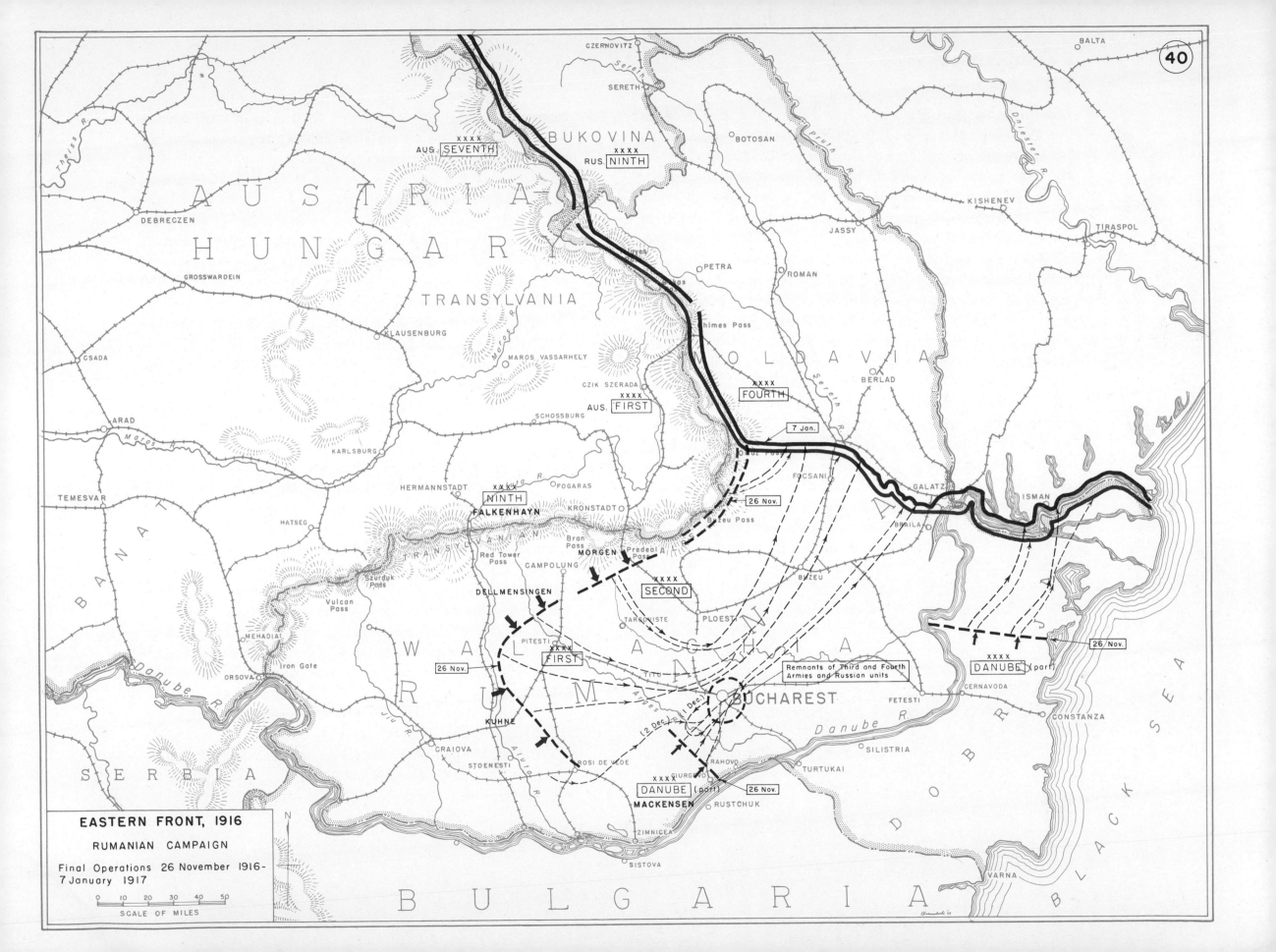

EASTERN FRONT, 1916

RUMANIAN CAMPAIGN

Final Operations 26 November 1916 -
7 January 1917

0 10 20 30 40 50
SCALE OF MILES

Morale in the Russian armies had deteriorated rapidly since August, 1916. The callous disregard of the top-level leadership for loss of life among the troops was the principal cause. Nor had the Czar, under Rasputin's sinister influence, yielded to demands for governmental reforms; instead, he became more autocratic and seemed bent on destroying the limited support he still enjoyed from the liberal middle class.

The Czar, reacting to Rasputin's assassination in December with unexpected ruthlessness, governed more than ever through mysticism. By then, all elements of the army were ripe for change, and, when rebellion broke out in St. Petersburg on 12 March, Nicholas was without major support. Three days later, he abdicated, and a liberal provisional government swept into power. Its avowed leader was the socialist Kerensky, but an organization, "The Soviet of Workmen and Soldiers Representatives," controlled much of the capital. This "Soviet," one of whose prime aims was the destruction of discipline in the army, took to its bosom the exiled Bolshevik revolutionaries, Lenin and Trotsky, upon their return to the country. Meanwhile, the Kerensky government had issued its famous "Order No. 1," designed to create a more democratic army. The result was complete chaos, the breakdown of discipline, mass desertions by peasants eager to claim land of their own, the murder of many officers, and the eventual disintegration of the army.

The Germans were quick to appreciate that the growing demoralization in Russian ranks would spread with inaction. So, during the spring and summer, they suspended offensive operations. Perhaps they might have been wiser to attack while Russia was so disorganized, force a peace, and then concentrate maximum strength in the West months earlier than Ludendorff finally did.

The Allies eventually pressed the Kerensky government to resume offensive operations to prevent Germany from taking advantage of the disastrous consequences of the Nivelle offensive in the West. Kerensky and Brusilov (now chief of staff) tried to whip up enthusiasm for an attack among the troops; but the seeds of Bolshevik propaganda, lack of discipline, and an earlier affirmation of a policy of peace were too strong. Nevertheless, the offensive was planned for 1 July.

Brusilov selected the most reliable formations (Finns, Siberians, and Poles) and launched the attack toward Lemberg (*sketch* a). Gains of thirty miles were made, but the troops soon became discouraged and rebellious. On the 19th, a well-prepared German counteroffensive—sparked by troops moved from the Western Front—struck the north flank of the Russian offensive and, by 3 August, had driven to the Galician border.

The Russian defeat was the signal for an unsuccessful attempt by Lenin to usurp control. Kerensky might have been able to retain his power, if Ludendorff had not decided to attack at Riga (*top center*) in order to force Russia into an armistice. This attack, on 1 September, was highly successful and was the initial test of a new German assault technique, eventually to be known as "Hutier tactics." The Riga attack had the desired effect on the Kerensky government: it toppled on 8 October. Lenin, vaulting into power, immediately asked for an armistice. On 2 December, hostilities were suspended, and in January, 1918, delegates met at Brest-Litovsk to agree on terms. For two months Trotsky haggled and propagandized, until Hoffman—introducing him to the cold realities of the situation—arranged for a German advance along the Gulf of Finland toward St. Petersburg. Russia, powerless to interfere, finally signed the treaty on 3 March. Germany occupied the territory shown (*sketch* b), thereby ensuring additional food supplies for a needy homeland.

The war on the Eastern Front was over. The Bolsheviks were free to carry on their first-priority task—subjugation of Russia—and Ludendorff had extra strength for the Western Front. But it had lasted long enough to prevent Germany from ever massing her total strength in the West to achieve a decisive victory.

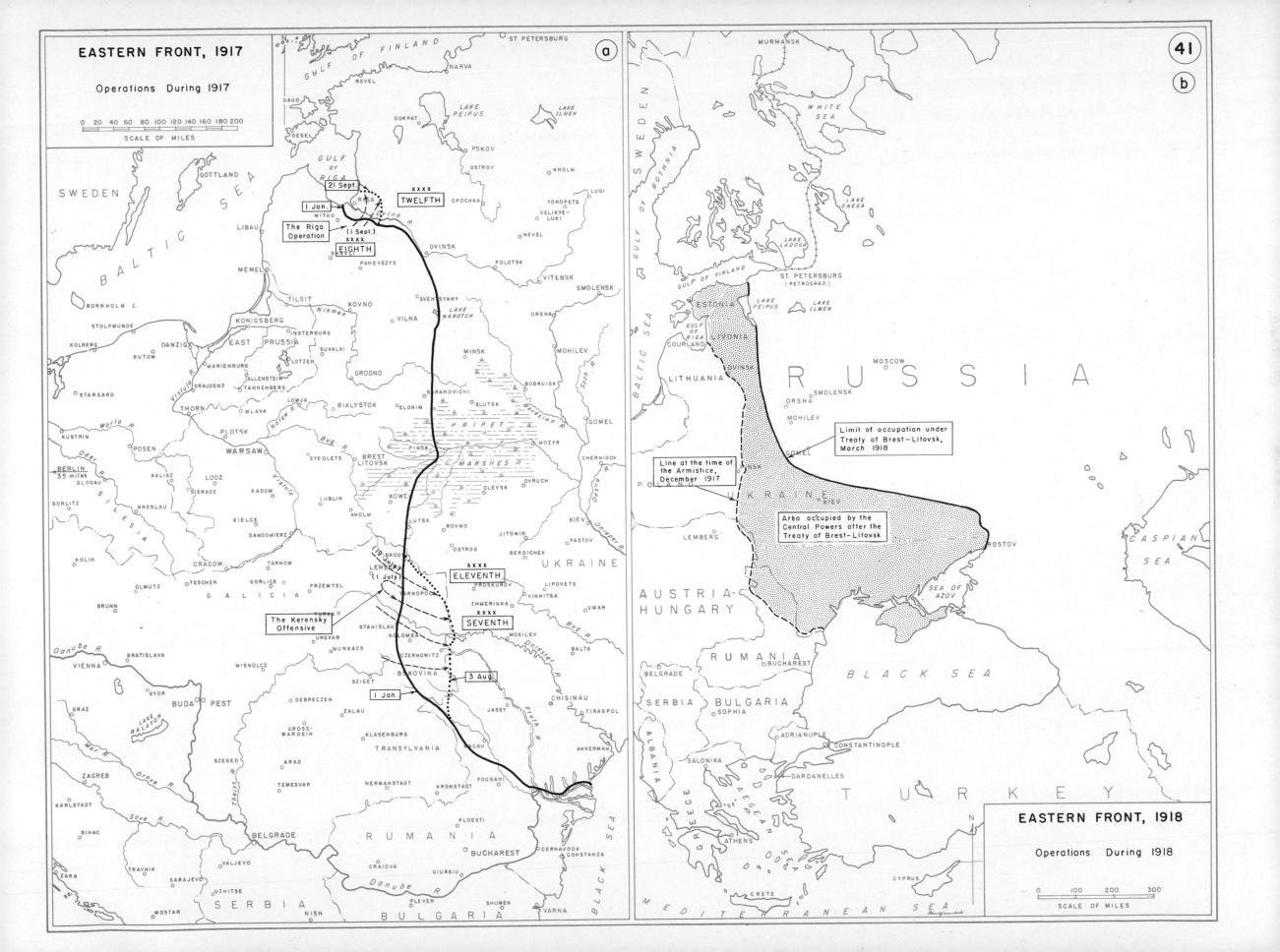

EASTERN FRONT, 1917

Operations During 1917

0 20 40 60 80 100 120 140 160 180 200
SCALE OF MILES

21 Sept.

1 Jan.

The Riga
Operation

(1 Sept.)

XXXX
TWELFTH

XXXX
EIGHTH

(15 July)

(1 July)

XXXX
ELEVENTH

The Kerensky
Offensive

XXXX
SEVENTH

3 Aug.

1 Jan.

SWEDEN

GULF OF FINLAND

ST. PETERSBURG

NARVA

DAGO

REVEL

LAKE
PEIPUS

LAKE
ILMEN

PSKOV

GULF
OF
RIGA

OSTROV

KHOLM

RIGA

Dvina R.

OPOCHKA

LUGI

TOROPETS

VELIKYE-
LUKI

OESEL

DORPAT

BALTIC SEA

GOTTLAND

LIBAU

MITAU

SERVEY

DVINSK

NEVEL

POLOTSK

VITEBSK

SMOLENSK

MEMEL

PANEVEZYS

SVENTSYANY

LAKE
NAROTCH

ORSHA

BORNHOLM I.

TILSIT

Niemen R.

KOVNO

VILNA

STOLPMUNDE

KONIGSBERG

INSTERBURG

SUVALKI

GRODNO

MINSK

MOHILEV

KOLBERG

DANZIG

EAST PRUSSIA

GUMBINNEN

BARANOVICHI

BOBRUISK

GOMEL

STARGARD

BUTOW

MARIENBURG

ALLENSTEIN

TANNENBERG

LOMJA

BIALYSTOK

SLONIM

South R.

Berezina R.

KUSTRIN

Warta R.

THORN

GRAUDENZ

MLAVA

Narew R.

PRIPET

Bug R.

PINSK

MOZYR

CHERNIGOV

Desna R.

POSEN

PLOTSK

WARSAW

BREST
LITOVSK

MARSHES

OVRUCH

BERLIN
35 miles

GLOGAU

KALISZ

LODZ

SIERADZ

RADOM

LUBLIN

KOWEL

OLEVSK

OVRUCH

GORLITZ

BRESLAU

KIELCE

SYEDLETS

KHOLM

LUTSK

ROVNO

JITOMIR

FASTOV

Dnieper R.

KOLIN

KRAKOW

TARNOW

SANDOMIERZ

OSTROG

BERDICHEV

KIEV

OLMUTZ

TESCHEN

GORLICE

PRZEMYSL

LEMBERG

TARNOPOL

PROSKUROV

VINNITSA

UMAN

BRUNN

GALICIA

BRODY

UKRAINE

LIPOVETS

ZHMERINKA

VIENNA

BRATISLAVA

UNGVAR

STANISLAU

KOLOMEA

MOGILEV

BALTA

GYOR

MUNKACS

CZERNOWITZ

Dniester R.

BUDA PEST

SZIGET

BUKOVINA

CHISINAU

GRAZ

GROSS-
WARDEIN

KLASENBURG

BACAU

Pruth R.

JASSY

TIRASPOL

ZALAU

ARAD

FOCSANI

AKKERMAN

ZAGREB

Drave R.

TEMESVAR

HERMANSTADT

KRONSTADT

TRANSYLVANIA

Danube R.

Theiss R.

Sava R.

KARLSTADT

BIHAC

ZARA

TRAVNIK

SARAJEVO

MOSTAR

BELGRADE

SERBIA

NISH

RUMANIA

BUCHAREST

CERNAVODA

CONSTANZA

PLOESTI

GIURGIU

Danube R.

PLEVEN

SHUMEN

VARNA

BLACK SEA

BULGARIA

a

41

b

EASTERN FRONT, 1918

Operations During 1918

MURMANSK

WHITE
SEA

SWEDEN

GULF OF BOTHNIA

LAKE
ONEGA

LAKE
LADOGA

ST. PETERSBURG
(PETROGRAD)

GULF OF FINLAND

ESTONIA

LAKE
PEIPUS

LAKE
ILMEN

BALTIC SEA

LIVONIA

GULF
OF
RIGA

COURLAND

DVINSK

MOSCOW

R U S S I A

LITHUANIA

ORSHA

SMOLENSK

MOHILEV

POLAND

MINSK

GOMEL

Limit of occupation under
Treaty of Brest—Litovsk,
March 1918

Line at the time of
the Armistice,
December 1917

UKRAINE

KIEV

LEMBERG

Area occupied by the
Central Powers after the
Treaty of Brest—Litovsk

ROSTOV

CASPIAN
SEA

AUSTRIA-
HUNGARY

SEA OF
AZOV

RUMANIA

BUCHAREST

BLACK SEA

BELGRADE

SERBIA

BULGARIA

SOPHIA

ALBANIA

ADRIANOPLE

CONSTANTINOPLE

SALONIKA

DARDANELLES

T U R K E Y

GREECE

ATHENS

AEGEAN SEA

CRETE

CYPRUS

MEDITERRANEAN SEA

N

0 100 200 300
SCALE OF MILES

Although a member of the Triple Alliance, Italy had remained neutral in 1914, on the grounds that the terms of the alliance required her to take action only if her partners were attacked. Actually, Italy had regarded that alliance merely as a means of ensuring German protection against Austria, her traditional enemy. She had long laid claim to Trieste (*lower right*), Istria, and Trentino (*left center*); now she insisted that Austria surrender them as the price of continued Italian neutrality. Austria refused; the Allies gladly promised Italy large sections of Austrian territory if she would join them against the Central Powers. On 23 May, 1915, therefore, Italy went to war.

By her geographical position, Italy flanked the Central Powers, but she suffered definite strategic and tactical handicaps. Except for a narrow, extremely rugged strip along the Isonzo River (*right center*; hereafter termed "the Isonzo") at the northeastern end of the Adriatic Sea, Italy's frontiers followed the southern slopes of the Alps, below the Austrian-held heights. Only two good passes led into Austria—one through the Isonzo, the other through Trentino. Both were fortified and had only limited road and rail facilities. Finally, northeastern Italy was largely flanked by Austrian territory; a successful Austrian attack from the Trentino could cut off Italian troops on the Isonzo front. Italy's one major advantage was her ability to shift troops between the Isonzo and Trentino more rapidly than the Austrians could over their circuitous railroads.

The Italian commander, General Count Luigi Cadorna, planned to make his main attack on the Isonzo front, attacking toward Trieste, meanwhile carrying out minor diversionary operations at various points along the front. His initial advance (*shaded blue areas*) was opposed largely by second-line Austrian troops, who withdrew slowly to their frontier defenses. There, Austrian resistance hardened. During the rest of 1915, Cadorna fought the first four battles of the Isonzo. Handicapped by lack of heavy artillery, he paid almost 250,000 casualties for imperceptible gains.

In March, 1916, as part of the coordinated Allied offensive planned for that year, the Italians fought their Fifth Battle of the Isonzo—again unsuccessfully. Conrad, in the meantime, had requested German help for an Austrian offensive from Trentino against Padua (*lower center*). Falkenhayn—then busy with the planning that led to his Verdun offensive—refused, stating that such an offensive would require more troops than the Trentino railroad system could supply; but Conrad stubbornly concentrated fifteen divisions and heavy artillery by stripping his Isonzo and Eastern fronts. Surprise was impossible because of the time required to assemble these troops, but the overconfident Italian First Army disobeyed Cadorna's orders to prepare defenses in depth. Consequently, Conrad's attack on 14 May (the so-called "Asiago offensive") threw it back; but supply problems, rugged terrain, and Italian reinforcements finally slowed the Austrian advance. On 4 June, however, the Russians answered an Italian appeal for help by launching the "Brusilov offensive" (*see map 36b*). Brusilov's success—made possible, in part, by Conrad's withdrawal of troops and artillery from the Eastern Front—forced Conrad to fall back to a strong defensive line (*this map, dashed red line*) on the Trentino front in order to return men and guns to the East. Cadorna, meanwhile, had organized the Italian Fifth Army for a counterattack. It advanced on 25 June (*action not shown*), but found the Austrians strongly entrenched.

Cadorna now rushed all available forces back to the Isonzo front, attacking before the Austrians could shift troops from the Trentino. In the Sixth Battle of the Isonzo, he won his first significant success, taking Gorizia, but three subsequent attacks during the autumn failed. He tried again in April, 1917, using heavy artillery supplied by his allies, but made only small gains in the Carso area. In August and September, 1917, a massive eleventh attack finally drove the Austrians out of their last defenses on the Bainsizza Plateau. The Italians, however, had outrun their artillery and supplies and were too exhausted to pursue.

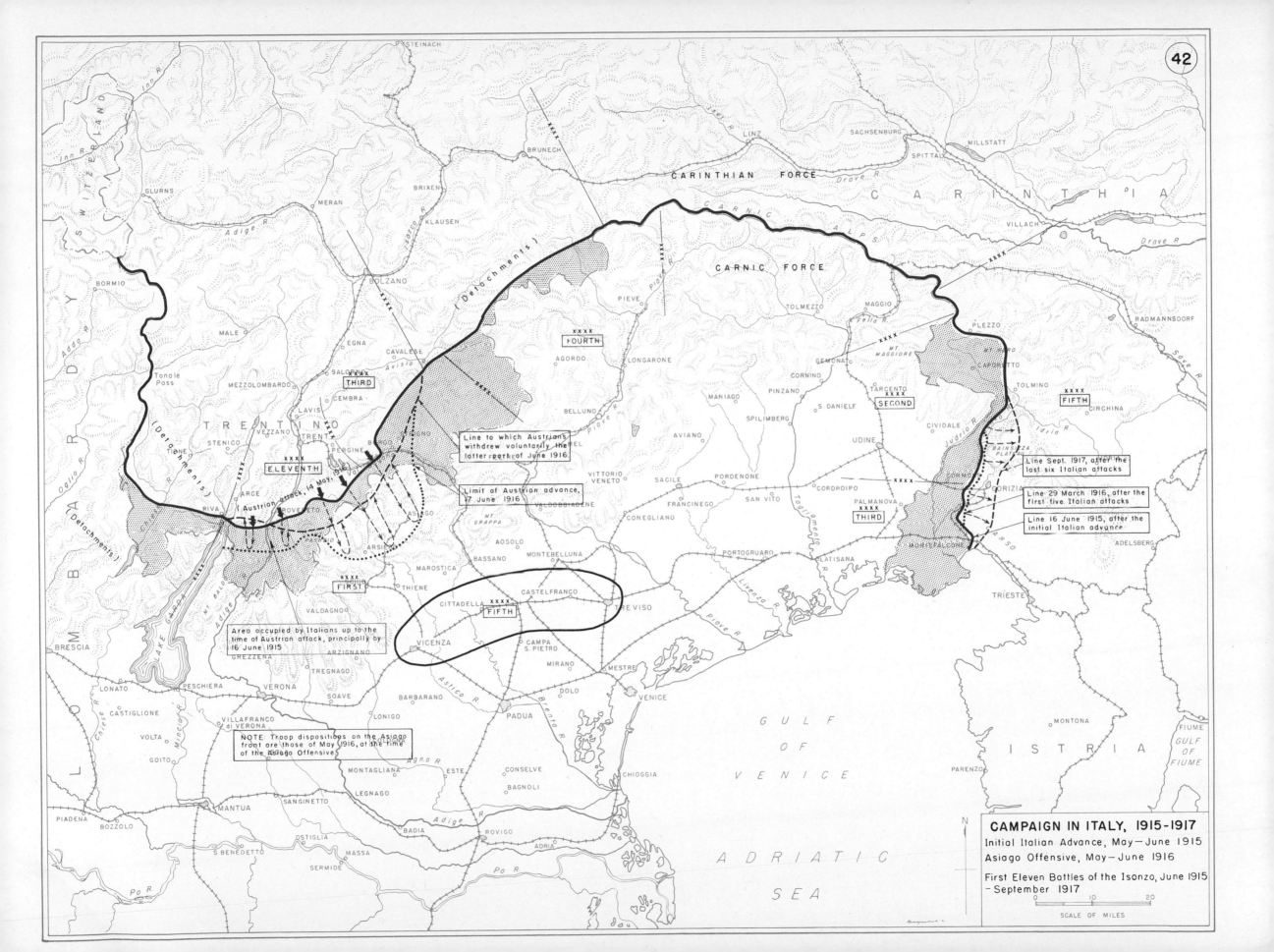

42

CARINTHIAN FORCE

CARINTHIA

CARNIC FORCE

(Detachments)

XXXX
FOURTH

XXXX
THIRD

(Detachments)

XXXX
ELEVENTH

(Austrian attack, 14 May)

XXXX SECOND

XXXX FIFTH

Line to which Austrians
withdrew voluntarily the
latter part of June 1916

Limit of Austrian advance,
7 June 1916

Line Sept. 1917, after the
last six Italian attacks

Line 29 March 1916, after the
first five Italian attacks

Line 16 June 1915, after the
initial Italian advance

XXXX
THIRD

XXXX
FIRST

XXXX
FIFTH

Area occupied by Italians up to the
time of Austrian attack, principally by
16 June 1915

NOTE: Troop dispositions on the Asiago
front are those of May 1916, at the time
of the Asiago Offensive.

GULF
OF
VENICE

ISTRIA

GULF
OF
FIUME

ADRIATIC

SEA

CAMPAIGN IN ITALY, 1915–1917

Initial Italian Advance, May–June 1915

Asiago Offensive, May–June 1916

First Eleven Battles of the Isonzo, June 1915
–September 1917

0   10   20

SCALE OF MILES

Repeated defeats on the Eastern Front had left the Austrians too weak to deal with the crisis resulting from the loss of the Bainsizza Plateau. German help was requested late in August; Hindenburg's available forces were then engaged in the Third Battle of Ypres (*see map 61*a), the Riga operation (*see map 41*a), and mopping-up operations in Rumania (*see map 40*), but he promised reinforcements as soon as possible, and meanwhile initiated the necessary reconnaissance and planning.

The Tolmino-Caporetto-Plezzo zone (*this map, right center*) was selected for the main Austro-German attack, to be delivered by the newly organized Fourteenth Army (which included seven German divisions) under General Otto von Below. The Austrian Fifth and Tenth Armies were to deliver secondary attacks on either flank of the main effort. The Fourteenth Army was held well behind the front until just before the offensive opened.

Cadorna, struggling to reorganize his forces for a renewed offensive in the Isonzo area, was soon aware of unusual enemy activity. Though larger and better armed and equipped than ever before, his forces were deeply discouraged. Most of their veteran officers and noncommissioned officers were dead or disabled; Communist and pacifist propaganda had rotted the discipline of some units; also, the Army reflected the considerable discontent and war-weariness among the civilian population. Cadorna—a rigid, devoted soldier with no sympathy for human weaknesses—accepted continual danger and hardship as a soldier's natural lot, without concerning himself particularly over methods of keeping up his men's morale. Consequently, it was low. In this situation, Cadorna decided to go on the defensive, ordering his army commanders to prepare defenses in depth all along the front. This the aggressive-minded commander of the Italian Second Army deliberately did not do. Cadorna himself misjudged the probable location of the coming attack; considering the Caporetto area too rugged for a large-scale offensive, he placed most of his reserves behind the Italian Third Army. Just before the attack, deserters brought the Italians detailed information on the enemy's plans, but it was then too late to do much more than warn the endangered Italian units.

At 0200, 24 October, 1917, massed Austro-German artillery opened a sudden surprise bombardment, using large quantities of gas and smoke shell mixed with high explosive. This quickly wrecked Italian signal communications, and demoralized many units. (Italian gas masks seem to have been relatively ineffective.) Six hours later, half-hidden by heavy rain and mist, the Fourteenth Army advanced, and the Italian front rapidly went to pieces.

The Germans were using the so-called "Hutier tactics," developed on the Russian front and now being given a major test. These featured short, violent artillery preparations, like the one described above, to blind the defenders. Thereafter, the leading units advanced rapidly, bypassing centers of resistance, which were reduced by reserve units. These tactics worked perfectly. The Italian Second Army was shattered, and much of the Carnic Force trapped. The Third and Fourth Armies withdrew in relatively good order. Cadorna had meant to make a stand behind the flooded Tagliamento River, and Below had not intended to pursue farther, but, during the night of 2-3 November, driving Austro-German advance guards forced a crossing upstream near Cornino. Late on 4 November, Cadorna ordered a retreat to the Piave River. Below then continued the pursuit. Had he possessed a force of cavalry and armored cars, Italian losses might have been crippling. Though the Piave was high from recent rains, the Austro-Germans seized several bridgeheads on the far bank, but here the attack had to pause. The attackers had outrun their supplies, were short of transportation, and found themselves encumbered with more than 275,000 Italian prisoners. Minor fighting continued along the Piave and in the mountains for several weeks more. (Among the German officers who especially distinguished themselves in this campaign was a first lieutenant of mountain troops named Erwin Rommel.)

Fearing the collapse of Italy, her allies managed to scrape together six French and five British divisions, the last of which reached Italy in mid-December.

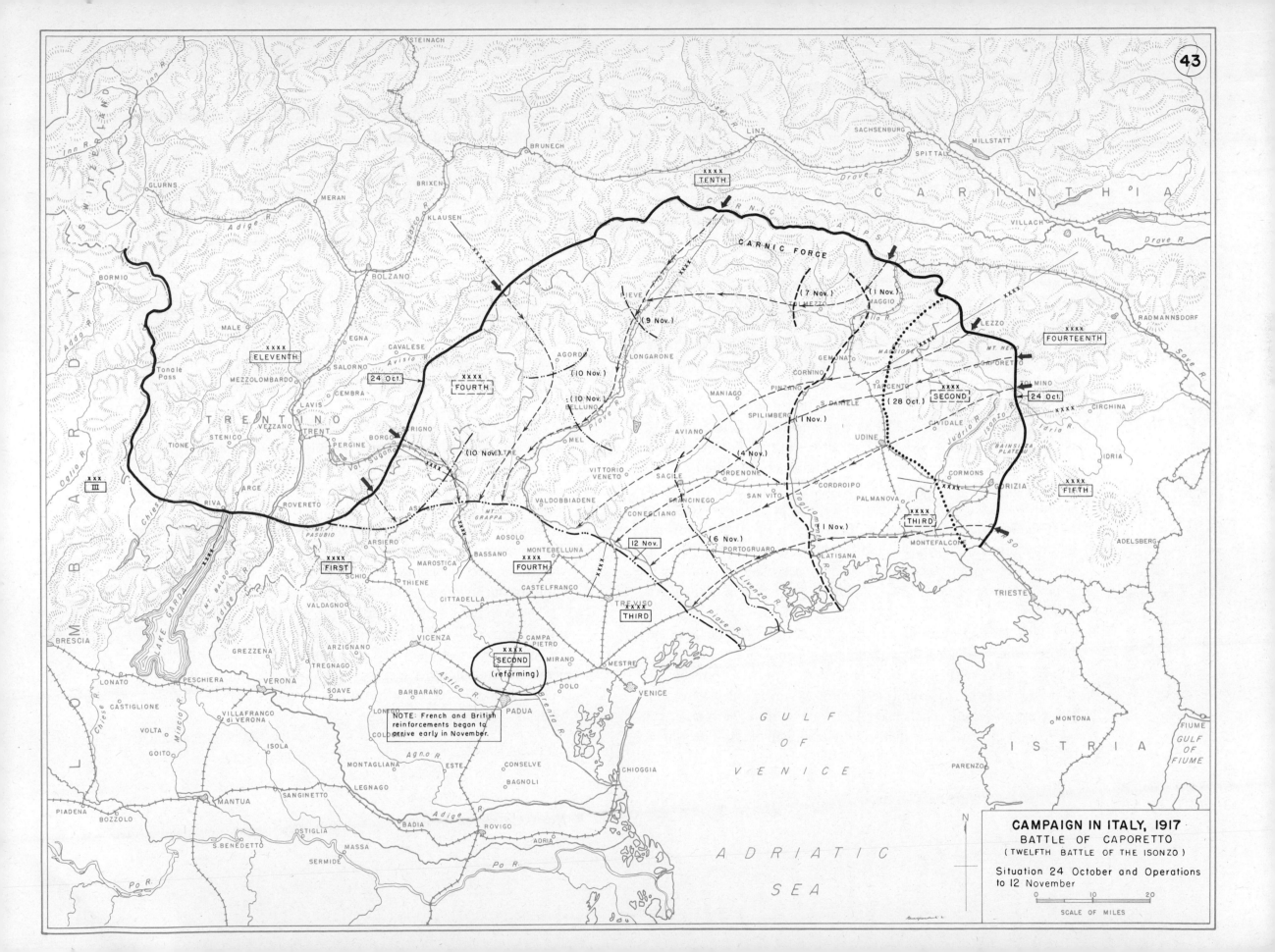

CAMPAIGN IN ITALY, 1917
BATTLE OF CAPORETTO
(TWELFTH BATTLE OF THE ISONZO)

Situation 24 October and Operations
to 12 November

SCALE OF MILES
0   10   20

NOTE: French and British
reinforcements began to
arrive early in November.

Though a costly and unpleasant defeat, the Caporetto disaster came to Italy as somewhat of a blessing in disguise. National pride was stirred to reassert itself; the army was reorganized, General Armando Diaz replacing General Cadorna. Foch, who had come to Italy with the French and British contingents, discreetly nursed this revival. Once it was apparent that the Austro-German offensive had exhausted itself at the Piave River, he refrained from putting his troops into the line there, allowing the Italians to reestablish themselves in order to demonstrate that, though defeated, they were not yet beaten. Late in November, some Allied divisions did take over positions along the foothills farther inland, where they shared in the last skirmishing of the campaign.

An important by-product of the Battle of Caporetto was the Allies' creation of a Supreme War Council at Versailles. This body was intended as the final authority on military policy, including the assignment of Allied forces to the various fronts. In practice, it proved somewhat ineffective, but it did represent a necessary initial move toward greater unity of command.

During the first part of 1918, the Germans completed the withdrawal of their troops from Italy, in preparation for their forthcoming major offensive on the Western Front. Two British and four French divisions were likewise withdrawn, their remaining units being stationed in the Asiago area. Late in April, as a complementary gesture, two Italian divisions were transferred to France.

With Russia out of the war after 3 March, 1918, the Germans felt that the Austrians alone should be capable of defeating Italy. They urged that this be accomplished as rapidly as possible, so that Austrian troops would be free to take over quiet sectors on the Western Front. The shaky Austrian government agreed, but its planning went awry in the tangle of palace politics which, throughout Austria's history as a nation, had snarled her military efforts. Conrad (recently relieved as chief of the Austrian General Staff) now commanded in the Trentino; General von Boroevic, on the Piave. Both insisted on the right to direct the decisive attack. A compromise solution allowed both of them to attack as shown, and divided the available forces almost equally between them, so that neither was strong enough to accomplish anything. In addition, there was to be a diversionary attack against Tonale Pass (*left center*). As usual, numerous deserters betrayed this plan to the Italians.

The Tonale Pass attack began on 13 June, 1918. On 15 June, both Boroevic and Conrad advanced. The latter struck the French and British contingents, but made slight gains during the first few hours. Counterattacks, however, drove him out again on the 16th—so roughly handled that he took little further part in the offensive. On the lower Piave, Boroevic forced a wide crossing, making gains of as much as three miles on the south bank. A combination of unexpected high water and aerial bombing attacks, however, played havoc with his bridges, and complicated the resupply of his bridgehead. Because of the lack of lateral communications, it was impossible to draw reinforcements from Conrad's army to maintain the momentum of the attack. Diaz rushed reinforcements into the area by truck. Boroevic therefore withdrew during the night of 22-23 June.

The collapse of this offensive cost Austria some 150,000 casualties and hurt Austrian morale badly. Foch—now charged with the coordination of all Allied armies—urged Diaz to attack immediately to exploit his success. Diaz refused, claiming he could expect no more success in an attack across the Piave than the Austrians had just experienced.

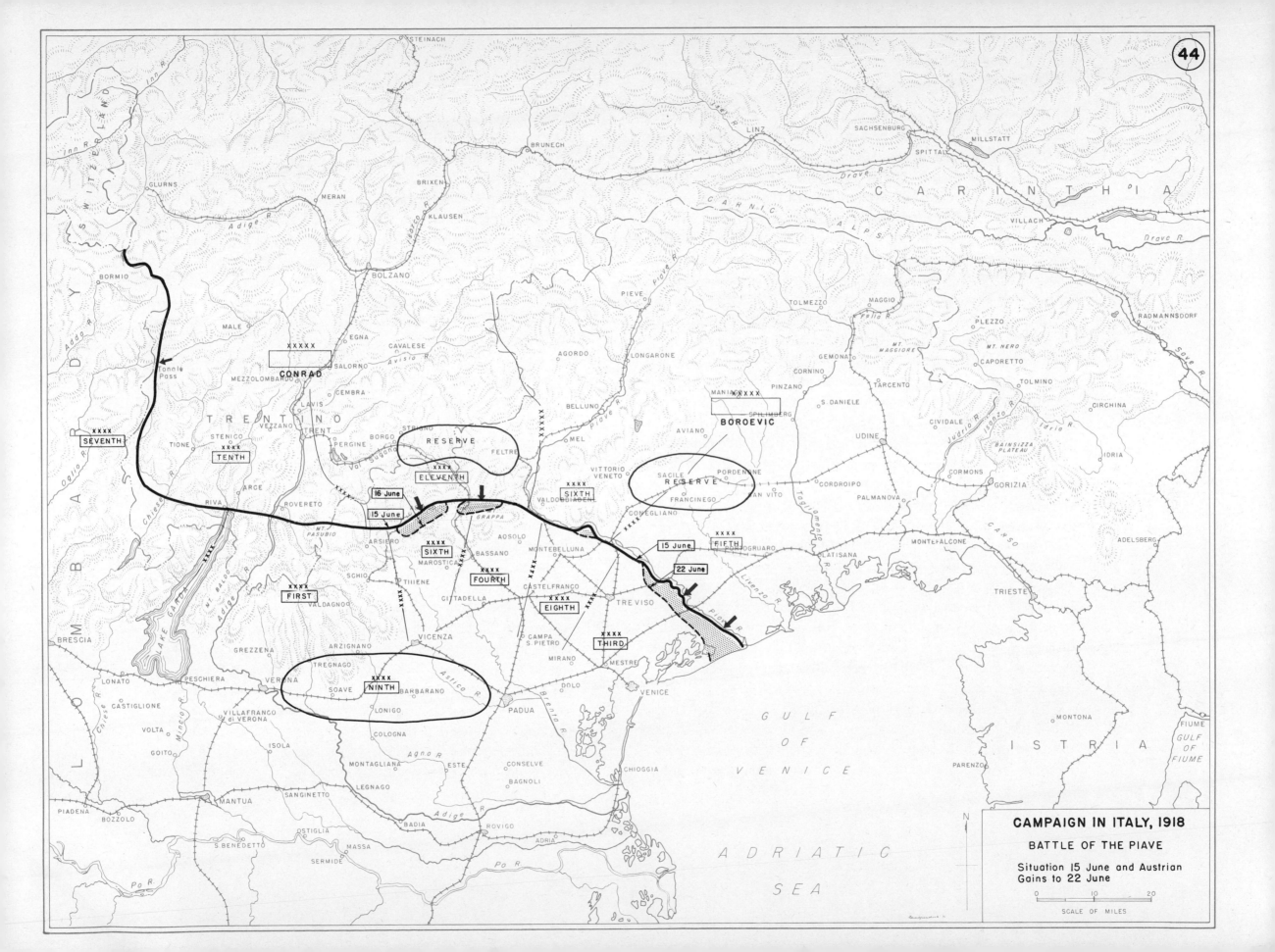

CAMPAIGN IN ITALY, 1918

BATTLE OF THE PIAVE

Situation 15 June and Austrian
Gains to 22 June

SCALE OF MILES
0   10   20

As the war turned definitely against the Central Powers during the latter half of 1918, Austria began to break up. Only along her frontiers—where her armies, though ragged and even hungry, kept their posts—was there any cohesion.

Nevertheless, Diaz was slow to act until Allied successes on the Western Front made it evident that Italy must move soon, if she hoped to profit at the eventual peace conference. Late in September, he began his preparations. Two new armies were activated and shifted to the Piave front. These were the Tenth (two British and two Italian divisions) under General Lord Cavan, commander of the British contingent, and the Twelfth (one French and three Italian divisions) under General Graziani of the French Army. One British and one French division were left in the Asiago sector to conceal the transfer of the rest of their contingents. A United States unit, the 332d Infantry Regiment of the 83d Division—sent to Italy as evidence of American participation in the war—originally formed part of the reserve. In view of the number of rivers in the objective area, large amounts of bridging equipment were provided.

Diaz's plan involved a double offensive. The Italian Fourth Army was to attack toward Feltre (*center*) to separate the Austrian army groups; the Eighth Army, supported on either flank by the Twelfth and Tenth Armies, was to attack across the Piave against Vittorio Veneto. After taking that town, part of its forces would advance westward to link up with the advancing Fourth Army, thus pocketing the Austrian Sixth Army. Such a dispersion of effort would have been foolhardy against this same Austrian Army a year earlier; now, Diaz apparently considered that he had sufficient combat superiority to risk it.

The offensive was scheduled for 0645, 24 October. Actual fighting began during the night of 23-24 October, when British troops of the Tenth Army, crossing a branch of the flooded Piave River in small boats handled by Italian rivermen, seized an important island. Thereafter, everything went otherwise than according to plan. The Austrian Imperial and Royal Army—short of ammunition, riddled by sickness—stood up to its last battle with a courage worthy of its greatest days. In the Mount Grappa area (*center, left; overprinted by blue arrow*), the Italian Fourth Army was beaten off with heavy losses. On the Piave front, high water aided the defenders in halting the Eighth Army. Eventually, during the night of 26-27 October, the Twelfth Army's French division won a small footing on the far bank. Some of its Italian units crossed on the 27th, while farther downstream Lord Cavan's English shattered the Austrian line, seizing a big bridgehead. Attacks out of this last position now linked up the different bridgeheads and cleared the fronts of the Eighth and Third Armies. The Austrian defense was further weakened by events at home; Austria-Hungary had been officially transformed from an empire into a group of separate states. Their former ties of allegiance thus canceled, Hungarian units mutinied and refused to fight; other nationalities deserted in mass. Even so, on 30 October, the Allied advance was checked at the Livenza River, but on 1 November, the Tenth Army (which now included the 332d Infantry Regiment) forced a crossing at Sacile. Austrian resistance crumbled. On the Sixth Army front, the remaining French division opened a gap on 1 November through which its British partner passed to capture Trent (*action not shown*) on 3 November, just before Italian armored cars arrived from the south. In the Fourth Army sector, the Austrians withdrew in time, but in the more open terrain to the east, Italian cavalry and armored cars and British and Italian aircraft hunted down their fleeing remnants.

The Austrians had been seeking an armistice since early October, but—incompetent to the last—their high command bungled the proceedings. As a result, it was not signed until late on 3 November, to take effect the next day. This delay gave the Italians time to send a naval expedition to force the surrender of Trieste.

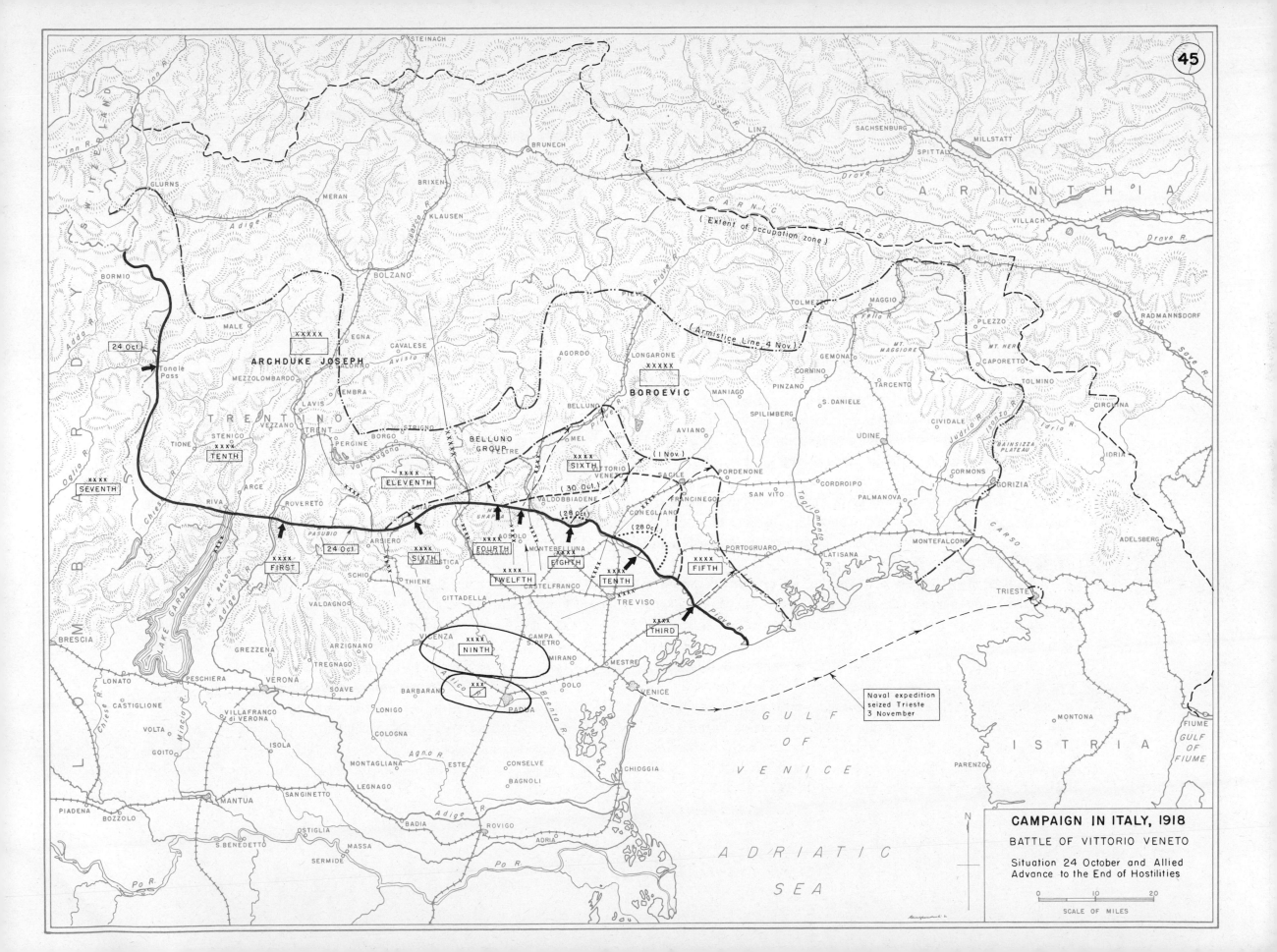

CAMPAIGN IN ITALY, 1918

BATTLE OF VITTORIO VENETO

Situation 24 October and Allied
Advance to the End of Hostilities

SCALE OF MILES
0   10   20

Naval expedition
seized Trieste
3 November

45

Since the immediate cause of the war—the murder of the Austrian Archduke Ferdinand—was the result of conflicting Serbian-Austrian ambitions, the Serbians knew that they could soon expect an Austrian invasion. Also, there would be more profound reasons behind the Austrian advance than simply a desire for vengeance. For one, the only feasible line of communications between the Central Powers and Turkey (their secret ally since 2 August) was by the Berlin-Belgrade-Nish-Adrianople-Constantinople railroad; Turkey would remain dangerously isolated until the portion of this line passing through Serbian territory could be cleared.

The Serbian Army was small (approximately 200,000 men) and lacked sufficient artillery and machine guns. Most of its supply trains were ox-drawn; it was dependent upon its allies for munitions and even food, which would have to be brought up the long haul from Salonika (*bottom center*). It was, however, a tough army of veterans from the two Balkan wars of 1913—men fired with a rough patriotism, accustomed to hardship. Their commander, Field Marshal Radomir Putnik, was a formidable semi-invalid who had a perfect knowledge of Balkan topography. The Montenegrin Army (Montenegro allied herself to Serbia at the beginning of the war) was a tiny, more primitive version of the Serbian Army.

The disparity of forces between the two opponents naturally forced the Serbs to wage a defensive war. In this, they had a strong ally in their rugged country. Any Austrian advance must cross either the Drina (*upper left*), the Save, or the Danube—all of them unfordable. Once beyond the river valleys, Serbia was a jumble of mountain ranges, where an invader's logistical problems multiplied with each mile he advanced, and his superior numbers were often more of an embarrassment than an asset. Putnik therefore left only an outpost line along the frontier, with the missions of determining the direction of the Austrian advance and of delaying it as long as possible. The main body of his army he held in a central position, ready to counterattack once the Austrians had committed themselves.

As described in the text of map 3, the Austrian plan for a war with Serbia alone (Plan B) specified that the Austrian Fifth and Sixth Armies would invade Serbia from the west, while the Second Army attacked from the north; whereas, the plan for war with *both* Serbia and Russia (Plan R) specified that the Second Army would be employed against the Russians. Blindly optimistic, the Austrians had mobilized according to Plan B on 25 July, 1914, only to discover that they had made the wrong choice.

Meanwhile, General Oskar Potiorek launched his Austrians across Serbia's northern frontier on 12 August. Only the Fifth Army, however, made noticeable progress. The Sixth Army, baffled by a screen of Serbian and Montenegrin frontier detachments, failed to push its attack. The Second Army had been warned that it would be transferred to the Galician front as soon as its rail transportation could be arranged; meanwhile, it was not to get "too deeply involved."

Putnik promptly identified the Austrian Fifth Army as the major threat, and moved the Serbian Second and Third Armies against it on 16 August (Battle of the Jadar). Initially, the Austrian XIII Corps drove the Serbian Third Army back, but the left-flank division of the VIII Corps was overwhelmed, and a demonstration by the IV Corps of the Austrian Second Army (its IX Corps had already moved north) ended in heavy losses. The IV Corps should then have followed the IX, but Potiorek begged for its retention on the Serbian front, and Conrad assented. The IV Corps managed to push the Serbians on its front back of the Dobrava River, but Putnik—reinforcing the Serbian Second Army with part of the Serbian First Army—completed the defeat of the Austrian VIII Corps. Meanwhile, the Serbian Third Army succeeded in checking the Austrian XIII Corps. Potiorek, his supplies exhausted by a week of heavy fighting, thereupon withdrew.

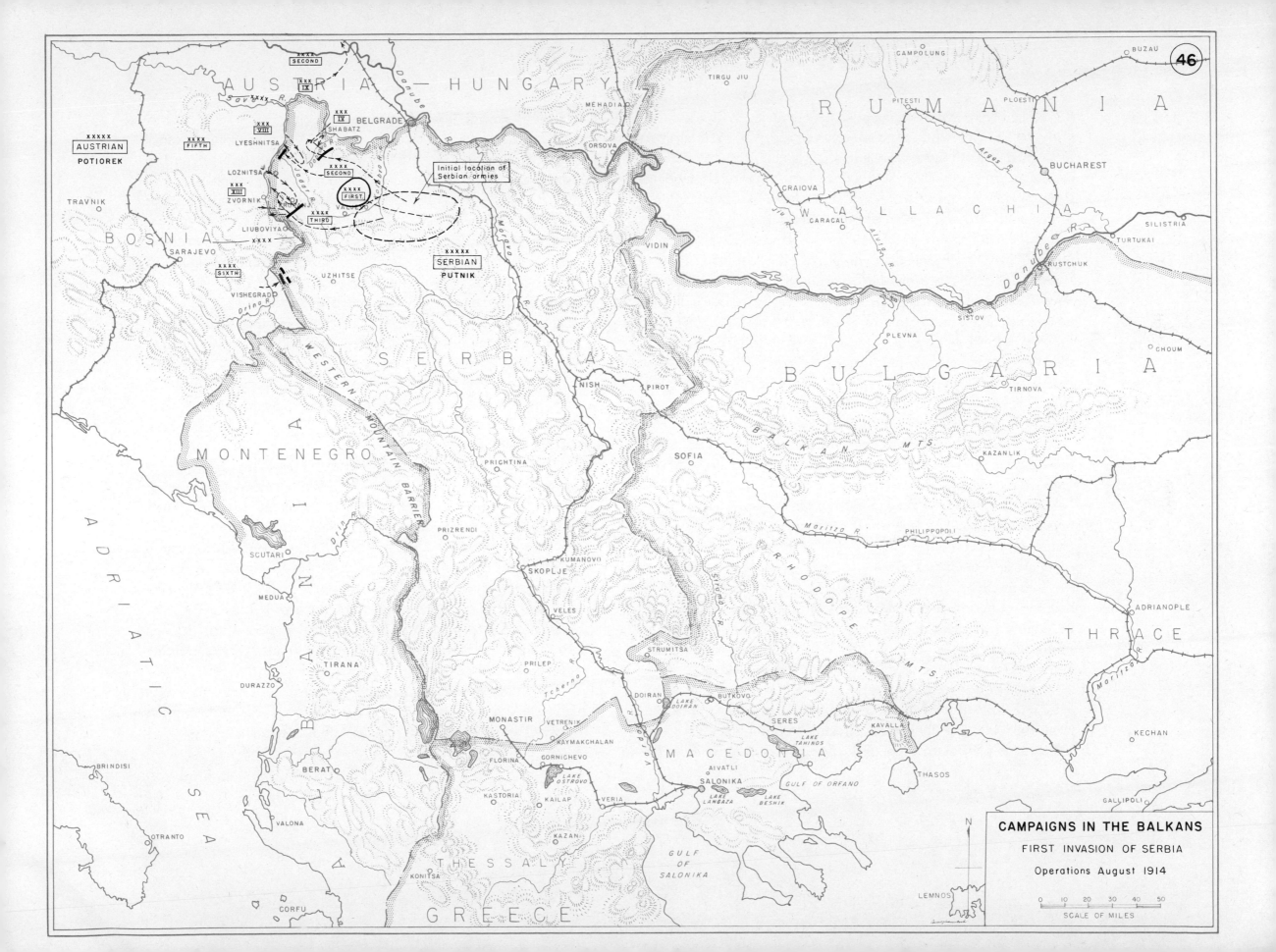

46

AUSTRIA - HUNGARY

RUMANIA

XXXX
SECOND

XXX
IX

XXX
IV   BELGRADE

XXX
VIII   SHABATZ

XXXXX
AUSTRIAN

XXXX
FIFTH

LYESHNITSA

AUSTRIAN
POTIOREK

XXX
XIII   LOZNITSA

XXXX
SECOND

ZVORNIK

XXXX
FIRST

Initial location of
Serbian armies

XXXX
THIRD

TRAVNIK

LIUBOVIYA

XXXX

BOSNIA

SARAJEVO

XXXXX
SERBIAN

SERBIAN
PUTNIK

XXX
SIXTH

UZHITSE

VISHEGRAD

TIRGU JIU

MEHADIA

ORSOVA

CRAIOVA

PITESTI

PLOESTI

BUCHAREST

CARACAL

WALLACHIA

SILISTRIA

TURTUKAI

VIDIN

RUSTCHUK

SISTOV

PLEVNA

CHOUM

SERBIA

BULGARIA

TIRNOVA

NISH   PIROT

KAZANLIK

BALKAN   MTS

MONTENEGRO

SOFIA

PRICHTINA

PRIZRENDI

SCUTARI

MORITZO R   PHILIPPOPOLI

RHODOPE

KUMANOVO

SKOPLJE

MEDUA

VELES

ADRIANOPLE

THRACE

TIRANA

PRILEP

DURAZZO

STRUMITSA

MONASTIR   VETRENIK

DOIRAN   LAKE
DOIRAN   BUTKOVO

KECHAN

MACEDONIA

KAYMAKCHALAN

SERES   KAVALLA

BRINDISI

FLORINA

GORNICHEVO

AIVATLI

LAKE
TAHINOS

THASOS

BERAT

LAKE
OSTROVO

SALONIKA

GULF OF ORFANO

GALLIPOLI

KASTORIA   KAILAP

VERIA

LAKE
LAMBAZA   LAKE
BESHIK

VALONA

KAZAN:

KONITSA

GULF
OF
SALONIKA

OTRANTO

CORFU

LEMNOS

GREECE

CAMPAIGNS IN THE BALKANS

FIRST INVASION OF SERBIA

Operations August 1914

0 10 20 30 40 50

SCALE OF MILES

Putnik had completely outgeneraled his opponent. With a smaller army, he had still managed to concentrate superior forces against the Austrian Fifth Army at the decisive point. Not only had he driven the Austrians from Serbian territory, but—by frightening Potiorek into retaining the IV Corps of the Austrian Second Army until 20 August—he had also forced them to fight their opening battles against the Russians in Galicia with insufficient forces. Then, on 6 September, the Serbs added insult to injury. Putnik sent his First Army north (*action not shown*) across the Save River into Austrian territory, hoping to inspire a revolt among the Slavic population of Bosnia.

Potiorek, who had shifted the Austrian Fifth Army north of the Save, countered this piece of impudence with a second invasion of Serbia during the night of 7-8 September. Putnik recalled his First Army, and again employed his defensive-offensive combination of delaying actions and heavy counterattacks. His success this time, however, was not so complete. Though he halted the Austrian advance, the invaders managed to hold bridgeheads (*dashed red line*) on Serbian territory.

Putnik immediately recognized the weakness of the new Serbian position (*dashed blue line*). Most of his army was concentrated in an exposed salient, dangerously vulnerable to any sudden Austrian attack through the Belgrade area. Also, the Serbian munitions expenditures during the first two invasions had not yet been made good by the Allies, and it would therefore be doubly hazardous to risk a major engagement in the near future. Consequently, Putnik ordered a withdrawal to more defensible terrain (*dotted blue line*).

Potiorek began his third advance on 5 November. The Serbs withdrew doggedly, through constant heavy rains that ruined the primitive roads and flooded the streams. Potiorek may have had some vague plan of enveloping the Serbian right flank; if so, he failed to execute it with sufficient force and energy. But the Serbian retreat went on. Valjevo fell, and the Austrian advance pushed on across the Kolubra River. The rain had changed to snow in the higher passes, and Austrian supply problems were increasing. Then, as the situation grew tenser, Potiorek diverted troops to seize Belgrade, the Serbian capital (according to contemporary opinion, he felt it would make an acceptable birthday gift for Emperor Francis Joseph of Austria). Putnik, valuing the safety of his army above the temporary possession of his nation's capital, ordered the city evacuated and pulled back his right flank. About 30 November, having drawn the Austrians far enough into the interior, he halted on a good defensive position (*solid blue line*). His retreat had brought his army near their bases of supply; behind the Austrians, the Kolubra River was now in full flood. On 2 December, the Austrians occupied Belgrade. That same day, Putnik issued his orders for a counterattack on 3 December.

There was little finesse to Putnik's plan. The three Serbian armies attacked abreast—the Belgrade Detachment covering their right flank, and the Uzhitse Detachment their left. Their naturally pugnacious patriotism inflamed by the example and exhortations of their King Peter and the sufferings of their noncombatant refugees, the Serbs went forward furiously. The First Army broke into the Austrian front in the direction of Valjevo. On 9 December, Potiorek again ordered a withdrawal. The Austrian Sixth Army fell back through Shabatz, the Fifth through Belgrade. The Serbians reoccupied their capital on the morning of 15 December.

An unpleasant aftermath of this masterful campaign was a great typhus epidemic which ravaged Serbia through the winter, until checked by medical missions from Serbia's allies.

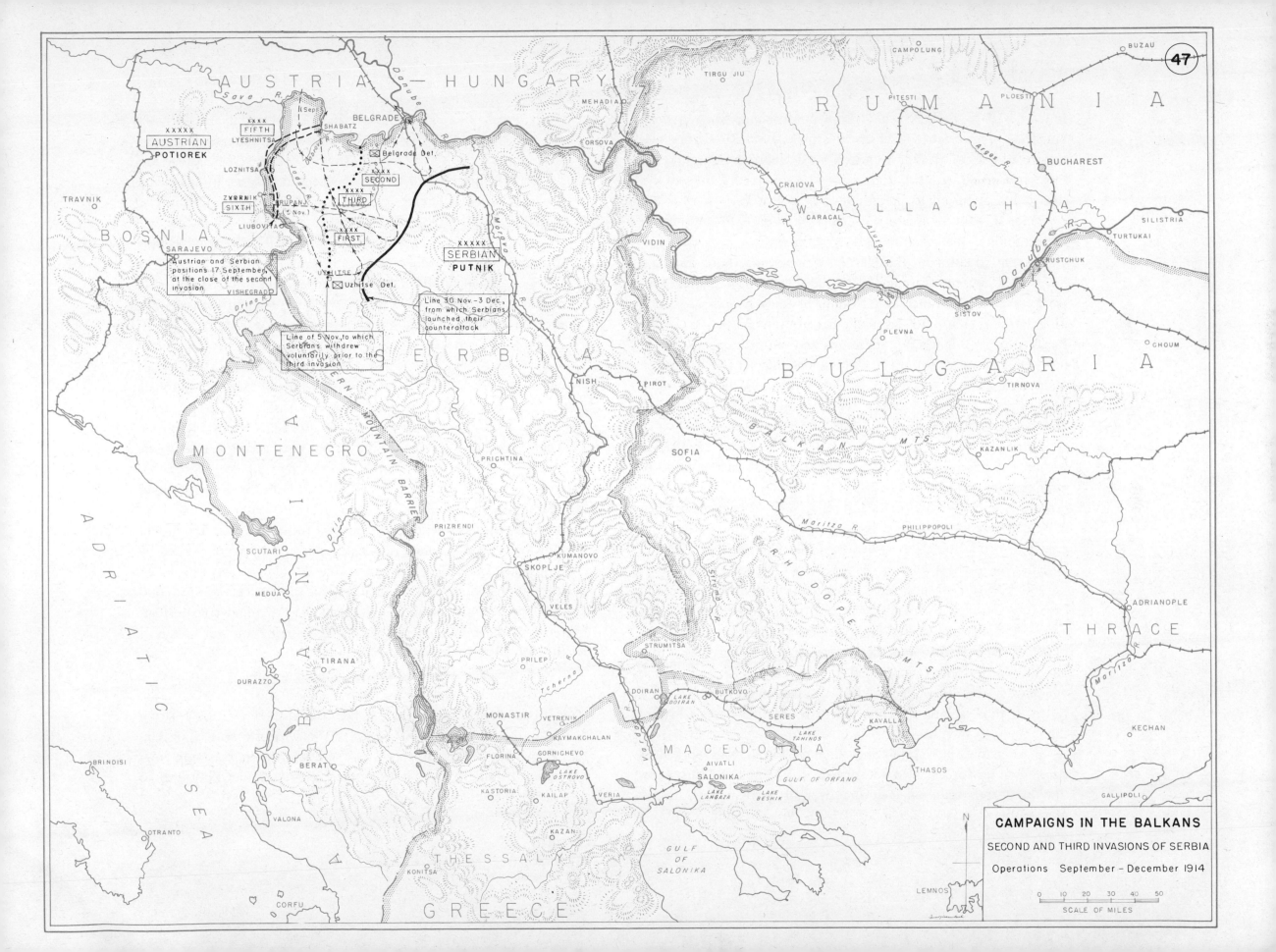

AUSTRIA — HUNGARY

RUMANIA

XXXXX
AUSTRIAN
POTIOREK

XXXX
FIFTH
LYESHNITSA

(Sep)
SHABATZ
BELGRADE
Belgrade Det.
XXXX
SECOND

XXXXX
SIXTH
ZVORNIK
KRUPANJ
(5 Nov.)
XXXX
THIRD
VIDIN

LOZNITSA

XXXX
FIRST

LIUBOVIIA

SERBIAN
PUTNIK

Austrian and Serbian
positions 17 September,
at the close of the second
invasion

Uzhitse Det.

Line 30 Nov.-3 Dec.,
from which Serbians
launched their
counterattack

Line of 5 Nov. to which
Serbians withdrew
voluntarily prior to the
third invasion

BOSNIA
TRAVNIK
SARAJEVO
VISHEGRAD

RUMANIA
CAMPOLUNG
BUZAU
TIRGU JIU
PITESTI
PLOESTI
MEHADIA
ORSOVA
CRAIOVA
BUCHAREST
CARACAL
WALLACHIA
SILISTRIA
TURTUKAI
RUSTCHUK
SISTOV
PLEVNA
CHOUM
TIRNOVA

S E R B I A

B U L G A R I A

MONTENEGRO

NISH
PIROT

SOFIA

BALKAN MTS.
KAZANLIK

PRIZRENDI

PRIGHTINA

ADRIATIC SEA

SCUTARI

MEDUA

KUMANOVO
SKOPLJE

VELES

RHODOPE MTS.

MARITZA R.
PHILIPPOPOLI

ADRIANOPLE

THRACE

A L B A N I A

TIRANA

PRILEP

STRUMITSA

DURAZZO

MONASTIR
VETRENIK
RAYMAKCHALAN
FLORINA
GORNICHEVO

DOIRAN
LAKE DOIRAN
BUTKOVO

SERES
LAKE TAHINOS
KAVALLA

KECHAN

BRINDISI

BERAT

LAKE OSTROVO

AIVATLI
SALONIKA
LAKE LANGAZA
LAKE BESHIK

GULF OF ORFANO

THASOS

GALLIPOLI

VALONA
KASTORIA
KAILAP
VERIA

M A C E D O N I A

OTRANTO

KAZAN

THESSALY

GULF
OF
SALONIKA

CAMPAIGNS IN THE BALKANS

SECOND AND THIRD INVASIONS OF SERBIA

Operations   September – December 1914

KONITSA

CORFU

G R E E C E

LEMNOS

0 10 20 30 40 50
SCALE OF MILES

47

In early 1915, Falkenhayn urged Conrad to consider a combined German-Austrian-Bulgarian attack to crush Serbia and restore direct rail communications with Turkey. Conrad being more concerned with the Isonzo front (*see map 42*), Falkenhayn turned his attention to mounting the Gorlice-Tarnow offensive (*see map 27*), but—as a precaution—sent a party of staff officers to reconnoiter the Austrian-Serbian frontier.

As the situation in the Dardanelles became more threatening for Turkey, the Germans increased their efforts to enlist Bulgaria as an ally. France and Britain, at the same time, exerted diplomatic pressure to persuade her to remain neutral. King Ferdinand of Bulgaria, an ambitious and crafty intriguer, would not commit himself—until it was evident that Russia had taken a shattering defeat at Gorlice-Tarnow and the Allies had failed at Gallipoli. Then he signed a treaty of alliance with Germany and Austria and began mobilizing on 23 September.

During this period, France and Britain had also engaged in tortuous negotiations with other Balkan states in the hope of gaining their support, and had discussed sending an expeditionary force to aid the Serbs. No definite action had been taken when news came of the Bulgarian mobilization. Then one French and one British division were rushed from the Dardanelles, reaching Salonika (*this map, bottom center*) on 3 October.

Field Marshal Mackensen led the fourth invasion of Serbia. The forces under his direct command consisted of the Austrian Third Army (which included three German divisions), the German Eleventh Army, and the Bulgarian First Army. The Bulgarian General Staff controlled the Bulgarian Second Army, which was to operate independently against the Salonika-Belgrade railroad, thus isolating Serbia. These four armies totaled more than 300,000 men.

During the quiet spring and summer, Putnik had worked to strengthen his forces. Two new armies, the Timok and the Macedonian, were organized, but the over-all Serbian strength remained between 200,000 and 250,000. Weapons and munitions of all types were lacking. Nevertheless, both Italy and Russia demanded that the Serbs launch offensives to relieve enemy pressure on the Isonzo and Galician fronts. This the Serbs refused to do. With Bulgaria ready to join the Central Powers, Putnik faced the problem of defending both his northern and eastern frontiers. The Bulgars—between whom and the Serbs there was an ancient, treasured feud—were tough mountain fighters. Eventually, Putnik adopted the cordon defense shown here, hoping to fight a delaying action until Allied help reached him from Salonika. It lacked depth and provided no reserves for a counteroffensive, but probably was the best solution available.

At 2030, 7 October, after a heavy artillery preparation, Mackensen's Austrian and German armies began successful assault crossings of the Save and Danube, surprising Serbian outposts on the south banks. Demonstrations at Vishegrad (*upper left*) and Orsova (*top center*) helped to confuse the defense. Belgrade was cleared on the 9th. As previously arranged, the Bulgarians attacked on the 11th; their Second Army cut the railroad at Kumanovo on 23 October. Thus cut off from Salonika, and forced back into the snow-covered mountains by Mackensen's relentless pressure, the Serbs chose to attempt a retreat through the mountains of neutral Albania, rather than surrender. Accompanied by thousands of civilian refugees, the Serbian Army struggled through the winter wilderness in an epic retreat; between 100,000 and 150,000 soldiers finally reached the Albanian coast. Here, the French Navy retrieved them. Mackensen's pursuit halted at the Albanian frontier on 4 December.

In the meantime, a French column had pushed northward from Salonika, but it was too weak and too late to save the railroad. Allied reinforcements then established a strong position in the Doiran area (*lower center*). This was held until 3 December, when growing Bulgarian pressure and the increasingly enigmatic attitude of the Greek government made a withdrawal to Salonika necessary.

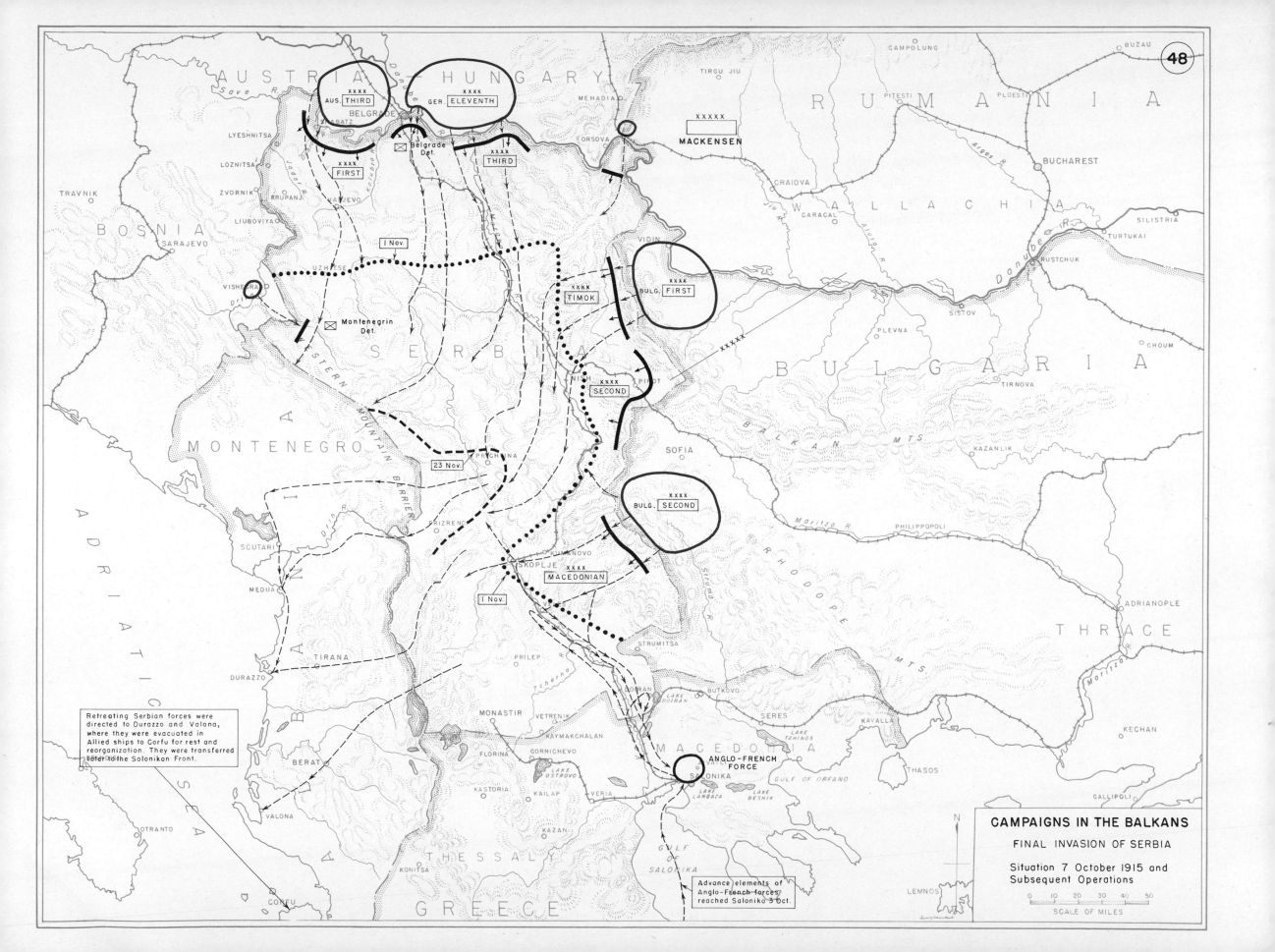

CAMPAIGNS IN THE BALKANS

FINAL INVASION OF SERBIA

Situation 7 October 1915 and
Subsequent Operations

0 10 20 30 40 50
SCALE OF MILES

Retreating Serbian forces were
directed to Durazzo and Valona,
where they were evacuated in
Allied ships to Corfu for rest and
reorganization. They were transferred
later to the Salonikan Front.

Advance elements of
Anglo-French forces
reached Saloniko 3 Oct.

Following their retreat from the Doiran area, the French and British occupied a strong position, known ironically as "the Bird Cage," around the port of Salonika (*solid blue line*). The British, who had regarded the operation as unwise from the start, now insisted on withdrawing. The French government reluctantly agreed, but French public opinion had been aroused, and it was finally decided that the Allied forces would remain.

On the side of the Central Powers, the Austrians and Bulgarians favored an all-out attack to drive the Allies into the sea, but Falkenhayn vetoed the idea. He feared that the presence of the Bulgarian troops in Greece would throw that country into the Allied camp. Also, the railroad from Nish to Salonika was single-tracked and could support only a limited body of troops. He therefore contented himself with holding the Greek frontier. The Austrians overran Montenegro and pushed southward through Albania (*action not shown*).

The political situation in Greece further complicated matters. The Allies had come into Salonika originally on the invitation of Eleutherios Venizelos, the Greek prime minister. King Constantine of Greece, however, was strongly pro-German. He succeeded in forcing Venizelos' resignation and began to talk of interning the Allied troops. The presence of strong Allied naval units off Athens forced him to decide otherwise, but he still kept the Central Powers fully advised as to Allied strength and activities.

Initially, the situation of the Allied forces was pure chaos. Theoretically, General Maurice P. E. Sarrail (a politically potent French officer whom Joffre had just removed from command of the French Third Army) was in full command. Actually, each contingent took its orders from its home government. Sarrail himself lacked the tact necessary to command a force of several nationalities. Logistics was another major problem: Salonika was a minor port; its hinterland had a limited road and rail net; in addition, it was necessary to construct all types of supply installations. The climate was vile, and a particularly virulent form of malaria was endemic. (The British alone reported 481,262 cases of sickness, as compared to 18,187 wounded during the campaign.)

During the late spring and summer of 1916, Sarrail, under pressure from Joffre to do something that would draw German troops away from Verdun, began moving forward (*dotted blue line*), nearer the Greek frontier. He now had approximately 250,000 men—French, British, Serbs (transferred from Corfu), Russians, and Italians. Rumania was expected to join the Allies in the near future, and Sarrail accordingly planned an attack up the Vardar Valley (*bottom center*) on 1 August. He hoped to link up with a possible Rumanian southward advance; but the Rumanians preferred to move northward into Hungary (*see map 37*). Supply difficulties forced a postponement until 20 August. On the 17th, the Bulgarians suddenly attacked. On the Allied right, a French cavalry screen (*not shown*) was driven in, but the British held the line of the Struma River (*this map, dotted blue line*). On the left flank, the Serbs were surprised and forced back to Lake Ostrovo, where the front stabilized on the 27th. That same day, Rumania entered the war.

Sarrail converted his planned offensive into a counteroffensive, attempting to pin down as many Bulgars as possible while the Rumanians opened their campaign; he now had about 350,000 men. Following a demonstration by the British toward Doiran on 10 September, the Serbs attacked northward on the 12th, while the French (with an attached Russian brigade) attempted to envelop the Bulgarian right flank. Rugged, wooded terrain slowed the Allied advance, but on 14 September the Serbians won a success at Gornichevo, and by 19 November the French enveloping movement had forced the Bulgars to retire behind Monastir. By this time, though, Rumania was obviously defeated, and Sarrail—furious because he had won no great victory—turned to quarreling with his subordinates. Operations dwindled away as the winter grew worse.

Meanwhile, the Italians carried out an independent operation in Albania in furtherance of their territorial ambitions in that area.

Note: On the map, bottom center, the date in the red box should be Aug. 1916, instead of Aug. 1917.

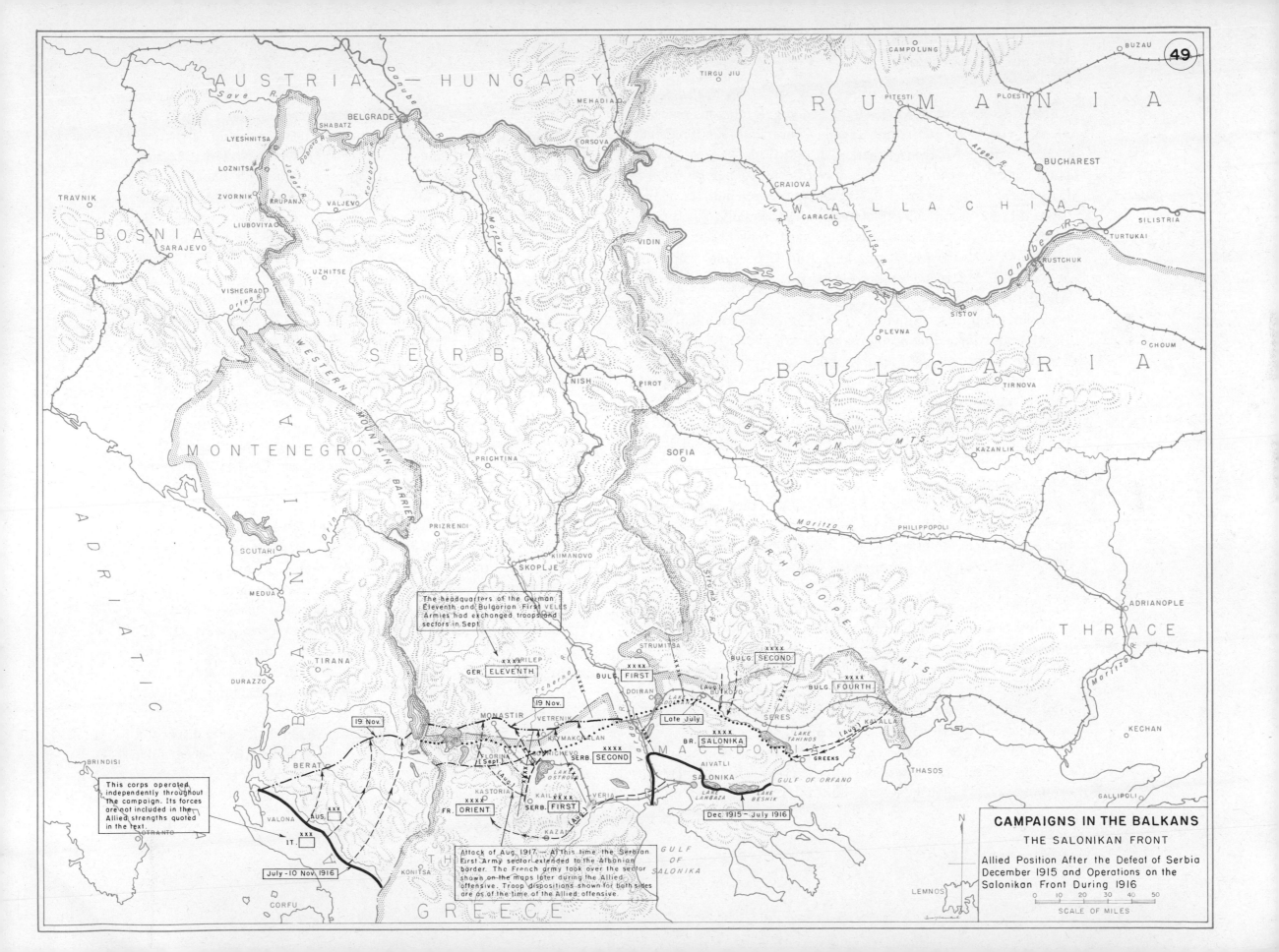

49

AUSTRIA — HUNGARY

RUMANIA

BOSNIA

SERBIA

BULGARIA

MONTENEGRO

ADRIATIC

THRACE

The headquarters of the German Eleventh and Bulgarian First Armies had exchanged troops and sectors in Sept.

GER. ELEVENTH

BULG. SECOND

BULG. FIRST

BULG. FOURTH

19 Nov.

19 Nov.

Late July

BR. SALONIKA

SERB. SECOND

MACEDONIA

Greeks

FR. ORIENT

SERB. FIRST

This corps operated independently throughout the campaign. Its forces are not included in the Allied strengths quoted in the text.

Dec. 1915 — July 1916

July — 10 Nov. 1916

Attack of Aug. 1917 — At this time the Serbian First Army sector extended to the Albanian border. The French army took over the sector shown on the maps later during the Allied offensive. Troop dispositions shown for both sides are as of the time of the Allied offensive.

GULF OF SALONIKA

GREECE

CAMPAIGNS IN THE BALKANS

THE SALONIKAN FRONT

Allied Position After the Defeat of Serbia
December 1915 and Operations on the
Salonikan Front During 1916

0   10   20   30   40   50

SCALE OF MILES

During the advance to Monastir, Allied-Greek relations reached a crisis. Greek troops around Kavalla (*lower right*) surrendered to the Germans. This led to an Allied naval blockade of Greek ports, which forced the Greek government to agree—on 14 December, 1916—to expel the diplomatic representatives of the Central Powers, surrender the Greek Navy, demobilize its forces, and withdraw its regular troops southward from Thessaly (*bottom center*). Meanwhile, Venizelos set up a government in exile at Salonika and began raising Greek troops to serve with the Allied forces.

Reinforcements continued to flow into the Salonika area; shortly afterward, the hospitals began to fill. In early 1917, Sarrail had over 600,000 men (in addition to Venizelos' units), but only some 100,000 were available for duty. He attempted another offensive on 26 April, and mismanaged it thoroughly. The British made a costly diversionary attack on their front on the night of 24-25 April—according to orders—only to find that the main attack had been postponed because of bad weather. When launched, the main attack broke down on 23 May because of the poor behavior of the Serbs, who felt that they had not been properly supported during the Monastir operation, and consequently suspected that they were to be sacrificed. For the rest of 1917, there was little fighting; the British transferred two divisions to Palestine.

Affairs behind the lines were somewhat livelier. King Constantine was discovered to be secretly mobilizing his army in Thessaly. The result was his enforced abdication and exile on 11 June. Venizelos again became prime minister of Greece, and the Greek Army was reorganized to take over part of the Salonika front. However, the most encouraging development of 1917 was the recall of Sarrail on 10 December.

Sarrail's successor, the capable General Guillaumat, made careful preparations for a major offensive—which, however, the Supreme War Council forbade him to launch because of the uncertain situation on the Western Front. During July, 1918, he was summoned back to France to take command of the garrison of Paris, again threatened by a German drive. His successor, General Franchet d'Esperey, adopted his plan. By September, with the Allies gaining ground everywhere, Franchet d'Esperey was allowed to attack. He had a total strength of 574,000 men—French, British, Serbs, Czechs, and Italians (not counting the Italian corps in Albania)—of whom approximately a third were available for duty. Opposing him, the Bulgarians had a total strength of about 400,000—many of them sick, all short of rations and ammunition, all with low morale. Practically all the German units that had formed the backbone of the Bulgarian Army had been withdrawn; in the German Eleventh Army, only the staffs were still German.

The Allied plan was for a French-Serbian force with heavy artillery support to penetrate the Bulgarian lines between the Vardar and the Tcherna (*lower center*), while the British made a secondary attack toward Doiran to prevent the Bulgarians from shifting troops westward against the flank of the breakthrough. The main attack was to be on 15 September; the secondary attack, on the 18th. One British division would feint an advance up the Vardar Valley on 1 September. Hard going was expected, because of the ruggedness of the terrain.

Almost from the first, Bulgarian resistance collapsed. By the 25th, the main attack had reached the Vardar River and split the Bulgarian front. The British entered Bulgaria, capturing Strumitsa; on the 26th, French cavalry passed through the infantry to exploit this success, taking Skoplje on the 29th. That same day, Bulgaria signed an armistice. Allied units, however, despite supply problems, kept up their advance until 11 November.

This campaign is a glaring example of unnecessary dispersion of effort. For three years, half the Bulgarian Army successfully pinned down from 300,000 to 600,000 Allied troops—troops that were urgently needed on the Western Front.

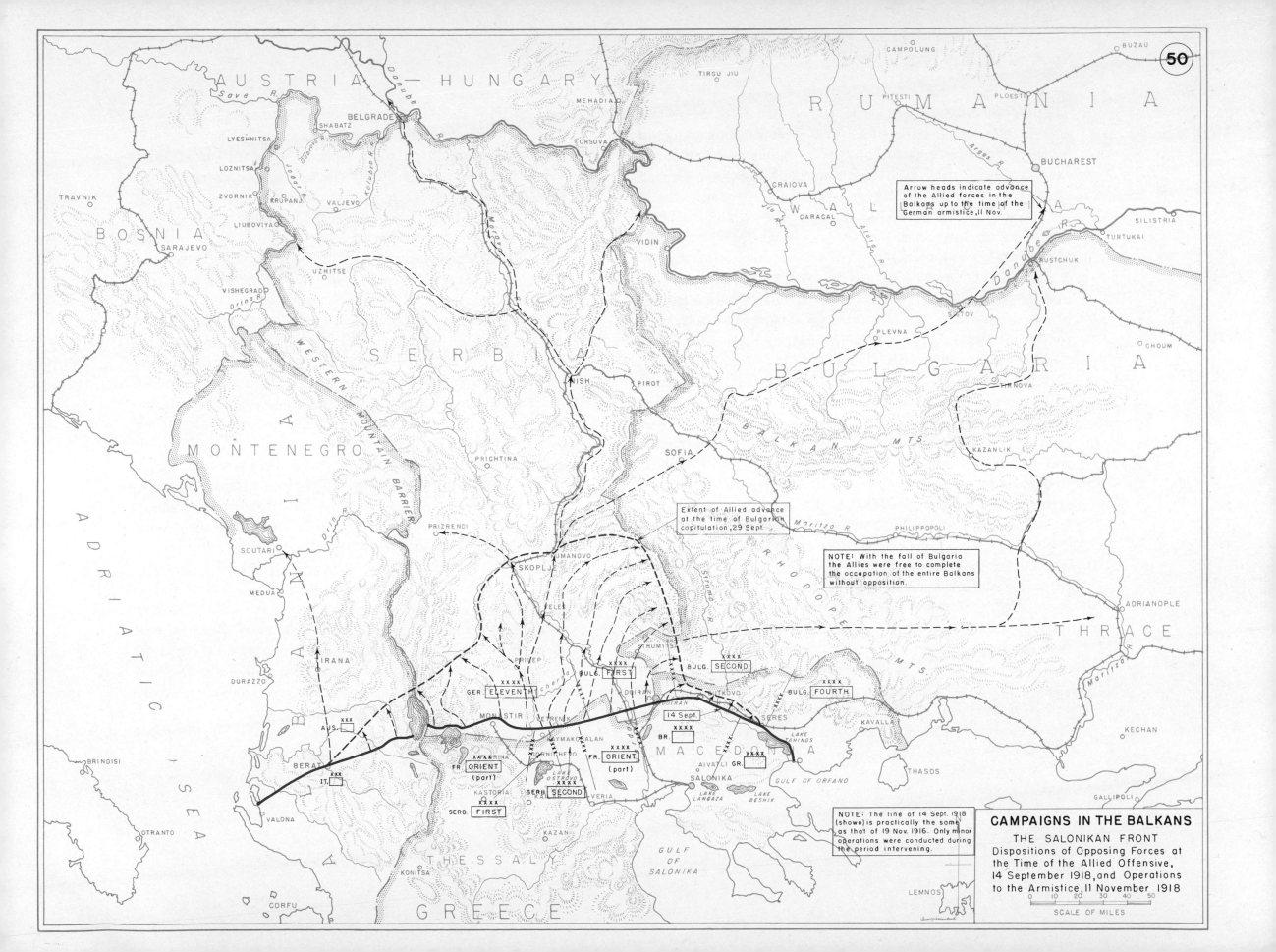

50

AUSTRIA — HUNGARY

RUMANIA

BOSNIA

SERBIA

BULGARIA

MONTENEGRO

ADRIATIC SEA

ALBANIA

MACEDONIA

GREECE

THESSALY

THRACE

Arrow heads indicate advance
of the Allied forces in the
Balkans up to the time of the
German armistice, II Nov.

Extent of Allied advance
at the time of Bulgarian
capitulation, 29 Sept.

NOTE: With the fall of Bulgaria
the Allies were free to complete
the occupation of the entire Balkans
without opposition.

NOTE: The line of 14 Sept. 1918
(shown) is practically the same
as that of 19 Nov. 1916. Only minor
operations were conducted during
the period intervening.

GER. ELEVENTH
BULG. FIRST
BULG. SECOND
BULG. FOURTH
14 Sept.
BR.
FR. ORIENT (part)
FR. ORIENT (part)
AIVATLI GR.
AUS.
IT.
SERB. CORINA
SERB. SECOND
SERB. FIRST

CAMPAIGNS IN THE BALKANS

THE SALONIKAN FRONT
Dispositions of Opposing Forces at
the Time of the Allied Offensive,
14 September 1918, and Operations
to the Armistice, II November 1918

0 10 20 30 40 50

SCALE OF MILES

That part of the Near East shown on the map encompasses two widely separated areas in which troops of the British Empire fought campaigns against Turkey. In the over-all pattern of strategy, these were secondary campaigns, though each had grown into a sizable and expensive affair by 1918, and at least one of them bid fair to become a major operation. The two areas are Mesopotamia (*center*)—now Iraq—and Palestine, on the Mediterranean opposite Cyprus, extending from Gaza northward.

The area known in 1914 as Mesopotamia was generally that drained by the Tigris and Euphrates Rivers. It was inhabited by Arab tribes, under local rulers who paid more or less allegiance to Turkey. From the Persian border to the eastern edge of the Syrian Desert is about 150 miles; the distance from the Persian Gulf to Mosul (*upper center*) is approximately 500 miles. These limits defined, in general, the extent of Mesopotamia. The area was practically barren of trees. There were very few roads and even fewer bridges; consequently, during the rainy season, traffic was largely confined to the rivers. The Tigris and Euphrates join at Basra (*center*) to form the Shatt-al-Arab (Shatt means river bank.) From the Persian Gulf to Basra, the river was navigable to ships of less than seventeen feet draft; above that point, the Tigris was navigable as far as Baghdad to small craft drawing less than three and a half feet. The Shatt-al-Hai (*center*), extending between Kut-al-Amara and Nasiriya, is a sizable stream during the rainy season. During the rest of the year, it gradually dries up. In the wet season (January-May), the rivers overflow their banks—unless well diked—and inundate the surrounding countryside. (The river banks are actually higher than the inland areas.) The climate fluctuates drastically between recorded extremes of 19° and 123° F. August is the hottest month, and January the coolest, respective mean temperatures being 92.5° and 48.8° F. This was not a healthful area in 1914, such diseases as cholera, plague, malaria, and dysentery being endemic.

In September, 1914, when it became obvious that relations with Turkey had seriously deteriorated, the British Foreign Office in India recommended the dispatch of a small force to the head of the Persian Gulf to counter Turkish designs. This force, it was hoped, would encourage the Arabs to throw off the yoke of Turkish oppression (Arab-Turkish relations were none too warm) and would safeguard the interests of the two local pro-British sultans. More important, it would protect the vital oil pipeline from Persia to Abadan Island (*center, opposite Fao; shown more clearly on map 52a*). The Indian government concurred, and dispatched the reinforced 16th Brigade (5,000 men) to Fao on 16 October. It might be noted here that the Indian Army (seven divisions plus supporting troops—deficient in artillery and lacking its full complement of British officers) was the only troop source in 1914 for this campaign. Further, it had to expect calls for troops elsewhere and still maintain order in India. On 23 October, the 16th Brigade arrived at the head of the gulf, where it remained on ships for two weeks until Britain declared war on Turkey. Then the brigade landed against negligible opposition (*action not shown*). Within a few days, the remaining troops of the 6th Indian Division arrived, and the Turks, who had made an ineffectual counterattack earlier, fell back to Basra.

From the Turkish viewpoint, Mesopotamia was a relatively unimportant area in 1914. The Dardanelles, the Caucasus, and Egypt received higher priorities. Thus, there were only two divisions in the area south of Baghdad. One of these, with a rifle strength of 5,000, was in the Basra area and opposed the initial British operations.

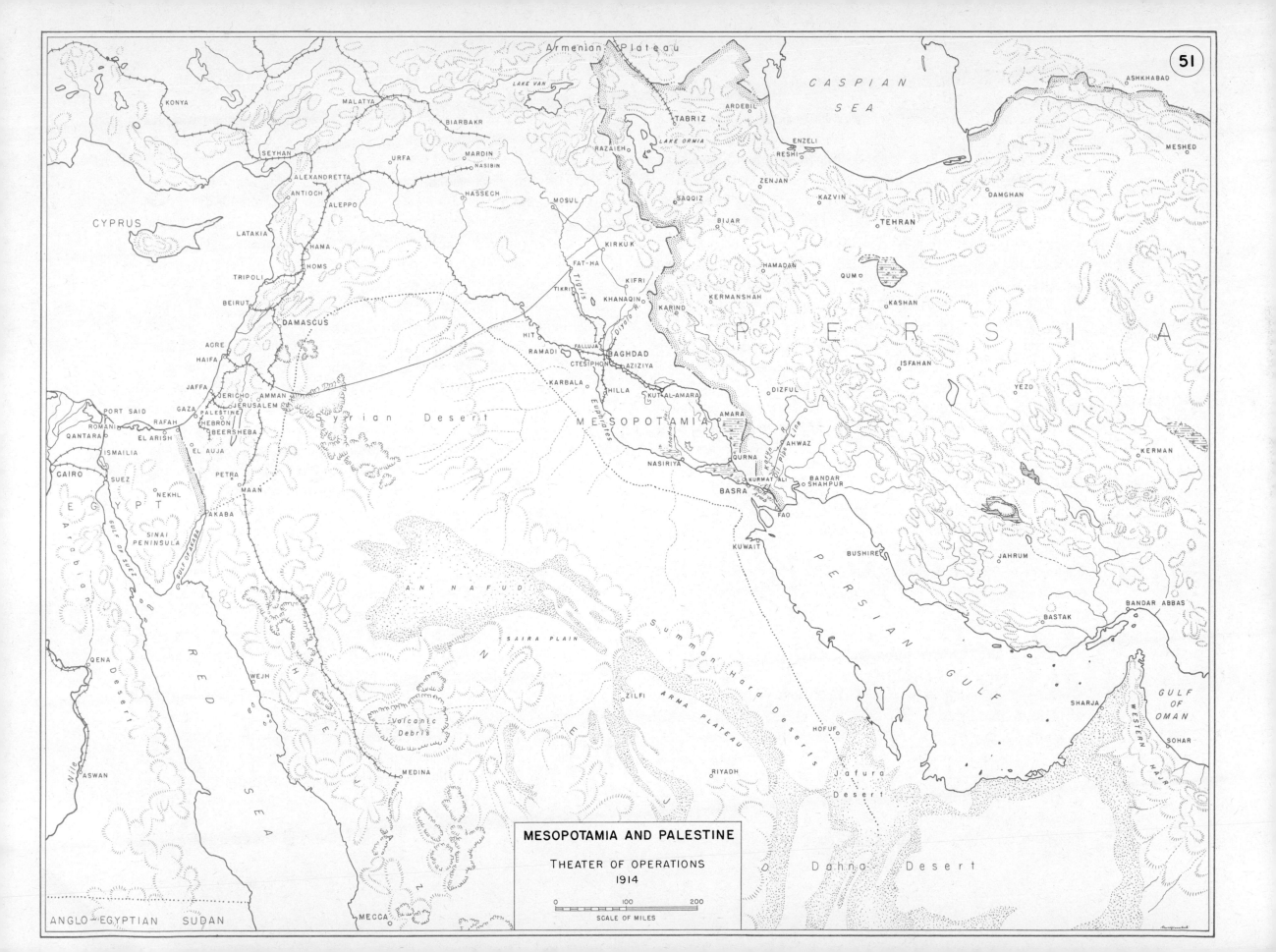

MESOPOTAMIA AND PALESTINE

THEATER OF OPERATIONS
1914

SCALE OF MILES
0   100   200

Brushing aside the weak Fao defenses upon landing, the 16th Brigade moved to secure Abadan Island (*sketch a, bottom right*). By 15 November, the rest of the 6th Division had arrived, and the British pushed upstream. A spirited fight occurred east of Khora on the 17th. Basra was occupied four days later, and a detachment moved forward to Qurna. Now, for several months, both sides built up strength. The Turks moved the 37 R Division to Baghdad (*top left*) and concentrated troops at Nasiriya (*lower center*), while the Indian government scraped together another division and a cavalry brigade. These, together with the 6th Division, formed a corps under General Sir John E. Nixon. A Turkish strike at Ahwaz (*right center*) in February, 1915, drove the two battalions there into their defenses. Nixon, fearful of this Turkish threat to the oil line, sent a strong detachment up the Karun River in May which forced an enemy retreat. In April, the Turks—reinforced by Arabs who were not yet impressed with British pledges—fiercely attacked Shaiba (*bottom center*), but were decisively beaten. In June and July, Nixon captured Amara and Nasiriya against considerable opposition, thus accomplishing the original mission of the expedition.

By now, the climate, disease, combat, and logistical deficiencies had made themselves felt, but Nixon, a cheerful optimist, argued convincingly that the seizure of Kut-al-Amara (*upper left*) was desirable and feasible. The Indian government reluctantly consented, and Townshend's reinforced 6th Division was given the assignment. The Turks had concentrated at Kut and entrenched a formidable position (*sketch b*). But there was a weakness: the position lay astride the river, and the nearest bridge for lateral communications was five miles to the rear. The British, benefiting from aerial reconnaissance, planned to turn the Turkish north flank. But, to entice Nur-ud-Din into positioning his reserve near the river, Townshend conducted demonstrations as shown. The attack on the 28th was entirely successful, the Turkish reserve arriving too late to stop the envelopment. But Townshend's troops were tired, the cavalry lacked water, and a mirage played tricks; thus, the majority of the Turks escaped northwest

to Ctesiphon (*sketch c, top left*). Townshend pursued with his few boats and the cavalry, halting at Aziziya on 5 October to reorganize.

Political considerations now exerted their influence. Nixon was authorized to advance to Baghdad if he felt his force was sufficient for the task. It was obvious that the government favored this advance: Persia was wavering, the Dardanelles venture had failed, and Baghdad appeared to be a fine political objective. Townshend dissented, pleading for more troops and a reliable line of communications; Nixon disagreed and ordered the advance. It got under way on 19 November. On the 22d, the well-entrenched Turks repulsed the vigorous British blow at Ctesiphon. Townshend—outnumbered and with no tactical advantage—withdrew to Kut, where he elected to accept investment. For five months, he stood off his enemy while hunger and disease decimated his force. Meanwhile, Nixon had sent a large force to relieve Townshend. All its efforts failed against floods and stubborn Turkish defenses; on 29 April, 1916, Townshend surrendered. The campaign to date had cost Britain 40,000 men.

In August, the competent General Sir Stanley Maude assumed over-all command in Mesopotamia and began improving the logistical arrangements. Reinforcements poured in, and by December he was ready to move on Kut. Maude spent two months clearing the Turks from the south bank of the river and then executed his well-conceived plan (*sketch d*). On 17 February, 1917, he attacked at Sannaiyat (*top right*), achieving few gains, but drawing some Turks north. Another attack was launched at Sannaiyat on the 22d, and that night a feint was made at Maqasis (*center*) and a demonstration at Kut. The next morning, the main crossing was successfully made at the lightly defended Shumran Peninsula (*left center*), compromising the Turkish position. On the 24th, the attacks at Dahra Ridge and Sannaiyat continued as the Turks withdrew. The pursuit encountered a skillfully employed Turkish rear guard and accomplished little. The Turks fell back to Diyala (*sketch a, top left*); Maude followed to Aziziya, where logistical problems forced a halt.

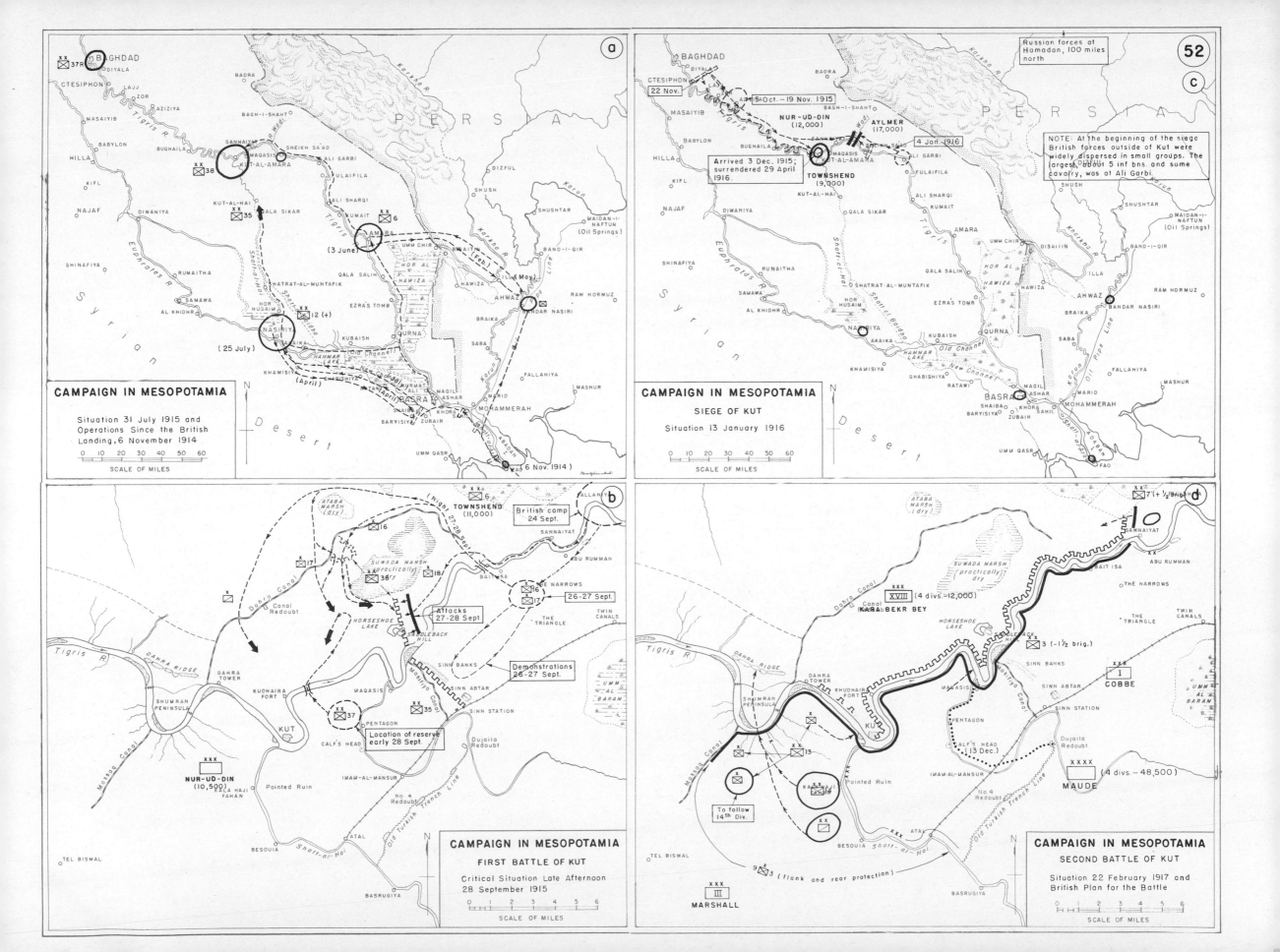

(a)

BAGHDAD

PERSIA

CAMPAIGN IN MESOPOTAMIA

Situation 31 July 1915 and
Operations Since the British
Landing, 6 November 1914

0 10 20 30 40 50 60
SCALE OF MILES

(c)

Russian forces at
Hamadan, 100 miles
north

BAGHDAD

Ctesiphon
22 Nov.

5 Oct. – 19 Nov. 1915

NUR-UD-DIN
(12,000)

AYLMER
(17,000)

4 Jan. 1916

Arrived 3 Dec. 1915;
surrendered 29 April
1916.

TOWNSHEND
(9,000)

PERSIA

NOTE: At the beginning of the siege
British forces outside of Kut were
widely dispersed in small groups. The
largest, about 5 inf bns and some
cavalry, was at Ali Garbi.

CAMPAIGN IN MESOPOTAMIA

SIEGE OF KUT

Situation 13 January 1916

0 10 20 30 40 50 60
SCALE OF MILES

(b)

TOWNSHEND
(11,000)

British camp
24 Sept.

Attacks
27-28 Sept.

26-27 Sept.

Demonstrations
26-27 Sept.

Location of reserve
early 28 Sept.

NUR-UD-DIN
(10,500)

CAMPAIGN IN MESOPOTAMIA

FIRST BATTLE OF KUT

Critical Situation Late Afternoon
28 September 1915

0 1 2 3 4 5 6
SCALE OF MILES

(d)

7 (+ ½ brig.)

XVIII (4 divs – 12,000)

KARA BEKR BEY

3 (– 1½ brig.)

I

COBBE

To follow
14th Div.

(13 Dec.)

MAUDE

XXXX (4 divs – 48,500)

9 3 (flank and rear protection)

MARSHALL

CAMPAIGN IN MESOPOTAMIA

SECOND BATTLE OF KUT

Situation 22 February 1917 and
British Plan for the Battle

0 1 2 3 4 5 6
SCALE OF MILES

On 4 March, 1917, the British renewed the advance toward Baghdad (*center*). After three days of difficult fighting at the Diyala River, they entered Baghdad on the 11th. The long-sought prize held no enchantment for Maude, however, and he quickly moved north to consolidate his conquest. Detachments moved up the Tigris, Diyala, and Euphrates Rivers; by May, Maude's hold on Baghdad was secure, and he now rested during the burning summer.

Turkish troop dispositions on 11 March show the high priority given the Caucasus (where the Turks were massing in anticipation of a Russian collapse) and Palestine. The relative weakness of the forces assigned to Mesopotamia, however, was in large part due to the logistical problems involved in supporting that theater. The Baghdad-Constantinople trip (1,255 miles) required twenty-two days, for the railroad was not yet completed between Biarbakr and Tikrit (300 miles). Nevertheless, in the summer, Turkey concentrated available reserves (*not shown*) at Aleppo (*upper left*) with a view toward recapturing Baghdad. However, the destruction of many of the supplies for this force (in an explosion near Constantinople), coupled with British successes in Palestine, thwarted the scheme.

On 18 November, General Maude died of cholera and was succeeded by General Sir William R. Marshall. In February and March, 1918, Marshall executed Maude's plan for a move on Mosul (*upper center*). He captured Kifri and Hit and then suspended operations for the summer.

Russia had moved about 20,000 troops into Persia in 1915, for political as well as military reasons. The next year, after Townshend surrendered at Kut, the Russians attempted a move down the Diyala River, but, when rebuffed by the Turkish XIII Corps, fell back to the positions shown. When Russia capitulated, this force disintegrated. As Turkey and Germany raced for the Caucasian oil fields, Britain became worried. She feared Bolshevik collaboration with Germany to invade Persia, Afghanistan, and then India; nor did she want Baku (*off map, top center; on western shore of Caspian Sea*) oil in German hands. Hence, General L. C. Dunsterville moved into Persia, logistically supported by Marshall, to rally the White Russian remnants and secure Baku. The tiny force, relying on British prestige rather than power, had little success; however, the fears of the British were never realized.

In October, 1918, Marshall's final campaign began. Though Turkish resistance was strong in places, the British eventually routed them at Fat-Ha (*upper center*) on the 24th and accepted the surrender of most of the Sixth Army on the 30th. The next day, Turkey signed an armistice—more because of her defeats in Palestine than her reverses in Mesopotamia. Marshall occupied Mosul on 14 November.

Thus ended the "sideshow" which cost the British Empire 92,501 men. Turkish casualties are not known, but 45,500 Turks became prisoners. When the war ended, the British had 414,000 men in the area, of whom only 112,000 were combat troops. The price for defending the oil line had indeed been high.

Concurrently with the Mesopotamian campaign, the British and Turks fought in Egypt and Palestine. The primary British concern here was the protection of the Suez Canal. When Turkey entered the war, Egypt became a British protectorate—somewhat against her will. By January, 1915, there were 70,000 British troops in the area, most of them Indians and Anzacs.

In 1915, a Turkish force of 20,000 crossed the waterless desert in an attempt to seize the canal; the Turks were handily repulsed and forced to withdraw. The British, now realizing that the Suez could not be defended from the west bank, made plans to move to the El Arish area where any Turkish advance could be directly opposed or taken in flank. By early 1916, there were 400,000 British troops in Egypt (many had just returned from Gallipoli for temporary billeting) and construction of the necessary rail and water lines leading east had started. Gradually, these logistical tools moved forward, governing the advance of the troops who fought an occasional engagement with the Turks. By 20 December, 1916, the British were established around El Arish as shown.

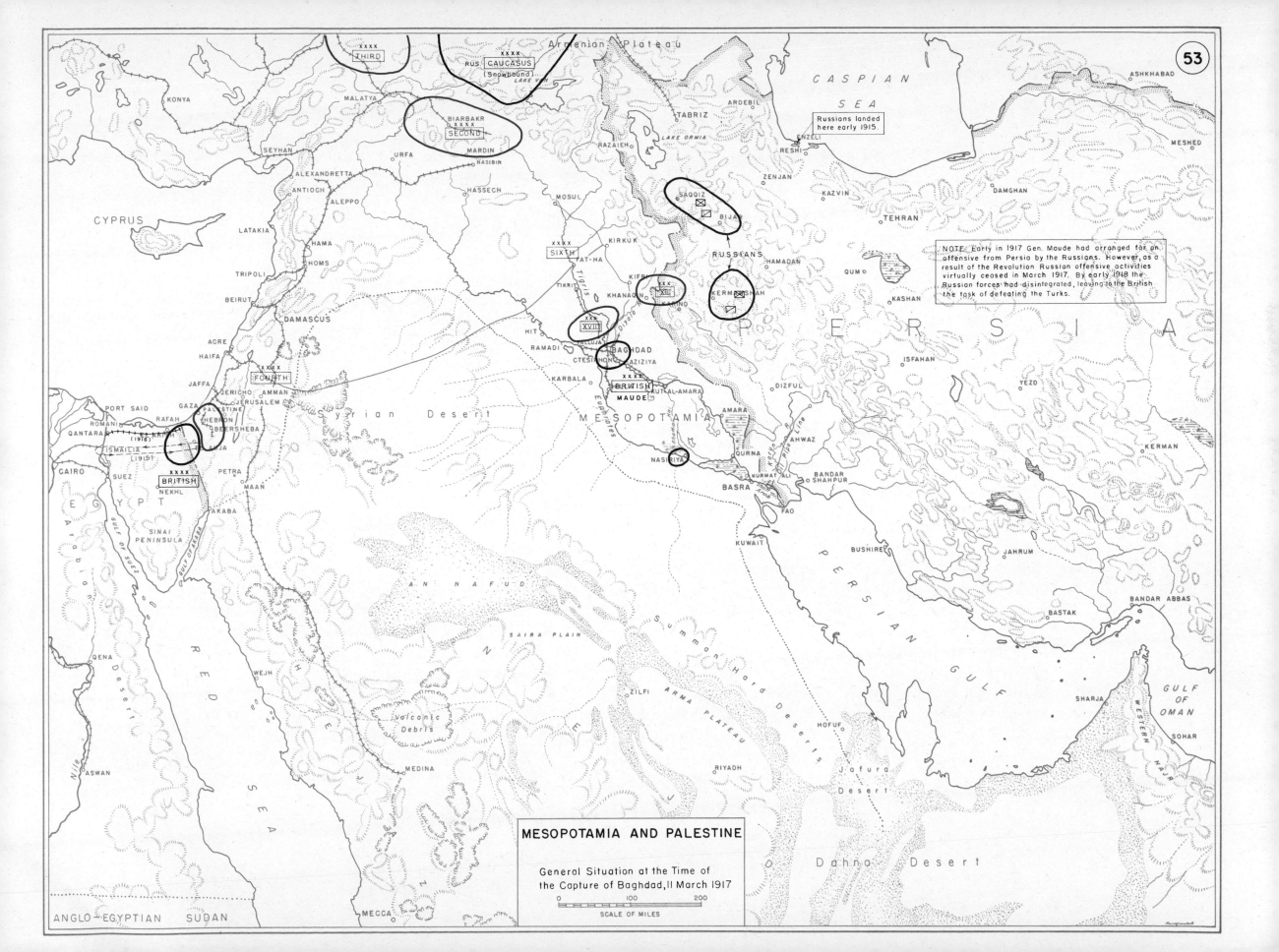

MESOPOTAMIA AND PALESTINE

General Situation at the Time of
the Capture of Baghdad, 11 March 1917

0 ___ 100 ___ 200
SCALE OF MILES

With the capture of El Arish (*off map, bottom left*), the British had attained their original objective of securing the Suez Canal against attack. General Sir Archibald Murray had sufficient troops to stop effectively any Turkish attempts to drive across the Sinai Peninsula, but he was not strong enough to mount a major offensive into Palestine. Nevertheless, this was to be his mission. (Murray maintained a lavish headquarters at Cairo, but moved to a more advanced, austere site at El Arish for the coming operations.)

In December, 1916, following the collapse of Rumania and the British-French failure to achieve any great gains in the Somme offensive, David Lloyd George—a man of vast energy, guile, and self-confidence—had come to power in England. The British prime minister was prone to think in terms of political objectives, and he stood firmly against battles of attrition like the Somme. He had been exploring the possibilities of peripheral war, and now urged an advance into Palestine. A victory here would add fuel to the flaming Arab revolt against the Turks—Lawrence ("of Arabia") was advising Hussein (the Sherif of Mecca) in this venture—and perhaps Jerusalem, an impressive objective, could be captured. Murray cautiously advised that he needed reinforcements to attempt a major advance. But none was forthcoming, for the Allies were scraping together all possible troops in preparation for the heralded Nivelle offensive (*see map 60*). So plans were prepared for an overland movement toward Gaza (*this map; center, left*). Paradoxically, the greatest sea power on earth was unable to exploit fully the strategic mobility conferred by its fleet; global commitments precluded it.

The advance to the border began in January, 1917; Rafah was seized by the British on the 9th. The railroad and pipeline were pushed forward, the railroad reaching the border in March. The Turks (whose forces in this area the British usually overestimated) gave up their forward positions and occupied the positions shown with about 16,000 men. Murray's army—only slightly superior to the Turks in total strength, but extremely dominant in cavalry—closed to the Wadi Ghazze (a sizable ravine, dry much of the time) and prepared to attack Gaza, the key to the enemy position.

The British field commander was General Sir Charles M. Dobell. He planned to move his two cavalry divisions around to the east and north of Gaza to prevent Turkish reinforcement of that locality; meanwhile, the 53d Division would seize the dominant Ali Muntar ridge and then rush the town. The 52d Division was to remain in reserve, and the 54th Division would protect the right flank.

The attack was launched on 26 March and, though initially delayed by a heavy fog, proceeded as planned. By 1830, the 53d Division had seized the ridge after a hard fight and was on the edge of the town; at the same time, one of the cavalry divisions was in the northern suburbs. But now confusion and misunderstanding, so frequent in war, set in to ruin British chances for what appeared to be a certain victory on the 27th. Through poor staff work and an inexplicable breakdown in communications, the commander of the cavalry was not aware of the success achieved by the 53d Division. Fearful that the Turks would attack his divisions from two sides—and also concerned over lack of water for his horses—he ordered the cavalry to withdraw that night. The 53d Division's flank was thus exposed, and it, too, withdrew to Wadi Ghazze. The next morning, attempts were made to retake Ali Muntar, but the reinforced Turks were too strong.

London, receiving an optimistic report on the outcome of the battle, now directed Murray to renew the offensive to capture Jerusalem. That commander had reported Turkish losses as 8,000 and his own as 3,500; actually, they were 2,447 and 3,967, respectively. The British had *not* won a great victory and were in no condition to plunge recklessly toward Jerusalem.

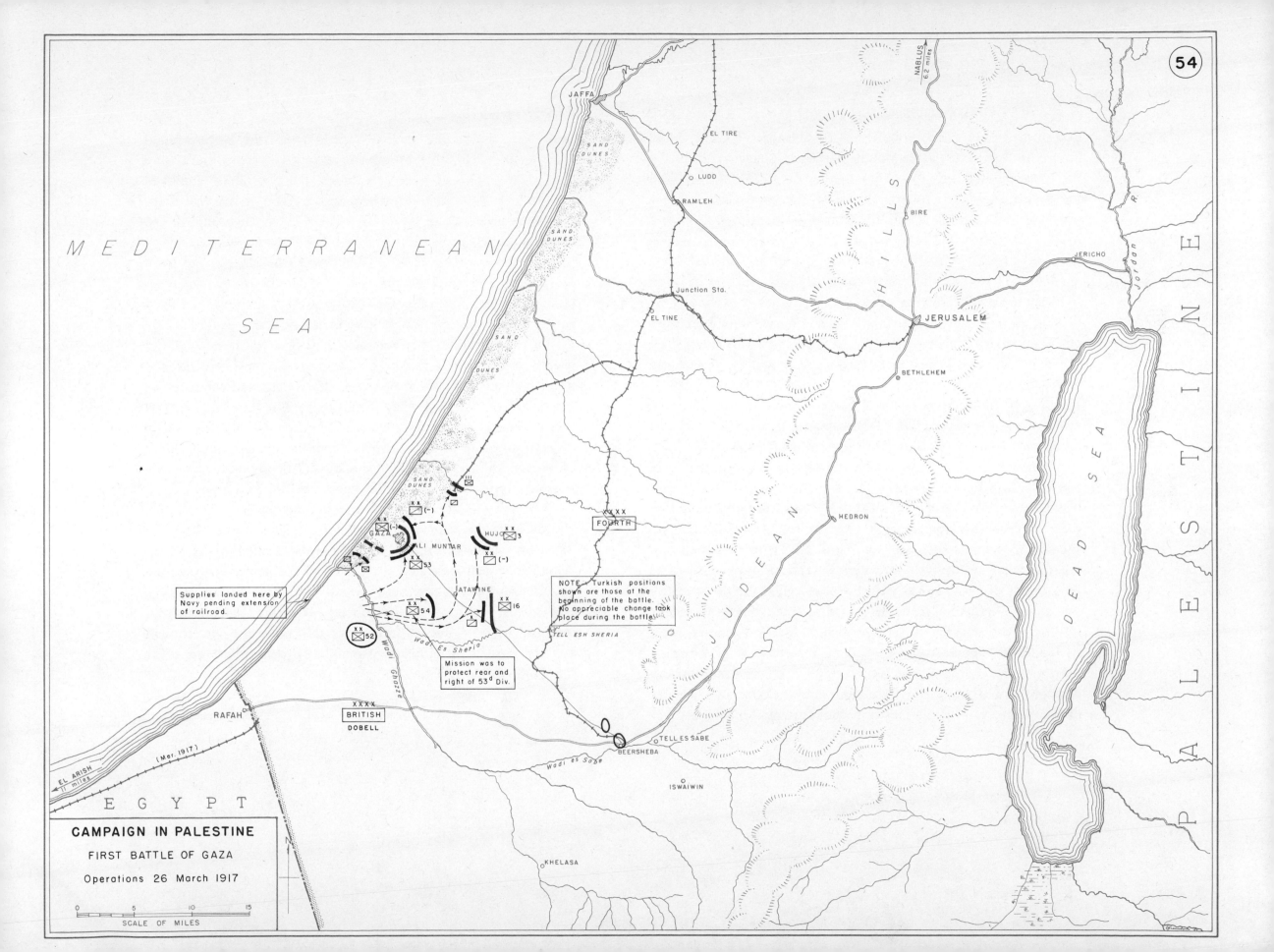

CAMPAIGN IN PALESTINE

FIRST BATTLE OF GAZA

Operations 26 March 1917

General Murray had not appreciated what extreme optimism his exaggerated report of success in the First Battle of Gaza would arouse in London. Consequently, he was somewhat surprised when immediately ordered to capture Jerusalem. He again asked for reinforcements, stressing the need for two more infantry divisions and additional artillery if such an ambitious task were to be accomplished. London replied that prompt action on his part was important and that the 74th Division would be made available. The implication of the necessity for a success to boost public morale was clear to Murray.

The task facing the British now was immeasurably more difficult than it had been previously. The Turks, soundly advised by Germans, had established a strong defensive position from Gaza to Beersheba (*lower center*), with the bulk of their troops in strong points at and southeast of Gaza. They also had adequate artillery and air support, the latter making it extremely difficult for Dobell to achieve secrecy in preparation for the attack.

Dobell learned that Beersheba was lightly held, but the problem of supplying a large force on that flank—particularly with water—precluded an envelopment there. Nor would the mounting pressure from Murray and London allow a delay to build up supplies to support such a move. Thus, the British resorted to a frontal attack on the well-prepared Turkish position—it was to be a battle of brute force. Dobell's plan called for an attack in two phases; in the first phase, he hoped to obtain an advantageous position from which the decisive assault (second phase) could be launched. The 53d Division, along the coast, was to be supported by naval gunfire; the 74th would be in reserve; the cavalry divisions would protect the right flank; and the other two infantry divisions, making the main effort, would attack Ali Muntar.

On 17 April, Dobell launched his offensive. The first phase went well, but in the decisive second phase the British failed everywhere. The three assaulting infantry divisions took little ground and suffered heavy casualties; the few tanks employed were of little assistance, either being picked off by Turkish artillery or stalled in the sand. At 1700, 19 April, Dobell broke off the attack and withdrew. He had lost 6,444 men, while Turkish casualties were about 2,000. Once more, the British had been given a convincing display of the Turk's ability to defend tenaciously a piece of terrain: Gallipoli and Mesopotamia had been earlier demonstrations whose lessons had not been heeded.

One of Murray's first acts after this Second Battle of Gaza was to relieve Dobell. But his own failure could not be condoned in a London which now looked upon the Palestinian campaign as the means of driving Turkey from the war. In June he, too, was recalled, being replaced by General Sir Edmund Allenby, a cavalryman who had recently achieved some prominence in the Battle of Arras. Before departing for Cairo, Allenby was given the mission "Jerusalem before Christmas" by Lloyd George.

The new commander was a forceful and energetic individual. He lived in the field with the troops, began overhauling the logistical establishment, and revitalized the command. After surveying the Gaza area, he concluded that the key to the position was Beersheba, the capture of which would enable him to turn the Turkish position. Allenby now asked for three more divisions, aircraft, artillery, and service units; this time, the government met the request of its field commander. Preparations began for the Third Battle of Gaza.

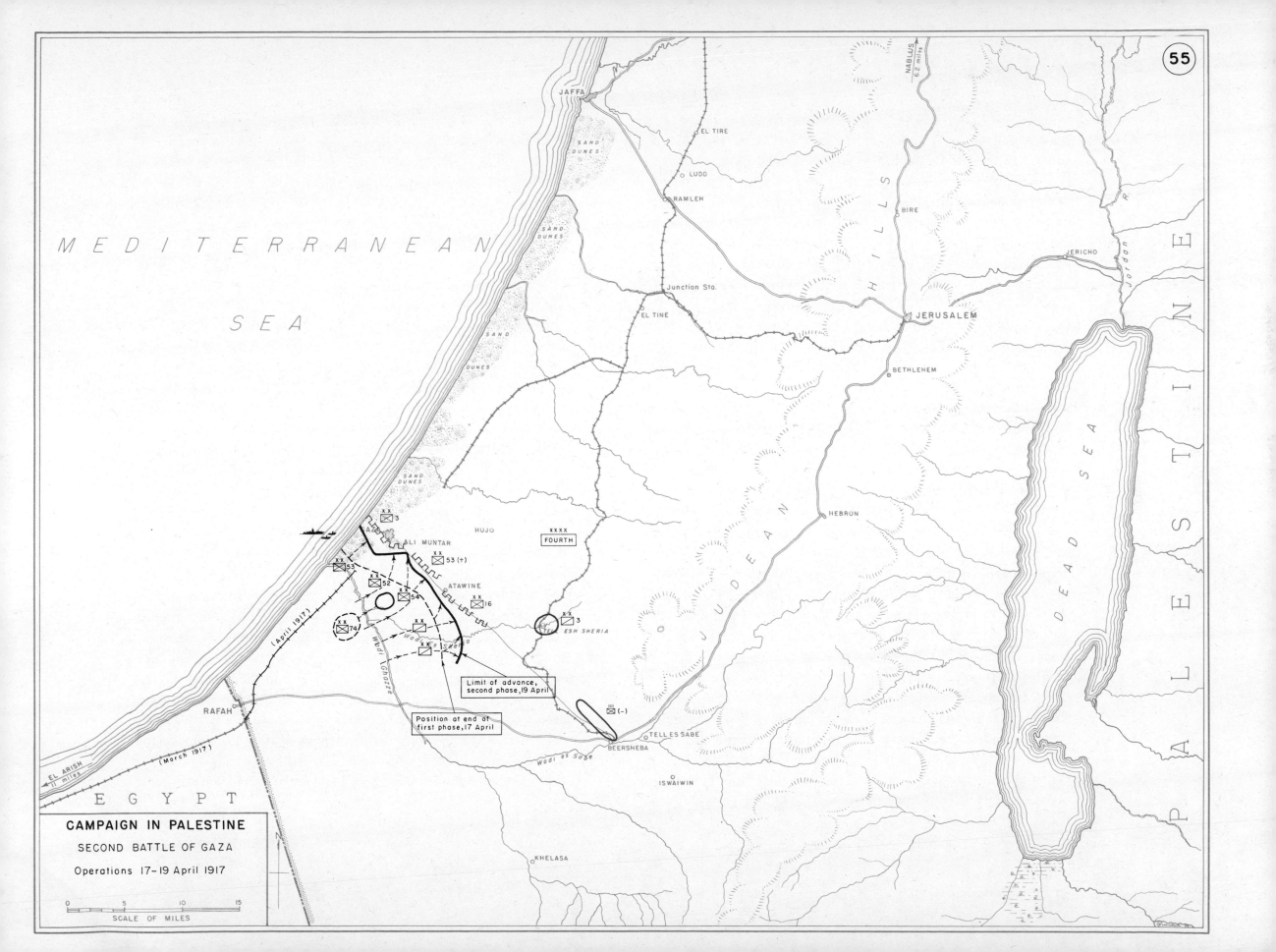

55

MEDITERRANEAN

SEA

JAFFA

EL TIRE

SAND
DUNES

LUDD

RAMLEH

BIRE

SAND
DUNES

NABLUS
62 miles

JUDEAN

HILLS

Junction Sta.

JERUSALEM

EL TINE

SAND

DUNES

BETHLEHEM

HEBRON

SAND
DUNES

XX
⊠ 3

HUJO

XXXX
FOURTH

XX
⊠ 53(+)

ALI MUNTAR

XX
⊠ 53

XX
⊠ 52

ATAWINE

XX
⊠ 54

XX
⊠ 16

XX
⊠ 3

ESH SHERIA

JUDEAN

XX
(74)

XX
⊠

Wadi Sheria

XX
⊠

Wadi Ghazze

(April 1917)

Limit of advance,
second phase, 19 April

Position at end of
first phase, 17 April

III
⊠ (-)

RAFAH

TELL ES SABE

Wadi es Sabe

BEERSHEBA

DEAD

SEA

PALESTINE

Jordan R.

JERICHO

(March 1917)

EL ARISH
11 miles

ISWAIWIN

EGYPT

CAMPAIGN IN PALESTINE

SECOND BATTLE OF GAZA

Operations 17-19 April 1917

KHELASA

0   5   10   15
SCALE OF MILES

In early 1917, Turkey's fortunes were declining. The rigors of the previous winter had taken a heavy toll of her troops in the Caucasus; in Mesopotamia, General Maude advanced relentlessly; Arab uprisings, sparked by Lawrence, were proving troublesome; and the Rumanian campaign had drained off some of her better troops. But, with the defeat of Rumania and the impending collapse of Russia, it became possible to reinforce the Palestine front. By September, 1917, 35,000 Turkish troops were in the Gaza area. These troops were disposed in three general fortified areas (Gaza, Tell Esh Sheria, and Beersheba) connected by outposts. They were organized into two armies whose actions were to be coordinated by Falkenhayn. (After his Rumanian triumph, the German had been dispatched to Turkey, and eventually went on to Jerusalem, arriving there on 1 November.) As mentioned earlier, Turkey had concentrated a force at Aleppo (*off map, north*) in March to be used to recapture Baghdad; but Allenby's preparations convinced Falkenhayn that the force should be used in Palestine. This force (called "Yilderim") was thus routed southward to form the nucleus of the Seventh Army, though not all of it had arrived by the time Allenby struck.

On 31 October, the British force numbered 88,000 and was well supplied and competently commanded. The key to Allenby's plan—to seize Beersheba and then drive northwest to the coast—was surprise founded on deception. Every means of misleading the Turks to expect the main attack on Gaza was employed—including a faked attack order which was allowed to fall into enemy hands—while the XX Corps (four divisions) and two cavalry divisions were moved secretly to the Beersheba area at the last moment. To support his sizable army, Allenby also built additional railroads and extended the pipeline. Aerial reconnaissance provided the Turks with information of the movement toward Beersheba, but they greatly underestimated its strength. When Allenby attacked at dawn on the 31st, the Turks were taken completely by surprise.

The XX Corps succeeded in seizing the outer position at Beersheba, with the 74th Division encountering the most difficulty. By nightfall, the 74th and 60th Divisions had almost reached Beersheba (*dashed blue line*), while the 53d Division continued to guard their left flank. Meanwhile, late in the afternoon, the Australian Cavalry Division had made a mounted charge which captured Beersheba and its vital water supplies; the Turks, who had fairly well contained the attack of the Anzac Cavalry Division, then withdrew to the position west of Tell Esh Sheria.

From 1 to 4 November, the British assaulted the Gaza position, making only minor gains, while the Turks reinforced the Sheria position to the east. As the 53d Division applied more pressure, more enemy troops were moved from the center of the line to oppose it, thus inviting attack by the divisions of Allenby's XX Corps (*small division symbols*) at Sheria. This attack came at 0400, 6 November; by 0600, Allenby had achieved such success that he ordered the cavalry to move through to the coast.

The Gaza defenders, in danger of being cut off, withdrew toward Junction Station (*upper center*). They arrived there by 11 November, despite pressure maintained by the British cavalry, hampered as it was by water shortages. To the east, the Seventh Army also withdrew.

Allenby gave his foe no respite, attacking Junction Station on the 13th and capturing it the following day. The Eighth Army fell back northward, and Allenby turned his attention toward Jerusalem. After one unsuccessful attack (*action not shown*), it became obvious that the XXI and the Cavalry Corps could not effect the capture alone. Hence, Allenby paused, regrouped, and prepared for a major attack. On 8 December, he pushed forward all along the line; the next day, the long-sought political prize—Jerusalem—was in British hands. Allenby, shrewdly and humbly, made his official entry into the city on foot.

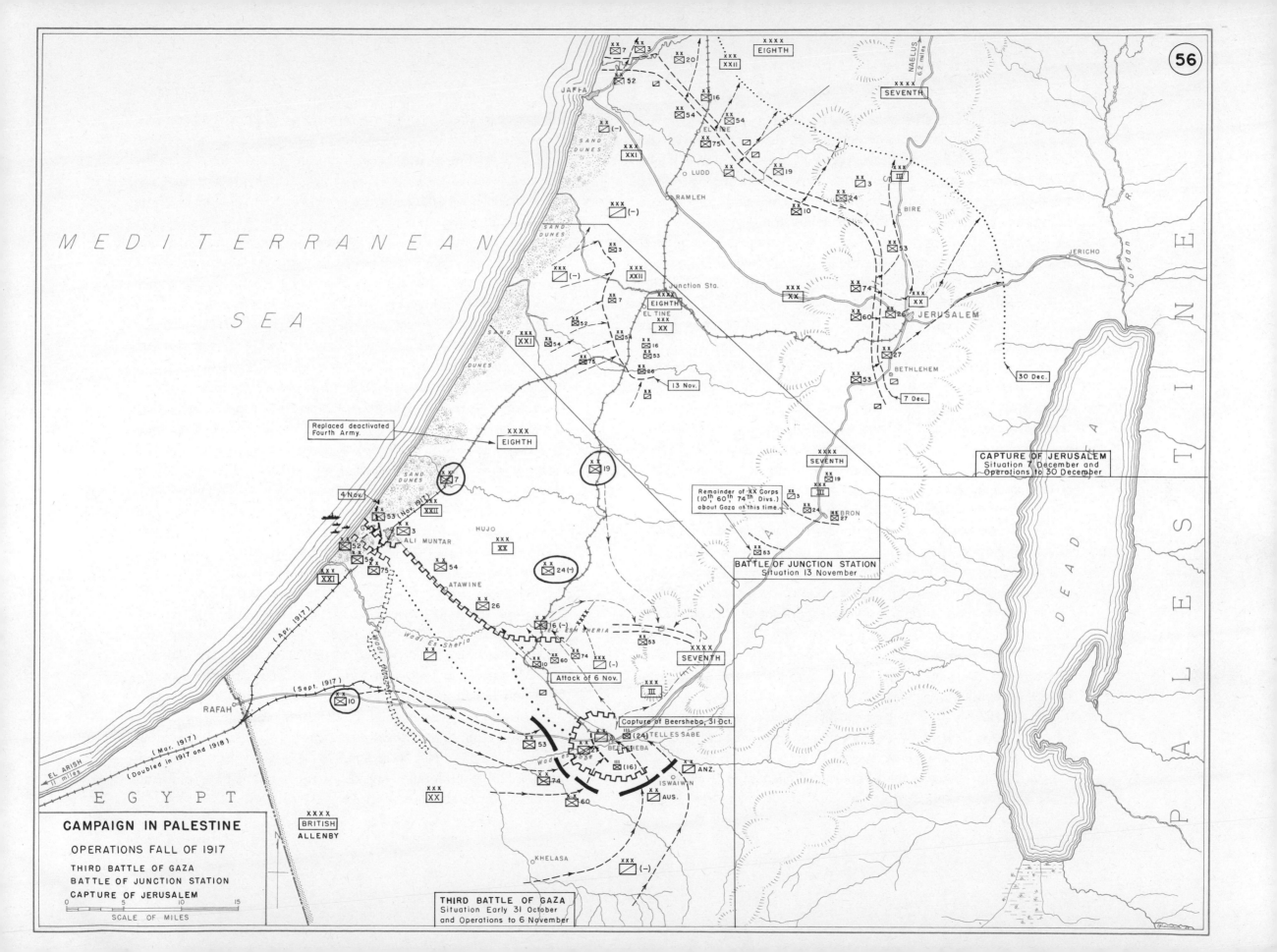

56

MEDITERRANEAN

SEA

JAFFA

NABLUS

EIGHTH

SEVENTH

JERICHO

Jordan R.

DEAD

SEA

PALESTINE

Replaced deactivated
Fourth Army.

EIGHTH

CAPTURE OF JERUSALEM
Situation 7 December and
Operations to 30 December

Remainder of XX Corps
(10th, 60th, 74th Divs.)
about Gaza at this time.

SEVENTH

BATTLE OF JUNCTION STATION
Situation 13 November

Junction Sta.

13 Nov.

7 Dec.

30 Dec.

BETHLEHEM

JERUSALEM

BIRE

LUDD

RAMLEH

EL TINE

4 Nov.

(Nov. 1917)

(Apr. 1917)

ALI MUNTAR

HUJO

ATAWINE

Wadi Es Sheria

TEL ESH SHERIA

Attack of 6 Nov.

Capture of Beersheba, 31 Oct.

TELL ES SABE

BEERSHEBA

ISWAIWIN

Wadi es Saba

(Sept. 1917)

RAFAH

(Mar. 1917)

(Doubled in 1917 and 1918)

EL ARISH
II miles

E G Y P T

KHELASA

CAMPAIGN IN PALESTINE

OPERATIONS FALL OF 1917

THIRD BATTLE OF GAZA
BATTLE OF JUNCTION STATION
CAPTURE OF JERUSALEM

XXXX
BRITISH
ALLENBY

SCALE OF MILES
0   5   10   15

THIRD BATTLE OF GAZA
Situation Early 31 October
and Operations to 6 November

The capture of Jerusalem and Maude's success in Mesopotamia provided the only bright spots in Allied operations in 1917. As such, they added fuel to Lloyd George's demands that Allenby be reinforced in order to eliminate Turkey from the war. This, he thought, would be the best means of applying pressure on Germany. He apparently chose to ignore the fact that the Germans, with their interior lines, could move troops between fronts more easily and quickly than the British. Nivelle's failure and the great losses in the Flanders battles preyed heavily on the prime minister's mind. Thus, against the advice of the Imperial General Staff, Allenby received two more divisions from Mesopotamia and was directed to undertake the offensive.

But Ludendorff's offensive on the Western Front (*see map 63a*), striking the weakened British line on 21 March, 1918, completely disrupted Allenby's plans. The British were forced to withdraw two divisions and supporting troops equivalent to three more from Palestine. Allenby postponed his attack and, during the spring and summer, resorted to training the green replacements received from India. He also conducted minor operations (*not shown*) east of the Jordan River—partly to secure bridgeheads, but primarily to deceive the Turks as to his eventual intentions: already, Allenby had decided to launch his main blow along the coast north of Jaffa (*this map, lower left*). Though these minor operations were tactically unsuccessful, they did direct Turkey's attention toward the vulnerability of the Amman-Dera railroad (*lower center*)—exactly as Allenby desired. Lawrence's Arabs added to the deception by increased forays on the railroad. British air power, by now, was so superior that the Turks were unable to conduct effective reconnaissance. Thus, by September, when the British were ready to attack, the Turks had one-third of their forces east of the Jordan and were poorly prepared for Allenby's devastating blow.

In March, Sanders had replaced Falkenhayn and had at once set about reorganizing the Turkish defenses to take full advantage of the Turkish forte for defense of prepared positions. Thus, most of his troops were moved into line, and reserves were held to a minimum. But Turkish morale was low (except in the German Asia Corps), desertion reached high proportions, and the government withdrew troops to pursue political aims in Persia and the Caucasus.

Allenby launched his attack—the famous Battle of Megiddo —at 0430, 19 September. The XXI Corps (five divisions) made the main attack without the customary preparatory bombardment. By 0730, the enemy line had been rent asunder, and the Cavalry Corps burst through in the exploitation to seize the Megiddo (*center*)–El Affule–Beisan area and block the northern exits from the Judean Hills (*lower center*). That evening, the XX Corps took up the attack, and Chaytor Force pushed across the Jordan. By nightfall on 21 September, the cavalry had blocked the retreat of the Seventh and Eighth Armies, 25,000 prisoners had been taken, and Turkish resistance west of the Jordan had been broken. British aircraft were particularly effective in strafing and bombing the defiles through which the Turks struggled to escape—a portent of the coming influence of tactical air power. During the period 22-30 September, the Turkish Fourth Army, harried by cavalry and Arabs, disintegrated on its way to Damascus, its survivors surrendering near that city.

Damascus fell to Allenby on 2 October, and Aleppo on the 28th. The Battle of Megiddo cost the British 5,666 casualties; total Turkish casualties are unknown, but the British captured 76,000 men. The Turks, routed also in Macedonia (*see map 50*) and Mesopotamia (*see map 53*), asked for an armistice on the 28th and signed the surrender papers on the 30th.

Thus ended the campaign in Palestine, concluded brilliantly by Allenby, but at great over-all expense. Total British casualties from 1 January, 1915, were 554,828—90 per cent of them nonbattle. This considerable subsidiary effort might have been put to better use on the more decisive Western Front.

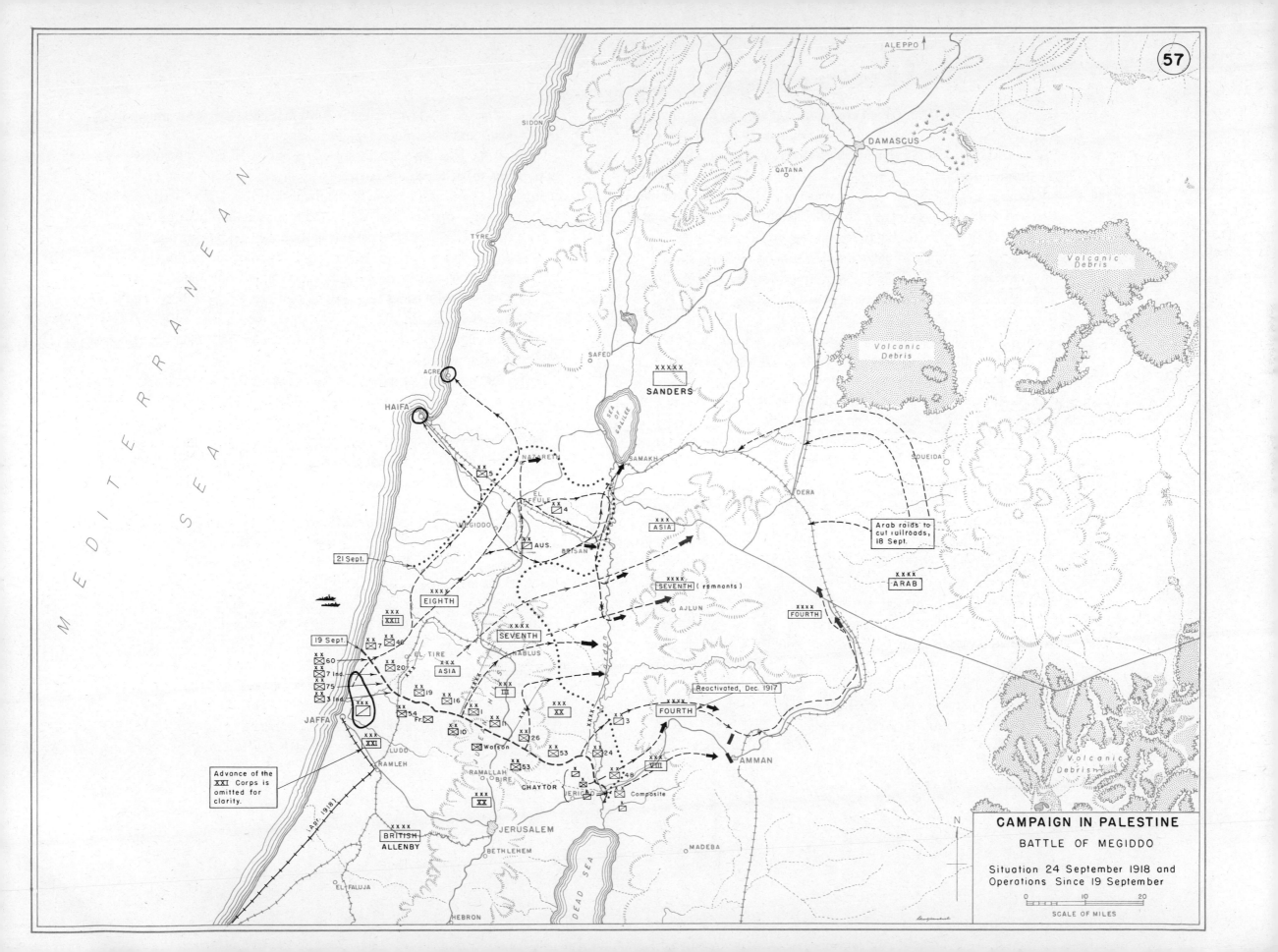

ALEPPO

DAMASCUS

QATANA

Volcanic Debris

Volcanic Debris

SIDON

TYRE

ACRE

HAIFA

SEA OF GALILEE

SAFED

SAMAKH

SUEIDA

XXXXX
SANDERS

NAZARETH

EL FFULE

XX
5

MEGIDDO

XX
4

DERA

XX
AUS.

BEISAN

XXX
ASIA

Arab raids to
cut railroads,
18 Sept.

21 Sept.

XXXX
SEVENTH (remnants)

XXXX
ARAB

AJLUN

XXXX
EIGHTH

XXX
XXII

XXXX
FOURTH

19 Sept.

XX 7   48
XX 60
XX 7 Ind.
XX 75
XX 3 Ind.

EL TIRE

XXX
20

XXX
ASIA

NABLUS

XX
19

XX
16

III

XXX
XX

Reactivated, Dec. 1917

XXX
FOURTH

JAFFA

XX
54 Fr.

XX
1

XX
1

XXX

XX
3

AMMAN

XXX
XXI

XX
10

Watson

XX
26

XX
24

XXX
VIII

LUDD

RAMLEH

XX
53

XX
53

XX
48

Composite

Advance of the
XXI Corps is
omitted for
clarity.

RAMALLAH
BIRE

CHAYTOR

JERICHO

XX

MEDITERRANEAN SEA

(Apr. 1918)

XXXX
BRITISH
ALLENBY

JERUSALEM

BETHLEHEM

MADEBA

EL FALUJA

DEAD SEA

HEBRON

Volcanic Debris

N

CAMPAIGN IN PALESTINE

BATTLE OF MEGIDDO

Situation 24 September 1918 and
Operations Since 19 September

0   10   20
SCALE OF MILES

57

In November, 1916, an Allied conference at Joffre's headquarters had decided to carry out coordinated offensives on the Western, Eastern, Italian, Salonika, and Palestine fronts during 1917, with the major effort on the Western Front. There, Joffre proposed to continue the attrition of the Somme with a massive combined British-French offensive from the Oise River (*left center*) north to Arras. This was to be followed, several weeks later, by a British-Belgian attack to clear the north coast of Belgium, where the Germans had established several important submarine bases. The Allied commanders were optimistic; except for the fall of Rumania, 1916 had gone generally in their favor. They now had definite numerical superiority on all fronts, and munitions production was increasing. They hoped that sometime during their 1917 operations the German lines would break. If not, they felt capable of grinding down the forces of the Central Powers through unremitting pressure on all fronts.

These decisions were immediately nullified by political changes in Britain and France during December, 1916. In England, the new prime minister, David Lloyd George, did not favor great battles of attrition like the Somme, preferring peripheral operations like his expanded Palestine campaign (*see map 54*). In France, the Chamber of Deputies, which resented Joffre's strictly professional conduct of the war, forced him into retirement and replaced him with General Robert G. Nivelle, an extrovert who had distinguished himself at Verdun. Nivelle spoke perfect English and so impressed the mercurial Lloyd George that, except for the vigorous protests of Haig and Robertson, he would have given Nivelle what amounted to complete command of the British forces. Finally, with relations badly strained, it was agreed that Haig should make his plans conform generally to those of Nivelle, but during the coming campaign only.

Nivelle's principal claim to fame was the skillful counterattack he had directed at Verdun. Now—proclaiming his belief in the effectiveness "of violence, of brutality, and of rapidity"—he boasted that he could repeat his Verdun operation on a much larger scale and obtain a complete breakthrough of the German lines in from twenty-four to forty-eight hours. Masses of heavy guns were to paralyze the enemy by a short, surprise bombardment; masses of infantry would then smash through the German trench system, opening the way for an all-out exploitation by large forces of cavalry. His operational plan provided for an initial, powerful British-French secondary attack between Bapaume and Arras, after which the French would make the main effort in the Chemin des Dames area (*this map; center, left*) between Reims and Soissons. In order to free sufficient French units for this offensive, the British were required to extend their right about twenty-five miles.

Meanwhile, the Germans withdrew from their long, unfavorable position in the Somme sector to the new Hindenburg Line (correctly, "the Siegfried zone"—a deep, complex, defensive system). This gave them a stronger front and—by shortening their line—enabled them to hold it with fewer divisions and thus form a badly needed reserve. Their organization of the Siegfried position and withdrawal to it were expertly handled, and took the Allies largely by surprise. The evacuated territory was devastated: all buildings were destroyed, all trees cut down, roads ruined, wells choked up or polluted, and booby traps, inundations, and demolitions arranged to slow the pursuit.

Nivelle's projected main attack was not particularly affected by this withdrawal, but in the sector of the secondary attack, it would take several months to close to and mount an offensive against the new German line. Nivelle contented himself with arranging for the British alone to make a strong attack near Arras. The French troops that had been originally assigned to the secondary attack in cooperation with the British were added to his Group of Armies of the Reserve, which was to make his main attack. Other French forces were to make minor attacks at St. Quentin and east of Reims (*small blue arrows*).

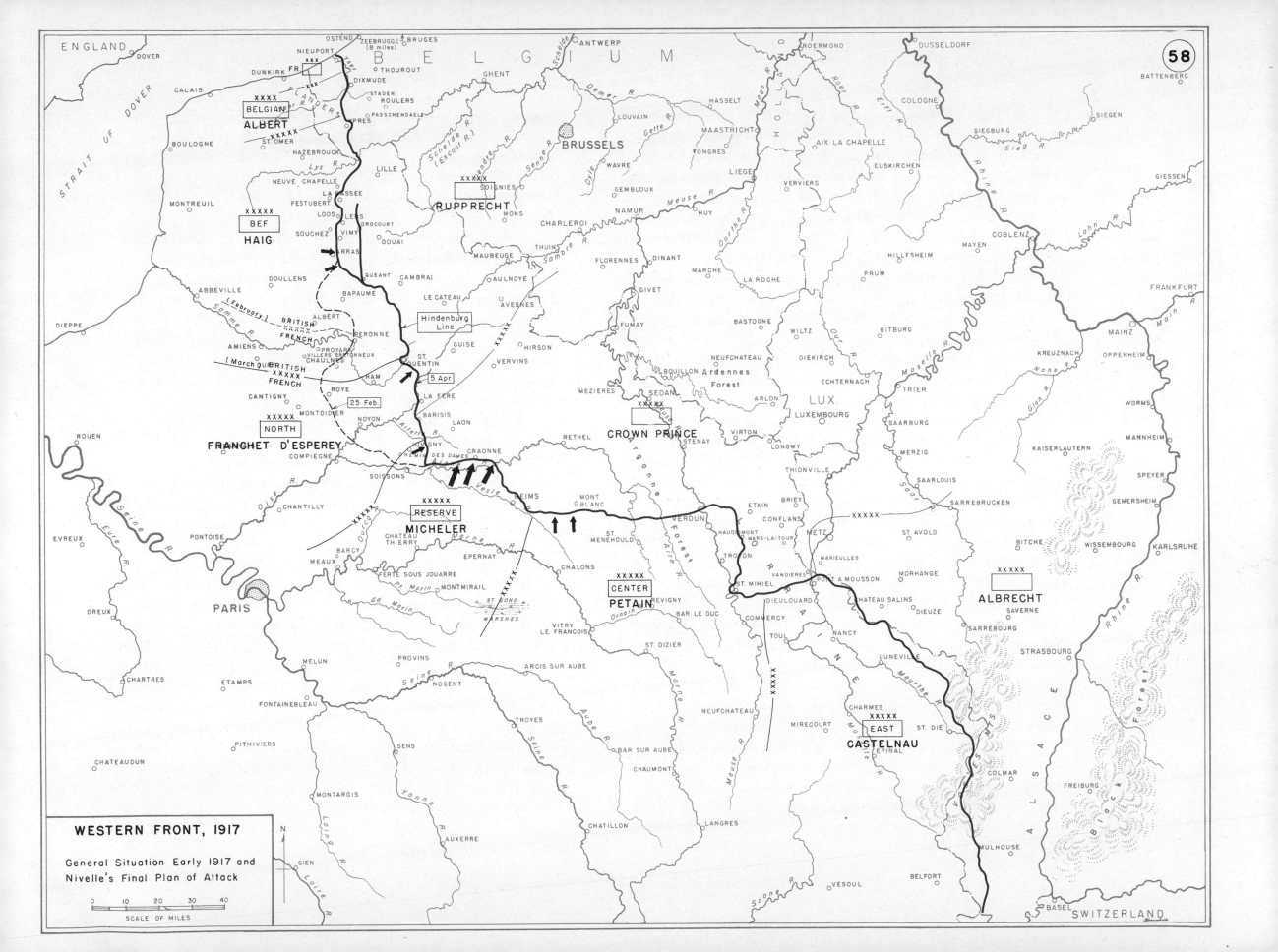

ENGLAND

BELGIUM

OSTEND ZEEBRUGGE BRUGES
(8 miles)

ANTWERP

ROERMOND

DUSSELDORF

58

DOVER

NIEUPORT

DUNKIRK FR. xxx
xxx

THOUROUT

GHENT

DIXMUDE

STADEN
ROULERS

YPRES

PASSCHENDAELE

BATTENBERG

COLOGNE

SIEGEN

CALAIS

xxxx
xxxx

BELGIAN
ALBERT

HASSELT

LOUVAIN R.

BRUSSELS

LIEGE

MAASTRICHT

TONGRES

VERVIERS

AIX LA CHAPELLE

EUSKIRCHEN

SIEGBURG

COBLENZ

BOULOGNE

ST. OMER

HAZEBROUCK

LILLE

NEUVE CHAPELLE

NAMUR

GEMBLOUX

MONS

CHARLEROI

HUY

MARCHE

LA ROCHE

HILLESHEIM

MAYEN

PRUM

MONTREUIL

LA BASSEE

FESTUBERT

xxxxx
BEF
HAIG

LOOS LENS

SOUCHEZ VIMY

DOUAI

MAUBEUGE

THUIN

SOMBRE

FLORENNES DINANT

GIVET

BASTOGNE

WILTZ

BITBURG

FRANKFURT

ABBEVILLE

DOULLENS

ARRAS

QUEANT CAMBRAI

LE CATEAU

AVESNES

AULNOYE

FUMAY

NEUFCHATEAU

DIEKIRCH

ECHTERNACH

TRIER

KREUZNACH

MAINZ

OPPENHEIM

WORMS

DIEPPE

(February)
BRITISH
xxxxx
FRENCH

BAPAUME

ALBERT

PERONNE

Hindenburg
Line

GUISE

HIRSON

VERVINS

MEZIERES SEDAN

BOUILLON Ardennes
Forest

ARLON

LUX.
LUXEMBOURG

VIRTON

TRIER

MANNHEIM

KAISERLAUTERN

SPEYER

AMIENS

PROYART
VILLERS BRETONNEUX
CHAULNES

(March)
BRITISH
xxxxx
FRENCH

HAM

ST.
QUENTIN

5 Apr.

LA FERE

BARISIS

LAON

RETHEL

xxxxx

CROWN PRINCE

STENAY

LONGWY

THIONVILLE

MERZIG

SAARLOUIS

SARREBRUCKEN

GERMERSHEIM

ROUEN

CANTIGNY

MONTDIDIER

xxxxx
NORTH

FRANCHET D'ESPEREY

ROYE

25 Feb.

NOYON

COMPIEGNE

SOISSONS

VOUGNY

CHEMIN DES DAMES

CRAONNE

REIMS

MONT
BLANC

VERDUN

ETAIN

BRIEY

CONFLANS

HAUDIOMONT
MARS-LA-TOUR

METZ

CHATEAU SALINS

xxxxx

ST. AVOLD

MORHANGE

DIEUZE

BITCHE

WISSEMBOURG

KARLSRUHE

EVREUX

CHANTILLY

xxxxx
RESERVE
MICHELER

CHATEAU
THIERRY

BARCY

MEAUX

ST.
MENEHOULD

TROYON

xxxxx
CENTER
PETAIN

MARIEULLES

PONT A MOUSSON

ST. MIHIEL

DIEULOUARD

VANDIERES

xxxxx
ALBRECHT

SAVERNE

SARREBOURG

STRASBOURG

DREUX

CHARTRES

PARIS

EPERNAY

FERTE SOUS JOUARRE
MONTMIRAIL

ST. GOND
MARSHES

CHALONS

REVIGNY

BAR LE DUC

COMMERCY

TOUL

NANCY

LUNEVILLE

CHATEAUDUN

ETAMPS

MELUN

PROVINS

NOGENT

ARCIS SUR AUBE

VITRY
LE FRANCOIS

ST. DIZIER

NEUFCHATEAU

xxxxxx

MIRECOURT

CHARMES

xxxxx
EAST
CASTELNAU

ST. DIE

COLMAR

FREIBURG

PITHIVIERS

FONTAINEBLEAU

SENS

TROYES

BAR SUR AUBE

CHAUMONT

EPINAL

MULHOUSE

MONTARGIS

AUXERRE

CHATILLON

LANGRES

VESOUL

BELFORT

BASEL

SWITZERLAND

GIEN

N

WESTERN FRONT, 1917

General Situation Early 1917 and
Nivelle's Final Plan of Attack

0   10   20   30   40
SCALE OF MILES

Not the least questionable of the features of Nivelle's plan was his selection of the Arras sector (*sketch* a) for the secondary attack which the British were to launch one week before his main attack, in order to draw the German reserves northward. The German defenses here were deep and strong; about five miles behind them lay the northward extension of the Hindenburg Line, running from Quéant to Drocourt (*see map 58*). The whole area was dominated by Vimy Ridge, which the Germans considered impregnable, and which gave them excellent observation of the British lines.

Despite its strength, Haig hoped to break through this entire German defensive system. The British Third and First Armies were to attack simultaneously, the Third making the main effort, while the First protected its left flank by taking Vimy Ridge. If their attacks progressed successfully, the British Fifth Army (*off this map, south*) would join in the offensive. If a breakthrough were achieved, Haig planned to exploit it by vigorous cavalry action. Otherwise, he proposed to cut the Arras operation short in favor of a major offensive farther north in Flanders.

Masses of artillery, including many heavy guns, fired a carefully organized, five-day preparatory bombardment, employing improved ammunition with greatly increased wire-cutting capability. (Plans called for a four-day preparation, which had to be lengthened when Nivelle's inability to attack on time caused a twenty-four–hour postponement of the British attack.) A limited number of tanks were available, and these—over the objections of the tank unit commanders—were distributed among the different corps.

Having learned during the Somme fighting that attempts to hold every foot of ground during heavy attacks resulted in extremely high casualties, Ludendorff had developed a new system of defensive tactics. Under it, an attacker first encountered a deep, lightly held outpost zone where a combination of dense wire entanglements and plentiful machine guns was designed to delay and disorganize him. Behind this was the first defensive position, consisting of several lines of mutually supporting strong points connected by trenches; behind that, a second one; and, behind that, waited specially trained counterattack divisions, ready to advance and recover any lost ground. The whole system was highly flexible and permitted a great deal of opportunity for initiative and aggressiveness in what had been a purely static defense.

In the Arras sector, however, the German Sixth Army commander either misunderstood this system or willfully ignored it. Possibly because of concern over Vimy Ridge, he held his front lines in great strength and, at the same time, posted his counterattack divisions too far to the rear.

The British jumped off at 0530, 9 April, following a heavy rolling barrage. Artillery support was so heavy that the Germans in the front lines were confused and demoralized. Gains were beyond all expectations, Canadian troops capturing most of Vimy Ridge at the first rush. But the weather now turned bad, and a series of costly new assaults brought little success. The Fifth Army attacked on the 10th, and was abruptly repulsed. It tried again in early May, but made only slight gains. Elsewhere, the Germans fell back skillfully when necessary. Operations continued until late May on a very reduced scale—in part, to divert attention from Haig's preparations around Ypres (*sketch* b).

No major offensive could well be undertaken at Ypres as long as the Germans held the long spur of Messines Ridge just south of that town. A limited attack was therefore launched by General Sir Herbert Plumer's Second Army. Since normal methods of obtaining surprise were impossible in the narrow Ypres salient, which was under constant German observation, Plumer's engineers had dug nineteen mines, packed with almost 1,000,000 pounds of high explosives, under the German-held ridge. A heavy preliminary bombardment began on 21 May. At 0310, 7 June, all mines were exploded; a barrage 700 yards deep was put down on the wrecked ridgeline, and nine divisions attacked with immediate success. Minor advances were made during the next few days to improve the newly won position.

Note: On Map b (and similarly on Map 61a), upper left, the symbol on the southern boundary of the Belgian Army should be XXXXX.

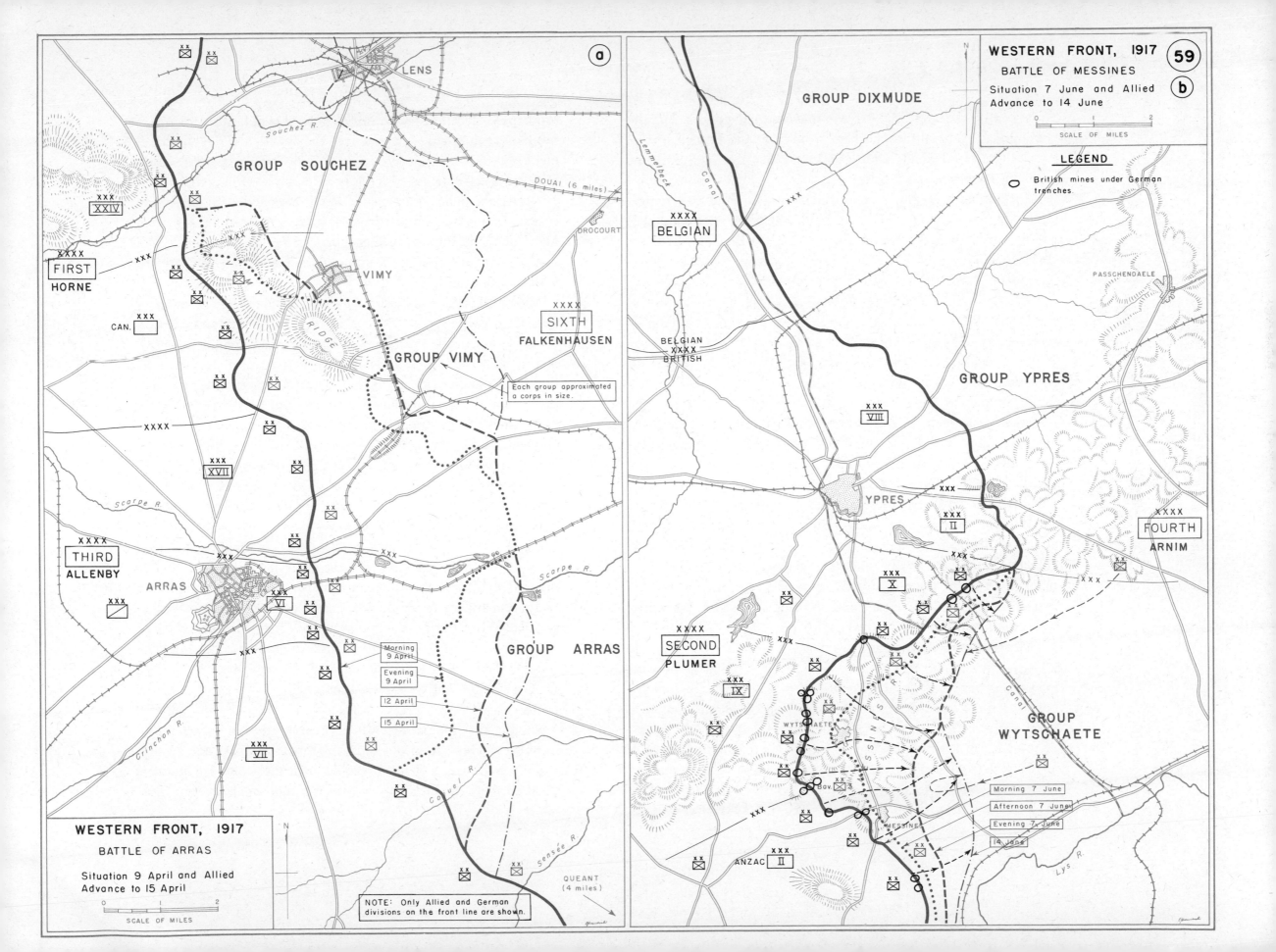

a

GROUP SOUCHEZ

LENS

Souchez R.

DOUAI (6 miles)

DROCOURT

GROUP VIMY

VIMY

RIDGE

XXXX
SIXTH
FALKENHAUSEN

XXXX
FIRST
HORNE

CAN. XXX

Each group approximated a corps in size.

XXXX
THIRD
ALLENBY

Scarpe R.

ARRAS

XVII

VI

Scarpe R.

GROUP ARRAS

Morning 9 April

Evening 9 April

12 April

15 April

Crinchon R.

VII

Cojeul R.

QUEANT (4 miles)

Sensée R.

WESTERN FRONT, 1917

BATTLE OF ARRAS

Situation 9 April and Allied Advance to 15 April

0 — 2
SCALE OF MILES

N

NOTE: Only Allied and German divisions on the front line are shown.

b

GROUP DIXMUDE

Lemmelbeck

Canal

XXXX
BELGIAN

BELGIAN
XXXX
BRITISH

GROUP YPRES

YPRES

PASSCHENDAELE

XXXX
FOURTH
ARNIM

LEGEND

◯ British mines under German trenches.

VIII

II

X

XXXX
SECOND
PLUMER

IX

WYTSCHAETE

MESSINES
RIDGE

Bav. 3

GROUP
WYTSCHAETE

Canal

Morning 7 June

Afternoon 7 June

Evening 7 June

14 June

ANZAC II

Lys R.

Strategically, the area that Nivelle had selected offered definite possibilities. A breakthrough here would put the French in the rear of the Hindenburg Line (*see map 58*), thus splitting the German front at a most vulnerable spot. Tactically, however, it was forbidding (*this map*). Any attack must surmount a series of steep and wooded parallel ridge lines, which the Germans had greatly strengthened. Victory here, against the new German elastic defense, could come only as the result of a skillful combination of surprise and concentrated force.

Nivelle could provide the force. The German withdrawal in the British sector had freed thirteen French divisions and 550 heavy guns. These Nivelle added to General Micheler's army group, along with the French forces originally designated to act with the British in the secondary attack. But surprise was a different matter; Nivelle himself made it impossible. For one thing, he talked too much, both in France and England. For another, detailed plans were widely circulated, even down to the front-line companies. The inevitable promptly happened: copies were captured by the Germans. When so informed, Nivelle stubbornly refused to make the slightest change in his plans.

Having confirmed the captured plans through agents and aerial reconnaissance, the Germans brought in a new army under General Fritz von Below and strengthened their lines. They planned to move their light artillery well to the rear when the French bombardment began, and to bring it forward promptly when the French infantry advanced.

Meanwhile, Nivelle found troubles in his rear. The French government had changed again, and the new minister of war mistrusted both Nivelle and his plan. In this, he was backed by Nivelle's three army group commanders, all of whom favored a more limited offensive. In a final conference, called by the President on 5 April, Nivelle still clung to his plan; rather than accept anything less, he offered his resignation. This the government lacked the courage to accept. However, Nivelle was instructed to suspend his offensive if it did not produce the rapid success he so firmly predicted. The preparatory bombardment began on 5 April; but bad weather repeatedly delayed the attack, and the bombardment had to be continued overtime, with a resulting severe drain on the French reserves of artillery ammunition. Finally, at 0600, 16 April, the main attack began. Pétain's secondary attack to the east of Reims was launched the next day. Whatever the French high command thought of their chances for success, Nivelle had inspired the rank and file. His infantry and tanks stormed forward with the old French fury.

Instantly, they met massed German machine-gun and artillery fire. Their own barrage, shifting too rapidly as they stumbled up the slippery hillsides, ran away from them. Communications collapsed. German aviators cleared the skies over the battlefield, knocking out the French artillery's aerial observation. In most places, the German first line was taken, but deeper penetrations were smashed by prompt counterattacks. French tank losses reached over 75 per cent, many of them having been caught in march column on the roads by German artillery.

Obstinately, Nivelle pushed his attack on the 17th. The weather remained stormy; but the Germans, finding the salient between Laffaux and Vailly (*top center*) under attack from both sides, began to evacuate it. Gradual, expensive gains continued at a few points along the line. On the night of 19-20 April, Nivelle ordered the Tenth Army committed between the Fifth and the Sixth, preparatory to another major attack. This produced another political-military crisis. Pétain was made chief of the general staff and thereafter limited the operations. A final offensive on 5 May brought only slight gains. The French cleared the Chemin des Dames summit, but the Germans still held high ridges just to the north. On 15 May, Pétain succeeded Nivelle. In the confused wrangling that followed, the French front-line armies broke out in mutiny. This Pétain put down by mixed firmness and justice, while a thin screen of loyal soldiers held the front. By amazing good fortune, the Germans remained in ignorance of the whole affair.

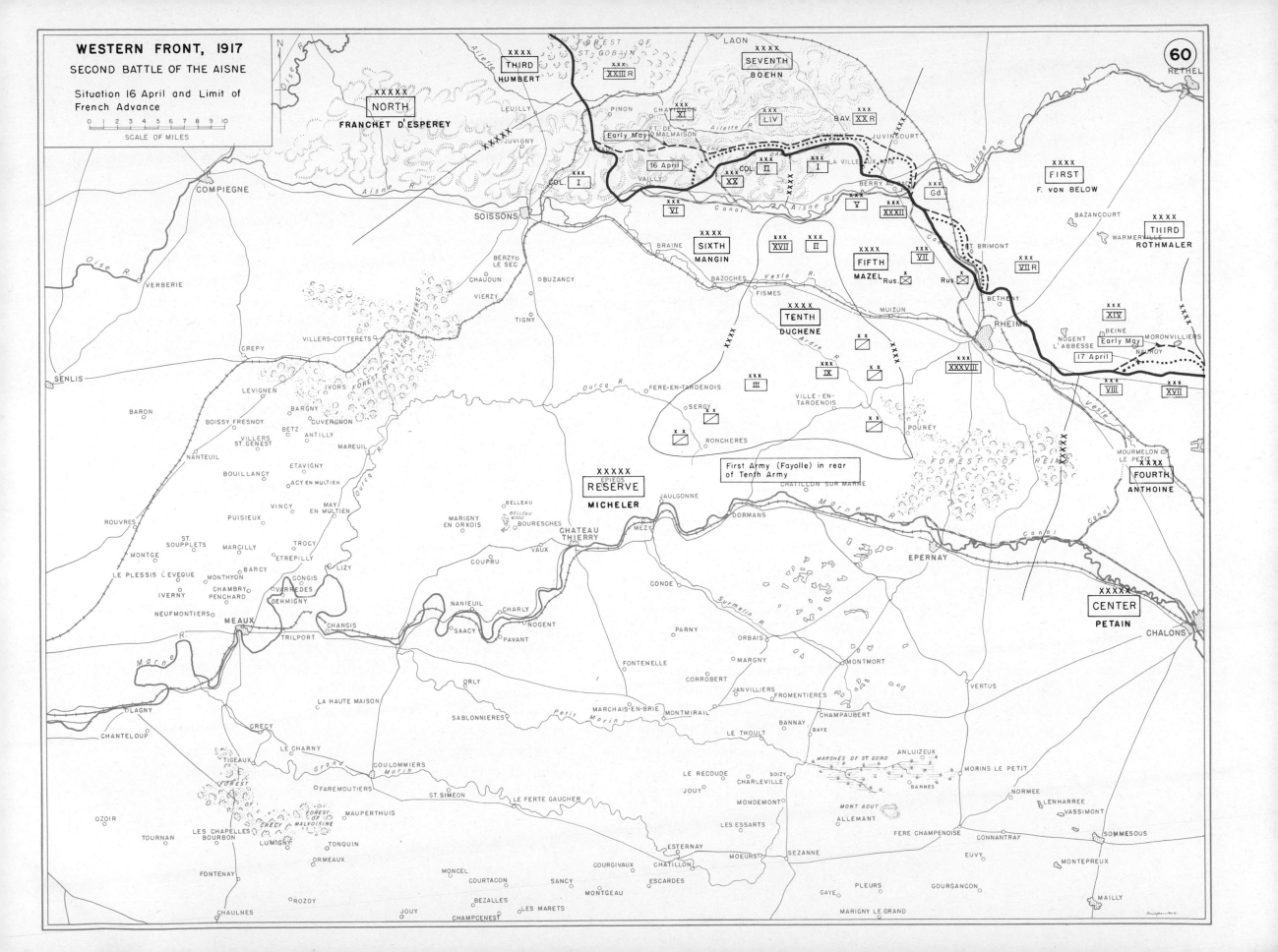

60

WESTERN FRONT, 1917

SECOND BATTLE OF THE AISNE

Situation 16 April and Limit of
French Advance

0 1 2 3 4 5 6 7 8 9 10
SCALE OF MILES

XXXX THIRD HUMBERT

XXXX SEVENTH BOEHN

XXXXX NORTH FRANCHET D'ESPEREY

XXXX FIRST F. VON BELOW

XXXX THIRD ROTHMALER

XXXX SIXTH MANGIN

XXXX FIFTH MAZEL

XXXX TENTH DUCHENE

XXXXX RESERVE MICHELER

First Army (Fayolle) in rear of Tenth Army

XXXXX CENTER PETAIN

XXXX FOURTH ANTHOINE

Early May
16 April
17 April

Places labeled on map: RETHEL, LAON, LEUILLY, PINON, CHAVIGNON, VAILLY, SOISSONS, COMPIEGNE, VERBERIE, OISE R., BRAINE, CHAUDUN, BERZY LE SEC, BUZANCY, VIERZY, TIGNY, VILLERS-COTTERETS, CREPY, SENLIS, BARON, LEVIGNEN, BARGNY, BETZ, ANTILLY, MAREUIL, CUVERGNON, NANTEUIL, VILLERS ST GENEST, BOISSY FRESNOY, ETAVIGNY, ACY EN MULTIEN, BOUILLANCY, ROUVRES, PUISIEUX, VINCY, MAY EN MULTIEN, BELLEAU, BELLEAU WOOD, BOURESCHES, MARIGNY EN ORXOIS, ST SOUPPLETS, MARCILLY, TROCY, ETREPILLY, LIZY, MONTGE, BARGY, MONTHYON, CHAMBRY PENCHARD, GONGIS, OVARREDES, GEHMIGNY, LE PLESSIS L'EVEQUE, IVERNY, NEUFMONTIERS, MEAUX, NANIEUIL, CHARLY, NOGENT, SAACY, PAVANT, CHANGIS, TRILPORT, MARNE R., OLAGNY, CRECY, CHANTELOUP, TIGEAUX, LE CHARNY, FOREST OF CRECY, FOREST OF MALVOISINE, LES CHAPELLES BOURBON, LUMIGNY, MAUPERTHUIS, TONQUIN, COULOMMIERS, FAREMOUTIERS, ST SIMEON, LE FERTE GAUCHER, OZOIR, TOURNAN, ORMEAUX, FONTENAY, MONCEL, COURTACON, BEZALLES, LES MARETS, CHAULNES, JOUY, CHAMPCENEST, ROZOY, MONTGEAU, SANCY, FORESTS OF VILLERS COTTERETS, IVORS, FERE-EN-TARDENOIS, SERGY, RONCHERES, VILLE-EN-TARDENOIS, POUREY, EPIEDS, JAULGONNE, DORMANS, CHATEAU THIERRY, MEZY, VAUX, COUPRU, CONDE, PARNY, ORBAIS, MARGNY, FONTENELLE, CORROBERT, MONTMORT, VERTUS, JANVILLIERS, FROMENTIERES, CHAMPAUBERT, MARCHAIS-EN-BRIE, MONTMIRAIL, BANNAY, BAYE, LE THOULT, MARSHES OF ST GOND, ANLUIZEUX, LE RECOUDE, SOIZY, CHARLEVILLE, JOUY, MONDEMONT, LES ESSARTS, ALLEMANT, MONT AOUT, ESTERNAY, SEZANNE, MOEURS, CHATILLON, ESCARDES, COURGIVAUX, CHAMPCENEST, GAYE, PLEURS, MARIGNY LE GRAND, GOURGANCON, EUVY, MONTEPREUX, MAILLY, SOMMESOUS, VASSIMONT, LENHARREE, NORMEE, FERE CHAMPENOISE, CONNANTRAY, MOURMELON LE PETIT, RHEIMS, BETHENY, BRIMONT, NOGENT L'ABBESSE, BEINE, MORONVILLIERS, NAUROY, MUIZON, FISMES, BAZOCHES, VESLE R., ARDRE R., OURCQ R., SURMELIN R., PETIT MORIN, GRAND MORIN, SABLONNIERES, LA HAUTE MAISON, ORLY, CHALONS, EPERNAY, BAZANCOURT, WARMERVILLE, JUVINCOURT, BERRY AU BAC, LA VILLE AUX BOIS, FT DE MALMAISON, FOREST OF ST GOBAIN, AISNE R., AILETTE R., JUVIGNY, LA FERE

Pétain begged Haig to keep the Germans occupied while he nursed his armies, crippled by mutiny, back to effectiveness. Accordingly, Haig went ahead with his Flanders offensive. This was to consist of three phases: first, an attack by the British Second and Fifth Armies to capture the rest of the high ground east of Ypres (*sketch* a); next, an amphibious landing on the Belgian coast between the Yser River and Ostend (*see map 58, top left*), in conjunction with an attack eastward from the Nieuport area; finally, a general advance toward Ghent. Exaggerated intelligence reports having caused him to overestimate the decline in German strength and morale, Haig planned an operation similar to Nivelle's recent failure, seeking a sudden breakthrough that would carry the war out of the trenches into the open. Accordingly, he entrusted the main attack (*this map*) to the aggressive General Sir Hubert Gough rather than the methodical Plumer, who had commanded the Ypres area for over two years and was familiar with the terrain. Gough was to attack northeast, making his main effort on his right. Plumer would cover Gough's right flank.

If this offensive could have been launched simultaneously with Nivelle's, greater results might have been possible. Now, time was lost while men and guns were brought north from Arras and the small French First Army was fitted into line. Consequently, the Germans had six weeks in which to prepare.

Allied aircraft eventually gained control of the air over the front, but the frequent bad weather largely nullified their success. The preparatory bombardment began on 18 July; zero hour was 0350 on the 31st. Unfortunately, the heavy rains soon filled the thousands of shell holes created by the long bombardment with water, forming a major obstacle. Most of the early British gains were lost to German counterattacks. When Gough proved unable to break through, Haig placed Plumer in command of the offensive. After careful preparations, Plumer advanced on 20 September, delivering a series of limited assaults on narrow fronts, with a pause after each one to get guns and supplies forward, and

reserves held ready to meet German counterattacks. By late September, he had won three battles. Then came the winter rains and the Battle of Caporetto (*see map 43*); five British divisions had to be rushed to Italy. Mud thwarted British advances in early October, but Canadian troops finally drove the Germans back to secure what Haig considered a good winter defensive position (*this map, dot-dashed red line*).

Meanwhile, seeking success before the Germans could be reinforced from the East, Haig revived an earlier plan for an attack in the Cambrai area (*sketch* b). This was to be a surprise attack without a preparatory bombardment. The artillery would open fire as the attack jumped off, using map and survey data. Tanks would be employed in mass, attacking with the infantry to break through the German position, seize bridges across the St. Quentin Canal (*lower center*), and breach the German second line behind it. Cavalry would strike through the gap thus created to isolate Cambrai and capture the wooded ridge just south of Bourlon (*center, left*) and the Senseé River crossings beyond.

At 0620, 20 November, a sudden deluge of fire dropped on the German positions, and more than 200 tanks lumbered forward, smashing gaps in the wire for the British infantry. Completely surprised and outnumbered, the Germans gave way, except around Flesquieres (*center, left*), where inept British tactics gave the defenders a chance to deal with tanks and infantry separately. But lack of infantry reserves—either casualties at Ypres or idle in Italy—finally slowed the assault; the longed-for breakthrough could not quite be achieved.

On 30 November, Ludendorff, having scraped together all available reserves, attacked both flanks of the British salient. To the south, the first German rush drove almost three miles into the original British position, but Gouzeaucourt (*lower center*) was saved by a tank counterattack, and farther north the British lines held firm. Haig, however, ordered a withdrawal (*dashed red line*) on the night of 4 December.

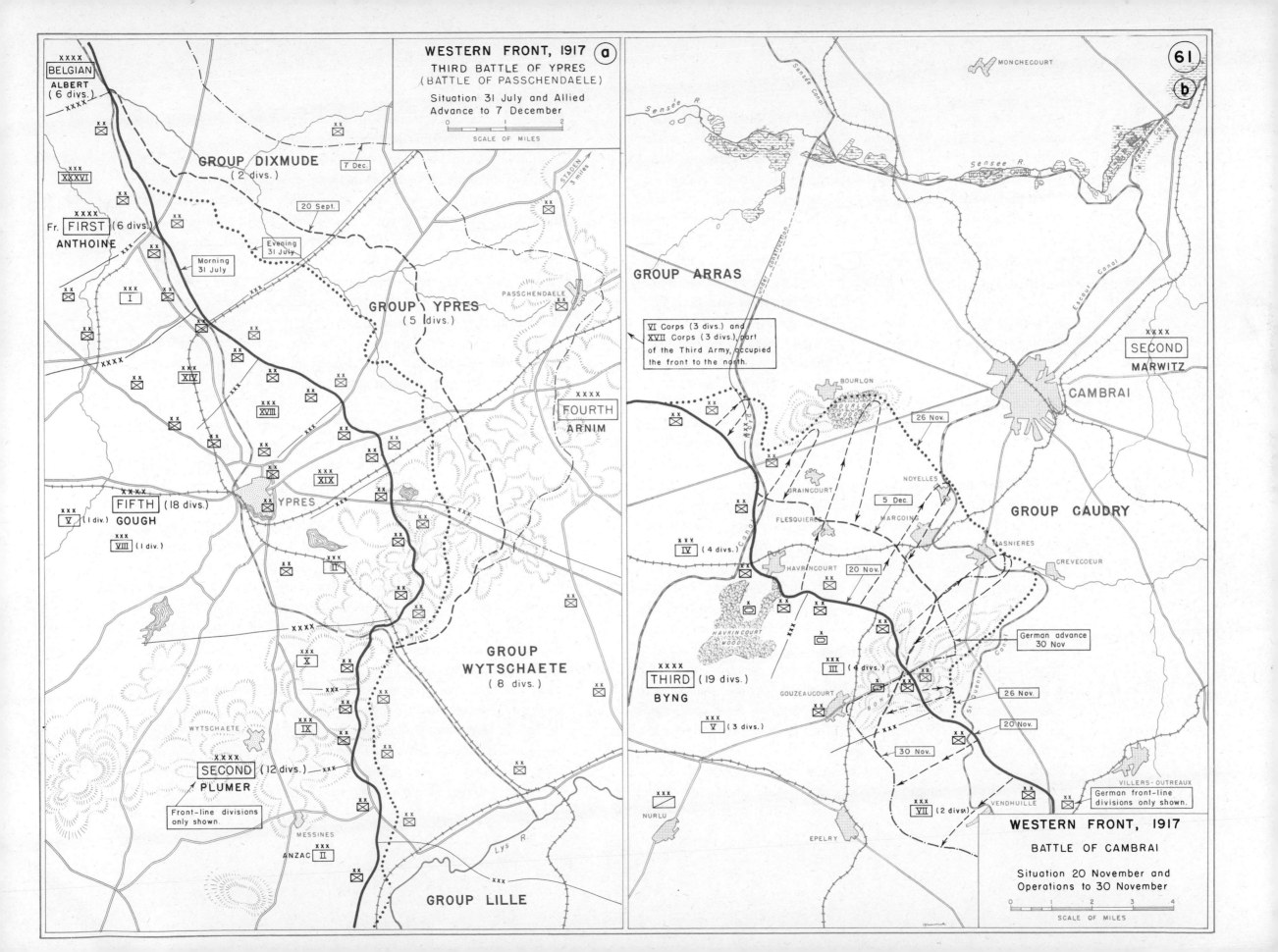

61

WESTERN FRONT, 1917 (a)

THIRD BATTLE OF YPRES
(BATTLE OF PASSCHENDAELE)

Situation 31 July and Allied
Advance to 7 December

0   1   2
SCALE OF MILES

XXXX
BELGIAN
ALBERT
(6 divs.)
XXXX

XX

GROUP DIXMUDE
(2 divs.)

XXX
XXXVI

7 Dec.

XX

20 Sept.

XXXX
Fr. FIRST (6 divs.)
ANTHOINE

XX

Evening
31 July

STADEN
3 miles

Morning
31 July

XXX
I

GROUP YPRES
(5 divs.)

PASSCHENDAELE

XX

XXX
XIV

XXXX
FOURTH
ARNIM

XXX
XVIII

XXX
XIX

XXXX
FIFTH (18 divs.) GOUGH

XXX
V (1 div.)

XXX
VIII (1 div.)

XXX
II

XXX
X

GROUP
WYTSCHAETE
(8 divs.)

XXX
IX

WYTSCHAETE

XXXX
SECOND (12 divs.)
PLUMER

Front-line divisions
only shown.

MESSINES

ANZAC
II

Lys R.

GROUP LILLE

MONCHECOURT

Sensée R.

Sensée Canal

Sensée R.

GROUP ARRAS

VI Corps (3 divs.) and
XVII Corps (3 divs.), part
of the Third Army, occupied
the front to the north.

BOURLON

26 Nov.

XXXX
SECOND
MARWITZ

CAMBRAI

BOURLON
WOOD

NOYELLES

GRAINCOURT

5 Dec.

GROUP CAUDRY

FLESQUIERES

MARCOING

MASNIERES

CREVECOEUR

XXX
IV (4 divs.)

HAVRINCOURT

20 Nov.

HAVRINCOURT
WOOD

German advance
30 Nov

XXXX
THIRD (19 divs.)
BYNG

GOUZEAUCOURT

XXX
III (4 divs.)

BON

26 Nov.

XXX
V (3 divs.)

30 Nov.

20 Nov.

VILLERS-
OUTREAUX

German front-line
divisions only shown.

NURLU

XXX
VII (2 divs.)

VENDHUILLE

EPELRY

WESTERN FRONT, 1917 (b)

BATTLE OF CAMBRAI

Situation 20 November and
Operations to 30 November

0   1   2   3   4
SCALE OF MILES

Early 1918 was a time of crisis for the Allies. The French Army's morale had been badly shaken. The Italians were still recovering from Caporetto. Russia had quit the war, leaving Germany free to mass in the West. By 1 March, the United States, though it had been a belligerent for almost a year, had only six divisions in France. The British Army had been weakened by its 1917 battles, and Lloyd George refused it further replacements, claiming that Haig would merely expend them in another offensive. Under these circumstances, Haig and Pétain planned to stand on the defensive, coming to each other's assistance promptly if attacked. They attempted to organize deep defensive systems on the German model, but these were never completed because of manpower shortages and the negligence of some subordinates.

Germany also felt the pressures of war. Her allies were faltering; the Allied blockade, plus internal transportation problems, caused hunger and discontent. Submarine warfare had failed either to starve England or to halt the arrival of American troops. Therefore, Ludendorff planned to conquer a peace. He had men and heavy guns enough to mount one major offensive, but not enough to launch a simultaneous, large-scale diversionary operation. This offensive must begin as early as possible, before American strength in France increased. It would strike against the British Army, the only strong Allied force still in the field.

Ludendorff envisaged a breakthrough in the Somme area on both sides of Péronne (*center, left*). This accomplished, the attack would wheel to the right, advancing northwest to separate the British and French and roll up the British line. He also began preparations for two attacks near Ypres (*top center*)—partly for deception, partly in case operations there became necessary to support the main attack. The British gradually developed a fair estimate of Ludendorff's intentions, but German deceptive measures along the French front convinced Pétain that any offensive would strike the Reims–Mont Blanc sector (*center*).

Ludendorff's planning included large-scale utilization of the Hutier tactics, which had been so successful in Russia and at Caporetto. Special, picked "shock" divisions were organized and given intensive training in them. The offensive would open with a relatively short bombardment, including much smoke and gas, designed to neutralize the enemy's defenses. Then the infantry would advance, keeping close behind the rolling barrage, and infiltrating between known enemy strong points. Initially, this action would be tightly controlled by higher headquarters, but once the infantry advanced beyond the range of its barrage, regimental and battalion commanders would take over, pushing as far and as rapidly as possible in a predesignated general direction. Centers of resistance were to be reported, bypassed, and later mopped up by supporting units. Fire support for the assault battalions would come from their trench mortars, attached accompanying guns, and ground-attack aircraft.

Ludendorff's preparations were impressive; German morale grew high. But his plans embodied several serious errors. He left an unnecessarily large force in the East—troops who could have at least garrisoned quiet sectors on the Western Front, thus releasing more good divisions for offensive missions. He made only feeble efforts to build up a tank force. Most serious of all, he did not adjust to the fact that he was no longer fighting Russians. In Russia, battles had ebbed and flowed over miles of open country; the Germans had always been superior in everything but numbers. France was a more difficult country, full of natural obstacles and stone villages; Allied weapons and equipment were excellent; the British, at least, had an innate toughness which the ill-led Russians had never displayed. Knowing this, Ludendorff's staff urged him to employ two or more limited offensives in rapid succession against different points on the British front, in order to throw the British off balance, before delivering his final blow in the Flanders area. Ludendorff, however, insisted on attempting an immediate breakthrough. The map shows (*shaded red areas*) the gains made in Ludendorff's initial offensive and in the two subsequent drives (*see text, maps 63 and 64*).

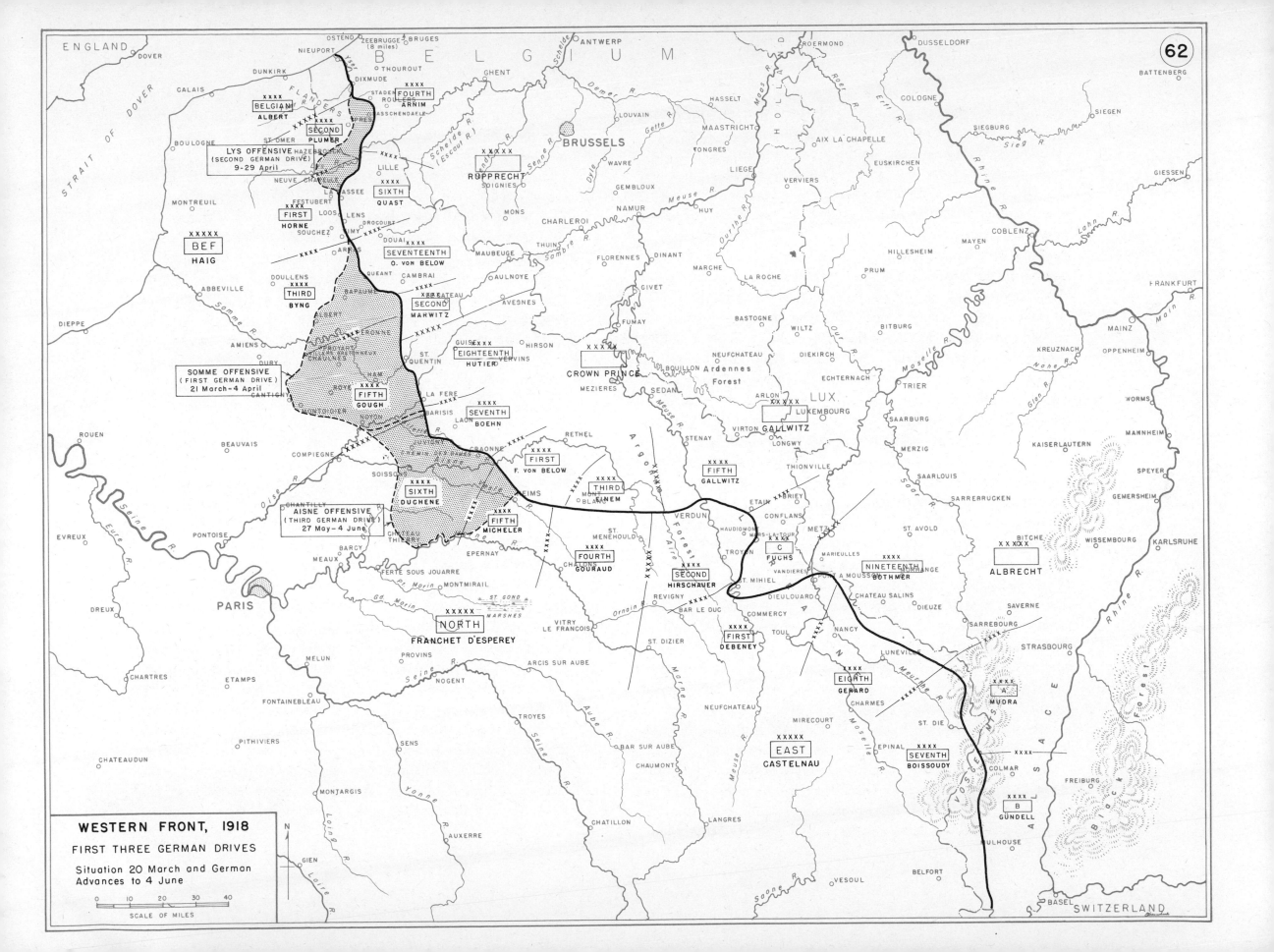

ENGLAND

BELGIUM

BRUSSELS

HOLLAND

DÜSSELDORF

62

STRAIT OF DOVER

DOVER

CALAIS

BOULOGNE

MONTREUIL

ABBEVILLE

DIEPPE

ROUEN

EVREUX

DREUX

CHARTRES

CHATEAUDUN

ETAMPS

FONTAINEBLEAU

PITHIVIERS

OSTEND ZEEBRUGGE BRUGES
(8 miles)

NIEUPORT

DUNKIRK

ST. OMER

HAZEBROUCK

NEUVE CHAPELLE

FESTUBERT

LOOS

SOUCHEZ

DOULLENS

ALBERT

AMIENS

DURY

BEAUVAIS

COMPIEGNE

PONTOISE

PARIS

MEAUX

MELUN

MONTARGIS

THOUROUT

DIXMUDE
STADEN
ROULERS
ASSCHENDAELE
YPRES

LILLE

LA BASSEE

LENS

VIMY

DOUAI

ARRAS

BAPAUME

PERONNE

HAM

ROYE

CANTIGNY

MONTDIDIER

NOYON

BARISIS

SOISSONS

CHATEAU THIERRY

FERTE SOUS JOUARRE

MONTMIRAIL

GHENT

ANTWERP

GEMBLOUX

MONS

CHARLEROI

MAUBEUGE

CAMBRAI

QUEANT

ST. QUENTIN

GUISE

VERVINS

LA FERE

LAON

CRAONNE

REIMS

EPERNAY

CHATEAU SALINS

□ **FOURTH**
ARNIM

□ **BELGIAN**
ALBERT

□ **SECOND**
PLUMER

LYS OFFENSIVE
(SECOND GERMAN DRIVE)
9-29 April

□ **FIRST**
HORNE

XXXXX **BEF**
HAIG

□ **THIRD**
BYNG

SOMME OFFENSIVE
(FIRST GERMAN DRIVE)
21 March-4 April

□ **FIFTH**
GOUGH

□ **SIXTH**
QUAST

RUPPRECHT

□ **SEVENTEENTH**
O. VON BELOW

□ **SECOND**
MARWITZ

□ **EIGHTEENTH**
HUTIER

□ **SEVENTH**
BOEHN

□ **FIRST**
F. VON BELOW

□ **SIXTH**
DUCHENE

AISNE OFFENSIVE
(THIRD GERMAN DRIVE)
27 May-4 June

□ **FIFTH**
MICHELER

□ **FOURTH**
GOURAUD

□ **SECOND**
HIRSCHAUER

□ **NORTH**
FRANCHET D'ESPEREY

□ **THIRD**
EINEM

□ **FIFTH**
GALLWITZ

CROWN PRINCE

Ardennes
Forest

BOUILLON

MEZIERES

SEDAN

RETHEL

STENAY

ARGONNE

VERDUN

□ **C**
FUCHS

□ **FIRST**
DEBENEY

□ **EIGHTH**
GERARD

□ **EAST**
CASTELNAU

□ **SEVENTH**
BOISSOUDY

NAMUR

LIEGE

LUXEMBOURG

LUX.

GALLWITZ

METZ

□ **NINETEENTH**
BOTHMER

NANCY

LUNEVILLE

ST. DIE

COLMAR

MULHOUSE

BELFORT

□ **A**
MUDRA

□ **B**
GÜNDELL

ALBRECHT

COLOGNE

COBLENZ

TRIER

FRANKFURT

MAINZ

WORMS

MANNHEIM

KARLSRUHE

STRASBOURG

FREIBURG

SWITZERLAND

BASEL

WESTERN FRONT, 1918

FIRST THREE GERMAN DRIVES

Situation 20 March and German
Advances to 4 June

0 10 20 30 40

SCALE OF MILES

During early March, tension steadily increased on the British front (*sketch* a). Gough's Fifth Army was spread thinly along a forty-two–mile front, the southern end of which had recently been taken over from the French as a result of political pressure. The British expected an attack here and had guessed the approximate date it would strike, but—lacking reserves—they could only brace themselves.

At 0440, 21 March, in a heavy fog, a five-hour German bombardment began. Then the highly trained battle groups of shock troops advanced. Three German armies struck the British Third and Fifth Armies. Once the British lines were broken, the Seventeenth Army was to advance to Bapaume (*center*) and then turn north toward Arras. The Second Army would capture Péronne (*center*), then push northwest through Doullens (*off map, upper left*). The Eighteenth Army would establish a defensive line at the Somme River, to guard the left flank of the offensive. (Note that the Eighteenth Army belonged to the Crown Prince's army group and the Second and Seventeenth to Rupprecht's—a peculiar version of the principle of unity of command, introduced by Ludendorff so that he might exercise greater personal control.)

From the start, Gough was in trouble. The trench system he had taken over from the French was unsuited to British tactics. (French defensive tactics emphasized massed artillery fire rather than infantry weapons.) By the end of 22 March, the skillful Hutier had broken through and was in open country. Farther north, the British Third Army, in its deeper defensive system, held the German Seventeenth and Second Armies to limited gains. Ludendorff now decided to exploit Hutier's success, and changed his plan: the Eighteenth Army would advance southwest across the Somme, the Second would attack toward Amiens (*off map, left center*), the Seventeenth would move northwest.

Hutier had followed Gough so closely that he captured some of the Somme River bridges. Gough's retreat uncovered the right flank of the British Third Army, forcing it to pull back. All available British reserves, including service troops, were committed, the cavalry (*not shown*) being put in to link the Fifth and Third Armies. Some French reserves began to arrive piecemeal (and short of artillery and ammunition), but Pétain's primary concern obviously was to form a new east-west defensive line south of the Somme to protect Paris. Haig immediately forced the convocation of a high-level Allied conference at Doullens on 26 March; this resulted in Foch's appointment as supreme commander.

On the 27th, Hutier took Montdidier (*bottom left*), actually opening a small gap between the French and British. But his troops were exhausted from the advance across the old Somme battlefield; their transport and artillery had not kept up with them. The gap was closed. A strong attack against Arras failed against stubborn British defense. Operations toward Amiens brought only slight gains, and by 4 April the line stabilized as shown (*dashed blue line*). Basically, logistical difficulties had thwarted the Germans.

Ludendorff now shifted his effort northward to Flanders (*sketch* b). Though his immediate objectives were none too clear, his basic purpose was to complete the destruction of the British Army. His own losses, however, forced him to restrict the scope of the new offensive. A Hutier-type assault on the morning of 9 April by the German Sixth Army struck the Portuguese 2d Division and gained over three miles, but was finally checked by the Lys River and stout British resistance on the flanks of the penetration. On 10 April, the German Fourth Army advanced; the attack the day before had pulled British reserves south, and another penetration was made. French units were sent up, though not immediately committed; Haig issued his famous "backs to the wall" order, demanding a fight to the last man. After 12 April, the force of the German attacks dwindled, 17 April being a day of bloody repulses for them. A surprise attack south of Ypres on 25 April took Mt. Kemmel (*upper center*). An Allied counterattack the next day failed. Plumer, his ranks badly thinned, withdrew the British line around Ypres behind the Yser Canal. On 30 April, Ludendorff halted his second offensive.

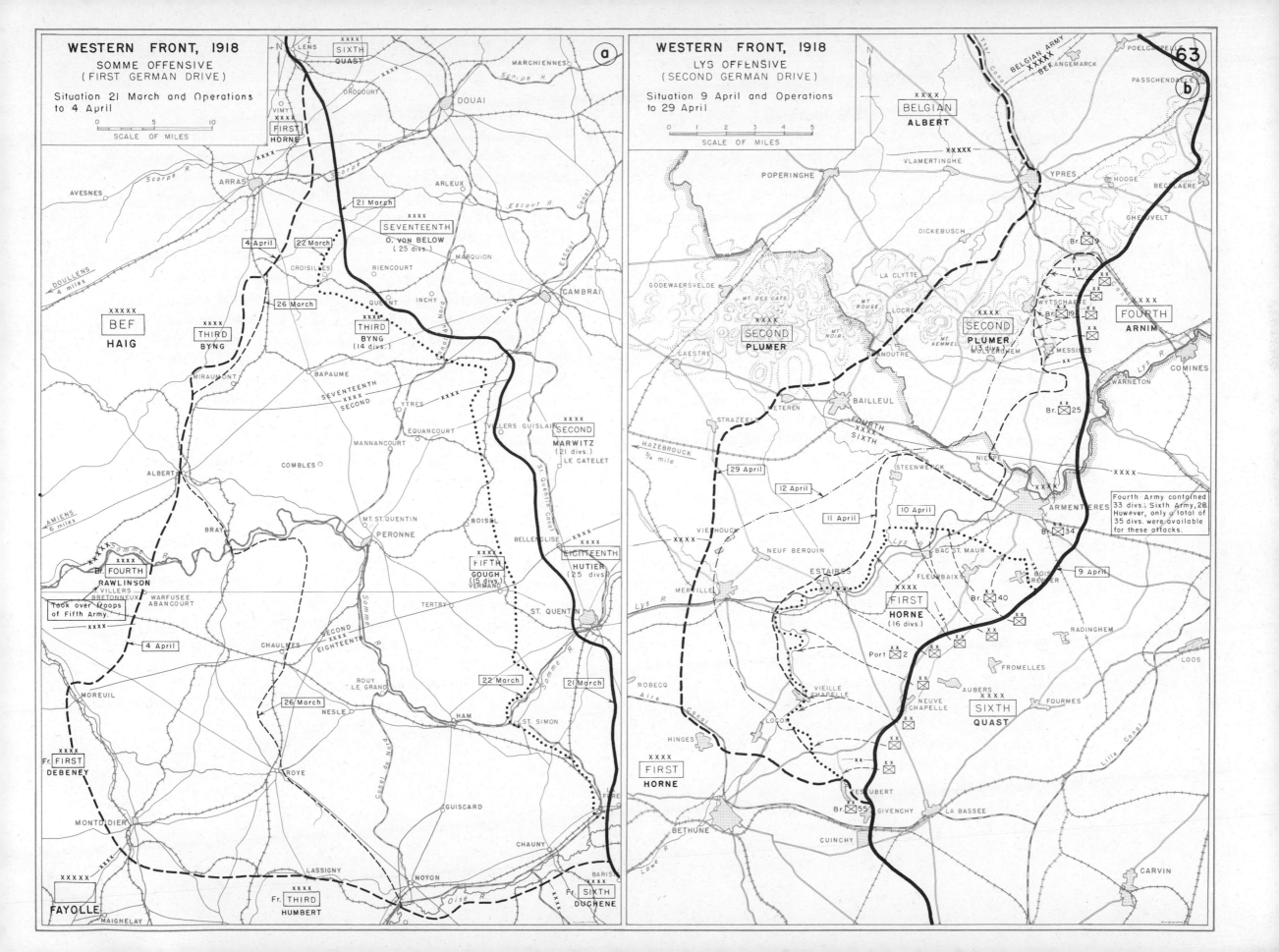

WESTERN FRONT, 1918
SOMME OFFENSIVE
(FIRST GERMAN DRIVE)

Situation 21 March and Operations
to 4 April

SCALE OF MILES
0   5   10

WESTERN FRONT, 1918
LYS OFFENSIVE
(SECOND GERMAN DRIVE)

Situation 9 April and Operations
to 29 April

SCALE OF MILES
0   1   2   3   4   5

63

Fourth Army contained
33 divs.; Sixth Army, 28.
However, only a total of
35 divs. were available
for these attacks.

Ludendorff had now twice attacked the British. Both offensives—especially the first one—had been brilliant tactical successes, but neither had produced the necessary general breakthrough. Still, he had reason to believe that one more such major attack would wreck the British Army as an effective fighting force. Rupprecht began the necessary preparations; Ludendorff meanwhile organized a diversionary operation designed to draw all French (and, if possible, some British) reserves from Flanders.

Desiring a quick, cheap victory which would have maximum effect on the Allies, Ludendorff chose the Chemin des Dames sector (*top center*) of the Aisne front. The French position here lay along a steep ridge, behind the swampy Ailette River. It was heavily fortified and naturally strong, though the presence of the Aisne and Vesle Rivers immediately behind it caused some Frenchmen to consider it a trap. Because of the formidable nature of its defenses, it was lightly held, part of its garrison consisting of English divisions which had lost two-thirds of their personnel during March and April and had therefore been temporarily exchanged for stronger French divisions. Ludendorff reasoned that, because of its strength, the French would not expect any large-scale activity in this area, and so would be vulnerable to a surprise attack. He also considered another factor: any advance here would directly threaten Paris (*off map, west*), a matter of the utmost sensitivity with the French.

The Germans had eleven divisions in line in this area; thirty more were quietly brought in under cover of darkness and hidden in the woods behind the German lines; 1,036 heavy guns were placed in concealed positions. At the same time, a variety of deceptive measures were carried out on the Flanders and Somme fronts. Foch, expecting another attack in the north, was readily convinced and concentrated most of his reserves around Amiens (*see map 62*), where they could counter any German attempt to split the British and French or to drive to the Channel ports.

So stringent were the German security measures that the first firm indication the Allies had of the imminent German attack came at about 1200 on 26 May, when two prisoners broke down under interrogation and stated that a heavy attack would be launched on either the 27th or 28th. Hasty preparations were begun, but the commander of the French Sixth Army (*this map*) insisted on holding his front lines in strength instead of waging an elastic defense.

At 0100, 27 May, the German bombardment began, smothering the Allied artillery. It was one of the heaviest yet employed, reaching back twelve miles to the Vesle River and extending on each flank well beyond the point selected for the attack. At 0340, still in darkness, seventeen German divisions poured across the Ailette. It was a small-scale Caporetto; the French lines dissolved. The Aisne bridges were captured intact, and by evening the Germans were up to or across the Vesle on a nine-mile front—a thirteen-mile advance, the longest day's drive in the West since the front had stabilized. Here, the attack should have stopped, but the momentum of victory swung it forward. By the next evening, Soissons (*upper center*), with large quantities of French supplies, had been captured, though an important railroad tunnel north of that town had been destroyed in time. Allied reserves arrived in dribbles, but could do little at first. Eventually, the Germans—who had never expected such a success—completely outran their supplies. Counterattacks by the American 2d Division against the nose of the salient stopped the German advance down the Château Thierry road (*center*) and eventually recaptured Belleau Wood; meanwhile, the American 3d Division repelled all enemy attempts to establish a bridgehead over the Marne near Château Thierry. (The first division-size American action had been the capture of Cantigny, near Montdidier [*see map 65*], on 28 May by the American 1st Division.)

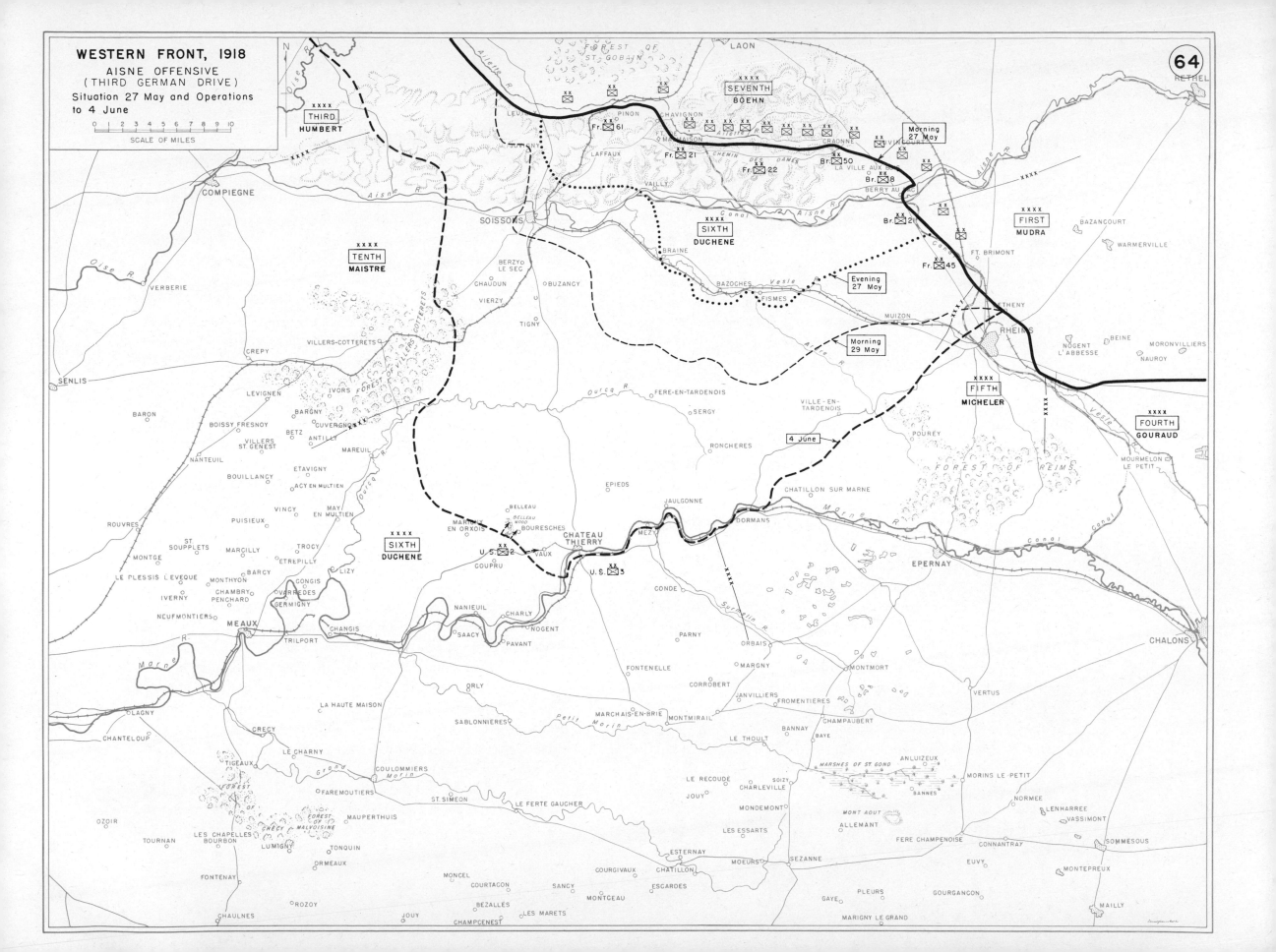

WESTERN FRONT, 1918

AISNE OFFENSIVE
(THIRD GERMAN DRIVE)
Situation 27 May and Operations
to 4 June

0 1 2 3 4 5 6 7 8 9 10
SCALE OF MILES

64

THIRD HUMBERT

SEVENTH BÖEHN

Fr. 61

Morning 27 May

Fr. 21

Fr. 22

Br. 50

Br. 8

BERRY AU BAC

Br. 21

FIRST MUDRA

TENTH MAISTRE

SIXTH DUCHENE

Fr. 45

FT. BRIMONT

Evening 27 May

Morning 29 May

FIFTH MICHELER

4 June

FOURTH GOURAUD

SIXTH DUCHENE

U.S. 2

U.S. 3

CHATEAU THIERRY

BELLEAU WOOD

BOURESCHES

VAUX

COMPIEGNE

SOISSONS

RHEIMS

EPERNAY

MEAUX

CHALONS

Lundendorff was now the worried possessor of three salients, which greatly increased the length of his front. His last drive, however—with its apparent threat to Paris—had considerably unsettled French opinion. Signs of defeatism appeared in French governmental circles (to be squelched by the ferociously patriotic Premier Georges E. B. Clemenceau). Foch and Pétain, the latter especially, urged that large numbers of British troops be transferred southward to aid in the defense of the French capital. Haig refused. He appears to have sensed the fact that the Aisne offensive had been a diversionary operation, designed to draw Allied forces from Flanders. Eventually, Foch agreed with him. The need for strong American reinforcements now being painfully obvious, the Allies took all possible measures to speed their arrival.

Ludendorff had planned his diversionary operation in two stages. The first—the Aisne offensive—had been only too successful. The second—an advance in the general area Soissons-Montdidier (*left center*)—now became increasingly important, since the only railroad into the new Aisne-Marne salient ran through Soissons and along that salient's western edge. Ludendorff hoped to eventually reach the line Montdidier-Compiègne. Preparations for this attack were rushed and open; in fact, the French at first suspected that they might be purely for the purpose of distracting Allied attention from Rupprecht's activities in Flanders. German deserters (their number had increased with declining German morale) furnished the date and the hour of the attack.

Forewarned, the French laid down an artillery counterpreparation at 2350 on 8 June, ten minutes before the German preparatory bombardment was scheduled to begin. Though both its artillery bombardment and infantry assault were consequently confused, the German Eighteenth Army still broke through the French first and second positions. On the 10th, the Germans made further advances. On the 11th, they did not attack; a French-American counterattack threw them on the defensive, though it made only slight gains. On the 12th, the German Seventh Army attacked from the Aisne-Marne salient, but made little progress.

During the subsequent month of relative inaction, a worldwide influenza epidemic struck both opponents, bearing harder on the poorly fed Germans. German morale began to crack noticeably, while American forces in France rapidly increased.

Ludendorff still clung to his plan for a decisive blow against the British in Flanders, but he felt that one final diversionary operation would be necessary to draw Allied reserves from that front. Consequently, he planned an attack on both sides of Reims (*center, left*) for 15 July. The German Seventh Army would take Epernay and advance up the Marne until it established contact with the German First Army, which was to take Châlons. This would pinch out the strongly fortified Reims area. The German Third Army was to cover the flank of the First. Once the preparatory bombardment was completed, the heavy artillery would proceed northward to get into position for Rupprecht's grand attack in early August.

Deserters, prisoners, and Allied aerial reconnaissance gradually disclosed Ludendorff's entire plan. Reinforcements were brought in, and Foch prepared a major counteroffensive for 18 July against the western face of the Aisne-Marne salient. Having learned the hour of the German attack, the French again employed an artillery counterpreparation, catching the German shock troops as they formed. East of Reims, the German attack collapsed against well-established defenses by 1100, 15 July. North of Epernay the defenses were weaker, and the German assault, pushed home with skill and daring, forced the Marne and established a sizable bridgehead. Only the American 3d Division held firm, fighting in three directions. Also, just southwest of Reims, the two Italian divisions which held the line there were driven back; British divisions were rushed to relieve them on the 19th. During the 16th and 17th, French resistance around the new Marne bridgehead stiffened. It became increasingly difficult for the Germans to push reinforcements and supplies across the Marne under Allied air and artillery bombardment.

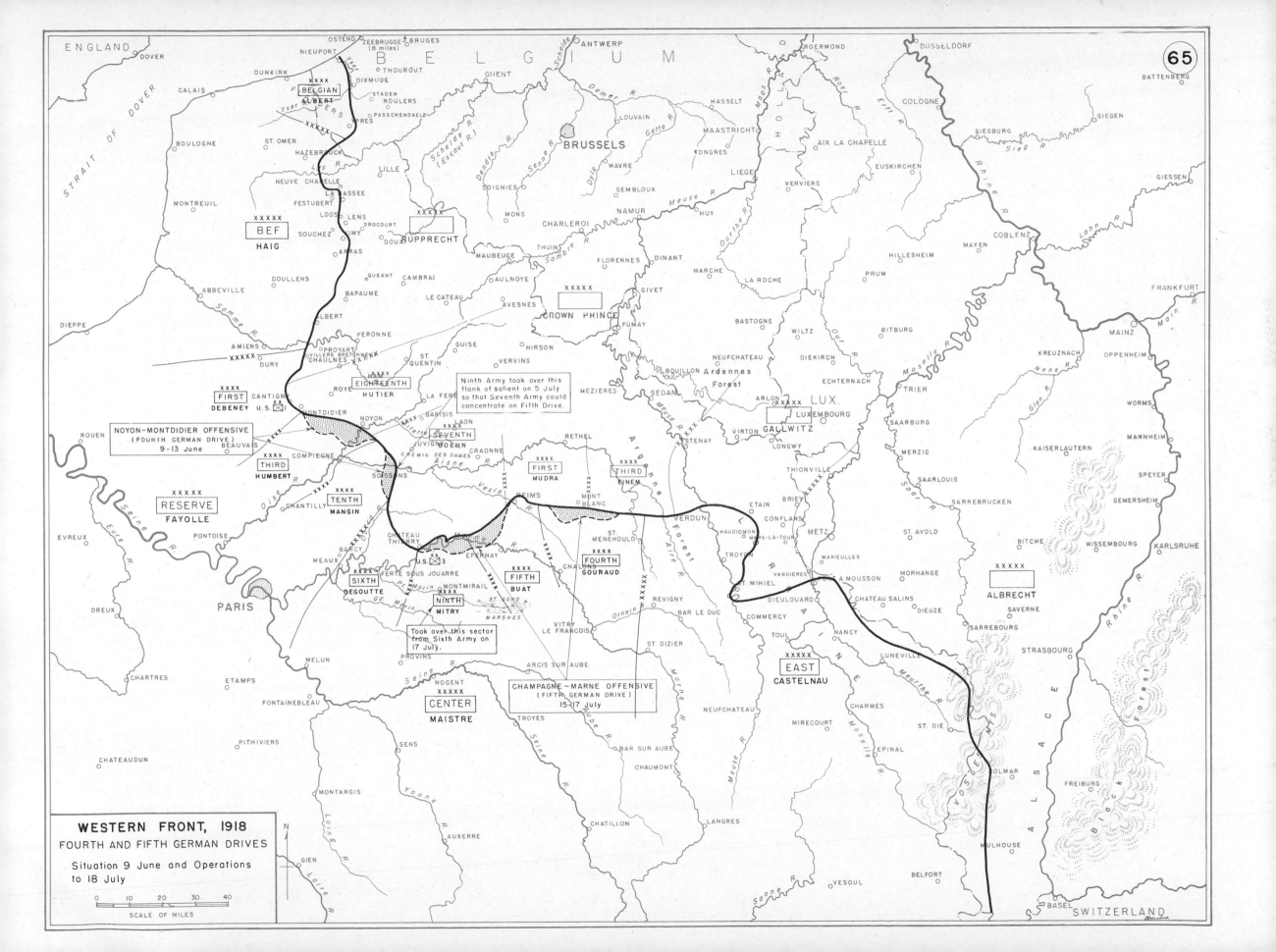

ENGLAND

BELGIUM

65

STRAIT OF DOVER

BRUSSELS

XXXX BELGIAN ALBERT

XXXXX

XXXXX BEF HAIG

XXXXX RUPPRECHT

XXXXX CROWN PRINCE

XXXXX

XXXXX LUXEMBOURG GALLWITZ

XXXX EIGHTEENTH HUTIER

XXXX FIRST DEBENEY U.S.

Ninth Army took over this flank of salient on 5 July so that Seventh Army could concentrate on Fifth Drive.

NOYON–MONTDIDIER OFFENSIVE (FOURTH GERMAN DRIVE) 9–13 June

XXXX SEVENTH BOEHN

XXXX FIRST MUDRA

XXXX THIRD EINEM

XXXX THIRD HUMBERT

XXXX TENTH MANGIN

XXXXX RESERVE FAYOLLE

XXXX FOURTH GOURAUD

U.S. 3

XXXXX ALBRECHT

XXXX SIXTH DEGOUTTE

XXXX FIFTH BUAT

XXXX NINTH MITRY

Took over this sector from Sixth Army on 17 July.

XXXXX EAST CASTELNAU

CHAMPAGNE–MARNE OFFENSIVE (FIFTH GERMAN DRIVE) 15–17 July

XXXXX CENTER MAISTRE

PARIS

SWITZERLAND

WESTERN FRONT, 1918
FOURTH AND FIFTH GERMAN DRIVES

Situation 9 June and Operations to 18 July

0 10 20 30 40
SCALE OF MILES

As early as 20 May, 1918, Foch had begun plans for a series of massive Allied counteroffensives, only to have them upset by the German third and fourth 1918 drives. In the lull that followed the fourth (Noyon-Montdidier) drive, he kept the French forces active in minor operations to rebuild their fighting spirit. One of these attacks (*not shown*), made by General Mangin's Tenth Army, scored a creditable local success west of Soissons. Mangin suggested enlarging this operation; Foch agreed and set up a large-scale counteroffensive for 18 July. Mangin was to make the main effort, while the other armies around the Aisne-Marne salient attacked on their fronts. A minor crisis occurred when Pétain, concerned over the fifth German drive (15 July), ordered all preparations suspended, but Foch promptly countermanded that order.

As noted (*see text, map 65*), the fifth German drive (on both sides of Reims) was obviously a failure by the evening of the 17th, and the position of the German divisions holding the bridgehead south of the Marne was becoming increasingly critical.

Mangin secretly concentrated his troops at the last moment under cover of the Forest of Villers-Cotterêts. (Some American units had to move up on the run to reach the jump-off line at the zero hour.) The attack (beginning at 0435 in the west, at 0500 in the east) was a complete surprise. German troops holding the western sector were second-line "trench" units of limited combat value. Pounded by a sudden, heavy artillery bombardment, and rushed by fresh American divisions and picked French colonial units supported by masses of tanks, they gave ground rapidly or surrendered in large numbers.

Ludendorff, meanwhile, had gone to Flanders to make final arrangements for Rupprecht's great offensive. He had drawn heavily upon Rupprecht's reserves for his fifth drive, but he felt that by using some "trench" divisions in place of shock troops, he would be able to proceed as originally planned. During a staff conference on 18 July, he learned of the Allied Aisne-Marne offensive. He at once sent reserves into the Soissons area and ordered the attack on Reims stopped.

On the 19th, German resistance stiffened. The French Tenth and Sixth Armies gained some ground, but the Ninth and Fifth made little progress. That night, the Germans evacuated their Marne River bridgehead. Thereafter, they began a deliberate, skillful withdrawal to the line of the Aisne and Vesle Rivers, covering their retreat with machine-gun and artillery rear guards, while the German Air Force swept the skies over the shrinking salient. (During this period, on 20 July, Rupprecht's Flanders offensive was canceled.)

On 24 July, Foch met with Haig and General John J. Pershing and developed his future plans. The Allies now had the initiative and must keep it, through a series of strong, closely spaced offensives that would give the enemy no chance to reorganize. The first objectives would be to free three strategic rail lines which would facilitate future operations: the Marne section of the Paris-Verdun line (to be accomplished by the current Aisne-Marne offensive); the Paris-Amiens line (to be freed by a British offensive in the Amiens sector [*see text, map 67*]); and the section of the Paris-Nancy line south of Verdun (to be carried out by an American attack on the St. Mihiel salient [*see map 68*]). These operations would be followed by others to free the coal-mining areas in northern France and force the German extreme right flank back along the Channel.

All unaware of this, Ludendorff released his own estimate of the situation on 2 August: no other Allied attacks were likely in the immediate future, though they might be expected thereafter south of Ypres, east of Reims, against the St. Mihiel salient, or in Lorraine; the Germans must pass temporarily to the defensive, while gathering forces for limited surprise offensives, designed to inflict casualties rather than to gain ground.

As indicated (*shaded blue areas*), eight American divisions took part in the Aisne-Marne offensive. It should be kept in mind that the United States infantry division of World War I had about twice the strength of contemporary French, English, and German divisions.

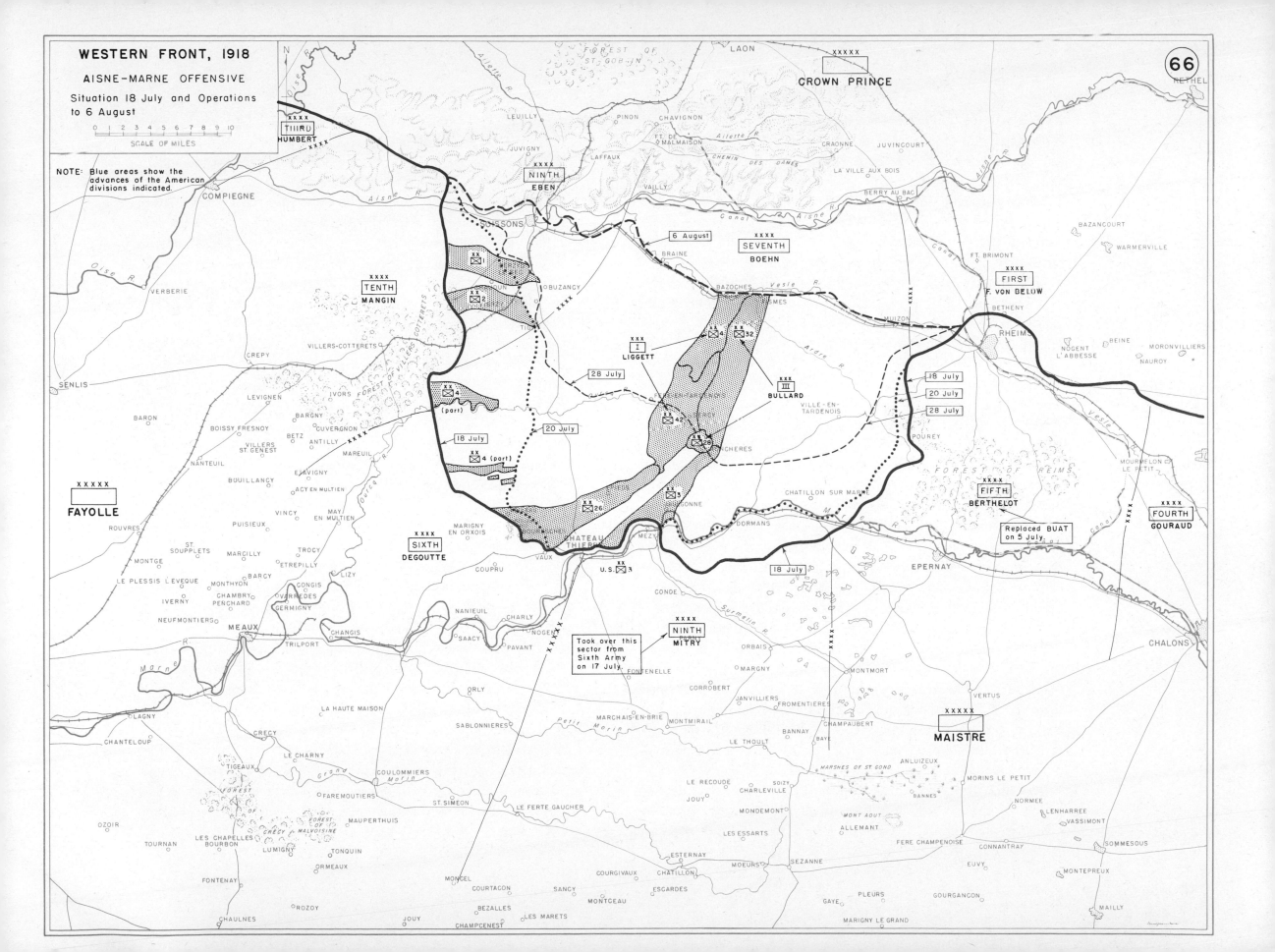

WESTERN FRONT, 1918

AISNE—MARNE OFFENSIVE

Situation 18 July and Operations
to 6 August

0 1 2 3 4 5 6 7 8 9 10
SCALE OF MILES

NOTE: Blue areas show the
advances of the American
divisions indicated.

Ludendorff did not expect an Allied attack in the immediate future; nor did he anticipate that, when it did come, it would be in the Amiens area. Consequently, the British offensive there was a total surprise.

Foch wanted a British offensive in Flanders from La Bassée north (*sketch* b, *bottom center*; this sketch is an extension northward of *sketch* a) in order to liberate important French coal-mining areas; but Haig, undoubtedly remembering his 1917 experiences in Flanders, objected on the grounds that the terrain was unsuitable and the general area of less strategic importance than that east of Amiens (*sketch* a). Foch not only accepted Haig's preference, but also placed the French First Army under his command for this operation.

General Sir Henry Rawlinson carried out his preparations with the greatest secrecy. His main effort was to be made by the Australian and Canadian Corps and the left-flank corps of the French First Army. Since the Canadian Corps and one Australian division had to be moved south from Flanders, elaborate deceptive measures were necessary. A skeleton of the Canadian Corps, including its headquarters radio, was left in its original position, and the Canadian troops took over their attack positions on the Amiens front only two hours before the attack began. These measures were entirely successful. Rupprecht's attention was concentrated on the Ypres area (Ludendorff had predicted an attack there); the Germans facing Rawlinson were lax and careless.

The British offensive, launched at 0420, 8 August, repeated the tactics that had been so successful at Cambrai. There was no preliminary bombardment. Just before zero hour, approximately 400 tanks (some of them speedy new Whippets) emerged from their assembly areas, reaching the front line as the rolling barrage came down, and the infantry rose and followed. On the right, the French—who had only a few tanks—opened a forty-five–minute bombardment, and then advanced.

At first, the assault was hampered by a dense ground fog, which also blinded the approximately 1,700 Allied aircraft concentrated to support it. Nevertheless, during the first day, the offensive gained up to nine miles (*lower shaded blue area*), being held up only on the flanks. Whippets, armored cars, and cavalry got among the fleeing Germans; approximately 15,000 prisoners and 400 guns were captured. Even more shocking to German commanders was the low morale, bordering on mutiny, shown by many retreating units. Still, between rallying stragglers and calling up reinforcements, they reestablished a line. On 9-10 August, the Allied attack and German defense were both disjointed and confused. Communications were fragmentary; almost two-thirds of the British tanks were out of action because of mechanical troubles, ditching, or enemy artillery fire; and the German Air Force was concentrating on the battlefield. However, also on the 10th, the French Third Army came into action on the south, and the Germans evacuated Montdidier (*bottom left*). By the 11th, the Germans were even beginning to counterattack. Haig decided that a pause was necessary on the Amiens front. This decision produced a clash with Foch, who was in favor of pushing ahead regardless of casualties. On the 11th, Haig had ordered his Third Army to begin probing the German lines below Arras.

The next phase of the offensive began on 21 August, when the French and the British Third Army attacked; on the 22d, the British Fourth Army advanced; on the 26th, the British First Army joined in. Advances over the battle-worn area were slow and methodical; tanks and low-flying aircraft were used against strong points.

Ludendorff now ordered a major withdrawal, and gave up the Lys salient (*see map 62*) in Flanders as well. However, on 30-31 August, the Australians crossed the Somme and took Péronne and Mt. St. Quentin (*this map, center*). On 2 September, the Canadians broke a strong position (*not shown*) between Quéant and Drocourt (*upper center*). Ludendorff thereupon ordered a second withdrawal (*heavy dashed red line*). His losses had been more than 100,000; morale had plummeted. However, for the time being, Haig had no fresh troops with which to exploit his success.

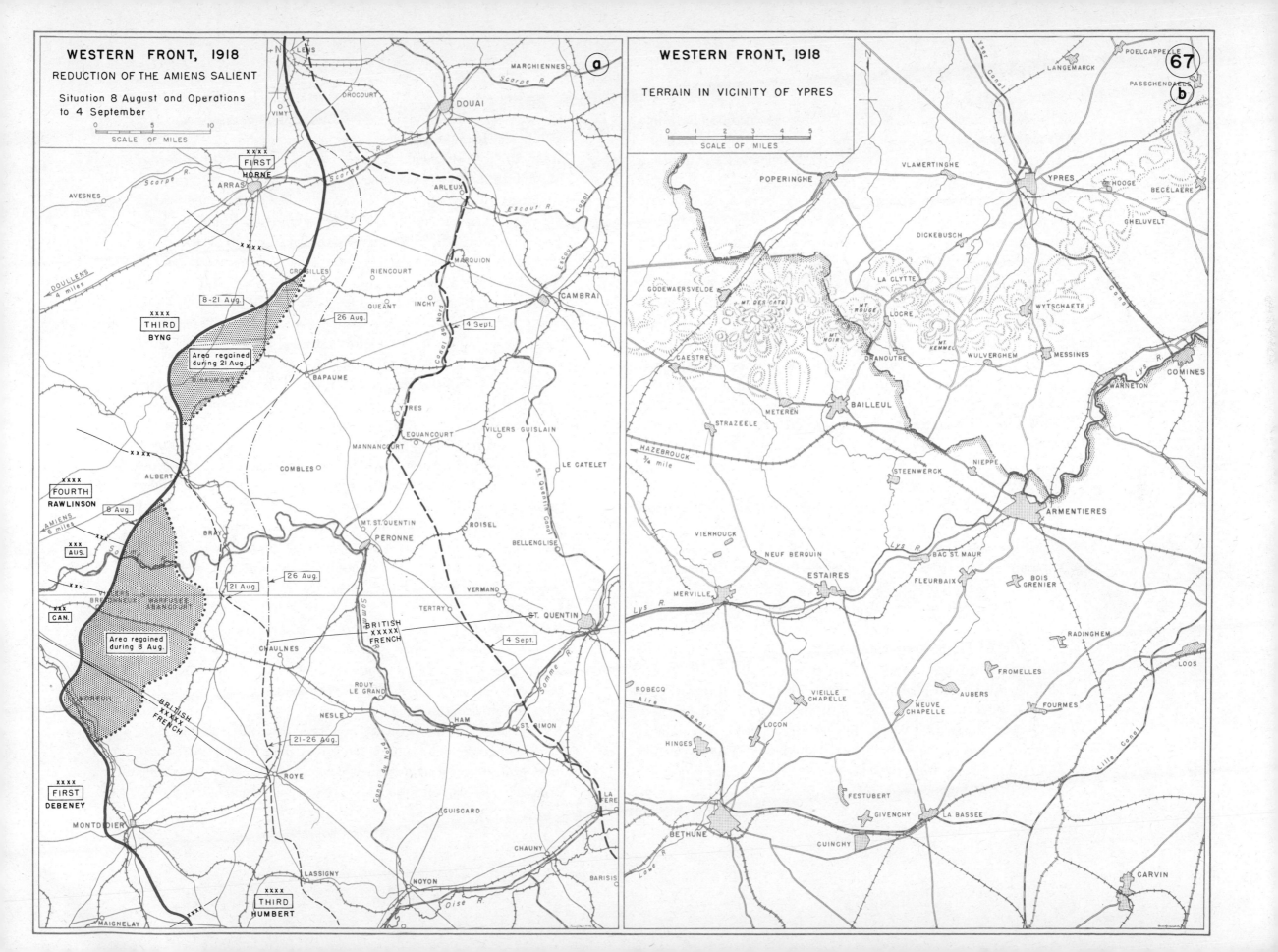

67

WESTERN FRONT, 1918

REDUCTION OF THE AMIENS SALIENT

Situation 8 August and Operations
to 4 September

SCALE OF MILES

WESTERN FRONT, 1918

TERRAIN IN VICINITY OF YPRES

SCALE OF MILES

The sector originally assigned the American Expeditionary Force was that between St. Mihiel and Pont-a-Mousson (*bottom right*). There were a number of reasons for its selection: first, it had long been a quiet sector, lightly held by both sides, hence suitable for advanced training; second, an offensive from this area would threaten the vital Metz-Longuyon-Sedan railroad, the Briey-Longwy iron-ore mining region, and the Saar's coal mines (*off map, right*)—also, an advance down the Moselle River would threaten the Rhine Valley; third, port congestion in northern France led to the basing of the American forces on western French seaports, such as Bordeaux and St. Nazaire, which had good, direct rail communications with the assigned area.

Pershing insisted upon a separate and distinct United States army, with its own assigned front. Its establishment was repeatedly delayed—partly because of British and French desire to keep American units under their command, partly by the crises created by the five German 1918 drives which made it necessary to put in available American units to halt the German advance. On 24 July, Foch finally accepted Pershing's plan for the reduction of the St. Mihiel salient; on 10 August, the United States First Army was activated, and on 30 August it formally took over the St. Mihiel sector. The French II Colonial Corps was assigned to it. Pershing's plans considered an advance to the general line Mari-eulles (*lower right*)–Mars-la-Tour–Etain. Success here would be followed by an offensive into Lorraine against Metz and the Briey mines.

But Haig persuaded Foch that the American effort should be directed at Mezieres (*top left*), so that it might converge with Haig's push toward Cambrai (*see map 69*). Foch therefore proposed (30 August) that the Americans make only a limited attack against the south face of the St. Mihiel salient; the remaining American forces would be divided between the French Second and Fourth Armies for an advance on Mezieres. This most peculiar proposition Pershing forcibly declined.

Finally, on 2 September, the two commanders compromised: the St. Mihiel operation would be carried out, but only to the line Vandières-Haudiomont (*this map, dashed red line*); the United States First Army would take over an enlarged sector from the Moselle to, and including, the Argonne Forest (*lower left*); the Americans would attack on the Argonne front immediately after the completion of the St. Mihiel operation; the French Fourth Army, reinforced by two American divisions, would attack to the west of the Argonne; these two offensives would converge on the Sedan-Mezieres area.

On 8 September, Ludendorff ordered the evacuation of the lightly garrisoned St. Mihiel position. On the 11th, the garrison began removing the heaviest guns and supplies. At 0100, 12 September, a heavy bombardment began. At 0500, in a heavy fog, American forces attacked the two faces of the salient, while the French II Colonial Corps made a holding attack against its nose. A mixed American, French, British, Italian, and Portuguese air force (some 600 planes) under Col. William Mitchell maintained air superiority and supported the attack. Some planes were attached directly to the ground forces; others acted as an independent group in tactical support against the enemy lines; and still other groups operated in the German rear, against logistical support installations and lines of communications. Their contribution to the success was substantial. The salient was cleared in thirty-six hours with a bag of some 15,000 prisoners and over 250 guns.

The roads to Longuyon (*upper center*) and to Lorraine (*lower right*) were open, and a drive against either probably would have shaken the Germans far worse than any threat to Mezieres. Sweating German reserves wondered why the Americans did not continue their advance.

The St. Mihiel operation had been excellent training for American commanders, staffs, and troops alike. It also deprived the Germans of an area from which they might have been able to attack the rear of American forces engaged in the Argonne.

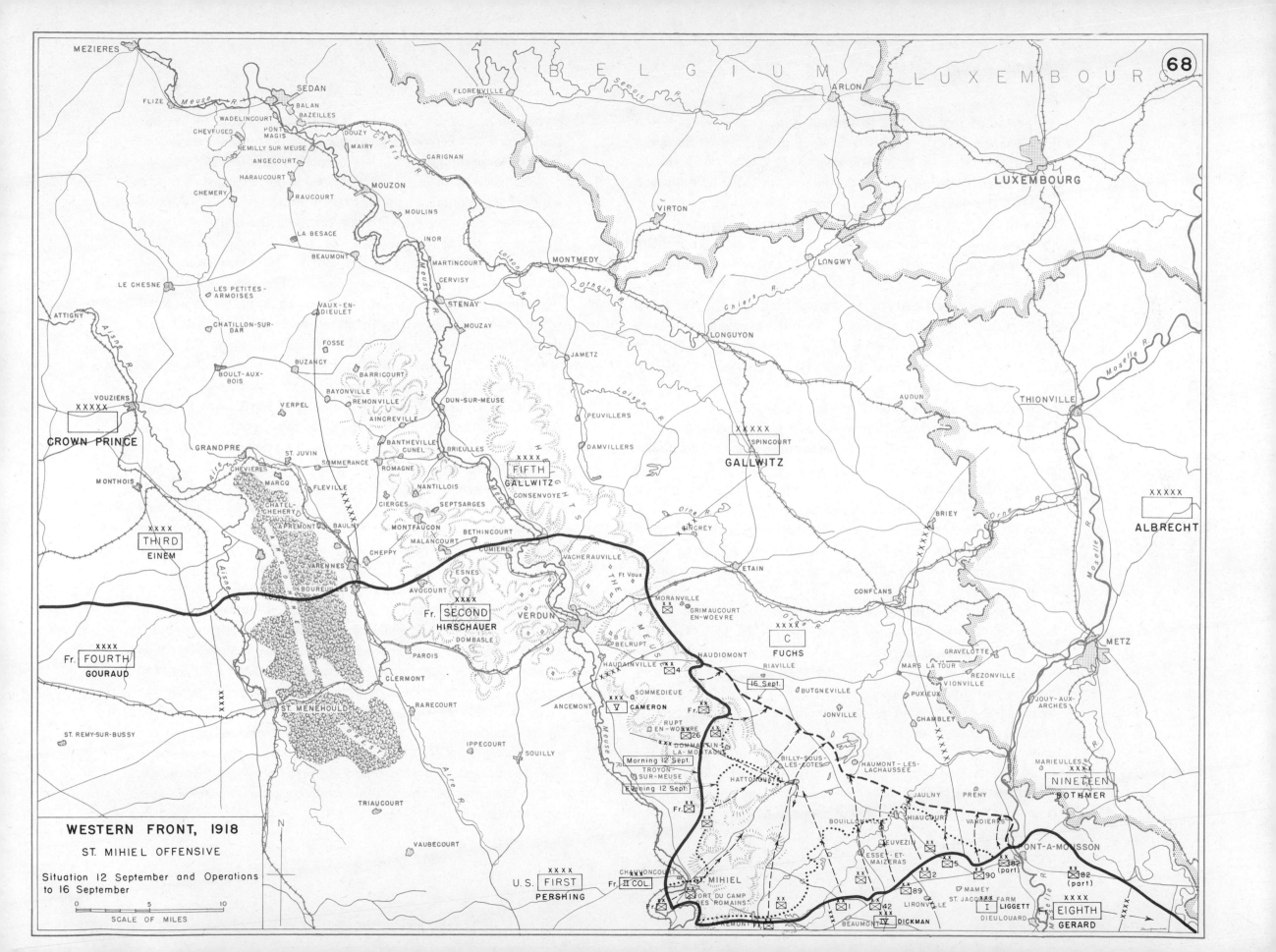

MEZIERES

SEDAN

BELGIUM LUXEMBOURG

68

FLIZE
WADELINCOURT
CHEVFUGED
PONT MAGIS
REMILLY SUR MEUSE
HARAUCOURT
CHEMERY
RAUCOURT

BALAN
BAZEILLES
DOUZY
MAIRY
MOUZON
MOULINS
INOR

FLORENVILLE

CARIGNAN

LUXEMBOURG

ARLON

LE CHESNE
LES PETITES-ARMOISES
ATTIGNY

BEAUMONT

MARTINCOURT
CERVISY

MONTMEDY

LONGWY

VAUX-EN-DIEULET

STENAY
MOUZAY

LONGUYON

THIONVILLE

VOUZIERS
XXXXX
CROWN PRINCE

CHATILLON-SUR-BAR
FOSSE
BUZANCY
BARRICOURT

JAMETZ

PEUVILLERS

AUDUN

GRANDPRE

BOULT-AUX-BOIS
VERPEL
BAYONVILLE
REMONVILLE
AINGREVILLE

DUN-SUR-MEUSE

DAMVILLERS

XXXXX
SPINCOURT
GALLWITZ

BRIEY

ST. JUVIN
SOMMERANCE
BANTHEVILLE
CUNEL
BRIEULLES

XXXX
FIFTH
GALLWITZ

XXXXX

MONTHOIS
CHEVIERES
MARCQ
FLEVILLE
CHATEL-CHEHERY
APREMONT
BAULNY

ROMAGNE
CIERGES
NANTILLOIS
SEPTSARGES

CONSENVOYE

LINCREY

BRIEY
ALBRECHT
XXXXX

THIRD
EINEM
XXXX

MONTFAUCON
BETHINCOURT
CHEPPY
MALANCOURT
CUMIERES

VACHERAUVILLE

ETAIN
CONFLANS

METZ

VARENNES
BOUREUILLES

ESNES
AVOCOURT

Ft VOUX

MORANVILLE
XX
4

GRIMAUCOURT EN-WOEVRE

GRAVELOTTE

Fr. SECOND
HIRSCHAUER
XXXX

VERDUN

DOMBASLE
BELRUPT

HAUDIOMONT

C
FUCHS
XXXXX

MARS LA TOUR
REZONVILLE
VIONVILLE

JOUY-AUX-ARCHES

Fr. FOURTH
GOURAUD
XXXX

PAROIS
CLERMONT

HAUDAINVILLE
XX 4

RIAVILLE

16 Sept.

BUTGNEVILLE

PUXIEU

CHAMBLEY

MARIEULLES
XXX

ST. MENEHOULD

RARECOURT

ANCEMONT
SOMMEDIEUE

V CAMERON
XXX
Fr. XX

JONVILLE

ST. REMY-SUR-BUSSY

IPPECOURT
SOUILLY

RUPT EN-WOEVRE
XX 26

DOMMARTIN LA-MONTAGNE

BILLY-SOUS-LES-COTES

HAUMONT-LES-LACHAUSSEE

PRENY

JAULNY

NINETEEN
BOTHMER
XXXX

Morning 12 Sept.

TRIAUCOURT

TROYON-SUR-MEUSE

Evening 12 Sept.
Fr. XX

HATTONVILLE

BOUILLONVILLE
THIAUCOURT
VANDIERES

PONT-A-MOUSSON

VAUBECOURT

WESTERN FRONT, 1918

ST. MIHIEL OFFENSIVE

Situation 12 September and Operations
to 16 September

U.S. FIRST
XXXX
PERSHING

CHAUVONCOURT
Fr. II COL.

ST. MIHIEL
FORT DU CAMP
DES ROMAINS

NEMONT FM.

KEUVEZIN

ESSE-ET-MAIZERAS

LIRONVILLE

BEAUMONT

89

42

1

IV
DICKMAN
XXX

2

15

90

182
(part)

MAMEY
ST. JACQUES FARM

I
LIGGETT

DIEULOUARD

182
(part)
XX

EIGHTH
GERARD
XXXX

N

0   5   10
SCALE OF MILES

By the end of September, with all the German salients recaptured or evacuated, Foch's armies had successfully accomplished the preliminary missions he had outlined on 24 July. Furthermore, at St. Mihiel, and especially at Amiens, the Allied troops had established a definite combat superiority. Their morale was high. With the arrival of more and more American divisions, they again had numerical superiority. In the tank, they had a weapon for which the Germans were unable to develop an effective countermeasure.

A great many Allied leaders were certain that the war could not be won before 1919, and Foch continued to plan for a massive final offensive through Lorraine. But he also planned to make the best possible use of the rest of 1918. His objectives were the rail lines (*shown in blue*), by means of which the Germans supplied their armies—or would evacuate them in case of defeat. Of these railroads, the northernmost—from Cologne to Aulnoye—was the best and therefore the most vital, since it carried the greatest share of supplies. The lateral line from Strasbourg north through Metz to Bruges (*top left*) was highly important for distribution and evacuation along the whole German front. It can readily be seen that if any important junction in this system—especially Aulnoye, Maubeuge, Longuyon, or Mezieres—were captured, the German situation would become exceedingly critical.

Ludendorff was fully aware of these facts. Personally, he was being rapidly worn down by his responsibilities. By 3 October, he and Hindenburg were insisting that negotiations for peace should be begun. (The Kaiser had come to the same conclusion in August.) Meanwhile, they proposed to retire as necessary, fighting delaying actions to inflict maximum delay and punishment. To accomplish this, the Germans would utilize the river and canal lines and a series of fortified positions. Their major problems would be to get their troops out of Flanders and the so-called "Laon bulge" (*center*) before the rail lines were cut. Some of Ludendorff's army group commanders had been in favor of a prompt withdrawal to the line Antwerp–Meuse River, but Ludendorff had vetoed that because it would force the abandonment of large quantities of irreplaceable supplies.

Foch now launched a series of major offensives: on 26 September, the Americans and French attacked in the Meuse-Argonne sector (*see map 70*); on the 27th, the British, between Péronne and Lens; on the 28th, the "Group of Armies of Flanders" (Belgian, British, French); on the 29th, the French and British, between La Fere and Péronne. The first two of these operations (*this map, shaded blue arrows*) should be considered main attacks; the over-all operation can best be described as a double penetration. Seven American divisions—the 2d, 27th, 30th, 36th, 37th, 91st, and 93d (Provisional)—served with the French and British in these offensives.

The remainder of the war consisted of hard, straight-ahead fighting, the Germans trading space for time in front of the English and holding doggedly in the rugged terrain of the Argonne against the Americans. The German retreat in most sectors was skillful, though the main British attack achieved considerable success west of Le Cateau. Up to mid-October, Ludendorff handled the situation well. Then, by 18 October, the Americans broke into the last German defensive position in the Meuse-Argonne. Between the 17th and the 23d, the British scored a breakthrough, advancing beyond Le Cateau. Nothing but further, immediate retreat was left for the Germans, but—aided by increasingly bad weather, which restricted the Allied advance guards to the roads—they succeeded in escaping any large-scale Allied envelopments. Tough little rear guards, mostly artillery and machine gunners, repeatedly delayed the pursuit. Farther to the rear, however, the German Army and government were falling apart. Ludendorff resigned on 27 October. The Navy mutinied on the 29th. On 9 November, a German republic was proclaimed. The Kaiser fled the next day, and the 11th brought the Armistice, under the terms of which Allied troops occupied strategic zones in Germany (*upper right*).

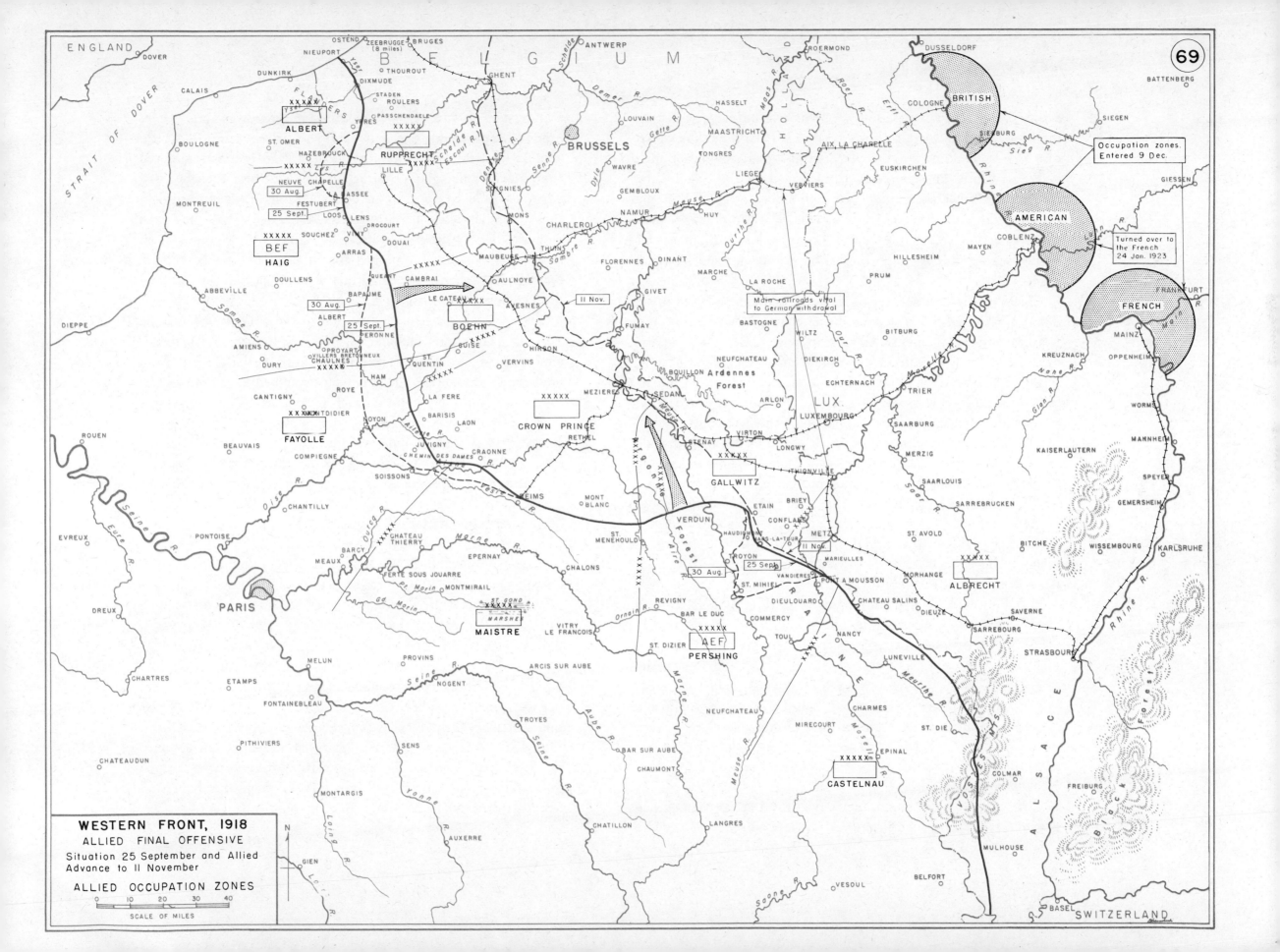

WESTERN FRONT, 1918
ALLIED FINAL OFFENSIVE
Situation 25 September and Allied
Advance to 11 November

ALLIED OCCUPATION ZONES

0   10   20   30   40
SCALE OF MILES

Basically, the Argonne was two roughly parallel river valleys—the Meuse and the Aire—separated by a broken ridge line which rose in commanding heights at Montfaucon, Romagne, Cunel, and Barricourt. This area was commanded on the east by the Heights of the Meuse, on the west by the hilly, tangled Argonne Forest. Across the area, the Germans had built a defensive network roughly twelve miles deep, tied together with mazes of barbed wire, mutually supporting strong points, and machine-gun nests.

The American take-over of this sector was a hurried affair, due to Foch's insistence on an immediate attack toward Mezieres. Somewhat more than 1,000,000 men were shifted, during the nights of a three-week period, over inadequate road and rail nets, through the careful planning of the United States First Army Assistant G-3, Col. George C. Marshall. This hurried preparation resulted in the more seasoned American divisions remaining at St. Mihiel while the Argonne attack was initiated by troops with little or no combat experience. Pétain was of immense help in making up American deficiencies in tanks, artillery, and transport.

There was little chance for maneuver in such a situation, but feints in the St. Mihiel area persuaded the Germans that the Americans planned to renew their suspended offensive there. It seems to have been 0200 of the 26th before they learned that American units were west of the Meuse.

Pershing had planned the offensive in three phases: first, a combined advance by the Americans and the French Fourth Army on both sides of the Argonne Forest, to link up at Grandpré (*left center*); second, a further advance to the line Le Chesne (*upper left*)–Stenay (*upper center*), to outflank the German position behind the Aisne River and thus clear the way for the American-French advance on Sedan-Mezieres; third, the capture of the Heights of the Meuse. The initial attack was to be a swift, massed double penetration to seize the heights of Montfaucon, Romagne, and Cunel.

The preparatory bombardment opened at 0230, 26 September; at 0525, the French Fourth Army jumped off, followed five minutes later by the Americans. Initial progress was good except around Montfaucon, where the Germans held out until the 27th, gaining time to pour in reinforcements. The Americans suffered from inexperience and a shortage of tanks. (Those that they had were rapidly used up; Col. George S. Patton, Jr., commanding a tank brigade, won the Distinguished Service Cross and was wounded here.) Replacing green divisions with veterans from St. Mihiel, Pershing continued the drive on 4 October. On 8 October, a Franco-American attack made important gains along the Heights of the Meuse (*dot-dashed red line*). By 10 October, attacking westward, the I Corps drove the Germans off the hills into Grandpré, enabling the French Fourth Army to advance up to the Aisne. Their flanks thus partially freed from enfilading German fire, the Americans resumed their grim battering, slowly gaining ground through Romagne, despite increasing German reinforcements and worsening weather. The Argonne Forest was cleared, adding to American military tradition the sagas of "the Lost Battalion" and of Sergeant York.

Meanwhile, in preparation for a renewed eastward advance from the St. Mihiel area, Pershing organized the United States Second Army under General Robert L. Bullard. General Hunter Liggett took over the First Army.

At daybreak on 1 November, Liggett—having rebuilt his communications and regrouped his forces—launched a new attack. Massed artillery and air support helped punch an opening in the last German defenses northeast of Buzancy (*left center*). On 2 November, the capture of Boult-aux-Bois (*west of Buzancy*) enabled the French Fourth Army to cross the Aisne. By that night, the Germans were retreating; and on the night of 6 November the Americans were before Sedan, and the vital railway was under artillery fire. The next day, the north end of the Heights of the Meuse was cleared, and Liggett was preparing an advance on Montmédy (*upper center*). On 10 November, the Second Army broke through on its front, but the Armistice halted all activity the next day.

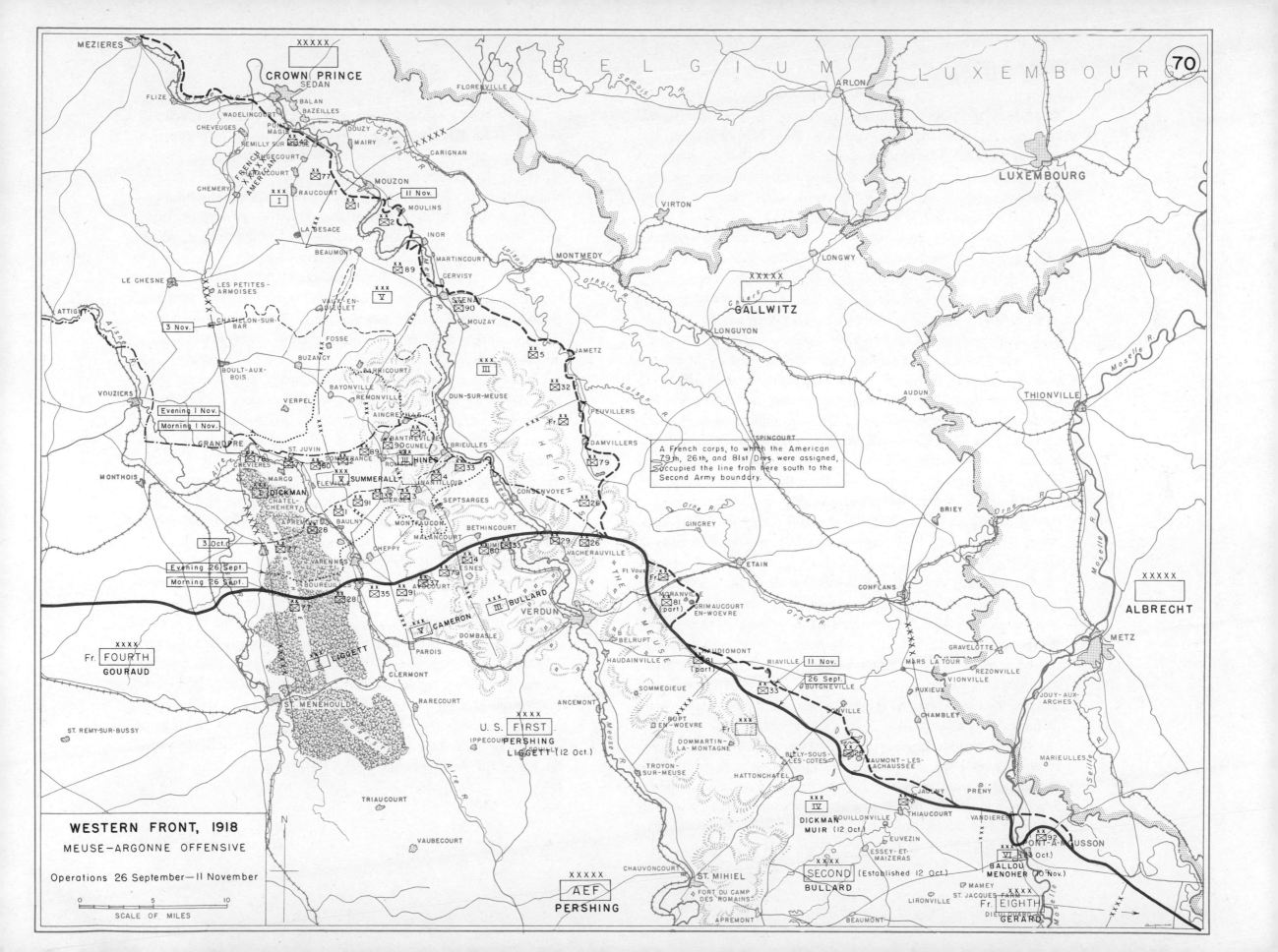

WESTERN FRONT, 1918

MEUSE-ARGONNE OFFENSIVE

Operations 26 September — 11 November

0   5   10
SCALE OF MILES

The Allies had poured military supplies of all types into Russia during late 1916 and 1917 through the ports of Murmansk, Archangel, and Vladivostok (*blue arrows*). Large quantities remained in the port areas after the Russian collapse, awaiting shipment to the front. (At Vladivostok alone, there was about 725,000 tons, valued at over $750,000,000.)

The Bolsheviks had overthrown the Kerensky government and signed a separate peace with the Central Powers. They had also, it must be remembered, openly (if informally) declared war on all existing governments through their call for world revolution —a war that Communist rulers of Russia continue even today by devious means against all non-Communist countries.

There was a definite danger that the Germans might seize— or force the weak Bolshevik government to surrender—the stockpiles at the ports. Further, since the Bolsheviks were openly and contemptuously hostile to the Allies, common sense forbade allowing them to retain such military equipment. The situation in Siberia was complicated by several other factors. A large force of Czechs (deserters and prisoners from the Austrian Army, who had joined the Czar's Army) were attempting to fight their way out of Russia along the Trans-Siberian Railway to Vladivostok. Also, the Japanese had large territorial ambitions in Siberia, which the United States considered it proper to thwart.

During July, August, and September of 1918, Allied forces landed in Russia. A sizable perimeter was established around Murmansk and Archangel under British command, though Bolshevik attacks later forced its contraction. American forces involved consisted of a reinforced regiment. In Siberia, operations were largely restricted to the line of the Trans-Siberian Railway; units of the two American regiments serving in that area operated as far west as Lake Baikal.

The immediate objectives of these expeditions were successfully accomplished: the masses of supplies were recovered, the Czechs extricated, and the Japanese kept from dismembering Siberia. Eventually, the American units were withdrawn—from northern Russia in August, 1919, and from Vladivostok in April, 1920.

World War I continued the technological trend, first seen in the American Civil War—the ability of a nation with superior industrial capacity to gain the victory (all other things being relatively equal) through superior and more abundant weapons and equipment, plus the understanding of organization and logistics which is an essential part of the industrialized society. Likewise, it was another war of mass, hastily trained armies, which only an industrialized nation could arm or equip.

Therefore, it is a war remembered chiefly for the mass employment of new weapons: the machine gun, modern artillery, poison gas, the airplane, and the tank. Both the airplane and the tank were still in their technical infancy—slow, mechanically unreliable, and of limited range.

Innovations in strategy and tactics were rare. The few that appeared were usually ignored or misunderstood, especially by the victorious Allies. The long, bloody battle on the Western Front, and the continual failure to ever obtain a decisive breakthrough, left the French and British with an obsessive belief in the power of the defense. From this was born the Maginot Line and the creed that the mission of the tank and the airplane was the direct support of the infantry. In 1940, they were prepared for another World War I. Meanwhile, the professional minds of the German General Staff, edged by the bitterness of defeat, considered their expensive lessons. In the East, against Russia and Rumania, they had won victory against great odds through superior organization, weapons, and mobility; in the West, they had seen victories snatched from their grasp because the momentum of an advance powered by men and horses could not be maintained across battle-wrecked terrain; finally, they had bitter knowledge of what even rudimentary tanks could do. Disarmed, and thus unencumbered with obsolescent weapons and equipment, they built anew around the airplane-tank spearhead team. Such was the genesis of the 1939 "Blitzkrieg."

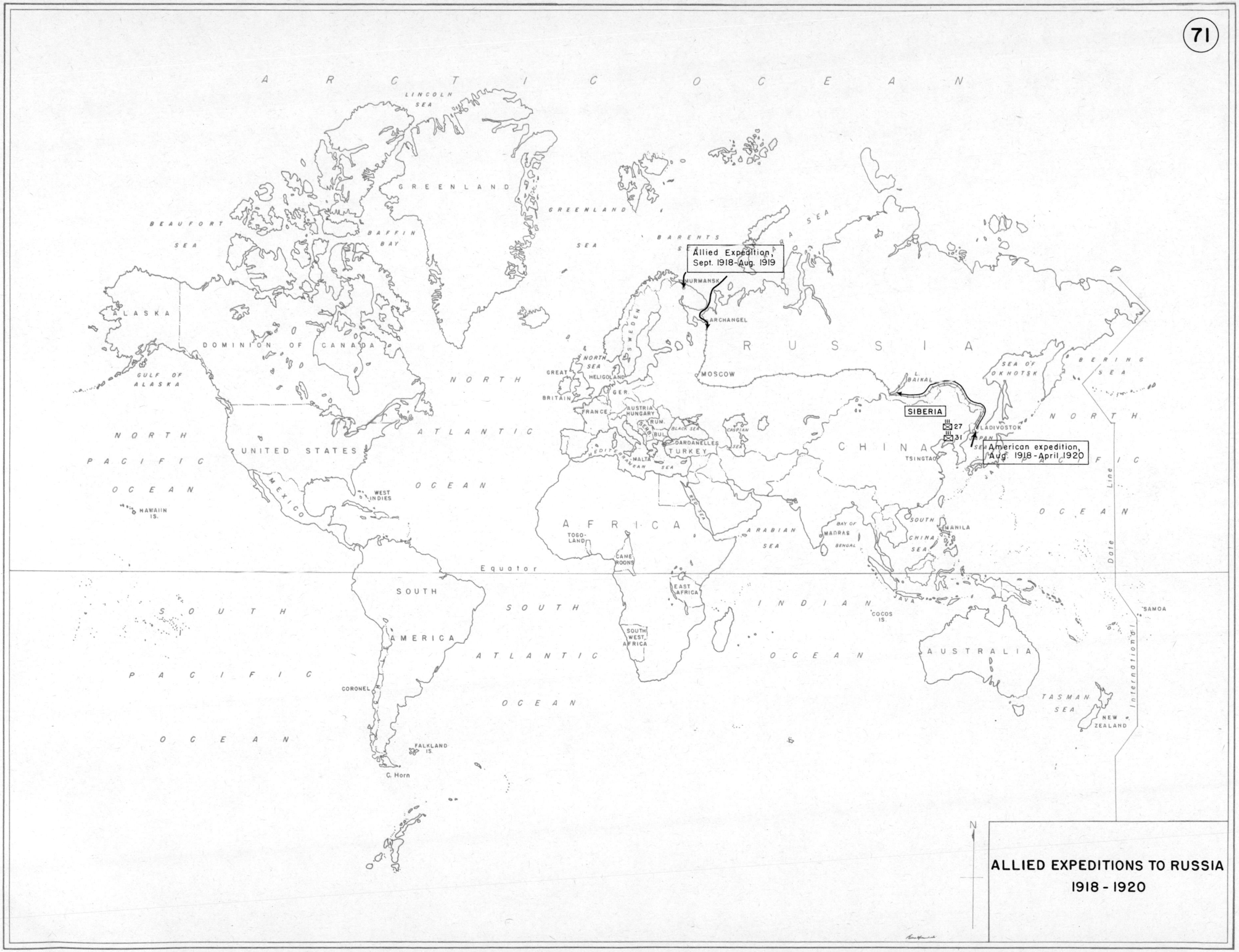

A R C T I C   O C E A N

LINCOLN
SEA

GREENLAND

GREENLAND

BEAUFORT
SEA

BAFFIN
BAY

BARENTS
SEA

SEA

ALASKA

DOMINION OF CANADA

Allied Expedition,
Sept. 1918-Aug. 1919

MURMANSK

ARCHANGEL

R U S S I A

SWEDEN

NORTH
SEA

GREAT
BRITAIN

MOSCOW

SEA OF
OKHOTSK

BERING
SEA

GULF OF
ALASKA

NORTH

ATLANTIC

GER.

HELIGOLAND

FRANCE

AUSTRIA
HUNGARY

L.
BAIKAL

NORTH

PACIFIC

UNITED STATES

OCEAN

BLACK SEA

CASPIAN
SEA

SIBERIA

27

VLADIVOSTOK

PACIFIC

RUM.
BUL.

JAP.

31

American expedition,
Aug. 1918-April 1920

OCEAN

MEXICO

MALTA

TURKEY

C H I N A

SEA

OCEAN

HAWAIIAN
IS.

WEST
INDIES

MEDIT.
SEA

TSINGTAO

Date

AFRICA

ARABIAN
SEA

BAY OF
MADRAS
BENGAL

SOUTH
CHINA
SEA

MANILA

Line

TOGO-
LAND

Equator

CAME-
ROONS

EAST
AFRICA

INDIAN

JAVA

COCOS
IS.

SAMOA

International

SOUTH

SOUTH

OCEAN

AUSTRALIA

AMERICA

SOUTH
WEST
AFRICA

ATLANTIC

OCEAN

TASMAN
SEA

PACIFIC

CORONEL

NEW
ZEALAND

OCEAN

OCEAN

FALKLAND
IS.

C. Horn

N

ALLIED EXPEDITIONS TO RUSSIA

1918 - 1920

SECTION 2 · WORLD WAR II

CONTENTS OF SECTION 2

1939	POLAND	NORWAY	WESTERN EUROPE	BALKANS	NORTH AFRICA	RUSSIA	JAPAN
SEPT.	⌐Invasion		⌐				
OCT.	└Surrender		│				
NOV.			│				
DEC.			│ Minor				
1940 JAN.			Operations				
FEB.			│				
MAR.			│				
APR.		⌐Invasion	│				
MAY		│	■German Invasion				
JUNE		└Allied Evacuation	■				
JULY			└French Surrender				
AUG.			⌐				
SEPT.			│ Battle of Britain		■Graziani's Advance		
OCT.			│				
NOV.			└	⌐			
DEC.				│	⌐		
1941 JAN.				│ Italian Invasion of Greece	Wavell's Offensive		
FEB.				│	└		
MAR.				│			
APR.				│	⌐		
MAY				└ German Invasion of Greece and Crete	─ Rommel's First Offensive		
JUNE					■Wavell's Counteroffensive	■Bialystok; Minsk	
JULY						■Smolensk	
AUG.						■Uman and Gomel	
SEPT.						■Kiev	
OCT.						■Vyazma and Bryansk	
NOV.					⌐	⌐ Approach to Moscow	
DEC.					│ Auchinleck's Offensive	└ Russian Counterattacks	⌐Pearl Harbor; Malaya; Philippines

1942	NORTH AFRICA	SICILY AND ITALY	RUSSIA	JAPAN
JAN.			Russian Counterattacks	
FEB.				Singapore
MAR.				
APR.	Rommel's Second Offensive			Fall of Bataan
MAY			Kharkov	Corregidor Retreat from Burma
JUNE			Sevastopol	Midway; Kiska
JULY				
AUG.			Caucasus	Guadalcanal Landing; Kokoda
SEPT.	Alam Halfa			
OCT.				
NOV.	El Alamein / Allied Invasion / Race for Tunis		Stalingrad	
DEC.				Buna-Gona
1943 JAN.			Russian Leningrad Offensive	
FEB.	Kasserine Pass		Russian Campaign in Ukraine	Japanese Evacuate Guadalcanal
MAR.	Mareth			
APR.				
MAY	Bizerte; Tunis Surrender			
JUNE				
JULY		Invasion of Sicily	Kursk; Orel	Salamaua New Georgia
AUG.				
SEPT.		Salerno / Naples; Volturno River	German Withdrawal	Lae
OCT.				
NOV.		Winter Line Campaign		Bougainville / Tarawa
DEC.			Russian Winter Offensive	Arawe / Cape Gloucester

1944	WESTERN EUROPE	ITALY	RUSSIA	JAPAN
JAN.		Anzio Landing		
FEB.			Leningrad	Kwajalein
MAR.		Attack on Cassino	Ukraine	Manus
APR.			Crimea	Imphal-Kohima / Hollandia
MAY				
JUNE	Normandy Landing	Rome Campaign		Biak
JULY	Avranches		Latvia; Warsaw	Saipan / Guam
AUG.	Southern France		Rumania	
SEPT.	Arnhem		Bulgaria	Palaus / Morotai
OCT.	Aachen — Westwall	Attacks on the Gothic Line		
NOV.	Metz			Leyte
DEC.			Budapest	Mindoro
1945 JAN.	Ardennes		East Prussia; Poland	Landing on Luzon
FEB.				
MAR.	Advance to the Rhine			Manila / Shimbu Line / Iwo Jima
APR.	Ruhr Encirclement / Advance to the Elbe	Allied Spring Offensive	Vienna	
MAY	German Surrender	German Surrender	Berlin / German Surrender	Okinawa / Shuri Line / Mindanao
JUNE				
JULY				
AUG.				
SEPT.				Japanese Surrender

BASIC SYMBOLS:

Battalion	II	Airborne	
Regiment	III	Air Force unit	
Brigade	X	Armor	
Division, air division	XX	Artillery	
Corps	XXX	Cavalry	
Army, air force	XXXX	Infantry	
Army group	XXXXX		

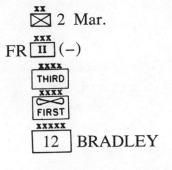

Examples of Combinations of Basic Symbols:

Small British infantry detachment   Br. ⊠

34th Regimental Combat Team   ⊠ 34 RCT

Combat Command C of
   1st Armored Division   C ⊡ 1

82d Airborne Division   ⊠ 82

1st Motorized Division   ⊠ 1 Mtz.

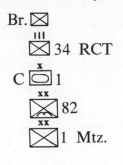

2d Marine Division   ⊠ 2 Mar.

French Second Corps
   less detachments   FR II (−)

Third Army   THIRD

First Air Force   FIRST

12th Army Group,
   commanded by Bradley   12 BRADLEY

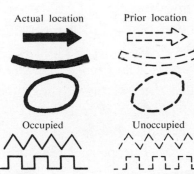

OTHER SYMBOLS:

Troops on the march

Troops in position

Troops in bivouac or reserve

Field works

Strong prepared positions

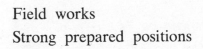

Troops displacing and direction

Troops in position under attack

Route of march or flight

Boundary between units

Fort

Fortified area

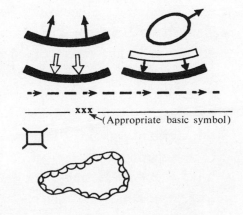

Several important changes marked the post–World War I map of Europe. The most noticeable of these was the fragmentation of Austria-Hungary into its major component parts. The passing of that onetime great power, at once massive and ramshackle, was not a completely unalloyed blessing. In its unique way, Austria-Hungary had given south-central Europe a certain economic and political stability. The collection of small, bickering states that replaced it frequently lacked both.

Russia had been pushed back toward Asia; the confusion of its Communist revolution had given Poland, Lithuania, Latvia, Estonia, and Finland the chance to regain their independence. Rumania had seized the opportunity to occupy Bessarabia. Behind this outpost line of struggling, reborn nations, a succession of callous Communist Party leaders was building the Union of Soviet Socialist Republics (hereafter called Russia) into a mighty industrial power with armed forces far stronger than any Czar could have ever mustered. The process, however, bore heavily upon the Russian people.

Germany had lost her colonies and had been almost completely demilitarized. Her nineteenth-century conquests—Alsace-Lorraine and Schleswig-Holstein—had been returned to France and Denmark, respectively; a small border district had been claimed by Belgium. These territorial losses were resented, but greater still was Germany's anger over the changes on her eastern frontier. Here, the Treaty of Versailles had given landlocked Poland a strip of German territory along the Vistula River (the so-called Polish Corridor) as an outlet to the Baltic Sea. Danzig, the German-populated seaport at the mouth of the Vistula, had been declared a "free city" under a commissioner appointed by the League of Nations, but Poland controlled its customs and foreign relations. Farther south, parts of Silesia also had passed to Poland—some as a result of local plebiscites, others as the result of unilateral Polish military seizure. These changes put large numbers of unhappy Germans under Polish rule, upset established channels of German economy, and left the "beloved outwork" of East Prussia isolated from the rest of Germany.

Finally, some of the various frontier "rectifications" and "adjustments" decreed at Versailles were as unjust as the situations which they supposedly corrected. Memories of ancient national glories, the desire for easily defended "strategic" frontiers, and the lack of definite ethnological boundaries in many areas combined to produce a smoldering collection of minority problems. Besides the German minority in Poland, thousands of Germans (or, originally, Austrians) found their ancestral homes suddenly a part of Italy (the southern Tyrol) or of Czechoslovakia (the Sudetenland). Likewise, Hungarians found themselves legally Czechs or Rumanians. Beyond this, there were unsolved differences between Yugoslavia and Italy, Poland and Czechoslovakia, Lithuania and Poland, and Greece and Bulgaria. Many of the new nations had their own internal tensions—in Czechoslovakia, between the Czechs and the Slovaks; in Yugoslavia, among the Serbs, Croats, and Slovenes. No one of these in itself was enough to cause a war; yet, under the hand of Adolf Hitler, each became a potent wedge for the splintering of Western civilization.

Two forces tried to give this pre–World War II Europe some sort of stability: one was the League of Nations; the other, France's system of military alliances. The League (which the United States failed to join) lacked authority, and the great powers generally ignored it in matters that affected their own interests. The French, fearful of an eventual German revival, had allied themselves with the other nations that had profited territorially from World War I—Yugoslavia, Czechoslovakia, Rumania, and Poland.

The Europe of 1938 had been sapped by World War I and again by the depression which followed it. England and France, remembering their shattering losses in men and wealth, could not bring themselves to consider another major war. The United States was far away and self-absorbed. Meanwhile, in Russia, in Italy, and in Germany, totalitarian governments tightened their regimes and looked abroad for other worlds to conquer.

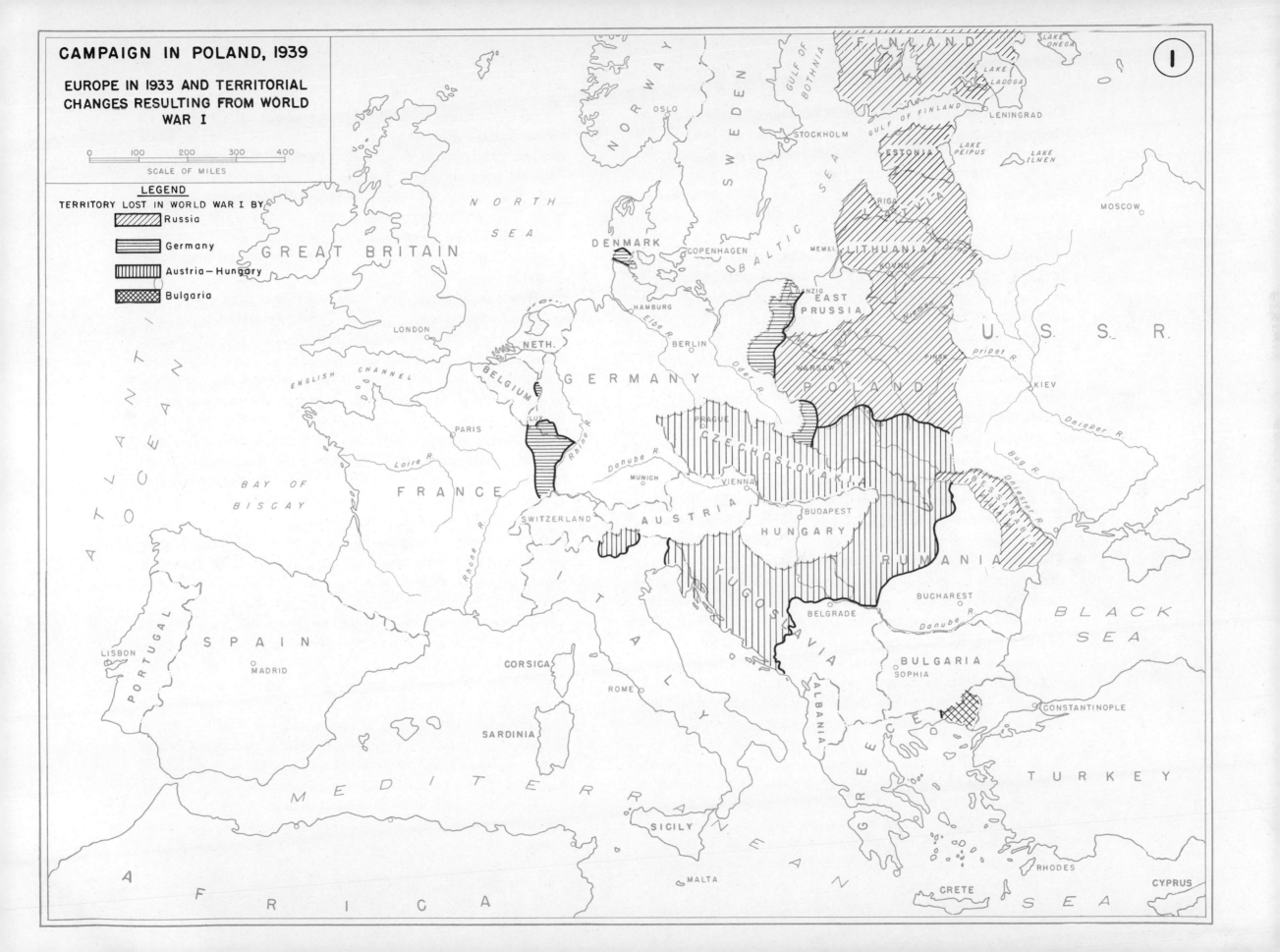

Of these totalitarian governments, Communist-ruled Russia was the oldest. Its threat, however, was principally the indirect one of subversion; its ruler, Joseph Stalin, preferred a waiting game.

Next was Benito Mussolini's Facist Italy—a petty despotism. Even Mussolini's attempt to revive the glories of Imperial Rome, through the conquest of Ethiopia (1935-36), merely accented a certain comic aspect of his regime.

In contrast, Adolf Hitler, who became chancellor of Germany in 1933, was a dangerous man who wanted quick results. His program was simple—". . . tomorrow, the whole world." But, possessing abundant low cunning, he realized the need for considerable preparation. Germany had only a tiny navy, a 100,000-man army, the covert nucleus of an air force, and the bare bones of an armament industry. Her Rhineland frontier had been demilitarized, so that there were neither fortifications nor troops between the Rhine Valley—Germany's commercial artery —and the French frontier.

Hitler did have several advantages. By careful selection and training, General Hans von Seeckt had made the German Army a school for future officers and noncommissioned officers, an expert cadre for the hosts Hitler would raise. Military research and development had gone on secretly (much of it in Russia). There were no stockpiles of obsolescent World War I weapons; thus, the new forces Hitler raised could receive equally new armaments. Finally, England and France, obviously anxious for peace at almost any price, might be bluffed into a policy of appeasement in any dispute that did not concern their most vital interests.

Accordingly, Hitler began by withdrawing from the League of Nations. In 1934, he signed a treaty of arbitration with Poland. This made him appear a reasonable person—and also immobilized the Polish Army throughout the period when it was still superior to Hitler's.

In 1935, Hitler took advantage of the crisis generated by Mussolini's invasion of Ethiopia by denouncing the clauses of the Versailles Treaty that limited German armament. Conscription was reintroduced, and an agreement reached with England allowing Germany to enlarge its navy. Aircraft and submarine construction was pushed. Alarmed, France sought an alliance with Russia. Hitler, claiming that this threatened Germany, remilitarized the Rhineland (March, 1936). This was a major gamble. France could have crushed him, but neither France nor England acted. In 1937, Hitler began construction of his "West Wall" (the "Siegfried Line" [see map 12]) to protect his back while he opened a campaign of subversion in Austria and the German-inhabited Sudeten area of Czechoslovakia.

The Spanish Civil War (1936-39) gave the Germans, who intervened to aid General Francisco Franco's "Nationalists" (and the Russians, who aided the leftist "Loyalists"), an opportunity to test new weapons and tactics and give their emerging air force considerable on-the-job training. In November, 1936, Germany, Italy, and Japan signed the Anti-Comintern Pact, directed against Communist Russia. Hitherto, Italy had opposed German absorption of Austria; now Mussolini stepped out in the path of his demoniac partner. During March, 1938, Hitler occupied Austria.

German possession of Austria left Czechoslovakia (see map 1) half-surrounded. Hitler's demands for the Sudetenland caused Czechoslovakia to mobilize. War threatened, but at the Munich Conference France and England—finding chances of Russian support equivocal—offered Hitler the Sudetenland (this map, center) in hopes of receiving "peace in our time." The Sudetenland secured, Hitler busily fomented a Slovakian independence movement, while Poland and Hungary seized slices of Czech territory.

During October, 1938, Hitler began to exert pressure on Poland over Danzig and the Polish Corridor. Poland refused any concessions, but in March, 1939, Hitler turned her southern flank by seizing the remainder of Czechoslovakia. This was his first conquest of territory inhabited by a non-Germanic people. England and France began to rearm and prepared to support Poland. Hitler persuaded Lithuania to return the onetime German district of Memel, and pressured Rumania into a pact guaranteeing Germany most of the Rumanian oil production.

Then, as tension grew constantly tighter, Hitler again outmaneuvered France and England. On 23 August, he and Stalin —sworn ideological enemies—announced a nonaggression pact.

CAMPAIGN IN POLAND, 1939

GERMAN AGGRESSIONS, 1936-39

SCALE OF MILES
0   100   200   300   400

2

MEMEL
March 1939

RHINELAND
March 1936

SUDETENLAND
September 1938

March 1939

March 1938

Poland is a vaster Belgium—an open, level country with few natural obstacles to the passage of large armies. Like Belgium, much of its history had been that of a roadway and a battleground for contending powers.

Its only natural defenses are the Tatra-Carpathian Mountains on the south; the lines of the Vistula, Narew (*upper center*), and San (*lower center*) Rivers; and the Pripet Marshes on the east. None is particularly formidable. The mountains reach heights of 8,700 feet, but there are several good passes—the Jablunka (*lower left*) being the most important—traversed by road and rail lines. Furthermore, the most defensible terrain in this area lies south of the Polish frontier. The rivers are generally broad and slow, practically impassable when in flood after heavy rains, but frequently low at the end of a hot summer. (In 1939, for example, the Vistula was fordable at many points upstream from Warsaw.) Finally, the Pripet Marshes are flanked to the north and the south by wide plains.

Military operations in Poland are highly dependent on the weather. Normally, the fall rains during September and October flood the rivers and turn the countryside into a quagmire which prohibits much activity until the ground freezes. The fall of 1939, however, remained warm and dry—"Hitler weather." Rivers were low, and the ground was hard, making a perfect arena for the German panzer (armored) and motorized troops. Advanced airfields could be easily improvised as the German advance swept forward.

Among the difficulties confronting the Polish high command were the shape of their western frontier and the location of their major industries. Troops in the Poznan area (*left center*) and the Polish Corridor were exposed to enveloping attacks; their main industries were in the exposed Lodz-Cracow area of southwestern Poland. Thus, if the Poles massed their troops west of the San-Vistula line, they occupied a salient, its flanks exposed to German advances from East Prussia and Slovakia. If they retired behind the rivers, they gave up the richest and most productive area of their country, as well as their one seaport, Gdynia.

Poland's fatal weakness, however, was its isolation. Its seaport faced the Baltic, which the Germans could easily block with mines, submarines, and aircraft against Allied entry. To the south, Germany was allied with Slovakia, and Hungary and Rumania were semi-vassals of the Germans. To the east waited an unfriendly Russia. To the north, Lithuania had an old score to settle with Poland over possession of Vilna (*top right*), the capital of the medieval Kingdom of Lithuania, before whose power the rulers of Moscow had walked softly. Under these circumstances, England and France could help Poland only indirectly—by exerting pressure on Germany in the West. Neither was prepared, militarily or emotionally, for such an effort. Memories of the Somme, of Flanders, of Verdun and Champagne had convinced them that the defense was the decisive form of warfare—a conviction that the French had embodied in the concrete and steel of the Maginot Line (*see map 12*). Hitler's West Wall might be of unproved strength and garrisoned largely by second-rate troops, but no French or British statesman or general was willing to chance a major offensive against it.

One thing became certain, however, as war crept closer through August's hot weather: the Poles would fight. They had seen the fate of Czechoslovakia, which had elected to surrender without a struggle. Their army might be small, its equipment scanty and antiquated, its mobilization seriously delayed as the result of heeding a final, futile sputter of Franco-British appeasement; but Poland had never lacked tough infantry and gallant horsemen. The Germans were an ancient enemy; the rains would surely come to bog the German tanks; England and France would not fail their ally. But—whatever came—it was better to die on their feet than to live on their knees.

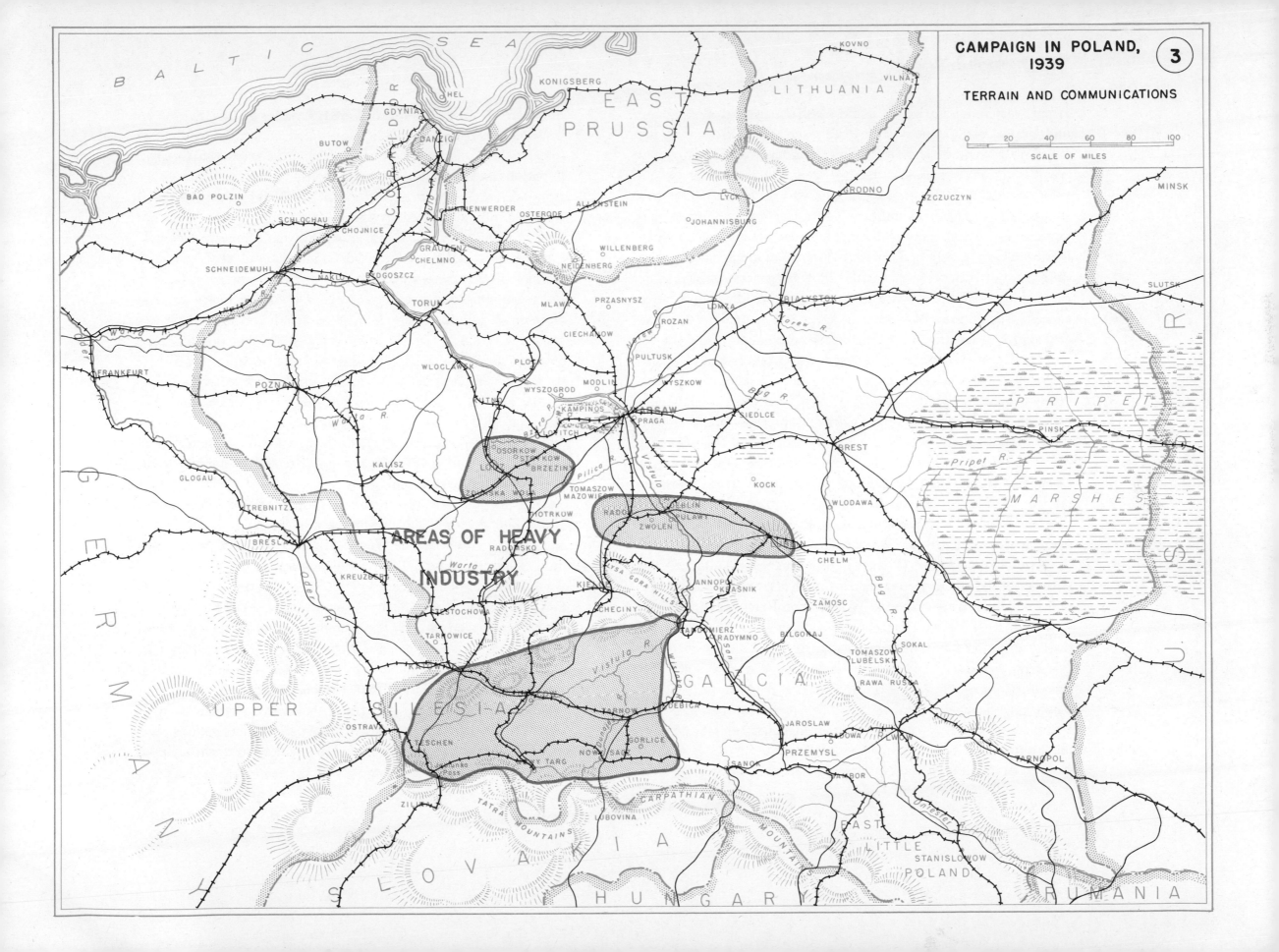

Hitler was confident that he could crush Poland before England and France could react. If they did attempt to aid Poland, the West Wall would hold them. A quick victory over Poland would cow the nations of southeast Europe, guaranteeing Germany continued access to Hungarian wheat and Rumanian oil. Hitler had successfully dragged his military leaders through a series of adventures—the Rhineland, Austria, the Sudetenland— all of which had been won largely by bluff and bluster. Poland promised to be different, but Hitler refused to even allow his generals to war game the coming operations. His intuition would provide a short-range success, but, in August, 1939, the chill professionals of his general staff had already made their accurate estimate of the future.

The German plan provided that Army Group North (General Fedor von Bock) would mount two major attacks. Its Fourth Army (General Guenther von Kluge) would advance immediately on Graudenz, cutting the Polish Corridor at its base and establishing communications between Germany proper and East Prussia; it would also seize Gdynia. The Third Army (General Georg von Kuechler) would make its main effort toward Warsaw, and also launch a secondary attack westward to help the Fourth Army seize the Vistula crossings. Once the Corridor was secured, Bock's whole force would drive on Warsaw.

Army Group South (General Gerd von Rundstedt) was the stronger of the two. It would make its main attack toward Warsaw with its Tenth Army (General Walther von Reichenau), covered on its left flank by the Eighth Army's (General Johannes Blaskowitz) drive on Lodz, and on its right by the Fourteenth Army (General Wilhelm List), which would move on Cracow. The link-up of Army Group North and the Tenth Army at Warsaw could cut off a large part of the Polish forces west of the San-Vistula-Narew line. (Note that most of the panzer units were with the Fourth and Tenth Armies.)

The area between the two army groups was largely filled by the Oder Quadrilateral fortified area. Frontier guards, reinforced by some reserve units, were concentrated here with instructions to carry out local attacks—both to deceive the Poles as to German intentions and to tie down as many Polish units as possible. Other frontier guard units covered the flank of the Third Army. Local reserve units, supported by the German Navy, were to secure Danzig. The Navy would also provide a small force to blockade the Polish coast, attack Polish naval installations at Gdynia and Hel, keep open the sea lanes to East Prussia, capture or destroy Polish shipping, and give Bock's forces all possible assistance. The German Air Force (hereafter called the Luftwaffe) deployed some 1,400 fighters and bombers against Poland, one air force being in support of each army group. The Luftwaffe placed first priority on the destruction of the Polish Air Force, in the air or on the ground. Thereafter, it would begin an interdiction campaign directed against Polish communications, troop movements, and concentrations. An efficient "fifth column" within Poland signaled the location of Polish headquarters and similar important targets to German airmen.

Against the possible threat of Franco-British intervention, Hitler had deployed the greater part of his navy in the North Sea and the Atlantic. The West Wall was garrisoned by infantry units, supported by relatively light air forces.

The Polish plan appears to have been an attempt to hold as much of Poland as possible by concentrating most of the available troops along the frontiers. It can only be surmised that the Poles —like their allies—expected to fight a World War I type of war, which would give them time to complete their mobilization. Also, they undoubtedly believed that French and British pressure in the West would limit the strength of the German armies of invasion. They had almost no armored forces. Field fortifications (*not shown*) were hastily erected along the frontier, but these—on the whole—were weak and incomplete.

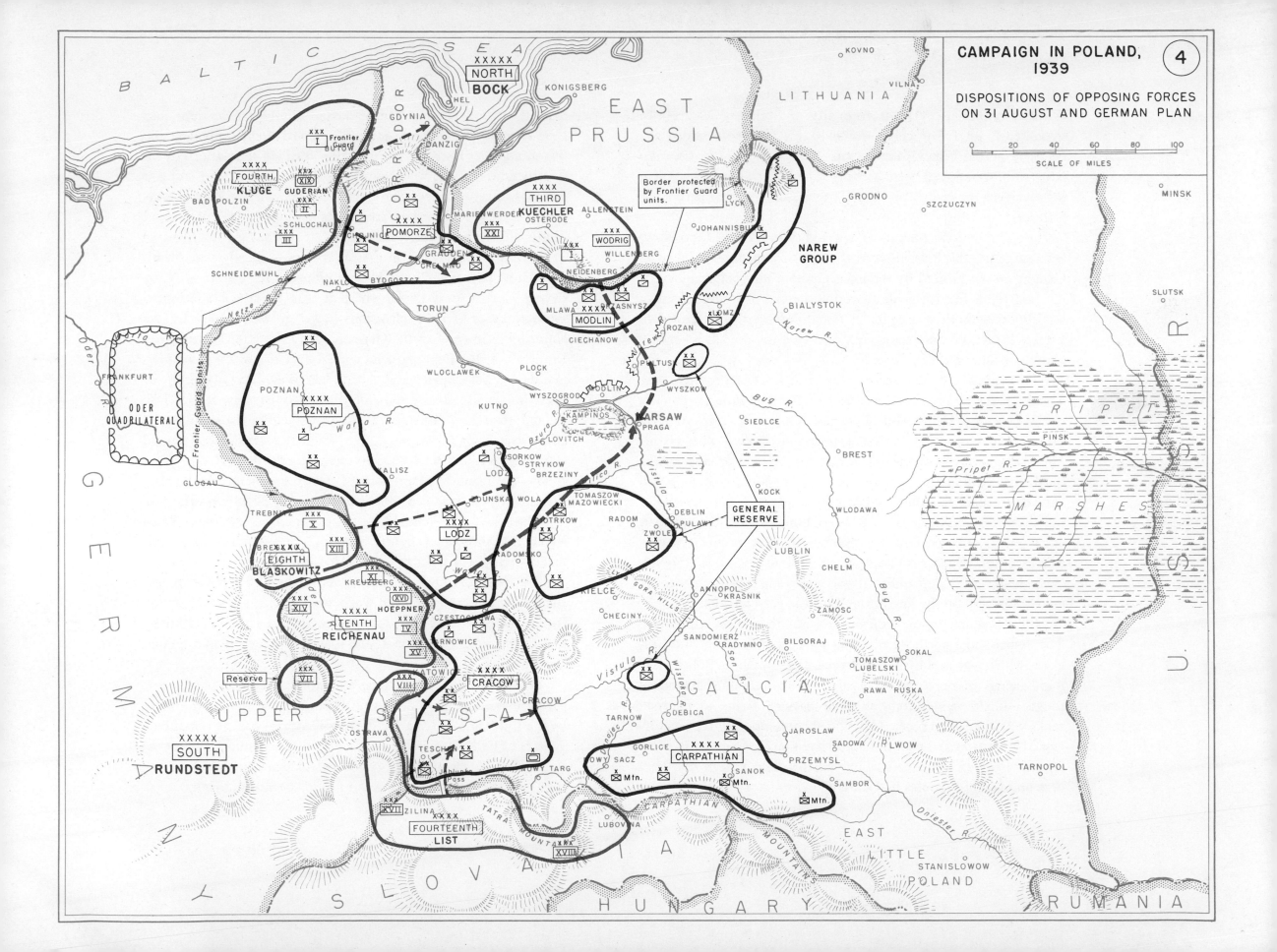

Without bothering over the formality of declaring war, Hitler struck early on 1 September. At 0440, his Luftwaffe raided airfields all across Poland; almost simultaneously, an old German battleship (which had been "visiting" Danzig) took nearby Polish fortifications under fire, and the German Army surged across the frontier.

Despite the long preliminary period of tension—or, possibly, because of it—this invasion took the Poles completely by surprise. Caught on the ground by the mass German air assault, much of the Polish Air Force was destroyed in the first few hours. Danzig fell almost without a struggle. A few Polish warships escaped to England; the rest were soon sunk or driven into Swedish harbors and there interned.

On the first day, the Fourth Army made good progress. The Third Army's I Corps was checked by a fortified Polish area (*not shown*) around Mlawa, but Kuechler reinforced Corps Wodrig (which broke through farther east the next day) with all his armor and swung it westward (*action not shown*) to envelop the town. Rundstedt's armies were equally successful, some units advancing up to fifteen miles by late afternoon of the 1st. The Poles relied on their rear guards and demolitions to slow the German advance, but panzer units—supported by dive bombers—were usually able to bypass such obstacles. Jablunka Pass was rapidly cleared, but by 2 September it was apparent that the Poles intended to stand on the line of the Warta River (*left center*).

By 3 September, the Polish Air Force had been wiped out. The Third and Fourth Armies had joined hands to cut the Corridor, which was rapidly being cleared, the remaining Polish units there being driven toward Gdynia. Polish resistance had been tough and desperate, some of their cavalry riding at German tanks with lance and saber. (Unofficial contemporary reports suggest these troopers had been told that the German tanks were fakes, "armored" with canvas or papier-mâché.) Both the Pomorze and Modlin Armies had suffered heavy losses. Polish cavalry

from the Narew Group had made several short incursions into East Prussia, but had not slowed the Third Army's advance. To the south, the Tenth Army took the fortified industrial city of Czestochowa on the morning of the 3d and moved on to seize several bridgeheads over the Warta. The next day, its panzer units drove beyond Radomsko. Several Polish units were cut off and destroyed; the rest retired hurriedly.

Meanwhile, Bock's Third Army continued its advance toward the Narew River, while the Fourth prepared for a shift to Army Group North's east flank, where it was to attack southward through Lomza. This operation, however, was vetoed by the commander in chief of the German Army, General Walther von Brauchitsch. England and France had declared war against Germany on 3 September; Brauchitsch feared an early attack in the West and consequently did not wish to move any deeper into Poland than was necessary to destroy the Polish Army as an effective fighting force. He would permit the transfer of General Heinz Guderian's XIX Panzer Corps to the left of the Third Army, but it must remain west of the approximate line Lomza-Warsaw. Bock appealed this decision unsuccessfully on the 5th.

That day, the Tenth Army had begun crossing the Pilica River, with only open country between it and Warsaw. The Fourteenth Army was meeting increasing resistance west of Cracow, and the Eighth Army was pushing across the Warta River. Rundstedt, however, had begun to worry about the Eighth Army's left flank. There, the Polish Poznan Army had been able to withdraw slowly and practically intact, and therefore represented a mounting threat.

Otherwise, the Polish Army's situation was increasingly desperate. Most available reserves had been committed, and attacks by the Luftwaffe had snarled the mobilization of those remaining. Worst of all, the Luftwaffe—guided by fifth columnists—kept the Polish General Headquarters under attack wherever it moved, disrupting communications between it and the Polish armies.

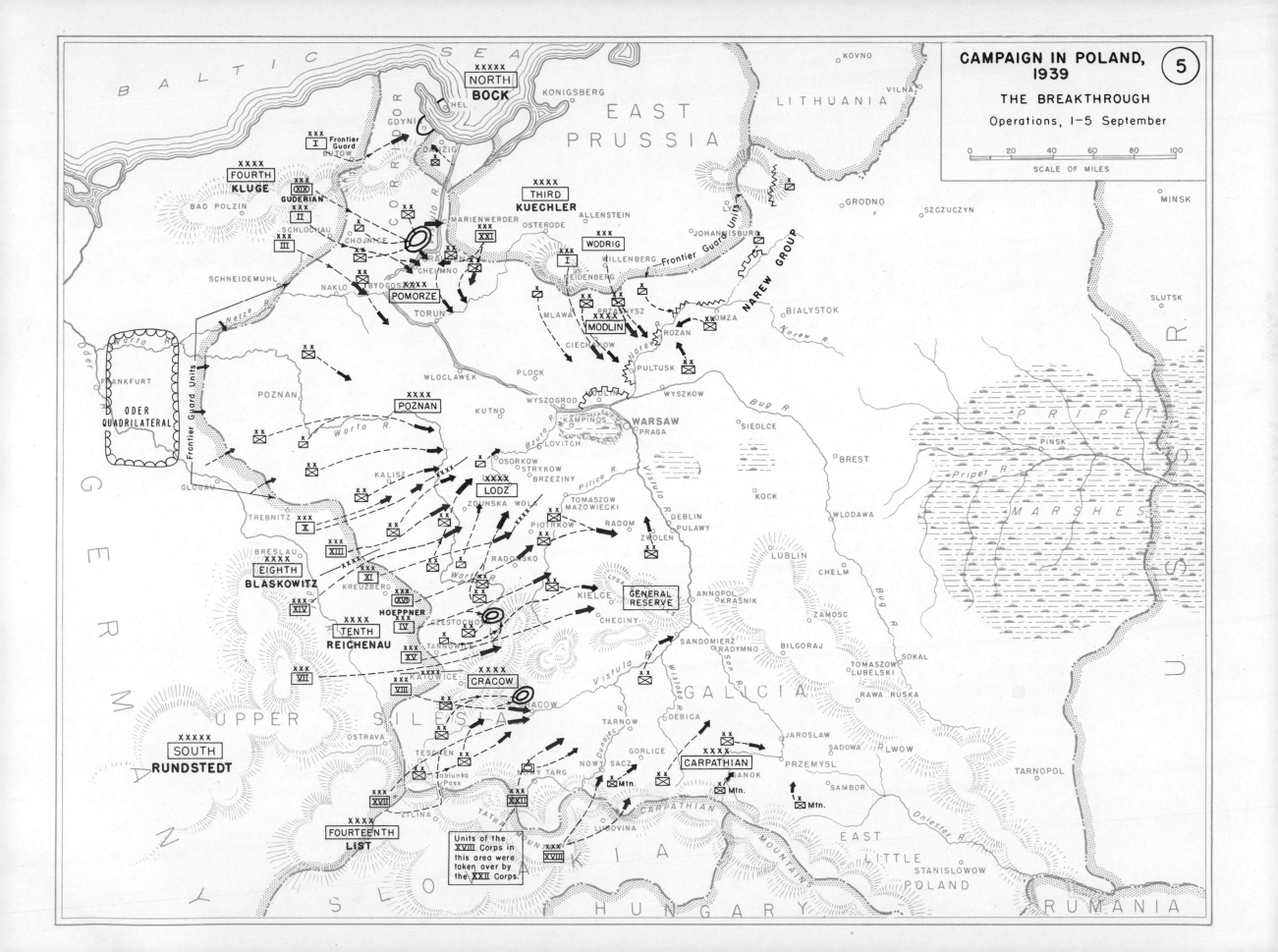

CAMPAIGN IN POLAND, 1939

⑤

THE BREAKTHROUGH

Operations, 1–5 September

SCALE OF MILES
0   20   40   60   80   100

BALTIC SEA

EAST PRUSSIA

LITHUANIA

KOVNO

KONIGSBERG

VILNA

NORTH
BOCK

GDYNIA

HEL

GRODNO

SZCZUCZYN

MINSK

I Frontier Guard

BUTOW

DANZIG

SLUTSK

FOURTH
KLUGE

BAD POLZIN

GUDERIAN

II

SCHLOCHAU

III

MARIENWERDER

XXI

THIRD
KUECHLER

ALLENSTEIN

OSTERODE

WODRIG

I

JOHANNISBURG

Frontier Guard Units

NAREW GROUP

CHOJNICE

GRAUDENZ

CHELMNO

WILLENBERG

NEIDENBERG

BIALYSTOK

SCHNEIDEMUHL

NAKLO

BYDGOSZCZ

POMORZE

TORUN

MLAWA

PRZASNYSZ

MODLIN

CIECHANOW

ROZAN

PULTUSK

LOMZA

Narew R.

ODER
QUADRILATERAL

FRANKFURT

Frontier Guard Units

Netze

WLOCLAWEK

PLOCK

WYSZOGROD

WYSZKOW

Bug R.

SIEDLCE

BREST

PRIPET

MARSHES

Pripet R.

PINSK

WLODAWA

POZNAN

POZNAN

Warta R.

KUTNO

KAMPINOS

WARSAW

PRAGA

LOVITCH

Bzura

Vistula R.

KALISZ

OSORKOW

STRYKOW

BRZEZINY

Pilica R.

DEBLIN

PULAWY

KOCK

TREBNITZ

X

LODZ

ZDUNSKA WOLA

PIOTRKOW

RADOM

ZWOLEN

LUBLIN

CHELM

BRESLAU

EIGHTH
BLASKOWITZ

XIII

RADOMSKO

Warta R.

KIELCE

GENERAL
RESERVE

ANNOPOL

KRASNIK

ZAMOSC

KREUZBERG

XI

HOEPPNER
IV

XVI

CZESTOCHOWA

TENTH
REICHENAU

TARNOWITZ

CHECINY

Lysa

SANDOMIERZ

RADYMNO

BILGORAJ

TOMASZOW
LUBELSKI

SOKAL

XIV

XV

VII

KATOWICE

VIII

CRACOW

CRACOW

Vistula

Wisloka R.

San R.

GALICIA

RAWA
RUSKA

LWOW

UPPER   SILESIA

SOUTH
RUNDSTEDT

OSTRAVA

TESCHEN

TARNOW

DEBICA

JAROSLAW

SADOWA

PRZEMYSL

SAMBOR

TARNOPOL

FOURTEENTH
LIST

XVII

ZILINA

Toblunka
Pass

NOWY TARG

XXII

Tatra Mtn.

GORLICE

NOWY SACZ

CARPATHIAN

Mtn.

SANOK

Mtn.

CARPATHIAN

MOUNTAINS

Dniester R.

EAST

LITTLE
POLAND

STANISLOWOW

Units of the
XVIII Corps in
this area were
taken over by
the XXII Corps.

XVIII

LUBOVINA

HUNGARY

RUMANIA

SLOVAKIA

GERMANY

On 6 September, Rundstedt's Tenth Army continued its relentless advance toward Warsaw, despite bitter Polish resistance. On its right, the Fourteenth Army took Cracow; thereafter, Brauchitsch directed that it advance northeast toward Lublin (*center, right*) to intercept any Polish units which might escape across the Vistula.

That same day, Rundstedt tried to secure more cavalry for reconnaissance and screening on the left of his Eighth Army. None being available, he dispatched two infantry divisions from the Army Group South reserve to fill the gap between the X Corps and the frontier guard formations farther to the northwest. Also on the 6th, since intelligence reports indicated that Polish troops were attempting to regroup at Lodz and Radom (*center*), he took measures to prevent their withdrawal east of the Vistula. The Eighth Army was to move directly on Lodz; Radom was to be enveloped by the Tenth Army.

In the north, Bock regrouped his XXI Corps and sent it toward Lomza on the 7th. On the 9th, the leading elements of Guderian's XIX Corps came into action on its left, Bock having meanwhile wrangled greater freedom of action for Guderian from Brauchitsch. Frontier guard units (*not shown*) moved eastward on Bialystok to cover Guderian's east flank. Two days later (11 September), because of reports that the Polish government had fled to Lwow (*lower right*) and was trying to set up a new defense line along the Bug and San Rivers, Brauchitsch directed that the Third Army advance be pressed to a line just below Kock and Wlodawa (*center, right*). Here, it would come into contact with the Fourteenth Army's advance to Lublin, thus completing a second envelopment of the Polish Army. Meanwhile, the I and Wodrig Corps crossed the Narew River, leaving bypassed Polish units encircled in their rear, and drove for the Bug, which Wodrig's leading elements crossed on the 10th.

It was also on 10 September that the Poznan Army struck its blow for Poland. Moving out of the Kutno area, it surprised the awkwardly handled German 30th Infantry Division (X

Corps), forcing the rest of the corps to change front to the north. German reinforcements (air transport was used to bring up one regiment) helped in checking the Polish attack, while the XI Corps swung north and west to take the attacking force in its flank and rear and cut it off from Warsaw. Converging attacks of the Eighth and Fourth Armies then compressed elements of the Pomorze, Poznan, and Lodz Armies—about one-third of the entire Polish Army—into a pocket around Kutno. A desperate Polish attempt to break out was thwarted on 12 September; thereafter, the reduction of the pocket continued relentlessly.

Farther south, the XVI Panzer Corps pushed one division to Warsaw by the 8th, but—its tanks being unsuited for street fighting—had to withdraw it to the suburbs. This deep penetration, however, crowded the Polish forces into either the Kutno-Warsaw area or the area around Radom.

The Tenth Army now made its major effort against the Polish units assembling around Radom, enveloping them from the north and south to clear its way to the Vistula. After bitter fighting, this mission was accomplished by 11 September, 60,000 prisoners being taken. To the southeast, mountain troops of the Fourteenth Army seized the dominating heights around Lwow on the 12th and 13th.

Continuing German advances on all fronts gave the Poles no chance to reorganize. Brauchitsch now directed the Third Army to envelop Warsaw from the north and east; Guderian was ordered to capture Brest (*center, right*); the Eighth Army, heavily reinforced, would reduce the Kutno pocket; and the Tenth Army was to move on Lublin from the west, to link up there with both Army Group North and the Fourteenth Army.

Considerable mopping up had to be completed, especially in the Radom area, where Polish units up to regimental size had retired into the woods. Frontier guard units occupied the Poznan area. To the north, bitter fighting went on around Gdynia and at Hel, where Polish naval troops put up a last-ditch defense.

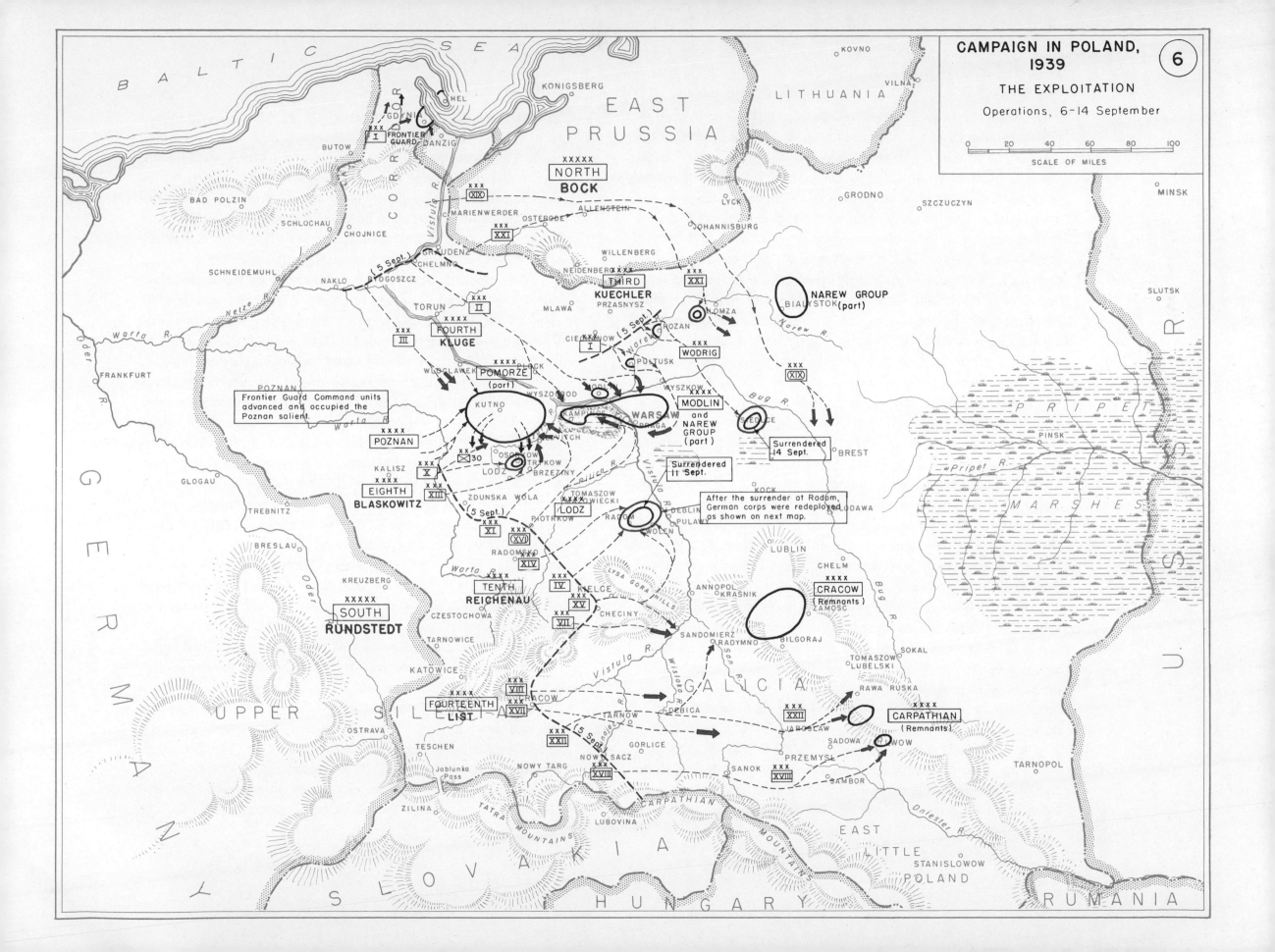

CAMPAIGN IN POLAND, 1939

THE EXPLOITATION

Operations, 6-14 September

SCALE OF MILES
0   20   40   60   80   100

6

Frontier Guard Command units advanced and occupied the Poznan salient.

After the surrender at Radom, German corps were redeployed as shown on next map.

Surrendered 14 Sept.

Surrendered 11 Sept.

NAREW GROUP (part)

MODLIN and NAREW GROUP (part)

WARSAW

NORTH BOCK

THIRD KUECHLER

FOURTH KLUGE

POMORZE (part)

POZNAN

EIGHTH BLASKOWITZ

TENTH REICHENAU

SOUTH RUNDSTEDT

FOURTEENTH LIST

CRACOW (Remnants)

CARPATHIAN (Remnants)

WODRIG

The Third Army now closed in on Warsaw and the nearby fortress city of Modlin from the north and east, its I Corps beginning the siege of the Praga suburb on 16 September, while Corps Wodrig cleared the country to the east. Bock shifted the Fourth Army headquarters (its corps were divided between the Eighth and Third Armies) to his east flank. Here, it took over the XXI Corps —plus an improvised corps (*not shown*) of frontier and fortress troops—and pushed east to Bialystok. At the same time, Guderian (XIX Panzer Corps) swept south to break into the fortified city of Brest on the 14th-15th. The Brest citadel held out until 17 September, but two of Guderian's divisions had meanwhile continued south through Wlodawa. These soon established radio contact with the leading elements of Army Group South. (The short gap between them was never closed.)

The Tenth Army, regaining control of its XVI Panzer and XI Corps (lent temporarily to the Eighth Army), took over operations against Warsaw from the south and west, and against the Kutno pocket from the east. The Polish forces in the pocket made another unsuccessful attempt to escape on the 16th. The next day, the Germans attacked with heavy air support, crushing all resistance. One Polish column did break out eastward through the closing German lines into the forests south of the Vistula, but it was intercepted and destroyed by the Tenth Army. About 52,000 Poles were captured.

Other Tenth Army units fought their way into Lublin on the 17th. The Fourteenth Army had taken Przemysl on the 15th, but heavy fighting continued at Lwow and farther north. Many Polish units, government officials, and the Polish high command were attempting to push through this area into Rumania. Lwow fell on 21 September; two large pockets farther north were liquidated during this same period.

The remaining centers of resistance were Warsaw and Modlin. Realizing that an infantry assault would mean heavy losses, Hitler ordered both cities kept under artillery and Luftwaffe bombardment, while repeated demands for their surrender were made and refused. Finally, on 26 September, the Eighth Army launched an attack on Warsaw from the west, the Third Army providing artillery support. Warsaw, already facing starvation and typhoid, capitulated on 27 September, and some 140,000 Polish troops became prisoners. The Third Army and the Luftwaffe then concentrated against Modlin, which surrendered with 24,000 men on the 28th. The isolated coastal fortress of Hel withstood heavy artillery, air, and naval bombardment until 1 October.

These final operations were complicated by the Russian advance into Poland. The agreement of 23 August had secretly assigned the Russians all territory east of the Narew, San, and Vistula (later changed to all territory east of the Bug). The Russians, however, were coy about occupying eastern Poland, apparently preferring to let the Germans conquer it for them. Eventually, they advanced on 17 September, after extremely short notice. Great confusion developed, especially in the south, where some German units were hotly engaged with die-hard Polish forces and had considerable trouble extricating themselves. There were a number of minor clashes between Germans and Russians during this period, but all were settled by the local commanders.

The Polish Army made its last organized stand at Kock (*center, right*), where, after a two-day fight, Tenth Army panzer units took 17,000 prisoners on 6 October. Guerrilla warfare (against both the Germans and the Russians), however, was never completely put down, and thousands of Poles escaped to fight another day.

Even before the campaign was fully over, Hitler had begun transferring forces to the West. It had been a spectacular accomplishment, from which he wrung full propaganda value. The new Luftwaffe-panzer team had proved itself, though both members still had much to learn. The main burden of the battle, however, had fallen—all unnoticed—on the hard-marching German infantry and their largely horse-drawn artillery and trains.

Possibly the most significant result of the campaign was that Hitler began to consider himself a military genius.

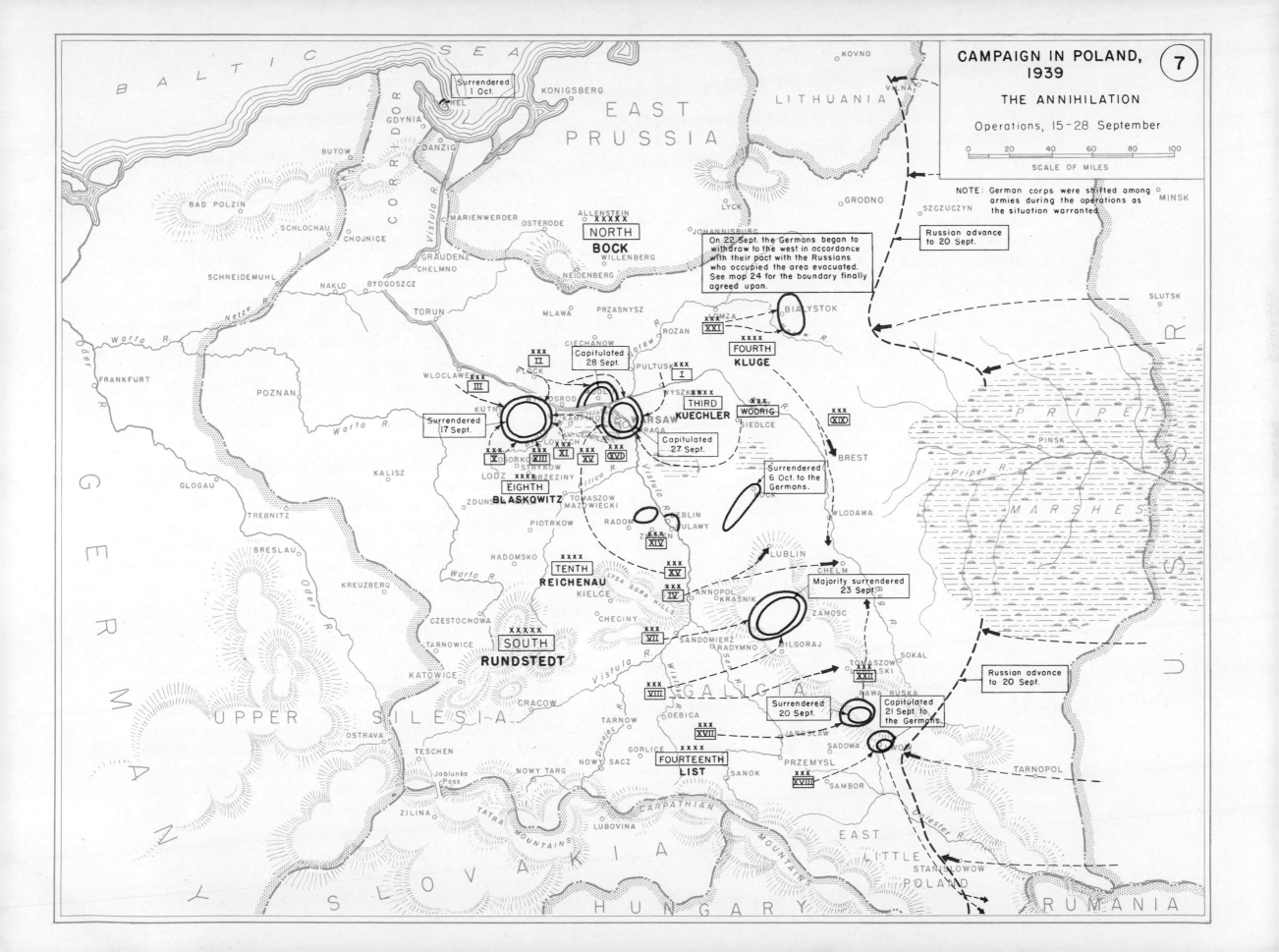

CAMPAIGN IN POLAND, 1939

7

THE ANNIHILATION

Operations, 15-28 September

0   20   40   60   80   100
SCALE OF MILES

NOTE: German corps were shifted among armies during the operations as the situation warranted.

On 22 Sept. the Germans began to withdraw to the west in accordance with their pact with the Russians who occupied the area evacuated. See map 24 for the boundary finally agreed upon.

Russian advance to 20 Sept.

Russian advance to 20 Sept.

Russian advance to 20 Sept.

Surrendered 1 Oct.

Capitulated 28 Sept.

Surrendered 17 Sept.

Capitulated 27 Sept.

Surrendered 6 Oct. to the Germans.

Majority surrendered 23 Sept.

Surrendered 20 Sept.

Capitulated 21 Sept. to the Germans.

BALTIC SEA

EAST PRUSSIA

LITHUANIA

CORRIDOR

GERMANY

SLOVAKIA

HUNGARY

RUMANIA

GALICIA

UPPER SILESIA

EAST LITTLE POLAND

PRIPET MARSHES

KOVNO
VILNA
KONIGSBERG
GRODNO
MINSK
SLUTSK
SZCZUCZYN
JOHANNISBURG
LYCK
BIALYSTOK
ALLENSTEIN
WILLENBERG
NEIDENBERG
OSTERODE
MARIENWERDER
GDYNIA
DANZIG
HEL
BUTOW
BAD POLZIN
SCHLOCHAU
CHOJNICE
GRAUDENZ
CHELMNO
SCHNEIDEMUHL
NAKLO
BYDGOSZCZ
TORUN
MLAWA
PRZASNYSZ
ROZAN
PULTUSK
CIECHANOW
PLOCK
WLOCLAWEK
KUTNO
WYSZKOW
WARSAW
PRAGA
SIEDLCE
BREST
WLODAWA
PINSK
FRANKFURT
POZNAN
KALISZ
LODZ
BRZEZINY
STRYKOW
LOWICZ
SOCHACZEW
SKIERNIEWICE
ZDUNSKA
PIOTRKOW
TOMASZOW MAZOWIECKI
RADOM
DEBLIN
PULAWY
LUBLIN
CHELM
ZAMOSC
BILGORAJ
SOKAL
GLOGAU
TREBNITZ
BRESLAU
RADOMSKO
KIELCE
CZESTOCHOWA
KREUZBERG
TARNOWICE
KATOWICE
CRACOW
TESCHEN
OSTRAVA
CHECINY
SANDOMIERZ
RADYMNO
ANNOPOL
KRASNIK
TOMASZOW LUBELSKI
RAWA RUSKA
LWOW
STANISLAWOW
TARNOPOL
JAROSLAW
PRZEMYSL
SADOWA
SAMBOR
DEBICA
TARNOW
GORLICE
SANOK
JABLUNKA PASS
NOWY TARG
NOWY SACZ
LUBOVINA
ZILINA

NORTH
BOCK

FOURTH
KLUGE

THIRD
KUECHLER

WODRIG

EIGHTH
BLASKOWITZ

TENTH
REICHENAU

SOUTH
RUNDSTEDT

FOURTEENTH
LIST

XXXXX

XXX II
XXX III
XXX I
XXXX
XXX XXMZA
XXXI
XXX
XIX
XXX XIII
XXX XI
XXX XV
XXX XVI
XXXX
XXX XIV
XXX XV
XXX IV
XXX VII
XXX VIII
XXX XXII
XXX XVII
XXX XVIII

Vistula R.
Warta R.
Netze R.
Oder R.
Warta R.
Narew R.
Bug R.
Vistula R.
Pilica R.
Lysa Gora Hills
San R.
Wisloka R.
Dunajec R.
Dniester R.
Pripet R.
Carpathian Mountains
Tatra Mountains

Finland—aptly described as a country consisting "almost entirely of natural obstacles to military operations" (*sketch a*)—was assigned to the Russian sphere of interest by the 1939 Russo-German treaty, along with Estonia, Latvia, and (later) Lithuania (*see map 1*). Hitler cynically threw these small nations to Russia as a means of keeping his temporary ally occupied while he dealt with France and England. Stalin rapidly absorbed Estonia, Latvia, and Lithuania by forcing "mutual defense" pacts upon them and then pouring in Russian troops to "defend" his new "allies." From Finland, Stalin demanded the Karelian Isthmus (*this map, bottom center*) up to Viipuri, four small islands in the Gulf of Finland, the Finnish portion of the Rybachi Peninsula (*top center*), and the use of Hango (*bottom left*) as a Russian naval and air base. These concessions, he declared, were essential for Russian security, particularly in the Leningrad-Kronstadt area. The Finns, with bitter memories of Russian misrule from 1809 to 1918, could see only that their country would be left entirely at the mercy of any future Russian aggression. They attempted negotiations. On 30 November, Stalin—also without a declaration of war—loosed his air force against Helsinki (*bottom left*) and Viipuri.

Knowing Russia to be their historical enemy, the Finns had prepared to the best of their limited means against the day the Russians would come again. Their armed forces (Army, Navy, Coast Guard) numbering approximately 300,000 were backed up by a Civic Guard (a force of 100,000, resembling the United States National Guard) and the Lotta Svärd (a 100,000-strong women's auxiliary, which took over administrative duties). They lacked heavy artillery and mechanized equipment, but were sensibly trained and armed for operations in their own land of forests, laced with lakes and swamps. The Mannerheim Line (*sketch b, bottom center*), which blocked the Karelian Isthmus, consisted of scattered strong points (groups of mutually supporting concrete pillboxes), connected by a World War I system of field fortifications. In strength, it did not compare to the German West Wall, but it had been cleverly constructed to take every advantage of the Isthmus' rugged terrain and heavy woods. In addition, there were lighter fortifications on the southern seacoast and across the roads to the northeast of Lake Ladoga. Along the rest of their eastern border, the Finns could depend only on the rough terrain.

The Finns knew that they had no hope of singlehandedly defeating Russia. They did hope, however, to hold out until other nations might be moved to come to their assistance or—that failing—to put the blood price of their conquest too high for even Muscovite stomachs.

The exact initial Russian plan remains unknown; apparently, it followed the classic Russian style—a mass onslaught along every possible avenue of approach, combined with energetic treason from within. There were to be landings on both the northern and southern coasts; air raids against Finnish communications, coupled with "terror raids" to break civilian morale; a ground attack all along the frontier; and a Communist revolution within the country.

Russian amphibious attacks along the southern coast failed dismally, with heavy losses. In the north, a combined amphibious–cross-country attack seized Petsamo and got as far as Nautsi. There, supply difficulties and one Finnish battalion stopped it for the rest of the war. Bad weather and poor Russian tactics rendered the air raids relatively ineffective. There was no revolt.

Russian attacks against the snow-cloaked Mannerheim Line, pushed with utter disregard for losses, ended in bloody failure in early February. Above Lake Ladoga, the Russians initially broke through on a wide front, but Finnish counterattacks at Pitkaranta (*lower right*) forced the surrender of a Russian division and tank brigade in February. (Another division barely held out until the fighting ended.) In other Russian operations (taken from south to north), two divisions were practically wiped out at Tolvajarvi; the Ilomantsi advance was blocked; the 54th Division, surrounded at Kuhmo, was almost destroyed; Suomussalmi was a disaster (*see map 9*); the 122d Division reached Kemijarvi, only to be chased back on the 88th Division, and the two stalled thereafter at Markajarvi.

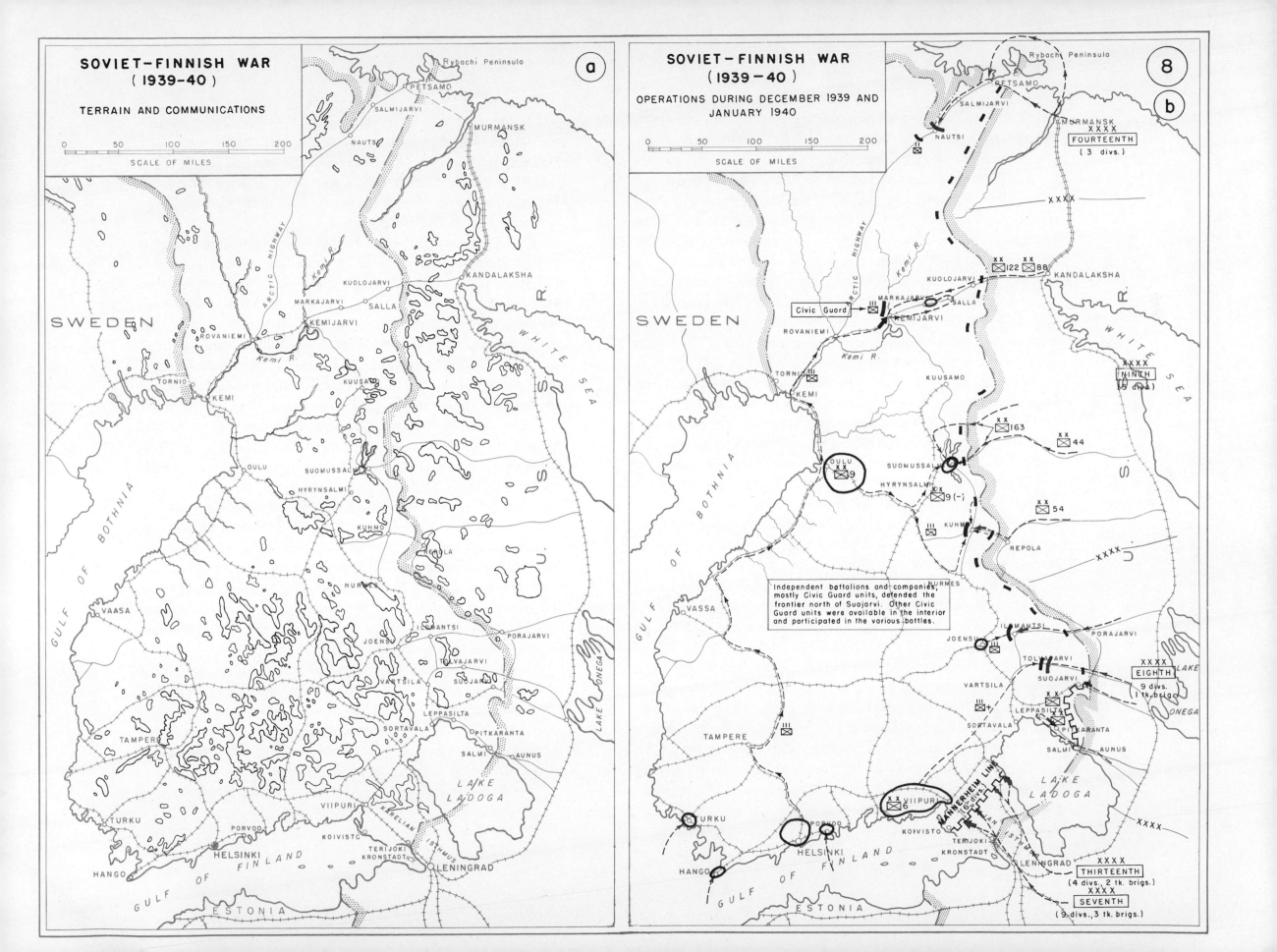

SOVIET–FINNISH WAR (1939–40)

TERRAIN AND COMMUNICATIONS

(a)

SCALE OF MILES
0   50   100   150   200

SOVIET–FINNISH WAR (1939–40)

OPERATIONS DURING DECEMBER 1939 AND JANUARY 1940

(8) (b)

SCALE OF MILES
0   50   100   150   200

Map (a) labels: Rybachi Peninsula, PETSAMO, SALMIJARVI, MURMANSK, NAUTSI, SWEDEN, ARCTIC HIGHWAY, Kemi R., KUOLOJARVI, KANDALAKSHA, MARKAJARVI, SALLA, KEMIJARVI, ROVANIEMI, WHITE SEA, Kemi R., KUUSAMO, TORNIO, KEMI, U.S.S.R., OULU, SUOMUSSALMI, HYRYNSALMI, GULF OF BOTHNIA, KUHMO, REPOLA, NURMES, JOENSU, ILOMANTSI, PORAJARVI, VAASA, TOLVAJARVI, SUOJARVI, VARTSILA, LEPPASILTA, SORTAVALA, PITKARANTA, TAMPERE, SALMI, AUNUS, LAKE LADOGA, LAKE ONEGA, TURKU, VIIPURI, KARELIAN ISTHMUS, KOIVISTO, PORVOO, TERIJOKI, KRONSTADT, LENINGRAD, HELSINKI, HANGO, FINLAND, GULF OF FINLAND, ESTONIA

Map (b) labels and unit markers: Rybachi Peninsula, PETSAMO, SALMIJARVI, MURMANSK XXXX FOURTEENTH (3 divs.), NAUTSI, SWEDEN, Kemi R., KUOLOJARVI 122 88, KANDALAKSHA, Civic Guard, MARKAJARVI, SALLA, KEMIJARVI, ROVANIEMI, WHITE SEA, NINTH (5 divs.), TORNIO, KEMI, KUUSAMO, OULU 9, 163, 44, SUOMUSSALMI, HYRYNSALMI 9(–), 54, KUHMO, REPOLA, NURMES, GULF OF BOTHNIA, VASSA, ILOMANTSI, JOENSU, PORAJARVI, TOLVAJARVI, VARTSILA, SUOJARVI, EIGHTH 9 divs. 1 tk. brig., LEPPASILTA, PITKARANTA, SORTAVALA, TAMPERE, SALMI, AUNUS, LAKE LADOGA, LAKE ONEGA, TURKU, VIIPURI 6, MANNERHEIM LINE, KOIVISTO, PORVOO, TERIJOKI, KRONSTADT, HELSINKI, FINLAND, HANGO, LENINGRAD THIRTEENTH (4 divs., 2 tk. brigs.), SEVENTH (9 divs., 3 tk. brigs.), GULF OF FINLAND, ESTONIA

Independent battalions and companies, mostly Civic Guard units, defended the frontier north of Suojarvi. Other Civic Guard units were available in the interior and participated in the various battles.

The Battle of Suomussalmi is a military classic—an outstanding example of what can be done by a handful of free men, intelligently trained, equipped, and led.

The Russian 163d Division entered Finland in two columns (*see map* 8b). Fresh from the Ukraine, it was neither trained nor equipped for subarctic service. Its heavy weapons and equipment were handicaps on the poor, one-way Finnish frontier roads. The terrain around Suomussalmi (*this map*) was a monotonous jumble of lake, forest, and swamp, where a stranger easily became lost. The woods were choked with four feet of snow, restricting movement and visibility; the temperature was frequently –40° F.; blizzards were common; daylight lasted only a few hours. The frozen lakes were the only open areas.

Local Civic Guard units—invisible in their white uniforms, swift and silent on their skis—haunted the Russian columns. Supply vehicles and field kitchens were their favorite targets—at forty below, a hot meal can mean the difference between life and death. Everything that could give the enemy shelter was burned.

This was the first phase of the Finnish *motti* tactics (*motti* translates roughly as a stack of wood, ready for chopping)— the reconnaissance and blocking of the enemy's movements. The second phase consisted of attacks to split up his immobilized forces; the third, their annihilation.

On 7 December, the two columns of the 163d Division linked up at Suomussalmi. Weather had blinded its supporting aerial reconnaissance; its own reconnaissance detachments seldom returned. While the Russians paused, the infantry units of the Finnish 9th Division began arriving. These attacked on the 11th, without waiting for their artillery. The Russians held doggedly to Suomussalmi, but the Finns blocked the road east of that village and turned the road north of it into one long ambush, through which supply was almost, but not quite, impossible. While awaiting the rest of the 9th Division, the Finns maintained constant pressure on the freezing, starving Russians, gradually wearing them down.

Then, on 22 December, the Russian 44th Division, reportedly a crack motorized unit, advanced on Suomussalmi from the east. A few companies of ski troops checked it, harassing it so savagely that its commander concluded he was being attacked by superior forces. Unable to deploy off the narrow road, he set up a perimeter defense along it.

On Christmas Eve, both Russian divisions attempted to break out, apparently with some air support. An elastic, aggressive Finnish defense—including tank traps cut in the frozen lakes, and hidden wire entanglements buried in snow—kept them penned. Meanwhile, the rest of the 9th Division arrived. Its artillery—shooting accurately from its detailed maps, while the Russian guns, lacking both maps and aerial observation, fired almost blindly—completed the discomfiture of the huddled Russians. On the 27th, the Finns attacked Suomussalmi from all directions; the next day, the Russians there tried to break out northward along Lake Kiantajarvi. Most of them died trying. By the 30th, the rest of the 163d Division, to the west of the lake, was mopped up.

Then it was the 44th Division's turn. The Finns plowed a road through the snow along a lake to the south of its position. From the road, trails led forward to assembly areas (where shelter and hot food were available) and on to attack positions opposite weak points in the Russian line. Assaulting suddenly from these, the Finns systematically cut the 44th Division into smaller and smaller groups, mopping up each one in turn, though the Russians resisted tenaciously to the last.

In this battle, the Russians had had a numerical superiority of about three to one. Their losses were approximately 27,500 killed or frozen to death. An additional 1,300 Russians—as well as more than fifty tanks and all the artillery and equipment of two divisions—were captured. The Finns had 900 killed and 1,770 wounded.

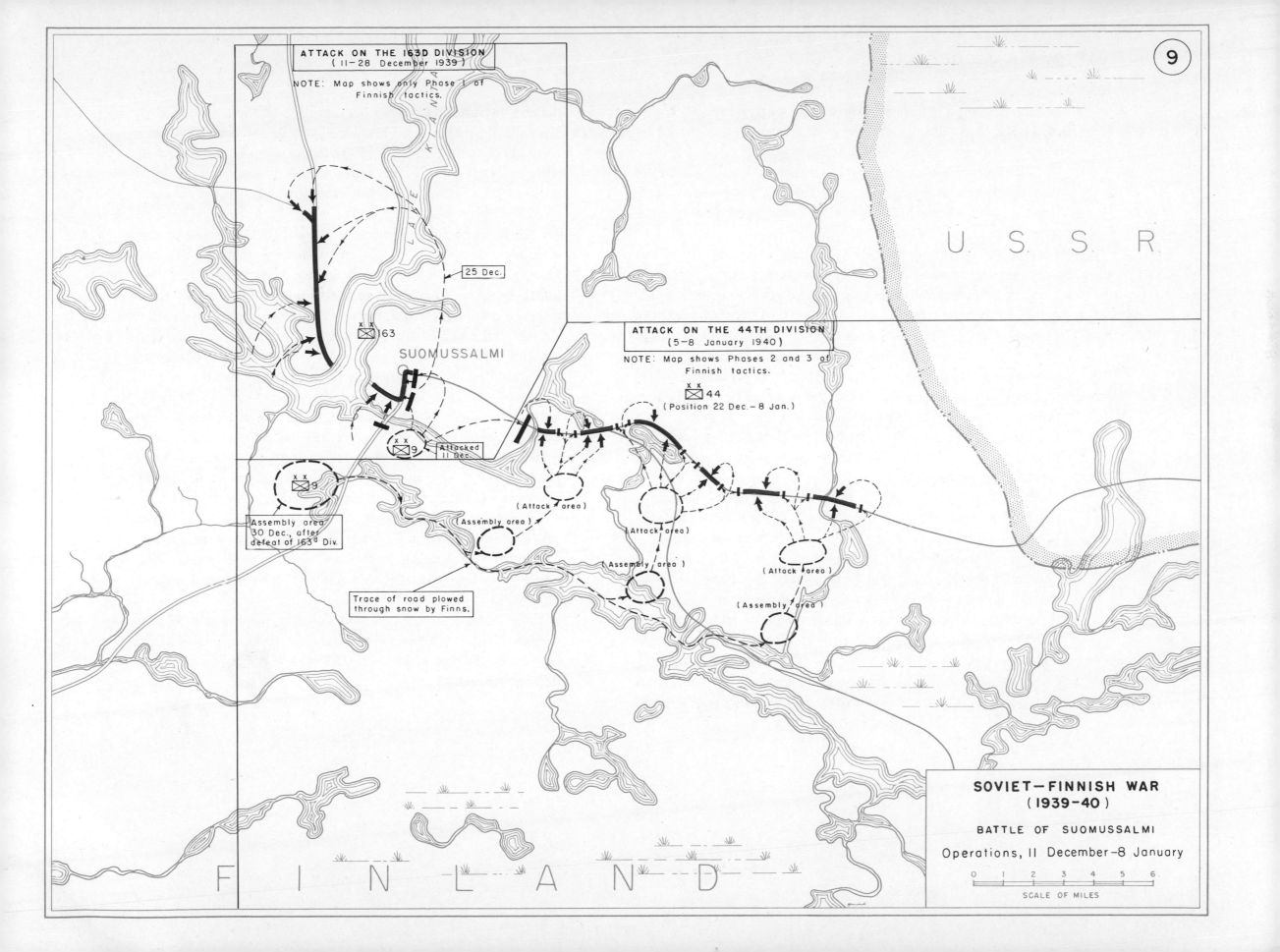

ATTACK ON THE 163D DIVISION
(11–28 December 1939)

NOTE: Map shows only Phase 1 of
Finnish tactics.

25 Dec.

XX 163

SUOMUSSALMI

ATTACK ON THE 44TH DIVISION
(5–8 January 1940)

NOTE: Map shows Phases 2 and 3 of
Finnish tactics.

XX 44
(Position 22 Dec.–8 Jan.)

XX 9

Attacked
11 Dec.

XX 9

Assembly area
30 Dec., after
defeat of 163ᵈ Div.

(Attack area)

(Assembly area)

(Attack area)

(Attack area)

(Assembly area)

(Attack area)

(Assembly area)

Trace of road plowed
through snow by Finns.

U. S. S. R.

F I N L A N D

9

SOVIET—FINNISH WAR
(1939–40)

BATTLE OF SUOMUSSALMI

Operations, 11 December–8 January

0 1 2 3 4 5 6

SCALE OF MILES

If Suomussalmi is a triumph of free men in arms, the final battles of the Karelian Isthmus are a grim reminder that naked courage alone is not enough.

The Russian failures during December and early January in this area were humiliating and costly. Infantry was pushed against Finnish machine guns in "human sea" attacks; tank-infantry-artillery coordination was poor.

After their early defeats, the Russians regrouped. It was evident that they could not match the Finns in forest fighting; the limited communications net along Finland's eastern frontier would not allow them to crowd in enough troops to overwhelm superior Finnish quality with sheer weight. The Karelian Isthmus, however, was a more promising theater. Leningrad's excellent rail connections would enable them to support as many divisions there as they desired. Furthermore, victory here would be an immediate threat to the heart of Finland.

The resulting operation was not subtle. Beginning on 1 February, there were four or five major attacks each day, wave after wave crowding forward, tanks frequently towing the infantry in armored sleds. Supporting artillery fire is reported as having reached the rate of 300,000 shells a day—one of the heaviest bombardments ever recorded. Large numbers of supporting aircraft were also employed. Thirteen divisions made the main effort between Lake Kuolema and Lake Muola. Casualties were extremely high but, characteristically, of no particular importance to the Russian high command, which was prepared to expend its men, tanks, and ammunition until the Finns could no longer endure the strain.

Eventually, on 13 February, the defenders gave way near Summa. The Russians pushed ahead, against stubborn rear-guard actions, to Johannes (*upper left*), cutting off the key fortress of Koivisto. By 1 March, the Finnish right wing and center had been forced back to the outskirts of Viipuri, and a Russian attack across the ice of the Gulf of Finland from Johannes was threatening this position. The Finnish Army was exhausted, whereas the Russians were still committing fresh units.

All hope of foreign intervention on behalf of Finland had vanished. Some 11,500 foreign volunteers—mostly Swedish, Danish, and Norwegian, but including a Hungarian battalion and a few Americans—had reached Finland, but most of these required considerable training and, therefore, never saw action. France and England had sent weapons and were preparing to dispatch a 100,000-man expeditionary force. Norway and Sweden, however, clinging desperately to their neutrality, would not permit its passage. Finland therefore was forced to yield. The terms inflicted on her—roughly, the original Russian demands—appeared lenient, but probably were inspired by the consideration that foreign intervention might still be possible if matters were pushed too far. Also, the prospect of a guerrilla war in the interior of Finland could hardly have been attractive to the Russians.

Ironically, Russia profited from the very magnitude of her mistakes and defeats in Finland. Hitler and many of his generals concluded that Russian leadership, weapons, and tactics were hopelessly inferior—that Russia could be easily defeated without any special preparations.

The Finns lost about 25,000 killed or missing and 43,500 wounded. Russian losses, as usual, are not accurately known; the best estimates give at least 200,000 killed and a proportionate number wounded.

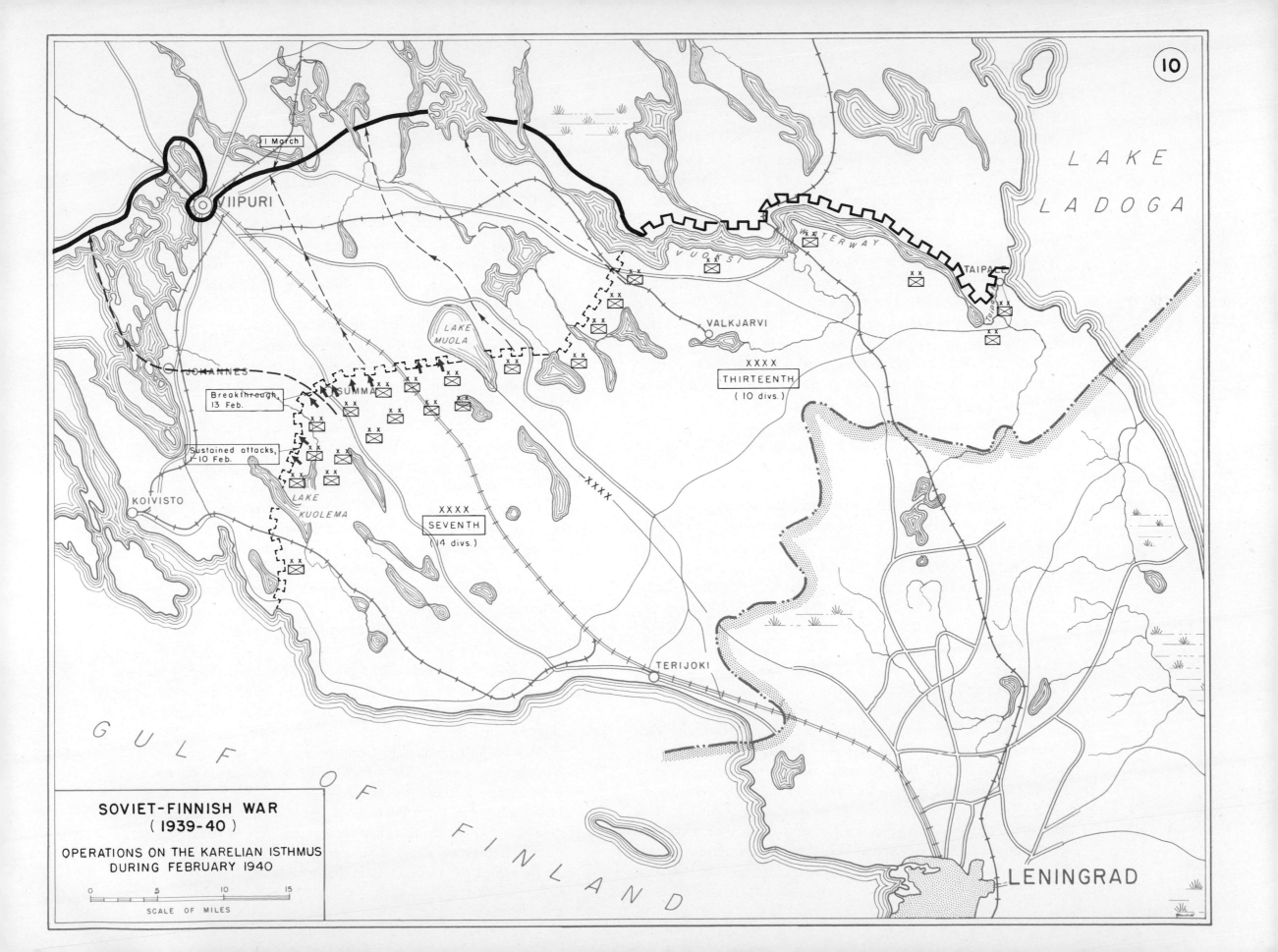

LAKE LADOGA

LAKE MUOLA

VUOKSI

WATERWAY

TAIPA[LE]

VIIPURI

I March

Breakthrough, 13 Feb.

Sustained attacks, 1-10 Feb.

JOHANNES

SUMMA

VALKJARVI

XXXX
THIRTEENTH
(10 divs.)

KOIVISTO

LAKE KUOLEMA

XXXX
SEVENTH
(14 divs.)

TERIJOKI

GULF OF FINLAND

LENINGRAD

(10)

SOVIET-FINNISH WAR
(1939-40)

OPERATIONS ON THE KARELIAN ISTHMUS
DURING FEBRUARY 1940

0   5   10   15

SCALE OF MILES

The German conquest of Norway (*sketch* a) was a daring and imaginative operation.

Remembering the World War I Allied naval blockade, German naval officers urged that bases along the Norwegian coast would give them greater freedom of action. Moreover, the German armament industry depended upon steady imports of Swedish iron ore. Much of this went from Kiruna (*top right*) by rail to Narvik; there, German freighters, hugging the coast to remain within Norwegian territorial waters, picked it up. Fearful that the British might block this traffic—or even occupy Norway as a base for future operations against Germany—Hitler decided, by early February, to seize Norway himself. A small joint staff began preliminary planning. On 21 February, General Nikolaus von Falkenhorst was designated commander of the army forces involved.

The German task force weighed anchor late on 7 April. (By coincidence, the British were then preparing to mine the entrance to Narvik harbor.) Scattered naval clashes during 8 April indicated a major German operation, but bad weather hindered British reconnaissance. Though warned, the Norwegian government failed to act decisively: coastal defense units were alerted, but were forbidden to lay defensive mine fields; nothing was done to defend key airfields; reservists were called up by ordinary mail. (Despite excited contemporary accounts, Vidkun Quisling's tiny pro-German party contributed very little to Norway's downfall.)

Early on 9 April, German warships put small, lightly equipped army units ashore at Oslo, Kristiansand, Bergen, Trondheim, and Narvik. Airborne troops seized Sola airport and Stavanger. Meanwhile, Denmark was swiftly overrun, to give the Luftwaffe advance bases to support the Norwegian operation.

Though surprised, the Norwegians fought. At Oslo, the German naval expedition was stopped, with heavy losses, by the coast defenses. This delay enabled the Norwegian government and royal family to escape, but Falkenhorst met the crisis by airlifting troops into Fornebu airport hours ahead of schedule. This handful of Germans overawed Oslo until the harbor forts were knocked out. Kristiansand and Bergen were captured after lively fighting; Stavanger, Trondheim, and Narvik fell quickly. A second wave, composed of supply ships and tankers, followed the naval task forces with heavy weapons and equipment. Subsequent naval engagements—at Narvik and elsewhere—cost the Germans heavily in warships and supply vessels, but Falkenhorst poured in reinforcements by sea and air, particularly into the Oslo area. German columns pushed out (*sketch* b) to link up their isolated forces and crush the mobilizing Norwegian Army.

This became a race against Allied efforts to reinforce the Norwegians. Rapid Luftwaffe utilization of Danish and Norwegian airfields gave the Germans air superiority from the start. Cooperation between Falkenhorst and the local German air and naval commanders was generous and effective. By 16 April, they had practically cleared southern Norway, and the British Navy had been forced by constant air attacks to withdraw its major ships north of Trondheim. Meanwhile, Allied troops—hastily assembled and poorly equipped—had landed at the minor ports of Andalsnes and Namsos in an effort to recapture Trondheim.

Almost immediately, however, the Andalsnes column was diverted southward to reinforce the Norwegians. En route (19 April), it captured a pocket of German paratroopers at Dombas, but was turned back just south of Lillehammer. The Namsos column was defeated (21 April) by the Trondheim garrison at Steinkjer. Despite stubborn Allied resistance in both cases, German superiority in armor, air support, artillery, training, and equipment was too great. By 3 May, the Allies had been forced out of central Norway; Norwegian forces remaining there soon surrendered.

Fighting continued around Narvik (*sketch* a). Allied forces recaptured that town, driving the Germans back into the mountains, but were withdrawn early in June because of the desperate situation in France.

This campaign brought Germany immense prestige, insured her supply of iron ore, and—by winning air and submarine bases in Norway—loosened the British blockade. The serious naval losses inflicted on the Allies by land-based German aircraft clearly demonstrated for the first time the vulnerability of naval vessels unprotected by air power. Conversely, the Norwegian campaign also crippled the German Navy for months.

Note: The Norwegian 6th Division (Map a, top right) had 7,000 men. On Map b, upper left, the correct Allied strengths in the large blue box are 13,000 at Namsos and Andalsnes, 25,000 at Narvik.

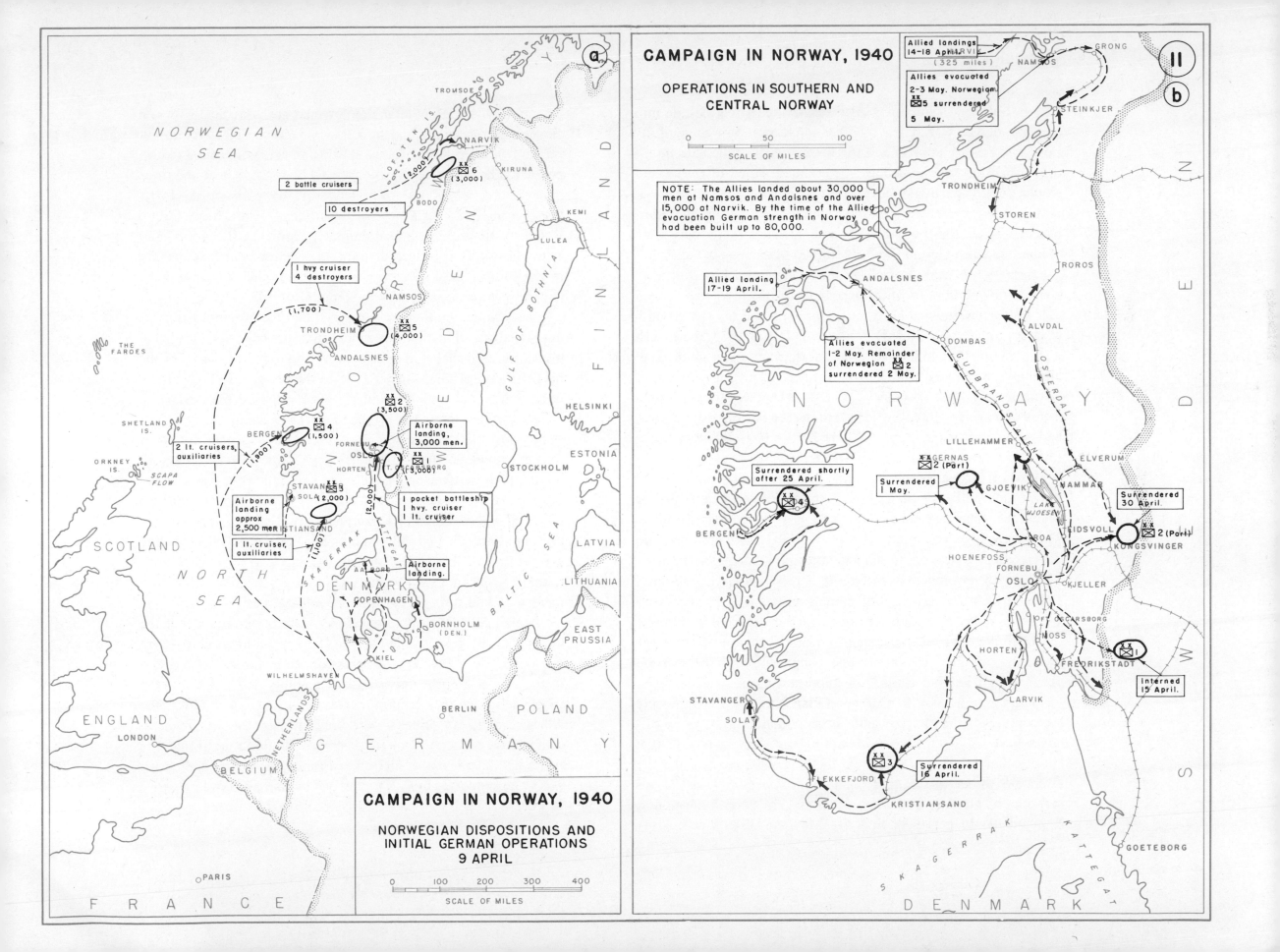

Hitler's invasion of Poland goaded France and Great Britain into a declaration of war. Their mobilization, however, was painfully slow, and neither appreciated the necessity for immediate industrial expansion. An immediate, determined Allied offensive into western Germany might have afforded Poland some relief, but only a weak, extremely tentative effort was made in the Saarbrücken area (*lower right*). (The slight gains made here were obliterated when German troops returned to the west in October.)

Instead, the Anglo-French planners relied upon blockade, economic strangulation, fortifications, and a defensive strategy which —it was believed—would exhaust Germany and lay the groundwork for an ultimate Allied offensive. As late as 1938, the British were planning that, in the event of a future war, only a small expeditionary force would be sent to France; naval and air power (strategic bombing specifically) were to be the decisive instruments of war. By 1939, the need for a larger British ground force had been accepted; in May, 1940, the British Expeditionary Force (BEF) in France numbered 394,165.

Except for patrol clashes, the fall and winter of 1939-40 passed uneventfully. In October, Hitler invited the Allies to negotiate a peace; upon being rebuffed, he resolved to crush them. The Army high command (known as OKH—Oberkommando des Heeres) was less optimistic and argued for a defensive posture. The controversy raged from October, 1939, through February, 1940, with Hitler insistent, his generals reluctant, and events conspiring to delay each date of attack set by the Führer. Finally, the offensive was postponed until spring, because of the poor prevailing weather and a possible compromise of the existing plan through Belgian capture of important German documents.

The German plan in October (Plan YELLOW) sought only the capture of the Belgian and Dutch channel coast, as an air-naval base for operations against England. It was based upon Hitler's fear of Allied occupation of the Low Countries and the attendant threat to the vital Ruhr (*see map 64*b)—just as his invasion of Norway had been prompted, in part, by fear that England would get there first. By May, at Hitler's and Army Group A's instigation, Plan YELLOW had been drastically revised as shown (*this map*) and now had a decisive objective: to cut off and destroy Allied forces north and west of Sedan (*lower center*). The major effort, spearheaded by seven panzer and three motorized divisions, was to be made by Army Group A (forty-five divisions) through the Ardennes Forest, while Army Group B (thirty divisions) applied frontal pressure in the north, and Army Group C (nineteen divisions)) remained on the defensive in the south. The Luftwaffe was to provide tactical air support and furnish airborne troops to Army Group B.

Meanwhile, the French, convinced that the Maginot Line was impregnable and that the Ardennes was impassable to large formations, disposed their forces as shown. The fortifications from the northern end of the Maginot Line to the coast were built at isolated points and were particularly weak opposite the Ardennes. Dutch fortifications—the Grebbe-Peel Line being the strongest —tied into the intricate system of rivers and depended for effectiveness upon flooding of the lowlands. The Belgians likewise relied upon the rivers and canals and had built Fort Eben Emael (*center, right*) to forestall a World War I type of drive through Liége. The strict neutrality maintained by Belgium and Holland prevented coordinated Allied planning; but the Allies, expecting a repetition of the Schlieffen Plan, prepared to move their four leftmost armies forward to the Dyle Line in Belgium if the Germans attacked through the Low Countries.

Numerically, the opposing armies were about equal, but the Germans had been combat-tested and—most important—were influenced by a few key, progressive leaders who appreciated tactical air power, the importance of mobility and speed, and the shock action of massed armor. Germany had 2,439 tanks, the Allies, 2,689; but Hitler's were concentrated for use in mass, while those of the Allies were dispersed all along the front. The Allies had 2,000 combat aircraft in France; the German offensive was to be supported by 3,700. Lastly, German *esprit* was superior to that of their foes—particularly the French.

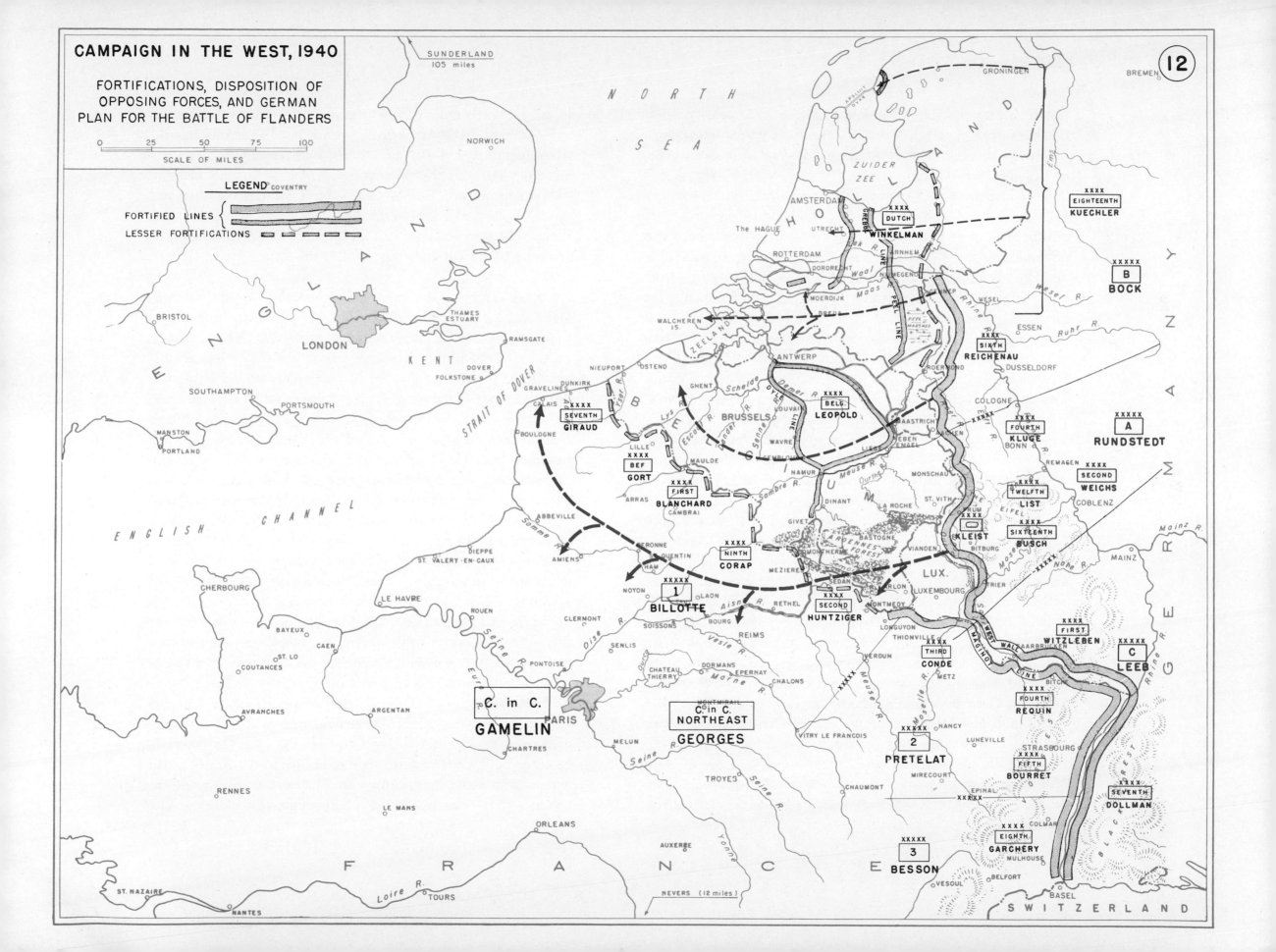

CAMPAIGN IN THE WEST, 1940

FORTIFICATIONS, DISPOSITION OF
OPPOSING FORCES, AND GERMAN
PLAN FOR THE BATTLE OF FLANDERS

SCALE OF MILES
0   25   50   75   100

LEGEND

FORTIFIED LINES
LESSER FORTIFICATIONS

Shortly after midnight, 9-10 May, Hitler struck. Intensive aerial bombardments of principal Allied airfields were followed at dawn by swift ground attacks across the border and airborne assaults in Holland and Belgium.

The conquest of Holland took only five days. Kuechler's Eighteenth Army (about ten divisions, including one armored) advanced in three columns (*see map 12*), while paratroops and air-landed elements landed at The Hague, Rotterdam, Moerdijk, and Dordrecht, seizing airfields and key bridges. Recovering from their surprise, the Dutch struck back at the airheads, but the Germans, superbly supported by the Luftwaffe, held on to most of their gains. The northernmost column reached Afsluit Dyke late on 11 May. The center column reached the Grebbe Line late on 10 May; here the Dutch held until the 13th, when events farther south forced their withdrawal. The southern column, Kuechler's main effort, seized the Gennep railroad bridge intact, and by nightfall on 10 May had forced Dutch evacuation of the Peel Line. On the 12th, panzer units of the southern column linked up with the airborne elements holding the key bridges at Moerdijk and Dordrecht (*this map, top center*). En route—at Breda—they had brushed aside advance elements of the French Seventh Army which had moved north to support the Dutch. On 13 May, the French withdrew to Antwerp, and the Dutch government departed for England. Isolated, and their cities threatened with destruction, the Dutch surrendered on 14 May. That day, the bulk of the French Seventh Army began moving south, as shown.

Army Group B's main attack was made by the Sixth Army (twenty-three divisions, including two armored) through the restricted Maastricht-Liége area. In a brilliantly executed operation, the Germans utilized airborne forces to capture Fort Eben Emael and key bridges over the Albert Canal, thus allowing armored elements to drive toward Liége and the Dyle River. On the 11th, the Belgians withdrew to the Dyle Line (*dashed blue line*), to which position the French and British advanced on 12 May. At Hannut (*center*), on the 13th, panzer elements de-

feated a French armored division, and by 15 May the Germans were probing the Dyle Line. Between Namur and Antwerp, the Allies had thirty-five of their best divisions (including practically all of the BEF), in the mistaken belief that the German main attack would be here. But, by that night, it was clear that the real threat lay farther south on the Ardennes front, where the weak French Second and Ninth Armies had been shredded. The Allies now elected to withdraw westward to the Escaut River (*center, left*).

While Bock was overrunning Belgium, the powerful German main attack force (Army Group A) moved by the three routes shown to the Meuse, arriving there by nightfall, 12 May. French cavalry and the rugged Ardennes terrain had only imperceptibly slowed the march. Leading the advance were General Evald von Kleist's Panzer Group (five panzer divisions under Guderian and Reinhardt, and three motorized divisions) and General Hermann Hoth's Panzer Corps (two panzer divisions). On the 13th, the river was forced at Houx (*center*), Monthermé, and Sedan, and the next day the bridgeheads were expanded against frantic French resistance and repeated air attacks. German armor poured across, and Guderian, securing high ground to the south, turned westward toward Montcornet (*lower center*). French counterattacks at Donchery and Stonne (*lower center, blue arrows*) were unsuccessful. That night, General André-Georges Corap ordered a withdrawal, but it was a futile gesture. His army and the left of the Second were shattered and unable to form a new line—a fifty-mile gap yawned invitingly. By the 16th, German spearheads had reached the line shown, and Rundstedt's infantry divisions were making forced marches to close up.

Meanwhile, on 12 May, General Maurice Gustav Gamelin had ordered divisions from his general reserve to the Ardennes area, but, moving slowly, they had been too late. On the 15th, he ordered divisions from the right of his line to the critical sector and activated the Sixth Army headquarters to command the troops which, being assembled, would supposedly close the gap.

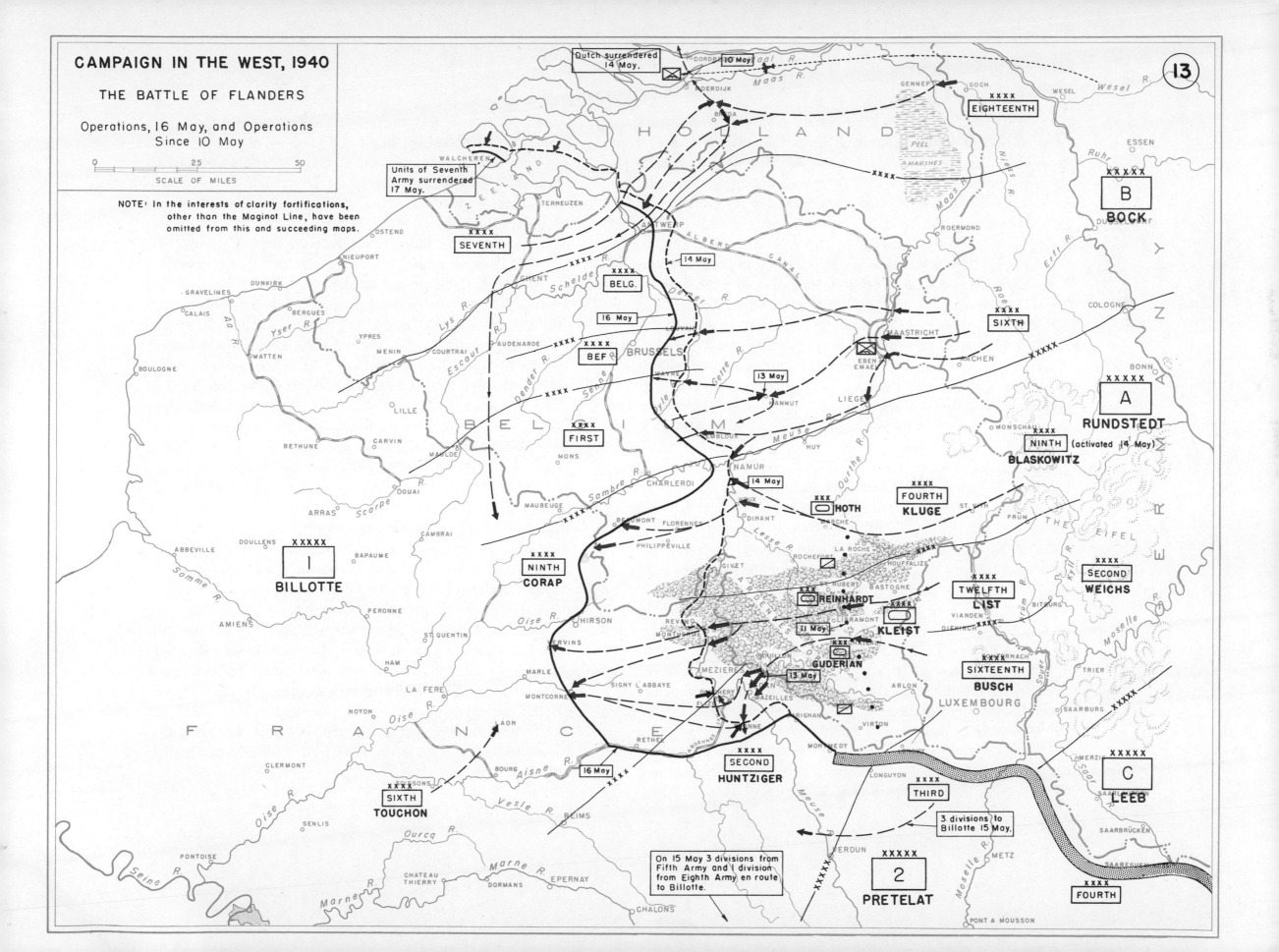

CAMPAIGN IN THE WEST, 1940

THE BATTLE OF FLANDERS

Operations, 16 May, and Operations
Since 10 May

SCALE OF MILES
0 — 25 — 50

NOTE: In the interests of clarity fortifications, other than the Maginot Line, have been omitted from this and succeeding maps.

Dutch surrendered 14 May.

Units of Seventh Army surrendered 17 May.

On 15 May 3 divisions from Fifth Army and 1 division from Eighth Army en route to Billotte.

3 divisions to Billotte 15 May.

Fear of a French counterstroke from the Verdun-Châlons area (*bottom center*) unnerved Army Group A and OKH on 17 May. As a result, Guderian, impatient to drive his divisions to the coast, was peremptorily ordered to halt. After a violent altercation with Kleist (which List had to come forward to resolve), Guderian received permission to conduct a "reconnaissance in force." He hurled his divisions westward and by 18 May had reached Péronne (*center, left*). It was during this advance that the French Ninth Army made one last futile effort to halt the onslaught. Also, General Charles de Gaulle launched counterattacks against Guderian's south flank, but his weakened armored division could not hold the limited gains made. Meanwhile, to the north, Hoth's Panzer Corps, spearheaded by Rommel's division, drove forward and seized Cambrai. In Belgium, Bock's depleted armies—his armor had already been dispatched to aid Rundstedt's drive to the coast—followed up the retreating Allies and by 18 May had reached the Dender River.

By the 19th, infantry from the Twelfth and Sixteenth Armies had lined the southern flank of the breakthrough as far west as Montcornet, and OKH now lifted the restrictions on Kleist's advance. Guderian, closely followed by the motorized infantry corps of Kleist's group, raced along the Somme River toward Abbeville. Late on the 20th, that town surrendered, and the corridor to the sea, though tenuous, was a reality. The BEF, its communications with Cherbourg severed, was forced to switch its base to the Dunkirk area. By the 21st, Kleist's other panzer corps had reached the line shown. Guderian had seized bridgeheads across the Somme River; the motorized infantry had closed up to relieve the panzers on the south flank; and infantry from the Second and Ninth Armies was rapidly moving westward to strengthen the extended south flank.

But on the north side of the penetration, German success was slower and was achieved at greater cost. After crossing the Meuse, in contrast to Kleist's drive in the south, Hoth still had to fight his way through the border fortifications. Rommel burst through relatively easily, but Kluge's following infantry corps had some bloody fighting in the "mop-up." Then, as they pushed toward Cambrai, the French First Army put up a vigorous resistance and took a heavy toll. Thus, when Guderian plunged forward on the 19th, Hoth restrained Rommel at Cambrai until more infantry could close up to protect the north flank. Early the next morning, Rommel pushed his leading elements to the vicinity of Arras. After closing up his division, he resumed his westward advance the afternoon of the 21st, soon colliding with the British attack being made by "Frankforce."

As Rundstedt's troops exploited their decisive breakthrough and the BEF withdrew to the Escaut River line, Lord Gort had realized that the French First Army could not protect his right and rear. Thus he had stationed some of his communications-zone troops in the gap between the Somme and the Scarpe—hoping to slow Guderian—and had begun organizing the canal line from Douai on the Scarpe to Watten (*upper left*). He also formed "Frankforce" (parts of two infantry divisions and a tank brigade) and gave it the mission of reinforcing Arras and blocking east-west roads to the south of it. On the 19th, General Maxime Weygand relieved General Gamelin. Now London ordered the BEF to move to the Somme, but Gort convinced his superiors of the impracticability of the move. The Allied high command then urged a joint French-British attack south toward the Somme, and the French agreed to aid Frankforce with an attack toward Cambrai. Frankforce was too weak to do more than bloody Rommel's nose. Hoth massed his other divisions and forced the British back to Arras on the 22d. The British attack disturbed OKH, however, and led to undue emphasis being placed upon securing Arras. Reinforcements were sent to the area, and Bock was ordered to transfer the main Sixth Army effort farther south to the Maulde area (*left center*).

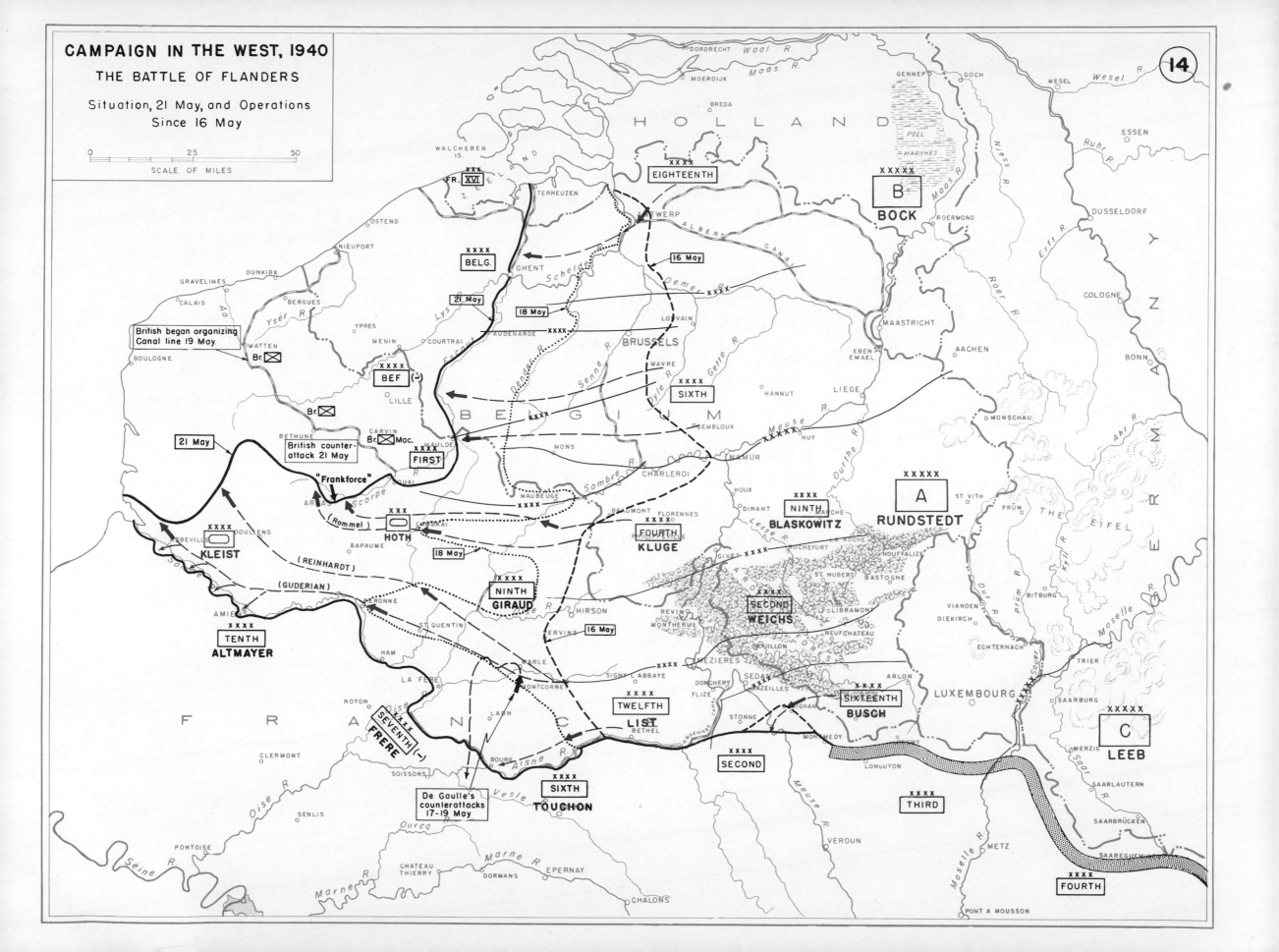

CAMPAIGN IN THE WEST, 1940
THE BATTLE OF FLANDERS

Situation, 21 May, and Operations
Since 16 May

SCALE OF MILES
25   50

14

HOLLAND

DORDRECHT   Waal R.
MOERDIJK   Maas R.
BREDA
GENNEP   GOCH   WESEL   Wesel R.
WESEL
ESSEN
DUSSELDORF
ROERMOND
WALCHEREN IS.
OSTEND
NIEUPORT
TERNEUZEN
ANTWERP
ALBERT CANAL
MAASTRICHT
Maas R.
Niess R.
Ruhr R.
COLOGNE
BONN
AACHEN
EBEN EMAEL
FR. XVI
EIGHTEENTH
BOCK   B
BELG.
GHENT
Scheldt R.
Demer R.
16 May
LOUVAIN
DUNKIRK
GRAVELINES
CALAIS
BERGUES
Aa R.
Yser R.
YPRES
MENIN
COURTRAI
Lys R.
21 May
AUDENARDE
18 May
Dender R.
Senne R.
BRUSSELS
WAVRE
Dyle R.
Gette R.
HANNUT
LIEGE
Meuse R.
Ourthe R.
MONSCHAU
British began organizing Canal line 19 May.
WATTEN
BOULOGNE
Br.
BEF (−)
LILLE
Br.
CARVIN
Br. Mac.
British counter-attack 21 May.
VAULDE
FIRST
SIXTH
GEMBLOUX
HUY
NAMUR
MONS
CHARLEROI
Sambre R.
Meuse R.
DINANT
HOUX
NINTH
BLASKOWITZ
RUNDSTEDT   A
ST. VITH
MARCHE
THE EIFEL
21 May
"Frankforce"
ARRAS
(Rommel)
HOTH
Scarpe R.
DOUAI
Scheldt R.
MAUBEUGE
BEAUMONT   FLORENNES
FOURTH
KLUGE
LA ROCHE
HOUFFALIZE
BASTOGNE
Prüm R.
PRÜM
BITBURG
VIANDEN
DIEKIRCH
21 May
DOULLENS
KLEIST
ABBEVILLE
BAPAUME
18 May
NINTH
GIRAUD
GIVET
ST. HUBERT
NEUFCHATEAU
SECOND
WEICHS
REVIN
MONTHERME
LIBRAMONT
BOUILLON
ECHTERNACH
Our R.
Sauer R.
LUXEMBOURG
TRIER
Moselle R.
(REINHARDT)
(GUDERIAN)
PERONNE
AMIENS
TENTH
ALTMAYER
ST. QUENTIN
HAM
Somme R.
HIRSON
VERVINS
16 May
MEZIERES
SIGNY L'ABBAYE
DONCHERY
FLIZE
SEDAN
BAZEILLES
ARLON
SIXTEENTH
BUSCH
SAARBURG
Saar R.
MERZIG
LEEB   C
NOYON
SEVENTH
FRERE (−)
Oise R.
LAON
MARLE
MONTCORNET
TWELFTH
LIST
RETHEL
Aisne R.
STONNE
Canal
CARIGNAN
MONTMEDY
LONGUYON
Ardennes Canal
SAARLAUTERN
SAARBRUCKEN
CLERMONT
De Gaulle's counterattacks 17-19 May
SOISSONS
Vesle R.
BOURG
SIXTH
TOUCHON
SECOND
Meuse R.
VERDUN
METZ
THIRD
Moselle R.
SAAREGUEMINES
SENLIS
PONTOISE
Seine R.
Ourcq R.
Marne R.
CHATEAU THIERRY
DORMANS
EPERNAY
CHALONS
FOURTH
PONT A MOUSSON
FRANCE
BELGIUM
GERMANY

Having driven Frankforce back into Arras on 22 May, Hoth pressed his attack northward. On that day, the Allied Supreme War Council approved the "Weygand Plan"—converging attacks on 23 May toward Bapaume (*left center*) from both Arras and the Somme. The decision was made without knowledge of the complete failure of the Frankforce attack on the 21st and of the tremendous power the Germans had crammed into the salient west of Cambrai-Péronne. Under these circumstances, the plan was decidedly unrealistic. On the 23d, Hoth forced the British back to Béthune; that day, the French counterattacks on the Somme failed. Still—as late as the 25th—Weygand persisted in his plan.

Meanwhile, Guderian (lacking part of his force, held back by OKH direction) fought his way against stiff resistance northward to Boulogne and Calais. Boulogne was captured on the 23d, but Calais, recently reinforced from England, held out until the 27th. By 24 May, five panzer divisions were exerting pressure on the canal line (*dotted blue line, dated 26 May*). Gort had reinforced this makeshift line with combat-tested troops from the Escaut line, but the chances of successfully holding the panzers appeared slim. Now, however, Hitler and Rundstedt intervened, and halted the attack of the armored elements for two days, allowing the British to stiffen their canal defenses and to begin a withdrawal to the Dunkirk beachhead. The halt order, one of the most controversial decisions of the war, was issued by Hitler over the protests of OKH; but the record reveals that Rundstedt—probably influenced by Kluge and Kleist—had recommended to the Führer on the 24th that the infantry continue the attack alone. The reasons for this incredible halt order are not clearly established, but it seems that Rundstedt, more cautious than the panzer leaders, was concerned with readying his troops for the campaign in southern France. Hitler considered the Dunkirk area unsuitable for armor; furthermore, he seemed almost frightened by the magnitude of his success. Underestimating the British, he considered the Luftwaffe capable of completing their destruction.

In the north, King Leopold had withdrawn by the night of the 23d to the Lys River and had taken over the front south to Menin, in order to allow the BEF to create a reserve with which to implement its part in the Weygand Plan. On 24 May, Bock launched a powerful offensive with his Sixth Army, which, on the 25th, created a gap between the Belgian right and the British left. Gort now committed all his available forces—none remained for the Weygand Plan—in an unsuccessful effort to close the gap. On the 26th, Gort decided to withdraw to Dunkirk, and that night the Royal Navy was ordered to begin evacuation of the BEF. That day, Leopold warned the Allies of the impending collapse of the Belgian Army. The next day, as his army was being pushed back toward Ostend, he asked Hitler for terms; on the 28th, he surrendered unconditionally.

Late on 26 May, Hitler's halt order was lifted, and the panzer divisions attacked the canal line. Near the coast, the improved defenses and flooded country held Guderian to negligible gains; but in the better terrain near Béthune Rommel's penetration, linking up with a Sixth Army column, sealed the fate of half of the French First Army, whose leaders had rebelled at the idea of withdrawal. By 30 May, most of the British and some French were within the Dunkirk perimeter; the previous day, most of the German armor had been withdrawn, and the reduction of the pocket was left to the Luftwaffe and ten infantry divisions under Kuechler's control. Now the well-organized evacuation proceeded under the cover afforded by the Royal Air Force, which, in general, kept the Luftwaffe from having its accustomed free hand. By 5 June, when the Germans finally reached Dunkirk, the Allies had evacuated 338,226 British, French, and Belgian troops.

South of the Somme, meanwhile, the French were lethargically preparing defenses along the river lines for the coming Battle of France. The Allies launched counterattacks at Abbeville and Amiens in an attempt to wipe out the German bridgeheads, but achieved only temporary gains.

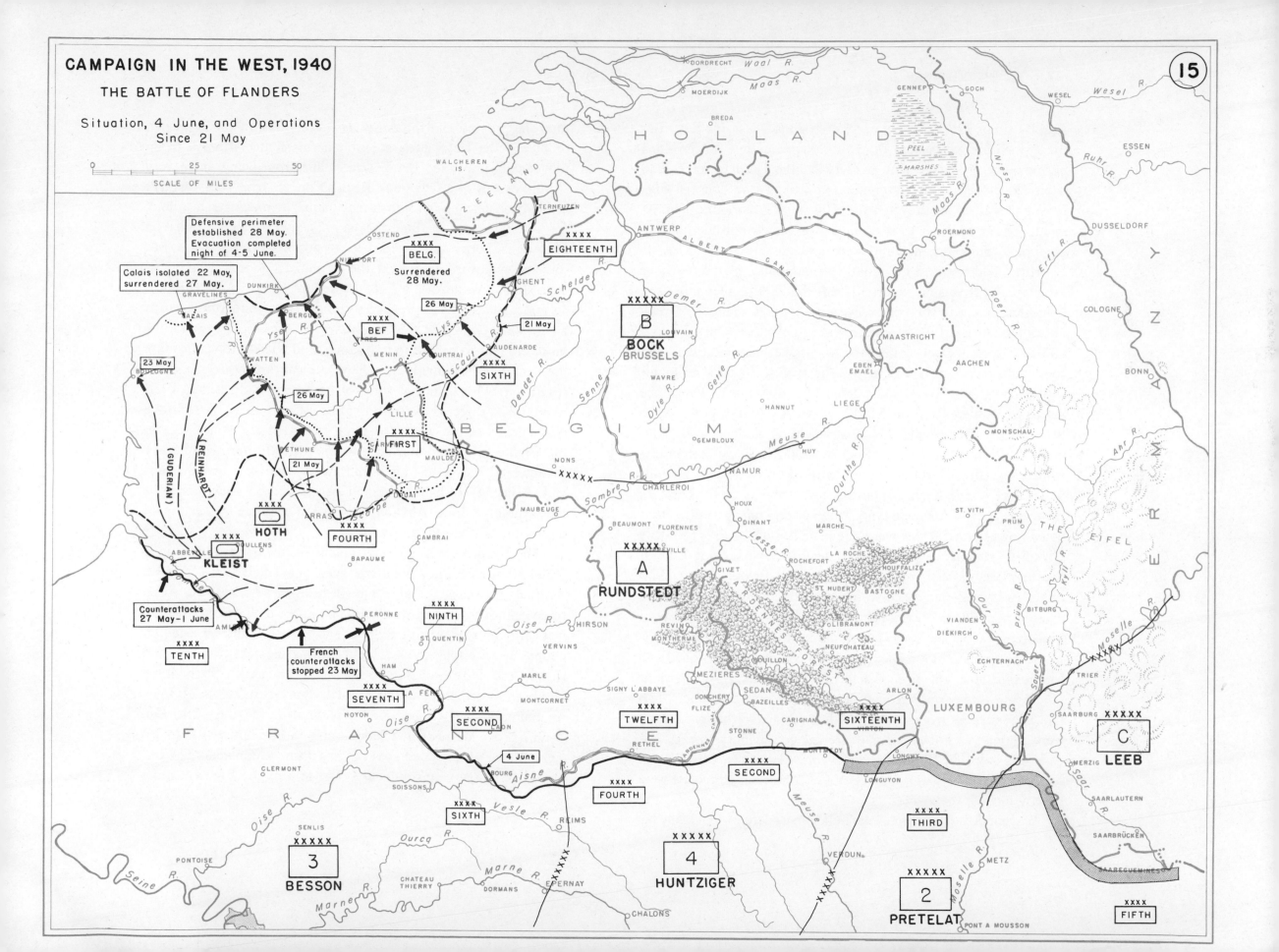

CAMPAIGN IN THE WEST, 1940
THE BATTLE OF FLANDERS

Situation, 4 June, and Operations
Since 21 May

SCALE OF MILES

Defensive perimeter
established 28 May.
Evacuation completed
night of 4-5 June.

Calais isolated 22 May,
surrendered 27 May.

Counterattacks
27 May–1 June

French
counterattacks
stopped 23 May

The Battle of France began early on 5 June—just one day after the British had completed the Dunkirk evacuation. In the short period since disengagement at Dunkirk, the German forces had been redeployed along the Somme and the Aisne (*dashed blue line*) and readied for the offensive. This was a remarkable achievement, for, in addition to the shifting of forces, considerable re-equipping and reorganization were necessary.

Hitler had received the initial German battle plan as early as 20 May, but it was not finalized until the 28th. Under this plan, Rundstedt (about forty-five divisions) would make the main attack east of Paris on 9 June to separate Army Groups 2 and 4 and to pin the former against the Maginot Line. Guderian, with four panzer divisions, was to spearhead this attack. The major secondary attack, by Bock (about fifty divisions), was to be launched west of Paris on 5 June. It was to drive rapidly to the Seine River, after which a decision would be made as to the ultimate direction of its attack. Bock was allocated six panzer divisions, two directly subordinated to the Fourth Army and four under Kleist; also, the Eighteenth Army, mopping up the Dunkirk area, was part of his command. Another secondary attack, itself consisting of two attacks, was to be launched on 14 June by Army Group C (twenty-four divisions) against the Maginot Line at Saarbrücken (*lower right*) and Colmar (*bottom right*). This attack was designed to link up with the main attack in the encirclement of the French behind the Maginot Line. Thus, about 120 divisions, backed up by twenty-three others in general reserve, would participate in the operations. To combat this seasoned and formidable host, the French had only about sixty-five divisions (including three armored), of which seventeen were either Maginot Line fortress troops or second-line reserve formations. Many were understrength, and some needed equipment; morale was generally low. The British had units equivalent to two divisions in line on the lower Somme. Under these conditions, the odds were greatly against the Allies.

Weygand had attempted to build up a defense in depth behind the Somme and the Aisne. However, lack of time and matériel and the Luftwaffe's constant harassment of French troop movements prevented the Weygand line from being made very strong, except in a few areas. Bock's Fourth Army took one day to establish a firm grip south of the Somme, then plunged headlong for the Seine. By 9 June, the panzers and General Erich von Manstein's corps had reached it. Now the German armor was directed westward to cut off the French IX Corps, which had been slow in withdrawing from the Somme west of Abbeville. On 12 June, Rommel accepted the surrender of the bulk of this corps at St. Valéry-en-Caux. The Sixth Army found the Weygand line more difficult to penetrate in its zone, and Kleist's tanks, leading the assault, were unable to achieve a clean breakthrough. As a result, on 8 June, though some of his troops had reached Clermont, OKH directed the shifting of Kleist's group eastward to the Ninth Army sector, where the going seemed easier. (On the 11th, the Eighteenth Army moved into line directly north of Paris.) Meanwhile, Weygand—his Tenth Army shattered, and the Seventh Army falling back—ordered Army Group 3 to withdraw to the Seine on 8 June. Already, the French were reeling, and now, on 9 June, Rundstedt attacked.

The French Fourth Army, defending in depth and making judicious use of local counterattacks, prevented List's Twelfth Army from securing a large enough bridgehead across the Aisne to accommodate the panzers until late in the day, when Guderian was able to cross west of Rethel. The French launched armored counterattacks against his columns during the next two days and slowed their advance. But, to the west, the French Sixth Army had been forced back, and the Fourth Army, bending its left back to maintain contact, became overextended. On the 12th, Guderian broke through at Châlons and raced southward; to his right, Kleist's armor had crossed the Marne at Château Thierry, and also was surging southward. The fate of the French armies was sealed.

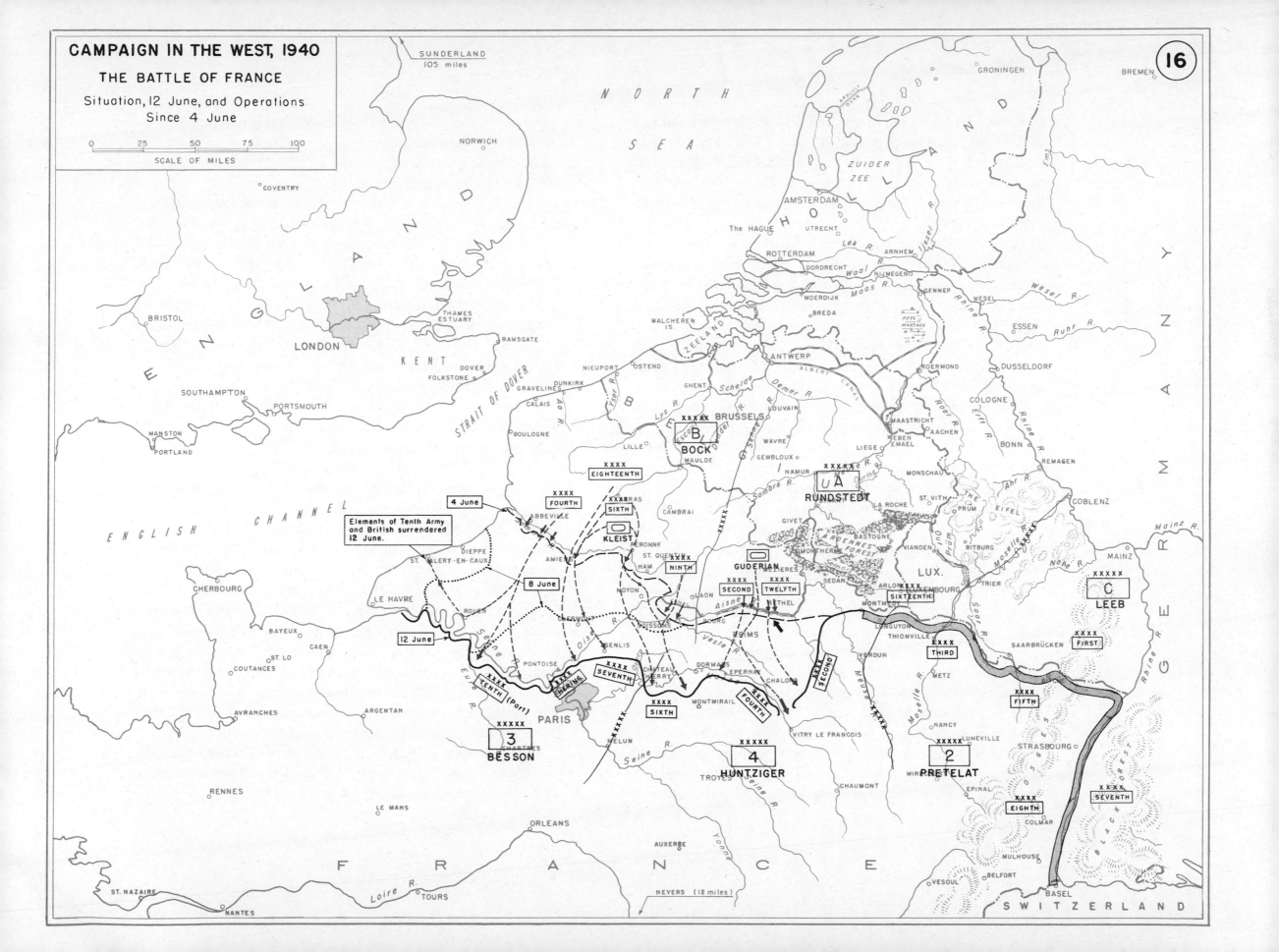

16

CAMPAIGN IN THE WEST, 1940
THE BATTLE OF FRANCE
Situation, 12 June, and Operations
Since 4 June

SCALE OF MILES

Elements of Tenth Army and British surrendered 12 June.

4 June

8 June

12 June

With Kleist's forcing of the Marne and Guderian's drive southeast from Châlons, the French retreat became a rout. The Germans at once launched the pursuit. As early as 12 June, Weygand had requested his government to seek an armistice, but not until Pétain became premier on the 16th was a surrender considered favorably.

Meanwhile, Bock's armies fanned out to the southwest while Rundstedt moved south and southeast. Hoth's panzer divisions overran Brittany and Normandy, arriving at Brest and Cherbourg on the dates shown. At Cherbourg, Rommel had a brisk encounter with the British, who were evacuating troops debarked there as recently as 14 June, when hope had still flickered for the French cause. In the meantime, Weygand had withdrawn his troops south of Paris on the 13th, and the Eighteenth Army moved into the city the following day. By the 17th, the remnants of the French armies had reached the general line shown (*dotted blue line*), but they had neither the time nor the inclination to organize it for effective defense. On that date, panzer elements from Kleist's and Guderian's groups (both now operating under Rundstedt) reached the Loire River at Nevers (*lower center*) and the Swiss border, respectively. Thus the French troops in and behind the Maginot Line were isolated. Guderian now turned his divisions north and east to assist in herding these forces into a pocket around Épinal. Kleist's troops drove on southward, as shown.

Between Hoth's panzers to the west and Kleist's group to the east, the infantry corps of five German armies pressed southward in a solid mass. (For purposes of clarity, only routes of representative corps are shown.) Farther east, List's Twelfth Army followed Guderian, and the Sixteenth Army swung in behind the Maginot Line to link up with the First Army, which had broken through the line at Saarbrücken on 14 June. The following day, the Seventh Army also broke through to assist in the ensuing encirclement operations. The Army Group C attacks on the Maginot Line, made against a weakened garrison lacking mobile reserves, were

extremely successful and less costly than might have been expected. The Germans utilized large quantities of artillery, bypassed strong points, and achieved surprise at Colmar by an unorthodox midmorning attack.

The last week of the campaign was an anticlimax. Pétain asked for an armistice on the 17th. It was signed with Germany on the 22d, but hostilities did not cease until after Italy had likewise signed on 25 June. Mussolini, eager to share in the spoils, had declared war on 10 June. But it was the 20th before his generals were able to attack. Stalled at the border by the much weaker but more determined French, the Italians begged Hitler to advance German troops from Grenoble toward the border. Only a halfhearted effort was made, and Italy went to the conference table without military conquests.

So ended the campaign in the West. In six weeks, the Allied armies in Western Europe had been shattered and pursued with a vengeance reminiscent of Napoleon.

Hitler now sought to inveigle Britain into suing for peace. When rebuffed, he ordered plans prepared for an invasion of England (Operation SEA LION). A plan was developed—and changed several times—amidst constant bickering between the Army and Navy; but it was never destined to be implemented, because the vital requirement for air superiority could not be met. In the critical Battle of Britain (10 July–31 October) the Luftwaffe was unable to sweep the Royal Air Force from the sky. On the contrary, Göring's vaunted air force—operating against newly developed radar and superior fighter planes, and employed less skillfully than it might have been—suffered a decisive defeat. The courage and sacrifices of the valiant handful of British fighter pilots probably spared England the ordeal of an invasion.

The attention of Hitler was now drawn eastward, where his partner in the dismemberment of Poland posed the only threat to German dominance of the Continent.

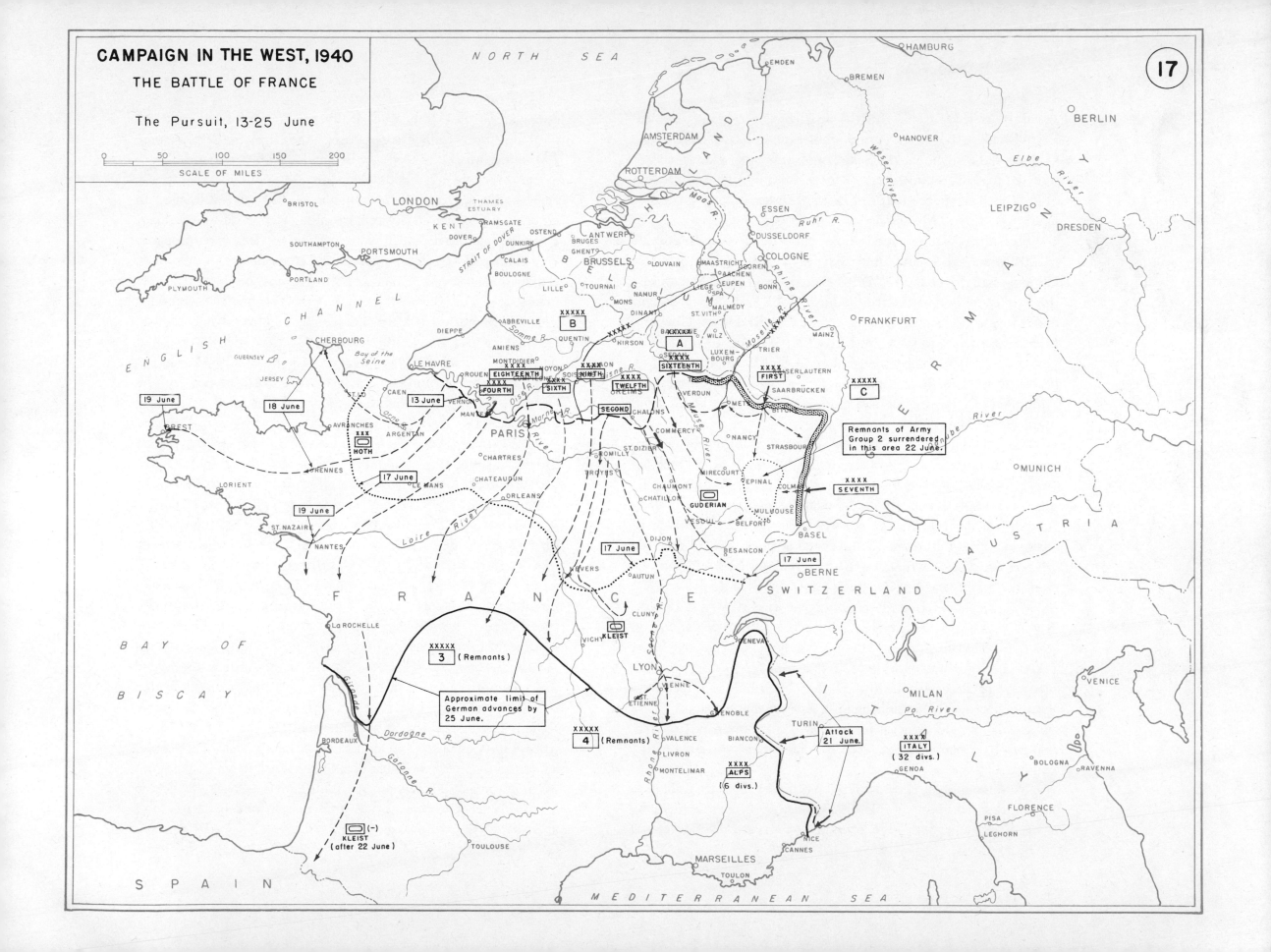

CAMPAIGN IN THE WEST, 1940
THE BATTLE OF FRANCE
The Pursuit, 13-25 June

SCALE OF MILES
0 50 100 150 200

17

NORTH SEA

ENGLISH CHANNEL

Remnants of Army Group 2 surrendered in this area 22 June.

Approximate limit of German advances by 25 June.

Attack 21 June.

BAY OF BISCAY

MEDITERRANEAN SEA

SPAIN

FRANCE

SWITZERLAND

AUSTRIA

GERMANY

BELGIUM

HOLLAND

ITALY

KLEIST (-) (after 22 June)

As early as July, 1940, Hitler—urged by Göring and Admiral Erich Raeder—began to consider operations in the Mediterranean against the British. At the same time, however, planners were directed to study an invasion of Russia. With the disastrous defeat of the Luftwaffe in the Battle of Britain, Hitler decided to transfer operations to the Mediterranean.

This new theater of operations had already seen action. A month after Italy's entry into the war, Italian troops based in Ethiopia had driven a token British force from British Somaliland (*inset sketch*) and had seized Gallabat and Kassala in the Sudan, and Moyale in Kenya. In Libya, Marshal Rodolpho Graziani, after months of prodding by Mussolini, invaded Egypt (*lower center*) on 13 September, but halted at Sidi Barrani to build an elaborate advance base. (This operation, as well as General Sir Archibald Wavell's subsequent offensive shown here, is discussed in the text of map 74.)

Hitler's concept of operations in the Mediterranean encompassed the seizure of Gibraltar, to be followed in 1941 by an Italian drive (stiffened by a German panzer corps) to the Nile. Such a plan—dependent upon Spain's cooperation and Vichy French resistance to British moves in North Africa—would virtually bar Britain from the Mediterranean. But General Francisco Franco was a hard bargainer. He desired major territorial concessions for Spain, and the German plan was stalled. In June, while the Wehrmacht (German Armed Forces) was involved in France, Russia had seized Bessarabia (*top center*) from Rumania. In August, when Bulgaria and Hungary clamored for like privileges, Hitler coerced Rumania into ceding parts of Dobrudja to the former, and of Transylvania to the latter. Then Italy and Germany jointly guaranteed Rumania against further transgressions. These upheavals brought General Ion Antonescu to power in Rumania, and on 7 October—at his request—German troops entered the country.

Now an indignant Mussolini, piqued by Hitler's unilateral action, decided upon an operation of his own which he had considered for some time—the conquest of Greece. Having seized Albania in 1939, Italy was ideally positioned for an invasion. On 28 October, Italian troops crossed the Greek border (*see map 19*). Hitler was vexed, for now Britain—committed to aid Greece in the event of aggression—had an excuse to move into the Balkans. From Greece, British bombers could strike at Rumanian oil fields, one of Germany's prime sources. Hence, on 4 November, Hitler directed that plans for an invasion of Greece be prepared (*see maps 20-21*). This necessitated movement through other Balkan countries, so Hitler applied pressure on Hungary, Rumania, and Yugoslavia to join the Axis. The first two complied in late November, 1940. Bulgaria, which had meanwhile allowed German troops to move secretly to the Greek border, did not join openly until 1 March, 1941. Yugoslavia joined on 25 March, but two days later an anti-German government seized power. The Germans feverishly revised their plans and scheduled Yugoslavia for invasion also (*see maps 20-21*).

In October, 1940, the British occupied Crete. In November, Mussolini suffered the humiliation of being repulsed by the much weaker Greeks. Royal Navy aircraft raided his timid fleet in its Taranto refuge (*this map, left center*), crippling half of it; and Wavell drove Graziani west to Agedabia. Franco, noting the British resurgence, refused to cooperate, and the Gibraltar scheme was dropped. In March, 1941, the British moved 50,000 troops into Greece; earlier, they had established air bases at Athens and Larissa, within bomber range of the Rumanian oil fields around Ploesti. Hitler now moved to eject the British from Greece.

Except for reverses in Greece (*see maps 20-22*) and in North Africa (*see maps 74-75*), the British successfully consolidated their positions in 1941. In East Africa, operating from the Sudan (*this map, inset sketch, blue arrows*), they liberated Ethiopia, Italian Somaliland, and Eritrea from the Italians; off Cape Matapan (*center, left*), the Italian fleet was soundly thrashed; in Iraq, a German-inspired revolt unseated the pro-British government but was put down by a sorely pressed Wavell; and in Syria, the hostile Vichy French government was forcibly removed from power—again by Wavell's troops.

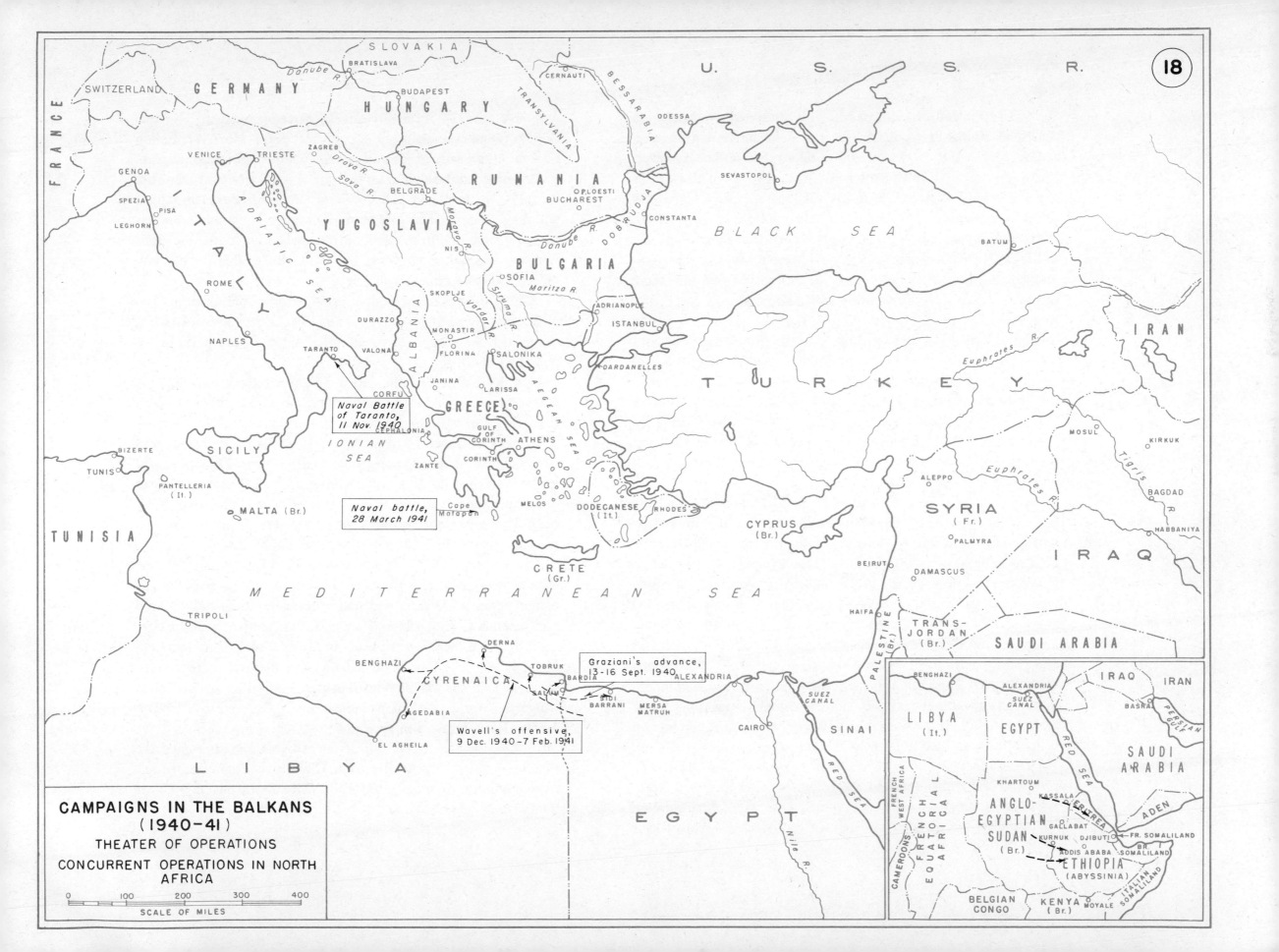

18

SLOVAKIA

FRANCE GERMANY

SWITZERLAND

Danube R.

BRATISLAVA

HUNGARY

BUDAPEST

CERNAUTI

U. S. S. R.

TRANSYLVANIA

BESSARABIA

ODESSA

VENICE TRIESTE

ZAGREB

GENOA

Drava R.

Sava R.

YUGOSLAVIA

SPEZIA

PISA

LEGHORN

BELGRADE

RUMANIA

O P LOESTI
BUCHAREST

Morava R.

Danube R.

DOBRUDJA

SEVASTOPOL

BLACK SEA

CONSTANTA

BATUM

ROME

ADRIATIC SEA

NIS

BULGARIA

I T A L Y

DURAZZO

NAPLES

TARANTO

VALONA

ALBANIA

SKOPLJE

SOFIA

Maritza R.

Vardar R.

Struma R.

MONASTIR

FLORINA

ADRIANOPLE

ISTANBUL

SALONIKA

IRAN

Naval Battle
of Taranto,
11 Nov. 1940

CORFU

JANINA

GREECE

LARISSA

AEGEAN SEA

DARDANELLES

T U R K E Y

Euphrates R.

MOSUL

CEPHALONIA

SICILY

IONIAN
SEA

ZANTE

GULF
OF
CORINTH

ATHENS

CORINTH

KIRKUK

BIZERTE

TUNIS

PANTELLERIA
(It.)

MALTA (Br.)

Naval battle,
28 March 1941

Cape
Matapan

MELOS

DODECANESE
(It.)

RHODES

CYPRUS
(Br.)

ALEPPO

Euphrates R.

SYRIA
(Fr.)

Tigris R.

BAGDAD

HABBANIYA

IRAQ

TUNISIA

CRETE
(Gr.)

M E D I T E R R A N E A N   S E A

PALMYRA

BEIRUT

DAMASCUS

TRIPOLI

HAIFA

PALESTINE
(Br.)

TRANS-
JORDAN
(Br.)

SAUDI ARABIA

DERNA

BENGHAZI

CYRENAICA

TOBRUK

SALUM

Graziani's advance,
13-16 Sept. 1940

BARDIA

SIDI
BARRANI

ALEXANDRIA

MERSA
MATRUH

SUEZ
CANAL

AGEDABIA

EL AGHEILA

Wavell's offensive,
9 Dec. 1940-7 Feb. 1941

CAIRO

SINAI

Nile R.

RED SEA

L I B Y A

E G Y P T

CAMPAIGNS IN THE BALKANS
(1940-41)
THEATER OF OPERATIONS
CONCURRENT OPERATIONS IN NORTH
AFRICA

0   100   200   300   400
SCALE OF MILES

BENGHAZI

ALEXANDRIA

SUEZ
CANAL

IRAQ

IRAN

BASRA

PERSIAN
GULF

LIBYA
(It.)

EGYPT

SAUDI
ARABIA

RED SEA

CAMEROONS

FRENCH
WEST AFRICA

FRENCH
EQUATORIAL
AFRICA

KHARTOUM

ANGLO-
EGYPTIAN
SUDAN
(Br.)

KASSALA

GALLABAT

KURNUK

ERITREA

DJIBUTI

ADEN

FR. SOMALILAND

BR.
SOMALILAND

ADDIS ABABA

ETHIOPIA
(ABYSSINIA)

BELGIAN
CONGO

KENYA
(Br.)

MOYALE

ITALIAN
SOMALILAND

Soon after the fall of France, Mussolini initiated a propaganda campaign aimed at establishing a pretext for an Italian invasion of Greece, but the Greeks refused to offer provocation. However, Mussolini seems to have preferred an attack on Yugoslavia as offering greater strategic advantages. Knowing this would require German assistance, he sought Hitler's opinion in July, 1940. With Hitler's emphatic refusal, Mussolini concentrated on events in Libya; but by August his eyes again were on Greece. His commander in Albania, General Visconti Prasca, assured him there would be no difficulty in securing Corfu and coastal Epirus (*bottom left*). However, Marshal Pietro Badoglio, Mussolini's chief of staff, disagreed and insisted upon sending four more divisions to Albania, making a total of nine there. (He actually believed twenty were needed to overrun Greece.) On 13 October, Mussolini decided to invade Greece, and Prasca's plan for securing Epirus was approved; the second phase was to be a drive on Athens. Seven Italian divisions were organized into two armies, while two other divisions stayed in northern Albania to watch the Yugoslavs.

Meanwhile, Greece continued to avoid provocation and did not mobilize. General John Metaxas, the premier, had only three and a half active divisions when the Italians struck on 28 October, after an ultimatum of three hours. These troops were disposed to guard the few passes through the mountains along the Albanian frontier. Mobilization of Greece's remaining divisions proceeded as rapidly as possible. Greek equipment was below Italian standards; there were shortages of antitank and antiaircraft weapons and transport. Metaxas had no tanks and only 160 obsolete aircraft. But Greek morale was high; the Greeks were skilled mountain fighters and they had good natural defensive positions. Their plan was to hold the Italians along the border until the completion of mobilization, then to launch a counteroffensive.

The Italians attacked at four points (*heavy red arrows*). The southernmost thrust reached the Kalamas River within a week. Had this success been exploited rapidly, Prasca might have gotten his one armored division into terrain suitable for action. But it was not, and Greek counterattacks forced a retreat. The two center Italian columns were initially successful. However, Italian neglect of security measures in moving through the mountain defiles afforded the skillful Greeks the opportunity to attack from the hills on the flanks. The Italians, suffering heavy casualties, withdrew. The advance of the northernmost Italian column was stopped short of Florina and Kastoria when its communications were endangered. By 8 November, Mussolini's offensive had collapsed, and the Greeks had seized the initiative.

On 3 November, the first Royal Air Force contingent arrived in Greece. By mid-November, as the Greeks drove into Albania, the British air groups struck at Italian airfields and ports in Albania.

On 18 November, the Greeks captured Ersek, cutting the main Italian lateral route, and on the 22d they took Koritsa. With the fall of Pogradec on 9 December, the Italians pulled their left flank back as shown (*dashed red line*). In the south, the Greeks were equally successful, seizing Porto Edda on 6 December and Himara on the 23d. But, by now, the shortage of supplies began to hamper them, and Italian resistance stiffened. The small RAF contingent labored to provide direct support to the heroic Greeks, who had been fighting in the face of Italian air attacks.

By 1 March, 1941, fighting had stabilized along the line shown. Mussolini, chagrined at his setback, had twice changed commanders in Albania and had relieved Badoglio. He poured reinforcements into Albania (by mid-March, there were twenty-eight divisions there, opposing about fifteen Greek divisions), and on 9 March the Italians launched a second offensive. After a week of slight gains, it was obvious that they had failed again. But in Bulgaria there were ominous indications of German troop movements. The Greeks, well aware of the danger of a German drive into Macedonia, shifted troops from Albania and shortened the line so that it ran generally from Himara to Pogradec. Hitler, having considered sending aid to the Albanian front, now felt it unnecessary.

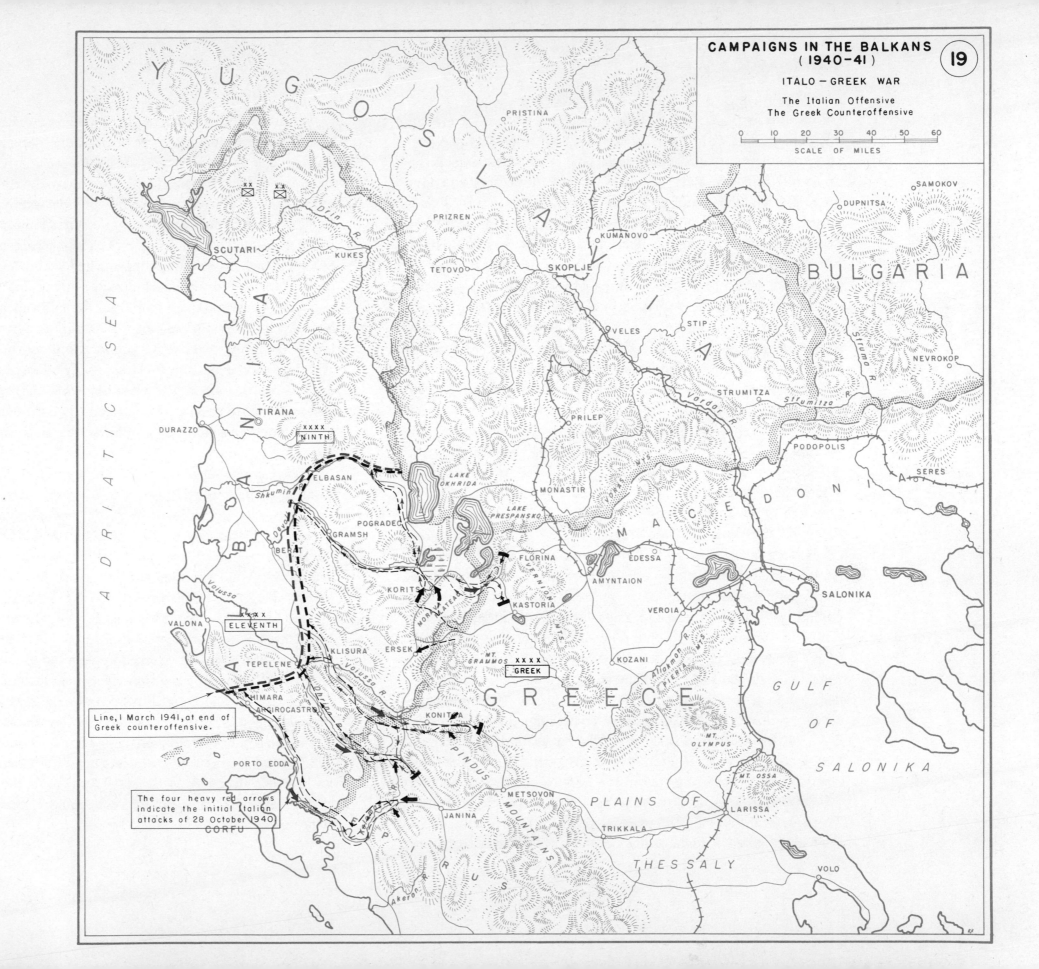

CAMPAIGNS IN THE BALKANS
(1940-41)

19

ITALO — GREEK WAR

The Italian Offensive
The Greek Counteroffensive

0   10   20   30   40   50   60
SCALE OF MILES

YUGOSLAVIA

BULGARIA

ALBANIA

MACEDONIA

GREECE

ADRIATIC SEA

GULF OF SALONIKA

PLAINS OF

THESSALY

PRISTINA

PRIZREN

KUMANOVO

SKOPLJE

SCUTARI

KUKES

TETOVO

VELES

STIP

SAMOKOV

DUPNITSA

NEVROKOP

STRUMITZA

PODOPOLIS

SERES

PRILEP

TIRANA

DURAZZO

XXXX
NINTH

ELBASAN

LAKE OKHRIDA

LAKE PRESPANSKO

MONASTIR

Din R

Shkumin R

Devoll R

POGRADEC

GRAMSH

BERAT

Vojussa R

FLORINA

EDESSA

KORITSA

AMYNTAION

SALONIKA

KASTORIA

VERORA

VEROIA

XXXX
ELEVENTH

VALONA

ERSEK

MT. GRAMMOS

XXXX
GREEK

KOZANI

MT. OLYMPUS

KLISURA

TEPELENE

HIMARA

ARGIROCASTRO

KONITSA

PINDUS MOUNTAINS

METSOVON

MT. OSSA

Line, 1 March 1941, at end of
Greek counteroffensive.

PORTO EDDA

JANINA

LARISSA

The four heavy red arrows
indicate the initial Italian
attacks of 28 October 1940

CORFU

TRIKKALA

VOLO

Vardar R

Struma R

Strumitza R

Aliakmon R

GULF OF SALONIKA

Akeron R

During the first quarter of 1941, Hitler had wooed Yugoslavia unceasingly, but with little success. Suddenly, on 18 March, the atmosphere brightened, and a week later Yugoslavia signed the protocol (Tripartite Pact). But it was never ratified, for two days later (27 March) a military *coup d'état* unseated the existing government; borne upon a wave of nationalism, anti-German demonstrations broke out in many places. That very day, Hitler conceded his diplomatic failure and ordered plans prepared for an invasion of Yugoslavia. He informed Mussolini of developments and requested that the Italian Second Army (*upper left*) protect the German right flank by an attack east across the border, then southeast into Dalmatia. The Italian chief consented, and directed his troops on the Albanian front to maintain a stout defense.

Meanwhile, the British had sent ground forces to Greece (*bottom center*) from North Africa. (Earlier, the Greeks had refused an offer of aid for fear of provoking Germany; now they accepted.) Thus, on 5 March, British troops began arriving at Athens; by the 27th, they had moved up to the Aliakmon Line, where they were joined by two Greek divisions. Farther east, about 70,000 Greeks—most of them in the Metaxas Line—defended the Bulgarian border.

Hitler's instructions to his planners specified that Yugoslavia be ground under quickly and unmercifully. OKH, under tremendous pressure, developed in one day a combined plan for operations against Greece and Yugoslavia. List's Twelfth Army, poised to invade Greece, would now also have to send forces into Yugoslavia. The German Second Army (*top left*) was formed from units rushed from Germany, France, and the Russian border, where troops were already assembling for the impending attack on that front. The OKH plan contemplated a two-pronged drive on Belgrade by divisions of the XLVI and XIV Panzer Corps and a drive on Zagreb by the rest of the German Second Army. (Hitler expected little resistance in the province of Croatia [*upper left*], where the Croats and dominant Serbs were at odds.) To the south, the Twelfth Army was to attack Greece and also send an armored column across southern Yugoslavia to isolate that country from Greece. Hitler added to the plan a third drive on Belgrade by the XLI Corps of SS troops. (SS indicates Schutzstaffel—that is, Nazi Party troops.) As previously described, the Italian Second Army was to advance along the route shown. The offensive was to open on 6 April with a devastating air attack on Belgrade and ground assaults by the First Panzer Group (while the rest of the Twelfth Army moved into Greece). The German Second Army, not yet fully concentrated, was to seize bridgeheads on the 6th, but not to launch a major attack until 10 April.

The Yugoslav Army's mobilized strength was 1,000,000—but on 6 April it was still mobilizing. Torn by Serb-Croat dissension, poorly equipped, weak in air support, and poorly led, the Yugoslavs were tremendously outclassed. Only token gestures had been made toward cooperative planning with Greece; instead, the Yugoslavs relied upon a cordon defense and the defensive strength of the mountains—terrain which the Germans avoided by using the river corridors.

The German plan was executed to perfection. The 6 April bombing of Belgrade paralyzed the Yugoslav high command and shattered communications. Belgrade was entered on 12 April almost simultaneously by the columns shown. On 11-12 April, the Hungarian Third Army attacked an already demoralized foe, and promptly incorporated the area it overran into Hungary. En route to Belgrade, elements of the XLVI Corps turned south and on the 15th joined the 14th Panzer Division at Sarajevo. The 14th Division had earlier taken Zagreb, receiving a liberator's welcome. Moving west, it linked up with the Italians, then turned southeast, followed by the slower-moving elements of the XLIX and LI Corps. The fighting for Sarajevo was vigorous, but the Yugoslavs could not long postpone the inevitable. On the 14th, they asked for a cease-fire, and capitulated unconditionally on 17 April. Total German losses in this lightning campaign in Yugoslavia were a mere 558.

Operations in southern Yugoslavia and Greece are described in the text of map 21.

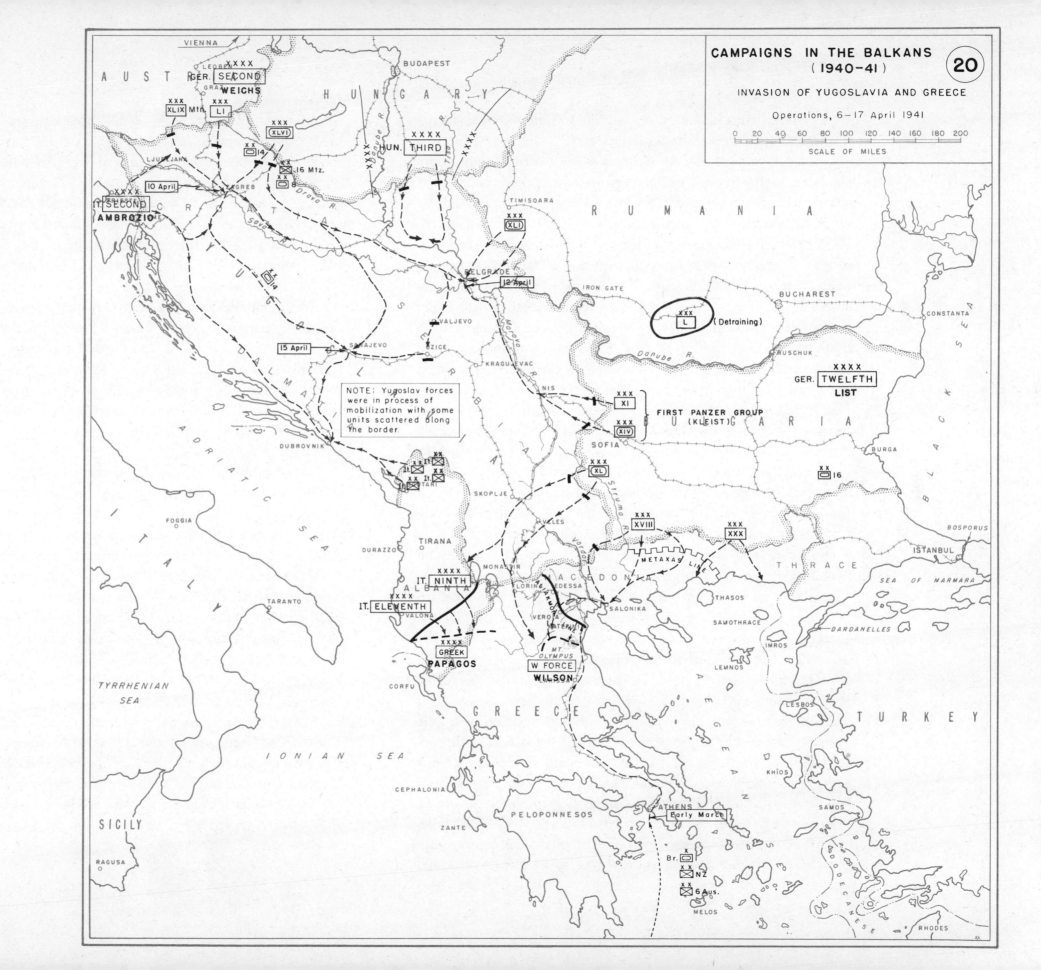

CAMPAIGNS IN THE BALKANS
(1940-41)

20

INVASION OF YUGOSLAVIA AND GREECE

Operations, 6-17 April 1941

0 20 40 60 80 100 120 140 160 180 200
SCALE OF MILES

By 27 March, the difficulties of coalition war had begun to plague the British in Greece. The weakness of the Aliakmon Line was obvious—it could easily be outflanked by a drive from Yugoslavia through Monastir (*center, left*)—but, underestimating the speed of German movement, the British expected to have time to withdraw their left to block Monastir Gap. Nor would General Papagos consider withdrawing the Greek First Army in order to block an enemy thrust through the gap. (The Greek Army's equipment was so run-down that a withdrawal under enemy pressure seemed impossible—not to mention its detrimental effect on morale.) Lt. Gen. Sir Henry Maitland Wilson had recognized that the Metaxas Line (concrete pillboxes, obstacles, and field fortifications) also could be turned easily on its left. He urged the Greeks to abandon it and to reinforce the Aliakmon Line. But Papagos was reluctant to surrender voluntarily any Greek territory; more important, Salonika (*center*) was the Greek First Army's major supply base and Yugoslavia's only link to outside help. Thus Wilson, feeling too weak to extend the Metaxas Line westward, had occupied the Aliakmon Line while making plans for a withdrawal to the south. After an unsatisfactory meeting with Greek and Yugoslav chiefs on 3 April, he had no doubts as to Yugoslav inability to prevent a rapid German thrust through Monastir, despite the optimism reflected in a preposterous Greek-Yugoslav plan for a joint attack on the Italians in Albania.

Early on 6 April, the Luftwaffe struck hard at the port of Piraeus (*bottom center*) and by nightfall had reduced it to a state of ineffectiveness. At the same time, columns from List's XL, XVIII, and XXX Corps crossed the Bulgarian border. Yugoslav resistance to the XL Corps was initially strong, but by nightfall it was diminishing, and on 7 April the key railroad center of Skoplje (*upper center*) was captured. During the drive, Kleist's 5th Panzer Division joined the XL Corps at Kumanovo. German troops now drove toward Monastir and Albania. This same day, Wilson withdrew his armored brigade to Amyntaion (*south of Monastir Gap*), where a Greek cavalry division joined it. Meanwhile, against fierce resistance, the XVIII Corps—its attack significantly spearheaded by mountain divisions—was fighting its way through

the Metaxas Line. By 9 April, all three infantry divisions had made clean penetrations, and the 2d Panzer Division had rounded the left of the Greek line and entered Salonika. The XXX Corps, on the east, subdued western Thrace. (Throughout the operations, the 16th Panzer Division kept a wary eye on neutral Turkey.) Now the entire eastern Macedonian front collapsed; the Greek Second Army surrendered; and the German XXX Corps, using commandeered fishing boats, invaded the islands off the Turkish coast, as shown.

The remainder of the fighting, though spirited in spots, was essentially a pursuit, once Wilson withdrew to a position north of Mt. Olympus (*center*). The Germans closed to this line, destroying the disorganized Greek 12th and 20th Divisions en route. On the 12th, Papagos ordered—too late—a withdrawal from Albania. Dispirited and exhausted after months of fighting, and cut off by German elements in its rear, the First Army surrendered.

In the meantime, Papagos had recommended to Wilson that the British evacuate Greece—if they did not intend to surrender. On 17 April, with Wavell's approval, W Force began to withdraw. A position at Thermopylae (*lower center*) was occupied on 20 April to gain time for the evacuation; it was abandoned on 24 April. During the withdrawal, the Luftwaffe, outnumbering the RAF almost ten to one, harried the British unmercifully; but poor weather intervened, as at Dunkirk, to provide some relief. The Isthmus of Corinth was seized by an airborne assault on 26 April, but most British troops had already moved into the Peloponnesos. By 30 April, the last British troops had been either evacuated or captured.

Total German casualties were 5,100; the British suffered 11,840. The Germans also took 270,000 Greek and 90,000 Yugoslav prisoners in the operations just described. Once again, bold, aggressive tactics and the skillful use of armor in supposedly impassable country had paid dividends. His south flank now secured, Hitler began to redeploy the troops for the imminent invasion of Russia.

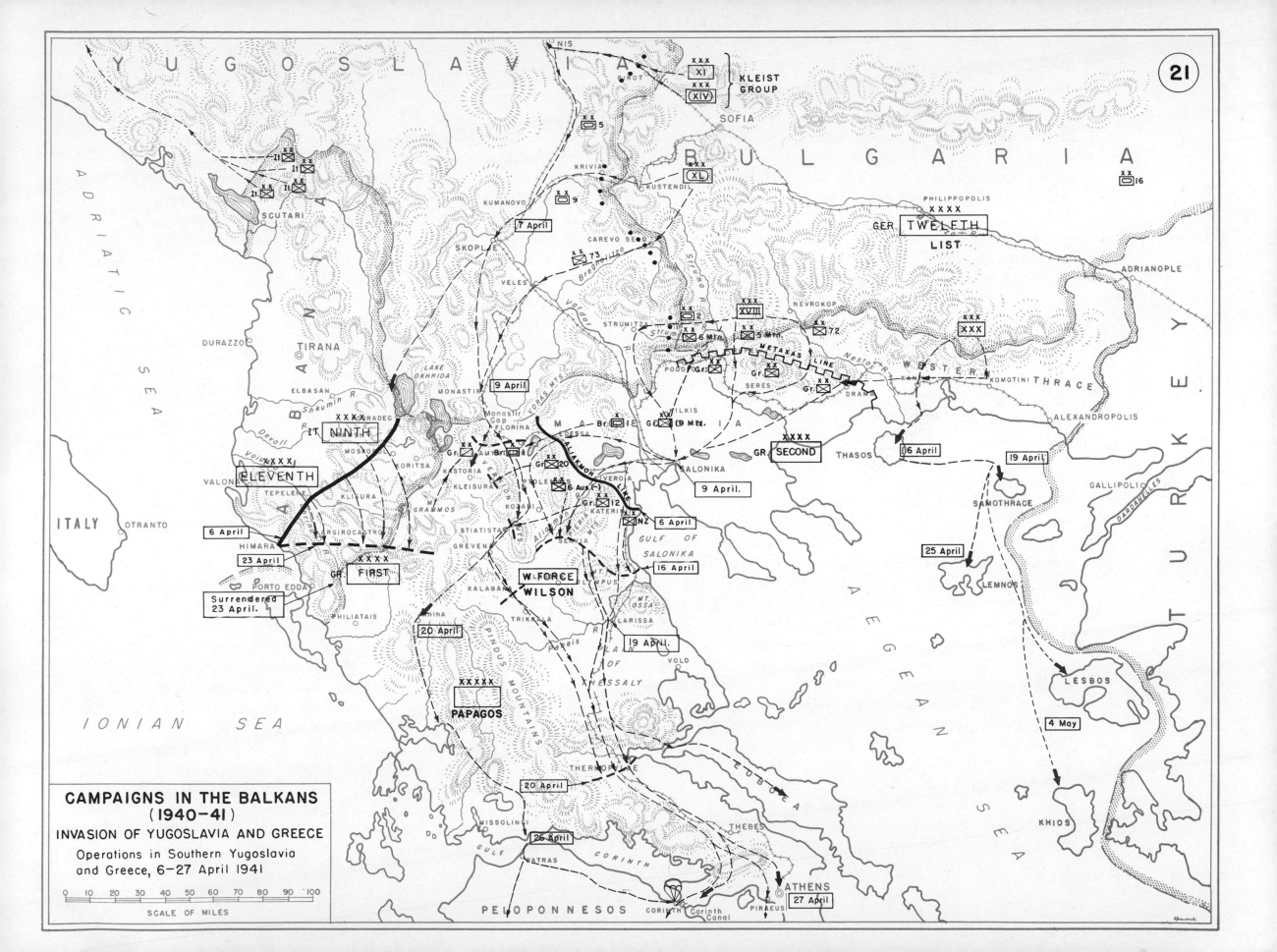

CAMPAIGNS IN THE BALKANS
(1940–41)

INVASION OF YUGOSLAVIA AND GREECE

Operations in Southern Yugoslavia
and Greece, 6–27 April 1941

0 10 20 30 40 50 60 70 80 90 100

SCALE OF MILES

The seizure of Crete in 1941 was the first major airborne operation executed independently of ground force support. It was a test of German air power against British sea power—won by the Germans when the Royal Navy, dispersed and operating in restricted waters, was forced to withdraw from the Aegean Sea (*see map 18*).

The British failure to garrison Crete strongly in early 1941 was not an oversight. They appreciated the importance of the island, but higher priority demands in Cyrenaica (*see map 74*) and in Greece (*see map 21*) sapped the limited resources locally available. The original garrison of Crete (*this map*)—one brigade and some naval elements sent there in November, 1940—received very little equipment or supplies and no sizable reinforcements, until the battered and tired remnants of W Force arrived from Greece in April. This conglomerate force, under Major General Bernard C. Freyberg, had few antiaircraft guns, only about twenty artillery pieces, and twenty-four tanks. No aircraft were based on the island, the RAF having withdrawn to Egypt in May. Worse still, the loss of airfields on Cyrenaica (*200 miles south*) precluded British fighters from offering more than token resistance to the Luftwaffe. The critical deficiency was Freyberg's lack of transport, which, coupled with the poor road net, prevented the creation of a central, mobile reserve. He therefore established four defense areas on the north coast of the island—at Maleme, Khania, Rethymnon, and Herakleion—and divided his troops among them.

After the operations in Greece, Hitler's attention focused on the coming Russian campaign. But Göring, with a vision of breaking British control of the eastern Mediterranean, pressed Hitler into agreeing to an airborne operation to capture Crete. The airborne forces—7th Parachute Division, reinforced, and 5th Mountain Division—were commanded by Lt. Gen. Kurt Student, Germany's airborne expert. These and all naval and tactical air support units were subordinated to the Fourth Air Force in Greece, thus ensuring unity of command.

After intensive air strikes, Student's assault elements—two parachute regiments, each preceded by two companies of glider-borne troops—began landing at 0800, 20 May, in the Maleme-Khania area. The defending New Zealanders, not taken by surprise, inflicted heavy casualties on the paratroops and by nightfall still controlled the Maleme airfield and Galatos. Meanwhile, Student's second wave (also two regiments) had been dropped at Rethymnon and Herakleion that afternoon. It had suffered even greater casualties than the first wave. Unable to capture the airfields, these regiments were surrounded and under considerable pressure by evening. Lacking an airfield and unable to air-land the 5th Mountain Division, Student sent in his last paratroop element early on 21 May to help capture Maleme airfield, but to no avail. By noon, the Germans controlled only part of the field. That afternoon, the Germans, in desperation, began landing the 5th Mountain Division at Maleme, even though the airfield was only partially controlled and under British fire. This tipped the balance. The Germans completely occupied the airfield and gradually drove the defenders into the mountains and toward Khania. Reinforcements poured in by air, but the small follow-up forces, coming by water, were destroyed or dispersed by the Royal Navy, which suffered heavily under air attacks. On 28 May, Freyberg directed a withdrawal to Sfakia (*south coast*) and ultimate evacuation. The German Herakleion airhead was reinforced from Maleme on that date, but a coordinated attack on the 29th found the British garrison gone. The Rethymnon defenders, unable to break out to the west, surrendered on the 30th. Meanwhile, the exhausted British force from Khania withdrew over the mountains to Sfakia, its discipline shattered. However, the Germans failed to pursue, in the mistaken belief that the British had withdrawn toward Rethymnon. On the 31st, they closed in on Sfakia, but by then the Royal Navy had evacuated much of the force.

British casualties totaled 17,325 (including 2,011 naval losses and 11,835 prisoners). The Germans lost 5,678 ground force personnel. Hitler, aghast at the high casualties and the shattering of the 7th Division, never again conducted a major airborne operation. Concerned with Russia, he withdrew air and ground elements and allowed Britain eventually to regain control over the eastern Mediterranean.

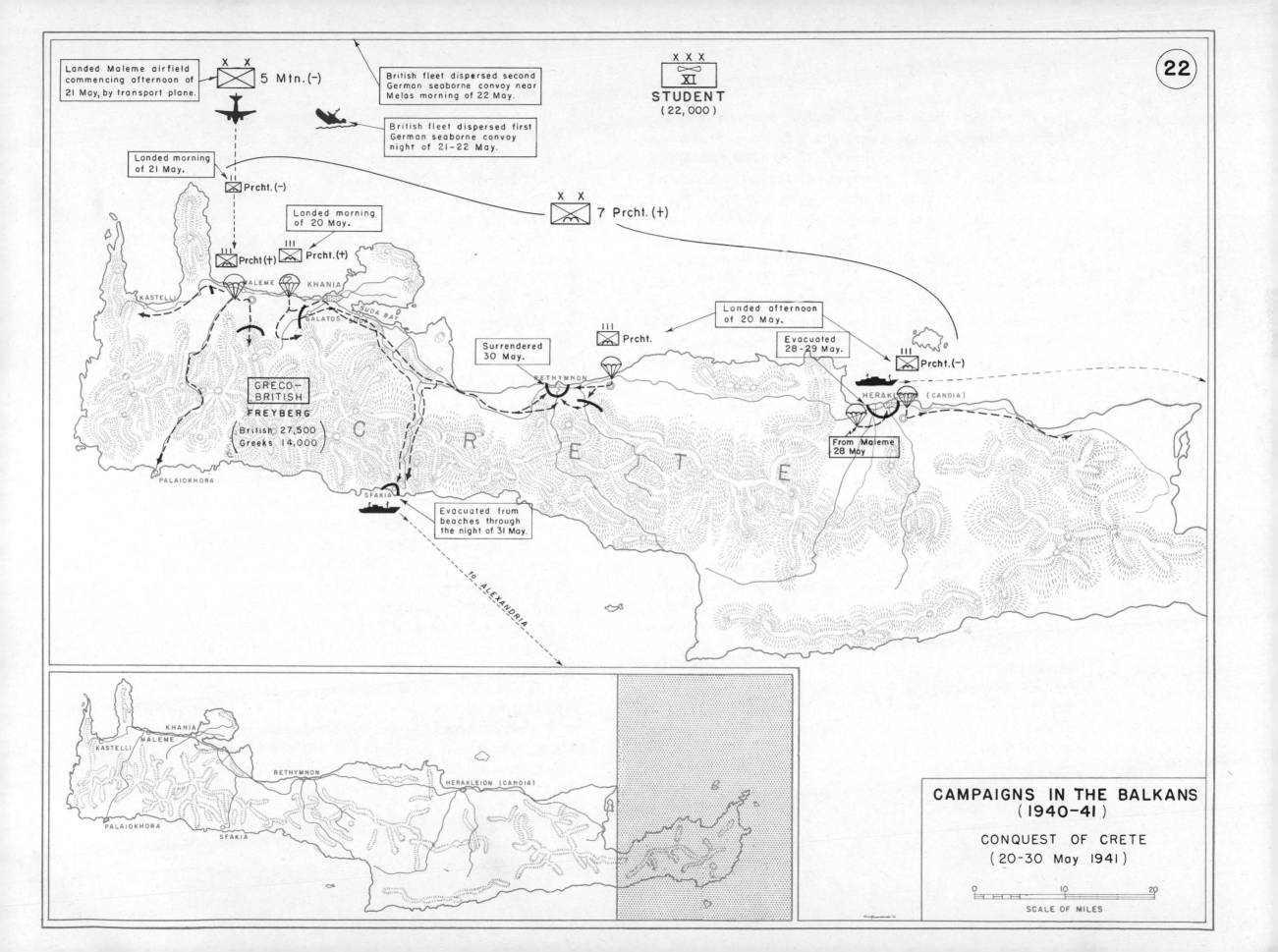

Landed Maleme airfield commencing afternoon of 21 May, by transport plane.

5 Mtn. (−)

British fleet dispersed second German seaborne convoy near Melas morning of 22 May.

British fleet dispersed first German seaborne convoy night of 21–22 May.

XXX
XI
STUDENT
(22,000)

Landed morning of 21 May.

Prcht. (−)

Landed morning of 20 May.

Prcht. (+)   Prcht. (+)

7 Prcht. (+)

Landed afternoon of 20 May.

Prcht.

Evacuated 28–29 May.

Prcht. (−)

KASTELLI

MALEME   KHANIA

GALATOS   SUDA BAY

Surrendered 30 May.

RETHYMNON

HERAKLI   (CANDIA)

GRECO–
BRITISH
FREYBERG
British 27,500
Greeks 14,000

C   R   E   T   E

From Maleme 28 May

PALAIOKHORA

SFAKIA

Evacuated from beaches through the night of 31 May.

To ALEXANDRIA

KHANIA
MALEME
KASTELLI

RETHYMNON

HERAKLEION (CANDIA)

PALAIOKHORA

SFAKIA

CAMPAIGNS IN THE BALKANS
(1940–41)

CONQUEST OF CRETE
(20–30 May 1941)

0   10   20
SCALE OF MILES

22

This map depicts the over-all results of the first year of Hitler's war with Russia. In some six months of fighting, the Germans and their satellites had overrun the fertile Ukraine and the Crimean Peninsula, had cut the railroad (*not shown*) to Murmansk, and had almost captured Moscow (*dotted blue line*). Winter, their own mistakes, and Russian endurance had finally brought them to a halt and forced them back (*solid blue line*), but only slightly. These operations are covered in detail in the following maps.

There probably will never be a full and accurate history of the war in Eastern Europe. German records are incomplete, and in some cases impossible to verify. The Communist dogma that history should indoctrinate, rather than elucidate, makes the relatively scanty Russian contributions thoroughly suspect. Finally, this was very much a private war—no competent outside observer was ever allowed more than a confused glimpse of it. This account will concentrate on reasonably established facts; speculation will be identified as such.

Hitler had always looked forward to the eventual dismemberment of Russia—just as Stalin had built up his forces in anticipation of the day when it would be profitable to intervene in an exhausted Western Europe. Once France was conquered, Hitler put his staff to work on plans for a Russian campaign. Having failed in the Battle of Britain, he also considered plans to cut the British life line through the Mediterranean by seizing the Suez Canal and Gibraltar. Franco's exorbitant price for Spanish assistance killed the Gibraltar plan. The capture of Suez by any means short of a major German campaign was thoroughly compromised by Italian failures in North Africa (*see map 18*) and by Mussolini's abortive attempt to conquer Greece (*see map 19*). At the same time, Stalin—apparently considering Hitler fully involved with England—began pushing the old Russian ambition of dominion over the Balkans and the Dardanelles (and, apparently, the complete absorption of Finland, to clear the way for further advances in the Baltic). Hitler failed to interest the Russians in

shifting their expansion toward India and the Far East; he did reach agreements with the anti-Communist governments of Finland, Hungary, Rumania, and Bulgaria. For some unknown reason, however, he did not disclose his plans to his Japanese ally. Consequently, the Japanese felt free to conclude a neutrality pact with the Russians (13 April, 1941). A few months later, this enabled the Russians to rush troops from Siberia to the defense of Moscow.

On 18 December, 1940, Hitler issued his first formal directive on the invasion of Russia, all preparations for which were to be completed by 15 May, 1941. This directive underwent a number of studies and revisions. Then, at the beginning of April, the invasion was postponed while the Germans cleared their Balkan flank (*see maps 20-22*). The Balkan campaign delayed the invasion of Russia by approximately three weeks. If properly utilized, this time should have allowed a decisive German victory before winter, but—as will subsequently appear—Hitler wasted even longer periods once the invasion was under way. The new date for the Russian attack was to be 22 June. Hitler and his military advisors felt that three or four months should suffice to defeat Russia; thereafter, they expected to drive the British out of the Mediterranean and, eventually, to invade the British Isles.

The German concentrations in Poland were detected by the Russians, but were explained away as diversionary measures to deceive the British, or as training exercises.

Note one important factor: the Germans had little reliable intelligence concerning Russia and its armed forces—and Hitler insisted on interpreting what there was according to his preconceived notions of Russian backwardness (bolstered, no doubt, by the poor Russian showing against Finland). Few military campaigns have been launched in more complete ignorance of the enemy's capabilities than Hitler's invasion of Russia. Nevertheless, it came amazingly close to success. Its failure can be attributed largely to Hitler's unswerving belief in his own military genius.

THE WAR
IN EASTERN EUROPE **23**
GERMAN AND RUSSIAN DISPOSITIONS
(June 1941)

GERMAN GAINS IN RUSSIA
(June 1941 — May 1942)

0   100   200   300   400   500   600
SCALE OF MILES

ARCTIC   OCEAN

ICELAND

KIRKENES
XXXX   PETSAMO
NORWAY   MURMANSK
FALKENHORST

WHITE
SEA   ARCHANGEL

BELOMORSK

FINLAND
June 1941   LAKE
ONEGA   KIROV   MOLOTOV

VIIPURI   LAKE
LADOGA   May 1942

NORWAY   GULF
OF
BOTHNIA   HELSINKI   VOLOGDA   MAGNITOGORSK

OSLO   SWEDEN   LENINGRAD   S O V I E T   S O C I A L I S T
TALLINN   Volga R.
ESTONIA   KAZAN
XXXXX   KALININ   XXXX   XXXX
NORTHWEST   (Reserve)   G. GORKI   (Reserve)
VOROSHILOV   MOSCOW   Ural R.
RIGA   VELIKIYE   KUIBYSHEV   CHKALOV
LUKI   RZHEV
NORTH
SEA   BALTIC   XXXXX   Dvina R.   VYAZMA   R E P U B L I C
SEA   NORTH   VITEBSK   SMOLENSK   Dec. 1941
IRELAND   LEEB   EAST   TULA
PRUSSIA   WHITE   MINSK   OREL
SCOTLAND   XXXXX   Niemen R.   RUSSIA   May 1942
CENTER   XXXXX   Don R.
ENGLAND   ENGLISH CHANNEL   BOCK   WARSAW   WEST   KURSK   VORONEZH
LONDON   BERLIN   TIMOSHENKO
ANTWERP   June 1941   Pripet R.   KIEV   STALINGRAD
BREST   BELG.   GERMANY   P O L A N D   Dnieper R.
LORIENT   PARIS   XXXXX   KORSUN   U K R A I N E   Don R.   Donets R.
WEST   Elbe R.   KHARKOV
BAY   WITZLEBEN   PRAGUE   LWOW   XXXXX   Bug R.   ASTRAKHAN
OF   Meuse R.   CZECHOSLOV.   SOUTHWEST   Dniester R.
BISCAY   FRANCE   Rhone R.   XXXXX   BUDENNY   ROSTOV
Rhine R.   SOUTH   Dniester R.   BESSARABIA   Kuban R.
SWITZ.   RUNDSTEDT   ODESSA   SEA OF   XXXXX
Loire R.   AUSTRIA   VIENNA   AZOV   CAUCASUS   GROZNY
Po R.   HUNGARY   BUDAPEST   CRIMEA   NOVOROSSISK   C A U C A S U S   M T S .
PORTUGAL   Garonne R.   R U M A N I A   SEVASTOPOL   CASPIAN
LISBON   MADRID   Danube R.   Danube R.   BATUM   TIFLIS   BAKU   SEA
SPAIN   CORSICA   YUGOSLAVIA   BELGRADE   B L A C K   S E A
ROME   BUCHAREST   LAKE
MARSEILLES   ADRIATIC SEA   BULGARIA   ARAL
GIBRALTAR   ITALY   SOFIA
PORTUGAL   XXXXX   DJULFA   PAHLEVI
SARDINIA   ALBANIA   SOUTHEAST   ISTANBUL   TABRIZ
SP. MOROCCO   M E D I T E R R A N E A N   LIST   GREECE   ANKARA   MIANEH   KAZVIN   TEHRAN
ORAN   ALGIERS   SICILY   T U R K E Y   I R A N
MOROCCO   ALGERIA   MALTA   ATHENS   CYPRUS   LEVANT   QUM
S E A   CRETE   HAIFA   STATES   BAGHDAD   AHWAZ
TUNISIA   TRIPOLI   JERUSALEM   Euphrates R.   KHORRAMSHAHR
BENGAZI   XXX   TOBRUK   PALESTINE   I R A Q   PERSIAN
LIBYA   ROMMEL   EL ALAMEIN   A R A B I A   GULF
E G Y P T   SUEZ

It is an ironic fact that neither the German nor the Russian Army began this campaign—probably, in terms of the numbers of men and the extent of territory involved, the greatest in history—with any definite over-all strategic concept.

Russian dispositions remain something of a puzzle. Initially, there appeared to be few, if any, preparations for a defense in depth or for delaying actions to draw the Germans deep into Russia before counterattacking. Masses of Russian troops had been concentrated close to the frontier, as if for eventual offensive action—which undoubtedly was Stalin's intention, whenever he considered the moment propitious for stabbing his fellow despot in the back. When he found himself completely out-scoundreled and surprised, it was necessary to invent the legend that the hasty Russian retreat which ensued was only the opening phase of Comrade Stalin's marvelous and farseeing strategy.

Hitler's 18 December directive had stressed that Russia was to be crushed in a "lightning campaign." The bulk of the enemy army in western Russia was to be destroyed in place, to prevent any organized units from retiring into the vastness of Russia's interior. This accomplished, the Germans would launch a rapid pursuit up to the general line Volga River (*right center*)–Kazan (*upper right*)–Archangel (*off map, 600 miles north of Moscow*).

Army Group South, operating below the Pripet Marshes, would make its main effort toward Kiev (*lower center*), as shown, in a strategic envelopment (*long red arrow*) designed to cut off all Russian forces in the western Ukraine before they could escape across the Dnieper River (*lower center*).

Army Group Center would make the main attack up the traditional Warsaw-Smolensk-Moscow invasion route, utilizing its two panzer groups to envelop and destroy the large Russian forces massed on its front.

Army Group North was to destroy the Russian forces in the Baltic area and then advance on Leningrad (*top center*).

Farther north, German and Finnish forces would operate toward Murmansk and the Murmansk railroad, while the main Finnish army advanced on Leningrad from the north.

Beyond these initial missions, Hitler and his military commanders were in profound disagreement. Hitler's chosen objectives were largely political and economic: Leningrad, the capture of which would enable the Germans and Finns to link up, and would turn the Baltic into a German lake; the Ukraine, with its wheat and coal; the industrial Donets River Basin (*lower right*); and, finally, the Caucasus oil fields (*off map, bottom right*). All of these would have been valuable conquests for an isolated Germany, but there were large Russian armies which must first be brought to battle and destroyed. The German generals' solution was to attack directly toward Moscow. That city was the political center of both Russia and Communism. It was also the site of much of the Russian armaments industry and the center of the Russian railroad system. For these reasons, the generals felt, the Russians would commit the flower of their army in Moscow's defense, giving the Germans the opportunity to destroy it in a relatively short period of aggressive fighting. No definite agreement was ever reached; the German advance was frequently on a day-to-day basis as Hitler vacillated and called upon his intuition.

Hitler had increased the number of his panzer divisions—largely by cutting the number of tanks in each division, thus reducing their capability for sustained combat. At this same time, Germany's armament industry operated at little more than peacetime tempo. Production of nonessential civilian goods was continuing, while Hitler refused to increase tank production. Many plants were being diverted from Army to Navy and Luftwaffe work—in preparation for the new offensive against England that was to follow the swift crushing of Russia.

Meanwhile, the Navy and much of the Luftwaffe were still engaged with the British. Hitler would have to fight a two-front war.

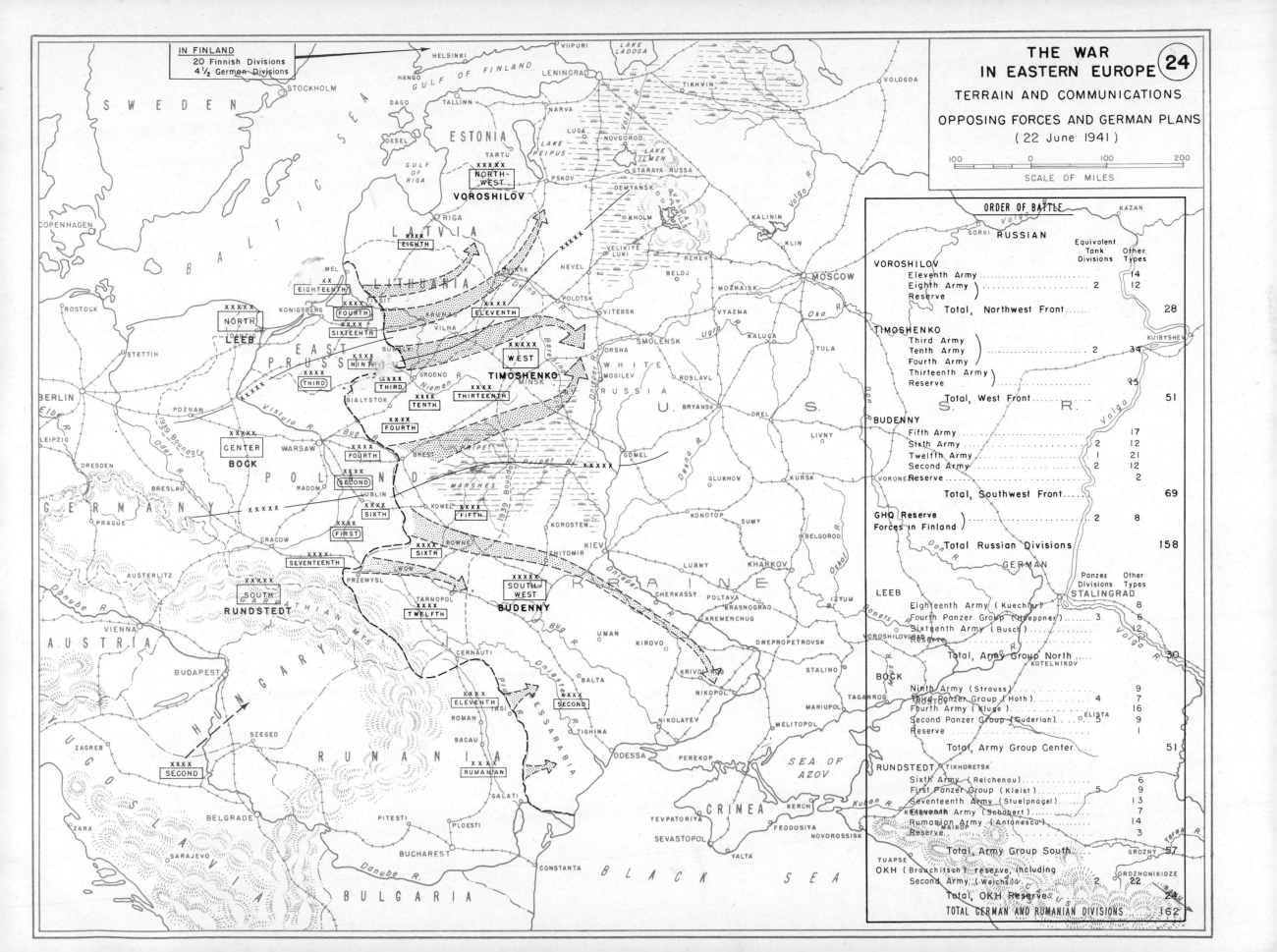

THE WAR IN EASTERN EUROPE (24)

TERRAIN AND COMMUNICATIONS
OPPOSING FORCES AND GERMAN PLANS
(22 June 1941)

100   0   100   200
SCALE OF MILES

IN FINLAND
20 Finnish Divisions
4½ German Divisions

ORDER OF BATTLE

RUSSIAN

	Equivalent Tank Divisions	Other Types
VOROSHILOV		
Eleventh Army		14
Eighth Army)		12
Reserve)	2	
Total, Northwest Front		28
TIMOSHENKO		
Third Army		
Tenth Army)	2	34
Fourth Army)		
Thirteenth Army)		
Reserve		15
Total, West Front		51
BUDENNY		
Fifth Army		17
Sixth Army	2	12
Twelfth Army	1	21
Second Army		12
Reserve		2
Total, Southwest Front		69
GHQ Reserve)		
Forces in Finland)	2	8
Total Russian Divisions		158

GERMAN

	Panzer Divisions	Other Types
LEEB		
Eighteenth Army (Kuechler)		8
Fourth Panzer Group (Hoeppner)	3	6
Sixteenth Army (Busch)		12
Reserve		1
Total, Army Group North		30
BOCK		
Ninth Army (Strauss)		9
Third Panzer Group (Hoth)	4	7
Fourth Army (Kluge)		16
Second Panzer Group (Guderian)	5	9
Reserve		1
Total, Army Group Center		51
RUNDSTEDT		
Sixth Army (Reichenau)		6
First Panzer Group (Kleist)	5	9
Seventeenth Army (Stuelpnagel)		13
Eleventh Army (Schobert)		7
Rumanian Army (Antonescu)		14
Reserve		3
Total, Army Group South		57
OKH (Brauchitsch) reserve, including Second Army (Weichs)	2	22
Total, OKH Reserves		24
TOTAL GERMAN AND RUMANIAN DIVISIONS		162

Another peculiar feature of this campaign was that Russia—despite its multiple spy systems, and though warned by England—was completely surprised by the onslaught Hitler loosed at 0300, 22 June (*sketch a*). Though many Russian units rallied quickly and fought stubbornly and well, many of the higher Russian headquarters seem to have completely lost control of the situation suddenly confronting them.

Russian units opposing Army Group South, however, waged determined delaying actions; the Russian Fifth Army's counterattacks southward from the Pripet Marshes were especially effective. During the first weeks of the offensive, Rundstedt's progress was disappointingly slow.

By contrast, Army Group Center was highly successful from the start. With effective Luftwaffe support, its two panzer groups smashed through the confused Russians to link up east of Minsk (*center*). The trapped masses made desperate but uncoordinated efforts to break out. Some escaped through the panzers' encircling net, but the German infantry, pressing forward behind the panzers, efficiently mopped up the remainder. This Minsk pocket yielded some 290,000 prisoners, 2,500 tanks, and 1,400 pieces of artillery. By mid-July, a second lunge forward by Army Group Center was closing another trap in the vital Smolensk-Orsha-Vitebsk area, which controlled the "dry" route to Moscow between the headwaters of the Dnieper and Dvina Rivers.

Army Group North likewise advanced steadily in a jolting series of penetrations and envelopments which destroyed between twelve and fifteen Russian divisions west of the Dvina. Moreover, the Russian Air Force had suffered crushing losses, the Luftwaffe having gained complete air superiority after a succession of massive air battles. Likewise, the Russian tank forces had been shattered. (The Russians had originally enjoyed great numerical superiority in tanks and planes, though their matériel—especially their aircraft—was qualitatively somewhat inferior. Superior German tactics and organization, however, had swiftly proved themselves decisive.)

By 19 July, Army Group Center had closed its trap near Smolensk (*sketch b*)—100,000 prisoners, 2,000 tanks, 1,900 guns. The Russian front here was highly disorganized; all sorts of improvised formations were being thrust into the line. But, on either flank, the drive was slow. Army Group North was hindered by difficult forested terrain and by Leeb's inept handling of his panzer units. Also, the German supply system was beginning to have trouble keeping up with the advance, while the rough, dusty roads had disabled a large number of tanks and vehicles. All the panzer divisions needed considerable rehabilitation.

On 19 July, Hitler ordered the Second Panzer Group diverted to Army Group South, and the Third Panzer Group to Army Group North. Army Group Center was to advance toward Moscow—where the Russians were known to be massing troops—with infantry only. This brainstorm produced violent protests from his generals and, in turn, a confused period of counterorders. Finally, on 21 August, Hitler reached a firm decision: Moscow was not important; it might be attacked *after* Leningrad was encircled, the Crimea and the Donets Basin occupied, and the Russians cut off from their Caucasus oil fields. (During that period of uncertainty the panzer groups had a brief opportunity to catch up on their maintenance problems.) Now, in obedience to Hitler's final decision, Guderian's Second Panzer Group and the Second Army turned south. The Russian high command appears to have been astounded at his failure to drive home Army Group Center's victorious advance—to them, it was a "miracle."

In the meantime, during early August, Army Group South had scored its first major successes, destroying between sixteen and twenty Russian divisions near Uman (*lower center*) and thereafter clearing the Dnieper bend. Rundstedt now swung his First Panzer Group northward to meet Guderian, the object being to trap the Russian forces that were resisting successfully around Kiev (*center*). The Second Army soon scored a major victory near Gomel, taking some 80,000 more prisoners. (Farther north, however, Russian counterattacks [*small blue arrows*] gained local successes against Army Group Center.)

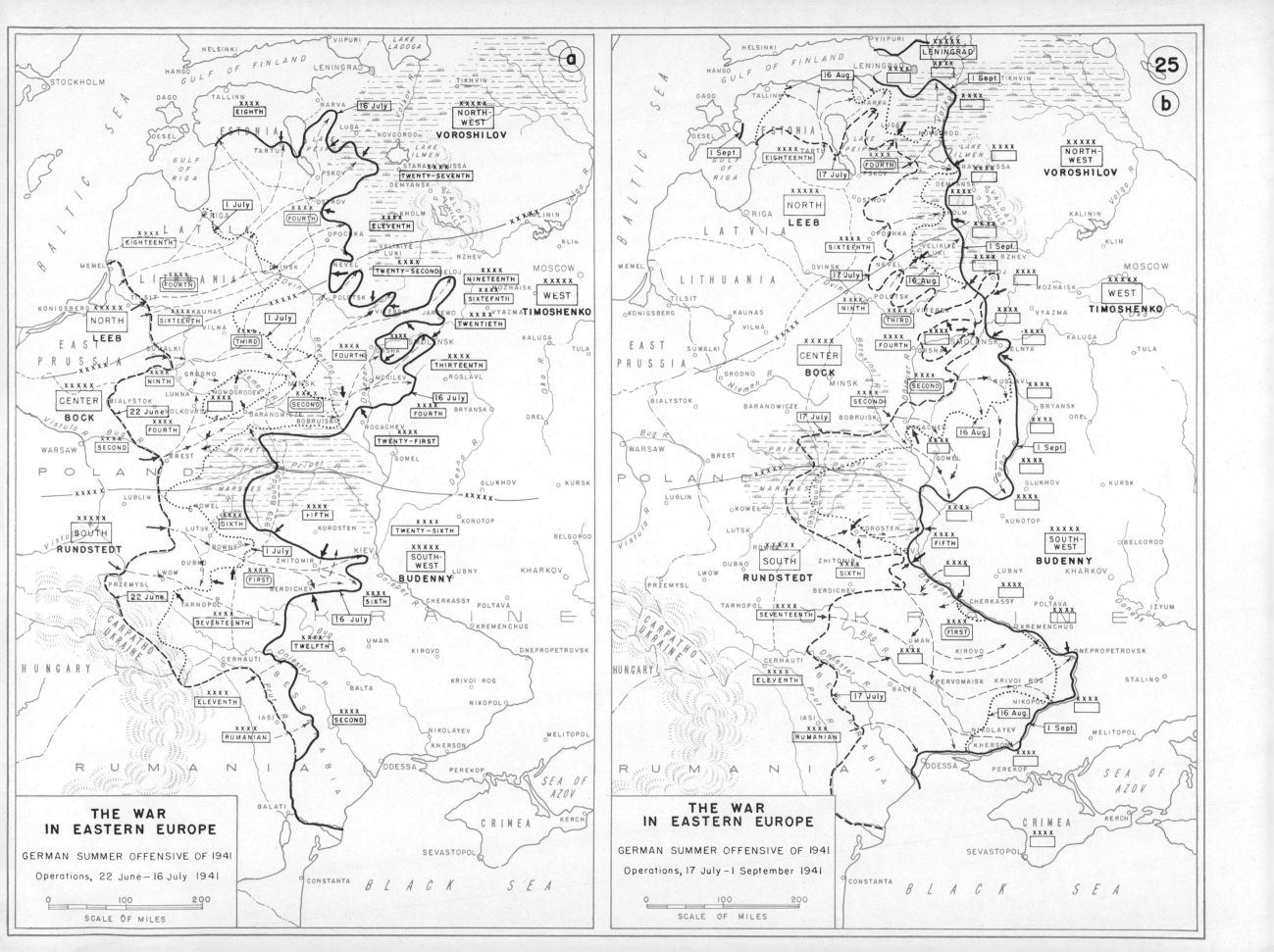

THE WAR
IN EASTERN EUROPE

GERMAN SUMMER OFFENSIVE OF 1941

Operations, 22 June – 16 July 1941

THE WAR
IN EASTERN EUROPE

GERMAN SUMMER OFFENSIVE OF 1941

Operations, 17 July – 1 September 1941

The southward march of Guderian's Second Panzer Group (*sketch* a, *center*) was risky, since its left flank was continuously exposed to Russian attacks from the east. Also, the weather was turning bad; heavy rains made "canals of mud" of the primitive Russian roads. Guderian met heavy opposition around Konotop and Romny, but, on 16 September, his leading elements made contact with those of the First Panzer Group advancing from the south. Kiev fell on the 19th, amid considerable confused fighting, with encircled Russian units attempting to break out and fresh Russian forces attacking westward to rescue them. Finally, on 26 September, the surviving Russians in the Kiev pocket surrendered: altogether, about 665,000 prisoners were taken. Meanwhile, the German Eleventh Army (*bottom center*) had pushed ahead to the Crimean peninsula, where it was preparing to assault the fortifications of the narrow Perekop Isthmus.

As a tactical operation, the creation and reduction of the Kiev pocket was outstanding. The greater part of the Russian forces in the zone of Army Group South had been destroyed, clearing the way for Rundstedt's subsequent drives on Kharkov and Rostov (*lower right*). But, from a strategic viewpoint, Hitler's diversion of forces to achieve this victory probably was one of his major blunders. It delayed the advance on Moscow, thus giving the Russians six weeks to fortify the approaches to their capital and to bring in tough new divisions from Siberia. Also, it seriously crippled the Second Panzer Group: a large percentage of its tanks and vehicles were worn out, and the remainder would not stand much more hard usage.

During early September, the Russians had continued their furious counterattacks in the Smolensk-Vyazma-Yelnya area (*upper center*), making slight gains at excessive cost, but giving the German command some anxious days. Bock lacked reserves because of the diversion of so many of his troops to assist Rundstedt and Leeb; also, increasing Russian partisan activity was beginning to hamper his supply system.

Leeb's advance, during early September, had finally closed up to Leningrad (*sketch* b), regarded by Hitler as "the cradle of Bolshevism," the capture of which would bring on Stalin's fall. Leeb had had to contend with difficult terrain—a mixture of swamps and thick forests—as well as with determined Russian resistance. His logistical situation, however, was better than that of the other army groups, since he could be supplied by sea. Moreover, there was very little guerrilla activity in his rear, the Baltic peoples having greeted the Germans as liberators. Once Leeb had reached Leningrad's inner defenses, Hitler forbade an assault on the city, preferring to destroy it by starvation and artillery fire. Leeb's attempt to seize the Valdai Hills south of Leningrad had very little success, because of terrain difficulties, Russian counterattacks, and steadily worsening weather. Of Leeb's various shortcomings during this campaign, the most significant, in the light of future events, was his failure to wipe out the isolated Russian Eighth Army.

In the far north (*sketch* c), Falkenhorst's German XXXVI and Mountain Corps had made initial gains, but soon stalled in the frontier wilderness, where climate and terrain were more formidable enemies than the Russians. By early September, Mannerheim's Finnish troops had reached their old frontier on the Karelian Isthmus (*bottom center*), had cut the Murmansk Railroad at Petrozavodsk, and had fought their way to the Svir River. By the end of October, they held generally the same front as that dated December (*solid blue line*). Here, the Finnish government, having regained the territory lost in 1939 (plus some east of Lake Ladoga, to which Finland had a historic claim), ordered its troops to halt. There was little change on this part of the front for the next two years. The Russians supplied Leningrad sketchily across Lake Ladoga by boat during the summer and by building a railroad on the ice during the winter. They also constructed a railroad from Belomorsk (*center*) to Plesetsk to detour the section of the Murmansk line held by the Finns.

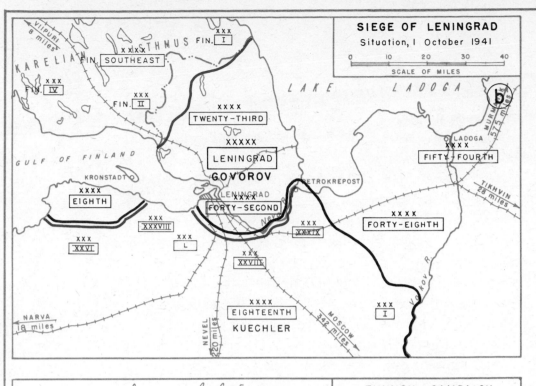

SIEGE OF LENINGRAD
Situation, 1 October 1941

0 10 20 30 40
SCALE OF MILES

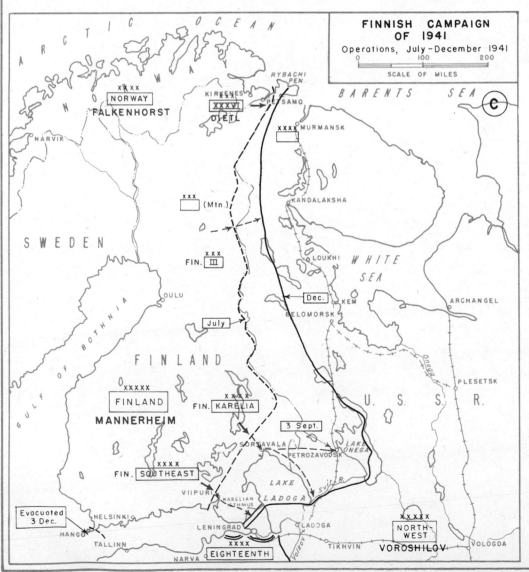

FINNISH CAMPAIGN OF 1941
Operations, July–December 1941

0 100 200
SCALE OF MILES

THE WAR IN EASTERN EUROPE
GERMAN SUMMER OFFENSIVE OF 1941
Operations, 2 September–1 October 1941

0 100 200
SCALE OF MILES

26

a

Back on 6 September—with Army Group North and the Finns tightening their ring around Leningrad, the Kiev pocket beginning to develop, and the Eleventh Army approaching the Crimea—Hitler at last had been willing to listen to his army commanders. Plans were drawn for a decisive offensive against Moscow. The Russian forces concentrated in the area Vyazma-Bryansk (*see map 26a, upper center*) were to be enveloped by the attack of Army Group Center, spearheaded by the Second, Third, and Fourth Panzer Groups (*this map, sketch* a). This was expected to clear the road to Moscow.

During the last of September, in preparation for this offensive, panzer and Luftwaffe units which had been temporarily transferred from Army Group Center to Army Group North were recalled. The Second Army and Second Panzer Group, previously transferred to Rundstedt, likewise reverted to Army Group Center. These movements, made insofar as possible during darkness to ensure secrecy, consumed considerable time. Many of the panzer divisions had to march several hundred miles to reach their assembly areas. (Guderian's moved some 400 miles.) Army Group Center's supply situation was becoming worse, and guerrilla activity in its rear was increasing. Furthermore, the season was growing late, a fact that haunted the more conscientious German commanders.

Army Group South was to continue its drives on Kharkov, Rostov, and the Crimea. Army Group North was to press its siege of Leningrad. Both army groups were to strengthen their inner flanks, to cover the advance of Army Group Center.

On 30 September, Guderian's Second Panzer Group attacked; two days later, the Third and Fourth Panzer Groups jumped off. The Russians were completely surprised. Bock's assault quickly shattered their well-established defensive position; in less than a week, masses of Russians were hopelessly trapped in pockets at Bryansk and Vyazma. These required time and hard fighting to liquidate, but the bag was enormous—658,000 prisoners. While the infantry cleared the pockets, Bock thrust his panzers forward to keep the offensive going. The Second Panzer Group was to advance through Tula on Moscow; the Third Panzer Group would move on Kalinin, preparatory to an attack on the Russian capital from the northwest; between them, the Fourth Panzer Group would spearhead a secondary frontal attack. Meanwhile, Army Group South was advancing steadily on Rostov, while its weak Eleventh Army methodically reduced the defenses of the Perekop Isthmus.

Then Russia's traditional ally, the weather, intervened. On 7 October, the autumn rains came, gradually choking the German advance, though it still drove doggedly forward against increasing opposition. Hard hit, the Russians threw in all available units to block the Moscow road, but Mozhaisk—the last major town before Moscow—fell on 20 October. By early November, Guderian was approaching Tula. However, it was on their flanks that the Germans made the greatest progress. In an attack through extremely difficult terrain (21 October–11 November), Leeb captured the bauxite-producing area of Tikhvin (*sketch* b). (It had been hoped that the Finns would advance southward to the east of Lake Ladoga to link up with the German forces at Tikhvin, but the Finnish government refused for political reasons.) Army Group South had taken Kharkov and Taganrog, and was on the outskirts of Rostov, "the gateway to the Caucasus." Furthermore, the Eleventh Army, under the skilled leadership of Manstein, had driven superior Russian forces out of their Perekop defenses on 8 November and was now clearing the Crimean peninsula.

With his troops only forty miles from Moscow, Hitler began his plans for its envelopment. Naturally, he ignored the mud in which his troops were floundering; somehow, he and his immediate staff had inspired themselves with the idea that the Russians were about to retreat from the Moscow front in order to save as many as they could of their remaining troops.

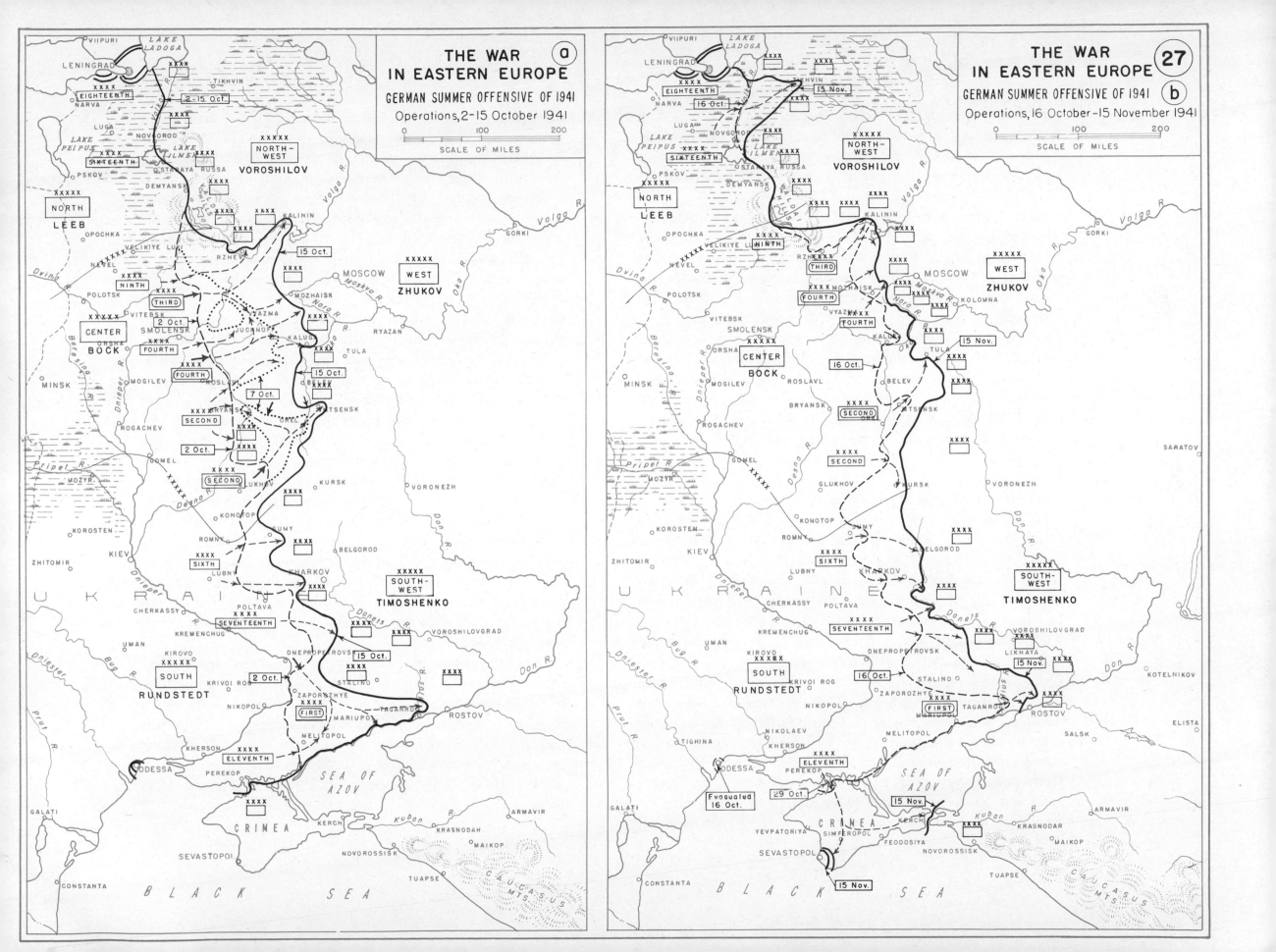

THE WAR
IN EASTERN EUROPE ⓐ

GERMAN SUMMER OFFENSIVE OF 1941

Operations, 2–15 October 1941

SCALE OF MILES
0   100   200

THE WAR
IN EASTERN EUROPE 27

GERMAN SUMMER OFFENSIVE OF 1941 ⓑ

Operations, 16 October–15 November 1941

SCALE OF MILES
0   100   200

Early in November, the rains dwindled. A short period of relatively clear, cold weather could be expected thereafter before the savage Russian winter began sometime in December. The Germans had but a few weeks in which to win a decisive victory in 1941.

The German armies were actually drawing on their last reserves of strength and resolution. They had just finished the greatest sustained offensive in military history, killing or capturing Russians in numbers at least equal to their own strength at the beginning of the campaign. But now their infantry divisions had only some 65 per cent of their original combat efficiency, their panzer divisions little more than 50 per cent. Their tank strength was less than one-third of normal (probably due more to Russian terrain than Russian armed resistance). Officer casualties had been very heavy, and supply was practically on a hand-to-mouth basis. All of Army Group Center's reserves had been committed.

Under these conditions, many German leaders urged the adoption of flexible defensive tactics until reinforcements and supplies could be accumulated for a renewed offensive. Hitler and his supporters spurned this idea. The Russians, they claimed, were almost exhausted, and one more hard blow would finish them. Moscow was only forty miles away. The Second Panzer Group (*main sketch*), on the right, was to advance northward from Tula, enveloping Moscow from the southwest. The Third Panzer Group would move up to the Volga Canal, then turn in on Moscow from the northwest, using the canal to cover its left flank. The Fourth Panzer Group and the Fourth and Ninth Armies would attack due east.

Meanwhile, Leeb's forces were consolidating their position in the Tikhvin area; Rundstedt's Eleventh Army had Sevastopol (*bottom center*) under siege and was clearing the Kerch peninsula, while his First Panzer Army (the First and Second Panzer Groups had been retitled "panzer armies" on 5 October) carried Rostov on 20 November. Elsewhere on the Army Group South front, the Russians appeared to be shifting troops northward. Rundstedt was severely hampered by his logistical situation. All the Dnieper River bridges had been destroyed, and the Russian Black Sea Fleet prevented supply by ship from Constanta.

Army Group Center began its offensive on 15 November with the Third Panzer Group and the Ninth Army. Two days later, Guderian attacked, bypassing Tula; on his right, the Second Army likewise began to pile up considerable gains. Astride the Mozhaisk-Moscow road, however, the Russians threw in attack after attack against the Fourth Army, holding it on the defensive until 1 December. One Russian unit committed against it was of evil portent for the Germans—an armored brigade equipped with British tanks, evidence that British and American aid was beginning to reach the Russians in appreciable quantities.

Russian resistance now stiffened throughout the Moscow area. The Russian Air Force, including several improved types of aircraft previously held in reserve, had been increasingly active for some time. Large numbers of Siberian troops, hardened by informal Manchurian border clashes against the Japanese, were now in action, as were substantial numbers of the new Russian T-34 tank (first identified in October), which was superior to even the best German tanks. It was the winter, however, that really crippled the German offensive. Temperatures suddenly fell to more than –40° F. Hitler having planned a short war, no supplies of winter clothing or of winter lubricants for vehicles were available at the front. Frostbite casualties soared. A final push carried the Third and Fourth Panzer Groups to within twenty-five miles of Moscow, but there, on 5 December, the great offensive ended (*inset sketch*).

In the meantime, the Russians had scored their first definite success. Overwhelming Russian forces had closed in around the exposed German spearhead at Rostov (*main sketch, lower right*). Rundstedt requested permission to evacuate that city. Hitler first agreed, then ordered Rostov held, relieving Rundstedt when he protested. Nevertheless, Rostov had to be abandoned on 28 November, Hitler finally consenting to a withdrawal to the Mius River.

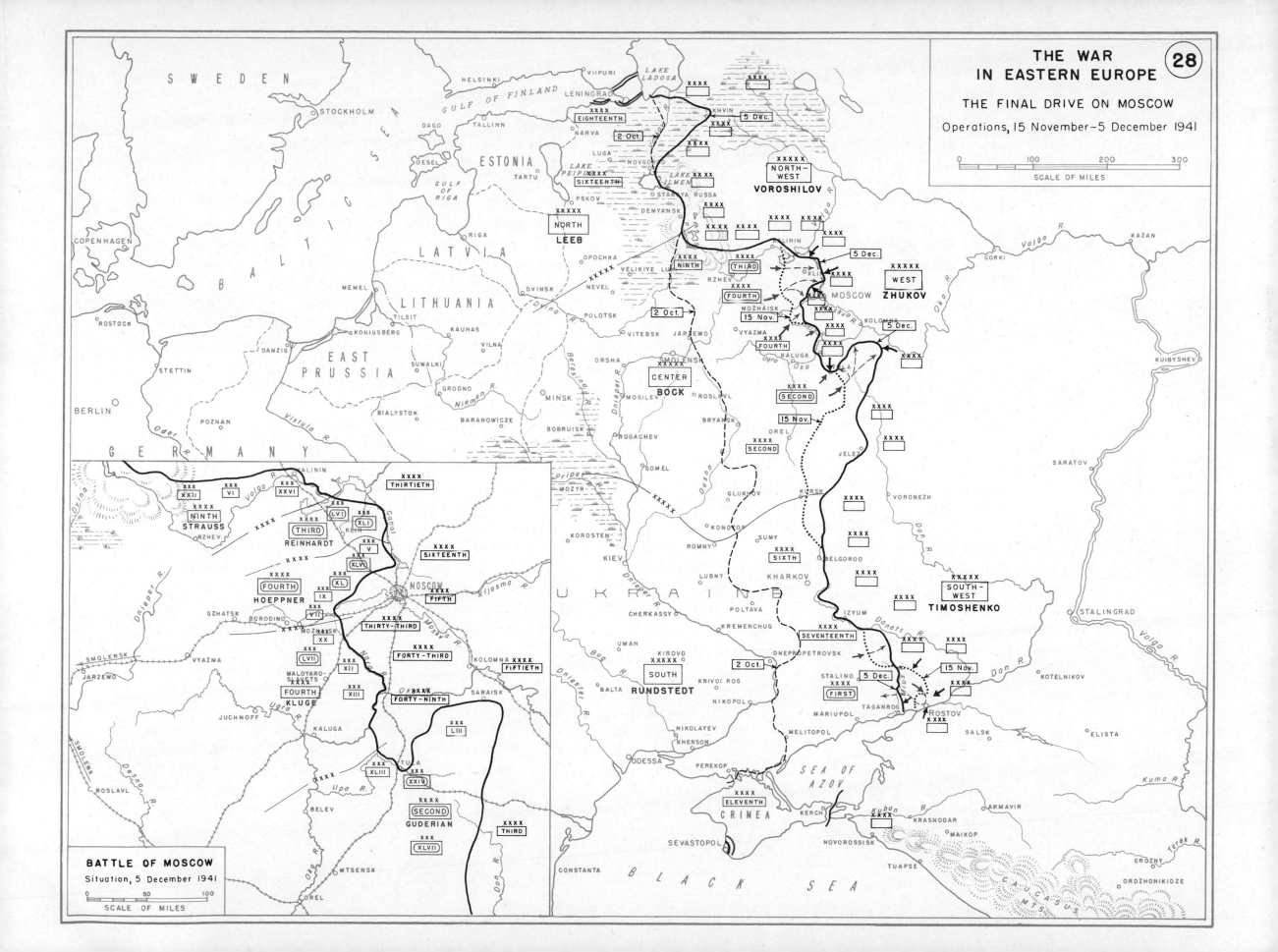

THE WAR
IN EASTERN EUROPE

28

THE FINAL DRIVE ON MOSCOW
Operations, 15 November–5 December 1941

100   200   300
SCALE OF MILES

SWEDEN

STOCKHOLM

COPENHAGEN

ROSTOCK

STETTIN

BERLIN

GERMANY

POZNAN

BALTIC SEA

DAGO

OESEL

GULF OF RIGA

DANZIG

KÖNIGSBERG

EAST PRUSSIA

BIALYSTOK

HELSINKI

VIIPURI

LAKE LADOGA

LENINGRAD

TALLINN

NARVA

ESTONIA

TARTU

LAKE PEIPUS

GULF OF FINLAND

XXXX EIGHTEENTH

2 Oct.

LUGA

NOVGOROD

LAKE ILMEN

PSKOV

RIGA

OPOCHKA

LATVIA

DVINSK

LITHUANIA

MEMEL

TILSIT

KAUNAS

VILNA

SUWALKI

GRODNO

Niemen R.

BARANOWICZE

MINSK

BOBRUISK

STARAYA RUSSA

DEMYANSK

VELIKIYE LUKI

NEVEL

VITEBSK

POLOTSK

Dvina R.

ORSHA

MOGILEV

ROGACHEV

GOMEL

XXXX SIXTEENTH

XXXX NORTH LEEB

XXXX NINTH

Berezina R.

SMOLENSK

XXXXX CENTER BOCK

ROSLAVL

Dnieper R.

BRYANSK

XXXX SECOND

Pripet R.

MOZYR

Desna R.

GLUKHOV

KONOTOP

KOROSTEN

ROMNY

KIEV

LUBNY

UKRAINE

KHVIN

XXXX

5 Dec.

XXXXX NORTH-WEST VOROSHILOV

XXXX XXXX XXXX XXXX

KALININ

XXXX THIRD

XXXX FOURTH

2 Oct.

15 Nov.

MOZHAISK

XXXX FOURTH

Ugra R.

KALUGA

Oka R.

15 Nov.

OREL

XXXX SECOND

KURSK

SUMY

SEA of AZOV

5 Dec.

XXXX

MOSCOW

XXXXX WEST ZHUKOV

Oka R.

KOLOMNA

5 Dec.

XXXX

XXXX

Volga R.

GORKI

KAZAN

KUIBYSHEV

SARATOV

VORONEZH

Don R.

JELEZ

XXXX

XXXX

BELGOROD

XXXX SIXTH

KHARKOV

POLTAVA

Donets R.

IZYUM

XXXX SEVENTEENTH

XXXXX SOUTH-WEST TIMOSHENKO

STALINGRAD

Volga R.

KOTELNIKOV

Don R.

KREMENCHUG

CHERKASSY

UMAN

KIROVO

XXXXX SOUTH RUNDSTEDT

2 Oct.

DNEPROPETROVSK

KRIVOI ROG

NIKOPOL

STALINO

XXXX FIRST

5 Dec.

TAGANROG

ROSTOV

15 Nov.

SALSK

ELISTA

BALTA

ODESSA

NIKOLAYEV

KHERSON

MELITOPOL

PEREKOP

MARIUPOL

CRIMEA

SEVASTOPOL

KERCH

CONSTANTA

BLACK SEA

NOVOROSSISK

TUAPSE

KRASNODAR

Kuban R.

ARMAVIR

MAIKOP

CAUCASUS MTS.

GROZNY

ORDZHONIKIDZE

Terek R.

XXXX ELEVENTH

Dvina R.

KALININ

Volga R.

XXII

VI

XXVI

XXXX THIRTIETH

XXXX NINTH STRAUSS

RZHEV

LVI

XLI

XXXX THIRD REINHARDT

V

XLVI

KLIN

Canal

XXXX FOURTH HOEPPNER

IX

XL

XXXX SIXTEENTH

MOSCOW

Kljasma R.

XXXX FIFTH

GZHATSK

BORODINO

VII

XX

MOZHAISK

Moskva R.

XXXX THIRTY-THIRD

SMOLENSK

VYAZMA

Dnieper R.

LVII

XII

XIII

XXXX FOURTH KLUGE

MALOYARO-SLAVETS

Ugra R.

JARZEWO

JUCHNOFF

Desna R.

ROSLAVL

KALUGA

XXXX FORTY-THIRD

KOLOMNA XXXX FIFTIETH

SARAISK

Oka R.

XXXX FORTY-NINTH

LIII

Oka R.

TULA

XLIII

XXIV

BELEV

XXXX SECOND GUDERIAN

Upa R.

XLVII

XXXX THIRD

MTSENSK

Don R.

OREL

On 6 December, the Russians opened their counteroffensive against overextended, freezing, disheartened Army Group Center. Army Group North and Army Group South were already under great pressure. By 8 December, as this Russian drive gained momentum, Hitler approved orders placing the German Army generally on the defensive for the winter. Panzer and motorized divisions were to be taken out of the line for rehabilitation. Incessant Russian local attacks, however, soon made that impossible. The Russian commanders had hordes of troops, accumulated for just this purpose, and no compunctions whatever about expending them. Their supply lines in the Moscow area were short and in good condition, their troops in high morale and reasonably well equipped for winter fighting. However, this was in large part a raw, new army, hastily assembled and short of all types of heavy weapons. Its commanders lacked the skill to carry out large-scale, coordinated operations; also, they had a hearty respect for their opponents.

Certain of the more primitive characteristics of this Russian Army were very much to its advantage in winter fighting. Using cavalry, infantry in sleighs, and their newly trained ski troops, the Russians were able to infiltrate the positions held by the Germans, whose heavy equipment made them roadbound in the deep snow. By late December, Leeb had been forced out of his Tikhvin salient, and Army Group Center had been pushed back generally to its 15 November line (*see map 27*b).

Hitler at first allowed some freedom of choice as to defensive tactics. But, on 18 December, irked by the loss of weapons and equipment during some local withdrawals, he ordered every inch of ground contested; officers were to inspire their troops to hold at all costs, even if surrounded. Concurrently, Hitler took direct command; Brauchitsch (whose functions Hitler had long usurped), Leeb, and others joined Rundstedt in retirement. Guderian was relieved on 25 December for withdrawing to a stronger line on his own initiative; General Erich Hoeppner (Fourth Panzer Group) was ignominiously discharged for remarks about "civilian leadership."

Late December and early January were times of crisis (*this map*). Russian attacks had gradually eroded gaps between the Second Panzer Army and the Fourth Army, and along the boundary between Army Group North and Army Group Center. Now, fresh Russian forces made deep penetrations in these areas; partisan attacks cut the railroad supplying the Ninth Army; attacks against Army Group North continued; and Russian amphibious operations poured troops into the Crimea, forcing the Eleventh Army to fight for its life. On 15 February, Hitler finally approved major "dignified" withdrawals by Army Group Center. Then, in late January, the Russians penetrated Army Group South's front near Izyum. In the north, the situation steadily worsened. Two corps of the Sixteenth Army were almost surrounded at Demyansk. Hitler chose to leave them in place to fix Russian forces which might otherwise have pushed on south and west, meanwhile supplying them by air.

Almost suddenly, in late February, the Russian offensive ran itself down. Army Group South had managed to contain the Izyum penetration, and Army Group Center had stabilized its right flank. The major Russian penetration, between Army Groups Center and North, still smoldered, but the Russians here were in logistical difficulties and had lost heavily in their assaults against the German "hedgehogs" (localities organized for all-around defense). Army Group North still held the key points of its lines, and, farther north (*off map*), a massive Russian counterattack in Finland had been a complete failure.

The Germans had lost heavily, but had suffered no really serious defeats. Their major misfortune, which was not immediately apparent, was that Hitler—far from being impressed by the results of his amateur meddling—now credited his own will power and his order to wage a static defense with having saved the German Army. Ironically, his "system," at great sacrifice, finally halted the Russians in the approximate area to which Army Group Center had originally wished to retire and wage a flexible defense.

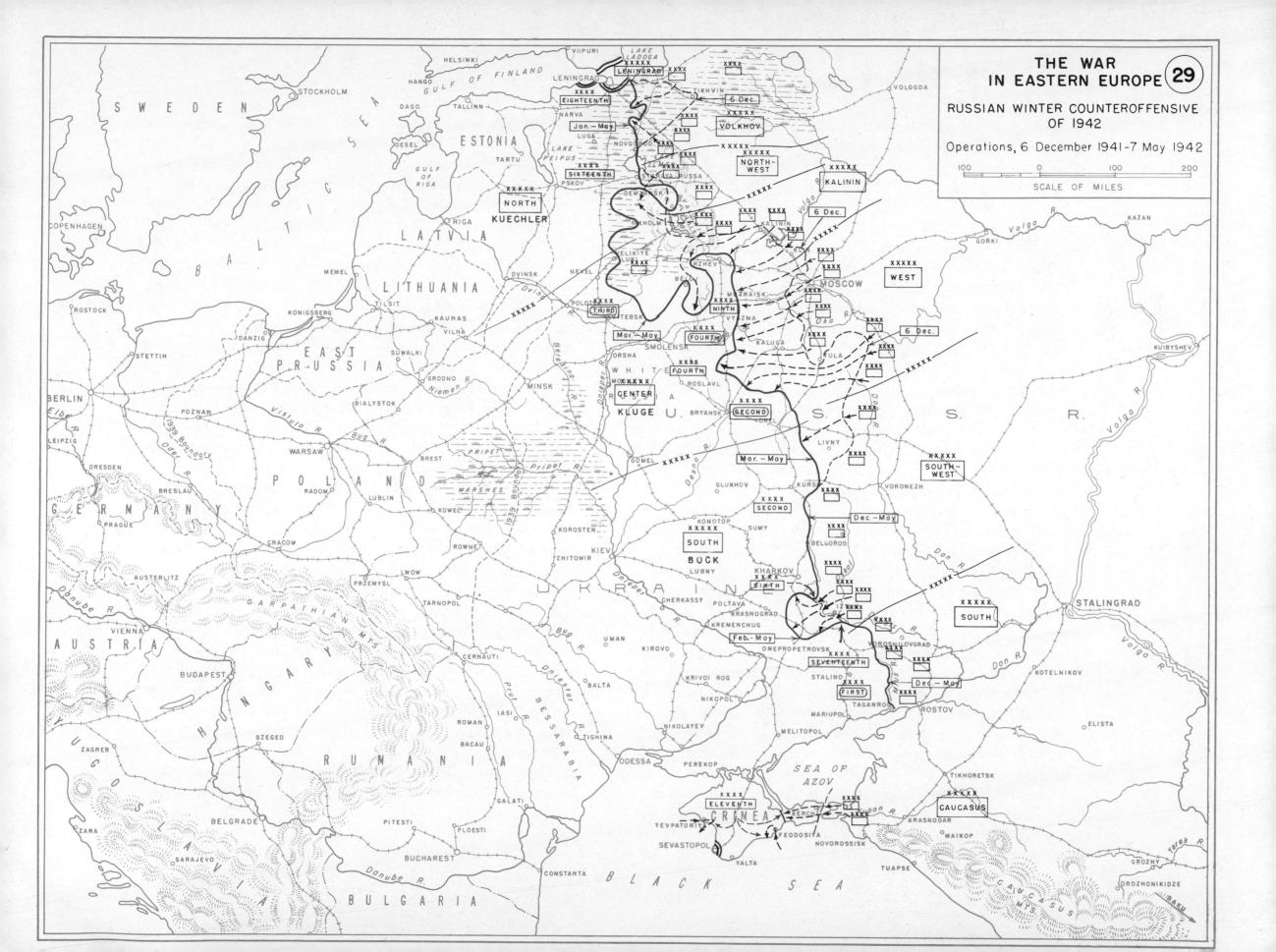

THE WAR
IN EASTERN EUROPE 29
RUSSIAN WINTER COUNTEROFFENSIVE
OF 1942

Operations, 6 December 1941-7 May 1942

100   0   100   200
SCALE OF MILES

As the Russian offensive slowly ebbed, Hitler turned to one of his pet projects—the seizure of the Caucasus oil fields. His choice of this objective is an example of his weakness for selecting economic objectives without considering the military problems involved.

March brought the spring thaws and the mud, which, until early May, enforced a general truce. The Russians were practically exhausted. Despite the arrival of increasing quantities of Lend-Lease supplies, they were even short of rifles. The Germans, however, were too worn down to mount a general counteroffensive. Hitler ordered the Luftwaffe to neutralize the Russian Black Sea Fleet and its bases. That accomplished, Army Group South was to drive the Russians from the Kerch peninsula (eastern Crimea), renew the siege of Sevastopol, and pinch off the Izyum salient. The other two army groups were to shorten their lines and clear up their rear areas.

The plan for the German 1942 offensive was issued on 5 April. (From all indications, Hitler himself prepared it.) Following the preliminary operations (described above), Army Group South would open an offensive to destroy all Russian forces in the bend of the Don River preparatory to seizing the Caucasus oil fields. Because of lack of rail facilities sufficient to get all the attacking troops into position for a simultaneous advance, this operation would be carried out in four principal phases (indicated on the map by circled numbers): (1) a double envelopment of Voronezh, followed by the establishment of a strong defensive line (*open red blocks*) from that city westward toward Orel; (2) an advance down the Don River from Voronezh to link up with a second German force advancing from Kharkov; (3) a continuing advance down the Don, to meet a third column which would drive eastward from the Mius River, simultaneously making secondary attacks southward to seize bridgeheads over the lower Don; (4) thereafter, operations to seize Stalingrad, while the main attack prepared to move southeast into the Caucasus. Army Group Center would remain on

the defensive, but—if Army Group South were successful—Army Group North would seize Leningrad.

The German Army of 1942 was far inferior to that of 1941. Only the divisions assigned to Army Group South had received the necessary number of replacements; elsewhere, the average German division was little over half strength. Fifty-one satellite divisions (Rumanian, Hungarian, Italian, and Slovak) and another of Spanish volunteers had been added, but these were poorly armed and of questionable value. The German war industry, still operating at a low level of efficiency, had failed to replace many of the motor vehicles lost during the winter. Even Army Group South's panzer divisions now had only 85 per cent of their organic vehicles.

Preliminary operations began on 8 May, with Manstein's attack on the Kerch peninsula. By the 19th, he had driven the Russians into the sea, inflicting 150,000 casualties. Meanwhile (12 May), the Russians broke through on either side of Kharkov, employing tanks in mass. Hitler countered by beginning the attack on the Izyum salient (17 May). After several weeks of confused fighting, this salient was cut off (25 June) and mopped up. The Russians lost 240,000 men and 1,249 tanks, but managed to withdraw the troops which had struck at Kharkov from the north. Manstein, in the meantime, had opened his attack against Sevastopol (*inset sketch*). Russian defenses were strong, and Russian resistance stubborn. To the end, reinforcements were pumped into the city, submarines being used after surface vessels were driven off. Supported by the Luftwaffe and superheavy siege artillery, the German assault teams fought their way to the north shore of Sevastopol harbor on 20 June. On the night of the 28th, they made a surprise amphibious assault across it, taking the defenses south of the city from the rear. Fighting ended on 1 July, the Russians having lost about 100,000 men. In the north, Army Groups Center and North had had considerable success in wiping out partisan groups in their rear areas.

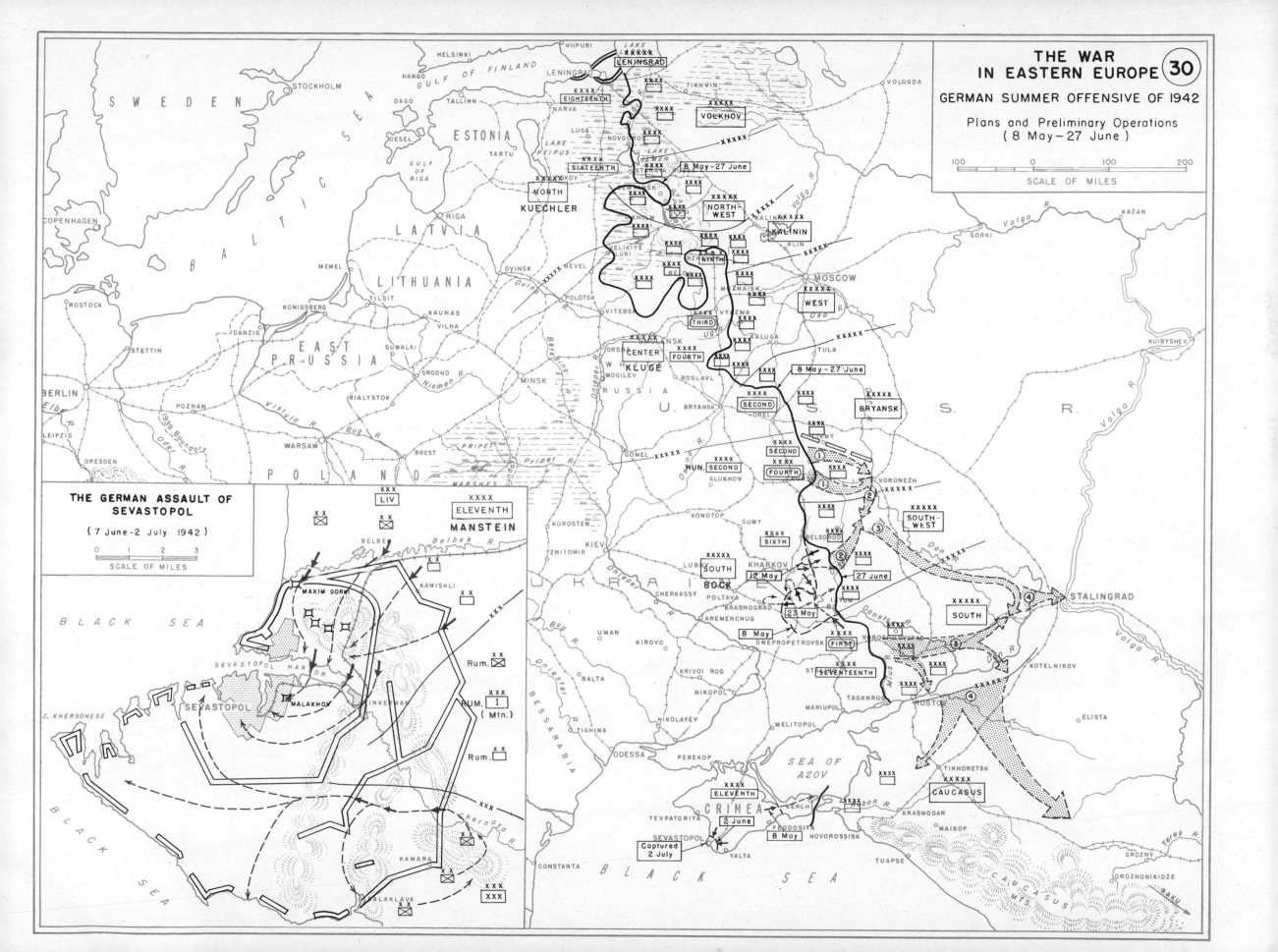

THE WAR
IN EASTERN EUROPE (30)
GERMAN SUMMER OFFENSIVE OF 1942

Plans and Preliminary Operations
(8 May — 27 June)

100   0   100   200
SCALE OF MILES

THE GERMAN ASSAULT OF
SEVASTOPOL

(7 June–2 July 1942)

0   1   2   3
SCALE OF MILES

As early as 2 May, a news agency report from Moscow indicated that the Russians expected a major German attack in the area Voronezh (*top center*)–Stalingrad. Hitler, however, was undisturbed. The results of the preliminary operations (*see map 30*) had confirmed his previous low opinion of the Russian Army. He now felt that his offensive aimed at Stalingrad and the Caucasus oil fields would meet little effective opposition. If he felt any worry, it was over a possible Anglo-American airborne operation against Western Europe.

His confidence soon had a rude testing. On 19 June, a staff officer of one of the panzer divisions to be employed during the first phase of the coming offensive—the drive on Voronezh—flew to the front in a liaison plane, which crashed behind the Russian lines. Against orders, he had carried with him several secret documents relating to the impending operations. Hitler's plans were now thoroughly compromised. It was too late in the season to change them; he either had to cancel the operation or go ahead with it as planned. Hitler chose to attack. Shortly thereafter, ominous signs appeared. German troops moving into their assembly areas around Kursk (*this map, top left*) were struck by heavy Russian air raids; reports from all along the front indicated that the Russians were pulling troops out of line, apparently to form reserves.

The attack against Voronezh (Second Army and Fourth Panzer Army) moved out on 28 June. Oddly enough, it seems to have surprised the Russians on this front. They recovered rapidly, however, and counterattacked vigorously, employing several tank brigades of which German intelligence had been unaware. Nevertheless, the Germans reached Voronezh on 2 July, capturing it four days later after violent fighting. German infantry then set up a defense line facing northeast from Livny to Voronezh, the Fourth Panzer Army turned south, and the Second Hungarian Army prepared to hold the line of the Don River south of Voronezh.

Next, the second-phase attack (the Sixth Army) advanced on 30 June, establishing contact with the leading elements of the Fourth Panzer Army on 7 July. Only a few enemy rear guards were cut off as they covered the withdrawal of the main Russian armies eastward across the Don. (Russian forces in this area probably were relatively weak because of their losses—roughly 400,000 men—in May and early June.)

Army Group South was reorganized during this period. On 7 July, the First Panzer, Eleventh, and Seventeenth Armies were assigned to the new Army Group A, under List. On the 9th, the remainder of the army group was redesignated Army Group B. On 13 July, Hitler relieved Bock—ostensibly because of his delay in taking Voronezh, but probably to replace him with the more pliable General Maximilian von Weichs.

List's attack (9 July) initiated the third phase. Russian troops opposing the First Panzer Army broke in disorder, many of them deserting. Then, on 13 July, Hitler promptly switched plans, thoroughly confusing the whole campaign (*compare maps 30 and 31*). Either anxious to speed up his planned invasion of the Caucasus or apprehensive over possible last-ditch Russian resistance at Rostov, he ordered List to wheel south and cross the Don River east of Rostov, reinforcing him for this maneuver with the Fourth Panzer Army from Army Group B. This left the Sixth Army alone to continue the advance toward Stalingrad and opened a gap between it and the Fourth Panzer Army through which approximately two-thirds of the Russians in the bend of the Don River were able to escape. It also complicated the already critical supply problem: Army Group B was hampered by gasoline shortages.

On 11 July, Hitler had directed that the Eleventh Army would attack across the Kerch Strait against the Russian naval base at Novorossisk and the Maikop oil fields (*lower center*). The Russians, meanwhile, were attacking heavily in the Voronezh area, with consistent lack of success, and maintaining considerable pressure along the rest of the front. Army Groups Center and North, however, reported their situations as steadily improving.

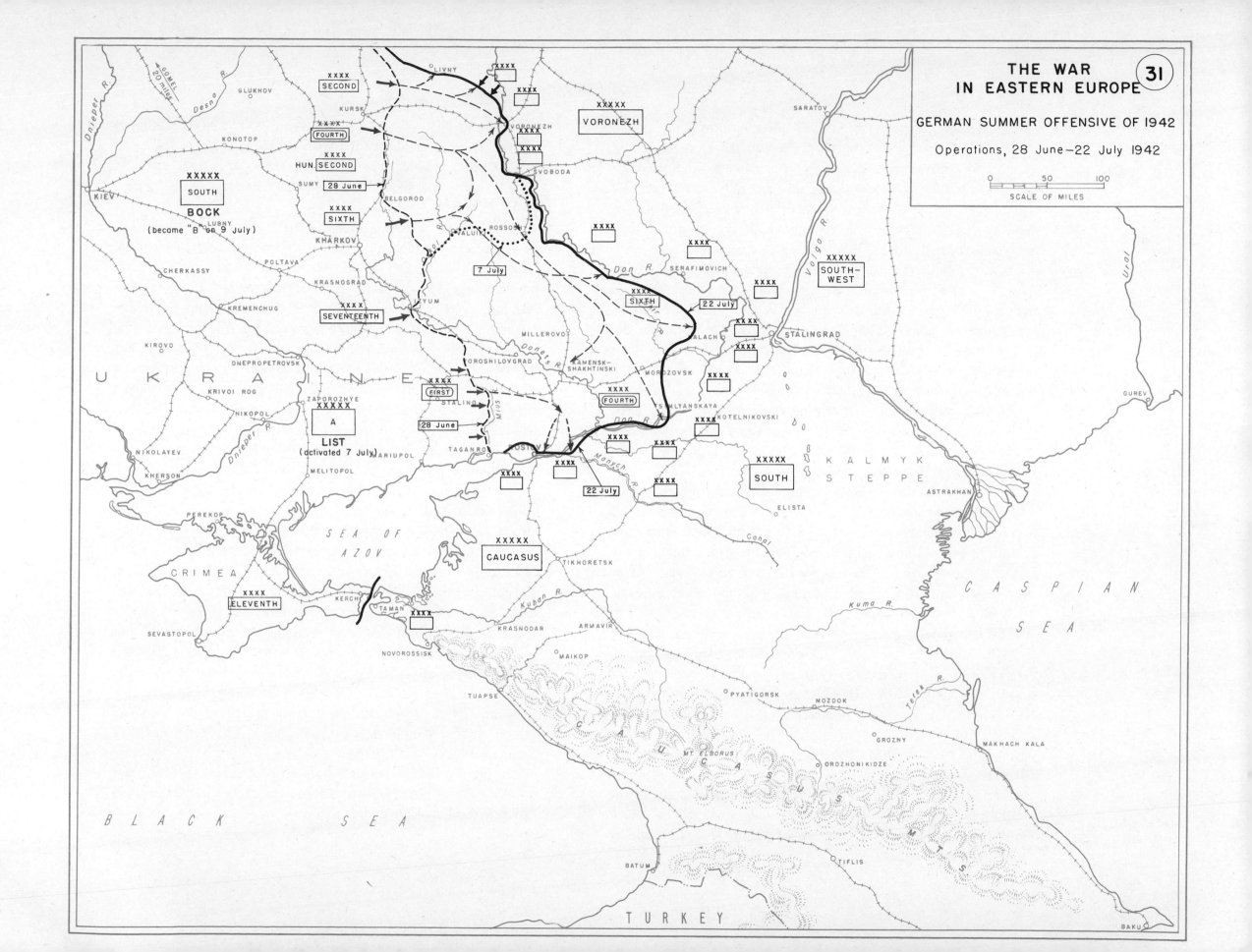

THE WAR
IN EASTERN EUROPE

31

GERMAN SUMMER OFFENSIVE OF 1942

Operations, 28 June–22 July 1942

0   50   100
SCALE OF MILES

Despite Hitler's anxiety, Rostov fell after a short battle. Both the First and Fourth Panzer Armies forced the Don River and established sizable bridgeheads. For the moment, the Russians here were somewhat demoralized and generally in retreat.

German supply problems and Hitler's military genius now came to Russia's rescue. By 25 July, both panzer armies had been stalled briefly by gasoline shortages; the Sixth Army, pushing toward Stalingrad, was without gasoline for a period of ten days, and had once momentarily run short of ammunition. In the time thus gained, the Russians worked frantically at fortifying Stalingrad. Some gasoline was airlifted forward, but the general shortage of transport aircraft, supply trucks, and even draft horses made it evident that no real relief could be expected until the railroad eastward from Stalino (*center, left*) was repaired.

Hitler's contribution was twofold. On 23 July, he ordered the Eleventh Army (less several divisions) and the siege artillery used against Sevastopol north to Leningrad, the capture of which Hitler now optimistically scheduled for September. Having thus sent the only available reserve behind his main attack to the other end of the Eastern Front, he then proceeded to scatter his attacking forces piecemeal across south-central Russia. For some reason, Stalingrad had begun to fascinate his erratic mind. Previously (*see text, map 31*), he had turned the Fourth Panzer Army away from that city when its capture should have been comparatively easy, and had allowed the Sixth Army's advance on it to stall for lack of supplies; he now suddenly detached a panzer corps from the Fourth Panzer Army and sent it back toward Stalingrad. Army Group A's new mission (also assigned on the 23d) was to destroy the Russian forces that had escaped across the Don from Rostov; cut the Stalingrad-Tikhoretsk (*this map, lower center*) railroad; seize the Black Sea coast to the Turkish frontier, thus leaving the Russian Black Sea Fleet without bases; capture the Maikop-Armavir oil-field area; and push a motorized force through Grozny (*lower right*) southeast along the shore of the Caspian Sea toward the Baku oil-producing center. The attack across the Kerch Strait was to be carried out on a reduced scale by the divisions left behind by the Eleventh Army. Army Group B was to advance to Stalingrad, destroy the Russian forces gathering in that area, establish a defensive front between the Don and Volga Rivers, and, finally, send a mobile column down the Volga to Astrakhan.

To date, the German offensive had been showily successful, despite inadequate logistical support. Russian leaders were more than somewhat shaken. Expert Communist propaganda in England and the United States furiously demanded an immediate "second front" in Western Europe. Hosts of impressionable American and English sympathizers echoed this demand. The British amphibious raid on Dieppe (19 August)—costly, but highly educational—seems to have been partly motivated by this clamor. Though unsuccessful, this Dieppe operation renewed Hitler's fears for Western Europe. Consequently, also on 23 July, he designated two elite motorized infantry divisions—one of them from Army Group A—for transfer to the West. Another crack division was later sent to Crete.

During late July, the Russian retreat on the Caucasus front continued, despite Stalin's order to fight to the end. List's advance, however, was hampered by Hitler's transfer of the entire Fourth Panzer Army to Army Group B, effective 1 August. Lack of gasoline slowed the German advance on all fronts. Russian resistance in the Caucasus was initially light, but eventually stiffened in the mountain passes. Army Group A was now badly overextended, with twenty understrength divisions spread out over a front of more than 500 miles. Army Group B, supported by most of the available Luftwaffe units, completed clearing the bend of the Don River by 18 August against growing Russian opposition. On 23 August, the Germans crossed the Don, repulsed Russian counterattacks, and reached the Volga north of Stalingrad.

In the north (*not shown*), considerable seesaw fighting went on along Army Group Center's front, diverting German air and ground reinforcements to that area.

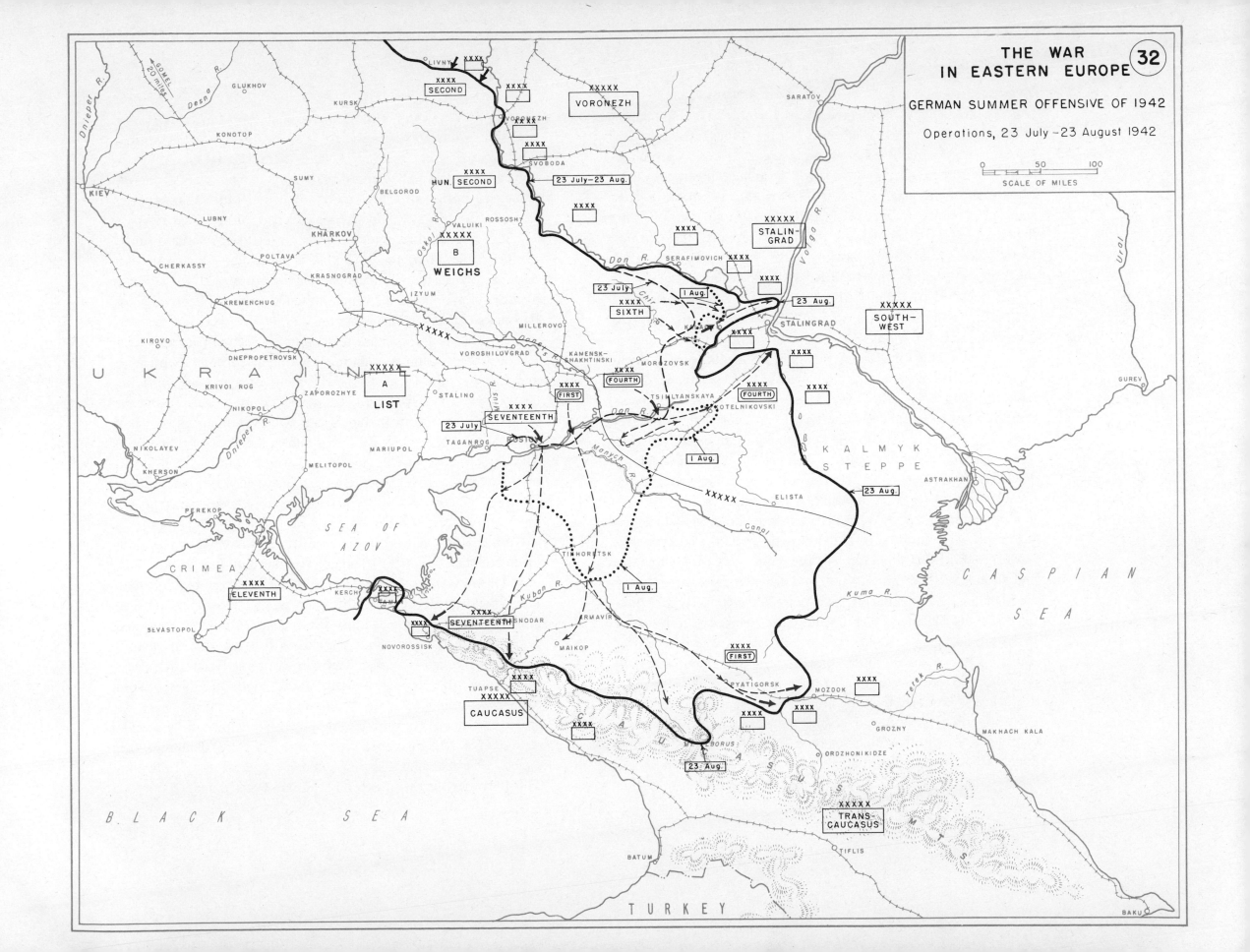

GERMAN SUMMER OFFENSIVE OF 1942

Operations, 23 July – 23 August 1942

0   50   100
SCALE OF MILES

During late August, September, and October, the momentum of the German offensive died away. In the Caucasus, List's panzer units were without gasoline for weeks at a time. Camel caravans had to be improvised to deliver gasoline and supplies. The Maikop oil fields had been wrecked by the withdrawing Russians; a special German "oil brigade" sent in to take over the fields was able to accomplish little. Furthermore, the German Navy failed to utilize the Black Sea as a supply line, even after the Luftwaffe had crippled the Russian Black Sea Fleet.

By the end of August, the Russian Trans-Caucasus Front ("front" was the Russian term for "army group") got its forces once more in hand. Many of the Caucasus hill tribes had reservations about dying for Russia, but reinforcements were brought in from central Russia (by boat across the Caspian Sea) and from northern Iran (where the Russians maintained large occupation forces to safeguard American Lend-Lease shipments [see map 37]). Digging in with their usual skill and speed, the Russians held the mountain passes, occasionally counterattacking. The diversion of most of the Luftwaffe to Stalingrad enabled them to achieve local air superiority. Nevertheless, in early September, German troops from the Crimea made an assault crossing of the Kerch Strait (this map), driving down the coast to take Novorossisk. Hitler, however, was becoming increasingly irritable and at odds with his military staff and army leaders, whom he accused of "intellectual conceit" and "complete incapacity for grasping essentials." Halder, chief of staff of the Army, was relieved for persisting in trying to talk sense to Hitler. List was relieved for lack of aggressiveness. Hitler himself took direct command of Army Group A—in addition to his other duties as commander in chief of the over-all German armed forces, commander in chief of the German Army, and civilian chief of state! Subsequent German attacks in the Caucasus made slight but indecisive gains. Some German motorized patrols even reached the Caspian.

By contrast to the Caucasus stalemate, the battle for Stalingrad grew in fury with Hitler's increasingly unbalanced obsession over the capture of that city. At Warsaw and Leningrad, Hitler had avoided street fighting because of the heavy casualties involved. Now he pulled more and more troops away from the Caucasus—originally his major objective—for a no-quarter struggle (a "rats' war," his troops called it) in a ruined town.

Stalingrad and its suburbs (inset sketch) stretched a distance of thirty miles along the west bank of the Volga. During the last days of August, the Germans had moved up through the suburbs against light opposition, which stiffened in early September as Russian reserves streamed into the city, finally checking the German advance in the business and industrial section near the river. Vicious house-to-house fighting continued through September and October, the Germans slowly gaining ground but suffering heavy losses. The Russian defense was devoted and expert; the defenders—fighting with the Volga River at their backs—had been told to hold or die. By 1 November, their position had been split into four separate bridgeheads, which could be reinforced only by ferry across the mile-wide river under German artillery fire. On 12 November, a final German attack (not shown) reached the Volga south of the city.

While this pointless battle of attrition raged, German intelligence officers warned of a major Russian build-up around Saratov (main sketch, top right), and of increasing activity around the Russian bridgehead on the south bank of the Don at Serafimovich (upper center). Luftwaffe reconnaissance flights failed to confirm their reports, but the known Russian skill at camouflage had frequently baffled German aviators. Even Hitler suspected that the Russians might attack south across the Don toward Rostov; he belatedly ordered one German panzer division extricated from the Stalingrad melee to provide a mobile reserve. On 12 November, German intelligence definitely predicted an impending Russian offensive against the Rumanian Third Army. But the attack on Stalingrad continued.

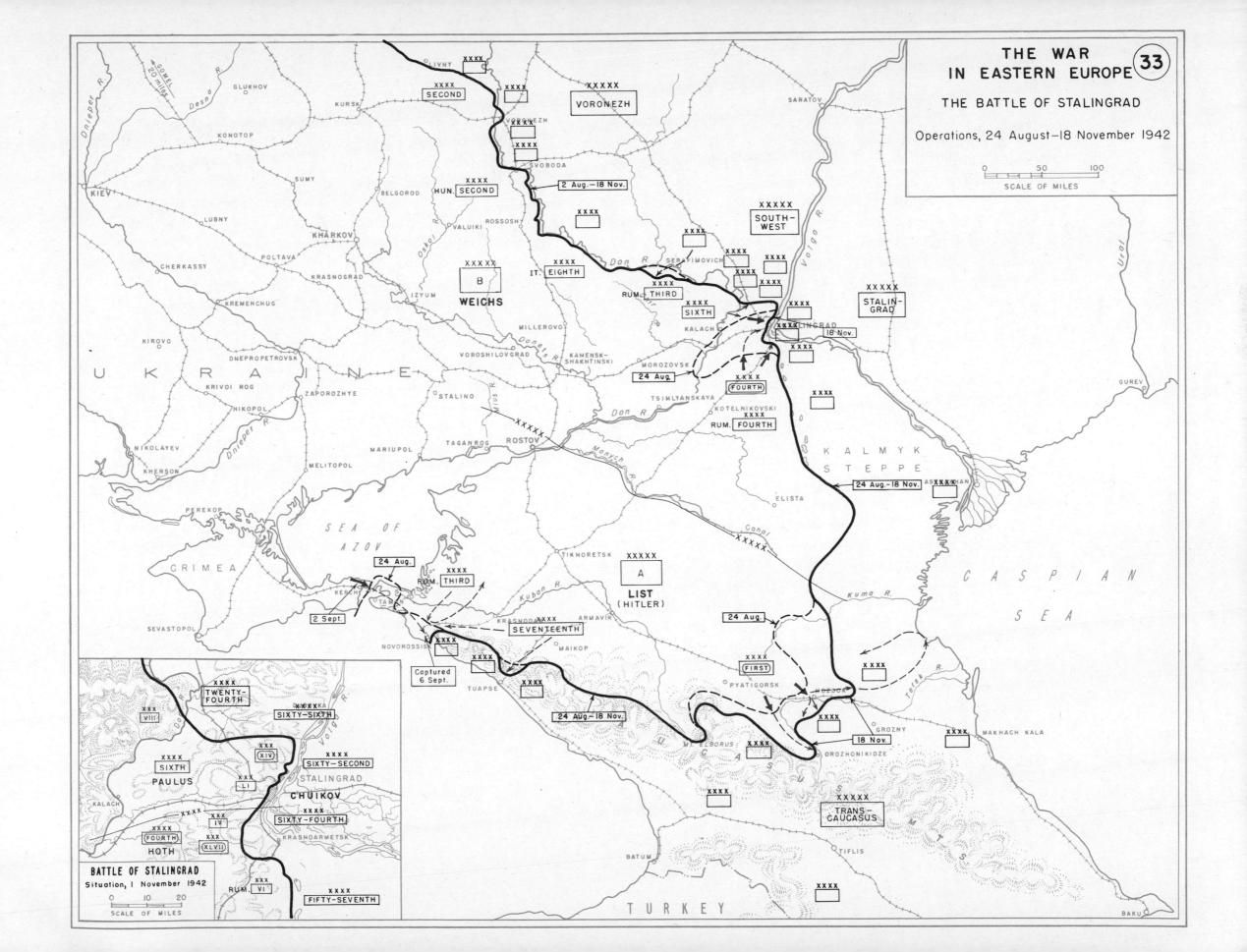

0   50   100
SCALE OF MILES

GOMEL R.
20 miles
Desna R.
Dnieper R.
OLIVNY
XXXX
SECOND
XXXX
VORONEZH
XXXXX
KURSK
GLUKHOV
KONOTOP
XXXX
VORONEZH
XXXX
SVOBODA
KIEV
SUMY
BELGOROD
HUN. SECOND
XXXX
VALUIKI
ROSSOSH
2 Aug.–18 Nov.
SARATOV
Volga R.
Oskol R.
Don R.
XXXX
LUBNY
POLTAVA
KHARKOV
KRASNOGRAD
IZYUM
XXXXX
IT. EIGHTH
XXXX
SOUTH-WEST
XXXXX
Serafimovich
XXXX
XXXX
XXXX
CHERKASSY
KREMENCHUG
B
WEICHS
XXXXX
MILLEROVO
Donets R.
RUM. THIRD
XXXX
SIXTH
XXXX
KALACH
STALINGRAD
XXXX
STALINGRAD
XXXXX
Dnieper R.
KIROVO
DNEPROPETROVSK
VOROSHILOVGRAD
KAMENSK-SHAKHTINSKI
MOROZOVSK
24 Aug.
FOURTH
XXXX
18 Nov.
XXXX
U K R A I N E
KRIVOI ROG
ZAPOROZHYE
NIKOPOL
STALINO
Don R.
TSIMLYANSKAYA
Kotelnikovski
RUM. FOURTH
XXXX
XXXX
K A L M Y K
GUREV
NIKOLAYEV
KHERSON
MELITOPOL
MARIUPOL
TAGANROG
ROSTOV
Mius R.
XXXXX
Manych R.
S T E P P E
24 Aug.–18 Nov.
ASTRAKHAN
XXXXX
PEREKOP
SEA OF
AZOV
Don R.
ELISTA
Canal
XXXXX
Kuma R.
C A S P I A N
CRIMEA
24 Aug.
XXXX
RUM. THIRD
TIKHORETSK
XXXXX
A
LIST
(HITLER)
S E A
SEVASTOPOL
KERCH
TAMAN
2 Sept.
Kuban R.
KRASNODAR
XXXX
ARMAVIR
SEVENTEENTH
MAIKOP
24 Aug.
XXXX
FIRST
24 Aug.
XXXX
NOVOROSSISK
XXXX
Captured 6 Sept.
TUAPSE
XXXX
24 Aug.–18 Nov.
PYATIGORSK
MOZDOK
Terek R.
XXXX
18 Nov.
GROZNY
XXXX
MAKHACH KALA
Mt. ELBORUS
XXXX
ORDZHONIKIDZE
XXXX
C A U C A S U S MTS.
TRANS-CAUCASUS
XXXXX
BATUM
TIFLIS
T U R K E Y
XXXX
BAKU

BATTLE OF STALINGRAD
Situation, 1 November 1942

0   10   20
SCALE OF MILES

Don R.
XXXX
TWENTY-FOURTH
XXX
VIII
XXXXX
SIXTY-SIXTH
XXXX
SIXTH
PAULUS
XXX
XIV
XXXX
SIXTY-SECOND
XXX
LI
Volga R.
STALINGRAD
CHUIKOV
KALACH
XXXX
XXX
IV
FOURTH
HOTH
XXX
XLVII
SIXTY-FOURTH
KRASNOARMETSK
RUM. VI
XXX
FIFTY-SEVENTH
XXXX

As of 0700, 19 November, most of the German elements of Army Group B were engaged around Stalingrad (*see map 33*). A screen of satellite troops—almost without armor, motor transport, or effective antitank guns—watched the line of the Don River to the northwest. South of Stalingrad, the Rumanian Fourth Army covered Army Group B's right flank, and between it and Army Group A stretched a 240-mile gap, guarded only by a single motorized division (*not shown*) at Elista (*this map; center, right*). Army Group A's front was stalemated. The logistical situation of both army groups was growing steadily worse. Army Group A, and most of Army Group B, depended on a single rail line which crossed the Dnieper River at Dnepropetrovsk (*left center.*)

The Russian plan was obvious. Hitler had obligingly jammed his troops into a tight corner at Stalingrad, where they would be automatically trapped by attacks through the Rumanians on their flanks. The Russian counteroffensive waited only for freezing weather (to permit cross-country tank movements) and the Anglo-American landings in North Africa (to pin down German reinforcements in Western Europe).

About 0720, 19 November, Russian artillery fire suddenly deluged the Rumanian Third Army (*center*). At 0850, Russian infantry, massed by divisions into human battering rams, surged out of the Serafimovich bridgehead. The badly overextended Rumanians held until past noon—a respectable fight, everything considered. By 1400, however, Russian tank columns, followed by swarms of cavalry, were driving through their broken front. The tanks headed directly for the vital bridge at Kalach (*west of Stalingrad*); the cavalry fanned out to the northwest. More infantry and armor cut southeast to isolate Stalingrad. No previous Russian offensive had shown such expert planning and execution.

South of Stalingrad, the Russians struck on 20 November. Here, the Fourth Rumanian Army panicked. Part of the Fourth Panzer Army was cut off and crowded into the city; the rest escaped, largely because of inept Russian staff work. Tanks from the northern Russian attack reached Kalach on the 21st; the southern attack linked up with them during the 22d. The trap was firmly closed the next day.

Late on the 22d, Paulus had requested authority to fight his way out. Weichs had urged him to act at once, but Paulus—aware of Hitler's feelings concerning Stalingrad—would not take the initiative and waited for Hitler's personal decision. Hitler customarily avoided firm decisions. Finally, on 24 November, he ordered Paulus to hold Stalingrad, promising to supply him by air. (Göring had grandiloquently pledged that the Luftwaffe would deliver 600 tons of supplies per day.)

On 20 November, meanwhile, Hitler had appointed Manstein commander of the newly formed Army Group Don (Fourth Panzer Army, Sixth Army, Third and Fourth Rumanian Armies), ordering him to "recapture the positions formerly held by us." Arriving on the 26th, Manstein found himself almost without troops. Fortunately, the Russians put most of their forces into attacks against Stalingrad. Bad weather, the slow arrival of reinforcements, and Russian pressure delayed Manstein's attempt to mount a relief expedition. The situation in Stalingrad grew desperate; the Luftwaffe's average daily supply delivery was only seventy tons. At last, on 12 December, a forlorn hope (two—later three—understrength panzer divisions) drove northeastward from Kotelnikovski (*center*). Wrecking one Russian unit after another, the panzers thrust to within thirty-five miles of Stalingrad on the 19th. Manstein thereupon ordered Paulus to break out and link up. Paulus quibbled; Hitler's definite authorization could not be secured. During this indecision, the front collapsed. On 16 December, farther north, the Russians had stampeded the Italian Eighth Army. On the 24th, fresh Russian tank units converged on the relief column, which fought its way back with difficulty.

Army Group A (commanded by Kleist since 22 November) had been under considerable pressure, but had held most of its ground. On 28 December, Hitler at last approved its withdrawal.

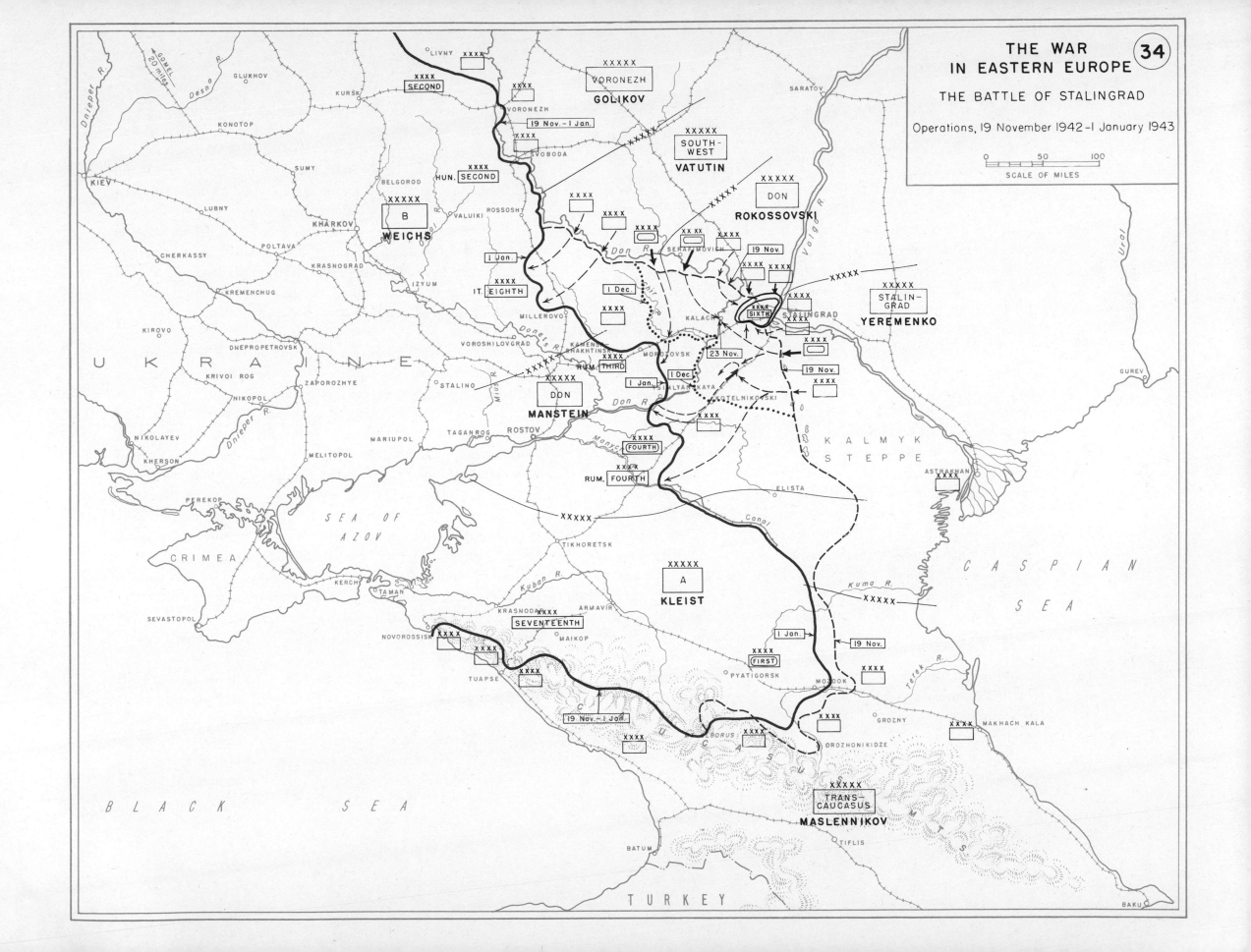

THE WAR
IN EASTERN EUROPE

34

THE BATTLE OF STALINGRAD

Operations, 19 November 1942–1 January 1943

0   50   100
SCALE OF MILES

Disaster now faced all the German forces in southern Russia. The furious offensive of the Russian Southwest Front threatened to turn the left flank of Army Group Don, seize the Donets and Dnieper River crossings behind it, and drive on to Rostov. Such a coup would cut Army Group A's line of retreat through Rostov and pocket Army Group Don against the Sea of Azov; the result would be a second, and greater, Stalingrad. (Note the relative distances from Rostov to Mozdok [*lower right*] and Rostov to Tsimlyanskaya [*center*].) Had Paulus, at any time before 25 December, been able to muster the moral courage to defy Hitler and throw the Sixth Army into a do-or-die attempt to break out of Stalingrad, he probably could have extricated the greater part of his troops. Thus reinforced, Manstein should have been able to wage a successful defensive-offensive campaign between the Don and the Donets, utilizing the superior German skill in mobile warfare.

But now—with Paulus cooped up in Stalingrad and the Luftwaffe bleeding itself white in an effort to fly in a mere trickle of supplies—Manstein, Weichs, and Kleist simply lacked sufficient troops to halt the Russians. Most of the Rumanians had been withdrawn, too shaken to be any longer reliable. The greater part of the Italian Eighth Army had practically evaporated. Large parts of the German "lines" were held only by isolated, improvised formations, created out of service troops, fugitives, and stray detachments.

In this swelling crisis, Paulus could render Germany one last service—to hold out, drawing as many Russians as possible against his famishing Sixth Army, until Army Group A completed withdrawing from the Caucasus. This Paulus did. His previous conduct is easily criticized, but few, if any, generals have ever faced so grim a set of alternatives as Paulus did, between Hitler and the Russians.

Stalingrad's story is quickly told. After the original Russian November offensive, the Sixth Army had had little trouble in beating off Russian infantry attacks. Early in January, the Russian Don Front, with considerable air support, was concentrated around Stalingrad. After Paulus had rejected two surrender ultimatums, the Russians attacked on 10 January. Short of ammunition, food, and fuel, the Sixth Army resisted stubbornly; however, by the 21st, both of the Stalingrad airports had been lost. On the 23d, Paulus reported the situation hopeless and requested permission to capitulate. Hitler ordered him to fight on. At 0840, 2 February, the last pocket of resistance reported it had done its duty "to the last man." Stalingrad cost Hitler approximately 300,000 men (including those lost in the earlier fighting around the town), leaving a gap in the German Army that could never be refilled. It inspired the Russians—somewhat prematurely—with self-confidence.

In the meantime, Manstein had been fighting Russians, weather, and Hitler to hold the Rostov gateway open for Kleist. The last of those three was by far the most dangerous and illusive. Hitler protested and delayed every backward step, even when he had previously authorized it. Finally, at last dissuaded (21 January) from attempting to hold the Maikop oil fields, he insisted upon at least retaining a bridgehead in the Taman-Novorossisk area (*lower center*). Consequently, the Seventeenth Army was pulled back into that area, while the First Panzer Army moved methodically back through Rostov, despite eager Russian attempts to cut it off. On 14 January, however, the situation again grew tense. A Russian attack south of Voronezh (*upper center*) dispersed most of the Hungarian Second Army. On the 25th, a second offensive caught the German Second Army retiring from Voronezh, mauling it badly. This shocked Hitler into transferring the First Panzer Army to Manstein.

Manstein was now fighting in three directions, against odds estimated at seven to one. Only by keeping his battered panzer units concentrated for counterattacks against Russian penetrations was he able to keep his front intact. By 1 February, however, a massive Russian armored offensive was crossing the Donets east of Voroshilovgrad (*center*); another was threatening to break into the German rear near Izyum to the northwest.

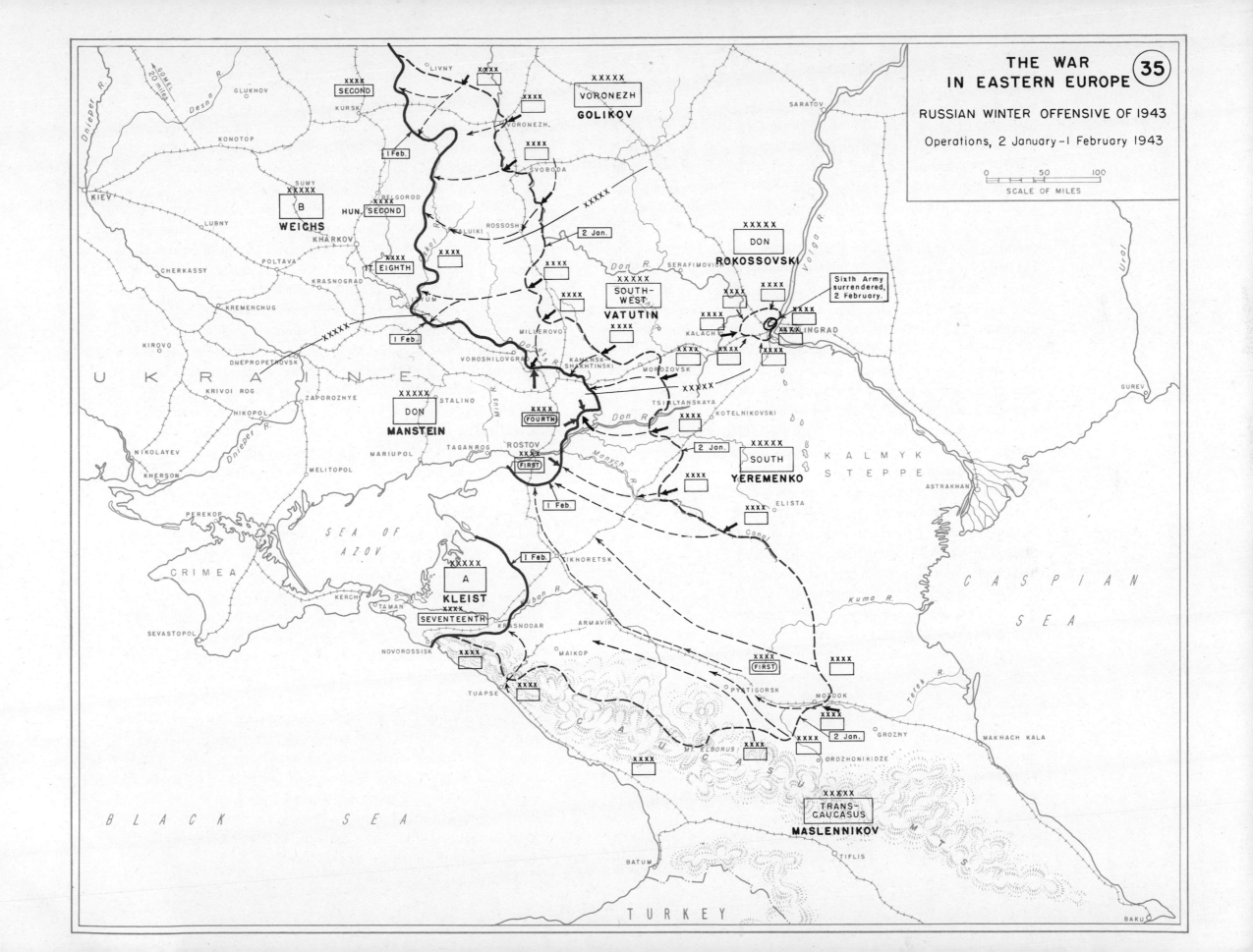

THE WAR
IN EASTERN EUROPE ㉟

RUSSIAN WINTER OFFENSIVE OF 1943

Operations, 2 January–1 February 1943

0   50   100
SCALE OF MILES

By early February, there appeared little hope for the Germans in southern Russia (*lower right, dashed red line*)—especially since Russian units released by the fall of Stalingrad were now joining in the attack. The defeat of the Second German Army near Voronezh (*right center*) had left a gap over 200 miles wide, extending south to Izyum. Izyum fell on 5 February. Vigorously prodded by Manstein, Hitler finally agreed that forces in the salient between Voroshilovgrad and Rostov (*lower right*) might withdraw to the line of the Mius River (*solid red line*). By 18 February, this line had been occupied, the Germans wrecking the mines and industrial plants of the Donets Basin as they withdrew.

Farther north, Hitler had been attempting to concentrate the SS Panzer Corps at Kharkov (*center, right*), with the farfetched idea of sending them to rescue Stalingrad, but this concentration was still incomplete. After an abortive counterattack on 11 February, those SS units which had reached Kharkov were forced out during 14-16 February by a combined civilian uprising and converging Russian attacks. A flood of Russian tank, cavalry, and motorized corps was cresting southward. By 20 February, Russian spearheads (*dotted red line*) were within twenty miles of Dnepropetrovsk (*lower center*) and had cut the railroad into Stalino, severing Manstein's supply line. Other Russian offensives had cracked the Mius River front at several points.

On 12 February, Hitler had abolished Army Group B, dividing its front and the remnants of its troops between Army Group Center and Army Group Don—now rechristened South. Manstein shifted his efficient Fourth Panzer Army headquarters westward to Dnepropetrovsk to take over the SS Panzer Corps (two divisions) and other available troops in that area. Hitler, finally shaken into action, had ordered Kleist to airlift as many troops as possible across the Sea of Azov to reinforce Manstein; had augmented General Wolfgang von Richtofen's Fourth Air Force, which was supporting Army Group South; and had ordered seven fresh divisions transferred to Manstein from the West by early March.

On 18 February, the Fourth Panzer Army began its counterattack, an SS panzer division striking south and east (*action not shown*) from Krasnograd, other Fourth and First Panzer Army units attacking north and west. The advancing Russians had failed to keep their forces concentrated; the German counterattack rapidly pocketed and destroyed unit after unit. Some Russian units panicked; others ran out of fuel. By 7 March, the Fourth Panzer Army had shifted its attack to the Kharkov area, racing an impending thaw. Kharkov was recaptured on the 14th, Belograd immediately thereafter. Except for the large bulge around Kursk (*center, right*)—which could not be cleared because of thawing weather and Army Group Center's refusal to help—the Germans had restored the general line (*solid red line*) from which they had begun their 1942 advance. Manstein's counteroffensive was a masterpiece of mobile warfare; it is sobering to consider what he might have accomplished if given a free hand from the beginning.

Fighting elsewhere in Russia during 1942 had been bloody, if less spectacular. Army Group North had weathered a series of crises. The projected attack on Leningrad had been abruptly halted when a major Russian attack on 4 September penetrated the Eighteenth Army south of Lake Ladoga. The Russian spearhead (approximately ten divisions) was destroyed by 21 September, but the Leningrad offensive was abandoned. On 12 January, 1943, the Russians again attacked in this area. Fighting lasted until early April, the Russians trading some 270,000 casualties for a corridor six miles wide—dominated by German artillery—along Lake Ladoga into Leningrad. Two hundred miles south, the salient around Demyansk (*upper center, dashed red line*) resisted constant attacks. Permission to evacuate it was eventually wrung from Hitler, and the withdrawal was successfully completed on 18 March.

Army Group Center's right flank was thrown back around Kursk. Farther north, on 25 November, the Russians launched a gigantic offensive (*not shown*)—rivaling their Stalingrad attack—against Rzhev (*upper center*), only to meet a complete and costly defeat. A hundred miles west of Rzhev, however, another offensive finally crushed the 7,000-man garrison of the Velikiye Luki hedgehog. After long wrangling, Hitler at last permitted the evacuation of the Rzhev-Vyazma salient.

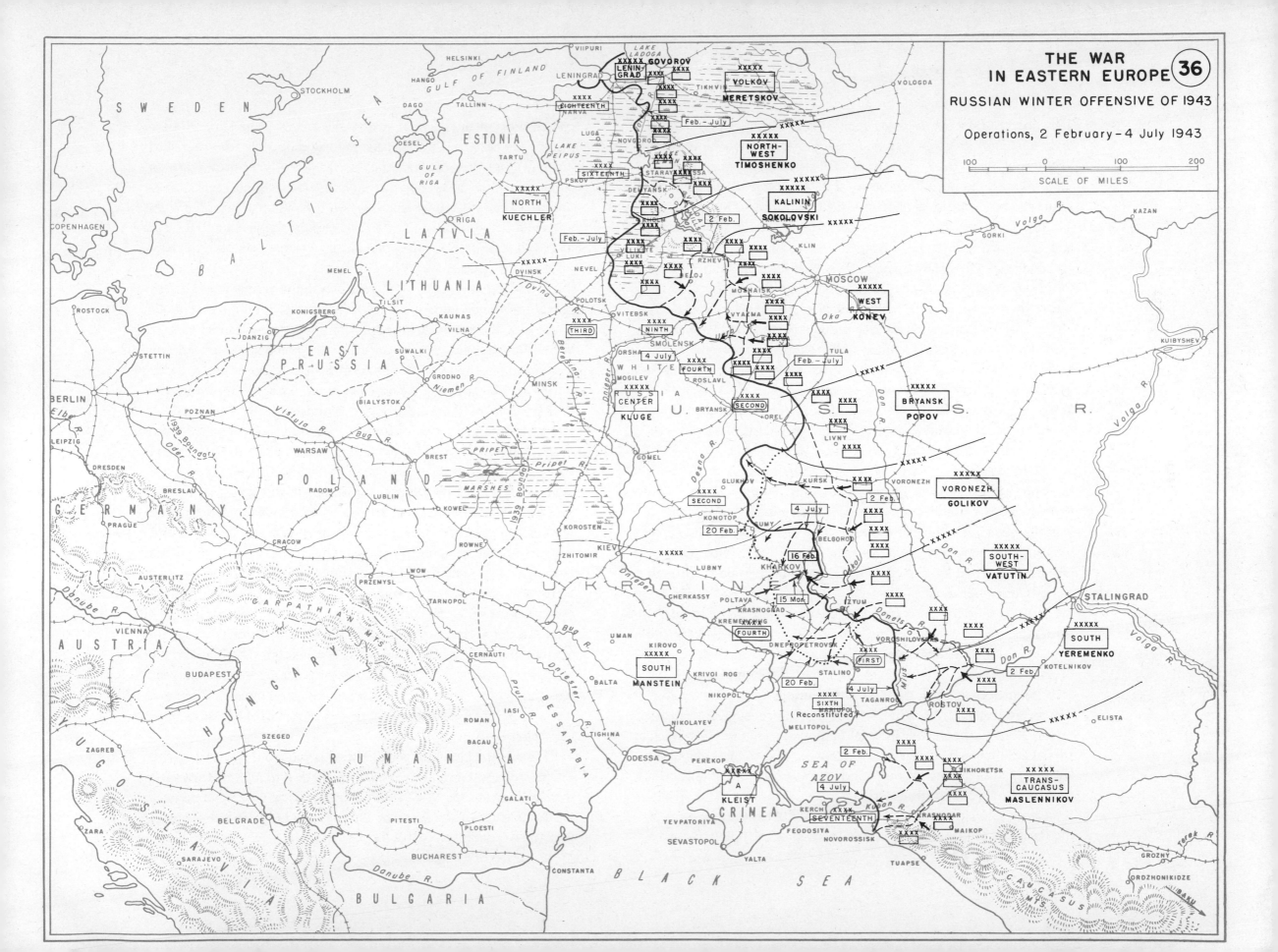

THE WAR
IN EASTERN EUROPE **36**
RUSSIAN WINTER OFFENSIVE OF 1943

Operations, 2 February – 4 July 1943

100   0   100   200
SCALE OF MILES

This map shows the frontier from which the Germans began their Russian campaign (*dashed blue line*), their position at the opening of their 1942 offensive (*dashed red line*), the extent of their greatest territorial conquest (*dotted red line*), and the front at the end of the early 1943 operations (*solid red line*).

The Germans still held vast areas of Russia, but Stalingrad had weakened them. The reasons for their failure had been many and complex. Hitler had invaded Russia with a fine flourish of optimistic ignorance. He had allowed his armament industry to idle, rather than arm or equip his troops properly. Assuming a quick victory, he had not prepared for the Russian winter. He had attacked without a definite plan, and—when one more major offensive toward Moscow might have given him a decisive victory—he had turned aside for a quick, cheap success in the Ukraine. In 1942, he had ignored the reality of the undefeated Russian armies to chase the will-o'-the-wisp of economic conquest. Thereafter, he had willfully sacrificed the Sixth Army at Stalingrad.

There were other factors. Russia was an endless country with few and primitive roads. The Russians were a tough people—and there were vast numbers of them. Their Communist government was all-powerful, highly centralized, shrewd, and utterly unscrupulous. Their generous—and gullible—allies were energetically building up Russian armed forces and industry alike through Lend-Lease shipments.

Hitler's military mistakes were compounded by his political errors. Not only in the Baltic states but in White Russia, the Ukraine, and the Caucasus, the Germans were welcomed as deliverers. Thousands of Russians volunteered for service with the German armies. Hitler could have come into Russia as a liberator. Instead, he turned the administration of the occupied territory over to Nazi Party officials for exploitation of its natural resources. In accordance with Nazi racial theories, the inhabitants were treated as subhumans. Many a friendly Russian was finally misgoverned into joining the guerrillas.

Large-scale guerrilla activity was a notable characteristic of the Russian campaign. Initially, the guerrillas, including many by-passed units of the Russian Army, operated in large bands. These proved too easy for the Germans to locate; by 1942, the guerrillas normally operated in small teams, principally against German communications. The Russian government took energetic measures to coordinate their activities with Russian army offensives and frequently supplied them by air. Despite the diversion of large forces to security missions, the Germans were never able to clean up their rear areas.

The German Army was seriously handicapped by Hitler's policy of "divide and rule." In addition to stripping his generals of most of their traditional authority (Kluge complained that he had to have Hitler's permission before he could order a battalion to attack), he steadily developed two private armies as a check on the regular army—and on each other. The SS units were the military arm of the Nazi Party, administratively controlled by Heinrich Himmler. The Luftwaffe Field Divisions, formed from excess Luftwaffe personnel, were similarly controlled by Hermann Göring. Units from these two forces normally served under Army command, but, if dissatisfied, could appeal directly to their respective chiefs. Moreover, because of the powers Göring and Himmler possessed, their private armies got the best recruits, equipment, and weapons—items which veteran regular units often lacked. At the same time—being officered by fanatical Nazis and Luftwaffe officers, respectively—they frequently suffered unnecessary casualties for lack of proper training.

Like the German Army, the Luftwaffe had not been intelligently equipped or organized for this campaign. Once again, the lack of a strategic air force, capable of reaching deep behind the Russian lines to strike war industries and communications centers, was a crippling weakness. Also, there was a lack of big, fast transport planes.

Finally, the Germans were fighting a two-front war. The greatest part of the German Navy and a large part of the Luftwaffe were engaged in the West and in North Africa, as was an increasing proportion of the German Army, especially after the Anglo-American landings in North Africa.

THE WAR
IN EASTERN EUROPE   37

CHANGES ON THE RUSSIAN FRONT
(May 1942–July 1943)

0 100 200 300 400 500 600
SCALE OF MILES

During the spring of 1943, both armies reorganized. The Germans gave special attention to rehabilitating their panzer divisions, which were reequipped with more powerful tanks. (The extremely able Albert Speer had successfully reorganized the German war production.) The Russians had vastly increased their artillery, their air force, and their armored units; in over-all numerical strength, they now had a four-to-one superiority over the Germans. Their morale was high, and their training had been much improved.

Hitler and his generals realized that another major offensive was beyond their capabilities, and that they did not have troops enough for a purely static defense of the Eastern Front. Anticipating an eventual Russian attempt to cut off the German salient from Kharkov south (*sketch* a), Manstein wished to mass his armor west of Kharkov, draw the Russian offensive toward the Nikopol-Kherson area (*lower center*), and then smash it against the Sea of Azov by a concentrated counterattack. Hitler—reluctant to abandon any territory, even temporarily, and probably secretly mistrustful of his own ability to wage a war of maneuver—refused. The plan finally adopted was to strike a quick, limited blow to inflict maximum casualties on the Russians and to upset their plans. The location selected for this operation was the Russian-held salient west of Kursk (*sketch* b, *center*). Massed German panzer units would attack north and south to cut off the salient and trap the considerable Russian forces there. This operation was scheduled for early May, as soon as the ground had dried out sufficiently. Hitler, however, postponed the operation until early July in order to finish equipping his units with the new tanks. Inevitably, the Russians learned of the long-delayed attack and prepared an elastic defense in depth, studded with mine fields and antitank weapons, and backed up by strong armored reserves. These preparations, likewise, were detected by German reconnaissance. Both Kluge and Manstein recommended that the offensive be abandoned, but Hitler—apparently egged on by his personal staff—ordered it launched as planned on 5 July.

The Ninth Army's attack in the north from the Orel salient (*upper center*) made slow progress (*dotted red line*) at considerable loss until the 9th, when it was halted by a secondary defense line. On 11 July, the Russians struck the Orel salient from the north and northeast, making considerable gains (*upper center, from dashed red line to solid red line*). The Ninth Army thereupon had to break off the attack to reinforce the Second Panzer Army. In the south, the attack likewise met determined opposition. Intensive Luftwaffe support for both attacks was met by massive Russian air activity, which inflicted severe losses on the German fliers.

On 13 July, Hitler announced that the Anglo-American invasion of Sicily (*see map 89*) had begun, and that it would be necessary to transfer several panzer divisions to the West. The Kursk attack therefore was to be broken off immediately.

With the cessation of the Kursk offensive, the Russians seized the initiative (*this map, sketch* a). Pressure on the Orel salient became critical, and Hitler approved its evacuation (in order to free troops for Italy) and the withdrawal of the Ninth Army behind the Desna River (*left center*). He insisted, however, that Manstein hold his larger, more exposed salient in the south. On 17 July, the Russians forced the Mius River, capturing Taganrog, and made some gains against the First Panzer Army. Manstein shifted his reserves south and defeated the Russians on the Mius River front. This transfer, however, weakened his left flank; a Russian attack (3 August) broke through toward Kharkov. Hitler ordered that town held at all costs, but Manstein deliberately abandoned it (23 August), and by rapid counterattacks succeeded in reestablishing his front. On 31 August, Hitler finally consented to limited withdrawals by Manstein's Sixth and First Panzer Armies.

In Army Group Center's sector, the Russians gained considerable ground against the Second Army, pushing west of Glukhov (*center*) and making appreciable advances southeast of Smolensk (*upper center*). The northern front remained static.

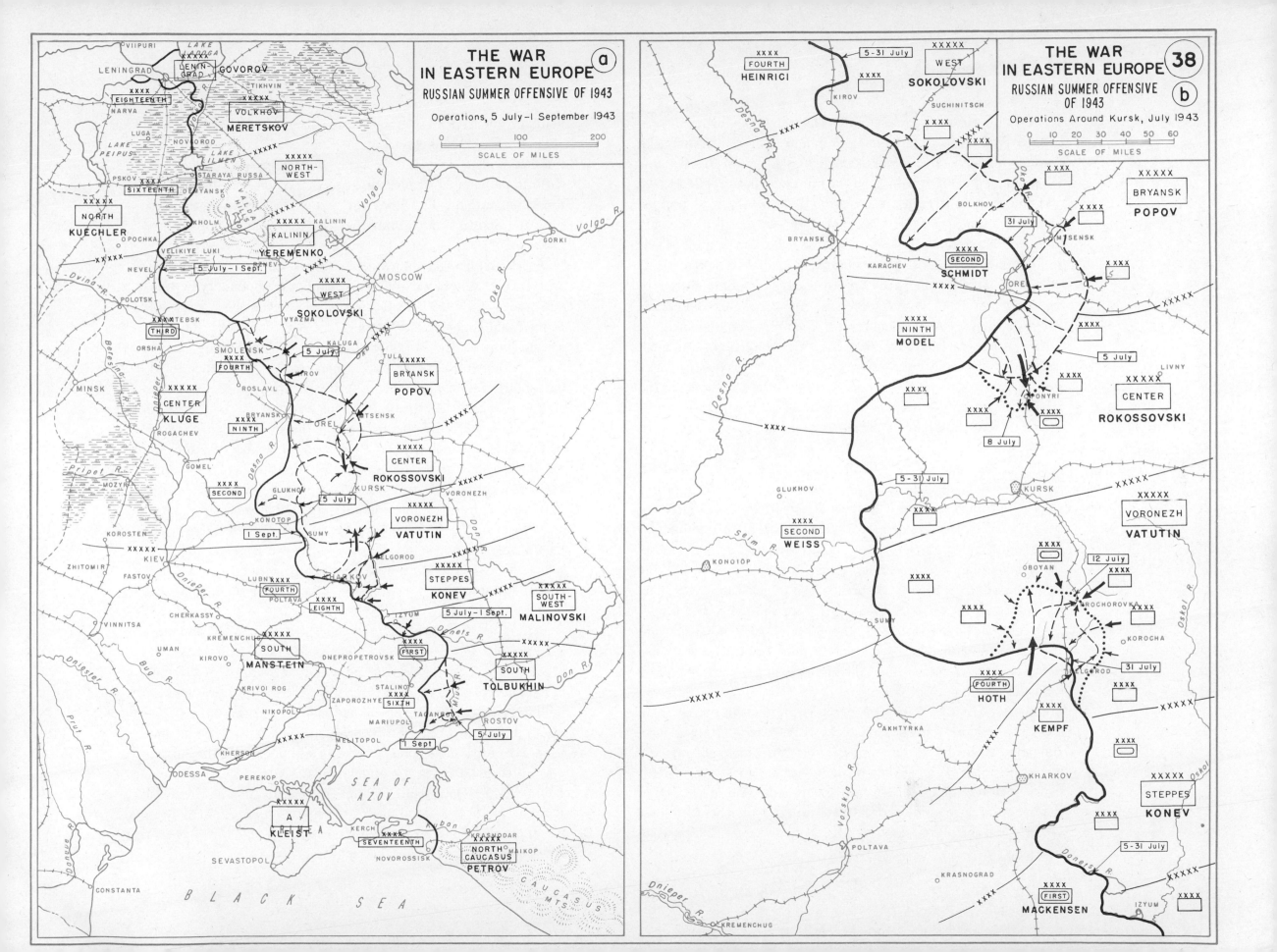

THE WAR IN EASTERN EUROPE — (a)
RUSSIAN SUMMER OFFENSIVE OF 1943
Operations, 5 July–1 September 1943

0   100   200
SCALE OF MILES

THE WAR IN EASTERN EUROPE — (b) 38
RUSSIAN SUMMER OFFENSIVE OF 1943
Operations Around Kursk, July 1943

0 10 20 30 40 50 60
SCALE OF MILES

There is no clear statement of Russian strategy during the period covered on this map, but both military and political considerations affected it: a breakthrough to the Lwow-Rowne area (*sketch* b, *left center*) would cut the railroads that supplied Kleist and Manstein; thereafter, their army groups might be trapped against the Black Sea (*sketch* a); also, victory in this area would fulfill the traditional Russian dream of a Balkan empire. Their great numerical superiority enabled the Russians to deliver a succession of massive offensives against widely separated sectors of the German front. When successful, these enveloped and destroyed considerable German forces; when repulsed, the Russians merely attacked elsewhere. They used masses of tanks and men, backed by enormous concentrations of artillery. Appalling losses were accepted stoically. The open terrain in the south offered the Germans few natural defensive positions; their panzer reserves, forced to shift rapidly from one crisis to the next, were soon worn down.

On 8 September, Hitler finally ordered the evacuation of the Kuban River bridgehead (*bottom right*) and approved in principal a withdrawal to the line Dnieper River–Melitopol (*dotted red line*). Nevertheless, he delayed the execution of this second decision until 15 September, when, the Fourth Panzer Army's situation having become desperate, Manstein forced his hand. Army Group South then began a desperate race to get behind the Dnieper before its overextended divisions were shattered. Good staff work and hard fighting saved it, though there were only five available crossing sites on Manstein's 440-mile front. The Germans devastated the country behind them, destroying or carrying off all foodstuffs.

The west bank of the Dnieper was unfortified, except for a few light defenses constructed recently by Army Group South, and ungarrisoned. (Hitler opposed the construction of rear defense positions, claiming they made his generals less aggressive.) Consequently, aggressive Russian spearheads were able to cross the river and seize small bridgeheads south of Kremenchug (*lower center*) and north and south of Kiev (*center, left*) before Man-

stein's troops could finish deploying along the west bank. These bridgeheads were quickly contained but could not be liquidated, Russian skill in defending such positions being proverbial. Two Russian parachute brigades were dropped on the west bank below Kiev, but were quickly wiped out. Army Group Center fell back from the Smolensk area under heavy pressure, but kept its front intact.

Repeated Russian attempts to break out of their Dnieper bridgeheads were bloody failures except at the boundary between Army Groups South and Center, where they made appreciable gains. Finally, during late October, the Russians drove out of the Kremenchug bridgehead, threatening to envelop the First Panzer Army. Counterattacks by the German reserves threw them back, but, south of the Dnieper bend, the Sixth Army was defeated and withdrew rapidly. Next, the Russians attacked out of their Kiev bridgeheads (3 November), mauling the Fourth Panzer Army badly. The Russians entered Kiev on 6 November. By the 7th, they had seized Fastov, and on the 13th they threatened Zhitomir. Manstein, shifting his reserves and wringing reinforcements from Hitler, replied with a panzer counterattack that smashed the Russians back on Kiev. An unexpected thaw (26 November) then halted operations. Meanwhile, five successive Russian offensives struck Army Group Center, concentrating on the Fourth Army. Here the terrain favored defensive tactics; gains were slight, and their price was high.

During early December (*sketch* b), Manstein's panzers made several effective spoiling attacks northwest of Zhitomir. Hitler was urged to evacuate the Crimea and authorize a limited withdrawal in the Dnieper bend to shorten the front and provide reserves for a mobile defense. Angrily, he insisted that the Nikopol area (*lower right*) and the Crimea must be held—the first because of its manganese deposits, the second because its loss would give the Russian Air Force good bases for attacks on the vital Ploesti oil fields (*bottom left*). During late December and early January, renewed Russian attacks made some gains, though one Russian force was trapped and largely destroyed north of Uman (*lower center*).

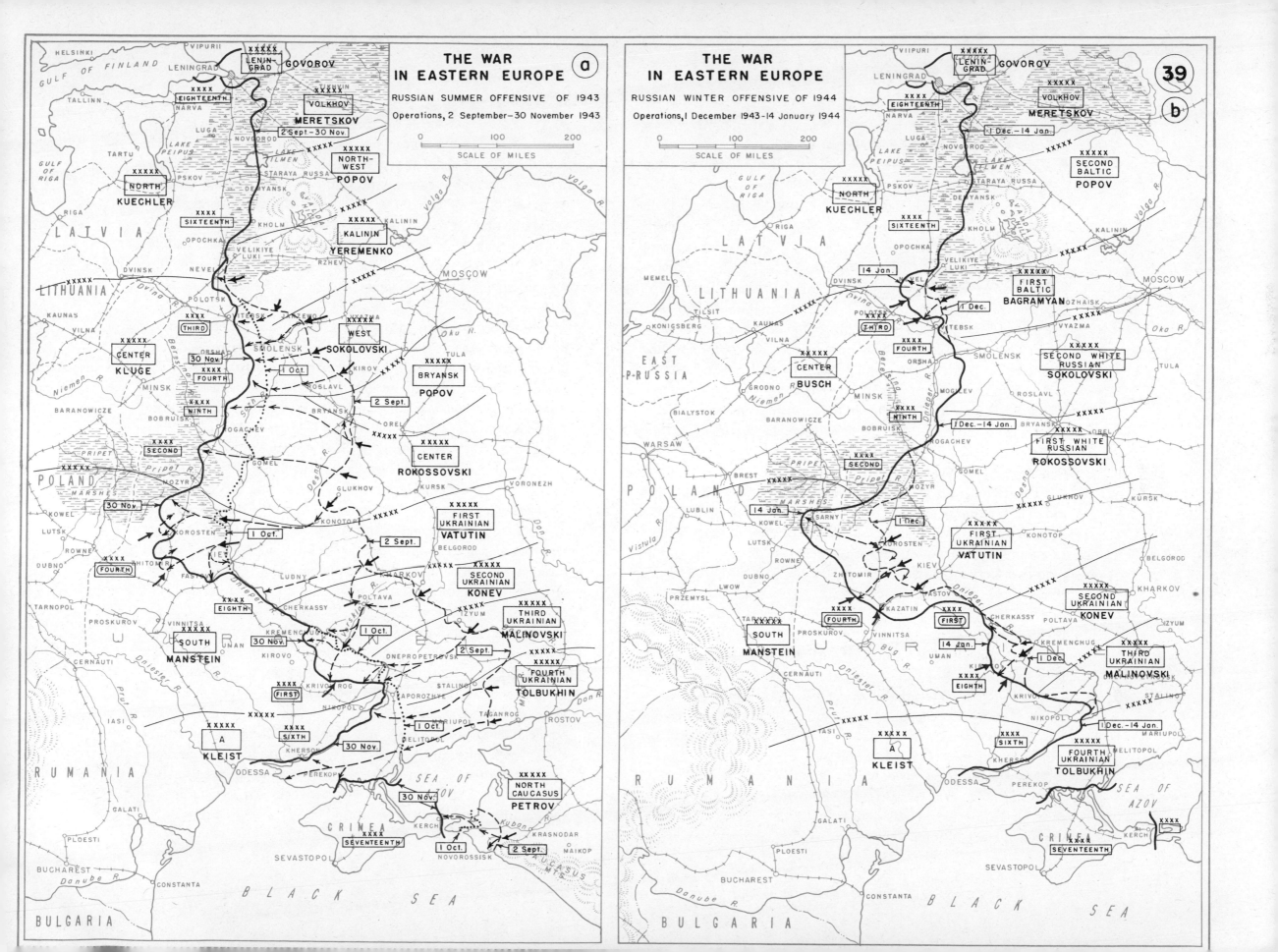

THE WAR IN EASTERN EUROPE (a)

RUSSIAN SUMMER OFFENSIVE OF 1943

Operations, 2 September–30 November 1943

SCALE OF MILES
0   100   200

THE WAR IN EASTERN EUROPE (b)

RUSSIAN WINTER OFFENSIVE OF 1944

Operations, 1 December 1943–14 January 1944

SCALE OF MILES
0   100   200

39

The Russians now abruptly shifted to the Leningrad sector (*sketch* a). The German Eighteenth Army had been static for a year there; its troops had become lax, and most of its reserves had been transferred elsewhere.

For their Leningrad offensive, the Russians mustered eight armies and masses of artillery. Their plan was clever: the Germans had originally failed to eradicate a Russian-held beachhead west of Leningrad. General Govorov built up a strong force here, moving his men in over the frozen Gulf of Finland. On 15 January, he attacked southwest out of this beachhead; simultaneously, General Meretskov pushed a converging attack across the ice of Lake Ilmen and its surrounding swamps. Surprise was total, and the German lines were quickly penetrated. Nonetheless, the Germans rallied quickly, withdrew skillfully, and established a new front through Luga (*dotted red line*). When the Second Baltic Front threatened to outflank the Luga position, the Germans retired westward (*solid red line*), where—aided by thawing weather—they stopped the Russian drive.

The Leningrad offensive had been a minor operation. Once more, the major Russian effort was concentrated in the south. Late in January, the converging attacks of the First and Second Ukrainian Fronts cut off the Korsun salient (*lower center*), trapping two German corps. The First Panzer Army and the Eighth Army at once counterattacked, but alternating blizzards and thaws bogged them down. Manstein then ordered the two corps to break out; about three-fourths did so, though most of their wounded and all of their artillery had to be abandoned. Other Russian attacks drove the Sixth Army out of the Nikopol area and seriously threatened the railroad near Lwow (*left center*). Army Group Center's sector was relatively quiet, except for one Russian offensive which got across the Dnieper and captured Rogachev. In early March, the thaws began.

Manstein utilized this period to sideslip his forces westward in order to build up the Fourth Panzer Army in the Lwow area, though this movement was hampered by the necessity for maintaining contact with the dangerously exposed Sixth Army (*sketch b*). The Russians, profiting from the greater flotation of their broad-tracked tanks and the cross-country capability of their American trucks, still drove vigorously forward in the Dubno-Tarnopol area (*left center*) and against Uman, where a German corps was badly defeated. On 11 March, the Eighth Army was ordered to withdraw, but a furious Russian pursuit overran much of it, forced back the First Panzer Army's right wing, and crossed the Bug River. Only the Fourth Panzer Army held firm. Eventually, the surviving units of the Sixth and Eighth Armies crossed the Dniester.

However, the Russian drive to the Dniester had isolated the First Panzer Army (*dotted red oval*). Manstein requested reinforcements for a breakthrough to extricate it. Hitler, after demanding that it stand its ground, finally furnished these, but almost immediately relieved Manstein and Kleist, replacing them respectively with Generals Model and Schoerner. Meanwhile, the one-armed General Hube kept his First Panzer Army concentrated and moved largely at will behind the Russian front, playing hob with Russian communications. Despite Russian air superiority, the Luftwaffe managed to organize an airlift to supply him. On 5 April, the Fourth Panzer Army drove eastward to extricate him. Hube attacked westward—fighting front, flank, and rear—and brought his command out with practically all its heavy equipment. After mid-April, the southern front stabilized as shown (*solid red line*).

In early April, the Russians unleashed a well-organized assault on the isolated garrison of the Crimea. Repulsed by German troops at the Perekop Isthmus, they succeeded in an amphibious attack across the lagoons to the east, where the front was held by Rumanians. Advancing from this beachhead and from the Kerch peninsula, they drove the Germans within the Sevastopol fortifications. These they attacked on 7 May, supported by 300 guns per mile of front, and cleared the town in two days. However, the Germans successfully evacuated most of their garrison, because of the timidity of the Black Sea Fleet.

Note: The symbol for German Army Group Center (Map b, upper left center) should be **XXXXX**.

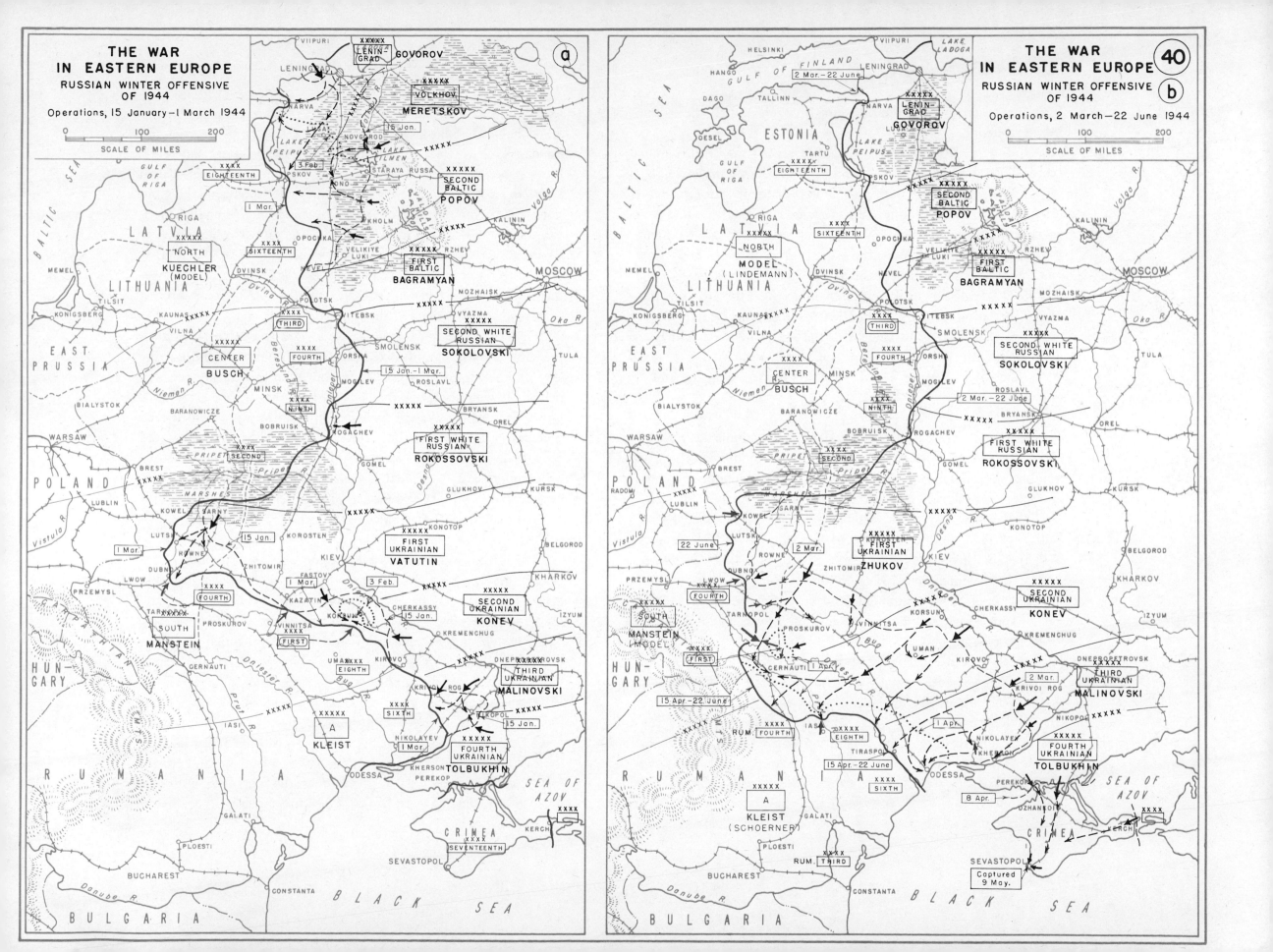

THE WAR IN EASTERN EUROPE

RUSSIAN WINTER OFFENSIVE OF 1944

Operations, 15 January–1 March 1944

SCALE OF MILES
0   100   200

THE WAR IN EASTERN EUROPE

RUSSIAN WINTER OFFENSIVE OF 1944

Operations, 2 March–22 June 1944

SCALE OF MILES
0   100   200

This map shows the relationship between the Eastern and Western Fronts.

On 5 July, 1943 (*dashed red line*), in the East, the Germans were launching their ill-fated Kursk offensive (*see maps 37-38*). In the West, the Allies were assembling for the invasion of Sicily (*see map 89*). On 23 June, 1944 (*dotted red line*), the Russians were breaking across the prewar frontiers of Poland and Rumania (*see map 40*); in the West, the Allied forces in Normandy were battling to expand their beachhead. On 15 December, 1944 (*solid red line*), the Russians, driving northwestward through the Balkans, had been halted by skillful German resistance around Budapest (*see map 43*b). In the West, the Allies likewise had been halted along the general trace of the German West Wall (*see map 59*). The solid blue line (7 May) shows the fronts at the end of the war.

The Russian offensives during 1943 had been marked by their greater speed, making it difficult for the Germans to rally or to establish new defense positions. The major factor in the increased mobility and efficiency of the Russian armies was Allied Lend-Lease. During the war, the United States alone provided Russia with 385,883 trucks, 51,503 jeeps, 7,056 tanks, 5,071 tractors, 1,981 locomotives, 11,158 freight cars, and 14,834 airplanes. Other supplies included 2,670,000 tons of petroleum products, industrial plants and equipment, and enough food to give (as a rough approximation) each Russian soldier over "one-half pound of fairly concentrated food per day."

Great difficulty was experienced in getting these supplies to Russia. The shortest route was across the North Atlantic into the White Sea ports of Murmansk and Archangel (*this map, top center*). Ships using it, however, were harried by German planes, submarines, and surface raiders operating out of Norwegian bases. Anglo-American losses in ships and sailors were heavy, some convoys being almost totally destroyed. A second route was by way of the Persian Gulf (*bottom right*) and the Iranian railways to Russian depots in northern Iran. (Iran had been occupied by the British and Russians in 1941.) Initially, supplies from the United States had to be sent around the Cape of Good Hope to reach the Persian Gulf. After the Mediterranean was cleared, however, these supplies could be sent via Gibraltar and the Suez Canal (*bottom center*), and the Persian Gulf therefore became the main port of entry for American Lend-Lease material. (A small American force, the Persian Gulf Command, was set up to handle these shipments.) A third route was from American West Coast ports via Vladivostok (*see map 113*) and the Trans-Siberian Railway to the Moscow area. Russian pilots also picked up American aircraft in Alaska and flew them to Siberian bases.

Generally speaking, Lend-Lease to Russia was carried out in the same atmosphere of mixed idealism, enthusiasm, and naïveté that characterized all Russo-American relations during the war period. It was necessary that Russia be aided in her early dark hours; frequently, American forces in training were denied adequate essential weapons and equipment so that the Russians could be supplied. After the Normandy landings and as the Russians rolled relentlessly westward, it was unrealistic to continue to build up the Soviet military and industrial might—especially when they refused explanation or justification of need.

The Finnish campaign of 1944 was short and relatively unimportant. The Finns had been inactive since 1941; since Stalingrad, they had been making diplomatic approaches through England and the United States in an effort to withdraw from the war. The Russians massed men, guns, and aircraft on Finland's southern and southeastern frontiers, establishing a preponderance of force which the Finns could not withstand. The offensive on the Karelian Isthmus began on 10 June; Viipuri fell ten days later. On 21 June, another Russian offensive began on either side of Lake Onega, but took almost a month to push the Finns back to their old eastern frontier. Hostilities between Finland and Russia ended on 4 September, 1944. In October, the light German forces in northern Finland were forced back into Norway.

THE WAR
IN EASTERN EUROPE (41)
ALLIED GAINS IN EUROPE
(July 1943 – May 1945)
LEND-LEASE ROUTES TO RUSSIA
FINNISH CAMPAIGN OF 1944

0   100   200   300   400   500   600
SCALE OF MILES

ICELAND

ARCTIC OCEAN

KIRKENES
PETSAMO
NARVIK   Oct. 1944   MURMANSK
27 Dec. 1944
WHITE SEA   ARCHANGEL
BELOMORSK
FINLAND   VLADOVOSTOK
July 1944   3750 miles
LAKE ONEGA
NORWAY   VIIPURI   LAKE LADOGA
OSLO   HELSINKI   KIROV   MOLOTOV
SWEDEN   GULF OF FINLAND   10 June 1944
GULF OF BOTHNIA   LENINGRAD   VOLOGDA   MAGNITOGORSK
TALLIN   S   O   V   I   E   SOCIALIST
ESTONIA   KAZAN
Volga   KUIBYSHEV   CHKALOV
NORTH   RIGA   KALININ   GORKI
SEA   VELIKIYE   MOSCOW
IRELAND   LUKI   RZHEV   REPUBLIC
VYAZMA
SCOTLAND   7 May 1945   Dvina   VITEBSK   SMOLENSK   URAL MTS
BALTIC SEA   EAST   WHITE   TULA   5 July 1943
ENGLAND   PRUSSIA   MINSK   OREL
Niemen   RUSSIA   23 June 1944   KURSK   VORONEZH
LONDON   BERLIN   WARSAW   Pripet   STALINGRAD
ENGLISH CHANNEL   15 Dec. 1944
ANTWERP   Vistula   KIEV   Donets   LAKE ARAL
BREST   BELG.   GERMANY   POLAND   U   K   R   A   I   N   E   ASTRAKHAN
LORIENT   PARIS   13 Dec. 1944   PRAGUE   LWOW   Dnieper R.   KHARKOV
23 June 1944   Meuse R.   KORSUN   Don R.
BAY   Rhine R.   Danube R.   CZECHOSLOVAKIA   Dniester   ROSTOV
OF   FRANCE   CARPATHIANS   Bug R.   SEA OF
BISCAY   SWITZ.   AUSTRIA   VIENNA   BESSARABIA   AZOV   Kuban R.   GROZNY
Po R.   HUNGARY   BUDAPEST   ODESSA   CAUCASUS MTS   CASPIAN SEA
15 Dec. 1944   Rhone R.   RUMANIA   CRIMEA   NOVOROSSISK   BAKU
MARSEILLES   YUGOSLAVIA   BUCHAREST   SEVASTOPOL   TIFLIS
15 Dec. 1944   ADRIATIC SEA   BELGRADE   Danube   BLACK   SEA   BATUM   DJULFA   PAHLEVI
MADRID   CORSICA   SOFIA   TABRIZ
LISBON   ROME   ITALY   ALBANIA   BULGARIA   MIANEH   KAZVIN
PORTUGAL   SPAIN   23 June 1944   GREECE   IRAN   TEHRAN
SARDINIA   ISTANBUL   QUM
MADRID   ANKARA
GIBRALTAR   5 July 1943   ATHENS   T   U   R   K   E   Y
SP. MOROCCO   SICILY   AEGEAN SEA   CYPRUS   LEVANT   BAGHDAD
ORAN   ALGIERS   MALTA   STATES   AHWAZ
TUNIS   CRETE   KHORRAMSHAHR
MOROCCO   ALGERIA   MEDITERRANEAN   HAIFA   PERSIAN GULF
SEA   PALESTINE   IRAQ   ARABIA
TUNISIA   JERUSALEM
TRIPOLI   EL ALAMEIN   SUEZ
BENGAZI   TOBRUK   EGYPT
LIBYA

The spring thaws gave the Germans one last chance to re-establish their Eastern Front. The irregular line (*dashed red line*) on which they had finally halted the Russian winter offensive was too long for the forces they now possessed. There was one obvious solution: to pull their front back to a shorter, stronger position—one suggestion was the line Riga (*upper center*)–Lwow (*center*)–Dniester River—and to fortify it in depth. This would make it possible to take enough divisions out of line to create a large, mobile reserve, which could be stationed in a central position, such as Warsaw.

Against such common-sense measures, Hitler set his face. His solution was to designate certain important communications centers (such as Vitebsk [*upper center*]) as "fortresses" which must be held to the last man. He still forbade the construction of any fortified zone behind the Eastern Front; also, he refused to recall any of the divisions on garrison duty in Norway, Greece, or Crete. Hitler seems to have expected that the Russians would continue to make their main effort between the Pripet Marshes and the Carpathian Mountains; most of his available panzer strength was concentrated in that area.

The Russians had other plans: the bulging, thinly defended German salient north of the Pripet Marshes invited a converging attack; the terrain along the axis Smolensk-Minsk-Warsaw (*center*) was especially favorable for armored action, and an offensive here would be easy to support logistically from the Moscow area. During the Teheran Conference (November, 1943), it had been agreed that the Russians would attack on the Eastern Front at about the same time that the Americans and English landed in northern France, so that the two offensives would be mutually supporting. On 6 June, 1944, the Anglo-American forces stormed the Normandy beaches.

During the night of 22 June, guerrilla activity erupted throughout the rear area of Army Group Center, crippling its communications. On the 23d, supported by artillery massed hub to hub (reportedly 400 cannon or heavy mortars per mile), the Russian Army rolled forward on a 350-mile front. The Russian Air Force had complete control of the air, the Luftwaffe having been practically neutralized by the Anglo-American air offensive.

Most of Army Group Center's forces were soon drawn into the defense of Hitler's fortresses—where they were rapidly encircled, as Russian armor poured past and around them. In ten days of wild, confused fighting, the Russians bludgeoned a 250-mile gap in the German front, overrunning twenty-five German divisions—the worst defeat that the Germans had yet suffered. Thereafter, increasing logistical difficulties slowed the Russian drive. Hitler placed the energetic Field Marshal Model, "the Führer's fireman," in command of the gap where Army Group Center had been. Army Group South Ukraine had a few German divisions in reserve; these were brought north. Model rallied the remnants of the Third Panzer and Second Armies and gathered up various improvised formations. With them, he counterattacked successfully near Radzymin (*center, left*).

Meanwhile, on 12 July, the Russian offensive spread to include Army Group North. In Estonia, the German front stood firm or gave slowly, but a flanking thrust by the Russian First and Second Baltic Fronts drove toward the sea near Riga. On 14 July, the Russians opened their attack south of the Pripet Marshes. Lwow fell on the 27th, and by 1 August the Russians had reached the Vistula River south of Warsaw. Most of the German troops here, thanks to their higher proportion of panzer units, avoided encirclement and fought their way out, though much equipment had to be abandoned. With their usual aggressiveness, the Russian advance guards established several bridgeheads on the west bank of the Vistula, but these were quickly destroyed or contained. By 7 August, most of the front (*solid red line*) was momentarily stabilized. But the Germans now had new troubles. On 1 August, as the Russian advance guards approached Warsaw, the Polish "underground," led by General Bor-Komorowski, seized control of most of that city.

THE WAR
IN EASTERN EUROPE **42**

RUSSIAN SUMMER OFFENSIVE OF 1944

Operations, 23 June–7 August 1944

0   100   200   300
SCALE OF MILES

The Polish underground forces in Warsaw were subordinate to the Polish government-in-exile, then in London. Therefore, the Russians, having fabricated their own Communist Polish government, watched cold-bloodedly (as in 1809) while hastily assembled SS and police units put down the uprising in a brutal house-to-house battle that lasted more than two months.

The destruction of most of Army Group Center was a mortal wound to the German forces on the Eastern Front. Its results were compounded by the attempted assassination of Hitler on 20 July. Hitler's previous distrust of his military leaders now turned to downright hatred; he interfered more than ever—if possible—in military operations. Guderian (made chief of the German General Staff on 21 July), wishing to fortify Germany's eastern frontier, thought it best to order the work begun on his own responsibility without seeking Hitler's approval. He also attempted to form fortress units from limited-service personnel, but these were largely diverted to the Western Front.

With the German forces in Poland still attempting to recover from their recent defeat—and the Russian armies in that area (*sketch* a) hampered by having largely outrun their logistical support during their 450-mile advance—Stalin now looked to his flanks. To the north, the German forces in the Baltic states were in a dangerously exposed position, but both sides there were regrouping after their battles in the Riga area. With the Germans obviously powerless to attempt a major counteroffensive, Stalin could now proceed with the acquisition of his Balkan empire.

On 20 August, the Russians launched a major offensive in Rumania (*lower right*). At the height of the battle (25 August), most of the Rumanians turned their coats and went over to the Russians. Sixteen German divisions—most of the Sixth Army and part of the Eighth—were trapped. The Russians entered Bucharest on 1 September. Since 26 August, Bulgaria had withdrawn from the war and begun negotiations. The Russians interrupted these on 5 September by overrunning that country; on 8 September, a new Bulgarian government declared war on Germany. Thus reinforced, the Russians turned northwest toward Budapest.

Guderian could see little hope unless the Eastern Front could be shortened, permitting him to build up a mobile reserve. Hitler consented to the long-overdue recall of Army Group F from the Aegean Islands and Greece (*off map, bottom center*), but it would take some time for this force, harassed by guerrillas and Allied air attacks, to make its way north. About the middle of September, therefore, Guderian began an offensive in the Riga area to reestablish communications with Army Group North. This drive was successful, but subsequent events are not clear. Guderian ordered General Schoerner to evacuate Estonia and Latvia. Schoerner began this movement, but—probably on orders from Hitler—suddenly suspended it. On 10 October, a renewed Russian offensive broke through to the Baltic (*sketch* b), leaving Schoerner stranded in northern Latvia with approximately twenty divisions. During the last half of October, the Russians launched an offensive against East Prussia. After slight gains, a combination of swampy terrain, bad weather, fortifications, and fanatical resistance by local troops halted it west of Insterburg. Limited German counterattacks (*not shown*) then overran the leading Russian units and forced the others on the defensive.

In Poland, there was only minor fighting. The Russian drive northwest across the Balkans continued, checked only briefly around Debrecen (*lower center*). The Russians captured Belgrade on 20 October, cutting the major north-south railroad available to Army Group F, which was forced to take the more western route through Sarajevo (*bottom left*). Tito's Communist guerrillas and the Bulgarians were given the mission of forcing the Germans out of Yugoslavia, while the Russians concentrated on the drive toward Budapest. They reached its outskirts on 29 October, won a bridgehead over the Danube on 24 November (at that date, Army Group F's rear guards were still in northern Greece), and by 15 December had reached the line shown (*solid red line*). To the south, a British expeditionary force had landed in Greece on 4 October, Churchill having decided that the Western nations should retain a Balkan foothold.

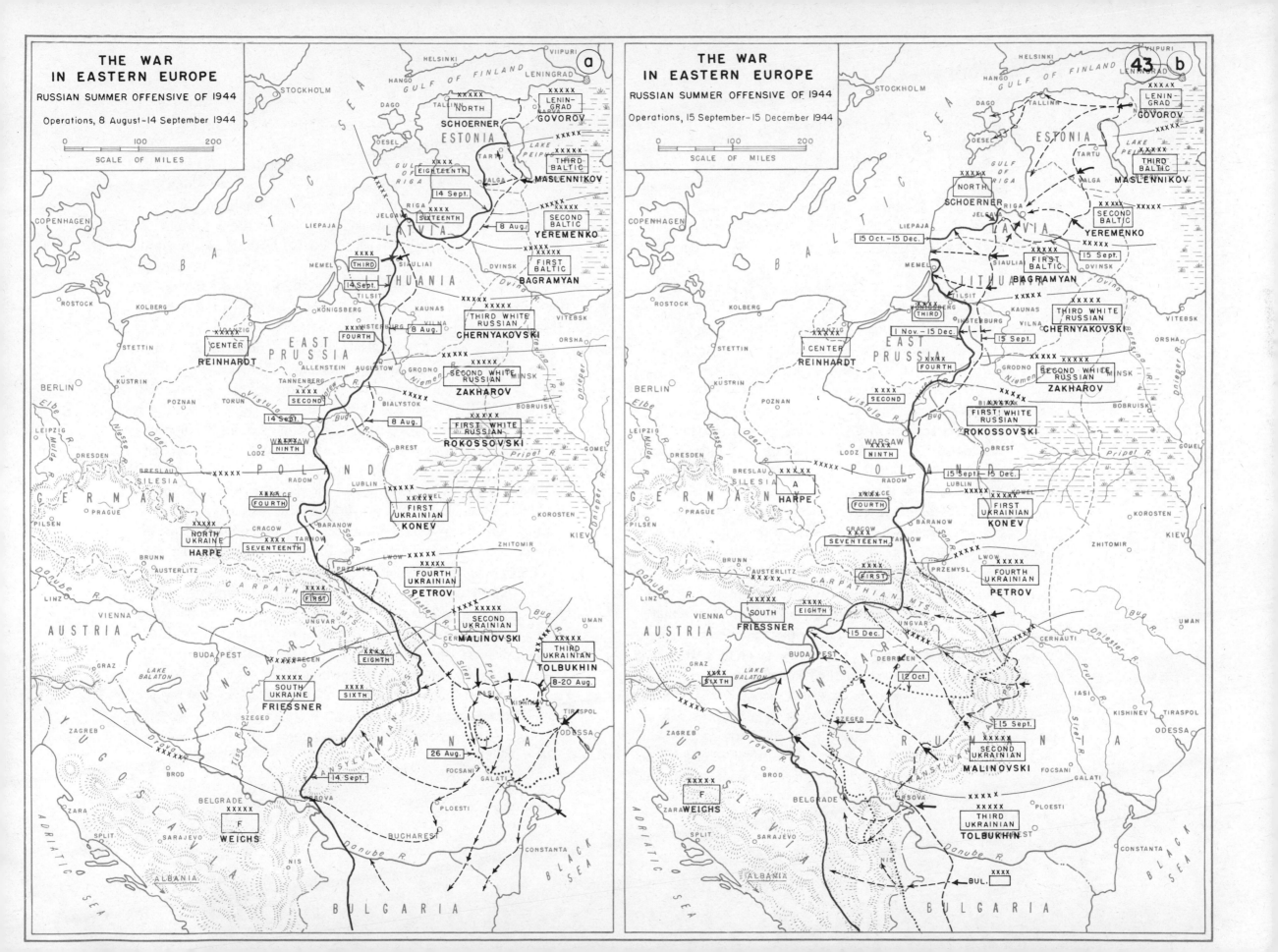

North of the Carpathian Mountains (*sketch* a, *center*), there was little fighting during November and December. While the Russians regrouped in preparation for their next offensive, the Germans began fortifying their front. Hitler again prevented its organization in depth. Meanwhile, he transferred the pick of his panzer units to the Western Front for his Ardennes offensive (*see maps 60-63*). He also insisted on maintaining Army Group North (*this map*), with over twenty veteran divisions, in its splendid isolation in northern Latvia—to protect the Baltic training area for submarine crews.

South of the Carpathians, fighting was constant and savage. Here, the Germans utilized the "twin" city of Budapest as a defensive outpost. (Buda, the portion of the city on the high west bank of the Danube, was a natural fortress; Pest, on the flat east bank, was of minor military value.) This city was strongly garrisoned and prepared for a siege, the German and Hungarian reserves being concentrated north of the city for a counteroffensive. By 24 December, the Russians finally succeeded in encircling the town. The momentum of their advance was such that the German counterattack was launched hurriedly; it almost succeeded, but superior Russian forces halted it just short of the beleaguered city. Pest fell on 18 January, but Buda held out until 13 February, blocking the main route into Austria.

Indications increased that the Russian offensive in Poland would soon be renewed. German intelligence predicted that it would begin about 12 January, and that the Russians would muster a superiority of eleven to one in infantry, seven to one in tanks, and twenty to one in both artillery and aircraft. Hitler, now living more than ever in his own dream world, derided this estimate. Even his personal military staff preferred to commit the few available reserves in an abortive attack in Alsace-Lorraine (*see map 64*a). As a climax, the Anglo-American bomber offensive (*see map 47*), by steadily wrecking the German communications and petroleum industry, had created a serious fuel shortage on the Eastern Front.

On 12 January, Marshal Konev broke out of his Baranow bridgehead (*this map, sketch* a) in overwhelming strength. The "fronts" on his right and left joined in the offensive during the next few days. Outnumbered and lacking a secondary defense line, the Germans could only attempt to maintain some semblance of order as they fell back. On 26 January, the Russians broke through to the Baltic east of Danzig; Marshal Zhukov's leading units reached the Oder River near Küstrin (*left center*), some forty miles east of Berlin, five days later. There he paused. Despite the increasing motorization of the Russian Army which Lend-Lease had made possible, he probably had outrun his supplies—especially since several old fortress cities, such as Torun (Thorn) and Poznan (Posen) still held out in his rear, blocking the main roads. It took until 23 February to complete their capture. Temporarily stalled along the Oder-Niesse Rivers, the Russians turned northward (*sketch* b), overrunning East Prussia. The German defense was grim, especially at Danzig (captured 30 March) and Königsberg (9 April), but there could be no new Tannenberg. Thousands of Germans were evacuated by sea, despite the Russian Navy's largely amateur efforts. To the south, the Russians overran most of southeastern Germany—the last remaining functioning major industrial area—but could not break Breslau's magnificent defense.

Early in January, Hitler ordered the crack Sixth Panzer Army (somewhat rehabilitated since the Ardennes campaign) transferred to Hungary, claiming that it was essential to hold the Lake Balaton oil fields (*lower left*). Because of the damaged condition of the railroads, its movement into Hungary was slow. Finally, in early March, its counterattack got under way with considerable success, almost reaching the Danube. A shortage of fuel reportedly checked it at a critical moment; however, the Russians soon managed to seize the initiative and, resuming their drive, captured Vienna on 13 April.

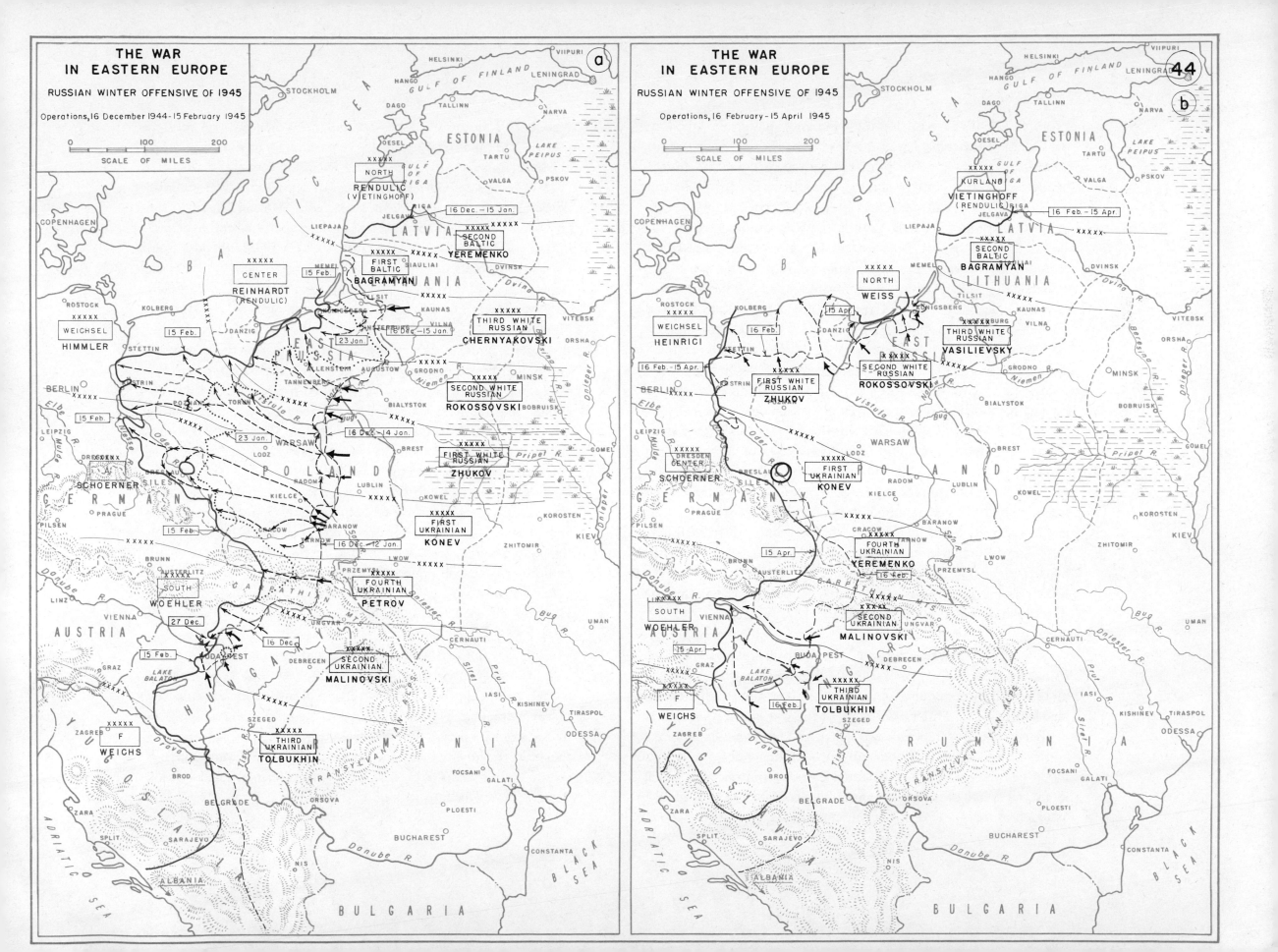

THE WAR
IN EASTERN EUROPE

RUSSIAN WINTER OFFENSIVE OF 1945

Operations, 16 December 1944-15 February 1945

SCALE OF MILES

THE WAR
IN EASTERN EUROPE

RUSSIAN WINTER OFFENSIVE OF 1945

Operations, 16 February-15 April 1945

SCALE OF MILES

44

From late February until 16 April, there was an uneasy lull along the Oder-Niesse front (*left center*). The Russians, in keeping with their usual commendable practice, had secured several bridgeheads on the west bank, including one at Küstrin, before halting their drive. Some, but not all, of these were knocked out by German counterattacks. Farther south, the Russian advance ground slowly forward across Austria and Czechoslovakia, slowed by mountainous terrain—for which the Muscovite has never displayed either talent or enthusiasm—and supply difficulties. The German divisions cut off in Latvia held their front, but otherwise remained helpless spectators. Hitler could have withdrawn them at any time, if he had been willing to sacrifice some of their heavy equipment, but he did not so choose. German forces in Yugoslavia —after holding on successfully through January and February, repulsing Russo-Bulgarian attacks from the east, and repeatedly defeating Tito—were involved in the failure of the Sixth Panzer Army's counteroffensive and forced to withdraw northward. At the same time, Stalin consolidated his conquests. Regardless of previous international agreements, a Communist government was forced upon Rumania at gunpoint; the Americans were refused the use of the Budapest airfields for "shuttle bombing" from Italian bases (an earlier attempt at using such fields in western Russia had been frustrated by Russian intransigence, plus one of the Luftwaffe's last brilliant strikes), and the Russians were intimating that Poland would have a Communist government, whatever America and England thought.

On 16-17 April, the northern Russian fronts renewed their advance. There was no hope of successful resistance, with American and English forces pouring across western Germany. All German leaders, including Hitler, realized that the war was lost. Hitler, in his Berlin headquarters air-raid shelter, did not care: he had long ago outlawed himself beyond all hope of surrender. Now, in a mood not uncommon in a defeated despot (and one which will haunt our world of nuclear weapons), he was anxious only to take as much of the world down in ruin with him as he possibly could.

And, to this insane end, he still commanded the loyalty of enough faithful and fanatic fools to make opposition by any German leader almost suicidal.

Consequently, German resistance, if scattered, was frequently desperate. The Russian advance reached Berlin on 22 April; the city was surrounded on the 25th; Hitler is believed to have committed suicide on the 30th, but it was 2 May before the last stubborn strong points surrendered. In the meantime, also on 25 April, American and Russian units had made contact near Torgau (*left center*) on the Elbe River. (General Eisenhower and the Russian high command had agreed on the line of the Elbe and Mulde Rivers [*see map 46*] as a general boundary between their forces in Germany to prevent incidents.) On 2 May, the Russians reached Wismar (*this map, upper left*), which British troops had just occupied, and the East and West Fronts soon came together along the length of the boundary in Germany. In Czechoslovakia and Austria, the Russian advance remained slow, in part because of determined German rear-guard actions. Nevertheless, the Russian high command insisted that the Americans should not advance appreciably eastward of Pilsen (*left center*). General Eisenhower acceded to their wishes, but some embarrassment resulted from this agreement: Czech underground forces in Prague rose in rebellion, only to find American troops inexplicably unable to advance to their rescue. On 7 May, Admiral Doenitz, named by Hitler as his successor, capitulated.

The war in the East had been marked by sufferings and a personal brutality rarely approached in the West. The major wonder is that, handicapped by Hitler's version of inspired leadership, the German commanders accomplished so much with so relatively little for so long a period. Even in defeat, the German was frequently the more deadly fighter. Statistics are fragmentary or untrustworthy, but it seems likely that the average German casualty took three or more Russians with him.

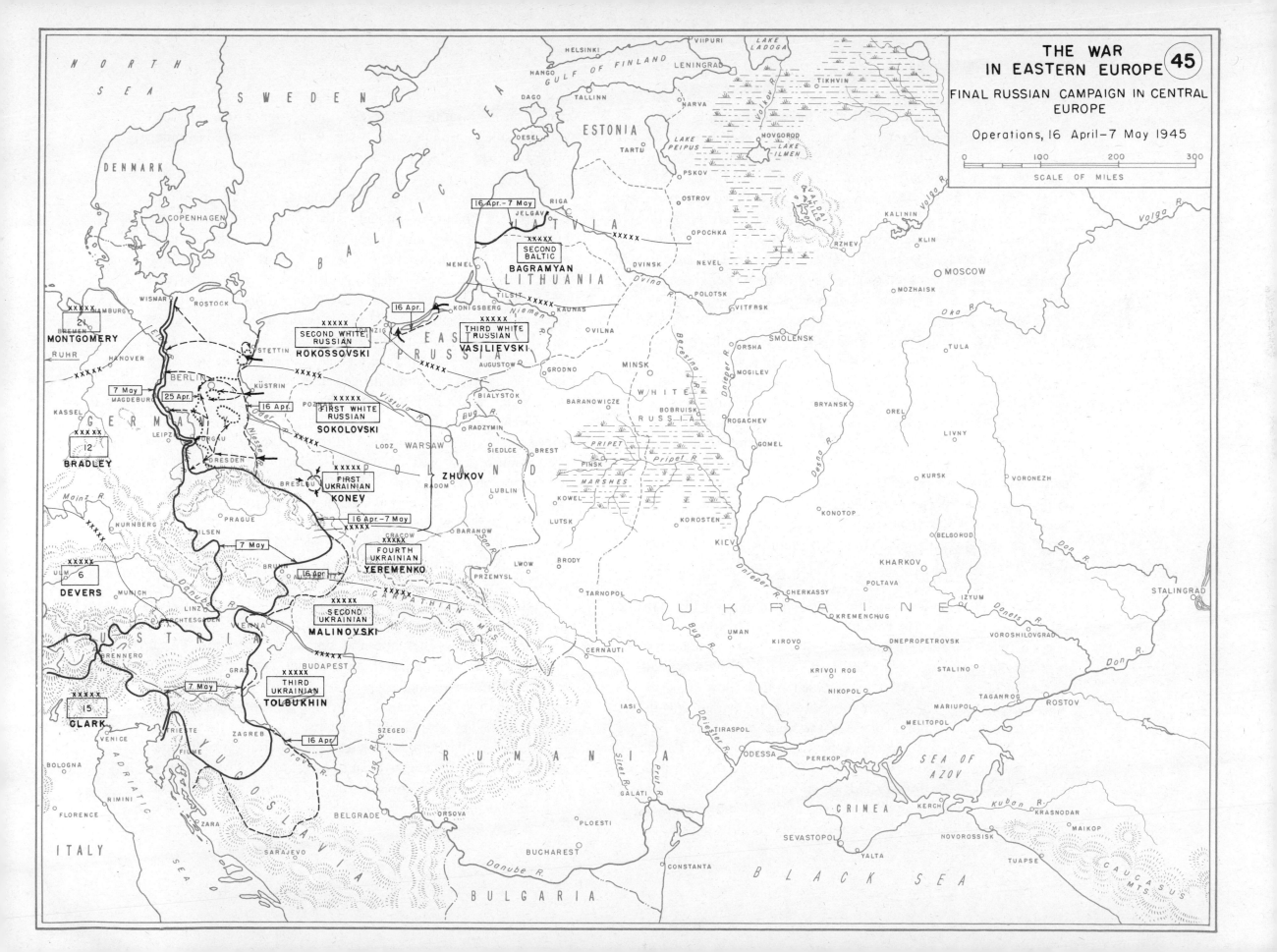

THE WAR
IN EASTERN EUROPE (45)

FINAL RUSSIAN CAMPAIGN IN CENTRAL
EUROPE

Operations, 16 April–7 May 1945

0   100   200   300
SCALE OF MILES

The area enclosed by dashed red lines indicates the approximate expansion of Hitler's Germany by means short of war up to the armed invasion of Poland in 1939. The succession of stunning triumphs from then to the summer of 1942, which practically made Germany master of the Continent, have already been described (*see maps 3-32*). By August, 1942 (*dotted red line*), the high tide of German aggression had been reached. The United States had entered the war (*see map 115*), and, though her military might had not yet been sampled by Germany, her enormous industrial machine had already begun to provide substantial aid to Russia and Britain. The German advances were stopped in the decisive battles of El Alamein (*see map 78*) and Stalingrad (*see map 34*), enabling the Allies to seize the initiative.

Two years later, Hitler's armies had been hurled back in the east and in the south (*solid red line*). The pendulum had not been reversed without much Allied "blood, sweat, and tears." Russia's renaissance, slow but inexorable, has been described (*see maps 34-41*); the succession of Allied victories in the Mediterranean is discussed on maps 77-104. Now, in June, 1944, a large Allied force stood poised in England ready to invade France, while fleets of bombers rained destruction on the German homeland. In the East, the Russians readied overwhelming forces to continue their drive westward.

The Anglo-American coalition for waging war on the Axis powers had been born in December, 1941. The historic conferences between the heads of state (six by June, 1944) settled major problems of strategy and guided the Combined Chiefs of Staff (CCS). (These conferences are discussed in the following pages, where applicable.) The CCS, in turn, directed the war effort within the framework of policy made by the heads of state (*see text, map 118*). Such major matters as the invasion of France, Pacific and Asiatic strategy, operations in the Mediterranean, coordination of the Anglo-American and Russian war efforts, and the allocation of major resources were resolved at these conferences, frequently through considerable compromise. Russia began to participate in the meetings in late 1943; prior to that time, she dealt with her allies through other channels, and from the beginning proved difficult to placate and satisfy.

While Germany was being forced on the defensive in Europe and Africa, a violent, less-publicized battle was raging—the Battle of the Atlantic (*this map*). One of the war's decisive battles, it began in 1939 and continued until Germany capitulated. The build-up of an invasion force in the British Isles—and, in fact, Britain's very survival—depended upon the outcome of this battle between German submarines and Allied naval and air power. The statistics reveal by how narrow a margin the Allies won. Not until 1943 did they succeed in countering the German submarines to the extent that new ship-construction tonnage exceeded the tonnage of ships sunk. Significantly, in that year the German submarine losses also skyrocketed. From that date onward, Allied superiority was maintained in spite of German efforts to reverse the tide by increased production of improved submarines. Nevertheless, by the end of the war, Germany had sunk 14,154,838 tons of Allied and neutral merchant shipping at a cost of 781 submarines. In spite of the lessons of World War I, she had begun the war with only 57 submarines; during its course, she employed 1,179 underseas craft, and had 398 remaining when the war ended (217 of these were scuttled). As Grand Admiral Karl Doenitz observed, it would be interesting to speculate as to the course of events if she had started the war with 1,000 submarines.

The map shows the pattern of submarine operations during the critical years (*see* Legend, *bottom left*). Note the division of the ocean into two major zones of responsibility and the further subdivision of the American seaboard into coastal zones, the latter being patrolled by air and naval elements.

Ultimately, the battle was won by the material contribution of such measures as the employment of escort carriers with convoys, air-sea cooperation, improved radar, and the bombing or capture of submarine bases.

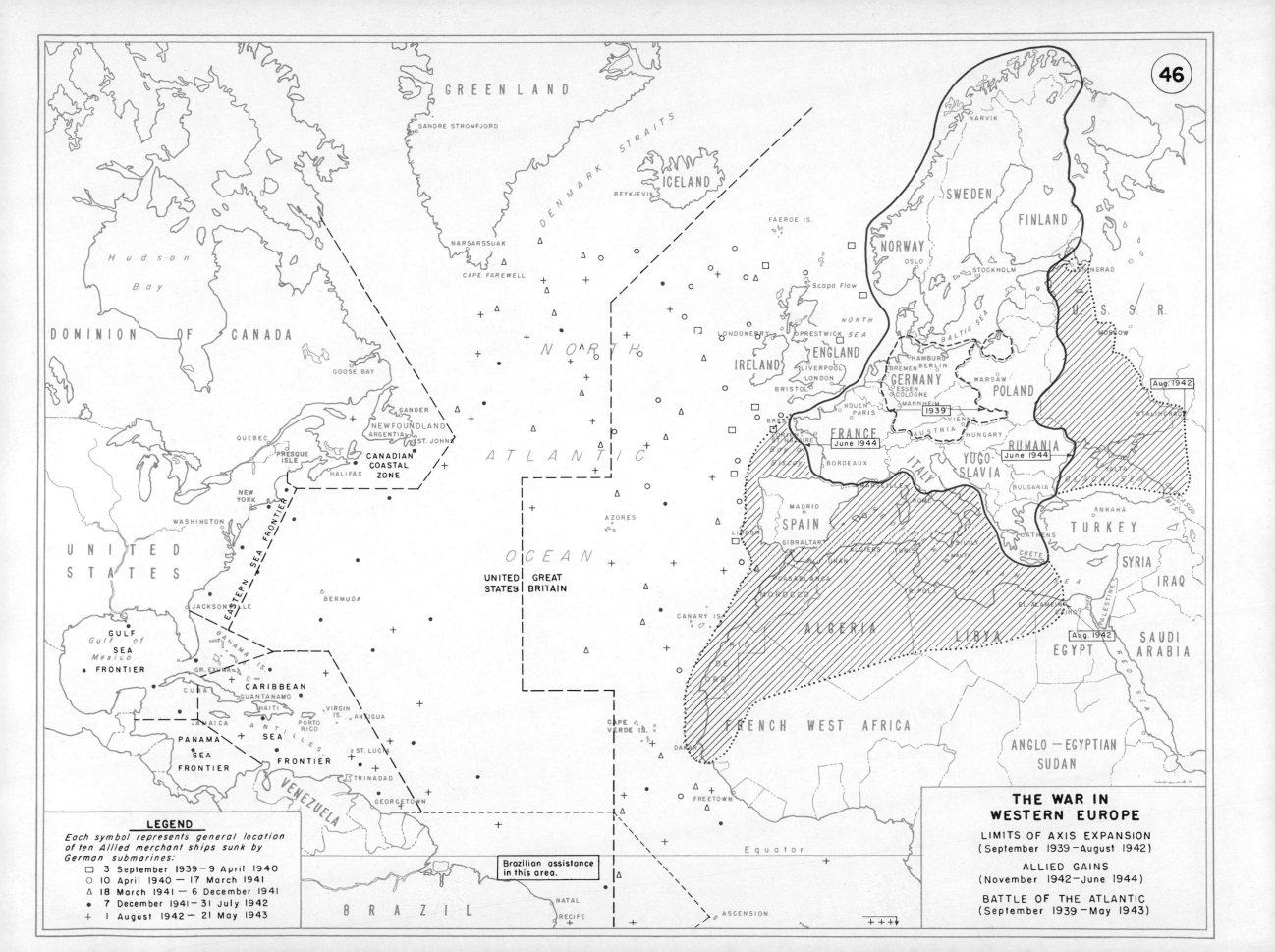

46

GREENLAND

SANDRE STROMFJORD

ICELAND

REYKJEVIK

DENMARK STRAITS

NARSARSSUAK

CAPE FAREWELL

Hudson Bay

DOMINION OF CANADA

GOOSE BAY

QUEBEC

PRESQUE ISLE

GANDER

NEWFOUNDLAND

ARGENTIA

ST. JOHN'S

HALIFAX

NEW YORK

WASHINGTON

UNITED STATES

JACKSONVILLE

BERMUDA

GULF of Mexico

GULF SEA FRONTIER

CUBA

GR. EXUMA

BAHAMAS

JAMAICA

GUANTANAMO

HAITI

PORTO RICO

VIRGIN IS.

ANTIGUA

ST. LUCIA

TRINIDAD

CARIBBEAN SEA FRONTIER

PANAMA SEA FRONTIER

GEORGETOWN

VENEZUELA

BRAZIL

NATAL

RECIFE

Equator

ASCENSION

CANADIAN COASTAL ZONE

EASTERN SEA FRONTIER

NORTH ATLANTIC OCEAN

UNITED STATES | GREAT BRITAIN

AZORES

CAPE VERDE IS.

FREETOWN

DAKAR

Brazilian assistance in this area.

FAEROE IS.

Scapa Flow

NORTH SEA

LONDONDERRY | PRESTWICK

IRELAND

ENGLAND

LIVERPOOL

LONDON

BRISTOL

NORWAY

OSLO

NARVIK

SWEDEN

STOCKHOLM

FINLAND

BALTIC SEA

LENINGRAD

U. S. S. R.

MOSCOW

HAMBURG

BREMEN

BERLIN

GERMANY

ESSEN

COLOGNE

MANNHEIM

WARSAW

POLAND

1939

VIENNA

AUSTRIA

HUNGARY

BREST

ST. NAZAIRE

ROUEN

PARIS

FRANCE

June 1944

BORDEAUX

Biscay

SPAIN

MADRID

LISBON

GIBRALTAR

CASABLANCA

MOROCCO

ALGIERS

ALGERIA

RUMANIA

June 1944

BULGARIA

YUGO-SLAVIA

ITALY

ROME

CRETE

ATHENS

TURKEY

ANKARA

Aug. 1942

STALINGRAD

BLACK SEA

CAUCASUS

CASPIAN SEA

SYRIA

IRAQ

SAUDI ARABIA

PALESTINE

CAIRO

EGYPT

EL ALAMEIN

Aug. 1942

RED SEA

TRIPOLI

LIBYA

TUNIS

FRENCH WEST AFRICA

RIO DE ORO

ANGLO—EGYPTIAN SUDAN

THE WAR IN WESTERN EUROPE

LIMITS OF AXIS EXPANSION
(September 1939—August 1942)

ALLIED GAINS
(November 1942—June 1944)

BATTLE OF THE ATLANTIC
(September 1939—May 1943)

As the Battle of the Atlantic was being fought, a similar battle raged in the European skies. But the roles were reversed; Allied strategic air power struck at German industry, while the Luftwaffe played the part of the defender.

The theory of strategic bombardment had been conceived during World War 1 and slowly nurtured thereafter—primarily by England. In 1940, with the British Army expelled from Western Europe, strategic bombing was given added impetus. The air battle seesawed as new defensive and offensive concepts vied for the ascendancy; but finally, in May, 1942, the British Bomber Command mounted a 1,000-plane raid against Cologne (*upper center*) which achieved considerable success without prohibitive losses.

Meanwhile, the United States Army Air Corps had likewise devoted considerable effort to developing strategic bombardment concepts. But whereas the British believed in area targets and night bombing, American fliers favored precision bombing from high altitudes in daylight. In March, 1942, the Eighth Air Force was formed in England as the nucleus of the American strategic air arm. The following August, in a small raid against Holland, the Eighth Air Force tested the feasibility of the American concept. The results were moderately successful. At the Casablanca Conference (January, 1943) the CCS recognized the potentiality of strategic bombing by directing the development of a coordinated plan for striking at the German military, industrial, and economic systems. By June, a plan had been conceived and was under implementation as the Combined Bomber Offensive. The key target areas are shown in green; in general, they encompassed the German industries designated for destruction—submarine construction, aircraft, ball bearings, oil, synthetic rubber, and military vehicles. The limit of daylight bombing operations was gradually extended as the Allies developed long-range fighter escorts and the German defenses were progressively weakened.

The Combined Bomber Offensive gathered momentum in 1943. In an effort to gain air superiority, the Allies hammered at the German aircraft industry by day and at cities by night. Overall results were disappointing. But in early 1944, new techniques and equipment began to tell, and by April air superiority had been achieved. By now, the U.S. Fifteenth Air Force, based in Italy, was participating in the air strikes; its operations were coordinated with those of the Eighth Air Force by United States Strategic Air Forces (USSTAF). Allied successes were due, in part, to German failure to concentrate—until too late—on fighter-plane production and, specifically, on their promising jet aircraft.

Meanwhile, an invasion force was being concentrated in England. In June, 1942, the United States had established the European Theater of Operations and sent Maj. Gen. Dwight D. Eisenhower to London to command it. The ultimate American-British aim had been an invasion of France in 1943, but circumstances combined to delay the amphibious assault and divert Allied resources to the Mediterranean area (*see maps 81-102*). As will be seen later, basic differences between American and British strategists developed in 1943. But, at the Casablanca Conference, a planning group was directed to begin work in London on an invasion plan, and at the Cairo-Teheran Conferences in November, 1943, the invasion plan (OVERLORD) was finally approved and given a target date. General Eisenhower, now in the Mediterranean theater, was designated supreme commander. In February, 1944, the planning group was absorbed into Supreme Headquarters Allied Expeditionary Force (SHAEF); during the next three months, SHAEF perfected the OVERLORD plan. Eisenhower's three immediate subordinates were British (*this map, upper left*). General Sir Bernard L. Montgomery, recently returned from Italy, initially commanded all ground forces (21st Army Group); ANCFX was the naval command, AEAF the air command. The U.S. Ninth Air Force initially was to support Lt. Gen. Omar N. Bradley's American First Army while the British Second Air Force supported the British Second Army.

The final OVERLORD plan involved a five-division amphibious assault (*small blue arrows*), supported by airborne landings. This map shows the German dispositions and SHAEF's planned limits of advance seventeen, thirty-five, sixty, and ninety days after landing. These subjects are discussed further in the text of map 48.

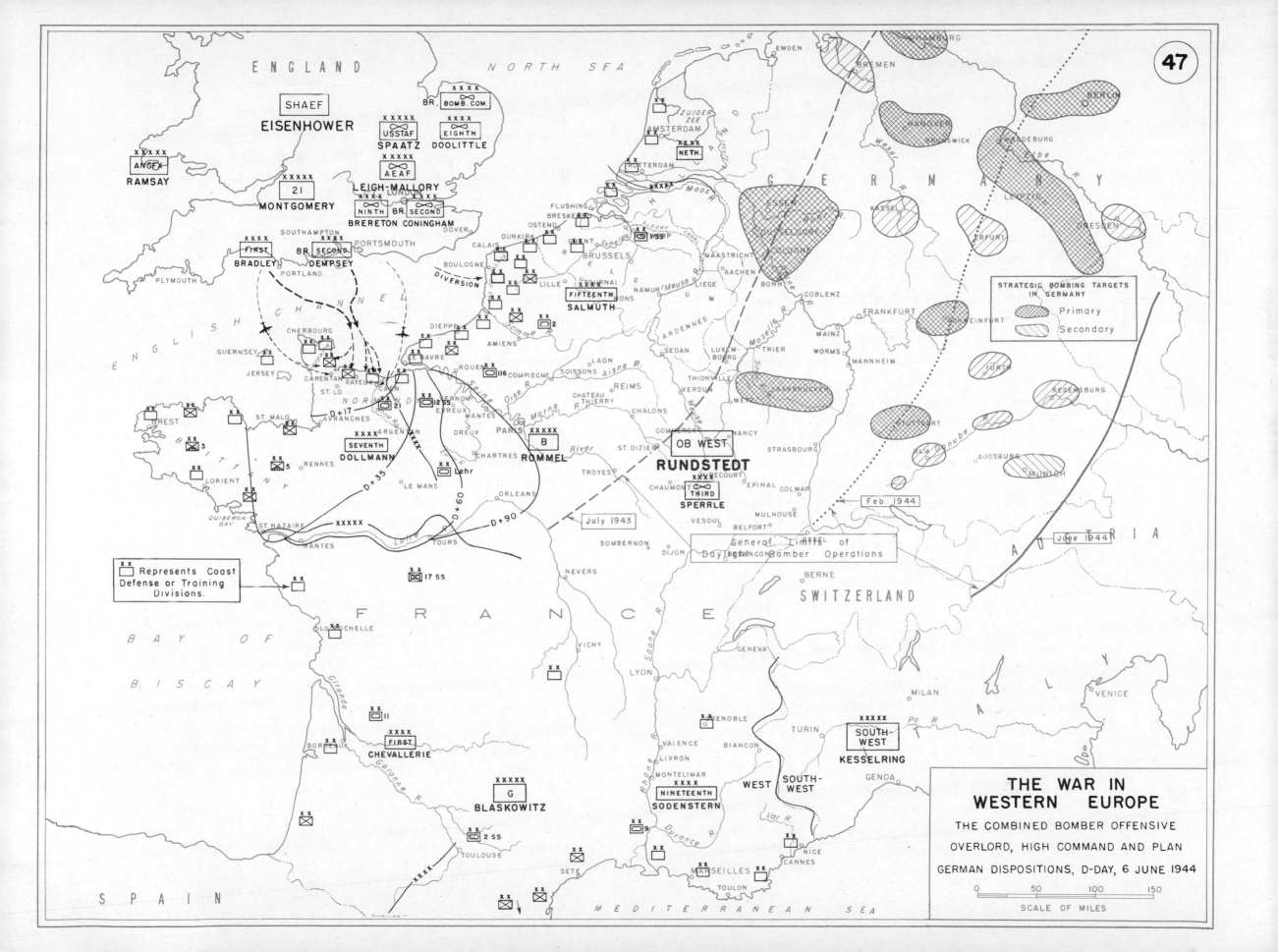

47

THE WAR IN WESTERN EUROPE

THE COMBINED BOMBER OFFENSIVE

OVERLORD, HIGH COMMAND AND PLAN

GERMAN DISPOSITIONS, D-DAY, 6 JUNE 1944

0   50   100   150

SCALE OF MILES

The preliminary invasion plan prepared by the staff designated at Casablanca did not satisfy Eisenhower. Both he and Montgomery deemed inadequate the three ground and one airborne divisions this plan allocated to the initial assault; they wanted five and three, respectively. Such an increase would require additional beaches, landing craft, and transport aircraft. So strong was Eisenhower's conviction that the assault had to be strengthened that, to secure the needed landing craft (shortages of which repeatedly plagued the Allies during the war), he recommended postponing OVER-LORD one month and delaying the landing planned for southern France. These changes the CCS approved. Consequently, in the final OVERLORD plan, the landing area was widened by including Utah Beach, thus causing the beachhead to be split by the estuary above Carentan. But this extension of the assault beaches closer to Cherbourg would force the Germans to defend a greater area, and the increased number of airborne troops would minimize the split.

In selecting the landing area, SHAEF planners considered many factors, the most important being the requirement for air cover, adequate beach and port capacity, German strength and dispositions, and availability of landing craft and transport aircraft. The choice was narrowed to the Le Havre–Calais and the Caen-Cherbourg areas; the second was eventually selected, primarily because of its better beaches and weaker defenses.

On 6 June, the strength of the Allied force (all services) was 2,876,000 men. The organization of the ground component, numbering forty-five divisions, is shown; only those divisions in the assault and follow-up forces are specifically indicated (corps organizations appear on *map 49*). The task of equipping and supplying this tremendous force had been staggering, but by virtually converting the United Kingdom into one huge military base, it had been accomplished.

Meanwhile, the Combined Bomber Offensive was intensified, and tactical air forces struck at German defenses and communications in France. Eisenhower insisted upon SHAEF control of the strategic bombers during the initial phases of OVERLORD. The CCS concurred, over the violent objections of the strategic air commanders. (Some airmen viewed strategic bombing as a satis-factory alternative to OVERLORD, confident that it alone could force Germany to surrender.) The weight of strategic air power was added to strikes at bridges, roads, and railroads leading into the lodgment area. By the time of the invasion, the area was virtually isolated.

On the Continent, the German forces waited, edgy and not nearly so well prepared as Nazi propaganda proclaimed. The bulk of their divisions were understrength, short of equipment, and filled with second-line troops. In contrast to the Allies, the German command structure (*see map 47*) bordered on chaos. Rundstedt, nominally the commander in all France, exercised no control over air (including antiaircraft artillery) or naval elements, and only limited control over SS and parachute units. Nor was Rommel completely subordinated to Oberbefehlshaber West (OB West). Hitler had sent him to France in December, 1943, to "inspect the Atlantic Wall." He had begun to vitalize the coastal defenses and subsequently had received command of the Seventh and Fifteenth Armies, though, by mutual agreement, he partially subordinated himself to Rundstedt. But, worst of all, the two generals disagreed on the best defense. Rundstedt wanted to hold the coast lightly and create a mobile striking force; Rommel, fearful of Allied air power, wanted a coastal defense backed up by strong local reserves. Hitler agreed with Rommel but established no policy. Thus, on 6 June, Rommel controlled three panzer divisions, Hitler four, Blaskowitz three, and Rundstedt none.

Nor was the fabled Atlantic Wall very strong (*this map*). In Rundstedt's opinion, these coastal fortifications were "sheer humbug." Some of the cities (those likely to be needed as Allied supply ports [*see* Legend, *lower right*]) were garrisoned by fanatically loyal troops under orders to resist to the last. Finally, the German dispositions indicate that the attack was expected in the Boulogne-Calais-Dunkirk area (*upper right*). Excellent Allied deception (a "cover plan") contributed materially to this before and after the invasion.

In short, Rundstedt was ill-prepared to resist the massive Allied assault. The Allies did not know this, but had wisely prepared to meet a typically professional German defense.

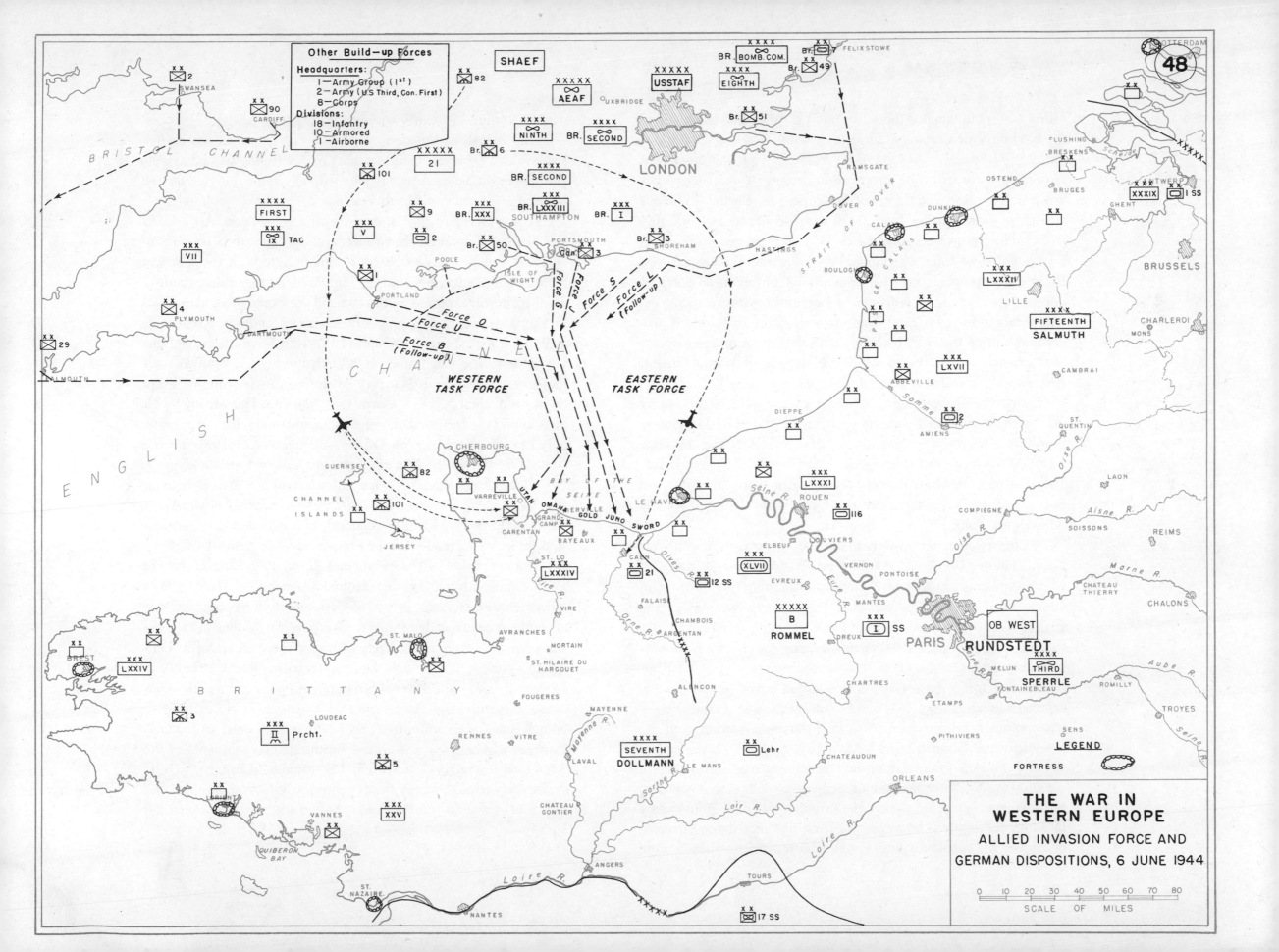

THE WAR IN
WESTERN EUROPE

ALLIED INVASION FORCE AND

GERMAN DISPOSITIONS, 6 JUNE 1944

0 10 20 30 40 50 60 70 80

SCALE OF MILES

Other Build-up Forces
Headquarters:
1—Army Group (1st)
2—Army (US Third, Con. First)
8—Corps
Divisions:
18—Infantry
10—Armored
1—Airborne

LEGEND

FORTRESS

Many factors influenced the selection of the date and the hours of the landings in Normandy. The major ones were tidal conditions (important because of German beach obstacles), the moonlight requirement for airborne drops, and acceptable weather. After much deliberation, the period of 5-7 June was selected. (H-Hour varied between beaches from 0630 to 0745 because of differing tides.) The troops were already loaded and preparations initiated for landing on 5 June, when unfavorable weather forecasts forced Eisenhower to postpone the operation. Continuing reports of questionable weather confronted Eisenhower with a crucial decision: Should the invasion be postponed again, or should it proceed, accepting the risk? Unhappy with the unfavorable prospects but appreciative of the many disadvantages of postponement, Eisenhower, at 0415, 5 June, designated 6 June as D-Day.

Shortly before midnight, 5 June, airborne units began taking off for their scheduled assaults between 0100 and 0200 the next morning. The primary missions of the three airborne divisions were: 82d—to secure a bridgehead across the Merderet River; 101st—to secure Utah Beach exits to aid the 4th Division; and 6th—to secure crossings over the Orne River and protect the Allied east flank.

Elements of five divisions made the OVERLORD amphibious assault landings. The initial follow-up divisions, and the dates on which they came ashore, are shown on the map. At dawn on 6 June, Allied air power (including 1,083 heavy bombers of the Eighth Air Force) struck hard at German beach defenses; shortly thereafter, naval gunfire began pulverizing the enemy positions. Particularly at Omaha (here, the aiming points were moved farther inland for troop safety because cloud cover forced the aircraft to bomb by instrument), the results of the aerial attacks were disappointing, but more effective than the assault troops realized —some of the German mine fields were detonated. By the end of D-Day, the Allies had established beachheads as shown (*solid blue lines*). Nowhere had they reached their planned objectives, but—except for Omaha, where the situation was precarious—they had firm footholds. The assault at Utah had met the least resistance; but the greatest success was achieved in the British zone where, landing in greater strength and against moderate opposition, the British had made sizable gains. (A factor in the British success was, however, their ingenuity in developing special assault equipment.) Charts A and B (*immediately following*) cover the fighting at Omaha and Utah Beaches.

To the Germans, the landings came as a surprise. Air attacks had destroyed much of their radar, and the German Navy considered the weather too rough for a landing. None of the German higher commanders believed the landing to be the main assault— all of them still expected that to come in the Boulogne-Calais-Dunkirk area. However, learning of the airborne landings, Rundstedt, at 0400, directed the movement of the 12th SS and Panzer Lehr Divisions to the Caen area. (OKW temporarily restrained their movement, however.) The fury of the assault fell upon the six divisions of the LXXXIV Corps (*see map 48*). Hamstrung by air attacks and the confused German command chain, the corps made only one counterattack on D-Day—an unsuccessful one by the 21st Panzer Division north of Caen (*this map, action not shown*). No attempt was made to wipe out the tenuous Allied hold at Omaha, because corps headquarters was erroneously advised that the landing there had been repulsed, and because the Germans were more concerned over the British advance toward Caen.

The expansion of the beachhead through 12 June (*solid red line*) entailed bitter fighting around Caen and Carentan. The movements and dates of arrival of German divisions concentrating around the beachhead are shown. Overpowering Allied air attacks caused heavy losses and severely restricted these movements. During this period, as the Allies built up their beachhead strength to sixteen divisions and feverishly poured supplies ashore, the Germans, concentrating their armor at Caen, were never able to launch a major counterattack. By 12 June, the center of the German line at Caumont was almost ruptured. The remnants of the 352d Division fell back toward St. Lô, and the 2d Panzer Division desperately tried to screen the gap; but the V Corps, cautious and aware of resistance on the flanks, halted the advance of the 1st Division.

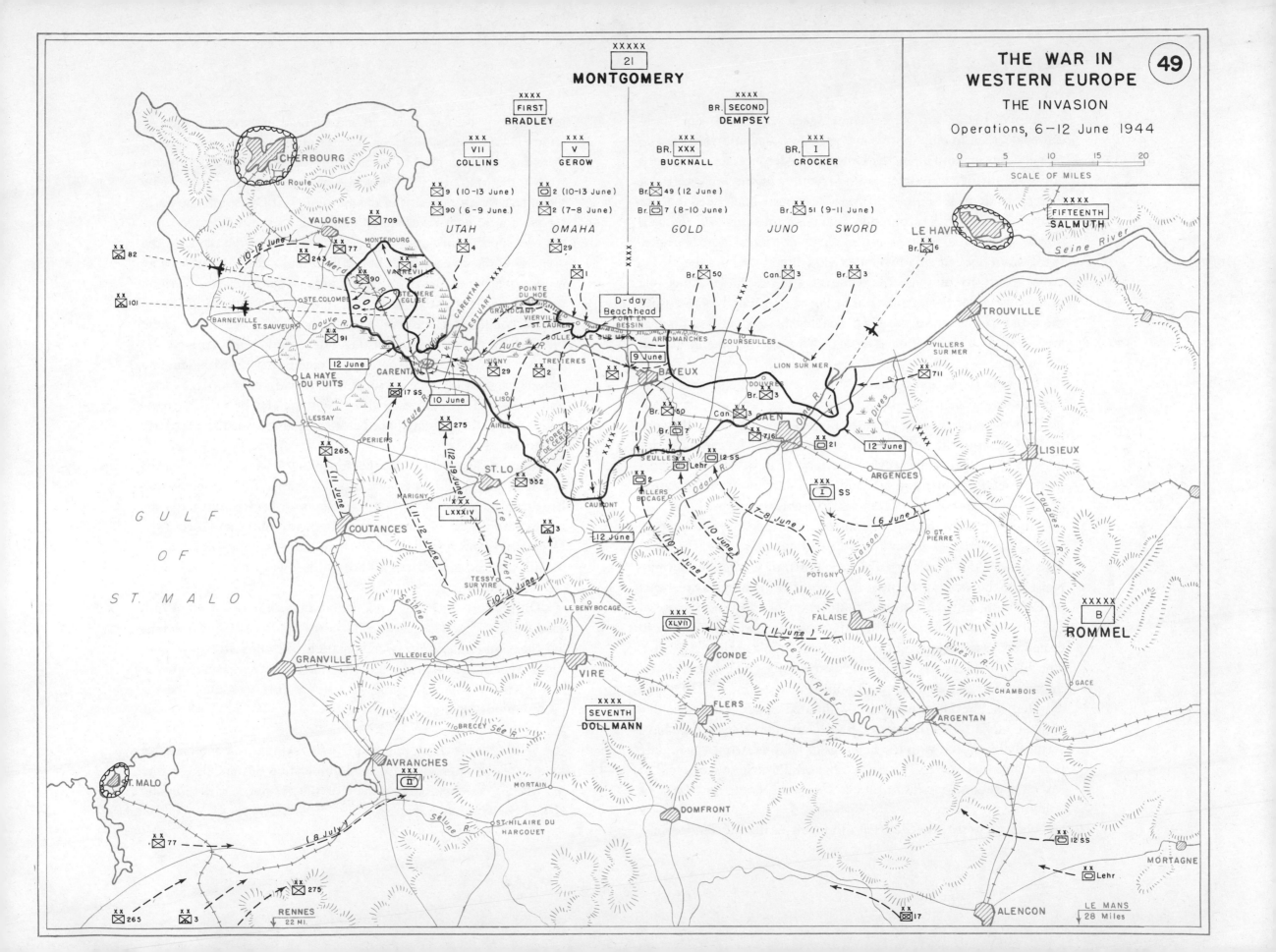

THE WAR IN
WESTERN EUROPE
THE INVASION
Operations, 6–12 June 1944

49

A study of the terrain behind Utah Beach will reveal why Eisenhower decided to employ two airborne divisions in that area. The marshy bottom land along the Douve and Merderet Rivers (which could be further inundated by destruction of the lock north of Carentan [*bottom center*]) formed an easily defended barrier across the base of the Contentin peninsula (*see map 49, the area north of the line Carentan–La Haye-du-Puits*). Furthermore, there was a flooded area two miles wide directly behind the beach, crossed only by four narrow causeways (*this chart*). Thus, the prime mission of both American airborne divisions was to ensure the rapid expansion of the Utah beachhead across these flooded areas, in preparation for a quick drive up the peninsula on Cherbourg.

Between 0100 and 0200, 6 June, the leading elements of six parachute regiments of the 82d and 101st Airborne Divisions jumped over Normandy. A careful study of chart A indicates that, in general, the airborne drops were poor. The excessive dispersion was due principally to German antiaircraft fire, inadequate briefing of many pilots, and cloud patches which obscured check points and caused aircraft to lose their bearings.

But, in spite of the lack of control, the dispersion, and the confusion, the 101st Division succeeded in capturing the important exits behind the beach and the lock north of Carentan. German resistance, however, prevented the seizure of the bridges northeast of Carentan and the planned destruction of those northwest of the city. By the end of D-Day, the division had suffered 1,240 casualties and had assembled only about 2,500 of the 6,600 men who had jumped early in the morning. (Fifty gliders, bearing reinforcements and supplies, had landed at daylight on D-Day.)

Had the Germans made a coordinated attack during the day against the weak position north of Carentan, they might have seriously interfered with the landings at Utah Beach. Instead, late that night, they merely dispatched the 6th Parachute Regiment to set up a defensive position at St. Côme-du-Mont, northwest of Carentan.

Farther north, the 82d Division, less scattered, landed in a more heavily defended area. It did succeed in capturing the key communications center of Ste. Mère-Eglise (*center*) and holding it against German attacks from the south. But the two regiments west of the Merderet River landed dispersed and were soon heavily engaged with elements of the German 91st Division. The paratroopers were hard-pressed and unable to secure the bridges over the Merderet to link up with the regiment east of the river. In the afternoon, the division's sea-borne tail (tanks and infantry) came ashore over Utah Beach. It was unable to penetrate the German position south of Ste. Mère-Eglise and reach the division; worse still, it could not clear the glider landing zone. As a result, the Germans took a heavy toll of the gliders landing at 2100. By the end of D-Day, the division, like its counterpart, had assembled only a fraction of its paratroopers and had suffered 1,259 casualties. It had no contact with either the 101st or 4th Divisions and faced a stiff two-day fight before crossings over the Merderet would be seized.

Meanwhile, about 0700, the 4th Infantry Division had landed —a mile south of the planned beach—against minor opposition. Pre-assault air and naval bombardments had softened up the defenses, and the operations of the airborne divisions had forced the Germans on the defensive. By the end of the day, the 4th Division, having suffered fewer than 200 casualties, was ashore and organized for offensive action.

During this day of fighting, the Germans had not reacted with their usual speed. The scattered airborne landings apparently misled them and caused an overestimation of Allied strength. Confused, uncertain of Allied intentions, and dispersed in small groups in the villages, the Germans were never able to mount the expected major counterblow.

(NOTE: This chart, and chart B following, are composites of a number of charts in the splendid publication of the Office, Chief of Military History, Department of the Army: *Cross Channel Attack,* by Gordon A. Harrison.)

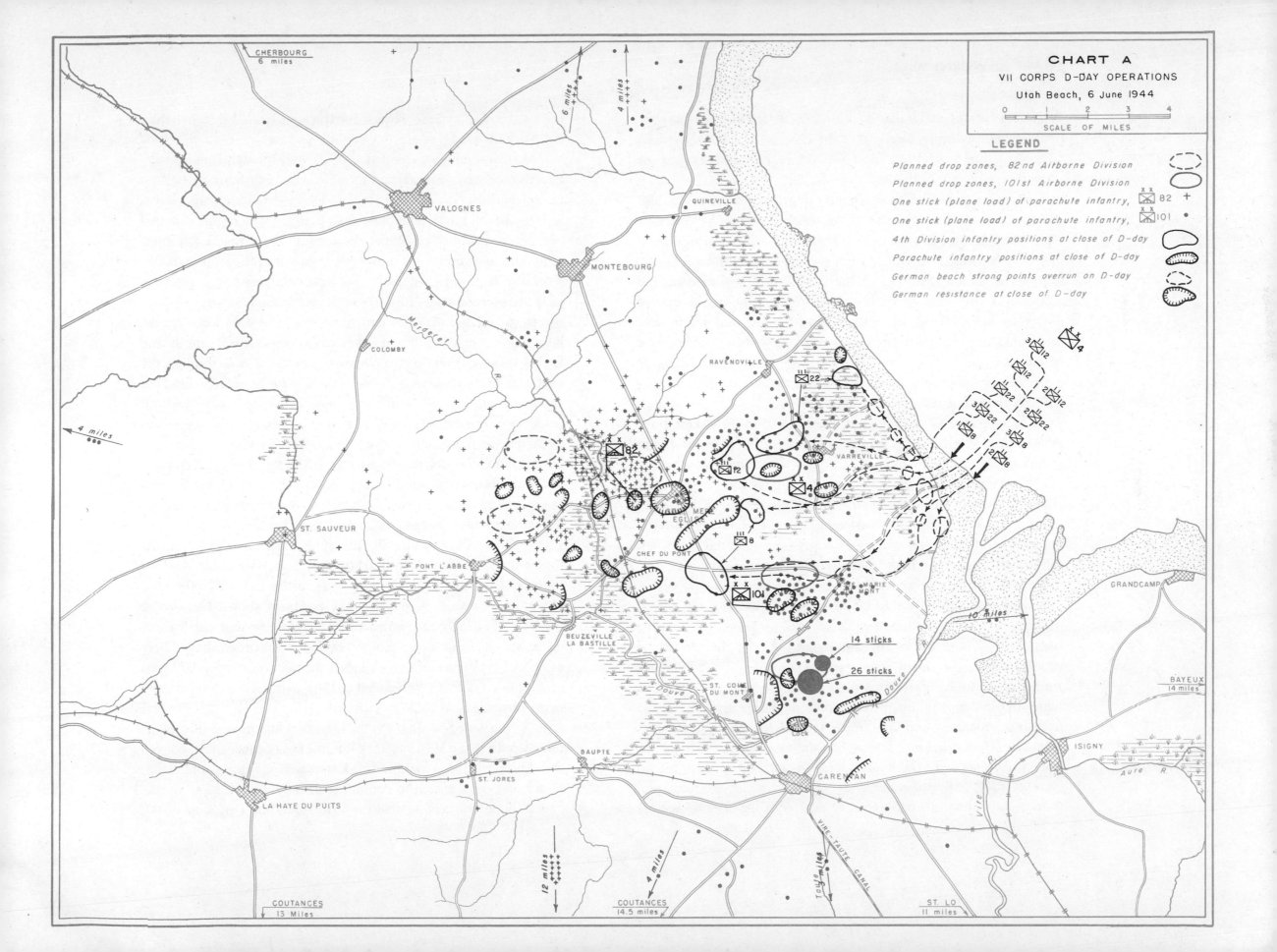

CHART A

VII CORPS D-DAY OPERATIONS
Utah Beach, 6 June 1944

0 1 2 3 4
SCALE OF MILES

LEGEND

Planned drop zones, 82nd Airborne Division

Planned drop zones, 101st Airborne Division

One stick (plane load) of parachute infantry, 82

One stick (plane load) of parachute infantry, 101

4th Division infantry positions at close of D-day

Parachute infantry positions at close of D-day

German beach strong points overrun on D-day

German resistance at close of D-day

CHERBOURG
6 miles

VALOGNES

QUINEVILLE

MONTEBOURG

COLOMBY

RAVENOVILLE

Merderet R.

ST. SAUVEUR

VARREVILLE

Ste. MERE EGLISE

CHEF DU PONT

PONT L'ABBE

Ste. MARIE MONT

GRANDCAMP

BEUZEVILLE LA BASTILLE

14 sticks

26 sticks

ST. COME DU MONT

Douve R.

BAYEUX
14 miles

LOCK

BAUPTE

ST. JORES

CARENTAN

ISIGNY

Aure R.

Vire R.

LA HAYE DU PUITS

Taute-Vire Canal

COUTANCES
13 Miles

COUTANCES
14.5 miles

ST. LO
11 miles

While operations at Utah Beach and in the British sector were progressing favorably, elements of the U.S. 1st and 29th Divisions were struggling to secure a foothold on Omaha Beach against the strongest resistance of the day.

A typical cross section of Omaha Beach is shown in the inset sketch. Note the imposing array of beach obstacles (covered at high tides, exposed at low), the shingle (impassable to vehicles), and the steep cliffs. Combined, they presented formidable obstructions to an assault landing. (Mine fields, both on the beach and offshore, are not shown.) The German strong points here were placed to defend the beach exits. Within these strong points were more than sixty light artillery pieces and many machine guns, sited to enfilade the beaches and their offshore approaches. Because many of the weapons were invisible from the sea, the preparatory naval bombardment was largely ineffective.

The intensive German resistance was in part due to the presence of the 352d Infantry Division, a first-line unit. In April, Hitler—intuitively, the Germans insist—had ordered the strengthening of the Normandy defenses. Allied intelligence, surprisingly enough, had not noticed the subsequent movement of the 352d Division into the area. Thus, instead of assaulting a four-battalion defensive front as expected, the V Corps encountered eight battalions with correspondingly increased depth of position.

The V Corps' plan specified that each of the assault regiments (the 16th and 116th) would land two battalions abreast—a total of eight infantry companies in the first assault wave (see landing plan, top). These troops, organized into special assault teams, were to reduce the enemy strong points protecting the exit roads. Immediately following them would come the special demolition teams to blow gaps in the obstacle zone; then the remainder of the assault regiments would land, to be followed by the normal divisional build-up echelons. To provide the vital support for the assault waves, special (DD) tanks which could "swim" ashore had been devised. All personnel had been thoroughly briefed, prepared, and trained to perfection to deal with the specific sectors shown. Herein lay a weakness, for if a unit landed in other than its assigned sector, confusion might—and did—reign.

As the initial waves landed at 0630, they found an enemy relatively unscathed from air and naval attacks. Furthermore, strong lateral currents and poor navigation brought the assault waves into the beach much differently than planned. (Compare planned and actual landings on map.) As a result, there was much intermingling, and, under the withering enemy fire, the right wing almost disintegrated. Disembarked too far out to sea, large numbers of the desperately needed tanks sank, as did many of the amphibious trucks loaded with 105-mm. howitzers. The demolition teams, laboring heroically, suffered heavy casualties (40 per cent during D-Day), but did manage to blast six gaps, as shown, through the obstacles. But the survivors of the assault wave huddled behind the shingle—demoralized, confused, and, in many cases, without leadership. Fortunately, in these desperate early hours when a determined German counterattack might have crushed the landing, a few courageous leaders rose to the occasion; their actions were decisive. Gradually, small groups worked their way inland—generally up the cliffs between the beach exits—and began to reduce the strong points. Naval gunfire took over the direct support mission; engineers began clearing the mine fields; and, by noon, the follow-up regiments (115th, 18th, and 26th) were landing. By the end of D-Day, the V Corps, having suffered about 2,000 casualties, had forward elements in the positions shown (solid blue ovals). The beachhead, nowhere more than one and a half miles deep, was far from secure, but the build-up was proceeding. There were still isolated German elements on the coast; only 100 tons of supplies (out of a scheduled 2,400) had been unloaded; and many obstacles had yet to be cleared.

As mentioned on map 49, the Germans had missed the opportunity to drive the V Corps back into the sea because they believed the Allies had been repulsed at Omaha. But a more important factor was the decision to commit their only reserve in an unsuccessful counterattack against the British landing (off map, east).

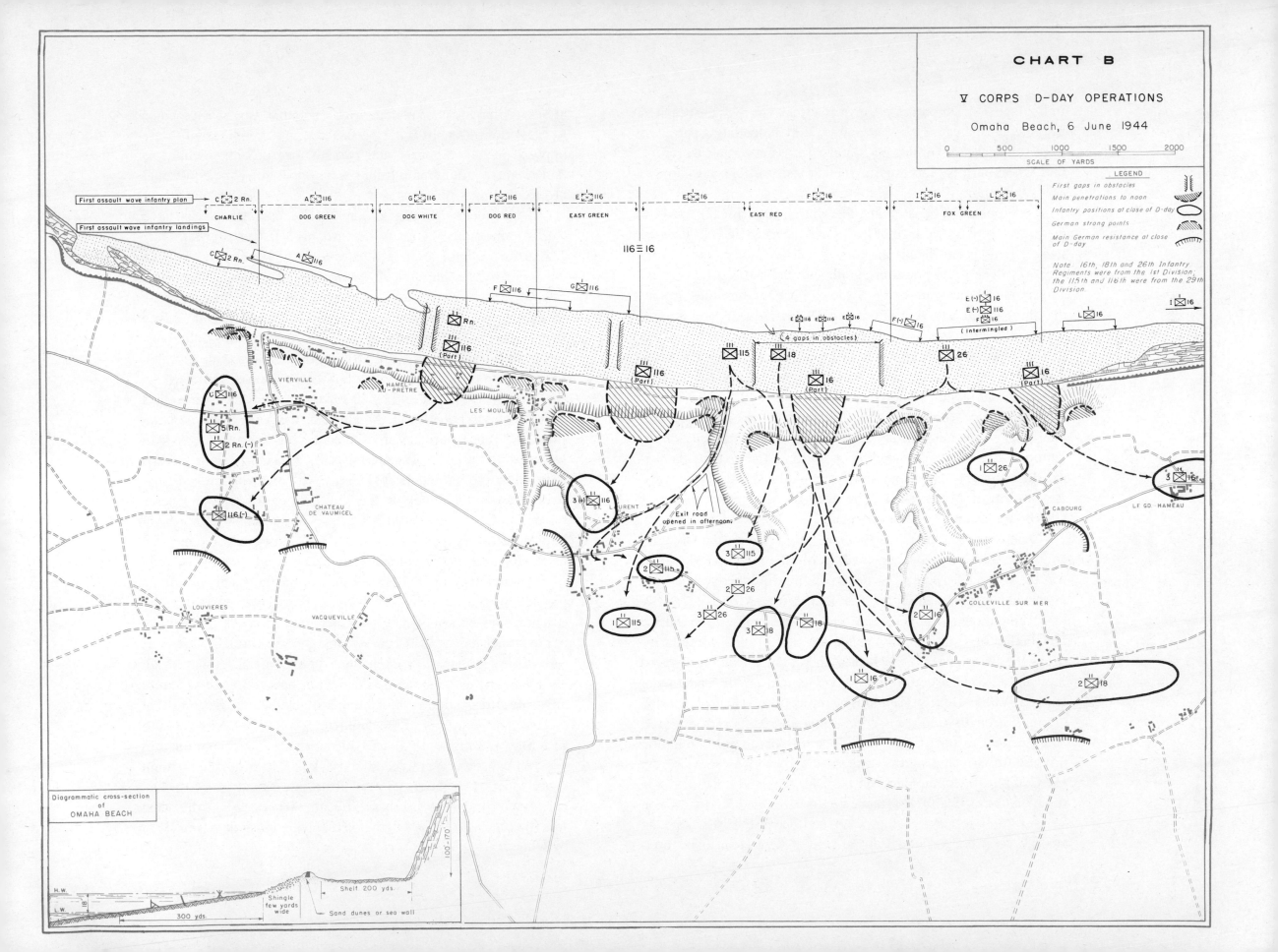

CHART B

V CORPS D-DAY OPERATIONS

Omaha Beach, 6 June 1944

0   500   1000   1500   2000
SCALE OF YARDS

LEGEND

First gaps in obstacles

Main penetrations to noon

Infantry positions at close of D-day

German strong points

Main German resistance at close of D-day

Note: 16th, 18th and 26th Infantry Regiments were from the 1st Division; the 115th and 116th were from the 29th Division.

First assault wave infantry plan

First assault wave infantry landings

CHARLIE   DOG GREEN   DOG WHITE   DOG RED   EASY GREEN   EASY RED   FOX GREEN

116 ☰ 16

(4 gaps in obstacles)   (Intermingled)

VIERVILLE

HAMEL AU-PRETRE

LES MOULINS

ST LAURENT

Exit road opened in afternoon.

CHATEAU DE VAUMICEL

CABOURG

LE GD HAMEAU

COLLEVILLE SUR MER

LOUVIERES

VACQUEVILLE

Diagrammatic cross-section of OMAHA BEACH

H.W.

L.W.

300 yds.

Shingle few yards wide

Sand dunes or sea wall

Shelf 200 yds.

100-170

Initial logistical support of the invasion was to be over the beaches. But the beach capacity was limited, and unloading operations were subject to disruption by storms. It was essential, therefore, that Cherbourg be captured at the earliest possible date for use as a supply port.

To supplement beach unloading during the critical period before ports were operable, the British had designed and constructed two ingenious artificial harbors (called "mulberries" [inset sketch]). Their "bombardons," "phoenixes," and "gooseberries" all served as breakwaters to provide still-water conditions around the clock. Mulberry A was off Omaha Beach near St. Laurent, and Mulberry B was in the British zone, off Arromanches. Each had an unloading capacity of 6,000 tons per day. Their construction was a major project and placed a heavy strain on British construction and towing resources.

On 19 June, three days after Mulberry A had been placed in operation, a severe four-day storm struck the Normandy coast, temporarily halting all unloading operations, and severely damaging the mulberry. Those parts which could be salvaged were used to supplement Mulberry B. The need for the early capture of Cherbourg became even more urgent.

Operations around Caen (center, right) and on the Cotentin peninsula were very closely related. In Montgomery's view, "Caen was the key to Cherbourg," since its capture would reduce German lateral-movement capabilities, free British forces for a shift westward, and allow more American forces to be employed in a drive on Cherbourg. Consequently, beginning on 13 June, Montgomery drove the British hard toward Caen and directed Bradley to speed the capture of Cherbourg; but when German armor reacted violently at Villers-Bocage (center), he settled for the idea of drawing German strength onto the Second Army and temporarily relaxed the attempts to take Caen. But—possibly because of mounting criticism of British progress contrasted to American successes on the Cotentin—Montgomery, on the 18th, directed renewal of the drive on Caen. This attack, made by the XXX and VIII Corps on 25 and 26 June (after being postponed because of the Channel storm), soon bogged down in the face of fierce panzer counter-attacks. Montgomery's plan to draw strength toward Caen seemed to be working—on 30 June, the British (on a 33-mile front) were opposed by seven panzer and two infantry divisions, while the Americans (on a 55-mile front) were opposed by the equivalent of seven infantry divisions.

Meanwhile, as Bradley's V and XIX (operational 13 June) Corps took up an aggressive defense, his VII Corps (Maj. Gen. J. Lawton Collins) drove westward to cut the peninsula. The going was costly in the difficult bocage country (small fields separated by hedges, banks, and sunken roads), but Collins, a veteran of fighting in similarly difficult terrain on Guadalcanal, solved the bocage problem by driving the VII Corps forward on narrow fronts with reserves in depth. Striking the disintegrating German forces on its front viciously, Collins' corps reached the coast on the 18th, turned north, and by 20 June was attacking Cherbourg's outer defenses (this map). Meanwhile, the VIII Corps (operational 15 June) occupied and defended the line from Carentan westward to the coast. The Germans at Cherbourg having refused a surrender ultimatum, the VII Corps, with overwhelming air support, renewed the attack on the 22d. Five days later, after fierce resistance, Cherbourg capitulated. The Germans had so thoroughly demolished the port that not until 7 August could the piers be used. However, beach unloading at Cherbourg began on 16 July.

The period of 13-30 June saw all German hopes of containing the Allies collapse. From the 16th on, Rundstedt, at Hitler's insistence, massed armor at Caen—not only to check the British, but to launch a drive to the coast. Montgomery's attacks, however, forced the Germans to commit their panzer divisions piecemeal. This, coupled with incessant Allied air attacks, doomed to failure any concentration for a major counterattack. Rundstedt and Rommel, seeing the futility of the "hold-at-all-costs" policy, wanted to withdraw as early as 17 June. Hitler forbade it and continued to issue unrealistic orders to counterattack. By 30 June, the German commanders, frustrated and pessimistic, had already conceded defeat; significantly, the German Fifteenth Army north of the Seine was still almost at full strength. On 3 July, Rundstedt was relieved by Kluge.

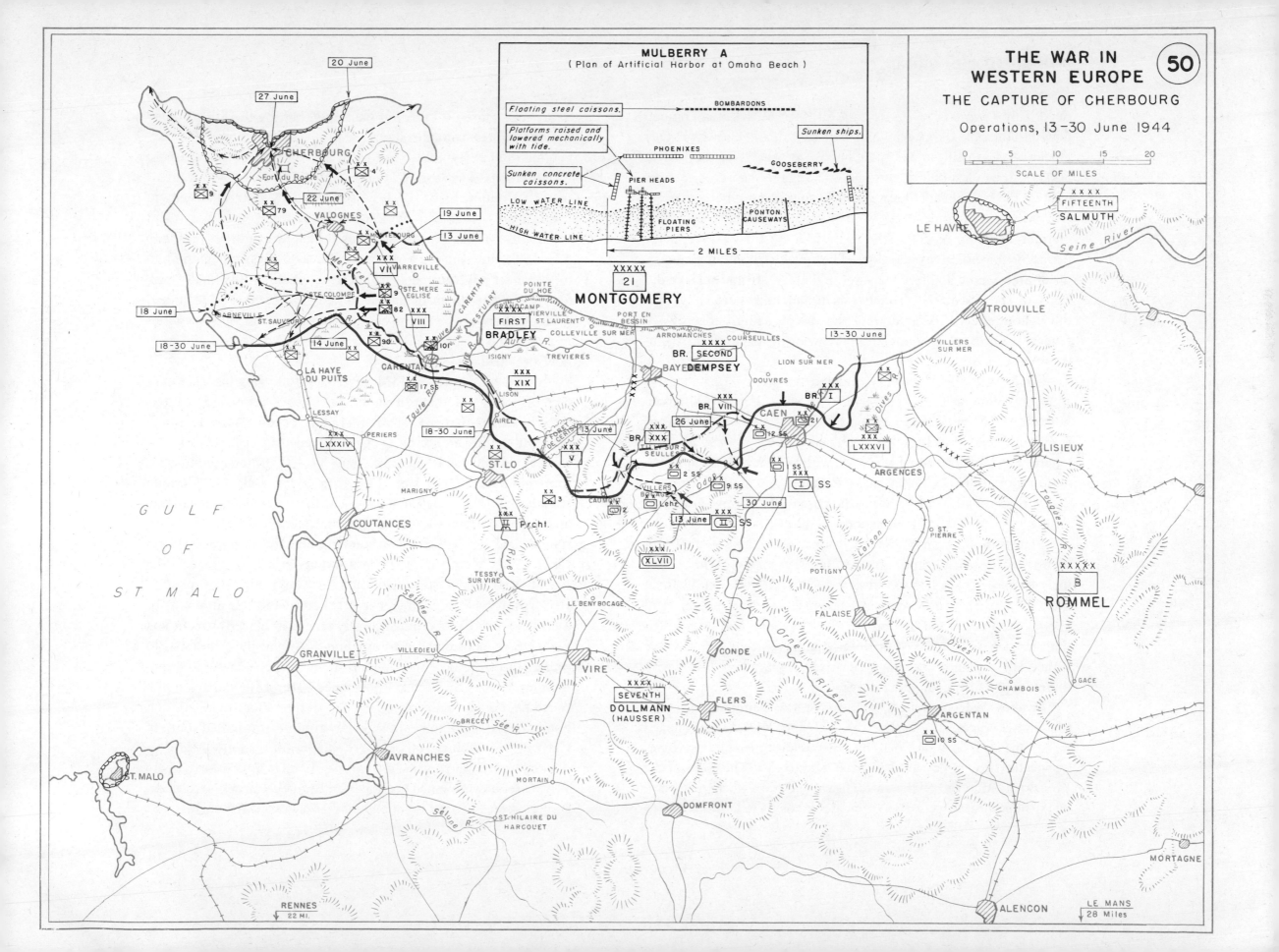

THE WAR IN WESTERN EUROPE
50
THE CAPTURE OF CHERBOURG
Operations, 13–30 June 1944

0 5 10 15 20
SCALE OF MILES

MULBERRY A
(Plan of Artificial Harbor at Omaha Beach)

Floating steel caissons. — — — — BOMBARDONS

Platforms raised and lowered mechanically with tide.

PHOENIXES

Sunken ships.

Sunken concrete caissons.

PIER HEADS

GOOSEBERRY

LOW WATER LINE

HIGH WATER LINE

FLOATING PIERS

PONTON CAUSEWAYS

2 MILES

20 June

27 June

CHERBOURG

Fort du Roule

XX 9

XX 79

VALOGNES

22 June

XX 4

19 June

13 June

Montebourg

VII

Barreville

STE. COLOMBE

9

Ste. Mere Eglise

18 June

82

VIII

18-30 June

14 June

90

St. Sauveur

Carneville

101

CARENTAN

LA HAYE DU PUITS

17 SS

LESSAY

XIX

Lison

PERIERS

LXXXIV

18-30 June

Airel

XXXXX
21
MONTGOMERY

FIRST
BRADLEY

POINTE DU HOE
GRANDCAMP
Vierville
ST. LAURENT
Isigny
Trevieres
COLLEVILLE SUR MER

PORT EN BESSIN
ARROMANCHES
COURSEULLES

BR. SECOND
DEMPSEY

BAYEUX

DOUVRES

LION SUR MER

13-30 June

VILLERS SUR MER

TROUVILLE

LE HAVRE

XXXX
FIFTEENTH
SALMUTH

Seine River

BR. I

LXXXVI

13-30 June

FORET DE CERISY

13 June

ST. LO

V

XXX
3

MARIGNY

XX 2

II Prcht.

XLVII

BR. VIII

26 June

BR. XXX

TILLY SUR SEULLES

2 SS

Lehr

VILLERS BOCAGE

CAUMONT

9 SS

30 June

13 June

II SS

CAEN

12 SS

21

I SS

ARGENCES

LISIEUX

Odon

Orne River

ST. PIERRE

B
ROMMEL

FALAISE

POTIGNY

Loison R.

Touques R.

GACE

CHAMBOIS

COUTANCES

TESSY SUR VIRE

LE BENY BOCAGE

GRANVILLE

VILLEDIEU

VIRE

CONDE

FLERS

SEVENTH
DOLLMANN
(HAUSSER)

ARGENTAN

10 SS

ALENCON

MORTAIN

DOMFRONT

AVRANCHES

ST. MALO

GULF

OF

ST. MALO

Seine R.

Selune R.

ST. HILAIRE DU HARCOUET

See R.

BRECEY

RENNES
22 MI.

LE MANS
28 Miles

MORTAGNE

Dives R.

On 1 July (*dashed red line*), only one-fifth of the area contemplated in the OVERLORD plan had been seized, and Caen, a D-Day objective, was still in German hands. About 1,000,000 men, 500,000 tons of supplies, and 150,000 vehicles had come ashore to cram the beachhead. Desired airfield sites had not been secured, and lateral communications were poor and subject to periodic German shelling. Nor was the terrain in the First Army sector favorable for offensive operations. The marshy Carentan plain was unsuitable for mechanized warfare; to the west, from La Haye-du-Puits to the coast, the ground was firmer and more hilly. But throughout the entire area were the discouraging hedgerows—fences of earth, hedge, and trees, varying in height from six to twenty-seven feet.

On 30 June, Montgomery directed the First Army to drive south, pivoting on Caumont (*center*). Earlier, Bradley, at Eisenhower's and Montgomery's urgings, had tried to get a southward push under way, but logistical problems and the priority given to Cherbourg had prevented it. Now, with pressure from above—news reports already hinted at "stalemate" and static warfare—and with German defenses along the base of the peninsula getting stronger daily, he could no longer delay the attack.

Elements of eleven German divisions (about 35,000 men with surprisingly high morale) opposed Bradley's First Army. They lacked supplies, but had excellent terrain to defend. On 28 June, the German front was reorganized as shown. SS General Paul Hausser took over the Seventh Army. (Dollman had been killed that day.) Now convinced of the impracticability of an offensive thrust, Hitler planned to fight defensively, replace his panzers with infantry, and form a mobile reserve.

Bradley designated the Coutances–St. Lô–Caumont line as the first-phase objective. Because the VII and XIX Corps needed more time and the VIII Corps had the greatest distances to cover, he specified an "oblique order" from west to east. The corps of the First Army attacked on the dates shown and everywhere met stern, unexpected resistance. All divisions took heavy, demoralizing cas-

ualties. La Haye-du-Puits fell on 7 July, but, by the 8th, Bradley—disappointed with the slight gains—began to contemplate accepting the Lessay–St. Lô line as an intermediate objective where he could mass—instead of attacking all along the line—for an attack to Coutances. By 13 July, the idea had matured, been enthusiastically endorsed by Eisenhower and Montgomery, and eventually became Operation COBRA, the breakthrough (*see map 53*). In the interim, the First Army slogged forward, beginning to meet panzer reinforcements from Caen, but on 18 July finally took St. Lô. Six days later, the attack halted (*this map, solid red line*). The five divisions attacking St. Lô had suffered 11,000 casualties in twelve days, but the Germans, too, had paid heavily and were now stretched very thin.

Meanwhile, to the east, Montgomery, following his basic concept of holding German strength near Caen—but now also interested in seizing that city—had ordered the Second Army to attack on 8 July. This attack (I Corps), preceded by a 2,300-ton "air carpet" (4,000 by 1,500 yards, laid by 470 strategic bombers), took that part of Caen west of the Orne River, soaked up German strength, and then bogged down. (The heavy bombs used had created many obstacles to movement, and there had been an unfortunate time lag between the bombing and the ground assault.) On the 13th, Montgomery ordered another attack, this time by the British VIII Corps (three armored divisions) and the Canadian II Corps, for 17 July. He apparently considered this attack to be a diversion for COBRA, but strangely no one at SHAEF, including Eisenhower, considered it as anything less than the Allies' bid to break out of the beachhead. Thus, there was considerable disappointment when the attack—postponed to the 18th and again preceded by a massive air carpet, which this time used fragmentation bombs in the sector to be traversed by armor—was halted south of Caen by Montgomery on 20 July (*solid red line, dated 24 July*).

As the British continued to probe German lines during 21-24 July, Eisenhower pinned his hopes on Bradley's attack—as Montgomery seems to have done all along—scheduled for 25 July.

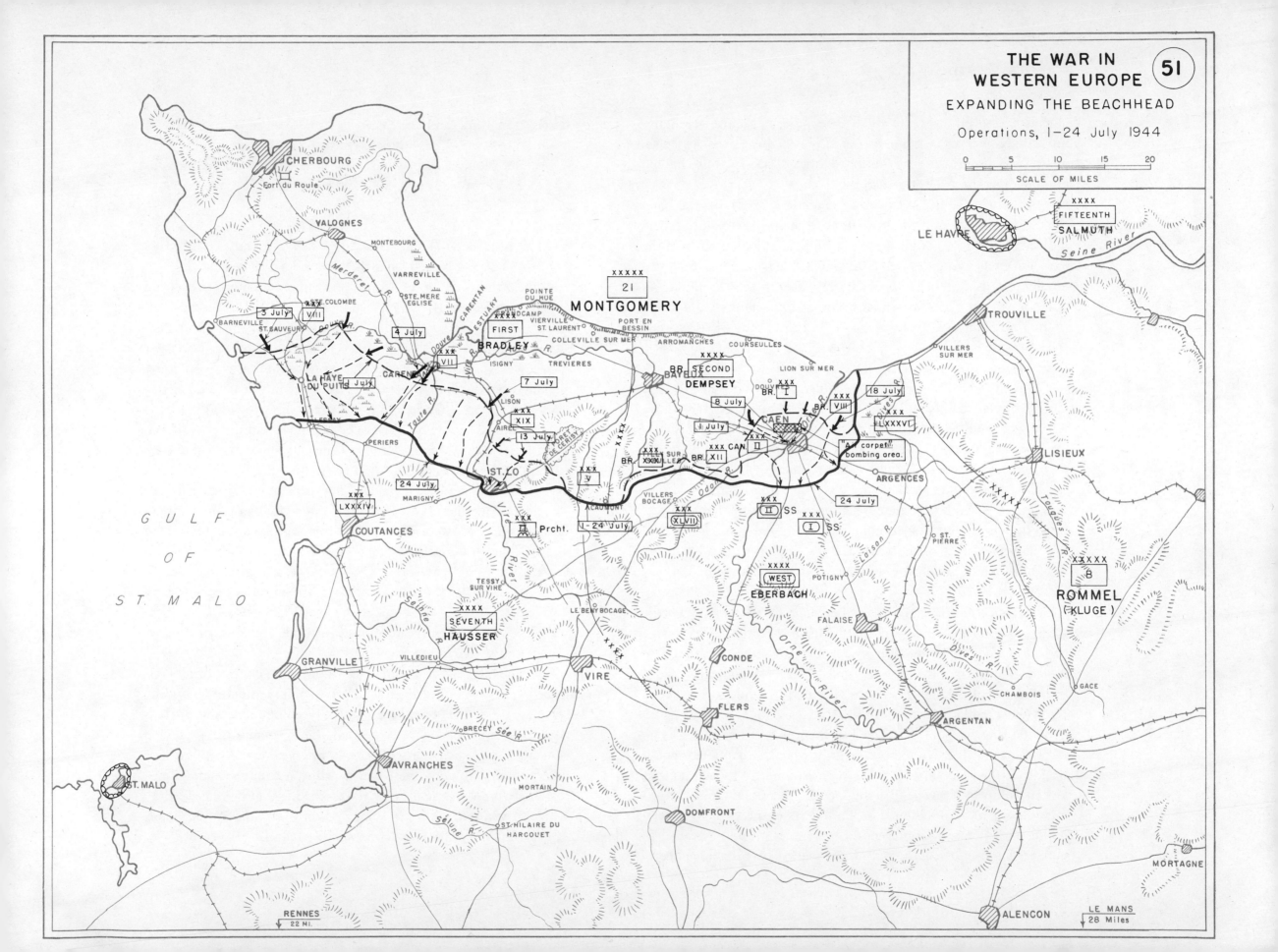

THE WAR IN
WESTERN EUROPE

51

EXPANDING THE BEACHHEAD

Operations, 1–24 July 1944

0   5   10   15   20
SCALE OF MILES

GULF

OF

ST. MALO

CHERBOURG
Fort du Roule

VALOGNES

MONTEBOURG

VARREVILLE

STE. COLOMBE

BARNEVILLE

ST. SAUVEUR

STE. MERE EGLISE

POINTE DU HUE

GRANDCAMP

VIERVILLE
ST. LAURENT

COLLEVILLE SUR MER

PORT EN BESSIN

ARROMANCHES

COURSEULLES

LION SUR MER

VILLERS SUR MER

TROUVILLE

LE HAVRE

Seine River

XXXX
FIFTEENTH
SALMUTH

XXXXX
21
MONTGOMERY

XXXX
FIRST
BRADLEY

ISIGNY   TREVIERES

BAYEUX

XXXX
BR. SECOND
DEMPSEY

DOUV

BR. I

BR. VIII

18 July

LXXXVI

LISIEUX

"Air carpet"
bombing area.

ARGENCES

24 July

XXXXX

ST. PIERRE

3 July
VIII

4 July

LA HAYE
DU PUITS

CARENTAN

July

7 July

XXX
VII

XXX
XIX

AIREL

13 July

LISON

FORET DE CERISY

ST. LO

XXX
V

ACAUMONT

VILLERS BOCAGE

XXX
XLVII

1–24 July

II SS

I SS

POTIGNY

WEST
EBERBACH

FALAISE

XXXXX
B
ROMMEL
(KLUGE)

Loison R.

Dives R.

Touques R.

Odon R.

Orne River

24 July

LXXXIV

COUTANCES

MARIGNY

XXX
II Prcht.

TESSY
SUR VIRE

XXXX
SEVENTH
HAUSSER

LE BENY BOCAGE

CONDE

GRANVILLE

VILLEDIEU

Seine R.

Vire River

VIRE

FLERS

ARGENTAN

ST. MALO

Selune R.

AVRANCHES

MORTAIN

BRECEY   See R.

DOMFRONT

ST. HILAIRE DU HARCOUET

CHAMBOIS

GACE

MORTAGNE

RENNES
22 MI.

LE MANS
28 Miles

ALENCON

Merderet R.

Taute R.

CAEN

CAN. II

BR. XII

During the seven weeks in which Eisenhower's armies were gaining a lodgment in Normandy (*shaded red area*), the war elsewhere was progressing favorably for the Allies. In Italy, having taken Rome, the Allies pursued Field Marshal Albert Kesselring's forces about 150 miles northward (*shaded red area*). On the Eastern Front, the Russians, in keeping with their agreement to create a diversion for OVERLORD, struck in Finland and then north of the Pripet Marshes (*shaded red area*). The Pacific offensive gained momentum as American forces seized bases in the Marianas, secured northeast New Guinea, and won an important naval victory in the Philippine Sea (*see map 143*). In Burma, the British forced the Japanese on the defensive (*see map 142*). Only in China (*see map 141*) did the enemy possess the initiative.

This map also shows (*shaded blue and green areas*) Allied gains between 25 July and 15 December, 1944. Some of these have already been discussed in detail; others will be described in subsequent maps. Russian operations during this period (*see maps 42-43*) were a succession of massive blows which steadily forced back the 200-odd German and satellite divisions opposing them. Hitler, insisting on an inflexible defense, sought to stem the Russian tide by desperately switching commanders along the line. (Note, during the second half of the year, Stalin's emphasis on subjugating the Balkans—as much for postwar political aims as for military reasons.)

Operations in Italy are covered on maps 105-106. Noteworthy is the obvious slackening of Field Marshal Harold Alexander's drive (*shaded blue and green areas*). Inextricably associated with Allied strategy in France, operations in Italy—much to the disgruntlement of the British—were relegated to a role secondary to the August landing in southern France (*see map 57*). The British deplored this decision. It seemed to them that Alexander was on the verge of a decisive victory in Italy which, if exploited, could well lead to an advance into Austria or southern France and thus aid Eisenhower (then still contained at the Caen–St. Lô line) more than another landing. The United States, however—remembering the Teheran Conference (November, 1943) promise to make a landing in southern France, fearful of becoming overly

involved in Italy, and convinced that the port of Marseilles was essential to support Eisenhower—insisted on the operation. With Alexander required to provide seven divisions for the landing, his advance was naturally slowed, and the idea of a move into Austria died.

The area occupied by the Allies in Normandy on 24 July (D + 48) encompassed what they had hoped to have on D + 5. However, the build-up of troops and supplies ashore proceeded almost as planned. By 24 July, though the Allies had already suffered some 122,000 casualties, the equivalent of thirty-four divisions was in the Allied beachhead. German estimates placed their own losses at about 117,000. The supply situation was generally satisfactory: personnel losses had been replaced; better guns to deal with superior German armor were being expedited from the United States; supply reserves were accruing; and the critical ammunition shortage was moderating. The map shows the rapid overrunning of France once the Allies broke out of the beachhead and also landed in southern France. They very quickly made up for lost time. Note that at D + 100 they were actually on the German border, whereas, according to their original plans, they expected at that time to be at the Seine. Naturally, with supply plans not geared to such a rapid advance, logistical difficulties arose. During this period, strategic bombing of the German oil industry was intensified (control of the bombers had reverted to the CCS in September), but the results were disappointing, as German production actually increased somewhat.

Meanwhile, Hitler assumed ever-tightening control of all German operations. Following the abortive 20 July attempt on his life, rebellious army leaders were ruthlessly eliminated, and Hitler's control became absolute. Note that the Germans still occupied isolated key French ports. This was in consonance with Hitler's determination to deny these to the Allies for much-needed logistical support purposes. Finally, on 27 July, Hitler acceded to Kluge's request to withdraw some divisions from the Pas de Calais (Fifteenth Army) for employment in Normandy.

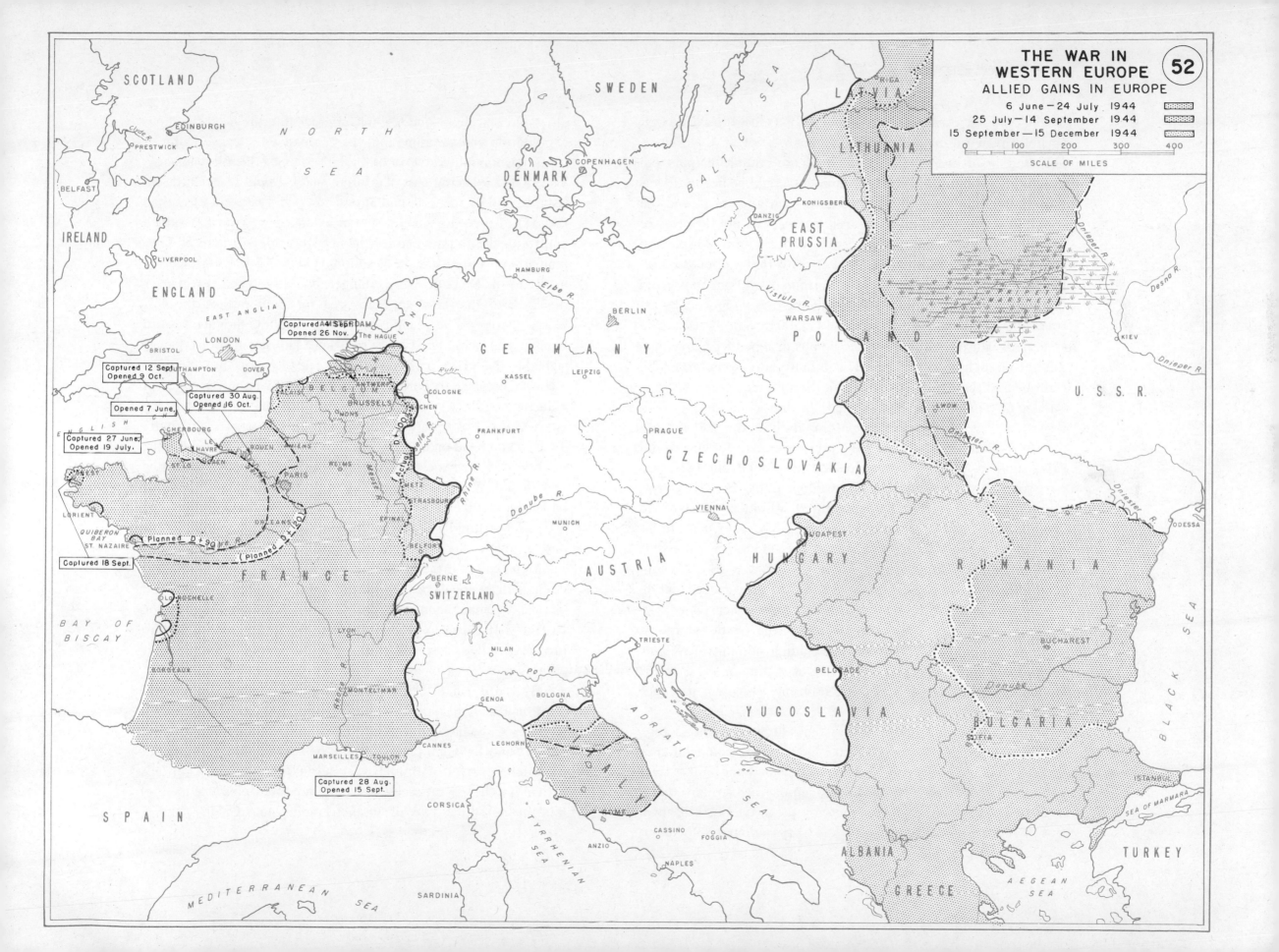

THE WAR IN
WESTERN EUROPE
ALLIED GAINS IN EUROPE
6 June—24 July 1944
25 July—14 September 1944
15 September—15 December 1944

52

0   100   200   300   400
SCALE OF MILES

SCOTLAND

EDINBURGH
PRESTWICK
Clyde R.

BELFAST

IRELAND

LIVERPOOL

ENGLAND

EAST ANGLIA

BRISTOL
LONDON
THAMPTON   DOVER

Captured 12 Sept.
Opened 9 Oct.

Opened 7 June.

Captured 30 Aug.
Opened 16 Oct.

Captured 27 June,
Opened 19 July.

CHERBOURG
LE HAVRE   ROUEN
AMIENS

REIMS

Captured 18 Sept.

LORIENT
QUIBERON
BAY
ST. NAZAIRE

Planned D-90

(Planned D-90)

Loire R.

ORLEANS

FRANCE

BAY OF
BISCAY

BERNE
SWITZERLAND

MONTELIMAR

SPAIN

MARSEILLES TOULON

Captured 28 Aug.
Opened 15 Sept.

CORSICA

MEDITERRANEAN SEA

SARDINIA

NORTH
SEA

SWEDEN

DENMARK
COPENHAGEN

Baltic Sea

HAMBURG

Elbe R.

BERLIN

AMSTERDAM
Captured 4 Sept.
Opened 26 Nov.
THE HAGUE

ANTWERP
BRUSSELS
MONS

Ruhr

KASSEL

LEIPZIG

GERMANY

COLOGNE

FRANKFURT

Moselle R.
Rhine R.

METZ

STRASBOURG

EPINAL

BELFORT

Danube R.

MILAN

Po R.

GENOA

BOLOGNA

LEGHORN

ITALY

ANZIO

ROME

CASSINO

NAPLES

FOGGIA

ADRIATIC SEA

TYRRHENIAN
SEA

LATVIA

LITHUANIA

EAST
PRUSSIA

DANZIG

KONIGSBERG

Vistula R.

WARSAW

POLAND

PRAGUE

CZECHOSLOVAKIA

VIENNA

MUNICH

AUSTRIA

BUDAPEST

HUNGARY

YUGOSLAVIA

BELGRADE

TRIESTE

ALBANIA

GREECE

Dnieper R.

Desna R.

KIEV

U. S. S. R.

Dnieper R.

Dniester R.

ODESSA

RUMANIA

BUCHAREST

BULGARIA

SOFIA

BLACK SEA

ISTANBUL

SEA OF MARMARA

TURKEY

AEGEAN
SEA

The U.S. First Army attack on 25 July (Operation COBRA), sought a penetration of German defenses west of St. Lô (*center, left*) and an advance to Coutances to secure suitable terrain from which the breakout, pivoting on Caumont, could be begun. It was thus to be a limited-objective operation—an attempt to end the bloody hedgerow fighting of the past two weeks—not the decisive breakout operation into which Bradley and Collins, displaying commendable flexibility of mind, later converted it. General Collins' VII Corps (three infantry, two armored, and one motorized infantry divisions) would make the main effort, supported by extra artillery and another bomb carpet (2,500 by 6,000 yards, to be saturated with over 4,200 tons of bombs dropped by heavy, medium, and fighter bombers). The infantry divisions, attacking right behind the carpet, would break through the defensive crust. Passing through the gap thus created, the motorized infantry division would seize Coutances; one armored division would envelop that town from the south; and the other armored division would drive southeast and establish blocking positions from Tessy-sur-Vire south to the Seinne River. To Collins' right, the VIII Corps, attacking after Coutances was captured, would move south to complete the encirclement of the German LXXXIV Corps; to his left, the XIX and V Corps would exert pressure to prevent a shift of German forces to the west.

German defenses west of St. Lô on 25 July lacked depth. Kluge, concerned with creating a mobile reserve near Caen, virtually ignored the Seventh Army front. On the eve of the attack, there were about 30,000 troops (including administrative and reserve echelons) opposite the VII Corps, but in or near the front line there were only about 5,000, most of them from the Panzer Lehr Division.

After a false start on the 24th, COBRA jumped off on 25 July. The bomb carpet—though "shorts" hurt the attacking infantry (558 casualties, 24-25 July)—practically wiped out Panzer Lehr and created such shock and confusion among the Germans that it must be considered the decisive factor in the initial breakthrough. But there was still resistance—the VII Corps suffered 1,060 casualties the first day—and Collins, appreciating the need for rapid exploitation and gambling that the German defenses were almost ruptured, committed two of his mobile columns the following day. The first, advancing east of Marigny (*left center*), met little resistance and by the 27th had almost reached Tessy-sur-Vire; then the XIX Corps, its zone of action extended westward, assumed control of the column and for the next three days fought off German attempts to restore the situation. (On the 27th, Kluge, alerted finally to the Seventh Army's danger, had dispatched two panzer divisions to the Tessy-sur-Vire area to counterattack the VII Corps' flank.) The second exploiting column, moving toward Coutances, encountered fierce resistance and saw its objective assigned to the VIII Corps on the 27th. The Germans, holding open a coastal escape corridor, evaded the planned Coutances trap; but Hausser, to Kluge's consternation, then ordered the withdrawing LXXXIV Corps toward Tessy-sur-Vire instead of straight south. Thus, it ran head-on into Collins' armor and was chopped to bits; many of the troops evaded capture, but most vehicles had to be abandoned. With the German line to the coast unhinged, Bradley had ordered full exploitation on the 28th. Elements of the VII and VIII Corps rapidly drove south, Coutances falling on 28 June and Granville and Avranches on the 30th.

Meanwhile, in the British sector the Canadian II Corps had made a diversionary attack on the 25th, successfully drawing a vicious German counterattack. Then Montgomery moved the British VIII Corps to Caumont, where it attacked on the 30th to protect Bradley's left, but this attack came too late to prevent Kluge's movement of armor to the Tessy-sur-Vire area.

By 31 July, the Allies were in good positions on the line shown. Two new army headquarters had arrived: Lt. Gen. Henry D. G. Crerar's Canadian First Army (now controlling the British I Corps) and Lt. Gen. George S. Patton's Third Army (prepared to assume control of Bradley's westernmost divisions). Patton's arrival had been kept secret, since his supposed presence in England furthered the hoax of another landing near Calais.

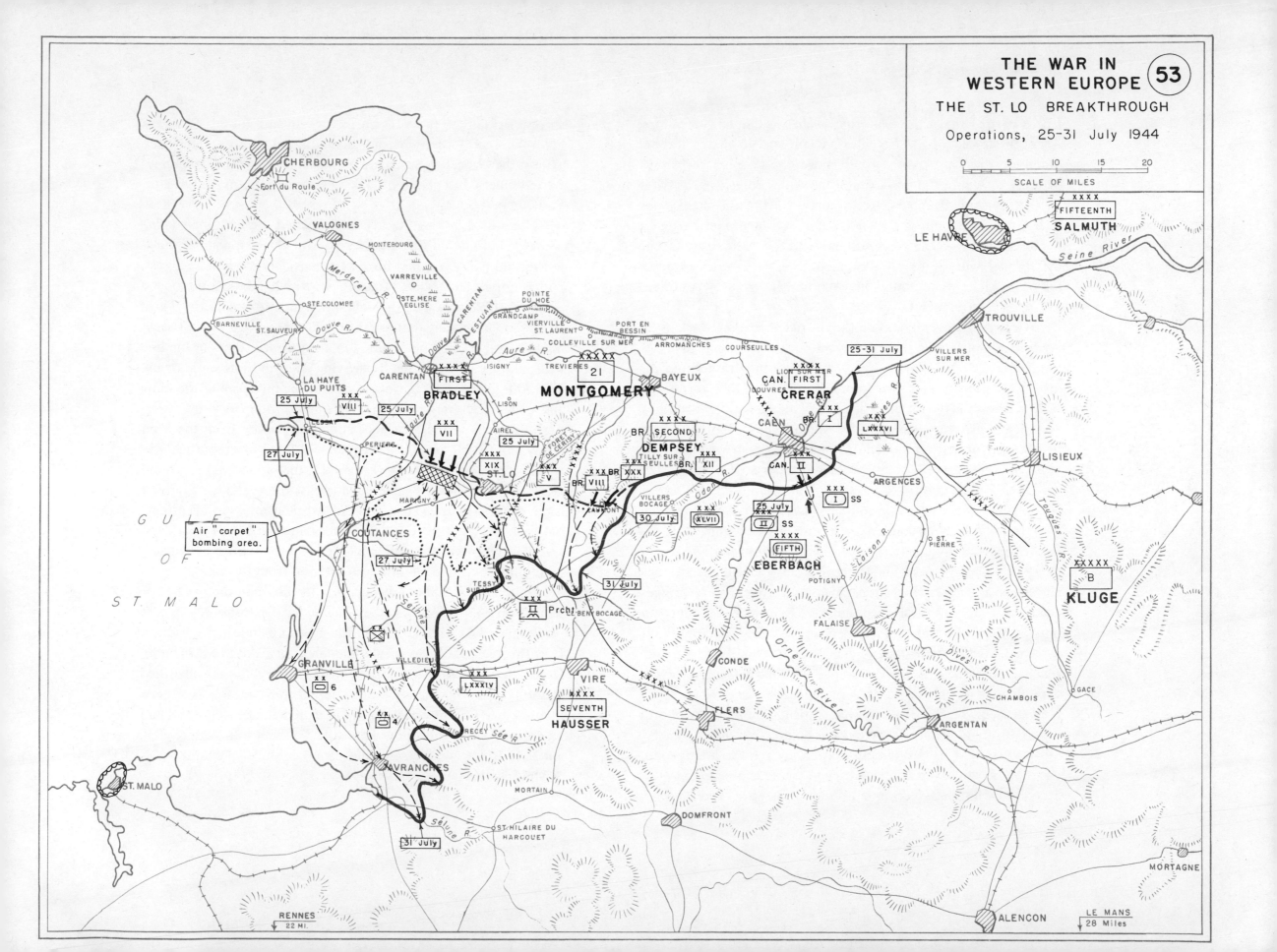

THE WAR IN WESTERN EUROPE 53
THE ST. LO BREAKTHROUGH
Operations, 25-31 July 1944

SCALE OF MILES
0   5   10   15   20

It was part of the Allied plan that when the United States First Army broke out of the Cotentin and pivoted to the east about Caumont, the Third Army would move one or more corps into Brittany to secure the ports which the Allies considered so vital for their logistical support. Accordingly, when the United States VIII Corps broke into the open south of Avranches on 1 August, the Third Army became operational, and the 12th Army Group was formed, with Bradley in command. Lt. Gen. Courtney Hodges took over the United States First Army. Montgomery continued to control operations.

While engineers labored on the restricted road network at the Avranches bottleneck, the flamboyant but boldly imaginative Patton drove the VIII Corps (spearheaded by the 4th and 6th Armored Divisions) westward into Brittany. His other corps—the XV, XX, and XII—he moved through the gap straight south of Avranches. Brittany was quickly overrun (most of the German field forces formerly stationed there had been destroyed in the defense of Normandy), except for its major ports (*see map 52*).

During the operations shown on this map, Allied close air support was superb. Tank columns had direct communication with the aircraft flying column cover, thus ensuring immediate tactical support and reconnaissance. The map illustrates another aspect of air support—the lines interdicted by tactical and strategic air power to isolate the battlefield. So effectively were bridges, roads, and railroads destroyed that the Germans were reduced to moving troops by night; supply deficiencies became acute.

On 4 August, the first major change in the OVERLORD plan took place. In June, 21st Army Group planners had considered how to capitalize on just such a set of German weaknesses as now existed. Near the end of July, Eisenhower, anticipating a great opportunity, had urged Montgomery to take bold action. Montgomery's answer was his 4 August directive ordering Crerar to attack southeast not later than the 8th, Dempsey to continue attacking toward Argentan, Hodges to continue his swing eastward, and Patton—

leaving Brittany to the VIII Corps—to advance toward Le Mans (*bottom center*). Montgomery's intention was to force Kluge back against the bridgeless Seine and destroy him. Airborne commanders were alerted to plan for blocking escape routes in the Orléans-Paris "gap."

The Allied armies quickly implemented the new plan (*blue arrows*), but late on 6 August a powerful German counterattack at Mortain (*lower center*) forced a reconsideration. On 2 August, Hitler himself had ordered this attack: it was to be a full-blooded armored stroke toward Avranches, designed to isolate the Third Army, and ultimately to turn north to crush the OVERLORD beachhead. Kluge readied his forces, replacing panzer units in the line with infantry divisions finally arriving from the Fifteenth Army. The 30th Division (VII Corps) caught the full force of the blow and reeled backward, but Bradley quickly stopped two of Patton's divisions in the area and, adding two more from the First Army, reinforced the 30th Division. Allied air power, particularly British rocket-firing Typhoons, rallied to the support of the ground elements, and Crerar's attack to the east forced Kluge to divert some panzers there. Thus, on 8 August, Kluge halted his attack, but was ordered by Hitler—then miles away in East Prussia—to renew it. Not until the 10th could he convince Hitler that it was more important to contain Patton's threat from the south.

On 8 August, in bold disregard of the German threat at Mortain, Montgomery and Bradley had turned Patton's XV Corps north toward Argentan. By the 13th, against increasing resistance, it had reached the army group boundary just south of Argentan. Here, much to Patton's disgruntlement, Bradley, fearing an Allied mix-up, ordered a halt. Meanwhile, Crerar's attack had been blunted by a skillfully conducted German defense. Kluge still had an escape route—if he moved quickly. To the south, Patton's XX and XII Corps were assembling near Le Mans, preparatory to driving on Chartres and Orléans.

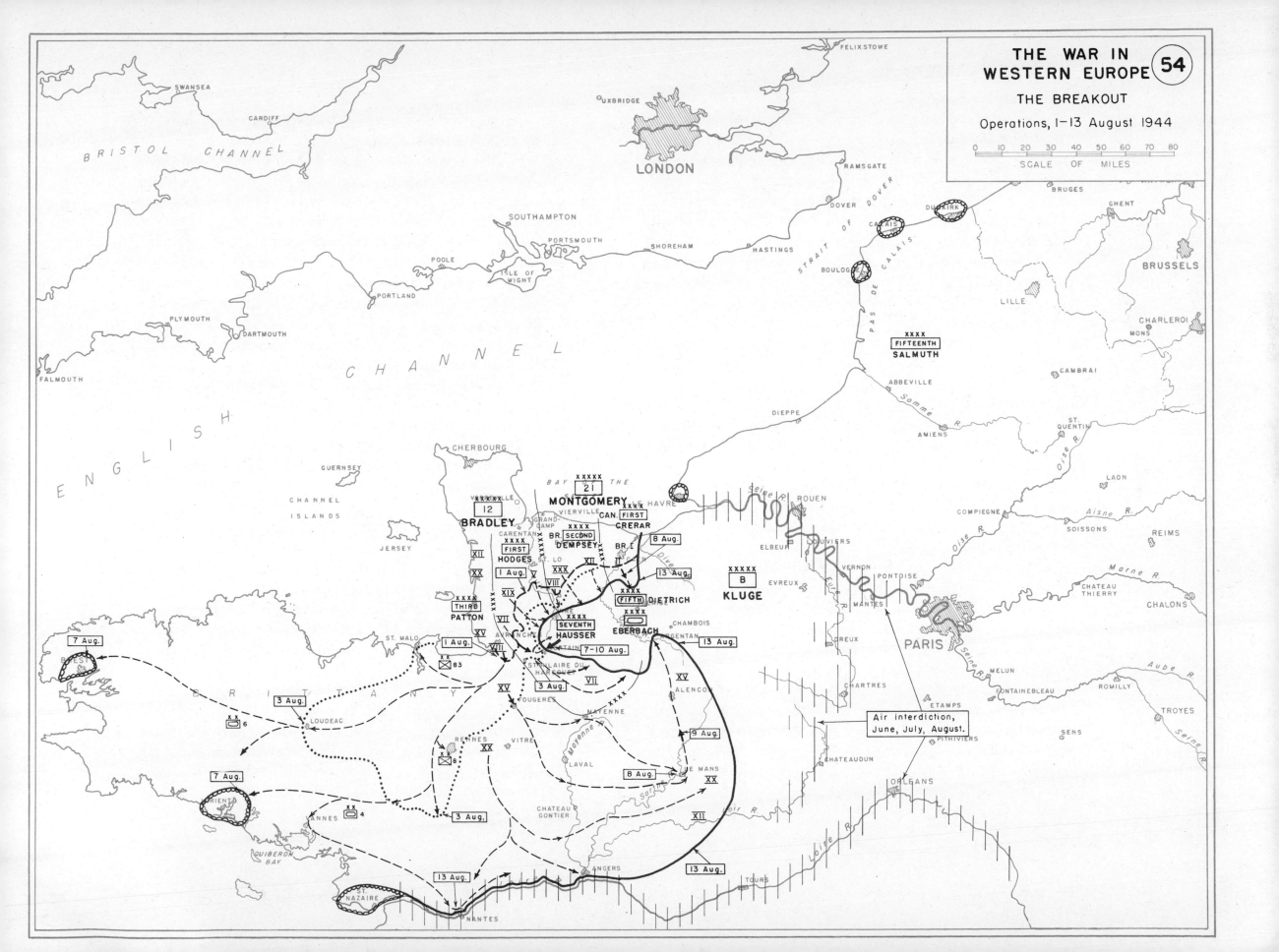

THE WAR IN
WESTERN EUROPE
54
THE BREAKOUT
Operations, 1–13 August 1944

0 10 20 30 40 50 60 70 80
SCALE OF MILES

BRISTOL CHANNEL

SWANSEA
CARDIFF

FELIXSTOWE

UXBRIDGE

LONDON

RAMSGATE

DOVER

Strait of Dover

BRUGES
GHENT

DUNKIRK

CALAIS

BRUSSELS

BOULOGNE

LILLE

CHARLEROI
MONS

SOUTHAMPTON
PORTSMOUTH
SHOREHAM
HASTINGS

POOLE
ISLE OF WIGHT

PORTLAND

PLYMOUTH
DARTMOUTH

FALMOUTH

E N G L I S H   C H A N N E L

XXXX
FIFTEENTH
SALMUTH

ABBEVILLE

CAMBRAI

DIEPPE

Somme R.

AMIENS

ST. QUENTIN

Oise R.

CHERBOURG

GUERNSEY

CHANNEL ISLANDS

JERSEY

BAY   THE

XXXXX
21
MONTGOMERY

XXXXXX
12
BRADLEY

VIERVILLE
GRAND CAMP

CARENTAN

XXXX
FIRST
HODGES

XII

XX

ST. LO

1 Aug.

XXXX
THIRD
PATTON

ST. MALO

XIX

VII

VII

XV

AVRANCHES

1 Aug.

XX 83

ST. HILAIRE DU HARCOUET

3 Aug.

FOUGERES

CAN. FIRST
CRERAR

BR. SECOND
DEMPSEY

BR I

8 Aug.

V

VIII

XII

13 Aug.

XXXX
FIFTH
DIETRICH

XXXX
SEVENTH
HAUSSER

XXXX
EBERBACH

CHAMBOIS

ARGENTAN

7–10 Aug.

VII

ALENCON

LE HAVRE

ROUEN

Seine R.

ELBEUF
LOUVIERS

XXXXX
B
KLUGE

EVREUX

VERNON

PONTOISE

MANTES

COMPIEGNE

Aisne R.

LAON

SOISSONS

REIMS

CHATEAU THIERRY

CHALONS

Marne R.

PARIS

Seine R.

13 Aug.

9 Aug.

XV

DREUX

CHARTRES

MELUN

FONTAINEBLEAU

Air interdiction,
June, July, August.

ETAMPS

7 Aug.

BREST

7 Aug.

LORIENT

XX 6

LOUDEAC

B R I T T A N Y

RENNES

XX 8

XX

VITRE

XV

Mayenne R.

LAVAL

Sarthe R.

8 Aug.

LE MANS

XX

13 Aug.

3 Aug.

VANNES

XX 4

3 Aug.

CHATEAU GONTIER

XII

Loir R.

CHATEAUDUN

ORLEANS

PITHIVIERS

SENS

Loire R.

QUIBERON BAY

13 Aug.

ST. NAZAIRE

NANTES

ANGERS

13 Aug.

TOURS

TROYES

Seine R.

Aube R.

ROMILLY

Bradley's decision to halt the northward drive of the XV Corps on 13 August has since become controversial. On 14 August, he authorized Patton to send the XV Corps with two of its divisions eastward toward Dreux (two others, joined by a third on the 15th, remained at Argentan). This move to Dreux was in consonance with Montgomery's instructions of the 11th that, if the Falaise-Argentan encirclement failed, a wider envelopment toward the Seine would be made. Several indications led Bradley to believe the encirclement had failed: the slowness of Crerar's advance seemed to have enabled Kluge to withdraw; Montgomery had not ordered Bradley beyond Argentan; and Hodges and Dempsey had wheeled eastward with relative ease. Actually, only slight opposition was met because Kluge, concerned over the XV Corps' northward advance toward Argentan, had withdrawn the panzer units from the Mortain sector to strike at the XV Corps' exposed flank between Argentan and Mayenne. (This attack never took place, for the VII Corps moved into the gap before the attack could be launched.)

It was now clear to Kluge that immediate retreat was his only salvation, and Hitler was bluntly so informed. Hitler gave his approval on the 16th; the next day, Model arrived from the Eastern Front to replace Kluge. In preparation for the withdrawal, the Germans moved considerable strength to Falaise and Argentan to hold open the shoulders of the gap. Whereas, on the 13th—with the bulk of the Germans in the pocket west of Argentan—a continuation of the northward advance might have succeeded in closing the gap, the attempt of the V Corps to do so on 18-19 August met with stiff resistance. (The V Corps having been pinched out of line during Hodges' eastward wheel, its headquarters was sent to Argentan to take over the three divisions left there by the XV Corps when it moved toward Dreux.) The Germans conducted an orderly withdrawal against overwhelming aerial and ground attack from three directions, and by the 19th, when the Americans and Poles (from Crerar's army) met near Chambois, many of the panzer forces had escaped. The remaining Germans made one last attack and then surrendered. Hitler lost 50,000 prisoners in the Falaise-Argentan pocket; 10,000 German corpses strewed the area.

When Patton moved toward Dreux with the XV Corps (two divisions) on 14 August, he ordered his XII and XX Corps to drive east also. The XIX Corps (pinched out with the V Corps by Hodges' wheel) moved toward the Seine on the 20th to aid Patton. Opposition to this general eastward advance was minor. Orléans and Dreux fell on the 16th; Chartres on the 18th, after some spirited resistance. Bradley now removed restrictions on any advance beyond the Dreux-Chartres-Orléans line, and Patton's corps, aided by emergency air supply, continued the eastward drive.

On 19 August, Eisenhower modified his pre-invasion plans. Taking a calculated risk on the adequacy of logistical support and on German deterioration, he ordered exploitation beyond the Seine. Montgomery now urged the encirclement of Army Group B remnants south of the Seine. All armies advanced as shown. Pincers closed at Elbeuf on the 26th, but most of the German infantry was in the bridgehead west of Rouen. During the next two days, many of them crossed to the north of the Seine, but the Seventh and Fifth Panzer Armies had been shattered; on 28 August, the latter reported its strength as 1,300 men, 24 tanks, and 60 pieces of artillery.

On the 19th, the XV Corps had seized a bridgehead at Mantes; by the 25th, three others had been established south of Paris by the XII and XX Corps. Free French uprisings in Paris on the 19th soon needed assistance; accordingly, the V Corps took the city on the 25th, the honor of the triumphal entry being given to the French 2d Armored Division.

Meanwhile, the laudable efforts of the VIII Corps in clearing Brittany came to nought. With the opening of the ports of Cherbourg and Marseilles (*see map 56*), surprisingly increased supply over the beaches, and the imminent prospect of the capture of the Channel ports, logistical planners saw little need to go back several hundred miles into Brittany for supply bases.

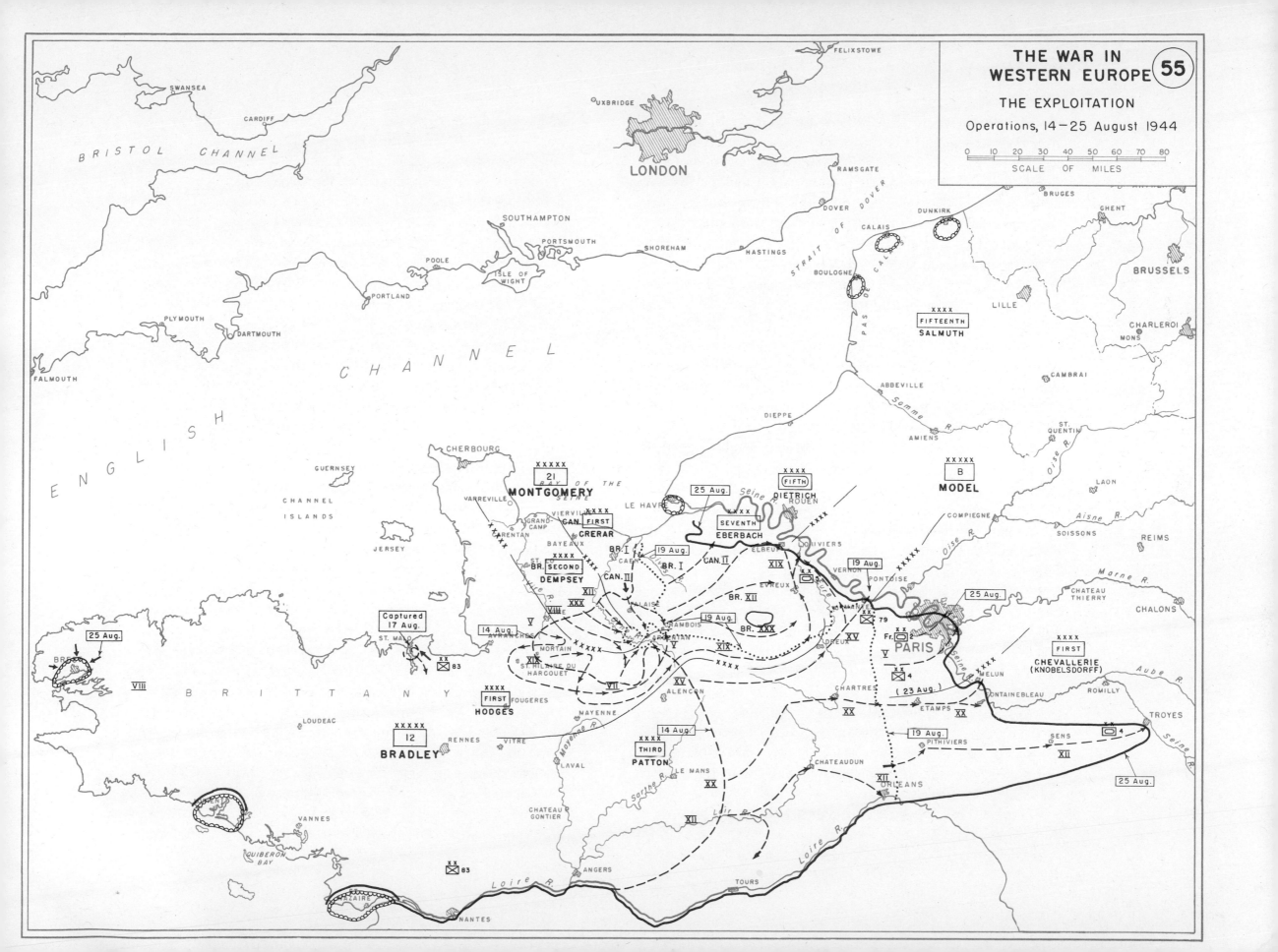

SCALE OF MILES
0 10 20 30 40 50 60 70 80

As the Allies raced from the Seine to the West Wall (*shaded red areas*), American and French forces landed in southern France and sped northward. The latter operations are covered in full on map 57; for the present, it is sufficient to know that the Germans successfully withdrew more than half of their forces from southern and southwestern France before the northern and southern Allied forces linked up at Sombernon (*center*) on 11 September. These troops helped bolster German defenses against the SHAEF advance. Alexander's operations during this period (*bottom right*) are covered in the text of map 106.

In northern France, Eisenhower's victory-flushed armies drove into the Low Countries and to the German border, while Lt. Gen. William H. Simpson's Ninth Army (activated on 5 September) protected the Allied flank along the Loire River and contained the German-held Brittany ports.

Back in May, SHAEF had decided upon the Ruhr (*upper center*, Dusseldorf-Essen industrial area) as the initial Allied objective in Germany. It had been concluded that the main advance would be made along the Amiens-Liége-Ruhr axis, supported by a secondary effort in the direction Verdun-Metz. A massive single thrust had been discarded as subject to canalization and concentrated counterattack. On 19 August, with the Allies nearing the Seine, this plan was reviewed. Conditions were not the same as had been assumed in May: German losses in Normandy had totaled 530,000 (Russia, meanwhile, had inflicted about another 700,000), only about 120 German tanks had recrossed the Seine, and the Fifth Panzer and Seventh Armies had almost ceased to exist. Now Montgomery and Bradley pressed for single thrusts into Germany, each in his own sector. But Eisenhower, reverting to the May plan, directed Bradley to support Montgomery's advance with the American First Army; Patton, much to his dismay, was to advance only if supplies would permit it after Hodges' needs were met.

Patton's forces debouched from their Seine bridgeheads on 26 August and, against spotty resistance, raced toward the Meuse, crossing it on the 30th. Here, they ground to a halt for lack of fuel.

(Actually, Patton's advance eastward from Orléans [*overprinted by Third Army symbol*] had been possible largely through herculean supply efforts, airlifted supplies, and the capture of considerable fuel.) Hodges attacked northeast on the 27th and, by 3 September, had pocketed 25,000 prisoners at Mons. Montgomery's armies attacked on 29 August. Dempsey grounded one corps west of the Seine to fully motorize his XXX Corps which, two days later, captured Amiens (and General Eberbach) and—in a remarkable advance—had secured Brussels by the 3d. The Canadians had the dubious task of driving up the coast and securing the garrisoned channel ports.

The 4th of September was a critical date for the Germans. That day, Dempsey entered Antwerp, the prize European port, seizing all facilities intact. The German First Parachute Army was rushed to the Albert Canal in desperation to plug the gap, and the Fifteenth Army was ordered to block the estuary leading to Antwerp and thus prevent the port's use. Meanwhile, Eisenhower had assumed control of the Allied ground forces on 1 September and, two days later, had authorized a continuation of Patton's advance. Hodges shifted the axis of his advance to the east and, by the 14th, had reached the German border. Patton's movement was slow, for the Germans, fearing his attack the most, had concentrated in his sector in late August many of the troops arriving from other theaters. Even if Patton had not been held idle for three days for lack of fuel, it is unlikely that he could have made a decisive penetration into Germany.

During the period of 4-10 September, Montgomery argued that, given unequivocal support, the 21st Army Group could reach the Ruhr. Eisenhower refused to halt Bradley's diverging attacks but gave Montgomery supply priority, while stressing the need for the latter to open Antwerp. The fettering effects of the lack of ports and the long supply hauls had created logistical problems which were exerting a deciding influence on Allied strategy.

On the German side, Rundstedt (recalled on 5 September)—with 63 divisions in line (each judged to be only 50 per cent effective)—contemplated the sad state of repair of the West Wall.

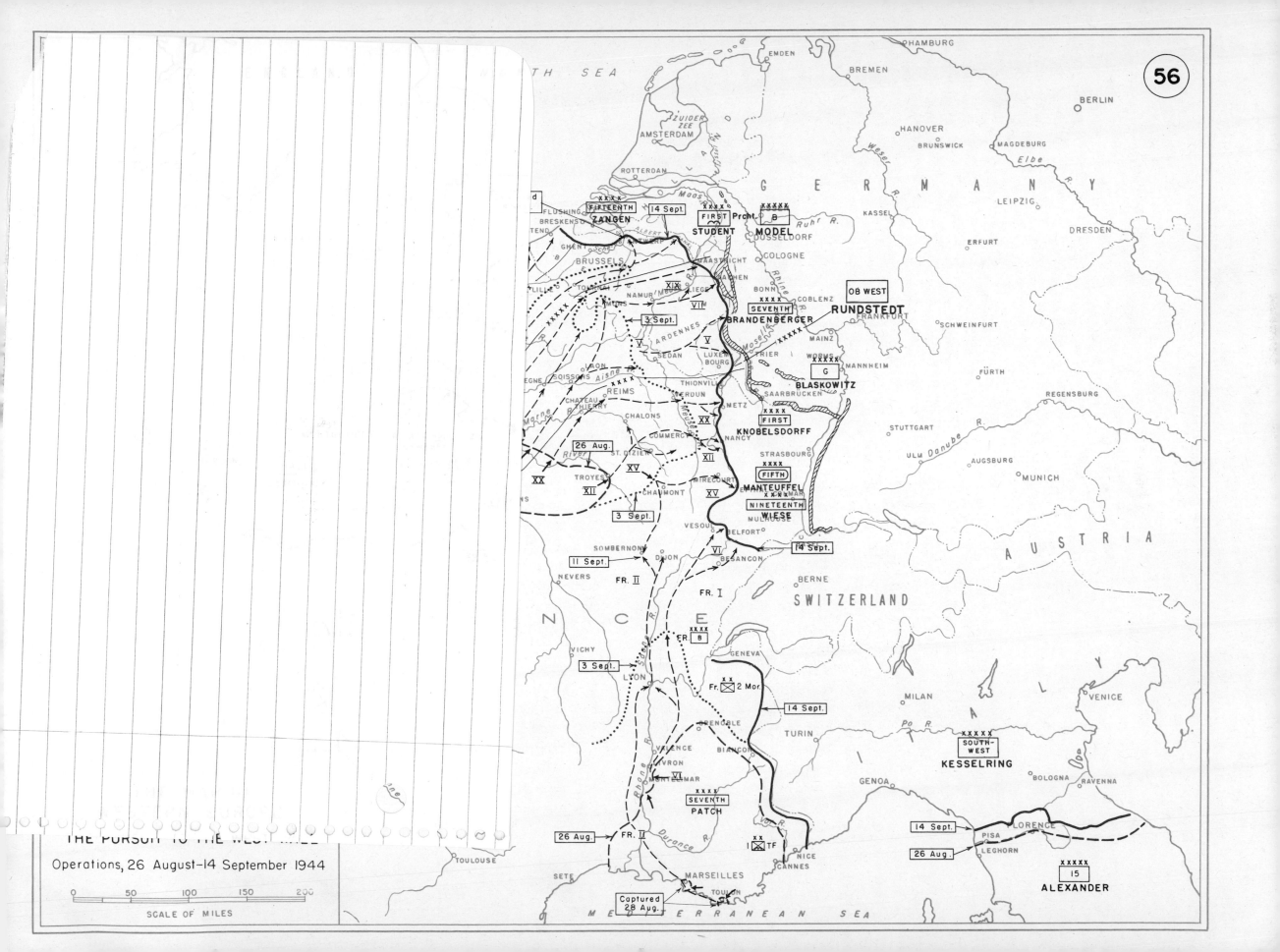

THE PURSUIT TO THE WEST WALL

Operations, 26 August–14 September 1944

SCALE OF MILES

0   50   100   150   200

As early as August, 1943, the CCS had considered a diversionary landing in southern France (Operation ANVIL) to precede OVER-LORD. At the Teheran Conference, three months later, the operation was finally confirmed. (Initially, American planners supported ANVIL, British planners preferred an operation toward Austria, and Stalin—not wanting troops of the Western Allies in the Balkans—sided with the American planners.) However, because of the demands for troops and logistical support in Italy and for the OVERLORD build-up, a definite date or size of force for ANVIL could not be established. Ultimately, ANVIL was scheduled to follow instead of preceding OVERLORD, primarily to enable Eisenhower to assemble sufficient landing craft for OVERLORD.

When the Allies broke out of the Normandy beachhead (*see map 53*) and, simultaneously, Alexander's campaign in Italy (*see map 105*) seemed on the verge of decisive results, the British again questioned the necessity for ANVIL. They believed the necessary forces could be employed more profitably elsewhere—in Italy, Austria, or possibly Brittany. But Generals Marshall and Eisenhower insisted upon the necessity for ANVIL to protect the southern flank of the Normandy invasion forces and to provide another critically needed supply port (Marseilles). The American position was finally upheld at the Roosevelt-Churchill level.

The inset sketch (*this map*) shows, generally, the origin, composition, and movements of the ANVIL assault and follow-up forces. All units, except some of the French, were veterans of the fighting in Italy. Besides the American VI and French II Corps, the force (designated United States Seventh Army, under Lt. Gen. Alexander Patch) included two special units: the 1st Airborne Task Force (1 TF), a composite, predominantly American force of parachute and glider infantry and artillery units numbering 8,000; and the 1st Special Service Force (1 SSF), an American-Canadian unit originally employed in specialized operations in the Aleutians. Air support was to be provided by the XII Tactical Air Command in Corsica and, to an extent, by strategic bombers of the Fifteenth Air Force in Italy. Naval support would come from Vice Adm. Henry K. Hewitt's Western Task Force.

Opposing this formidable force was the German Nineteenth Army—seven second-line infantry divisions and the 11th Panzer Division. Coastal defenses were similar to those in Normandy, but neither as extensive nor as well-manned.

On the night of 14 August, naval and airborne demonstrations (the latter consisting of the dropping of dummies equipped with noise devices and demolition packets) were made as shown (*main sketch*) on the flanks of the landing area. Also, French commandos landed to block the coastal highway, and the 1 SSF seized Port Cros and Levant in order to destroy suspected gun emplacements (found to be dummies). At 0800 the next morning, the assault force (Maj. Gen. Lucian K. Truscott's VI Corps) began landing. The landing was preceded by intensive aerial and naval bombardments and one of the most effective and best-executed airborne operations (1 TF at Le Muy) of the war. Only Camel Force met much resistance. The follow-up force (French II Corps) landed in the wake of the VI Corps. By noon, 17 August, all units had crossed the beachhead line (*solid blue line*). The French II Corps began the task of capturing Toulon and Marseilles, while the American VI Corps set off in pursuit of the retreating Germans.

In accordance with Truscott's bold plan, the 3d Division drove up the Rhône as a direct pressure force, while other units as shown (spearheaded by Task Force Butler, specially created for the purpose) raced to capture the defile at Montélimar (*upper center*) and encircle the Germans. However, failure of the 36th Division to seize a critical height in time, potent German counterattacks, and growing Allied supply difficulties enabled a considerable portion of the Nineteenth Army to escape (57,000 were taken prisoner).

The pursuit continued up the Rhône, as shown on map 56. Meanwhile, the build-up force (French I Corps, from Italy and Africa) joined the French II Corps, and the two were formed into French Army B (General Jean de Lattre de Tassigny), which for the time being operated under Patch.

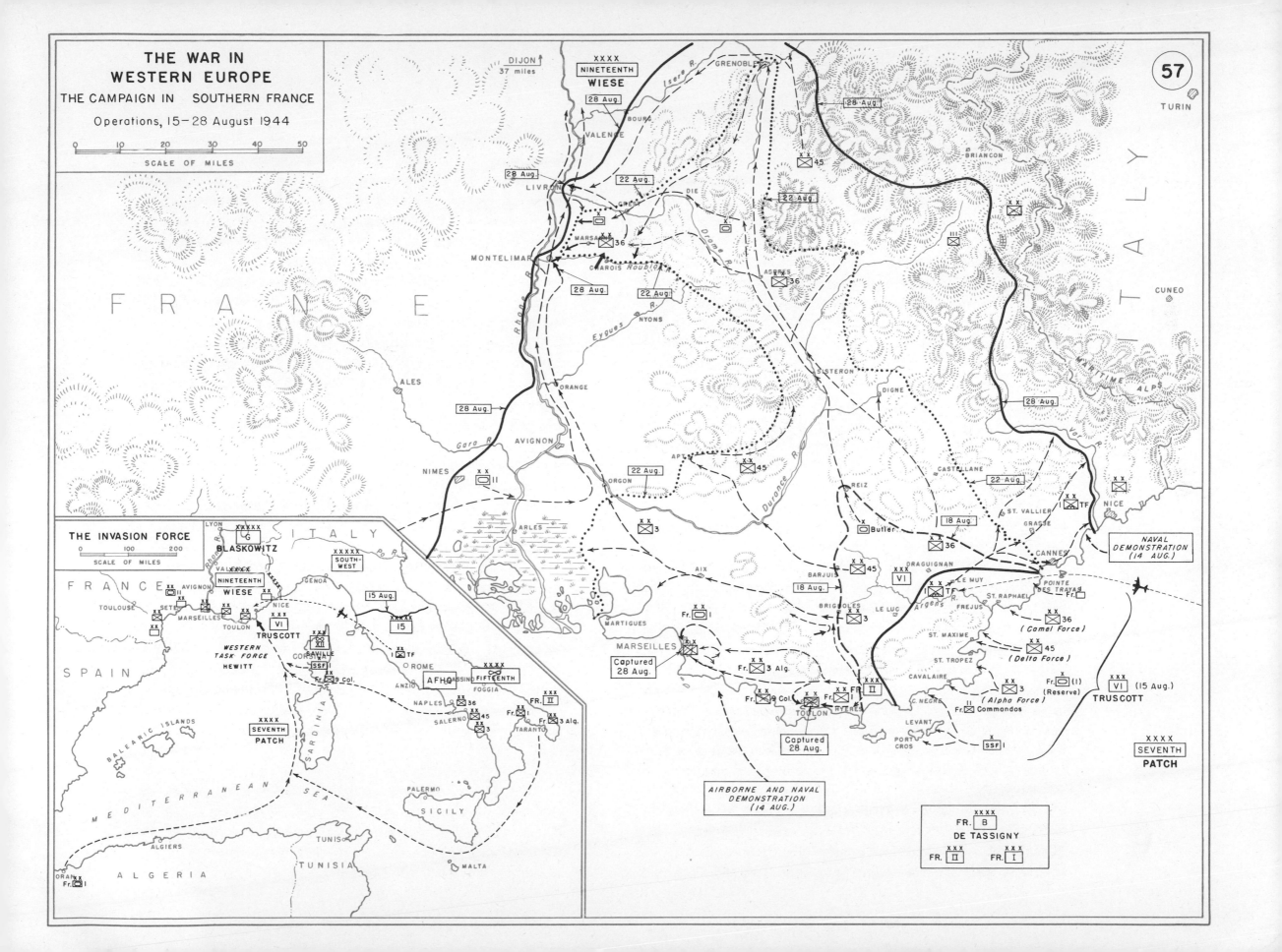

THE WAR IN WESTERN EUROPE

THE CAMPAIGN IN SOUTHERN FRANCE

Operations, 15-28 August 1944

SCALE OF MILES
0   10   20   30   40   50

57

TURIN

THE INVASION FORCE

SCALE OF MILES
0   100   200

NAVAL DEMONSTRATION (14 AUG.)

AIRBORNE AND NAVAL DEMONSTRATION (14 AUG.)

Logistically, the Allies were unprepared for the rapid advance to and beyond the Seine in August; their supply build-up had been predicated upon a more orderly advance which would allow the rebuilding of railroads, laying of pipelines, opening of ports, and accrual of supplies. Thus, though every expedient to support the advance was exploited, Hitler's intransigent policy of port denial had its effects as logistics began to govern operations. By October, the daily discharge tonnage was far behind the original SHAEF estimates, shipping awaiting discharge was mounting, and transportation means for moving supplies forward were proving inadequate.

As the Allies fought the logistical battle, Rundstedt drew his armies together and stabilized a defensive line (*solid red line in the north, dashed red line southward*). He decided to hold the advanced position along the Dutch Schelde and the Meuse-Escaut Canal as long as possible. A key element of the defense was the West Wall (*shaded red area*)—dilapidated, stripped, and outmoded in June, but being rehabilitated feverishly since the Allied breakout from Normandy.

While the 6th and 12th Army Groups struggled to reach and penetrate the West Wall (*see text, map 59*), Montgomery, contending with an intricate maze of waterways in Belgium and Holland, sought to turn its north flank. In early September, hopeful of securing a Rhine bridgehead and willing to postpone operations to open Antwerp, Eisenhower authorized Montgomery to mount an attack toward Arnhem (*top right*). Montgomery planned to drop the three airborne divisions allotted him as shown (Operation MARKET), and to make a ground attack with the Second Army (Operation GARDEN) to link up the airheads and cross the Lek River. Extremely bold in its conception, the plan envisioned a single corps' advance along a narrow corridor, sixty-four miles to Arnhem, over seven major bridges secured by paratroopers—all during a season when weather is normally bad in northwest Europe.

At 1400, 17 September, the airborne divisions began landing, and at 1430 the XXX Corps attacked toward Eindhoven. The 101st Division captured several assigned bridges, but the 82d was unable to seize the vital Nijmegen bridges until the 20th. The British 1st Division, landing seven miles west of Arnhem, could only secure the north end of the Arnhem bridge. German reaction was prompt; Student and Model—near Eindhoven and Arnhem, by chance—immediately organized counterattacks and moved reinforcements into the area. Poor weather during the next five days upset plans for air reinforcement and supply, while German attacks on the airheads and corridor slowed the link-up. The XXX Corps' advance is shown on the map. On the 21st, the element of the British 1st Division at the Arnhem bridge—German counterattacks had driven a wedge between it and the rest of the division—was forced to surrender. A XXX Corps spearhead reached the Lek the next day but could not force its way across, and, on the 25th, the remnants of the British 1st Division had to withdraw across the river. The two American divisions continued to fight (with heavy losses) until relieved on 6 November, but MARKET-GARDEN had failed. Poor weather, the inability of the Second Army to move north rapidly or widen the corridor, Allied failure to concentrate enough strength at Arnhem, and the rapid German reaction had spelled its doom.

Montgomery now concentrated on widening the corridor. Eventually, he began operations—using the Canadian First Army—to reduce the Schelde area and open Antwerp. The British I Corps attacked from Antwerp on 2 October and slowly fought its way into South Beveland, while the Canadian II Corps cleared the Schelde's south bank. In mid-October, Montgomery ordered Dempsey to assist Crerar's forces and also obtained help from Hodges. An amphibious operation (1-8 November) cleared the last resistance—on Walcheren Island—but German mines prevented ships from reaching Antwerp until 28 November. Elements of the German Fifteenth Army, given time to prepare positions, had defended skillfully and exacted a heavy toll in casualties and time.

With Montgomery concentrating on the Schelde estuary operations and too weak to make a strong attack toward the Rhine, Eisenhower had assigned Bradley the main effort in October. To support Bradley, Montgomery attacked on 14 November and cleared the area west of the Maas.

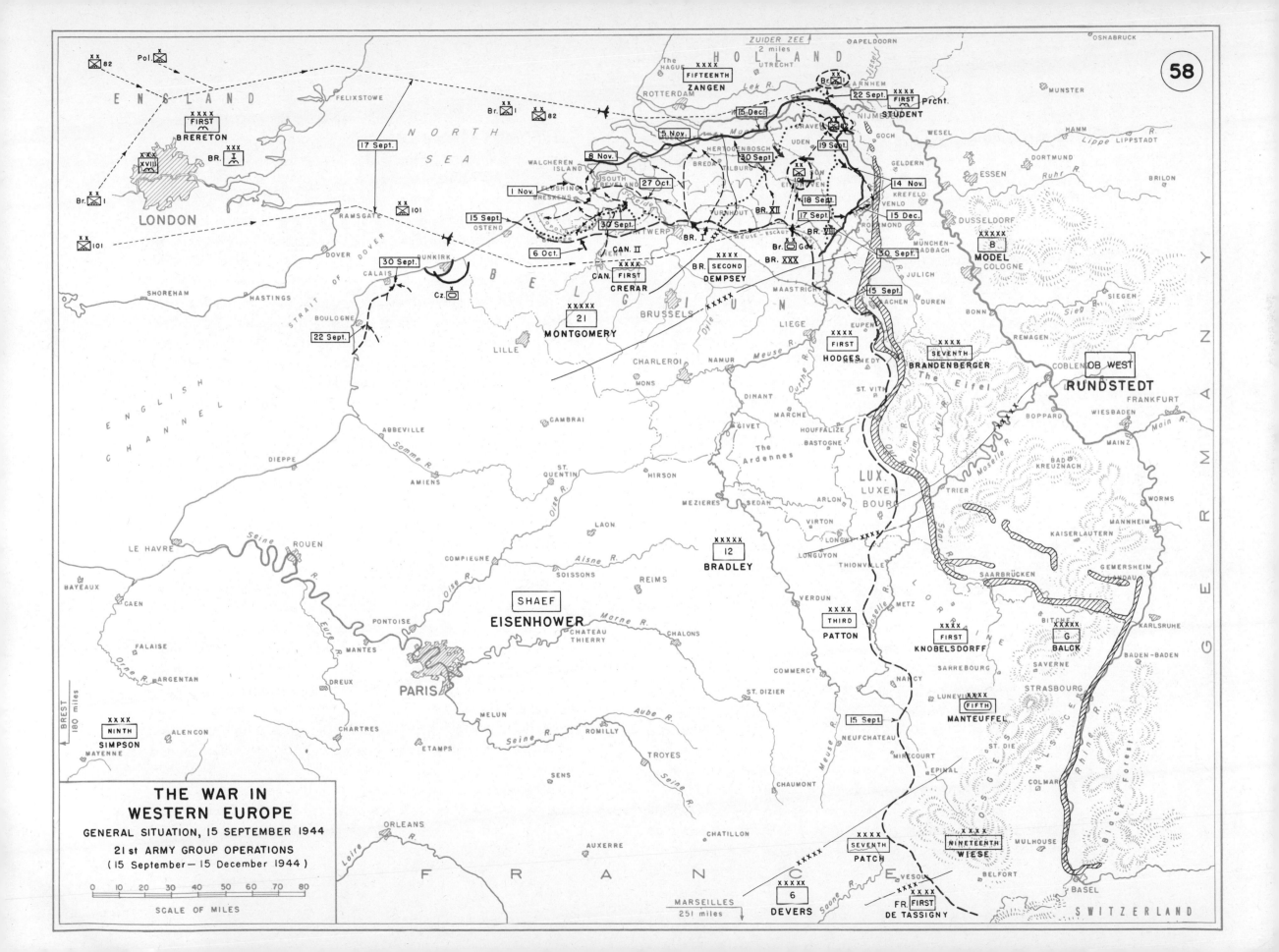

58

THE WAR IN
WESTERN EUROPE

GENERAL SITUATION, 15 SEPTEMBER 1944

21st ARMY GROUP OPERATIONS

(15 September — 15 December 1944)

0 10 20 30 40 50 60 70 80

SCALE OF MILES

During Montgomery's operations in the north (*see map 58*), Bradley's 12th Army Group and Lt. Gen. Jacob L. Devers' 6th (the reorganized southern France invasion force) slowly advanced to the east (*this map, sketch* a). On 22 September, Eisenhower had directed Bradley to support Montgomery's thrust toward the Rhine with a First Army drive toward Cologne; Patton was to operate within the limits of his supply quota; and Devers would drive toward Mulhouse and Strasbourg.

In some of October's most vicious fighting, Hodges' VII and XIX Corps moved through the West Wall at Aachen, entered the city on 13 October, and, after severe house-to-house fighting, captured it on the 21st. The Ninth Army (recently arrived, after capturing Brest) engaged in patrol activities.

Patton's efforts were forestalled by a German attack on 18 September. Hitler, aiming to drive a wedge between Patch and Patton and force the latter back on Reims, ordered the Fifth Panzer Army to attack. It was roughly handled by the XII and XV Corps. The German First Army joined in on the 24th with equally poor results. By 1 October, even Hitler finally realized the futility of the German efforts and stopped the attacks. Now Patton took the offensive. A XX Corps attack on Metz on 3 October captured a key fort, but the corps was forced to withdraw on 17 October. Meanwhile, the XII and XV Corps pushed forward to the line marked 7 November.

Farther south, Devers' troops, fighting in mountainous terrain and increasingly bad weather, forced the Germans back into the Vosges.

By the middle of October, Eisenhower appreciated that Montgomery, burdened with the Schelde operation, was too weak to make the SHAEF main attack toward the Rhine simultaneously. Hence, he temporarily assigned Bradley's northern armies the main effort for the November offensive (*sketch* b); Montgomery, Patton, and Devers were to make secondary efforts. All armies were to close to the Rhine on a broad front, destroying Germans and—if possible—seizing bridgeheads. Ultimately, Eisenhower expected to shift the main effort back north to Montgomery's sector in order to use the better avenue of approach into Germany.

The Ninth and First Armies launched the main attack on a narrow front on 16 November. (Bradley, anticipating the eventual loan of an army to Montgomery, had shifted the greener Ninth northward so that he could retain the veteran First.) Preceded by the heaviest air preparation yet used in the West, the advance moved through the West Wall against bitter opposition, particularly in the dense Hurtgen Forest (*overprinted by West Wall, V and VII Corps' zones*), where the V Corps had been attacking since 2 November. By 1 December, the advance had reached the Roer River (*along solid red line*) against stiffening German defenses. To prevent flooding of the river, Bradley now directed the First Army to seize the Roer River dams near Schmidt (*better exposed on sketch* a) before driving to the Rhine. The German Ardennes offensive canceled this effort.

Meanwhile, the Third Army had encircled strategically located Metz by 18 November. The city capitulated on the 22d, but the last of the outer forts did not fall until 13 December. At the same time, the XII and XX Corps forced the Germans back into the West Wall, took Sarreguemines on 6 December, and, by the 15th, had several small bridgeheads across the Saar River. The driving Patton, finally fighting with adequate supplies but in abominable weather which hampered bridging operations, was in position to plunge into Germany.

In the south, Devers' troops made the greatest gains of the period. The Seventh Army attacked in a snowstorm on the 13th and took Sarrebourg on the 20th; then the XV Corps sent the 2d French Armored Division (*not labeled*) eastward. Outflanking, then clearing the Saverne Gap, that unit entered Strasbourg on the 23d and repelled a German counterattack the next day. Concurrently, the French First Army took Mulhouse and closed to the Rhine at the Swiss border. In early December, Patch reoriented his forces to the north and, against increasing opposition, closed to the 15 December line (*solid red line*). De Tassigny, weakened by detachments sent to southwestern France, was unable to undertake the reduction of the German salient about Colmar.

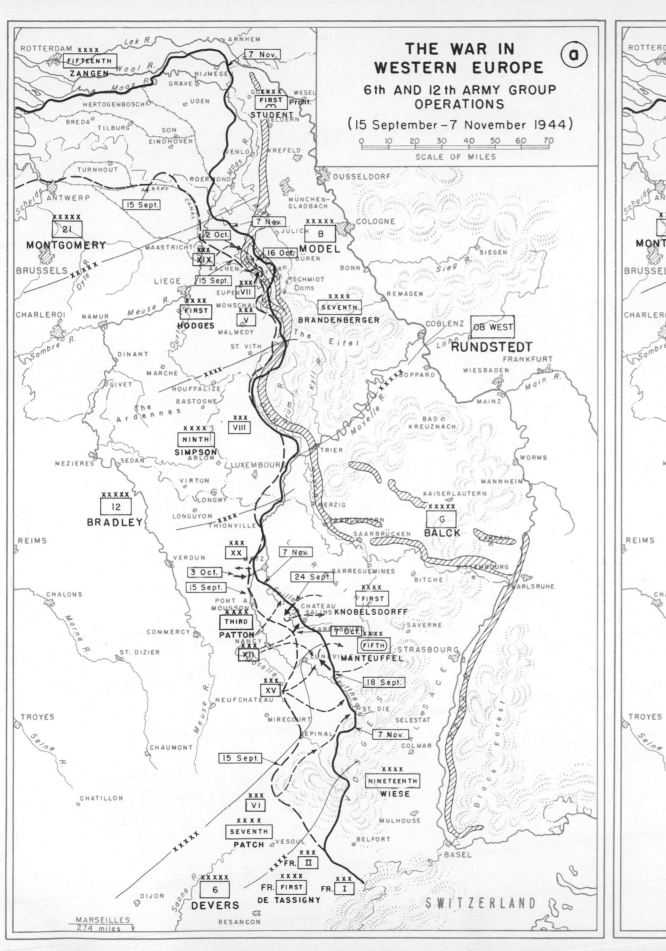

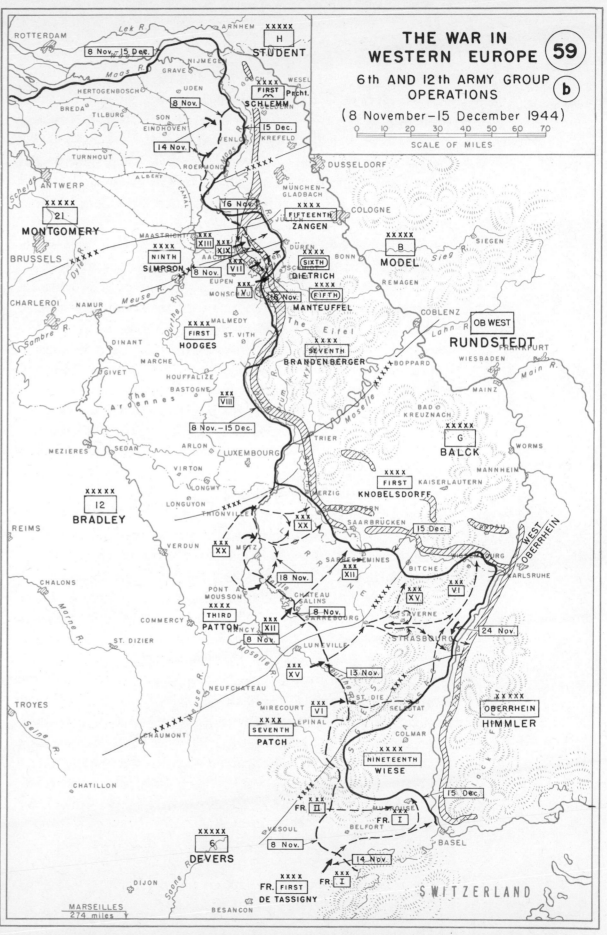

THE WAR IN
WESTERN EUROPE (a)

6th AND 12th ARMY GROUP
OPERATIONS

(15 September – 7 November 1944)

0 10 20 30 40 50 60 70
SCALE OF MILES

THE WAR IN
WESTERN EUROPE (59)

6th AND 12th ARMY GROUP
OPERATIONS (b)

(8 November – 15 December 1944)

0 10 20 30 40 50 60 70
SCALE OF MILES

The advances in November, though they brought the Allies closer to the Rhine, had not lived up to expectations. Considerable damage had been inflicted upon the hard-pressed Germans—in November-December, the Allies took about 75,000 prisoners—but at considerable cost to Eisenhower's armies. Nor were the Allies much closer to a Rhine crossing in the critical northern sector in December than they had been in November.

The logical outcome of this disappointment was a renewal of Mongomery's argument for a single, well-supported thrust in the north. Eisenhower steadfastly refused to accept it. The apparent stalemate caused some apprehension at the Roosevelt-Churchill level, the latter displaying concern over Allied strategy. The period of misgiving was augmented by the pessimistic voicings of Allied airmen in November. General Spaatz expressed concern over the possible revitalization of the Luftwaffe, and Doolittle warned that the Eighth Air Force might have to shift from strategic bombing back to reconquering the Luftwaffe. Nevertheless, on 5 December, the Allies agreed to bombing priorities in the order of oil, ground support, and transportation facilities.

In spite of the disappointing results in November, Eisenhower expected to launch a decisive offensive in early 1945. On 7 December, he met with Montgomery and Bradley and outlined his plans: a major attack north of the Ruhr (Montgomery) and secondary attacks farther south (Bradley and Devers). The "broad front" strategy was not to be modified, though the main effort was to revert to the extreme north. The supreme commander expected to conduct this offensive in three phases—close to the Rhine, seize bridgeheads, and advance to the east.

Eisenhower had good reason to be optimistic about the logistical situation. As the map shows (*items in green*), the U.S. and French armies were now being supported by an extensive Communications Zone (headquarters at Paris). Of major importance in the improvement of logistical support was the opening of the major ports of Marseilles and Antwerp, particularly the latter. Nor were ammunition and fuel supply any longer critical, for with the repair of the transportation lines and construction of pipelines, the forward depots had sizable stocks. Advance Section (ADSEC, *upper center*) and Continental Advance Section (CONAD, *center*) supported the 12th and 6th Army Groups, respectively. They were backed up by intermediate sections (in the case of ADSEC) and ultimately by base sections which operated the ports and base depots. In December, 830,000 tons of supplies were moved forward by the Communications Zone (not including Delta Base Section, but inclusive of the British portion of Antwerp's tonnage). Thus, though there were still some shortages, the supply status could be termed acceptable and capable of supporting the projected offensive.

The headquarters of Eisenhower and Spaatz had moved forward to Paris by 15 December; each army group now had a tactical air force in direct support. Along the Bay of Biscay, German port garrisons were merely being contained, while at the front the Allies were preparing for the coming offensive. Only in the Ardennes (VIII Corps) sector were they defensive-minded—here, Middleton's troops were spread very thinly.

Hitler met this situation with a counteroffensive (*inset sketch*). This attack would thrust through the Ardennes, repeating his 1940 offensive (*see map 12*) on a smaller scale. Its objective (*this map*) was the capture of Antwerp and the destruction of Allied forces north of the line Bastogne-Brussels-Antwerp. The Sixth Panzer Army, flanked by the Fifth Panzer Army, would make the main effort as shown. The Fifteenth and Seventh Armies, advancing as indicated, would form defensive flanks for the panzers. Rundstedt and Model considered this plan too ambitious, and recommended a limited offensive to pinch off the Aachen salient (*center*). Hitler rejected their advice. Apparently, he counted on winning a decisive, quick victory in the West; then, shifting his reserves eastward, he would crush the next Russian offensive. Thereby, he might either gain a negotiated peace or win time to put large numbers of his various new weapons into action.

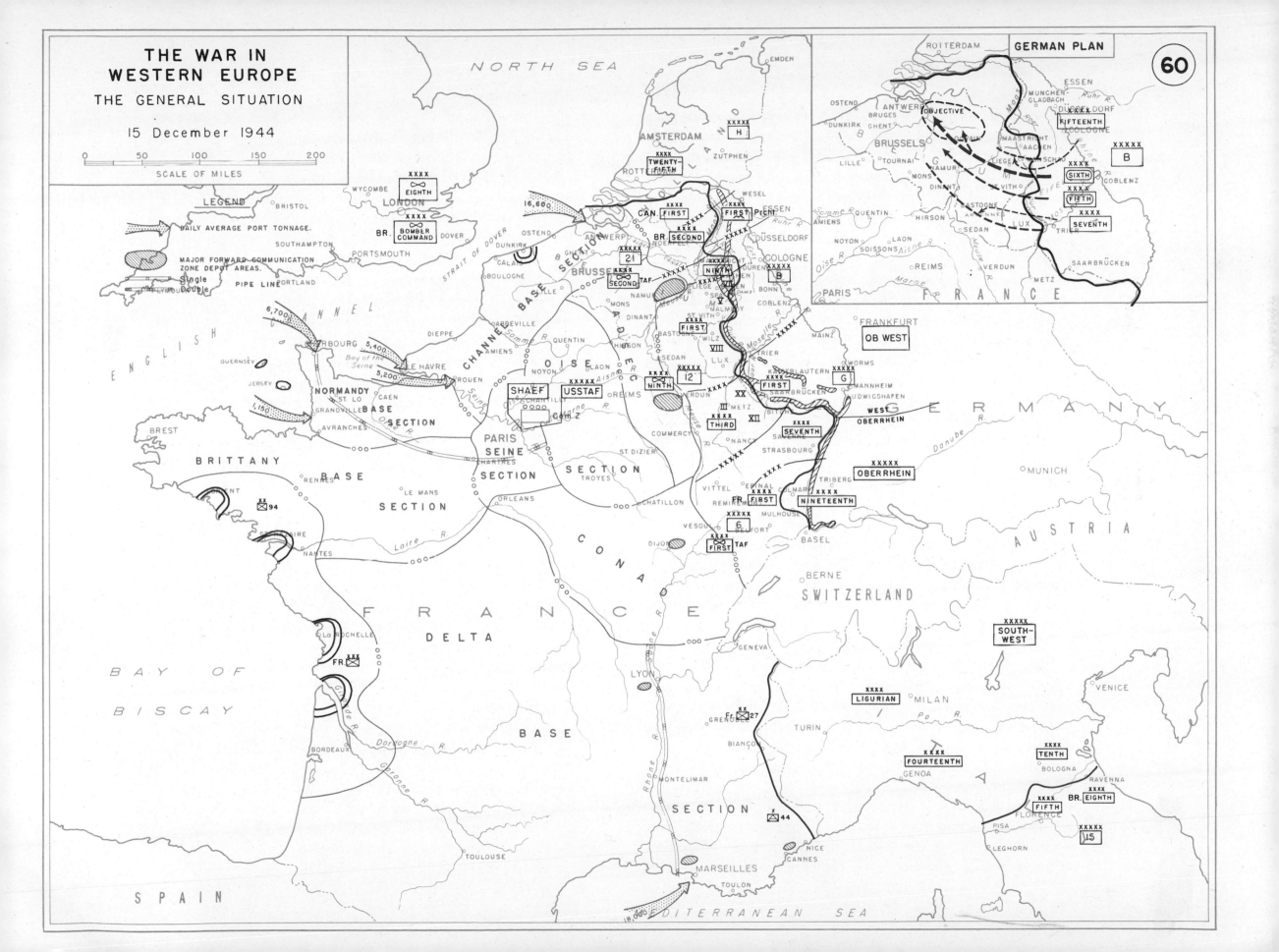

THE WAR IN WESTERN EUROPE

THE GENERAL SITUATION

15 December 1944

SCALE OF MILES
0   50   100   150   200

LEGEND

DAILY AVERAGE PORT TONNAGE.

MAJOR FORWARD COMMUNICATION
ZONE DEPOT AREAS.
Single
Double

PIPE LINE

GERMAN PLAN

60

Hitler's plans included two subsidiary operations: a small parachute unit would be dropped to block the roads north of the Ardennes, and Lt. Col. Otto Skorzeny's special force (partially equipped with American vehicles) would pass through the German advance guard to seize the Meuse bridges. (Skorzeny's unit included a detachment of English-speaking volunteers, in American uniforms, for commando-type missions behind the American lines.)

Though preparations were screened by strict secrecy, Allied intelligence detected most of the German movements. It is one thing, however, to collect information, and another to evaluate it correctly. Allied commanders were preoccupied with their offensive plans. Bradley knew his Ardennes sector was weak, but took few precautions there beyond leaving his major supply depots west of the Meuse. His reserves were either on the Saar front—where Patton was readying an offensive—or around Aachen, waiting for the capture of the Roer dams. It was accepted that the Germans lacked fuel for an offensive, and that Rundstedt was too sensible to risk one. The fact that Hitler, not Rundstedt, directed the German Army was overlooked.

The Germans had waited for a period of bad weather to minimize Allied air attacks. At 0530, 16 December, their infantry struck the American front from Monschau south to Echternach. The Sixth Panzer Army immediately snagged on the U.S. V Corps. Hitler had assigned the Sixth Panzer Army the main effort; its SS troops had the highest morale and best equipment in the German Army. But its Obergruppenführer Sepp Dietrich, picked by Hitler for his bravery and personal loyalty, could not handle large panzer forces—especially in this terrain. Traffic jammed; one advance guard got through and almost reached a large fuel depot near Stavelot, but it was checked and then cut off by the 30th Division. The Fifth Panzer Army—better led and with more room—shattered the 28th and 106th Divisions. The Seventh Army made slight gains.

Confusion was immediate and impressive. Late on 16 December, Eisenhower and Bradley received fragmentary reports. Bradley considered it a spoiling attack, designed to forestall Patton's offensive, but Eisenhower was concerned. Consequently, the 7th

and 10th Armored Divisions were ordered into the Ardennes. That night, the German paratroopers dropped northwest of Spa (*upper center*). The air drop was ineffective, but it added to the psychological shock produced by Skorzeny's volunteers. Exaggerated security measures were taken as far west as Paris.

Late on 17 December, the 7th Armored Division occupied the important road junction of St. Vith. Here, it blocked Dietrich until the 23d, then withdrew to escape encirclement. Also on the 17th, Eisenhower committed the theater reserve (82d and 101st Airborne Divisions): the 101st was sent to Bastogne, another important road center; the 82d joined the XVIII Corps in the north. By 21 December, the 101st, with parts of the 9th and 10th Armored Divisions, was encircled in Bastogne.

The night of the 18th, Bradley ordered Patton to suspend the Saar offensive and shift his Third Army north. Two days later, Eisenhower transferred command of all American forces north of the line Givet (*left center*)–Houffalize–Prum to Montgomery.

With Dietrich blocked and Gen. Hasso von Manteuffel successfully advancing northwest, Model proposed to reinforce the latter with all available panzer units, including Dietrich's two uncommitted SS panzer divisions. Hitler insisted that Dietrich must strike the decisive blow. On 22 December, Patton began his drive to relieve Bastogne. Warned by intercepted American radio messages, the Germans were ready, and Patton made little progress. But the weather began to clear on the 23d, permitting aerial resupply of Bastogne. Model now urged that the offensive be reduced to a limited drive against Aachen. Hitler again refused. Meanwhile, Manteuffel had launched a series of unsuccessful attacks to clear the Bastogne garrison from his line of communications. Most of his spearhead units had been halted by lack of gasoline for some thirty-six hours in the positions shown (*solid red line*). On Christmas, the American 2d Armored Division struck the 2d Panzer Division near Celles (*center, left*). The battle ended on 26 December when the 2d Armored crushed the 2d Panzer's immobilized advance guard and beat back other German units attempting to extricate it. Late that same day, Patton's 4th Armored Division punched a narrow corridor into Bastogne.

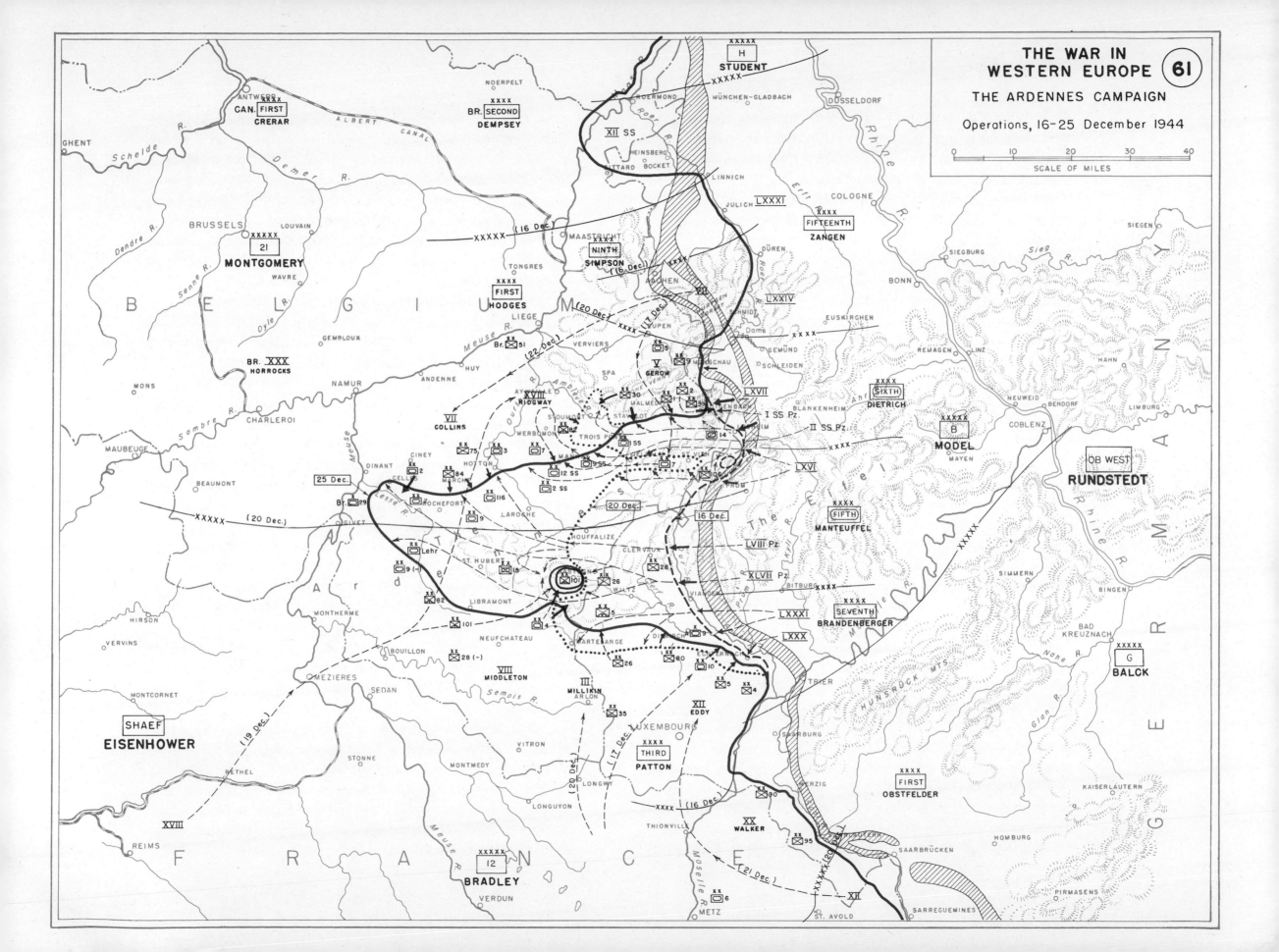

THE WAR IN 61
WESTERN EUROPE
THE ARDENNES CAMPAIGN
Operations, 16-25 December 1944

SCALE OF MILES
0   10   20   30   40

On the 26th, German supply trains, restricted to two narrow roads west of St. Vith, were pounded by Allied tactical aviation; Allied tactical and strategic air elements carried out heavy interdiction missions against Model's communications. At the same time, the Third Army's increasing pressure along the southern flank of the salient began to force the German Seventh Army back, despite stubborn fighting.

Rundstedt now intervened, proposing that the offensive be suspended, the German lines reestablished along the high ground running generally southwest from St. Vith to Wiltz, and the panzer units pulled back into reserve. Hitler's reaction was at least consistent—Model would hold his ground and regroup to continue the offensive to the Meuse; at the same time, he would take Bastogne (part of the Sixth Panzer Army would be transferred to Manteuffel for this attack). An offensive was to be launched in northern Alsace (*off map, lower right; see map 64*a) on 1 January to take advantage of the transfer of most of the Third Army to the Ardennes.

On the Allied side, the heaviest combat during 27-30 December was along the corridor into Bastogne (*this map*), which the Germans made repeated efforts to cut. Bradley was eager for an immediate counteroffensive, but Montgomery demurred, declaring that his American units had lost heavily and that he expected the Germans to launch at least one more major attack against the northern flank of the pocket. Meanwhile, he was moving British divisions into line so that the American VII Corps could be withdrawn and regrouped for a counterattack as soon as the expected German assault had been repulsed. Eisenhower's final decision was that—barring such a renewed German attack—Montgomery would begin his counteroffensive on 3 January. In the meantime, Bradley was given the newly reestablished theater reserve—the 87th Infantry, 11th Armored, and 17th Airborne Divisions—all new units without combat experience. As they arrived, Patton immediately pushed them into the battle; Manteuffel, correspondingly reinforced by divisions from the Sixth Panzer Army, sent repeated coordinated attacks against Bastogne and its corridor. Savage, hammer-and-tongs fighting, with heavy losses on both sides, raged in this area through 4 January, without any great change of position; increasing masses of American artillery and the XIX Tactical Air Command (which carried out its missions under abominable flying conditions) intervened effectively at every crisis. By the end of the 4th, it was obvious to Patton that only a coordinated attack with fresh troops could make appreciable headway; he therefore ordered the 90th Division northward and organized a major assault by the III and VIII Corps, to be launched 9 January.

Montgomery meanwhile had tidied up his front and regrouped. By 2 January, he had brought the British XXX Corps into line on his west flank, mopped up isolated German units in the area Marche-Hotton-Manhay (*center, left*), and concentrated the VII Corps. On 3 January, his counteroffensive began. As noted, much of Dietrich's strength had been diverted to Bastogne. Driving through bitter German opposition, storms, and waist-deep snow, the VII Corps cut the vital Laroche-Vielsalm road on the 7th. This left the Germans only the road through Houffalize. Model demanded permission to withdraw. Hitler granted this on the 8th, directing that the Sixth Panzer Army be withdrawn immediately for rehabilitation.

The Germans, by now hardened to winter warfare in the Russian school, waged a fighting retreat, taking their price in Allied casualties for every foot of ground. (Patton's advance was slowed somewhat by the transfer of the 4th Armored Division to the Saar.) On 13 January, patrols of the 87th Division and the British 6th Airborne Division established contact northwest of St. Hubert. Allied pressure increased, and at 0905, 16 January, the 2d and 11th Armored Divisions linked up in Houffalize, reestablishing a solid front.

On 1 January, the Luftwaffe had made a skillful, large-scale attack on Allied airfields in Holland and Belgium, knocking out 156 Allied planes, but losing heavily itself.

There were two principal results of Hitler's Ardennes offensive: it delayed Allied operations in the West by about six weeks; and it consumed the German mobile reserves which might otherwise have balked the coming Russian spring offensive.

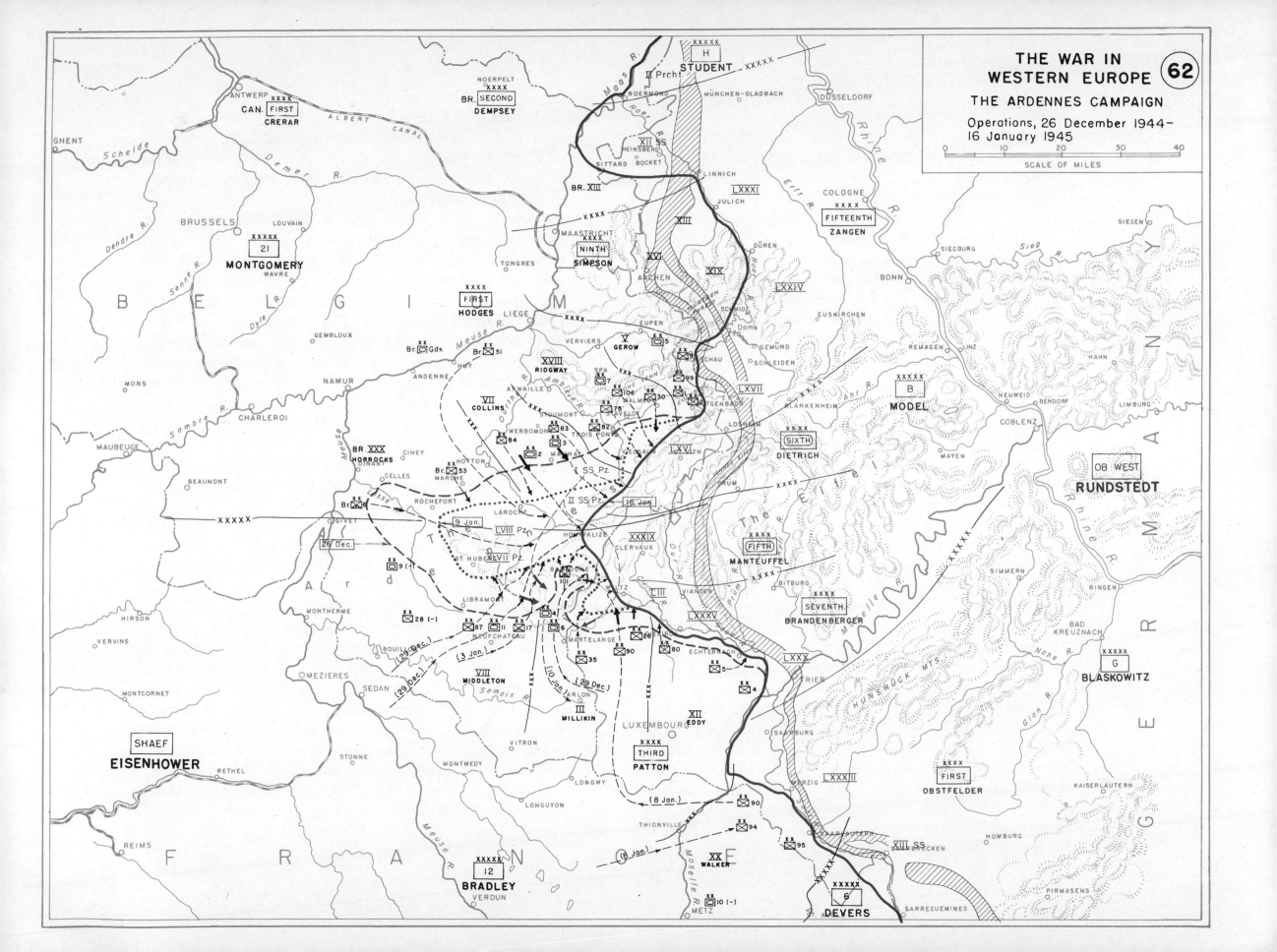

THE WAR IN
WESTERN EUROPE 62
THE ARDENNES CAMPAIGN
Operations, 26 December 1944–
16 January 1945

SCALE OF MILES
10   20   30   40

With the restoration of the American front in the Ardennes, Eisenhower returned the United States First Army to Bradley's command, but left the Ninth under Montgomery. He directed that Bradley continue to attack the German position in the Ardennes, seeking to inflict maximum casualties and—if possible—to penetrate the West Wall. If successful, Bradley then was to attack northeast on the axis Prüm (*center*)–Euskirchen. Such an advance, it was hoped, would capture the Roer dams, as well as draw German forces away from Montgomery's front. The latter was to regroup for an advance to the Rhine north of Düsseldorf (*top right*). The recently activated Fifteenth Army (*bottom left*) was assigned to the 12th Army Group.

Bradley maintained pressure on the Ardennes front, where the Germans—though suffering appreciably from American artillery and tactical air strikes—nevertheless fell back in good order. No enemy units of any size were cut off. On 24 January, Bradley curved the boundary between the First and Third Armies to the northeast, along the line St. Vith–Losheim–Ahr River. The First Army was to break through the West Wall to seize the commanding terrain around Blankenheim; the Third Army was to cover the First Army's right flank.

Rundstedt, meanwhile, was making every effort to reestablish the German front along the West Wall. (The West Wall's pillboxes and shelters formed only a framework for a defensive system, most of its weapons and signal equipment having been previously transferred to the Atlantic Wall.) Hitler was now stripping the Ardennes front: the Sixth Panzer Army had been transferred to Hungary, and other troops to the German First Army (*lower right*) for its Alsace offensive. Nevertheless, the stubbornness of the German defense was matched only by the drive of the American attacks. The West Wall was finally pierced, west of Prüm and in the Gemünd area farther north, though the going was scarcely easier in the rough terrain behind it. On 7 February, Eisenhower ordered all attacks halted except for those (V Corps) directed at the Roer dams. Farther north, from 15 through 26 January, the British XII Corps eliminated the Roermond Triangle (*inset, top center*)—the bridgehead which the XII SS Corps held on the west bank of the Roer River.

In retrospect, Hitler's Ardennes offensive was a daring gamble. Achieving complete surprise, it struck and shattered the weakest portion of the Allied front. It was foredoomed to failure, however, because it did not have assured logistical support to sustain a speedy, uninterrupted drive to its objective—Antwerp—before the Allies could react in force on its flanks. When fuel ran out, the advance stopped. Once halted, the force engaged was too small to withstand the full Anglo-American power. Secrecy was carried to extremes. Company commanders were briefed only the day before the attack; previous ground reconnaissance of the Ardennes had been strictly limited, and aerial reconnaissance prohibited. Thus, exact American dispositions were unknown, and there was considerable hesitation during the initial attacks. Furthermore, the capture of American fuel depots was vital to the plan, but the German commanders did not know their location. Hitler's prime error in the operation was his refusal to shift Dietrich's reserve panzer divisions promptly to support Manteuffel's successful advance. Finally, the German failure to achieve success before the weather improved permitted the effective intervention of Allied air power.

One by-product of this battle remained to haunt future Allied operations. Eisenhower's decision (20 December) giving Montgomery command of the First and Ninth Armies (and typically indiscreet remarks made by that British commander) infuriated Bradley and some of his subordinates. Their reactions affected Eisenhower's subsequent plans. During the Ardennes campaign, the contrast between Bradley's and Montgomery's conduct of operations is interesting—the first attacking immediately and energetically with all available troops; the second keeping his forces concentrated, holding out a reserve, willing to let the Germans exhaust themselves overrunning unneeded territory before he counterattacked. As for Eisenhower, his rapid appreciation of the seriousness of the German attack, his quick perception of Bastogne as the key point to hold, and his calmness throughout the whole operation displayed a high order of military skill and instinct.

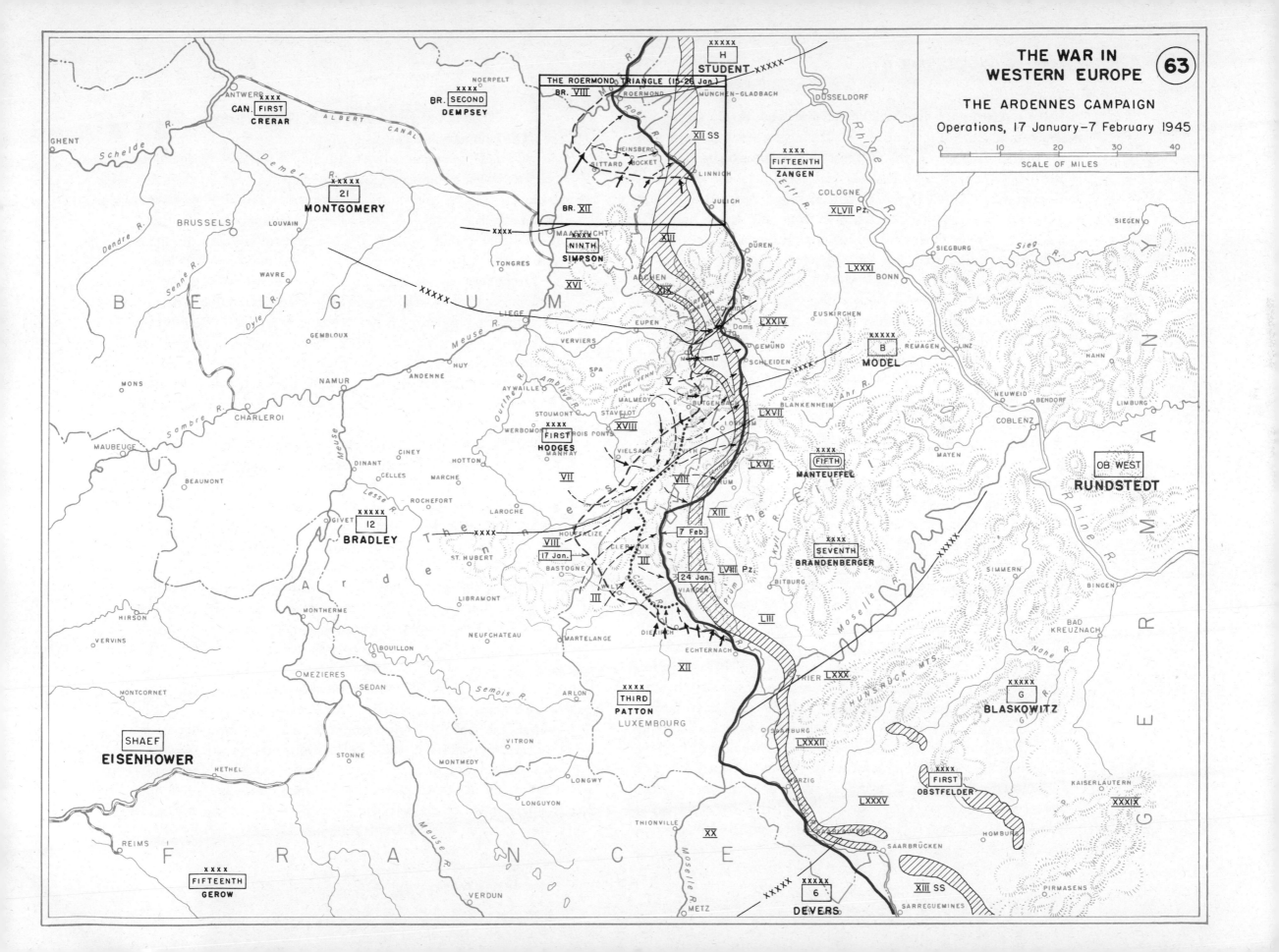

THE WAR IN
WESTERN EUROPE
63

THE ARDENNES CAMPAIGN
Operations, 17 January–7 February 1945

SCALE OF MILES
0   10   20   30   40

THE ROERMOND TRIANGLE (15-26 Jan.)

XXXXX
H
STUDENT
XXXXX

BR. VIII

ROERMOND

NOERPELT

XXXX
BR. SECOND
DEMPSEY

MÜNCHEN-GLADBACH

DÜSSELDORF

ANTWERP
XXXX
CAN. FIRST
CRERAR

ALBERT CANAL

XII SS

HEINSBERG

SITTARD BOCKET

XXXXX
21
MONTGOMERY

BRUSSELS

LOUVAIN

WAVRE

GHENT

Scheldt R.

Demer R.

Senne R.

Dyle R.

Dendre R.

LINNICH

XXXX
FIFTEENTH
ZANGEN

COLOGNE

Rhine R.

BR. XII

XXXX

MAASTRICHT

XXXXX
NINTH
SIMPSON

XVI

TONGRES

JÜLICH

XIII

Roer R.

DÜREN

Zerfft R.

XLVII Pz.

SIEGEN

SIEGBURG

BONN

Sieg R.

AACHEN

XIX

LXXXI

XXXXX
BELGIUM

LIÈGE

Meuse R.

VERVIERS

EUPEN

SPA

GEMBLOUX

HUY

ANDENNE

MONS

NAMUR

Sambre R.

CHARLEROI

MAUBEUGE

BEAUMONT

DINANT

CINEY

HOTTON

MARCHE

LAROCHE

ROCHEFORT

CELLES

GIVET

XXXXX
12
BRADLEY

St. HUBERT

LIBRAMONT

Lesse R.

Ourthe R.

Ambleve R.

HOHE VENN

MONSCHAU

MALMÉDY

STOUMONT

STAVELOT

WERBOMONT

TROIS PONTS

MANHAY

VIELSALM

XXXX
FIRST
HODGES

VII

VIII

17 Jan.

BASTOGNE

HOUFFALIZE

CLERVAUX

WILTZ

III

III

7 Feb.

24 Jan.

DASBURG

VIANDEN

DIEKIRCH

ECHTERNACH

BÜTGENBACH

V

XVIII

VII

LXVII

LXVI

XXXX
FIFTH
MANTEUFFEL

LXVII

The Eifel

XIII

LVIII Pz.

LIII

PRÜM

BITBURG

Kyll R.

XXXXX
B
MODEL

REMAGEN

LINZ

BLANKENHEIM

Ahr R.

SCHLEIDEN

GEMÜND

EUSKIRCHEN

MAYEN

NEUWIED

BENDORF

LIMBURG

NEUWEID

COBLENZ

Moselle R.

XXXX
SEVENTH
BRANDENBERGER

XXXXX
OB WEST
RUNDSTEDT

Rhine R.

SIMMERN

BINGEN

BAD KREUZNACH

Nahe R.

HUNSRÜCK MTS.

TRIER

LXXX

XXXX
G
BLASKOWITZ

XII

LXXXII

XXXXX
THIRD
PATTON

LUXEMBOURG

MARTELANGE

ARLON

Semois R.

NEUFCHATEAU

BOUILLON

SEDAN

MÉZIÈRES

MONTHERMÉ

HIRSON

VERVINS

MONTCORNET

STONNE

VITRON

MONTMÉDY

LONGWY

LONGUYON

THIONVILLE

Moselle R.

SAARBRÜCKEN

XXXXX
G

ZWEIBRÜCKEN

KAISERSLAUTERN

XXXX
FIRST
OBSTFELDER

HOMBURG

XXXIX

XIII SS

PIRMASENS

SHAEF
EISENHOWER

REIMS

FRANCE

Meuse R.

METZ

VERDUN

XX

SARREGUEMINES

XXXXX
6
DEVERS

XXXX
FIFTEENTH
GEROW

Hitler's Ardennes offensive found Devers' 6th Army Group engaged in a successful offensive (*sketch* a), its Seventh Army having broken into the German defenses between Sarreguemines and Karlsruhe (*upper right, dashed red line*). On 20 December, Eisenhower directed Devers to halt his attack, extend to his left to take over part of the Third Army's front, and defend his sector against any major German attack. Within limits, he was to give up territory rather than risk having his forces cut off by an enemy advance.

Having seen the fate of the unsuspecting and complacent vividly illustrated in the Ardennes, 6th Army Group intelligence was alert. The Seventh Army organized a rear defensive position along the trace of the old Maginot Line (Sarreguemines-Bitche-Lembach-Hatten-Sessenheim) and a final line along the eastern slope of the Vosges Mountains.

Hitler's reasons for launching his second offensive are variously given, but they were probably based on a desire to retain the initiative in the West. A German success over the weakened American forces in this area—for example, an advance southward from Bitche to seize the Saverne-Sarreburg pass through the Low Vosges (the "Saverne Gap")—would force Eisenhower to draw troops from the Ardennes sector to reinforce the 6th Army Group. Hitler's plans, however, as usual, discounted facts. German divisions in this area were generally badly understrength and short of equipment.

Early on 1 January, Blaskowitz attacked southward toward the Saverne Gap. His XIII SS Corps was halted after a ten-mile advance, but his XC Corps broke into the American position around Bitche. The American VI Corps began a withdrawal to its second position during the night of 2 January. The XC Corps' breakthrough to Wingen on the 4th threatened the flank of this line. De Gaulle, fearing that the Americans would fall back to their final line, abandoning Strasbourg, insisted violently that that city must be defended. To avoid a French political crisis, Eisenhower was forced to order Devers to hold the city at all costs. Early on 5 January, the Germans launched a surprise Rhine cross-

ing to seize and hold a bridgehead in the Drusenheim-Gambsheim area. On 7 January, the Germans struck north at Rhinau (*center*), but were finally contained by the French. A series of German attacks at Hatten (7 January) and Sessenheim (17 January) finally linked up with the bridgehead. The Americans retired behind the Moder River the night of 20 January, and a final German attack at Haguenau failed on the 25th-26th. Several German divisions were now sent to the Eastern Front, and the offensive died down.

Eisenhower then ordered the "Colmar Pocket" (*lower center*) eliminated. The French First Army, which had attempted unsuccessfully to do so in early December, was heavily reinforced by American divisions. Between 20 January and 9 February, the pocket was pinched off from the river after heavy fighting. Hitler again delayed authorizing the evacuation of the pocket, and the German Nineteenth Army therefore suffered unnecessarily heavy losses.

With major German bridgeheads eliminated in the Colmar and Roermond areas (*sketch* b), the Allies could prepare to close up to the Rhine River from Switzerland to the sea.

This Rhineland campaign was visualized as consisting of three phases. The first phase would consist of Operation VERITABLE (an attack southeast from its Nijmegan bridgehead by the Canadian First Army), which would link up at Mörs with Operation GRENADE (a converging advance by the Ninth Army). While these operations were progressing, Bradley was to seize the Roer dams (*not shown*) and cover Montgomery's right flank. The second phase would be Operation LUMBERJACK (an advance to the Rhine by Bradley's 12th Army Group). The last phase would be UNDERTONE (an advance to the Rhine by the 6th Army Group). These operations completed, Montgomery—reinforced by the United States Ninth Army—would launch Operation PLUNDER (the principal assault crossing of the Rhine) to envelop the Ruhr from the north. Originally, this was to be followed by a drive, north of the Ruhr, to Berlin. Later, when it appeared that the Russians might reach Berlin first, the objective of this northern drive was tentatively shifted to Hamburg (*see map 52*).

Note: On Map b (and similarly on Map 66b), top center, the river running north-south through Zutphen is the Ijssel R., not Issel.

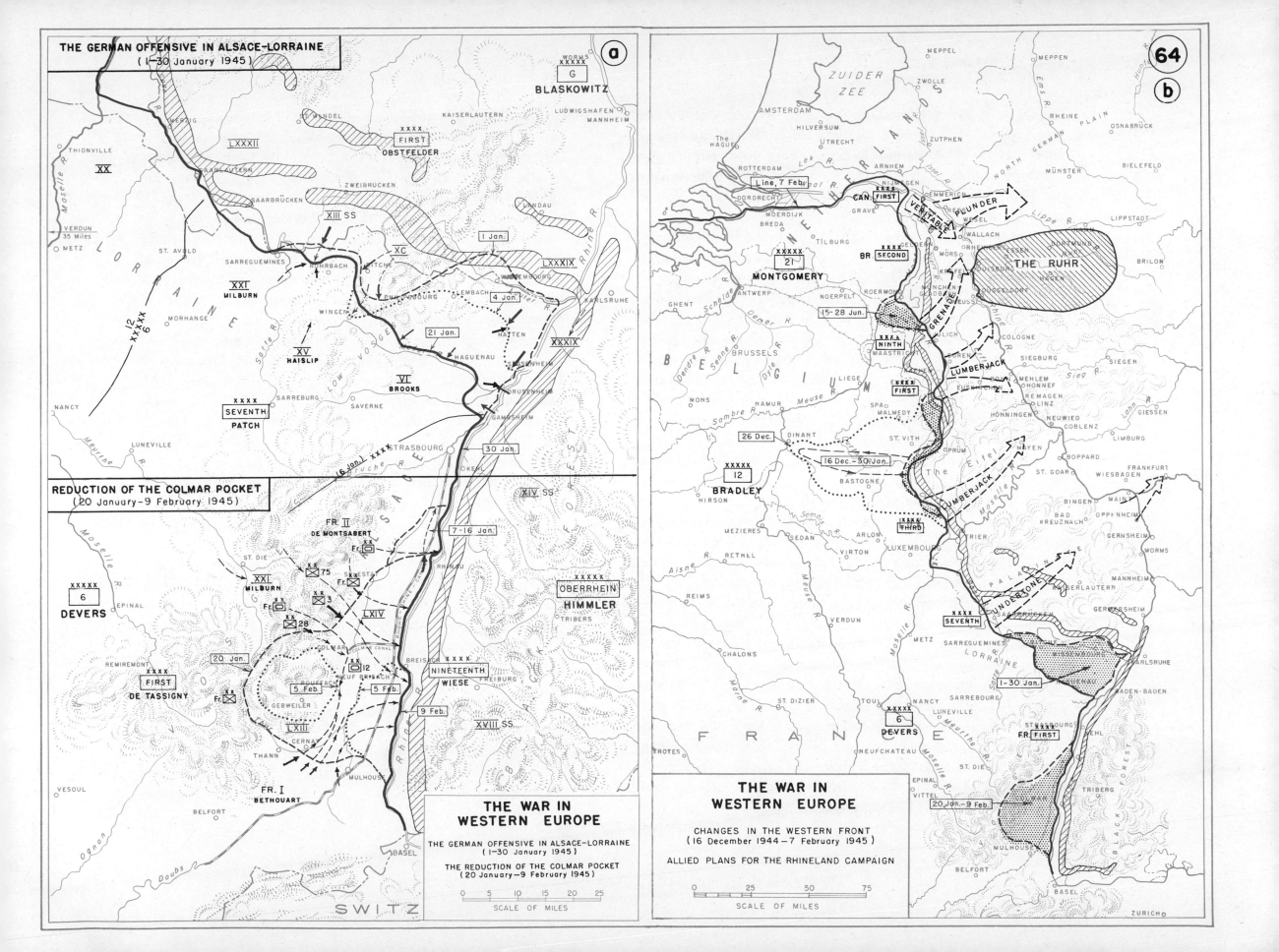

THE GERMAN OFFENSIVE IN ALSACE-LORRAINE
(1-30 January 1945)

64

a

b

BLASKOWITZ

REDUCTION OF THE COLMAR POCKET
(20 January-9 February 1945)

DEVERS

THE WAR IN
WESTERN EUROPE

THE GERMAN OFFENSIVE IN ALSACE-LORRAINE
(1-30 January 1945)

THE REDUCTION OF THE COLMAR POCKET
(20 January-9 February 1945)

SCALE OF MILES

THE WAR IN
WESTERN EUROPE

CHANGES IN THE WESTERN FRONT
(16 December 1944-7 February 1945)

ALLIED PLANS FOR THE RHINELAND CAMPAIGN

SCALE OF MILES

Operation VERITABLE faced deep German defenses. The first was the Reichswald (*sketch* a, *top left*), thoroughly organized in depth; behind it, Cleves and Goch had been converted into major strong points; behind them, a third position extended from Geldern northward toward Rees. The Germans had flooded the low ground along the rivers.

Montgomery planned to launch VERITABLE on 8 February, GRENADE on the 10th. On the night of 7 February, the RAF Bomber Command pounded Cleves, Goch, and other targets in that area. At 0500, 8 February, British artillery put down a five-and-a-half-hour bombardment; at 1030, the XXX Corps, reinforced by special assault tank regiments, advanced. Though clogged by a sudden thaw and rising flood waters, the attack reached Cleves on the afternoon of the 9th. There it found that the Bomber Command had used high explosive bombs against the town, rather than the incendiaries requested, and a wilderness of craters and debris halted all progress.

Bradley, meanwhile, had been battering toward the Roer dams since 2 February. (As previously mentioned, the Ninth Army could not risk an assault across the Roer River so long as the Germans held these dams and thus retained the capability to flood out the Roer Valley.) After bitter fighting, the V Corps won control of the dams late on 10 February—only to discover that the Germans had wrecked the discharge valves the previous evening, thus creating a steady flooding that would halt the Ninth Army for two weeks.

This left Blaskowitz free to concentrate against the British attack. German parachute units, composed of fanatical young Nazis, fought literally to the last man. Continued rains and floods put most of the battlefield under water; amphibious vehicles were needed to resupply the troops and evacuate the wounded; attacks struggled through waist-high water. But neither German courage nor foul weather stopped the British and Canadians. By 23 February, they had overrun the first two German positions and were regrouping (*dotted red line*) to attack the third.

The Ninth Army had taken advantage of its enforced pause to perfect its preparations for crossing the Roer. Simpson secured surprise by employing only a short preparatory bombardment and by attacking at 0245, 23 February, before the flood waters had finished subsiding. Fighter-bombers protected the first bridgeheads against confused counterattacks, until bridges could be built to enable American armor to cross. On the 25th, the Ninth Army attacked out of its bridgeheads; by the 28th, it had broken loose. Most of the Germans in this area were struggling vainly to check the British, who had resumed their offensive on the 26th. On 3 March, American and British troops linked up at Geldern. Two days later, the Germans held only the Xanten-Wesel bridgehead (*top center*), which Hitler insisted must be held. However, on 10 March, Canadian attacks forced its evacuation (*sketch* b). Montgomery now began concentrating for Operation PLUNDER. Simpson proposed an immediate assault crossing in the Düsseldorf-Duisburg sector, which he knew to be unfortified and lightly defended; but Montgomery refused, stating that—even if successful—a crossing there would only entangle the Ninth Army in the industrial jungle of the Ruhr.

Bradley, meanwhile, had carried out his pre-LUMBERJACK mission of covering the Ninth Army's right flank. Attacking on 23 February, the First Army scored considerable gains, as shown. Farther south, from 8 to 23 February, Patton—assigned the temporary mission of "active defense" until LUMBERJACK began—had gnawed his way through the West Wall. By 5 March, Bradley was ready to close to the Rhine from the Moselle River north. His advance swept through confused German resistance. On 7 March, leading units of the 9th Armored Division discovered the Rhine bridge at Remagen still standing and seized it by a daring rush. This unexpected fortune changed the entire balance of the Allied offensive. Eisenhower ordered the bridgehead reinforced.

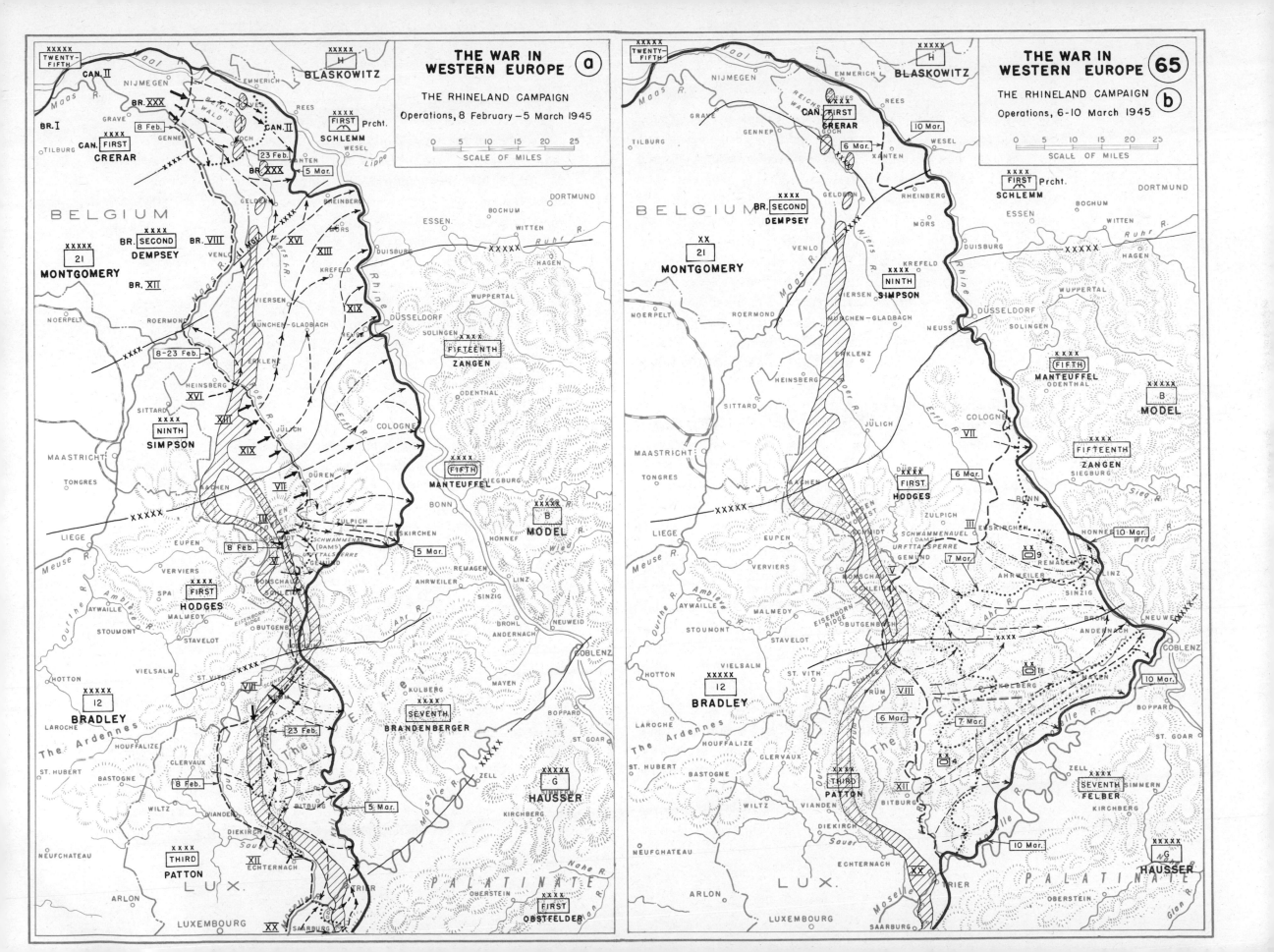

THE WAR IN WESTERN EUROPE (a)

THE RHINELAND CAMPAIGN

Operations, 8 February – 5 March 1945

SCALE OF MILES
0 5 10 15 20 25

THE WAR IN WESTERN EUROPE 65 (b)

THE RHINELAND CAMPAIGN

Operations, 6-10 March 1945

SCALE OF MILES
0 5 10 15 20 25

The first German counterattacks against the Remagen bridgehead (*sketch* a, *top center*) were piecemeal and futile, using up most of the available panzer units. American reinforcements poured across the shaky Remagen Bridge (considerably damaged when some of the German demolition charges were set off during the American attack). Once the bridgehead was sufficiently enlarged, ponton bridges were installed (11 March); a number of ferries, including small Navy-operated landing craft, were likewise employed. The Germans made determined efforts to wreck the bridge—including air attacks, artillery fire, V-2 missiles, floating mines, and frogmen—but all were thwarted by the elaborate American defenses. By 21 March, the bridgehead was approximately twenty miles long and eight miles deep, and six bridges connected it to the west bank.

The rapid success of Operation LUMBERJACK led to a modification of UNDERTONE (the 6th Army Group's advance to the Rhine). Under this revised plan, Patton would attack southward across the Moselle River to strike the German Seventh Army's north flank as Devers assailed its front. If successfully carried out, this maneuver would crush the German First and Seventh Armies and liquidate the last German foothold on the west bank of the Rhine.

The German commanders involved were only too conscious of the weakness of their position. A large part of their forces consisted of the recently organized, poorly officered Volksgrenadier divisions. Fuel and ammunition were both in short supply. They pleaded for permission to withdraw; Hitler's answer was the same as it had always been: defend in place.

Devers concentrated most of his strength in his Seventh Army for an attack on 15 March, with the main effort toward Kaiserlautern (*center, right*). Patton, meanwhile, had begun his attack across the Moselle on 13 March, his infantry leading through the rough terrain on the south bank. On the 15th, his armored divisions began to pass through the infantry; thereafter, they drove swiftly through collapsing resistance, leaving bypassed German units for their infantry to mop up. The Seventh Army's advance was slower, since it had to fight its way through some of the strongest sections of the West Wall. The smooth coordination between the Third and Seventh Armies and their supporting tactical air commands was outstanding. By 21 March, most of the German Seventh Army had been destroyed, and the German First Army was struggling for its life in a shrinking salient.

The Rhineland campaign had been one of the greatest defeats inflicted on Hitler. Exact figures are not available, but approximately a quarter of a million Germans were taken prisoner, with possibly an additional 60,000 killed or wounded. The effect was to destroy the German Army in the West, so that no effective forces remained available to defend long stretches of the east bank of the Rhine. Militarily, Hitler's conduct appears to have been another piece of sheer lunacy. He might have utilized the West Wall as a delaying position while withdrawing his heavy equipment behind the Rhine during January and February, when the prevalent bad weather would have offered considerable protection from Allied air attacks. The Rhine was a formidable natural barrier, behind which he could have waged an effective defense for some time. Various reasons have been advanced for his decision to make his stand west of the Rhine: for example, the importance of that river and its tributary rivers and canals as a communications network, now that the German railway system was so badly damaged; or the value of whatever production could still be achieved in the badly damaged Ruhr, now that the Russians had occupied most of the Silesian industrial area. But there was also the fact that Hitler was already turning his back on life— on 19 March, he had decreed that the battle should be conducted without any consideration for the population of Germany, and that Nazi Party leaders were to begin the destruction of everything in Germany that might be of use to his enemies.

(In sketch *b*, the blue numbers in parentheses under each United States army symbol represent that army's losses in killed during this campaign. The numbers in the red boxes indicate the German losses in prisoners during this same period.)

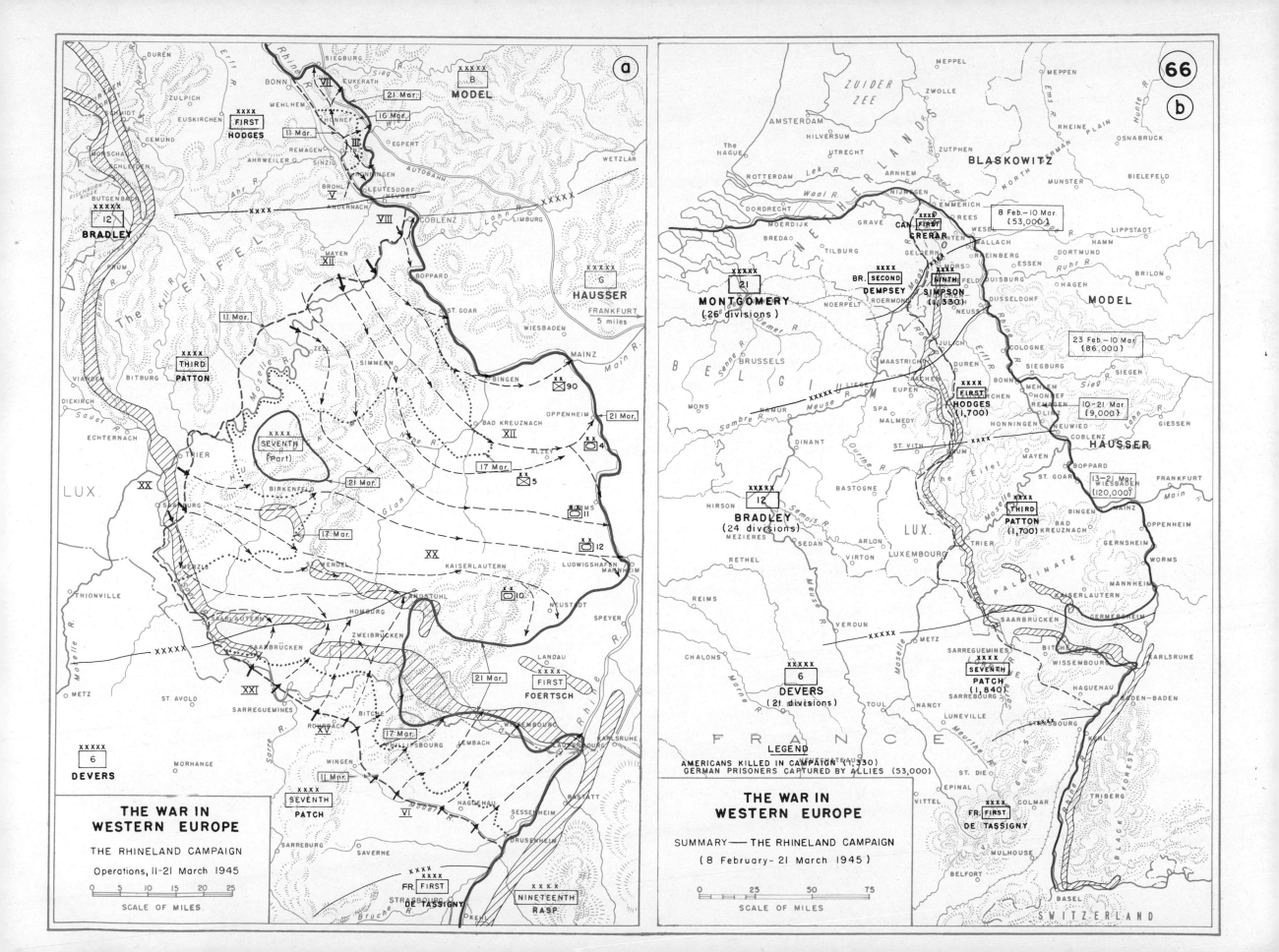

(a)

XXXXX
B
MODEL

XXXX
FIRST
HODGES

XXXXX
12
BRADLEY

XXXXX
G
HAUSSER
Frankfurt

XXXX
THIRD
PATTON

XXXX
SEVENTH
(Part)

XXXXX
6
DEVERS

XXXX
SEVENTH
PATCH

XXXX
FR. FIRST
DE TASSIGNY

XXXX
XXXX
NINETEENTH
RASP

FR. FIRST
FOERTSCH

THE WAR IN
WESTERN EUROPE

THE RHINELAND CAMPAIGN

Operations, 11-21 March 1945

0 5 10 15 20 25

SCALE OF MILES

(b)

66

BLASKOWITZ

XXXXX
21
MONTGOMERY
(26 divisions)

XXXX
FIRST
CRERAR

BR. SECOND
DEMPSEY

NINTH
SIMPSON
(1,330)

MODEL

8 Feb.- 10 Mar.
(53,000)

23 Feb.- 10 Mar.
(86,000)

XXXX
FIRST
HODGES
(1,700)

10-21 Mar.
(9,000)

HAUSSER

XXXXX
12
BRADLEY
(24 divisions)

13-21 Mar.
(120,000)

XXXX
THIRD
PATTON
(1,700)

XXXXX
6
DEVERS
(21 divisions)

XXXX
SEVENTH
PATCH
(1,840)

XXXX
FR. FIRST
DE TASSIGNY

LEGEND
AMERICANS KILLED IN CAMPAIGN (1,330)
GERMAN PRISONERS CAPTURED BY ALLIES (53,000)

THE WAR IN
WESTERN EUROPE

SUMMARY — THE RHINELAND CAMPAIGN

(8 February - 21 March 1945)

0   25   50   75

SCALE OF MILES

This map shows the three general stages of the final extinction of Hitler's empire. The first (*shaded red area*) had seen the Russians capture Budapest and drive to the Oder River in Germany, while the Americans and British first defeated Hitler's offensives in the Ardennes and Alsace-Lorraine and then advanced to the Rhine. In the second (*shaded blue area*), Anglo-American columns poured across the Rhine, closing up to the line of the Elbe and Mulde Rivers, while the Russians built up their bridgeheads on the west bank of the Oder and absorbed more territory in Czechoslovakia, Hungary, Austria, and Yugoslavia. During the third and last phase (*shaded green area*), the British and Americans—instead of continuing their drive across central Germany to Berlin—turned their efforts north and south (and also rapidly overran northern Italy); the Russians took Berlin and moved forward to the Elbe. At the time of the German capitulation (7 May), out of the thousands of German troops still under arms, practically all stood on foreign soil—Norway, Denmark, Latvia, Czechoslovakia, Austria, and Yugoslavia. Their German homeland had been conquered behind them.

As outlined in the text of map 64b, Eisenhower had originally intended to make his main Rhine crossing north of the Ruhr, enveloping the Ruhr from the north, and to continue this attack across the plains of northern Germany toward Berlin. At the same time, he had hoped to mount a secondary offensive across the Rhine south of the Ruhr. (In fact, a large part of his insistence on closing to the Rhine on a broad front was based on his conviction that only by thus covering the inactive portions of his front with a strong natural barrier could he accumulate the necessary forces for a secondary attack.) This secondary attack, he believed, would give his operations a greater degree of flexibility, since the Germans might manage to contain a single drive.

During early March, however, a variety of reasons led Eisenhower to alter this original plan. For one thing, by 11 March, Zhukov's Russians were reported nearing Berlin, thus—in Eisenhower's mind—decreasing that city's importance as an objective for his forces. Also, much of the Ruhr's armament industry reportedly had been shifted deeper into Germany during recent months; a drive south and east of the Ruhr would be required to overrun Germany's remaining industrial capacity. Furthermore, one of history's most potent frauds was beginning to prey upon the imaginations of Allied commanders. This was the so-called "National Redoubt," a subject requiring much further research. (This "redoubt" reputedly was the mountainous area south of Munich [*lower center*], including Alpine sections of western Austria and northern Italy. It was to be organized into a vast fortress—garrisoned by picked fanatics and defended by secret weapons—from which Nazi guerrillas would sally forth to bushwhack Allied troops. Hitler had once mentioned some such plan, but in 1945 there were neither troops, materials, nor the time for it. Nevertheless, this fable powerfully influenced American planning, pulling American strength southward to crush a nonexistent threat. In the final analysis, the acceptance of this fable was one of the major failures of American intelligence in World War II.)

One final consideration undoubtedly also influenced Eisenhower. The Remagen, Oppenheim (*see text, map 68*), and Boppard bridgeheads were clear evidence of the aggressiveness of Bradley and his army commanders, in contrast to Montgomery's conservatism. Whatever his exact reasons, once across the Rhine, Eisenhower entrusted the final main effort to Bradley.

During March, Allied air forces had carried out a vigorous interdiction campaign east of the Rhine. By 24 March, the Ruhr area was practically isolated, all rail lines leading into it being effectively cut. Strategic bombers continued their pounding of the German fuel industry and communications systems, while engineers rapidly repaired captured German airfields along the west bank of the Rhine to ensure continuous tactical air support for the next phase of the Allied offensive. Allied logistical support was operating at maximum efficiency, and a new influx of replacements had brought Allied divisions up to full strength.

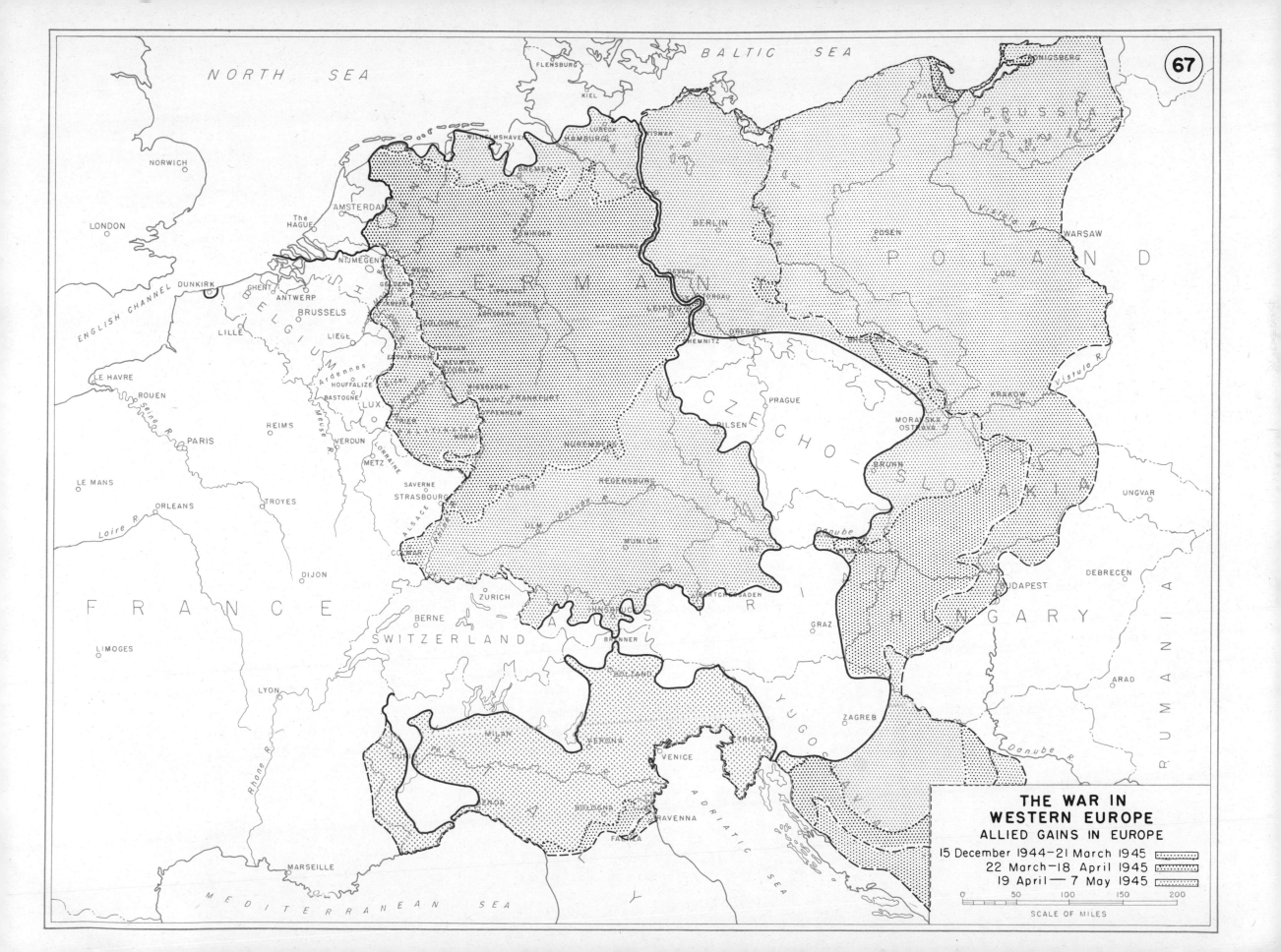

THE WAR IN
WESTERN EUROPE
ALLIED GAINS IN EUROPE
15 December 1944–21 March 1945
22 March–18 April 1945
19 April – 7 May 1945

SCALE OF MILES
0   50   100   150   200

67

Patton's participation in Operation UNDERTONE (*see map 66a*) hit its climax at 2200, 22 March, when one of his divisions (the 5th), abruptly changing its direction of march from south to east, made a surprise assault crossing of the Rhine at Oppenheim (*this map, center*). Having long planned a crossing in this area, Patton had bridging equipment and a Navy detachment with landing craft close up behind his infantry. By the evening of 24 March, his bridges were in, and four of his divisions had crossed to the east bank of the Rhine. German forces in this area were weak and demoralized; American losses were very light. Also on the 24th, Patton's VIII Corps seized another bridgehead near Boppard. Thus Bradley's troops held three large bridgeheads on the central Rhine—a factor that no doubt deeply influenced Eisenhower's future planning.

On paper, the Germans had more than sixty divisions east of the Rhine. Over twenty of these, however, were mere fragments, four consisting of their staffs alone. Their total numerical strength may have equaled that of twenty-six normal divisions, but their ranks were full of untrained, often unwilling recruits. Ammunition, fuel, and weapons were lacking; the Luftwaffe had practically disappeared. Against this shadow army, Eisenhower deployed eighty-five full-strength divisions (five airborne, twenty-three armored, fifty-seven infantry), reinforced by dozens of additional artillery, tank, tank destroyer, antiaircraft, and engineer battalions. Allied air power was still increasing—and beginning to run out of targets. The hopelessness of the German cause was starkly evident, except apparently to Hitler, but, while he still ruled, it would be suicidal for any German general to attempt to surrender.

Montgomery had originally planned his Rhine crossing for 15 March, but Eisenhower later postponed it until the 23d. As usual, Montgomery's preparations were detailed and meticulous, accumulating sufficient supplies and equipment to enable him to thrust deep into Germany. The British Second Army launched its crossing against Wesel at 2100, 23 March, with massive artillery support (3,300 guns on a 25-mile front) and a heavy air attack on Wesel. The Ninth Army began crossing near Dinslaben at 0200, 24 March. Later that morning, one American and one British airborne division, flown in from France and England respectively, began landing north of Wesel. Both linked up with British ground forces by midafternoon. (With memories of the final failure of the Arnhem operation, Allied planners chose to drop the airborne units during daylight, close enough to the main attack to permit their support by its artillery and, consequently, an early link-up.) Resistance was rapidly overwhelmed, though some German paratroopers died hard—one battalion held out in Rees for three days. Once again, Allied progress was slowed by wreckage resulting from overheavy Allied air bombardment, but on the 26th twelve bridges were in operation. Two days later, British tanks and American airborne infantry broke through the German lines near Haltern, opening the North German Plain to Montgomery's advance.

Southward, Bradley's troops broke out of their bridgeheads (*dotted red lines*) on 25 March. The First Army struck eastward through Giessen and Siegen—completely surprising Model, who had expected an attack northward against the Ruhr—and southward to link up with the Third Army. Scattering light opposition, both armies then swung toward Kassel (*upper center*). On the 6th Army Group's front, the XV Corps forced the Rhine north and south of Worms on the 26th, against brief but bitter resistance.

On 28 March, Eisenhower startled Montgomery with his sudden change of plan. The Ninth Army would remain under Montgomery's command until the Ruhr was encircled. Thereafter, it would revert to Bradley. Bradley's 12th Army Group would mop up and occupy the Ruhr, while making the main Allied effort northeast along the axis Erfurt-Leipzig-Dresden. Montgomery would cover Bradley's left flank. Devers was to cover Bradley's right and be prepared to advance down the Danube.

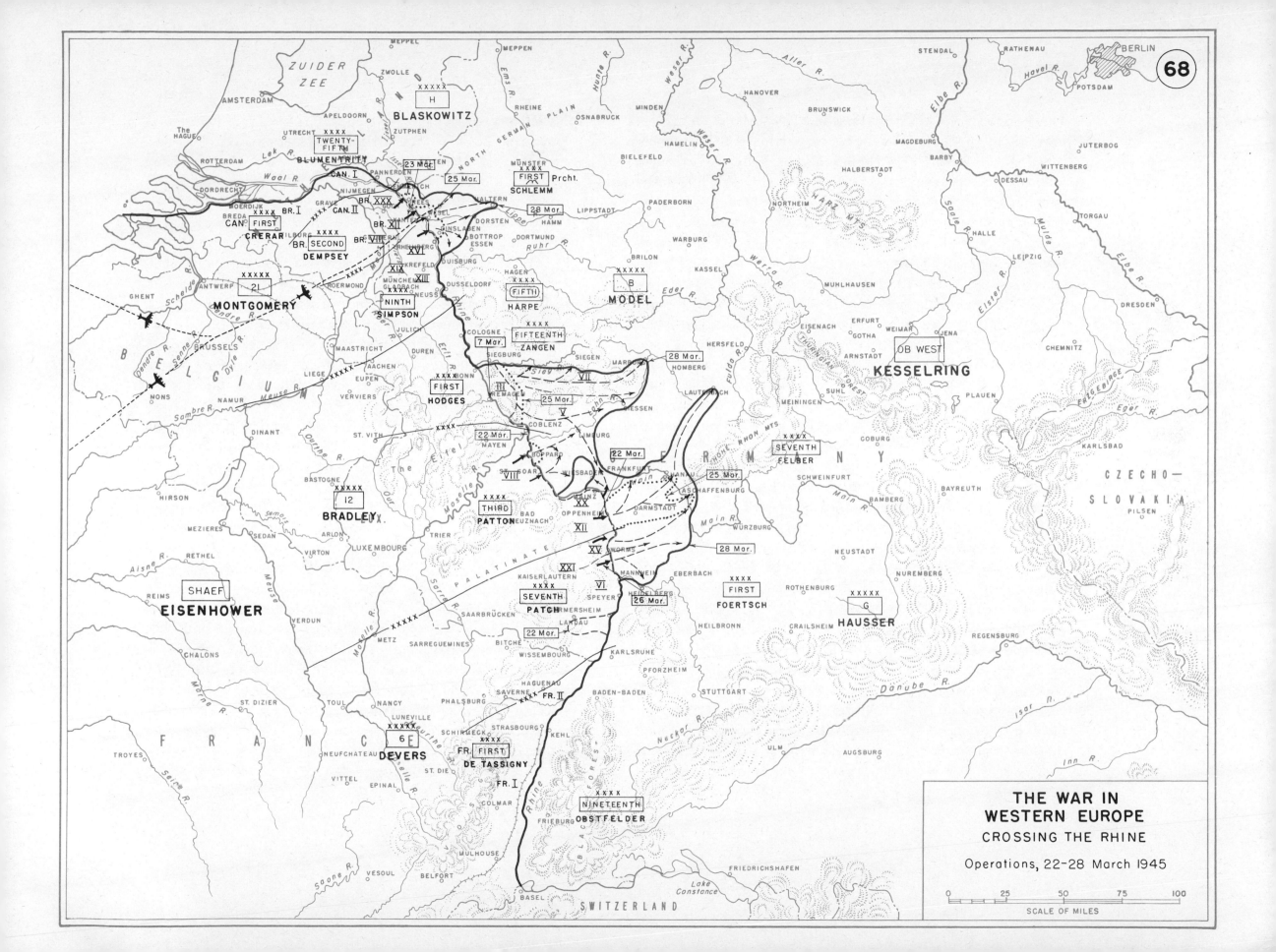

THE WAR IN
WESTERN EUROPE

CROSSING THE RHINE

Operations, 22-28 March 1945

SCALE OF MILES

0   25   50   75   100

The advance of the American First and Third Armies during the next few days was hindered more by rough terrain than by German troops. By 29 March, they had linked up laterally at Wiesbaden (*center*), and their armor was plunging forward, averaging thirty miles a day. On 28 March, Bradley had shifted the First Army's axis of advance from northeast to almost due north; the Third Army was ordered to attack toward Kassel (*upper center*) and Hersfeld, driving the Germans east of the line Hohe Rhön Mountains (*center*)–Werra River–Weser River (*upper center*). On 29 March, Simpson directed elements of the Ninth Army toward Paderborn (*upper center*) to meet the First Army. The latter became involved in furious fighting in the SS panzer training area near Paderborn, but had the superior combat power necessary to break through. On the afternoon of 1 April, units of the Ninth Army's 2d Armored Division made contact with the First Army's 3d Armored Division near Lippstadt. The Ruhr was surrounded.

To the south and east, the Third Army was in Kassel by 2 April and held several bridgeheads over the Werra River. The French First Army, which had crossed the Rhine at Speyer and Germersheim on 31 March, turned southward on Karlsruhe, Pforzheim, and Stuttgart. In the north, the Canadian First Army was turning northward to cut off the German forces in Holland and clear the German coastline, while the British Second Army drove eastward to the Elbe. On its right flank, Simpson likewise moved eastward with his XIII and part of his XIX Corps, while maintaining pressure on the Ruhr pocket with the XVI Corps and the rest of the XIX. The American Fifteenth Army had been brought up to hold the west bank of the Rhine opposite the Ruhr pocket and to be prepared to take over control of the Rhineland provinces as the rest of the 12th Army Group advanced farther to the east. By 4 April, the Allied offensive had reached the line shown (*heavy red line*). On that date, Patton had paused to allow his infantry divisions to close up behind his armor before continuing the attack; the 6th Army Group reported effective German resistance at Heilbronn (*lower center*) and Aschaffenburg (*center*); Montgomery was delayed somewhat by skillful German demolitions; and the Ninth Army reverted to the 12th Army Group's control. The final drive eastward to crush Germany could now begin.

The German chain of command was now thoroughly shattered, many of the higher headquarters having lost contact with their subordinate units. Nevertheless, Hitler continued a deluge of orders for counterattacks and for resistance to the end—still promising new miracle weapons which were to snatch victory out of total defeat. In the south, Army Group G managed to hold the semblance of a front together while falling back through the mountains toward the Danube (*lower right*). In the center, Model held a pocket of some 4,000 square miles with most of his Fifth Panzer and Fifteenth Armies, plus elements of the First Parachute Army and some 100,000 miscellaneous troops (many of slight military value). He had food for three or four weeks, and ammunition enough for two or three weeks—if he could avoid a major battle. He also had Hitler's orders prohibiting further withdrawals or loss of inhabited areas, on pain of death; additional orders instructed him to destroy all of the Ruhr's industrial and communications facilities. The first orders he could not obey; the second he would not. Army Group H, with the exception of its Twenty-Fifth Army, had been shattered by Montgomery's offensive. Blaskowitz had requested permission to withdraw enough troops from Holland to reestablish his front along the Weser River and regain contact with Model. He received the usual orders to hold in place. Lacking reinforcements, Hitler accelerated his recent policy of meeting each crisis by replacing the German commander concerned.

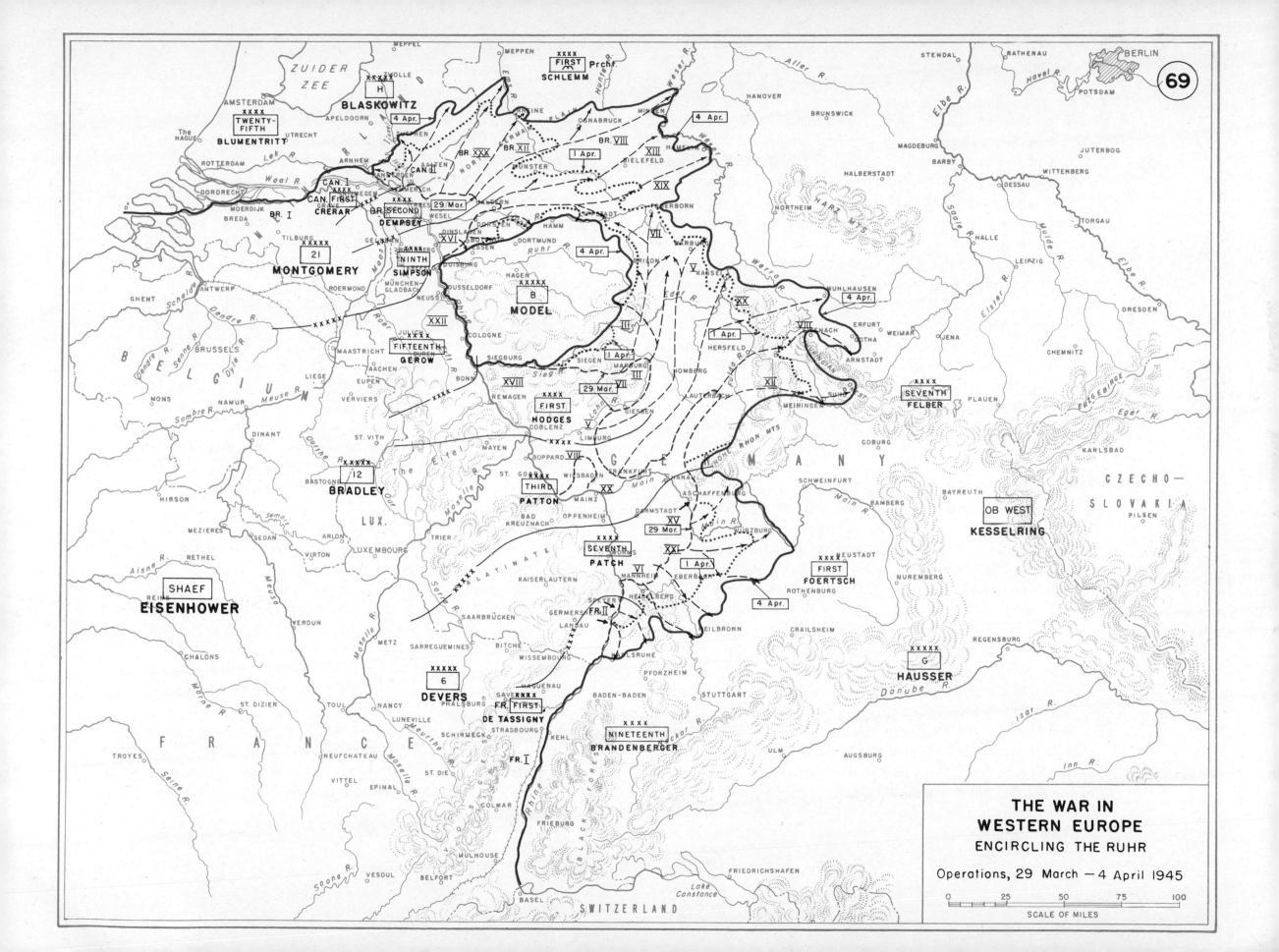

THE WAR IN
WESTERN EUROPE

ENCIRCLING THE RUHR

Operations, 29 March – 4 April 1945

SCALE OF MILES

0   25   50   75   100

While the Allied front surged eastward, the Ruhr pocket was methodically reduced. Model knew his situation was hopeless, but refused to surrender as long as he could divert American forces away from the main offensive. Initially, he tried to reinforce the eastern face of his pocket, hoping that help might come from that direction or that some of his troops might be able to escape, but it was soon obvious that the ring about him was too strong. While the Fifteenth Army's XXII Corps secured the west bank of the Rhine in this sector, the Ninth Army's XVI Corps (reinforced by part of the XIX Corps) attacked the northern front of the pocket, and the First Army's III and XVIII Corps moved against the east and southern fronts, respectively. Generally speaking, the Germans fought a careful, often skillful delaying action, avoiding pitched battles. By 14 April, however, all of the pocket north of the Ruhr River had been occupied, and the remaining portion split by a north-south attack. (It was at this state of affairs that Hitler's headquarters ordered Model to break out.) As the Americans widened their north-south corridor, Model disbanded his army, and reportedly committed suicide. Resistance ended on 18 April; more than 317,000 prisoners were gathered in—the largest mass surrender of German troops during the war.

Other German forces were swept ahead of the tide. Blaskowitz took over the German troops in Holland, reorganized into Army Group Netherlands, and prepared to stand siege behind that country's water barriers. A new Army Group Northwest was created to take over the First Parachute Army and other remnants trying to halt Montgomery. Kesselring attempted to maintain control of Army Group G and other fragments to the south. The German Eleventh Army—a grab-bag collection of new units, hastily assembled with some vague idea of relieving Model—had been ordered to hold the Harz Mountains area. The Nazi Party's effort to organize a guerrilla movement under the bloodcurdling title of "Werewolves" was an outstanding failure.

As the Allied armies plunged headlong toward the Elbe, a clash of opinion arose between the British and American leaders. The British, more politically astute and more experienced in the uses of war as an instrument of national policy, urged an all-out advance on Berlin. Eisenhower—reflecting the policy of the American Joint Chiefs of Staff—considered his task as military commander in the field to be the achievement of a quick and decisive military victory. Though aware of the political implications, he intended to halt his advance on the line of the Elbe and Mulde Rivers and concentrate on the destruction of the German forces on his flanks. He would move against political objectives only if directed to do so.

Actually, insofar as Germany was concerned, the political objectives had already been delimited at the highest level by an agreement on occupation zones (*see map 72*), confirmed at the Yalta Conference in February, 1945. American forces moving beyond the zones would have to withdraw later. Any failure on their part to do so would have raised howls of protest from the American public, which—conditioned by a mixture of idealism and skillful Communist propaganda—looked upon their Russian big brother with compassion, if not with love. More important, the blame for the "cold war" would have been placed squarely upon the Western Allies.

On the whole, the advance during this period was delayed more by terrain and traffic jams than enemy opposition. The Canadians had some stiff fighting on the approaches to Emden and Wilhelmshaven (*this map, top center*). The Ninth Army reached the Elbe near Magdeburg (*upper right*) on 11 April, seized one bridgehead on the 12th and another, south of Magdeburg, on the 13th. The northern bridgehead was driven into the river by a sudden German counterattack on the 14th, but the southern one held. Also on the 14th, Patton's troops were near the Czech frontier, patrols crossing it on the 17th. The 6th Army Group, meanwhile, still was meeting determined resistance at Nuremberg (*lower right*).

(During this period, the Russians launched their final offensive [16 April], and the final Allied attack in Italy [launched 14 April] was gaining rapidly.)

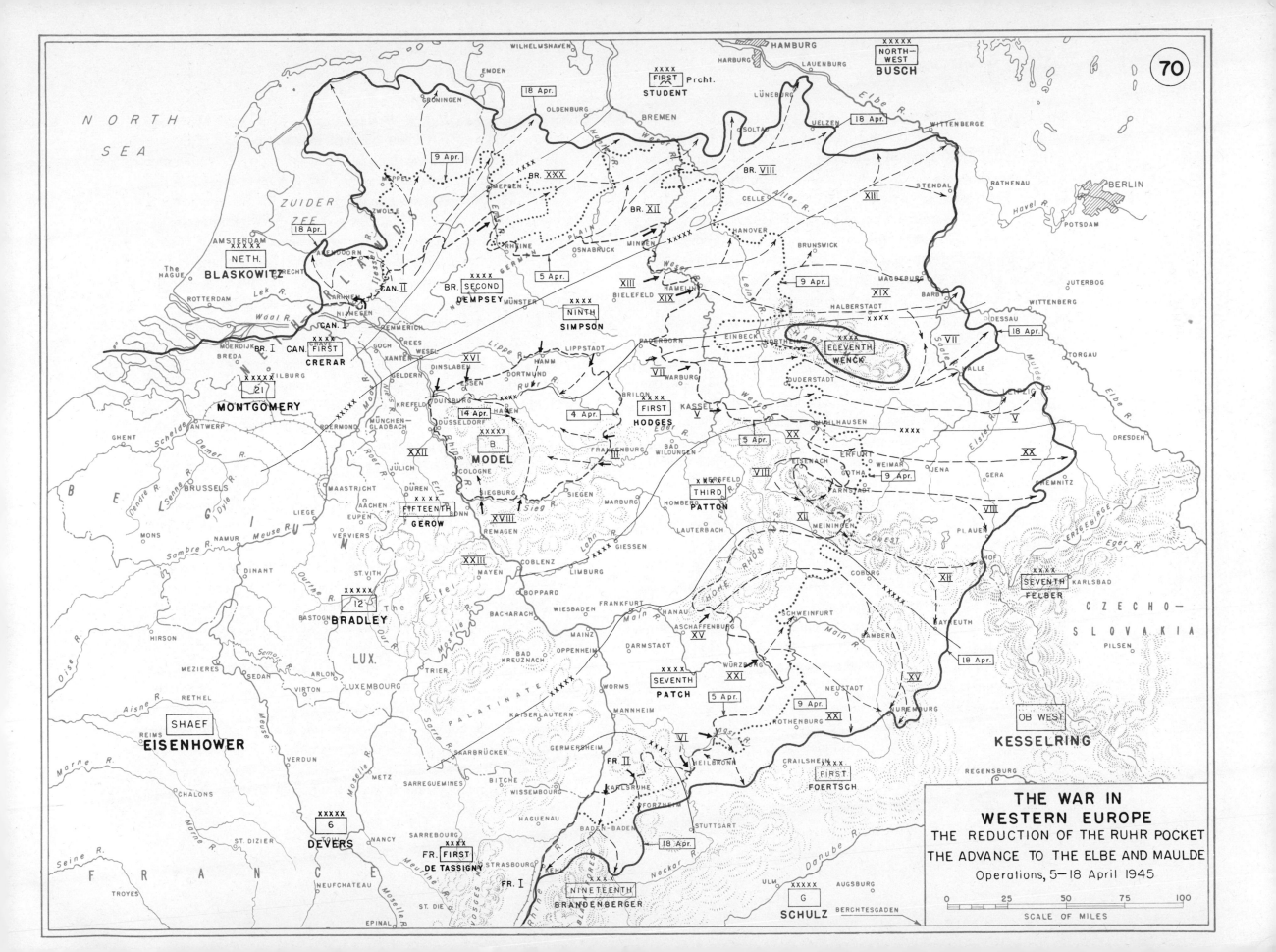

THE WAR IN
WESTERN EUROPE
THE REDUCTION OF THE RUHR POCKET
THE ADVANCE TO THE ELBE AND MAULDE
Operations, 5—18 April 1945

SCALE OF MILES
0   25   50   75   100

The danger of accidental clashes, as his forces came into contact with the Russians, now became one of Eisenhower's major concerns. Also, he was anxious to destroy the German forces on his flanks, especially in the "redoubt" area to the south, where 100 German divisions were rumored to be concentrating. He therefore ordered Bradley to hold the line Elbe River–Mulde River–Erzgebirge Mountains (*center*) with two armies, and to send the Third Army through Nuremberg and Regensburg (*lower center*) and down the Danube Valley. Montgomery, reinforced by the American XVIII Corps, would advance northward across the Elbe to the Lübeck area (*top center*). Devers would swerve slightly westward to clean out the "redoubt."

Remaining operations were minor. In Holland, the Canadian First Army halted its advance on 22 April, when the German occupational authorities promised not to flood additional farmland. Many of the Dutch inhabitants in the occupied area were near starvation. Hostilities here were suspended on 28 April; subsequent negotiations resulted in food deliveries to the inhabitants, beginning 1 May. The German authorities, however, refused to surrender.

The British Second Army had cleared most of the west bank of the Elbe in its sector by 26 April. On 1 May, it drove northward, seizing Lübeck and Wismar on the 2d. (Russian troops approached Wismar shortly after an American unit had occupied it.) On 3 May, Hamburg surrendered.

In the Allied center, Simpson had urged a renewed advance toward Berlin, but Bradley disapproved the idea. (Most of the German forces on the east bank here had meanwhile been recalled to join the fighting around Berlin.) By 6 May, the Russians had closed up to the Elbe, and the Ninth Army turned its bridgehead over to them.

Meanwhile, the First Army had cleared Leipzig (*center*) on 19 April, liquidated the Harz Mountains pocket on 21 April, and closed to the Mulde River. On 25 April, its V Corps' patrols met Russian detachments near Torgau (*center*)—the first contact between the Eastern and Western Fronts. The Third Army had spent several days moving units south to take over part of the 6th Army Group's front. On 22 April, Patton renewed his advance, moving rapidly against scattered opposition. On 4 May, the Third Army took Linz, Austria (*lower center*), and was approaching Pilsen, Czechoslovakia, under new orders from Bradley to advance to the line Budejovice–Pilsen–Karlsbad (*all lower center*). Eisenhower now proposed to the Russian High Command that Patton continue eastward to liberate Prague, but canceled the movement because of their anguished protests.

The 6th Army Group had finally cleared Nuremberg (*lower center*) on 20 April and Stuttgart (*lower left*) on the 23d. Thereafter, traffic jams inflicted more delay than German opposition. Munich (*lower center*) surrendered on the 30th, Salzburg and Berchtesgaden on 4 May. Also on the 4th, Seventh Army troops advanced through the Brenner Pass to meet leading units of the Fifth Army advancing northward from Italy.

During this period, the German forces in the West surrendered piecemeal. On 5 May, all German forces in Holland, Denmark, Schleswig–Holstein, and northwest Germany, including the coastal islands (*all top left and center*), surrendered to Montgomery. Army Group G (*see map 70*) surrendered to Devers that same day. Thousands of individual German soldiers fled across the Elbe before the Russian advance. At the same time, Admiral Doenitz (designated by Hitler as his successor on 29 April) began the negotiations that ended on 7 May at Reims with the final surrender of Germany.

During April, logistical problems had hampered the Allies more severely than had enemy action, supply trains of some units having to make round-trip hauls of over 700 miles. The rapid extension of the railroad system across the Rhine maintained the flow of essential supplies, and air resupply became increasingly important. When the strategic air forces ran out of targets (16 April), many heavy bombers were modified to serve as additional transport aircraft.

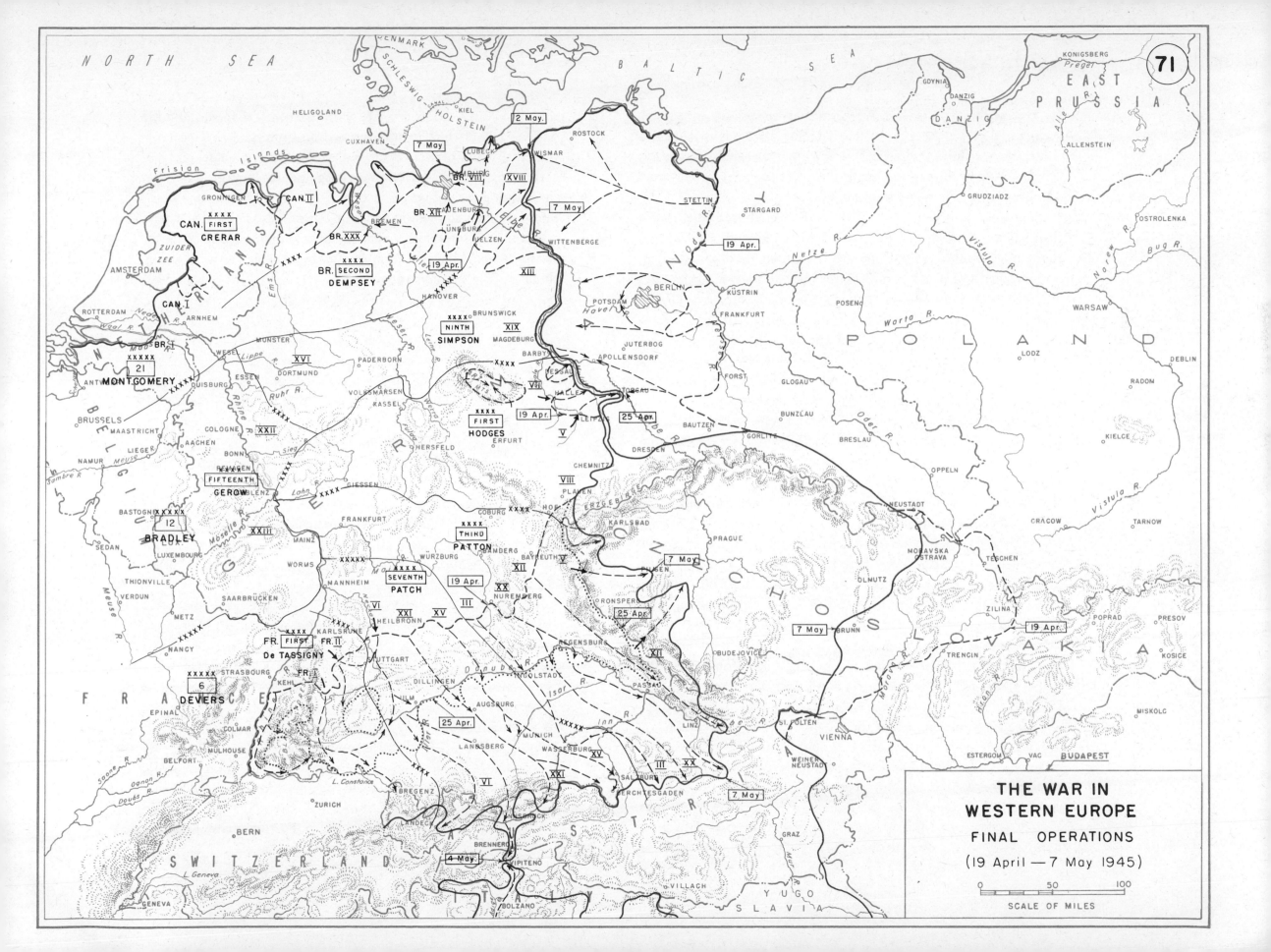

THE WAR IN
WESTERN EUROPE
FINAL OPERATIONS
(19 April — 7 May 1945)

SCALE OF MILES
0   50   100

Following Doenitz's surrender, hostilities in Europe ended officially at 2301, 8 May. (At the demand of the Russians, this surrender was formally ratified on 9 May in Berlin.) Thereafter, Allied forces began regrouping to take over their respective occupation zones in Germany and Austria.

The general organization of these zones had been worked out through negotiations during 1944 to give England, Russia, and the United States occupation areas with approximately equal populations and resources. Berlin (and, by a later agreement, Vienna) was to be similarly divided into three sectors. The United States was to have an enclave around the port of Bremen (*upper left*) and certain rights over road and railroad communications between that enclave and its zone. At the Yalta Conference (February, 1945), Roosevelt, Stalin, and Churchill had reached general agreement on this subject. Churchill and Roosevelt had also urged that France be given a zone; Stalin reluctantly concurred, but made it plain that such area would have to be made up from territory relinquished by the Americans and British. As can be seen by comparing maps 71 and 72, during the last weeks of the war the British and Americans had advanced well into the future Russian occupation zone. This led the ever-suspicious Russians into a period of delays and minor squabblings, but on 1 July the American and British troops were finally able to begin their withdrawal. At the same time, the Russians at last permitted their allies to occupy their assigned sectors in Berlin. One major mistake marred the agreement under which this last movement was carried out; instead of obtaining definite control of surface communications between their zones and Berlin, the Anglo-American command naïvely entrusted the safety of these communications to the Russians.

Meanwhile, even before the war in Europe was completely done, the English and American commands had begun the rapid redeployment of air and ground forces to the Far East for the final attacks against Japan. This was a logistical operation of stupendous magnitude.

Also, the Allied forces found themselves involved in a large number of "tidying-up" missions. German troops in Norway, Denmark, Holland, Czechoslovakia, various French seaports, and the Channel Islands had to be disarmed and returned to Germany. Allied prisoners of war, displaced persons, and civilian refugees of all nationalities required processing and evacuation. Land and sea communications were reopened. Intelligence and technical teams rounded up senior German officers, Nazi Party leaders, suspected war criminals, scientists, and weapons technicians for interrogation. Allied military government agencies were busily rebuilding the administrative and economic machinery of Germany.

The Allied victory in Western Europe—like most of history's other great victories—was won by the greater force with the better means. The Allied forces were superior in numbers of men, weapons, and aircraft; they had almost unlimited resources behind them. Their leadership, if generally cautious and conservative, was also steady and unrelenting.

The Germans fought with their supply lines cut and their armament industries shattered behind them by the Allied air offensive. Their every movement, during daylight and good weather, brought down Allied tactical aircraft and massed artillery fire. As in Russia, Hitler's insane demand that every position must be held trapped them repeatedly in untenable positions. Yet, they fought well.

Allied intelligence was poor. It overlooked the defensive potentialities of the *bocage* country in Normandy; it failed in the Ardennes; it bemused itself with its fable of the "National Redoubt." Despite its many accomplishments, the Allied logistical system lacked flexibility to provide support for the pursuit after the breakout. On the highest levels, Allied psychological warfare was a dismal failure; instead of attempting to split Hitler and the German people, it drove them together by schemes such as the Morgenthau Plan to convert Germany into an agrarian state. Finally, Americans as a nation were only gradually awakening to the stark reality that cessation of armed conflict does not end war, but that war as an instrument of policy has many forms.

THE WAR IN
WESTERN EUROPE

ALLIED OCCUPATION ZONES

SCALE OF MILES
0   50   100

North Africa played an important role in the war. It was the only area, other than the British Isles, from which the Western Allies could approach the German-controlled continent. Its possession was necessary for the control of the Mediterranean, the vital Suez Canal, and the Middle East (Turkey, Syria, Palestine, Trans-Jordan, Arabia, Iraq, and Iran) with its oil. But Germany, though evincing some interest in operations in this area (see text, maps 18-22), eventually turned toward Russia in 1941 and relegated the Mediterranean to a secondary role until too late.

After the fall of France, the disposition of the French fleet became a major concern of the British. Hitler, in not demanding the surrender of this fleet, placed a strain on Franco-British relations. Britain was determined that the French fleet must not join the Axis navies and, after confused diplomatic dealings with Vichy France, decided to take positive action. Consequently, the Royal Navy interned all French warships which were in British-controlled ports and disabled many others in attacks (July, 1940) at Oran and Dakar.

Meanwhile, Mussolini, taking advantage of the weakness of British forces in East Africa, sought to expand his empire (inset) by seizing frontier posts in Kenya and Sudan and invading British Somaliland (see text, maps 18-22).

In September, 1940, the British supported an abortive attempt by De Gaulle to occupy Dakar and bring the French colonies in West and Equatorial Africa (see map 46) under the control of the embryonic Free French Forces. From these bases, it was hoped that De Gaulle could extend his authority to Algeria and Tunisia and aid the British in securing North Africa. However, the Dakar garrison, loyal to Vichy France, repelled the token landing force, and the grand scheme came to nought. September also brought the long-awaited invasion of Egypt by the Italians (this map).

Egypt was the key to British success in the Middle East. This country, a British protectorate until 1922 and thereafter virtually a sovereign state, had signed a treaty with England in 1936 pledging aid in case of war and authorizing the stationing of British troops in key areas. With the fall of France and Turkey's avowed neutrality policy, Egypt's importance became accentuated. Algeria and Syria, under Vichy control, might allow entry of Axis troops which, together with the Italians in Libya, could strike at the Suez Canal. Alexandria also became more important as a British naval base in the eastern Mediterranean; the Royal Navy alone now would have to control that sea. The small island of Malta likewise was of great strategic importance. This imposing British air and naval base, lying midway between the eastern and western entrances to the Mediterranean, dominated the air and sea passages between Italy and North Africa.

The Western Desert (center) is, in the words of German General von Ravenstein, "a tactician's paradise and a quartermaster's hell." It stretches 1,400 miles from Tripoli to Alexandria, with no major road except the coastal highway and only one major port (Benghazi) between the terminal ports of Tripoli and Alexandria. In the ensuing operations, the opposing forces, operating from the two major bases at the desert's extremities, seesawed back and forth. Thus, as one advanced and its supply line became tenuous, the other, falling back toward its base, became stronger and repelled the weakened aggressor. The terrain, ideal for the maneuver of armored forces—there is only one natural defensive position between El Agheila and El Alamein—is not the sandy waste the name implies. Except for the coastal strip, it is underlaid by limestone, while plateaus and escarpments rise farther inland. A significant characteristic of the area was that it produced nothing for the support of the armies. Though the major fighting took place along the coastal strip, the little-known British Long Range Desert Group operated in the interior —in the forbidding inner desert where the Italians had established posts and airfields.

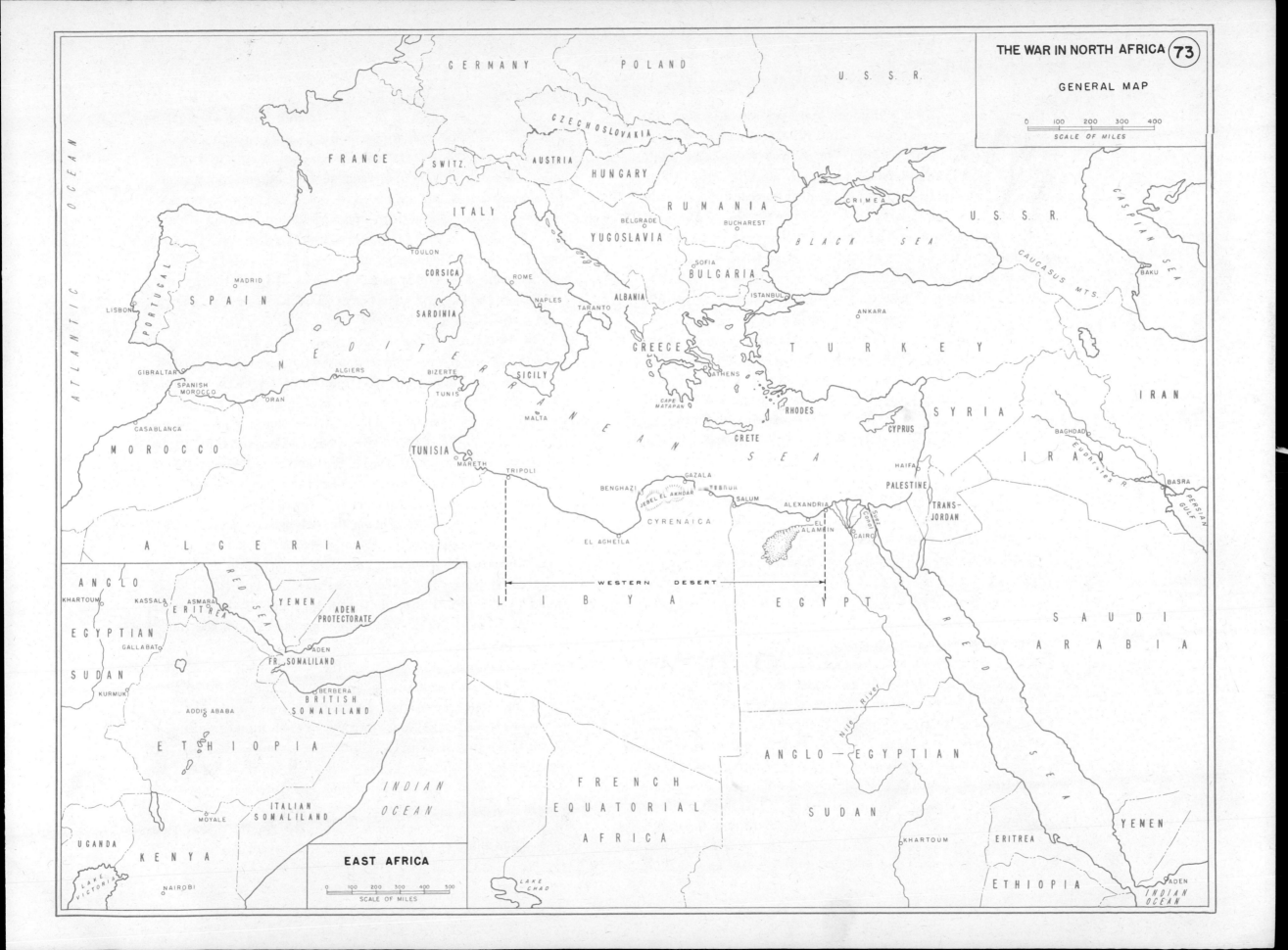

GENERAL MAP

0 100 200 300 400
SCALE OF MILES

GERMANY   POLAND   U. S. S. R.

CZECHOSLOVAKIA

FRANCE   SWITZ.   AUSTRIA   HUNGARY

ITALY   RUMANIA   CRIMEA   U. S. S. R.

BELGRADE   BUCHAREST

YUGOSLAVIA   BLACK   SEA

TOULON   SOFIA

CORSICA   ROME   BULGARIA   CAUCASUS MTS.   BAKU

NAPLES   ALBANIA   ISTANBUL

SARDINIA   TARANTO   ANKARA

GREECE   T U R K E Y

M   ATHENS   IRAN

SPAIN   BIZERTE   SICILY   CAPE   RHODES   SYRIA

MADRID   ALGIERS   MATAPAN

GIBRALTAR   TUNIS   MALTA   CRETE   CYPRUS   BAGHDAD

SPANISH   ORAN   IRAQ

MOROCCO   EUPHRATES R.

CASABLANCA   HAIFA   BASRA

TUNISIA   PALESTINE

MOROCCO   MARETH   TRIPOLI   GAZALA   HAIFA

BENGHAZI   TOBRUK   PERSIAN

JEBEL EL AKHDAR   SALUM   ALEXANDRIA   TRANS-   GULF

ALGERIA   CYRENAICA   EL   CAIRO   JORDAN

EL AGHEILA   ALAMEIN

WESTERN   DESERT

L I B Y A   E G Y P T

S A U D I

A R A B I A

F R E N C H

E Q U A T O R I A L   A N G L O - E G Y P T I A N

A F R I C A   S U D A N

LAKE   KHARTOUM   ERITREA   YEMEN

CHAD

E T H I O P I A   ADEN

INDIAN

OCEAN

PORTUGAL   LISBON   ATLANTIC OCEAN

MEDITERRANEAN SEA   RED SEA

East Africa inset

A N G L O   RED SEA   YEMEN   ADEN

KHARTOUM   KASSALA   ASMARA   PROTECTORATE

ERITREA

E G Y P T I A N   ADEN

GALLABAT   FR. SOMALILAND

S U D A N   BERBERA

KURMUK   BRITISH

ADDIS ABABA   SOMALILAND

E T H I O P I A

ITALIAN   INDIAN

MOYALE   SOMALILAND   OCEAN

UGANDA

K E N Y A

LAKE   EAST AFRICA

VICTORIA

NAIROBI   0 100 200 300 400 500

SCALE OF MILES

In the summer of 1940, although hard-pressed at home, the British struggled to reinforce General Sir Archibald P. Wavell's Middle East Command. By July, Wavell had 100,000 men with which to defend the entire Middle East. Around Bardia, in Libya (*sketch* a), Marshal Rodolfo Graziani mustered some 250,000 Italian troops and an air force several times the size of Wavell's. But the marshal, pleading a lack of tanks, transport, and artillery, would not advance into Egypt until peremptorily ordered to do so by Mussolini on 29 August.

On 13 September, five Italian divisions moved across the border against a light British screening force. The bulk of Wavell's two available divisions were at Mersa Matruh, his elected defensive position. By the 16th, Graziani had occupied Sidi Barrani, but then he decided to settle his troops in fortified camps (*dashed red circles*) stretching fifty miles from the coast to Sofafi. There was little mutual support, no depth to the position, and a twenty-mile gap between the two southernmost camps. Mussolini, planning to attack Greece and wanting the British fully committed in Africa, urged a continuation of the advance, but Graziani, constructing roads and pipelines eastward, opined that this would not be feasible before December. The discussions were interrupted by Wavell's seizure of the initiative.

Since September, he had been planning this counterstroke, but the necessity for sending aid to the Greeks in November had delayed an attack. By 9 December, however, he was ready. The Western Desert Force, commanded by Lt. Gen. Richard O'Connor, attacked through the gap in the Italian defenses and one day later was in Sidi Barrani. Surprised, cut off, and demoralized, some 38,000 Italians surrendered. By 16 December, Graziani had been driven from Egypt. Pausing to reorganize and resupply his forces, O'Connor moved westward. Subjected to land, sea, and air attack, heavily garrisoned Bardia and Tobruk surrendered on the dates shown. Maintaining relentless pressure, O'Connor struck the remaining Italians at Mekili and Derna and boldly sent his armor across the unreconnoitered desert to block their retreat at Beda Fomm. Graziani's troops, after trying unsuccessfully to break out of the trap, surrendered on 7 February. The British captured 130,000 men, 845 guns, and 380 tanks; their losses were 1,928.

Wavell now wanted to drive on Tripoli, but was ordered to hold near Benghazi with minimum forces and dispatch maximum support to the Greeks. He left only one green armored brigade and an infantry division in Cyrenaica. This seemed enough under the circumstances, but he had discounted German intervention. Mussolini, facing disaster in Libya and disappointed in Albania, now reluctantly accepted Hitler's offer of two divisions. The Luftwaffe had already begun operations from Sicily and, by 1 March, had neutralized Benghazi as a port. General Irwin Rommel and part of his Deutsches Afrika Corps (D.A.K.) arrived in Tripoli during March.

On 24 March, Rommel launched a heavy raid against El Agheila (*sketch* b, *bottom left*) and, upon discovering how weak the British were, boldly pressed the advance. By 11 April, he had driven the British, except for the Tobruk garrison, out of Libya. This advance by the German 5th Division and elements of two Italian divisions, characterized by dynamic and forceful leadership on Rommel's part, resulted in the capture of General O'Connor, the destruction of most of the British armored brigade, and consternation in Cairo and Berlin. (OKH was aghast at Rommel's disregard of orders to remain on the defensive.) Wavell rushed reinforcements westward as Egypt's defense took priority over Greece. Meanwhile, Rommel, launching a hasty and ill-prepared attack on Tobruk (10-14 April), received a nasty rebuff. Reinforced by the 15th Panzer Division, he renewed the attack on the 30th and again failed. Meanwhile, his forces occupied Bardia and Salum.

Wavell, under pressure to strike back, made an abortive attack in May and another, employing two divisions, on 15 June. His second attack was repulsed with heavy tank losses. Here, for the first time, the British were introduced to Rommel's skillful use of antitank gun screens, including the dreaded 88-mm. gun. Wavell, plagued with problems everywhere (Crete, Syria, Iraq, and Libya), had mounted the attack too hurriedly. His troops were ill-prepared, his equipment inferior to that of Rommel, and his plan encouraged piecemeal commitment. The defeat shattered Churchill's confidence in him and led to his relief and transfer to India in July.

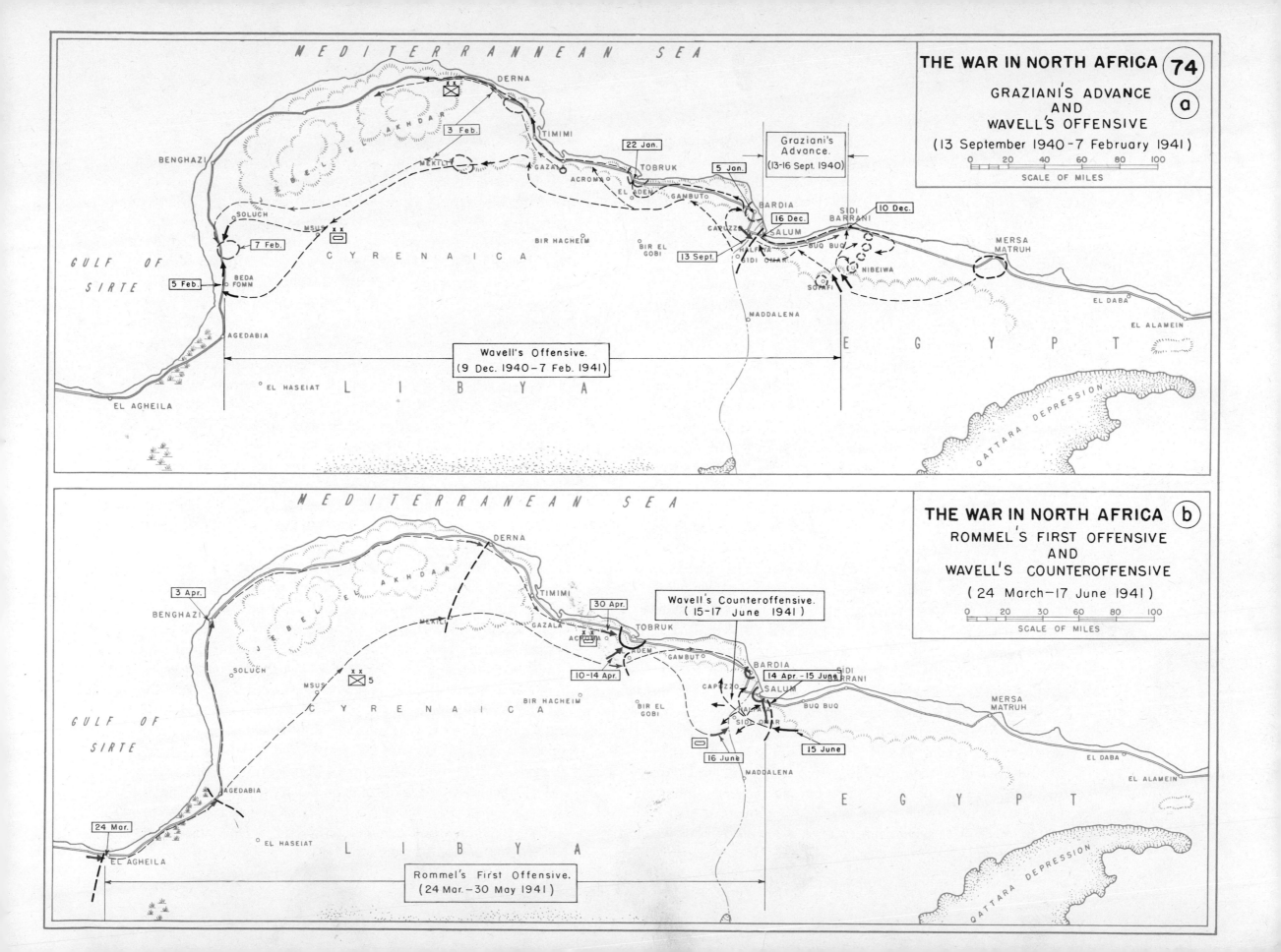

THE WAR IN NORTH AFRICA 74

a

GRAZIANI'S ADVANCE
AND
WAVELL'S OFFENSIVE

(13 September 1940 – 7 February 1941)

SCALE OF MILES
0   20   40   60   80   100

MEDITERRANNEAN SEA

DERNA

DJEBEL EL AKHDAR

3 Feb.

TIMIMI

22 Jan.

BENGHAZI

Graziani's
Advance.
(13-16 Sept. 1940)

MEKILI

GAZALA

ACROMA

TOBRUK

5 Jan.

EL ADEM

GAMBUT

BARDIA

10 Dec.

SOLUCH

MSUS

16 Dec.

CAPUZZO

SALUM

SIDI
BARRANI

BIR HACHEIM

BIR EL
GOBI

HALFAYA

BUQ BUQ

MERSA
MATRUH

7 Feb.

C Y R E N A I C A

SIDI OMAR

13 Sept.

NIBEIWA

5 Feb.

BEDA
FOMM

SOFAFI

EL DABA

GULF OF
SIRTE

AGEDABIA

MADDALENA

EL ALAMEIN

Wavell's Offensive.
(9 Dec. 1940 – 7 Feb. 1941)

E G Y P T

EL HASEIAT

L I B Y A

EL AGHEILA

QATTARA DEPRESSION

THE WAR IN NORTH AFRICA **b**

ROMMEL'S FIRST OFFENSIVE
AND
WAVELL'S COUNTEROFFENSIVE

(24 March – 17 June 1941)

SCALE OF MILES
0   20   30   60   80   100

MEDITERRANEAN SEA

DERNA

3 Apr.

DJEBEL EL AKHDAR

TIMIMI

30 Apr.

Wavell's Counteroffensive.
(15-17 June 1941)

BENGHAZI

MEKILI

GAZALA

ACROMA

TOBRUK

ADEM

GAMBUT

BARDIA

SIDI
BARRANI

SOLUCH

MSUS

XX 5

10-14 Apr.

14 Apr. – 15 June

CAPUZZO

SALUM

BUQ BUQ

BIR HACHEIM

BIR EL
GOBI

SIDI OMAR

MERSA
MATRUH

C Y R E N A I C A

16 June

15 June

EL DABA

GULF OF
SIRTE

AGEDABIA

MADDALENA

EL ALAMEIN

24 Mar.

EL HASEIAT

E G Y P T

L I B Y A

EL AGHEILA

Rommel's First Offensive.
(24 Mar. – 30 May 1941)

QATTARA DEPRESSION

General Sir Claude Auchinleck succeeded Wavell in July. Though the Defence Committee in London wanted an immediate offensive to help Russia, the state of training, lack of equipment, and problems in Syria and Iraq precluded such action until November. By then, the forces in North Africa (now reorganized as the Eighth Army under General Alan Cunningham) comprised seven divisions, some 700 tanks—mostly inferior to German models—and about 1,000 operational aircraft.

Auchinleck's plan (*sketch* a) visualized an advance through Maddalena by the armor-heavy XXX Corps, designed to draw Rommel's panzers south, while the XIII Corps encircled the Salum and Bardia garrisons and then drove to the relief of Tobruk. Exploitation to recover Cyrenaica would follow.

Meanwhile, Rommel, appreciating the danger of his position in the Bardia-Salum area should the British launch simultaneous attacks from Tobruk and Egypt, readied plans to take Tobruk. (Capture of its port facilities also would improve his logistical support.) But, with the Germans fully engaged in Russia, Rommel could not expect additional troops and supplies. Concurrently, British air and naval power began to reassert themselves in the Mediterranean. Thus, as November neared, the situation of Rommel's command (now called Panzer Group Afrika) steadily worsened. When Auchinleck attacked, Rommel had three German divisions (two panzer and one motorized), a two-division Italian motorized corps (Ariete and Trieste), and four Italian infantry divisions. He had 414 tanks (including 154 Italian) and 320 aircraft (including 200 Italian).

The British attack achieved tactical surprise, but Rommel, reacting quickly, committed most of his German troops against the XXX Corps. The battle raged for two weeks south of Tobruk in a series of small independent actions, with the British employing armor piecemeal. The Tobruk garrison broke through the investing Italian divisions on the 21st (*not shown*), but German troops soon sealed off the penetration. By the 23d, Cunningham's armor had been badly mauled, and he contemplated retreat. Auchinleck would not sanction such action, and three days later replaced Cunningham with Maj. Gen. Neil Ritchie.

Meanwhile, on 24 November, in an attempt to cause a British panic, Rommel led most of the panzers on a raid as shown. It did not accomplish its purpose, and when the British renewed the attack toward Tobruk, the German armor had to backtrack. On the 27th, the New Zealand Division linked up with the Tobruk garrison which had again broken out. Now Rommel bent all his efforts to restoring the ring around the port. By 1 December, the New Zealanders had been chopped to pieces and the investment restored. But the reinforced XXX Corps was applying pressure on the Italians at Bir El Gobi, and—though for two more days Rommel tried to aid the Bardia-Salum defenders—on 4 December he withdrew all of his panzers to the 1-7 December line. Failing to defeat the XXX Corps armor in the next two days, and fearful of being enveloped from the south, he began a retirement to the Gazala line on the 7th. Threatened with envelopment there, he withdrew on the 15th and was back at El Agheila on the 31st. By 17 January, the Bardia-Salum defenders had surrendered.

There was a lull in the action as both sides refitted and replenished supply stocks—Rommel, being closer to his base, now had the advantage. On 5 January, a sizable Axis convoy arrived at Tripoli; on the 21st, Rommel attacked (*sketch* b). The Eighth Army was caught off balance and forced to withdraw to the Gazala–Bir Hacheim line, abandoning large stocks of supplies which helped sustain Rommel's advance to Gazala. For four months, the opposing forces faced each other on this line, while they tried to gather strength. Finally, in May, aware that the British build-up was exceeding his own, Rommel attacked and drove the British from the Gazala–Bir Hacheim position. Reaching Tobruk on the 19th, he rapidly organized an assault and, by the 21st, had forced the garrison to surrender. Rommel, rewarded with a promotion to field marshal, now boldly continued the pursuit into Egypt. Having captured immense stores at Tobruk, he believed that he could destroy the Eighth Army. But Auchinleck's personal intervention and exemplary leadership, and a typically tenacious stand at Mersa Matruh, saved the battered British. By 7 July, both armies had arrived at El Alamein, exhausted and in need of reorganization.

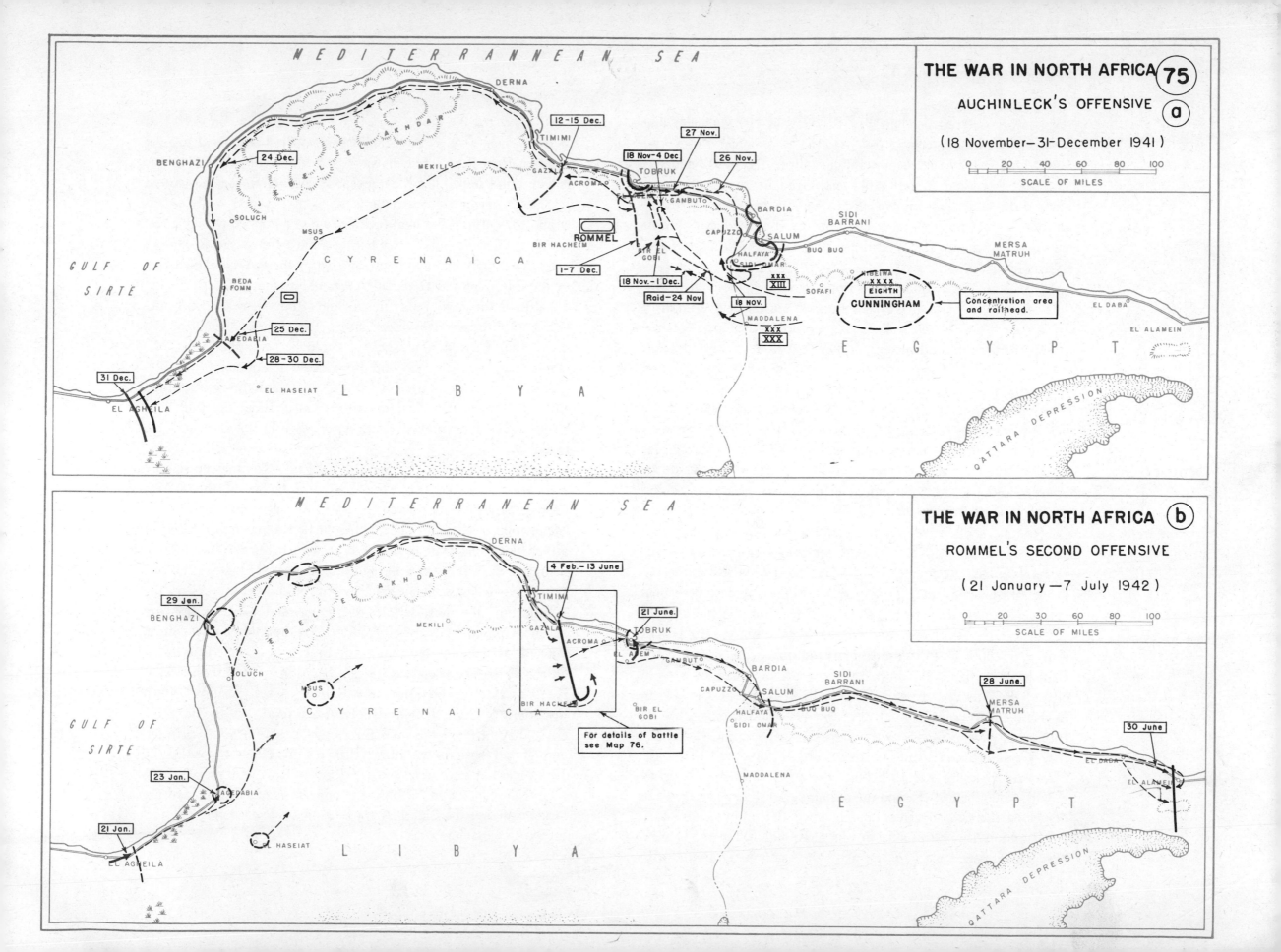

THE WAR IN NORTH AFRICA 75

AUCHINLECK'S OFFENSIVE a

(18 November – 31 December 1941)

0 20 40 60 80 100
SCALE OF MILES

THE WAR IN NORTH AFRICA b

ROMMEL'S SECOND OFFENSIVE

(21 January – 7 July 1942)

0 20 30 60 80 100
SCALE OF MILES

Axis forces entered the battle at the Gazala–Bir Hacheim line with 560 tanks (240 were Italian); the British had about 700 (an additional 200 were brought up before the battle ended). The 200 American Grant tanks employed by the British outgunned the German armor, while the Italian tanks were virtually useless in battle. Rommel's salvation, as it turned out, lay in superior tactics and the skillful use of his fifty-odd dual-purpose 88-mm. guns.

Opposing forces and dispositions are shown here in detail. The Italian XXI and X Corps contained a total of five infantry divisions, but these, as well as the motorized Italian elements, were considerably understrength. The British 1st and 32d Tank Brigades, equipped with slow-moving "I" tanks, were designed to support the infantry divisions. Ritchie's position consisted of a series of strong points ("boxes"), anchored on the south by the Bir Hacheim fortress. The whole line was interwoven with extensive mine fields (approximately 500,000 mines were in the area outlined by the blue mine symbol [*circles connected by lines*]), and backed by armored elements concentrated behind the open southern flank.

Rommel's offensive was initiated on 26 May with a frontal attack by the X and XXI Corps, ostensibly supported by panzer elements which Rommel had detached to deceive Ritchie as to the location of his main attack. Early in the evening, he sent a motorized column toward Gazala as if to reinforce the assault, but after dark all of these mobile elements rejoined their parent units. At 2200, he started all of his motorized units toward the British south flank. By morning, these forces (Rommel's main effort) had moved around Bir Hacheim—part of the Ariete Division turned off to attack that fortress—and engaged the 3d Indian Brigade, which slowly withdrew. After a short rest, the Italo-German force swung north toward Acroma and the coast. The 90th Division was to protect the right flank by seizing El Adem, while the D.A.K. and the remainder of the Ariete Division dispersed the British armor and isolated the infantry divisions.

By noon, the 90th Division was in El Adem, but the D.A.K. was still engaged with the British 7th Armored Division, with both sides taking heavy losses. By nightfall, the panzers had worked their way to the Knightsbridge–El Adem road against the two British armored divisions, while the 90th Division was isolated and under heavy attack at El Adem. Rommel renewed his attack the next day, pulling the 90th Division westward to support his armor, but again Ritchie's tanks stopped the advance. By now, German tank losses had become serious, and Rommel's extended supply line was being harried by the RAF and elements of the 7th Armored Division. Accordingly, the X Corps having penetrated the mine fields meanwhile, Rommel realistically decided to withdraw his armor into a "bridgehead" (*shaded red area*—the "Cauldron"), where it could be resupplied while the penetration was widened and Bir Hacheim reduced. The withdrawal was begun on the 30th, but heavy tank fighting continued for two days around Knightsbridge. On 1 June, the 90th and Trieste Divisions moved south (*not shown*) to surround Bir Hacheim.

After ten days of the hardest fighting—Rommel personally supervised some of the assaults—the survivors of the valiant French Brigade surrendered, a few having escaped to the west. Meanwhile, as Rommel had anticipated, Ritchie had refused to attack the weak Italian XXI Corps with his armor for fear of being taken in the rear and flank by the D.A.K. Instead, he had continued to fritter away his armor in piecemeal attacks on the "Cauldron," the most serious one being made and repulsed on 5 June. Consequently, when Rommel, his supply line now secure, massed his rehabilitated armor and broke out of the "Cauldron" on the 11th (the 90th and Trieste Divisions joined the attack), Ritchie's outnumbered forces withdrew to the position shown just south of the Knightsbridge–El Adem road. For the next two days, they held off the Axis forces while the 1st South African and 50th Divisions withdrew. British tank losses rose—by the 13th, Ritchie had only sixty-five tanks left—but most of his infantry escaped. On 13 June, the panzers reached the coast; the battle ended as the Eighth Army streamed eastward and Rommel turned toward Tobruk.

Note: On this map, lower right, the German 90th Division should be shown as an infantry division.

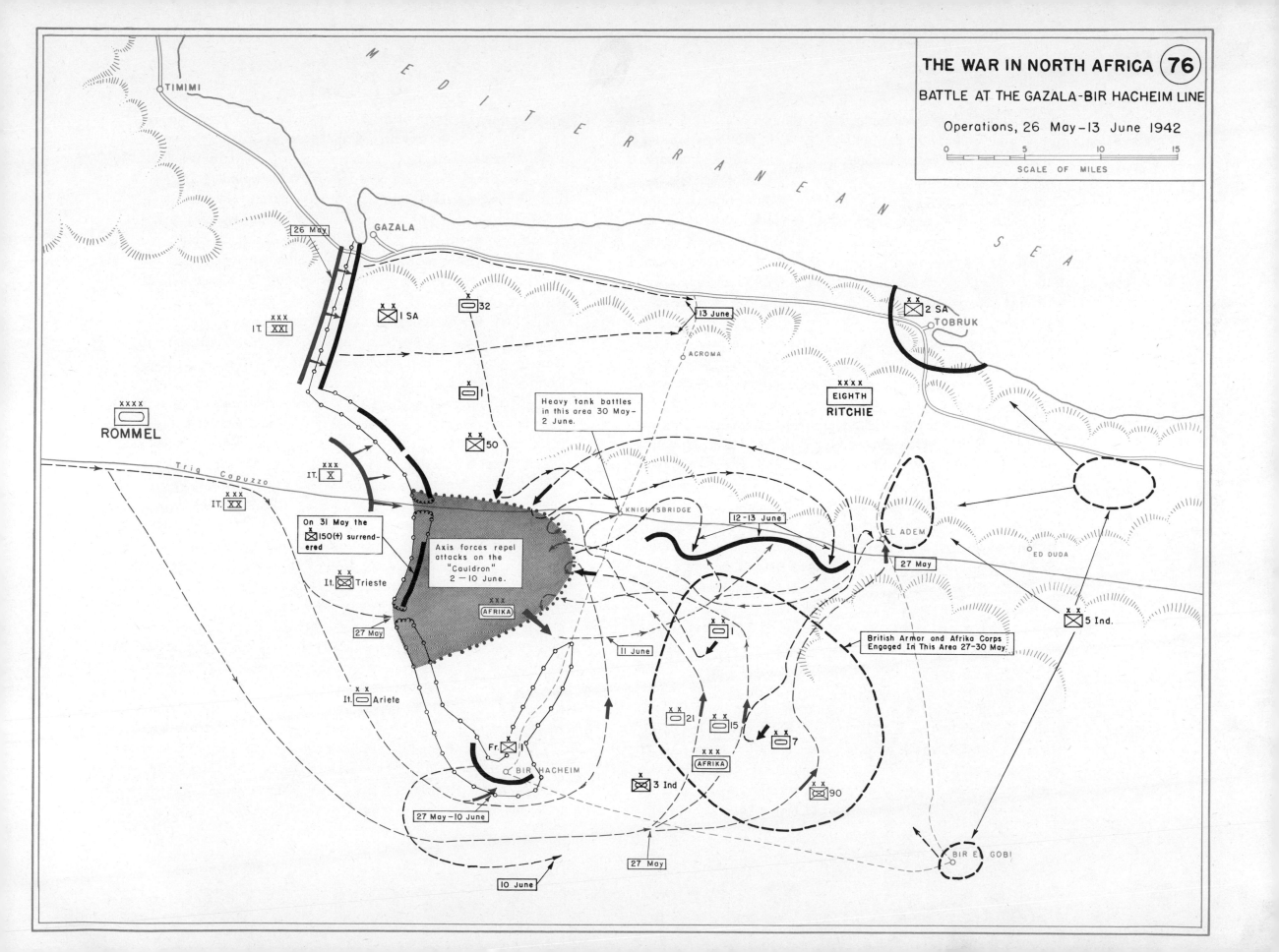

0   5   10   15
SCALE OF MILES

MEDITERRANEAN SEA

TIMIMI

26 May

GAZALA

IT. XXX XXI

XX 1 SA

XX 32

XX 2 SA
TOBRUK

ACROMA

XXXX
ROMMEL

XX 1

EIGHTH
RITCHIE

Trig Capuzzo

IT. XXX X

XX 50

Heavy tank battles
in this area 30 May–
2 June.

IT. XXX XX

On 31 May the
XX 150(†) surrend-
ered

Axis forces repel
attacks on the
"Cauldron"
2 – 10 June.

KNIGHTSBRIDGE

12-13 June

EL ADEM

27 May

ED DUDA

IT. XX Trieste

XXX
AFRIKA

11 June

British Armor and Afrika Corps
Engaged In This Area 27-30 May.

27 May

XX 5 Ind.

IT. XX Ariete

XX 1

XX 21   XX 15   XX 7

Fr. XX 1

BIR HACHEIM

XXX
AFRIKA

XX 3 Ind   XX 90

27 May–10 June

27 May

BIR EL GOBI

10 June

During July, the opposing forces at El Alamein exchanged feeler thrusts and limited attacks. Neither side was able to gain an advantage. By 1 August, Auchinleck had admitted a stalemate. Though the July battles had cost him 13,000 casualties, he had captured 7,000 enemy troops, including about 1,000 Germans. With the arrival of reinforcements, Auchinleck was urged to attack again; but, needing time to acclimatize his troops, he demurred. As a result, on 13 August, the gifted team of General Harold R. L. G. Alexander and Lt. Gen. Bernard L. Montgomery arrived to take over the Middle East Command and Eighth Army, respectively.

To Rommel, the worsening logistical situation was of more ominous purport than the July stalemate. As the Germans in Russia drove toward Stalingrad, Rommel's forces in Africa and Luftwaffe elements in the Mediterranean received less and less support. At the same time, Britain poured supplies and reinforcements into Africa, Malta grew stronger, the RAF ranged almost unchallenged in the sky, and Axis shipping en route to Africa stood only one chance in four of getting through. Even Rommel despaired of success; but the Suez was too tempting, and Hitler absolutely forbade a withdrawal. The OKW staff, completely ignorant of the true conditions, blandly urged Rommel to attack. He finally agreed, but with the stipulation that he must have 6,000 tons of fuel. This was promised—only a fraction of it ever arrived.

Having received several new units during July, Rommel reorganized his army in late August as shown here. His troops, particularly the Italians, had undergone some rehabilitation, and he had 440 tanks (240 of them Italian). Montgomery had immediately available the forces shown, though more were near Alexandria in rehabilitation centers. He had 480 tanks for the battle. His infantry occupied the position shown (*31 August line*), which was well fortified except for the section in the south (*dashed blue line*). Here, it was heavily mined and screened by the 7th Armored Division. Expecting Rommel to seek a penetration in the weak southern portion of his line, Montgomery defended Alam Halfa Ridge in great strength to stop the almost certain subsequent envelopment toward the coast. On the ridge, he dug in two tank brigades—which he considered too green for mobile warfare—and positioned a third farther north in a central position.

Rommel's plan was strikingly similar to that he used at Bir Hacheim. Apprised of the British weakness in the south, he launched his main attack there about midnight on 30 August; diversionary attacks were also made along the coast and at Ruweisat Ridge, the second achieving some success before being halted by a British counterattack at dawn. Rommel expected to breach the mine fields quickly and to have his armor east of Gabala by dawn; then it would turn north, bypass most of Alam Halfa Ridge to the east, and strike for the coast. Meanwhile, part of the Italian armor and the 90th Division would make a shorter penetration, turn north at Deir El Muhafid, and protect the corridor thus created. But the mine fields proved unexpectedly difficult, and it was not until 0930 that the D.A.K. was ready to drive east. By then it was under heavy air attack. Having lost his chance for surprise, Rommel considered calling off the attack, but finally decided to make the shallower envelopment shown. Fighting the withdrawing 7th Division and harassed by air power, the panzers did not reach Alam Halfa Ridge until late afternoon. Here, they were stopped by the 22d Tank Brigade. Rommel was now short of fuel, and his troops were harried all night by air attacks. He therefore ordered only local attacks for 1 September; these, made by the 15th Panzer Division, were easily stopped as Montgomery moved more armor to the ridge nose. On 2 September, the D.A.K. began to withdraw. Montgomery, fearing one of Rommel's traps, did not pursue, but did order the New Zealand 2d Division to attack on the 3d; this assault was a costly failure.

Rommel's withdrawal came to a halt on 7 September (*lower center, solid blue line*). Montgomery, feeling that the Eighth Army was not yet ready for the decisive showdown, was content to let his foe withdraw to nurse his wounds.

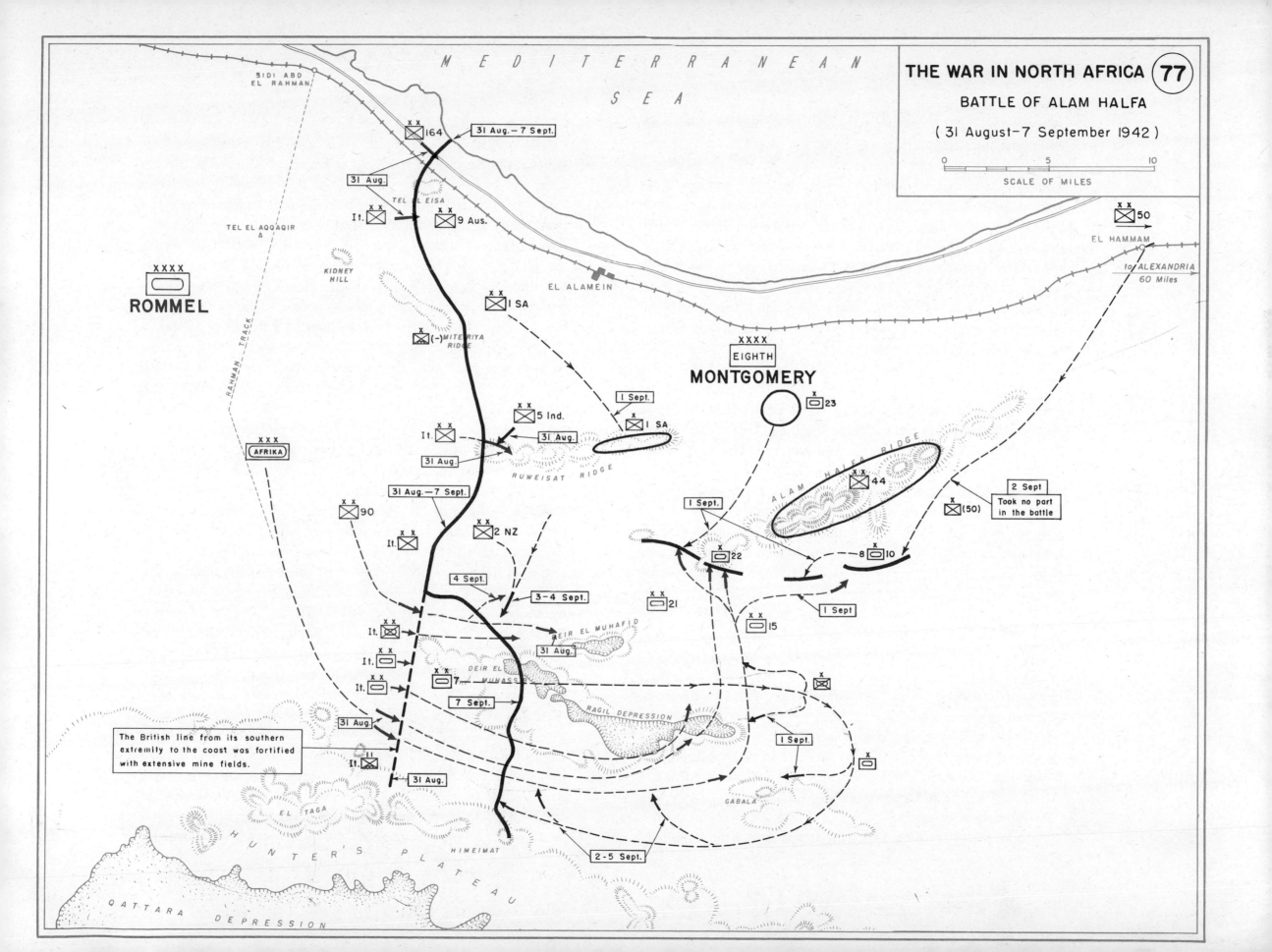

MEDITERRANEAN
SEA

0   5   10
SCALE OF MILES

SIDI ABD
EL RAHMAN

XX 164   31 Aug. – 7 Sept.

31 Aug.

TEL EL AQQAQIR △

TEL EL EISA

It. XX   XX 9 Aus.

XXXX
ROMMEL

KIDNEY
HILL

XX 50
EL HAMMAM

to ALEXANDRIA
60 Miles

RAHMAN TRACK

XX 1 SA

XX (-) MITEIRIYA RIDGE

EL ALAMEIN

XXXX
EIGHTH
MONTGOMERY

X 23

XXX
AFRIKA

XX 5 Ind.

It. XX

1 Sept.

X 1 SA

31 Aug.

31 Aug.

RUWEISAT RIDGE

ALAM HALFA RIDGE

XX 44

2 Sept
Took no part
in the battle

X (50)

XX 90

31 Aug. – 7 Sept.

It. XX

XX 2 NZ

1 Sept.

X 22

8 X 10

X 21

4 Sept.   3–4 Sept.

It. XX

X 15

1 Sept

It. X

DEIR EL MUHAFID

31 Aug.

It. X

DEIR EL MUNASSIB

X 7

7 Sept.

RAGIL DEPRESSION

X

7 Sept.

31 Aug.

1 Sept.

The British line from its southern
extremity to the coast was fortified
with extensive mine fields.

It. XX

31 Aug.

GABALA

X

EL TAGA

31 Aug.

HIMEIMAT

2–5 Sept.

HUNTER'S PLATEAU

QATTARA   DEPRESSION

After Alam Halfa, Montgomery resumed his program of training, equipping, and revitalizing the Eighth Army. The troops' confidence returned quickly under their dynamic leader's influence. Meanwhile, supplies continued to pour in, new Sherman tanks arrived from America, huge forward supply dumps were established, and elaborate deception plans were implemented. Again, pressure built up for an attack. Allied landings were scheduled for early November in Algeria and Morocco (*see map 81*), and —to impress the French—it was considered desirable to have decisively defeated Rommel before then; but Montgomery insisted upon an adequate period of preparation. Finally, on 6 October, he issued orders for the attack on the 23d. These orders prescribed a main attack by the XXX Corps in the north to drive two corridors (*this map, bounded by dashed blue lines*) through Rommel's mine fields, while the XIII Corps simultaneously launched a secondary attack in the south to deceive Axis forces and hold the 21st Panzer Division in that area. The X-Armored Corps would pass through the corridors created by the XXX Corps and block enemy armor, while the XXX Corps eliminated the Axis infantry. Then it would destroy Rommel's panzers. Probably because he questioned the capability of his armored units in a mobile, fluid situation, he chose this conservative plan—rather than seeking out the panzers at once in an attempt to destroy them, without the costly subsidiary infantry attacks.

Rommel used the period from 7 September to 23 October to build defenses for the inevitable attack. Logistical support continued to be inadequate, while Montgomery built up a two-to-one preponderance in men, tanks, artillery, and air power. Rommel's deep, static defenses were held by the Italian infantry divisions, stiffened by German paratroops, except in the vital coastal sector which was defended by German infantry. On 22 September, a very sick Rommel flew to Germany for rest and medical treatment. In the hospital when Montgomery struck, he at once returned to Africa, arriving on 25 October.

The British offensive opened at 2140, 23 October, with a tremendous artillery preparation, followed twenty minutes later by the infantry assault. The XXX Corps' effort was made by four divisions on a seven-mile front and was accompanied by feints along the coastal road and at Ruweisat Ridge. Four hours later, the X Corps armor moved into the expanding corridors. Heavy fighting continued all night as the Axis troops, recovering from their initial shock, concentrated artillery fire on the corridors and struck back with the 15th Panzer Division. In the south, the XIII Corps achieved moderate gains during the night and held the 21st Panzer Division on that flank. By morning, Montgomery's troops had made gains as shown (*dotted red lines*), but the armor had not reached the hoped-for blocking positions.

Now began the "dogfight," as Montgomery characterized the ensuing week of bitter fighting designed to destroy Rommel's infantry. Meager gains were made on 24-25 October. When the 50th Division attack (24 October) collapsed, and it became evident that gains in the extreme south were too costly, Montgomery ordered the XIII Corps to suspend its attacks (25 October). The same day, he switched his main effort from the corridors to the 9th Australian Division sector, but ordered the 1st Armored Division to fight its way beyond Kidney Hill. Throughout the period 26-29 October, the Australians made good progress, but the armor, though finally taking Kidney Hill, met violent opposition as Rommel repeatedly counterattacked. On the night of the 26th, he moved the 21st Panzer Division north for an attack the next day. Montgomery countered by moving the 7th Armored Division north, and withdrew the 1st Armored and New Zealand 2d Divisions into reserve, preparatory to regrouping for his final "breakout." During the "dogfight," Rommel's tank losses mounted rapidly as, desperately short of fuel and under constant overwhelming aerial attack, he was forced to commit armor piecemeal.

On 29 October, learning of the concentration of the 90th Division near Sidi Abd El Rahman, Montgomery elected to make his breakout in the Kidney Hill area instead of along the coast road. While he readied his forces, the Australians reached the coast (31 October). Aided by 21st Panzer Division counterattacks, most of the German 164th Division escaped encirclement.

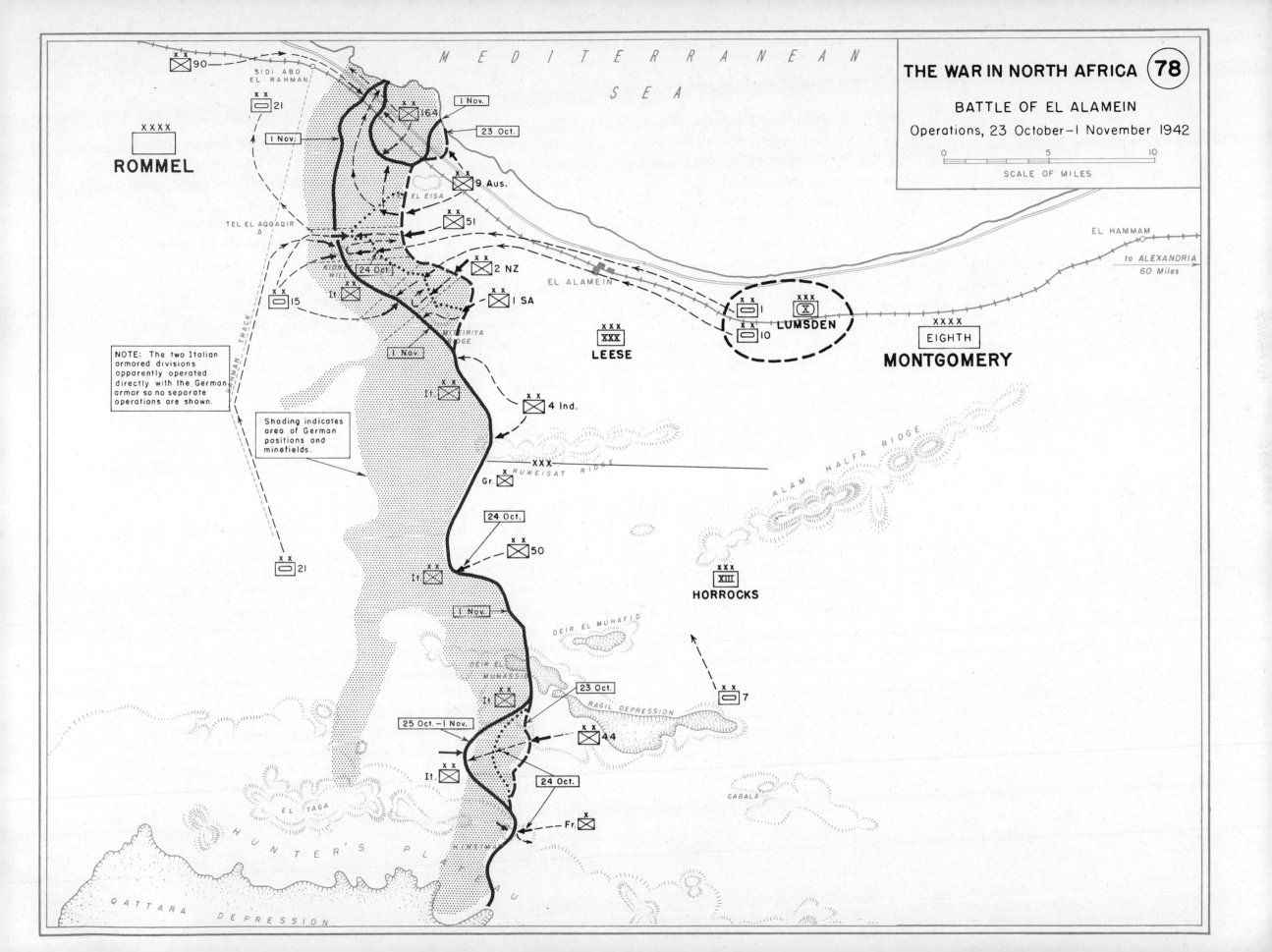

MEDITERRANEAN

SEA

XXXX

ROMMEL

XX 90
SIDI ABD EL RAHMAN

XX 21

1 Nov.

1 Nov.

XX 164
23 Oct.

XX 9 Aus.
EL EISA

TEL EL AQQAQIR

XX 51

XX 2 NZ

24 Oct.
It. XX

XX 15

XX 1 SA

1 Nov.

MITEIRIYA RIDGE

NOTE: The two Italian armored divisions apparently operated directly with the German armor so no separate operations are shown.

Shading indicates area of German positions and minefields.

It. XX

XX 4 Ind.

Gr. X RUWEISAT RIDGE

XXX

24 Oct.

XX 21

XX 50

It. XX

1 Nov.

DEIR EL MUHAFID

DEIR EL MUNASSIB

It. XX

23 Oct.

RAGIL DEPRESSION

25 Oct.–1 Nov.

XX 44

It. XX

24 Oct.

EL TAGA

GABALA

Fr. X

HUNTER'S PLATEAU

QATTARA   DEPRESSION

EL ALAMEIN

XXX
LEESE

XX 1

X
LUMSDEN

XX 10

XXX

XXXX
EIGHTH

MONTGOMERY

XXX
XIII
HORROCKS

XX 7

EL HAMMAM

to ALEXANDRIA
60 Miles

ALAM HALFA RIDGE

The final phase of the battle began at 0100, 2 November. Montgomery's plan provided for an infantry penetration of the Axis lines just north of Kidney Hill, to be followed by armor which would fan out into the open country and complete the destruction of Rommel's army. He selected this location because most of Rommel's German formations were now along the coast, leaving weaker, less mobile, predominantly Italian units farther south.

The stalwart New Zealand 2d Division, rested and reinforced since its earlier, costly action, led the attack behind a heavy rolling barrage. By dawn, a new corridor had been carved out, and the supporting 9th Armored Brigade had established a "bridgehead" (*dotted red line*) across Rahman Track. But in attempting to expand it, the brigade ran into another of Rommel's skillfully placed antitank screens, suffered 75 per cent casualties, yet managed to hold the salient. Meanwhile, the 1st Armored Division debouched from the bridgehead and collided head-on with the 15th Panzer Division. A violent tank battle ensued for the rest of the day in which elements of the 21st Panzer Division and Italian armor joined. Rommel finally sealed off the penetration, but the attrition rate was reaching catastrophic proportions for the Axis. When the day ended, the D.A.K. had only thirty-five serviceable tanks. Equally critical was the fuel and ammunition situation, which restricted Rommel's freedom of action. Lastly, his highly effective antitank guns were slowly being eliminated.

That night (2 November), acknowledging defeat, Rommel decided to withdraw. The Italians on the southern front pulled back (*action not shown*) to the line occupied before the battle of Alam Halfa (*see map 77, dashed blue line*) during the night. But early on the 3d, Rommel made the mistake of asking Hitler for freedom of action; in the meantime, he commenced withdrawing infantry units from the line on either side of the British penetration when it became obvious that Montgomery was not pressing his advantage. At 1330, he received the unequivocal answer: stand fast.

Dejected, he ordered the withdrawal halted; but by now confusion reigned in the rear on the clogged coastal road as British aerial attacks took their toll—few of the withdrawn Italians went back into line. Meanwhile, the Australian 9th Division mopped up remnants of the 164th Division in the coastal pocket (*this map*).

On the night of 3 November, Montgomery, unwilling to continue his breakout efforts in the established bridgehead, ordered an attack astride Kidney Hill. It was launched just before dawn, 4 November, by the 51st and Indian 4th Divisions and achieved a clean breakthrough. (The area had been partially evacuated in Rommel's abortive withdrawal the previous day.) Montgomery poured the 7th and 10th Armored Divisions through the gap and diverted the 1st Armored and New Zealand 2d Divisions to this sector also. The full onslaught fell upon the Ariete Division, recently moved from behind the southern front; by midafternoon, it had been surrounded and destroyed while the D.A.K.'s futile attempts to come to its assistance were repulsed.

At 1530, in defiance of Hitler's edict, Rommel ordered a withdrawal. The next day, permission to withdraw arrived from the Führer, two days too late. The Italian divisions in the south, now isolated, were abandoned; in the next few days they were rounded up by XIII Corps. The remainder of the beaten army struck out westward on a broad front near the coast road, on foot or in whatever vehicles would run. British armor started west that evening, but was soon halted, Montgomery apparently being unwilling to risk a night pursuit. The next day he regrouped while Rommel continued to move westward. Similarly, the results of the RAF's attacks on the withdrawing Axis forces were disappointing.

The Battle of El Alamein was over; British arms had removed the Axis threat to the Suez with finality. This battle, in conjunction with the German failure at Stalingrad, stopped the German march of conquest.

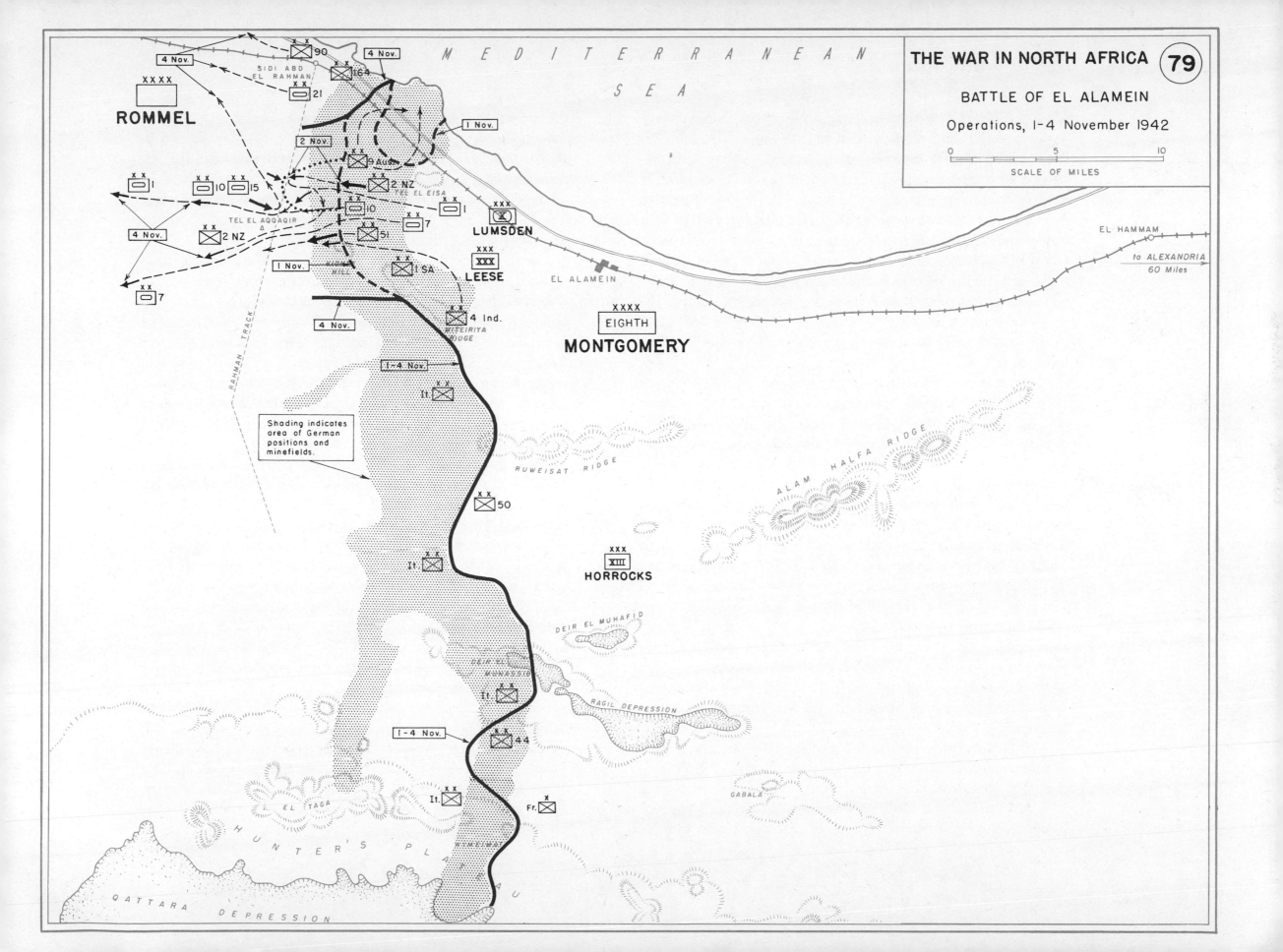

MEDITERRANEAN SEA

ROMMEL

SIDI ABD EL RAHMAN

4 Nov.

4 Nov.

1 Nov.

2 Nov.

9 Aus.

TEL EL EISA

2 NZ

TEL EL AQQAQIR

10

51

7

1

LUMSDEN

KIDNEY HILL

1 SA

LEESE

2 NZ

4 Nov.

7

1 Nov.

4 Ind.

MITEIRIYA RIDGE

EL ALAMEIN

to ALEXANDRIA 60 Miles

EL HAMMAM

EIGHTH

MONTGOMERY

1-4 Nov.

It.

Shading indicates area of German positions and minefields.

RUWEISAT RIDGE

ALAM HALFA RIDGE

50

XIII

HORROCKS

DEIR EL MUHAFID

It.

DEIR EL MUNASSIB

It.

RAGIL DEPRESSION

GABALA

1-4 Nov.

44

EL TAGA

It.

Fr.

HUNTER'S PLATEAU

QATTARA DEPRESSION

SCALE OF MILES
0   5   10

After the halt for regroupment on 5 November, Montgomery began a determined pursuit, with the X Corps (1st and 7th Armored Divisions, New Zealand 2d Division) acting as the encircling force and the XXX Corps applying direct pressure. In spite of the respite granted by Montgomery's initial delay, the Axis retreat bordered on chaos. The coast road was choked with Italian and German transport, and the battered German divisions (most of the Italian units had been destroyed or captured) had considerable difficulty organizing for any kind of a defense. Allied air attacks compounded the confusion—though, considering the lack of opposition and some of the defiles Rommel's troops had to traverse, the air arm seems to have lacked proficiency in low-level attacks.

On the 5th, the New Zealand 2d Division almost blocked the retreat at Fuka. An even greater opportunity came two days later at Charing Cross–Mersa Matruh, where the X Corps armor, already to the west of Rommel's combat elements, frustratingly found itself bogged down on the desert trails when supply columns were immobilized by torrential rains. The Germans on the better coastal road were able to keep moving, even though, on the 6th, the 21st Panzer Division—for lack of fuel—was forced to form a hedgehog and withstand heavy British attacks east of Mersa Matruh. Its few remaining tanks were finally abandoned, and the division, using wheeled transport, fought its way westward to join the other divisions in the position at Mersa Matruh.

Montgomery now gave up hopes of quickly trapping Rommel and organized for a long race. From this date, his operations were governed by three factors: Rommel must be given no rest; forward airfields must be established along the route of advance (*small blue circles*); and ports must be opened to sustain the pursuit logistically.

On 8 November, the British continued the pursuit, paring down their encircling force to one division (7th Armored) to ease the supply problem. That same date, Allied forces were landing in Algeria and French Morocco (*see map 82*). On the 11th, Axis forces were ejected from Egypt, and Rommel refueled with his last stocks in Cyrenaica; for the next two weeks, he depended upon aerial resupply. The New Zealand 2d Division paused at Bardia to regroup, but British armor pressed westward, the 7th Armored Division plunging across the neck of Cyrenaica in an attempt to get behind Rommel at Agedabia (*this map*). The effort failed—again, partially because of rain—and Montgomery closed up to his foe's old position east of El Agheila.

Here, the pursuit stopped while the British built up their forward supply stocks and concentrated on opening the port of Benghazi. Montgomery brought two fresh divisions forward to augment the elite "Desert Rats" (7th Armored), and assigned continuation of the pursuit to the XXX Corps. Rommel, too, was finally receiving some supplies, equipment, and a few replacements. Much too late, the logisticians in Italy had reacted to his pleas for aid, and by now Hitler was alerted to the likelihood of losing North Africa. Most of the German troops and equipment were going to Tunisia, however.

Montgomery attacked the El Agheila position on 11 December, but Rommel promptly withdrew when threatened with encirclement. In spite of frantic appeals from the Italian African Command (Rommel's superior headquarters), Tripolitania was being overrun rapidly. Pausing again at Buerat to tidy up the supply situation, Montgomery outflanked that position and entered Tripoli on 23 January, using the grounded X Corps' transport to help surmount his critical logistical problem. In three months, the Eighth Army had driven Rommel 1,400 miles and had entered the capital of Italian Colonial Africa.

On 14 January, as a result of the Casablanca Conference, Montgomery had been subordinated to Lt. Gen. Eisenhower's Allied Forces Headquarters. With Rommel obviously moving into Tunisia to join Axis forces there, Montgomery sent the 7th Armored Division westward—logistics would not support a larger force—and prepared to close up against an old French position (the Mareth Line), behind which Rommel was waiting. As the Allies would discover, he did not wait long.

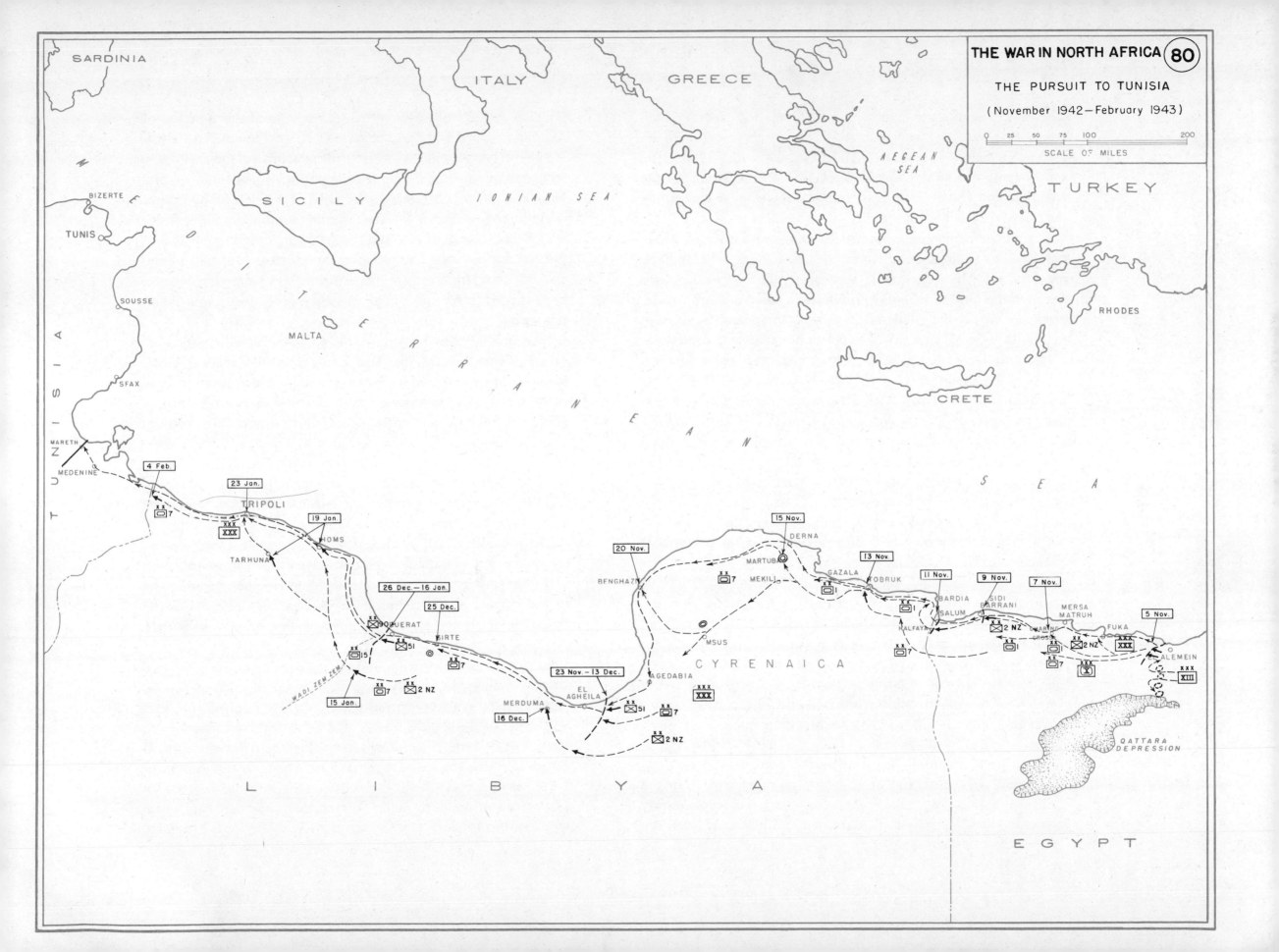

SARDINIA

ITALY

GREECE

AEGEAN
SEA

TURKEY

BIZERTE

TUNIS

SICILY

IONIAN SEA

RHODES

SOUSSE

MALTA

MEDITERRANEAN

SEA

SFAX

CRETE

MARETH

MEDENINE

4 Feb.

23 Jan.

TRIPOLI

19 Jan.

HOMS

TARHUNA

26 Dec. — 16 Jan.

25 Dec.

BUERAT

90

51

SIRTE

7

15

15 Jan.

WADI ZEM ZEM

7   2 NZ

16 Dec.

MERDUMA

EL
AGHEILA

51   7

2 NZ

23 Nov. — 13 Dec.

AGEDABIA

MSUS

CYRENAICA

20 Nov.

BENGHAZI

MEKILI

7

15 Nov.

DERNA

MARTUBA

GAZALA

13 Nov.

TOBRUK

1

11 Nov.

BARDIA

SALUM

HALFAYA

7

9 Nov.

SIDI
BARRANI

2 NZ

7 Nov.

MERSA
MATRUH

FUKA

5 Nov.

2 NZ

1

XXX

7

X

ALEMEIN

XIII

1

2 NZ

1

L I B Y A

QATTARA
DEPRESSION

E G Y P T

The Allied landings in North Africa (Operation TORCH) on 8 November were the culmination of almost a year of Anglo-American debate regarding Allied strategy for 1942. The evolvement of a strategy evoked the first serious strain on the coalition and revealed areas of future disagreement concerning the role of the Mediterranean.

From the beginning, a North African invasion had the support of both Churchill and Roosevelt, the indispensable requirement for any Allied operation. Accordingly, decisions taken bore as much the imprint of political influences as of military considerations. But, if the heads of state were in general agreement, their military staffs were not. At the first heads-of-state conference (ARCADIA; December, 1941), a North African operation was broached by the British as a relatively cheap means of seizing the initiative from Hitler. They stressed the desirability of bringing French forces back into the war against Germany, and the amount of shipping which would be saved as opposed to the much longer Cape of Good Hope route. Not yet stressed by Churchill —but present, and to emerge in the next two years in ever-expanding scope—was the possibility of securing a route for the invasion of Continental Europe. Roosevelt liked the idea of the North African operation because it promised early commitment of American troops against Germany.

On the other hand, the U.S. Joint Chiefs of Staff (JCS) opposed the operation as a secondary, dissipative venture, preferring instead to mass Allied strength in Great Britain for an early attack against Western Europe. Nevertheless, at ARCADIA, the Combined Chiefs of Staff agreed to begin planning for an invasion of North Africa. By 1 April, 1942, as resources became more plentiful, a build-up in England (BOLERO), preparatory to an invasion of France, had supplanted the Mediterranean venture in Allied priorities. But, though the British agreed in principle to a landing in northwest France, they questioned Allied ability to successfully make one—even by 1943. For the next four months the argument raged, with new factors constantly appearing—such as Rommel's successes in Libya and Egypt, the

German summer offensive in the Caucasus, and the shortage of shipping. At one stage, the chagrined JCS contemplated switching the major American effort to the Pacific, as their Allies— schooled in the traditional British policy of containment and peripheral war, and remembering 1940 (and 1917) in France —continued to urge a Mediterranean operation. In July, President Roosevelt finally resolved the matter by ordering the JCS to prepare for TORCH. This decision, as General Marshall appreciated, effectively killed any hopes for a 1943 landing in France, since the North African landings would require diverting BOLERO resources.

Accordingly, on 14 August, the CCS appointed Eisenhower (then in command of the American forces in England) Commander, Allied Expeditionary Force, and directed him to prepare plans for the landings. Mindful of the importance of unity of effort, Eisenhower established his Allied Force Headquarters (AFHQ) as a combined team of British and American officers, with the best men, irrespective of nationality, heading the various sections. AFHQ planners encountered many problems, including a basic disagreement between American and British strategists concerning the locale of the landings. (The British wanted to land some forces well to the east—near Bône—to ensure rapid seizure of Tunisia; the Americans, fearing Spanish intervention and German air power, advocated landings on the western coast of Morocco only.) A compromise resolved this difficulty, as the final plan illustrates. Equally thorny was the complicated French political structure in North Africa, wherein three different factions existed. Secret negotiations, aimed at eliminating resistance to the landings, were only partially successful, and, as will be seen, the political problem was never completely solved.

In the final plan, the Center and Western Task Forces were wholly American, the latter sailing directly from the United States. The Eastern Task Force was a composite British-American force, elements of which would eventually become the British First Army and advance into Tunisia while the other two forces combined to forestall any German move into Spanish Morocco.

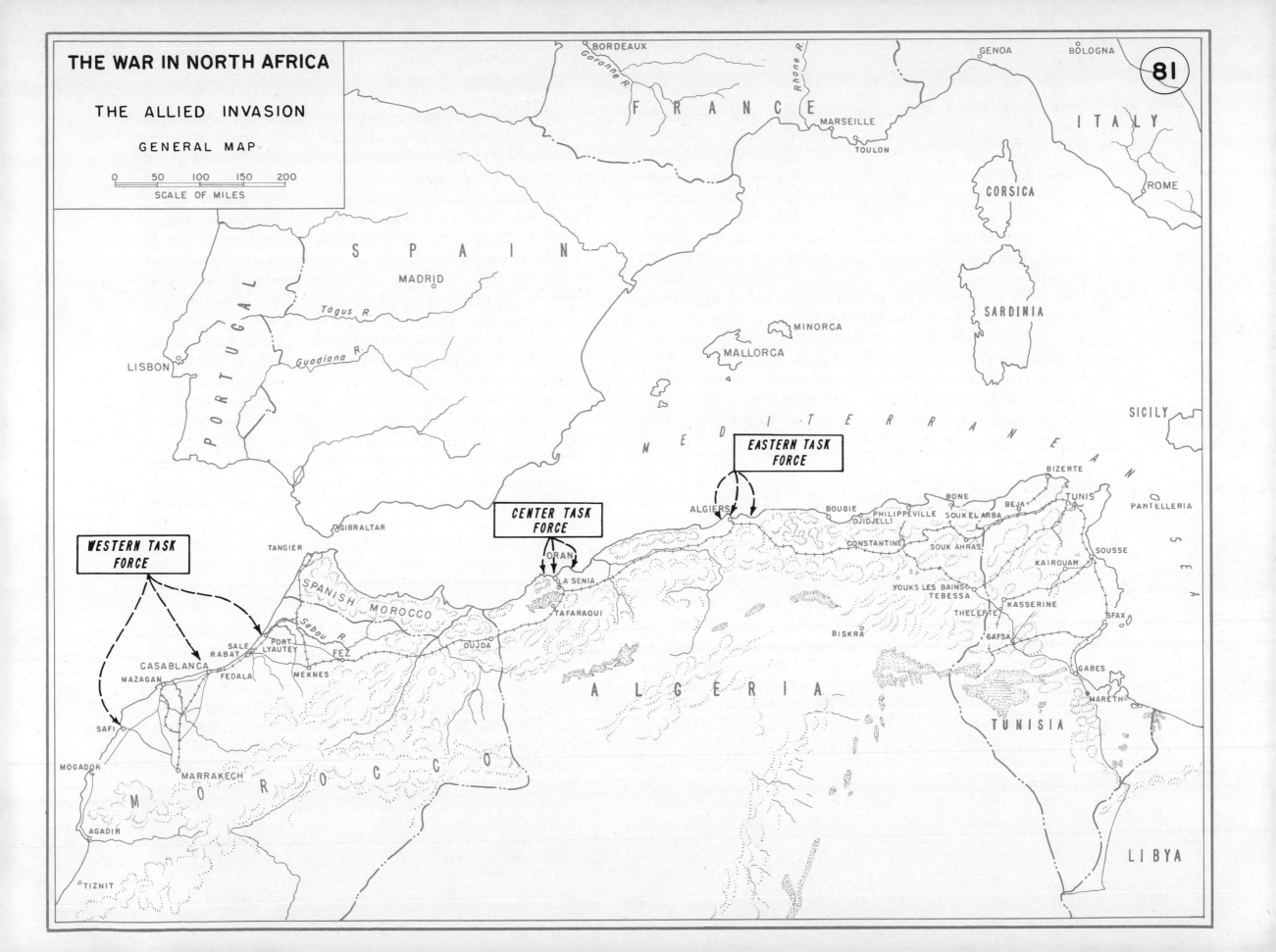

THE WAR IN NORTH AFRICA

THE ALLIED INVASION

GENERAL MAP

0   50   100   150   200
SCALE OF MILES

81

WESTERN TASK FORCE

CENTER TASK FORCE

EASTERN TASK FORCE

FRANCE

ITALY

SPAIN

PORTUGAL

SPANISH MOROCCO

MOROCCO

ALGERIA

TUNISIA

LIBYA

MEDITERRANEAN SEA

CORSICA

SARDINIA

SICILY

PANTELLERIA

MINORCA

MALLORCA

BORDEAUX

GENOA
BOLOGNA

ROME

MARSEILLE

TOULON

MADRID

LISBON

Tagus R.

Guadiana R.

Garonne R.

Rhone R.

Sebou R.

GIBRALTAR

TANGIER

SALE
RABAT
PORT LYAUTEY
FEZ
MEKNES
FEDALA
CASABLANCA
MAZAGAN
SAFI
MOGADOR
MARRAKECH
AGADIR
TIZNIT

ORAN
LA SENIA
TAFARAOUI
OUJDA

ALGIERS
BOUGIE
DJIDJELLI
PHILIPPEVILLE
SOUK EL ARBA
CONSTANTINE
SOUK AHRAS
BONE
BEJA
BIZERTE
TUNIS
SOUSSE
KAIROUAN
YOUKS LES BAINS
TEBESSA
THELEPTE
KASSERINE
SFAX
GAFSA
BISKRA
GABES
MARETH

Before dawn on 8 November, the three Allied task forces landed in North Africa (*main sketch*), their H-Hours varying because of tidal fluctuations. Each force sought the capture of the major city, port facilities, and key airfields in its area. The plans adopted were strikingly similar, each being designed to pinch out the major city by landings on either side of it. Carrier-based aircraft supported the initial assaults; it was expected that, by D + 3, RAF and United States Army Air Corps planes would have been flown in from Gibraltar to the captured fields. Naval support for the landings at Oran and Algiers was provided by the Royal Navy, for Casablanca by the United States Navy.

Elements of Maj. Gen. George Patton's Western Task Force landed between 0400 and 0600. It had been hoped that pro-Allied officers in Morocco would seize control and allow unopposed landings, but they failed, and Patton's forces met the strongest resistance of the day from tough French colonial troops. However, Maj. Gen. Ernest Harmon's force secured Safi by 1015, established a beachhead, and concentrated upon bringing armor ashore. Operations were slowed somewhat by French aircraft, but by 9 November carrier planes had nullified that threat, and a tank force had moved southeast toward Marrakech to block the observed movement of French forces toward Safi and Casablanca. Attacked by Allied aircraft on 8 November and by the tanks on the 9th, the French withdrew and dispersed. Early on 10 November, Harmon, in consonance with his major mission, left the 47th RCT (9th Division) to protect Safi and started Combat Command B (2d Armored Division) toward Casablanca. Capturing Mazagan the next morning, the force halted as shown when informed that French resistance in Morocco had ceased. Meanwhile, north of Casablanca, the other two landing forces were encountering stiffer resistance. Fire from shore batteries—soon neutralized by naval gunfire—plus failures to land at planned beaches caused considerable confusion, but by 1500 the 3d Division had captured Fédala. At Casablanca, French naval vessels took heavy losses in an engagement with the American fleet. On 9-10 November, General Truscott's 60th RCT (9th Division), admirably supported by the Navy, took the Port Lyautey airfield in hard fighting along the city's waterways. After difficulty in building up adequate supplies, the 3d Division closed in on Casablanca. At 0700, 11 November, having refused several armistice offers the past two days, the French commander surrendered upon orders from Algiers.

Meanwhile, the Center and Eastern Task Forces, entering the Mediterranean on 5-6 November, had veered sharply southward at the last minute to their landing areas. Axis intelligence agencies were aware of the convoys, but estimated their destination as Malta, Tripoli, or the Suez. Thus, only minor damage was inflicted on the convoys by Axis air and naval forces.

At Oran, Maj. Gen. Lloyd Fredendall's force began landing at 0135, 8 November, against sporadic resistance. The Rangers (*left inset sketch*) quickly seized coastal batteries, and by noon the three RCT's of the 1st Division had secured Les Andalouses and Arzeu. The two armored task forces seized the Lourmel and Tafaraqui airfields before 1200, and started toward La Senia. A small landing force aboard two cutters attempted to surprise the harbor defenses at Oran about 0300, but the ships came under fire. Casualties were heavy, and the survivors had to surrender. The airborne landing likewise was ineffective, as the troops destined to seize Tafaraqui airfield landed well off target on the Sebkra (dry salt lake). On 9 November, after repelling French counterattacks near Arzeu and Tafaraqui, Fredendall's troops tightened the ring around Oran. At 1230, 10 November, the French capitulated.

At Algiers, the Allies met the least resistance, primarily because of the temporary seizure of control of the area by friendly, pro-Allied forces. By 1000, 8 November, when Vichy adherents regained control, the Allies were closing in on Algiers; by 1900, all opposition had been put down. Fortunately, Admiral Jean François Darlan, commander of the Vichy armed forces, was in Algiers and was taken into protective custody. After delicate negotiations, Darlan assumed governmental authority in North Africa and ordered a cessation of hostilities.

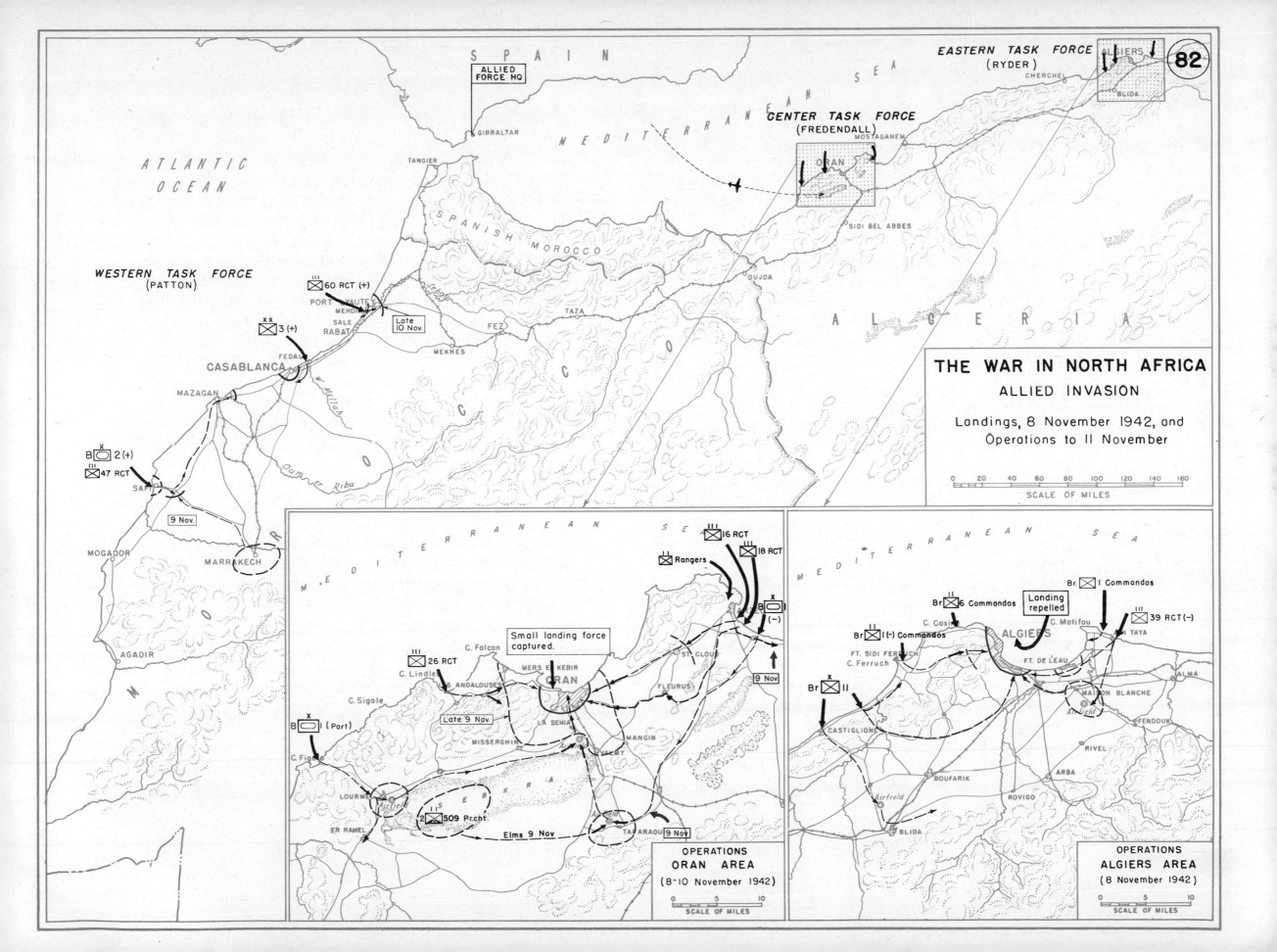

THE WAR IN NORTH AFRICA
ALLIED INVASION

Landings, 8 November 1942, and
Operations to 11 November

SCALE OF MILES
0 20 40 60 80 100 120 140 160

82

ATLANTIC OCEAN

SPAIN

MEDITERRANEAN SEA

ALLIED FORCE HQ

GIBRALTAR

EASTERN TASK FORCE (RYDER)

ALGIERS
CHERCHEL
BLIDA

CENTER TASK FORCE (FREDENDALL)

MOSTAGANEM
ORAN
SIDI BEL ABBES

WESTERN TASK FORCE (PATTON)

TANGIER

SPANISH MOROCCO

60 RCT (+)

PORT LYAUTEY
MEHDIA
SALE
RABAT
Late 10 Nov.

3 (+)

FEDALA
CASABLANCA

MAZAGAN

B 2 (+)
47 RCT

SAFI
9 Nov.

MOGADOR

MARRAKECH

AGADIR

TAZA
FEZ
MEKNES

OUJDA

ALGERIA

OPERATIONS ORAN AREA
(8-10 November 1942)

SCALE OF MILES
0 5 10

MEDITERRANEAN SEA

16 RCT
18 RCT
Rangers

B II (−)

Small landing force captured.

26 RCT
C. Falcon
C. Lindle

MERS EL KEBIR
ORAN

ST. CLOUD

9 Nov

FLEURUS

US ANDALOUSES
Late 9 Nov.
LA SENIA
MANGIN

B I (Part)

MISSERGHIN
VALMY

C. Sigale

C. Figa

LOURMEL
Airfield

2 509 Prcht.

ER RAHEL

Elms 9 Nov
TAFARAOUI
9 Nov

OPERATIONS ALGIERS AREA
(8 November 1942)

SCALE OF MILES
0 5 10

MEDITERRANEAN SEA

Br I Commandos

Br 6 Commandos

Landing repelled

C. Caxine

ALGIERS
C. Matifou

39 RCT (−)

Br I (−) Commandos
FT. SIDI FERRUCH
C. Ferruch

FT. DE L'EAU
TAYA

Br II

CASTIGLIONE

MAISON BLANCHE
Airfield

ALMA

FENDOUK

BOUFARIK
RIVEL

Airfield

ARBA

BLIDA
ROVIGO

The race for Tunisia began on 9 November when Hitler—anticipating an Allied occupation of that colony, followed by a drive on Rommel's rear—began moving troops into Bizerte. On the 10th, in keeping with the second phase of TORCH, British forces (the floating reserve of Eastern Task Force) were dispatched to Bougie as the first step in a rapid advance to Tunis.

To appreciate the complicating factors in the race for Tunisia, an understanding must be had of the Allied-Darlan and Hitler-Vichy negotiations. Maj. Gen. Mark W. Clark (AFHQ Deputy Commander) and Darlan first conferred on 10 November, the result being the cease-fire order from Darlan. But Clark was under pressure to obtain more—active French support and French resistance to Axis movements into Tunisia. Darlan was equally hampered because political concessions had to bear Marshal Pétain's concurrence. Late on the 10th, Pétain, under pressure from Vichy Premier Pierre Laval, withdrew his earlier approval of Darlan's cease-fire order. Darlan then revoked the order, further confusing some French commanders who now felt they must oppose the Allies. On the same day, Laval met with Hitler at Munich in an attempt to save the tottering Vichy government. Pétain, on 9 November, had authorized German use of Tunisian airdromes, but Hitler demanded full authority to move large bodies of troops into Tunisia, under the guise of aiding the French in defending against Allied attack. Laval hedged, and the conference closed with Hitler having decided to occupy the rest of France. German and Italian divisions began moving into southern France that night, while Italy occupied Corsica. Meanwhile, Clark insisted that Darlan reinstate his original cease-fire order—which the latter did, claiming to have received a secret authorization from Pétain. With the German move into southern France, Darlan broke with Vichy and ordered the French to resist Axis forces in Tunisia. Under German pressure, Vichy stripped Darlan of his authority on the 12th and disavowed his orders. Again, some commanders in Tunisia accepted Vichy's authority, and Axis troops in ever-increasing numbers continued to enter Tunisia unopposed. In the next week, the French army commander in Tunisia, General Georges Barré, gradually withdrew his forces westward into the mountains (*upper right, dotted blue line*) as Vichy tried to force him to collaborate with the Germans. The Axis commander was as confused about French intentions as the Allies earlier had been and lacked the strength to contest the move. Barré, following orders from Algiers, established contact with Allied columns at Beja on 17 November. The acceptance of Darlan as the French commissioner in North Africa raised a public clamor in England and the United States and incensed De Gaulle. But the decision, made in the interests of military practicality, was ultimately accepted as a temporary measure.

The Allies had originally planned to seize airfields at Bône, Bizerte, and Tunis with airborne and commando troops, but, with the French reaction uncertain, a more conservative approach was used. The force landing at Bougie tried to disembark some troops at Djidjelli, but failed because of heavy surf. Thus, the airfield at the latter town was not operational for two more days; and meanwhile, lacking carrier air support, the Bougie landing force lost several ships to German air attack. The commando-paratroop landings at Bône, both unopposed, were likewise designed to secure forward airfields. Advance spearheads were now sent across the Tunisian border with orders to contact the French and reconnoiter to the east. Meanwhile, the main body of the British 78th Division would start moving overland from Algiers on 15 November. By 17 November, Allied forces were in close proximity to Axis forces in northern Tunisia, and the race for Tunisia was about to be decided by a clash of arms.

The terrain in Tunisia is easily defended. The Eastern and Western Dorsals of the Atlas Mountains form an inverted "V" running southwest from Tunis; they are traversed by the few roads and railroads indicated. In the extreme north, the mountains are cut by rivers and streams, but these valleys are easily blocked.

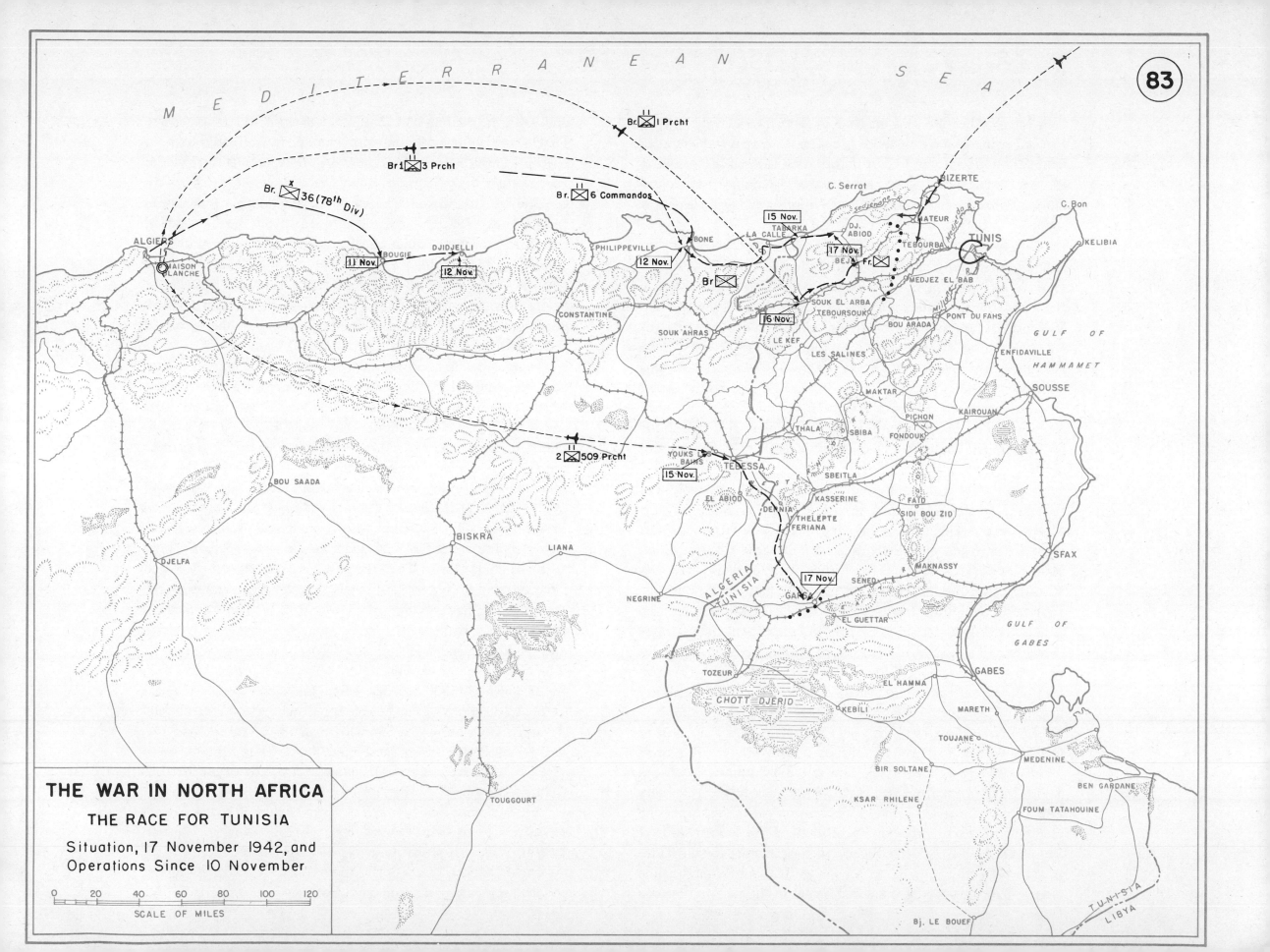

MEDITERRANEAN SEA

Br. ⊠ I Prcht

Br I ⊠ 3 Prcht

Br. ⊠ 36 (78ᵗʰ Div)

Br. ⊠ 6 Commandos

BIZERTE

C. Serrat

C. Bon

ALGIERS

MAISON BLANCHE

BOUGIE

DJIDJELLI

PHILIPPEVILLE

BONE

LA CALLE

TABARKA

15 Nov.

DJ. ABIOD

MATEUR

TEBOURBA

TUNIS

KELIBIA

11 Nov.

12 Nov.

12 Nov.

Br ⊠

17 Nov.

BEJA   Fr. ⊠

MEDJEZ EL BAB

CONSTANTINE

SOUK AHRAS

16 Nov.

SOUK EL ARBA

TEBOURSOUK

BOU ARADA

PONT DU FAHS

GULF OF HAMMAMET

LE KEF

LES SALINES

ENFIDAVILLE

SOUSSE

MAKTAR

PICHON

KAIROUAN

2 ⊠ 509 Prcht

YOUKS LES BAINS

15 Nov.

TEBESSA

THALA

SBIBA

FONDOUK

SIDI BOU ZID

SFAX

BOU SAADA

EL ABIOD

DERNIA

KASSERINE

THELEPTE FERIANA

FAID

MAKNASSY

BISKRA

LIANA

SENED

DJELFA

NEGRINE

ALGERIA TUNISIA

17 Nov.

GAFSA

EL GUETTAR

GULF OF GABES

GABES

TOZEUR

EL HAMMA

TOUGGOURT

CHOTT DJERID

KEBILI

MARETH

MEDENINE

TOUJANE

BIR SOLTANE

BEN GARDANE

KSAR RHILENE

FOUM TATAHOUINE

TUNISIA LIBYA

Bj. LE BOUEF

83

THE WAR IN NORTH AFRICA

THE RACE FOR TUNISIA

Situation, 17 November 1942, and
Operations Since 10 November

0   20   40   60   80   100   120
SCALE OF MILES

General Walther Nehring arrived in Tunis (*sketch* a) on 16 November to assume command of the small German-Italian forces there. He was expected to expand the Axis bridgehead westward to gain room for the deployment of the 10th Panzer, Hermann Göring Panzer, and 334th Infantry Divisions which were expected soon.

During the period of 17-23 November, aggressive German columns—primarily tough paratroop units—pushed westward (*not shown*) and fought minor engagements with British advance elements and the French. On 18 November, Blade Force (a mobile task force consisting of armor, infantry, artillery, and engineers) arrived from Algiers to reinforce the front. By 23 November, the line of contact was as shown. These initial actions convinced General Kenneth A. N. Anderson (British First Army commander) that the British 78th Division and Blade Force were too weak to seize Tunis and Bizerte. Thus, Combat Command B of the United States 1st Armored Division, the British 6th Armored Division, and several American artillery battalions were dispatched from Oran and Algiers to the First Army. On the 25th, Anderson launched an attack along three axes toward Mateur and Djedeida. Forward air support was furnished from the three airfields shown. In spite of the aid of Combat Command B (CCB) elements and the extra artillery—the 6th Armored Division did not arrive in time—the results were disappointing; Nehring's troops held at the 30 November line. An amphibious "end run" and an airborne attack (*neither shown*) contributed nothing to the operations. Supply difficulties, aggravated by the beginning of the winter rains, had hindered Anderson; but the most influential factor had been the Allied inability to gain air superiority over the Luftwaffe.

Eisenhower ordered a continuation of the attack as soon as forward airfields had been established and supplies and reinforcements had arrived, but Nehring now seized the initiative. Between 1 and 10 December, he forced the Allies back to the 1 January line. (On 9 December, General Juergen von Arnim assumed command of the Axis forces, now called the Fifth Panzer Army.) In late December, Anderson made one last attempt to take Tunis by a thrust (*not shown*) near Medjez el Bab, but Arnim was too strong. Eisenhower now conceded defeat in the race for Tunisia

and, with the coming of winter rains, decided to strengthen the First Army with units from Morocco and switch operations to central Tunisia against the Germans at Sousse, Sfax, and Gabes (*upper right to lower right*).

The II Corps began arriving in the Sbeitla area (*center*) in early January. It was to attack toward Sfax to cut the Axis coastal corridor connecting Arnim and Rommel. But when Eisenhower learned (at the Casablanca Conference) that Montgomery could not reach Tunisia until mid-February, he canceled the plan as being too risky—the weak II Corps would be exposed to flank attacks from the north and south. Fredendall was then directed to defend the Eastern Dorsal.

Meanwhile, Arnim continued to launch attacks. On 2 January, he captured Fondouk (*sketch* b, *center*) from the French XIX Corps (formed of Algerian units moved east in December and some of Barré's battalions—the rest of Barré's division continued to operate between Bou Arada and Robaa [*both upper center*]; some French units were also in the United States II Corps zone). On 18 January, Arnim switched his attack back north and by the 25th had penetrated (*dotted red line*) the undermanned French sector. (In an attempt to solve command problems, Eisenhower subordinated the XIX and II Corps to Anderson's First Army on 25 January.) CCB and elements from the 6th Armored Division were moved to the French sector and eventually forced the Germans back to the 14 February line. But the German attack had so weakened the French that part of the 1st Division and the lead elements of the 34th Division were moved into the XIX Corps line to relieve them.

Meanwhile, on 30 January, Arnim attacked to secure the pass at Faid (*center*). Again, the blow fell on the French. The 1st Armored Division, which had been planning an attack on Maknassy, moved to reinforce the French, leaving a provisional force (CCD) to undertake the Maknassy attack. It was repulsed at both places.

By 14 February, Arnim had severely punished the French forces and had secured commanding positions along the Eastern Dorsal. Worse, II Corps units were badly intermingled, the 1st Armored Division was widely dispersed, and Rommel was about to join Arnim in an attack on the II Corps.

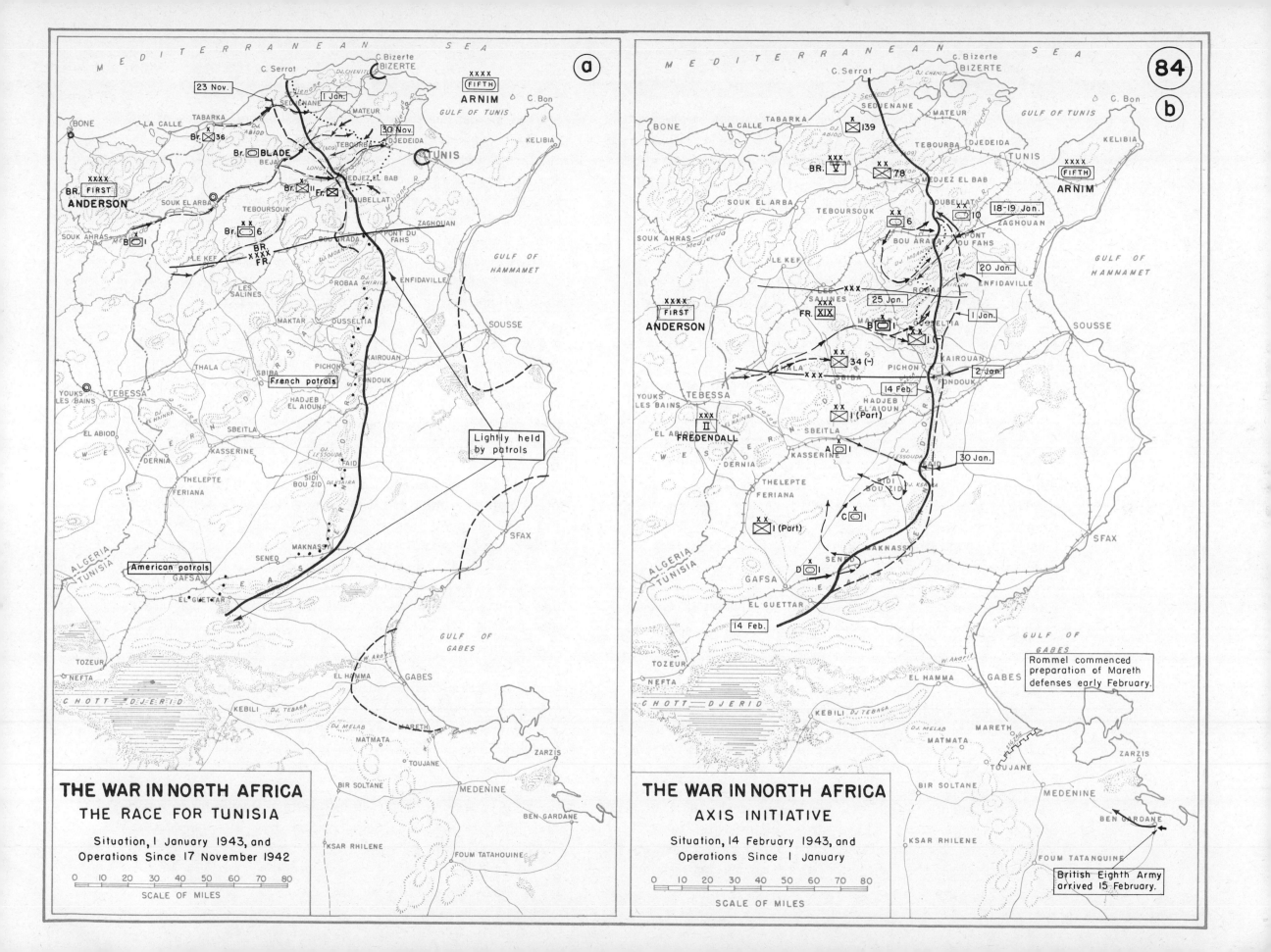

THE WAR IN NORTH AFRICA
THE RACE FOR TUNISIA

Situation, 1 January 1943, and
Operations Since 17 November 1942

0 10 20 30 40 50 60 70 80
SCALE OF MILES

THE WAR IN NORTH AFRICA
AXIS INITIATIVE

Situation, 14 February 1943, and
Operations Since 1 January

0 10 20 30 40 50 60 70 80
SCALE OF MILES

Rommel commenced
preparation of Mareth
defenses early February.

British Eighth Army
arrived 15 February.

Lightly held
by patrols

French patrols

American patrols

Early in February, at Rommel's suggestion, the Germans planned a limited dual offensive. Arnim was to attack first to seize Sidi Bou Zid (*center, right*), and then send Rommel part of the 21st Panzer Division to assist the Afrika Corps (D.A.K.—now a composite German-Italian force of divisional size) in taking Gafsa (*bottom center*).

Early on 14 February, the 10th and 21st Panzer Divisions moved through the passes shown and attacked toward Sidi Bou Zid. The Americans were expecting an attack, but not in such strength. As previously noted, the II Corps' major striking force, the 1st Armored Division, was badly dispersed, and its best unit (CCB) was still attached to the XIX Corps at Maktar (*top center*). Only CCA (with the 168th Regimental Combat Team attached) was immediately available to oppose the powerful panzer thrust. Supported by dive-bomber and strafing attacks, the panzer columns quickly overcame forward motorized patrols and by noon had outflanked Sidi Bou Zid and cut off the 168th RCT on the two heights. That afternoon, CCA withdrew to the 15-16 February line, having suffered heavy tank losses and barely avoided encirclement. Underestimating the German strength, Maj. Gen. Orlando Ward (1st Armored Division) planned to counterattack the next day with CCC, reinforced by one battalion from CCB.

The counterattack by CCC on the 15th was disastrous. The veteran panzers, again ably assisted by the Luftwaffe, enveloped the advancing column, practically wiped out one tank battalion, and sent the rest of the force scurrying back to the 15-16 February line. The 168th RCT, cut off and short of food and water, was trapped. (It attempted to break out on 17 February, but very few men escaped.)

On 15 February, Anderson, finally releasing the remainder of CCB to Ward, ordered the II Corps to withdraw to the Western Dorsal but still to secure Sbeitla, Kasserine, and Feriana (*all center*). By early evening, 16 February, the 1st Armored Division was concentrated at Sbeitla. Meanwhile, the weak Allied force at Gafsa (*bottom center*) had withdrawn on the 14th; Rommel's entry into the town the next day thus made unnecessary the planned transfer of the 21st Panzer Division. Accordingly, Arnim ordered his panzers to lay waste to Sbeitla and then move to Fondouk (*upper right*) to trap Allied forces there.

The panzer attack on the American position near Sbeitla started the night of 16 February. Some of the American troops panicked in their first night combat, and a rout was barely averted. But CCB, in particular, fought well until the town was evacuated on the 17th. Ward's division now moved back to the vicinity of Tebessa as other units moved in to block the passes at Sbiba and Kasserine. This same day, most of the 10th Panzer Division moved toward Fondouk, but failed to trap any Allied troops.

Having occupied Feriana on the 17th, Rommel concluded that a quick thrust through Tebessa northward might force a major Allied withdrawal. Since Arnim refused to provide assistance, Rommel took the matter to Kesselring (Arnim's superior), who concurred in the plan. But the order, coming to Rommel through his confused Italian superiors on the 18th, specified that the drive would be through the Thala-Sbiba area (*upper center*)—not through Tebessa. Rommel would be in command and would have control of all the panzers. Consequently, on the 19th, Rommel ordered attacks toward both Sbiba and Kasserine Pass, intending to exploit the more successful one. Additionally, he directed the 10th Panzer Division to move from the Fondouk area to Kasserine. Neither drive achieved much success on 19 February: the D.A.K. tried to force Kasserine Pass without seizing the heights and failed, while at Sbiba the Allies had too much strength. The next day, the 10th Panzer Division joined the attack at Kasserine, and, though the outnumbered defenders were outflanked and forced back, the decisive thrust toward Thala was stopped by a tenacious British defense aided by 9th Division artillery. Overworked CCB and the 1st Division stopped the D.A.K. drive toward Tebessa (which was only intended to secure Rommel's flank). On the 22d, Rommel conceded failure and began to withdraw (*note, lower right*). Primarily because of an unduly complicated II Corps chain of command—the Allies had handled this matter poorly since 14 February—Rommel was able to withdraw unmolested. On the 23d, he became over-all commander in Tunisia—two weeks too late.

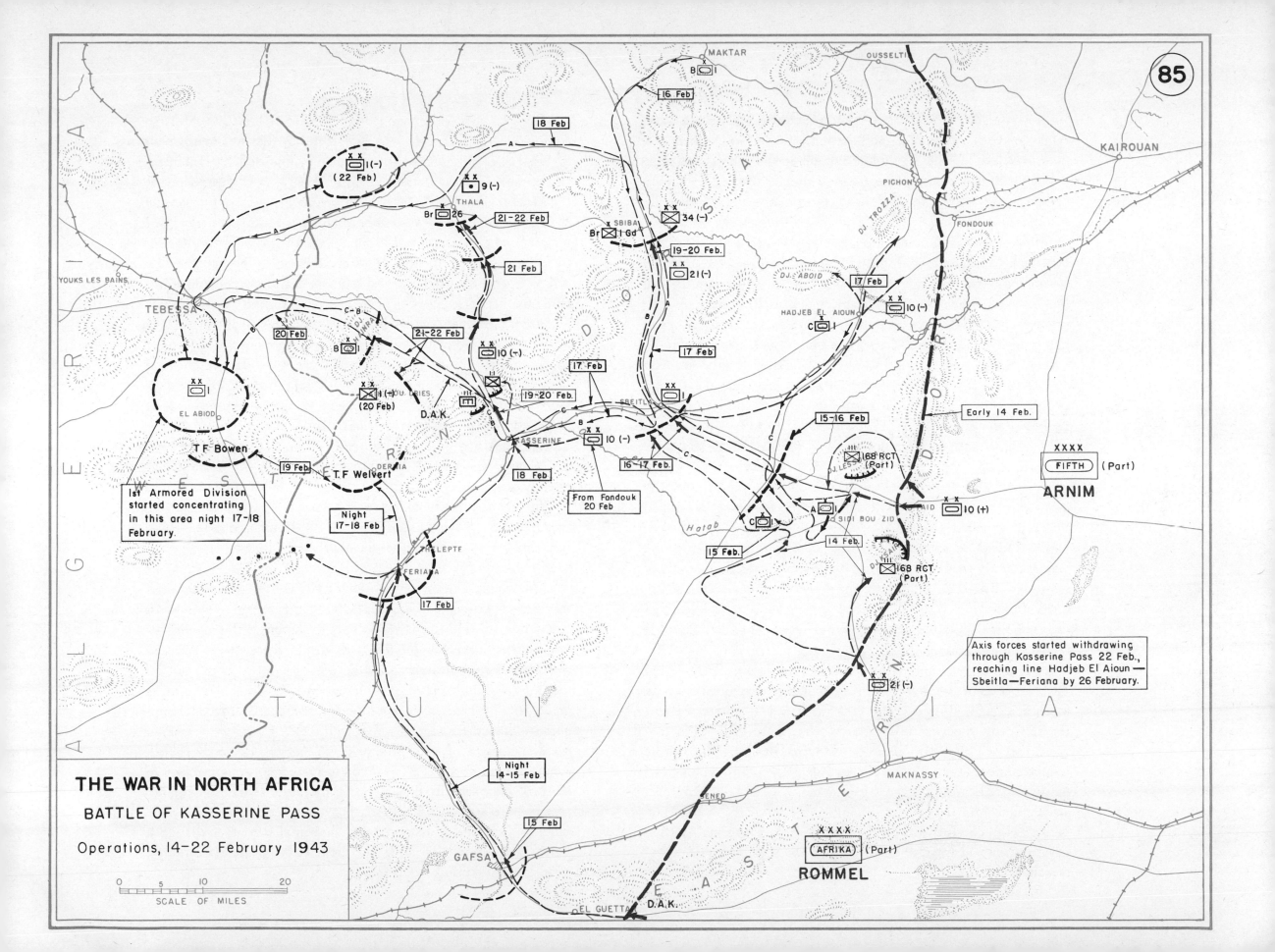

85

THE WAR IN NORTH AFRICA

BATTLE OF KASSERINE PASS

Operations, 14-22 February 1943

0 5 10   20
SCALE OF MILES

1st Armored Division started concentrating in this area night 17-18 February.

Axis forces started withdrawing through Kasserine Pass 22 Feb., reaching line Hadjeb El Aioun — Sbeitla — Feriana by 26 February.

MAKTAR
KAIROUAN
OUSSELTIA
PICHON
FONDOUK
KAIROUAN
THALA
SBIBA
HADJEB EL AIOUN
DJ. TROZZA
DJ. ABIOD
TEBESSA
YOUKS LES BAINS
EL ABIOD
T F Bowen
T.F Welvert
FERIANA
D.A.K.
KASSERINE
SBEITLA
DJ SIDI BOU ZID
GAFSA
MAKNASSY
EL GUETTAR
D.A.K.

ARNIM
ROMMEL

XXXX
FIFTH (Part)

XXXX
AFRIKA (Part)

16 Feb
18 Feb
21-22 Feb
21 Feb
20 Feb
19 Feb
Night 17-18 Feb
17 Feb
Night 14-15 Feb
15 Feb
14 Feb
15 Feb
17 Feb
18 Feb
16-17 Feb
15-16 Feb
Early 14 Feb.
19-20 Feb.
17 Feb
19-20 Feb.
21-22 Feb
From Fondouk 20 Feb

With Rommel's voluntary retirement from the Western Dorsal, the Allies made plans for regaining the initiative. Alexander's immediate problems were to sort out the scattered troop units, organize distinct national sectors, and create a mobile reserve. His more far-reaching task was to ensure the coordination of offensives by Montgomery and the forces in Tunisia (*sketch* a).

Meanwhile, as Rommel moved toward Mareth (*lower right*) to attack Montgomery's Eighth Army before it was completely assembled, Arnim launched a spoiling attack against the British V Corps (*top center*). This attack, much to Rommel's disgust, was soon enlarged into a full-blown offensive. By 3 March, Arnim had gained some ground (*dotted red line*), but, having suffered severe losses—particularly in armor—he called a halt. Later in the month, heavy Allied pressure all along the front and British counterattacks (28 March) drove him back to the original line (*solid red line*).

In the meantime, Rommel attacked the British at Médenine (*bottom right*) on 6 March. Only Montgomery's XXX Corps was present, but it had 300 tanks, 350 artillery pieces, and 450 antitank guns, and was in a strong position. Rommel, inferior in matériel, attacked with the 10th, 15th, and 21st Panzer Divisions, without adequate reconnaissance or strong infantry support. He was decisively repulsed, suffering the loss of more than a third of his tanks. Three days later Rommel—a sick man—left Africa, never to return.

On 6 March, Patton assumed command of the United States II Corps and immediately began to revitalize it. The corps now consisted of the 1st, 9th, and 34th Infantry Divisions and 1st Armored Division; two of the divisions, as indicated, had detached a regiment apiece for duty elsewhere. Alexander was convinced that the II Corps—because of its poor performance in the Sidi Bou Zid–Kasserine fighting—needed additional training and battle indoctrination. Accordingly, Patton was given a limited mission: to divert Axis troops from Montgomery's front at Mareth by seizing Gafsa for a supply point; and to reconnoiter toward Maknassy, being careful to avoid becoming heavily engaged. Patton naturally wanted to drive all the way to the coast, but Alexander remained firm.

Rommel had recommended withdrawal of the First Army to Enfidaville (*upper center*) to permit more efficient employment of Axis forces, but Kesselring, strongly supported by Hitler, refused, and directed a stand against the British Eighth Army at the Mareth Line. By 20 March, Montgomery—with a four-to-one tank preponderance—was ready to attack. (Patton had occupied undefended Gafsa on the 17th and was now probing to the east, thus pinning down the 10th Panzer Division on his front.) The XXX Corps was to make the main attack on a narrow front, while the New Zealand Corps swung south around the mountains and then moved up across the Axis rear. Behind a tremendous artillery bombardment, the XXX Corps' moonlight attack made some progress, but counterattacks by the 15th Panzer Division finally drove it back on the 23d. With the failure of his main attack to breach the line, Montgomery, showing great command flexibility, abandoned his original plan. He sent the X Corps headquarters with the 1st Armored Division to reinforce the New Zealanders, who were deep in the enemy rear by the 22d and had already begun to siphon off Axis strength from the main position. On the 26th, a combined New Zealand–X Corps attack broke through Axis defenses southwest of El Hamma, but the Italo-German forces evaded encirclement and withdrew to the 31 March line.

Meanwhile, Patton's attacks in the El Guettar–Maknassy area so worried Arnim that he ordered the 10th Panzer Division to counterattack. The 1st Division handily repulsed this panzer attack on the 23d. Now the 9th and 34th Divisions were released to Patton for employment, and he was ordered to break out on the coastal plain west of El Guettar and Fondouk. His attacks made little progress against stubborn resistance. But when Montgomery lunged forward on 6 April (*sketch* b), Gen. Giovanni Messe withdrew toward Enfidaville, so that the II Corps–Eighth Army link-up north of El Hamma ensnared no Axis forces. On 8 April, the 34th Division, temporarily under British command, renewed the attack on Fondouk, but made little progress. By the time the British 6th Armored Division finally contacted Eighth Army elements on the 12th, the great bulk of the Axis forces, withdrawing skillfully, had escaped.

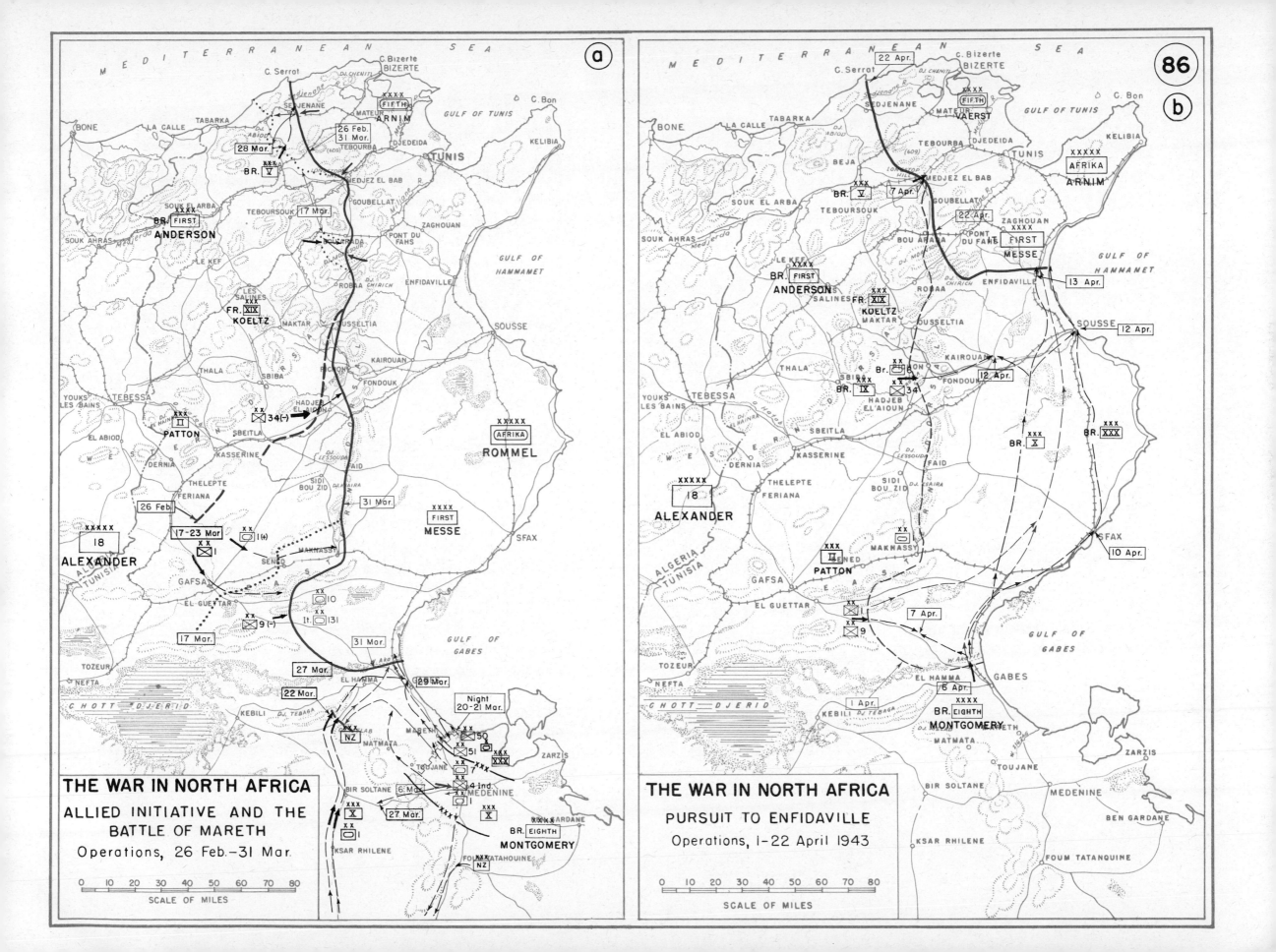

THE WAR IN NORTH AFRICA

ALLIED INITIATIVE AND THE
BATTLE OF MARETH

Operations, 26 Feb.–31 Mar.

SCALE OF MILES
0 10 20 30 40 50 60 70 80

THE WAR IN NORTH AFRICA

PURSUIT TO ENFIDAVILLE

Operations, 1–22 April 1943

SCALE OF MILES
0 10 20 30 40 50 60 70 80

Since the Allies had decided at the Casablanca Conference (January, 1943) to invade Sicily in July of 1943, it was essential that the Axis forces in Tunisia be eliminated as quickly as possible. Any delay would postpone the Sicilian operation beyond summer and into poorer weather.

By 16 April, the United States II Corps had moved to the Allied north flank and had relieved the British V Corps, which then shifted south. Alexander had reluctantly authorized the redeployment of the II Corps, having done so only after Eisenhower had indicated a desire to see it assigned an aggressive role. Maj. Gen. Omar N. Bradley had assumed command of the II Corps on the 15th, so that Patton could return to Morocco and complete the planning for the Sicilian invasion. The transfer of the 100,000 American troops across the rear of the British lines and the creation of a new logistical base were considerable administrative feats.

Alexander's plan for the final phase of the Tunisian campaign specified that the First Army—reinforced with one of Montgomery's armored divisions—would make the main effort, while the Eighth Army and the II Corps (and later the French XIX Corps) would mount secondary attacks. The Allied air force, having gained superiority over the Luftwaffe by now, would provide close support and continue to interdict Axis supply lines from Italy.

Montgomery kicked off the offensive with a night attack on 19 April; two days later, his gains having been negligible and costly, he decided to regroup and concentrate along the coast. The regroupment took time—four days—and came just as the main attack was about to commence. Alexander had hoped that Montgomery's attack would mislead Arnim and cause him to withdraw forces from Anderson's front, but, with Montgomery's attack stopped, the hoped-for deception was ephemeral. Thus, before Anderson could attack, Arnim made a spoiling attack against the British V Corps on 21 April (*not shown*) which created some confusion among the British, but did not deter their attacks. On the 22d, the IX Corps moved forward, and the following day the V Corps joined the attack. For four days, amidst bloody fighting, Anderson's troops inched ahead, but the Germans moved reserves up, counterattacked, and prevented Anderson from breaking loose his armor toward Tunis. By 1 May, the Germans south of the II Corps stood on the 3 May line. To bolster the front opposite Anderson, they had so weakened the sector in the south facing the French that the XIX Corps' attack on the 25th had met little opposition. Already, on 29 April, Alexander had realized that Anderson's army was too weak to crack the Axis defenses, and on the following day he ordered Montgomery to move additional divisions to the First Army. The 7th Armored and Indian 4th Divisions were chosen and moved as shown. The second Allied offensive was to be a power thrust by the V Corps.

While the British and eventually the French were being held by a tenacious defense, Bradley's lightly regarded II Corps was achieving—admittedly, against weaker opposition—the greatest gains of the period. On 23 April, the 1st and 9th Divisions attacked in practically independent operations. The 1st Division was stopped short of Hill 609 (*upper left*) by 26 April. At this time, Bradley committed the 34th Division with the mission of seizing that domineering height. By the 30th, the hill was in American hands, and the 34th Division, having regained its self-respect, repulsed the feverish German counterattacks. To the north, the 9th Division likewise disdained moving down the valleys and committed most of its strength in the hills above Jefna (*upper left*). By 1 May, the Germans, still holding Jefna, were in danger of being cut off from Bizerte. Bradley had secured the commanding terrain and was in position to commit the 1st Armored Division down the Tine River valley to seize Mateur. That night, and the next, the Germans quietly withdrew to a new position (*solid red line*). On 3 May, the 1st Armored, eager to advance during the past week, raced down the valley as shown and entered Mateur that afternoon.

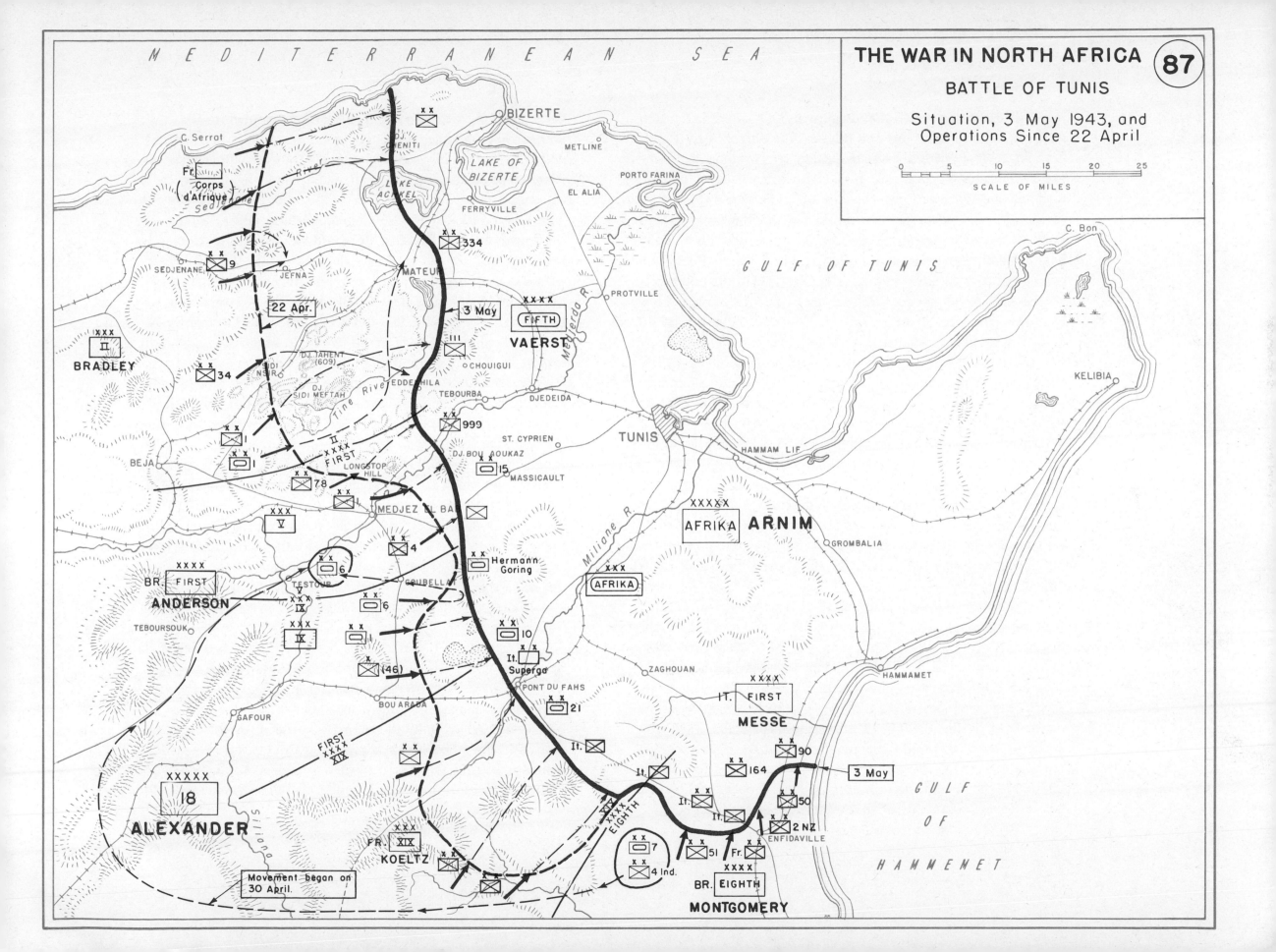

THE WAR IN NORTH AFRICA 87

BATTLE OF TUNIS

Situation, 3 May 1943, and
Operations Since 22 April

0   5   10   15   20   25

SCALE OF MILES

MEDITERRANEAN SEA

C. Serrat

BIZERTE

DJ. CHENITI

LAKE OF BIZERTE

METLINE

PORTO FARINA

Fr. Corps d'Afrique

EL ALIA

LAKE ACHKEL

FERRYVILLE

SEDJENANE

JEFNA

MATEUR

XX 334

PROTVILLE

GULF OF TUNIS

C. Bon

22 Apr.

3 May

XXXX FIFTH VAERST

KELIBIA

BRADLEY

XX 34

DJ. TAHENT (609)

SIDI NSIR

DJ. SIDI MEFTAH

Tine River

EDDEKHILA

O CHOUIGUI

III

TEBOURBA

DJEDEIDA

BEJA

XX 1

XXXX FIRST

XX 999

ST. CYPRIEN

TUNIS

HAMMAM LIF

LONGSTOP HILL

XX 78

MEDJEZ EL BAB

XX 1

DJ. BOU AOUKAZ

15

MASSICAULT

XXX V

XX 4

XX 6

Hermann Goring

XXXXX AFRIKA ARNIM

GROMBALIA

BR. FIRST ANDERSON

TESTOUR

XXX V IX

XX 6

GOUBELLAT

AFRIKA

TEBOURSOUK

XXX IX

XX 1

XX 10

XX It. Superga

XX (46)

BOU ARADA

XX 21

ZAGHOUAN

HAMMAMET

It. FIRST MESSE

GAFOUR

FIRST XXXX XIX

Siliana R.

It.

It.

XX 164

XX 90

3 May

GULF

XXXXX 18 ALEXANDER

XX It.

It.

XX 50

Fr. XIX KOELTZ

XX 7

XX 4 Ind.

XXX EIGHTH

It.

2 NZ

ENFIDAVILLE

OF

Movement began on 30 April.

XX 51

Fr.

BR. EIGHTH MONTGOMERY

HAMMEMET

Alexander's plan specified that the British IX Corps (Indian 4th and 4th Infantry Divisions and 6th and 7th Armored Divisions, concentrated at Medjez El Bab [center, left]) would make the main attack on a 3,000-yard front, with overwhelming air and artillery support toward Massicault and Tunis. The two infantry divisions would open the hole through which the armor would pour in the exploitation. After seizing Tunis, the First Army would rapidly move east and south to meet the Eighth Army and prevent an Axis withdrawal to the Cape Bon peninsula (northeast of the line Hammam Lif–Hammamet). The IX Corps' blow would be preceded by a French XIX Corps attack and a British V Corps assault on Djebel Bou Aoukaz (center, left). This V Corps attack was designed to protect the north flank of the IX Corps. Meanwhile, Bradley's II Corps would continue to advance in its zone to prevent the shifting of German units southward and to seize Bizerte (top center).

Allied deception measures did not mislead Arnim as to the location of the impending main effort, but he could do little to counteract the Allied build-up. The fighting through 1 May had forced him to commit all of his mobile reserves, and, even though on 1-3 May he tried to shift units to the sector he knew to be threatened, the transport and fuel shortages severely restricted his efforts. Furthermore, the Luftwaffe moved almost all of its aircraft to Sicily about this time.

Alexander's offensive got underway as planned on 4 May with the attacks by the XIX and V Corps, the latter seizing the key height of Djebel Bou Aoukaz on the 5th. At the same time, in the extreme north, the 9th Division drove toward Djebel Cheniti (top left), the last remaining defensive position west of Bizerte. Employing enveloping tactics, the division took possession of the dominating hill on 6 May. In the meantime, behind a 600-gun artillery preparation and the most devastating air attack yet launched in Africa, the British IX Corps had rolled forward at 0330, 6 May. At 1100, the armor passed through the infantry and had advance elements in Massicault that night. The battered

Germans fell back toward Tunis and attempted to establish another line, but their lack of mobility soon reduced them to a desperate state. This same day, Bradley's three southernmost divisions launched their attacks. The 1st Armored, against moderate resistance, sent two columns in the directions shown, while the 34th slugged its way toward Chouigui against stiff resistance. In the center, the 1st Division, disregarding instructions to merely apply pressure, tried an all-out attack across the Tine River, received a nasty repulse, and was forced to withdraw that night. On 7 May, Tunis and Bizerte fell to the 7th Armored and 9th Divisions, respectively. The following day, with German resistance slackening everywhere, Allied units began to fan out in exploitation. On the 9th, the 1st Armored Division cut the Tunis-Bizerte road and linked up with the British at Protville (upper center). By now, encircled Axis forces, desperately short of ammunition and fuel and despairing of evacuation, were surrendering all along the front (dashed red circles). North of Tunis, 40,000 eventually surrendered to Bradley. On the 11th, the 6th Armored Division, smashing the last enemy rear guard near Hammam Lif, drove south to cut off any major withdrawal toward Cap Bon. On 13 May, Messe surrendered his Italian First Army, the last major force, to the Eighth Army. In all, the Allies took a total of about 275,000 prisoners—including the top commanders—in the last week of fighting. The Italian Navy, much to the Royal Navy's disappointment, made no attempt at evacuating the Axis forces.

The conquest of North Africa substantially cleared the Mediterranean for Allied shipping, and provided air bases for heavy bomber attacks against southern Europe. Equally important, Tunisia had taught the Americans valuable combat lessons and had welded Allied unity in the first experiment in combined operations. Hitler had lost a complete army, but he managed to convince himself that the campaign had delayed an Allied invasion of Europe and had prevented an Italian surrender.

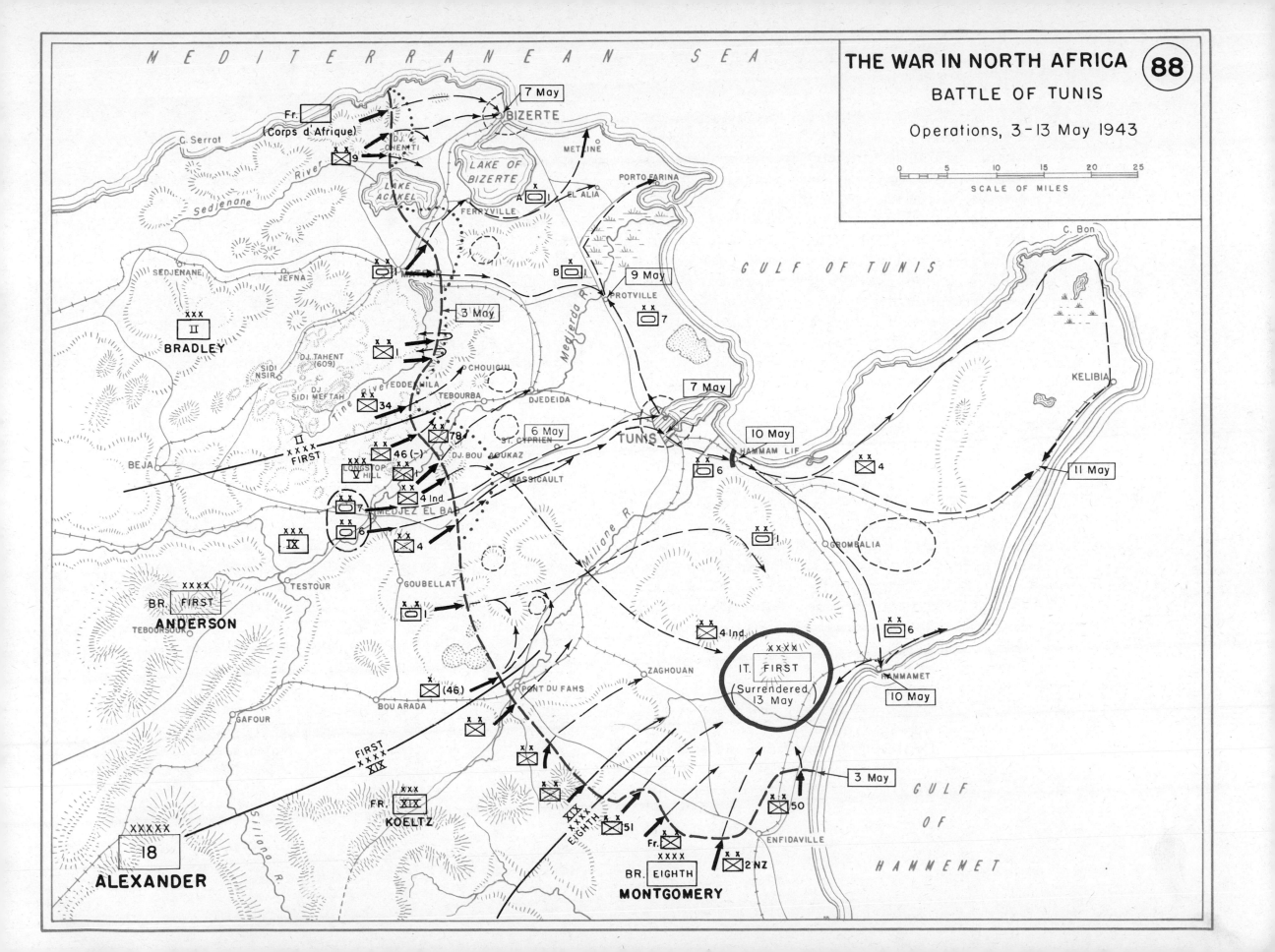

THE WAR IN NORTH AFRICA 88
BATTLE OF TUNIS
Operations, 3–13 May 1943

0 5 10 15 20 25
SCALE OF MILES

MEDITERRANEAN SEA

GULF OF TUNIS

GULF OF HAMMAMET

C. Serrat
C. Bon
BIZERTE
LAKE OF BIZERTE
LAKE ACHKEL
METLINE
PORTO FARINA
EL ALIA
FERRYVILLE
PROTVILLE
KELIBIA
MATEUR
DJ. CHEMTI
7 May
9 May
SEDJENANE
JEFNA
DJ. TAHENT (609)
SIDI NSIR
DJ. SIDI MEFTAH
TEDDER HILA
CHOUIGUI
TEBOURBA
DJEDEIDA
ST. CYPRIEN
DJ. BOU AOUKAZ
MASSICAULT
3 May
6 May
TUNIS
7 May
HAMMAM LIF
10 May
11 May
GROMBALIA
BEJA
LONGSTOP HILL
MEDJEZ EL BAB
TESTOUR
GOUBELLAT
TEBOURSOUK
HAMMAMET
10 May
ZAGHOUAN
PONT DU FAHS
BOU ARADA
GAFOUR
ENFIDAVILLE
3 May

BRADLEY — II (xxx)
FIRST (xxxx)
IX (xxx)
BR. FIRST (xxxx) — ANDERSON
FR. XIX (xxx) — KOELTZ
FIRST XIX (xxxx)
18 (xxxxx) — ALEXANDER
BR. EIGHTH — MONTGOMERY
EIGHTH (xxxx)

Fr. (Corps d'Afrique)
9
1
34
78
46 (−)
1
4 Ind.
7
6
4
1
1
7
A 1
B 1
6
4
1
6
4 Ind.
(46)
1
50
51
Fr.
2 NZ

IT. FIRST (xxxx)
(Surrendered 13 May)

At the Casablanca Conference, Eisenhower was directed to invade Sicily (Operation HUSKY) in July, 1943. Reflected in the strategy discussions leading to this directive was the continuing divergence of American and British viewpoints on how best to prosecute the war against the Axis powers. The Americans, still hoping for a cross-channel invasion of France in 1943, wanted to reduce the Allied commitments in the Mediterranean in favor of continuing the build-up in England. The British had already concluded that a channel crossing in 1943 would be premature and wanted to exploit the North African success with operations aimed at weakening Italy. Both groups of planners finally agreed that the Tunisian campaign was not likely to be concluded before late spring. Consequently, troops and shipping could not be concentrated in England before September, and even then would not have reached parity with the German strength in France. Prospects of a 1943 channel crossing therefore disappeared.

British planners accordingly urged the maintenance of pressure on the Germans in the Mediterranean in order to weaken the Wehrmacht. General Marshall, however, wary of the British opportunistic and flexible approach, feared the creation of a Mediterranean vacuum which would consume the resources for the cross-channel operation. If a landing in France were not possible in 1943, he argued (ably supported by Admiral King), then some Allied resources should be diverted to the Pacific to enable the Allies to retain the initiative there. The ultimate outcome was a compromise, with limited operations in both the Mediterranean and Pacific being authorized.

In consonance with American insistence that HUSKY be an end in itself and not a stepping stone to further operations in the Mediterranean, the avowed fourfold purpose of the operation was stated as: to secure the Mediterranean line of communications (Tunisia alone could not accomplish this), to divert German divisions from Russia, to apply pressure to Italy, and to create "a situation in which Turkey can be enlisted as an active Ally." (At the next conference—*TRIDENT*, in May—Churchill obtained American consent for Eisenhower to plan for the exploitation of HUSKY with the object of eliminating Italy from the war; Eisenhower was, however, to do this with the forces he then had, less some which would be withdrawn to England.)

With the concurrent campaign in Tunisia demanding the time of the key commanders who would ultimately lead HUSKY, the development of the final plan was long delayed. D-Day (10 July) had to satisfy airborne planners who wanted moonlight and ground planners who wanted a landing in darkness; it was not fixed until 13 April, and the final plan was not firm until 3 May. Army and naval commanders were considerably indignant over air force reluctance to prepare a specific air-support plan for the landings. (The airmen maintained that the logical air targets—Axis planes and airfields—would have been eliminated by the time of the landings.) Similarly, the navy sought in vain to convince the army that a pre-invasion naval bombardment should be used, even though it compromised the attainment of tactical surprise.

Two factors exerted the major influence on the HUSKY plan: early seizure of ports and rapid capture of airfields to be used for close-support missions. The initial plan envisioned Montgomery landing on D-Day along the southeastern coast, followed by American landings two and five days later near Marsala and Palermo, respectively. (This staggering of assaults would enable captured airfields to be used to support the succeeding landings.) Montgomery objected to the Allied dispersion of effort and the failure to plan the initial capture of enough airfields, and when the logisticians reluctantly ventured that beach supply might compensate for the lack of adequate ports, Eisenhower decided to adopt the plan shown. The naval diversions were designed to contain Axis forces in western Sicily and to threaten western Greece. An elaborate hoax—involving a corpse washed ashore in Spain and bearing alleged plans for an invasion of Sardinia and Greece—apparently fooled only Hitler, who reinforced these two localities. Axis commanders pinpointed Sicily as the Allied target.

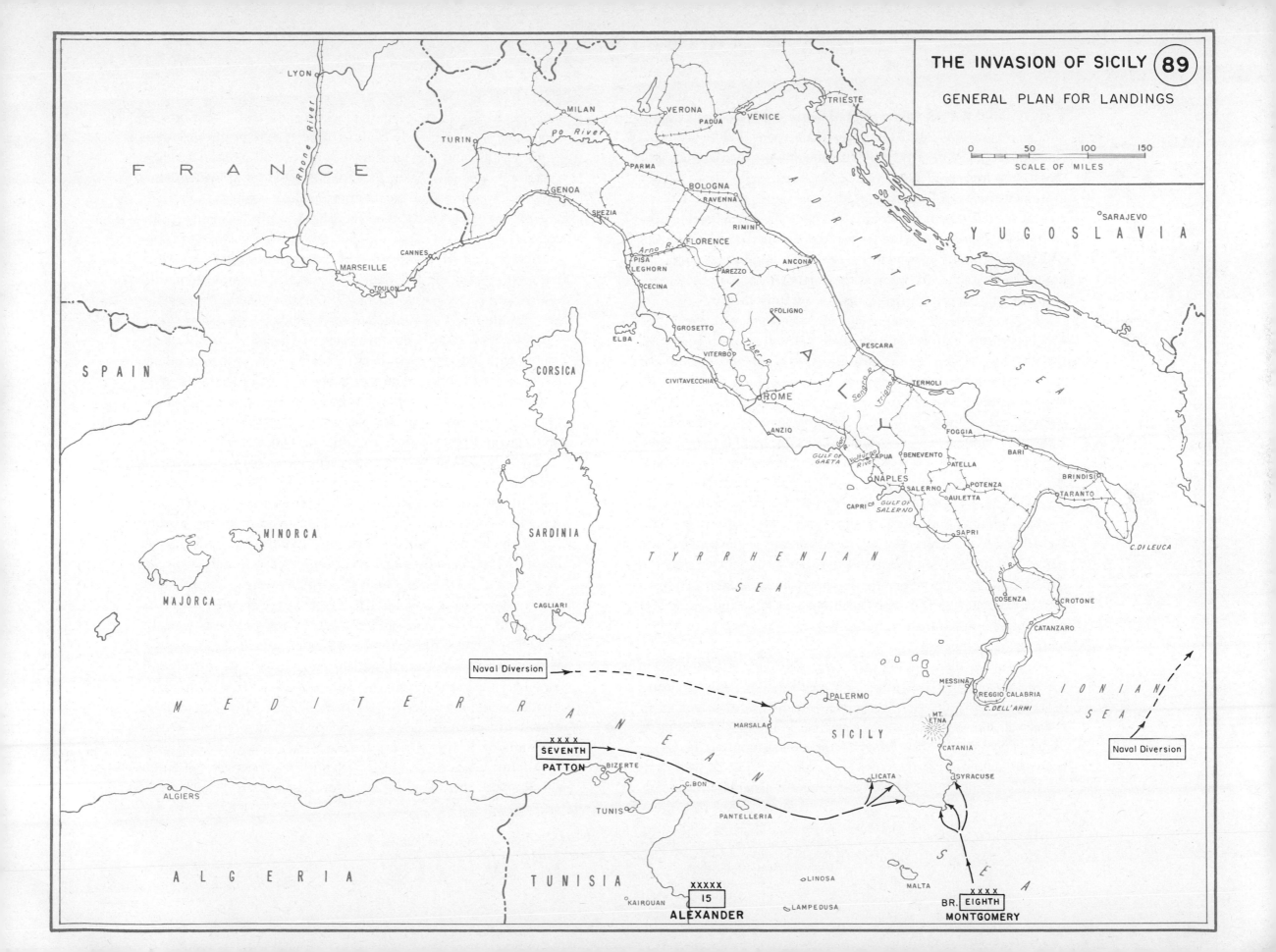

THE INVASION OF SICILY 89

GENERAL PLAN FOR LANDINGS

0   50   100   150
SCALE OF MILES

FRANCE

LYON

MILAN   VERONA   TRIESTE
PADUA   VENICE
TURIN   Po River
PARMA
GENOA   BOLOGNA
SPEZIA   RAVENNA
RIMINI
Arno R.   FLORENCE
CANNES   PISA   AREZZO   ANCONA
MARSEILLE   LEGHORN
TOULON   CECINA

YUGOSLAVIA
SARAJEVO

SPAIN

CORSICA

ELBA   GROSSETO
VITERBO   FOLIGNO   PESCARA
CIVITAVECCHIA   ROME   TERMOLI

ITALY
Tiber R.   Sangro R.   Trigno R.
FOGGIA   BARI
ANZIO   GULF OF   Volturno   CAPUA   BENEVENTO
GAETA   River   NAPLES   ATELLA   BRINDISI
CAPRI   SALERNO   POTENZA   TARANTO
GULF OF   AULETTA
SALERNO   SAPRI

MINORCA

SARDINIA

MAJORCA

CAGLIARI

TYRRHENIAN

SEA

COSENZA   CROTONE

CATANZARO

Naval Diversion

MESSINA   IONIAN
PALERMO   REGGIO CALABRIA   SEA
C. DELL'ARMI
MARSALA   Naval Diversion
SICILY
MT.
ETNA
MEDITERRANEAN   CATANIA

XXXX
SEVENTH
PATTON   BIZERTE   LICATA   SYRACUSE
C. BON
ALGIERS   SEA

TUNIS   PANTELLERIA

ALGERIA   TUNISIA   LINOSA   MALTA
XXXXX   XXXX
KAIROUAN   15   LAMPEDUSA   BR. EIGHTH
ALEXANDER   MONTGOMERY

Sicily is about the size of the state of Vermont. It is largely mountainous, hence movement except by main roads is difficult. Near Catania (*right center*) there is a sizable plain which merges into the 10,686-foot–high Mt. Etna to the north. Mt. Etna restricts movement between Catania and Messina (*top right*) to a narrow coastal stretch. The main mountain range runs along the northern coast, with spurs emanating from it toward the south. The rivers and streams, many of which dry up in the hot July climate, are not major obstacles. Messina, at the northeastern tip of the island, is just a short ferry trip from the toe of Italy proper.

As soon as the Tunisian campaign was concluded, the Allied Mediterranean air forces turned their full attention to preparing the way for HUSKY. To deprive the Axis of advanced air bases, the islands of Lampedusa, Linosa, and Pantelleria (*see map 89, bottom center*) were all captured by amphibious operations following heavy bombings. Enemy air bases in Sicily, Sardinia, and Italy were subjected to constant attacks by medium and heavy bombers. In daily raids during the month preceding the landing, Allied air power hammered at Axis fields so that, by 1 July, enemy aircraft available for the defense of Sicily numbered only 1,400 (including 600 inferior Italian craft). The Allies had 3,680. By 10 July, the German-Italian air forces had evacuated the permanent airfields on the island in order to avoid complete destruction. The night before the landing, the crescendo of Allied air attacks reached its peak as airdromes, installations, command posts (and, unfortunately, some innocent towns) were struck with savage efficiency.

The final Allied landing plan (*this map*) for HUSKY concentrated the might of two armies on southeastern Sicily. Patton's Seventh Army units were assembled, trained, and staged from Bizerte all the way west to Algiers, while Montgomery used ports between Syria and Sfax. Most of the units employed had seen previous action in North Africa, but some had just arrived from the United States or the United Kingdom. In general, Alexander's plan specified seizure of initial beachheads and the ports of Licata and Syracuse, early capture of key airdromes in the south of the island, and the juncture of the two armies along their common boundary. After the establishment of a wider base, Catania, Augusta, and the Gerbini airfield complex (*all right center*) would be seized; then the island would be methodically reduced. Though Messina was not mentioned, it was generally understood that Montgomery would move upon that city while Patton protected his left flank. The details of implementation would await future developments. Within this general framework, the Seventh Army designated Line Yellow (*dashed blue line*) as the first objective—this protected the beaches and airfields from enemy long-range artillery. Line Blue, along commanding terrain to forestall Axis counterattacks, was the second objective. Both armies planned to employ airborne forces (near Ponte Olivo [*lower center*] and Syracuse) to secure strategic points which would facilitate the advance from the beachheads.

The Axis defenders were disposed as shown, with their greatest potential combat strength in the six mobile Italian and German divisions (those not labeled "Coast"). General Alfred Guzzoni wanted to concentrate the two German divisions in the eastern half of the island, ready for a strong counterattack, but the optimistic Kesselring advocated a cordon defense to defeat the invader on the beaches; the final dispositions were a compromise. The coastal divisions, composed principally of Sicilian reservists who hated the Germans and considered the war lost, were of dubious reliability. Furthermore, Allied air attacks had seriously crippled the transportation system and had cut off intercoastal shipping, the prime means of supply. Nevertheless, Guzzoni's situation was not hopeless: Hitler had offered—Mussolini initially refused—three more divisions, and on 10 July reinforcements were moving to the Messina ferries, which were still operating. On 10 July, Axis forces on the island totaled between 300,000 and 365,000; the Allied invasion force numbered 478,000.

Note: The two brigades of Royal Marines (this map, bottom right corner) actually had been reorganized into a Royal Marine Commando Brigade. This brigade landed on the left flank of the 1st Canadian Division.

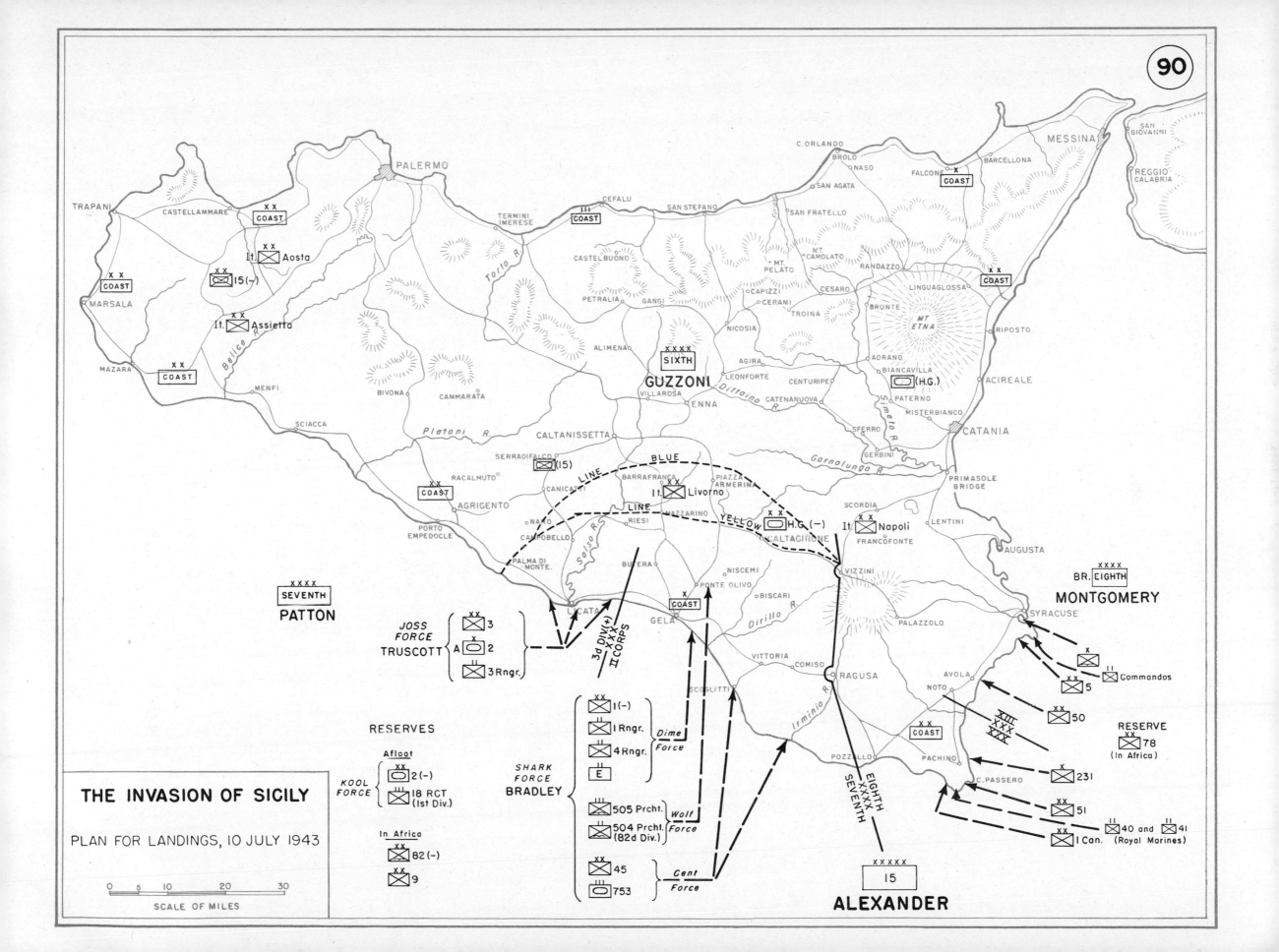

THE INVASION OF SICILY

PLAN FOR LANDINGS, 10 JULY 1943

SCALE OF MILES
0 5 10 20 30

As the convoys made their silent way toward Sicily on 9 July, a strong wind came out of the west to belabor the hundreds of ships. The heavy seas threw some of them off course and, for a time, threatened to force a postponement of HUSKY. But late that night the winds subsided somewhat, and landings began as scheduled, about 0230, 10 July. Apparently, the bad weather had thrown the defenders off guard, for the landings, in general, did not encounter serious opposition. By nightfall, the assault divisions had secured their assigned beachheads (*dashed blue lines*). The movement and landing of the 3d Division at Licata (*lower center*) was a shore-to-shore operation—the first large-scale test of the new beaching craft (LST, LCI, and LCT) which allowed the movement of a large force directly to beaches without intermediate transfer to small landing craft. It was a resounding success.

The airborne assaults, however, were not so successful. Taking off from Tunisian airfields shortly after dusk, 9 July, both airborne forces (the United States 505th Parachute Infantry Regiment and a brigade of the British 1st Airborne Division) were blown off course by the high winds. The paratroopers (gliders, in the case of the British) were scattered all over the southeastern end of the island. Amazingly enough, however, elements of the 505th managed to seize high ground near Vittoria and Ragusa (*lower right*), set up road blocks, demoralize the defenders—who overestimated their numbers—and assist in blocking the Axis counterattack on 10 July. Similarly, a small force from the British brigade captured its assigned objective—a bridge near Syracuse (*lower right*)—and held on long enough to enable the British 5th Division to move up and secure it permanently. Subsequent airborne operations took place on the nights of 11 and 13 July. On the 11th, the 504th Regiment was dropped to reinforce the 505th, and in the process suffered heavily from friendly antiaircraft fire; on the 13th, British paratroopers came in to seize a bridge south of Catania, and likewise suffered losses to friendly fire. Opinions vary as to the overall value of the four airborne drops. Admittedly, inexperience in planning and mounting such complex operations—as well as lack of coordination among services—contributed materially to the questionable results. Nevertheless, the airborne elements played an important part in the success of HUSKY.

General Guzzoni ordered the Hermann Göring Panzer and the Livorno Divisions to counterattack the Gela beachhead on 10 July. Some Italian tanks attempted to carry out the order, but were stopped by infantry units and naval gunfire. They had, however, disconcerted the II Corps troops who were having great difficulty getting supplies and equipment ashore. The Luftwaffe added to the confusion by harassing the unloading almost at will, and might have seriously crippled the landing force had its bombing been more accurate. The failure of the pre-invasion planning to provide an Allied air umbrella over the beachheads was responsible for the Luftwaffe having a free hand. Fortunately, the new amphibious truck (DUKW) proved of tremendous help in bringing supplies and artillery ashore. That night, Patton began landing his floating reserve.

The 11th of July was the critical day of the campaign for the Allies. On this date, the German armor launched a counterattack (*not shown*) toward Gela. It was repelled by the combined efforts of superb naval gunfire, artillery, dogged infantry action, and American tanks; but the Seventh Army suffered more casualties than in any other twenty-four–hour period of the campaign. On 13 July, Guzzoni, with Kesselring's approval, ordered most of his remaining mobile elements out of western Sicily and began to concentrate his strength to cover the Catania plain; henceforth, his tactics would be those of delay and attrition. Hitler concurred and, concluding that the Italians would soon collapse, authorized the dispatch of additional German troops to Sicily.

Between 12 and 15 July, the Allies joined their beachheads, established a continuous line, and advanced northward against spotty resistance, capturing several key airfields. By the 15th, Patton had the 2d Armored and 82d Airborne Divisions in reserve near Gela—the 9th Division was still in Africa—and Montgomery was meeting stiffer resistance as he moved toward Catania.

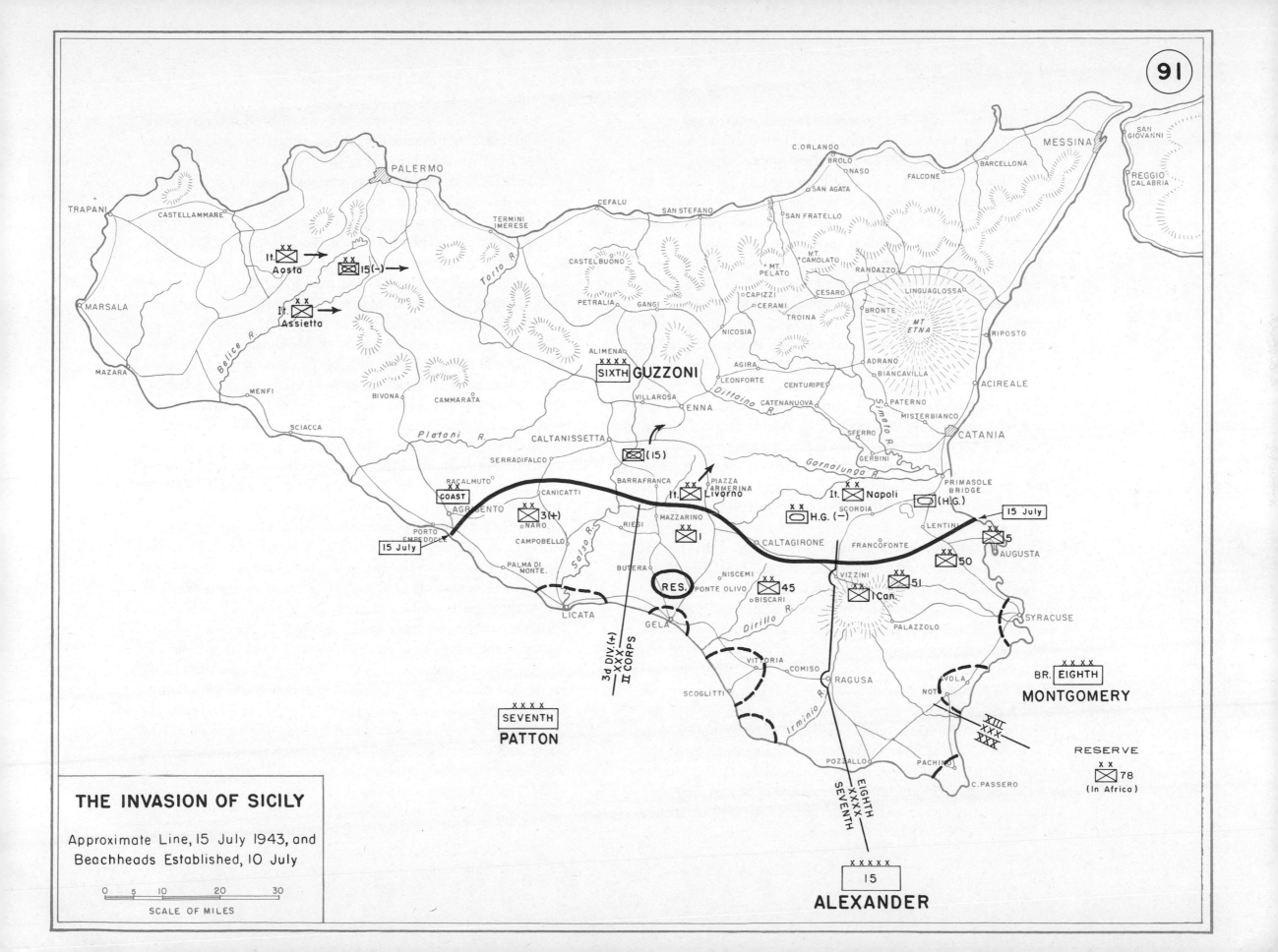

THE INVASION OF SICILY

Approximate Line, 15 July 1943, and
Beachheads Established, 10 July

0 5 10   20   30
SCALE OF MILES

Possessing a more definitive appreciation of Axis dispositions by now, Alexander issued a directive on 15 July outlining his plan for securing the island. The Eighth Army was to advance northward on either side of Mt. Etna, with Messina as its ultimate objective. The Seventh Army would protect Montgomery's rear as he pivoted northeastward, push a force north to the coast to cut the island in two, and eventually mop up western Sicily.

Patton initially implemented the directive by seizing Agrigento and additional port facilities at Porto Empedocle (*center, left*), and by sending the II Corps northward toward Villarosa (*center*). In order to move the Canadian 1st Division inland, the road through Caltagirone had been reserved for Montgomery's use. This necessitated a westward shift of the boundary between armies. This arrangement left Bradley (II Corps) no choice but to sideslip the 45th Division to the west in a difficult move through a congested area. Upon the capture of Agrigento on 17 July, Patton obtained Alexander's approval for an immediate drive on Palermo (*top left*). The next day, he created the Provisional Corps (Maj. Gen. Geoffrey Keyes); assigned to it the 2d Armored, 3d Infantry, and 82d Airborne Divisions; and ordered Keyes to overrun western Sicily. This proved to be an easy task, for Guzzoni's mobile elements had largely evacuated that part of the island, and the coastal divisions did not offer much resistance. Truscott's 3d Division, in a march reminiscent of Stonewall Jackson's "foot cavalry," made the 100-mile advance to Palermo in four days, despite rugged country and skillful rear-guard action by the mobile forces withdrawing to the east. The shattered city —a previous Allied air target—surrendered on 22 July; the next day, the 2d Armored Division, bearing Patton in triumph, arrived. By the 24th, the 82d Airborne Division had mopped up its zone, capturing 20,000 Italians at Trapani and Castellammare (*top left*). In the II Corps' zone, the 45th Division met little opposition in its drive to the coast east of Palermo (23 July); but the 1st Division, encountering the stiffest resistance of any of the American units, moved more slowly, reaching Enna (*center*) on 20 July and Petralia three days later.

Meanwhile, the Eighth Army had encountered stiff opposition in its drive toward Catania, as Guzzoni shifted his better divisions to that front. A British airborne force (*see text, map 91*) had seized the Primasole Bridge (*this map, right center*) on the 13th, but was dislodged the next night; by the time the 50th Division recaptured the bridge on the 15th, Guzzoni had shifted all of the Hermann Göring Division to that sector. For the next four days, Montgomery struggled unsuccessfully to expand his bridgehead and take Catania. On the 19th, he tried to outflank the German position by moving the 5th and 51st Divisions inland as shown. but success still proved elusive.

On 20 July, Alexander, aware of Montgomery's reluctance to continue the costly frontal attack along the coast, again modified his strategy. Patton was now ordered to change front and drive eastward along the north coast toward Messina. Montgomery would make a sharper hook around Mt. Etna with the Canadians to afford the Seventh Army the necessary room; meanwhile, he would refrain from active offensive operations south of Catania until the other troops were in position for the final push. Perhaps it would have been less costly in the long run—and more rewarding in prisoners—to accept high initial casualties in an all-out attempt to break through on the Catania front. Thus, the Germans might not have been able to organize so strong a position in the mountains and bring in as many reinforcements as the week of grace enabled them to do. The Allied amphibious capability might also have been exploited.

Upon receiving Alexander's directive, Patton turned the 1st, 3d, and 45th Divisions eastward. By 23 July, as the Allies stood on the line shown, Kesselring had already moved the 29th Panzer Grenadier Division and two regiments of the 1st Parachute Division (*not shown, but with the Hermann Göring panzers*) to Sicily, and General Hube had arrived to exercise command over the German troops.

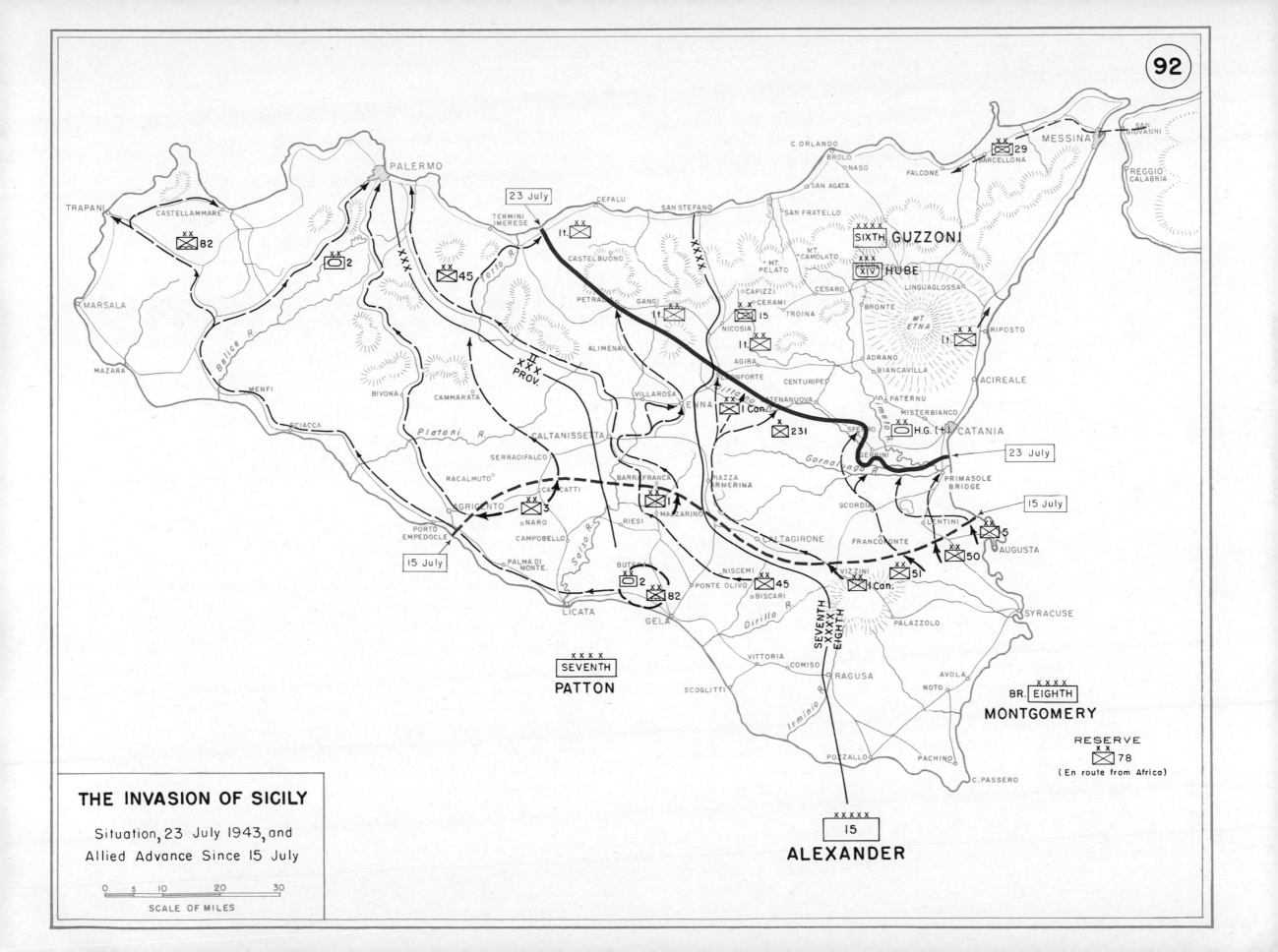

92

THE INVASION OF SICILY

Situation, 23 July 1943, and
Allied Advance Since 15 July

0 5 10   20   30
SCALE OF MILES

SEVENTH
PATTON

BR. EIGHTH
MONTGOMERY

RESERVE
78
(En route from Africa)

15
ALEXANDER

Patton wasted no time in implementing Alexander's 20 July directive. Utilizing the only two feasible axes of advance in the difficult mountainous terrain—the coastal route and the Gangi-Nicosia-Randazzo road (*upper center*)—the 1st and 45th Divisions pushed to the east. By 2 August, they had reached the line shown, where it became obvious that Axis resistance was stiffening. The 3d Division relieved the 45th and prepared to assault the strong position at San Fratello, while the 1st, now reinforced with a combat team from the 9th Division, made plans for the capture of Troina. Patton spared no effort to support Bradley: additional artillery was provided; the remainder of the 9th Division, unloaded at Palermo on 1 August, was prepared for movement to the 1st Division sector; and naval aid was enlisted for the coastal operations.

Meanwhile, in the Eighth Army sector, Montgomery had side-stepped the 5th and 51st Divisions westward and given them five days to prepare for attacks out of their small bridgeheads. The attacks came on 31 July and, in conjunction with thrusts by the newly arrived 78th Division and the Canadians, forced the Germans back to the Simeto River (*center, right*).

Their key position at Adrano now threatened, the Germans began to pull back from the Catania position. Already—on 31 July—Guzzoni had decided to evacuate the Italian troops (*note, top right*), and shortly thereafter Kesselring authorized Hube to exercise his own judgment as to when to begin evacuating the Germans. Hube had already selected five positions upon which to delay while the evacuation took place; the first of these was the San Fratello–Troina–Bronte–Adrano line, which the Allies had just begun to probe. As events will show, the Allies did not seriously upset his delaying schedule or evacuation.

On 3 August, the 1st and 3d Divisions launched attacks in their respective areas. In the north, Truscott's troops broke through to the Furiano River, but here they were stopped for three days. At Troina, the 1st Division, in spite of overwhelming artillery and air support, was unable to crack the German defenses. The enemy made skillful use of the rugged terrain and augmented it with mine fields, road blocks, and demolitions. On the 5th, the 9th Division attacked through the mountains toward Cesaro; probably, the success it achieved forced the outflanked Germans to evacuate Troina that night. The 1st Division promptly occupied it and was then relieved by the 9th Division. On 6 August, Hube also abandoned the San Fratello position in time to evade the amphibious envelopment by an American reinforced battalion on the 8th. As shown, Patton made two more of these "end runs" in an attempt to exploit naval superiority, and Montgomery belatedly tried one. None of these succeeded in trapping sizable Axis forces.

By 8 August, the Allies were advancing slowly all along the front. Montgomery had finally occupied an abandoned Catania on the 5th and Adrano on the 7th. The British threat to Bronte forced the Germans to pull back from the 9th Division front; Randazzo was occupied by that unit on the 13th. Too late, the Allies entered Messina on 17 August to find Hube's force gone.

The Germans had delayed skillfully and methodically as the evacuation from Messina proceeded in an orderly manner. In spite of Allied naval and air superiority, the Axis evacuated some 100,000 troops, 9,800 vehicles, and 47 tanks during the period of 3-17 August. The haphazard Allied attempts to stop the evacuation only succeeded in sinking seven boats and damaging an equal number. The three German divisions which escaped would make their presence painfully felt in the coming Italian campaign.

Two events associated with the conquest of Sicily exerted considerable influence on Allied global strategy. Three days after the fall of Palermo, Mussolini was ousted as Italy's ruler. News of Mussolini's overthrow triggered the second event: on 26 July, the CCS ordered Eisenhower to plan for landings at the bay of Salerno (*see map 94*).

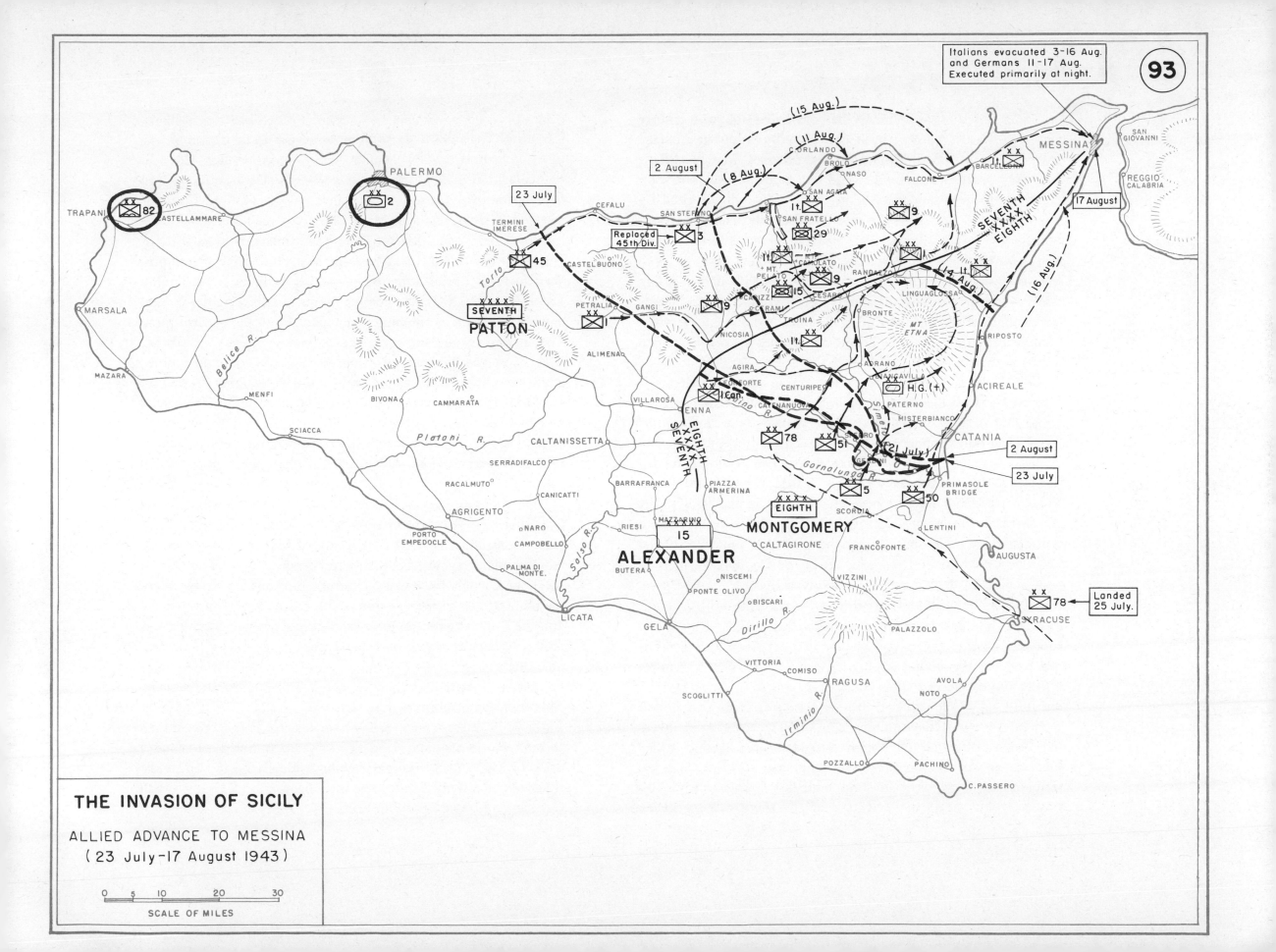

THE INVASION OF SICILY

ALLIED ADVANCE TO MESSINA
(23 July–17 August 1943)

On 24-25 July, 1943, with the Sicilian campaign still being bitterly contested, Italian war-weariness unexpectedly produced a palace revolt which overthrew Mussolini. His successor, Marshal Pietro Badoglio, pledged that Italy would continue the war, but soon began secret negotiations with the Allies. Though surprised by Mussolini's sudden fall, Hitler reacted decisively: German troops fighting in Sicily were ordered to prepare for a withdrawal back into Italy; German divisions already in that country laid plans to seize control and disarm the Italian forces there; and a strong reserve was gradually moved into northern Italy, since it was feared that the first sign of Italian desertion would be an attempt to block the Alpine passes in northern Italy and so cut off German troops in the south.

The Allies were hampered by conflicting strategic objectives. The British, with their traditional interests in the Mediterranean, urged that past Allied successes be exploited by an invasion of Italy or the Balkans. General Marshall wanted to withdraw maximum forces from the Mediterranean to speed the build-up for the projected invasion of northern France. The United States Navy, its primary interest being in the war in the Pacific, demanded the transfer of scarce assault (amphibious) shipping to the Far East. Finally, during the TRIDENT and QUADRANT Conferences (May and August, 1943) the Combined Chiefs of Staff agreed on the major European operations for 1944. Operation OVERLORD would be the primary United States–British effort in Europe and, as such, it would command priority in men and supplies. Operations in the Mediterranean, therefore, must be designed to immobilize enough German divisions to enable OVERLORD to succeed. This could best be accomplished by forcing Italy out of the war and by threatening Germany's southern frontier; these objectives, in turn, could best be achieved by invading Italy. Possession of Italian airfields would enable Allied bombers to strike industrial areas—hitherto relatively inaccessible—in southern Germany and southeast Europe. Italy's surrender would cause the defection of the thousands of Italian troops on occupation duty in southern France and the Balkans, forcing the Germans to garrison those areas with their own forces. Finally, later operations would occupy Sardinia and Corsica, tightening the Allied grip on the western Mediterranean and opening the way for an eventual invasion of southern France.

On 27 July, Lt. Gen. Mark Clark, commanding the American Fifth Army, was directed to prepare plans for the capture of Naples (*right center*) as a base for future offensive operations. Two factors restricted the scope of his planning: the limited (approximately 200-mile) combat radius of Allied fighter planes, and the shortage of shipping. This map shows his general plan. The invasion would be preceded by intense Allied air strikes, which would concentrate on enemy airfields and communications, and a naval task force would carry out a diversionary attack in the Gulf of Gaeta (*right center*). Initial planning had included an American airborne operation—originally to hold the Volturno River (*north of Naples*) against German reinforcements; later, to seize Rome's (*center, right*) airfields. This operation was abandoned after complex secret negotiations with the Italians.

The Italians signed a secret armistice on 3 September. At 0430 that same day, two British divisions (from the Eighth Army) made an assault crossing of the Straits of Messina (*lower right*), moving inland against negligible resistance. (This operation, it was hoped, would draw German forces into southern Italy, where the main attack might cut them off.) From the 3d through the 7th, the convoys carrying the Fifth Army stood out from various ports to rendezvous late on 8 September, preparatory to an amphibious assault in the Salerno area early on the 9th (*see maps 95 and 96*). At the last minute, another secondary attack (amphibious) was improvised to seize the Italian naval base at Taranto (*this map, right center*) on the 9th. When the Italian surrender was announced on the 8th, the Italian fleet made a dash for Malta (*bottom right*), enthusiastically belabored by the Luftwaffe as it went. At the same time, fighting broke out between German and Italian troops in Rome.

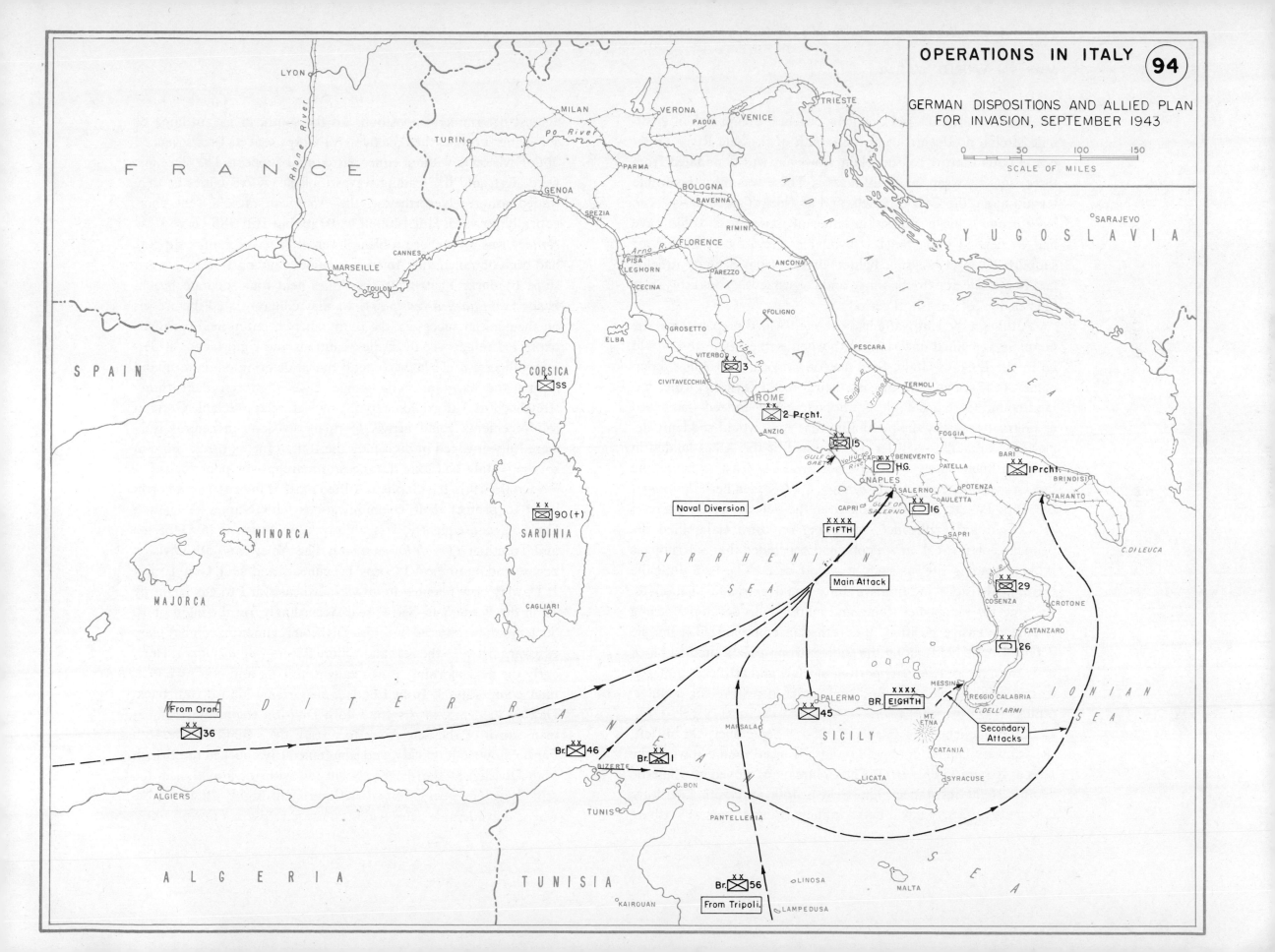

FRANCE

LYON

RHONE RIVER

MILAN VERONA TRIESTE

TURIN PADUA VENICE

PO RIVER

PARMA

GENOA BOLOGNA RAVENNA

SPEZIA RIMINI

MARSEILLE ARNO R. FLORENCE ANCONA

CANNES PISA AREZZO

TOULON LEGHORN

CECINA

OFOLIGNO

SPAIN GROSETTO

ELBA PESCARA

VITERBO TERMOLI

CORSICA CIVITAVECCHIA

SS ROME FOGGIA

2 Prcht. BARI

ANZIO BENEVENTO 1 Prcht.

15 CAPUA BRINDISI

GULF OF GAETA HG. PATELLA

SARDINIA VOLTURNO RIVER NAPLES POTENZA

90(+) SALERNO AULETTA

CAPRI GULF OF SALERNO 16 TARANTO

CAGLIARI SAPRI C. DI LEUCA

Naval Diversion FIFTH

MINORCA

TYRRHENIAN SEA

29 COSENZA CROTONE

Main Attack

MAJORCA CATANZARO

26

MESSINA

PALERMO REGGIO CALABRIA IONIAN

BR. EIGHTH C. DELL'ARMI SEA

From Oran. 45 MT. ETNA Secondary Attacks

36 MARSALA SICILY

CATANIA

MEDITERRANEAN

Br. 46 LICATA SYRACUSE

Br. 1

ALGIERS BIZERTE

C. BON

ALGERIA TUNISIA PANTELLERIA MALTA SEA

TUNIS

Br. 56 LINOSA

KAIROUAN From Tripoli. LAMPEDUSA

YUGOSLAVIA

SARAJEVO

ADRIATIC SEA

The Salerno area offered excellent beaches, except for an eight-mile stretch northward from the mouth of the Sele River (*right center*). Its narrow coastal plain, however, was dominated from three sides by steep, high hill masses. There was more favorable terrain along the Gulf of Gaeta and at Anzio (*see map 94, both right center*), but a landing in either of those areas would have had to depend upon the few available aircraft carriers for air support. Even at Salerno, fighter aircraft from Sicilian airfields had to operate at extreme range and consequently could stay over the beaches for only short periods.

Although the Luftwaffe had detected Allied preparations, the Germans remained uncertain as to whether their objective would be in the Balkans, Italy, Sardinia, or Corsica. The Allies' command of the sea and the air gave their forces a flexibility which the land-bound Germans could not hope to equal. Indeed—menaced as Germany was by the possibility that Italy would suddenly declare for the Allies—Hitler had planned, if the Allies landed in Italy, to immediately withdraw northward at least as far as the line Grosetto-Ancona (*upper center*). On 6 September (*this map*), the 16th Panzer Division took over the defense of the Salerno area. German intelligence, reckoning on the usual Allied dependence on tactical air support, had concluded that Salerno was a likely landing site; as such, it would have to be held until the German divisions in southern Italy could extricate themselves. Lacking the manpower, time, and materials to develop a strong coastal defensive position, the 16th Panzer organized a mobile defense: mine fields along the shore; strong points sited to block exits from the beaches; supporting mortars and artillery emplaced to cover the whole area; and tank units in reserve for counterattacks.

Clark launched his assault at 0330, 9 September. On his left, the Rangers landed unopposed and advanced inland toward the pass at Nocera (*upper left*). The Commandos moved into Salerno against slight resistance. The British 46th and 56th Divisions, covered by a heavy naval bombardment, fought their way ashore against determined opposition. To the south, in a vain hope of achieving surprise, the American VI Corps sent its inexperienced 36th Division in without either naval or air support. The Germans were alert, and the leading waves took heavy casualties as they waded ashore. Nevertheless, the American attack went energetically forward. Hill 140 fell by 0730, but Hill 386 (*both right center*) was a tougher problem. Even after naval gunfire support had been obtained, the Americans gained only part of its forward slope by dark. That night, the Allies held four separate beachheads (*thin dashed red lines*). As they congratulated themselves on their initial successes, the outnumbered, outgunned Germans expressed relief over the Allies' cautious and rigid tactics. (German officers would later contend that a determined drive inland during the early morning would have shattered their thinly stretched line.) It would be some time before appreciable German reinforcements could arrive. German divisions in central Italy were fully engaged in disarming the Italian forces there; those in southern Italy had long distances to march, over poor roads.

On the 10th, the Germans shifted most of their strength northward to protect their communications with Naples. The 36th Division, consequently, was able to push forward to Ogliastro and Trentinara (*both lower right*). The American 45th Division began landing in the VI Corps' beachhead, and Maj. Gen. Ernest J. Dawley now planned to attack northeastward to cut Highway 19 in the Ponte Sele–Serre area. Accordingly, on the night of 10 September, he ordered one 45th Division regimental combat team eastward between the Sele and Calore Rivers (*right center*). Here, early the next morning, it was caught in flank and rear by a German counterattack from Eboli (*upper right*) and driven back. Dawley then moved a second 45th Division regimental combat team north of the Sele River to restore the situation. The 16th Panzer stopped it quickly, and simultaneously checked the British 56th Division at Battipaglia. Night fell with the situation in the Allied center (*heavy dashed red line*) still highly "fluid." Elsewhere, considerable gains had been made (*solid red line*).

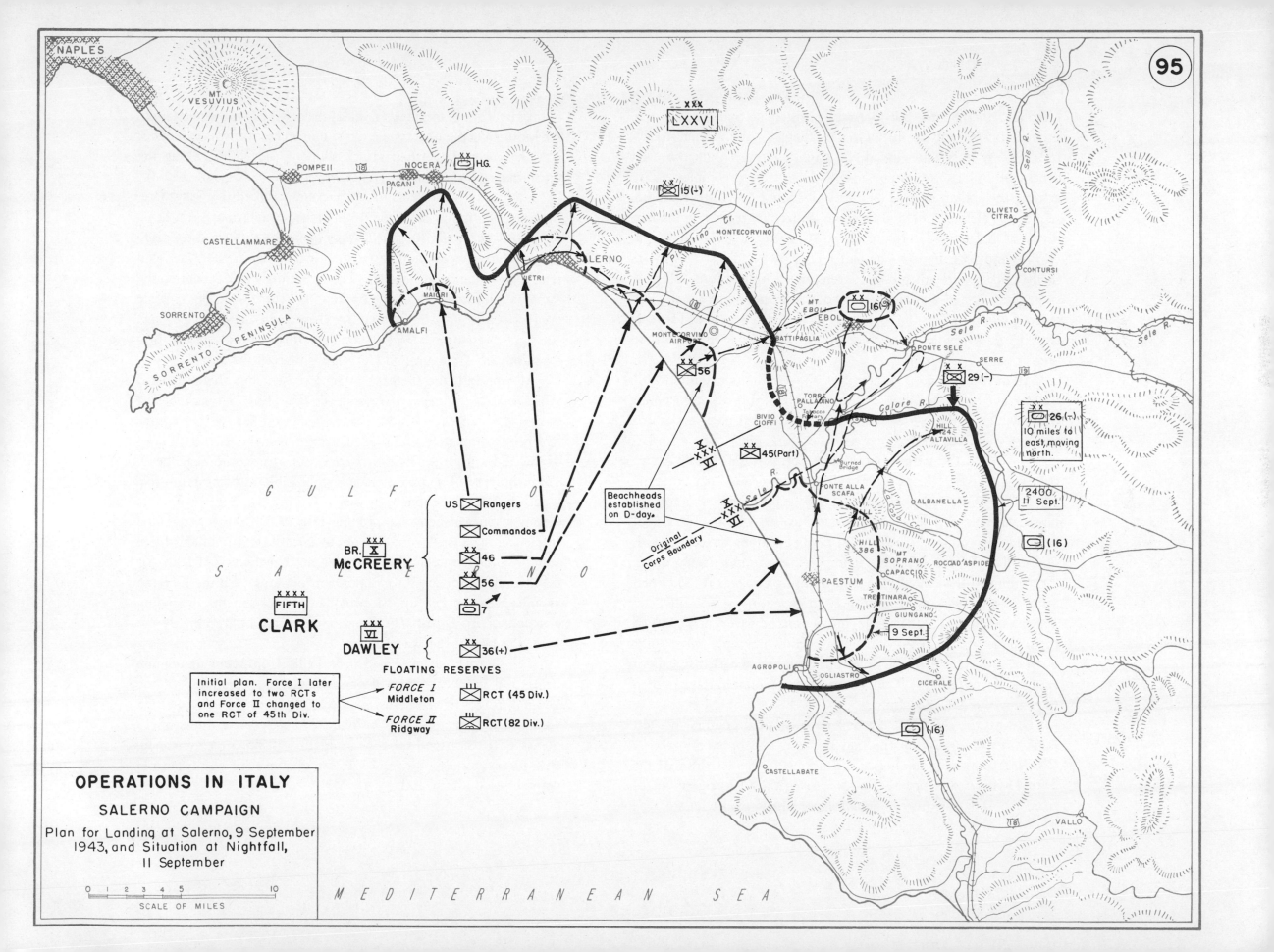

NAPLES

MT VESUVIUS

POMPEII

NOCERA

PAGANI

CASTELLAMMARE

SORRENTO

SORRENTO PENINSULA

AMALFI

MAIORI

VIETRI

SALERNO

XXX
LXXVI

XX
H.G.

XX
15(-)

MONTECORVINO

OLIVETO CITRA

CONTURSI

MT EBOLI

EBOLI

XX
16(-)

Sele R.

XX
56

MONTECORVINO AIRPORT

BATTIPAGLIA

PONTE SELE

SERRE

XX
29(-)

TORRE PALLADINO

Galore R.

XX
26(-)
10 miles to east, moving north.

BIVIO CIOFFI

XX
XXX
VI

XX
45(Part)

HILL 424
ALTAVILLA

2400
11 Sept.

Sele R.

Burned Bridge

PONTE ALLA SCAFA

ALBANELLA

(16)

GULF

OF

SALERNO

US   Rangers

Commandos

BR. X
McCREERY

46

56

7

XXXX
FIFTH
CLARK

XXX
VI
DAWLEY

36(+)

Beachheads established on D-day.

Original Corps Boundary

XXX
VI

PAESTUM

HILL 386

MT SOPRANO

CAPACCIO

ROCCAD ASPIDE

TRENTINARA

GIUNGANO

9 Sept.

(16)

FLOATING RESERVES

Initial plan. Force I later increased to two RCTs and Force II changed to one RCT of 45th Div.

FORCE I
Middleton   RCT (45 Div.)

FORCE II
Ridgway   RCT (82 Div.)

AGROPOLI

OGLIASTRO

CICERALE

(16)

CASTELLABATE

VALLO

OPERATIONS IN ITALY

SALERNO CAMPAIGN

Plan for Landing at Salerno, 9 September 1943, and Situation at Nightfall, 11 September

0 1 2 3 4 5   10
SCALE OF MILES

MEDITERRANEAN   SEA

Despite Allied gains, the German position at Salerno had improved considerably by the night of 11 September. German troops in southern Italy had eluded the Eighth Army, while those in central Italy had, by prompt and decisive action, completed disarming the Italian ground and air units concentrated there. Consequently, elements of five German panzer or panzer grenadier divisions had arrived to reinforce the 16th Panzer. (The Hermann Göring and 15th Panzer Grenadier Divisions had lost heavily in Sicily, and so were much below strength.) With this force, Kesselring, the German commander in southern and central Italy, decided it might be possible to destroy the Salerno beachhead before the Eighth Army could advance up the Italian peninsula to that area.

At daybreak on 12 September, the Germans assaulted Hill 424 (*right center*), finally recapturing it during the afternoon. Meanwhile, in the center, the battle had surged back and forth through the Tobacco Factory area (*center, right*). The 45th Division held it at nightfall, but contact between the British X and the American VI Corps remained tenuous in this area, a sector some five miles wide being held largely by a screen of reconnaissance units. (The weakness of the Allied line at this critical point had its origin in the fact that sand bars along the coast north of the Sele River had made it impossible to land troops there. According to the Allied plan, the resulting gap was to be closed quickly by converging British and American drives to Ponte Sele. The 16th Panzer's skillful delaying action, however, had stopped them short of that town, preventing a firm link-up.) After dark on the 12th, a driving German attack threw the British out of Battipaglia, further weakening this sector. Counterattacks failed to restore the Allied position.

During the day, Dawley had decided to strengthen his left flank, in order to close the gap between his forces and the X Corps. Accordingly, he began shifting his troops northward: the 36th Division was ordered to take over the Calore-Sele sector from the 45th, and also to detach troops from the Ogliastro area to take over the extreme left flank of the corps around Bivio Cioffi. At 1530, 13 September, while this sidling maneuver was still under way, a powerful German attack suddenly developed along the north bank of the Sele River. Beating the right flank of the 45th Division away from Persano, the Germans forced the Sele there, overran a battalion from the 36th Division, and drove southeast for a ford (*near the Burned Bridge; center, right*) on the Calore River. Once across the Calore, they would be in the American rear areas along the beaches. The situation was desperate; the American infantry lines were broken; and there was considerable confusion, verging on panic. But American artillerymen, just south of the Burned Bridge, standing to their guns in the best traditions of Antietam and Gettysburg, barred the way.

At nightfall, the German attacks ceased, but the exhausted Allies had to struggle to reestablish their lines along the best available defensive position. Losses had been heavy; many units had been completely scattered. During the night, two battalions of the 82d Airborne Division were dropped into the beachhead. (The shortage of shipping made it impossible to bring reinforcements in rapidly enough by sea.) During 14 September, the Germans pushed constant probing attacks all along the Allied front, seeking a weak spot. Thanks to splendid naval and air force support (the Strategic Air Force of the Northwest African Air Command was diverted to tactical air missions), all the German assaults were broken up. More Allied reinforcements, including elements of the British 7th Armored Division, poured in. By the 15th, the beachhead was safe.

The German defense had been skillful, inflicting maximum delay and casualties. Had Rommel (then in command of the German forces in northern Italy) seen fit to reinforce Kesselring with two or three divisions in time for the German attack on 13 September, the Allied beachhead might well have been crushed. But, fortunately for the Allies, Rommel could see no purpose in defending southern Italy.

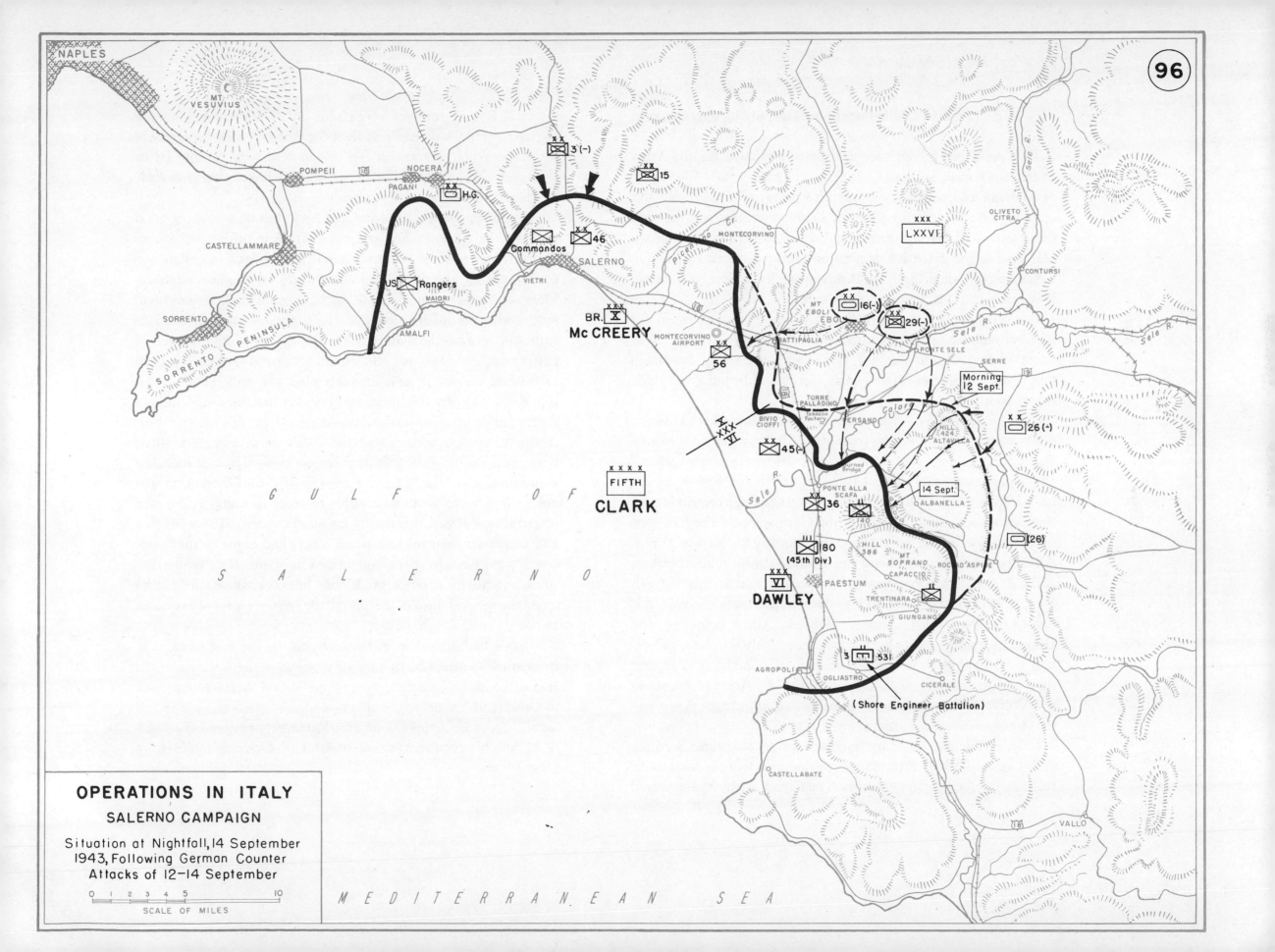

OPERATIONS IN ITALY

SALERNO CAMPAIGN

Situation at Nightfall, 14 September
1943, Following German Counter
Attacks of 12–14 September

SCALE OF MILES
0 1 2 3 4 5   10

MEDITERRANEAN SEA

This map summarizes Allied operations in Italy up to 8 October, 1943.

As previously noted (*see text, map 94*), two Eighth Army divisions (British 5th and Canadian 1st) had crossed the Straits of Messina and begun a long march northward through difficult country. (Because of the shortage of shipping, this was the only feasible way of getting them into Italy.) Small, mobile German rear guards and extensive demolitions delayed their advance. On 9 September, when the Fifth Army struggled ashore at Salerno, they were still 130 miles to the south.

Also on the 9th, the British 1st Airborne Division carried out its improvised amphibious assault on Taranto (*this map, right center*), only to find that the Germans had already evacuated that town. Pushing north and east, it occupied Brindisi and Bari; subsequently, it was strongly reinforced.

On 16 September, leading elements of the British 5th Division made contact with a Fifth Army patrol forty miles southeast of Salerno. Kesselring, therefore, began a deliberate disengagement and withdrawal from the Salerno area on 18 September, falling back from one delaying position to the next through terrain ideally suited for such tactics. Initially, the Germans held the hill mass north of Salerno to gain time enough to destroy the Naples harbor. Allied forces in the beachhead had received sizable reinforcements and now pushed vigorously after the German rear guards, without —generally speaking—hurrying them appreciably. Naples was finally occupied on 1 October. Between Allied bombings and German demolitions, its harbor was thoroughly wrecked, but expert work by American engineers soon had it operating at greater than prewar capacity. By 6 October, the Fifth Army had reached the Volturno River (*right center*), to find all bridges down and the stream swollen by autumn rains.

Meanwhile, the Germans had successfully evacuated Sardinia and Corsica, while Kesselring cobbled together a continuous front across the Italian peninsula. The Eighth Army had captured the vital Foggia complex of airfields on 27 September, but the Germans made a determined fight for Termoli (28 September– 6 October) before being at last driven across the Trigno River —in part, through a small-scale amphibious envelopment of their left flank by a commando brigade.

On 26 September, believing that his forces were making good progress, Eisenhower had ordered that their offensive be continued to seize Rome (*center, right*). Alexander's intention was to follow that operation with an advance to the line Leghorn- Florence (*upper center*). Both of these commanders were planning under the assumption that the Germans still intended to withdraw into northern Italy. (Allied intelligence had learned of Hitler's original plan, and all German actions so far had appeared to confirm the impression that this plan was still operational.) But Kesselring, by this time, had decided that he could wage a successful defense for a considerable period south of Rome. Furthermore, he felt certain that the Allies, with Foggia in their possession, would now halt their Italian campaign and launch a major invasion of the Balkans. Consequently, the Germans should hold a line as far south as possible in order to hamper any such preparations. Hitler, apparently far more concerned over his Balkan conquests than for southern France, had come to that same conclusion; Kesselring was authorized to organize a "Winter Position" (actually a series of defense lines, organized in depth) along the general trace of the Garigliano (*right center;* abbreviated as "Gar.") and Sangro Rivers.

Italy's withdrawal from the war had, in the meantime, confronted the Germans with a major problem in the Balkans, as the Italian troops on occupation duty there turned their weapons over to Greek and Yugoslav guerrillas—and, on occasion, even joined them. Vigorous German counteraction largely restored the situation, but this required further transfer of German forces from other fronts.

Note: On this map, the boxed note north of Corsica (top center) and that east of Sardinia (center), together with their adjoining arrows, should be red.

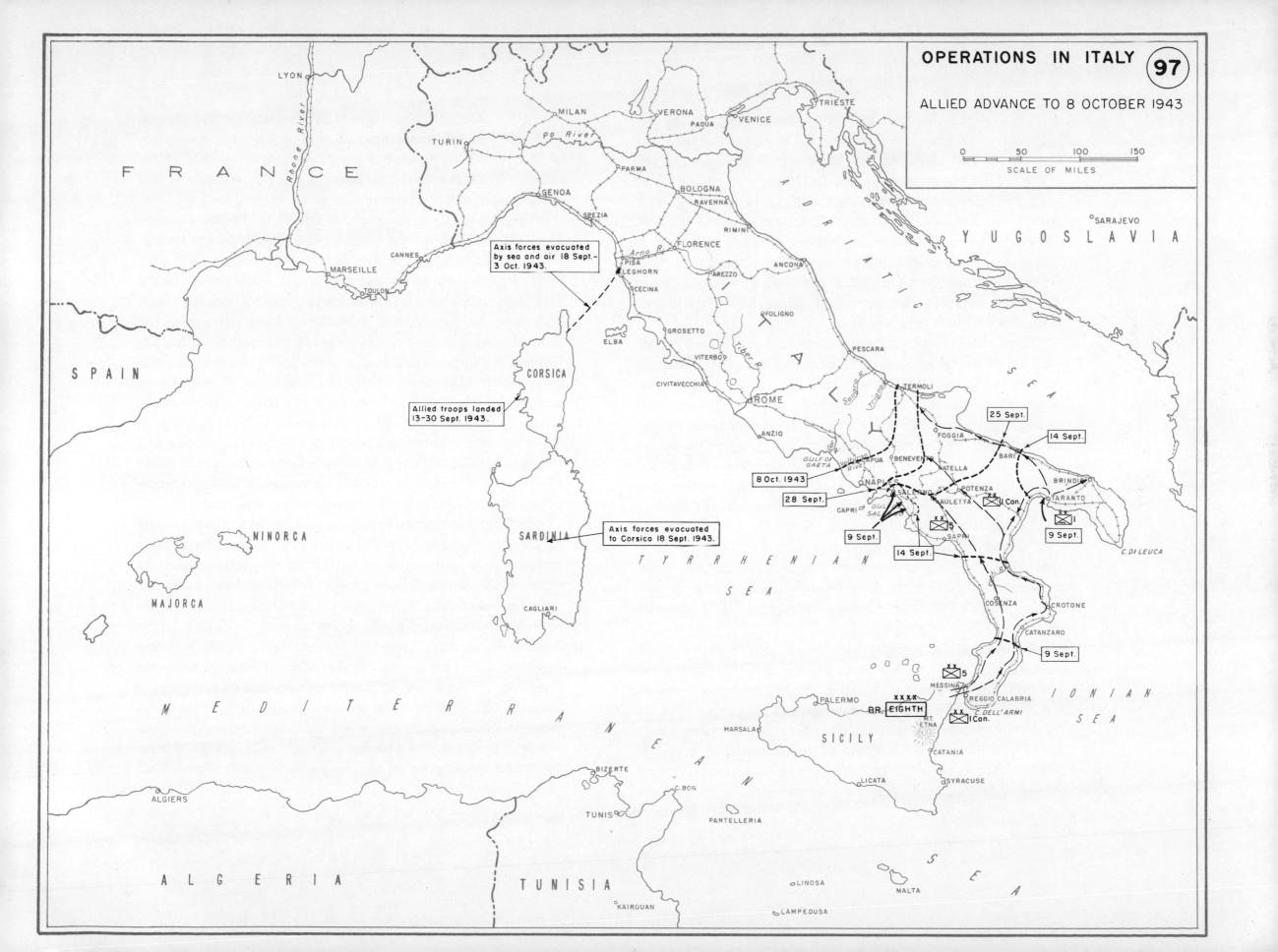

FRANCE

LYON

Rhone River

MILAN
TURIN
Po River
VERONA
PADUA
VENICE
TRIESTE

GENOA
SPEZIA
PARMA
BOLOGNA
RAVENNA
RIMINI

Arno R.
PISA
LEGHORN
CECINA
FLORENCE
AREZZO
ANCONA

Axis forces evacuated
by sea and air 18 Sept.–
3 Oct. 1943.

SPAIN

CORSICA

ELBA

GROSETTO

FOLIGNO

Tiber R.

VITERBO

PESCARA

CIVITAVECCHIA

ROME

Sangro R.

Trigno R.

TERMOLI

25 Sept.

Allied troops landed
13-30 Sept. 1943.

ANZIO

FOGGIA

14 Sept.

GULF OF
GAETA

VOLTURNO
RIVER

CAPUA

BENEVENTO

ATELLA

BARI

8 Oct. 1943

NAPLES

SALERNO

POTENZA

I Can.

BRINDISI

TARANTO

28 Sept.

CAPRI

GULF OF
SALERNO

AULETTA

SARDINIA

Axis forces evacuated
to Corsica 18 Sept. 1943.

MINORCA

9 Sept.

SAPRI

5

14 Sept.

I

9 Sept.

C. DI LEUCA

MAJORCA

T Y R R H E N I A N

S E A

CAGLIARI

COSENZA

CROTONE

CATANZARO

9 Sept.

5

I O N I A N

S E A

M E D I T E R R A N E A N   S E A

PALERMO

BR. EIGHTH

MESSINA

REGGIO CALABRIA

C. DELL'ARMI

I Can.

MARSALA

MT.
ETNA

SICILY

CATANIA

BIZERTE

C. BON

LICATA

SYRACUSE

ALGIERS

TUNIS

PANTELLERIA

ALGERIA

TUNISIA

LINOSA

MALTA

S E
A

KAIROUAN

LAMPEDUSA

A D R I A T I C   S E A

YUGOSLAVIA

SARAJEVO

By early October, the Allies had achieved their initial objectives: Italy had surrendered; the Germans had evacuated Sardinia and Corsica; the port of Naples was being rapidly restored; and the capture of the Foggia airfields gave the Allied air forces excellent bases for raids against the "underbelly" of Hitler's temporary empire. Furthermore, the Germans had been forced to rush additional troops into Italy and the Balkans, including many panzer and panzer grenadier divisions which would be sorely missed from the Russian front. With the wisdom conferred by hindsight, some critics have suggested that the Allied ground forces should now have gone on the defensive in Italy.

There were, however, definite reasons for a continued advance. The first, previously mentioned, was Allied knowledge of the original German plan to withdraw into northern Italy; some pressure would probably hurry this movement along. Rome was an important political objective; its liberation would mean prestige for the Allies, loss of face for the Germans. Capture of the numerous airfields around Rome would increase the reach of the Allied air forces. Finally, when, in early October, it became only too plain that the Germans proposed to make a fight of it between Naples and Rome, the Allies had to reconsider their obvious success in drawing large numbers of good German troops into Italy. Once they gave up their initiative—failed, in Alexander's words, to "keep the enemy 'on his heels' "—they could expect a German counteroffensive which might wipe out much of their hard-won gains.

There were also forceful arguments against a continued advance. From the Volturno River (*lower center*) to Rome was over 100 miles of jumbled mountains, deeply cut by swift streams which usually ran east or west across the Allied line of advance. Such country was naturally designed for delaying actions, especially so in view of the Allied lack of troops trained for mountain warfare. Autumn was the wettest season in Italy; coastal swamps would be flooded, and mountain streams would run in torrents.

Allied navies might control the Mediterranean, but the chronic shortage of assault shipping would severely limit the exploitation of this superiority for future amphibious envelopments of the German front. But, in the judgment of those responsible at that time, it seemed the best decision to go ahead.

To gain time for the construction of his Winter Position, Kesselring had ordered the Volturno River held until 15 October. After much careful reconnaissance to locate good crossing sites, the Fifth Army opened its offensive across the Volturno on the night of 12 October, each of its corps attacking simultaneously with three divisions abreast. In generally bitter fighting, five of these six divisions finally won bridgeheads during the 13th, but German artillery fire held up the construction of bridges behind them until the 14th and 15th. By 15 October, the Allied advance had reached the lines shown (*dotted red lines*). The Germans gradually fell back from one natural strong point to another. In this, they were greatly aided by the terrain, yet the effectiveness with which their delaying actions were carried through revealed a high order of leadership and skill—especially when it is remembered that the Allies possessed complete air superiority.

The Eighth Army had become somewhat overextended during its drive to Termoli (*upper right*); consequently, Montgomery busied himself with his usual methodical preparations until 22 October. On that date, he began another of his characteristically deliberate offensives, forcing the Trigno River against vigorous opposition and closing to the south bank of the Sangro River. Meanwhile, the Fifth Army had found German resistance stiffening again along the outposts of the Winter Position (*heavy red line*). On 13 November, exhausted and drained by casualties, it halted in obedience to orders to rest and regroup. Constant rains turned roads into bogs and washed out the temporary bridges which had replaced those blown up by the withdrawing Germans (who had developed a murderous proficiency with demolitions, mines, and booby traps).

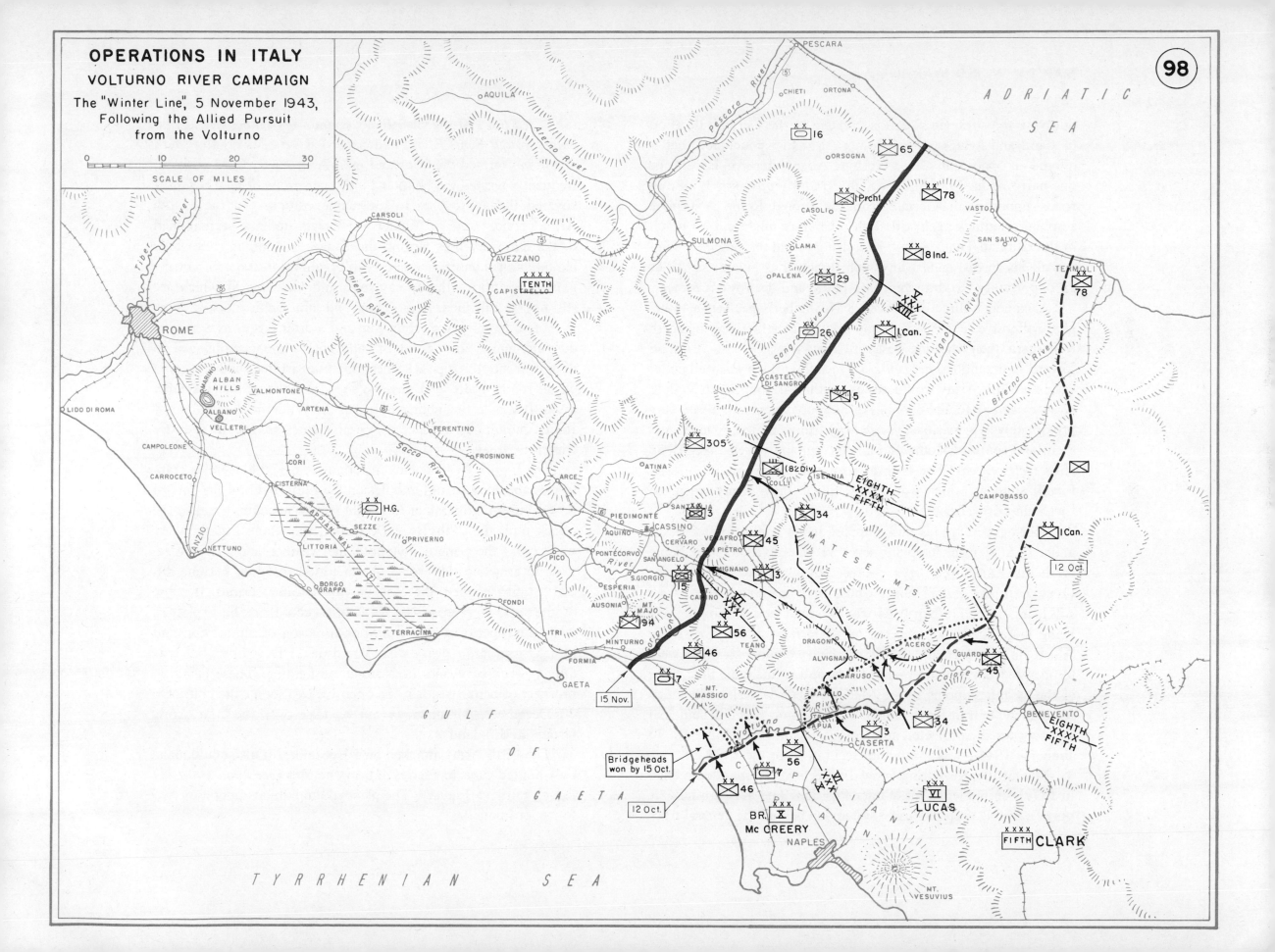

98

OPERATIONS IN ITALY

VOLTURNO RIVER CAMPAIGN

The "Winter Line", 5 November 1943,
Following the Allied Pursuit
from the Volturno

SCALE OF MILES

0   10   20   30

ADRIATIC SEA

TYRRHENIAN SEA

GULF OF GAETA

ROME

PESCARA

AQUILA

CARSOLI

AVEZZANO

CAPISTRELLO

SULMONA

CHIETI

ORTONA

ORSOGNA

CASOLIO

OLAMA

PALENA

OPALENA

CASTEL DI SANGRO

ISERNIA

CAMPOBASSO

TERMOLI

VASTO

SAN SALVO

TENTH

EIGHTH
XXXX
FIFTH

ALBAN HILLS

MARINO

DALBANO

VELLETRI

VALMONTONE

ARTENA

FERENTINO

FROSINONE

ATINA

ARCE

AQUINO

CASSINO

PIEDIMONTE

CERVARO

SAN PIETRO

VENAFRO

COLLI

SANTA MARIA

MT. MAJO

AUSONIA

CAIRO

ESPERIA

S.GIORGIO

MIGNANO

TEANO

DRAGONI

ALVIGNANO

ACERO

GUARD

BENEVENTO

EIGHTH
XXXX
FIFTH

MINTURNO

FORMIA

GAETA

ITRI

PICO

PONTECORVO

FONDI

TERRACINA

MT. MASSICO

CAPUA

CASERTA

NAPLES

MT. VESUVIUS

LUCAS

FIFTH CLARK

BR. X
McCREERY

Bridgeheads
won by 15 Oct.

12 Oct.

15 Nov.

15 Oct.

12 Oct.

16

65

1 Prcht.

78

8 Ind.

29

26

1 Can.

5

305

(82 Div.)

34

3

45

3

15

56

94

46

7

3

34

45

1 Can.

78

7

56

46

H.G.

MATESE MTS.

Studying the strategic situation created by the German decision to stand and fight south of Rome, Alexander concluded that it offered an opportunity for a crushing Allied offensive. Except for one narrow-gauge rail line through Pescara (*top center*), all railroads supporting the German front ran through Rome. A surprise amphibious attack against that city therefore might cut off much of the German Tenth Army. Kesselring would undoubtedly commit all his forces against any such threat, thus giving the Allies an opportunity "to draw him into battle and destroy his forces."

Alexander's directive, issued 8 November, specified a three-phase offensive. The Eighth Army would attack first, driving north to Pescara, then wheeling westward along the good east-west road toward Avezzano (*upper center*). Once this attack was well under way, the Fifth Army would attack up the Liri and Sacco Valleys (*lower center*) to Frosinone. An amphibious assault force (approximately two divisions, *not shown*) from the Fifth Army would then land south of Rome and advance inland to seize the Alban Hills (*left center*). The Eighth Army would have initial priority for air support, which would shift to the Fifth Army when the Liri Valley drive began.

Shortages of troops and shipping made it difficult for Alexander to implement his plan: seven veteran divisions were being gradually transferred from the Mediterranean to England for OVERLORD; the French units which were to replace them were still being trained in North Africa; the usual lack of shipping was being increasingly complicated by the arrival in Italy of strong Allied air force formations—mostly heavy bombers—which were to operate from the captured airfields; and, at the same time, most of the assault shipping in the Mediterranean was also scheduled for immediate transfer to England. Permission to retain sufficient shipping for the projected amphibious assault—but only until 15 January, 1944—was eventually secured from the CCS.

Meanwhile, Kesselring (now the German commander in chief in Italy) strengthened his Winter Position. The most formidable portion of this deep defensive system lay behind the general trace (*solid red line*) of the Garigliano, Rapido (*not labeled, but running through Sant' Elia*), and Sangro Rivers; its southwestern sector was termed the "Gustav Line." A strong forward position, frequently termed the "Winter Line" (*generally, dashed red line*) covered the approaches to the main position. (In the Eighth Army's zone, the term "Winter Line" seems to have been applied to the main defenses beyond the Sangro.) Actually, the whole mountainous countryside had been organized into a series of defensive positions—the exact names and locations of which are still not well defined. Demolitions and mine fields blocked every avenue of approach; machine-gun and mortar positions were well dug in—many blasted out of solid rock—and camouflaged to disappear into the rugged scenery; German artillery had registered on all roads, trails, and possible sites for bivouac and assembly areas. It was to be another Battle of the Wilderness, with craggy Italian mountains in place of Virginia thickets, fought in bitter winter weather.

The Eighth Army opened its offensive on 20 November, rapidly establishing small footholds on the north bank of the Sangro River, but an outbreak of torrential rains immediately stalled the attack until the 27th. By 2 December, the whole Eighth Army was across the Sangro, but both the weather and German resistance grew steadily worse. Ammunition resupply became difficult, tanks bogged, the casualty rate became serious. Because of the lack of reserves, local victories could not be exploited, while air superiority meant little in a season of almost constant rain. Ortona (*top right*) was cleared on 27 December, but only after a week of vicious house-to-house fighting. There being no prospect of better weather, the offensive was soon called off. (On 30 December, Montgomery left to take over the 21st Army Group in England.)

The Fifth Army attacked on 1 December. It also could make only limited gains in a series of heavy actions (*see maps 100-102*) lasting until 15 January. The planned amphibious operation had to be postponed.

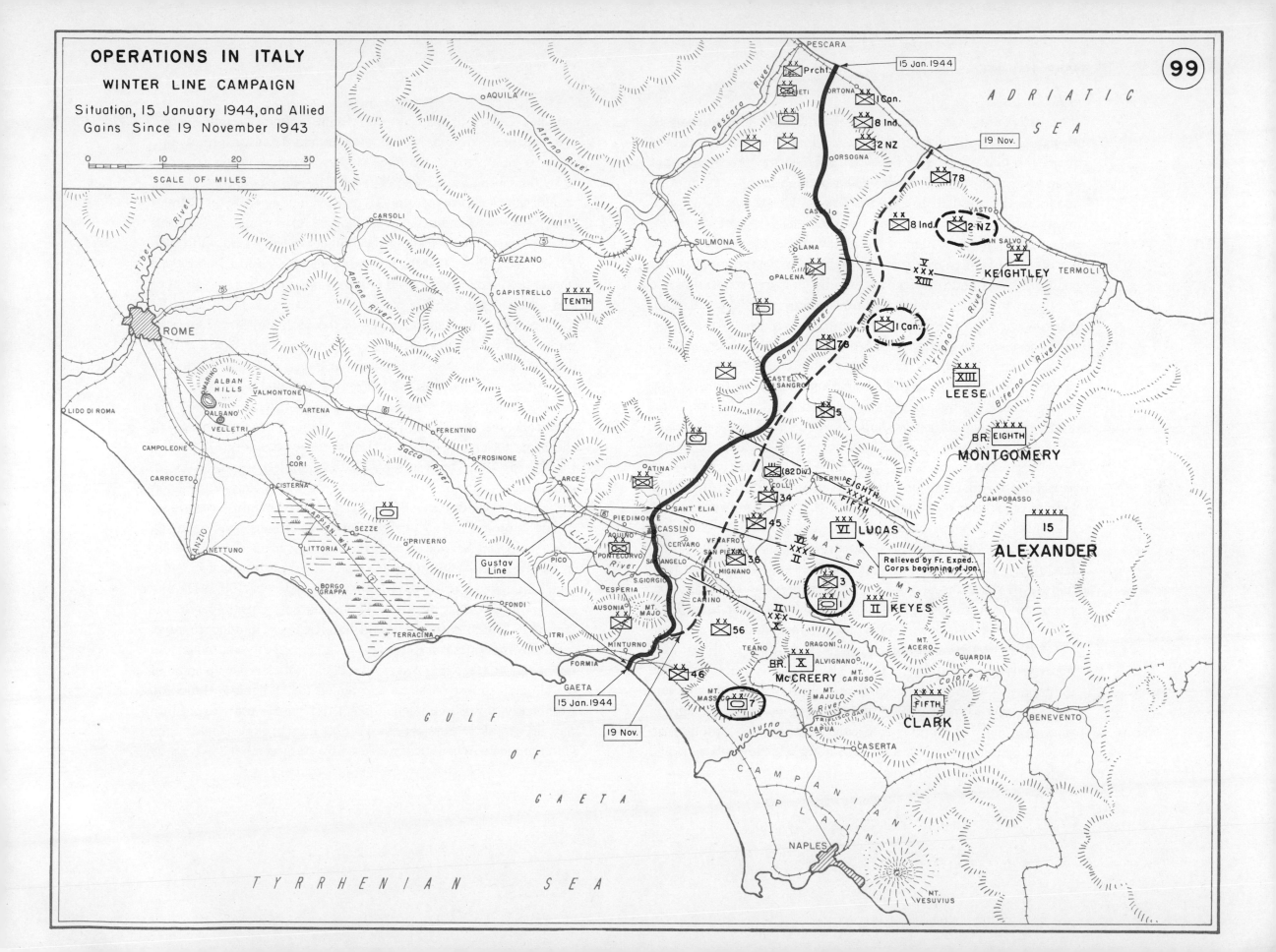

OPERATIONS IN ITALY
WINTER LINE CAMPAIGN
Situation, 15 January 1944, and Allied
Gains Since 19 November 1943

SCALE OF MILES

0   10   20   30

99

The Liri Valley (*left center*) has been termed "the gateway to Rome." It was not an inviting portal. The Fifth Army's X Corps faced the Garigliano River (*lower left*)—a narrow stream, but deep and swift, its west bank walled by high mountains from its junction with the Liri to the sea. The VI Corps was confronted by a major hill mass, extending from the main ridge of the Apennine Mountains (*off map, top*) southward to Mount Sammucro (*center*). This was a particularly rough and barren region, studded with tall peaks and traversed by only two narrow, crooked roads. In the center, a mile-wide natural corridor, the Mignano Gap (*astride the road running northwest from Mignano*), opened before the newly organized II Corps. This gap, however, is dominated from the south by the Mount Camino hill mass; to its north are the even higher crests of Mount Sammucro. Within the gap itself, Mount Lungo rises abruptly from the level valley floor. Farther west, as the gap widens, are two steep, isolated hills— Mount Porchia and Mount Trocchio. All of these features had been organized as parts of the Winter Line, the Mignano Gap especially having been converted into an ideal killing ground. The Germans had blocked it with mine fields, wire entanglements, and log-and-earth bunkers, and had converted the hillside villages— such as San Pietro (*center*)—into strong points which could enfilade any Allied advance through the gap. The frustrating feature of these defenses was that nowhere was there any key point, the capture of which would shatter the Winter Line. Each hill, valley, or village had to be fought for—and paid for.

Against defenses of this type, Fifth Army operations were necessarily slow and methodical. The X Corps would simulate preparations to force the Garigliano near its mouth, plus an amphibious envelopment of the German right (southwest) flank in that area. The VI Corps would carry out aggressive probing attacks all along its front and, beginning 29 November, would launch a limited offensive in the Mount Pantano (*upper center*) area. These operations would test German defenses in this area, prior to phase two of the offensive, and would—it was hoped— draw the German reserves northward. In phase two, the II Corps would attack north of the Mignano Gap against the Mount Lungo–Mount Sammucro area. The VI Corps would support this offensive by an attack along the Filignano–Sant' Elia and Colli-Atina roads, directed at the hills northwest of Cassino. In the third phase, the Fifth Army would crush remaining German resistance and advance into the Liri Valley.

According to plan, elements of the 45th and 34th Divisions jumped off on 29 November. Terrain and an aggressive German defense held them to inconsiderable gains, amounting to little more than a toehold on one corner of Mount Pantano.

To the south, the main attack began on the night of 1 December as the British 46th Division attacked the southern tip of the Mount Camino hill mass. Late on the afternoon of the 2d, the British 56th Division took up the assault (supported by an artillery concentration that dumped over 1,900 tons of shells on the Mount Camino area) in a head-on drive against the ridges of the Mount Camino peak. With the Germans thus engaged, the 1st Special Service Force attacked that night. The 142d Infantry Regiment (36th Division) advanced on Mount Maggiore (*at the northwest tip of the Camino hill mass*) at 0300, 3 December, and captured it by 1700. Though largely outnumbered, the Germans fought savagely, the 142d Regiment having to repel several counterattacks. Resupply was a major problem, the terrain here being so steep that even mules could not clamber up some of the slopes. Almost constant rain added to the general difficulty. Frequently, it was impossible for Allied air force units to get into the air, let alone support the ground attack. Nevertheless, the Camino area was completely cleared by 10 December.

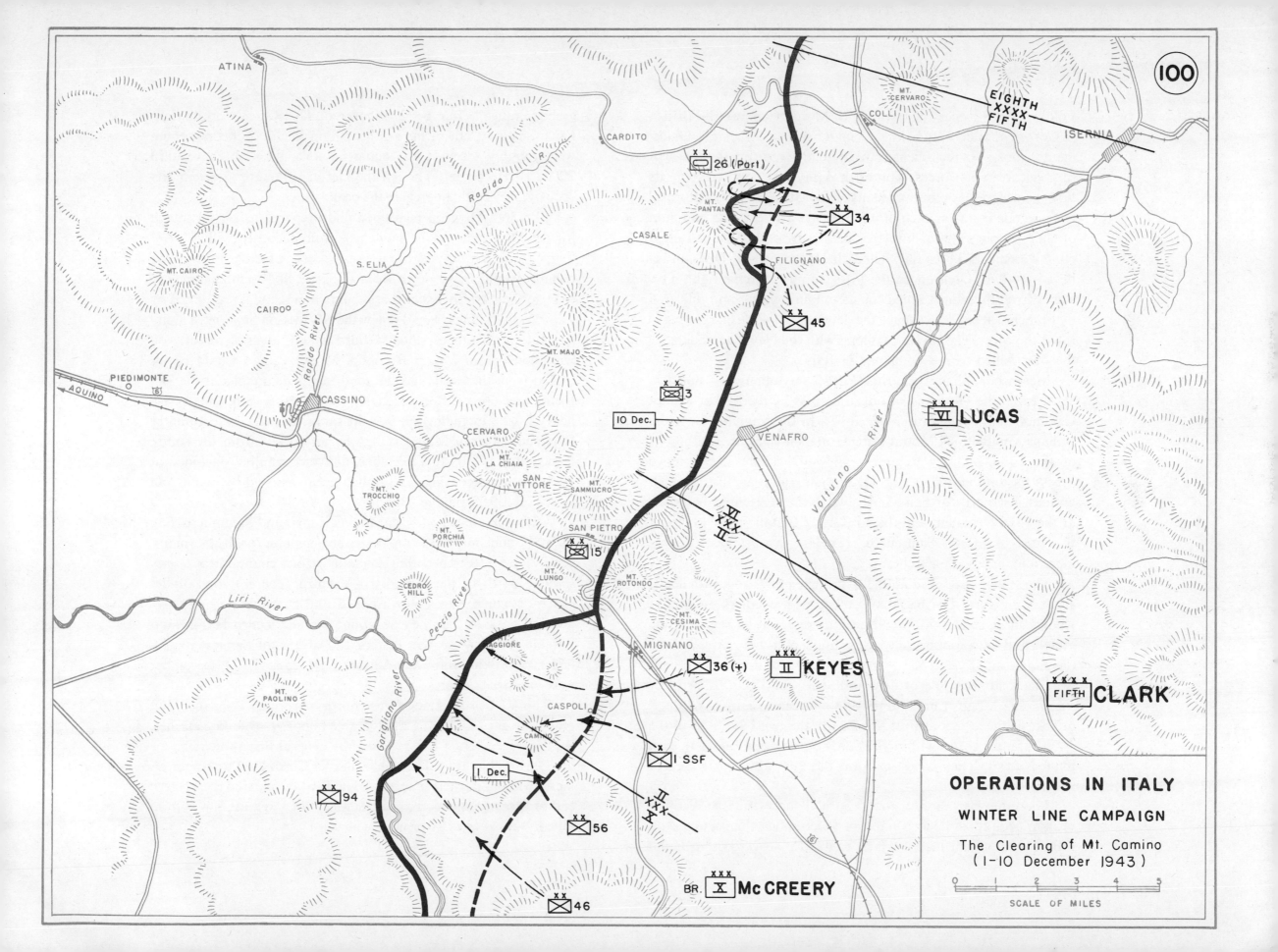

ATINA

MT. CERVARO

COLLI

EIGHTH
XXXX
FIFTH

ISERNIA

CARDITO

Rapido River

R.

XX 26 (Part)

MT. PANTAN

CASALE

FILIGNANO

XX 34

MT. CAIRO

S. ELIA

CAIROO

XX 45

MT. MAJO

Rapido River

PIEDIMONTE

CASSINO

10 Dec.

XX 3

VENAFRO

Volturno River

VI LUCAS

AQUINO

CERVARO

MT. LA CHIAIA

SAN VITTORE

MT. SAMMUCRO

VI
XXX
II

MT. TROCCHIO

MT. PORCHIA

SAN PIETRO

XX 15

MT. LUNGO

MT. ROTONDO

CEDRO HILL

MT. CESIMA

Liri River

Peccia River

AGGIORE

MIGNANO

XX 36(+)

XXX
II KEYES

MT. PAOLINO

CASPOLI

XXXX
FIFTH CLARK

Garigliano River

MT. CAMINO

X I SSF

XX 94

1 Dec.

II
XXX
X

XX 56

OPERATIONS IN ITALY

WINTER LINE CAMPAIGN

The Clearing of Mt. Camino
(1–10 December 1943)

BR. XXX
X McCREERY

XX 46

0 1 2 3 4 5

SCALE OF MILES

100

Following the successful storming of Mount Camino, the British X Corps (considerably below strength because of lack of replacements) took over the defense of that area, permitting the II Corps to concentrate its forces. The Fifth Army was now receiving its first considerable reinforcements. The Italian 1st Motorized Group (one regiment each of infantry and artillery, one battalion of sharpshooters) went into the lines in front of Mount Lungo on 7 December. Three days later, the Moroccan 2d Division relieved the 34th Division on the Fifth Army's extreme right. This was a fresh division, trained for mountain fighting and officered by Frenchmen eager to avenge the defeats of 1940. (The Germans rated the Moroccan divisions, along with the New Zealanders, as the best Allied troops employed in Italy.)

Meanwhile, phase two of the Fifth Army offensive—timed so as to catch the Germans still disorganized by the loss of Mount Camino—had opened on 8 December. In the Mignano Gap, the Italians would attack Mount Lungo; on their right, two battalions of the 143d Infantry Regiment (36th Division) would move across the southern slopes of Mount Sammucro against the high ground just north of San Pietro, while the remaining battalion of the 143d Regiment and the 3d Ranger Battalion would attack the crest of Mount Sammucro. The last two attacks involved night-long approach marches.

The Italians attacked at 0630, through a thick fog, with heavy artillery support. The battalion of panzer grenadiers on Mount Lungo, in its strong position, had little difficulty in repelling the attack, and found opportunity to use much of its fire power against the American drive on San Pietro. By early afternoon, the Italians were back at their line of departure, with the II Corps' artillery smothering Mount Lungo to prevent a possible German counterattack. In the attack against San Pietro, the two battalions of the 143d Infantry got to within 400 yards of the town, but were then pinned down. They tried again on the 9th, with equal lack of success.

The other battalion of the 143d had successfully rushed the peak of Mount Sammucro at dawn, 8 December, thanks to a skillfully led approach march which enabled it to get within hand-grenade range before being discovered. The Rangers on its right flank, however, advancing against the north end of the mountain, were roughly received and could not take their objective until 2000, 10 December. Though the Germans counterattacked vigorously, they could not regain the peak.

The 36th Division regrouped and prepared a heavier attack for 15 December, to be launched simultaneously with the VI Corps' secondary attack along the two roads farther north. One column would move down from the crest of Mount Sammucro to seize the western end of that mountain; a second, reinforced by a company of tanks, would renew the advance on San Pietro along Sammucro's southern slope; a third would advance directly on San Pietro from Mount Rotondo. Mount Lungo would be attacked from the south and the southeast. The attacks in the San Pietro area, pressed courageously through the 16th, failed with heavy losses, including most of the tanks. But the 142d Infantry Regiment overran Mount Lungo by an assault from the south, launched at 1730, 15 December, and successfully concluded at 1000 the next morning. The Italian group assisted by making an attack at 0915 on the 16th.

With Americans on both Mounts Lungo and Sammucro, San Pietro became more of a trap than a strong point for the Germans. Late on 16 December, they made a vicious counterattack (*not shown*) north of the San Pietro–Venafro (*center*) road, under cover of which they booby-trapped and evacuated San Pietro, and fell back to their next position: the line Cedro Hill–Mount Porchia–San Vittore–the western end of Mount Sammucro. Allied attempts to storm San Vittore on 19 and 20-21 December were expensive failures.

The VI Corps' attack in the north met tough resistance, but gradually got forward in innumerable minor, yet bloody, clashes. By 21 December, it had reached the general line shown.

During the last of December, the VI Corps kept up minor attacks, without particular success. The II Corps cleared the western end of Mount Sammucro, but renewed efforts against San Vittore failed. New Year's Eve brought a blizzard.

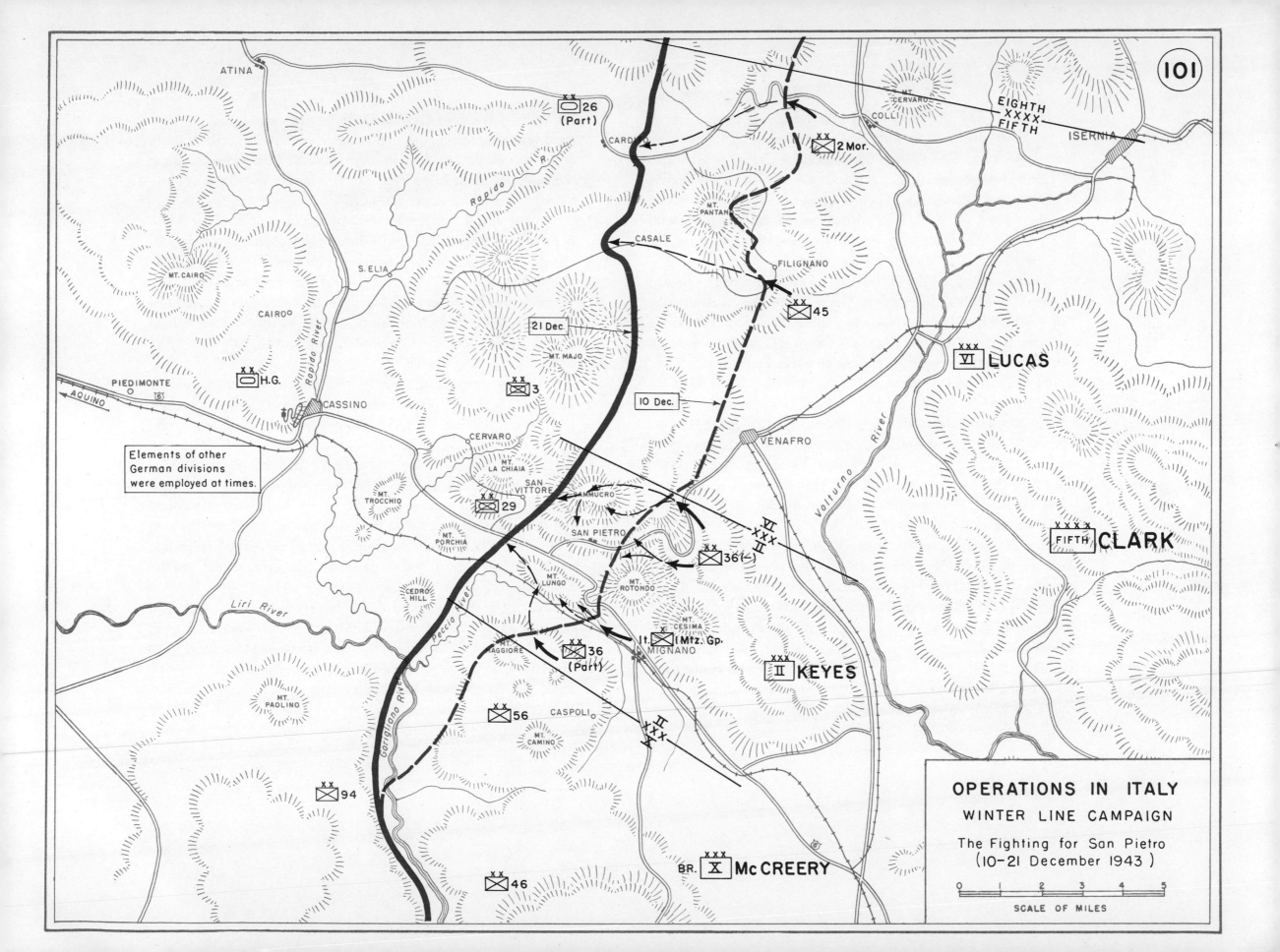

ATINA

MT. CAIRO

CAIRO

S. ELIA

Rapido River

PIEDIMONTE

AQUINO

6

CASSINO

H.G.

Rapido R.

26
(Part)

CARD...

CASALE

21 Dec.

MT. MAJO

10 Dec.

3

MT. PANTANO

2 Mor.

FILIGNANO

45

Volturno River

VI LUCAS

Elements of other
German divisions
were employed at times.

CERVARO

MT. LA CHIAIA

SAN VITTORE

MT. TROCCHIO

29

MT. PORCHIA

SAMMUCRO

SAN PIETRO

MT. LUNGO

CEDRO HILL

MT. ROTONDO

36(-)

Peccia River

MT. CESIMA

It. I Mtz. Gp.

MIGNANO

VI
XXX
II

FIFTH CLARK

II KEYES

Garigliano River

MT. MAGGIORE

36
(Part)

56

CASPOLI

MT. CAMINO

MT. PAOLINO

II
XXX
X

94

MT.
CERVARO

COLLI

EIGHTH
XXXX
FIFTH

ISERNIA

Venafro

OPERATIONS IN ITALY

WINTER LINE CAMPAIGN

The Fighting for San Pietro
(10-21 December 1943)

0   1   2   3   4   5

SCALE OF MILES

BR. X McCREERY

46

101

Early in January, the Fifth Army regrouped. The 34th Division relieved the hard-worked 36th, and the Algerian 3d Division replaced the 45th. The French Expeditionary Corps, commanded by General Alphonse P. Juin, replaced the VI Corps. The arrival of the veteran 1st Armored Division gave General Clark a strong mobile reserve. (This division's 6th Armored Infantry Regiment, reinforced, formed the Task Force A shown here as part of the II Corps.)

The third phase of the Fifth Army offensive had been intended to break through the remaining German defenses and into the Liri Valley. The II Corps would again make the main attack, along the general axis of Highway 6; the X Corps and the French would deliver supporting secondary attacks on either flank. In its attack, the II Corps planned to make its main effort with the 34th Division against Mount La Chiaia (*center, left*), outflanking that mountain stronghold from the north. Still farther north, the 1st Special Service Force would strike across the mountains to clear out the dominating peaks in the Mount Majo area (*center*). On the south flank of the main attack, Task Force A would seize Mount Porchia. The weather had cleared sufficiently to permit considerable air support for the attack.

The 1st Special Service Force began its advance at 2120, 3 January, moving swiftly forward in two columns along the twisting ridges. Two infantry battalions (one, the 100th Battalion, was composed of Japanese-Americans) were attached on the 6th, to consolidate and defend the ground gained. A pack train—approximately 700 mules—carried the necessary supplies. At 0520, 7 January, the right-flank column of the Special Service Force overran Mount Majo. Its left-flank column had pushed toward the ridges north of Cervaro (*center, left*). Reaching them early on

the 7th, it was forced back by counterattacks, but outmaneuvered the Germans during the night and seized its objectives early on the 8th. Repeated German counterattacks (*not shown*) against the peak of Mount Majo from 7 to 10 January were broken up— usually by massed American artillery fire.

In the meantime, the 34th Division had jumped off at 0550, 5 January. The Mount La Chiaia terrain was extremely rugged, the defense expert and determined, but San Vittore fell on the 6th and Mount La Chiaia itself on the 7th. Farther south, Task Force A finally occupied Mount Porchia that same day, after rough, costly fighting. The German garrison on Cedro Hill held off the British 46th Division until the night of the 8th, then evacuated the hill as untenable.

Quickly regrouping, the II Corps drove forward again on the 10th, with Mount Trocchio as its objective. First, it was necessary to clear out the remaining German positions in the Cervaro area, which still flanked any Allied debouchment from the Mignano Gap. Even with heavy air and artillery support, this took three more days. On 14 January, the II Corps was closing against Mount Trocchio; a massive attack against it the next day found the position abandoned, the Germans having withdrawn behind the Rapido River during the night. Farther north, the French had made considerable advances, as shown, through desolate mountain country.

All of this fighting, difficult and bloody as it was, actually had been only the result of a German delaying action waged to gain time. Both the Eighth and Fifth Armies had failed to achieve their objectives; both were temporarily fought out. The Fifth Army now faced the main Gustav Line. Its outpost skirmishings were over; the real battle for Rome was about to begin.

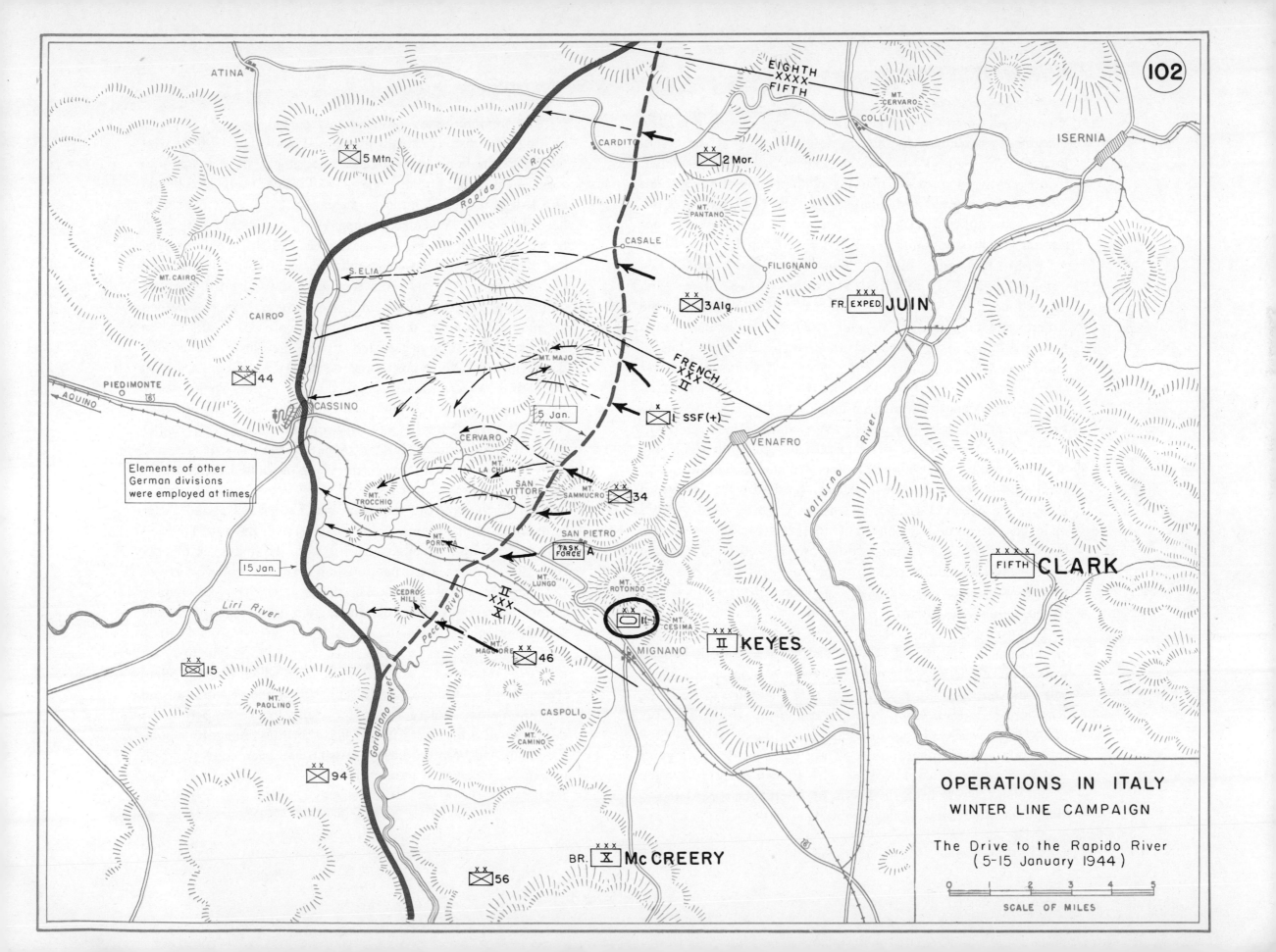

ATINA

EIGHTH
XXXX
FIFTH

MT. CERVARO

COLLI

ISERNIA

5 Mtn.

CARDITO

2 Mor.

MT. PANTANO

FILIGNANO

CASALE

Rapido R.

MT. CAIRO

S. ELIA

3 Alg.

FR. EXPED. JUIN

CAIROO

MT. MAJO

FRENCH
XXX
II

PIEDIMONTE

44

5 Jan.

CASSINO

I SSF(+)

AQUINO

VENAFRO

Volturno River

Elements of other
German divisions
were employed at times.

CERVARO

MT. LA CHIAIA

SAN VITTORE

MT. SAMMUCRO

34

MT. TROCCHIO

SAN PIETRO

FIFTH CLARK

15 Jan.

MT. PORCIA

TASK FORCE A

Liri River

CEDRO HILL

MT. LUNGO

MT. ROTONDO

MT. CESIMA

II KEYES

II
XXX
X

It(-)

Peccia River

15

MT. MAGGIORE

46

MIGNANO

MT. PAOLINO

CASPOLI

Gorigliano River

94

MT. CAMINO

BR. X McCREERY

56

OPERATIONS IN ITALY

WINTER LINE CAMPAIGN

The Drive to the Rapido River
(5-15 January 1944)

0   1   2   3   4   5

SCALE OF MILES

102

The prospect confronting the Fifth Army was not alluring. The battle for the Winter Line had made it obvious that any breakthrough of the Gustav Line would be costly and time-consuming. Consequently, the previous plan for an amphibious landing south of Rome was revived and enlarged. Because of OVERLORD's priority, it was difficult to secure the necessary shipping for this operation, but a bare minimum was finally collected.

Unlike the Winter Line, the Gustav Line had a definite key point—the massively built town of Cassino (*lower center*) lying at the foot of the Mount Cairo hill mass, at the junction of the Rapido and Liri Valleys (*see map 102*). Alexander's new plan provided for an initial secondary attack across the lower Garigliano River (*this map, lower center*) by the X Corps, to pull the German reserves out of position. The II Corps would then attack up the Liri Valley toward Frosinone (*center, left*) while the French worked their way across the mountains into the peaks north of Cassino. When these operations were well begun, the VI Corps would make an amphibious landing in the Anzio-Nettuno area (*left center*). Once ashore, it would drive northward to seize the Alban Hills, thus cutting the German Tenth Army's main line of communications. This threat—it was hoped—combined with the frontal attacks, would force Kesselring to evacuate the Gustav Line and retreat north of Rome. The Eighth Army, though weakened by the transfer of troops to the Fifth Army, would continue its offensive toward Pescara.

Late on 17 January, the X Corps stormed the Garigliano, establishing a considerable bridgehead; by the 20th, it had attracted all of Vietinghoff's available reserves—and had its hands full. Also on the 20th, the 36th Division attempted to force the Rapido, two miles below Cassino, in one of the strongest sectors of the Gustav Line. Its assault was poorly organized and ended in bloody and complete failure. The French made some gains east of Cassino. Clark now ordered a French-American attack to envelop Cassino from the north, the French being ordered to shift their attack toward Piedimonte (*center*).

The amphibious expedition sailed from Naples on 21 January, making a surprise, practically unopposed landing at 0200 the next morning. An immediate bold advance might have swept into Rome—but probably, thereafter, would have been cut off and crushed. Maj. Gen. John P. Lucas paused to organize his beachhead thoroughly. When he attempted to move inland on the 30th, he found himself penned against the sea. Kesselring had foreseen and planned for such an emergency. German reserves were rushed in from the north, and quiet sectors of the Gustav Line were stripped of troops. Waiting until bad weather hampered Allied air and naval support, the German Fourteenth Army attacked on 15 February. Its initial assault (16-17 February) penetrated deeply into the Allied position along the Anzio-Albano road; on the 18th, however, Mackensen failed to commit his whole reserve for a knock-out blow. Reinforced only by driblets, his offensive rapidly lost momentum; a VI Corps counterattack (19 February) checked it. Subsequent German assaults in the Cisterna area had little success. Early in March, the Germans halted their attacks and began to fortify their positions.

The fortunes of war had been even harder at Cassino. After some initial gains north and east of that town, the 34th Division launched a major attack against it during the first week of February. By 12 February it had to admit defeat. The newly arrived New Zealand Corps then took up the assault, with great courage but with equal lack of success. In an attempt to break the rapidly solidifying Italian stalemate, the Allies organized a third attack on Cassino. This was to be a limited operation, designed to gain a secure bridgehead over the Rapido, from which a major offensive up the Liri Valley could be launched at a later date. Massed air power and artillery battered Cassino for hours before the infantry and armor went in—to find that this preparatory bombardment had been too heavy. Cassino had been converted into an almost impenetrable maze of capsized masonry, in which the fanatical Nazis of the 1st Parachute Division had fought the Allies to a standstill by 23 March.

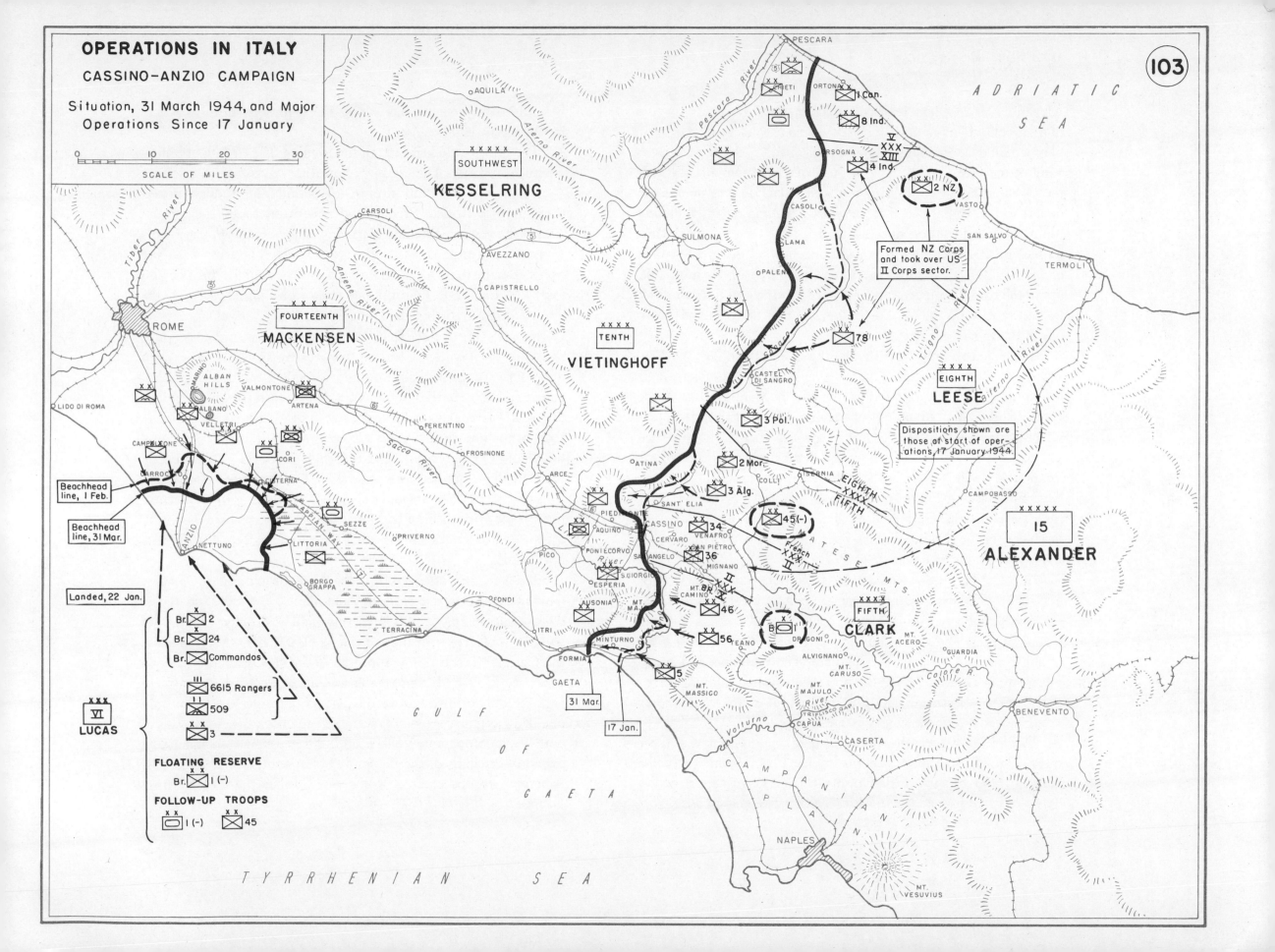

Alexander at last had secured sufficient reinforcements to give him a definite numerical superiority over Kesselring. He now planned an overwhelming offensive, designed to "destroy the right wing of the German Tenth Army; to drive what remains of it and the German Fourteenth Army north of Rome; and to pursue the enemy to the Rimini-Pisa line [*off map, 150 miles north*], inflicting the maximum losses on him in the process." To accomplish this, he had reorganized his forces and concentrated the greatest part of them—under conditions of extreme secrecy—on his left flank, along the twenty-mile front from Cassino to the sea. Furthermore, he had reinforced the VI Corps, literally packing men and weapons into its narrow Anzio beachhead.

The Eighth Army would make the main attack, against Cassino and up the Liri and Sacco Valleys, along the general axis of Route 6 to Valmontone (*left center*). Simultaneously, the Fifth Army would attack out of the Garigliano bridgehead (previously established by the X Corps) toward Anzio to link up with its VI Corps. The VI Corps would hold itself ready to attack inland to Valmontone, on or after D + 4, thus trapping the Germans retreating before the Eighth Army. An elaborate cover plan deceived the Germans into believing that the Allies were mounting a large amphibious operation against Civitavecchia (*off map, on the coast north of Rome*).

In late May, the Allied air forces initiated an effective day-and-night offensive against German communications in Italy. Railways, highway bridges, truck convoys, and coastal shipping were systematically sought out and destroyed. The effect of these attacks, naturally, was not immediate. The Germans had stockpiled supplies during the winter, and their line-of-communications personnel were both energetic and resourceful. Initially, the enemy never lacked ammunition and essential supplies.

During the winter, the Germans had begun two new defense lines: the Hitler Line (still incomplete) ran from Terracina (*center, left*) inland to Piedimonte (*center*), with its strongest defenses extending across the Liri Valley. The Caesar Line (apparently barely begun) lay across the highways south of Rome in the Alban Hills region.

The Allies attacked late on the evening of 11 May, attaining complete surprise. The German, however, was too good a soldier —and his defenses too strong—to permit any sudden breakthrough. The British, French, and Americans found their initial gains followed by stiffening German resistance; the Polish Corps was defeated in its spirited attempt to envelop Cassino from the north. But in the Mount Majo area (*lower center*; this is a different Mount Majo than the one shown on *maps 100-102*), the French discovered that the Gustav Line was relatively weak, the Germans having decided that the rugged terrain would not require extensive fortification. Clearing this area by 13 May, the French drove forward the next morning across roadless mountain country. Spearheaded by parties of goumiers (Moroccan irregulars), their progress was unexpectedly swift; by 17 May, they threatened the road running north from Itri (*lower center*), thereby dislocating the whole German front. The British XIII Corps, supported by the Canadians, pushed forward west of Cassino, which fell at last to a renewed Polish assault (17-18 May). Failing in an attempt to rush the Hitler Line (18 May), the XIII Corps breached it by a coordinated attack on the 23d. The Germans retired doggedly northward.

The VI Corps attacked from the Anzio beachhead on 23 May, making good progress toward Valmontone. On the 25th, the II Corps—advancing against relatively light resistance—linked up with the VI Corps near Borgo Grappa (*lower left*). Momentarily, the German Tenth Army appeared doomed. On the 26th, however, Clark abruptly shifted the weight of the Fifth Army's advance to the northwest, toward Rome. As a result, small, skillfully handled German rear guards were able to check the Americans at both Valmontone and Velletri until 2 June. Then, their mission gallantly discharged, the Germans broke contact and withdrew. American troops entered Rome on 4 June; the Tenth Army escaped.

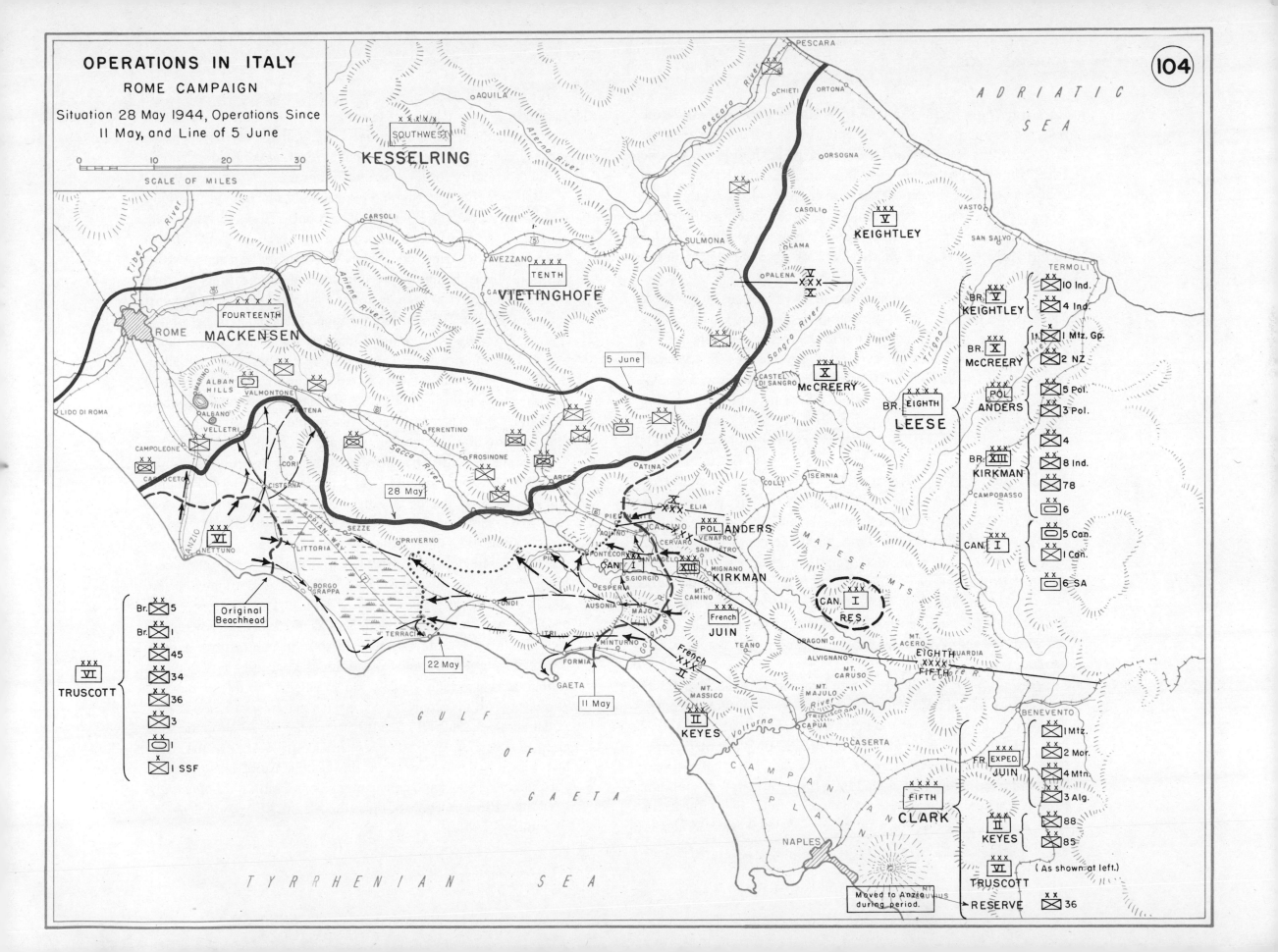

OPERATIONS IN ITALY
ROME CAMPAIGN
Situation 28 May 1944, Operations Since
11 May, and Line of 5 June

SCALE OF MILES
0   10   20   30

104

Kesselring now faced a double problem: he must withdraw the battered remnants of his Tenth and Fourteenth Armies into the last remaining German defensive system in Italy—the Gothic Line, running generally from Pisa northeast to Rimini (*both upper center*); at the same time, construction of the Gothic Line being far from complete, he would have to conduct his withdrawal so as to inflict maximum delay upon the pursuing Allies. All this would have to be done in the teeth of absolute Allied aerial superiority.

Initially, the Allied pursuit swept the Germans northward, especially in the flat coastal district north of Rome. Civitavecchia fell on 7 June; German demolition teams had wrecked its harbor, but American engineers had it operating a week later. The Viterbo complex of airfields was overrun on the 9th. The French, previously pinched out by the converging Americans and British below Rome, now came forward again to seize the island of Elba from a stubborn garrison on 17-18 June. Everything promised a major triumph in Italy. The Allied forces had tasted victory; strong, ably led, and well supplied, they had the Germans outnumbered and on the run. Alexander was confident that his forces could shatter the unfinished Gothic Line and break into the Po Valley (*top center*) during August. Once there, he could attack either westward into southern France or eastward through Venice into Austria. British leaders favored the latter as offering the most direct threat to Germany. They recommended that the plans for the long-delayed landing in southern France (*see maps 56-57*) be canceled and that Alexander proceed with the destruction of the German forces in Italy.

This proposal ran head-on into American opinion in favor of the invasion of southern France. American military leaders considered the capture of the port of Marseille (*this map, upper left*) essential for the support of operations in Western Europe. Also, at the Teheran Conference (November, 1943), Roosevelt, Churchill, and Stalin had agreed on a future invasion of southern France. (Churchill had pressed for operations in southeastern Europe, but Stalin did not want troops of the Western Allies in

that area.) Now Roosevelt felt that this operation could not be canceled without Stalin's consent. Finally, there was considerable serious feeling that the French would insist that their troops should be used primarily for the liberation of France.

Following prolonged (and occasionally sharp) consultations, Churchill yielded to Roosevelt's insistence. Seven divisions, including all of the French Expeditionary Force, were withdrawn from the Fifth Army, completely unbalancing Alexander's dispositions—and jamming his lines of communications as they moved southward to prepare for the amphibious assault against southern France. This transfer stripped Alexander of his best—in fact, his only—mountain troops; as replacements, he could expect the American 92d Division in September and a Brazilian division in late October. One group of bombers and twenty-three squadrons of fighters were likewise diverted to southern France. Alexander was then instructed to continue his advance to the approximate line Verona-Padua-Venice (*all top center*).

Meanwhile, Hitler had reinforced Kesselring with eight more divisions of varying quality (one each from Denmark, Holland, and Russia; two from the Balkans; and three—hitherto earmarked for the Russian front—from Germany). He also allowed Kesselring to retain the redoubtable Hermann Göring Panzer Division, previously scheduled for transfer to France. Thus reinforced, Kesselring reestablished his front, approximately along the line shown (*dashed blue line, dated 17 June*). Thereafter, covering his front with hasty mine fields and demolitions, sacrificing his second-rate units ruthlessly to gain time to concentrate and reorganize his crack divisions, exploiting the natural strength of the Italian terrain with its many stone villages and farm houses, Kesselring and his subordinates waged a masterly delaying action. A deliberate assault (9-16 July) was necessary to clear the road and rail center of Arezzo (*upper center*). By 4 August, the Allies had reached the outworks of the Gothic Line, but winter, a pertinacious enemy, and exhaustion halted them (*solid blue line*). (See map 106 for details of operations from 26 August, 1944, to 15 January, 1945.)

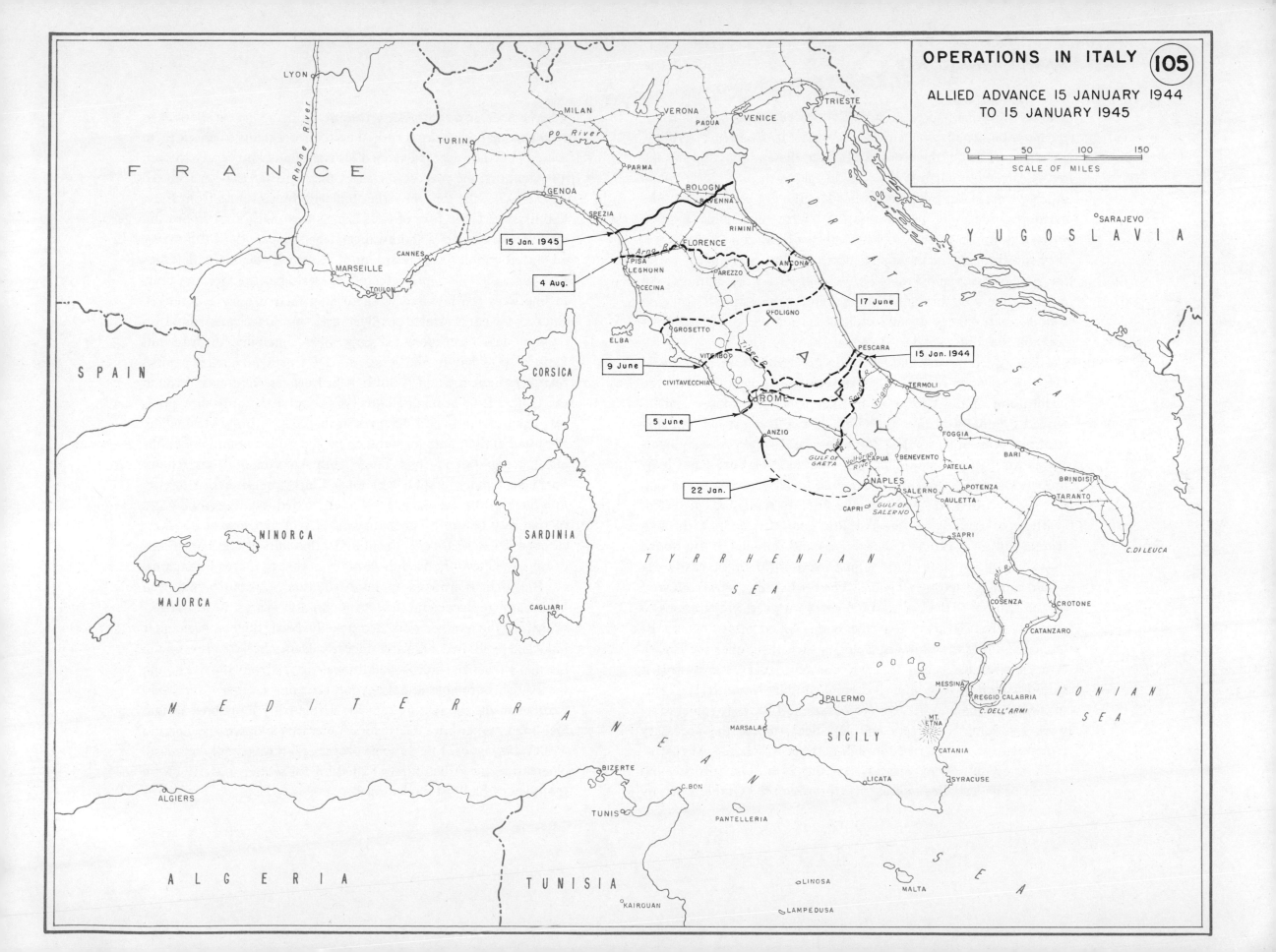

OPERATIONS IN ITALY 105

ALLIED ADVANCE 15 JANUARY 1944
TO 15 JANUARY 1945

0   50   100   150
SCALE OF MILES

LYON
MILAN
VERONA
PADUA
VENICE
TRIESTE
TURIN
Po River
PARMA
GENOA
BOLOGNA
RAVENNA
SPEZIA
RIMINI
15 Jan. 1945
Arno R.
FLOREN E
ANCONA
PISA
LEGHORN
AREZZO
4 Aug.
CECINA
17 June
FOLIGNO
GROSSETO
ELBA
Tiber
PESCARA
VITERBO
15 Jan. 1944
9 June
CIVITAVECCHIA
Trigno
ROME
TERMOLI
5 June
FOGGIA
ANZIO
Volturno River
CAPUA
BENEVENTO
PATELLA
BARI
GULF OF
GAETA
22 Jan.
NAPLES
SALERNO
AULETTA
POTENZA
BRINDISI
CAPRI
GULF OF
SALERNO
TARANTO
SAPRI

FRANCE

SPAIN

CORSICA

YUGOSLAVIA

SARAJEVO

A D R I A T I C   S E A

MINORCA

SARDINIA

CAGLIARI

T Y R R H E N I A N   S E A

MAJORCA

M E D I T E R R A N E A N

COSENZA
CROTONE
CATANZARO

PALERMO
MESSINA
REGGIO CALABRIA
C. DELL'ARMI

I O N I A N   S E A

MARSALA
MT. ETNA
SICILY
CATANIA
C. DI LEUCA

BIZERTE
C. BON
LICATA
SYRACUSE

ALGIERS

TUNIS
PANTELLERIA

S E A

A L G E R I A

T U N I S I A
KAIROUAN
LINOSA
MALTA
LAMPEDUSA

The Gothic Line had been shrewdly located to take advantage of the mountain chain which divides central Italy from the Po Valley. On the west coast, the corridor between these mountains and the sea is extremely narrow; the corridor along the east coast, while much wider, is cut by many rivers. Though not yet complete, the existing defenses of the Gothic Line were formidable enough. From a point on the west coast southeast of Spezia (*left center*), they ran through the mountains north of Pistoia (*center, left*) to the Foglia River and Pesaro (*right center*) on the Adriatic. An outpost line ran through Pisa and along the Arno River (*left center*); particularly strong fortifications guarded Futa Pass (*center*), on the direct road to Bologna.

The Allied pursuit had halted on 4 August (*dashed red line*), after an advance of 270 miles in sixty-four days, including the penetration of the Gustav and Hitler Lines. Alexander had intended originally to take the Gothic Line in his stride, utilizing his Moroccan units to clear the Florence-Bologna road by operations through the mountains on either side of Futa Pass. Now too weak for such measures, he paused for three weeks to regroup for a new offensive. Most of the Eighth Army was diverted, swiftly and secretly, to the Adriatic coast for a drive through Rimini toward Ravenna (*upper right*) and Bologna. It was hoped that this sudden shift of the Allied main effort to the east coast would catch Kesselring off guard. The Fifth Army, now reinforced by the British XIII Corps, would carry on overt preparations to convince the Germans that the main Allied attack would be launched along the Florence-Bologna axis; then, once the Eighth Army's offensive began to draw German reserves eastward, it would launch its own offensive, employing its II and XIII Corps, toward Bologna and Ferrara (*top center*). Thanks to remarkable work by Allied engineers and logistical troops, the necessary redeployment was carried through between 15 and 23 August.

The Eighth Army attacked on the 25th. The surprise and weight of its initial assault carried it through the Gothic Line; by 4 September, it was attacking Rimini. Utilizing his excellent east-west road net, Kesselring rushed up reinforcements to check them there. This, however, weakened his right flank and center to such an extent that the outpost line along the Arno had to be evacuated. (Hitler, knowing that the Allies had withdrawn forces from Italy, had likewise taken four of Kesselring's best divisions.) Following up this unexpected withdrawal on 1 September, the Fifth Army advanced rapidly northward until it struck the main defenses (13 September). Fighting there was stern, but the German units in line were too few and weak to man their extensive defenses. Backed by concentrated artillery fire, the Americans found an opening near Firenzuola (18 September), enabling them to outflank Futa Pass. In the west, the IV Corps advanced against relatively light resistance. Both Allied armies were now through the Gothic Line at many points, but could make only slow progress against improvised defenses in the hills beyond. Meanwhile, the usual Italian autumn weather eroded Allied communications and hampered operations. The Eighth Army finally took Rimini on 21 September, and on 1 October Clark committed his reserve in a final bid for Bologna. His attack carried to within nine miles of that city before a concentration of picked German divisions stopped it (20 October). Profiting by this shift of German troops to oppose Clark, the Eighth Army was able to increase its gains.

Both Allied armies were now exhausted. Casualties had been heavy and replacements few. Ammunition stocks were dangerously low; the weather worsened steadily. Nevertheless, Alexander launched a limited offensive in early December to prevent the Germans from transferring additional troops from Italy. Though the British were able to get beyond Ravenna (*upper right*), bad weather in the mountains kept the Fifth Army immobile. In late December, a surprise German counterattack down the Serchio Valley (*left center*) made some progress, but was finally repulsed. Thereafter, the Allied forces halted for the winter, bitterly aware that victory had just eluded them.

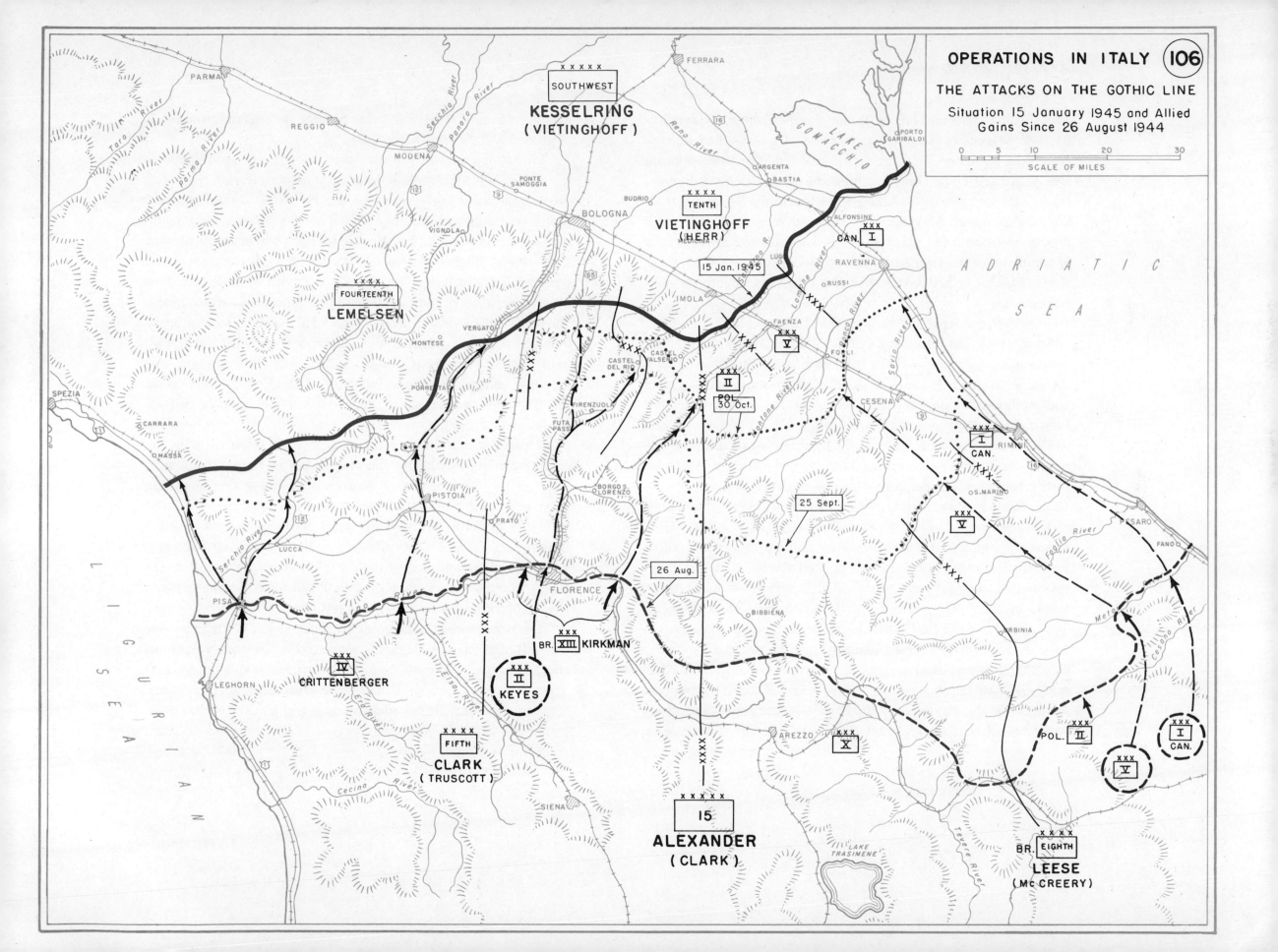

OPERATIONS IN ITALY 106

THE ATTACKS ON THE GOTHIC LINE

Situation 15 January 1945 and Allied
Gains Since 26 August 1944

SCALE OF MILES
0   5   10   20   30

KESSELRING
(VIETINGHOFF)
SOUTHWEST

TENTH
VIETINGHOFF
(HERR)

FOURTEENTH
LEMELSEN

15 Jan. 1945

CAN. I

30 Oct.

II
POL.

25 Sept.

26 Aug.

CRITTENBERGER
IV

BR. XIII KIRKMAN

II
KEYES

FIFTH
CLARK
(TRUSCOTT)

15
ALEXANDER
(CLARK)

X

POL. II

V

I
CAN.

BR. EIGHTH
LEESE
(McCREERY)

ADRIATIC
SEA

LIGURIAN SEA

The ensuing stalemate on the Italian front—from early January through March—was the longest period of quiet it had known. Numerous command changes took place in the two opposing armies. Kesselring had been summoned home to try his skill at delaying actions against the Allied offensive on the Western Front. On the Allied side, Alexander had replaced Wilson as commander of the Mediterranean theater; Clark had succeeded Alexander in command of the 15th Army Group; and Truscott and Lt. Gen. R. L. McCreery had taken over the Fifth and Eighth Armies, respectively.

Though the Russians were within forty miles of Berlin on 1 April, 1945—and the armies of the Western Allies were thrusting deep into Germany—Hitler still clung to northern Italy. There, the understrength divisions of Army Group Southwest stoically and methodically strengthened their front and built new defense lines to their rear along the Po and Adige Rivers (*lower center*), while Fascist Italian troops of the Ligurian Army guarded the passes into France—and deserted at every opportunity. Allied air forces kept the German communications under constant attack. (The Allies had approximately 4,000 aircraft in Italy; the Luftwaffe there could muster less than 200 planes of all types.) Consequently, supplies of motor fuel and ammunition were dwindling toward the danger point. Losses of motor vehicles had been so severe that the Germans were sometimes reduced to using ox teams in their supply trains. In view of these facts, General Vietinghoff had concluded that his forces had neither the strength to withstand a major Allied offensive nor the necessary mobility to withdraw successfully across the Po after one began. Accordingly, he had requested authority to begin a secret withdrawal north of the Po, leaving only small, mobile rear guards in contact with the Allies along his front line (*solid red line*). Hitler gave him the standard reply: hold that position and defend every inch of ground.

The Allied armies—rested, reorganized, and reequipped—knew that only a few more miles of mountainous terrain separated them from the open country of the Po Valley, where massed armor could operate effectively. They were a polyglot command: three veteran Canadian and British divisions had been transferred from the Mediterranean to the Western Front; they had been replaced by new Italian formations, a Jewish brigade, the Japanese-Americans of the famous 442d Regimental Combat Team, and a Brazilian division. Since the 15th Army Group already included American, British, New Zealand, Canadian, Newfoundland, South African, Gurkha, Indian, and Polish units, the language difficulties can be imagined. The logistical support of this force, with its varied dietary requirements, provided an assortment of unique problems.

Alexander and Clark planned their 1945 offensive with the objective of destroying the German forces in Italy—if possible, south of the Po. The Eighth Army would attack first along the Adriatic coast, pushing northwestward toward Ferrara (*lower right*). The Fifth Army would then drive northward, capture Bologna, and continue its advance to Bondeno (*near Ferrara*), where it would link up with the Eighth Army. Thereafter, the Allies would strike north across the Po to seize Verona (*center, right*), blocking the last escape routes into Germany.

The result seemed a foregone conclusion. Yet German morale was still high, and Vietinghoff's command was probably the most effective army group remaining in the German service. Its position might seem hopeless, but it had made a career of forlorn hopes. It would meet this Allied offensive as it had met the earlier ones.

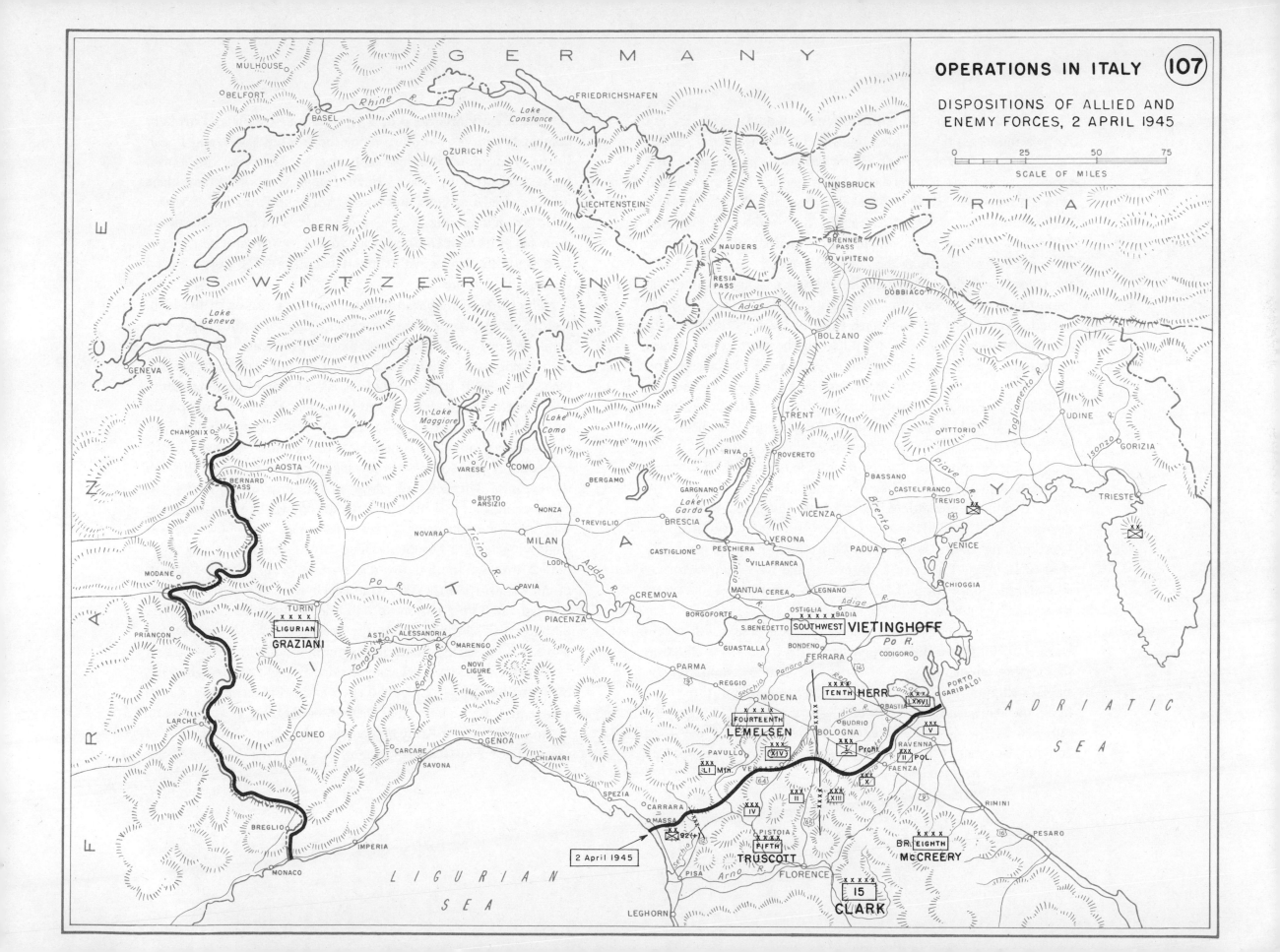

GERMANY

MULHOUSE
BELFORT
Rhine R.
BASEL
FRIEDRICHSHAFEN
Lake Constance
INNSBRUCK
LIECHTENSTEIN
AUSTRIA

BERN
ZURICH

SWITZERLAND

BRENNER PASS
VIPITENO
NAUDERS
RESIA PASS
DOBBIACO
Adige R.
BOLZANO

Lake Geneva

GENEVA

CHAMONIX
Lake Maggiore
Lake Como
TRENT
RIVA
ROVERETO
VITTORIO
Piave R.
Tagliamento R.
UDINE
GORIZIA
Isonzo R.

AOSTA
ST. BERNARD PASS
VARESE
COMO
BERGAMO
Lake Garda
GARGNANO
BASSANO
CASTELFRANCO
TREVISO
TRIESTE

MODANE
BUSTO ARSIZIO
MONZA
Ticino R.
BRESCIA
VICENZA
PADUA
VENICE

PRIANCON
TURIN
LIGURIAN
GRAZIANI
NOVARA
MILAN
TREVIGLIO
Adda R.
PESCHIERA
VERONA
VILLAFRANCA
CHIOGGIA

Po R.
PAVIA
LODI
MANTUA
CEREA
LEGNANO
Adige R.

ASTI
ALESSANDRIA
Tanaro R.
PIACENZA
BORGOFORTE
OSTIGLIA
BADIA
S. BENEDETTO
SOUTHWEST VIETINGHOFF

LARCHE
MARENGO
NOVI LIGURE
Bormida R.
PARMA
GUASTALLA
BONDENO
FERRARA
Po R.
CODIGORO

CUNEO
Tanaro R.
REGGIO
Secchia R.
MODENA
Panaro R.
TENTH HERR
PORTO GARIBALDI

ADRIATIC SEA

CARCARE
SAVONA
GENOA
CHIAVARI
FOURTEENTH
LEMELSEN
XIV
BOLOGNA
Idice R.
BUDRIO
Reno R.
XXVI
V

BREGLIO
SPEZIA
PAVULLO
LI Mtn.
Prcht.
RAVENNA
II POL.
FAENZA
RIMINI

LARCHE
CARRARA
MASSA
II
XIII
X
PESARO

IMPERIA
92(+)
2 April 1945
PISTOIA
FIFTH
TRUSCOTT
BR. EIGHTH
McCREERY

MONACO
PISA
Arno R.
FLORENCE

LIGURIAN SEA
LEGHORN

15
CLARK

FRANCE

The critical phase of the Allied offensive would be the Eighth Army's initial assault astride Highway 16 through the so-called "gap" at Argenta (*top right*), where a corridor of relatively high ground carried the highway through a flooded, swampy region between the Reno River and Lake Comacchio. A breakthrough here would unhinge the entire German line, and would place the Allies in a position to cut off much of Vietinghoff's force from its final defense line along the Adige River (*off map, top*). Since the Germans could be depended upon to be equally aware of the importance of this sector, a hard fight for it was only to be expected. To confuse the Germans, therefore, several diversionary operations were planned: an attack up the west coast toward Spezia (*left center*), a commando attack on the Comacchio Spit (the narrow strip of land between Lake Comacchio and the Adriatic Sea), and a naval demonstration to simulate a large-scale amphibious assault against the east coast north of the mouth of the Po (*off map, top*).

As finally approved, the plan provided for an initial attack by the British V Corps (three divisions) along the axis of Highway 16 and by the Polish Corps (two divisions, reinforced) northwestward toward Bologna. The Fifth Army would attack later, putting all its strength into an offensive aimed generally west of Bologna. Each army, in turn, would have priority for air support, including strong forces of heavy bombers, as its respective offensive opened.

The naval demonstration pulled one panzer division northward, but not for a long enough period to have much effect on the coming offensive. On 2-4 April, Commandos, supported by the British 56th Division, cleared the Comacchio Spit; three days later, the American 92d Division (two of its organic regiments replaced by the 442d Regimental Combat Team and the 473d Infantry Regiment) attacked along the west coast toward Spezia through extremely rugged country.

In the early afternoon of 9 April, a massive air and artillery bombardment was put down along the front of the V and Polish Corps. The infantry attack, supported by flame-throwing tanks, jumped off at 1900. The Germans fought stubbornly from their well-prepared positions, but by 14 April the British V Corps—aided by an amphibious envelopment across Lake Comacchio by elements of its 56th Division—had forced its way into the Argenta Gap while the Poles, with support from the XIII Corps, seized Imola (*upper center*).

The Fifth Army began its attack on the morning of the 14th, sending its IV Corps forward behind the heaviest air support yet employed in Italy. Truscott had massed practically all his troops on a twenty-five–mile front south of Bologna, with only two detached regiments from the 92d Division holding the long mountain front between this concentration and the 92d Division on the west coast. Furthermore, he now had troops trained for mountain warfare—the American 10th Mountain Division, which immediately proved its worth by snaking its way rapidly through the German defenses, well ahead of the units on its flanks. On the evening of the 15th, the II Corps joined in the attack, but was held for slight gains. German resistance here, however, was fruitless. The 10th Mountain Division was working its way down out of the last foothills by the evening of 17 April; Truscott promptly switched the 1st Armored Division across its rear and brought the 85th Division up into line on its right. On the 20th, the Americans broke out into the open country, the 10th Mountain Division seizing Ponte Samoggia by midnight.

Meanwhile, McCreery, having added weight to his right flank by inserting the XIII Corps between the Polish and V Corps (*movement not shown*), had cleared the Argenta Gap. All along its front, the Eighth Army had reached the plain. Vietinghoff had committed his last reserves, but all in vain.

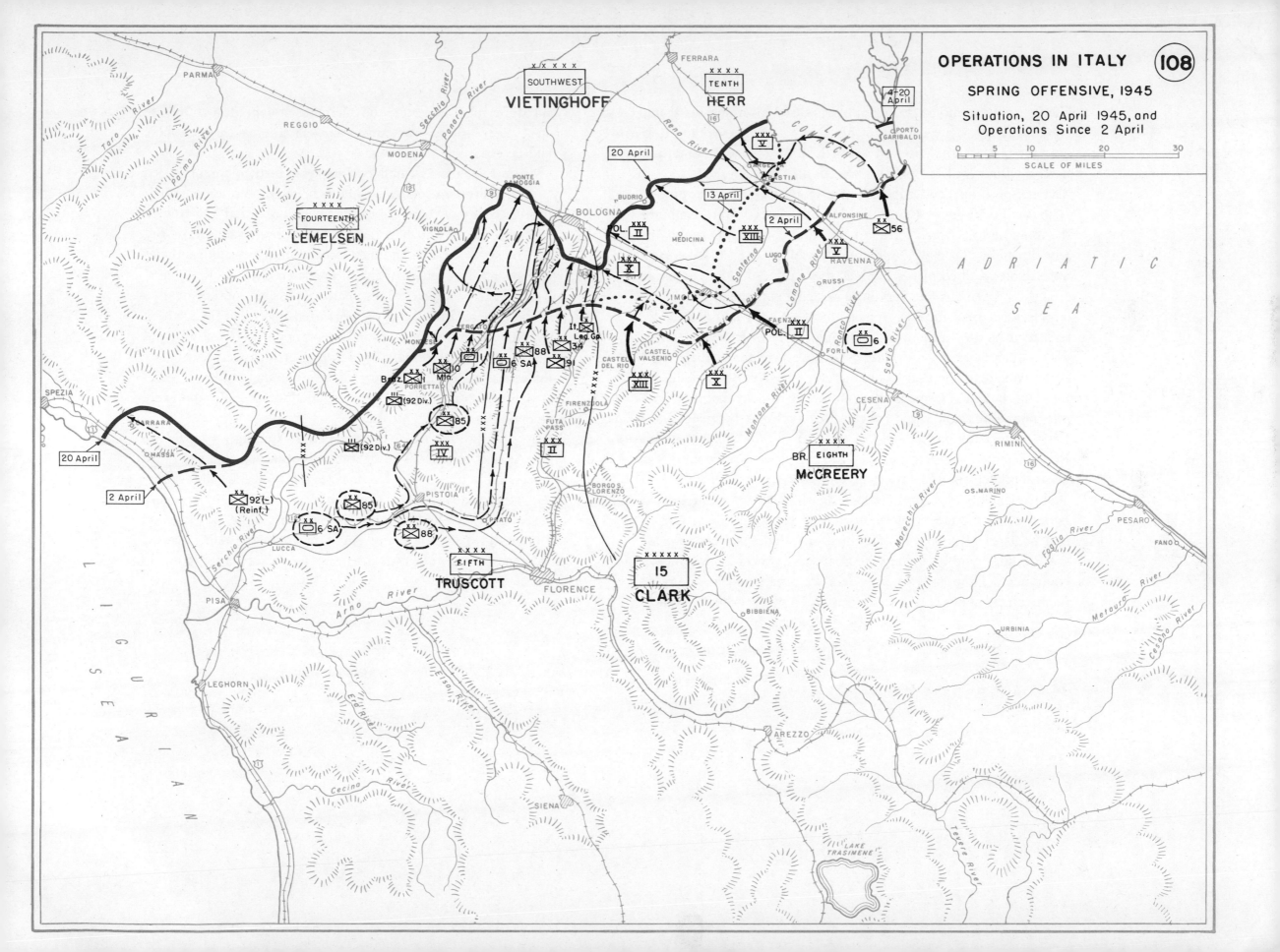

OPERATIONS IN ITALY 108

SPRING OFFENSIVE, 1945

Situation, 20 April 1945, and
Operations Since 2 April

SCALE OF MILES
0   5   10   20   30

Vietinghoff, his mountain defenses ruptured all along his front, could only try to get enough of his troops back across the Po to hold the prepared defenses on its north bank. This was a daunting task: a withdrawal across flat, open country that offered few good delaying positions, under the constant scourge of Allied air power. Also, the Po Valley possessed the finest road net in Italy, enabling the more mobile Allied forces to shift and concentrate rapidly in any direction. To cap Vietinghoff's problem, the Po River was unfordable—Allied planes had destroyed all the bridges across it —and the Germans had very little bridging equipment.

German opposition in front of the IV Corps had practically collapsed on 19 April; units opposing the II Corps withdrew in good order when the IV Corps' advance threatened their right flank. American and Polish columns converged on Bologna during the 21st, but the Germans made no effort to hold that city. The pursuing Allies now raced for the Po, which the 10th Mountain Division reached on the night of the 22d and forced on the 23d. Roads jammed with wrecked German vehicles and a die-hard rear guard checked the II Corps near Finale (*center*) long enough to enable elements of several German divisions to escape the closing Allied trap at Bondeno (*center*). Using ponton bridges, ferries, and boats of all kinds, the Germans strove desperately to cross the Po, but could do so only by abandoning most of their heavy equipment. Thousands of prisoners were gathered in, many of them caught unaware of the sudden speed of the Allied advance.

Around Ferrara, however, the Germans fought desperately to protect their withdrawal, since an Allied breakthrough here would be especially disastrous.

Meanwhile, the German position was further compromised by a major eruption of Italian partisan bands throughout their rear area. Many of these groups had been organized and trained by Allied officers who had been dropped by parachute or put ashore by small craft behind the German lines; arms and supplies had been air-dropped to them in considerable quantity. On 1 April, Allied headquarters estimated (possibly optimistically) that there were 50,000 active, organized guerrillas in northern Italy. Now, with the Germans in retreat, opportunists of all types joined the partisan formations. These guerrillas were extremely valuable as guides and sources of information, but they represented a wide spectrum of clashing political beliefs and were frequently difficult to control.

By 23 April, the Allies had reached the line shown (*solid red line*). Against all odds, Vietinghoff had succeeded in saving most of his men, but it would be too much to say he had saved his army group. Units were scattered; ammunition was low; heavy weapons, tanks, and vehicles had been largely lost south of the Po. He could not hope to reestablish a coherent front unless the Allies paused to reorganize and replenish their supplies before attempting to cross the Po.

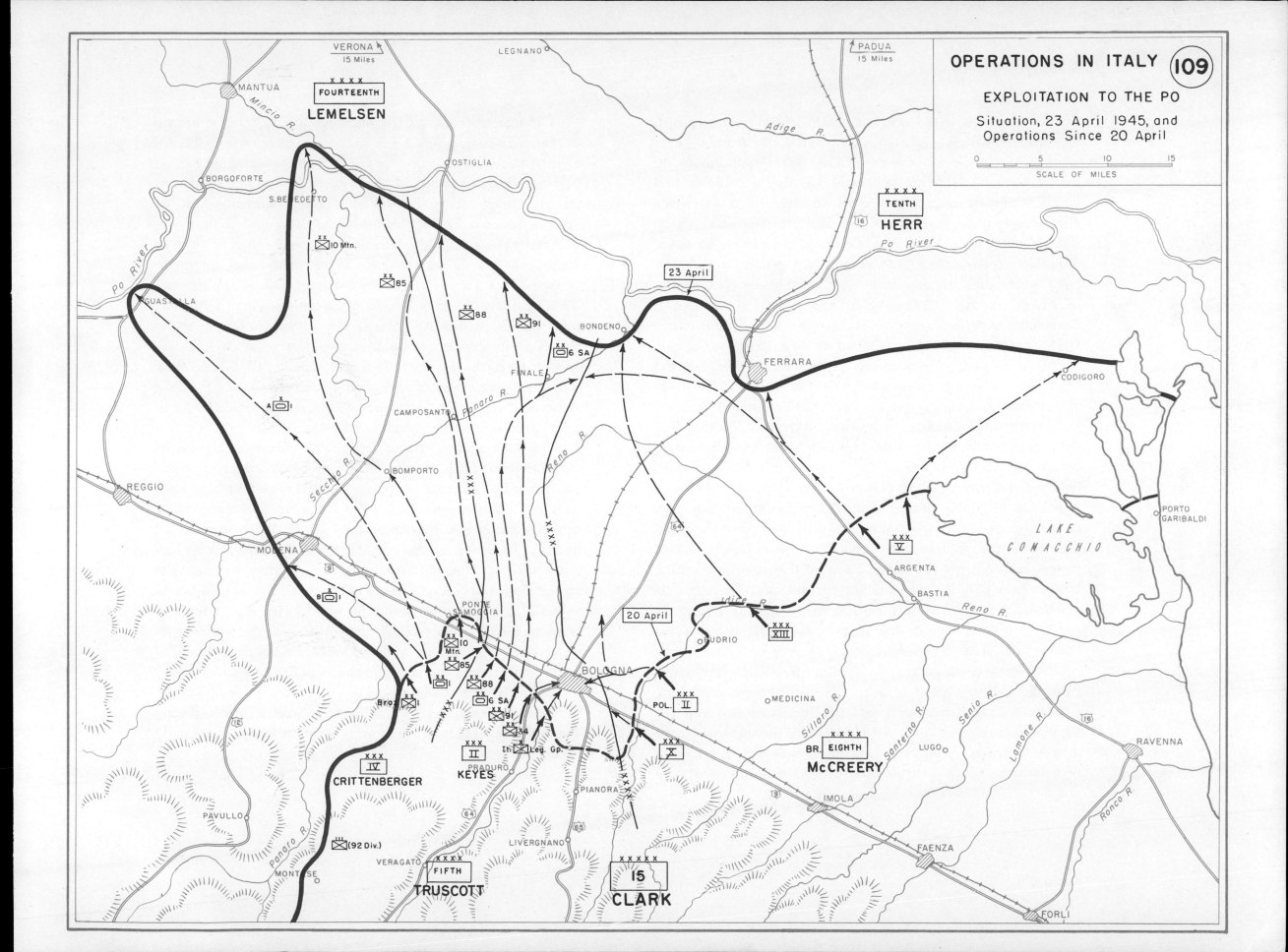

OPERATIONS IN ITALY (109)

EXPLOITATION TO THE PO

Situation, 23 April 1945, and
Operations Since 20 April

0   5   10   15
SCALE OF MILES

VERONA
15 Miles

PADUA
15 Miles

MANTUA

XXXX
FOURTEENTH
LEMELSEN

Mincio R.

BORGOFORTE

S. BENEDETTO

OSTIGLIA

Adige R.

TENTH
XXXX
HERR

Po River

Po River

XX 10 Mtn.

GUASTALLA

23 April

XX 85

XX 88

XX 91

BONDENO

FERRARA

CODIGORO

XX 6 SA

A X 1

FINALE

Ponaro R.

CAMPOSANTO

REGGIO

Seccia R.

BOMPORTO

Reno R.

64

LAKE COMACCHIO

PORTO GARIBALDI

MODENA

9

B X 1

XXX V

ARGENTA

BASTIA

Reno R.

PONTE SAMOGGIA

XX 10 Mtn.

Idice R.

20 April

BUDRIO

XIII

XX 85

Brio

XX 1

XX 88

XX 6 SA

BOLOGNA

MEDICINA

Sillaro R.

Santerno R.

Senio R.

16

RAVENNA

XX 91

XX 34

POL. II

BR. EIGHTH
XXXX
McCREERY

LUGO

Lamone R.

XXX II
KEYES

It. Leg. Gp.

PBADURO

XXX X

PIANORA

9

IMOLA

Ronco R.

XXX IV
CRITTENBERGER

18

Panaro R.

PAVULLO

LIVERGNANO

65

64

FAENZA

III (92 Div.)

MONTESE

VERAGATO

FIFTH
XXXX
TRUSCOTT

XXXXX 15
CLARK

FORLI

The Italian campaign ended with exploiting Allied columns thrusting through collapsing resistance all across northern Italy. These apparently reckless drives were, in fact, based upon months of careful planning. Bridging equipment was always available, and logistical support never failed. As shown here, Allied spearheads drove deeply to seize important communications centers, possession of which would block any large-scale German withdrawals. Thereafter, the bypassed German units were rounded up. At any point where the Germans were weak, partisan bands normally seized control, as in Genoa, Milan, and Venice. (One band of Communist guerrillas captured and butchered Mussolini on 27 April, appropriating his private hoard for their party's war chest.)

Major German resistance had evaporated by the 25th, the Eighth Army having crushed the hard core of the Tenth Army against the Po east of Ferrara on the 24th. The strong Adige Line was passed, almost without opposition, on the 27th. By the 29th, the Italian Fascist troops of the Ligurian Army began to surrender, all of them giving up on the 30th. A small German corps held out northeast of Turin (*lower left*) until assured of Hitler's death. On 29 April, Vietinghoff agreed to an unconditional surrender, effective at noon, 2 May. This was the first of the large-scale German capitulations that ended the war in Europe. Allied troops, however, pressed forward toward the Austrian frontier, troops of the 88th Division establishing contact at Vipiteno (*upper right*) with the American Seventh Army, advancing from the north, on 4 May. Two days previously, New Zealand units had received the surrender of the German garrison of Trieste (*right center*). Peace came to Italy in a guise scarcely distinguishable from the last few weeks of war: Tito was attempting to seize considerable portions of northeastern Italy and southern Austria, while a French expedition (*not shown*) had occupied the Aosta area (*left center*). To the rear, much of Italy was in a state of high ferment, which—on occasion—required firm, careful handling.

Throughout the war, Italy had been a poor relation among the various theaters. The Allies' primary purpose there had been, bluntly, to attract and consume German units which might otherwise have been employed on the Western Front or in Russia. In this, the Italian campaign—with all its disappointments—was an obvious success. Fighting in Italy was slow and difficult—in Alexander's words, "only one more mountain range or river to cross in the face of an enemy resistance which never seemed to weaken." It was a war fought with what was left over, with what could be spared. Veteran British, American, and French divisions were steadily withdrawn from it for service elsewhere, to be replaced with odd lots of troops gathered up from the four corners of the earth. It is doubtful that Alexander, Clark, and their subordinate commanders have received sufficient credit for their ability to carry forward an aggressive, eventually victorious campaign with such heterogeneous contingents.

The success of the Italian campaign reached far beyond its mountain battlefields. Behind the Allied soldiers, doggedly fighting forward to the next ridge, Italy formed a vast air base from which the Allied Combined Bomber Offensive delivered some of its weightiest blows. Furthermore, to Hitler, the limited Allied forces in Italy were always a threat to the Balkans, forcing him to divert troops from the battlefronts to stand guard there against an invasion which never came. And, by his original decision to fight for Italy south of Rome, he was forever forced to keep divisions idle in northern Italy to guard both coasts against possible Allied amphibious landings, while his Atlantic Wall remained only a shell and his commanders in Russia pleaded vainly for reinforcements.

In no small way, Italy was to Hitler as Spain was to Napoleon —an "ulcer" steadily draining away strength from a weakening empire.

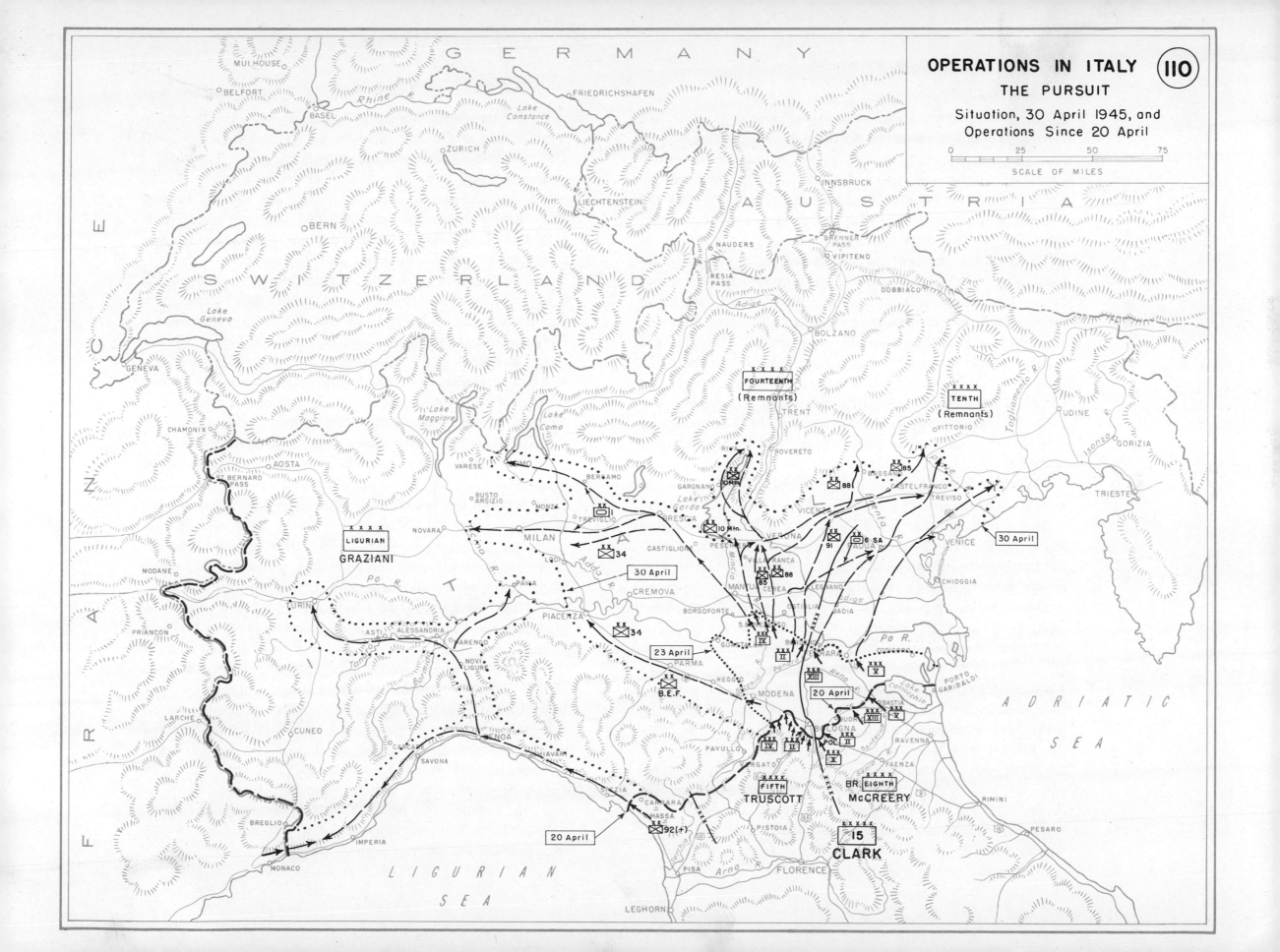

OPERATIONS IN ITALY (110)
THE PURSUIT

Situation, 30 April 1945, and
Operations Since 20 April

SCALE OF MILES
0   25   50   75

Japan exhibited the aggressive and expansionist traits which had generally characterized its growth as a nation by attacking China in 1894-95 and seizing Formosa (*lower right*) and the Kwantung Peninsula (*upper right*). International pressure nullified the Kwantung seizure, but after the Russo-Japanese War (1904-05) —her first war with a European power—Japan reclaimed that peninsula, which Russia had meanwhile leased from China. In 1910, Korea was annexed, and Japanese nationals promptly occupied all the responsible governmental and professional positions in the country. Token participation in World War I gave Japan the opportunity to claim former German rights in the Shantung Peninsula (*right center*) and in the Caroline, Marshall, and Marianas (except Guam) Islands (*see map 113, center*). The League of Nations gave Japan a mandate over these islands, but the wary United States and Great Britain pressed the Japanese at the Washington Nine-Power Conference (1922) to recognize China's territorial integrity, thereby forcing her to withdraw from Shantung.

Japanese acquiescence in this territorial setback, as well as her earlier acceptance of inferior naval status (the five-five-three ratio at the Washington Naval Conference in 1921), was due to the emergence of a liberal government which clamped a restraining hand on the militaristic clique. However, the militarists (led by the Army), aided by social unrest and economic depression, plotted their way to power in 1931 on the heels of the "Mukden Incident" (the alleged bombing of a section of the Japanese-controlled Mukden-Harbin railroad [*this map, upper right*]). Here was Japan's excuse for overrunning Manchuria (renamed Manchukuo) on the pretense that the Chinese could not control their "bandits." When the League of Nations protested this occupation, Japan resigned from the League, and promptly incorporated Jehol into Manchukuo (1933). Meanwhile, China had retaliated with an anti-Japanese boycott—particularly in Shanghai. Attendant riots in that city led to bloodshed, and the Japanese landed 50,000 troops to enforce demands for reparations. They withdrew in May, 1932, after driving the Chinese Army inland.

During the next four years, Japan plagued China with ever-increasing demands, all intended to extend Japanese domination over the hapless Chinese. The Chinese Central Government of Generalissimo Chiang Kai-Shek, striving desperately to unite a nation previously torn by civil war, at first acceded to the demands; but, as Chiang built an army, resistance stiffened. Finally, the Japanese decided to use force. War came with the manufactured "China Incident" (a clash between Japanese and Chinese troops at the Marco Polo Bridge near Peiping) on 7 July, 1937.

Japan—with an industrial base geared for a minor war—had a well-trained, recently modernized 300,000-man regular army backed up by 2,000,000 reserves. An efficient navy and surprisingly effective army and navy air forces supported them. China's Army numbered 2,000,000, but only 100,000 were reasonably well equipped. Chiang—dependent upon outside sources for supplies—had no navy, very little artillery, and only a few obsolete aircraft; his subordinates lacked real military ability.

Japan decided to make a main attack from Manchukuo and a secondary effort at Shanghai. This plan took advantage of the existing base in Manchukuo and might lead to Chiang's encirclement between the two attacks before he could withdraw into mountainous western China.

In the north, the Japanese secured their right flank by the capture of Paotow (*upper center*) in August and then regrouped. The three-pronged drive south down the railroads in September stalled by November as the Chinese defended stubbornly and used guerrillas to harass Japanese communications at night. More telling, however, had been the reduction in Japanese strength occasioned by the need for troops at Shanghai. There, the fighting—beginning in August—had been bitter; Chiang's German-trained 88th Division contained the attack until reinforcements enabled the Japanese to pinch out the city by landing on either side of it. Then they crossed Lake Tai easily (using armored motorboats) and captured Nanking on 13 December; the infamous rape of that city continued for days. By the end of the year, the Japanese had made gains as shown (*solid red lines*). Meanwhile, their aircraft had rained destruction on China's cities in a campaign of terror.

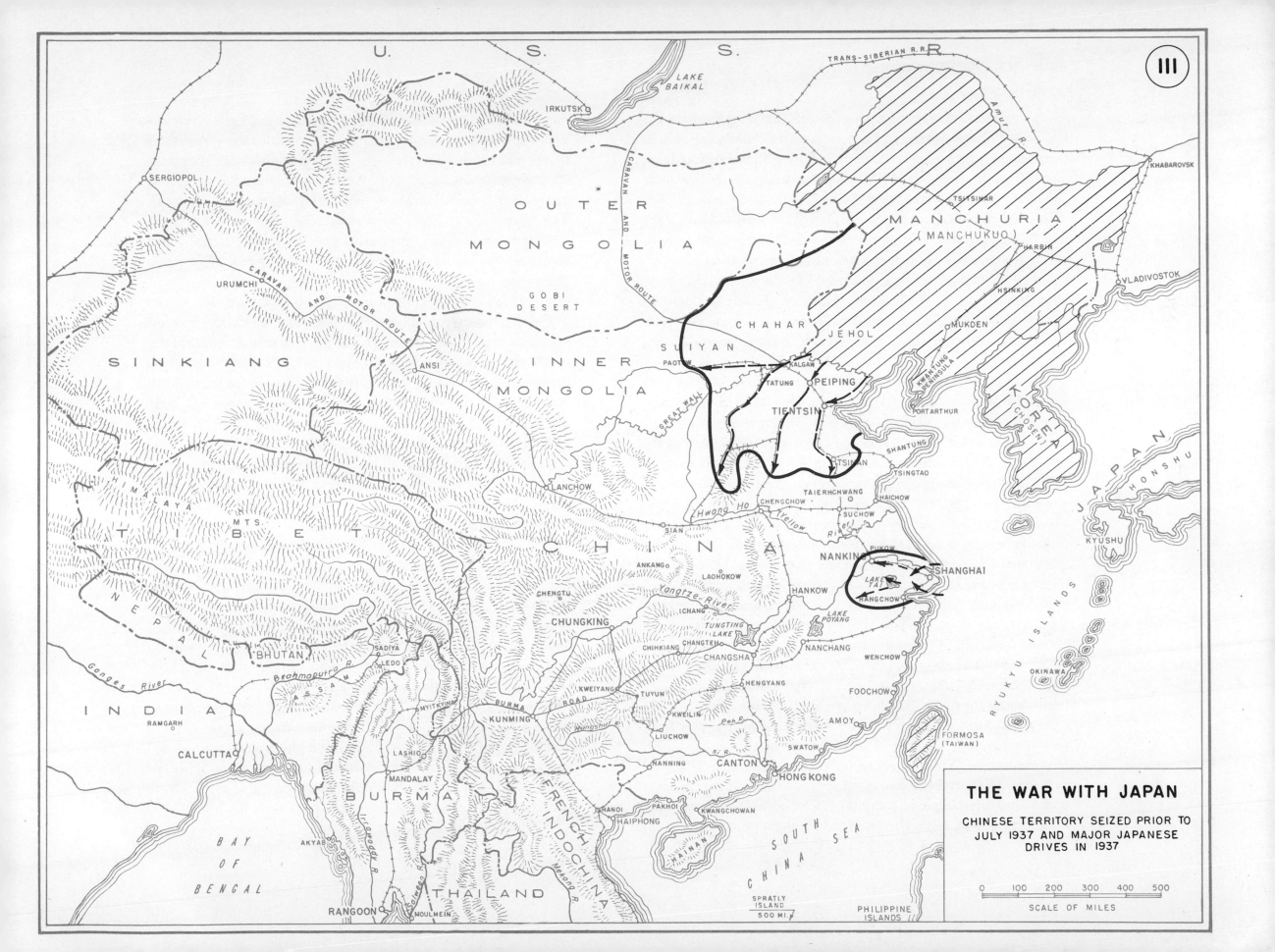

THE WAR WITH JAPAN

CHINESE TERRITORY SEIZED PRIOR TO
JULY 1937 AND MAJOR JAPANESE
DRIVES IN 1937

0   100   200   300   400   500

SCALE OF MILES

Japan's strategists were disappointed with the gains made in the first year of the war. They had hoped to defeat Chiang's organized forces quickly before he could unite the several factions in China, and before the war imposed an excessive drain on the Japanese economy. But they had been frustrated by the Chinese, who desperately traded space for time and avoided decisive battle. Nor had Chiang's ability to import desperately needed supplies been materially limited. Though the loss of Shanghai was a blow, he still controlled most of the seaports and the four remaining overland routes out of China: the Haiphong-Kunming (*bottom center*) railroad; the Rangoon-Lashio-Kunming railroad and road; and the two caravan and motor routes to Russia (*upper left and top center*).

Japan's initial operations in 1938 were designed to close the Lunghai Corridor (*center, right*)—the area still under Chinese control between the two fronts. Süchow, an important rail center, was the first objective. Chinese resistance was stubborn, but the twin drives from north and south ultimately captured the city in May. The northern prong had met serious resistance at Taierhchwang, where 60,000 Japanese troops were cut off in April; two-thirds cut their way out of the trap but were forced to leave large quantities of equipment and supplies behind. This success stimulated the morale of the Chinese and stiffened their determination to resist the invader. In June, the Japanese began a drive on Chengchow (*center, right*) to sever the railroad to Hankow. This advance bogged down when the Chinese demolished the Yellow River dikes, allowing the swollen river to inundate the countryside. The drive on the Chinese capital (Hankow) was now reinforced while, in October, a 40,000-man force landed twenty miles above the British crown colony of Hong Kong (*lower right*), and easily occupied Canton, thus cutting off Hankow from its major source of supply. Consequently, in November—after five months of bloody fighting—Chiang abandoned Hankow, moved its industrial machinery inland, adopted a scorched-earth policy, and reestablished his capital at Chungking (*lower center*).

By the end of 1938, the Japanese occupied an important segment of China (*solid red lines*). But within this area, they continued to meet smoldering resentment; armed bands—professing to be guerrillas—increased Japanese administrative problems. Meanwhile, relations with the Western powers had deteriorated, and the Japanese militarists lobbied for an alliance with Germany. The United States began to provide more supplies for Chiang, moving them primarily via Lashio and the Burma Road. Japan countered by expressing her intention of creating a "Co-Prosperity Sphere" in east Asia.

In 1939, Japan, having been unable to obtain a quick victory in China in two years, adopted a policy of strangulation, employing minimum forces at strategic places. This met with the wholehearted approval of Japan's naval leaders, who had been urging the government to move southward in preparation for the domination of the Netherlands East Indies (*off map, bottom*). Consequently, only limited offensives were conducted in 1939. In the interior, these were unsuccessfully aimed at securing control of the Canton-Hankow railroad. But along the coast, Chiang's remaining ports were seized, and the capture of Nanning (*lower center*) placed the Haiphong-Kunming railroad within range of Japanese bombers. French Indochina was threatened and Hong Kong isolated by the seizure of Hainan Island in February.

In 1939, stern treatment of foreign nationals in occupied China indicated a stiffening Japanese attitude toward the Western powers. In July, the United States, exasperated with Japan's aggressions in China, declared its intention to abrogate the 1911 Trade Treaty, thereby threatening to cut off United States exports to Japan after 1 January, 1940. Then, without warning, Hitler concluded a neutrality pact with Russia in September. Coming after months of fruitless German efforts to get the Japanese to commit themselves to war against the Anglo-French bloc, it seemed to repudiate the 1936 Anti-Comintern Pact, and caused grave concern in Japan about Russia's future actions in Asia. The Army went into temporary political eclipse, and a more liberal group of politicians sought better relations with the West.

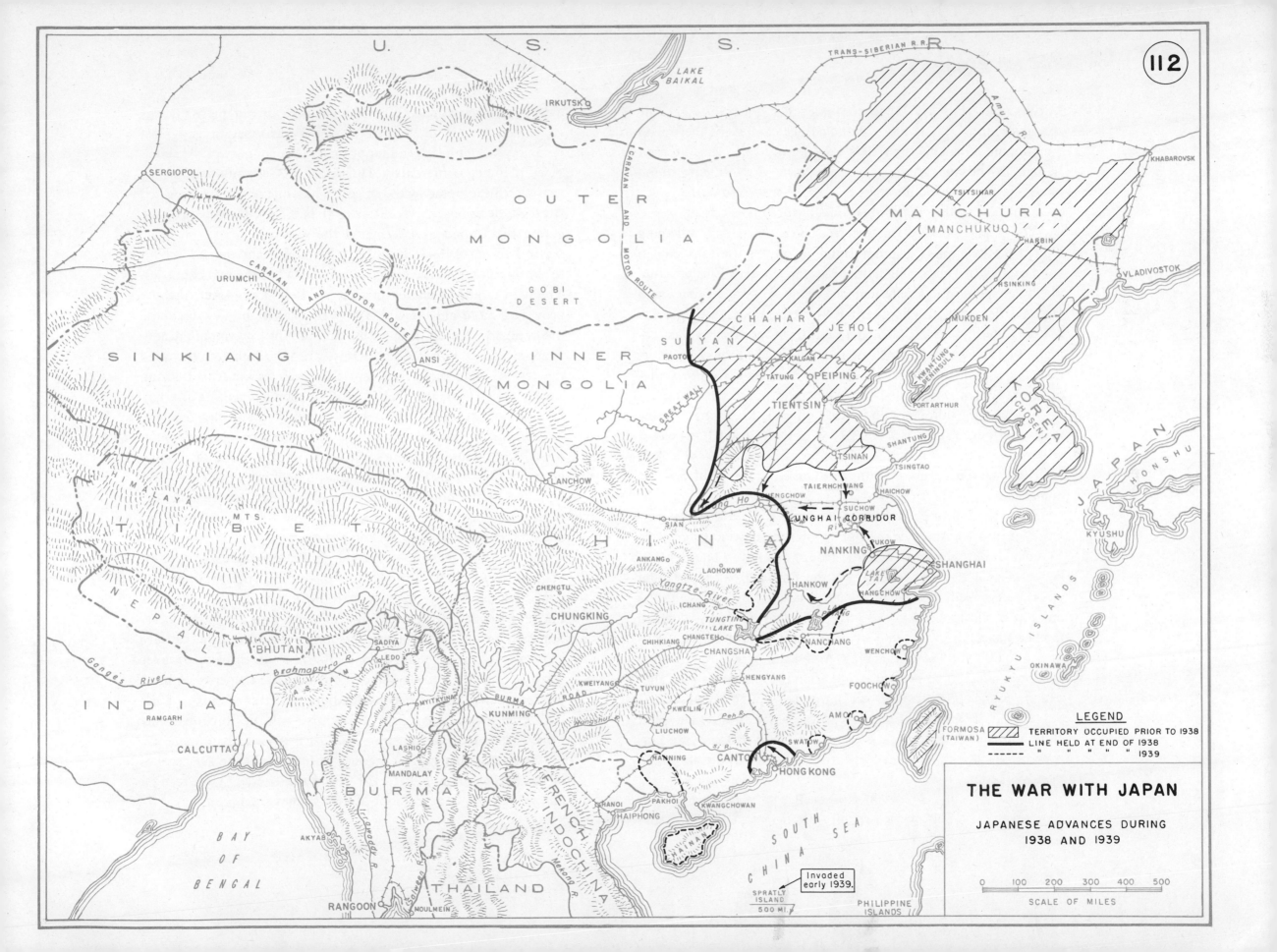

112

LEGEND

▨ TERRITORY OCCUPIED PRIOR TO 1938
━━━ LINE HELD AT END OF 1938
╌╌╌ " " " " 1939

THE WAR WITH JAPAN

JAPANESE ADVANCES DURING 1938 AND 1939

```
0   100   200   300   400   500
```
SCALE OF MILES

Invaded early 1939.

SPRATLY ISLAND
500 MI.

Throughout 1940–41, Japan continued her policy of economic strangulation of China and conducted her campaigns there with a minimum of men and materials. All the while, the armed forces, though in the background, were preparing for ultimate domination of the rich Southern Resources Area (*left center*)—by peaceful penetration if possible, but by force if necessary.

The Japanese were not deterred even when an awakening United States applied a minor embargo on exports to Japan in January, 1940. That spring, Hitler overran Western Europe, completely changing the Pacific balance of power. With France and Holland defeated, the Southern Resources Area lay helpless—if the United States could be deterred from interfering. Accordingly, in July, a new cabinet, dominated by the Army, set as its goal the establishment of the Greater East Asia Co-Prosperity Sphere (generally intended to include the Southern Resources Area, plus the Philippines and New Guinea). Preliminary measures were to be a successful conclusion of the war in China, closer alliance with the Axis, and negotiation of a nonaggression pact with Russia. That same month, the United States tightened the embargo.

After the fall of France, Japan coerced the weak Vichy government into granting her the right to move troops into northern Indochina (*left center*). Japanese troops entered in late September, and secured bases from which the Burma Road into China could be bombed. The United States retaliated by increasing the amount of aid to Chiang. Also, in September, Congress enacted the first peacetime Selective Service Act and authorized a strength of 1,400,000 for the burgeoning American Army. Meanwhile, Japanese attempts to press the Netherlands East Indies into allocating practically their entire oil output to Nippon failed. On 27 September, Japan signed the Tripartite Pact with Germany and Italy, effecting a diplomatic coup which—unrealistically and erroneously—was expected to deter the United States from taking positive action.

About this time, President Roosevelt, vitally concerned over developments in Europe, leased fifty destroyers to England, and a reappraisal was made of existing American war plans. It was concluded that, in the event of a global war, operations against Germany would be given first priority. In a January, 1941, combined planning conference (*ABC-1*), this "Germany-first" policy was heartily accepted by the British. Thus, one of the major Allied strategic decisions of World War II had, in effect, been made before the United States entered the war.

In February, 1941, Japan sent Admiral Kichisaburo Nomura to Washington to settle disagreements between the two countries. The next month, Congress passed the Lend-Lease Act, thereby providing more aid for China as well as Britain. The Japanese theoretically secured their north flank in April by signing a nonaggression pact with Russia. In July, when the Japanese occupied the rest of Indochina, President Roosevelt reacted by freezing Japanese assets in the United States—thereby making the embargo complete. Some Japanese now panicked and urged reaching agreement with the United States, but the Army leaders maintained that oil reserves were sufficient to wage war and that Japan must not turn back. The die was cast; though negotiations would continue in Washington in an attempt to reach agreement, the Army and Navy leaders—for the first time—sat down to evolve a comprehensive strategy for the coming war.

Japan's war plan—based upon limited objectives—consisted of three phases. The first phase (expected to take five months) would consist of a surprise attack to neutralize the United States Pacific Fleet so that it could not interfere with Japanese operations; seizure of the Southern Resources Area; and the capture of strategic areas required to establish a defensive perimeter (*dashed red line*) around the proposed Co-Prosperity Sphere. Phase two would be the consolidation and strengthening of the perimeter. Phase three would be defensive—the destruction of any forces attempting to penetrate the perimeter. The ultimate expectation was that long and costly operations in the far reaches of the Pacific would destroy the will of the United States to fight and would lead to acceptance of the Japanese conquests.

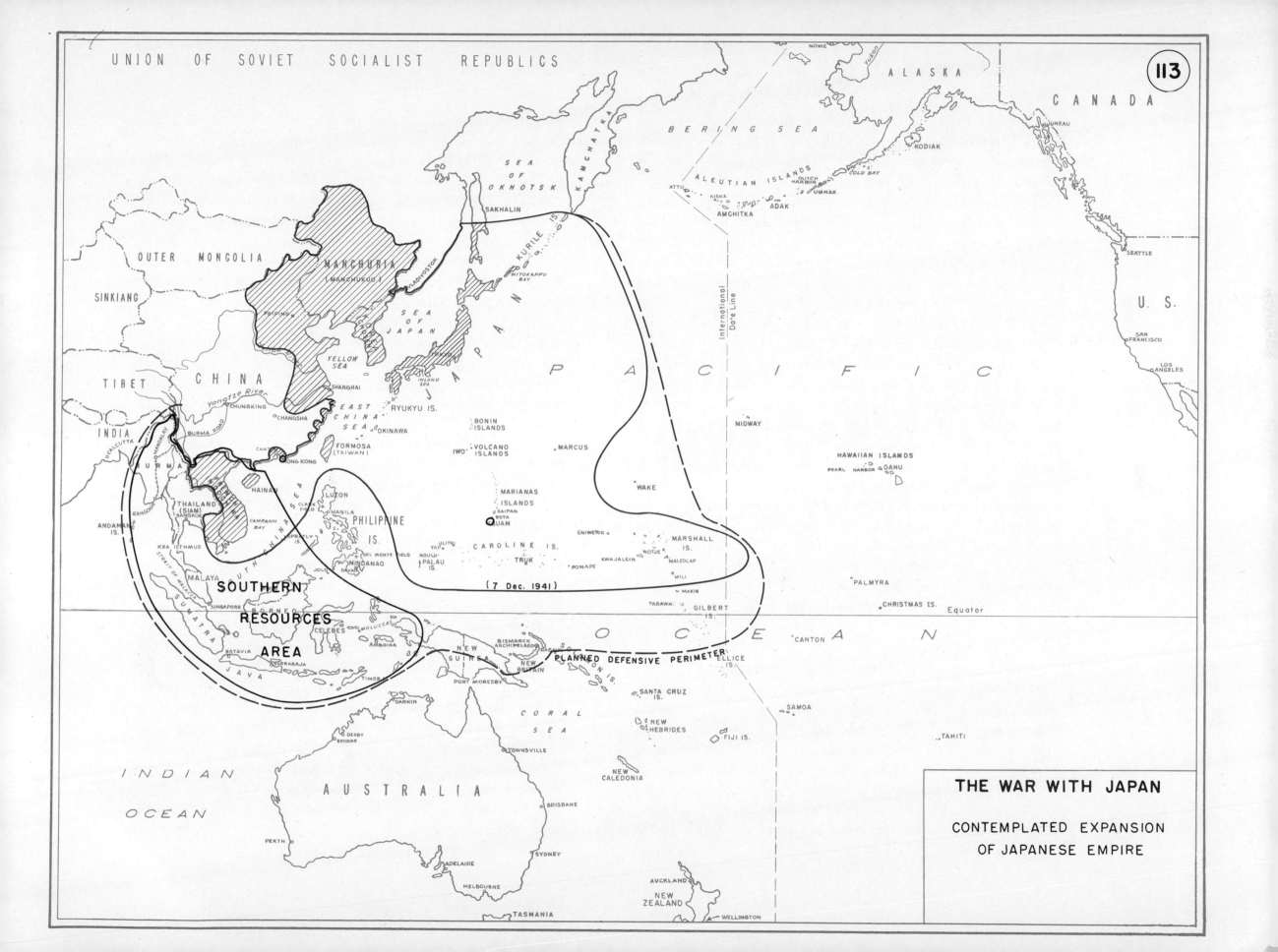

THE WAR WITH JAPAN

CONTEMPLATED EXPANSION
OF JAPANESE EMPIRE

Negotiations continued in Washington during the late summer and early fall of 1941 in an atmosphere of frustration, for neither side would compromise. In Japan, the Army and Navy leaders stressed the growing shortage of resources and the need for a decision as to Japan's future course of action. The premier, Prince Konoye, argued for an extension of the secret 15 October deadline Japan had set for negotiations with the United States, and even suggested acceding to United States demands to withdraw from China; but the war minister, General Hideki Tojo, refused. The cabinet resigned, and, on 18 October, Tojo became premier. On 5 November, he authorized continuation of negotiations until 25 November (later extended to the 29th). But Japan's new proposals, though they contained conditional agreement to a Japanese withdrawal from China, could not be accepted by America without condoning Japan's policy of aggression. Consequently, the proposals were rejected, and the United States submitted a counterproposal to Nomura on the 26th. The Japanese, considering both their own proposals and the American counterproposals as ultimatums, now made final preparations for war. As early as 6 November, field commanders had been alerted to prepare detailed plans to implement the war strategy, and, on the 25th, the Pearl Harbor Striking Force had departed the Kurile Islands (*upper left*). On 1 December, the date for initiation of hostilities was selected—8 December, a Sunday (7 December) at Pearl Harbor. (Dates given in the text recognize the International Date Line.)

Japan's operation plan for the execution of phase one of the war plan was based upon a finely calculated distribution of forces. Of the fifty-one divisions and fifty-nine brigades comprising the Army ground forces in December, only ten and four, respectively, were allocated to the four offensive armies; the remaining units were held in Japan and China in the event that alternative courses of action had to be adopted. The primary objective of the offensive was the rich Southern Resources Area, whose seizure—the Japanese believed—would not be possible without also capturing the Philippines and neutralizing the United States Pacific Fleet. Operations would begin with a surprise air attack on Pearl Harbor (*center, right*), to be followed immediately by similar strikes against the Philippines and Malaya (*center, left*). Then landings would be made in the Philippines and Malaya to initiate a two-pronged drive on Java (*lower left*). Concurrently, Thailand would be occupied; Guam, Wake (*both center*), and Hong Kong seized; and Borneo (*lower left*) invaded. These comprised the initial operations planned for the first phase. (The concluding operations in this phase—subjugation of the Philippines, Burma, and the Netherlands East Indies—are covered on subsequent maps.) The almost simultaneous execution of operations against the widely separated objectives attests to the thoroughness of Japanese planning. Surprisingly, in none of the joint operations was there unity of command—army and navy elements merely "cooperated."

The idea of attacking Pearl Harbor had been conceived in January, 1941, by Admiral Isoruku Yamamoto, commander of the Combined Fleet; but its very boldness scared his navy superiors who did not finally incorporate it into the over-all plan until October. Meanwhile, Yamamoto selected elite personnel, thoroughly trained them, and gathered intelligence on Pearl Harbor. His task force was ready when it was alerted for the operation in mid-November. The nucleus of this Pearl Harbor Striking Force consisted of six aircraft carriers bearing 414 aircraft, of which 360 made the attack. A northerly route (*upper center*) was selected in spite of the refueling difficulties created by prevailing poor weather, since a more southerly route would expose the force to discovery by American planes or ships. By 0600, 7 December, the force had arrived—exactly as scheduled—at the launching point 200 miles north of Oahu. To the west, two of its destroyers were nearing Midway to carry out a scheduled naval bombardment. United States forces in the Hawaiian Islands were completely unaware of the location of this potent carrier task force and had no premonition of the destruction it would soon loose upon them.

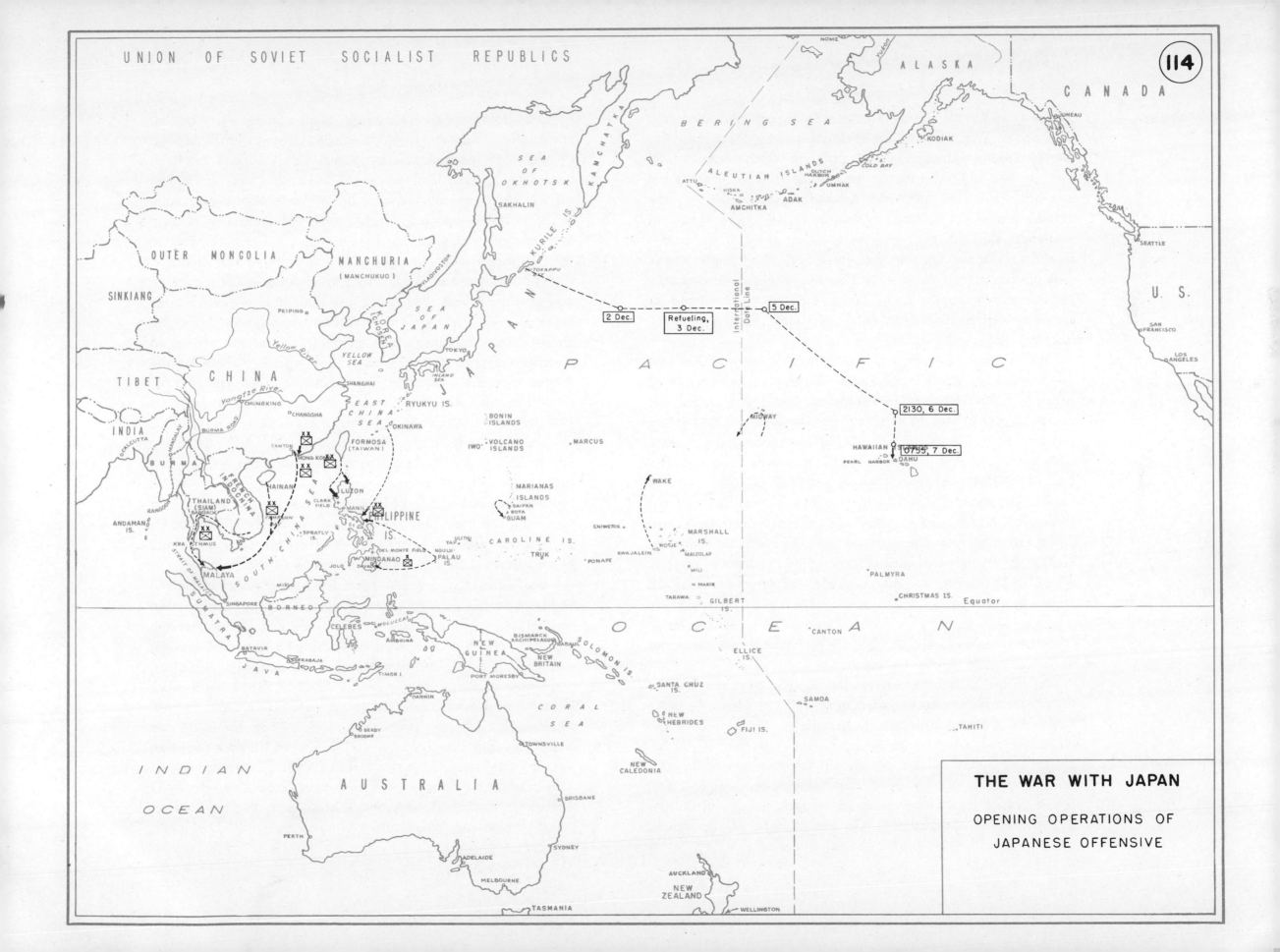

THE WAR WITH JAPAN

OPENING OPERATIONS OF
JAPANESE OFFENSIVE

The early 1930's were years of isolation and economic depression in America. The armed forces, in drastic need of modernization, struggled along with military appropriations which were naturally meager. Not until Germany's threatening actions alarmed the administration was attention directed toward enlarging the nation's armed forces. Thus, by December, 1941, the Army had a strength of 1,500,000, but the great majority of the troops lacked training and equipment. (Lend-Lease to Britain and Russia took priority in some cases.) The Hawaiian Islands were probably garrisoned by as well-equipped and trained army ground and air forces as were available; the Navy, of course, had its imposing Pacific Fleet based there.

With the adoption of the "Germany-first" strategy in January, 1941, initial operations in the Pacific Ocean areas were relegated to purely defensive roles. The Philippines would be defended, but no reinforcements would be sent there; the Navy would capture positions in the Marshall Islands, but only prepare for further advances to the west. Under this plan (RAINBOW-5), a powerful base in the Hawaiian Islands was essential.

The defenses of Hawaii were the joint responsibility of the local army and navy commanders; unity of command did not exist. A defense plan—periodically tested—was in being, but its implementation depended upon close cooperation between services, which, in December, was not completely effective. Nor was the army aircraft warning system in the islands fully developed by 7 December, because of shortages of trained personnel and radar equipment. Offshore air patrols were maintained, but they, too, were inadequate on the critical day.

After the United States rejected Japan's final proposal in Washington, the two commanders in Hawaii (Lt. Gen. Walter C. Short and Admiral Husband E. Kimmel) were notified on 27 November that war was imminent. Neither commander put his forces on a full war alert. Additional information—some of it rather nebulous—was received from Washington prior to 7 December which could have indicated an attack, but still the defenses were not fully alerted. On the morning of the attack, ominous signs appeared. Unidentified submarines were spotted, and one radar indicated the approach of a large unidentified group of planes. In the holiday atmosphere of that Sunday morning, these signs aroused little reaction. The Pacific Fleet—minus the carriers which, fortunately, were at sea—rode at anchor exactly as the Japanese expected. Aircraft were likewise neatly lined up on runways throughout Oahu. At the time, the critical threat in the Hawaiian Islands, in General Short's opinion, was sabotage.

The Japanese had planned well; their execution of the attack was equally efficient. The attack was made in two waves following the general routes shown. The fighters were expected to attain air superiority and then attack grounded aircraft, but when no American aircraft appeared aloft, they turned to those on the ground. The first wave of fighters struck at all the airfields (*blue circles*) except Haleiwa (*upper left*), while the bombers attacked Pearl Harbor. The highly skilled torpedo-bomber pilots inflicted the heaviest damage on the fleet. By 0825, most of the first wave had departed. A few American planes rose from the stricken fields, only to be smothered by the incoming second wave. Its bombers—armed with light bombs destined for the missing carriers—did less damage to the fleet than the first wave. By 0945, all Japanese planes had left Oahu, and the Pearl Harbor Striking Force—never detected—quickly withdrew to the west.

The United States Pacific Fleet and the air forces in Hawaii had been dealt a shattering blow. Eighteen ships were sunk or so seriously damaged that they would be out of action for months; included were seven of the eight battleships. Of some 394 aircraft, 188 were destroyed and an additional 159 damaged. American casualties, predominantly naval, totaled 3,581 (2,403 were killed). The Japanese lost only twenty-nine aircraft and six submarines (five of them midget types). The Japanese made one error: they failed to destroy the oil-storage and harbor facilities, so that Pearl Harbor soon resumed its function as a base.

Far to the west, the isolated garrison of Guam (*see map 114*) was soon overcome. United States Marines at Wake Island repelled one landing, but succumbed to a second on 23 December.

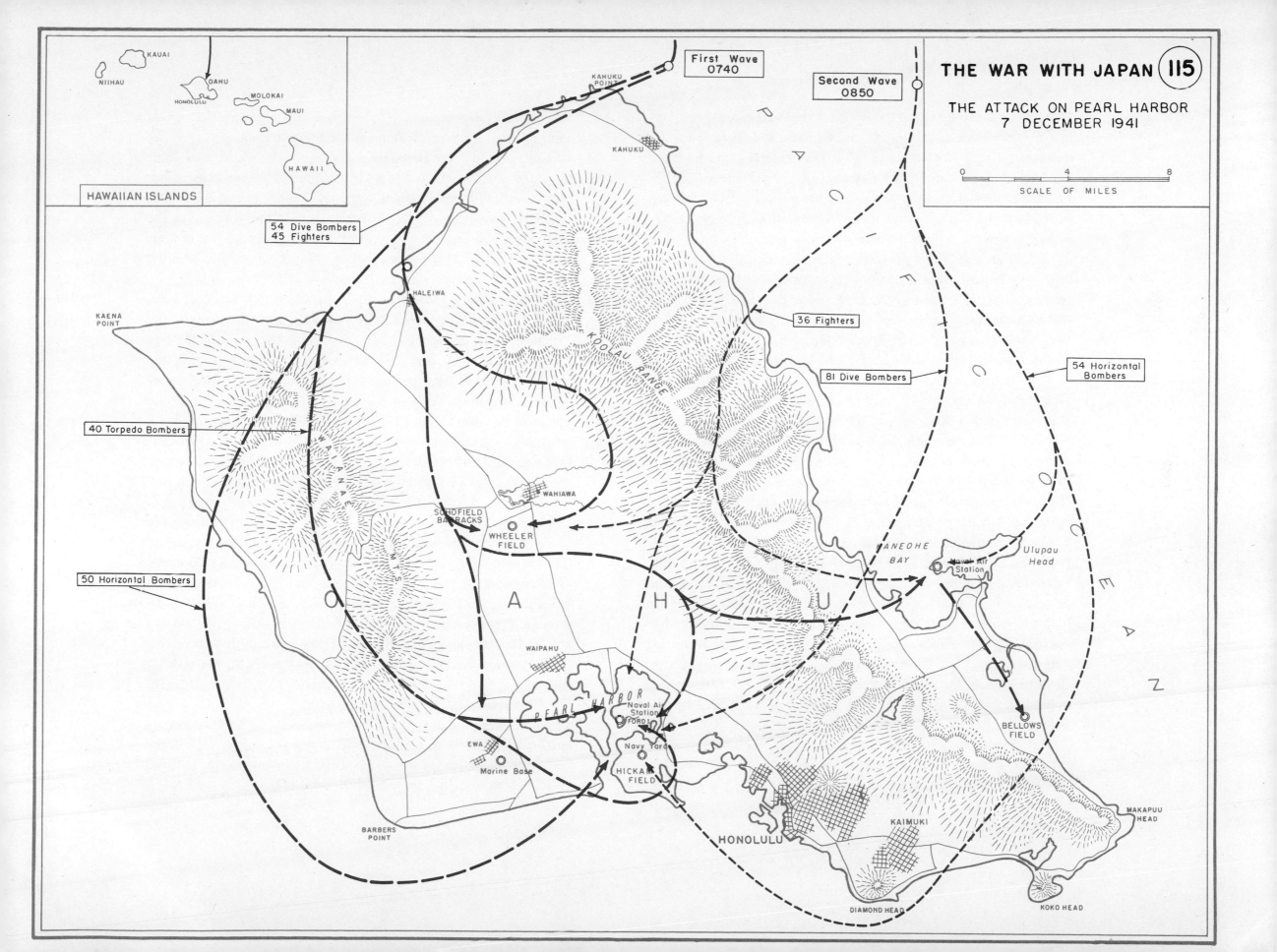

THE WAR WITH JAPAN 115

THE ATTACK ON PEARL HARBOR
7 DECEMBER 1941

0   4   8
SCALE OF MILES

HAWAIIAN ISLANDS

KAUAI
NIIHAU
OAHU
HONOLULU
MOLOKAI
MAUI
HAWAII

First Wave
0740

Second Wave
0850

54 Dive Bombers
45 Fighters

36 Fighters

81 Dive Bombers

54 Horizontal
Bombers

40 Torpedo Bombers

50 Horizontal Bombers

KAHUKU
POINT

KAHUKU

HALEIWA

KAENA
POINT

KOOLAU RANGE

WAIANAE RANGE

WAHIAWA

SCHOFIELD
BARRACKS

WHEELER
FIELD

KANEOHE
BAY

Naval Air
Station

Ulupau
Head

O A H U

WAIPAHU

PEARL HARBOR

Naval Air
Station
FORD I.

Navy Yard

EWA

Marine Base

HICKAM
FIELD

BELLOWS
FIELD

BARBERS
POINT

KAIMUKI

MAKAPUU
HEAD

HONOLULU

DIAMOND HEAD

KOKO HEAD

P A C I F I C

O C E A N

Hong Kong—consisting of the island of that name, Kowloon Peninsula, and leased territory on the Chinese mainland—was acquired by Great Britain in 1841. It gradually became an international shipping center and a symbol of British influence in the Far East. In 1941, Hong Kong was not so important militarily to Japan as it was politically: should the British be forcibly ejected from the colony, it would mean a serious loss of face for them in the Orient. This was well understood by the British who, though regarding the colony as an untenable outpost, recognized that the harbor should be denied to the Japanese as long as possible. Two Canadian infantry battalions were sent to the colony in November, 1941, as a calculated show of force, making a total of six battalions available for defense.

The British plan of defense envisioned occupation of the Gin Drinker's Line (*center*) by three battalions, while the other three occupied beach defense positions on Hong Kong Island. It was recognized that the mainland line was too long to be manned in sufficient strength to repel a strong attack; but the three battalions were expected to hold for about a week before withdrawing to the island, where the main battle would be fought. The island had twenty-nine coastal guns, some of which could fire on mainland targets, but only token naval forces (one destroyer, eight torpedo boats, and four gunboats) remained in Hong Kong waters after war broke out. The army troops, only partially trained, were short of transport and lacked adequate mortar ammunition. But the greatest armament weakness was in aircraft—the garrison had only six obsolete planes. The Japanese were undoubtedly familiar with British military defense measures, for in the prewar months the members of the Japanese Consulate moved about freely, and unhindered traffic to and from the mainland facilitated the activities of Japanese agents.

In November, 1941, the British commander moved the three mainland defense battalions from training camps into the Gin Drinker's Line, where they set to work improving the defenses. By this time, a false sense of confidence existed among the troops and many of the civilians. The island was impregnable, it was said, and the Japanese equipment, troops, and tactics were decidedly inferior; they were inept at night operations, and their aircraft were obsolete. Nor was British intelligence on 7 December very reliable: reports of 20,000 Japanese concentrating near Sham Chun Hu (*top center*) were discounted. Actually, this was the Japanese 38th Division, preparing to attack across the border. Fortunately, the British commander, Maj. Gen. C. M. Maltby, took no risks and manned all his defenses.

About 0800, 8 December, the Japanese struck without warning. Air raids destroyed the British aircraft, and concurrently the Japanese 38th Division moved across the border toward the Gin Drinker's Line. By dusk, 9 December, they were probing the British position. That night, their strength massed in the west, they ripped a hole in the defenses by seizing and holding the key strong point, Shing Mun Redoubt. The British failed to make any counterattack to recapture the redoubt, and, on the 10th, the Japanese exploited their success by widening the gap and forcing a British withdrawal. On 11 December, with his troops being driven southward, Maltby ordered a withdrawal to the island. By the 13th, it had been successfully executed. That day, and again on the 15th, the Japanese summoned Maltby to surrender and, upon being refused, unleashed intensive artillery and aerial bombardments. On the night of 18 December, the 38th Division crossed to the island as shown. By nightfall of the 19th, they had split the defenders in two groups—Maltby had erred in failing to hold the key Wong Nai Chong Gap (*lower right*) in strength, and his belated counterattacks were unavailing. By the 24th, their water supply almost exhausted, the disorganized British were beaten. On Christmas Day, Maltby surrendered.

In just eighteen days, an efficient, well-trained, and adequately led Japanese division, supported by an equally effective air force and navy, had overrun the stately British crown colony. Its total casualties were 2,754; the British lost 11,848.

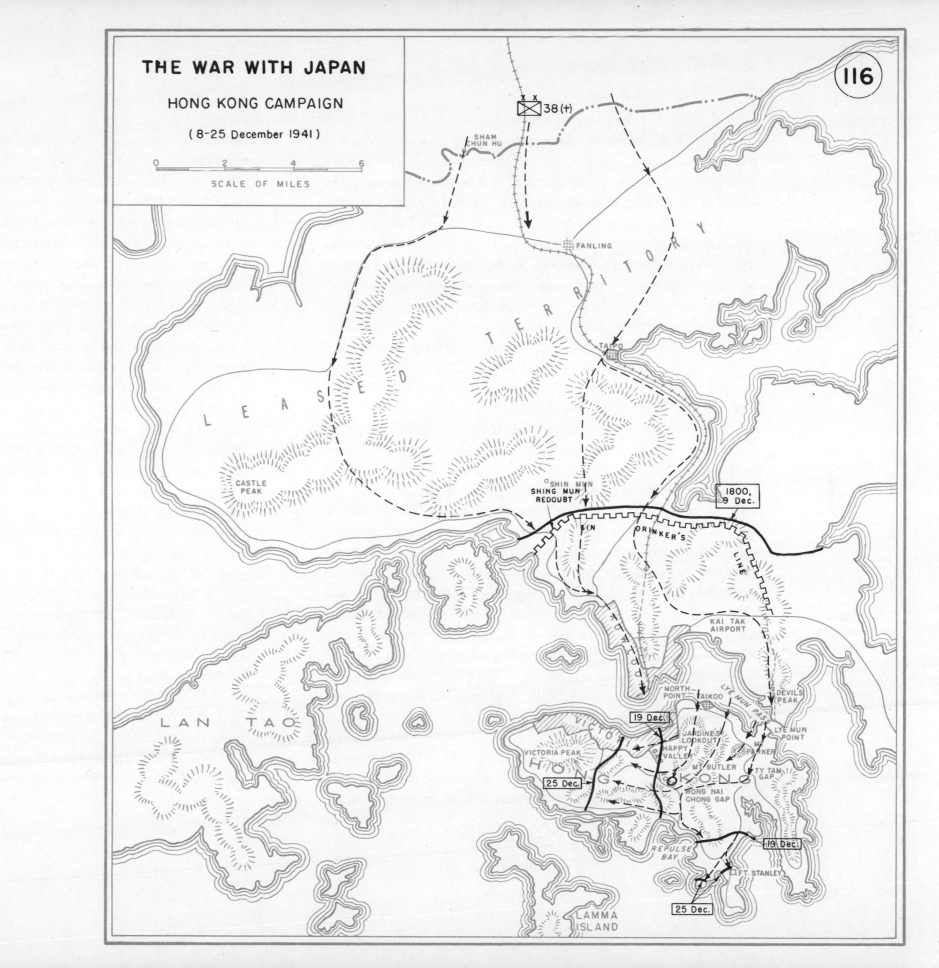

THE WAR WITH JAPAN

HONG KONG CAMPAIGN

(8-25 December 1941)

SCALE OF MILES

0   2   4   6

38 (†)

SHAM CHUN HU

FANLING

L E A S E D   T E R R I T O R Y

TAIPO

CASTLE PEAK

SHIN MUN
SHING MUN REDOUBT

1800, 9 Dec.

GIN   DRINKER'S   LINE

KAI TAK AIRPORT

NORTH POINT   TAIKOO   DEVILS PEAK

LAN TAO

19 Dec.

VICTORIA PEAK

JARDINE'S LOOKOUT   LYE MUN POINT

HAPPY VALLEY   MT. PARKER

25 Dec.

MT. BUTLER   TY TAM GAP

H O N G   K O N G

WONG NAI CHONG GAP

19 Dec.

REPULSE BAY

FT. STANLEY

25 Dec.

LAMMA ISLAND

One of Japan's earliest targets for conquest in 1941 was Malaya, the rich British possession lying between the Strait of Malacca and the South China Sea (*right sketch*). It is bordered on the north by Thailand, and in 1941 extended southward to include the island of Singapore. A mountain range, crossed by very few east-west roads, runs down the center of the peninsula and occasionally reaches 7,000 feet in height. The many streams, choked by tropical vegetation and belabored by the heavy rainfall, overflow and create sizable jungle swamps. The equatorial climate is extremely humid; until troops are acclimatized—requiring at least two months—physical exertion in the steaming jungle will quickly sap their energy. In 1941, more than half of Malaya was covered by dense, luxuriant jungle, broken by occasional areas under cultivation. Extensive tin deposits, rubber plantations, and rice paddies abound along the western plain.

At the southern extremity of the peninsula lies the island of Singapore, site of a naval base large enough to service a sizable fleet and so strongly fortified as to be considered impregnable by many Britishers. Upon the completion of this base in the 1920's, the mission of the army garrison became that of defending the base until a fleet arrived from European waters; this fleet was expected to isolate any hostile forces invading Malaya. As air power developed, however, the mission was broadened in 1933 to include the protection of air bases. By 1940, the British had concluded that air power was to be the primary weapon of defense, but—under tremendous pressure in Europe and North Africa—they were never able to station sufficient modern aircraft in Malaya to implement this policy. Consequently, the army, dispersed by its mission to defend the scattered air bases, bore the brunt of defense against the Japanese attack.

The ground forces commander (Lt. Gen. A. E. Percival) assigned the defense of air bases in the north to the Indian 9th and 11th Divisions (forming the III Corps), while the Australian 8th Division defended Johore. Fortress troops garrisoned Singapore, and the Reserve Brigade (*not shown*) was near Port Swettenham (*lower center*). Percival did not overlook the possibility of a Japanese attack on Singapore from the north, but he expected the jungle to seriously impede such a move. To defend Malaya, he had about 80,000 troops (seventeen infantry battalions and two tank regiments short of his estimated requirements). The air force had only 158 first-line aircraft of the 336 considered a minimum requirement. Ground troops were short of artillery and tank support, but their greatest deficiency was lack of realistic training in jungle warfare. On 2 December, the battleship *Prince of Wales* and the battle cruiser *Repulse* arrived in Singapore to join the Far Eastern Fleet; this intended show of force no more impressed Japan than had the earlier reinforcement of Hong Kong.

Japan's occupation of Indochina in 1941 was an important strategic step toward the conquest of Southeast Asia. It provided her with air and naval bases near Malaya which—coupled with Thailand's complacent attitude—thoroughly compromised the British plans for the defense of Malaya. The Japanese Twenty-Fifth Army (Lt. Gen. Tomoyuki Yamashita) was selected to seize Malaya. It consisted of four divisions, two of which had seen combat in China and had recently received thorough training in jungle warfare. This army was well supported by the Japanese Second Fleet and the Third Air Army. Yamashita's plan envisioned initial air strikes, followed by landings at Singora and Patani in Thailand and at Kota Bharu in Malaya (*all top*). These forces, seizing air bases for early Japanese use, would then drive down the east and west coasts toward Singapore. Later, they would be joined by a third force which initially would move through Bangkok (*left sketch, top;* this sketch is an extension northward of the right sketch) to overawe the Siamese, and then down the peninsula into Malaya.

(It should be noted that a Japanese [or Chinese] "army" corresponded roughly to a corps of the Western powers.)

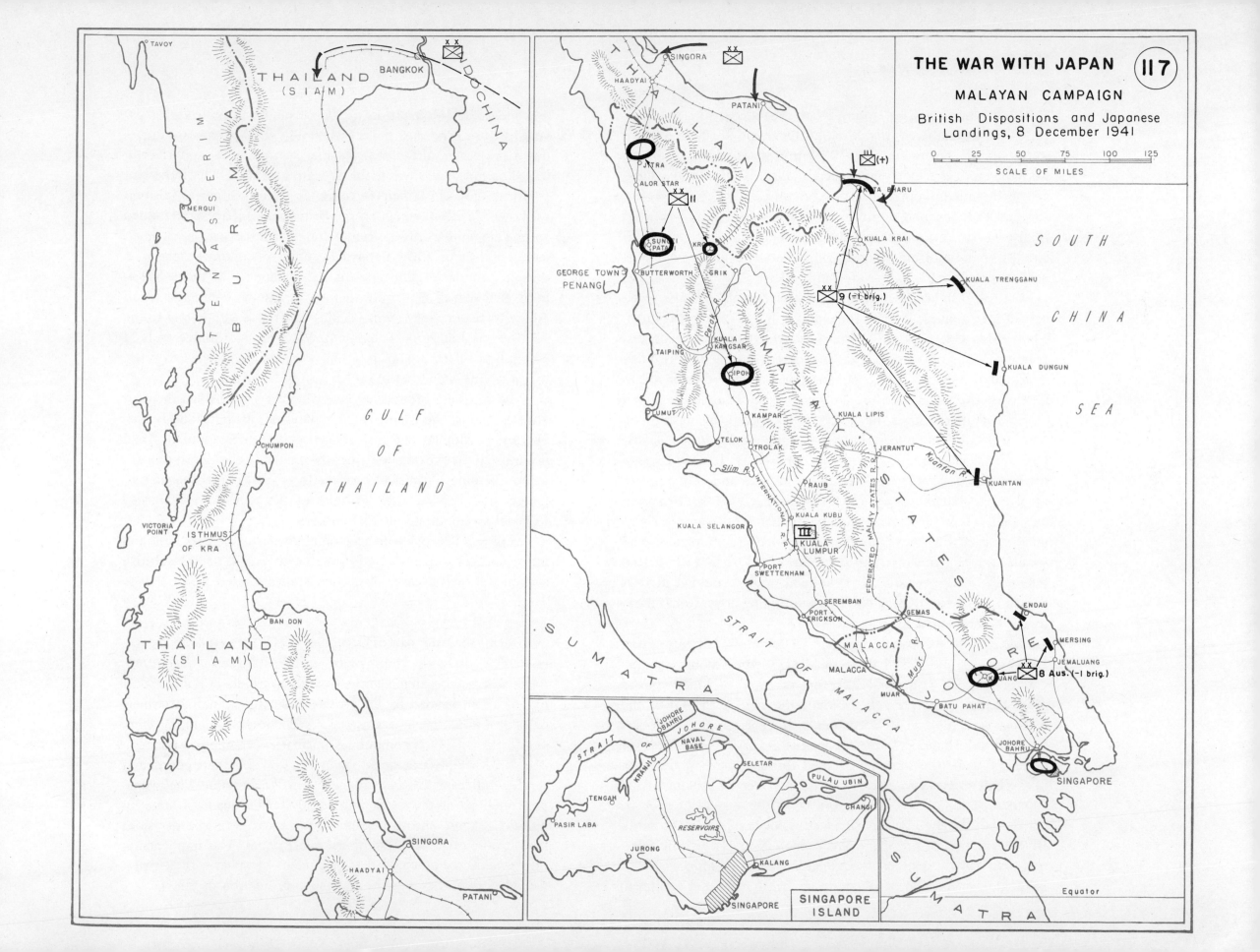

THE WAR WITH JAPAN (117)

MALAYAN CAMPAIGN

British Dispositions and Japanese
Landings, 8 December 1941

SCALE OF MILES
0   25   50   75   100   125

SINGAPORE ISLAND

The Japanese attack on Malaya came with startling swiftness early on 8 December. Airfields in Singapore and northern Malaya were bombed, beginning at 0430. Within three days, the British were forced to evacuate the northern fields. Meanwhile, the Japanese had landed unopposed at Singora and Patani (*right sketch, top*) in Thailand and established air bases. A landing at Kota Bharu had to overcome considerable opposition. Supported by aircraft operating from Singora and Patani, two ground columns quickly struck out for the Malayan border.

On 6 December, a British reconnaissance plane had sighted part of the Japanese landing force at sea, but it then lost contact. The convoy's destination was not discovered until it began disgorging troops at Singora two days later. During this two-day interlude, the British high command pondered whether or not to adopt MATADOR (a plan for movement into Thailand if Japan violated that country's neutrality)—hampered by restraining notes from London, uncertainty concerning the Japanese convoy, and the delicate political situation concerning Thailand. As a result, MATADOR was never attempted; instead, an alternate plan, involving a short advance across the frontier (*top left*) to commanding defensive terrain, was undertaken. The Siamese vigorously resisted this move, until reinforced by the Japanese who soon drove the British back to Jitra. The 11th Division was forced out of the Jitra position on 10 December; nor could it hold at Sungei Patani, for the Japanese column coming down from Patani to Kroh threatened its rear.

Meanwhile, a Japanese regiment landed at the Isthmus of Kra (*left sketch*) and seized the airfield at Victoria Point, thereby cutting the British aerial reinforcement route to Malaya. And off Kuantan (*right sketch, center*), the *Prince of Wales* and *Repulse* were sunk on 10 December by Japanese torpedo bombers based in Indochina. Despite their lack of air cover—either carrier or land-based—the ships had sallied forth in the true tradition of the British Navy to assist the ground forces by striking at the Japanese landing force at Singora.

By the 23d, the 11th Division was in position behind the Perak River, and most of the 9th was at Kuala Lipis. Already the Japanese had clearly demonstrated their superior training and skill in jungle warfare. Their soldiers were lightly clad and equipped,

and moved phantomlike in the dense jungle to infiltrate or envelop British positions; tanks were boldly used in surprise moves down the roads; aircraft played the role of direct-support artillery; and liberal use was made of night attacks. Under persistent pressure, the British were forced back from position to position as shown. In efforts to cut off the British, the Japanese attempted several amphibious envelopments along the west coast, using small, captured fishing craft. Percival wanted to continue fighting a delaying action to gain time for reinforcements to reach Singapore, but Wavell (en route to Java to assume command of all Allied forces in the western Pacific) ordered a withdrawal to the province of Johore on 8 January. When he was unable to hold Yamashita at the Johore position, Percival was forced to retire to Singapore Island (*inset sketch*) on 31 January.

The Japanese brought up heavy artillery, intensified their air attacks against the island, and prepared an assault. The British had ample supplies and a sizable defending force, but they had not utilized the previous two months diligently enough to prepare against landings. Yamashita crossed three divisions as shown, outflanked the British, and—in spite of fierce resistance—forced Percival to capitulate on 15 February.

Malaya's loss opened the Indian Ocean to the Japanese and imperiled Sumatra, Java, and Borneo (*see map 126*). The British sustained 138,708 casualties; Yamashita's totaled 9,824.

During the latter part of December, 1941, the first Allied heads-of-state conference took place in Washington (ARCADIA). From this meeting stemmed the Combined Chiefs of Staff (CCS) organization, headed by the British and American Joint Chiefs of Staff (JCS). Members of the respective JCS planning committees met as CCS committees on matters of mutual concern. The British Chiefs actually sat in London, but had permanent representatives at CCS Headquarters in Washington. The principal functions of the CCS were to advise the heads of state on military matters and to implement the broad strategic decisions made at the periodic international conferences. This implementation generally concerned the assignment of spheres of activity, the allocation of resources, and the coordination of effort.

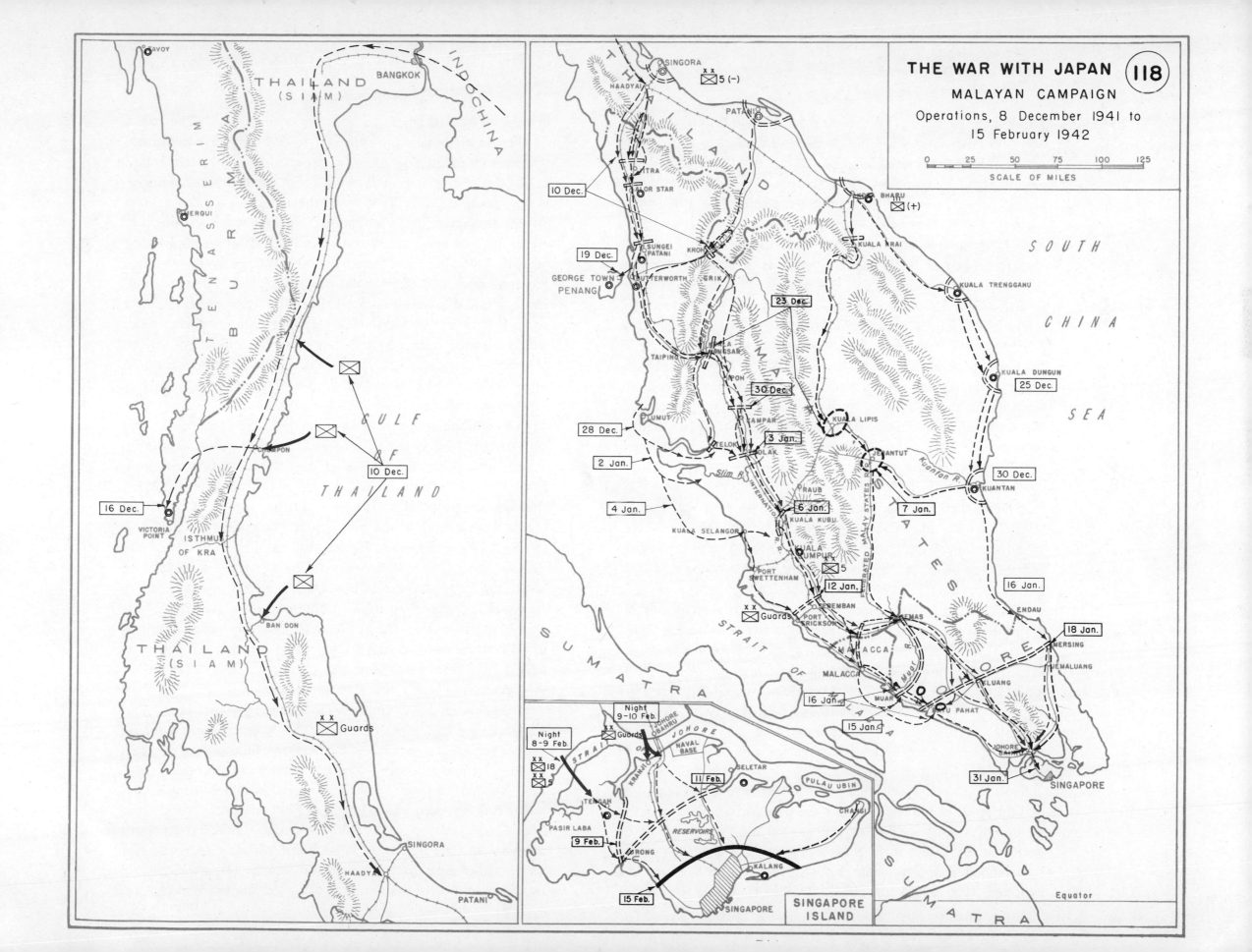

THE WAR WITH JAPAN **118**

MALAYAN CAMPAIGN

Operations, 8 December 1941 to
15 February 1942

SCALE OF MILES
0   25   50   75   100   125

The Philippine Archipelago, comprising some 7,000 islands, lies only 500 miles from the China coast and dominates the eastern approaches to the South China Sea (*see map 114*). Luzon is the largest island and, in 1941, was the most important militarily. Under foreign influence since the third century, the Philippines harbored a conglomeration of oriental and occidental institutions when the United States seized them from Spain in 1898 (*see text, map 158, Volume I*). In the ensuing years, a benevolent policy —including a promise of full independence in 1946—won the loyalty of the Filipinos to an unusual degree.

In 1935, General Douglas MacArthur was designated military advisor to the Philippine Commonwealth. Ably assisted by a small group of military men—including Major Dwight D. Eisenhower—MacArthur prepared plans for a Philippine defense establishment, designed for maturity in 1946. But implementation was slow and costly, and by 1941 the Philippine Army was neither prepared nor equipped to repel the Japanese onslaught. Nor were the American armed forces' contingents in the Philippines sufficient for the task.

Under the "Germany-first" strategy conceived in January, 1941, Japan would be contained with a minimum defensive effort. In effect, the over-all war plan (RAINBOW-5) accepted likely defeat in the far-away Philippines and held out no hope for major reinforcements.

When relations with Japan worsened, American and Filipino ground and air forces were consolidated into the United States Army Forces Far East (USAFFE) under MacArthur (recalled to active duty on 26 July). As shown (*this map, lower left*), USAFFE contained only a few American troops—primarily the Philippine Division (USAFFE's only adequately trained and equipped division) and artillery, tank, and service units. Now, primarily because of MacArthur's stature and overly optimistic claims for the offensive capabilities of the new B-17 bomber, the defensive policy suddenly changed. MacArthur injected optimism and the spirit of the offensive into the plan for the defense of the Philippines (ORANGE-3): defeat was no longer conceded, the enemy would be met at the beaches, the entire archipelago would be defended. Reinforcements began moving to Luzon, and it was expected that by April, 1942, USAFFE would be strong

enough to hold the islands. But the Japanese had other ideas.

The Fourteenth Army planned to use only two reinforced divisions to conquer Luzon, and expected to complete the task in fifty days; thereafter, most of the troops would be used in operations elsewhere. Concurrent with the initial air strikes against American aircraft and installations, landings would be made at Aparri, Vigan (*both top*), and Legaspi (*bottom right*) to seize airfields. Operating from these fields, army planes would complete the destruction of American air and naval forces. Then the main landing would be made at Lingayen Gulf (*left center*), and a secondary attack at Lamon Bay (*lower center*); these forces would advance to seize Manila, and thereafter the rest of Luzon. (Coincident with the early landings, a reinforced battalion would seize Davao in Mindanao [*see map 114*] as a springboard for future operations in Borneo.)

The Philippine garrison went on full war alert on 27 November. By 10 December, its forces were disposed as shown. Shortly after noon on 8 December, Japanese navy bombers from Formosa struck MacArthur's air force a devastating blow. In spite of being alerted by the Pearl Harbor attack, most of the planes were caught on the runways. By the end of the day, half of the B-17's and modern fighters had been destroyed, and the striking force of the small American Asiatic Fleet was steaming southward from Luzon and Cebu. During the next week, Japanese air power hammered at Luzon air bases and the Cavite naval base near Manila. On the 11th, the remaining bombers were withdrawn to Mindanao and, six days later, to Australia—without ever having been able to mount one effective strike. By 15 December, the fighters had been reduced to a handful.

Meanwhile, the preliminary Japanese landings on 10 and 12 December had been successful. The Japanese moved inland against very light resistance as MacArthur, still awaiting the main landing, refused to commit forces in strength to stop these small detachments. However, the 11th Division, Philippine Army (PA), sector was extended along Lingayen Gulf to San Fernando, the 26th Cavalry Regiment (Philippine Scouts) was moved north to that area, one regiment of the 71st Division (PA) was sent northward to intercept the Kanno and Tanaka Detachments, and two companies were committed to delay the Kimura Detachment.

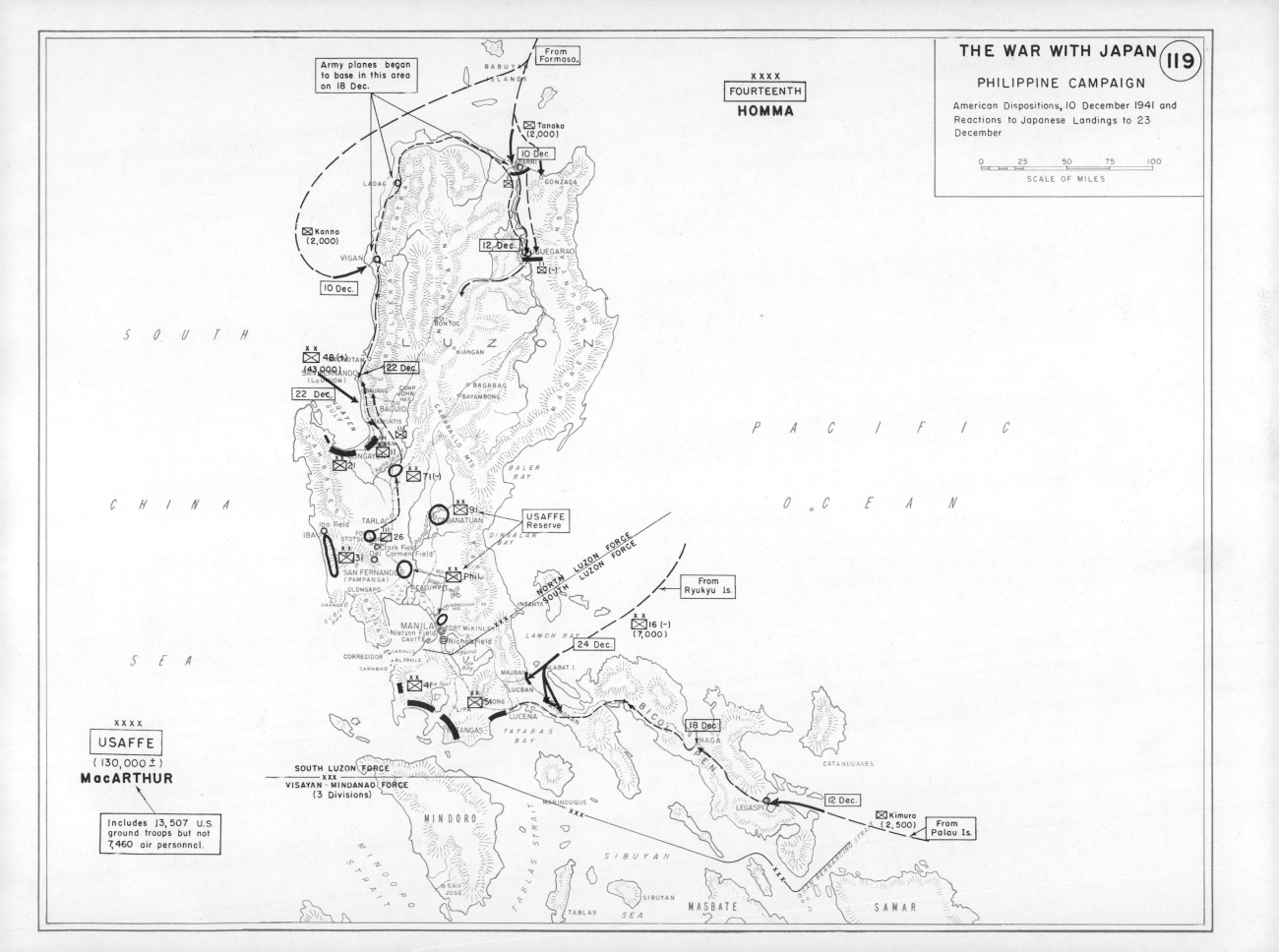

XXXX
FOURTEENTH
HOMMA

Army planes began
to base in this area
on 18 Dec.

From Formosa.

BABUYAN ISLANDS

Tanaka
(2,000)

10 Dec.

GONZAGA

LAOAG

Kanno
(2,000)

VIGAN

10 Dec.

12 Dec.
TUGUEGARAO

0   25   50   75   100
SCALE OF MILES

S O U T H

C H I N A

S E A

BONTOC

L U Z O N

KIANGAN

48 (NOTAN)
(43,000)
SAN FERNANDO
(La UNION)

22 Dec.

BAGABAG
BAYAMBONG

CAMP
JOHN
HAY

BAUANG

BAGUIO

22 Dec.

ARORTIS

11

LINGAYEN

21

71 (-)

91
CABANATUAN

USAFFE
Reserve

TARLAC

DINGALAN
BAY

BALER
BAY

P A C I F I C

O C E A N

Iba Field

FORT
STOTSENBERG

26

Clark Field
Del Carmen Field

3

SAN FERNANDO
(PAMPANGA)

CALUMPIT

Phil

OLONGAPO

NORTH LUZON FORCE
SOUTH LUZON FORCE

INFANTA

From
Ryukyu Is.

MANILA
Nielson Field
CAVITE
Nichols Field

FORT McKINLEY

LAMON BAY

16 (-)
(7,000)

24 Dec.

CORREGIDOR
CARABAO

EL FRAILE

Laguna

MAUBAN
ALABAT I.

4

e Toal

51
LONG

LUCBAN

LUCENA

18 Dec.

BATANGAS

LIPA

TAYABAS
BAY

BICOL PEN.

NAGA

CATANDUANES

USAFFE
(130,000 ±)
MacARTHUR

Includes 13,507 U.S.
ground troops but not
7,460 air personnel.

SOUTH LUZON FORCE
XXX
VISAYAN - MINDANAO FORCE
(3 Divisions)

MARINDUQUE

LEGASPI

12 Dec.

Kimura
(2,500)

From
Palau Is.

MINDORO

SAN
JOSE

MINDORO
STRAIT

TABLAS
STRAIT

SIBUYAN
SEA

TABLAS

MASBATE

SAMAR

SAN BERNARDINO STRAIT

Shortly after midnight, 22 December, eighty-five heavily escorted Japanese troop transports dropped anchor in Lingayen Gulf. Seas were heavy and there was a slight drizzle, but, by 0800, assault elements were ashore at the four points shown. This area, recently occupied by elements of the 11th Division (PA), was not held in strength. Only at Bauang did the Japanese meet any resistance, for though the landing did not surprise USAFFE—the convoy had been detected as early as 18 December, and Maj. Gen. Jonathan Wainwright had been alerted—it had been expected at the head of the gulf.

The regiment of the 71st Division (PA), moving north to intercept the Tanaka-Kanno Detachments, was struck in flank by the Japanese 9th Regiment, and (along with 11th Division [PA] elements) part of it was forced into the mountains toward Baguio. (Wainwright ordered this composite force to rejoin the North Luzon Force [NLF] at Rosario, but it delayed overnight at Baguio and was forced to withdraw eastward when the Japanese cut Route 11 near Rosario.) By 1700, the 9th Regiment had secured Bauang and started a column up the twisting road to Baguio.

Farther south, the Japanese 48th Division assault elements aggressively expanded the beachhead. One regimental column struck out for Rosario, while the other two columns moved along Route 3 toward Damortis. (Meanwhile, rough weather had forced the transports farther south into the gulf, thus temporarily exposing them to fire from emplaced 155-mm. guns at San Fabian and Dagupan. American submarines and three B-17's also attacked Japanese shipping, but with disappointing results.) When the 11th Division (PA) troops opposing the landing of the Japanese 48th Division fled in rout southward beyond Damortis, Wainwright ordered the 26th Cavalry Regiment (horse-mounted, with some light scout cars) forward from Rosario and instructed it to hold Damortis. At 1300, this regiment came under heavy attack; three hours later, it was forced to withdraw toward Rosario. Fighting a skillful delaying action, the regiment—by now reinforced with a company of USAFFE's precious tanks—held off the superior Japanese force until the enemy column coming from Agoo made its position untenable. The American tankers, operating much too independently, had not been of much assistance; nor had the 71st Division (PA) (sent forward by

Wainwright) arrived in time to aid the gallant cavalrymen.

Homma's troops continued their relentless drive south on the 23d. That afternoon, the 71st Division (PA) fled when attacked near Sison, and that night the 91st Division (PA) regimental combat team that had reached Pozorrubio also broke under attack. Earlier that day, the hard-hit 26th Cavalry had gone into reserve at Binalonan, where it had established an outpost line. Here, on 24 December, while the demoralized 71st Division (PA) was withdrawn for reorganization and the 91st Division (PA) moved into the D-2 line, the heroic cavalrymen held off the Japanese; late that afternoon, they withdrew to the east to Tayug.

Meanwhile, on the afternoon of the 23d, Wainwright had asked permission to withdraw to the Agno River; from here—if given the Philippine Division—he wanted to launch a counterattack. But the demonstrated inability of the green Philippine Army divisions to hold the Japanese, and the sighting of an enemy convoy moving toward Lamon Bay, caused MacArthur to adhere to an older plan for the last-ditch defense of Luzon: withdrawal to Bataan (*see map 119, lower left*). This plan hinged upon the NLF delaying at the previously selected positions marked D-1 to D-5 (*this map*), while the South Luzon Force withdrew into Bataan. The first four lines were to be held lightly, and only to force the Japanese to deploy for attack; the D-5 line was to be organized in strength.

On the 24th, Wainwright's troops were on the D-1 line. That night, he ordered a withdrawal to the D-2 line. By Christmas night, the NLF was along that line, but on the right—where the 26th Cavalry had fought all day—it had been touch and go holding the Japanese. The next night, the troops withdrew to the D-3 line, but the 11th Division (PA) and USAFFE's two tank battalions took heavy losses in disengaging near Rosales. While Homma paused to regroup, Wainwright withdrew to the D-4 line and—contrary to his original plan—decided to hold there as long as possible. The Japanese moved most of their strength toward Cabanatuan on the 28th; only the 9th Regiment moved on Tarlac, on the direct road to Bataan. Outflanked by a Japanese tank column, the 91st Division (PA) withdrew from Cabanatuan on the night of 29 December, just as Japanese infantry began to cross the Pampanga River.

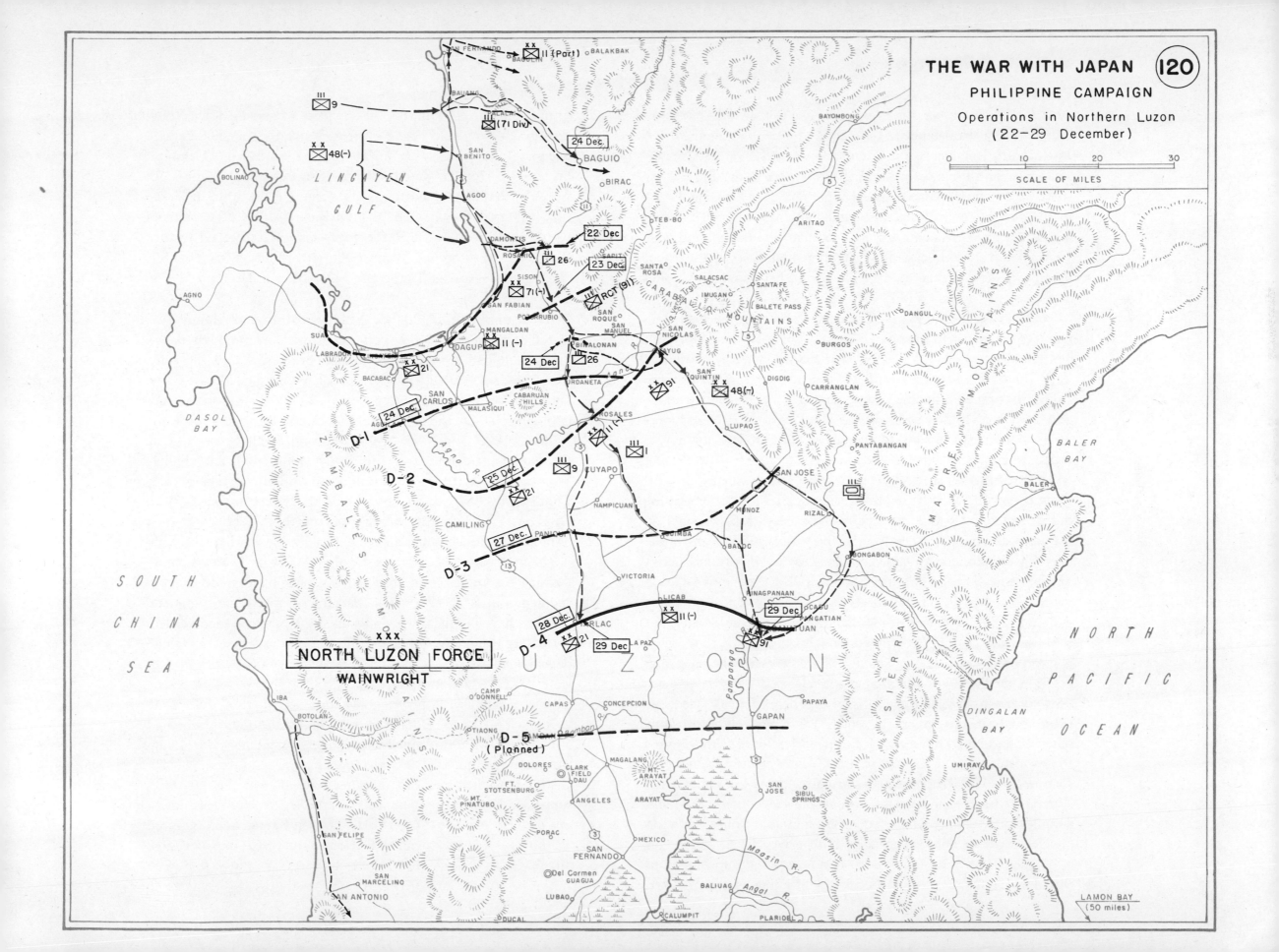

THE WAR WITH JAPAN (120)
PHILIPPINE CAMPAIGN
Operations in Northern Luzon
(22–29 December)

SCALE OF MILES
0   10   20   30

NORTH LUZON FORCE
WAINWRIGHT

At 0200, 24 December, the Japanese began to land at Lamon Bay (*lower right*). Resistance to the landing by two battalions of the 1st Infantry Regiment (1st Regular Division [PA]) at Mauban was fierce, and Japanese gains for the day were slight. But farther south, the main Japanese force caught the 51st Division (PA) in the process of shifting units and had little difficulty taking Atimonan and advancing toward Lucena. One of its units (*not shown*) moved southeast and cut off a battalion on the Bicol Peninsula—located there to oppose the earlier Japanese landing at Legaspi (*see map 119*).

On the 24th, Maj. Gen. George M. Parker relinquished command of the Southern Luzon Force (SLF) to Maj. Gen. Albert M. Jones and was given the mission of preparing defensive positions on Bataan (*this map; center, left*), utilizing forces already there (elements of the Philippine Division and a few supporting troops) and other units as they arrived. The 31st Division (PA) and most of the 41st began moving to Bataan at once. Jones, now under orders to block the Japanese advance but to withdraw to Bataan when forced to do so, had no previously selected delaying positions, though he was favored by excellent defensive terrain. Utilizing accepted retrograde techniques—no easy task, considering his green and poorly armed troops—he withdrew as the Japanese aggressively pushed two major columns eastward beyond Lucena and Lucban. The 1st Infantry squandered a good tank platoon west of Lucban in an ill-advised counterattack and had to be stiffened with a 300-man force of retired Philippine Scouts, but it slowed the northern enemy column. In the south, Jones leapfrogged battalions back to Taiong, where he established a strong position on the 28th. But that night, alarmed by the Japanese advance against Wainwright, USAFFE ordered Jones to clear the Calumpit bridges (*center*) by 0600, 1 January. (The previous date set had been 8 January.) Reluctantly, Jones withdrew his forces to the edge of Laguna de Bay (*lower center; dashed blue line, dated 29 December*) and started elements toward Bataan. Then USAFFE equivocated—probably because there were still supplies in Manila to be evacuated—and told Jones early on 30 December to hold his position until driven back.

A glance at the map (*center*) indicates the importance of Plaridel, Calumpit, and San Fernando. If either of the first two were to fall into the hands of the Japanese advancing down Route 5, Jones' force would be cut off from Bataan (strangely enough, Japanese air power made no attempt to destroy the Calumpit bridges); if Homma were to capture San Fernando, Wainwright would have difficulty moving into Bataan. On the 30th, the Japanese captured Gapan, the 91st Division disintegrated, and an unexpected thrust to La Paz (*upper center*) threatened to turn the D-4 line, forcing Wainwright to withdraw to the line Bamban–Mt. Arayat. That night, MacArthur ordered the SLF to start north at once.

The night of the 30th, the SLF moved around Manila (declared an open city on the 26th) and toward Plaridel. By dawn, much of it had crossed the Calumpit bridges. About the same time, the demoralized 91st Division (PA) reached Baliuag, two battalions of the 51st Division (PA) took up a position at Plaridel, and 71st Division (PA) elements arrived to reinforce the 91st. At 1000, Jones was given command of all troops east of the Pampanga River, but, apparently unaware of this change, Wainwright told the troops at Baliuag to withdraw in time to clear Calumpit by 0600, 1 January. At 1200, 31 December, the 91st Division (PA) began its withdrawal; shortly thereafter, the 71st did likewise. Jones, when apprised, futilely tried to halt the withdrawal. Desperate because the Japanese—now in Baliuag—were massing for an attack, he ordered two tank platoons to make a spoiling attack at 1700. The tankers surprised the Japanese, wreaked havoc in the town, and gained the precious time needed. By 0500, 1 January, all USAFFE troops—except a few small detachments—had crossed the Pampanga; at 0615, the bridges were destroyed.

On 1 January, Wainwright withdrew the 11th and 21st Divisions (PA) to the Borac-Guagua line, where these decimated units held off the two attacking Japanese regiments until 4 January, and then pulled back into Bataan. The reinforced 71st Division (PA) held one last delaying position, but the Japanese, supported by overwhelming air and artillery, cracked this line in one day. By 7 January, USAFFE—now on Bataan and organized as shown—was improving its defenses to resist the inevitable attack.

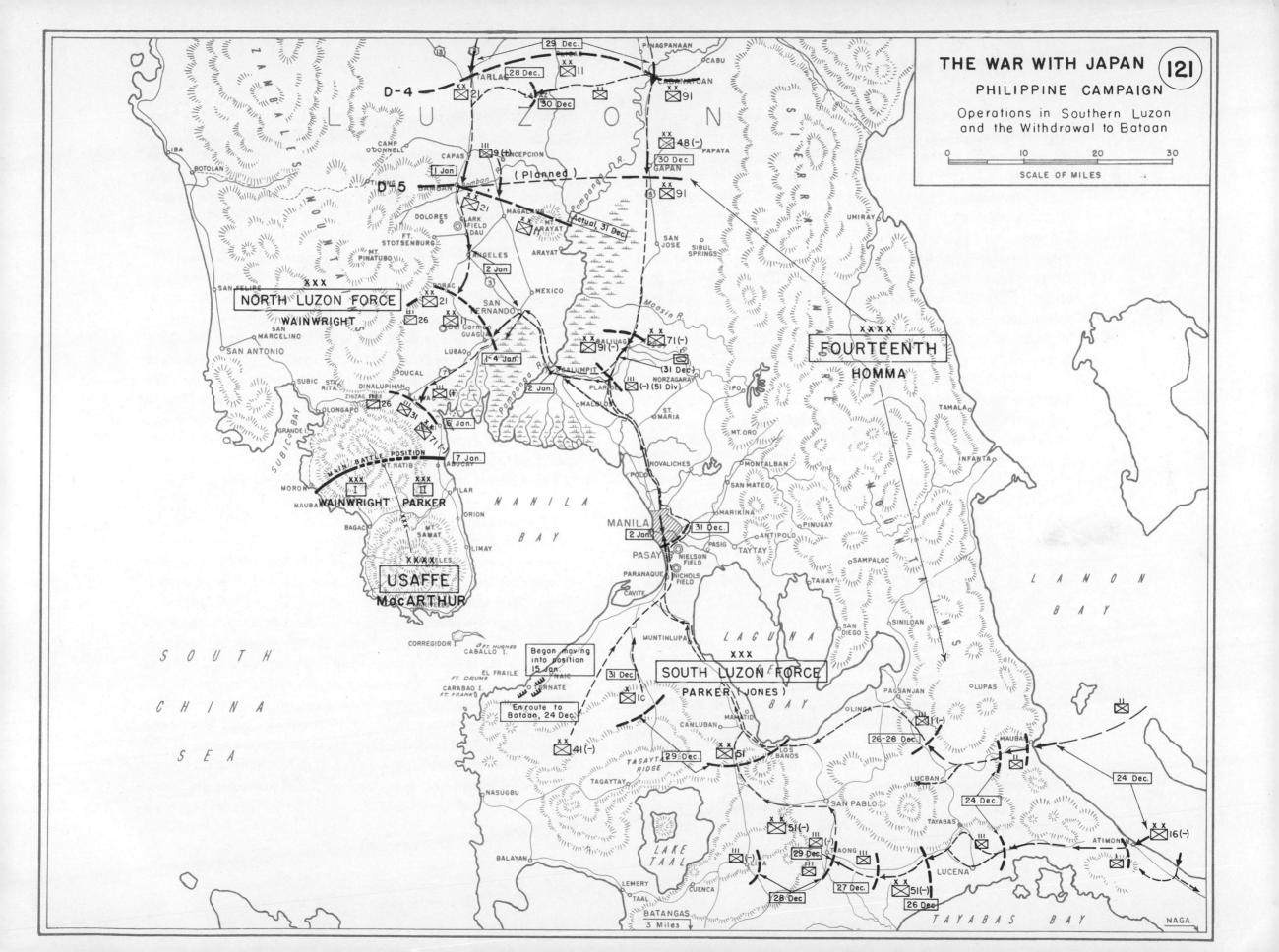

THE WAR WITH JAPAN 121

PHILIPPINE CAMPAIGN

Operations in Southern Luzon
and the Withdrawal to Bataan

0   10   20   30
SCALE OF MILES

The Bataan peninsula is mountainous and covered—particularly on its west—with dense jungle. The mountains run generally down the middle of the peninsula, the dominant heights being Mt. Natib (in the north) and the rugged Mariveles Mountains (in the south). Emanating from these towering terrain masses, many small streams have cut steep gullies as they wind their way to the coast. In the west, the mountains drop off abruptly at the coast, forming high cliffs which dominate the narrow coastal corridor; on the opposite coast, between Abucay and Orion, the terrain is flat and water-logged, but farther south it resumes the mountainous pattern. The only good beaches are along the Manila Bay shore. At the peninsula's tip, a cove provides a natural harbor for the small port of Mariveles. In 1941, though many small trails existed, there were only two roads generally suitable for vehicular use. These were: the perimeter road running down the east coast from Abucay to Mariveles (one lane, all weather) and thence north to Moron (dry weather); and the Pilar-Bagac road, the only lateral communication route for USAFFE forces.

The USAFFE defense plan provided for defense in depth, utilizing main and reserve battle positions. Provision was also made for defending the beaches. Though the prewar plans had selected the Orion-Bagac line as the main battle position, MacArthur had chosen the Mauban-Abucay line as the initial position in order to gain more time to prepare the rearward line, and to protect the best means of lateral communication—the Pilar-Bagac road.

Fortifications along Parker's front were much stronger than in Wainwright's sector because the relatively open terrain in the east had dictated first priority when preparations began in late December. Parker held the vital coastal sector with the fresh and well-trained 57th Regiment (Philippine Scouts) of the Philippine Division. Wainwright, likewise, concentrated on the coastal corridor in his sector, stationing most of the 1st Regular Division (PA) near Mauban. (Elements of the 26th Cavalry and 1st Infantry Regiments [not shown] occupied the likely enemy concentration area between Moron and Mauban.) His reserve was not as strong as it appears; the 71st and 91st Divisions (PA) had taken a severe beating in the withdrawal from Lingayen, and the 26th Cavalry was similarly greatly reduced in strength. Both corps enjoyed substantial artillery support. In addition to divisional artillery, Wainwright had about thirty-five corps artillery pieces (mostly 75-mm.) and Parker had about sixty (half of 155-mm. caliber). The greatest defect in the main battle position was the inability of the corps to establish firm contact in the fantastically rugged Mt. Natib area, which was held primarily with patrols.

Of critical influence in the defense of Bataan was the supply situation. It was unsatisfactory in the beginning and—growing steadily worse—probably had as much effect on the ultimate capitulation as any other single factor. Some supplies were stored on Bataan when war came, and every attempt was made to transfer more there beginning 23 December. But the number of troops—and civilians—eventually moved to the peninsula far exceeded the prewar planning figures. Further, the scarcity of ships (the prime means of movement) and vehicles, coupled with Japanese air superiority, severely handicapped movement.

Some efforts were made in December to provide relief for MacArthur's harried forces. When war came, a supply convoy was en route to Manila. After considerable debate in Washington, it was diverted to Australia, but General Marshall ordered that every effort be made to move its vitally needed artillery, airplanes, and ammunition northward. Naval planners, shocked by the Pearl Harbor disaster, conceded the loss of the Philippines and were unwilling to risk the small Asiatic Fleet in an attempt to escort ships through the tightening Japanese naval blockade. Attempts at supply by submarine were generally fruitless. A disappointed MacArthur, grasping better than anyone else how thinly spread the Japanese were, continued to urge attempts at reinforcement and even limited offensive strikes at the Japanese home islands. But the Pacific theater had second call on Allied resources. By 7 January, it was clear that USAFFE would have to fight with what it had.

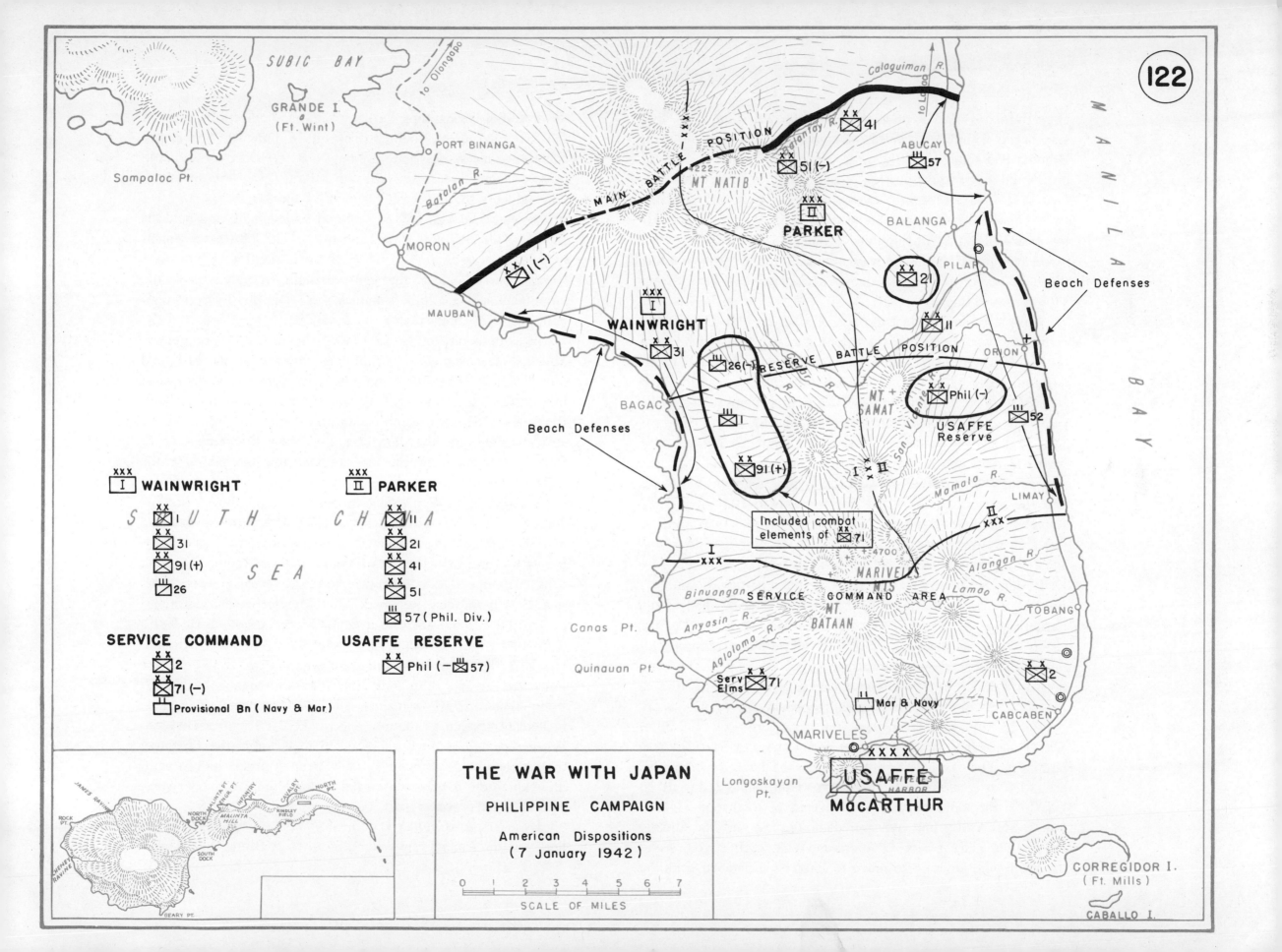

SUBIC BAY

GRANDE I.
(Ft. Wint)

Sampaloc Pt.

PORT BINANGA

to Olongapo

to Lubao

Calaguiman R.

⊠⊠ 41

MT NATIB

222

MAIN BATTLE POSITION

⊠⊠ 51 (–)

ABUCAY

⊠⊠ 57

MANILA

Batalan R.

MORON

XXX
Ⅱ
PARKER

BALANGA

PILAR

⊠⊠ 21

MAUBAN

XXX
Ⅰ
WAINWRIGHT

⊠⊠ 31

⊠⊠ 1 (–)

Beach Defenses

⊠⊠ 11

Beach Defenses

⊠⊠ 26 (–)   RESERVE BATTLE POSITION

ORION

⊠⊠ Phil (–)

BAGAC

San Vicente R.

MT
SAMAT

USAFFE
Reserve

⊠⊠ 1

⊠⊠ 52

BAY

⊠⊠ 91 (+)

Ⅰ × × Ⅱ
XXX

Included combat
elements of   ⊠⊠ 71

+ 4700

Mamala R.

LIMAY

Ⅱ
XXX

Binuangan R.

SERVICE   COMMAND   AREA

Ⅰ
XXX

MARIVELES
MTS

Lamao R.

Alangan R.

Anyasin R.

MT.
BATAAN

Canas Pt.

TOBANG

Agloloma R.

Quinauan Pt.

Serv
Elms   ⊠⊠ 71

⊠⊠ 2

Ⅰ Ⅰ
Mar & Navy

CABCABEN

MARIVELES

Longoskayan
Pt.

XXXX
USAFFE
MacARTHUR

122

CORREGIDOR I.
(Ft. Mills)

CABALLO I.

XXX
Ⅰ WAINWRIGHT   XXX
Ⅱ PARKER

⊠⊠ 1   S O U T H   C H I N A   ⊠⊠ 11

⊠⊠ 31   ⊠⊠ 21

⊠⊠ 91 (+)   S E A   ⊠⊠ 41

⊠⊠ 26   ⊠⊠ 51

                                         ⊠⊠ 57 (Phil. Div.)

SERVICE COMMAND   USAFFE RESERVE

⊠⊠ 2   ⊠⊠ Phil (– ⊠⊠ 57)

⊠⊠ 71 (–)

□ Provisional Bn (Navy & Mar)

THE WAR WITH JAPAN

PHILIPPINE CAMPAIGN

American Dispositions
(7 January 1942)

0 1 2 3 4 5 6 7
SCALE OF MILES

ROCK PT.

JAMES RAVINE

NORTH DOCK

MALINTA PT.

TOPSIDE PT.

CAVALRY PT.

NORTH PT.

MALINTA HILL

KINDLEY FIELD

SOUTH DOCK

CHENEY RAVINE

BEARY PT.

On 5 January—earlier than originally planned—the 48th Division began withdrawing from the Philippines for duty in Java. Homma had some misgivings, but, anticipating slight resistance on Bataan, he gave the mission of reducing that peninsula to Lt. Gen. Akira Nara's recently arrived and poorly trained 65th Brigade (about 6,500 men). Supporting artillery, tanks, and air units, as well as the 9th Infantry Regiment (16th Division), were made available to Nara. He was ordered to make his main effort down the east coast toward Balanga, and a secondary attack from Moron toward Bagac.

Nara advanced against the II Corps on the 9th. He initially employed two regiments—one along the east coast, while the other (the veteran 9th Infantry) moved inland against Parker's left flank, seeking to turn it and drive the defenders against the east coast. A third regiment (the 122d Infantry) moved across the peninsula to attack down the west coast, and the fourth regiment (*not shown*) was positioned in reserve behind the 9th Infantry. North of Abucay, the advance came under heavy artillery fire, whereupon Nara shifted most of the coastal regiment westward into the zone of the 41st Division (PA). On 10 January, the Japanese finally encountered the right of the II Corps' outpost line (*not shown*) and forced it back. For the next four days, savage fighting took place in the zones of the 57th Infantry and 41st Division as Japanese penetrations of the main battle position (*not shown*) were wiped out by counterattacks. During this period, Parker had been forced to commit his corps reserve, the 21st Division (PA). By the 13th, Nara had shifted all except one battalion of his coastal regiment farther inland, where it was exerting pressure against the 51st Division (PA). Meanwhile, his reserve regiment was moving into the sector opposite the 41st Division.

On 15 January, the Japanese attacked vigorously (*top center; red arrow, dated 12-22 January*) along the 41st-51st Division boundary. The 41st held firmly, but Jones' 51st was forced to give ground after committing all its reserve. That night, Parker asked USAFFE for additional troops to bolster the weakened 51st Division. MacArthur had anticipated the request and had already ordered the 31st Division (PA) (from Wainwright's sector) and the Philippine Division to move to Parker's assistance. Pending the arrival of these troops, Parker, over Jones' objections, ordered the 51st Division to counterattack on 16 January. The attack achieved some success initially, but Nara applied overwhelming pressure from three sides—the 9th Infantry was now in line—and suddenly the rightmost regiment of the 51st broke and fled to the rear. The 41st Division refused its left flank and held off the fierce assaults now turned against it. The leftmost regiment of the 51st was ordered to fall back to the southwest into the I Corps' zone. (Some of the men eventually struggled across the mountains to Bagac; others managed to rejoin the division's remnants reforming in the rear.)

In a desperate effort to restore the line, Parker counterattacked piecemeal with the Philippine Division on the 17th, and after five days of vicious fighting had almost recouped his losses; but, on the 22d, heavy artillery and air attacks drove the weary Philippine Division back to its starting point. The 9th Infantry, struggling through the difficult terrain, now threatened the II Corps' left flank, and Parker's position became untenable. On the night of the 22d, he was ordered to withdraw.

Meanwhile, in Wainwright's zone, the 122d Infantry had occupied Grande Island and then moved by water and overland on Moron. It entered this town on 17 January after two days of fighting with elements of the 26th Cavalry and 1st Regular Division (PA). Homma, disconcerted over Nara's slowness, now sent part of the 20th Infantry Regiment from Manila to this sector, attached the 122d Infantry to it, and assigned the command—directly under the Fourteenth Army—to Maj. Gen. Naoki Kimura. On the 19th, Kimura attacked as shown, and two days later had infiltrated the 3d Battalion, 20th Infantry Regiment, through Wainwright's lightly held inner flank to the coastal road. This movement severed the supply line of the 1st Regular Division. When repeated counterattacks failed to dislodge the Japanese, the 1st Regular Division, also under frontal attack, had to withdraw along the narrow coastal flats, abandoning its artillery and vehicles in the process.

By morning, 26 January, both corps were on the Bagac-Orion line, and the Japanese were closing up to continue the attack.

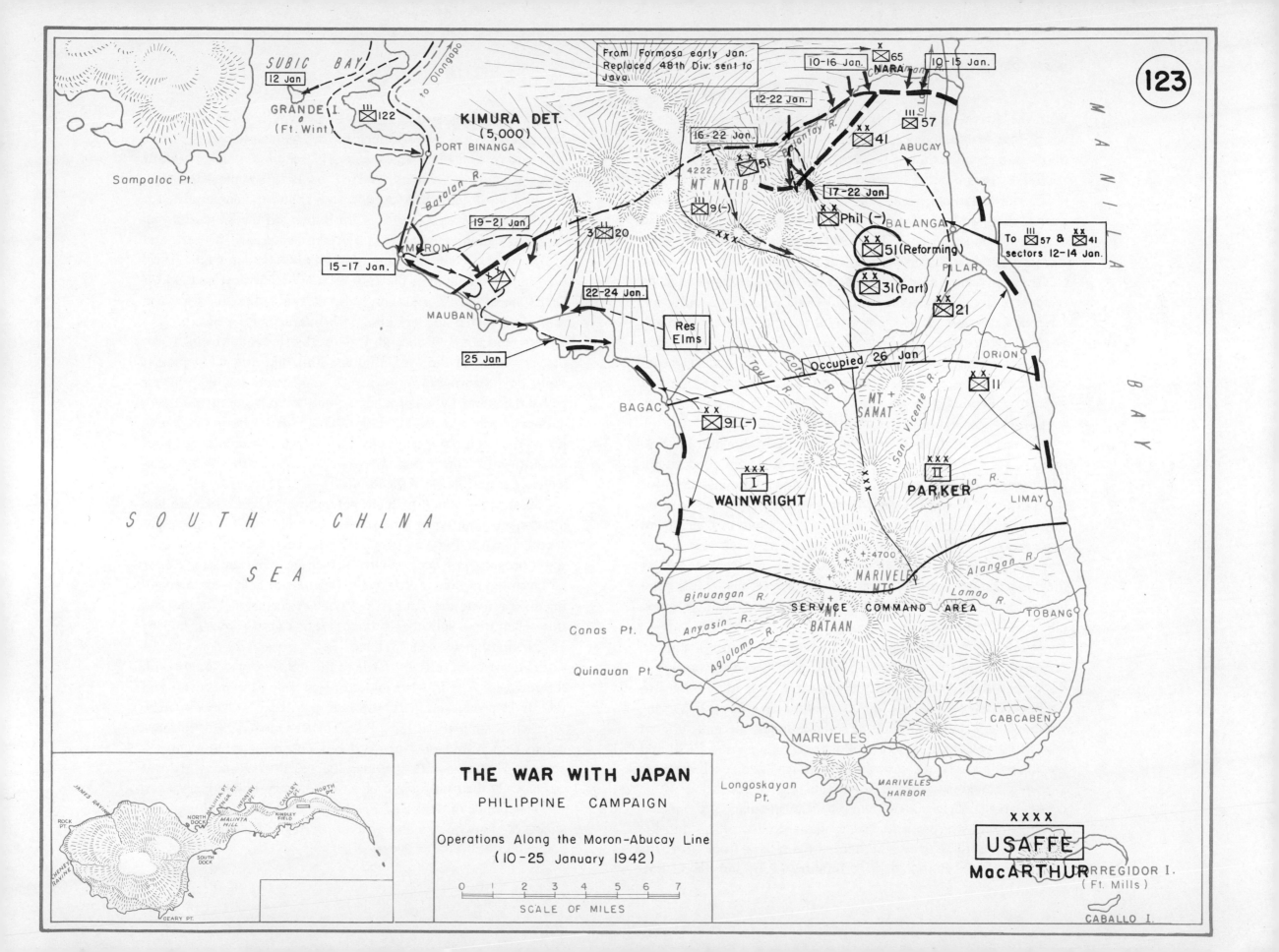

SUBIC BAY
12 Jan

GRANDE I.
(Ft. Wint)

☒ 122

Sampaloc Pt.

KIMURA DET.
(5,000)

PORT BINANGA

From Formosa early Jan.
Replaced 48th Div. sent to
Java.

10-16 Jan.   ☒ 65   10-15 Jan.

NARA

12-22 Jan.

16-22 Jan.

MT NATIB
4222

☒ 51

☒ 41

☒ 57

ABUCAY

17-22 Jan.

19-21 Jan

☒ 9(-)

☒ Phil (-)   BALANGA

3 ☒ 20

☒ 51 (Reforming)

To ☒ 57 & ☒ 41
sectors 12-14 Jan.

15-17 Jan.

☒ I

☒ 31 (Part)

PILAR

MAUBAN

22-24 Jan.

☒ 21

Res
Elms

25 Jan

Occupied 26 Jan

ORION

☒ 11

BAGAC

☒ 91 (-)

MT.
SAMAT

I
WAINWRIGHT

II
PARKER

LIMAY

S O U T H   C H I N A

S E A

+4700

MARIVELES
MTS

Alangan R.

Lamao R.

TOBANG

Binuangan R.

SERVICE   COMMAND   AREA

MT.
BATAAN

Canas Pt.

Anyasin R.

Quinauan Pt.

Agloloma R.

CABCABEN

MARIVELES

THE WAR WITH JAPAN

PHILIPPINE CAMPAIGN

Longoskayan
Pt.

MARIVELES
HARBOR

Operations Along the Moron-Abucay Line
(10-25 January 1942)

XXXX
USAFFE
MacARTHUR

ORREGIDOR I.
(Ft. Mills)

0 1 2 3 4 5 6 7
SCALE OF MILES

CABALLO I.

ROCK PT.

JAMES RAVINE

MALINTA HILL

INFANTRY PT.

CAVALRY PT.

NORTH PT.

NORTH DOCK

KINDLEY FIELD

SOUTH DOCK

GEARY PT.

MANILA BAY

123

With the arrival of USAFFE troops at the Bagac-Orion line—where MacArthur intended "to fight it out to complete destruction"—the organization of the defense underwent a change. The Service Command was relieved of responsibility for beach defense, each corps absorbing that function in its area. The organization along the main battle position was also modified. Because of the attrition in units and the dearth of qualified officers, defense sectors were established containing a conglomeration of units. Consequently, unit designations became less meaningful as some sectors controlled elements of two divisions. (To avoid confusion, the sectors are not shown; nor are all the units which were disposed along the position.) On 25 January, the Philippine Division was again withdrawn into USAFFE reserve; the division headquarters took over a sector command, and the three regiments were initially positioned as shown—the 31st near Limay, the 45th south of Bagac, and the 57th north of Mariveles.

The new battle position allowed the establishment of a continuous, shorter line across the peninsula. It lacked good lateral communications, but local trails were immediately improved for this purpose. The Mariveles Mountains dominated the position (which ran through dense jungle), and Mt. Samat provided good observation over the entire front. Neither Wainwright nor Parker was able to assemble more than a regiment as a corps reserve. As they desperately shuttled units to fill the gaps created by the withdrawal of the Philippine Division, the Japanese, sensing a quick kill, launched their attack.

Previously (on the night of 22 January), Kimura, hoping to secure his right flank after he took Bagac and turned eastward, had dispatched the 2d Battalion, 20th Infantry, in landing barges to Caibobo Point (*not shown, but five miles below Bagac*). Moving without adequate preparation or suitable maps, the unit suffered losses to a patrolling American PT boat, became dispersed, and landed erroneously at the two points shown. The beach defenses —then manned by Service Command troops, consisting of air corps, naval, marine, and Philippine Constabulary personnel—contained the two forces, but were unable to drive them into the sea. On the 27th, Wainwright secured the release from USAFFE reserve of the 2d Battalion, 57th Infantry (PS), and the 3d Battalion, 45th Infantry (PS). The Longoskayan Point force was quickly eliminated by the former, but at Quinauan Point the latter took heavy casualties and eventually required the support of tanks, Corregidor artillery, and PT boats to complete the task. Meanwhile, Homma had sent the 16th Division commander (Lt. Gen. Susumu Morioka) to western Bataan on the 25th with two additional infantry battalions. Morioka superseded Kimura and at once sent a company to reinforce the Quinauan Point force. Moving out the night of the 26th, it, too, became lost and landed near Canas Point. The air corps unit defending the area was soon reinforced by the 2d Battalion, 45th Infantry (PS), but the Japanese would not be dislodged. Prodded by Homma, Morioka sent the remainder of the 1st Battalion, 20th Infantry, to Quinauan Point on 1 February. Wainwright's troops were waiting and repelled the attempted night landing, but the Japanese turned north and came ashore at Canas Point. The 57th Infantry (PS) now joined the fight, but the tenacious enemy was not eliminated until the 13th, thus concluding the series of engagements known collectively as the "Battle of the Points."

Meanwhile, along the main battle position, the Japanese had attacked in both corps sectors. Nara, continuing to make night assaults, struck Parker's line on 27 January, but he made only slight progress in five days. On 2-3 February, Parker struck back and restored his line. To the west, Japanese attacks were unavailing except along the Toul River. Wainwright eventually blocked this penetration, split it into three pockets (*not shown*), and by 15 February had reduced them.

The last week of this "Battle of the Pockets" was fought with the Japanese withdrawing under orders from Homma, who had ruefully accepted the fact, on 8 February, that he was too weak to crack the USAFFE line. The Japanese moved back to more defensible terrain, and Homma asked Tokyo for reinforcements. Some of Homma's units had literally ceased to exist; by his own estimate, he had only three effective infantry battalions.

The morale of the USAFFE troops was high. But already the effects of short rations and general shortage of all supplies were being felt.

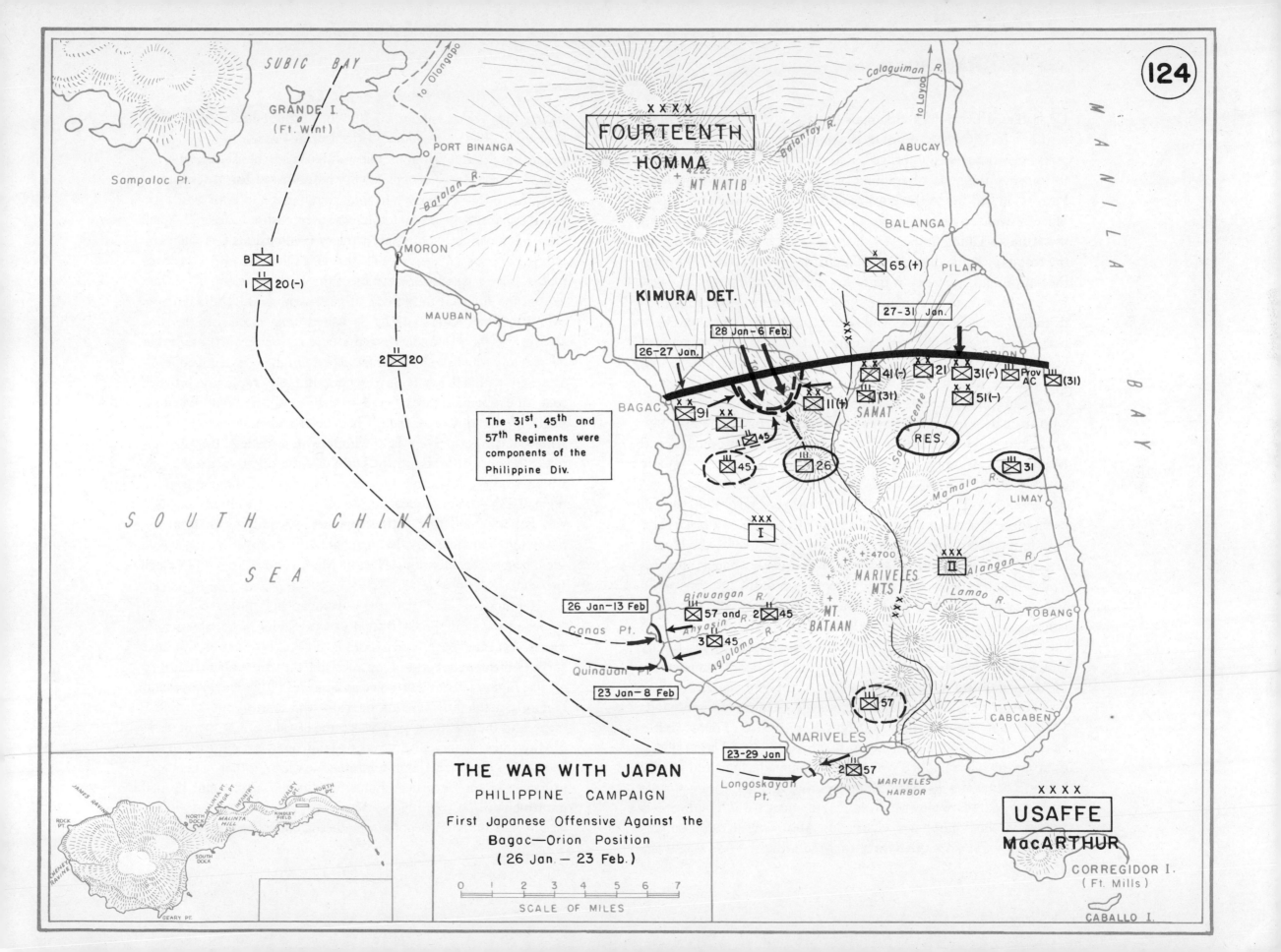

124

SUBIC BAY

GRANDE I.
(Ft. Wint)

Sampaloc Pt.

PORT BINANGA

to Olongapo

Calaguiman R.

to Layac

XXXX
FOURTEENTH
HOMMA
+ 4222
MT NATIB

ABUCAY

BALANGA

PILAR

MORON

B ☒ 1

1 ☒ 20(-)

MAUBAN

2 ☒ 20

KIMURA DET.

27-31 Jan.

X
☒ 65 (+)

28 Jan–6 Feb.

26-27 Jan.

ORION

BAGAC

The 31st, 45th and 57th Regiments were components of the Philippine Div.

XX
☒ 91

XX
☒ 1

II ☒ 45

III ☒ 45

II ☒ 11(+)

III ☒ 26

XX
☒ 41(-)

☒ (31)

XX
☒ 21

XX
☒ 51(-)

XX
☒ 31(-)

III ☒ Prov AC

☒ (31)

SAMAT

RES.

☒ 31

MAMALA R.

LIMAY

SOUTH CHINA SEA

XXX
I

XXX
II

+ 4700

MARIVELES MTS

Alangan R.

Lamao R.

TOBANG

26 Jan–13 Feb

Canas Pt.

Binuangan R.

Ahyasin

☒ 57 and 2 ☒ 45

3 ☒ 45

MT. BATAAN

Quinauan Pt.

Aglaloma R.

23 Jan–8 Feb

☒ 57

CABCABEN

MARIVELES

23-29 Jan

Longoskayan Pt.

2 ☒ 57

MARIVELES HARBOR

THE WAR WITH JAPAN
PHILIPPINE CAMPAIGN
First Japanese Offensive Against the
Bagac—Orion Position
(26 Jan. — 23 Feb.)

0 1 2 3 4 5 6 7
SCALE OF MILES

XXXX
USAFFE
MacARTHUR

CORREGIDOR I.
(Ft. Mills)

CABALLO I.

ROCK PT.
JAMES RAVINE
MALINTA HILL
INFANTRY PT.
CAVALRY PT.
NORTH PT.
NORTH DOCK
KINDLEY FIELD
CHEESE RAVINE
SOUTH DOCK
GEARY PT.

Upon the suspension of Homma's offensive on 8 February, MacArthur's forces settled down to the dreary existence of a besieged army. Positions were improved, and concerted efforts were made to improve the state of training of the Philippine Army troops. Patrols ranged far to the north, and some of the more optimistic officers even advocated launching a counteroffensive to regain the Abucay-Mauban line. All the while, the fighting efficiency of the troops continued to ebb as malnutrition set in. (On 6 January, the ration had been cut in half—to thirty ounces per man—and by 1 April it had been halved again.) Also, as medical supplies dwindled, dreaded diseases (malaria, dengue, dysentery, and beriberi) made greater inroads; sanitation standards dropped; convalescent periods lengthened; and, significantly, nerve fatigue—in the absence of rest areas—became more serious.

Meanwhile, attempts to supply the beleaguered garrison met with dismal failure. Only three ships pierced the tightening Japanese blockade, and only a fraction of their cargo ever reached Manila Bay. Attempts to use aircraft and submarines were equally disappointing.

As early as February, Washington had concluded that, though every effort to sustain them would be made, the USAFFE garrison was doomed. Accordingly, MacArthur, whose talents the United States could ill afford to sacrifice, was queried concerning his evacuation. He declared his intent to remain to the last, but on 23 February President Roosevelt ordered him to Australia to assume command of Allied forces in the Southwest Pacific. Therefore, on the night of 12 March, MacArthur, accompanied by his family and some of his staff, left Corregidor via PT boats, transferring at Mindanao to B-17's for the last leg of the journey. Just before departing, MacArthur reorganized his forces into four commands (Mindanao, Visayas, Harbor Defenses, and Luzon Force), all to be responsible to him in Australia through an advance headquarters on Corregidor. Wainwright assumed command of the Luzon Force. But Marshall knew nothing of these arrangements and designated Wainwright as commander of United States Forces in the Philippines (USFIP). After considerable embarrassment—and an explanation to MacArthur—Wainwright assumed that command on 20 March, and appointed Maj. Gen. Edward P. King to command the Luzon Force.

In the interim, Homma had refitted his exhausted army, absorbed the reinforcements shown, and prepared for an estimated hard, four-week offensive. In mid-March, Japanese air and artillery bombardments began to increase in intensity. Late on 3 April, after the most devastating air-artillery bombardment of the campaign, Homma savagely struck the 41st Division (PA) in three places. There was little resistance; the bombardment alone had caused the division to break and flee to the rear. The Japanese, overestimating King's strength, halted that night on the line shown. On the 4th and 5th, the attack rolled onward as Parker desperately sought to hold his left flank. On the 6th, King counterattacked with all available reserves, but the Japanese brushed aside the opening thrusts and surged southeastward. By now, many of the II Corps' troops had been overrun and captured; King's only alternative was to withdraw. On the left, the I Corps, under less pressure, began to pull back the night of the 8th, by which time the II Corps' remnants were well to the south. That night, King—under orders to attack—decided that his position was hopeless and that further resistance would mean total annihilation. The next day, he surrendered the Luzon Force, which then began the infamous "Death March" to Camp O'Donnell (*see map 121, upper left*).

Homma, angered that the surrender had not included all troops in the Philippines, turned to Corregidor. The island forts (*lower left*) had been under sporadic air and artillery attack since early February, but now they received the concentrated fire of all the Japanese heavy artillery and aircraft. By early May, Corregidor's defenders were dazed from the continuous bombardment, and their water supply was critically short. On the night of 5 May, the Japanese managed to land one battalion as shown (*this map, inset*) and soon reinforced it with another. Their plan to land a larger force near James Ravine the next night, though implemented, proved unnecessary, for by noon on 6 May, Wainwright had initiated negotiations to surrender the island forts.

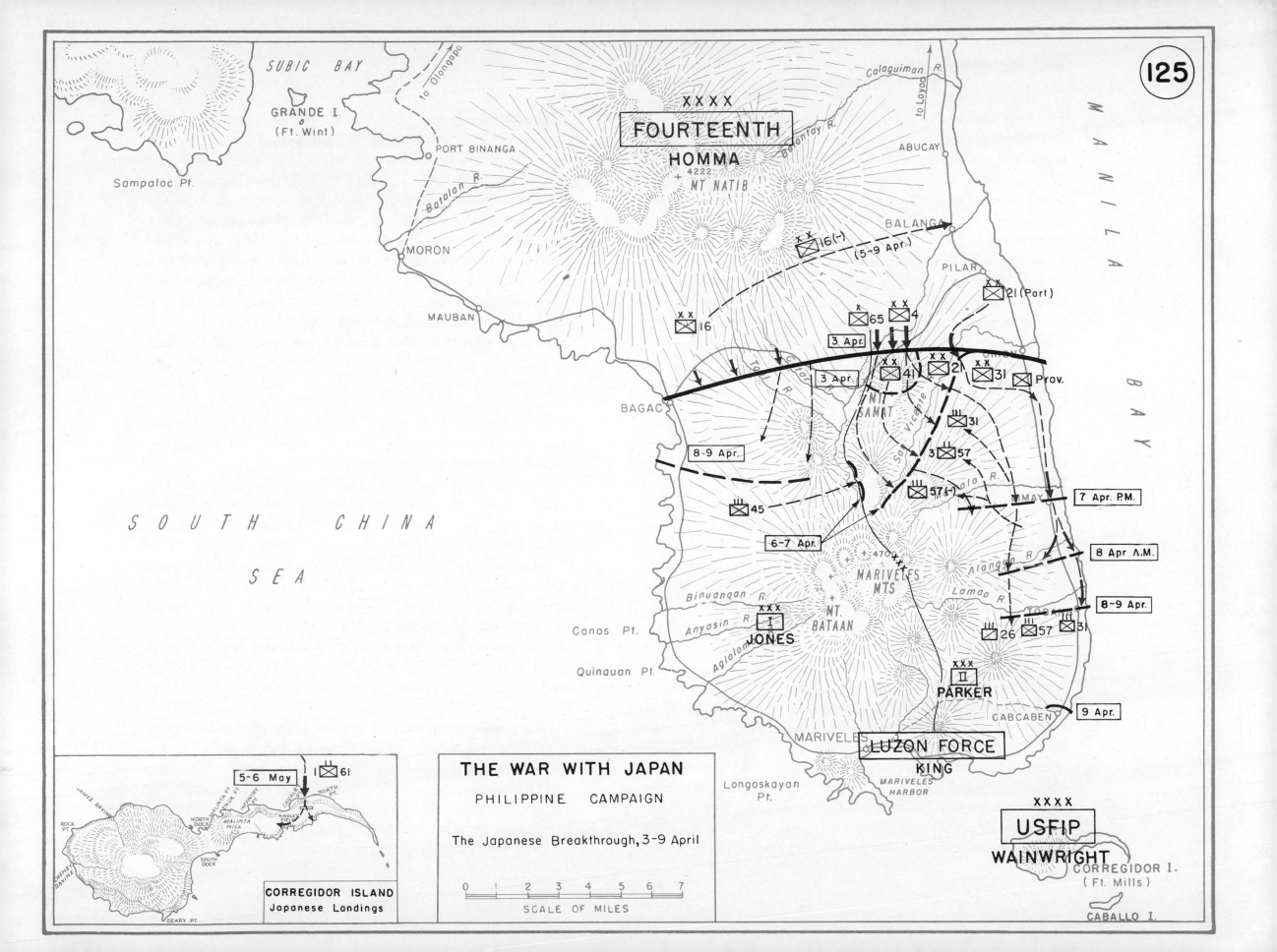

THE WAR WITH JAPAN

PHILIPPINE CAMPAIGN

The Japanese Breakthrough, 3-9 April

0 1 2 3 4 5 6 7
SCALE OF MILES

CORREGIDOR ISLAND
Japanese Landings

XXXX
FOURTEENTH
HOMMA
+4222
MT NATIB

SUBIC BAY

GRANDE I.
(Ft. Wint)

Sampaloc Pt.

PORT BINANGA

MORON

MAUBAN

to Olongapo

ABUCAY

BALANGA

PILAR

XX 16(-) (5-9 Apr.)

XX 21 (Part)

XX 16

X 65   XX 4

3 Apr.

3 Apr.

XX 41   XX 2   XX 31   Prov.

MT
SAMAT

III 31

III 3 57

III 57(-)

8-9 Apr.

BAGAC

XX 45

6-7 Apr.

+4700
MARIVELES
MTS

XXX
I
JONES

MT.
BATAAN

Canas Pt.

Quinauan Pt.

Binuangan R.

Anyasin R.

Agloloma R.

S O U T H   C H I N A

S E A

MANILA BAY

7 Apr. P.M.

8 Apr. A.M.

8-9 Apr.

III 26   III 57   31

XXX
II
PARKER

LUZON FORCE
KING

9 Apr.

CABCABEN

MARIVELES

Longoskayan Pt.

MARIVELES
HARBOR

XXXX
USFIP
WAINWRIGHT

CORREGIDOR I.
(Ft. Mills)

CABALLO I.

5-6 May   I 61

125

This map generally sums up Japanese landings in Southeast Asia and the Philippines in implementation of the first phase of the master war plan. In support of operations in Burma (*see text, map 127*), additional troops were landed near Rangoon (*this map, top left*) in April. The landings at Sarawak in British Borneo (*center*) were made by a brigade-size force principally to gain control of oil fields and to facilitate the coming attacks on Java and Sumatra.

It will be recalled (*see text, map 119*) that the Japanese had landed a reinforced battalion at Davao, on Mindanao, on 20 December. Philippine Army troops offered only slight resistance before withdrawing into the hills. This Miura Detachment was reinforced by a regiment, which moved on to seize Jolo Island on Christmas Eve. Very cheaply, the Japanese had gained air and naval bases from which to support operations against Dutch Borneo.

Brig. Gen. William F. Sharp's Visayan-Mindanao Force was responsible for the defense of all the Philippines except Luzon. (The islands between Luzon and Mindanao are known as the Visayas.) When war broke out, his command (elements of three Philippine Army divisions, a Philippine Scout regiment, and miscellaneous units) was in the same—if not a worse—state of unpreparedness as the troops on Luzon (*this map*). In view of his weakness and dispersion, Sharp's mission was to oppose the Japanese as long as practicable and then retire to the hills and conduct guerrilla operations.

In late December, MacArthur, concerned over the defense of the important Del Monte airfields, ordered Sharp to concentrate the bulk of his troops on Mindanao. Then—just before leaving Corregidor—he made Sharp responsible for Mindanao only, and created the Visayan Force (Brig. Gen. Bradford G. Chynoweth) to control the Cebu, Panay, Negros, Leyte, and Samar garrisons. Sharp, commanding a larger force, made plans to fight vigorously any landings, while Chynoweth's garrisons realistically stocked supplies in mountain hideouts in preparation for guerrilla warfare.

When Homma received reinforcements in March after his Bataan campaign had stalled, he sent two brigade-size forces to subjugate the southern islands. On 10 April, one detachment landed on Cebu and in three days established control over the island; similarly, Panay was invaded on 16 April and subjugated in four days by the other detachment. Both island garrisons, after taking moderate losses, had fallen back to their mountain retreats. Homma then sent the two detachments to Mindanao, where they landed on 29 April and 3 May. Assisted by Miura's detachment, they quickly routed Sharp's forces and forced them into the mountains. (A small Japanese force had occupied Zamboanga on 2 March to establish a seaplane base.) On 10 May, Sharp was given a message carried by one of Wainwright's staff officers (flown by the Japanese from Manila) directing that he surrender his force —or the 11,000 captives on Corregidor would suffer the consequences.

Just before Wainwright surrendered, on 6 May, he had released Sharp from his command, but Homma would not deal with him unless he surrendered all troops in the Philippines. Thus, Wainwright was forced to surrender Corregidor to the local Japanese commander, and then—fearing reprisals against his erstwhile garrison—he reassumed command over Sharp and agreed to surrender the latter's forces as well. Sharp, who had been ordered by MacArthur in the interim to ignore any orders from Wainwright, now had a difficult choice. He elected to surrender and was then compelled to do exactly what Wainwright had done: reassume command over the Visayan garrisons he had released, and order their surrender. Several of Chynoweth's commanders balked, the Japanese having occupied only two of the Visayas, but they all ultimately surrendered; many of their troops simply melted into the hills, some to operate as guerrillas, but most to return to their homes.

For General Homma, victory in the Philippines had been hollow; he was soon relieved of command and ordered to Tokyo. For Wainwright, there would be no victories until 1945, when, gaunt and sickly, he would return to Luzon to witness the surrender of the Japanese at Baguio. But he could take solace in the knowledge that his troops had proved to a Western world awed by Japanese victories that the Japanese were not invincible.

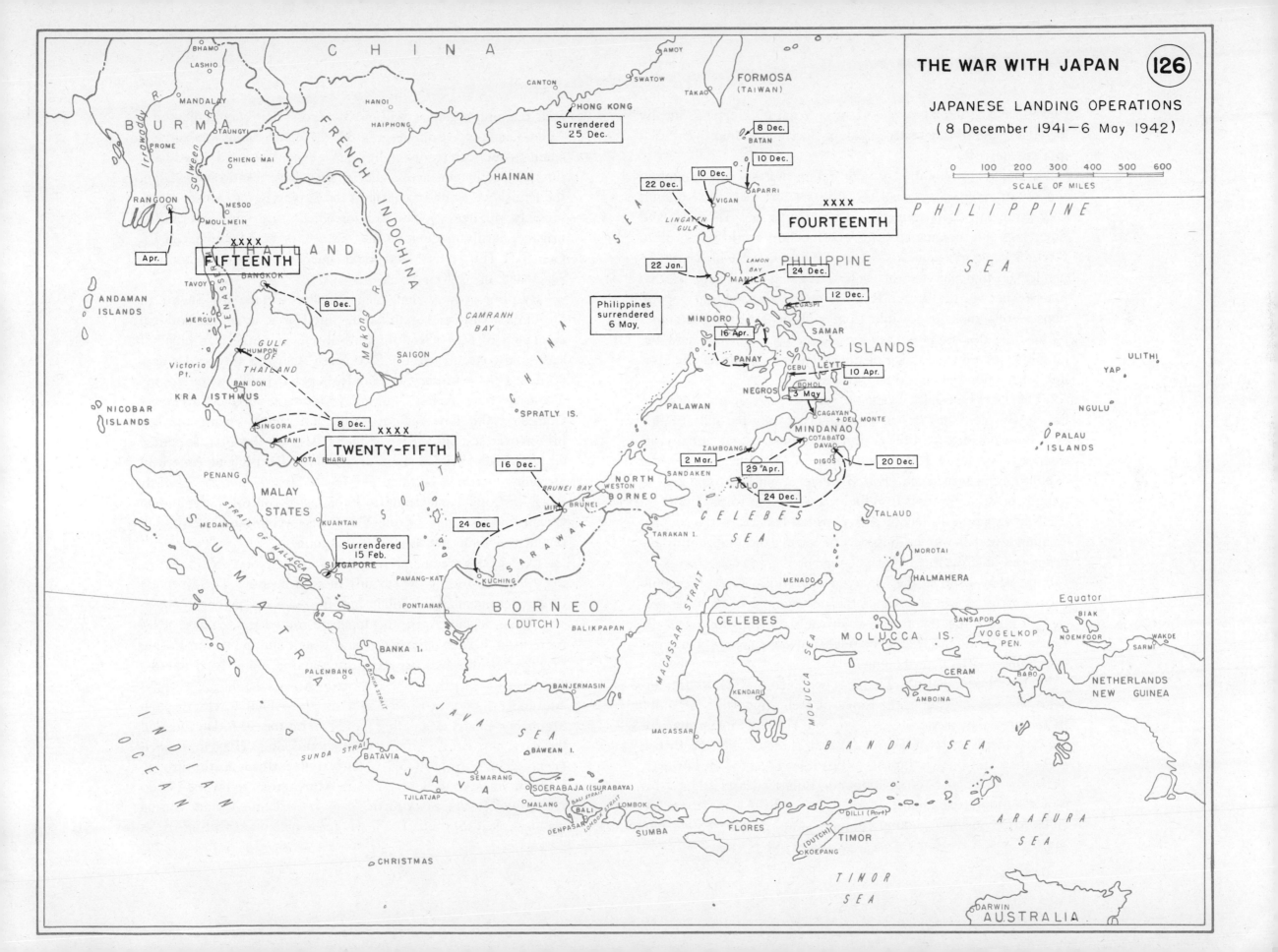

THE WAR WITH JAPAN 126

JAPANESE LANDING OPERATIONS
(8 December 1941 — 6 May 1942)

0   100   200   300   400   500   600
SCALE OF MILES

CHINA

BHAMO
LASHIO
MANDALAY
BURMA
PROME
TAUNGYI
CHIENG MAI
MESOD
Irrowaddy R.
Salween R.
RANGOON
MOULMEIN
PMOULMEIN
Apr.
FIFTEENTH
XXXX
BANGKOK
8 Dec.
TAVOY
TENASSERIM
MERGUI
ANDAMAN ISLANDS
GULF OF THAILAND
CHUMPON
THAILAND
Victoria Pt.
BAN DON
KRA ISTHMUS
NICOBAR ISLANDS
SINGORA
PATANI
8 Dec.
TWENTY-FIFTH
XXXX
KOTA BHARU
PENANG
MALAY STATES
MEDAN
KUANTAN
Surrendered 15 Feb.
SINGAPORE
PAMANG-KAT
SUMATRA
STRAIT OF MALACCA
PALEMBANG
BANKA I.
PONTIANAK
BORNEO (DUTCH)
Equator
BANJERMASIN
BALIKPAPAN
BATAVIA
JAVA SEA
SEMARANG
SOERABAJA ((SURABAYA)
TJILATJAP
MALANG
BALI
DENPASAR
SUMBA
FLORES
INDIAN OCEAN
CHRISTMAS
Sunda Strait
Bali Strait
Lombok Strait
TIMOR SEA

CANTON
SWATOW
AMOY
HONG KONG
Surrendered 25 Dec.
HANOI
HAIPHONG
FRENCH INDOCHINA
HAINAN
Mekong R.
SAIGON
CAMRANH BAY
SPRATLY IS.
SOUTH CHINA SEA
16 Dec.
24 Dec.
NORTH BORNEO
WESTON
BRUNEI BAY
MIRI
BRUNEI
SARAWAK
KUCHING
TARAKAN I.
SANDAKEN
MACASSAR STRAIT
CELEBES
MACASSAR
KENDARI
MOLUCCA SEA
MENADO
BANDA SEA
CERAM
AMBOINA
TAKAO
FORMOSA (TAIWAN)
8 Dec.
BATAN
10 Dec.
10 Dec.
APARRI
VIGAN
22 Dec.
LINGAYEN GULF
FOURTEENTH
XXXX
PHILIPPINE SEA
22 Jan.
LAMON BAY
PHILIPPINE
MANILA
24 Dec.
12 Dec.
LEGASPI
Philippines surrendered 6 May.
MINDORO
16 Apr.
SAMAR
ISLANDS
PANAY
CEBU
LEYTE
10 Apr.
NEGROS
BOHOL
3 May
CAGAYAN
DEL MONTE
MINDANAO
COTABATO
DAVAO
DIGOS
20 Dec.
ZAMBOANGA
2 Mar.
29 Apr.
JOLO
24 Dec.
CELEBES SEA
TALAUD
MOROTAI
HALMAHERA
SANSAPOR
VOGELKOP PEN.
BIAK
NOEMFOOR
WAKDE
SARMI
NETHERLANDS NEW GUINEA
BABO
ULITHI
YAP
NGULU
PALAU ISLANDS
DILLI (Port)
(DUTCH) TIMOR
KOEPANG
ARAFURA SEA
DARWIN
AUSTRALIA
BAWEAN I.

Burma, as the Japanese saw it, was a natural fortress, ideally situated to guard the western flank of their new empire—and rich in rice and oil.

Burma is a country of alternating north-south mountain ranges and river valleys. In 1942, it was a curiously isolated land; only a few hill trails connected it with India and Thailand, and practically all commerce with the outside world took place through Rangoon (*bottom center*). Beleaguered China also depended on that port for the American Lend-Lease supplies that reached her via the Burma Road (*upper right*). Military operations were almost impossible from mid-May to late September because of the monsoon rains; malaria was endemic; and the jungle which covered much of the country reduced the effectiveness of air power and motor transport.

The forces initially available for the defense of Burma— largely Burmese and Indian troops—were only partially trained and almost without artillery, signal equipment, and antiaircraft weapons. Air support was scant; most of the airfields lay in the exposed Tenasserim area (*bottom center*), but had to be held as long as possible in order to refuel planes bound to Singapore.

The Japanese Fifteenth Army, which had recently occupied Thailand, had the initial missions of seizing the Tenasserim airfields and of protecting the right rear of the Japanese forces invading Malaya. Once the Malayan operations were proceeding satisfactorily, it would advance through Moulmein (*bottom center*) to take Rangoon. Japanese air raids on Rangoon began 23 December, doing little actual damage, but slowing port operations by panicking the longshoremen.

During December, the Japanese occupied the Tenasserim airfields, thereby extending the range of their supporting air units. In January, they advanced on Rangoon. Hoping to gain time for reinforcements to reach Burma, Wavell directed that the British make their first stand as far east as possible. Their forces, however, were too weak and too roadbound. Equipped and trained for jungle fighting, the Japanese would fix the British by frontal attacks while pushing flanking columns across country to get into

their rear and organize road blocks across their communications. (The Chinese Communists used the same tactics effectively against American troops eight years later in Korea.) Forced back through Moulmein, across the Salween River, and out of Bilin, the British were almost cut off at the Sittang River bridge, escaping only with heavy losses. Reinforcements, including an armored brigade, hardly made good the wastage. Alexander replaced Lt. Gen. T. J. Hutton as Allied commander in Burma; Rangoon was evacuated on 7 March.

By prior arrangement, Generalissimo Chiang Kai-Shek sent the Chinese Fifth and Sixth Armies into Burma under the nominal command of Maj. Gen. Joseph Stilwell, his American chief of staff, and concentrated the Sixty-Sixth Army on the border as a reserve. Thus reinforced, Alexander hoped to hold the line Prome-Toungoo (*lower center*), but on 21 March the Japanese drove the Chinese 200th Division out of the latter city, seizing the key bridge over the Sittang River there. Also on the 21st, Japanese air raids overwhelmed the few remaining British and American air units, then concentrated at Magwe (*lower center*). In early April, a strong Japanese naval force seized control in the Indian Ocean, and two more Japanese divisions—reinforced by two tank regiments—were put ashore at Rangoon.

Despite the gradual arrival of the Chinese Sixty-Sixth Army, the Allied position grew steadily more desperate. The Burmese civil government began collapsing; Burmese troops began to desert. Then, in late April, the Japanese routed the Chinese Sixth Army near Loikow, chasing it into China and capturing Lashio (*center*) on the 29th. By exhausting marches and hard fighting (and timely help by the Sixty-Sixth Army's leading division), Alexander finally extricated most of the Allied forces through Mandalay, finally evacuating that town on the 30th. He then led the surviving British troops through the Chin Hills to Imphal (*center, left*). Stilwell led a party out farther north through Homalin; most of the Chinese Fifth Army retreated through Ledo (*top center*). The Sixty-Sixth Army retired into China. Burma was lost. Said Stilwell: ". . . we got a hell of a beating."

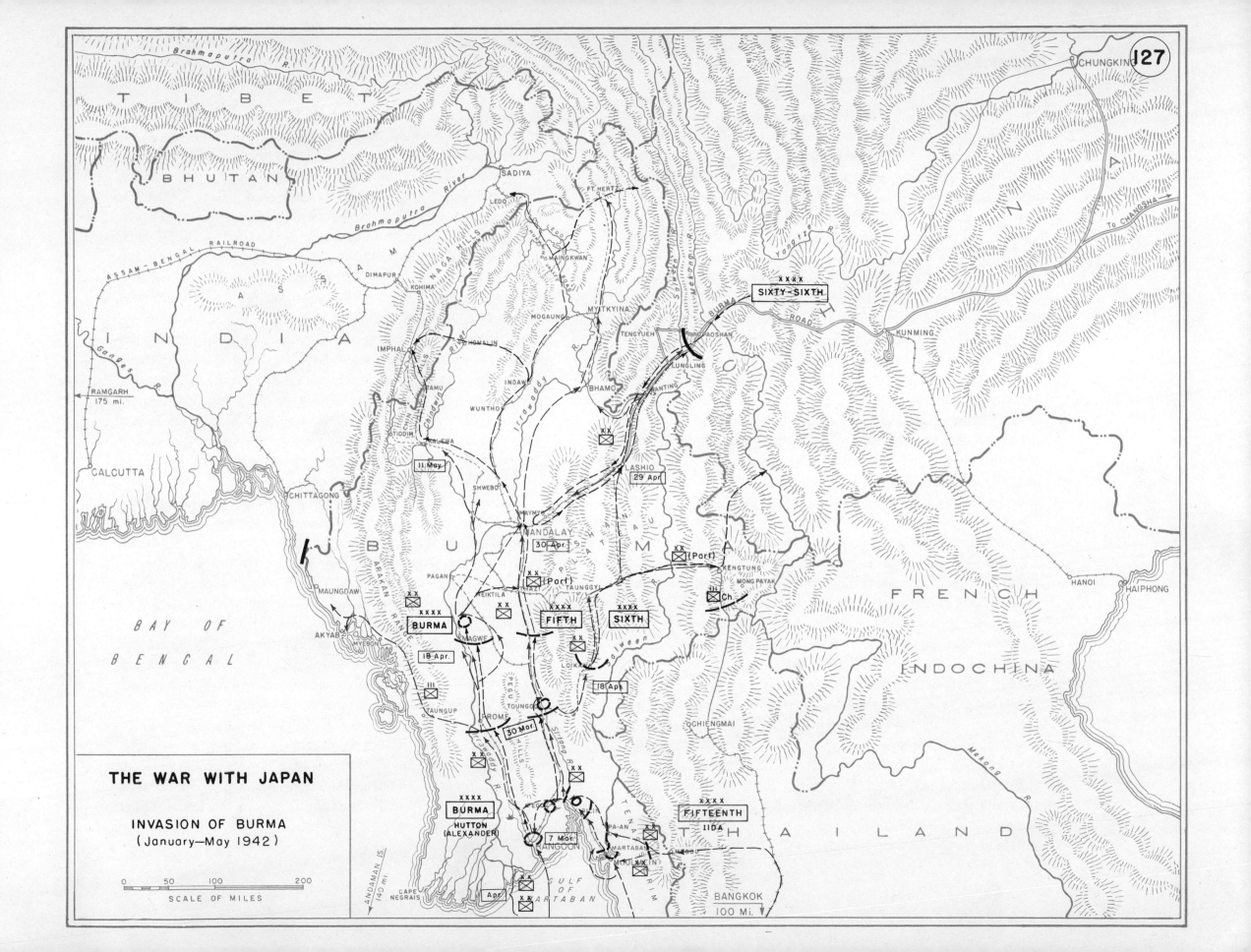

127

THE WAR WITH JAPAN

INVASION OF BURMA
(January—May 1942)

0   50   100   200
SCALE OF MILES

The Netherlands East Indies—rich in oil, rubber, and other strategic materials—were to be the treasure house of Japan's Greater East Asia Co-Prosperity Sphere. Once the Japanese had cleared their flanks by seizing Malaya and the Philippines, and crippling the United States Pacific Fleet at Pearl Harbor, the East Indies were their major objective.

The vast expanse of the East Indies, the great number of their islands, and the lack of good roads on most of the larger islands, made their defense extremely difficult. The Dutch had built an excellent system of airfields throughout the East Indies, but since the Allies had only a handful of planes, mostly obsolescent, these airfields could not be exploited, except by the Japanese. In an area where communication was normally by water, the Allies had only a small, hastily assembled fleet of light Dutch, American, and British warships. Available ground forces were chiefly Dutch (most of them native troops, armed and trained for internal security duties); the strongest concentration was on Java (*lower left*), but large numbers of troops were scattered on garrison duty at major ports throughout the East Indies. The Dutch had not endeared themselves to their native subjects; only in the Amboina (*lower right*) area was the population loyal.

The East Indies had been placed under the improvised joint American-British-Dutch-Australian Command (ABDACOM). General Wavell received the unenviable task of commanding it. ABDACOM's creation, however, did not produce a unified Allied strategy, for the British were concerned with Singapore, the Americans with the Philippines, and the Dutch and Australians with self-defense.

The Japanese invasion built up swiftly. In December, with Luzon still unconquered, they had developed bases at Jolo, Brunei (*both center*), and Davao (*center, right*). At least two naval task forces were formed for the invasion (Central Force may have been a subdivision of Eastern Force); the Sixteenth Army provided the necessary troops. The Carrier Striking Force would assist Eastern Force in cutting ABDACOM's communications with Australia.

Japanese tactics were both aggressive and cautious. Selecting an objective—usually a seaport with an adjoining airfield—the Japanese concentrated their land-based aircraft and wiped out Allied air units stationed there. That accomplished, a naval task force (always including aircraft carriers) landed sufficient marines or troops to overwhelm the local Allied ground forces. The captured airfield was made operational; land-based planes were leapfrogged forward, and the cycle was repeated. Japanese naval task forces seldom moved beyond the combat range of their supporting land-based planes. At Menado (*center, right*) and other critical objectives, small naval paratroop units were employed. Meanwhile, major Allied bases, such as Soerabaja (*bottom center*), were kept under constant air attack. Allied air reconnaissance was smothered; consequently, Allied naval forces operated blindly, and Allied ground forces had little warning of impending attacks. This combination of mass and mobility was more than the isolated Allied garrisons of the outlying islands could withstand; their piecemeal destruction rapidly reduced Allied air and ground strength. Single Allied ships were quickly picked off by the superior Japanese air and naval forces.

Japanese operations proceeded as shown, without a check. At Balikpapan (*lower center*), American destroyers surprised a Japanese convoy, sinking five ships, but did not delay the Japanese a single day. An attack on a convoy in Lombok Strait (*bottom center*) was unsuccessful. The Japanese Carrier Striking Force wrecked the growing Allied base at Darwin (*bottom right*); the capture of Timor and Bali (*bottom center*) enabled the Japanese to control the sea route from Australia to Java. Realizing that the situation was hopeless, Wavell left Java on 25 February. ABDACOM collapsed; British and American forces began evacuating. As the Japanese Eastern and Western Forces converged on Java, Dutch Rear Admiral K. W. F. M. Doorman took his worn-down Allied fleet out to meet them, but was overwhelmed in the Battle of the Java Sea. The Japanese then swarmed ashore on Java, forcing a Dutch capitulation on 9 March. A Japanese wedge had been driven between the British in the Indian Ocean and the American forces in the Pacific.

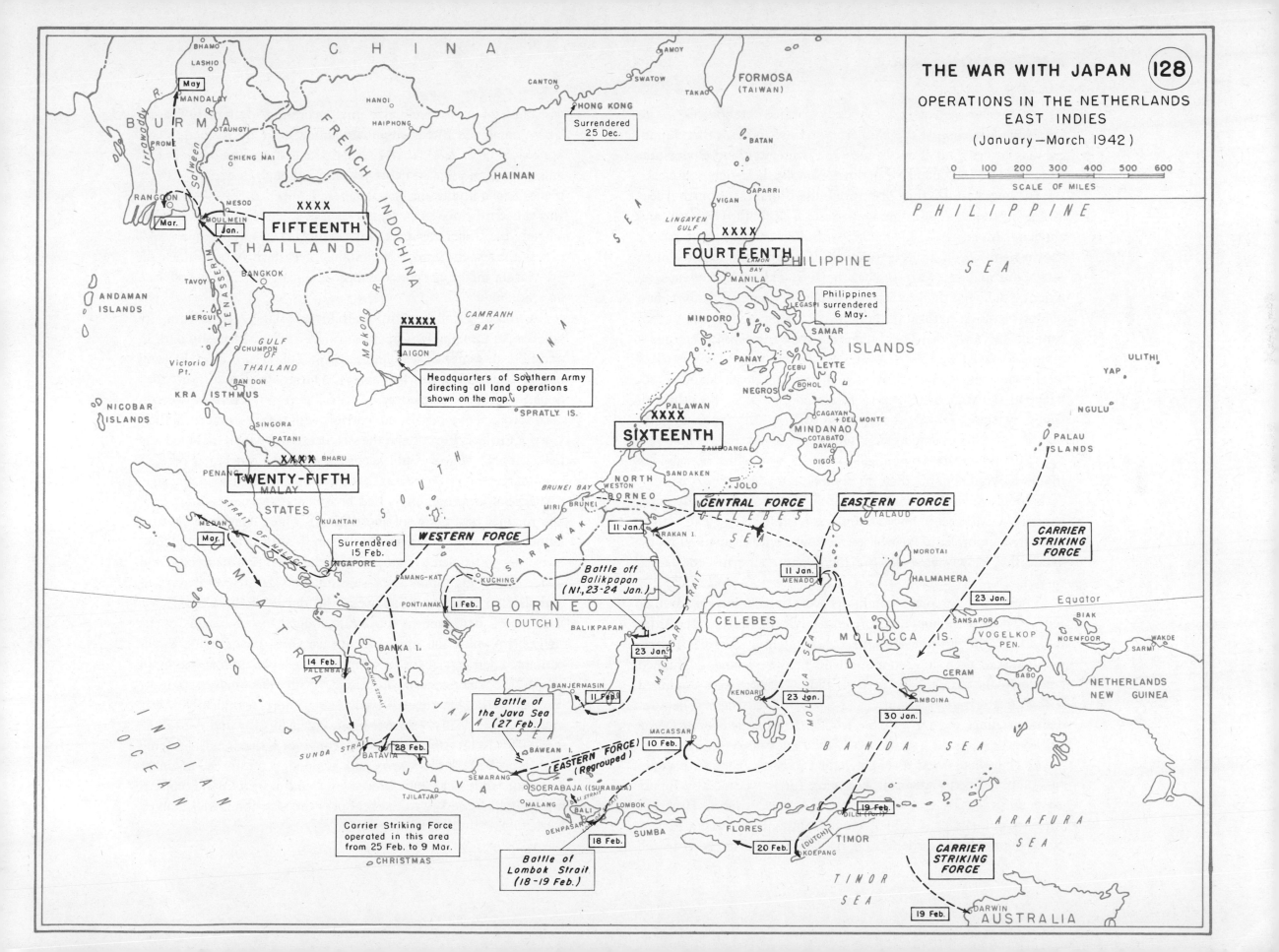

THE WAR WITH JAPAN 128

OPERATIONS IN THE NETHERLANDS
EAST INDIES

(January—March 1942)

0 100 200 300 400 500 600
SCALE OF MILES

CHINA

BURMA

FRENCH INDOCHINA

THAILAND

May
MANDALAY
LASHIO
BHAMO
PROME
RANGOON
Mar.
Jan.
MOULMEIN
MESOD
FIFTEENTH XXXX

TAVOY
TENASSERIM
MERGUI
Victoria Pt.
GULF OF THAILAND
BAN DON
KRA ISTHMUS
SINGORA
PATANI

ANDAMAN ISLANDS

NICOBAR ISLANDS

TWENTY-FIFTH XXXX
MALAY STATES
PENANG
BHARU
KUANTAN
Medano
Mar.
STRAIT OF MALACCA

Surrendered 15 Feb.
SINGAPORE

WESTERN FORCE

SUMATRA

14 Feb.
PALEMBANG

BANKA I.

INDIAN OCEAN

CHRISTMAS

Carrier Striking Force
operated in this area
from 25 Feb. to 9 Mar.

SUNDA STRAIT
28 Feb.
BATAVIA

JAVA
TJILATJAP
MALANG
SEMARANG
SOERABAJA (SURABAYA)

**Battle of
Lombok Strait
(18-19 Feb.)**

18 Feb.
DENPASAR
BALI STRAIT
LOMBOK
20 Feb.
SUMBA
FLORES

HAINAN

HONG KONG
Surrendered
25 Dec.

AMOY
SWATOW
CANTON
TAKAO
FORMOSA (TAIWAN)

BATAN

CAPARRI
VIGAN
LINGAYEN GULF
LAMON BAY
MANILA
FOURTEENTH XXXX
PHILIPPINE

Philippines surrendered 6 May.

MINDORO
SAMAR
PANAY
LEYTE
NEGROS
CEBU
BOHOL
PALAWAN

XXXXX
SAIGON
CAMRANH BAY

Headquarters of Southern Army
directing all land operations
shown on the map

SPRATLY IS.

SOUTH CHINA SEA

SIXTEENTH XXXX
CAGAYAN + DEL MONTE
MINDANAO
ZAMBOANGA
COTABATO DAVAO
DIGOS
JOLO

PHILIPPINE SEA

ULITHI

YAP

NGULU

PALAU ISLANDS

BRUNEI BAY
NORTH BORNEO
WESTON
MIRI BRUNEI
SANDAKEN
11 Jan.
TARAKAN I.
CENTRAL FORCE
CELEBES SEA
TALAUD
EASTERN FORCE

CARRIER STRIKING FORCE

11 Jan.
MENADO

23 Jan.
Equator

MOROTAI

HALMAHERA

**Battle off
Balikpapan
(Nt., 23-24 Jan.)**

SARAWAK
KUCHING
KAMANG-KAT
PONTIANAK
1 Feb.
BORNEO (DUTCH)
BALIKPAPAN
23 Jan.
BANJERMASIN
11 Feb.
MACASSAR STRAIT
CELEBES
KENDARI
23 Jan.
MACASSAR
10 Feb.

MOLUCCA SEA
SANSAPOR
BIAK
NOEMFOOR
WAKDE
SARMI
VOGELKOP PEN.
CERAM
BABO
NETHERLANDS NEW GUINEA
AMBOINA
30 Jan.
MOLUCCA IS.

**Battle of
the Java Sea
(27 Feb.)**

BAWEAN I.
(EASTERN FORCE)
(Regrouped)
BANDA SEA

ARAFURA SEA

(DUTCH) TIMOR
DILI
19 Feb.
KOEPANG

CARRIER STRIKING FORCE

TIMOR SEA

19 Feb.
DARWIN
AUSTRALIA

As the Japanese invasion relentlessly crushed the hopelessly gallant Allied defense of the Netherlands East Indies, other Japanese task forces fanned out to seize the strategic island chains that were to form the defensive perimeter about their rich conquests.

As one part of this operation, the Japanese Fourth Fleet steamed south in late January to seize Rabaul (*center*) and Kavieng. Most of the available Australian forces (the territory shown here was under Australian jurisdiction) had been sent to Singapore and the East Indies; the few soldiers and planes remaining did what they could, and were overwhelmed. Rabaul had one of the finest natural harbors in the Pacific and ample terrain suitable for airfields. The Japanese rapidly developed it into a major advanced base.

From Rabaul, they continued their methodical, leapfrog advance as shown, constructing airfields as they moved southward, island by island. During the first part of 1942, the Japanese planners decided to extend their planned perimeter (*see map 113*) to include Port Moresby (*this map, lower left*), since air bases in that area would enable them to dominate northeastern Australia. A bold move in February or March would undoubtedly have overrun it with ease, but the Japanese preferred to carry their protective umbrella of land-based air power with them at all times. While they slowly chopped out their jungle airstrips, the Allies rallied.

These new Japanese conquests were incomplete in another sense. The Australians had forehandedly organized a special intelligence agency known as the Coastwatching Service. Picked men, most of them long-time residents of these islands, remained behind as the Australian forces withdrew. They were equipped with two-way radios; usually, the natives aided them. Their radioed warnings were invaluable to the scanty Allied forces. As a sideline, they rescued shot-down Allied aviators.

During this period, the Americans were struggling to secure their supply line to Australia (*see map 130*). Alarmed by Japanese activity in New Guinea and the Solomons, Admiral Ernest J. King—Commander in Chief, United States Fleet, and Chief of Naval Operations—ordered a carrier task force to move to the assistance of Australian naval units operating south of that area. These combined forces attempted an air strike on Rabaul. Their approach (*this map, center*) was detected by Japanese reconnaissance planes on 20 February, and—though American carrier planes broke up the ensuing Japanese bomber attacks—the strike was called off since surprise had been lost. Reinforced by another carrier, the American task force launched a surprise air strike across the Owen Stanley Mountains of eastern New Guinea on 10 March, inflicting some damage on Japanese shipping off Lae and Salamaua.

A more serious operation followed. The Japanese finally launched an amphibious operation to seize Port Moresby and, in addition, to establish seaplane bases at Tulagi (*lower right*) and in the Louisiades (*lower center*). During this operation, they hoped to trap the Allied naval forces opposing them between a carrier force (two big aircraft carriers with their escorts from their Carrier Striking Force) and the strong escort (which included one light carrier) which would accompany their Transport Force.

Intercepted radio messages warned the Allies of this offensive. (American cryptographers had broken the Japanese codes even before the beginning of hostilities.) One American carrier launched its planes against Tulagi on 4 May. Most of the Japanese ships assigned to that phase of the operation had come and gone; a few small craft were sunk or damaged. Several days of complicated maneuvers followed (the Battle of the Coral Sea). This was a new type of sea battle, waged by exchanges of air strikes, in which the opposing surface ships never made direct contact. Their carrier forces crippled (the Japanese lost one small carrier, the Americans one large one), both sides finally withdrew. Tactically, the Americans were the worse hurt; technically, it was a draw; strategically—since it saved Port Moresby and the Louisiades—it was an Allied victory. Unconvinced, the Japanese Army took over the task their Navy had fumbled; a reinforced engineer regiment landed at Gona (*lower left*) and moved inland, capturing Kokoda—the key to the best pass through the Owen Stanley Mountains—by 29 July.

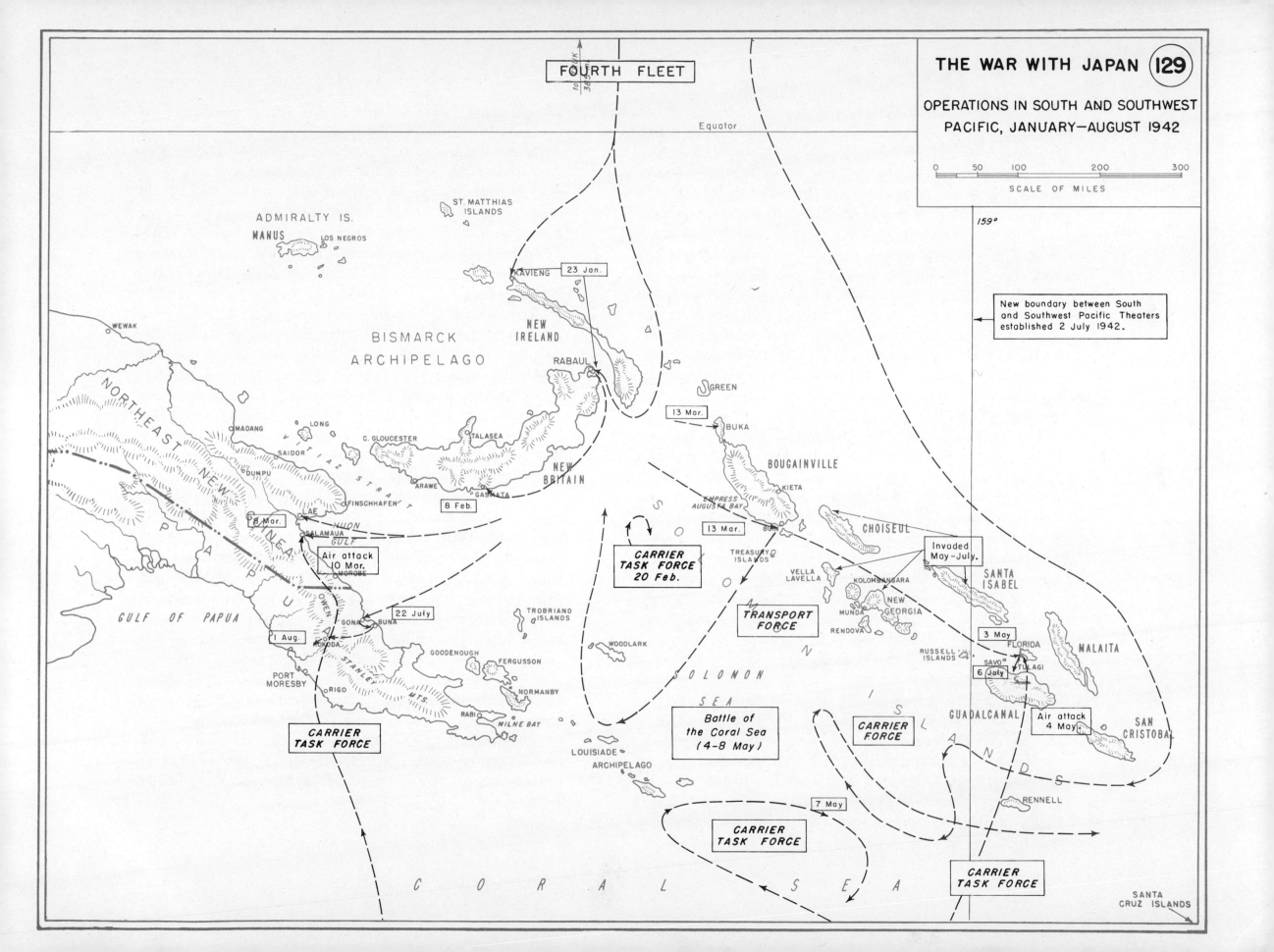

FOURTH FLEET

THE WAR WITH JAPAN 129

OPERATIONS IN SOUTH AND SOUTHWEST PACIFIC, JANUARY–AUGUST 1942

Equator

0   50   100   200   300
SCALE OF MILES

159°

New boundary between South and Southwest Pacific Theaters established 2 July 1942.

ADMIRALTY IS.
MANUS
LOS NEGROS

ST. MATTHIAS ISLANDS

WEWAK

KAVIENG
23 Jan.

NEW IRELAND

BISMARCK ARCHIPELAGO

RABAUL

GREEN

13 Mar.
BUKA

NORTHEAST NEW
MADANG
LONG
SAIDOR
DUMPU
C. GLOUCESTER
TALASEA
ARAWE
GASMATA
8 Feb.

NEW BRITAIN

BOUGAINVILLE
KIETA

EMPRESS AUGUSTA BAY

13 Mar.
BUIN

CHOISEUL

Invaded May–July.

FINSCHHAFEN
LAE
8 Mar.
SALAMAUA
HUON GULF
Air attack 10 Mar.
MOROBE

CARRIER TASK FORCE 20 Feb.

TREASURY ISLANDS

VELLA LAVELLA

KOLOMBANGARA

SANTA ISABEL

PAPUA

OWEN

22 July
GONA BUNA
1 Aug.
KOKODA

STANLEY MTS.

TROBRIAND ISLANDS

WOODLARK

TRANSPORT FORCE

MUNDA
RENDOVA
NEW GEORGIA

3 May
FLORIDA
RUSSELL ISLANDS
SAVO
6 July TULAGI
MALAITA

GULF OF PAPUA

PORT MORESBY
ORIGO
RABI
MILNE BAY

GOODENOUGH
FERGUSSON
NORMANBY

SOLOMON SEA

Battle of the Coral Sea (4–8 May)

CARRIER FORCE

GUADALCANAL

Air attack 4 May.

SAN CRISTOBAL

CARRIER TASK FORCE

LOUISIADE ARCHIPELAGO

7 May

RENNELL

I S L A N D S

CARRIER TASK FORCE

C O R A L   S E A

CARRIER TASK FORCE

SANTA CRUZ ISLANDS

The break-up of ABDACOM forced a reorganization of the Allied command in the Pacific. The Japanese advance had cut off the British in India from Australia and New Zealand. At the same time, American forces were building up in Australia. Discussions among Allied leaders produced the system shown here. The United States assumed responsibility for the Pacific, the British for India and the Indian Ocean. China remained a special case— an area of American strategic responsibility, where Chiang Kai-Shek retained the supreme command, with Stilwell as his chief of staff. (The American creation, for administrative reasons, of a China-Burma-India Command Area resulted in something of a command monstrosity, wherein Stilwell—commanding general of United States Army forces in that area, and commander of the Chinese forces in India and Burma—could be simultaneously responsible to his American superiors, Chiang, and the British commander in India.)

The Pacific was divided into three commands: the Southwest Pacific Area, under MacArthur; the Pacific Ocean Areas, under Admiral Chester W. Nimitz; and the minor Southeast Pacific Area (*off map, east*). Nimitz's area was subdivided as shown. This organization remained largely unchanged for the first two years of the war. The one major boundary change (*lower center*) was made to give Nimitz responsibility for the southern Solomons at the beginning of the Guadalcanal campaign (*see map 132*).

The American supply line to Australia was rapidly strengthened in early 1942. Hawaii was heavily reinforced, and strong Allied garrisons were established at islands along and astride this route. This involved construction of a whole series of air, naval, and logistical bases.

The Japanese triumphs over England, Holland, and the United States had come far sooner and far more cheaply than they had dared to hope. Possessed by a conviction of invincibility, they began to consider expanding their perimeter, instead of rapidly consolidating its defenses. This desire was stimulated by Lt. Col. James H. Doolittle's surprise air raid on Tokyo (*not shown*) on 18 April with sixteen air corps medium bombers, launched by an American carrier task force. Realizing that their capital was vulnerable to air attacks, the Japanese planners took action: a major expedition would be launched against Midway, to draw the American Pacific Fleet into battle and destroy it. As a diversion, a smaller Japanese force would seize Attu and Kiska in the western Aleutians (*this map, upper center*), making its strike one day ahead of the main force. Later, once the Japanese had established bases at Port Moresby and Tulagi, further operations could be launched to isolate Australia and New Zealand by capturing New Caledonia, Fiji, and Samoa.

The Japanese fleets put to sea, confident of quick and overwhelming victory. But—while facing their greatest battle—they split their formidable Carrier Striking Force. Two of their big carriers had gone to the Coral Sea. The four that were assigned to the Midway operation had just returned from a highly successful raid into the Indian Ocean (25 March–8 April), which had, however, apparently resulted in the loss of a considerable number of veteran naval aviators. According to Japanese accounts, their replacements were relatively untrained.

Once again, intercepted radio messages alerted the Americans; Nimitz quickly concentrated and readied his three available carriers. The Battle of Midway was another intricate struggle between distant aircraft carriers, the American ships being supported by marine and army aircraft from the Midway field. Japanese tactics were clumsy—they had overwhelming superiority in battleships and cruisers, but failed to commit them while the carrier battle was deadlocked. That battle ended with all four Japanese carriers and their planes lost. One American carrier was sunk. The Japanese Navy had lost its long-range striking power; except for the Battle of the Philippine Sea, it would never again venture far beyond the protection of land-based aircraft.

The Japanese did have one consolation. Under cover of a hit-and-run raid on Dutch Harbor (*upper right*), their Aleutian expedition occupied the empty islands of Attu and Kiska on 6-7 June.

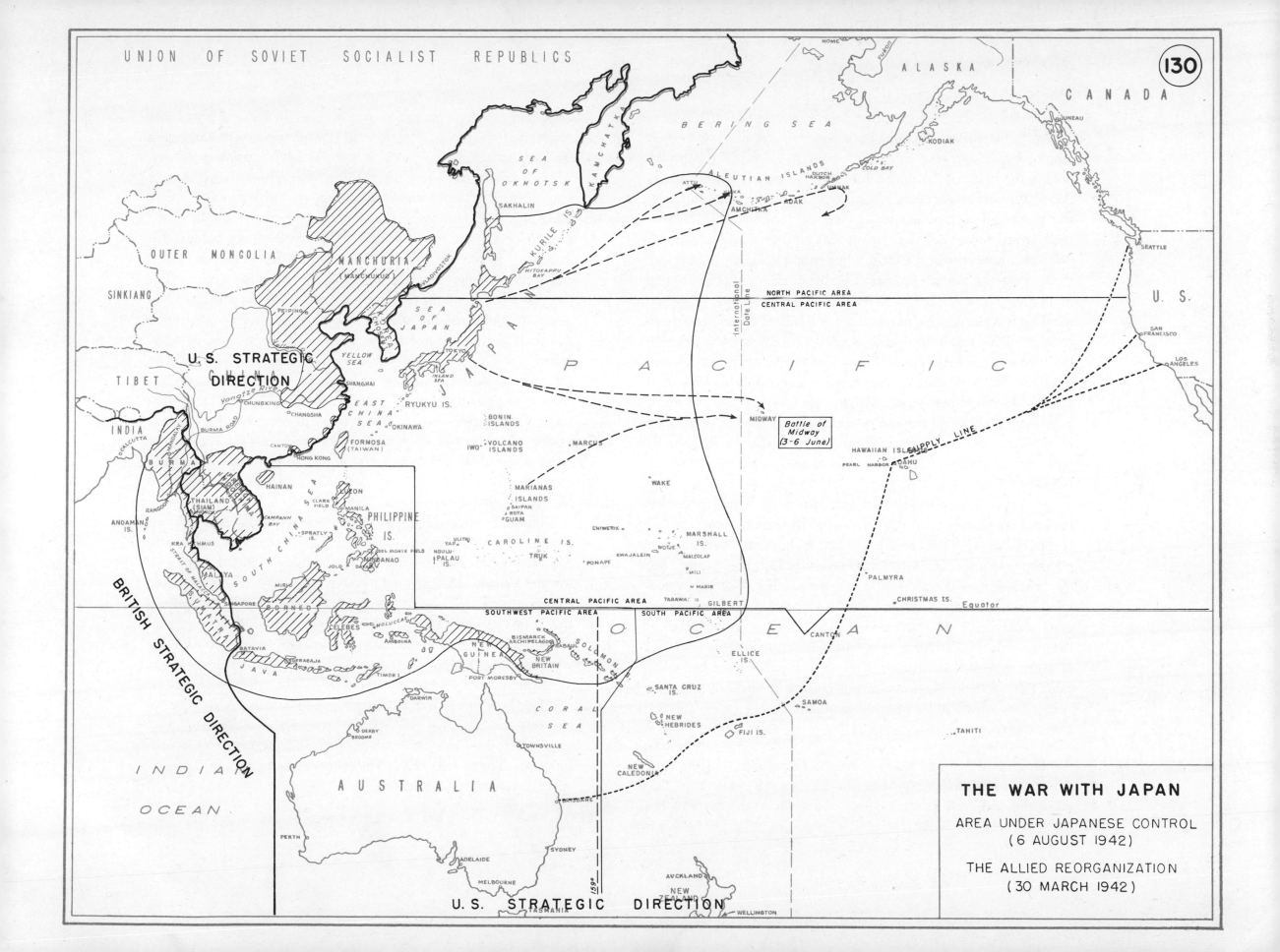

THE WAR WITH JAPAN

AREA UNDER JAPANESE CONTROL
(6 AUGUST 1942)

THE ALLIED REORGANIZATION
(30 MARCH 1942)

The Japanese wave of conquest had come on in full flood to Midway; thereafter, it could only ebb. On the map, their new empire looked impressive; in cold actuality, it was a patchwork imperium, built of far more ramshackle materials than either Allied or Japanese leaders recognized. To begin with, Japanese war plans had been predicated upon a short, limited war. Neither their armed forces nor their armament industry had been organized for a long war of attrition. (For example, Japan had begun the war with an aircraft industry capable of doing little more than maintaining her air force at its prewar strength, let alone expanding it.) Her merchant marine was weak; it could manage its mission of hauling troops and supplies on outbound voyages to her far-flung perimeter, and of returning loaded with the raw materials so badly needed by Japanese industry, only so long as it suffered merely minor losses. Finally, the loss of the big carriers, with their planes and trained pilots, had abruptly thrown Japan on the defensive on its ocean front. New ships would have to be built, which meant a hopeless race against superior American industry.

However, there remained one front where the Japanese felt capable of continuing their offensive—the Bismarck–New Guinea–Solomons area. They could no longer hope to launch their planned operation against New Caledonia, Fiji, and Samoa, but the possession of Port Moresby and the southern Solomons now was even more important. From such bases, their land-based aircraft could strike at the American supply line to Australia, or at Allied counteroffensives in that area. Consequently, the overland advance against Port Moresby (*see text, map 129*) began. At the same time, airfield construction was pushed throughout this area; one of the new fields was located on Guadalcanal (*see map 132, lower right*).

The Allied build-up in the Pacific had been rapid. Most of the Australian troops serving in the Middle East were ordered home; Australia and New Zealand raised new forces. American troops and planes likewise poured in. Approximately four times as many Americans went to the Pacific as to Europe in early 1942, despite the fact that Germany had been proclaimed the primary enemy. This diversion of troops involved an even greater diversion of scarce shipping, since to land and support an American unit in Australia took over twice the ship tonnage that a similar force bound for Europe would require. The driving force behind this American mustering was the United States Navy, as personified by Admiral King. Through long years of planning and service, the Navy had come to regard the Pacific as its own theater and any war against the Japanese as its particular war. To wage such a war, it wanted an immediate, massive concentration of army troops and aircraft, even if this meant the delay of the European offensive against Germany. Army planners, generally speaking, were willing to oppose any further Japanese advances which might imperil American interests, but wished to commit only the necessary minimum of ground and air forces. The Navy pressed for more aggressive operations—the Japanese must be constantly engaged and kept off-balance until the United States was ready to launch its major Pacific offensive.

This difference of opinion was further perplexed by irritations resulting from the division of the Pacific into two major commands. MacArthur was emotionally, as well as geographically, oriented toward a campaign that would involve the early liberation of the Philippines. The Navy, following its prewar planning, visualized the coming major Pacific offensive as driving due west from Hawaii. MacArthur and Nimitz were in constant competition for whatever forces were available; each regarded his area as the vital one.

This lack of unity of command was to confuse American operations in the Pacific. Nevertheless, considering the powerful interests and personalities involved, it is difficult to see how such unity could have been achieved. Fortunately, the enemy was even more divided in his counsels.

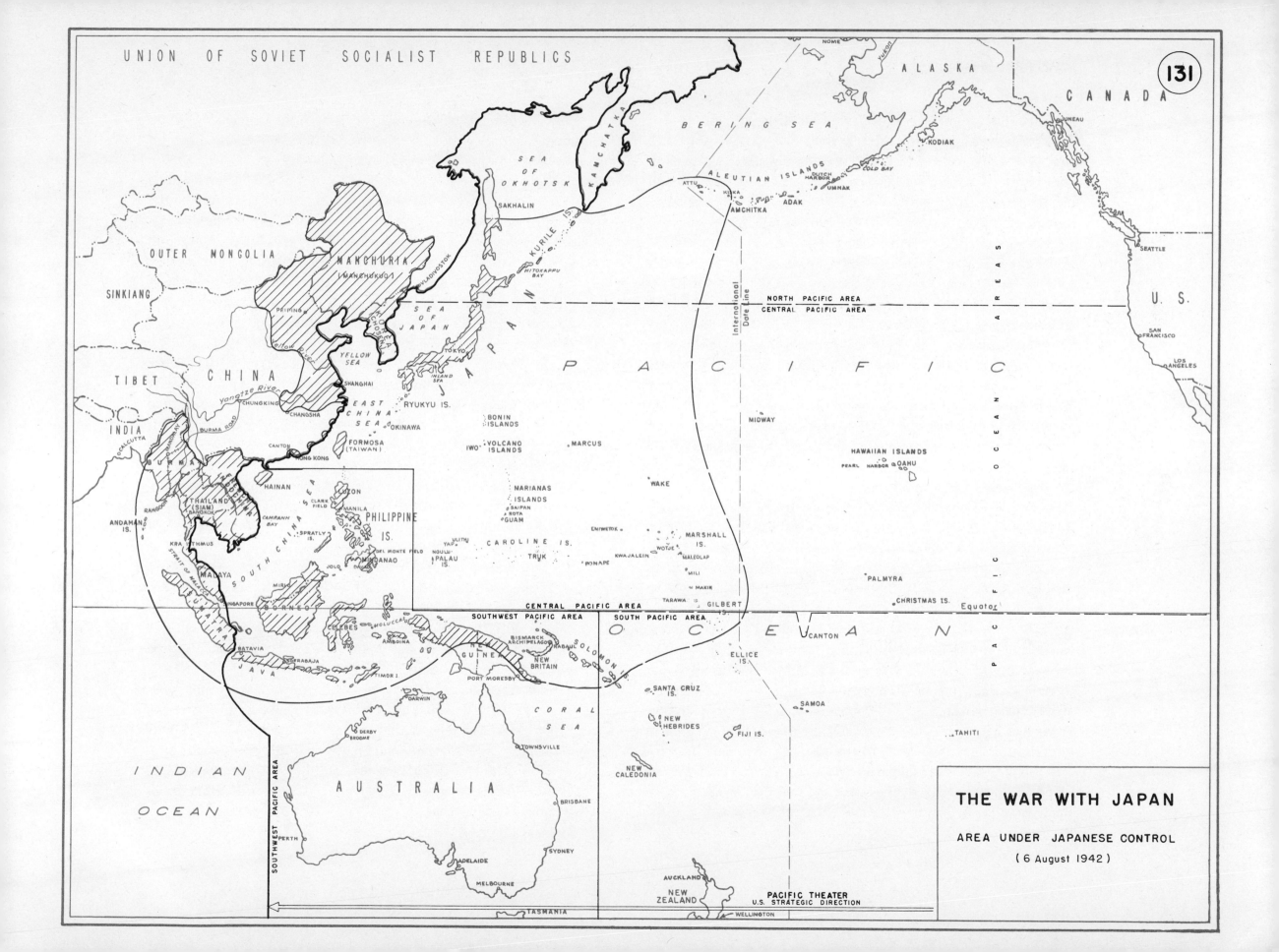

THE WAR WITH JAPAN

AREA UNDER JAPANESE CONTROL

(6 August 1942)

In demanding prompt offensive action in the Pacific, the United States Navy was only preaching what it had already practiced. Shortly after Pearl Harbor, it had used its few available ships in raids against Japanese-held islands in the central Pacific. Though these did the Japanese no appreciable damage, they were valuable training exercises in the handling of carrier task forces and had an excellent effect upon American public morale. In the Battles of the Coral Sea and Midway, American fleets had closed boldly with stronger Japanese naval forces.

After Midway, for the first time since Pearl Harbor, the Americans possessed a degree of naval superiority in the Pacific. This superiority was, however, so marginal that the loss of one or two aircraft carriers would come close to canceling it; consequently, the Navy could not yet launch its long-planned major Pacific offensive. American planners therefore sought to develop an operation by which the modest forces at their disposal could inflict maximum punishment upon the Japanese, while improving the over-all Allied strategic position in the Pacific.

King and MacArthur urged an offensive in the Bismarck–New Guinea–Solomons area to destroy the growing Japanese threat to the American supply line to Australia. But, aside from agreeing that such action would be desirable and should be taken as soon as possible, the Army and Navy found themselves completely at odds as to how this was to be done, and who was to do it. The Army favored a quick, direct blow at Rabaul; since the action would take place within the Southwest Pacific Area, MacArthur would naturally command the forces involved. The Navy proposed to fight its way up the Solomons, island by island, to Rabaul; since the operation would be primarily of a naval and amphibious character, Nimitz would command. (King's plan provided that Nimitz was to take over all of MacArthur's ships and aircraft; it assigned the Army the mission of garrisoning the various islands after the Navy and Marines had captured them.) General Marshall needed all his tact and patience to reach a solution, placed as he was between the outraged MacArthur and the irascible King. On 2 July, he and King finally signed a joint directive, ordering that an offensive be mounted at once to seize the New Britain–New Guinea–New Ireland area.

This offensive was to consist of three "tasks." The first—to be carried out by Vice Adm. Robert L. Ghormley, commanding the South Pacific Area—would be the seizure of the Santa Cruz Islands (off map, bottom right corner), Tulagi (lower right), and adjacent islands. This would begin as soon as possible after 1 August. Ghormley would be reinforced by some of MacArthur's aircraft and warships; other aircraft from Australian bases would interdict Japanese air and naval activity west of Ghormley's objectives.

MacArthur would take command for Task Two (the seizure of the rest of the Solomons, Lae and Salamaua [left center], and the northwest coast of New Guinea [off map, west]) and Task Three (the capture of the Rabaul area). The Joint Chiefs of Staff reserved the authority to withdraw any naval units after the completion of any phase of the operation, in case the carriers were in jeopardy or an emergency developed elsewhere. Finally, the boundary between the Southwest and South Pacific Areas (see map 130) was shifted westward to facilitate Ghormley's control of Task One.

Both Ghormley and MacArthur objected that this offensive was being launched too soon with insufficient forces, but the discovery that the Japanese were building an airfield on Guadalcanal caused the JCS to reject their protests. Preparations were rushed, and shipping was in short supply. As a result, D-Day had to be postponed until 7 August.

Ghormley organized his forces into three major commands: the supporting land-based aircraft; the Amphibious Force (a convoy—carrying the reinforced 1st Marine Division—and its escort, fire support group, and mine sweepers); and the Air Support Force (three aircraft carriers and their escorting battleship, cruisers, and destroyers). Early on 7 August, this armada approached Guadalcanal.

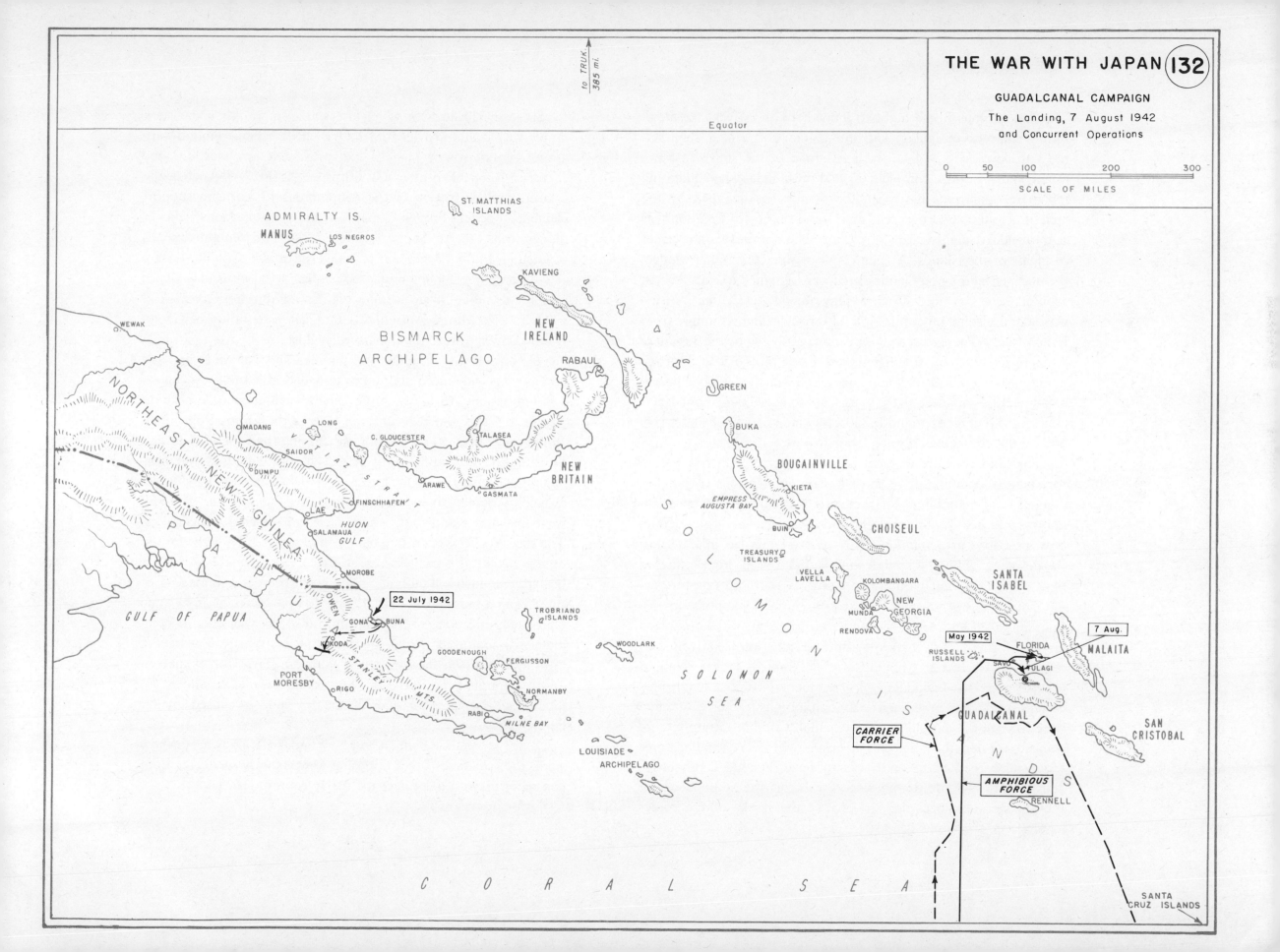

0   50   100   200   300
SCALE OF MILES

to TRUK.
385 mi.

Equator

ST. MATTHIAS
ISLANDS

ADMIRALTY IS.
MANUS   LOS NEGROS

KAVIENG

BISMARCK
ARCHIPELAGO

NEW
IRELAND

WEWAK

RABAUL

GREEN

MADANG   LONG

NORTHEAST   NEW   GUINEA

SAIDOR

C. GLOUCESTER   TALASEA

BUKA

BOUGAINVILLE

DUMPU

VITIAZ STRAIT

KIETA

PAPUA

ARAWE   GASMATA

NEW
BRITAIN

EMPRESS
AUGUSTA BAY

LAE   FINSCHHAFEN

HUON
SALAMAUA   GULF

BUIN

CHOISEUL

TREASURY
ISLANDS

MOROBE

S   O   L   O   M   O   N

SANTA
ISABEL

VELLA
LAVELLA

KOLOMBANGARA

22 July 1942

TROBRIAND
ISLANDS

MUNDA

NEW
GEORGIA

OWEN

GONA   BUNA

KOKODA

RENDOVA

May 1942   7 Aug.

FLORIDA

MALAITA

GOODENOUGH

FERGUSSON

WOODLARK

RUSSELL
ISLANDS

SAVO   TULAGI

STANLEY

PORT
MORESBY

RIGO

MTS.

NORMANBY

S   O   L   O   M   O   N

I

GUADALCANAL

SAN
CRISTOBAL

RABI

MILNE BAY

S   E   A

S

CARRIER
FORCE

GULF OF PAPUA

LOUISIADE
ARCHIPELAGO

N

D

AMPHIBIOUS
FORCE

S

RENNELL

C   O   R   A   L   S   E   A

SANTA
CRUZ ISLANDS

The Amphibious Force had two immediate objectives: the small island complex of Tulagi-Tanambogo-Gavutu, which sheltered the best-developed and largest anchorage in the southern Solomons, and the still incomplete airfield on Guadalcanal. Planning for these operations had been thoroughly handicapped by the lack of adequate hydrographic charts and maps. Information was scanty and frequently erroneous, even when obtained from former residents of the islands. As one result of this lack of knowledge, the marines landing on Guadalcanal were assigned Mount Austen (*lower center*) as one of their D-Day objectives. (Mount Austen was actually some nine miles inland through tangled jungle from Beach Red.) There was equal misinformation as to the Japanese strength in this area. Intelligence estimates placed it at approximately 7,000, 5,000 of whom were believed to be on Guadalcanal. Actual Japanese strength appears to have been about 1,500 men in the Tulagi area and 2,230 on Guadalcanal; of these, 600 and 1,700, respectively, were labor troops.

The Solomons are tropical islands, covered with heavy rain forests, and combining the most unpleasant features of jungles, swamps, and mountains. Their climate is dominated by heat, humidity, and heavy rain; malaria and dengue fever are endemic; skin infections are common. Only native trails led inland from the beaches, though Guadalcanal had a rough track running through the coconut plantations along its northern coast.

Since this operation would require several simultaneous assault landings, Maj. Gen. Alexander A. Vandegrift had organized his 1st Marine Division and its attached units into relatively self-contained task forces. Combat Groups A and B (these "combat groups" were the equivalent of a regimental combat team, plus certain specialized units such as an amphibious tractor company) were to seize the airfield on Guadalcanal. Combat Group C (*not shown*) formed the division's floating reserve. A smaller force (four reinforced battalions) was to seize Tulagi, Tanambogo, and Gavutu. (Some dominating terrain on the south coast of Florida was also occupied, to protect the flanks of the forces landing on the three islands.)

Since the haste with which the whole operation had gotten under way—plus providential bad weather which blinded Japanese reconnaissance planes—had prevented any warning, the Japanese were taken utterly by surprise. At 0613, 7 August, the cruisers and destroyers of the Amphibious Force's fire support elements opened fire on Japanese shore installations; carrier planes from the Air Support Force, which had remained south of Guadalcanal (*see map 132*), joined the attack. Combat Group A (*this map*) began an unopposed landing at Beach Red at 0650; at 0930, Combat Group B followed, passing through Group A at 1115 to seize Mount Austen. About 1330, a battalion of Group A moved west toward the Ilu River. By dusk, each group—its men heavily loaded with weapons and supplies, short of water and salt tablets—had advanced about a mile. General Vandegrift, realizing that Mount Austen was too distant, thereupon ordered both groups to attack the next morning to seize the Lunga Point area Jumping off at 0930 on the 8th, the marines had the airfield and the situation well in hand by 1600. The outnumbered Japanese had offered only the slightest resistance before fleeing, leaving the airfield undamaged and abandoning large quantities of food, weapons, and equipment. There were no American casualties. The success of this operation had been dimmed only by the failure of the logistical arrangements at Beach Red, where a lack of beach personnel and suitable landing craft left the unloading of supplies in a muddle. The result was that the beach soon became congested, and none of the waiting transports was able to completely discharge its cargo—a state of affairs that was to have a grim aftermath on the 9th, when Japanese naval forces arrived and precipitated the Battle of Savo Island (*see text, map 134*). Small-scale Japanese air raids on the 7th and 8th caused further delay.

But, for the time being, General Vandegrift, unaware of how small the Japanese forces opposing him actually were, set up a perimeter defense to protect the newly captured airfield.

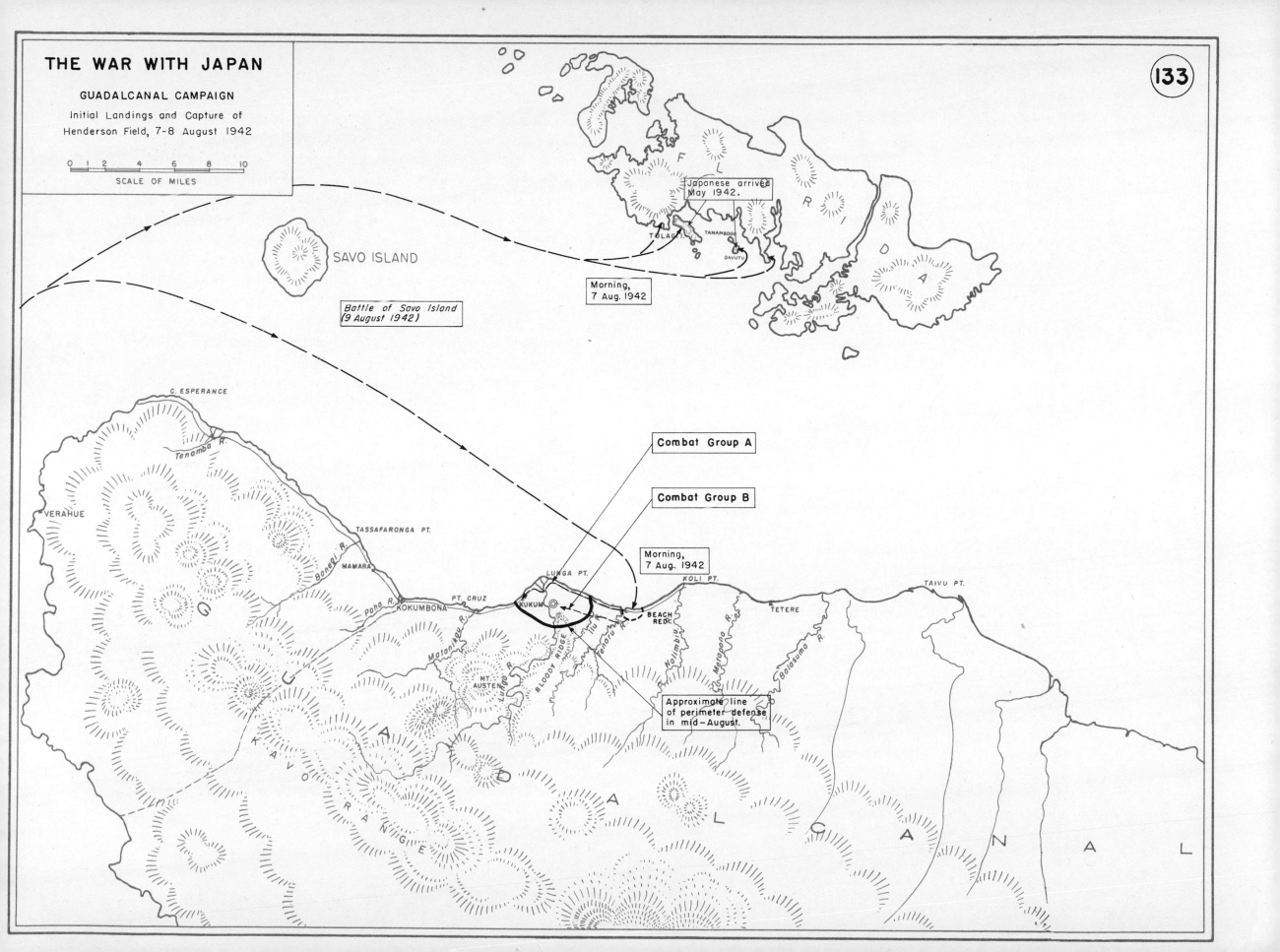

THE WAR WITH JAPAN

GUADALCANAL CAMPAIGN

Initial Landings and Capture of
Henderson Field, 7-8 August 1942

```
0  1  2    4    6    8    10
SCALE OF MILES
```

133

SAVO ISLAND

*Battle of Savo Island
(9 August 1942)*

Japanese arrived
May 1942.

TULAGI   TANAMBOGO

GAVUTU

F   L   O   R   I   D   A

Morning,
7 Aug. 1942

C. ESPERANCE

Tenambo R.

VERAHUE

TASSAFARONGA PT.

Banegi R.

MAMARA

Combat Group A

Combat Group B

Morning,
7 Aug. 1942

LUNGA PT.

KOLI PT.

TAIVU PT.

Poha R.

PT. CRUZ

KOKUMBONA

KUKUM

TETERE

BEACH
RED

Matanikou R.

MT.
AUSTEN

Lunga R.

BLOODY RIDGE

Tenaru R.

Ilu R.

Nalimbu R.

Metapona R.

Balosuna R.

Approximate line
of perimeter defense
in mid-August.

K   A   V   O   R   A   N   G   E

G   U   A   D   A   L   C   A   N   A   L

On Guadalcanal, there had been little to fight besides jungle, insects, and heat; in the Tulagi area, it was different.

The assaults on Tulagi, Gavutu, and Tanambogo formed an intricate pattern—in part, because the shortage of landing craft made it impossible to attack all objectives simultaneously. The assault on the causeway-linked islands of Gavutu and Tanambogo was further complicated by offshore reefs which forced the adoption of the circuitous approach shown here.

Initially, the attack went according to plan. Elements of a re-inforced battalion (detached from the floating reserve) landed on Florida Island and seized the Haleta and Halavo peninsulas as shown. They found no Japanese (and were withdrawn in the late afternoon of 7 August). At H-Hour (0800), the Marine 1st Raider Battalion began splashing ashore on Tulagi at Beach Blue, followed by a battalion previously detached from Combat Group A. Once ashore, the Raiders pushed toward the southeastern end of the island, while the other battalion advanced toward its northwestern tip. There was little resistance at first; then, about a mile from its objective, the Raider Battalion developed an extensive system of Japanese cave and dugout positions. Here, the marines got their first lesson in the brutal facts of war in the Pacific theater: the Japanese was an expert burrower; his defenses could absorb amazing amounts of bombing and shelling; however hopeless his position, he did not surrender; and—once he was dug in—killing him was a slow and difficult job. When it became obvious that Tulagi could not be cleared before dark, the Raider Battalion set up a defensive position (*dashed red line*) across the island, holding it against several uncoordinated Japanese counterattacks during the night.

Meanwhile, the Marine 1st Parachute Battalion (serving as infantry) had cleared most of Gavutu after a stiff fight, but could not force the causeway between Gavutu and Tanambogo. The detachment that had been withdrawn from the Haleta area therefore attempted to land on the north shore of Tanambogo, but was repulsed with severe casualties.

Attacks were renewed on the morning of 8 August. Tulagi was cleared by 1500, and the last Japanese strong points on Gavutu wiped out, but Tanambogo's garrison held out until two light tanks were brought into action. American losses were reported as 144 killed and missing and 194 wounded.

So far—except for the unloading problem on Guadalcanal—the operation had been competently handled. The Japanese had launched a number of air attacks during the 7th and 8th, but—forewarned by a coastwatcher on Bougainville (*off map, northwest*)—American carrier planes and antiaircraft fire had beaten them off. Nevertheless, the expedition commander, Vice Adm. Jack Fletcher, apprehensive over the safety of his aircraft carriers, abruptly withdrew the Air Support Force southeastward on the evening of 8 August. (Fletcher had previously warned Rear Adm. Richmond K. Turner, the Amphibious Force commander, that he would withdraw the carriers before 10 August—even though Turner had protested that it would take four days to unload the transports. No one had warned Vandegrift.) Thus abandoned, Turner announced that he would be forced to withdraw the ships of the Amphibious Force on the morning of 9 August.

To increase Turner's worries, aerial reconnaissance had warned him during the day that a large Japanese naval task force was moving southward from Rabaul (*off map, northwest*). Turner's defensive dispositions for the night of the 8th were clumsy, and some of his subordinates lax. The Japanese squadron slipped through his inadequate patrols, completely surprised the unready Allied cruisers, and sank four of them in the Battle of Savo Island. Fortunately, the Japanese commander—like Fletcher—feared a possible trap; he failed to push home his attack and destroy the huddled and defenseless transports, which represented most of the available shipping in the South Pacific. Turner was tougher; regardless of the risks of further Japanese air and surface attack, he held his shattered fleet off Guadalcanal until the afternoon of the 9th, unloading what additional supplies he could.

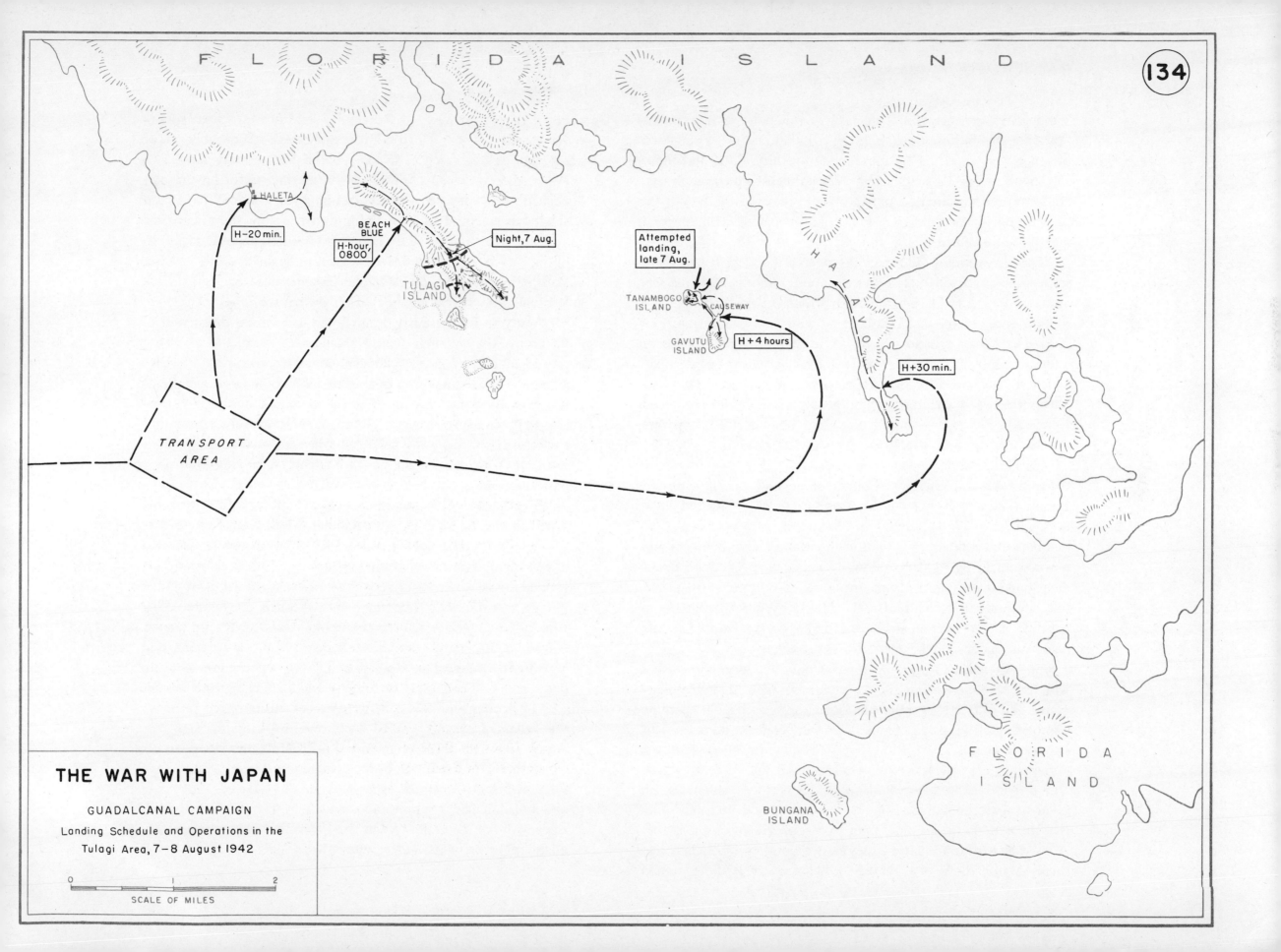

FLORIDA ISLAND

134

HALETA

H-20 min.

BEACH BLUE

H-hour, 0800

Night, 7 Aug.

TULAGI ISLAND

Attempted landing, late 7 Aug.

TANAMBOGO ISLAND

CAUSEWAY

GAVUTU ISLAND

H + 4 hours

HALAVO

H+30 min.

TRANSPORT AREA

BUNGANA ISLAND

FLORIDA ISLAND

THE WAR WITH JAPAN

GUADALCANAL CAMPAIGN

Landing Schedule and Operations in the
Tulagi Area, 7–8 August 1942

0   1   2
SCALE OF MILES

Vandegrift's marines found themselves isolated—with ammunition enough for four days of heavy combat, rations (one-third of which were captured Japanese food) for thirty days, and eighteen spools of barbed wire. Their coastal defense guns, radar sets, and heavy construction equipment were in the holds of the vanishing transports. As a climax, the fleet had departed with approximately 1,400 marines still aboard!

Though Admiral Ghormley considered Vandegrift's position serious, he approved Fletcher's premature withdrawal of the aircraft carriers, considering them too irreplaceable to risk in the routine support of the Guadalcanal garrison. He began (12 August) to get a trickle of supplies to Vandegrift by means of a few attack transports (old destroyers converted to cargo ships) which ran in and unloaded under cover of darkness. He overlooked the urgency of developing the captured airfield (renamed Henderson Field) as a base from which bombers could operate against the Rabaul area.

On Guadalcanal, meanwhile, Vandegrift put his marines on reduced rations, strengthened his defenses, and—using captured Japanese equipment—lengthened and roughly completed Henderson Field (17 August). On 20 August, Marine Corps dive bombers and fighters took station there; navy dive bombers and obsolescent army fighters followed. These fliers operated under great handicaps, Ghormley having supplied only the most primitive equipment. Planes had to be fueled by hand pumps from gasoline drums—a time-devouring and risky process when the field was under attack.

Initially, the marines experienced only a few minor clashes with the Japanese remaining on Guadalcanal, though enemy planes and warships kept the American beachhead under sporadic bombardment. Japanese commanders were concentrating on their operation against Port Moresby; the hasty withdrawal of the American fleet and the lack of air support subsequently given Vandegrift had convinced them that American operations on Guadalcanal represented only a reconnaissance in force—and that there might not be more than 1,000 Americans on the island. Almost as a routine matter, they began building up their forces there. About 18 August, the first echelon of the so-called Ichiki Force (approximately 1,000 men) landed from Japanese cruisers and destroyers near Taivu Point (*center, right*). Probably out of arrogant self-confidence, Colonel Ichiki immediately moved to attack the American position; or—a marine patrol having ambushed one of his detachments on the 19th—he may have considered it essential to seize the initiative before the Americans attacked him. Assaulting the American position behind the mouth of the Ilu River at about 0310, 21 August, he met a costly repulse. Later that morning, an American counterattack enveloped his left flank and almost annihilated his little force.

A strong Japanese naval task force had moved down well to the east of the Solomons from Rabaul on 19 August to cover the movement of a second Guadalcanal-bound troop convoy. Fletcher engaged the Japanese fleet in another long-range clash (Battle of the Eastern Solomons, 24 August) in which neither side displayed much aggressiveness. The Japanese, however, lost another carrier—a loss that was balanced when a Japanese submarine sank an American carrier on 15 September, leaving Ghormley with only one serviceable warship of that type.

By gradual infiltration, the Japanese built up a force of some 5,000 in the Taivu area, with another 1,000 near Kokumbona (*center, left*). Their commander, General Kawaguchi, planned a coordinated air-naval-ground attack on the beachhead; his ground forces would strike it on three sides, as shown. Kawaguchi put his men to work chopping a trail through the jungle to the Bloody Ridge sector (*lower center*) of Vandegrift's perimeter. Native scouts, patrols, and aircraft detected the movement, and Vandegrift stationed his Raiders and paratroopers (now consolidated into one battalion) on Bloody Ridge. Kawaguchi's assault (13-14 September) was a masterpiece of mismanaged ferocity: the Japanese aircraft arrived early and did little damage; the attack across the Ilu River withered in front of the American defenses there; the assault on Bloody Ridge was beaten off in savage night fighting; the attack from Kokumbona arrived a day late and failed quickly; supporting Japanese warships shot at both sides with fine impartiality. On the 14th, the Japanese retreated, abandoning weapons and equipment.

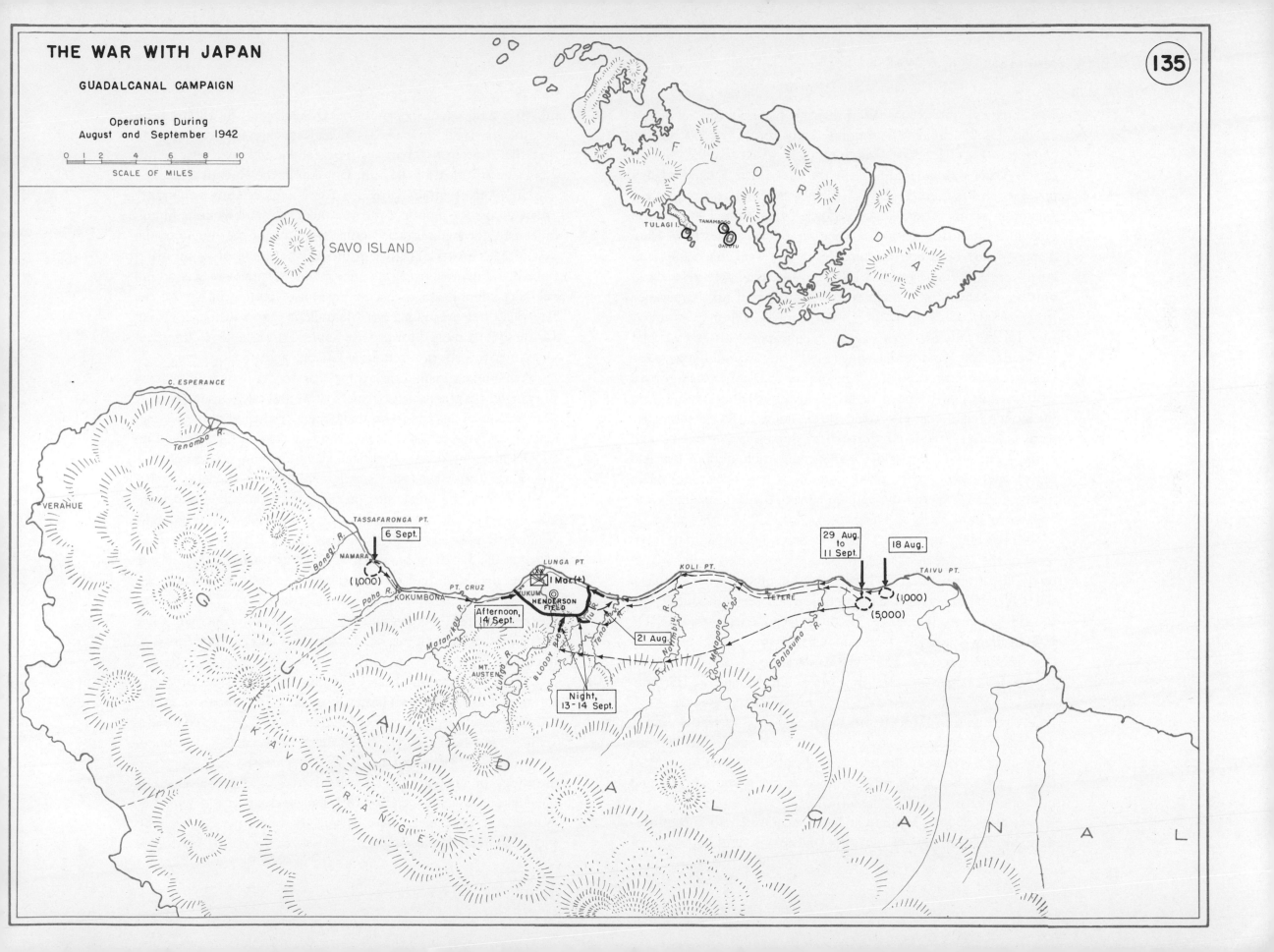

135

THE WAR WITH JAPAN

GUADALCANAL CAMPAIGN

Operations During
August and September 1942

0 1 2 4 6 8 10
SCALE OF MILES

SAVO ISLAND

FLORIDA

TULAGI
TANAMBOGO
GAVUTU

C. ESPERANCE

Tenambo R.

VERAHUE

Bonegi R.

TASSAFARONGA PT.

6 Sept.

MAMARA

(1,000)

Poha R.

KOKUMBONA

PT. CRUZ

LUNGA PT

I Mar. (+)

KUKUM

HENDERSON FIELD

Afternoon,
14 Sept.

KOLI PT.

29 Aug.
to
11 Sept.

18 Aug.

TAIVU PT.

TETERE

(1,000)

(5,000)

Matanikau R.

MT. AUSTEN

Lunga R.

BLOODY RIDGE

Tenaru R.

21 Aug.

Nalimbiu R.

Metapona R.

Balasuna R.

G   U   A   D   A   L   C   A   N   A   L

KAVO RANGE

Night,
13-14 Sept.

The Japanese now reconsidered their problems in the Southwest Pacific. Guadalcanal was draining away forces needed for the capture of Port Moresby. Therefore, General Hyakutake's Seventeenth Army was ordered to clear the island; the Japanese Navy promised full support. Through September and early October, Japanese troops moved steadily down from Rabaul to land on Guadalcanal during the night, when American planes from Henderson Field could not interfere. Since the weakened American naval forces seldom ventured into the Solomons area after dark, only one convoy was intercepted (Battle of Cape Esperance [*upper left*]). This method of reinforcement, however, was too slow for the Japanese, who began a determined effort to knock out Henderson Field so that they could bring in and unload large cargo vessels during the day. Air and naval bombardments were reinforced by newly landed Japanese medium artillery, firing from the Kokumbona area. (Fortunately, Japanese artillery techniques were primitive.) A bombardment by Japanese battleships and cruisers during the nights of 13-14 October actually put the field out of operation, but the few remaining planes—operating off a newly opened grass runway and fueled with the last gasoline available—somehow remained in action.

Meanwhile, the 7th Marine Regiment (the remaining regiment of the 1st Marine Division) was put ashore on Guadalcanal on 18 September, along with considerable quantities of supplies, the first reinforcements and ammunition Vandegrift had received. On 13 October, the 164th Infantry Regiment (Americal Division) likewise arrived. (Ghormley had wanted to use any available ground forces to establish a new base in the Santa Cruz Islands [*off map, southeast*], but Maj. Gen. Millard F. Harmon, who commanded the Army forces in the South Pacific Area, finally persuaded him to reinforce Guadalcanal instead.) Knowing that this regiment was en route, Vandegrift extended his perimeter to command the mouth of the steep-banked Matanikau River (*center, left*), the only point where heavy equipment could be gotten across it.

By mid-October, Hyakutake had concentrated all of the Japanese 2d Division, part of the 38th Division, several battalions of infantry, and a tank company on Guadalcanal; in addition, he had the survivors of Ichiki's and Kawaguchi's forces. Believing that the American forces on the island numbered only about 7,500, he left most of the 38th Division in the Rabaul area.

His plan of attack provided for a tank-infantry secondary attack across the mouth of the Matanikau to seize Kukum. Simultaneously, the main attack would strike out of the jungle to the east of Mt. Austen. (Either in the original plan, or as an afterthought—Japanese accounts are extremely vague—a second enveloping column was given the mission of cutting in behind the American defenses along the Matanikau.) Meanwhile, a strong Japanese fleet moved toward the Santa Cruz Islands to intercept any American effort to reinforce Guadalcanal.

Hyakutake's main attack forces had to cut their way through the jungle; progress was extremely slow, and all weapons heavier than machine guns had to be abandoned; contact with the secondary attack force seems to have been lost. The latter attacked on 23 October, hit strong American defenses, and was butchered. The main force (and the smaller column on its left) finally emerged from the jungle late on the 24th. It attacked that night and the next, was defeated, and staggered back into the jungle. Vandegrift now advanced toward the Poha River (*center, left*) to force the Japanese back out of artillery range of the airfield, but this operation had to be suspended to mop up some 1,500 Japanese who landed near Tetere on 2 November. The Japanese fleet, meanwhile, had met and defeated a weaker American force north of the Santa Cruz Islands on 26 October, but failed to pursue.

Subsequent action around Guadalcanal consisted largely of a series of naval and air clashes, brought on by Japanese efforts to land more troops. A series of clashes from 12 through 15 November (Battle of Guadalcanal) ended in the defeat of a major Japanese task force and the destruction of the convoy it was covering. In another night clash (Battle of Tassafaronga, 30 November), a small squadron of Japanese destroyers defeated an American cruiser task force. During this same period, elements of the 2d Marine and Americal Divisions reinforced Vandegrift.

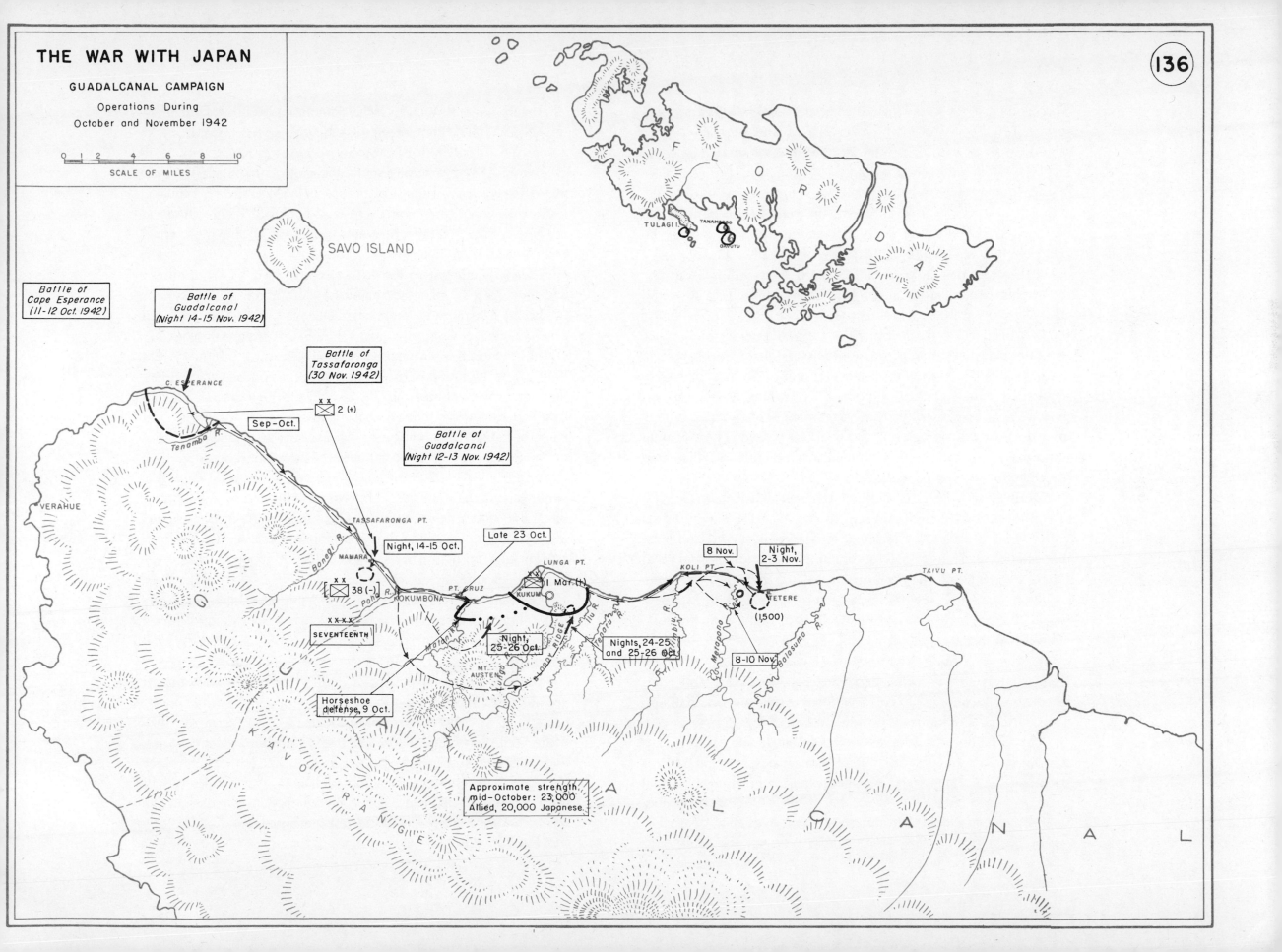

THE WAR WITH JAPAN

GUADALCANAL CAMPAIGN

Operations During
October and November 1942

0 1 2 4 6 8 10
SCALE OF MILES

136

FLORIDA

TULAGI
TANAMBOGO
GAVUTU

SAVO ISLAND

Battle of
Cape Esperance
(11-12 Oct. 1942)

Battle of
Guadalcanal
(Night 14-15 Nov. 1942)

Battle of
Tassafaronga
(30 Nov. 1942)

Battle of
Guadalcanal
(Night 12-13 Nov. 1942)

C. ESPERANCE

Tenamba R.

Sep-Oct.

XX
2 (+)

VERAHUE

TASSAFARONGA PT.

Bonegi R.

MAMARA

Night, 14-15 Oct.

Late 23 Oct.

LUNGA PT.

8 Nov.

Night,
2-3 Nov.

TAIVU PT.

KOLI PT.

Poha R.

PT. CRUZ

KOKUMBONA

XX
38 (-)

XXXX
SEVENTEENTH

KUKUM

XX
1 Mar (+)

Tiu R.

Night,
25-26 Oct.

BLOODY RIDGE

MT.
AUSTEN

Nights, 24-25
and 25-26 Oct.

Metapona R.

TETERE
(1,500)

8-10 Nov.

Balasuna R.

Horseshoe
defense, 9 Oct.

KAVO RANGE

G   U   A   D   A   L   C   A   N   A   L

Approximate strength,
mid-October: 23,000
Allied, 20,000 Japanese.

The opening of the Guadalcanal campaign coincided with preparations for the invasion of North Africa and the build-up of American air power in England. As the situation on Guadalcanal and New Guinea worsened, King, MacArthur, and Harmon called for additional reinforcements, especially aircraft, for the Pacific. This led to a long controversy over the priorities to be assigned the various theaters, the Navy demanding that the Pacific be reinforced, if need be, at the expense of the other theaters. The crisis raised by the Japanese Seventeenth Army offensive in October tipped the decision in favor of the Pacific. The 25th and 43d Divisions were ordered to the South Pacific Area; Nimitz sent all available aircraft from the Central Pacific; and repair work on damaged warships was speeded up. On 18 October, Vice Adm. William F. Halsey replaced Ghormley. Great efforts were made to secure sufficient shipping. Meanwhile, Vandegrift repulsed Hyakutake, the Japanese Navy failed to press its advantage after the Battle of Santa Cruz, and the crisis passed. The incoming reinforcements and supplies created a mammoth logistical jam throughout the South Pacific's rudimentary ports.

During early December, the 1st Marine Division was withdrawn from Guadalcanal and sent to Australia for rehabilitation (after which it was to be assigned to MacArthur, who had been requesting a division trained for amphibious operations). General Patch, commanding the Americal Division, took over the command on Guadalcanal with the mission to "eliminate all Japanese forces" there. His forces (reorganized on 2 January as the XIV Corps) consisted of the Americal, 2d Marine, and 25th Divisions, plus some smaller units. Allied air strength had increased, Henderson Field was being expanded and improved, and additional air strips were under construction at Koli Point and Kukum. The logistical situation was gradually improving.

The situation of the Japanese had grown steadily worse. Furtive night runs by destroyers and submarines brought only a trickle of replacements and supplies; disease and hunger riddled them. By December, they were incapable of offensive action, but—to the end—held their defenses with a fatalistic bravery.

Patch planned to capture the dominating terrain of Mt. Austen immediately. That accomplished, one division would move across the ridges from Mt. Austen to envelop Kokumbona, another would drive westward along the shore, and the third would guard the airfields. Initial operations (17 December–3 January; *not shown*) by the Americal Division pocketed the Japanese in the Mt. Austen area, where troops from the 25th Division wiped them out (10-23 January).

Meanwhile, most of the 25th Division (Maj. Gen. Collins) had moved off in the attack against Kokumbona, while elements of the 2d Marine and Americal Divisions passed through each other in successive attacks down the coastal trail. The 25th Division reached the sea west of Kokumbona on 23 January, but only a few Japanese were trapped, and it soon became evident that they were retreating toward Cape Esperance. Though troubled by reports that another Japanese force was massing at Rabaul, Patch sent a reinforced regiment toward Cape Esperance in pursuit, while a reinforced battalion was embarked on landing craft and landed at Verahue (*left center*) to drive on Cape Esperance from the southwest. The two columns met on 9 February, but found only a few stragglers. The Japanese Navy had carried out a brilliant evacuation during the nights of 1, 4, and 7 February, picking up between 11,000 and 13,000 troops at Cape Esperance, despite air attacks.

Guadalcanal was the first major defeat the Japanese Army had suffered. For the Americans, it was an operation launched on the proverbial shoestring—one that could have easily been a disastrous failure. That it was not was due in large measure to Japanese mistakes. Possessing a definite preponderance in air, ground, and naval strength in the beginning, they had never brought it to bear effectively. Strategically and tactically, they committed their forces piecemeal, failed to exploit their victories, and persisted stubbornly in their misconceptions. Their Navy expected their Army to recover Guadalcanal—yet it failed to halt the build-up of American ground forces on that island, with the result that they always outnumbered the Japanese.

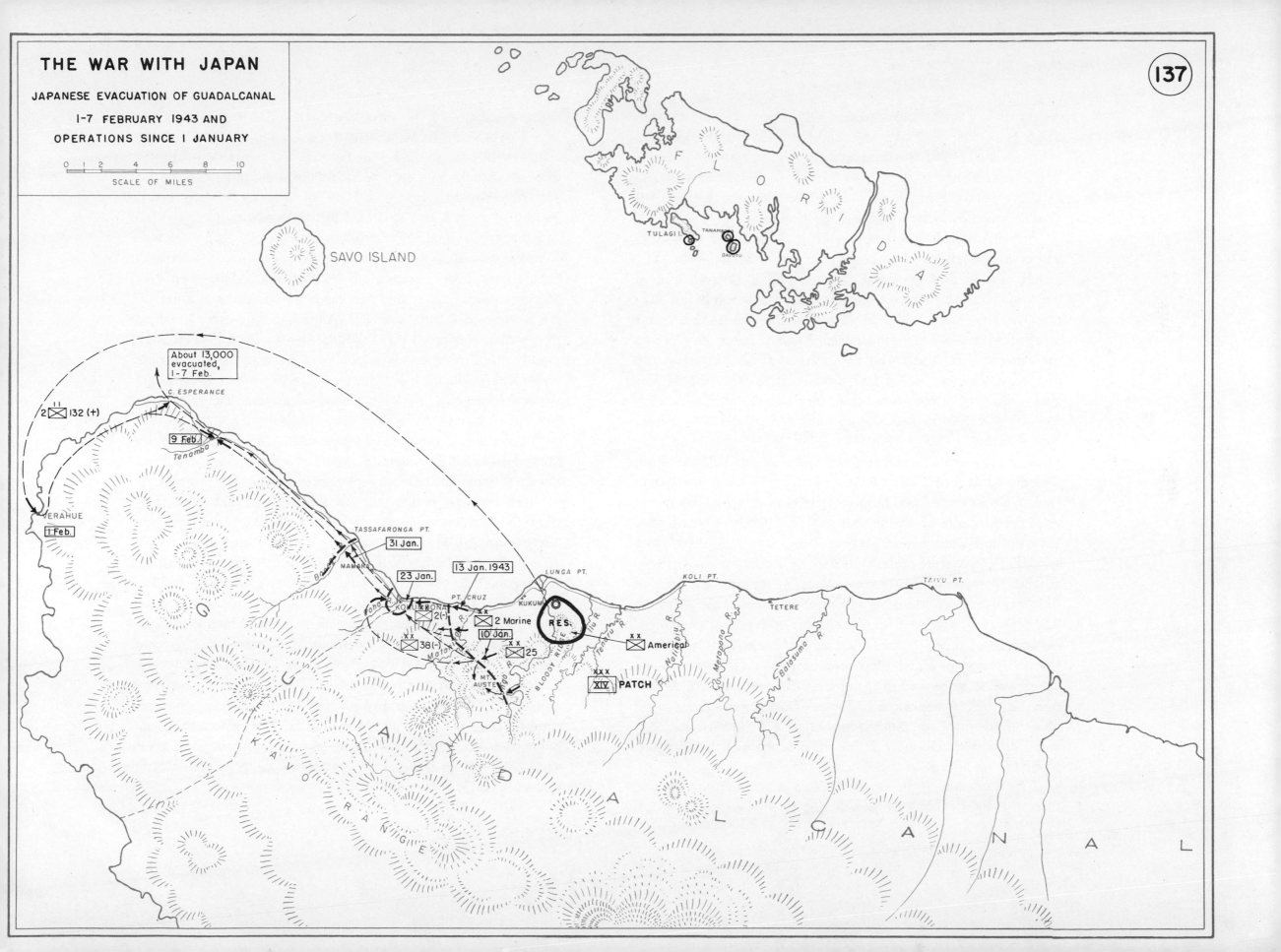

THE WAR WITH JAPAN

JAPANESE EVACUATION OF GUADALCANAL
1-7 FEBRUARY 1943 AND
OPERATIONS SINCE 1 JANUARY

0 1 2   4   6   8   10
SCALE OF MILES

137

SAVO ISLAND

FLORIDA

TULAGI I.   TANAMBOGO
GAVUTU

About 13,000
evacuated,
1-7 Feb.

C. ESPERANCE

2 ☒ 132 (+)

9 Feb.

Tenamba

VERAHUE

1 Feb.

TASSAFARONGA PT.

31 Jan.

MAMARA

Bonegi R.

23 Jan.

13 Jan. 1943

LUNGA PT.

KOLI PT.

TAIVU PT.

Poha R.

KOKUMBONA

PT. CRUZ

KUKUM

XX
2(-)

XX
2 Marine

RES.

Ilu R.

TETERE

Metapona R.

Balasuna R.

10 Jan.

XX
38(-)

Matanikau R.

XX
25

MT.
AUSTEN

Tenaru R.

Nalimbiu R.

XX
American

BLOODY RIDGE

XXX
XIV   PATCH

G U A D A L C A N A L

KAVO RANGE

As previously noted, the Japanese had occupied Lae and Salamaua (*both center, left*) in March, 1942. Having strengthened these advance bases, they prepared for an amphibious offensive, based on Rabaul, to seize Port Moresby (*bottom center*). In Japanese hands, Port Moresby would be a serious threat to the vital Brisbane-Melbourne sector of Australia.

Initial American troop movements to Australia in early 1942 had consisted largely of air corps units and their supporting elements, in the vain hope that these would enable Wavell to hold the Netherlands East Indies. These forces, plus a handful of Australian troops, were all that were available when MacArthur reached Australia (17 March) from Bataan. Later, he received the American 32d and 41st Divisions and the Australian 6th and 7th Divisions (which had been recalled from the Middle East). MacArthur considered these forces insufficient, but—even so—decided that the best way to defend Australia was to hold New Guinea.

The Japanese advance on Port Moresby was delayed about a month while their Carrier Striking Force raided into the Indian Ocean. On its return, two large carriers were detached to support the Port Moresby operation, but this first offensive was turned back in the Battle of the Coral Sea (*see map 129*). Plans for a second offensive were nullified by Japanese aircraft carrier losses at Midway. MacArthur took advantage of the time thus gained to strengthen Port Moresby and develop a new base at Milne Bay (*this map, bottom center*). With the initiation of the American offensive in the South Pacific (*see text, map 132*), he pressed the occupation of Buna (*this map, lower center*) and the development of an airfield in the adjacent Dobodura area, to support the projected attacks on Lae and Salamaua during the second phase of that offensive. Air and naval forces of MacArthur's command supported Ghormley during the first phase of the offensive, chiefly by air strikes on the Rabaul area.

The Japanese, however, forestalled him at Buna, landing there the night of 21 July and driving inland—against the desperate resistance of the tiny Australian forces in the area—to seize Kokoda and its small airstrip on 12 August. Then, to the complete surprise of Allied intelligence, the Japanese continued their advance through the wild mountains south of Kokoda. They got to within thirty miles of Port Moresby by 13 September, but Allied aircraft had disrupted their communications, and the situation of the Japanese forces on Guadalcanal had worsened. Consequently, they were recalled to Buna until the situation on Guadalcanal could be restored. As part of their drive on Port Moresby, the Japanese had also made an unsuccessful amphibious assault on Milne Bay (25 August–5 September). Allied troops then converged on the Buna area by air (airfields were rapidly improvised at Wanigela and Pongani [*both bottom center*]), by difficult mountain trails, and by small boats along the northern coast. Fighting continued around Buna from 19 November through 22 January (*see map 139*).

Elsewhere, a Japanese attempt (9-30 January; *action not shown*) to seize the mountain airfield at Wau (*center, left*) was thwarted when Australian troops were flown in at the last minute. A large Japanese convoy, bound for Lae and Salamaua, was shattered (*action not shown*) by Allied aircraft in the Bismarck Sea during 2-4 March. From June through September, MacArthur cleared the Lae-Salamaua area by feinting an attack on the Japanese forces at Salamaua and then seizing Lae behind them with a skillful converging airborne-amphibious-ground attack. Exploiting his success, he next seized the Huon Peninsula.

Meanwhile, amphibious operations, as shown, had covered the north flank of the Allied advance. On 26 December, the rehabilitated 1st Marine Division seized Cape Gloucester, and army units occupied Long Island (*both center*), threatening communications between Rabaul and New Guinea. Throughout this campaign, the Allied air forces did magnificent work in gaining air superiority and in transporting troops and supplies across New Guinea's jungle mountains.

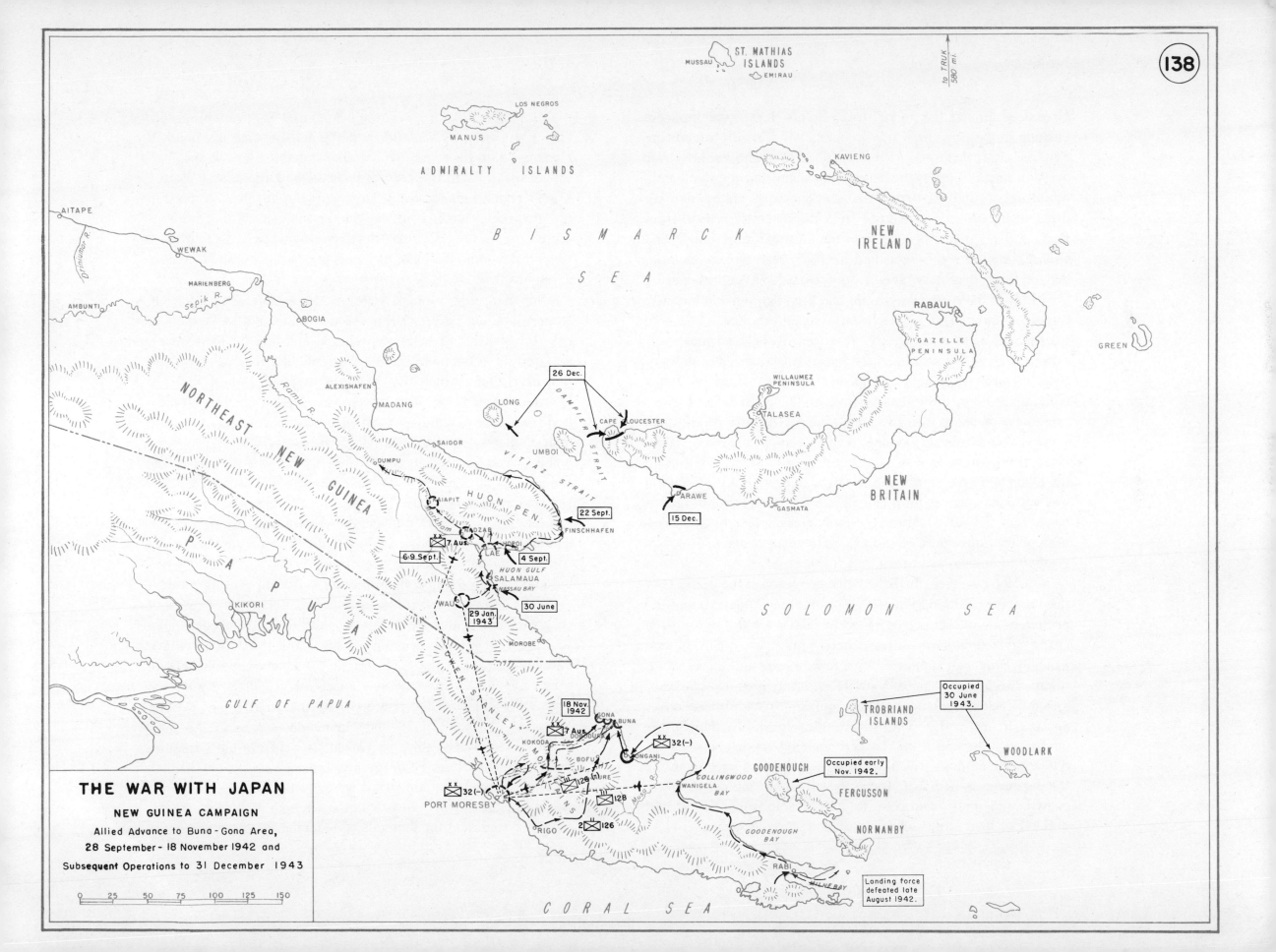

THE WAR WITH JAPAN

NEW GUINEA CAMPAIGN

Allied Advance to Buna-Gona Area,
28 September - 18 November 1942 and
Subsequent Operations to 31 December 1943

0   25   50   75   100   125   150

Organized around the major strong points shown, the Japanese position in the Buna area was a complex of mutually supporting bunkers, concealed by dense tropical vegetation and sited to cover every avenue of approach. Its garrison numbered approximately 6,500—about half of them exhausted survivors of the abortive drive on Port Moresby, the rest fresh troops newly arrived from Rabaul. This area was a hot and humid mixture of jungle and swamp, infested with insects and leeches. Scrub typhus, malaria, dengue fever, dysentery, and skin infections were endemic.

Many of the Australian troops had been fighting continuously for two months. The 32d Division went into its first battle here with many of its men already weakened by sickness and short rations. Practically untrained for jungle warfare, it was short of both engineer equipment and medical supplies. Initially, it was without artillery, until the Australians loaned it several guns; eventually, one of its own howitzers was sent forward. Its logistical support was extremely sketchy. At first, supplies came by small boats from Milne Bay or were air-dropped. Later, airstrips in the Dobodura area (*lower center*) were utilized, but the situation was never satisfactory until late December, when small freighters began bulk deliveries. An early supply crisis, created when Japanese planes sank most of the available small boats (16-17 November), handicapped operations for weeks.

On 18 November, the Allied advance reached the outposts of the Japanese position. The next morning they attacked, and immediately found themselves halted by heavy fire from an unseen enemy. Allied infantry—armed only with rifles, grenades, and machine guns, and supported by a few mortars and pieces of artillery—were thrust against a strong, carefully prepared defensive system. Lack of training and the confusing terrain made direct air support ineffective. The Navy refused to risk its ships in the uncharted waters off Buna. Lateral communications between the different Allied units was blocked by swamps and streams, while the Japanese shifted their forces swiftly along the coastal trail, or by landing craft from point to point. Radio equipment proved unreliable; losses and sickness mounted; morale sagged.

Maj. Gen. Edwin F. Harding organized his available forces (the 127th Infantry was still en route, and Lt. Gen. Edmund F. Herring had transferred two battalions of the 126th to the Australian sector) into two combat teams—the Urbana and Warren Forces (*note, bottom right*). He could gain but little ground; in the Australian zone, however, one of the American battalions scored the first appreciable Allied success when it established a roadblock behind the forward Japanese position on 30 November as shown.

Impatient for a quick victory, MacArthur sent Lt. Gen. Robert L. Eichelberger to Buna to take command of the American forces there. Eichelberger relieved Harding (2 December), replaced the commanders of the Warren and Urbana Forces, and put Brig. Gen. Albert W. Waldron in command of the 32d Division. Eichelberger was an aggressive leader, but he also profited from the gradual improvement taking place in the logistical system, the fact that the surviving Allied troops were becoming combat veterans, and the inroads starvation was making in the Japanese ranks. During a generally unsuccessful attack on 5 December, a platoon of the Urbana Force penetrated to the sea east of Buna. On 9 December, the Australians stormed Gona. The decisive attack, however, was launched on the 18th in the Cape Endaiadere sector, Warren Force being reinforced by two battalions of fresh Australian infantry and eight Australian light tanks. The tanks cracked line after line of bunkers in a series of coordinated assaults. By 3 January, the Buna-Endaiadere area was pinched out between this advance and the Urbana Force (now reinforced by the 127th Infantry), which had punched another corridor to the sea on 29 December. Subsequently, the Australian 7th Division, reinforced by the 163d Infantry (41st Division), finished clearing the Sanananda area by 22 January.

It was a costly campaign: in addition to normal casualties (Australian and American, 8,546; Japanese, probably 13,000-15,000), some 2,334 Americans were disabled by disease. But it was also educational—as to both the strength of a Japanese defensive system and the methods of reducing it.

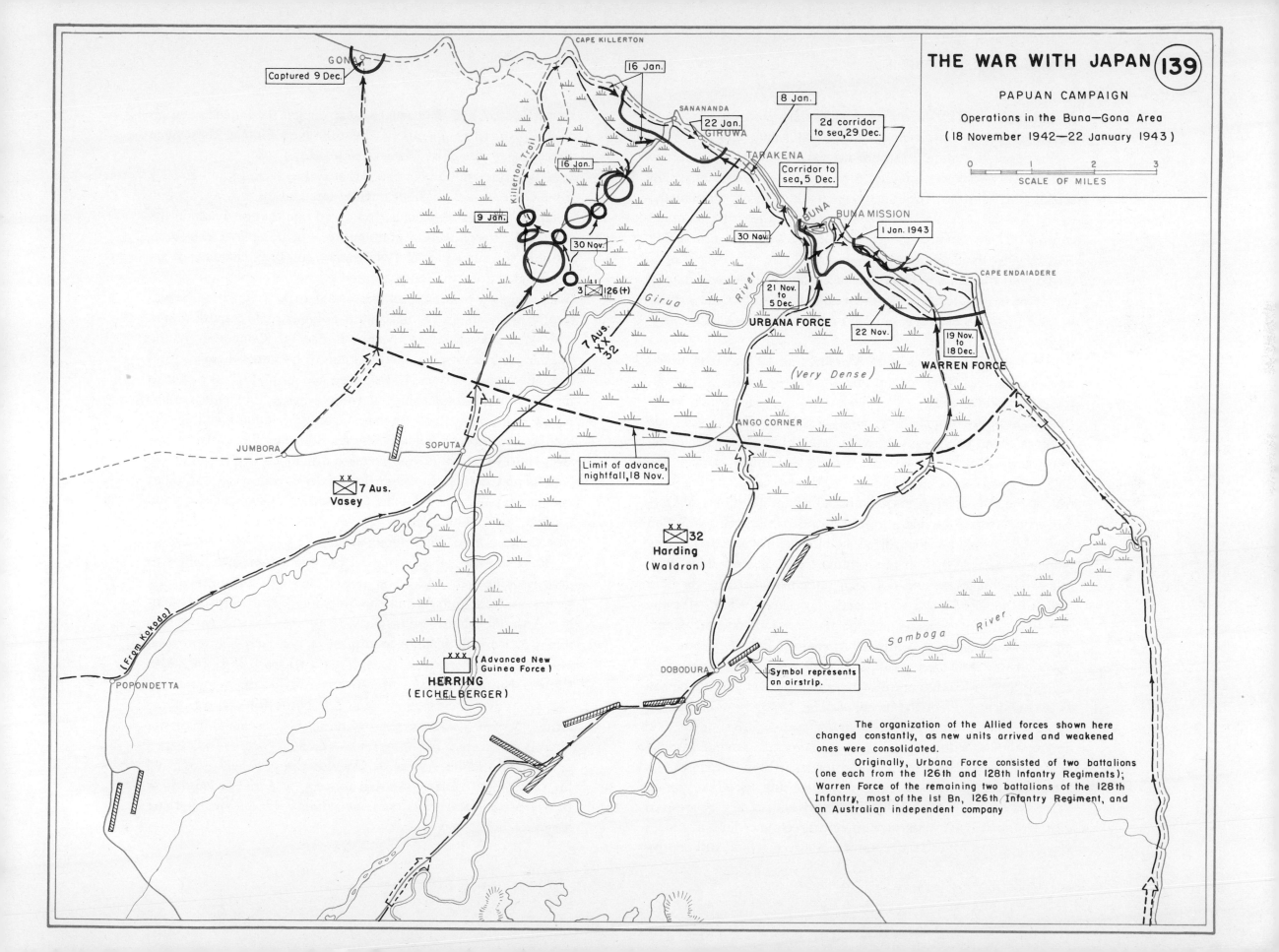

THE WAR WITH JAPAN (139)

PAPUAN CAMPAIGN

Operations in the Buna—Gona Area
(18 November 1942—22 January 1943)

SCALE OF MILES

CAPE KILLERTON

Captured 9 Dec.

GONA

16 Jan.

SANANANDA

22 Jan.

GIRUWA

8 Jan.

2d corridor
to sea, 29 Dec.

TARAKENA

Corridor to
sea, 5 Dec.

BUNA MISSION

16 Jan.

9 Jan.

30 Nov.

30 Nov.

1 Jan. 1943

CAPE ENDAIADERE

3 ⊠ 126(†)

21 Nov.
to
5 Dec.

URBANA FORCE

22 Nov.

19 Nov.
to
18 Dec.

7 Aus.
XX
32

WARREN FORCE

Girua

River

(Very Dense)

ANGO CORNER

Limit of advance,
nightfall, 18 Nov.

JUMBORA

SOPUTA

XX
7 Aus.
Vasey

XX
32
Harding
(Waldron)

Samboga
River

XXX
(Advanced New
Guinea Force)

HERRING
(EICHELBERGER)

DOBODURA

Symbol represents
an airstrip.

(From Kokoda)

POPONDETTA

The organization of the Allied forces shown here
changed constantly, as new units arrived and weakened
ones were consolidated.
    Originally, Urbana Force consisted of two battalions
(one each from the 126th and 128th Infantry Regiments);
Warren Force of the remaining two battalions of the 128th
Infantry, most of the 1st Bn, 126th Infantry Regiment, and
an Australian independent company

In November, 1942, before the Allies had achieved complete victory in Papua (*left center*) and Guadalcanal (*lower right*), Japan adopted a more determined defense in both New Guinea and the Solomons as a prelude to recapturing Guadalcanal and seizing Port Moresby. Ground and air reinforcements were moved to the Rabaul area, and a new army (the Eighteenth) assumed control of New Guinea operations—the Seventeenth now being restricted to the Solomons. In January, 1943, this overly optimistic plan was scuttled by Allied successes at Buna and Guadalcanal; now the Japanese—more realistically—decided to hold in the Huon Gulf area (*center, left*) and at New Georgia (*center, right*).

On the Allied side, General Marshall, on 1 December, urged implementation of the second and third tasks of the 2 July directive (*see text, map 132*). This set off a debate which raged for four months—primarily among JCS planners. The major issue revolved about command—already assigned in the earlier directive to MacArthur, in whose area the operations in both the Solomons and New Guinea would lie. But to Admiral King, control of the Pacific Fleet and command were indivisible: if MacArthur controlled the operations, the strategic flexibility afforded by the fleet would be jeopardized, he inferred. Exasperated Army planners observed that air and ground forces also provided flexibility. The argument had not been settled by the time the JCS went to the Casablanca Conference (January) where—for the first time—the Americans adopted the policy of counterbalancing British demands for continued Mediterranean operations with proposals for expanded Pacific operations. The conference gave a green light to continuation of the drive on Rabaul, which the JCS confidently predicted would fall in 1943. But, in March, upon receipt of MacArthur's plan for such a drive, it became apparent that, without sizable reinforcements (not authorized at Casablanca), MacArthur could not take Rabaul in 1943. As a result, a less ambitious program was substituted: CARTWHEEL (an advance in 1943 to Bougainville by Halsey and to western New Britain by MacArthur). Strategic direction of both advances was assigned to MacArthur; Nimitz, however, would still control Halsey's forces and the fleet. The map depicts the implementation of this plan. (The operations along the New Guinea coast have already been discussed [*see text, map 138*].)

MacArthur initially intended that Halsey would jump directly from Guadalcanal to Bougainville, but Halsey, having already occupied the Russell Islands, convinced him that air bases in the central Solomons were a prerequisite to a Bougainville assault. Thus, in the latter part of 1943, Halsey, utilizing elements of six army and marine divisions, executed a series of amphibious operations designed to secure air bases and bypass Japanese Seventeenth Army forces in the central Solomons. The battles were typical of operations in the South Pacific. Hampered by the weather, unhealthy climatic conditions, a resourceful enemy, and lack of communications, Halsey exploited air and naval power to the maximum in establishing a string of bases (*this map; center, right*) pointing toward Rabaul. Operations culminated in the landing at Empress Augusta Bay on Bougainville in November, after Halsey had misled the Japanese with an earlier, diversionary landing on Choiseul. In the northward drive, Halsey's naval forces and the Japanese had fought four surface engagements (Vella Lavella, Vella Gulf, Kolombangara, and Kula Gulf). On the whole, the honors were about even.

Back in April, the Japanese I-Go operation (an attempt to destroy Allied air and naval power through concentrated air strikes in New Guinea and the Solomons) had failed to blunt MacArthur's offensives. In early November, worried over the threat to Rabaul, Japan moved most of her carrier aircraft and powerful surface elements from Truk (*off map, top center*) to Rabaul. But Halsey's and MacArthur's air forces, supported by carriers provided by Nimitz, won this battle for control of the air and forced the Japanese to withdraw their remaining carrier aircraft and surface forces to Truk. Allied air forces now stepped up their attacks on Rabaul. In August, the JCS had recognized the possibilities of isolating that fortress, and had ordered it to be bypassed. MacArthur could now contain Rabaul and continue his drive north and west.

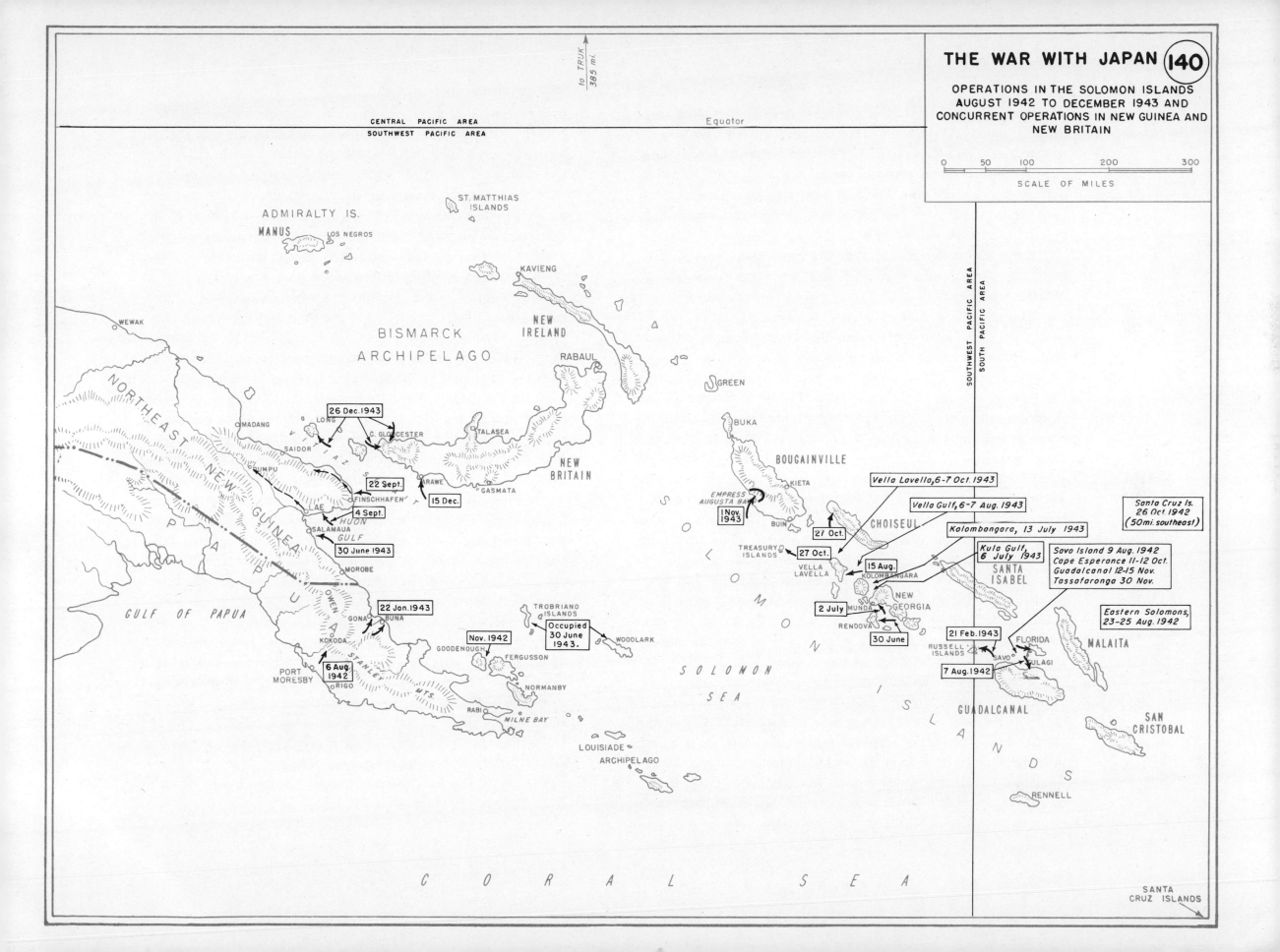

THE WAR WITH JAPAN (140)

OPERATIONS IN THE SOLOMON ISLANDS
AUGUST 1942 TO DECEMBER 1943 AND
CONCURRENT OPERATIONS IN NEW GUINEA AND
NEW BRITAIN

SCALE OF MILES
0   50   100   200   300

to TRUK 385 mi.

CENTRAL PACIFIC AREA   Equator
SOUTHWEST PACIFIC AREA

SOUTHWEST PACIFIC AREA
SOUTH PACIFIC AREA

ST. MATTHIAS ISLANDS

ADMIRALTY IS.
MANUS   LOS NEGROS

KAVIENG

NEW IRELAND

BISMARCK ARCHIPELAGO

RABAUL

GREEN

BUKA

BOUGAINVILLE

KIETA

Empress Augusta Bay
1 Nov. 1943

BUIN

Vella Lavella, 6-7 Oct. 1943

Vella Gulf, 6-7 Aug. 1943

Santa Cruz Is. 26 Oct. 1942 (50 mi. southeast)

WEWAK

MADANG

26 Dec. 1943

LONG

C. GLOUCESTER

TALASEA

NEW BRITAIN

GASMATA

27 Oct.

CHOISEUL

Kolombangara, 13 July 1943

SAIDOR

NORTHEAST NEW GUINEA

DUMPU

22 Sept.

ARAWE

15 Dec.

4 Sept.

FINSCHHAFEN

LAE

HUON GULF

SALAMAUA

30 June 1943

MOROBE

TREASURY ISLANDS

27 Oct.

VELLA LAVELLA

15 Aug.

KOLOMBANGARA

Kula Gulf, 6 July 1943

2 July

MUNDA

NEW GEORGIA

RENDOVA

30 June

Savo Island 9 Aug. 1942
Cape Esperance 11-12 Oct.
Guadalcanal 12-15 Nov.
Tassafaronga 30 Nov.

SANTA ISABEL

Eastern Solomons, 23-25 Aug. 1942

PAPUA

GULF OF PAPUA

OWEN

22 Jan. 1943

GONA

BUNA

KOKODA

STANLEY MTS.

6 Aug. 1942

PORT MORESBY

RIGO

TROBRIAND ISLANDS

Nov. 1942

Occupied 30 June 1943.

WOODLARK

GOODENOUGH

FERGUSSON

NORMANBY

RABI

MILNE BAY

21 Feb. 1943

RUSSELL ISLANDS

7 Aug. 1942

FLORIDA

SAVO

TULAGI

MALAITA

GUADALCANAL

SAN CRISTOBAL

SOLOMON SEA

SOLOMON   SEA

SOLOMON ISLANDS

LOUISIADE ARCHIPELAGO

RENNELL

C O R A L   S E A

SANTA CRUZ ISLANDS

The Japanese conquests of Burma (*see map 127*) left China practically isolated. Allied leaders consequently feared that general war-weariness and the cessation of foreign aid might force China out of the war. Great plans to reestablish land communication between India and China therefore were set afoot. This required the liberation of Burma—an operation of considerable magnitude in itself (*see maps 142 and 151*).

In the meantime, an air transport system was organized to fly in the most essential supplies from bases in the Assam region of India (*this map, lower left*) to Kunming (*lower center*) across the "Hump"—some 500 miles of Himalayan Mountain wilderness. For some unknown reason, the Japanese never made a serious effort to break up this vulnerable system.

Operations in China proper are poorly documented, and so can be covered only in the most general fashion. Even available American accounts are frequently highly partisan. It should be remembered that in many ways the struggle between China and Japan was hardly "war" in the Western understanding of the word —just as the Chinese Army was far from being a modern army. Throughout this period, a constant, fluctuating struggle went on between Chiang Kai-Shek and the Chinese Communists, who were based in the Sian area (*center*). The latter, while presenting themselves to the outside world as pure-hearted "agrarian reformers" devoted only to freeing China from the Japanese, applied most of their energy to undermining Chiang, who replied in kind. The average American, anxious to get on with the war, and innocent of any real knowledge of China or Communism, was at a major disadvantage in this environment.

The one American combat force in China was Maj. Gen. Claire Chennault's United States China Air Task Force (later the Fourteenth Air Force). Beginning in July, 1942, Chennault carried on a growing air offensive against Japanese shipping off the China coast and Japanese installations in China, Burma, Thailand, Indochina, and Formosa. In early June, 1944, B-29's of the XX Bomber Command began operating from bases deep in China, striking targets as distant as southern Japan. All these American air operations were strait-jacketed by the fact that all supplies—especially aviation gasoline—had to be flown in over the Hump.

Other than the American air activity, the over-all situation had hardly changed since 1939. The Japanese held most of the railroads, major ports, and important industrial and agricultural areas. Occasionally they conducted minor offensives to seize crops, suppress guerrilla outbreaks, or give new troops combat indoctrination. Chinese operations were largely limited to guerrilla activity, vastly publicized at the time, but apparently of no great importance. In some areas, there had been no fighting for years—allegedly, the opposing commanders sometimes reached mutually profitable understandings. Anxious to develop an efficient Chinese Army, Stilwell requested the allocation of a large part of the Hump system's cargo space for weapons and equipment. This put him at loggerheads with Chennault, who managed to retain control of most of the cargo capacity, claiming that the existing Chinese forces would suffice, if given sufficient air support.

In April, 1944, the China stalemate exploded. Apparently fearful that the defeats they had suffered in the Southwest Pacific would endanger their control of the South China Sea, the Japanese launched a series of offensives to consolidate their position on the Asiatic mainland. These offensives (*striped red areas*) swept the Chinese off the principal north-south rail lines in central and southern China, giving the Japanese continuous land communications between northern Manchuria and Singapore. Seven of Chennault's airfields were overrun, forcing him farther into the interior. During these painful reverses, Stilwell was recalled to the United States; his former command was divided into the India-Burma theater (under Lt. Gen. Daniel I. Sultan) and the China theater (Maj. Gen. Albert C. Wedemeyer). Late in November, the Japanese advanced on Kweiyang (*lower center*), but were checked by American-trained Chinese troops flown in from Burma.

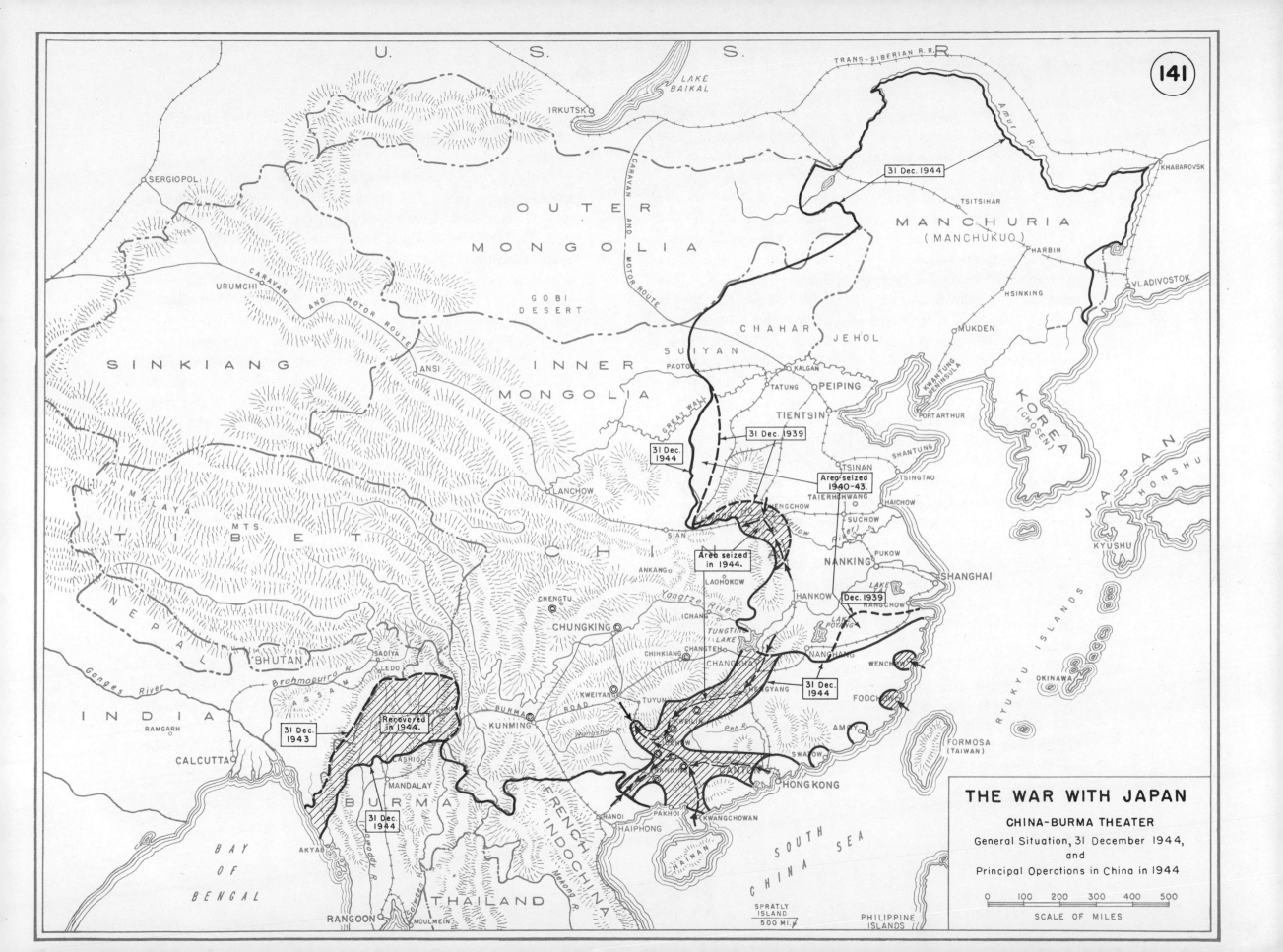

THE WAR WITH JAPAN

CHINA-BURMA THEATER

General Situation, 31 December 1944,
and
Principal Operations in China in 1944

Following the Allied retreat from Burma (*see map 127*), Wavell attempted a counteroffensive (September, 1942–May, 1943; *action not shown*) down the coast against Akyab (*this map, lower left*), but was unsuccessful.

The Allies then slowly gathered strength. The American Tenth Air Force had begun moving into India in March, 1942. In December, 1942, American engineers began the construction of a highway from Ledo (*upper center*) into northern Burma. Throughout India, a vast complex of improved road and rail communications, airfields, and supply installations proliferated. Concurrently, Stilwell reorganized and trained the Chinese troops that had retreated into India after the fall of Burma, flying in replacements from China. Brigadier Orde C. Wingate, an eccentric specialist in irregular warfare, now urged the use of small columns of specially trained troops—supplied by air drops—in operations against Japanese communications deep in Burma. Wavell authorized this force, and Wingate led these "Chindits" on a foray (February-April, 1943) against the railroad north of Mandalay. Air resupply proved highly effective, but Wingate's erratic tactics resulted in the loss of a third of his force, without compensating damage to the Japanese. Allied air forces carried out vigorous raids against the Japanese communications.

The *QUADRANT* Conference (Quebec, 1943) resulted in the decision to clear northern Burma and reestablish land communication with China as soon as the 1943 monsoon season ended. In its final form, this plan included four operations: an attack toward Akyab by the XV Corps, the seizure of Myitkyina (*upper center*) by Stilwell, a deep penetration by Wingate's Chindits to aid Stilwell's advance, and an advance to the Chindwin River by the IV Corps. Wingate's activities had greatly impressed the JCS, who hastily improvised the 5307th Composite Unit (Provisional)—better known as Merrill's Marauders—for service in Burma. The Japanese, meanwhile, strengthened their forces in Burma. Expecting an Allied offensive, they decided to strike first to seize the British bases at Imphal and Kohima (*center, left*).

Stilwell's attack opened in October, 1943. In February, when the Marauders came into line, Stilwell used them in a series of wide enveloping movements to get in the rear of the Japanese opposing his Chinese. These maneuvers were successful, the Marauders capturing Myitkyina airfield on 17 May, but the Japanese waged an indomitable fight for the town itself. The Chindits had blocked the southern approaches to Myitkyina, but were finally forced to withdraw.

The Akyab offensive began in November. In February, the Japanese delivered a major counterattack, but were roughly repulsed. In early March, the Japanese Fifteenth Army struck at Imphal and Kohima, isolating both towns. The British garrisons, supplied by air, held out successfully, and counterattacks threw the Japanese back. Their advance, as usual in Japanese operations, had combined aggressive tactics with shoestring logistical support. By 1 July, sickness, hunger, and battle casualties had crippled them; as the monsoon season worsened, they retreated in growing confusion.

During this period, fresh Chinese forces attacked down the Burma Road, but were checked at the walled towns of Lungling and Tengchung. Myitkyina finally fell on 3 August. Thereafter, operations paused until the end of the rains. The Marauders were disbanded, but the newly created Mars Force took their place. On 2 December, the British captured Kalewa (*center, left*), linking up the next day with Sultan's right flank. (Sultan had succeeded Stilwell.) Bhamo (*center*) fell on the 15th. The Chinese had previously, with help from the Fourteenth Air Force, stormed Tengchung and Lungling. By the end of the year, the Japanese were withdrawing along most of the front (*heavy red line*), and Allied pressure was steadily increasing.

Note: On this map, upper center, Tengyueh *should be* Tengchung.

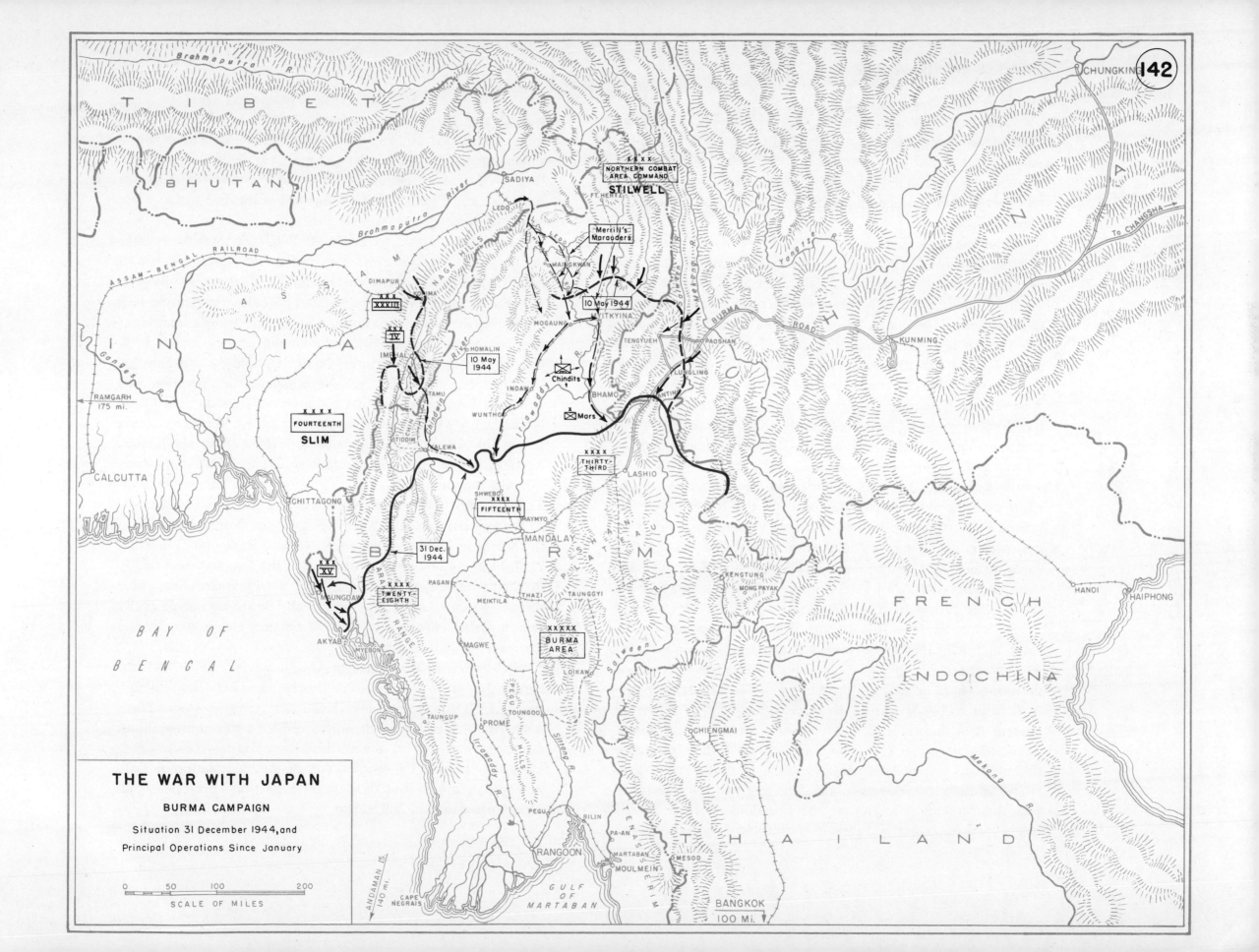

THE WAR WITH JAPAN

BURMA CAMPAIGN

Situation 31 December 1944, and

Principal Operations Since January

0   50   100   200
SCALE OF MILES

By approving CARTWHEEL in March, 1943, the JCS gave impetus to the Allied drive back to the Philippines. But, as yet, no Allied advance had been initiated in the Central Pacific. At the TRIDENT Conference (Washington) in May, the JCS presented an over-all plan for operations in the Pacific, which the CCS generally accepted.

This basic strategic plan specified the seizure—in conjunction with the British and Chinese—of a foothold on the China coast near Hong Kong as a base from which Japan could be taken under air attack, and invaded if necessary. American forces would get to Hong Kong by opening a line of communications to the Celebes Sea (center, left) and recapturing part of the Philippines. The plan specified that the main drive westward should be made through the Central Pacific, and a subsidiary one up through New Guinea. For the next nine months, this approach was debated between the JCS and MacArthur. The latter felt firmly that the Central Pacific advance was too long, could gain no vital strategic objectives, would entail costly island assaults, and would fail to exploit land-based air power; he wanted the major effort made up through New Guinea. But the JCS believed the central route would be easier to support logistically, was better hygienically, would exploit the fleet's mobility, and would strike Japan's vulnerable eastern flank. In October, the JCS added another reason—the Army Air Corps' new B-29 bomber could strike Japan proper from the Marianas.

So, ultimately, the Allies returned to the Philippines by the two routes delineated on the map. (MacArthur's operations from 15 February to 22 April [see text, map 144] and the meeting of the two-pronged advance in the Philippines on 20 October [see text, maps 145-148] will be described subsequently.) After the landing at St. Matthias (this map; center, right) on 20 March, the South Pacific Area was pinched out, and Halsey, returning to the Central Pacific Area, assumed command of the Third Fleet.

Meanwhile, in September, the Japanese had reluctantly revised their strategy. Recognizing the tremendous growth in American air and sea power and their own excessive losses in shipping and aircraft, they decided to contract their defensive perimeter to gain time for rebuilding an offensive capability. The new line would extend from the Kuriles (off map, top center) through the Bonins–Marianas–Carolines–western New Guinea–Netherlands East Indies to Burma. Outposts forward of this line would trade space for time.

Admiral Nimitz's drive across the Pacific began with landings in the Gilberts (right center) in November, 1943. Unable to obtain sufficient troops to implement the TRIDENT decision to seize the Marshalls, he had substituted the Gilberts when the JCS made available one marine division from MacArthur's area. Japanese concern for Bougainville had immobilized their fleet at Truk just when it might have caused Nimitz trouble by attacking his landing force in the Gilberts. Nevertheless, the operation was costly; at Tarawa, the marines had a vicious fight on their hands before finally wiping out the Japanese defenders. But the Gilberts taught the Americans many valuable lessons about amphibious warfare, and the subsequent seizure of Kwajalein in January was a model amphibious landing. About this time, carrier raids on Truk revealed that island's weakness and partial abandonment, so the western Carolines were bypassed, and Nimitz moved into the Marianas instead. It was while Admiral Raymond Spruance's Fifth Fleet lay off Saipan (center) that the Japanese fleet finally decided to give battle. The Battle of the Philippine Sea ended disastrously for Japan, for it practically destroyed her painfully rebuilt carrier pilot groups. Most of the fleet escaped, but it was no longer a serious threat.

Before seizing the Saipan bastion, however, Nimitz had lent carrier support to MacArthur so that he could leap beyond land-based aircraft range and take Hollandia (lower center). Then, while MacArthur—in a brilliantly executed series of amphibious landings—moved along the northern New Guinea coast, Nimitz swung south to the Palaus, thus completing the isolation of Truk and getting into position to support MacArthur's projected landing on Mindanao in November.

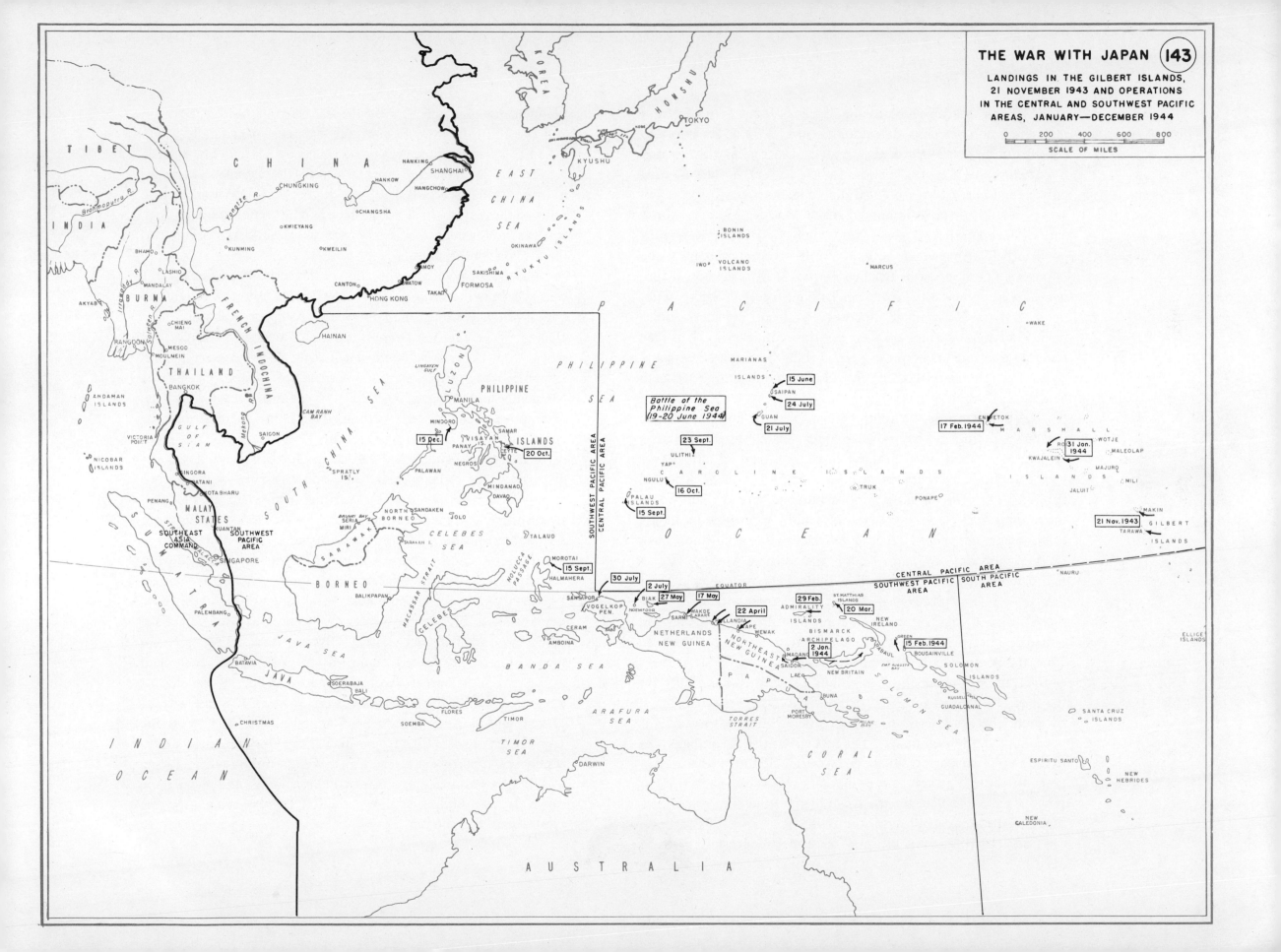

THE WAR WITH JAPAN 143

LANDINGS IN THE GILBERT ISLANDS,
21 NOVEMBER 1943 AND OPERATIONS
IN THE CENTRAL AND SOUTHWEST PACIFIC
AREAS, JANUARY—DECEMBER 1944

0   200   400   600   800
SCALE OF MILES

TIBET

CHINA

INDIA

BURMA

THAILAND

FRENCH INDOCHINA

MALAY STATES

SOUTHEAST ASIA COMMAND

SOUTHWEST PACIFIC AREA

KOREA

HONSHU

KYUSHU

TOKYO

EAST CHINA SEA

NANKING
SHANGHAI
HANGCHOW
HANKOW
CHUNGKING
CHANGSHA
KWEIYANG
KUNMING
KWEILIN
AMOY
SWATOW
CANTON
HONG KONG
TAKAO
FORMOSA
HAINAN

OKINAWA
RYUKYU ISLANDS
SAKISHIMA

BONIN ISLANDS
IWO
VOLCANO ISLANDS
MARCUS
WAKE

PACIFIC OCEAN

PHILIPPINE SEA

MARIANAS ISLANDS
SAIPAN   **15 June**
24 July
GUAM   **21 July**
23 Sept.

Battle of the Philippine Sea (19-20 June 1944)

ULITHI
YAP
NGULU
CAROLINE ISLANDS
TRUK
PONAPE

17 Feb. 1944   ENIWETOK

MARSHALL ISLANDS
31 Jan. 1944   WOTJE
KWAJALEIN   MALEOLAP
MAJURO
JALUIT   MILI

21 Nov. 1943   MAKIN
TARAWA   GILBERT ISLANDS

PALAU ISLANDS   **15 Sept.**
16 Oct.

PHILIPPINE ISLANDS
MANILA
MINDORO   **15 Dec.**
VISAYAN IS.   LEYTE   **20 Oct.**
PANAY   SAMAR
NEGROS
PALAWAN
MINDANAO
DAVAO

SOUTH CHINA SEA
LINGAYEN GULF
LUZON
CAM RANH BAY
SAIGON

SPRATLY IS.
SARAWAK
BRUNEI BAY
SERIA
MIRI
NORTH BORNEO
SANDAKEN
JOLO
TALAUD

BORNEO
BALIKPAPAN
CELEBES

MACASSAR STRAIT
CELEBES SEA
MOLUCCA PASSAGE
MOROTAI   **15 Sept.**
HALMAHERA
CERAM
AMBOINA

JAVA SEA
BATAVIA
SOERABAJA
BALI
JAVA

CHRISTMAS

INDIAN OCEAN

SUMATRA
PALEMBANG
SINGAPORE
PENANG

ANDAMAN ISLANDS

NICOBAR ISLANDS

GULF OF SIAM
BANGKOK

CENTRAL PACIFIC AREA

EQUATOR

CENTRAL PACIFIC AREA
SOUTHWEST PACIFIC AREA   SOUTH PACIFIC AREA

NAURU

ELLICE ISLANDS

VOGELKOP PEN.   **30 July**
SANSAPOR
2 July   BIAK   **27 May**
NOEMFOOR   **17 May**
SARMI   SARARE   WAKDE
NETHERLANDS NEW GUINEA
HOLLANDIA   **22 April**
SAWAR   AITAPE   WEWAK
NORTHEAST NEW GUINEA
MADANG   **2 Jan. 1944**
SAIDOR
LAE
PAPUA
BUNA
PORT MORESBY
MILNE BAY

ADMIRALTY ISLANDS   **29 Feb.**
ST. MATTHIAS ISLANDS
20 Mar.
NEW IRELAND
BISMARCK ARCHIPELAGO
RABAUL
GREEN   **15 Feb. 1944**
NEW BRITAIN
EMP. AUGUSTA BAY
BOUGAINVILLE
SOLOMON ISLANDS
RUSSELL IS.
GUADALCANAL

BANDA SEA

ARAFURA SEA

TIMOR SEA
TIMOR
FLORES
SOEMBA

DARWIN

TORRES STRAIT

CORAL SEA

SANTA CRUZ ISLANDS

ESPIRITU SANTO

NEW HEBRIDES

NEW CALEDONIA

AUSTRALIA

MacArthur's first amphibious landing in 1944 was made by a regimental combat team at Saidor (*center, left*) in an effort to cut off the Japanese who had retreated from Lae and Salamaua. Eventually, this sizable Japanese force (12,000)—starving, dispirited, and harried by the Australian advance from Finschhafen —was forced to move inland to reach Madang. Saidor, whose earlier occupation had given Maj. Gen. George C. Kenney a good airfield from which he could support operations on Cape Gloucester (*center*), was reached by the Australians on 10 January. In February, the American landing force at Saidor withdrew, and the Australians, opposed by strong Japanese forces from Madang, consolidated their position until April. Then they renewed their advance up the coast, having been joined en route by an Australian battalion which had moved out of the Markham Valley to Dumpu.

Halsey's troops in the South Pacific spent the first few months of 1944 isolating and neutralizing enemy bases. On 15 February, he landed a small New Zealand force at Green Island (*upper right*) to obtain a site for an air base. A month later, he occupied Emirau (*top center*), after MacArthur had already jumped to the Admiralties (*top center*) and Halsey's projected landing at Kavieng (*top center*) had been canceled. Meanwhile, back on Bougainville (*off map, right*), the bulk of Halsey's forces had a real fight on their hands to hold their perimeter against determined—but piecemeal—Seventeenth Army attacks. Nevertheless, by May, the Japanese—cut off from Rabaul and starving —had reached desperate straits; wholesale desertion followed. In June, the South Pacific Area operations came under MacArthur's control. In November, the Australians assumed responsibility for the area, as well as for New Britain and eastern New Guinea; by then, the American troops were being moved forward for operations in the Philippines. The task given the Australians was to mop up the bypassed Japanese. No strategic threat, these Japanese—in sizable groups and in inaccessible places—nevertheless posed a nasty problem for the Australians. When the war ended, many of these Japanese were still in hiding.

Early 1944 was not pleasant on Cape Gloucester. Fighting the elements as much as the Japanese, the 1st Marine Division and the 112th Cavalry Regimental Combat Team finally established a common front across the island by March. The marine landing on Willaumez Peninsula forced the Japanese to begin a withdrawal toward Rabaul which the 40th Division, having relieved the marines in April, hastened. When relieved by the Australians in November, the Americans had the Japanese contained on the Gazelle Peninsula.

The most spectacular operation of this series was MacArthur's seizure of the Admiralties. After the JCS decision in August to bypass Rabaul, MacArthur planned to complete Rabaul's encirclement by seizing the Admiralties and Kavieng in March. But when Nimitz stated he could not provide the necessary assault shipping and carrier support because of operations in the Marshalls in February, the date was changed to April. In the meantime, Allied aircraft continued to bomb Rabaul and the Admiralties. On 23 February, Kenney was advised that aerial reconnaissance flights indicated that the Japanese had practically abandoned the Admiralties. The Southwest Pacific intelligence section disagreed, maintaining that the enemy had about 4,000 troops there (a remarkably accurate estimate). MacArthur made a characteristically bold decision to dispatch a 1,000-man reconnaissance force to Los Negros to verify the report, and decided to accompany the troops himself. The landing took place on 29 February (*top center*) and quickly established that, indeed, Kenney's estimate of 300 Japanese was wrong. But MacArthur ordered the rest of the 1st Cavalry Division forward and directed the reconnaissance force to hold "at any cost." This accelerated action advanced operations in the Southwest Pacific by at least a month. Quickly, the Admiralties were overrun, Kavieng was bypassed, and in April MacArthur jumped all the way to Aitape (*upper left*) and Hollandia beyond. Thus, the Japanese Eighteenth Army, surprised at the leap beyond land-based air range, was caught between the advancing Australians and the Aitape force. It was ultimately left—isolated and starving—for the Australians to mop up.

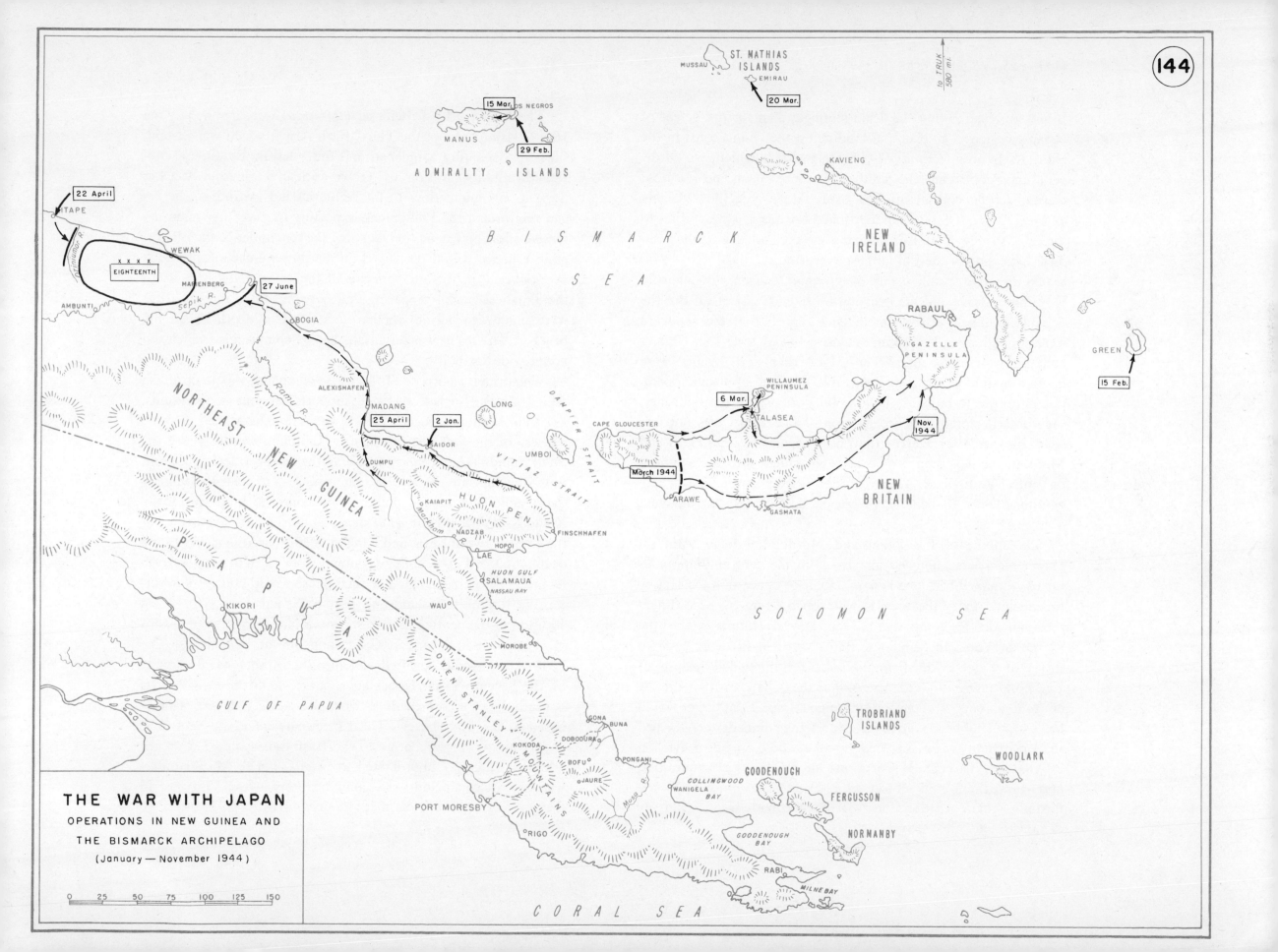

THE WAR WITH JAPAN

OPERATIONS IN NEW GUINEA AND

THE BISMARCK ARCHIPELAGO

(January — November 1944)

0   25   50   75   100   125   150

It will be recalled that the 1943 strategic plan for the defeat of Japan envisioned an eventual landing on the China coast in the Hong Kong area (*see map 143*). Since that lodgment would depend upon controlling the South China Sea, Luzon and Formosa merited serious consideration as likely Allied objectives. As late as June, 1944, JCS planners felt that Formosa was more vital to the basic strategy than Luzon, and some even advocated the complete bypassing of the Philippines. Nevertheless, in March, 1944, a JCS directive specified that MacArthur land on Mindanao in November; it avoided the question of the next objective. But the debate continued, fed by intelligence reports that the Japanese were strengthening Formosan defenses, and by fears that China's collapse was imminent. When MacArthur and Nimitz were queried in June concerning a possible speed-up of Pacific operations in order to facilitate landing on Formosa before February, they both declared that acceleration of operations was not feasible. Further, they averred that, after seizure of the Palaus and Morotai, the next step should be a movement into the southern or central Philippines. This operation was approved, but debate continued over the choice of Luzon or Formosa as the next objective.

In support of the Palau and Morotai landings, Admiral Halsey's carriers launched air strikes in the central Philippines on 12-14 September. The lack of Japanese opposition led Halsey to conclude that "the area is wide open," and he accordingly recommended to Nimitz that the scheduled operations against the islands of Yap and Mindanao be canceled in favor of a direct thrust at Leyte. Concurring, Nimitz recommended seizure of Leyte and offered to lend MacArthur the XXIV Corps (already en route to Yap) and carrier air support—since the target would be beyond land-based air range. MacArthur immediately grasped the opportunity, and reported that he would invade Leyte on 20 October. The XXIV Corps was shunted to the Admiralties, and MacArthur's staff set to work revising plans. Once again, the flexibility of operations in the Pacific had been strikingly demonstrated.

The Japanese Leyte defenses (*this map*) were manned by the 16th Division, part of the Thirty-Fifth Army, which was responsible for defending Mindanao and the Visayas. By June, 1944, Japan's military position had grown critical. To help protect her lines of communications to the Netherlands East Indies, she began reinforcing the Philippines, expecting to make her main defensive effort on Luzon. In defending the remainder of the islands, main reliance would be placed on air power—a concept which overlooked American superiority in the skies. On Leyte itself, the Japanese began preparing defensive positions in April, but were unable to decide whether to defend in depth or on the beaches. The result was an unsatisfactory compromise which did not provide flexibility.

The primary purpose of the Leyte campaign was to establish Allied air and logistic bases to support subsequent operations. Lt. Gen. Walter Krueger's plan of operations consisted of three phases. In the first, the 6th Ranger Battalion would secure the small islands (*right center*) guarding the entrance to Leyte Gulf, thus allowing safe passage for mine sweepers to clear the way for the assault. The second phase would comprise landings by the X and XXIV Corps (*upper center*), establishment of control over the strait between Leyte and Panaon Island (*bottom center*), and occupation of Leyte Valley (running from Carigara [*upper center*] to Abuyog [*center*]). The final phase would consist of securing the rest of the island and part of Samar (*top center*). In addition to the floating reserve shown, Krueger had two divisions in general reserve (one at Guam and one at Hollandia). The Sixth Army would be lifted and furnished direct naval support by the Seventh Fleet. Direct air support would be provided by Seventh Fleet escort carriers, while Kenney's bombers, China-based B-29's, and Halsey's Third Fleet carriers would neutralize enemy air power on Formosa, the East Indies, and Luzon. In addition, Halsey—subordinated to Nimitz, not to MacArthur—was to protect air and sea communications in the Visayas and destroy the Japanese fleet if it ventured forth to give battle.

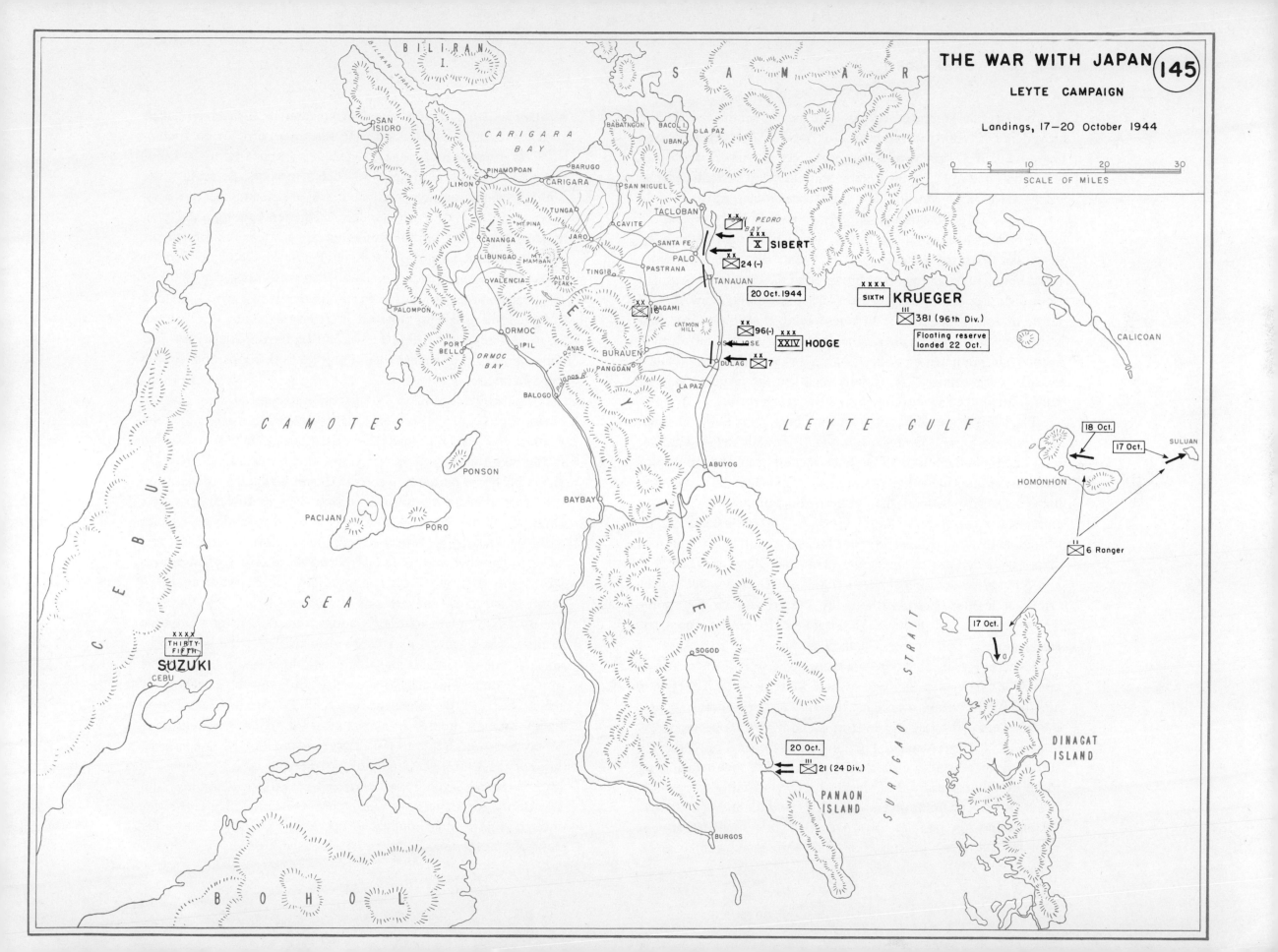

0   5   10   20   30
SCALE OF MILES

BILIRAN I.

SAMAR

BILIRAN STRAIT

CARIGARA BAY

SAN ISIDRO

BABATNGON   BACOL I.   LA PAZ
UBAN

PINAMOPOAN
BARUGO
LIMON
CARIGARA
PSAN MIGUEL
TUNGA
MT. PINA
TACLOBAN
CANANGA
JARO
CAVITE
SANTA FE
PEDRO BAY
X X
XXX   X   SIBERT
PALO
XX   24 (-)
PASTRANA
LIBUNGAO
MT. MAMBAN
TINGIB
TANAUAN
20 Oct. 1944
VALENCIA
ALTO PEAK
PALOMPON
PAGAMI
XX   8
XXXX   SIXTH   KRUEGER
CATMON HILL
III   381 (96th Div.)
ORMOC
XX   96(-)
XXX   XXIV   HODGE
Floating reserve landed 22 Oct.
PORT BELLO
IPIL
SN JOSE
ANAS
BURAUEN
DULAG   XX   7
ORMOC BAY
PANGDAN
POLONGS R.
LA PAZ
CALICOAN
BALOGO

CAMOTES

LEYTE GULF

PONSON

18 Oct.
17 Oct.   SULUAN
HOMONHON

ABUYOG

PACIJAN
PORO

BAYBAY

II   6 Ranger

SEA

17 Oct.

SOGOD

SURIGAO STRAIT

CEBU

XXXX   THIRTY-FIFTH   SUZUKI
CEBU

20 Oct.
III   21 (24 Div.)

PANAON ISLAND

DINAGAT ISLAND

BURGOS

BOHOL

As the largest American convoy yet assembled in the Pacific moved north from the Admiralties, Halsey's carriers struck at Formosa and Luzon, while Seventh Fleet carrier aircraft protected the convoy and hit enemy shipping and airfields in the Visayas. Kenney's Morotai-based air forces joined in the attacks on Visayan targets within range. Exaggerated reports by Japanese airmen of losses inflicted on the Third Fleet off Formosa led to a false sense of security and the belief that the Philippines could not be invaded for two more months. (Actually, Halsey had dealt Japanese air power on Formosa a crippling blow.) As a result of this belief and a Japanese predisposition to consider Mindanao as the next Allied objective (even though naval intelligence had predicted an Allied landing in the Philippines for late October and surmised that Leyte might be the target), MacArthur's landing achieved complete strategic surprise.

The Rangers landed as planned on Dinagat and Suluan Islands (*see map 145, right center*), but rough weather delayed the assault on Homonhon until 18 October. Resistance was encountered only on Suluan, the other islands being unoccupied. Navigation lights were installed on the islands, and mine sweepers began clearing the entrances to Leyte Gulf. At 1000, 20 October, following a two-hour naval bombardment, assault waves of four divisions landed (*this map, center*) between Dulag and Tacloban and quickly secured beachheads. The 24th Division met considerable opposition, but elsewhere Japanese resistance was spotty. Thirty minutes earlier, the 21st Regimental Combat Team had easily secured Panaon Strait (*off map, south*).

General Krueger's troops quickly moved inland the next four days. The 1st Cavalry Division captured Tacloban (*upper center*) and its airfield (*red block*), landed at La Paz (on Samar), secured the northeastern coast of Leyte as far as Babatngon, and drove inland toward San Miguel. The 24th Division continued to meet stiff resistance until it took Palo and Hill 522; then it advanced more rapidly toward Jaro. The 96th Division initially bypassed the enemy strong point on Catmon Hill (*center*) and drove across swamps and rice paddies toward Dagami; the Japanese on Catmon Hill withdrew on the 26th when threatened with encircle-

ment. The 7th Division seized Dulag and its airfield and then struck out for Burauen, capturing the three airfields en route.

Everywhere, the Japanese defense had appeared to be uncoordinated, though resistance was fierce in spots. In reality, the 16th Division—outnumbered and still organizing defense positions when the Sixth Army landed—had been fighting a delaying action back to the central mountain range, while reinforcements came ashore at Ormoc (*center, left*). On 21 October, General Yamashita (the Japanese commander in the Philippines) had decided to fight the battle for the Philippines on Leyte, and had ordered reinforcements moved there from Luzon and the Visayas. (Between 23 October and 11 December, the Japanese sent nine convoys to Ormoc and landed about 45,000 troops and 10,000 tons of matériel.)

Meanwhile, the Sixth Army continued its advance. In the north, the X Corps captured Carigara (*upper center*) on 2 November and then ran head-on into the strong Japanese position in the mountains southeast of Limon; in the south, the 7th Division pushed a battalion through Abuyog to Baybay (2 November) and then north toward Ormoc. But in the center, after Dagami fell on 30 October, the XXIV Corps made only slight gains against strong defenses in the mountains. During the last week in October and in early November, heavy tropical storms struck the area and turned many of the roads—already being taxed to the limit—into ribbons of mud.

By 7 November, Krueger's troops were poised for a drive on Ormoc, while Yamashita continued to reinforce the island. The construction of airfields and the logistic base had fallen well behind schedule. The airfield sites near Burauen were technically unsuitable, and the Tacloban and Dulag strips were unable to handle enough aircraft. As a result, there were insufficient ground-based planes on Leyte to either prevent the flow of Japanese reinforcements through Ormoc or provide the desired support of ground troops. Seventh Fleet carriers were of little assistance after the Battle for Leyte Gulf (*see map 147*), and Halsey's fleet, though it gave some support to operations on Leyte, could not compensate for the shortage of land-based aircraft.

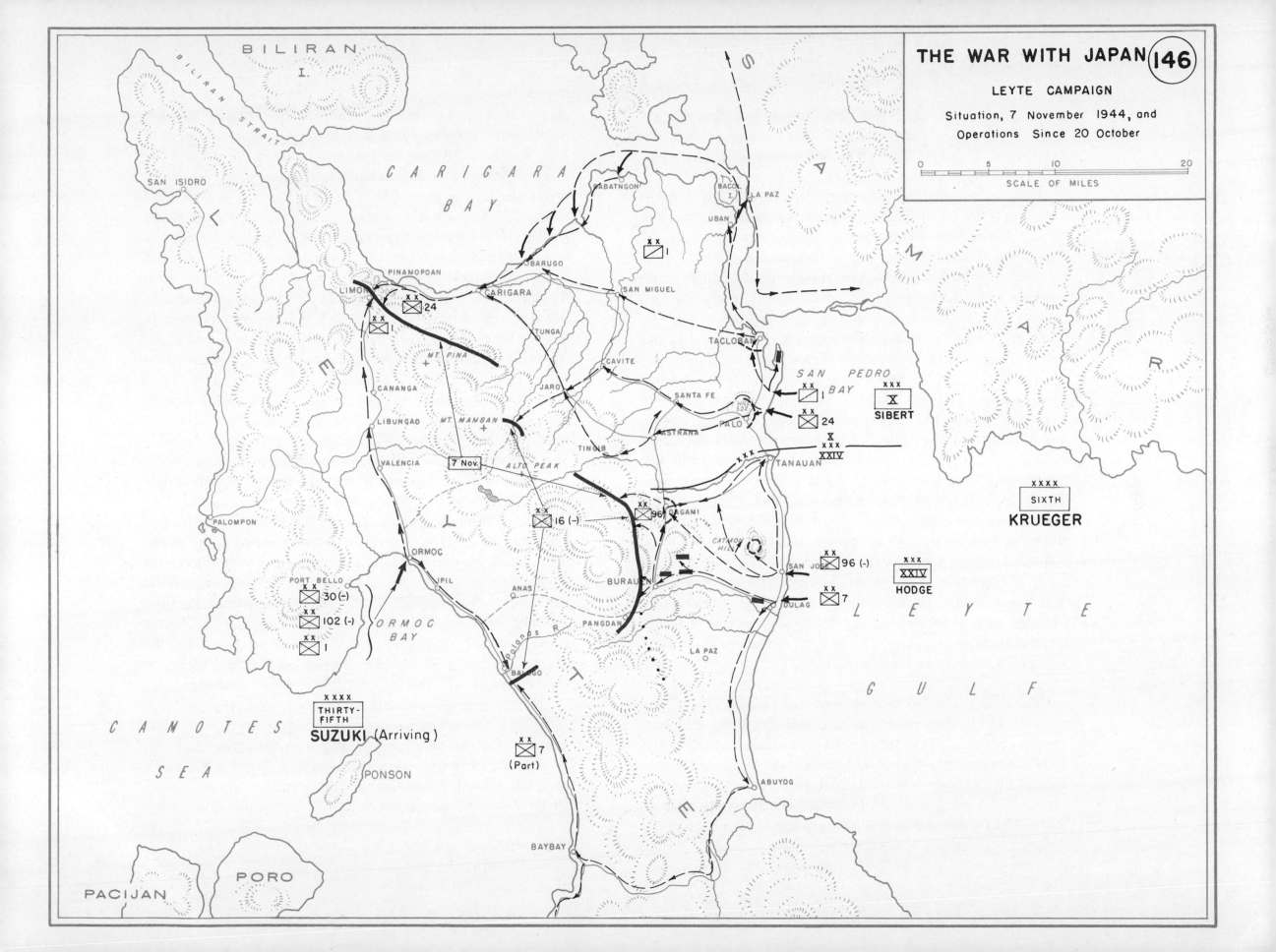

THE WAR WITH JAPAN (146)

LEYTE CAMPAIGN

Situation, 7 November 1944, and
Operations Since 20 October

SCALE OF MILES

BILIRAN I.

BILIRAN STRAIT

SAN ISIDRO

CARIGARA BAY

BABATNGON

BACOL I. LA PAZ

UBAN

PINAMOPOAN

BARUGO

LIMON

CARIGARA

SAN MIGUEL

XX 24

XX 1

TUNGA

TACLOBAN

MT. PINA

CAVITE

SAN PEDRO BAY

CANANGA

JARO

SANTA FE

XX 1

XXX X SIBERT

LIBUNGAO

MT. MAMBAN

HILL 522

XX 24

VALENCIA

7 Nov.

ALTO PEAK

TINGIB

ASTRANA

PALO

X XXX XXIV

PALOMPON

TANAUAN

XX 16 (-)

XX 96 DAGAMI

SIXTH

KRUEGER

CATMON HILL

ORMOC

IPIL

BURAUEN

SAN JOSE

XX 96 (-)

XXX XXIV

PORT BELLO

XX 30 (-)

ANAS

XX 7

HODGE

XX 102 (-)

ORMOC BAY

PANGDAN

DULAG

XX 1

LA PAZ

LEYTE

CAMOTES SEA

XXXX THIRTY-FIFTH

SUZUKI (Arriving)

BALOGO

XX 7 (Part)

GULF

PONSON

ABUYOG

PACIJAN

PORO

BAYBAY

While the 16th Division was withdrawing before Krueger's superior forces, the weakened Japanese Navy was moving toward Leyte under orders to destroy the American landing forces and their supporting ships.

Imperial General Headquarters had devised the Sho-Go (meaning "Victory Operation") plan to meet probable American attacks. It had four variations; Sho-1 applied to an attack on the Philippines. This plan, recognizing the great inferiority of Japanese carrier air power, provided for support of the fleet by land-based aircraft. Accordingly, the Japanese made every effort to transfer large quantities of aircraft to the Philippines in late October, but Halsey's crippling strikes against Formosa and Luzon seriously impaired the effectiveness of this program.

The Sho-1 plan was based upon deception. The Main Body (*top center*) would lure Halsey's Third Fleet north, while the main surface elements (divided into 1st Attack Force [*left center*] and C Force [*bottom center*]) would come up from Borneo to close a giant pincer on the amphibious forces in Leyte Gulf. The 2d Attack Force (*lower center*) would join the southern prong. The Main Body contained all the carriers as bait (without many aircraft, however). Its sacrifice was considered justified if it succeeded in diverting Halsey's attention so that the surface elements could destroy the American ships in Leyte Gulf.

It is important to note that the Seventh Fleet was under MacArthur and the Third Fleet under Nimitz. Halsey had orders to support the landings—but also to destroy the enemy fleet if the opportunity arose. As will be seen, he considered this second part of his mission the more important.

The first naval action took place west of Palawan (*lower left*) early on 23 October, when two Seventh Fleet submarines sank two heavy cruisers of the 1st Attack Force. Alerted by this action and later submarine sightings off Mindoro, Halsey's search planes soon located C Force and the 1st Attack Force. At once, Third Fleet aircraft were launched in strikes against both Japanese forces. The 1st Attack Force suffered enough damage (one battle-ship sunk, other ships hit) in the Sibuyan Sea (*center*) to cause its commander (Vice Adm. Takeo Kurita) to reverse course. This movement affected the battle in two ways: it delayed the northern prong of the Japanese pincer, and—coupled with overly optimistic damage reports by Third Fleet pilots—it convinced Halsey that Kurita was no longer a threat. Halsey, having finally located the Main Body, then decided that it was the major threat and moved the entire Third Fleet (less one task force, 300 miles to the east refueling) northward that night. While Halsey took the bait, the Seventh Fleet battleships and cruisers—warned of the approach of the C and 2d Attack Forces—took position in Surigao Strait (*lower right*) and, in a brilliant action, practically wiped out C Force. The 2d Attack Force withdrew without giving battle.

Meanwhile, Kurita had again reversed course, moved through San Bernardino Strait, and surprised the Seventh Fleet escort carriers off Samar. (The Seventh Fleet thought Halsey was guarding San Bernardino Strait.) The slow carrier force tried to outrun Kurita, but though it put up a magnificent fight, was in danger of annihilation when Kurita suddenly broke off the action and withdrew. Misunderstanding, fear of land-based aircraft, and knowledge of C Force's destruction all contributed to this amazing decision. Meanwhile, Halsey, in answer to Seventh Fleet calls for help, finally sent his battleships south—but they arrived too late to engage Kurita. Aircraft from the task force returning from refueling did strike Kurita's force, however, as did the rest of Halsey's aircraft on the 26th and 27th. In the meantime, the Third Fleet had inflicted heavy damage on the Main Body off Cape Engano (*top center*).

Withdrawing the remnants of their once-proud fleet, the Japanese could take consolation only in having come perilously close to reaching MacArthur's soft-skinned transports. They had also revealed the desperateness of their situation by using Kamikaze tactics (suicide dive bombing) for the first time: against Halsey on the 24th, and against the Seventh Fleet on the 25th.

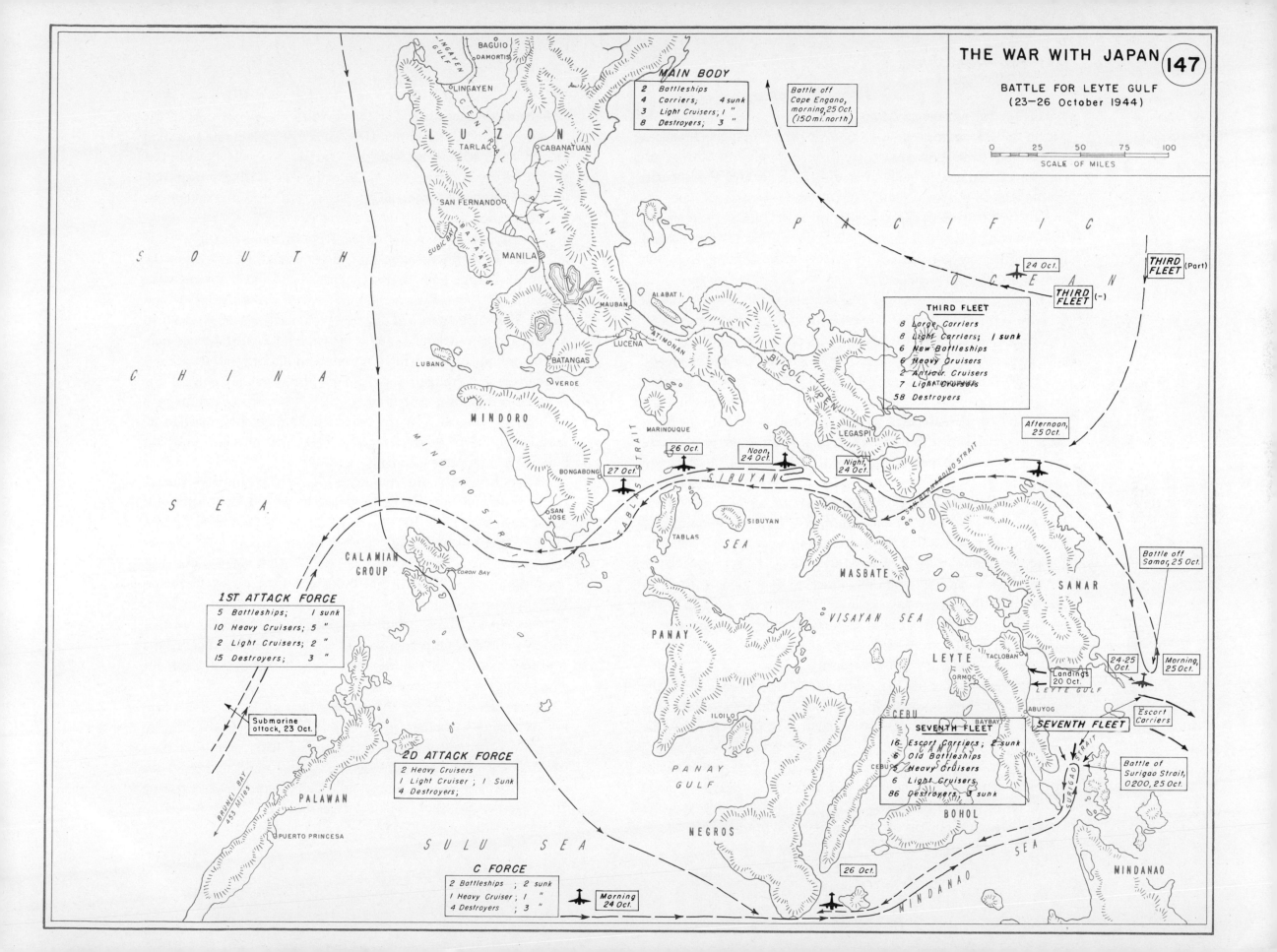

THE WAR WITH JAPAN (147)

BATTLE FOR LEYTE GULF
(23–26 October 1944)

0   25   50   75   100
SCALE OF MILES

MAIN BODY

2	Battleships	
4	Carriers;	4 sunk
3	Light Cruisers;	1 "
8	Destroyers;	3 "

Battle off Cape Engano, morning, 25 Oct. (150 mi. north)

THIRD FLEET

8	Large Carriers
8	Light Carriers; 1 sunk
6	New Battleships
6	Heavy Cruisers
2	Antiair. Cruisers
7	Light Cruisers
58	Destroyers

24 Oct.

THIRD FLEET (Part)

THIRD FLEET (-)

Afternoon, 25 Oct.

Battle off Samar, 25 Oct.

1ST ATTACK FORCE

5	Battleships;	1 sunk
10	Heavy Cruisers;	5 "
2	Light Cruisers;	2 "
15	Destroyers;	3 "

26 Oct.   Noon, 24 Oct.   27 Oct.   Night, 24 Oct.

Submarine attack, 23 Oct.

BRUNEI BAY 453 Miles

2D ATTACK FORCE

2	Heavy Cruisers
1	Light Cruiser; 1 Sunk
4	Destroyers;

Landings 20 Oct.

24-25 Oct.   Morning, 25 Oct.

Escort Carriers

SEVENTH FLEET

16	Escort Carriers; 2 sunk	
6	Old Battleships	
6	Heavy Cruisers	
6	Light Cruisers	
86	Destroyers; 3 sunk	

Battle of Surigao Strait, 0200, 25 Oct.

C FORCE

2	Battleships	; 2 sunk
1	Heavy Cruiser	; 1 "
4	Destroyers	; 3 "

Morning 24 Oct.

26 Oct.

SOUTH CHINA SEA

LUZON

LINGAYEN GULF
BAGUIO
DAMORTIS
LINGAYEN
TARLAC
CABANATUAN
SAN FERNANDO
SUBIC BAY
BATAAN
MANILA
BATANGAS
LUBANG
VERDE
MINDORO
BONGABONG
SAN JOSE
MINDORO STRAIT
MARINDUQUE
MAUBAN
ALABAT I.
LUCENA
ATIMONAN
BICOL PEN.
LEGASPI
TABLAS STRAIT
SIBUYAN
TABLAS
SIBUYAN SEA
SAN BERNARDINO STRAIT
MASBATE
SAMAR
CALAMIAN GROUP
CORON BAY
PANAY
VISAYAN SEA
ILOILO
LEYTE
TACLOBAN
ORMOC
LEYTE GULF
ABUYOG
BAYBAY
CEBU
CEBU
CAMOTES SEA
NEGROS
PANAY GULF
BOHOL
SURIGAO STRAIT
PALAWAN
PUERTO PRINCESA
SULU SEA
MINDANAO SEA
MINDANAO

PACIFIC OCEAN

Yamashita fully appreciated the implications of the Japanese defeat in the Battle of Leyte Gulf and suspected that the Japanese air arm had been seriously crippled. Accordingly, on 10 November, he recommended abandonment of Leyte and the concentration of strength for a defense of Luzon. But when his superiors balked, he renewed his efforts to reinforce Lt. Gen. Sosaku Suzuki. The latter planned to recapture Carigara and move forces down Leyte Valley to join up with another thrust coming from the mountains west of Dagami.

Meanwhile, Krueger was making plans for a two-pronged drive on Ormoc. However, apprehensive over the demonstrated Japanese capability to reinforce the island despite American air and naval superiority, he feared they might land in the X Corps' rear near Carigara. Consequently, when Krueger learned Suzuki's plan from a captured Japanese order, he postponed moving the rest of the 7th Division across the island to Balogo until the Sixth Army was reinforced. But the X Corps, leaving some troops along the coast to protect its rear, attacked the Japanese north of Limon (*upper left*). By 14 November, the 24th Division had managed to move two battalions to positions (*not shown*) in rear of the Japanese near the road leading south from Limon. Holding there against repeated counterattacks, they seriously interfered with Japanese supply efforts. On the 16th, the 32d Division relieved the tired 24th and continued the attack to seize Limon. By now, Suzuki had abandoned his optimistic plan for an offensive, but he fought desperately to hold Limon, the northern gateway to Ormoc. Not until 10 December was the 32d Division able to capture the village.

In the meantime, the 11th Airborne Division (arriving on the island to stage for another operation) had been assigned to the Sixth Army, and the 77th Division had arrived from Guam. While the 96th Division continued to press the remnants of the 16th Division west of Dagami, the 7th Division turned over its sector at Burauen to the 11th and moved across the island to Balogo on 22 November. The Seventh Fleet finally scraped together enough assault shipping to lift the 77th Division to Ipil (*lower center*) on 7 December. Three days later, the major part of the division entered Ormoc after a vigorous fight, while one battalion moved south to link up with the 7th Division, which had been slowly edging forward. On 9 December, an 11th Division column met a battalion from the 7th Division at Anas and completed the destruction of the Japanese 26th Division.

Suzuki, meanwhile—on orders from Tokyo—had made one final, but futile, offensive gesture. Fearing that aircraft from the Burauen, Dulag, and Tacloban airfields would soon interdict the vital lines of communications between the East Indies and Japan, Tokyo planners had directed that an offensive be launched to seize the Burauen fields and destroy facilities at the other two. Suzuki complied by making a ground and airborne attack on 6-7 December; but, though Japanese paratroopers did control the Burauen strips for a short time, the attack was too weak to be a real threat. Ironically, by the time of the attack, Krueger had already canceled plans to develop the Burauen airfields, and was building a new one at Tanauan.

After the seizure of Ormoc and Limon, the campaign moved swiftly to its conclusion. The 1st Cavalry and 32d Divisions drove south to link up with the 77th Division on 20 December at Libungao. On Christmas Day, the last Japanese port (Palompon) was seized by a battalion from the 77th Division. (This same day, Yamashita advised Suzuki that the Thirty-Fifth Army forces on Leyte had been written off as lost.) On the 26th, General Eichelberger's Eighth Army assumed responsibility for Leyte, so that Krueger could begin preparations for the next operation. For the next four months, the Eighth Army "patrolled" Leyte and Samar, eliminating isolated bands of Japanese.

Leyte never provided the major Allied air bases envisioned, but its seizure had other, more important results. By electing to fight a decisive battle there, the Japanese had committed their carefully hoarded fleet and a major part of their air arm; both suffered crippling losses. Nor could Yamashita afford the some 70,000 casualties the ground forces suffered. Total American Army casualties were 15,584.

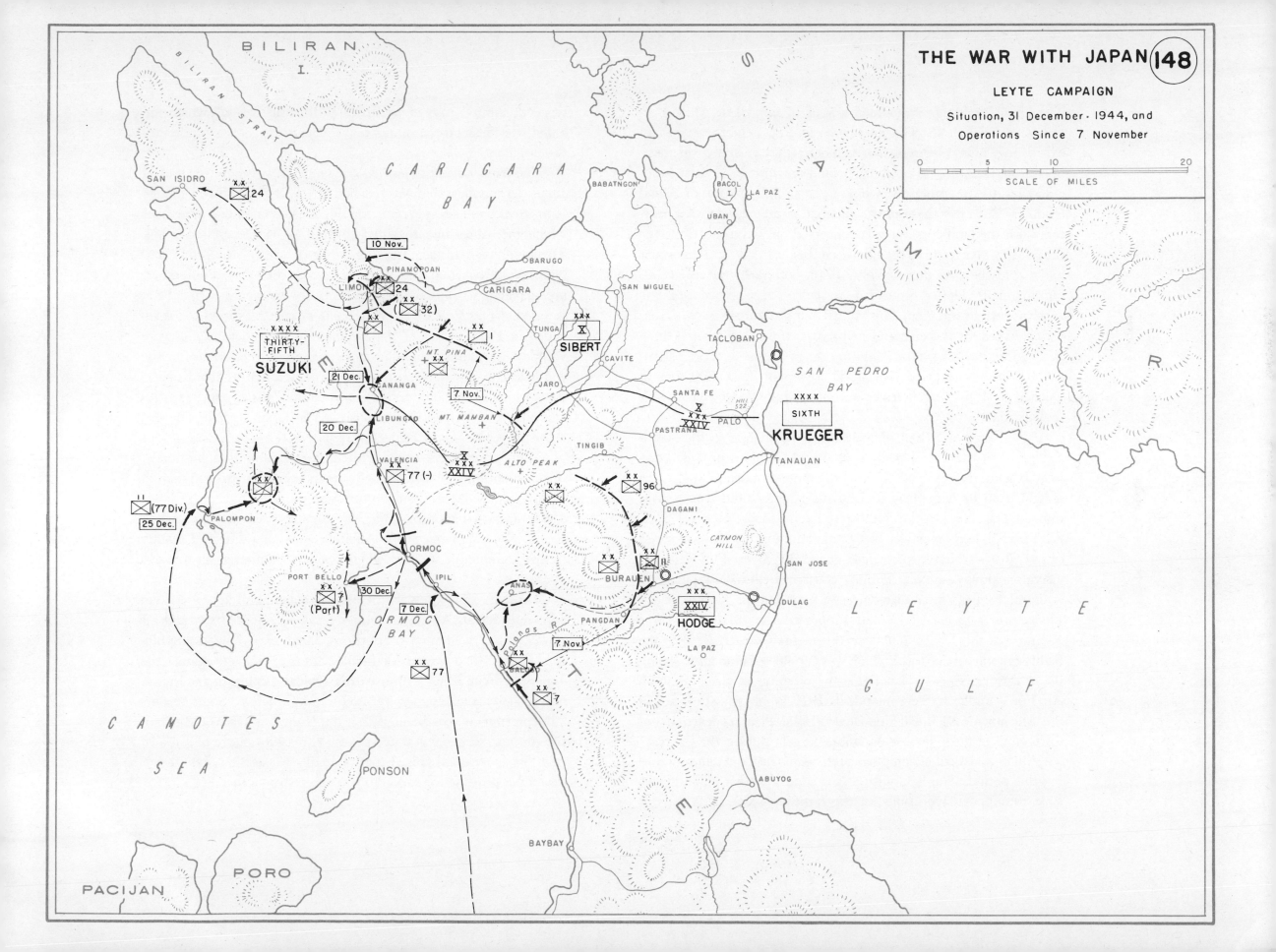

THE WAR WITH JAPAN 148

LEYTE CAMPAIGN

Situation, 31 December - 1944, and
Operations Since 7 November

SCALE OF MILES

The Leyte campaign concluded a year of unbroken Allied successes in the Pacific. The Japanese suffered defeat everywhere except in China (*see map 141*). There, they resumed offensive operations designed to establish a land corridor to French Indochina and to strengthen the China coast in anticipation of Allied landings. But even these operations had strategic defensive overtones, for the land corridor was conceived only as a substitute for the better water route to the Southern Resources Area. This route had already become unreliable by 1944—primarily because of attacks made by United States submarines on Japanese shipping—and was further threatened by MacArthur's seizure of Leyte, from which Allied air power could be projected over the South China Sea. (Japan's merchant shipping had declined from about 6,000,000 tons in December, 1941, to about 2,500,000 tons in December, 1944—submarines accounted for 60 per cent of this destruction.)

Allied air power had played an important role in the Allied string of victories in 1944. In Burma and China, it provided tactical support for ground forces but, more important, began to demonstrate its capability for moving supplies and troops over difficult obstacles. In the Southwest Pacific Area, General MacArthur exploited air power to the maximum in his brilliant series of operations which leapfrogged—generally covered by Kenney's aircraft—along the New Guinea coast into the Philippines. In Admiral Nimitz's area, army aircraft pounded the Kurile Islands (*this map, upper center*) and supported the drive across the Pacific, but more spectacular achievements were credited to the highly mobile carrier force which was capable of launching 1,000-plane attacks. Finally, 1944 saw the creation of the Twentieth Air Force under JCS command; its B-29 bombers—stationed in the Marianas and the China-Burma-India theater—carried out thirty-nine attacks against Japanese targets during the year.

Allied logistical accomplishments were truly outstanding during this period. The flexibility of the supply system made it possible to support operations on the far-flung battlefields. In this respect, Nimitz's use of small-scale "floating bases," which enabled the fleet to stay at sea longer, was a revolutionary development.

The map indicates (*dashed red line*) the maximum extent of Japanese conquest that was reached in 1942; also shown (*shaded blue areas*) are the parts of the Japanese-dominated area over which the Allies had regained control by 31 December, 1944. The Japanese-held localities (*red circles*), which MacArthur and Nimitz had bypassed in their respective drives to the Philippines, are depicted to illustrate how effectively these areas had been isolated. (The Volcano Islands [*center*] were destined to be invaded in 1945. A few of the Japanese in the other islands were withdrawn by submarine, but most of them surrendered after the war.) Except for those in the Aleutians, the many Allied operations which contributed to the contraction of the Japanese perimeter have been discussed previously. (The Japanese had occupied Attu and Kiska [*upper center*] in June, 1942. Though these troops posed no great threat to the United States, public indignation at this occupation of American soil was too persistent to be ignored. Consequently, Attu was recaptured by the 7th Division in May, 1943, and two months later the Japanese secretly evacuated Kiska. The campaign in the Aleutians was characterized mainly by the abominable weather which severely hampered all military operations.)

Thus, as 1944 drew to a close, all signs pointed to eventual Japanese defeat. American industry had augmented sea and air power to overwhelming proportions; huge, experienced amphibious forces stood poised for further advances—even against the Japanese home islands. But, with a typical display of fanaticism and tenacity, the Japanese refused to admit defeat. Some leaders still entertained a vague hope that the United States would tire of the war and seek a negotiated peace. Yamashita, more of a realist than his superiors, realized that after the disaster at Leyte it was no longer possible for Japan to win a decisive victory.

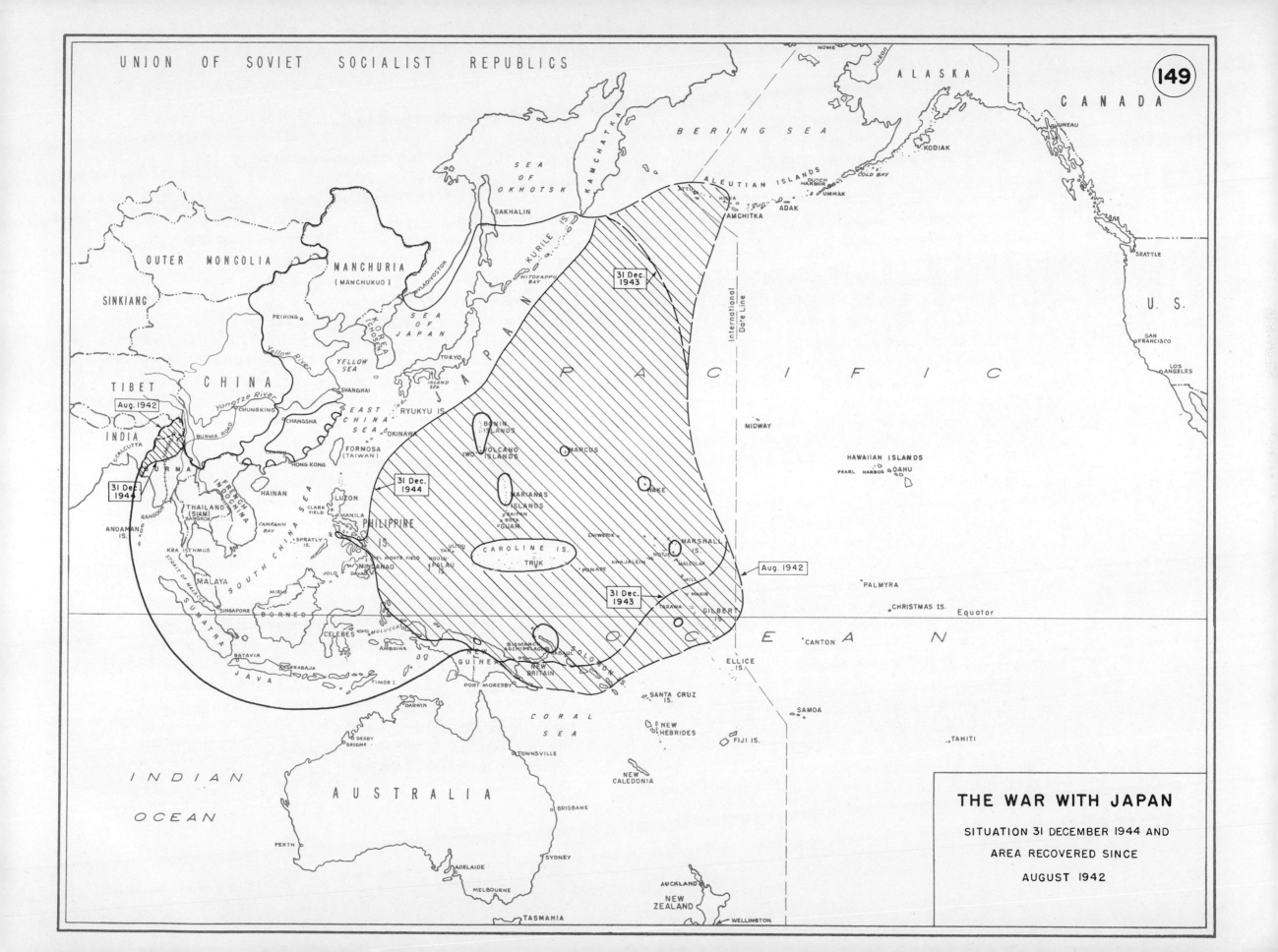

UNION OF SOVIET SOCIALIST REPUBLICS

149

ALASKA

CANADA

BERING SEA

NOME

YUKON

SEA
OF
OKHOTSK

KAMCHATKA

ALEUTIAN ISLANDS

JUNEAU

KODIAK

COLD BAY
DUTCH HARBOR
UMNAK

ATTU
KISKA
AMCHITKA
ADAK

OUTER MONGOLIA

MANCHURIA
(MANCHUKUO)

SAKHALIN

KURILE IS.

HITOKAPPU
BAY

31 Dec.
1943

SINKIANG

VLADIVOSTOK

SEA
OF
JAPAN

KOREA

PEIPING

TIBET

CHINA

Yellow River

CHUNGKING

Yangtze River

Aug. 1942

CHANGSHA

SHANGHAI

YELLOW
SEA

TOKYO

INLAND
SEA

J A P A N

P A C I F I C

International Date Line

U. S.

SEATTLE

SAN
FRANCISCO

LOS
ANGELES

MIDWAY

HAWAIIAN ISLANDS

PEARL HARBOR OAHU

BURMA ROAD

INDIA

CALCUTTA

31 Dec.
1944

BURMA

RANGOON

ANDAMAN
IS.

KRA ISTHMUS

Strait of Malaya

MALAYA

SINGAPORE

EAST
CHINA
SEA

RYUKYU IS.

OKINAWA

FORMOSA
(TAIWAN)

CANTON

HONG KONG

FRENCH
INDOCHINA

THAILAND
(SIAM)

BANGKOK

HAINAN

CAMRANH
BAY

SOUTH CHINA SEA

SPRATLY IS.

JOLO

MIRI

BORNEO

LUZON

CLARK
FIELD

MANILA

PHILIPPINE
IS.

DEL MONTE FIELD

MINDANAO

DAVAO

31 Dec.
1944

BONIN
ISLANDS

IWO

VOLCANO
ISLANDS

MARCUS

WAKE

MARIANAS
ISLANDS

SAIPAN
ROTA
GUAM

ULITHI

YAP

NOUMU

PALAU
IS.

CAROLINE IS.

TRUK

PONAPE

ENIWETOK

KWAJALEIN

MARSHALL
IS.

WOTJE

MALOELAP

MILI

Aug. 1942

PALMYRA

CHRISTMAS IS. Equator

MARKIN

CANTON

E A N

SUMATRA

BATAVIA

JAVA

SOERABAJA

CELEBES

MOLUCCAS

AMBOINA

TIMOR I.

31 Dec.
1943

TARAWA

GILBERT
IS.

NEW
GUINEA

BISMARCK
ARCHIPELAGO

RABAUL

NEW
BRITAIN

SOLOMONS

ELLICE
IS.

PORT MORESBY

SANTA CRUZ
IS.

SAMOA

DARWIN

DERBY
BROOME

CORAL
SEA

NEW
HEBRIDES

FIJI IS.

TAHITI

INDIAN

OCEAN

AUSTRALIA

PERTH

TOWNSVILLE

NEW
CALEDONIA

BRISBANE

SYDNEY

ADELAIDE

MELBOURNE

AUCKLAND

NEW
ZEALAND

TASMANIA

WELLINGTON

THE WAR WITH JAPAN

SITUATION 31 DECEMBER 1944 AND

AREA RECOVERED SINCE

AUGUST 1942

This map depicts (on a larger scale than map 149) the extent to which the Allies had reestablished control—by 1 January, 1945—over the empire Japan had carved out in the first year of the war. It was in the New Guinea–Bismarck Archipelago–Solomons area that the bypassing technique had isolated the most Japanese. There, some 135,000 members of the armies which had opposed MacArthur and Halsey were hopelessly cut off and under pressure from Australian forces.

As the new year dawned, the Allies were readying new offensives against Japan's inner defenses. MacArthur was preparing to land on Luzon, while Halsey's powerful fleet was already launching strikes to cover this assault. The remainder of the Pacific Fleet was raiding to the north in the Bonin and Volcano Islands (*upper center*), concentrating on Iwo Jima—the next target for Nimitz's amphibious forces. Australian forces were preparing offensives against Borneo and the bypassed Japanese in New Guinea and the Solomons. In Burma, the British were slowly pushing Japanese forces back on Mandalay. The Americans now had twenty-seven divisions deployed in the Pacific (Australia provided four more; New Zealand, one), and MacArthur's combined command alone numbered almost 1,500,000 men. The bulk of the United States Navy (some 37,000 aircraft and 61,000 vessels) was under the control of Nimitz. In the air, the Allies had overwhelming superiority. (Japan's desperate answer was the suicide mission—the Kamikaze.) But perhaps more important than the individual build-up of ground, air, and naval forces was the welding of these services into an efficient fighting machine, which the Japanese were powerless to stop. Japan, however, was not willing to quit; the war would last only eight more months, but in this short period the Allies would encounter some of the bitterest fighting of the entire conflict.

The Joint Chiefs of Staff had decided, in July, 1944, to invade Leyte, but the debate over the next objective—Luzon or Formosa —was by no means resolved by then. Until September, opinion in Washington was predominantly in favor of Formosa; in the field, Nimitz—apparently somewhat reluctantly—preferred Formosa, while MacArthur was solidly in favor of Luzon.

MacArthur believed that if Luzon were seized, Formosa could be bypassed; but, failing that, he averred that Formosa, in any event, could not be taken until Luzon was in Allied hands. He also pointed out that the liberation of all the Philippines was an American obligation—if not a political necessity. Admiral King, on the other hand, held that a seizure of Formosa would facilitate MacArthur's return to Luzon. He argued that the basic strategic plan of 1943 could not be implemented without seizing Formosa. Finally, he maintained—and General Marshall at first agreed— that if Formosa were bypassed, the next objective should be Japan itself. Army Air Corps planners, who wanted B-29 bases in eastern China, sided with King.

Events in September had a decisive influence on the debate. When the Leyte invasion date was advanced to October, MacArthur at once stated that he could land on Luzon in December, thus not interfering with a projected February operation in Formosa. When Nimitz's plan for a Formosa–China coast operation was received in Washington, the logisticians immediately pointed out that it could not be supported logistically without withdrawing troops from Europe and possibly canceling a Luzon assault as well. Then Stilwell advised the JCS that the Japanese were rapidly overrunning the Allied airfields in China which the air planners had expected to use for B-29 bases. The combination of these factors killed the Formosa operation. Only King continued to oppose a landing in Luzon, and eventually—when reassured by MacArthur that the carrier forces would not be tied up in support of the Sixth Army longer than the assault phase—he agreed to the operation. Hence, on 3 October, the JCS directed MacArthur to invade Luzon about 20 December, 1944.

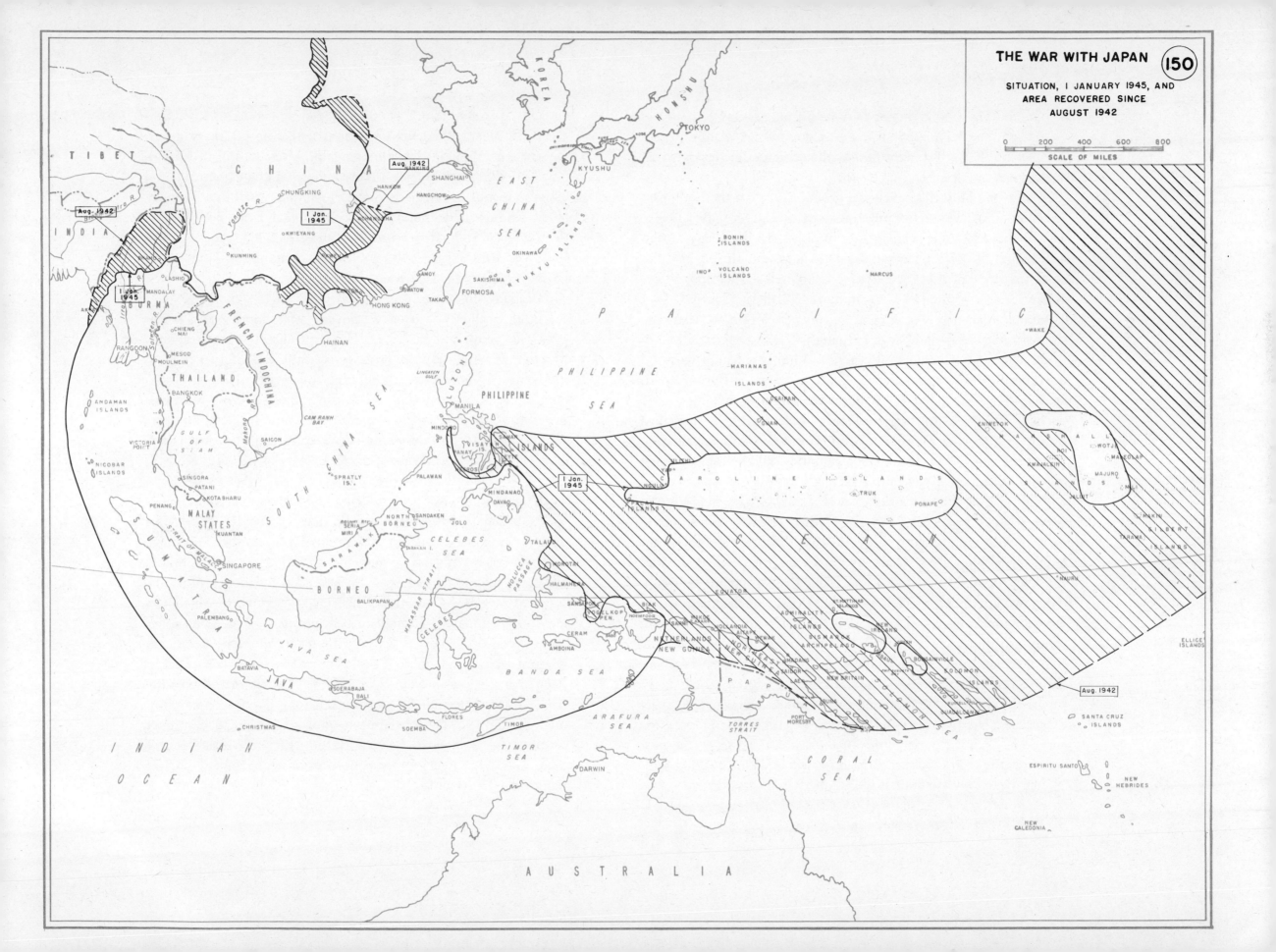

THE WAR WITH JAPAN 150

SITUATION, 1 JANUARY 1945, AND
AREA RECOVERED SINCE
AUGUST 1942

0   200   400   600   800
SCALE OF MILES

The situation on New Year's Day in Burma (*heavy dashed red line*) found the Japanese in retreat, except around Wanting (*center*), where they still fought fanatically to maintain their grip on the western end of the Burma Road.

Following Stilwell's relief, the ground forces of the Southeast Asia Command were reorganized under Lt. Gen. Sir Oliver Leese, who at the same time commanded the British 11th Army Group (consisting of the Fourteenth Army in northern Burma and the detached XV Corps in the Akyab coastal area). The other forces under Leese's command were Sultan's Northern Combat Area Command (British, American, and American-trained Chinese troops) and Marshal Wei-Li-Huang's Chinese Expeditionary Force (about twelve weak divisions). The Allied plan involved operations by Sultan and Wei-Li-Huang to open the Burma Road; an offensive by Lt. Gen. Sir William J. Slim on Mandalay—to be pushed, if possible, to Rangoon; and a drive down the west coast by the XV Corps. This last operation aided Slim's advance by capturing airfield sites from which supplies could be rapidly flown in to his advancing Fourteenth Army.

Slim had hoped that the Japanese would make a stand in the open country north of Mandalay, where British armor could operate with great effectiveness. Instead, the new Japanese commander in Burma, Lt. Gen. Hyotaro Kimura, decided to hold the line Akyab-Mandalay-Lashio. Any British assault on Mandalay would therefore first have to force the broad Irrawaddy River. Kimura apparently felt that, by catching the Fourteenth Army astride the river at the end of a long and tenuous supply line, he could inflict a crushing defeat similar to that the Japanese themselves had suffered at Imphal. Such a victory would leave him free to deal with Sultan and the Chinese, with every prospect of success. His plan was theoretically sound, but it ignored the supply and combat capabilities of the Allied air forces, the now superior jungle craft of the British troops, and the amazing feats of logistical improvisation which Allied staffs could achieve on short notice.

Wei-Li-Huang took Lashio on 7 March. The Ledo Road and a parallel pipeline had already been extended to Myitkyina; convoys began rolling into Kunming again. After the fall of Lashio, however, Chiang Kai-Shek ordered most of the American and Chinese troops in northern Burma to return to China. This enabled Kimura to withdraw troops from that front and employ them against Slim. He also recalled most of the Japanese troops from the west coast, but here British amphibious attacks repeatedly cut the coastal road, inflicting heavy casualties on the withdrawing columns.

In the center, once he was aware of Kimura's actual dispositions, Slim sent his XXXIII Corps directly south against Mandalay, while the IV Corps—practically building its road as it advanced—moved secretly through the jungle hills west of that city, crossed the Irrawaddy at Pagan (*lower center*), and surprised the Japanese supply center at Meiktila. This cut Kimura's supply line; his most desperate efforts to regain the town failed, and Mandalay meanwhile fell (20 March) to the XXXIII Corps.

Kimura had lost heavily. Quickly regrouping, Slim swept south, his main force following the axis of the Rangoon-Mandalay railroad, a secondary attack moving down the Irrawaddy. It was a race with the coming monsoon season and Kimura's ability to rebuild his defenses. Spearheaded by their armor, and supplied largely by air, the British attacks quickly gained momentum. A Japanese attempt to concentrate at Toungoo (*lower center*) was broken up by Karen tribesmen under British officers. Kimura stripped southern Burma of troops for a last stand at Pegu, but this was broken by 1 May, just as the monsoon rains began. Left undefended, Rangoon fell to a XV Corps amphibious operation on the 2d. Some mop-up campaigning continued as Japanese isolated in western Burma tried to break out, but there were no more major operations prior to the Japanese capitulation on 15 August.

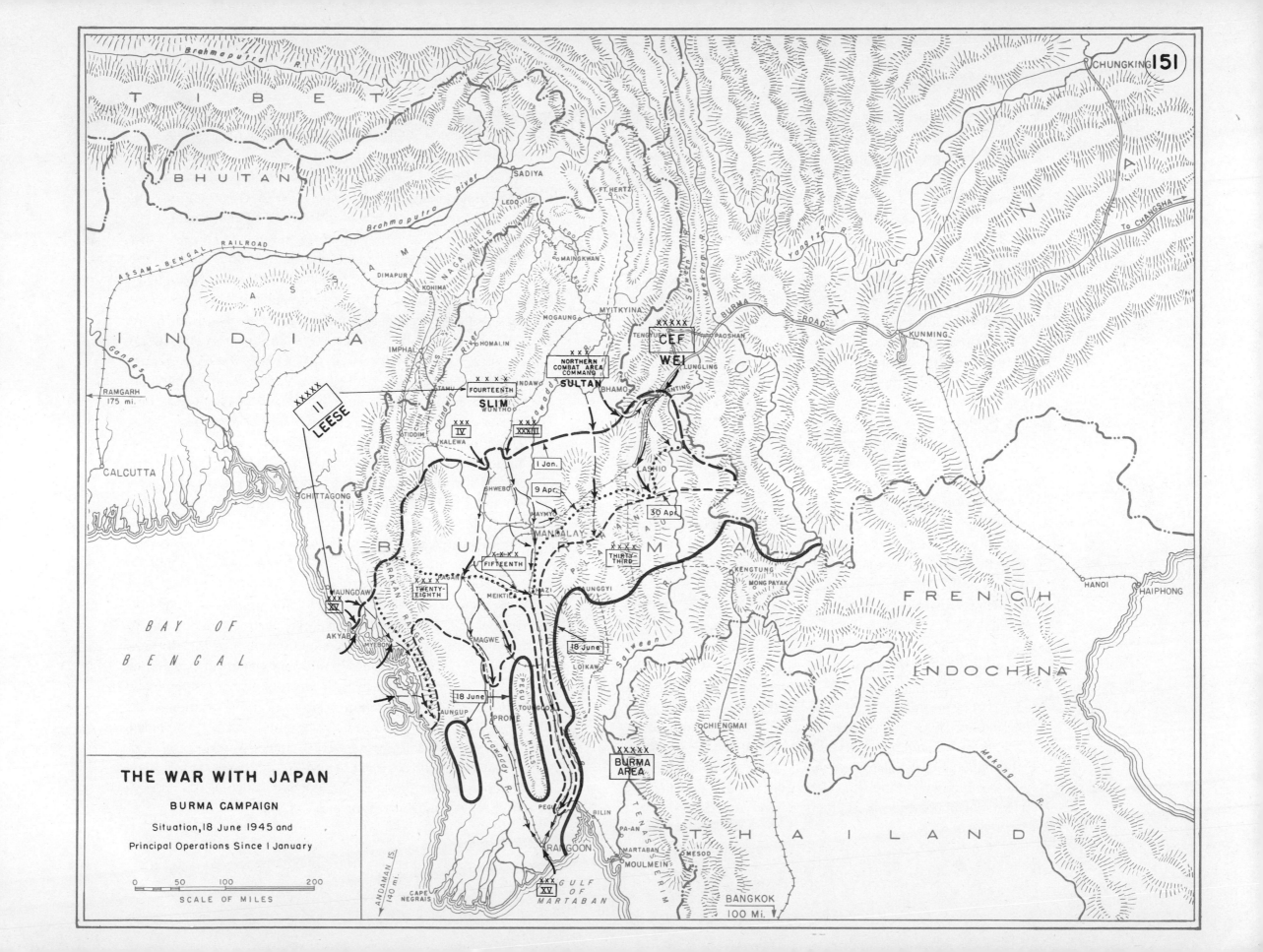

151

THE WAR WITH JAPAN

BURMA CAMPAIGN

Situation, 18 June 1945 and

Principal Operations Since 1 January

0   50   100   200

SCALE OF MILES

During early 1945, the Japanese continued to consolidate their position in southeastern China (*compare this map and map 141*), clearing the Canton-Hengyang railroad (*lower center*) by 5 February. The Fourteenth Air Force and the XX Bomber Command, hampered by periodic fuel shortages and the loss of their forward bases, carried the major burden of the Allied war effort. They were especially active in mid-January, in support of the American Third Fleet's raid into the South China Sea (launched to cover the American invasion of Luzon; *see map 154*) and in late March and early April (to support the American landing on Okinawa; *see map 163*).

To further strengthen their grip on southeast Asia, the Japanese seized full control of Indochina in early March. (The Japanese had occupied this French colony in 1940, but—by agreement—the French had continued to control its internal administration. Some of the weak, hopelessly isolated French garrisons appear to have waged an equally hopeless resistance.) In late March, the Japanese attacked in considerable force in central China, overrunning an American air base at Laohokow (*this map, lower center*) and seizing the ripening crops in this fertile area. A second such operation, directed at Changteh and Chihkiang (*lower center*) was thrown back in early May by a strong Chinese–Fourteenth Air Force counterattack.

This was the last large-scale Japanese offensive. Elsewhere, it was already obvious that Japan had lost her war. Germany had capitulated, Okinawa was largely in American hands, the Japanese forces in Burma had been destroyed, the Japanese Navy was a memory, and the remaining Japanese air power was bleeding itself to death in Kamikaze attacks. Furthermore, Stalin—having obtained his immediate objectives in Europe—had made it plain that he intended to follow a similar policy in the Far East. Japanese forces in Manchuria—the one-time crack Kwantung Army—had declined greatly in strength and quality, due to the transfer of veteran units during the war. Consequently, by mid-May, the Japanese began evacuating southern China to reinforce their

Manchurian defenses. This withdrawal was followed up—but, apparently, not appreciably troubled—by the Chinese. The Fourteenth and Tenth Air Forces (the latter recently transferred from Burma and India) harried the Japanese by strikes against their roads, railroads, and coastal shipping. No decisive actions took place in this area, however, before the end of the war.

Russia declared war on Japan on 8 August. The next day, the Russians launched their main attack from the west, advancing along the railroad toward Tsitsihar and Harbin and, farther south, along the ancient caravan route Kalgan (*center, right*)–Peiping–Tientsin. Secondary attacks pushed eastward and south from Khabarovsk and Vladivostok (*both upper right*). Using masses of armor and motorized troops, the Russians flooded across the Manchurian plains; the Japanese—lacking both modern armor and effective antitank weapons—could offer only spotty resistance, their most effective stands apparently being made southwest of Vladivostok. (Practically nothing is known concerning the details of this campaign, which the Russians presented to the world as *the* decisive blow that defeated Japan, after years of indecisive American fumbling among the Pacific Islands.) Although the war ended officially on 15 August, the Russians kept up their advance until the 20th. (For operations in Burma during 1945, *see map 151*.)

Operations in India, Burma, and China represent, above all, a logistical triumph. Supplies, in large part originating in the United States, were moved into remote corners of the Burmese jungle and the hills of China in sufficient quantity to maintain major air and ground offensives. In this, the transport plane and the bulldozer changed the entire concept of transportation in the Far East. Yet, at the same time, pack mules, porters, elephants, and improvised river shipping were frequently invaluable. This was a war fought for extended periods in unhealthy, rain-sodden, insect-ridden areas—probably the loneliest, most alien, and most primitive war Americans have ever faced.

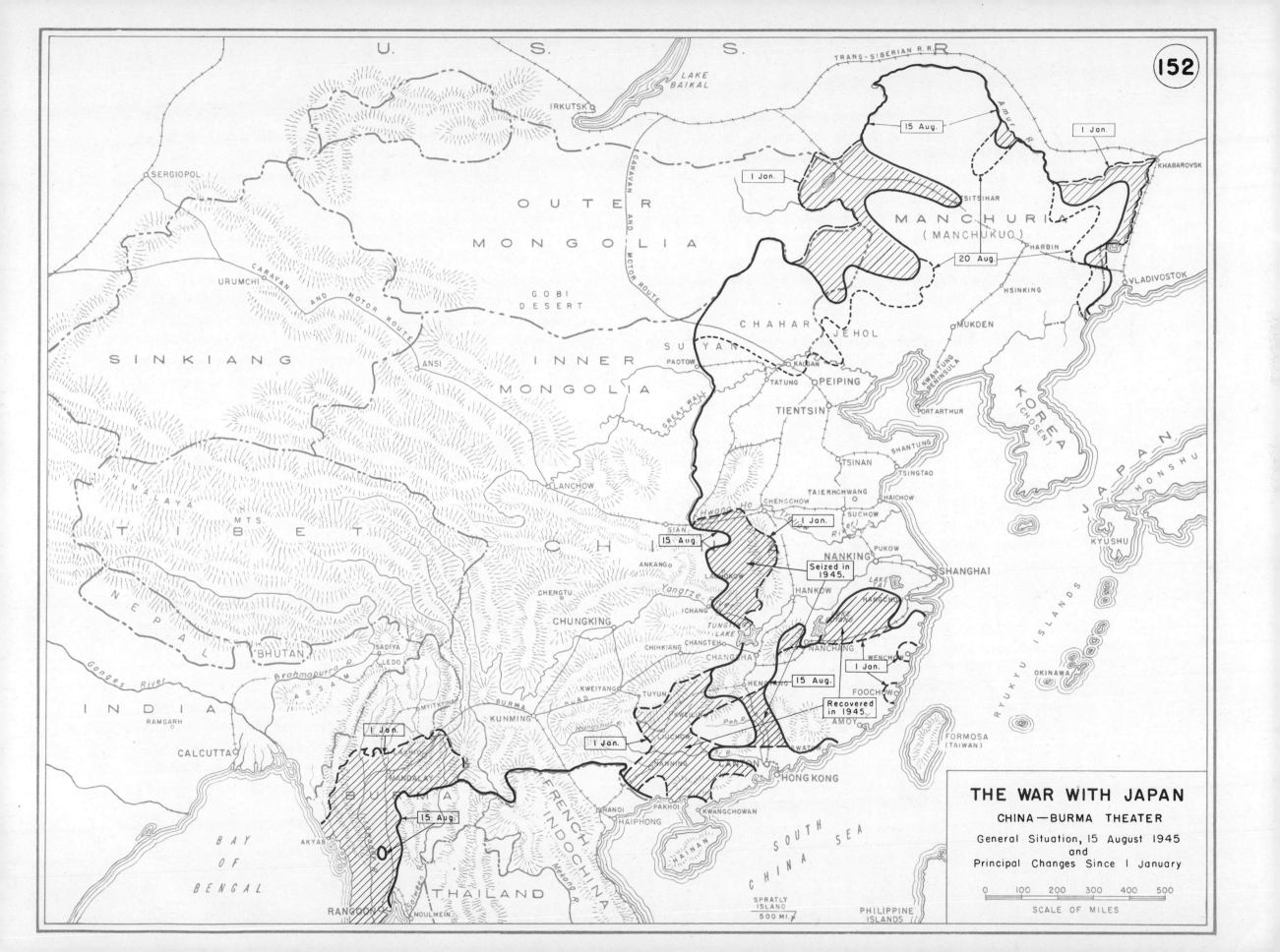

THE WAR WITH JAPAN

CHINA—BURMA THEATER

General Situation, 15 August 1945
and
Principal Changes Since 1 January

152

With the decision to invade Luzon rather than Formosa (*see text, map 150*), MacArthur began formulating his final plan. Originally, he expected to route the assault convoy from Leyte along the eastern coast of Luzon, around its northern end, and then to Lingayen Gulf (*this map, top center*). But to protect any convoy following this route, land-based air cover would first have to be established at Legaspi (*center, right*) and Aparri (*see map 156, top center*); and such a requirement would almost certainly entail postponing the projected 20 December landing at Lingayen Gulf. When naval planners also called attention to the poor weather conditions that normally prevailed off northern Luzon in December, MacArthur decided to use the route shown (*this map, dashed blue line*). (He had decided earlier to use this route for reinforcement convoys, providing them air cover from bases he planned to seize on Mindoro [*center, left*] on 5 December.)

The dates for the Mindoro and Luzon operations had to be reconsidered in light of the prolongation of the Leyte campaign and the delay in establishing airfields on Leyte to support the Mindoro landing. Additionally, Halsey pointed out that his fleet would have to have badly needed repair and rest before it could provide support for a Luzon landing. Consequently, MacArthur decided to augment land-based air support for the Mindoro operation with Seventh Fleet escort carriers and to postpone the landings on Mindoro and Luzon to 15 December and 9 January, respectively.

A brigade-size task force landed near San Jose on Mindoro early on 15 December, drove the small Japanese garrison inland, quickly occupied the southwestern part of the island, and established a defensive perimeter (*shaded blue area*). Two airfields were built; by the end of the month, Kenney's aircraft based there were striking Japanese installations on Luzon. On 1 January, 1945, the Eighth Army assumed responsibility for the island of Mindoro.

Japanese air power in the Philippines had been reduced to such a state of impotency in the last few months of 1944 that, by 1 January, 1945, there were only about 150 aircraft on Luzon —and practically all of these were destined to be destroyed by 13 January. But Yamashita's ground forces on Luzon were more formidable; as shown, he had 250,000 troops, poorly equipped though they were. Though actually wanting to counterattack any Allied landing, Yamashita reluctantly concluded that he would have to adopt a static defense, designed to delay the conquest of Luzon as long as possible. Consequently, he organized three groups: the Shobu Group would defend against a landing at Lingayen Gulf, and ultimately withdraw into a rugged mountain redoubt north of Baguio (*top center*); the Kembu Group would defend Clark Field (*upper left, near San Fernando*) and then withdraw westward into the mountains; and the Shimbu Group, though responsible for all of southern Luzon, would concentrate its strength in the mountains east of Manila—it was specifically directed not to defend the capital.

MacArthur's concept for the invasion envisaged an amphibious landing at the base of Lingayen Gulf and rapid consolidation of a beachhead; the establishment of air and base facilities; the securing of the Central Plain; and the capture of Manila. Before Krueger's Sixth Army undertook the accomplishment of this mission, the Eighth Army would seize northeastern Mindoro, naval and air elements would conduct demonstrations along the southern Luzon coast, and guerrillas would destroy communications in southern Luzon. (As it turned out, none of these attempts at deception [*blue arrows*] misled Yamashita as to the location of the main landing.) The Seventh Fleet would provide direct naval (surface and air) support while Halsey—operating independently of MacArthur—would cover the invasion force by hitting Formosan and northern Luzon targets. Kenney's aircraft, flying from Leyte and Mindoro, would pummel Luzon targets, and China-based B-29's would strike Formosa.

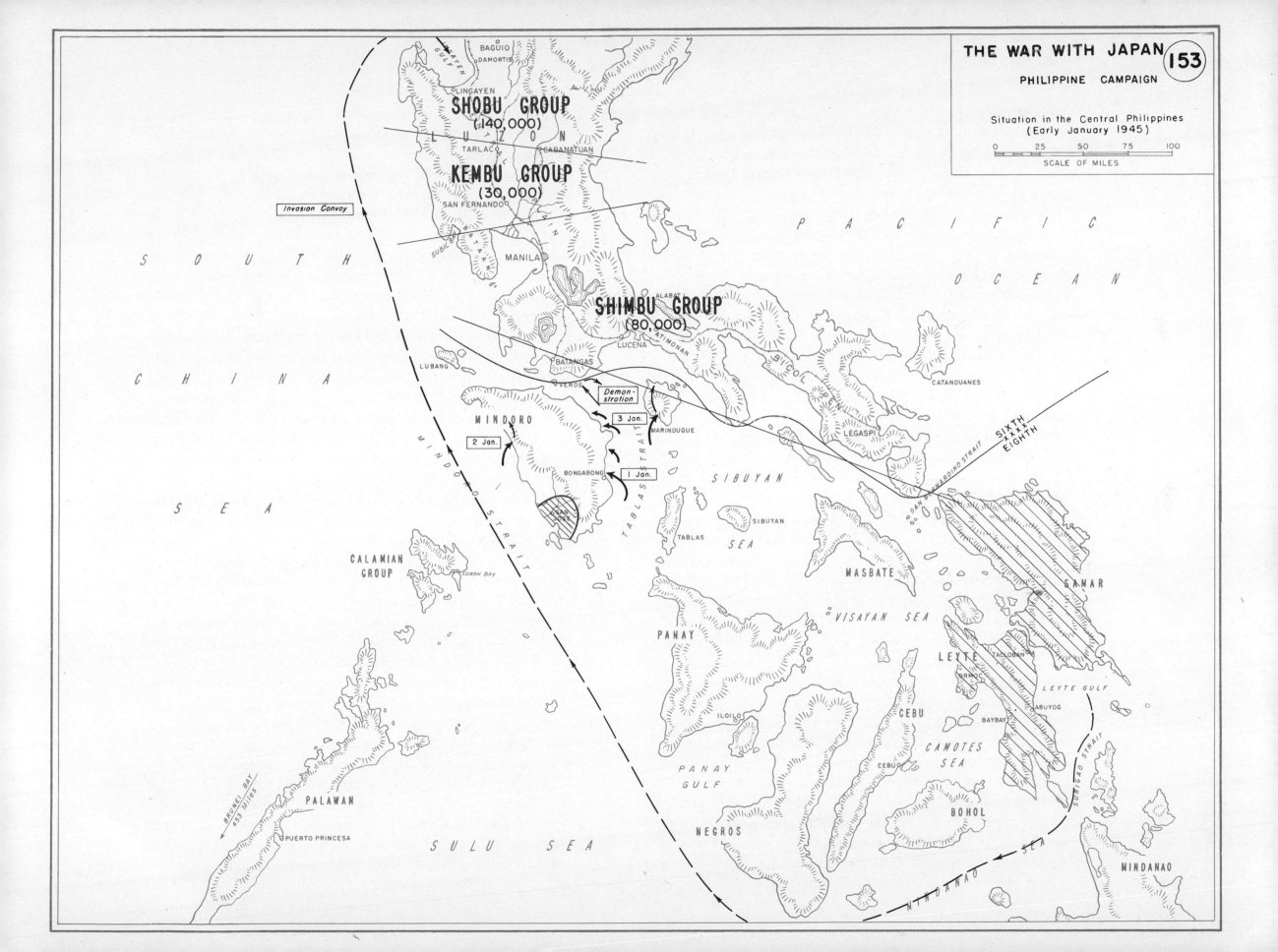

THE WAR WITH JAPAN (153)

PHILIPPINE CAMPAIGN

Situation in the Central Philippines
(Early January 1945)

0   25   50   75   100

SCALE OF MILES

SHOBU GROUP
(140,000)

KEMBU GROUP
(30,000)

SHIMBU GROUP
(80,000)

Invasion Convoy

Demonstration

3 Jan.

2 Jan.

1 Jan.

SIXTH
XXXX
EIGHTH

PACIFIC OCEAN

SOUTH CHINA SEA

LUZON

BAGUIO

DAMORTIS

LINGAYEN

LINGAYEN GULF

TARLAC

CABANATUAN

SAN FERNANDO

SUBIC

BATAAN

MANILA

LUBANG

BATANGAS

VERDE

LUCENA

ATIMONAN

ALABAT

BICOL

LEGASPI

CATANDUANES

MINDORO

SAN JOSE

BONGABONG

MARINDUQUE

TABLAS STRAIT

MINDORO STRAIT

CALAMIAN GROUP

CORON BAY

TABLAS

SIBUYAN

SIBUYAN SEA

MASBATE

SAN BERNARDINO STRAIT

SAMAR

VISAYAN SEA

PANAY

ILOILO

PANAY GULF

NEGROS

CEBU

CEBU

CAMOTES SEA

LEYTE

TACLOBAN

ORMOC

BAYBAY

ABUYOG

LEYTE GULF

BOHOL

SURIGAO STRAIT

BRUNEI BAY
453 Miles

PALAWAN

PUERTO PRINCESA

SULU SEA

MINDANAO SEA

MINDANAO

On 2 January, the first elements of the Luzon Attack Force departed Leyte for Lingayen Gulf. Three days earlier, Halsey's carriers had left Ulithi for the scheduled strikes against Formosa. Now—as MacArthur's force moved north through the Visayas—Japan's few remaining aircraft in the Philippines were committed in desperate Kamikaze strikes against the convoy. By the 7th, the Allies had sustained such damage that the naval commanders were very seriously disturbed over the practicability of landing the next day. Kenney and Halsey—the latter now in position off Luzon—intensified their attacks on Japanese airfields on Luzon, and the Kamikaze attacks began to taper off on 9 January. On the 13th, they ceased—not because the Allies had devised an effective defense, but because the Japanese high command refused to replace its aircraft losses on Luzon. Beginning with attacks on the convoy carrying the Mindoro landing force on 13 December and lasting through 13 January, Kamikaze attacks sank twenty ships, heavily damaged twenty-four, and lightly damaged thirty-five.

For the assault at Lingayen Gulf, the Sixth Army was organized as shown (*upper left*). Because the divisions it was to employ were so widely dispersed in the southern Pacific islands in late 1944, the mounting of the operation posed major problems in operational and logistical planning. The reinforcements shown (*top left*) were tentatively allocated to Krueger when November intelligence estimates forecast a larger enemy force on Luzon than had been originally expected. Of these units, the 33d and 41st Divisions were MacArthur's theater reserve. In addition, the Eighth Army (Lt. Gen. Robert L. Eichelberger) was preparing to execute a subsidiary landing on Luzon, after which the troops employed (XI Corps) would come under Krueger's control. (This landing was made later near San Antonio [*bottom left*].) Ultimately, the Luzon campaign became the largest of the Pacific war and, comparatively speaking, employed more American forces than did operations in North Africa or Italy.

Krueger landed with four divisions abreast at 0930, 9 January. He chose the relatively poor beaches shown, rather than the better ones on the eastern side of the gulf, in the hope of achieving tactical surprise. Also, they were less heavily defended, and behind them was an airstrip which Krueger wished to seize quickly. Opposition to the landing was light; by nightfall, the Sixth Army had landed 68,000 men and established a beachhead as shown (*dashed red line*).

The advance, superbly supported by engineer units, made good progress the next two days. Only the 43d Division met substantial resistance as it encountered the forward positions of the Shobu Group. On 11 January, Krueger landed his floating reserve and immediately sent the 158th RCT north to secure Damortis. By the 20th, the Sixth Army reached the line shown (*dotted red line*); the major resistance was encountered in the north (*heavy dotted section*). The XIV Corps' advance was being governed primarily by logistics, Japanese resistance being spotty; by contrast, the I Corps was meeting bitter opposition in its eastward advance. The 6th Division had encountered a strong position in the Cabaruan Hills which was not completely overrun until the 28th; meanwhile, the 25th Division had been committed on 17 January, and the 43d Division—threatening to break into Yamashita's planned redoubt area—continued to meet fierce resistance.

On the 17th, Kenney's aircraft had begun operating from the Lingayen airfields, thus releasing Kincaid's escort carriers which were still standing by. That same date, MacArthur—with characteristic boldness—had urged Krueger to speed his drive on Manila, but Krueger, fearing a Japanese attack on his east flank, preferred to wait until he could strengthen the I Corps. He did, however, push the XIV Corps forward; it promptly encountered the Kembu Group near Bamban (*lower center*) on 23 January and for the next week engaged in its stiffest fight to date in overrunning Clark Field and driving the Japanese westward. One regiment continued south to seize Calumpit. Meanwhile, the I Corps, reinforced by the 32d Division (30 January), pushed east and south as Yamashita—resisting stubbornly to hold the approaches to his redoubt and gain maximum time to bring supplies up Route 5—slowly gave ground. By the 31st, Krueger had moved the recently arrived 1st Cavalry Division to Guimba (*center*) and had forced the Japanese back far enough to feel secure at both Clark Field (*lower center*) and Rosario (*upper left*). He was now ready to rush columns to Manila.

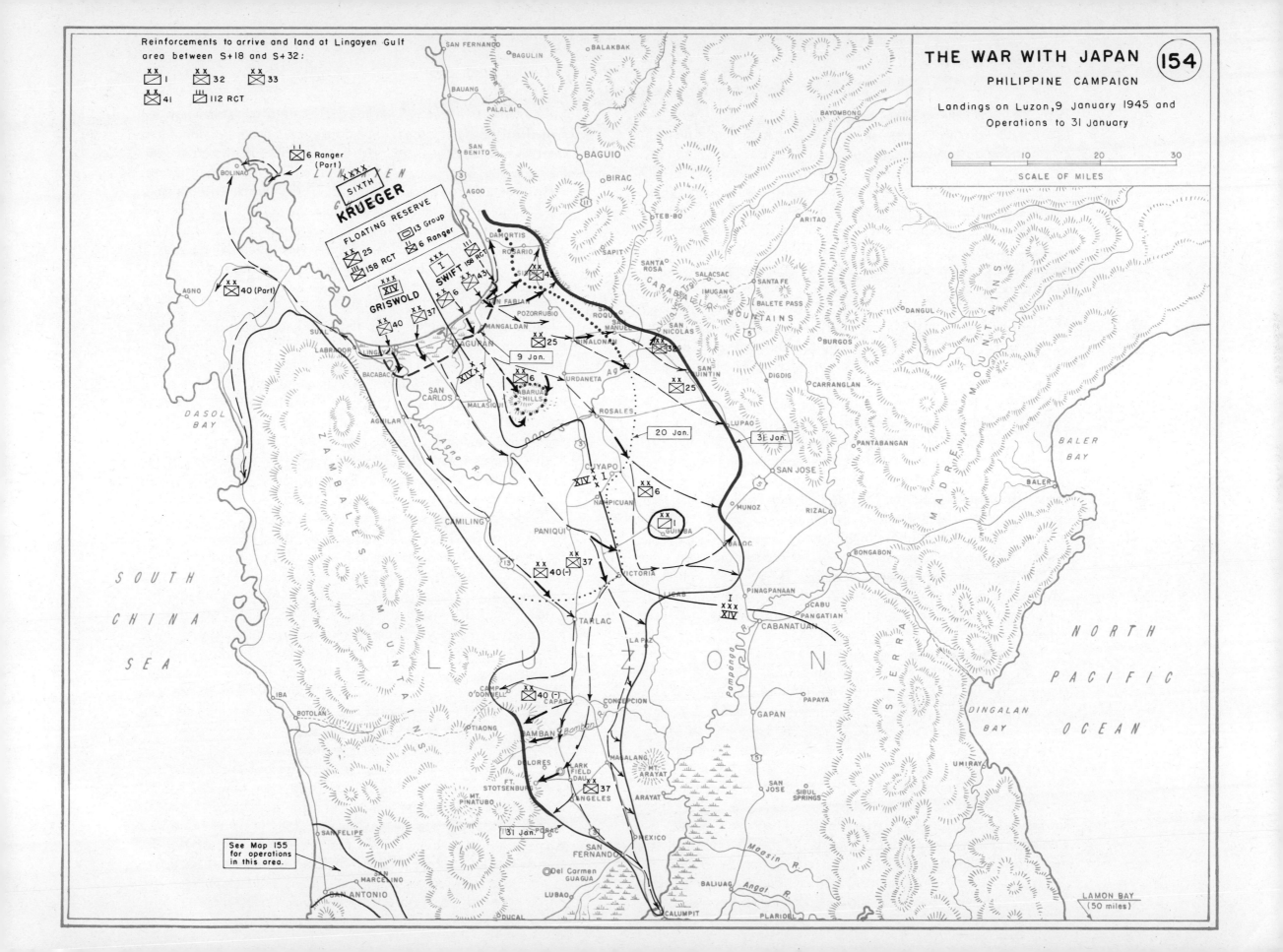

SCALE OF MILES

0   10   20   30

Reinforcements to arrive and land at Lingayen Gulf
area between S+18 and S+32:

1   32   33
41   112 RCT

6 Ranger
(Part)

SIXTH
KRUEGER

FLOATING RESERVE
13 Group
25   6 Ranger
158 RCT
SWIFT   158 RCT
GRISWOLD   43
6
40   37

40 (Part)

6 Ranger
(Part)

BOLINAO

AGNO

LINGAYEN
GULF

DAMORTIS
ROSARIO

SAN FABIAN
POZORRUBIO
MANGALDAN
DAGUPAN
BINALONAN
URDANETA
9 Jan.
CABARUAN
HILLS
ROSALES

SAN FERNANDO
BAGULIN
PALALAI
BAUANG
SAN BENITO
BAGUIO
BIRAC
AGOO
BALAKBAK

SANTA
ROSA
SALACSAC
IMUGAN   SANTA FE
BALETE PASS

CARABALLO
MOUNTAINS

40
25
6
25
1
37

25
32
SAN
NICOLAS
SAN QUINTIN
DIGDIG

LUPAO
PANTABANGAN

20 Jan.
31 Jan.

SAN JOSE

BALER
BAY

BALER

CUYAPO
XIV   1
NAMPICUAN
6
GUIMBA
I
BALOC
MUNOZ
RIZAL

BONGABON

PANIQUI
CAMILING

40(-)
37

VICTORIA
LICAB
LA PAZ
PINAGPANAAN
CABU
PANGATIAN
I
XXX
XIV
CABANATUAN

PAPAYA
GAPAN

SAN JOSE
SIBUL
SPRINGS

SIERRA MADRE

DINGALAN
BAY

TARLAC

DASOL
BAY

SOUTH
CHINA
SEA

ZAMBALES MOUNTAINS

L U Z O N

CAMP
O'DONNELL
CAPAS
40 (-)
CONCEPCION

IBA
BOTOLAN

TIAONG
BAMBAN
DOLORES
CLARK
FIELD
DAU
FT.
STOTSENBURG
ANGELES
37

MT.
PINATUBO
SAN FELIPE

SAN
MARCELINO
SAN
ANTONIO

See Map 155
for operations
in this area.

31 Jan.

PORAC
CALUMPIT

N O R T H

P A C I F I C

O C E A N

MAGALANG
MT.
ARAYAT
ARAYAT

MEXICO
SAN
FERNANDO
GUAGUA
DEL CARMEN
LUBAO
DUCAL

MOASIN R.
BALIUAG
ANGAT R.
PLARIDEL

Pampanga

UMIRAY

LAMON BAY
(50 miles)

Before Krueger loosed the XIV Corps on its quick dash for Manila, the Eighth Army—as part of MacArthur's strategy to keep the Japanese off balance and to seal off Bataan—made two amphibious landings on Luzon. The first was executed on 29 January by the XI Corps near San Antonio (*upper left*). These troops met no initial opposition—friendly guerrillas controlled the area—and quickly moved inland, seizing Olongapo and Grande Island on the 30th. On the 31st, the XI Corps (now under Krueger's control) began its drive eastward to block the Bataan peninsula.

The second landing took place on the 31st when one glider regiment of the 11th Airborne Division (soon followed by the second glider regiment) made an amphibious landing at Nasugbu (*lower left*) against slight opposition. Originally planned as a reconnaissance in force to be exploited—if practicable—by seizing Tagaytay Ridge and then patrolling north and east to contain elements of the Shimbu Group in southwestern Luzon, the operation soon developed into a headlong dash for Manila. Presumably having received MacArthur's permission, Eichelberger decided to exploit the landing and ordered the division's parachute regiment to jump on Tagaytay Ridge. This jump (3 February)—unopposed but poorly executed—gave Eichelberger a fresh regiment which he quickly motorized and dispatched toward Manila; simultaneously, the glider regiments fought their way to Tagaytay and prepared to follow. By late on 4 February, advance elements of the division had reached Paranaque (*center*), where they were abruptly halted by strong Japanese defenses.

Meanwhile, Krueger—prodded by MacArthur—had initiated the drive by the XIV Corps on Manila. On 2 February, elements of the 1st Cavalry and 37th Divisions met at Plaridel. The 1st Cavalry Division now organized two "flying columns" and sent them racing toward Novaliches and Manila; these columns entered the outskirts of the capital the next night (3 February). The rest of the division followed more slowly, leaving one regiment (later relieved by the 112th RCT) on the flank near Norzagaray. The 37th Division, meeting more resistance, smashed its way into the city on the 4th. Then, for a month, the Japanese fanatically defended Manila in fighting subsequently described (*see text, map 157*).

By 14 February (*this map, dotted red line*), the Japanese in Manila had been isolated from the remainder of the Kembu Group.

Most of the 1st Cavalry Division and the 6th Division (now assigned to the XIV Corps) advanced eastward and encountered the two independently organized fortified lines shown (*red symbols*). On 12 March, the 43d Division relieved the exhausted 1st Cavalry, and three days later the XI Corps assumed responsibility for the attack on these positions; the XIV Corps retained responsibility for liberating southwestern Luzon. The 11th Airborne Division (under the Sixth Army since 10 February) and the 158th RCT had already begun operations toward this end, and by 15 March held the lines shown (*bottom center, solid red lines*).

In the meantime, the 40th Division had been slowly forcing the Japanese back into the mountains west of Clark Field, and had also linked up with the 38th Division at Dinalupihan (*center, left*). This latter division, fighting in extremely rugged terrain, had badly mismanaged the attack to clear Zigzag Pass, but finally opened the Olongapo-Dinalupihan road and eliminated the last enemy resistance on 15 February. The 43d Division relieved the 40th (now assigned to the Eighth Army for operations in the Visayas) on 2 March, but was itself assigned to the XIV Corps and dispatched to the front east of Manila on 11 March. The 38th Division assumed sole responsibility for mopping up the remnants of the Kembu Group west of Clark Field.

Operations for liberating Bataan and Corregidor were begun early. As shown, the 151st RCT landed at Mariveles on 15 February, and, assisted by the 1st RCT (6th Division), eliminated the token resistance on the peninsula by the 21st. On 16 February, a spectacular amphibious-airborne assault was made on Corregidor. The extremely difficult airborne landing was well executed and surprised the Japanese. But they were in much greater strength than expected and fought fiercely before succumbing to troops of the 24th and 38th Divisions and the paratroopers on 27 February.

During the period covered by this map, two spectacular rescue missions were undertaken successfully. In January, several hundred Allied prisoners held under light guard at Cabanatuan (*top center*), well behind the Japanese lines, were released in a daring raid (*not shown*) by a reinforced company of the 6th Ranger Battalion. In February, civilian internees at Los Baños (*lower center*) were rescued in an equally bold amphibious-airborne operation by 11th Airborne Division elements.

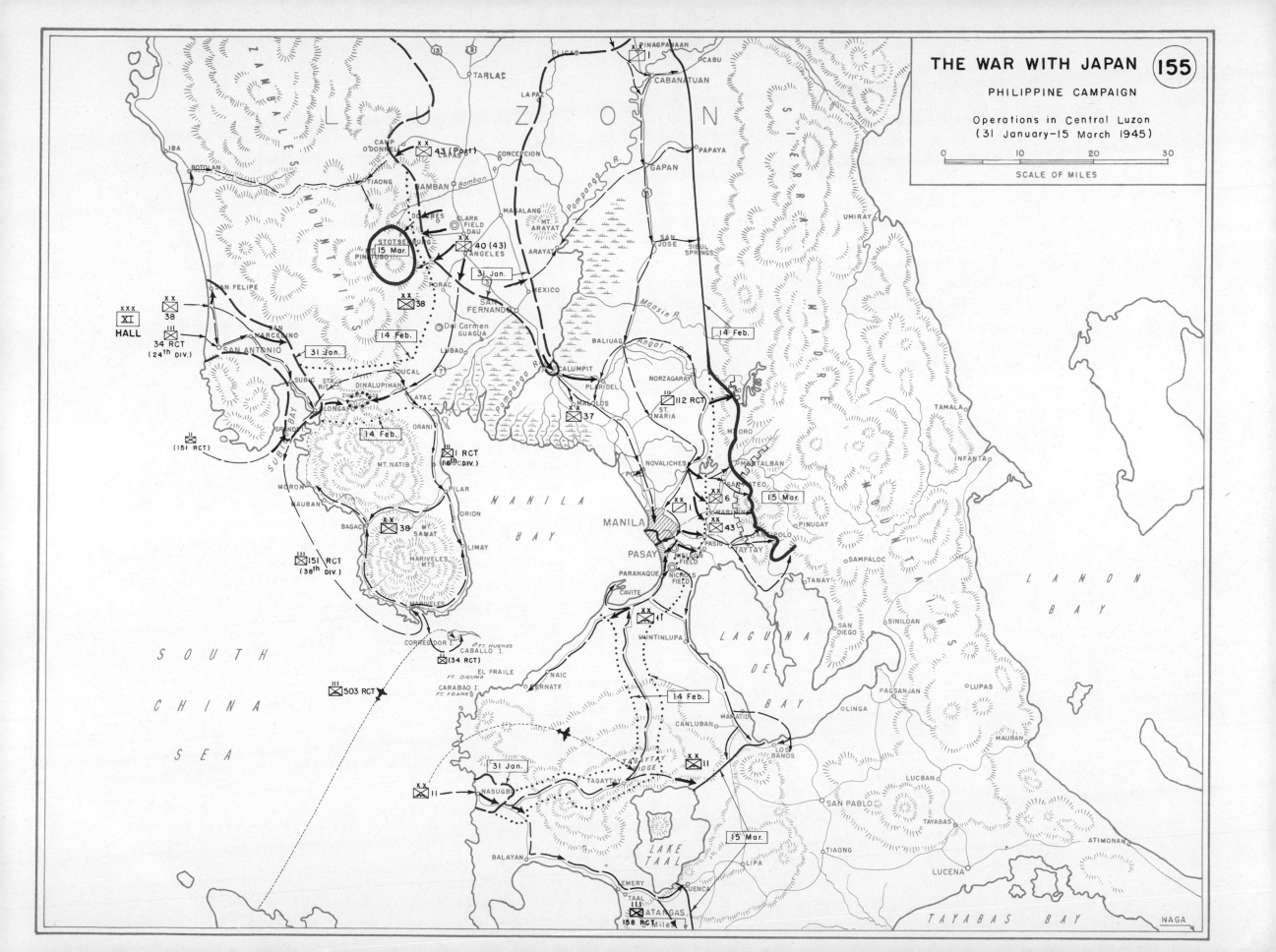

THE WAR WITH JAPAN 155

PHILIPPINE CAMPAIGN

Operations in Central Luzon
(31 January–15 March 1945)

SCALE OF MILES
0   10   20   30

LUZON

ZAMBALES

SIERRA   MADRE

IBA

BOTOLAN

CAMP O'DONNELL

CONCEPCION

TARLAC

LA PAZ

(13)

PINAGPAAAAN

OCABU

CABANATUAN

PAPAYA

UMIRAY

TIAONG

BAMBAN   Bomban

43 (Post)

GAPAN

SAN JOSE

SIBUL SPRINGS

DOLORES

CLARK FIELD
DAU

MAGALANG

MT. ARAYAT

Pampanga R.

STOTSENBURG

15 Mar.

PINTUBO

40 (43)
ANGELES

31 Jan.

ARAYAT

SAN FERNANDO

MEXICO

Maasin R.

14 Feb.

SAN FELIPE

XXX
XI
HALL

XX
38

38

14 Feb.

DEL CARMEN
GUAGUA

GUAGUA

SAN MARCELINO

34 RCT
(24th DIV.)

SAN ANTONIO

31 Jan.

LUBAO

DUCAL

SUBIC STA.
RITA

DINALUPIHAN

Angat

CALUMPIT

PLARIDEL

NORZAGARAY

14 Feb.

INFANTA

TAMALA

ZIGZAG

LAYAC

MALOLOS

ST. MARIA

112 RCT

(151 RCT)

LONGAPO

GRANDE I.

14 Feb.

ORANI

I RCT
(6th DIV.)

MT. NATIB

ORANI

PILAR

MT. ORO

MARIKINA

NOVALICHES

MANILA
BAY

ORION

MORON

MAUBAN

BAGAC

38

MT.
SAMAT

PILIMAY

MANILA

PASAY

PARANAQUE

NICHOLS
FIELD

XX
1

XX
6

15 Mar.

XX
43

PINUGAY

151 RCT
(38th DIV.)

MARIVELES
MTS.

MARIVELES

NIELSON
FIELD

PASIG

TAYTAY

ANTIPOLO

SAN
DIEGO

SINILOAN

LAMON
BAY

CAVITE

CORREGIDOR I.

O FT. HUGHES
CABALLO I.

(34 RCT)

EL FRAILE
FT. DRUM

CARABAO I.
FT. FRANK

NAIC

TERNATE

MUNTINLUPA

LAGUNA

DE

BAY

PAGSANJAN

OLUPAS

MAUBAN

503 RCT

XX
11

14 Feb.

CANLUBAN

MAMATID

LOS
BANOS

OLINGA

S O U T H

C H I N A

S E A

31 Jan.

NASUGBU

TAGAYTAY RIDGE

TAGAYTAY

XX
11

XX
11

LAKE
TAAL

15 Mar.

SAN PABLO

LUCBAN

TAYABAS

ATIMONAN

BALAYAN

EMERY

TAAL

CUENCA

OLIPA

LUCENA

BATANGAS

158 RCT

Miles

TAYABAS   BAY

NAGA

This map depicts the situation on the eve of General Krueger's final drive on Manila. During the three weeks of fighting to date, about 15,000 Japanese had been killed while American casualties totaled 5,754 (including 1,297 killed).

Since 9 January, the Sixth Army had expanded its initial beachhead rapidly and pushed southward down the Central Plain toward the Philippine capital. Obviously, the salient thus produced was an inviting target for a Japanese counterattack. It was for this very reason that Krueger was hesitant about plunging ahead rapidly to seize Manila. Until the I Corps could force Yamashita back into the mountains northeast of San Fabian (*center, left*) and secure defensible terrain, he had misgivings about advancing too far while his supply dumps at Lingayen were—in his view—susceptible to enemy seizure. MacArthur, on the other hand, viewed the operation in the light of strategic considerations. Desirous of securing Manila within the six-week period which he had assured the Joint Chiefs of Staff would suffice, and anxious to open Manila's port—one of the best in the Orient—MacArthur felt that the advance was too slow. He may have been influenced by his headquarters' underestimate of Japanese strength on Luzon (in contrast to the more accurate Sixth Army estimate). Another important consideration was the desirability of securing Clark Field (there were actually fifteen separate fields at this ideal airfield complex) to enable aircraft to support Nimitz's future operations as well as to intensify interdiction of Japanese communications to the East Indies.

In reality, the threat to Krueger's east flank was not serious, for—as we now know—Yamashita had no intention of making a major counterattack. Hamstrung by Allied air attacks and struggling to improve his deteriorating logistical situation, he was quite content to fight a defensive action. Furthermore, even if he had considered making a limited counterattack, it could not have been very effective, since he had frittered away the nucleus of any counterattack force (his 2d Tank Division) in costly piecemeal actions.

After MacArthur's forces had established a firm foothold on Luzon, Halsey's Third Fleet moved westward into the South China Sea to attack any elements of the Japanese fleet which might venture forth in an attempt to reestablish control over the sea lanes to the East Indies. Halsey met only insignificant opposition and, securing unchallenged control of the South China Sea, ranged at will throughout its length. On 12 January, his aircraft struck coastal Indochina (*see map 150, left center*), and three days later they launched attacks on Hong Kong, Hainan, Canton, and Formosa. On the 21st, in a parting attack, Halsey struck the Ryukyu Islands and Formosa again before returning to his base at Ulithi (*center*). By now, it had become equally clear to both sides that the Japanese fleet could not contest American control of the seas; the Kamikaze Corps was its only remaining threat, and this weapon was presumably being retained to defend the Japanese homeland.

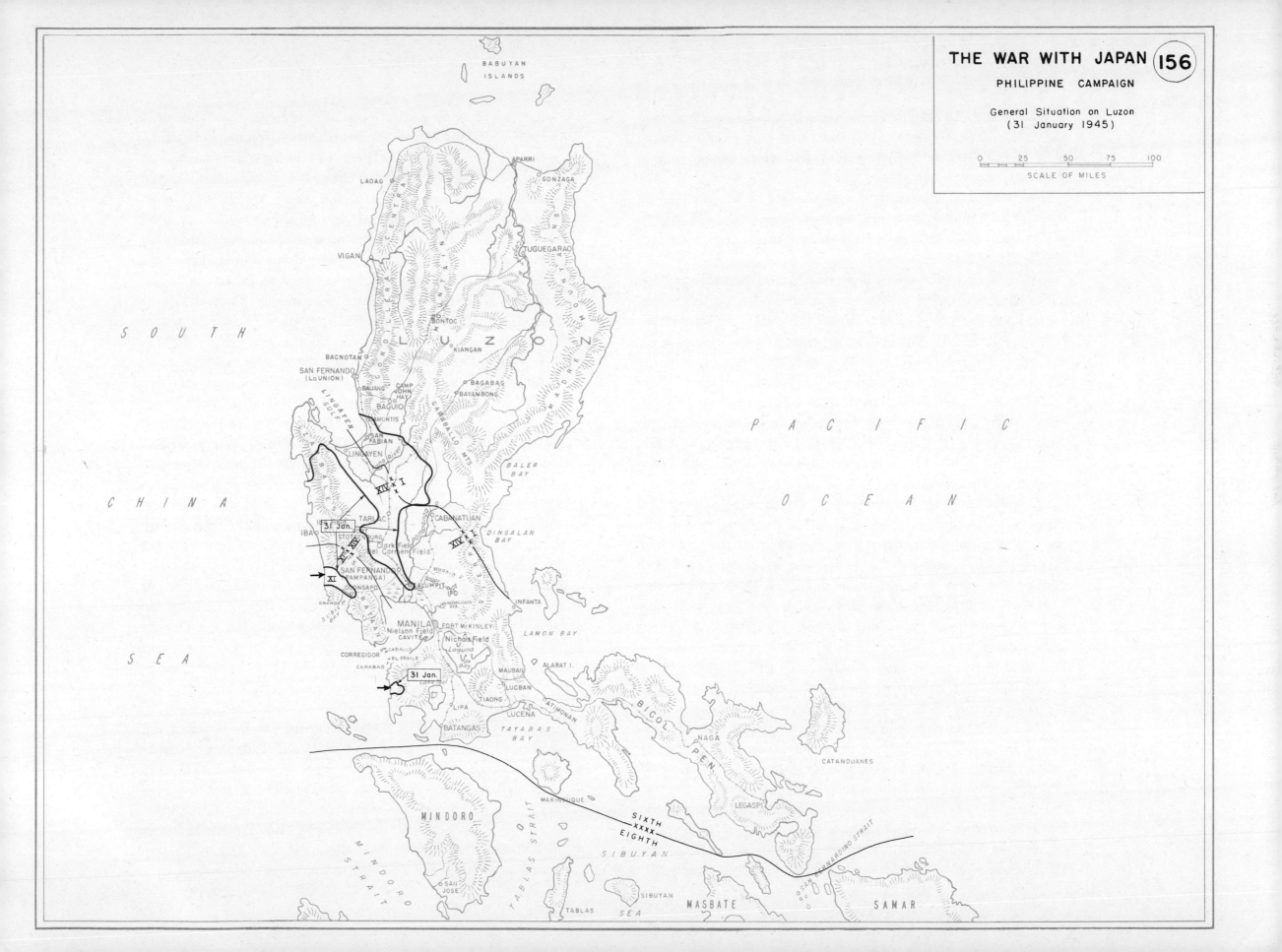

0   25   50   75   100
SCALE OF MILES

BABUYAN
ISLANDS

APARRI

LAOAG   GONZAGA

TUGUEGARAO

VIGAN

S O U T H

C H I N A

BONTOC

L U Z O N

BACNOTAN   KIANGAN

SAN FERNANDO
(La UNION)   BAGABAG
          BAUANG   CAMP   BAYAMBONG
                   JOHN
                   HAY
          DAGUPAN BAGUIO
          AMORTIS
LINGAYEN GULF
          SAN
          FABIAN
          LINGAYEN

S E A

BALER
BAY

P A C I F I C

O C E A N

XX I
XIV XX I

IBA   TARLAC
31 Jan.
STOTSENBURG   CABANATUAN
Clark Field   XIV I
El Carmen Field   DINGALAN
                         BAY

XI
SAN FERNANDO
(PAMPANGA)
OLONGAPO
CALUMPIT   INFANTA

GRANDE I.

SUBIC BAY   NOVALICHES
                   RES.

MANILA   FORT McKINLEY
Nielson Field
CAVITE   Nichols Field   LAMON BAY

CORREGIDOR   CABALLO   Laguna
             EL FRAILE Bay
CARABAO   MAUBAN
          31 Jan.
                   LUCBAN
                   TIAONG
                   LIPA   LUCENA   ATIMONAN   ALABAT I.
                   BATANGAS
                            TAYABAS
                            BAY   BICOL PEN.   NAGA

                                                      LEGASPI
MINDORO
                   MARINDUQUE   SIXTH
                                       XXXX
                   TABLAS STRAIT   EIGHTH

SAN JOSE
                   SIBUYAN
MINDORO STRAIT   TABLAS   SEA   MASBATE   SAMAR

The final dash for Manila began on 2 February (*see text, map 155*). Maj. Gen. Oscar W. Griswold (XIV Corps) expected the 37th Division to enter the city first; but when a cleverly conducted delaying action slowed that unit—while 1st Cavalry Division flying columns raced to the outskirts of the capital—he shifted the boundary between divisions westward and ordered the troopers into the city. (To avoid confusion, this boundary shift is not shown.)

Against negligible opposition, 1st Cavalry elements reached Santo Tomas University (*this map; center, left*) late on 3 February, liberated 3,500 Allied internees there and then seized Malacanan Palace. An attempt to capture Quezon Bridge (*not shown; near Intramuros, left center*) over the Pasig River on the 4th met with failure; that night, the Japanese destroyed all three of the bridges spanning the river. This same night, the 37th Division—bypassing and leaving the strong enemy position at Polo (*upper left*) for later reduction—pushed a regiment into Manila which seized Bilibid Prison and liberated some 1,300 Allied prisoners and civilian internees.

Griswold side-stepped the 1st Cavalry Division eastward on 5 February. Both divisions then closed to the Pasig, as the Japanese—executing their demolition program with ruthless abandon—withdrew south of the river. The greater part of both divisions was now in Manila, though the 1st Cavalry (the only "Square"—four regiment—division still in the Army) had detached one regiment at Norzagaray (*off map, top*) and another at Novaliches (*top center*). The latter had been given the important task of seizing Manila's water-supply facilities: the Novaliches Dam and Reservoir, the Balara Filters (*center*), and connecting pipelines.

The 37th Division skillfully crossed the Pasig near Malacanan Palace on 7 February, and three days later the 1st Cavalry crossed farther upstream. The advance faltered as Japanese resistance stiffened; MacArthur reluctantly lifted restrictions on the use of artillery in the city when it became clear that the enemy had organized buildings into strong points and had no intention of surrendering. This turnabout in Japanese strategy resulted from a lack of unity of command: Yamashita only partially controlled the Japanese naval troops in the Manila area; though he ordered abandonment of Manila, the naval commander decided to defend it rather than withdraw to join the Shimbu Group.

In bitter house-to-house fighting, Griswold's divisions compressed the Japanese into a pocket along Manila Bay by 14 February (*center, left; dashed red line*). Meanwhile, in south Manila, the 11th Airborne Division, encountering strong defenses near Paranaque (*lower left*), had made only slight gains since 4 February. By the 10th, it was hammering at the "Genko Line" at Nichols Field. There, permanently emplaced large-caliber guns, mine fields, and fire from automatic weapons took a heavy toll of the Americans; but, by the 14th, the position had been overrun, and contact had been made with the 1st Cavalry Division.

Griswold now left the reduction of Manila to the 37th Division and ordered the 1st Calvary Division to take Fort William McKinley and then move east to develop the Japanese position in the mountains. The 1st Cavalry (less one regiment helping the 37th Division) overran McKinley on 19 February and three days later entered Taytay. But then it smashed into the strong "Shimbu Line" (*fortified area shown*) and stalled. To the north, the 6th Division encountered similar resistance, but almost reached Montalban (*top right*) by the 24th. A lull in the fighting followed while the Americans reconnoitered the Shimbu Line. An attack was launched on 8 March in which the 1st Cavalry succeeded in turning the Japanese southern flank, but 6th Division gains were slight. By 15 March, when the XI Corps assumed control of operations east of Manila, the Japanese were holding the position shown (*solid red line*), and it was clear that dislodging them would be difficult.

Meanwhile, the 37th Division had forced the fanatical Japanese back to the Intramuros (the ancient walled city built by the Spanish) and a few government buildings near it. The thick walls of the Intramuros were breached by fire from heavy artillery in two places, and on 23 February the infantry moved inside to eliminate the last bitter resistance. Fighting continued for the government buildings until 4 March, when the battered and ruined city was finally declared secure.

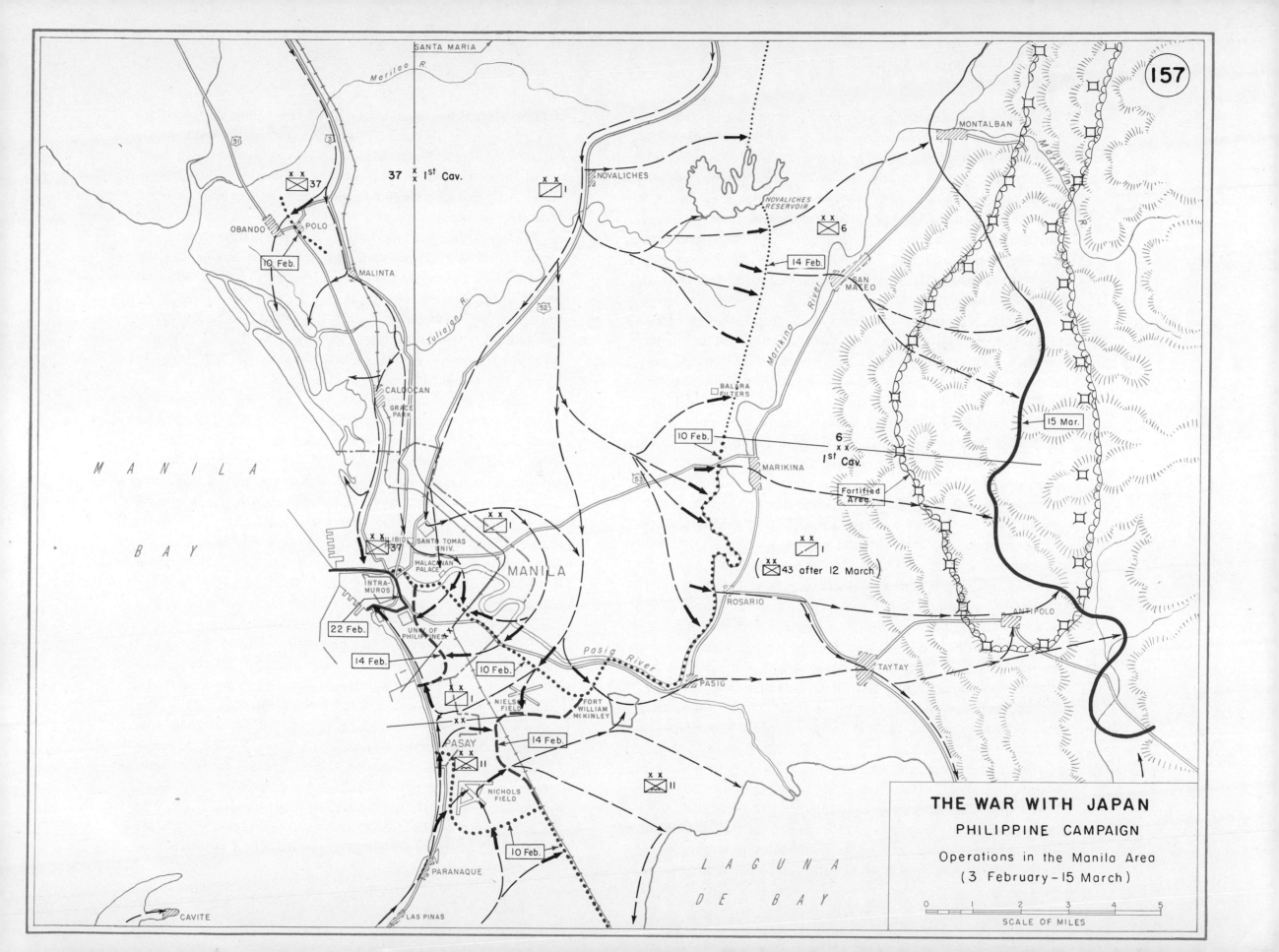

THE WAR WITH JAPAN

PHILIPPINE CAMPAIGN

Operations in the Manila Area
(3 February–15 March)

SCALE OF MILES
0   1   2   3   4   5

At the same time that the XIV Corps began its final drive on Manila (the 1st Cavalry Division is shown concentrated at Guimba [center], from which it started southward), the I Corps renewed its attack against the Shobu Group's positions (dashed red line) from Baloc (center) to Rosario (upper left). Krueger ordered the major effort to be made by the 6th Division—to secure the line of the Pampanga River north of Cabanatuan (center, right), thus isolating the Shobu Group and removing the threat of a possible Japanese counterattack against the left flank of the Sixth Army.

The 6th Division encountered fierce resistance at Muñoz (center) from dug-in tanks, direct artillery fire, and thoroughly entrenched infantry. One of its regiments enveloped the town from the north, while another applied frontal pressure; the rest of the division bypassed the town and took San Jose (4 February) and Rizal (7 February) against lesser opposition. Cut off, the Muñoz garrison attempted to withdraw the night of the 6th, but it was almost completely destroyed en route to San Jose. Columns of the 6th Division then moved through Bongabon to the east coast, which they reached on 14 February. As we have seen, the bulk of the division was then transferred to the XIV Corps.

Meanwhile, the 25th Division was engaged in a bitter fight for Lupao (center), while the 32d Division pushed up the Villa Verde Trail (upper center) against increasing resistance. With the fall of Lupao on 8 February, the Japanese 2d Tank Division practically ceased to exist. But 32d Division gains became slight as the division moved into extremely rugged, mountainous country—reminiscent of fighting in Italy—where the Japanese had excellent observation, innumerable caves, and well-sited artillery. On the left of the line, the recently arrived 33d Division relieved the 43d Division (not shown) and prepared to advance on Baguio.

In late February, the I Corps began an all-out offensive to destroy the Shobu Group: the 25th Division moved on Balete Pass (upper center) in two columns (on Route 5 and up the Pampanga River valley); the 32d Division concentrated primarily on the Villa Verde Trail, but also sent columns into the mountains on either side of the trail; and the 33d Division directed two columns toward the Baguio stronghold and a third up the coast. By 15 March, the I Corps' advance had reached the limit shown (dotted red line). Nowhere had a decisive breakthrough been made; Japanese resistance was as fanatical as ever. (Meanwhile, the 40th Division had been concentrated near Dagupan in preparation for movement to the Visayas.)

In early April, the 37th Division (less one combat team) was ordered from Manila to Bauang (top left). Thus augmented, the 33d Division, which had earlier (20 March) linked up with the North Luzon Guerrilla Force at San Fernando (top left), renewed its drive on Baguio. Superbly supported by aircraft, tanks, and artillery, the two divisions closed on the city which Yamashita now began to evacuate. On 27 April, the 37th Division entered the mauled Philippine summer capital.

Farther south, the 32d Division turned over its Sapit and Teb-bo sectors to elements of the newly organized Philippine Army and concentrated its greatly understrength units on the Villa Verde Trail. Here, the advance was slow, costly, and demoralizing as the division slugged its way toward Imugan. The 25th Division faced similar terrain problems as it grimly ground under one Japanese position after another. Finally, on 13 May, the key Balete Pass was captured, and two weeks later the 25th Division entered the important communications center of Santa Fe. The next day, the exhausted 25th and 32d Divisions made contact near Imugan; both divisions were then withdrawn for a well-earned rest.

The 37th Division, previously withdrawn from Baguio and reunited with its third combat team, pushed up Highway 5 on 31 May. The division seized Bayombong on 7 June and continued its advance northeastward toward the Cagayan Valley (off map, top right). Yamashita, having lost his key San Jose position, desperately tried to stem the 37th Division advance; but his troops, defending only partially completed positions, were unequal to the task. By 30 June, his positions were as shown (dashed red lines). As the Americans and Filipinos smashed at his mountain stronghold from the west, south, and north (see map 159), Yamashita withdrew deeper into the Cordillera Central (this map, solid red line).

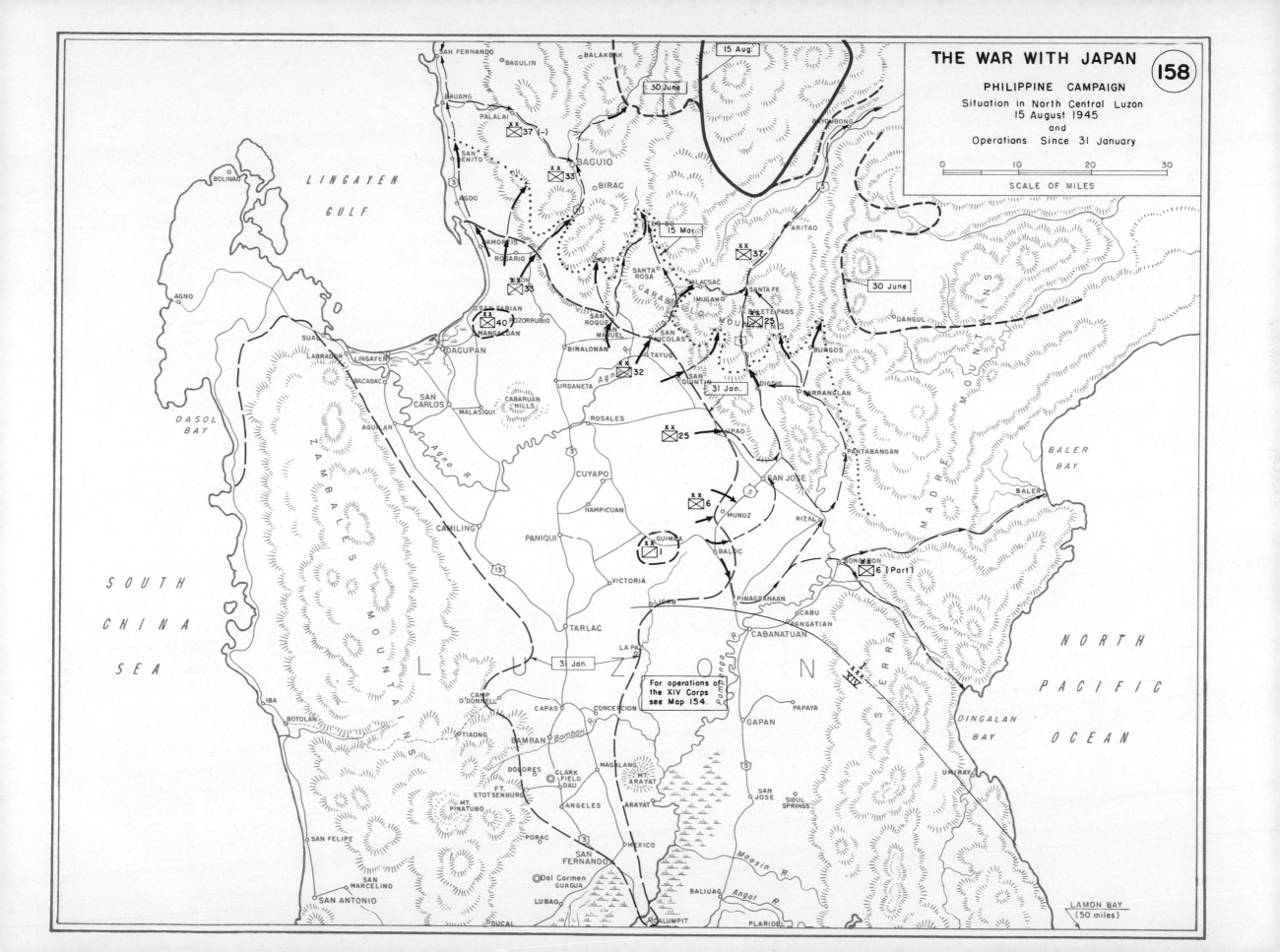

THE WAR WITH JAPAN

158

PHILIPPINE CAMPAIGN

Situation in North Central Luzon
15 August 1945
and
Operations Since 31 January

0   10   20   30
SCALE OF MILES

For operations of
the XIV Corps
see Map 154.

LAMON BAY
(50 miles)

This map portrays the over-all Sixth Army situation on 15 March. By that date, the Japanese had been pocketed into three separate groups—almost as Yamashita had expected—and the three American corps were conducting independent operations against the isolated Japanese forces. The I Corps had the most difficult task (already partially described in the text, *map 158*), but the other corps still faced some hard fighting before Yamashita's capitulation on 15 August. Meanwhile, Manila's port was being rehabilitated in one of the war's most extensive salvage tasks, and the build-up for the ultimate invasion of Japan gathered momentum.

In southern Luzon, the XIV Corps drove southeastward on either side of Lake Taal (*lower left*). The 11th Airborne and 1st Cavalry Divisions executed a series of pincer movements on Lipa, Tiaong, and Lucban, the last occurring on 9 April. Two days later, they reached the coast at Antimonan and Mauban. Then, as the 11th Airborne Division stayed behind to mop up the overrun areas, the 1st Cavalry Division sent a small force toward Infanta (*lower center*), while the bulk of the division moved down the Bicol Peninsula. On 1 May, cavalry troopers met the 158th RCT a few miles south of Naga (*lower center*). (In order to secure the northern exits of San Bernardino Strait [*bottom center*], the 158th RCT—directly under Sixth Army control—had been landed at Legaspi, as shown, on 1 April; after eliminating Japanese resistance in the southern part of the peninsula, it had moved north toward Naga.) On 25 May, Infanta was occupied. One week later, organized resistance ceased in the XIV Corps' zone.

In central Luzon, the 38th Division (*located at this time near Clark Field, not as shown*) hunted down the remnants of the Kembu Group in the mountains, and some of its units seized the island forts near Corregidor (13-16 April). Meanwhile, the 6th Division (*not shown, but actually where the 38th Division symbol is located*) and the 43d Division continued the bitter struggle with the Shimbu Group east of Manila; slowly, the Japanese were forced back to the position shown (*solid red line*). (The 38th Division relieved the 6th Division on 30 April; the latter unit moved into a rest area until 12 June, when it was committed in the I Corps' zone.) On 1 July, the 43d Division was withdrawn from the line to prepare for future operations; until the war ended, the 38th Division continued the fight against the Shimbu Group.

In northern Luzon's rugged mountain wilderness, the I Corps continued to apply pressure on the Shobu Group. The 37th Division, moving down the Cagayan Valley, entered Tuguegarao (*upper center*) on 25 June, pushed on north, and the next day met an American-Filipino column moving south from Aparri. (This column consisted of Connolly Force [*not labeled*], which had seized Aparri on 21 June, and a reinforced parachute battalion which had been dropped at Aparri on the 23d.) The Japanese were now split into two groups, one on either side of the Cagayan Valley. The smaller group on the east—disorganized and poorly armed—fled into the mountains; patrols from the 37th Division probed its weak defenses until the war ended on 15 August. But to the west of the valley, Yamashita—personally in command—still had a sizable force. The 6th and 32d Divisions (the 33d had been relieved), the guerrillas, and part of the 37th Division compressed this force into an ever-shrinking pocket. On 1 July, the Eighth Army (employing the XIV Corps, consisting of the 6th, 32d, 37th, and 38th Divisions) assumed responsibility for operations on Luzon; Krueger began preparing his troops for the projected invasion of Japan.

In the remaining days of the war, Yamashita's main force was split into three pockets with the seizure of Kiangan (*upper left*) on 12 July. But when the war ended on 15 August, Yamashita still had an organized force of 50,000 troops, about 40,000 of them in the Kiangan area. No longer capable of offensive action, they were, nevertheless, effectively tying down three American divisions. It cannot be denied that the Japanese had fought an effective delaying action as planned; similarly, it is clear that MacArthur had not been delayed materially in establishing a logistical base on Luzon and preparing the Sixth Army for an invasion of Japan.

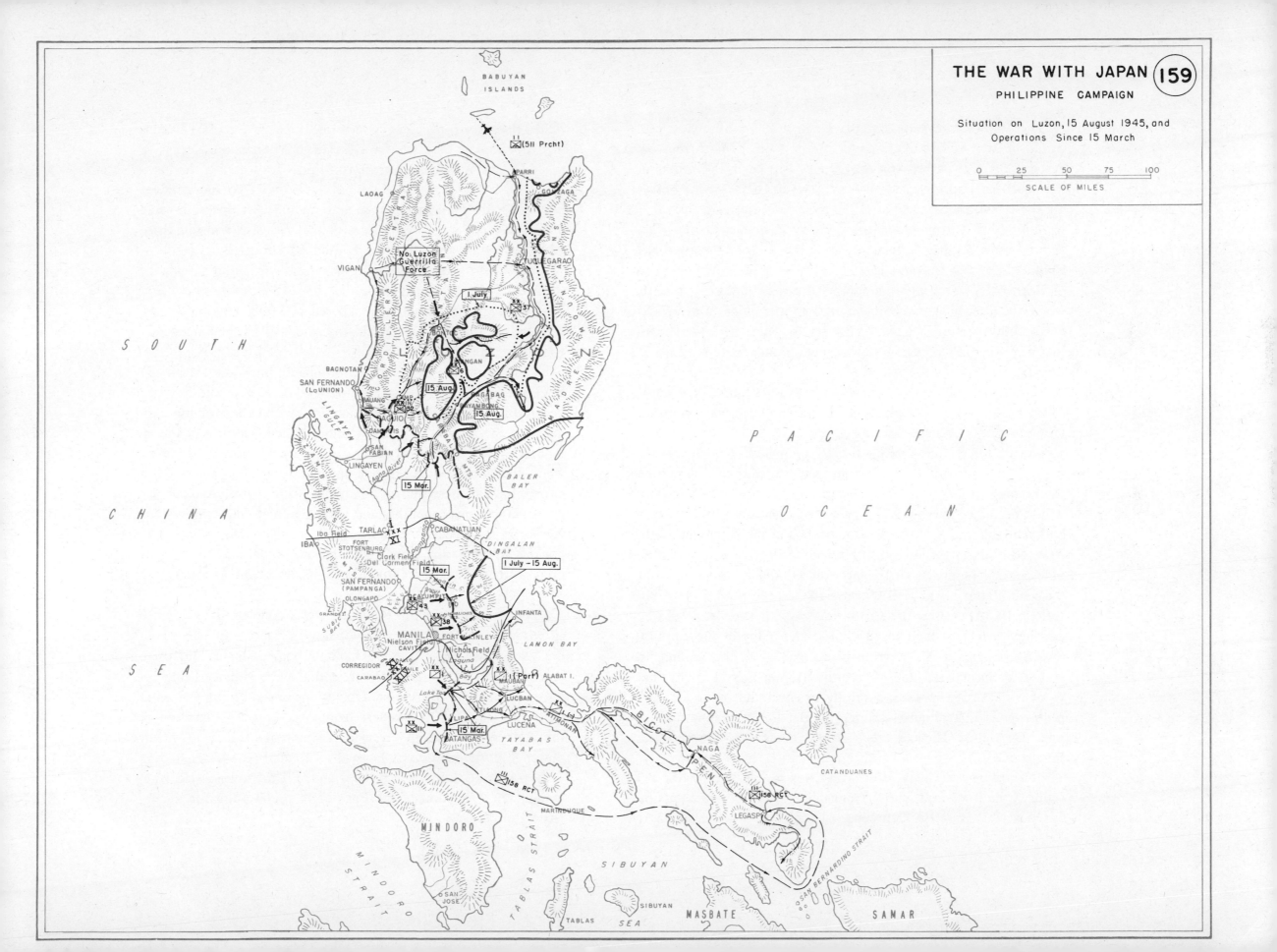

0   25   50   75   100
SCALE OF MILES

BABUYAN
ISLANDS

11
(511 Prcht)

APARRI

GONZAGA

LAOAG

TUGUEGARAO

VIGAN

No. Luzon
Guerrilla
Force

1 July

XX
37

BONTOC

BAGABAG

BANGAN

6

BACNOTAN

15 Aug.

SAN FERNANDO
(La UNION)

BAUANG

XX MP
152

ARITAO

BAGABAG

15 Aug.

BAGUIO

DAMORTIS

SAN
FABIAN

15 Aug.

LINGAYEN
GULF

LINGAYEN

Agno River

BALER
BAY

SOUTH

15 Mar.

CHINA

TARLAC   XX

Ibo Field

XX

CABANATUAN

DINGALAN
BAY

IBA

FORT
STOTSENBURG

Clark Field
Del Carmen Field

1 July – 15 Aug.

15 Mar.

SAN FERNANDO
(PAMPANGA)

SEA

OLONGAPO

XX CALUMPIT
43

GRANDE I.

INFANTA

XX
38

SUBIC
BAY

MANILA
Nielson Field
CAVITE

FORT McKINLEY
Nichols Field

LAMON BAY

CORREGIDOR

Laguna

CARABAO

CAVITE

XX
I

Bay
Lake Taal

XX
I (Part)

MAUBAN

ALABAT I.

XX II

15 Mar.

LIPA

LUCBAN

BATANGAS

LUCENA

TIMONAN

XX
II (-)

BICOL

NAGA

TAYABAS
BAY

PEN.

CATANDUANES

III
158 RCT

III
158 RCT

LEGASPI

MARINDUQUE

MINDORO

TABLAS
STRAIT

SIBUYAN
SEA

SAN BERNARDINO STRAIT

MINDORO
STRAIT

SAN
JOSE

TABLAS

MASBATE

SAMAR

PACIFIC

OCEAN

Waiting only to be sure that the Central Plain–Manila region would be secured in a reasonable length of time, MacArthur ordered the Eighth Army—on 6 February—to begin operations in the southern Philippines. There were several reasons for hurrying these operations, in spite of the attendant diversion of Allied strength from Luzon: Japanese communications with the East Indies could be more effectively interdicted from the southern islands than from Luzon; airfields had to be secured within range of Borneo (*lower left*) to support Australian landings there; it would be desirable to complete major operations and airfield construction before summer rains set in; and there was some fear for the fate of the Filipino inhabitants on the bypassed islands.

The first landings were to be made at Palawan (*upper left*), followed closely by occupation of the Zamboanga peninsula (*lower center*) and the Sulu Archipelago (*bottom center*). The seizure of the islands around the Visayan Sea (*top right*)—to secure a shorter supply route from Leyte to Manila—was to be the second-priority task. Then operations to liberate Mindanao would be undertaken. For the projected operation, Eichelberger had available the X Corps headquarters and the Americal, 24th, 31st, 40th, and 41st Divisions: He could also count on considerable guerrilla support, particularly on Mindanao. Since most of the amphibious lift and all the carriers had returned to the Central Pacific Area after the Luzon landing, air support would be provided solely by land-based planes, and many of the amphibious movements would have to be conducted by the 2d and 3d Engineer Special Brigades. Accordingly, the Eighth Army had to plan the many landings carefully to ensure adequate air, amphibious, and naval gunfire support. (Between Christmas, 1944, and 15 August, Eichelberger's troops made fifty-two separate landings.)

The Japanese Thirty-Fifth Army was responsible for the defense of the southern islands. Yamashita gave it the same mission he chose for himself in defending Luzon—to pin down as many Allied divisions for as long as possible. General Suzuki (eventually killed while en route from Leyte to Mindanao) elected to make his major defense on eastern Mindanao, where he had two divisions and a large body of naval troops. Two independent brigades garrisoned Zamboanga and the Sulu Archipelago, while a third division was responsible for the Visayas. None of these units was up to strength or well equipped (primarily because of reinforcements which had been sent to Leyte), and they were war-weary, complacently expecting the Allies to ignore them. Nevertheless, their strength numbered 102,000, and before the war ended, these troops would inflict considerable damage on Eichelberger's units.

The extent of the Eighth Army operations is shown on the map. Except on Mindanao, the pattern of each operation was generally the same: an assault landing, withdrawal of the Japanese to the interior to make a stand, Allied securing of the island, and withdrawal of American forces for future landings, while guerrillas conducted mop-up operations. On eastern Mindanao, the Japanese put up a harder fight; but, by judicious use of its amphibious capability and hard marching and fighting, the X Corps managed to compress the enemy garrison into two pockets by mid-July. Here—starving and under unremitting air attack—they remained until Japan's surrender on 15 August.

The campaign in the Philippines was concluded by Japan's surrender, and at a time when operations were still being conducted against some 100,000 Japanese still at large. But these enemy forces were no great threat and were rapidly being reduced to a state of starvation. Operations in the Philippines eliminated about 450,000 Japanese troops, led to the destruction of the Japanese Navy, and tremendously weakened Japanese air power. MacArthur's ground casualties totaled 62,143 (including 13,700 killed). And when the war ended, Luzon was rapidly becoming the "England of the Pacific" in preparation for the invasion of Japan.

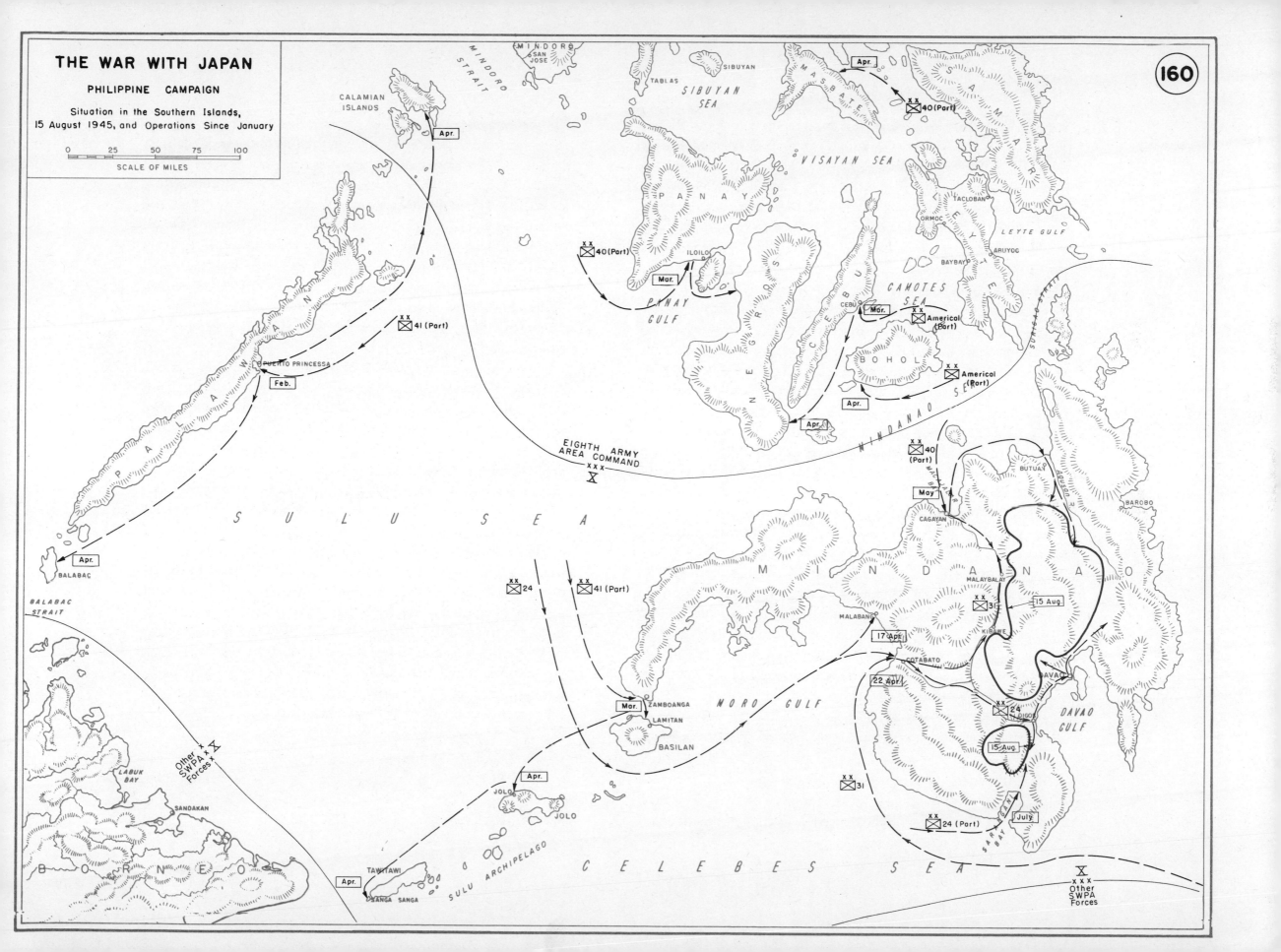

THE WAR WITH JAPAN

PHILIPPINE CAMPAIGN

Situation in the Southern Islands,
15 August 1945, and Operations Since January

SCALE OF MILES
0   25   50   75   100

160

While MacArthur's American forces were liberating the Philippines, his Australian troops continued mop-up operations against the isolated Japanese garrisons in New Guinea, New Britain, and Bougainville (*all lower center*). At the same time, General Sir Thomas Blamey, the Australian ground force commander, made preparations to implement MacArthur's instructions pertaining to the recapture of the Netherlands East Indies. The operations shown on the map (*small blue arrows*) are those which the Australians conducted in 1945.

The Japanese who had been bypassed in MacArthur's drive to the Philippines, though no longer a threat to future Allied operations, immobilized Allied troops which had to protect bases in proximity to the isolated enemy. This task ultimately fell to the Australians. By 1945, the Australian government had become somewhat exasperated with the mission assigned its troops, feeling that the mop-up operations lacked prestige and that Australian troops should be associated with the final drive on Japan proper. But, pending consideration of the Australian complaint by the Combined Chiefs of Staff, Blamey was still faced with the very real problem of the bypassed garrisons. He elected merely to contain the Japanese on New Britain, but to undertake full-blown offensives against those on Bougainville and New Guinea. Thus, until the end of the war, Australian troops continued to take casualties in their attempts to eliminate fanatical Japanese who could not affect its outcome. In defending this policy, Blamey contended that the adoption of a passive defensive would have been ruinous to the morale of his troops and that, if merely contained, the Japanese would have continued to dominate the natives, thereby lowering Australian prestige.

The operations against Borneo (*center, left*) were part of MacArthur's plan to recapture Java and reestablish the right-ful government in the islands. In the original plan, landings at Brunei Bay were to be the last step in the reconquest of the East Indies, but the plan was modified—presumably because of the great oil-producing fields in the Brunei Bay area. Admiral King stated that the Borneo operations were designed to "deny the enemy the fruits of his conquests in the Netherlands East Indies. . . ." However, since in 1945 the Japanese were scarcely capable of transporting fuel to Japan from the East Indies, it seems likely that Nimitz's desire to obtain Borneo oil for the Pacific Fleet may have been a more important factor. Significantly, the three operations conducted in Borneo were aimed at oil-producing centers.

On 1 May, Blamey landed a brigade of the Australian 9th Division, reinforced with a company of the Royal Netherlands East Indies Army, at Tarakan Island (*center, left*). Organized resistance ceased a month and a half later, after the Allies had suffered quite heavy casualties, but the engineers were unable to rehabilitate the captured airfield—one of the major objectives—because of unforeseen construction difficulties. The Brunei Bay landings in June were easier; important oil fields were quickly seized, and airfields were soon established. The last landing—at Balikpapan—was MacArthur's largest amphibious operation since Luzon. It was preceded by a devastating aerial bombardment which leveled the town, oil installations, and Japanese defenses. Opposition was light, the major objectives in the area having been seized by 10 July. In all three of the Borneo operations, Blamey's assault troops were supported by elements of the Seventh Fleet and the Royal Australian Navy as well as by Kenney's air forces (primarily their Australian components). In the remaining month of the war, the Australians contained the Japanese who had withdrawn into the interior of Borneo.

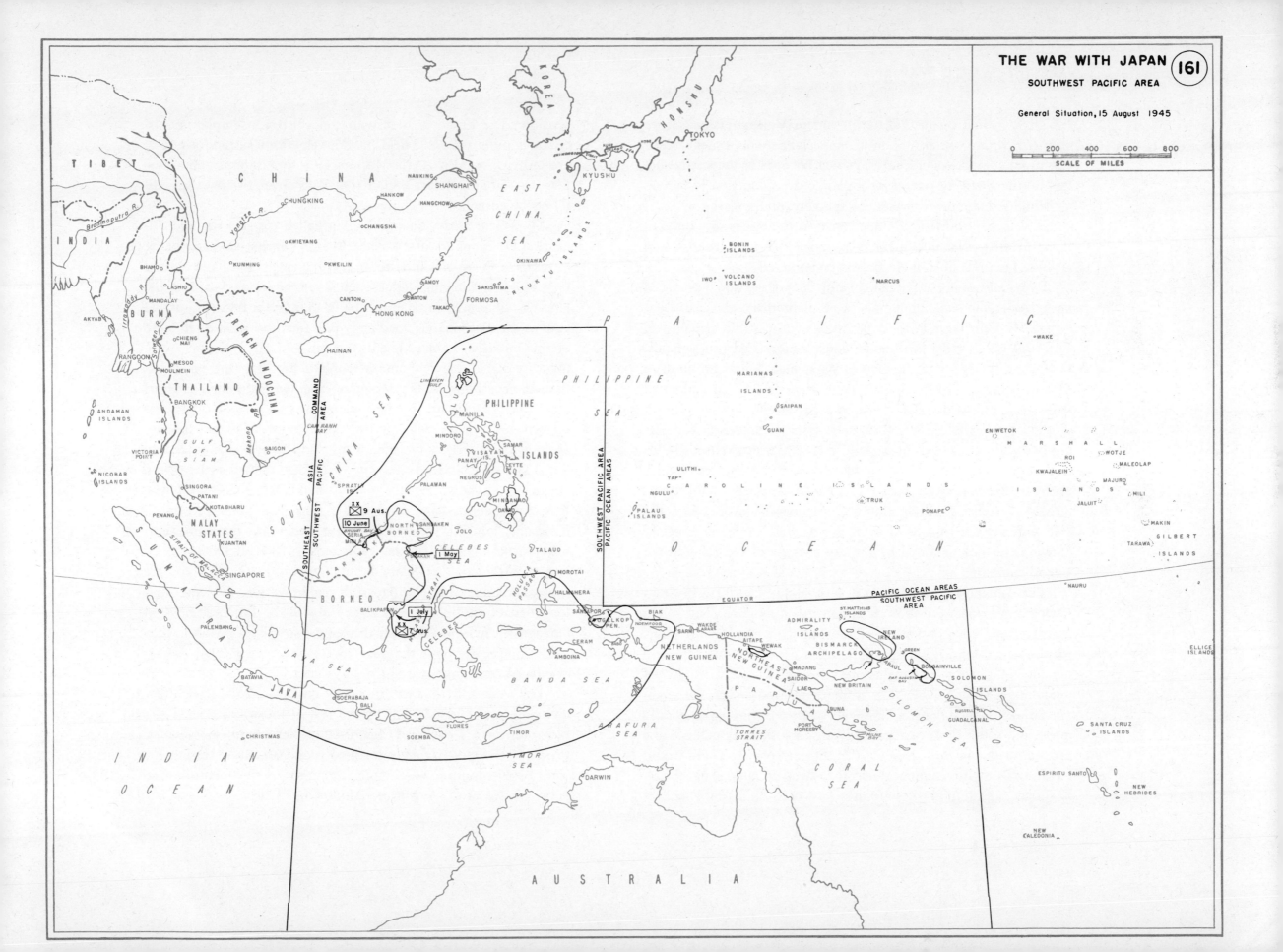

SCALE OF MILES
0   200   400   600   800

Iwo Jima (Jima means "island"), in the Volcano Islands (*see map 161, upper center*), is only about eight square miles in size. It is practically devoid of natural cover because of the sterile soil, and, in the words of one of its Japanese defenders in 1945, "was an island of sulphur, no water, no sparrow, and no swallow. . . ." But it was of considerable importance to the Allies, for only on Iwo—of all the islands in the Volcano and Bonin groups—can air-base facilities of suitable size be constructed.

Lying midway between Saipan and Tokyo, the island provided bases from which medium bombers and fighters could strike either target. By February, 1945, Japan had two operable airfields on Iwo (*this map*) and a third under construction. From these fields, they had already launched some raids against American bases in the Marianas, but by the date of the invasion, Allied air and naval strikes had eliminated the Japanese capability for basing aircraft on the island. There were other, more important reasons for seizing Iwo: fighters based there could escort Marianas-based B-29's to Japan; naval operations could be covered from the island; and crippled Superfortresses, returning from Japan, could use its airfields for emergency landings. Consequently, in October, the JCS ordered the seizure of Iwo; the original target date of 20 January was changed to 19 February because of the delay in the Luzon campaign.

The Japanese defended Iwo with about 21,000 army and navy troops, under the resolute command of Lt. Gen. Tadamichi Kuribayashi. These troops were thoroughly briefed in the plans for the island's defense and were imbued with the usual Japanese tenacity of purpose and willingness to die. Kuribayashi elected to employ a static defense with his main position on Mt. Suribachi (*lower left*) and along a line (*not shown*) running generally north and south through Airfield No. 2; a secondary defense line (*not shown*) ran just to the east of Airfield No. 3. There would be no costly all-out counterattacks to destroy an Allied beachhead, but local tank-infantry counterattacks would be made whenever

possible. The island bristled with concealed gun emplacements, concrete pillboxes, mine fields, and an elaborate system of underground caves and shelters. Mortars (90- to 320-mm.) and guns (20- to 150-mm.) were expertly sited to cover the beaches and all occupied areas.

Maj. Gen. Harry Schmidt's plan called for the 4th and 5th Marine Divisions to land abreast, the 3d Marine Division being in reserve. There was little room for maneuver; the battle would be a head-on slugging match. For seventy-four days before the landing, air power smashed at the island, and a three-day naval gunfire bombardment immediately preceded the assault. In spite of this intensive bombardment, the 4th and 5th Divisions were taken under a heavy volume of enfilade and flanking fire when they came ashore, as the Japanese emerged from their shelters after the pre-assault bombardment lifted. Wheeled vehicles bogged down in the volcanic ash as they moved inland, landing craft were destroyed by enemy fire, and heavy surf added to unloading difficulties. By the end of D-Day, the island had been cut in two as shown, but the marines had taken 2,420 casualties. In vicious hand-to-hand combat, Mt. Suribachi was taken on 23 February, but still the beaches were under fire from positions near Airfield No. 2. By the 24th, most of the 3d Division had been committed, and Schmidt, making his main effort in the center, was battering Kuribayashi's main position. A week later, the worst of the fighting was over, but still the Japanese held on tenaciously, fighting for every inch of ground. By 11 March, they were compressed into the two areas shown (*solid red lines*); organized resistance ceased five days later.

The conquest of Iwo Jima was costly—24,891 casualties, including 6,821 killed—but by the end of the war 2,251 B-29's (carrying 24,761 crewmen) had used its airfields in emergencies. Probably the most strongly fortified island assaulted during the war, Iwo's conquest was ample testimony to the fortitude and perseverance of the V Marine Amphibious Corps.

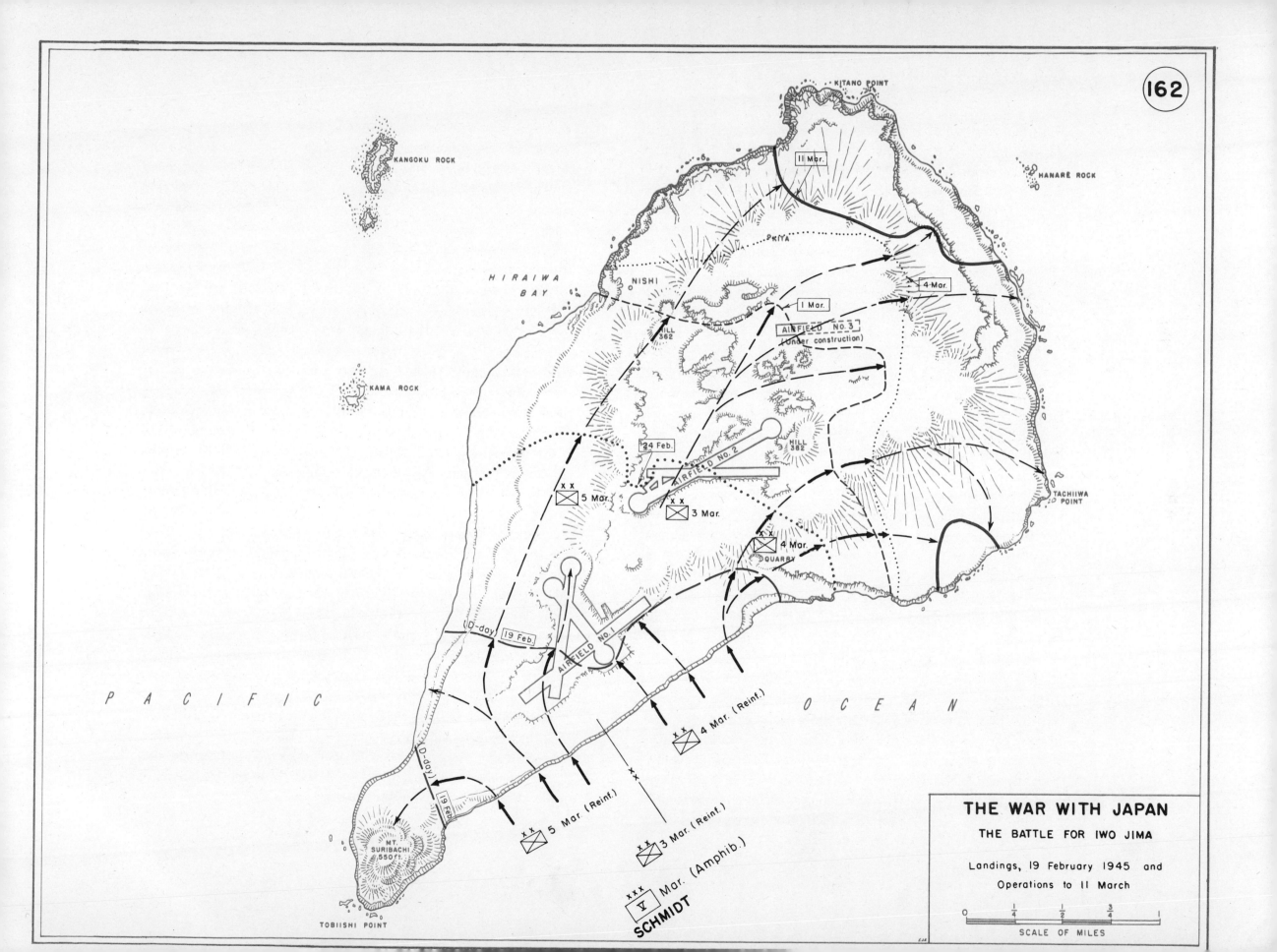

KANGOKU ROCK

KITANO POINT

HANARE ROCK

11 Mar.

HIRAIWA BAY

NISHI

KITA

4 Mar.

HILL 362

1 Mar.

AIRFIELD No. 3
(Under construction)

KAMA ROCK

24 Feb.

HILL 362

AIRFIELD No. 2

TACHIIWA POINT

XX 5 Mar.

XX 3 Mar.

XX 4 Mar.

QUARRY

P A C I F I C

AIRFIELD No. I

O C E A N

(D-day) 19 Feb.

XX 4 Mar. (Reinf.)

(D-day)

19 Feb.

MT. SURIBACHI 550 ft.

XX 5 Mar. (Reinf.)

XX 3 Mar. (Reinf.)

XXX Mar. (Amphib.)

XXX
V SCHMIDT

TOBIISHI POINT

THE WAR WITH JAPAN
THE BATTLE FOR IWO JIMA

Landings, 19 February 1945 and
Operations to 11 March

0   1/4   1/2   3/4   1
SCALE OF MILES

162

With the abandonment of Formosa as an objective, Nimitz was directed to invade the Ryukyu Islands (*see map 161*) in March, 1945 (later postponed to 1 April). A lodgment was desired in these islands for several reasons: bases for support of an invasion of Japan could be established; medium bombers could strike Japan from the Ryukyus; and Japanese communications to the south could be very effectively interdicted from Ryukyu bases. Okinawa (*this map*) was selected as the specific target because it is the only one of the islands large enough to accommodate several airfields; it also affords naval anchorages and adequate space to stage sizable ground forces.

In developing plans for the operation, Nimitz was faced with several complicating factors. Not only was Okinawa to be seized, but bases for future operations were to be developed there concurrently with the conduct of operations. This requirement compounded the magnitude of the logistical problem. The huge forces and resultant supply requirements, the distance from friendly bases to the objective, the limited availability of shipping, and the procurement of supplies (some directly from the United States) created a logistical nightmare for the planners. Also, Okinawa was within aircraft range of southern Japan, where the remaining Japanese air power could be massed, but it was relatively remote from Allied air bases. Consequently, the brunt of the likely air battle would have to be borne by carrier forces which would be required to remain in the combat area for a considerable period of time.

After balancing all considerations, Nimitz decided to sacrifice strategic surprise in an attempt to isolate Okinawa; the Tenth Army plan, however, was designed to achieve tactical surprise. The conquest of Okinawa was originally expected to follow three phases: the capture of the southern half of the island; seizure of the northern half and the island of Ie (*center, right*); and exploitation, to include the domination of other islands in the Ryukyus. Prior to the main landing, the Kerama and Keise Islands (*both bottom center*) would be seized—the former to obtain an anchor-age and seaplane base, the latter to provide positions for long-range field artillery to support the main landings. These would be made near Hagushi (*lower center*), where the best beaches existed and from which Yontan and Kadena airfields could be quickly seized. Then the XXIV Corps would swing south to establish a line through Kuba, while the III Marine Amphibious Corps drove northward to Ishikawa Isthmus to seal off the central portion of the island. From these positions (*dashed red lines*), the first phase of the general plan would be undertaken.

Early in March, the fast carrier forces, MacArthur's air forces, and B-29's began striking Japan, Hong Kong, and Formosa, in furtherance of the isolation program. By 1 April, the Japanese—resisting stubbornly—had inflicted some damage on the carrier force but had taken heavy aircraft losses in return. The Amphibious Support Force moved into Okinawan waters on 26 March, and began underwater demolition, mine-sweeping, and bombardment operations. The 77th Division quickly captured the Kerama and Keise Islands against minor opposition. On the Keramas, some 350 suicide boats were found—a portent of further desperate Japanese plans. The main landings, too, met only slight resistance; by 4 April, the two corps had reached the planned initial positions. But when the XXIV Corps encountered fierce opposition five days later, the Tenth Army commander, Lt. Gen. Simon B. Buckner, Jr., decided to initiate the second phase of the operation. As shown, the 6th Marine Division quickly overran the northern part of the island against token opposition. By the 19th, most of the Japanese had been eliminated in their last stand on Motobu Peninsula. The 77th Division had a harder fight before finally capturing Ie Shima on 21 April. Meanwhile, a battalion from the 27th Division (the floating reserve) seized Tsugen Island on 10 April, thus opening Nakagusuku Bay to Allied shipping. During June, elements of the 2d Marine Division seized the outlying islands of Kume, Aguni, and Iheya for establishment of radar installations to replace destroyer picket ships.

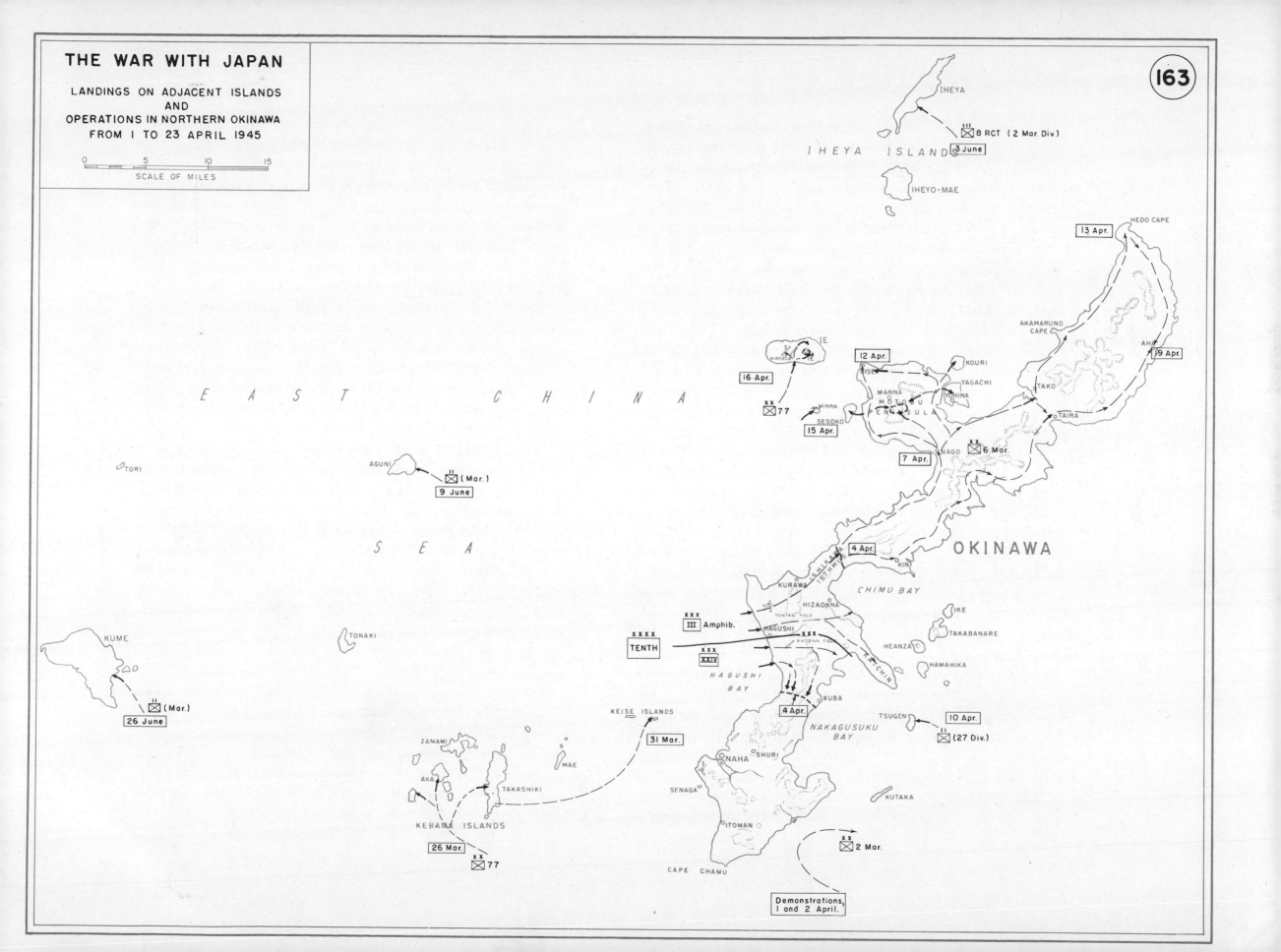

THE WAR WITH JAPAN

LANDINGS ON ADJACENT ISLANDS
AND
OPERATIONS IN NORTHERN OKINAWA
FROM 1 TO 23 APRIL 1945

0   5   10   15
SCALE OF MILES

163

IHEYA

IHEYA ISLAND

8 RCT (2 Mar. Div)
3 June

IHEYO-MAE

HEDO CAPE

13 Apr.

AKAMARUNO CAPE

AHA
9 Apr.

EAST   CHINA

IE
AIRFIELD   IE
16 Apr.

12 Apr.
BISE
KOURI
MANNA   YAGACHI
MOTOBU   YOHINA
PENINSULA
TAKO

77
MINNA
SESOKO
15 Apr.

TAIRA

NAGO   6 Mar.
7 Apr.

AGUNI

TORI

(Mar.)
9 June

SEA

OKINAWA

4 Apr.
KIN

ISHIKAWA ISTHMUS
KURAWA   CHIMU BAY

KUME

HIZAONNA
YONTAN FIELD

IKE
TAKABANARE

III Amphib.

XXXX
TENTH

MAGUSHI

KADENA FIELD

HEANZA
HAMAHIKA

XXX
XXIV

KATCHIN

(Mar.)
26 June

KEISE ISLANDS

31 Mar.

HAGUSHI
BAY

KUBA

4 Apr.

NAKAGUSUKU
BAY

TSUGEN   10 Apr.

(27 Div.)

TONAKI

ZAMAMI
MAE

AKA
TAKASHIKI

NAHA   SHURI

SENAGA

KUTAKA

KERAMA ISLANDS

26 Mar.

77

ITOMAN

2 Mar.

CAPE CHAMU

Demonstrations,
1 and 2 April.

Following the heaviest pre-assault naval and aerial bombardment of the Pacific war, the four assault divisions began landing near Hagushi (*upper center*) at 0830, 1 April. At the same time, the 2d Marine Division conducted such a realistic demonstration off the Minatoga beaches (*bottom center*) that the Japanese boasted of repelling a landing. (This division repeated the demonstration on 2 April and then returned to Saipan to prepare for other operations.) Surprised at the complete lack of ground opposition at the Hagushi beaches, the Americans rapidly advanced inland, and by nightfall of L-Day (landing day) had reached the originally scheduled L + 3 line. This early seizure of the important Yontan and Kadena airfields—halfheartedly defended by a makeshift, second-line regiment—enabled land-based aircraft to operate from Okinawa sooner than expected. Only in the air had the Japanese offered any resistance, and these attacks—made against invasion shipping—were not very successful.

Buckner's troops continued their rapid advance on 2 April, cutting the island in two when the 7th Division reached the eastern coast. The following day, the XXIV Corps regrouped for an advance southward, while the III Amphibious Corps continued to advance practically unopposed. By 4 April, the 6th Marine Division had secured the planned L + 15 line (*top right, solid red line*), but the XXIV Corps had begun to meet more resistance.

The Japanese Imperial Headquarters was determined to hold Okinawa and hoped that the Navy's Special Attack Corps (Kamikaze)—supported by a large portion of the surface fleet and small suicide boats—could destroy the covering forces of the American Fifth Fleet and the support shipping off Okinawa. This accomplished, Lt. Gen. Mitsuru Ushijima's Thirty-Second Army would attack the invasion force—now shorn of its support—and drive it into the sea. In keeping with this strategy, Ushijima did not defend the beaches but occupied the rugged terrain around Shuri (*lower center*), whence he could sally forth or defend. More realistic than his superiors, he did not expect to defeat the Americans, but intended to levy a heavy price for Okinawan territory.

The first major Kamikaze attack came on 6 April and inflicted considerable damage on American shipping. The same day, a Japanese surface naval task force moved toward Okinawa, but it was detected and almost totally destroyed by Admiral Spruance's carrier aircraft on the 7th. The Kamikaze attacks continued, but elaborate air defense measures and a Japanese tendency to concentrate on radar picket destroyers blunted their effectiveness. Nevertheless, during April, 20 American ships were sunk and 157 damaged—a large proportion by Kamikaze attacks. These suicide tactics continued through June, but with rapidly diminishing intensity. (In the entire campaign, the Japanese flew 1,900 suicide sorties and 3,700 orthodox sorties.) Actually, by 1 May, Japan's desperate gamble had failed. The Kamikaze Corps had been decimated, the surface fleet was no longer a threat, most of the suicide boats had been captured, and Spruance showed no inclination to withdraw the American fleet.

Meanwhile, the XXIV Corps had smashed headlong into Ushijima's strong defenses—the Machinato Line. (Oddly enough, American intelligence knew nothing of these defenses until after the landings.) The 96th Division took very heavy casualties in an unsuccessful assault on Kakazu Ridge (*center*), and the 7th Division had a difficult time farther east. Buckner then released the 27th Division from Tenth Army reserve (the 81st Division was still in area reserve in New Caledonia) and assigned it to the XXIV Corps; on 19 April, the corps launched a coordinated attack. Five days later, Ushijima abandoned the Machinato Line; his defense had been skillful, but it had cost the 62d Division heavily. To hold the Shuri Line, he now had to move most of the 24th Division (from the extreme south) and the 44th Independent Brigade (from Minatoga) northward to reinforce the badly weakened 62d Division. By 30 April, the XXIV Corps had reached the line shown (*solid red line*), but its divisions were exhausted, the Japanese still held all the key approaches to the Shuri Line, and Maj. Gen. John R. Hodge now knew that his XXIV Corps could not overrun southern Okinawa very quickly or easily.

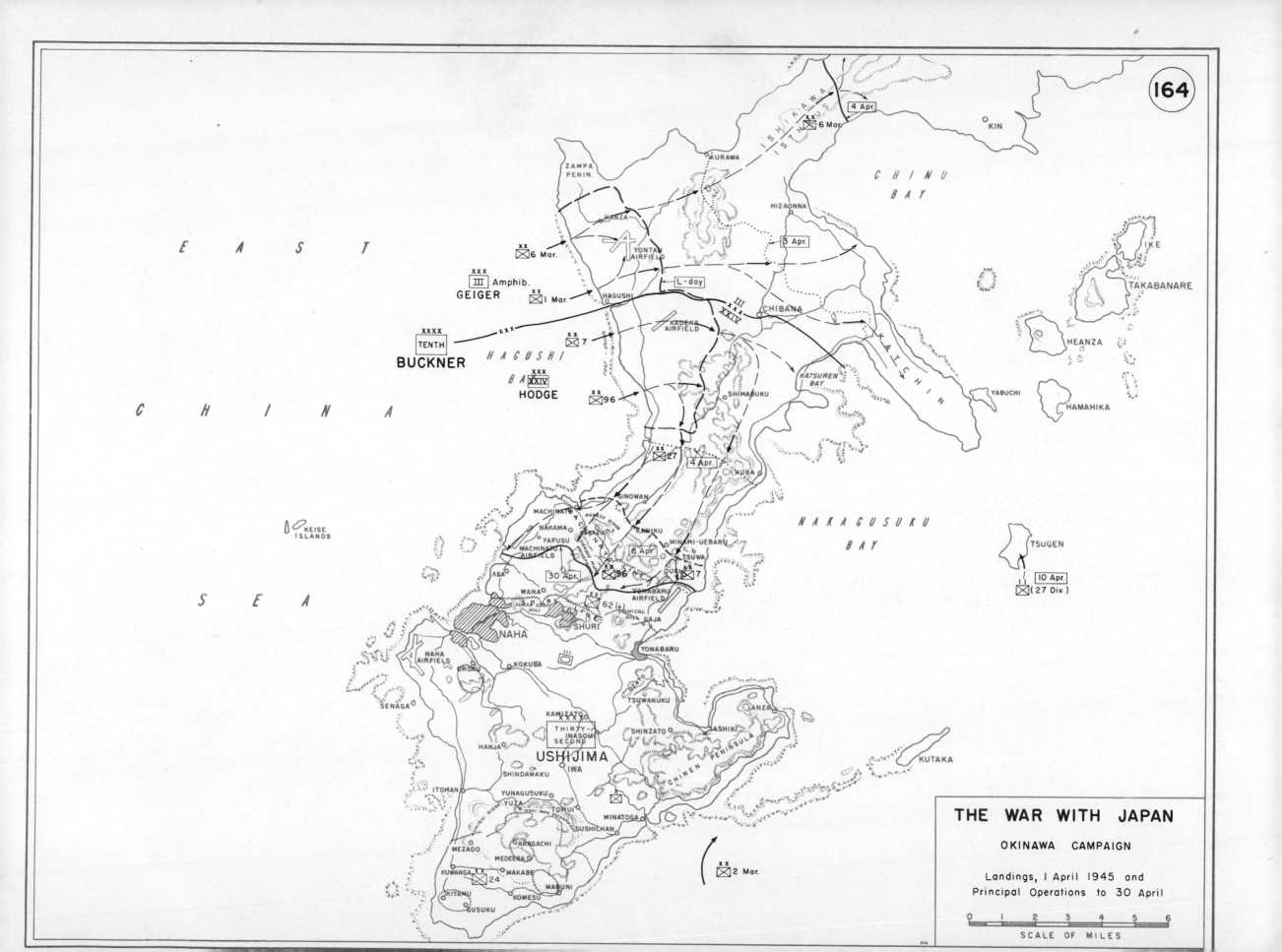

164

THE WAR WITH JAPAN

OKINAWA CAMPAIGN

Landings, 1 April 1945 and
Principal Operations to 30 April

SCALE OF MILES
0 1 2 3 4 5 6

Toward the end of April, the commander of the 77th Division (then mopping up on Ie Shima) recommended that his division be employed as it had been on Leyte—to make an amphibious envelopment. About the same time, Buckner was notified that the III Marine Amphibious Corps (being held relatively free for possible use in the third phase of the original plan) could now be fully committed on Okinawa. Immediately, the marine commanders similarly urged employing their troops in amphibious envelopments. Though Buckner was aware by this time that Ushijima had moved part of the 24th Division north, he rejected all of these proposals, primarily on the basis that landings could not be supported logistically and that Japanese artillery dominated the possible landing sites. Further, the divisions of the XXIV Corps were exhausted and in need of relief. Consequently, Buckner decided to strengthen the Shuri front, make penetrations on either side of Shuri, and then execute a double envelopment of that key town. About 1 May, the 27th Division relieved the 6th Marine Division of its security mission in northern Okinawa, the 77th Division spelled the 96th Division (the hardest hit of all divisions to date), and the 1st Marine Division took over the westernmost part of the line.

Hodge continued to attack, but gains were negligible and casualties heavy. On 4 May, Ushijima—against his better judgment —yielded to aggressive-minded subordinates and launched a major counteroffensive (not shown). Overly ambitious in conception, it failed dismally and was discontinued on the 5th. The Japanese took heavy casualties (about 5,000), consuming most of the slight reserve strength they had left at the time. Additionally, they brought out into the open much of their artillery, thus revealing many hitherto unsuspected positions. Buckner assumed direct command of the operations on 7 May with the establishment of both marine divisions on the western end of the front. On the 10th, the 96th Division relieved the 7th, and the next day an all-out offensive was launched.

The advance was slow and costly, for by now the Americans were up against the incredibly strong Shuri Line. Here, Ushijima had constructed a system of defenses in depth, employing mutually supporting strong points, pillboxes, and elaborate caves with connecting tunnels and several entrances. Many burial shrines were utilized, artillery and mortars were emplaced in caves, and reverse slopes were skillfully organized. It was probably the strongest position the Americans encountered in the Pacific war. Major activity centered around Sugar Loaf and Conical Hills as Buckner's troops inched forward. Torrential rains made the advance all the more difficult, but between 11 and 21 May the turning point of the battle occurred when the 96th Division succeeded in taking Conical Hill. The 7th Division was committed down the coastal corridor thus opened, and at last the Shuri Line was outflanked. Meanwhile, the marines edged forward into Naha and Shuri.

On 21 May, Ushijima decided to withdraw from the Shuri Line, but he did it so skillfully—aided by the abominable weather —that Buckner was unable to turn the withdrawal into a rout. The Japanese naval troops around Naha airfield (lower left) stayed in position and had to be rooted out by the two marine divisions, but in the XXIV Corps sector the advance was more rapid. By 14 June, the Americans had partially breached Ushijima's last organized position along the Yaeju Dake Escarpment (bottom center). The remaining Japanese were quickly compressed into three pockets, and on the 21st Okinawa was declared secured, though mopping up continued for another week. Neither commander survived the campaign—Buckner was killed by artillery fire on the 18th, and Ushijima committed hara-kiri on the 22d.

Okinawa was expensive to both sides. This last major battle of World War II cost the United States 49,151 casualties (12,520 killed) and Japan 117,472 (110,071 killed). American ship losses were 36 sunk and 368 damaged, while Japan lost a total of 7,830 aircraft. Most important of all, the Allies acquired a base only 350 miles from Kyushu, the southernmost of the Japanese home islands (see map 167).

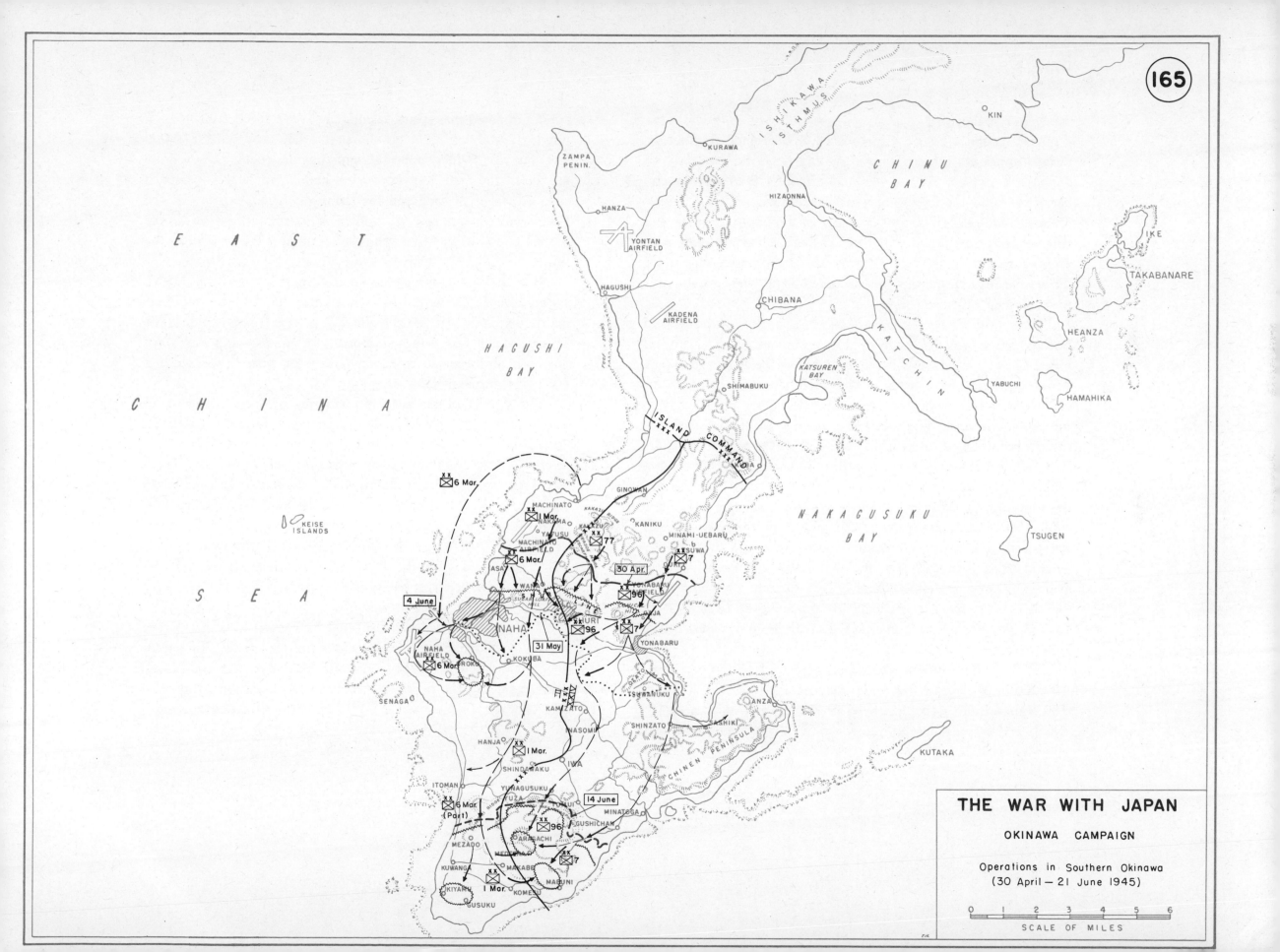

THE WAR WITH JAPAN

OKINAWA CAMPAIGN

Operations in Southern Okinawa
(30 April — 21 June 1945)

SCALE OF MILES
0 1 2 3 4 5 6

Strategic bombing of Japan prior to the spring of 1945 was more a nuisance than a threat. China-based B-29's made the first attacks, but not until the capture of the Marianas did the tempo of the assault increase. Tokyo was first struck by B-29's in November, 1944, and the following month the Marianas-based Superfortresses dropped 1,700 tons of bombs on Japan. But results were still far from satisfactory: the planes bombed at altitudes over 25,000 feet, the weather obscured targets, bombing by radar lacked the desired accuracy, and crippled planes were seldom able to reach their Marianas bases.

The capture of Iwo Jima for use as an emergency landing field boosted the morale of bomber pilots considerably and also provided fields from which fighters could escort the B-29's to Japan. More important, however, was Maj. Gen. Curtis E. LeMay's decision to bomb Japan's major cities at night from altitudes averaging 7,000 feet and using incendiary bombs. Tokyo was the first city to be attacked under these conditions. On 9 March, 1945, 234 B-29's dropped 1,667 tons of incendiaries which burned out almost sixteen square miles in the heart of the city. In quick succession, Japan's other major cities (Nagoya, Osaka, Kobe, and Yokohama) were subjected to the same type of raids. The air campaign picked up momentum—both night and day—as improved radar, fighter escorts, and increased bomb loads made the bombing operations more effective. By mid-June, the planned destruction in the five major cities had been achieved (Tokyo alone had 3,100,000 persons homeless), and the bombers switched to other targets.

By the end of the war, the Superfortresses had dropped about 100,000 tons of incendiaries on sixty-six Japanese cities. About 169 square miles were destroyed or damaged, with almost 100 square miles being burned out in the five major cities. The Jap-anese estimated that strategic bombing killed 260,000 people, injured 412,000, left 9,200,000 homeless, and destroyed 2,210,000 dwellings. Without a doubt, this appalling destruction lowered the morale of the Japanese people; but coming in 1945—by which time shortages of food and the string of Allied victories in the Pacific had already severely shaken the confidence of the people in their war leaders—it served more as an accelerator than as the prime force.

Had the war continued beyond August, Japan would have suffered under the weight of even greater attacks than had Germany. Okinawa was being readied as a base for the Eighth Air Force—which was being equipped with B-29's—and the Marianas bomber force had expanded to the point where it was sending 800 planes on single raids.

The climax of the strategic bombing of Japan came on 6 August when a single B-29 dropped an atomic bomb (with destructive power equal to that of 100 bombers) on Hiroshima (*see map 167, lower center*), destroying 60 per cent of the city. Three days later, a second bomb fell on Nagasaki, wreaking just slightly less destruction. The decision to use the atomic bomb had not been taken lightly, though it has since been criticized on moral and military grounds. It alone did not force Japan to surrender, but it helped convince the Japanese government that further resistance was hopeless. It had been used primarily as an alternative to an invasion of Japan proper.

The dogged resistance displayed by Japanese troops during the war to date had caused some sound thinkers to envision a massive suicidal defense of the beaches of the Japanese home islands (not excluding the horrible specter of participation by women and children), which would cost 1,000,000 Allied casualties.

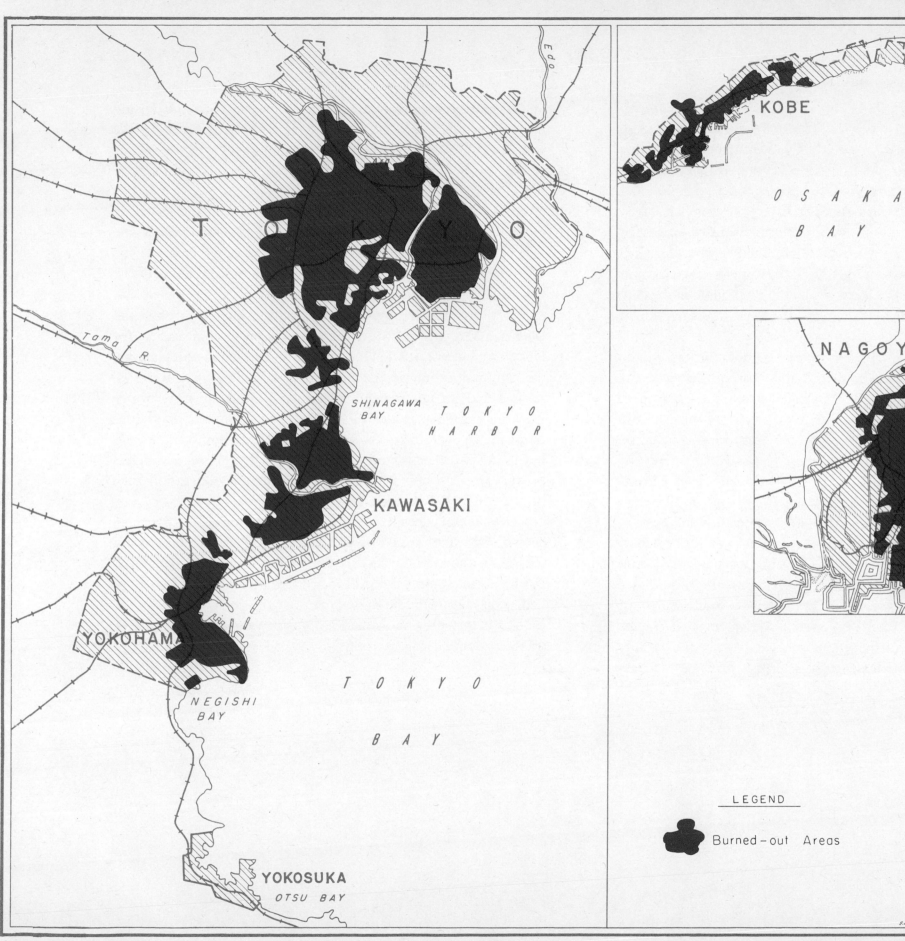

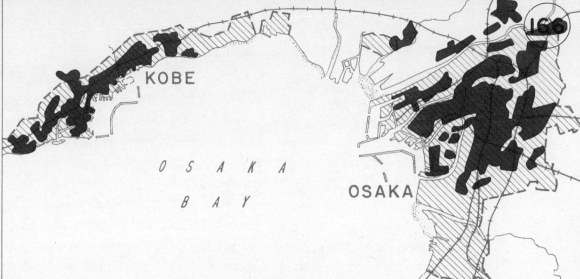

KOBE

O S A K A

B A Y

OSAKA

NAGOYA

T O K Y O

SHINAGAWA
BAY

T O K Y O

H A R B O R

KAWASAKI

YOKOHAMA

N E G I S H I

BAY

T O K Y O

B A Y

YOKOSUKA

OTSU BAY

LEGEND

Burned-out Areas

THE WAR WITH JAPAN

THE BOMBING OF JAPAN

Extent of Destruction by Bombing
of Principal Cities

0   5   10

SCALE OF MILES

As early as December, 1944, the Joint Chiefs of Staff contemplated operations against Kyushu (*bottom left*) and a landing near Tokyo (*center, right*). Accordingly, MacArthur and Nimitz were directed to initiate preliminary planning. In addition, the JCS specified that planning should continue for a possible lodgment on the China coast. By June, however, the war had developed to the point whereby future operations could be envisaged more precisely. Following discussions with the President, the JCS now subordinated all operations to the seizure of objectives in Japan proper, dropped the idea of a landing in China, and established a target date of 1 November, 1945, for the invasion of Kyushu (OLYMPIC).

Planning for the invasion of Japan was complicated by the need for coordination with the British and Russians. In 1943, the JCS had taken the position that Russian entry into the war against Japan was essential, and, indeed, that view still prevailed as late as February, 1945—as evidenced by the territorial concessions Stalin won at the Yalta Conference (*ARGONAUT*). But by June, the Americans—shocked by Russian behavior in Europe and no longer interested in establishing B-29 bases in Siberia—were not so desirous of ensuring Russian participation at any cost. They still wanted Stalin to attack the Japanese in Manchukuo, but as we have seen (*see text, map 152*), the Russians needed no urging in this regard. The British—foreseeing their ability to provide forces—desired to participate in the final operations against Japan, but found the Americans somewhat reluctant. A British fleet had participated in the Okinawan campaign, and by July arrangements were being made to base British strategic bombers on Okinawa. A combination of factors, however, precluded using a British ground force larger than three divisions; ultimately, the Combined Chiefs of Staff agreed to the employment of such a force—a Commonwealth Corps (*this map, not shown*) in Operation CORONET.

In an attempt to create a more workable command structure in the Pacific for the decisive operations against Japan proper, the JCS established a system of command by service on 6 April, 1945: MacArthur would control all army forces; Nimitz, all navy forces; and the JCS, the United States Strategic Air Forces (a new headquarters, commanded by General Spaatz, which controlled the B-29's). MacArthur was assigned primary responsibility for OLYMPIC, but was ordered to "cooperate" with Nimitz in planning the amphibious phase. Both commanders, however, were informed that the requirements of the land campaign were of primary importance in OLYMPIC. Thus, in the climactic operations of the Pacific war, there was to be no unity of command—at least, not as developments stood in July. MacArthur, though assigned primary responsibility, would have to rely upon cooperation from the navy and the strategic air forces.

The general concepts of the OLYMPIC and CORONET plans are shown. OLYMPIC would secure a firm foothold in Japan, but CORONET was to be the decisive operation. It was anticipated that the Japanese would resist with their usual fanaticism and that Allied casualties would be high. Note that the First Army—in the process of redeploying to the Philippines when the war ended—was to be employed in CORONET.

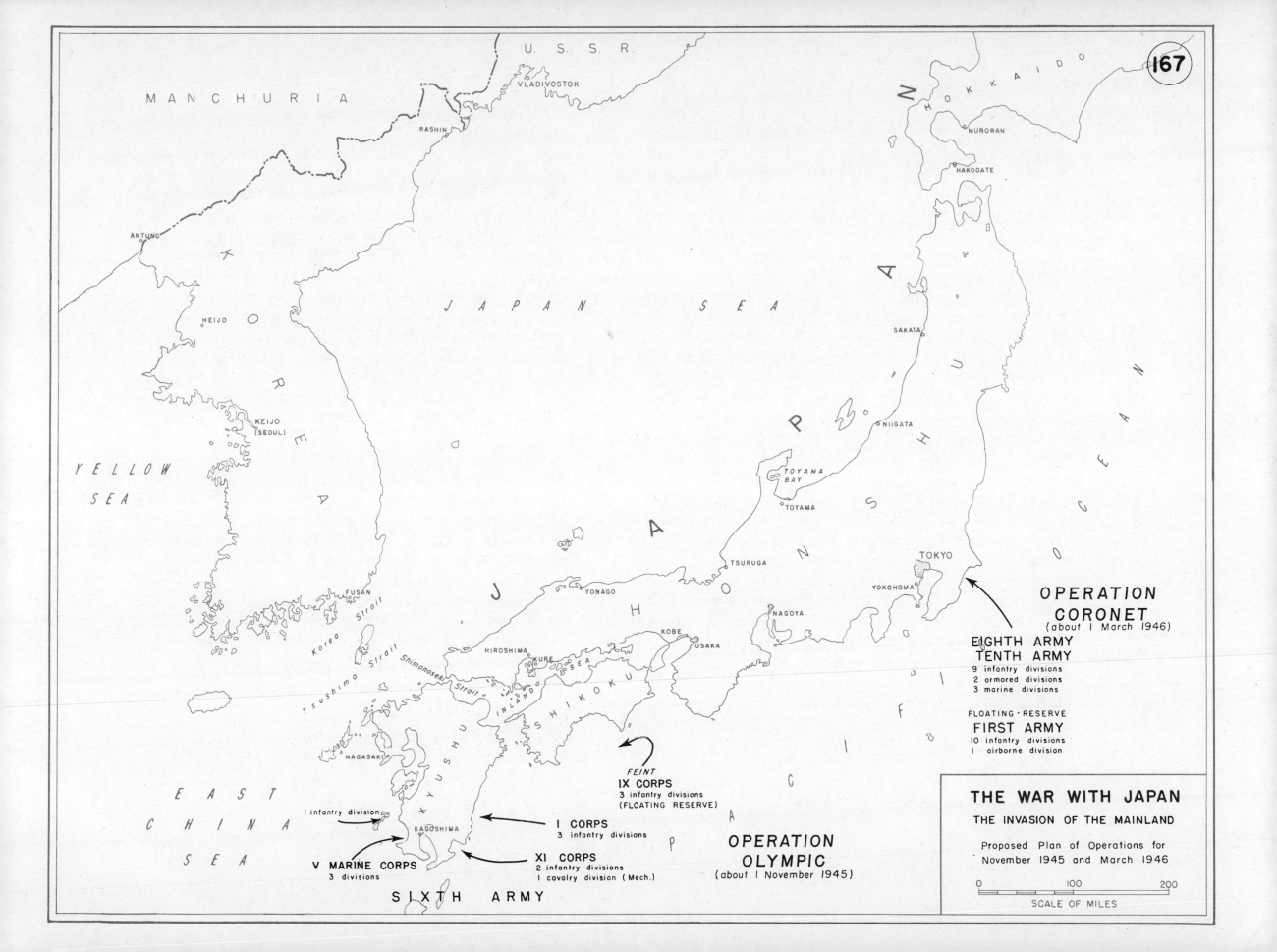

U. S. S. R.

MANCHURIA

VLADIVOSTOK

RASHIN

HOKKAIDO

MURORAN

HAKODATE

ANTUNG

K
O
R
E
A

HEIJO

JAPAN SEA

SAKATA

KEIJO
(SEOUL)

YELLOW
SEA

N
I
P
P
O
N
S
H
U

NIIGATA

TOYAMA
BAY

TOYAMA

J
A
P
A
N

TSURUGA

TOKYO

YOKOHOMA

FUSAN

YONAGO

NAGOYA

Korea Strait

Tsushima Strait

Shimonoseki Strait

HIROSHIMA

KURE

KOBE

OSAKA

INLAND SEA

SHIKOKU

**OPERATION
CORONET**
(about 1 March 1946)

**EIGHTH ARMY
TENTH ARMY**

9 infantry divisions
2 armored divisions
3 marine divisions

FLOATING·RESERVE
FIRST ARMY
10 infantry divisions
1 airborne division

NAGASAKI

E A S T

C H I N A

S E A

1 infantry division

KYUSHU

KAGOSHIMA

V MARINE CORPS
3 divisions

FEINT
IX CORPS
3 infantry divisions
(FLOATING RESERVE)

I CORPS
3 infantry divisions

XI CORPS
2 infantry divisions
1 cavalry division (Mech.)

**OPERATION
OLYMPIC**
(about 1 November 1945)

P
A
C
I
F
I
C

O
C
E
A
N

SIXTH ARMY

THE WAR WITH JAPAN

THE INVASION OF THE MAINLAND

Proposed Plan of Operations for
November 1945 and March 1946

0   100   200

SCALE OF MILES

In July, shortly after the fighting ended on Okinawa, Halsey boldly took his Third Fleet into Japanese waters and struck at targets throughout the length of the Japanese home islands. Launching raids with as many as 1,000 carrier aircraft and shelling east coast installations at will, Halsey's forces contributed materially to the destruction of Japanese industry and the blockade of the home islands. Opposition was light, and it became obvious that Japan was hoarding her precious aircraft for the expected Allied invasion.

About this same time, the B-29's were intensifying their mining operations—begun in March, 1945—to help tighten the blockade. This use of aerial mines was on a scale heretofore unequaled and achieved considerable success. Though the majority of the mines were employed in Shimonoseki Strait (*see map 167, lower left*), Japan's shipping bottleneck, the bombers also mined other areas off southern Japan and Korea. Meanwhile, American submarines, continuing their unheralded campaign against Japanese shipping, helped draw the noose ever tighter about a starving and industrially crippled Japan.

On 26 July, the Allies, meeting at Potsdam in Germany, publicly called for Japan's armed forces to surrender unconditionally. Though this Allied declaration offered some leniency—in that it specifically refrained from subjecting the Emperor to any terms distasteful to the Japanese—it was rejected. Secretly, however, the Japanese made a last attempt to get Russia to mediate; Stalin's delayed answer was a declaration of war. (As early as May, the Suzuki government, appointed with the mission of securing peace, had approached Russia; but inasmuch as Stalin was planning the attack in Manchukuo and the Japanese insisted on a conditional surrender, nothing came of these efforts.)

Thus the Allies, considering that they had no alternative, brought the full weight of their military power to bear upon the hapless Japanese. As already noted, two atomic bombs were dropped in early August. Russia invaded Manchukuo (*this map, upper left*), Halsey returned on 9 August to make another devastating attack on Honshu, and an 800-plane B-29 raid struck that same island on the 14th. The Japanese government at last capitulated unconditionally, but only under great pressure from the Emperor; the Army was adamant to the last and even sought to resist the Emperor's order to surrender. After three and one-half years of war, Japan had been beaten to her knees, not by any one factor but by a combination: the blockade, the succession of lost campaigns, air raids, the threat of invasion, the atomic bomb, and Russia's entry into the war.

The map shows the general situation at the time of Japan's surrender, as well as the limit of the Japanese advance in 1942.

Embarking upon a global war with an overly ambitious plan which was based upon the faulty premise that America would seek a negotiated peace, Japan never really had a chance of winning. Among her greatest mistakes were: attacking Pearl Harbor, failure to increase her merchant marine tonnage, insistence on expanding the basic perimeter, and her failure to concentrate strength at decisive points.

From the Allied viewpoint, the Pacific war was remarkable for its development of a supply system which could support such widely scattered operations, the use of the revolutionary atomic bomb, and the development of a coordinated air-naval-ground team.

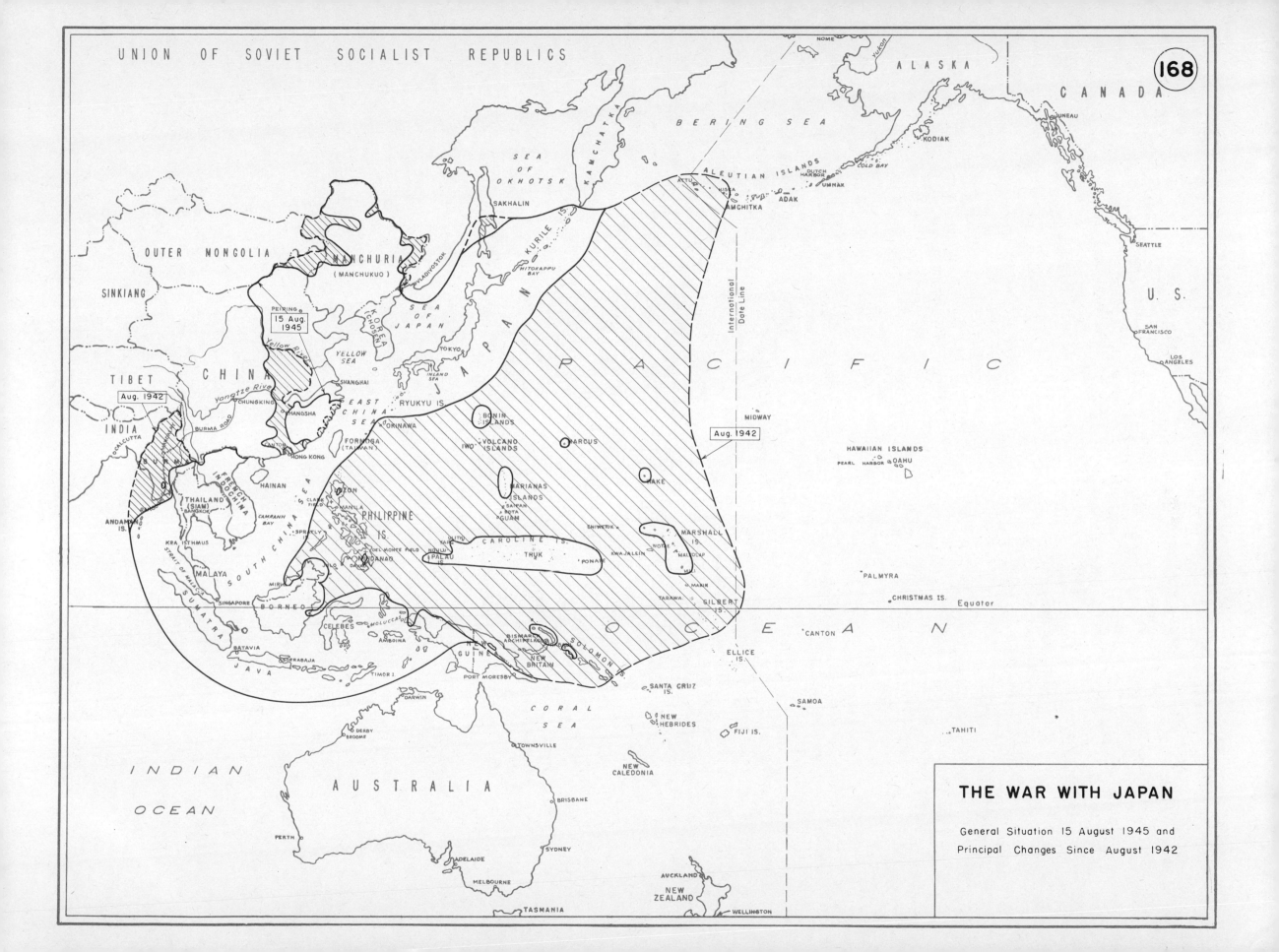

THE WAR WITH JAPAN

General Situation 15 August 1945 and
Principal Changes Since August 1942

SECTION 3 • KOREAN WAR

The ancient Hermit Kingdom of Korea—Chosen, "the Land of the Morning Calm"—was, in its day, the cultural mentor of both China and Japan. Its location, however, made it a traditional road of war between those two nations, either for an invasion of Japan or for a Japanese invasion of the Asiatic mainland. Despite repeated Japanese attempts at conquest, Korea remained a Chinese vassal state until 1894-95, when a newly westernized Japan shattered the antique armies of a declining China. Japan found her claim to Korea still disputed, however, for an expanding Russian imperialism was clutching at Korea, Manchuria, and northern China. Ten years of underhanded competition ended in the Russo-Japanese War (1905). Then, the Russians disposed of, the Japanese proceeded to absorb their prize. In such matters as roads, railroads, reforestation, and industry, they were diligent in improving their new property. For the rest, they exploited their new Korean subjects mercilessly, making every effort to stamp out their language, their customs, and their very national identity. Never a docile people, the Koreans (sometimes termed "the Irish of the Orient") nursed their hatred and waited.

At Cairo (1943) and Potsdam (1945), England, China, and the United States joined in pledging Korea eventual independence; Russia likewise endorsed this promise in her declaration of war against Japan (August, 1945). After the Japanese surrender, it was agreed among the American, British, and Russian governments that—as a matter of convenience—Japanese troops in Korea north of the 38th Parallel would surrender to the Russians, those south of it to the Americans. Almost at once, the Russians began organizing northern Korea into another Communist satellite state; the 38th Parallel was converted into a sealed political boundary, completely disrupting the normal workings of the Korean economy. An American-Russian joint commission, charged with the organization of a provisional democratic government for all Korea, wrangled unproductively, while the Koreans—chiefly in the south, where such conduct was safe—clamored for their promised independence. Finally, the United States laid the problem before the United Nations, which—after due debate—decreed that Korea should hold nationwide elections, under U.N. supervision, to elect a national assembly. This election was accordingly held in southern Korea; Russia refused the U.N. commission authority to enter northern Korea. South Korea promptly adopted a constitution, elected Syngman Rhee its president, and took over authority from the U.S. military government on 15 August, 1948. The General Assembly of the U.N. recognized it as the only valid Korean government. Above the 38th Parallel, the Russians expertly set up a puppet government, the "Democratic People's Republic of Korea," which claimed authority over the whole country. Russian troops reportedly evacuated North Korea on 25 December, 1948; the last American troops withdrew on 29 June, 1949.

Syngman Rhee, handicapped by the lack of associates with any experience in government and by a war-shattered economy, soon found that these routine problems were actually the least of his worries. North Korea, backed by Communist China and Russia, waged a war—no less vicious for being undeclared—against him and his government. In accordance with Communist strategy, it took many forms: economic pressure, all-out propaganda and psychological warfare, subversion and terrorism, and constant border clashes. The United States, then engaged in disarming in the interests of economy, was distant and not too interested.

As this map shows, the situation appeared perfect for a sudden Communist coup. Russia had added southern Sakhalin (*top right*) and the Kurile Islands (*upper right*) to her prewar empire in this area. In addition, she had military bases at Darien (*center*) and nearby Port Arthur (*not shown*). China was newly in the hands of a savage Chinese Communist government, with Chiang Kai-Shek relegated to Formosa and a few tiny offshore islands. The Communist-sustained revolt in Indochina was getting beyond the ability of the French to contain; there was guerrilla fighting in the Philippines and in Malaya (*off map, bottom left*). The seizure of Korea would almost encircle Japan; if the United States could be forced out of Japan, by one method or another, all Asia would probably go Communist.

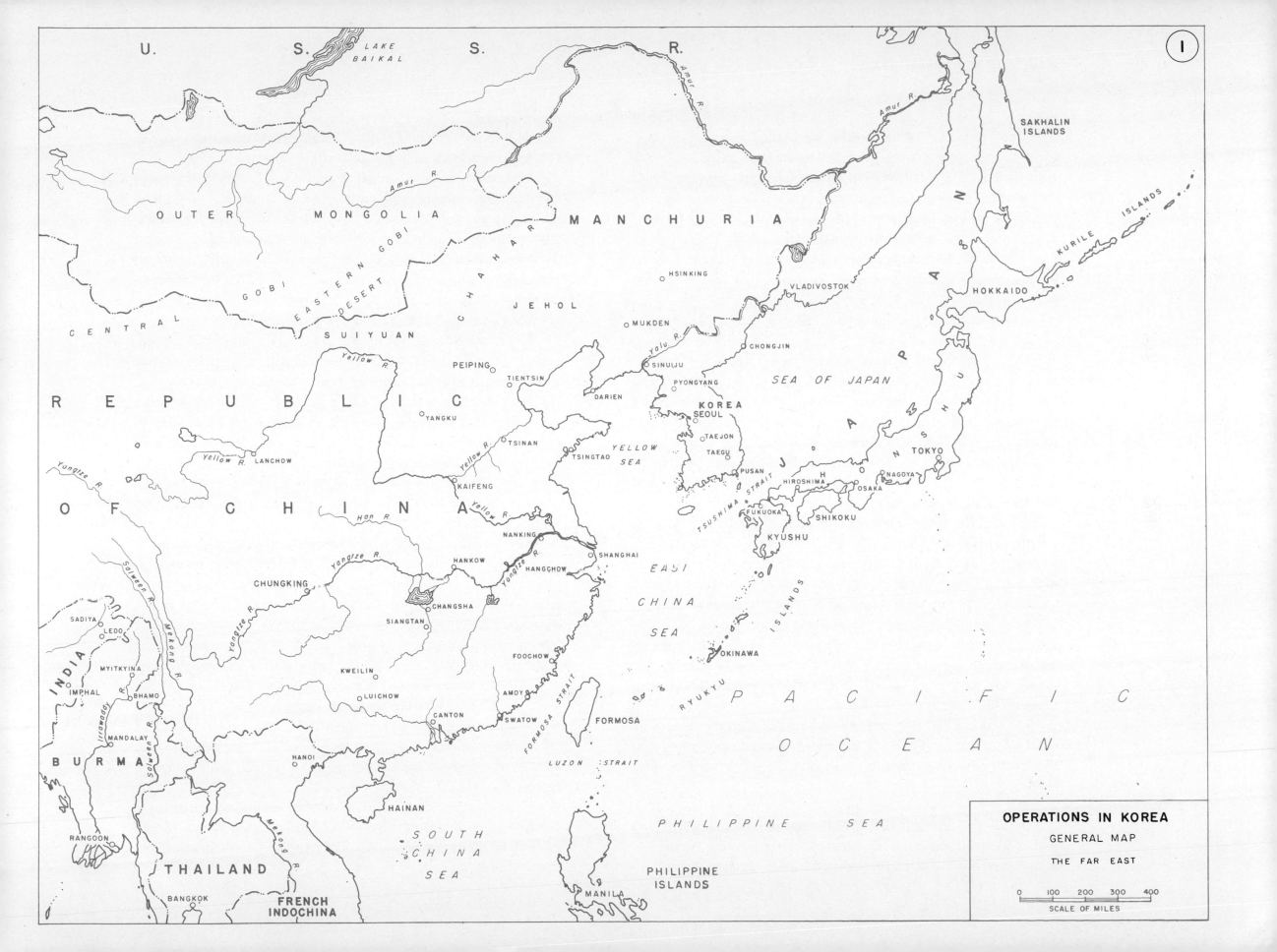

U. S.   S.   R.

LAKE
BAIKAL

OUTER   MONGOLIA   MANCHURIA

SAKHALIN
ISLANDS

Amur R.

Amur R.

KURILE ISLANDS

GOBI
EASTERN GOBI DESERT

CENTRAL

CHAHAR

JEHOL

HSINKING

VLADIVOSTOK

HOKKAIDO

SUIYUAN

MUKDEN

CHONGJIN

Yellow R.

PEIPING

TIENTSIN

Yalu R.
SINUIJU

PYONGYANG

SEA OF JAPAN

REPUBLIC

DARIEN

KOREA
SEOUL

YANGKU

TAEJON

TAEGU

TOKYO

Yellow R.

TSINAN

TSINGTAO

YELLOW
SEA

LANCHOW

Yellow R.

PUSAN

NAGOYA

Yellow R.

HIROSHIMA

HONSHU

OF   CHINA

KAIFENG

Han R.

NANKING

FUKUOKA

OSAKA

SHIKOKU

TSUSHIMA STRAIT

Yangtze R.

HANKOW

SHANGHAI

KYUSHU

Yangtze R.

HANGCHOW

CHUNGKING

EAST

Solween R.

Yangtze R.

CHANGSHA

CHINA

Mekong R.

SIANGTAN

SEA

SADIYA

LEDO

RYUKYU ISLANDS

MYITKYINA

KWEILIN

FOOCHOW

OKINAWA

PACIFIC

IMPHAL

INDIA

Irrawaddy R.

BHAMO

LUICHOW

AMOY

RYUKYU

MANDALAY

Solween R.

CANTON

SWATOW

FORMOSA STRAIT

FORMOSA

OCEAN

BURMA

HANOI

LUZON   STRAIT

RANGOON

Mekong R.

HAINAN

PHILIPPINE   SEA

THAILAND

Mekong R.

SOUTH
CHINA
SEA

PHILIPPINE
ISLANDS

BANGKOK

FRENCH
INDOCHINA

MANILA

OPERATIONS IN KOREA

GENERAL MAP

THE FAR EAST

0   100   200   300   400

SCALE OF MILES

Korea is basically a great mountain range, sloping southward from the headwaters of the Yalu River (*sketch* a, *upper center*). From this range, spurs run generally to the southeast, creating—with their companion rivers—a series of barriers to north-south movement. The largest of these lateral ranges slants across southern Korea toward the seaport of Mokpo (*bottom center*), forming a wild and desolate region which was historically the refuge of guerrilla bands. Especially when in flood, the main rivers (*sketch* b) are serious military obstacles, running wide and deep and heavy with silt.

On the east coast, the mountains fall steeply to the sea in most places, leaving barely room for the coastal road and railroad. With the exception of Wonsan (*center, right*), there are few harbors of any size. The Japan Sea is deep, and large vessels can operate easily close off the coast. There are several harbors along the broken southern coastline, but Pusan is the only one capable of handling large amounts of cargo. Westward, the Yellow Sea is comparatively shallow; mud banks and an unusual tidal reach (thirty-two feet—the second highest in the world—at Inchon [*center*]) hamper navigation.

In 1950, Korea had a population of approximately 30,000,000 people, 21,000,000 of whom lived south of the 38th Parallel, where the population density reached 586 persons per square mile. South Korea was primarily agricultural; the north possessed some industry and large reserves of strategic minerals, plus a highly developed hydroelectric power system. The major cities were connected by a reasonably adequate standard-gauge rail net, single-tracked for the greater part. The road net, however, was inadequate, consisting largely of narrow dirt tracks. There were few airfields.

The Korean summers are hot and humid; winters are bitterly cold. From late June to early September, the monsoon rains turn the country into a quagmire, dissolving the unsurfaced country roads.

During the first half of 1950, Russia and Communist China had cooperated to double the strength of the existing North Korean Army: the Russians furnishing weapons, equipment, and in-structors; the Chinese transferring thousands of Korean nationals who had served with the Chinese Communists during the war. The result was a tough, well-trained force, numbering approximately 127,000, stiffened with combat veterans and backed by a fanatically Communist-indoctrinated Border Constabulary of 18,600. This army was well provided with light artillery, mortars, and antitank weapons. It included a tank brigade with some 150 Russian T-34 medium tanks—a rugged and maneuverable vehicle, mounting an 85-mm. gun. The North Korean Air Force had approximately 180 Russian-built aircraft, about 110 of which were combat types; the North Korean Navy was minuscule.

The South Korean Army, as of June, 1950, numbered approximately 98,000 men. Four of its eight divisions were reasonably well equipped with American weapons, though they had no tanks, no heavy mortars, and no effective antitank weapons. The other four divisions had a mixture of light weapons, a large part of them obsolescent Japanese models. There were only five battalions of field artillery (a sixth was being formed) in the entire army, and these were equipped with a light 105-mm. howitzer that was easily outranged by the North Korean artillery. Supplies of ammunition and of weapon and vehicular spare parts were very low. The South Korean Air Force had twenty-two liaison and advance-trainer aircraft. A few old pursuit planes were available, but no Korean pilots were as yet qualified to fly them. The South Korean Navy consisted of a few small patrol craft. There was a National Police of approximately 48,000, but—unlike the North Korean Border Constabulary—it was not trained or armed for military service. Approximately 500 United States Army officers and enlisted men (the United States Korean Military Advisory Group to the Republic of Korea [KMAG]) were assisting in the development of the South Korean armed forces. In this, since General Douglas MacArthur was no longer responsible for the defense of Korea, they operated under the control of the American ambassador to Korea, Mr. John J. Muccio.

(In the succeeding texts, abbreviations will be used as follows: NKA—North Korean Army; ROK—Republic of Korea [South Korea]; ROKA—Republic of Korea Army; CCF—Chinese Communist Forces.)

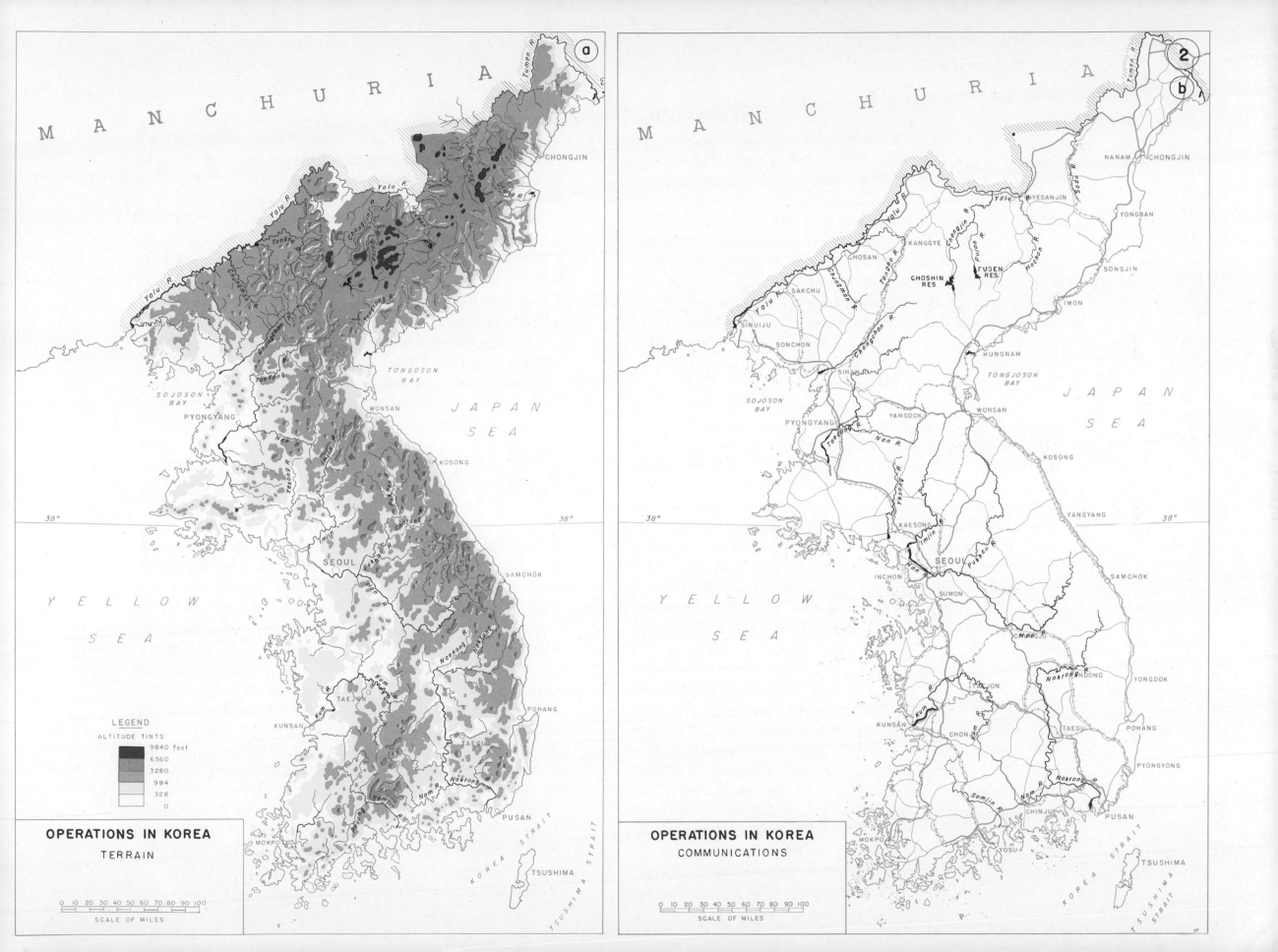

MANCHURIA

CHONGJIN

Yalu R.
Tumen R.
Chongjin R.
Hochon R.
Tongro R.
Tongjong R.

TONGOSON
BAY

JAPAN
SEA

WONSAN

SOJOSON
BAY

PYONGYANG

Taedong R.

Nan R.

KOSONG

Yesong R.

Imjin R.

Pukhan R.

Chojong R.

38°   38°

SEOUL

Pukhan R.

Han R.

SAMCHOK

YELLOW

SEA

Naesong R.

Naktong R.

POHANG

Kum R.

TAEJON
KUNSAN

Kum R.

TAEGU

LEGEND

ALTITUDE TINTS

	9840 feet
	6560
	3280
	984
	328
	0

Nam R.
Somjin R.
Naktong R.

PUSAN

MOKPO

KOREA
STRAIT

TSUSHIMA

TSUSHIMA STRAIT

OPERATIONS IN KOREA
TERRAIN

0 10 20 30 40 50 60 70 80 90 100
SCALE OF MILES

2

b

MANCHURIA

Tumen R.

NANAM CHONGJIN

PYESANJIN

YONGBAN

Yalu R.
Chongjin R.

KANGGYE

Pujon R.

Hochon R.

SONGJIN

CHOSAN

Changjon R.

CHOSHIN
RES

FUSEN
RES

IWON

Chungman R.

SAKCHU

SINUIJU

Chongchon R.

HUNGNAM

Yalu R.

SONCHON

SINAN

TONGJOSON
BAY

YANGDOK

WONSAN

SOJOSON
BAY

PYONGYANG

Taedong R.

Nan R.

KOSONG

Yesong R.

YANGYANG

KAESONG

Imjin R.

38°   38°

SEOUL

Pukhan R.

Han R.

INCHON

SUWON

SAMCHOK

YELLOW

SEA

CHUNGJU

Kum R.

Naktong R. ANDONG

YONGDOK

Kum R.

TAEJON

Kum R.

TAEGU

POHANG

KUNSAN

CHON

PYONGYONG

Nam R.

Somjin R.

Naktong R.

CHINJU

PUSAN

MOKPO

YOSU

KOREA
STRAIT

TSUSHIMA

TSUSHIMA
STRAIT

OPERATIONS IN KOREA
COMMUNICATIONS

0 10 20 30 40 50 60 70 80 90 100
SCALE OF MILES

Despite increasing rumors of an imminent invasion, the ROK had only four divisions near the frontier, plus a detached regiment on the Onjin peninsula (*upper left*). Another division garrisoned Seoul (*upper center*), and the remaining three were scattered through the interior. KMAG did not expect an invasion, but considered the ROKA capable of repelling one.

Between 15 and 24 June, the NKA concentrated seven infantry divisions, an armored brigade, and supporting troops near the 38th Parallel. Most of their infantry and armor were between Kaesong and Chorwon (*both upper center*), massed for a converging offensive through the Uijongbu gap against Seoul. Apparently the NKA—or, rather, its Russian creators—expected to seize Seoul and rapidly overrun all South Korea, thereby confronting the world with an accomplished fact.

About 0400, 25 June (Korean time), 1950, the NKA offensive struck—accompanied by radio broadcasts claiming that the ROKA had invaded North Korea, and that the NKA therefore had begun a "righteous invasion" in self-defense. At most points, the tank-spearheaded NKA broke through the hurriedly manned ROK defenses with comparative ease, though there was fierce and sustained resistance at Chunchon (*upper center*) and elsewhere. Parties of Communist guerrillas were landed along the east coast. Seoul fell on the 28th; in the confusion of the retreat, the bridges over the Han River were blown up while most of the ROK forces defending the capital were still north of the river. The greater part escaped by boat, badly disorganized and without their vehicles and heavy weapons.

MacArthur was first authorized to supply the ROK with ammunition and to protect the evacuation of American dependents. On the 26th (Washington time), he was authorized to employ air and naval forces against NKA units in South Korea. The next night, the U.N. Security Council called on its members to give South Korea military aid. Having personally inspected the ROKA forces along the Han River, MacArthur recommended the employment of American ground forces. Accordingly, President Truman (who had already approved their commitment to hold the Chinhae-Pusan [*lower right*] area) sanctioned this action, authorized the United States Air Force to strike specific military targets in North Korea, and ordered a naval blockade of North Korea.

England, Australia, Canada, New Zealand, and Holland began assigning naval and air forces to MacArthur's command. (On 7 July, President Truman—at the request of the U.N. Security Council—named MacArthur as Commander in Chief, United Nations Command.)

MacArthur ordered the 24th Division from Japan to Korea. A small delaying force (Task Force Smith), composed of elements of the 1st Battalion, 21st Infantry Regiment, was flown to Pusan, while the rest of the division followed by ship. A small American antiaircraft unit had preceded it on the 29th, to protect the Suwon (*upper center*) airfield.

Attacking south across the Han River, the NKA met bitter resistance (30 June–3 July) until it could get tanks across. Thereafter, its advance picked up speed, capturing Suwon on 4 July. Task Force Smith, reinforced by a battery of American field artillery, made its stand just north of Osan (*center*), astride the vital Seoul-Taejon-Pusan axis, on 5 July. Lacking effective antitank weapons, it was overrun after a hard fight. As other elements of the 24th Division became available, its commander, Maj. Gen. William F. Dean, committed them in a series of delaying actions (*dated dashed blue lines*)—sometimes heroic, usually desperate, and always confused. In the stand at Taejon, Dean was captured. On 13 July, the American Eighth Army (Lt. Gen. Walton H. Walker) took command of all United States Army forces in Korea. On 18 July, the 1st Cavalry and 25th Divisions arrived, followed on the 26th by the 29th Regimental Combat Team from Okinawa. Concurrently, ROK units fought a series of delaying actions in the mountains to the east of the Americans, winning several creditable minor actions. Though opposed only by a ROK reinforced regiment, the NKA advance down the east coast was particularly slow and hesitant—in part, probably because of active support given the ROKA by American warships and aircraft. By 5 August, however, the U.N. forces had been pushed back to the general line of the Naktong River (*solid blue line*).

By 10 July, the United States Air Force, with Australian assistance, had eradicated the North Korean Air Force. Because of communications difficulties, poor joint training, and the chaotic tactical situation, American and ROK ground forces were frequently attacked by U.N. aircraft during the first few weeks.

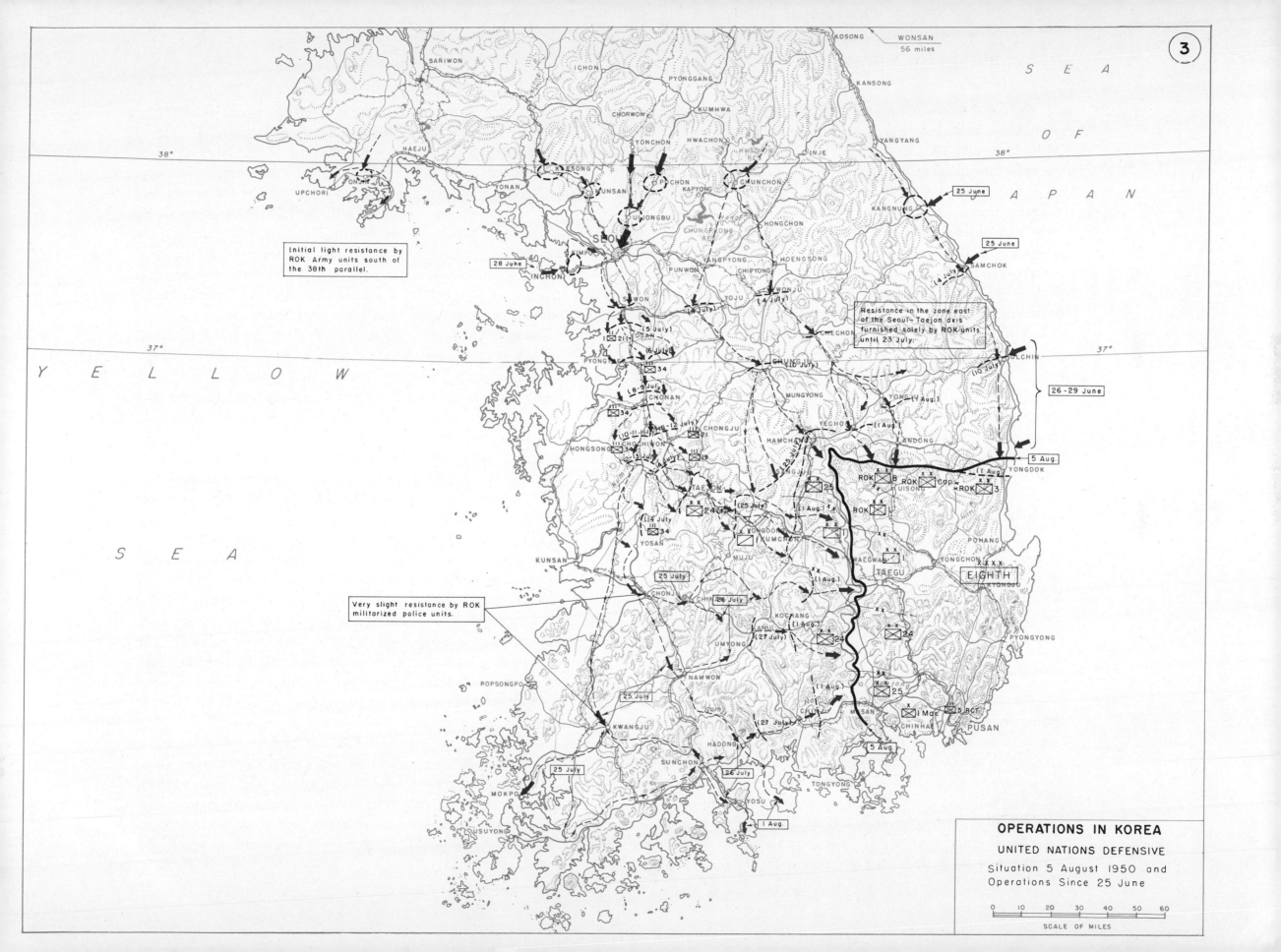

WONSAN
56 miles

Initial light resistance by
ROK Army units south of
the 38th parallel.

Resistance in the zone east
of the Seoul–Taejon axis
furnished solely by ROK units
until 23 July.

Very slight resistance by ROK
militarized police units.

OPERATIONS IN KOREA

UNITED NATIONS DEFENSIVE

Situation 5 August 1950 and
Operations Since 25 June

SCALE OF MILES

0   10   20   30   40   50   60

The NKA invasion of South Korea found the United States with almost a third of its ground forces in the Far East—the 7th, 24th, 25th, and 1st Cavalry Divisions in Japan, the 5th Regimental Combat Team (RCT) in Hawaii, and the 29th RCT in Okinawa. All of these units were filled with young replacements and were understrength: with the exception of one infantry regiment and one field artillery battalion in the 25th Division, all infantry regiments had been reduced from their normal three battalions to two; all artillery battalions, from three firing batteries to two. The troops in Japan had been scattered on occupational duties; there was a shortage of suitable training areas, and some units had not yet satisfactorily completed their battalion training programs. Physical and psychological conditioning left a good deal to be desired. Weapons and equipment were practically all of World War II vintage, in poor condition and badly worn. Spare parts and ammunition were in short supply; some ammunition proved unreliable. Many radios were reported inoperable. Divisional tank units were equipped only with the M-24 light tank, since medium tanks were too heavy for Japanese bridges and roads.

As habitual, the United States had been caught unprepared. Unlike World War I and World War II, it had no allies capable of holding off the enemy while it armed. Victory in two wars against major powers had left Americans with an unjustified feeling of superiority. Consequently, they had to see their troops driven in disorder before the veterans of a semicivilized minor nation, and to find many of their weapons and fighting skills inferior to the enemy's.

The last days of July had seen the development of a new enemy threat (*see map 3*). While the main enemy thrust continued along the axis Taejon-Taegu-Pusan, some of the NKA units which had overrun southwestern Korea now turned eastward for a drive on Pusan through Chinju (*lower center*). Committed to meet this threat, the 29th RCT (*not shown*) had one of its battalions badly cut up in an NKA ambush. Walker therefore shifted the 25th Division from the northwest corner of his perimeter to the Masan area (*lower left*). The battered 24th Division was kept

in line, though desperately in need of rehabilitation, while the 1st Cavalry Division spread itself thin to hold a front of 103,600 yards with approximately 7,000 riflemen. (Ten thousand yards was considered a satisfactory frontage for a full-strength division.)

General Walker waged a flexible, aggressive defense (*this map, sketch* a); on 7 August, he thrust Task Force Kean (most of the 25th Division, the 1st Marine Provisional Brigade, and the 5th RCT) toward Chinju (*lower left*) in a spoiling attack. This ran into the NKA attack toward Pusan and drove it back in several days of hard fighting. Later, however, the task force had to be withdrawn to reinforce other parts of the perimeter.

During the general period 6-26 August, the NKA launched several successive attacks at different points along the perimeter. In the west, they established several bridgeheads (*dotted blue lines*) over the Naktong River, but these were contained and later wiped out. Along the eastern coast, the NKA had better fortune, infiltrating through the mountains west of Yongdok (*upper right*) to seize Pohang. The ROK 3d Division was cut off and had to be evacuated by sea. ROK forces, however, soon reestablished their front. Around 15 August, a final NKA drive bent in the northwest corner of the perimeter, but was finally checked below Tabu (*upper center*). Walker exploited his interior lines to shift reserves rapidly from one threatened sector to another. To counteract these tactics, the NKA next launched (*sketch* b; approximately 27 August–10 September) assaults all around the perimeter, trying for a victory before the continuing build-up of U.N. forces made that impossible. In the west, they were held for limited gains and then thrown back; but in the north they appeared on the verge of victory until Walker committed the 24th Division (which had been relieved in the south by the 2d Division), and the ROK II Corps counterattacked.

Generally speaking, the NKA had displayed a questionable level of generalship from the time they had crossed the Han River. When one concentrated drive should have carried them to Pusan, their efforts had been piecemeal and generally poorly coordinated. Also, their communications were now under a concentrated attack by U.N. air power, which had increased rapidly in strength and effectiveness.

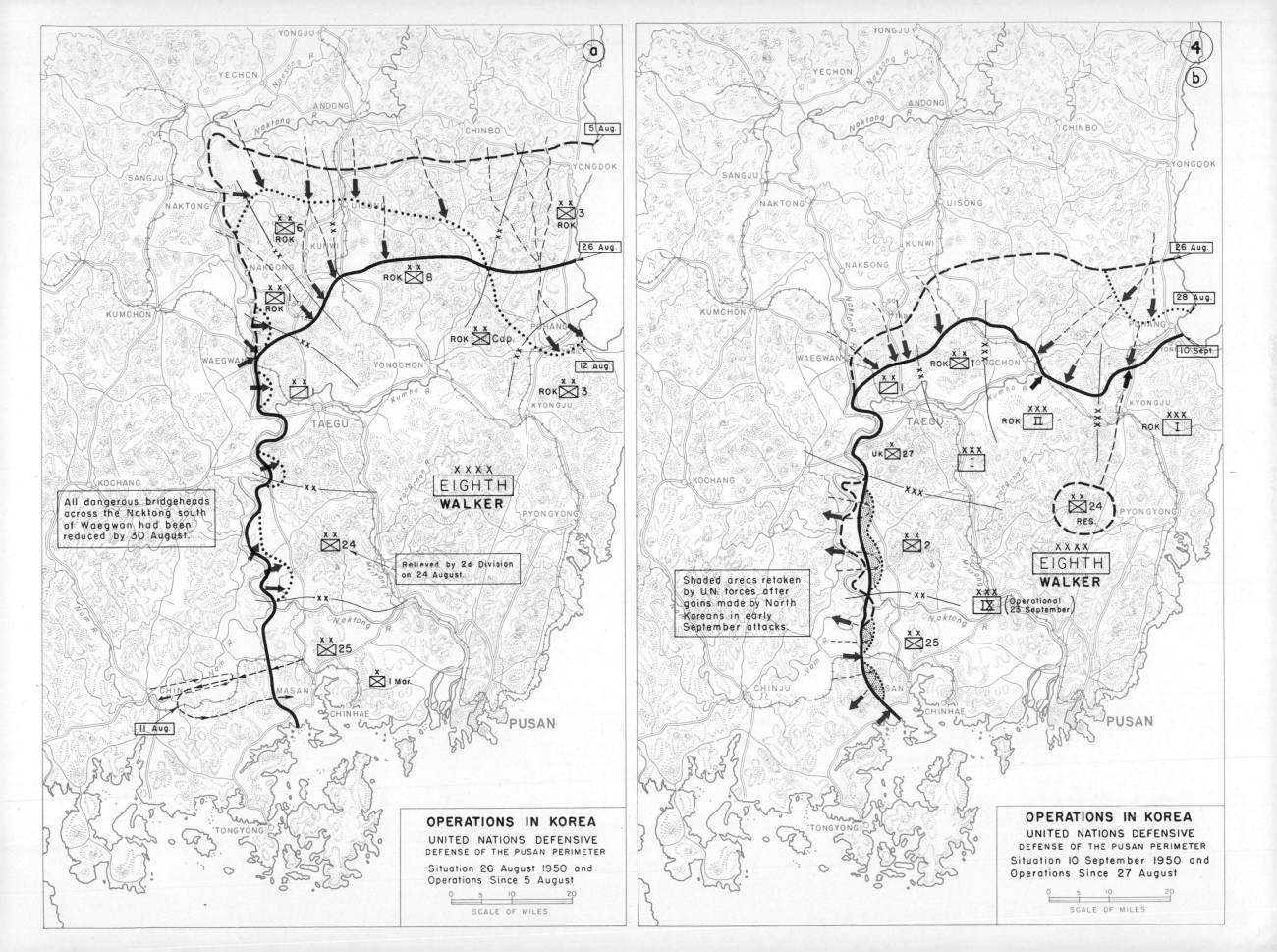

a

4

b

5 Aug.

26 Aug.

12 Aug.

XX 6 ROK

XX ROK 8

XX ROK

ROK XX Cap.

XX 3 ROK

XX 3 ROK

XXXX
EIGHTH
WALKER

XX I

All dangerous bridgeheads across the Naktong south of Waegwan had been reduced by 30 August.

XX 24

Relieved by 2d Division on 24 August.

XX 25

X I Mar.

11 Aug.

OPERATIONS IN KOREA

UNITED NATIONS DEFENSIVE
DEFENSE OF THE PUSAN PERIMETER

Situation 26 August 1950 and
Operations Since 5 August

0   5   10   20
SCALE OF MILES

26 Aug.

28 Aug.

10 Sept.

XX I

XX ROK Yongchon

ROK XXX II

XXX I

UK X 27

XXX I

XX 24 RES.

XXXX
EIGHTH
WALKER

XXX ROK I

Shaded areas retaken by U.N. forces after gains made by North Koreans in early September attacks.

XX 2

XXX IX (Operational 23 September)

XX 25

OPERATIONS IN KOREA

UNITED NATIONS DEFENSIVE
DEFENSE OF THE PUSAN PERIMETER

Situation 10 September 1950 and
Operations Since 27 August

0   5   10   20
SCALE OF MILES

Throughout the grim struggle to hold the perimeter west and north of Pusan, MacArthur had been gathering forces in Japan to mount his counteroffensive. Most of the NKA was now committed to the offensive against Pusan with only light forces covering its rear and flanks. Its principal supply lines from North Korea converged at Seoul, from which city they spread out again across South Korea. The NKA garrison in the Seoul area was weak, though reportedly busy constructing coastal defenses.

MacArthur therefore planned to seize the Seoul area by an amphibious operation against Inchon (*upper center*), Seoul's seaport. The Eighth Army would then break out of the Pusan perimeter, making its main effort to the northwest to link up with the Inchon landing force. Since it would be impossible to conceal preparations for the amphibious operation—there was a strong Communist Party in Japan, and a Russian mission with normal freedom of movement—preliminary aerial bombardments and raids were carried out against the west coast port of Kunsan (*lower center*), as if in preparation for a landing there. ROK marine units followed this with a feint at Kunsan and a landing at Mokpo (*bottom center*), plus additional feints near Pohang and Yongdok (*both right center*) on the east coast. U.N. naval units demonstrated off Samchok (*upper right*). U.N. air forces carried out a heavy interdiction campaign, beginning in North Korea in early August and thereafter spreading to South Korea. This hampered the NKA's attacks on the Pusan perimeter and so disrupted its communications as to limit severely its mobility and flexibility during the coming U.N. counteroffensive.

To carry out the Inchon operation, MacArthur activated the X Corps under Maj. Gen. Edward M. Almond, who had headed the joint staff which had planned that operation. This corps consisted of the 1st Marine Division (the 1st Marine Provisional Brigade, withdrawn from Korea, plus six marine battalions transferred from the Mediterranean and the United States) and the 7th Division (the last of the four occupational divisions in Japan,

its skeletonized ranks fleshed out with some 8,000 partially trained Korean replacements). By great exertions, the Navy assembled sufficient assault shipping to lift it.

Although the NKA was still stubbornly pressing its offensive against Pusan, it was becoming steadily weaker. Personnel casualties had been made at least partially good by the forcible conscription of available South Koreans, but these replacements were both unwilling and untrained. U.N. air interdiction had forced the NKA to operate its railroads only after dark and had destroyed a large part of its available motor vehicles, compelling it to place increasing reliance upon impressed civilian bearers. Supplies of food, clothing, and equipment were therefore low—though the NKA seldom ran short of ammunition or of fuel for its remaining tanks.

On 15 September, the X Corps made a successful amphibious assault landing at Inchon, and rapidly extended its beachhead (*see text, map 6*). Though the NKA was still attacking toward Taegu, the Eighth Army opened its offensive on the 16th (*this map*). NKA resistance was most determined and their defenses strong, but their position lacked depth, they had no general reserve to reinforce crumbling sectors of it, and they were hampered by poor signal communications. By 20 September, the U.N. forces were breaking through all along the front; except in the extreme south, NKA opposition collapsed. The American I Corps (1st Cavalry, 1st ROK, and 24th Divisions, plus the British 27th Brigade) broke out northwest of Taegu; on 26 September, elements of the 1st Cavalry Division thrust more than 100 miles ahead in eleven hours to link up with elements of the 7th Division near Osan.

All or part of eight NKA divisions were cut off by this advance, and most of the other divisions had to abandon the greater part of their tanks, heavy weapons, and supplies as they attempted to escape.

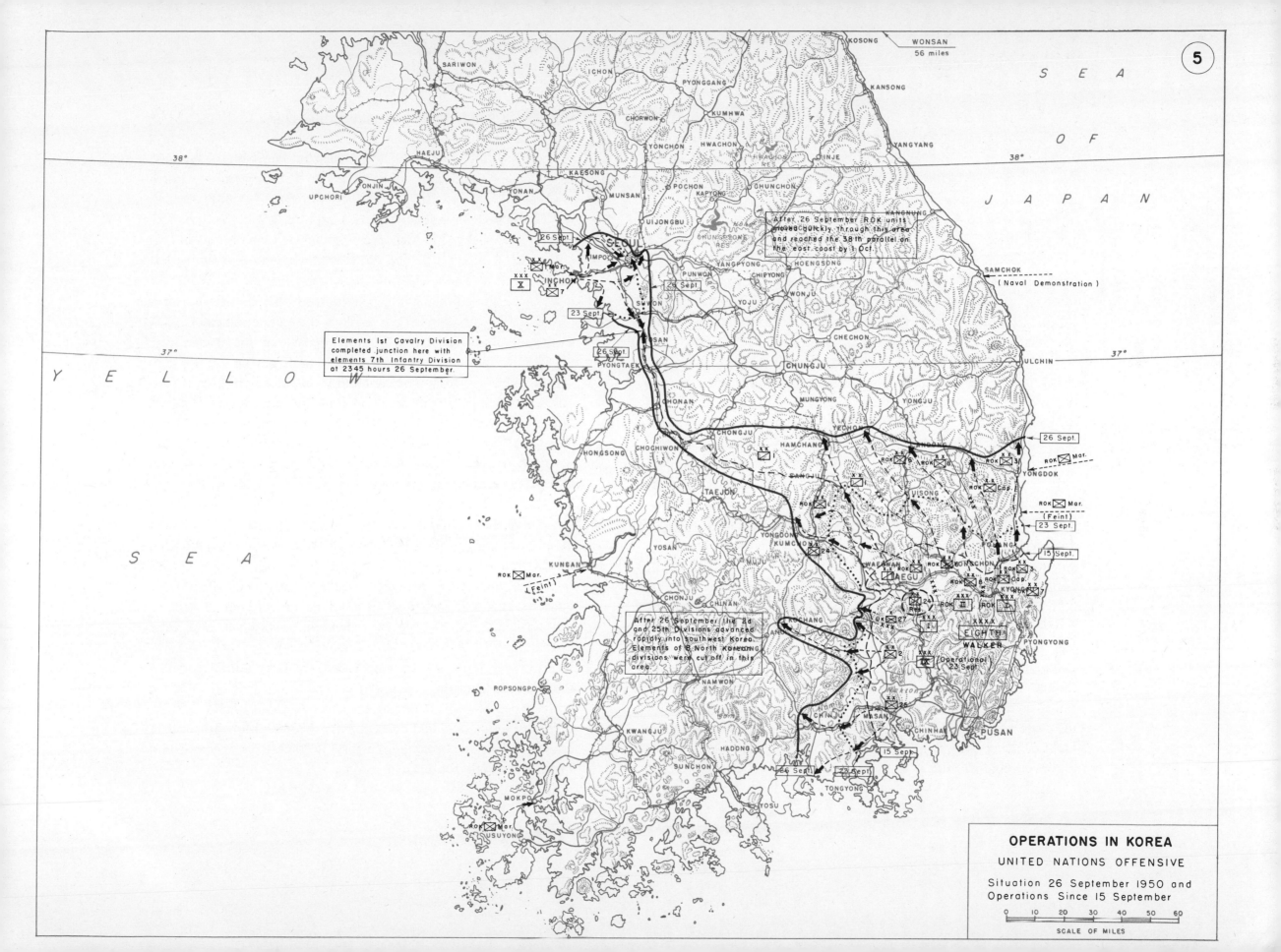

OPERATIONS IN KOREA

UNITED NATIONS OFFENSIVE

Situation 26 September 1950 and
Operations Since 15 September

MacArthur selected the Inchon-Seoul area as the objective of his amphibious counteroffensive primarily because its capture would enable him to cut the NKA's principal north-south supply lines. A secondary, yet important, consideration was Seoul's psychological importance as the traditional capital for all Korea.

As an objective, Inchon (*sketch* a) was a planner's nightmare. It was a relatively small port which had to be approached along a narrow channel through a maze of mud banks. As previously noted, it had extremely variable tides; the landing would have to be made at high tide, and there were only three days during the fall of 1950 when the tidal conditions would permit the proper beaching of assault shipping—15 September, 11 October, or 3 November. MacArthur insisted on the first date because he feared that further delay would enable the NKA to complete the coastal defenses they were constructing. The Joint Chiefs of Staff were dubious as to the practicality of this operation, but finally consented. Planning and preparations were completed in record time.

Two days before the landing, a naval task force (including two British cruisers) struck at the Inchon area with carrier aircraft, guns, and rockets. At dawn, 15 September, approximately one hour before high tide, a marine battalion stormed Wolmi Island (*left center*), an abrupt little peak, connected to the mainland by a causeway, which dominates Inchon harbor. That accomplished, on the next high tide (1730), the 1st Marine Division (reinforced by four battalions of ROK marines) seized Inchon against light resistance and pushed inland. The airfield at Kimpo (*upper left*) was taken on the 17th; by the 18th, the Far East Air Force's Combat Cargo Command had it in operation as a major airhead, the big transport planes flying out the seriously wounded on their return trips. Also on 18 September, the 7th Division landed and took over the south flank of the beachhead. The enveloping attacks of the two divisions rapidly closed in on Seoul, but the NKA had been able to shift at least a part of its 9th Division into that

city, which it thereupon sold stubbornly, house by house. MacArthur announced its capture on the 26th, but several more days of street fighting were necessary to clear it. The 7th and 1st Cavalry Divisions had meanwhile linked up (26 September) north of Osan (*lower center*).

To further strengthen the X Corps as rapidly as possible (*sketch* b), the 187th Airborne Regimental Combat Team was flown into Kimpo on 24 and 27 September. It took over the left flank of the X Corps, clearing the Kumpo Peninsula. While the marines expanded their bridgehead north of the Han River, most of the 7th Division fanned out to block the escape routes of NKA troops attempting to retreat from the debacle around Pusan.

Despite the large number of NKA units cut off by the converging advances from the Seoul and Pusan areas, the bag of prisoners was comparatively small. It must be remembered that the link-up of elements of the 1st Cavalry and 7th Divisions did not mean that the U.N. forces had been able to form a tight cordon across Korea from coast to coast. Aided by the broken terrain and the general confusion, thousands of enemy soldiers, singly or in small groups, infiltrated northward. Many of them changed into civilian clothing; elements of six NKA divisions drifted into the mountains, where they resorted to guerrilla warfare, confronting MacArthur with a new problem. (One valuable lesson, strongly reaffirmed during this period, is that personnel assigned to headquarters and rear logistical installations—regardless of arm or service—must be capable of defending themselves and their installations.)

However, if enemy personnel escaped in large numbers, below the 38th Parallel the NKA had ceased to exist as an effective army. Apparently its commanders had never considered the possibility of defeat and had consequently made no plans for a withdrawal. When one became necessary, it quickly degenerated into a rout and a flight for survival.

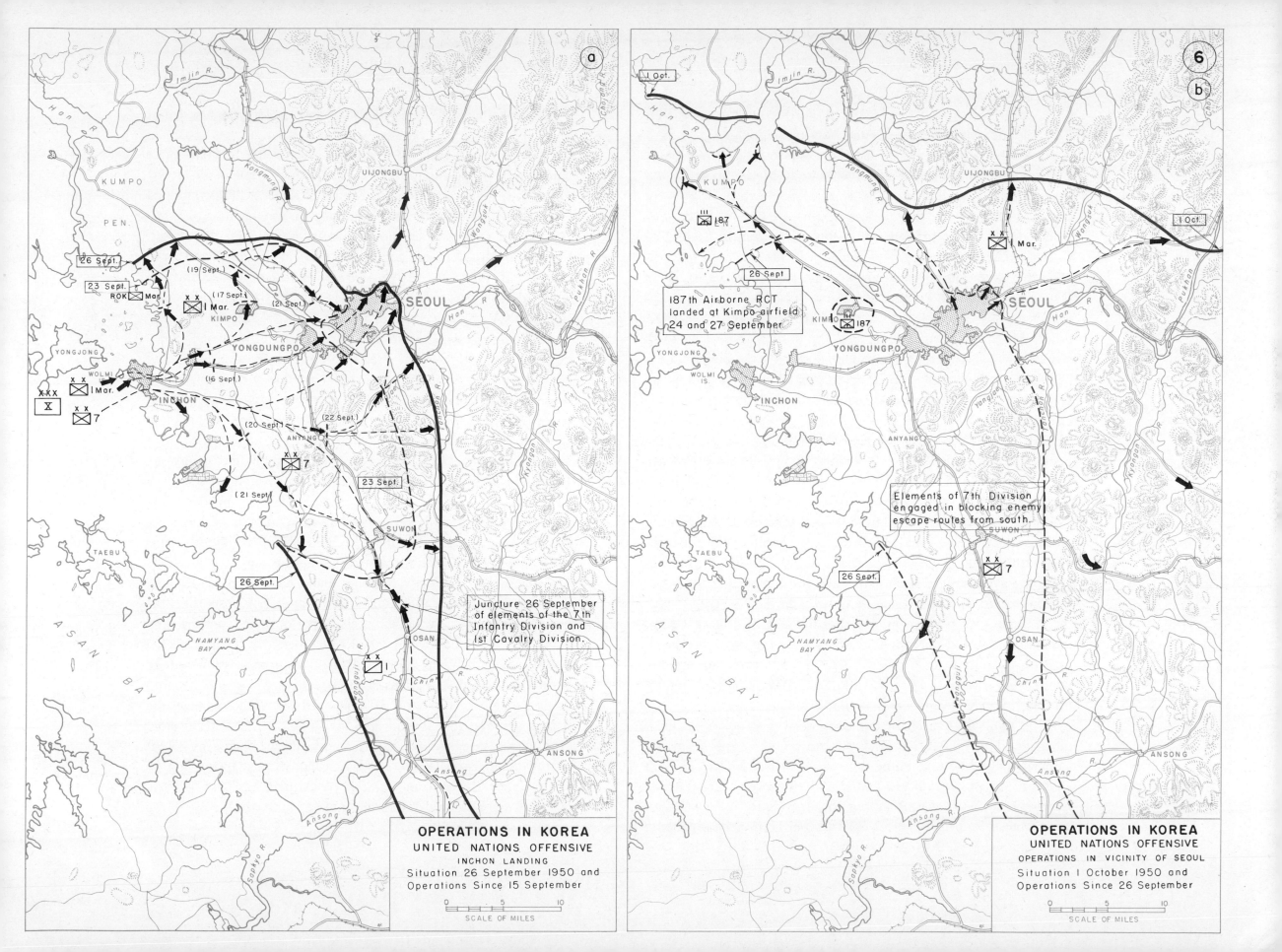

OPERATIONS IN KOREA
UNITED NATIONS OFFENSIVE
INCHON LANDING
Situation 26 September 1950 and
Operations Since 15 September

SCALE OF MILES
0   5   10

Junction 26 September
of elements of the 7th
Infantry Division and
1st Cavalry Division.

OPERATIONS IN KOREA
UNITED NATIONS OFFENSIVE
OPERATIONS IN VICINITY OF SEOUL
Situation 1 October 1950 and
Operations Since 26 September

SCALE OF MILES
0   5   10

187th Airborne RCT
landed at Kimpo airfield
24 and 27 September

Elements of 7th Division
engaged in blocking enemy
escape routes from south.

MacArthur now urged that he be authorized to cross the 38th Parallel and complete the destruction of the NKA. The JCS approved such action—provided there was no danger of major Chinese Communist or Russian intervention. MacArthur received the necessary Presidential authority on 29 September. There were certain storm signals: the Chinese Communists warned that they would not "tolerate foreign aggression"; India opposed any "invasion" of North Korea; Rhee announced his intention to complete the liberation of his country. (On 1 October, the ROK 3d Division crossed the Parallel on the east coast.) The U.N. General Assembly approved an advance into North Korea on 6 October. MacArthur twice demanded the surrender of the North Korean armed forces (1 November and 9 November), but received no official reply. On the 9th, the U.N. forces—now increased by a battalion each of Australian and Philippine troops—crossed the Parallel.

MacArthur's plan was to send the Eighth Army north from Seoul along the axis Kaesong-Sariwon-Pyongyang (*all lower center*). The X Corps was to carry out an independent amphibious assault against Wonsan, and then move westward on Pyongyang. This decision, which resulted in the establishment of two separate field commands in Korea—both of them equally subordinate to MacArthur—has caused considerable discussion. MacArthur appears to have reasoned that Inchon and the damaged Pusan-Seoul railroad could not support an offensive by the Eighth Army—plus the X Corps—in western Korea; that the lack of east-west communications would make it too difficult for Eighth Army headquarters to control the X Corps' operations on the east coast; and, finally, that it would be best for him to keep the control of operations in Korea firmly in his own hands.

The immediate result of this decision was to delay the U.N. offensive. The 1st Marine Division and the X Corps troops reembarked at Inchon, jamming that port for several days. The 7th Division moved overland to Pusan and embarked there. During this period, Eighth Army supply was frequently on a hand-to-mouth basis, and its logistical reserves were seriously depleted.

Meanwhile, all ROK divisions (except the 1st, which was part of the U.N. I Corps) had crossed the frontier. It was a driving pursuit. The 3d Division, averaging fifteen miles a day against considerable opposition, took Wonsan (*lower center*) on 11 October, with some help from the Capital Division, which continued north to seize Hungnam and Hamhung on the 17th.

The I Corps attacked northward from Seoul on 9 October, the 1st Cavalry Division leading. (Logistical shortages and guerrilla activity by bypassed NKA troops had made it necessary to leave the IX Corps [2d and 25th Divisions] deep in South Korea.) Initial NKA resistance was determined, but frequently inexpert; by 14 October, the I Corps was through most of the enemy's fortified positions on its front. NKA troops became confused, and there were several instances of mass surrenders. Pyongyang fell on 19-20 October, pinched out between the 1st Cavalry and 1st ROK Divisions. On 20 October, the 187th Airborne Regimental Combat Team jumped at Sukchon and Sunchon (*center, blue ovals*), hoping to block NKA forces retreating from Pyongyang. (This was the first time heavy equipment was dropped in combat.) The jump, however, was too late and too close in, hence no appreciable number of NKA personnel were trapped. Enemy opposition continued to dwindle. On 26 October, leading elements of the ROK 6th Division reached the Yalu River.

Meanwhile, X Corps elements finally had been loaded and supplied at Inchon and Pusan by 16 October. Considering the means available, this was an impressive performance, but the campaign had not waited on it. On 19 October, the 1st Marine Division arrived off Wonsan to find ROK units in possession and the harbor full of Russian mines of the latest type, laid under the direction of Russian experts. It took until the 25th to sweep the harbor clear so that the marines could land. The 7th Division, after waiting for ten days aboard ship in Pusan harbor, was sent northward to Iwon (*center, right*), where it finished landing on 9 November. Recognizing that this check made his plan to move the X Corps westward impracticable, MacArthur shifted the corps' axis of advance northward.

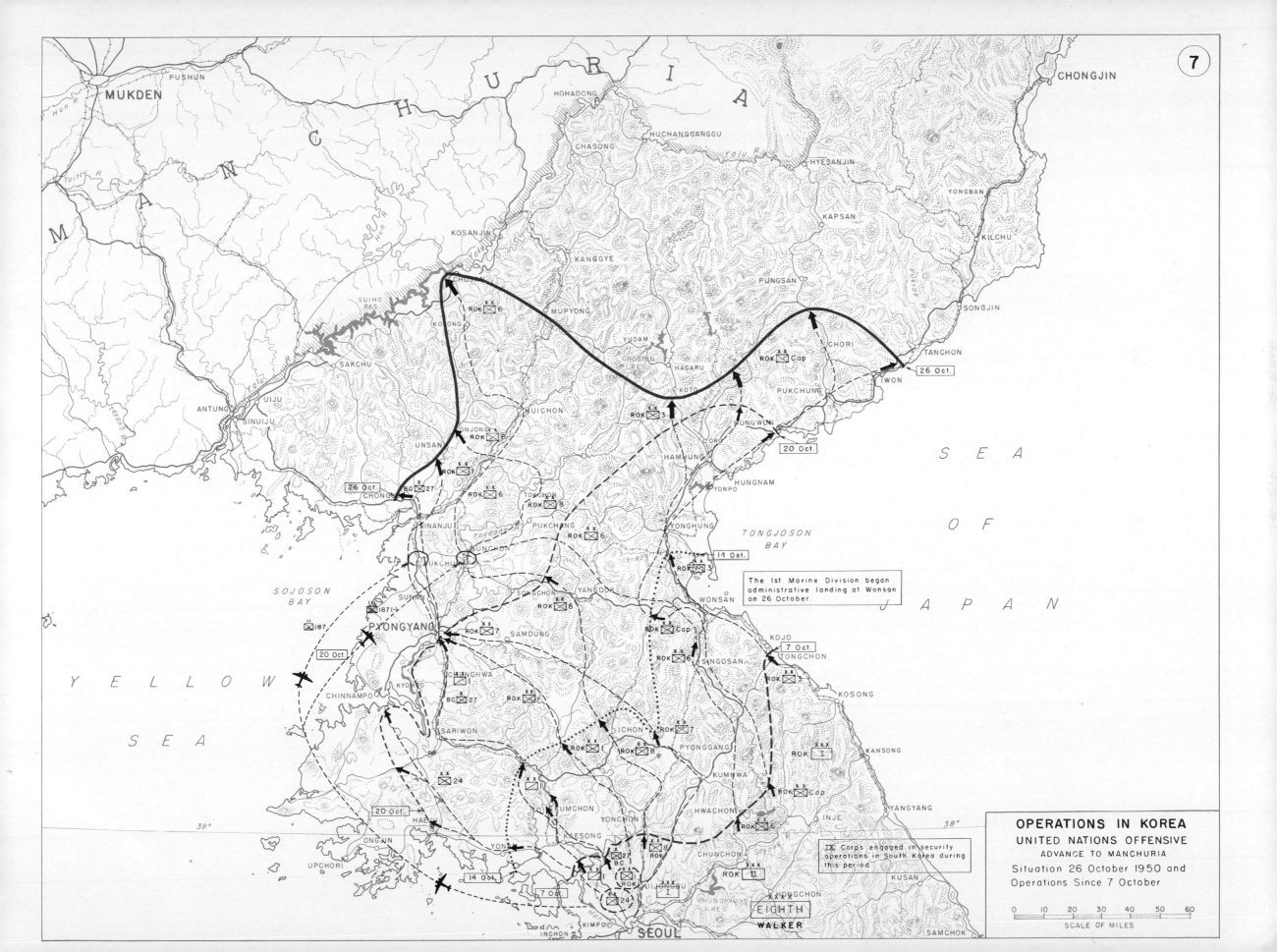

OPERATIONS IN KOREA
UNITED NATIONS OFFENSIVE
ADVANCE TO MANCHURIA
Situation 26 October 1950 and
Operations Since 7 October

The 1st Marine Division began administrative landing at Wonsan on 26 October.

IX Corps engaged in security operations in South Korea during this period.

SCALE OF MILES
0   10   20   30   40   50   60

The logistical situation of the pursuing U.N. forces was steadily worsening. Railroad reconstruction had failed to keep pace with their advance; unit motor transport was wearing out on the rudimentary Korean roads. The only alleviating factor was the imaginative and aggressive employment of air transport.

More U.N. contingents were arriving: the British 29th Brigade, a Turkish brigade, and Canadian, Thailand, and Netherlands battalions. Many thought them too late. From MacArthur downward, the U.N. forces were brashly optimistic. Requisitions for replacements and ammunition were cut back. MacArthur first modified and then canceled earlier orders (based on a 27 September JCS directive) prohibiting the advance of U.N. ground forces—other than ROK units—north of the line Chongju (*center, left*)–Hamhung. All U.N. forces now would close to the Yalu.

Then, during 25-30 October, elements of the 6th and 8th ROK Divisions, advancing out of supporting distance through broken country, fell into a series of CCF traps in the general area Onjong (*center*)–Kojong (*upper center*). Following up these successes, the CCF drove the ROK II Corps south of the Chongchon River in disorder. Simultaneously, the ROK 1st Division had come into contact with CCF units around Unsan (*center*), taking several prisoners. These prisoners talked freely, stating that large CCF forces had entered Korea. Though their nationality was definitely established, American intelligence was reluctant to accept their statements as reliable indications of a Chinese Communist decision to intervene in the almost-finished Korean campaign. Walker ordered the 1st Cavalry Division to pass through the 1st ROK Division and drive to the Yalu. Farther west, the British Commonwealth Brigade (the 27th Brigade, reinforced by the Australian Battalion) and the 24th Division won several engagements, driving to within eighteen miles of Sinuiju (*left center*) before—much to their surprise—they were recalled. A heavy CCF night attack (1 November) had shattered the 8th Cavalry Regiment near Unsan. The I Corps went on the defensive, re-

taining only a bridgehead over the lower Chongchon River; the CCF attacked this position on 5-6 November, was repulsed, and withdrew northward. Russian-built jet aircraft began appearing over North Korea.

Meanwhile, Almond had assumed command (20 October) of all troops in the X Corps' assigned area. On 25 October, his ROK 3d Division encountered CCF units south of the Choshin Reservoir (*upper center*). The marines then relieved the ROK division; in subsequent engagements they practically destroyed the CCF 124th Division. Despite snow and sub-zero cold, ROK troops— effectively supported by naval gunfire and marine aircraft— fought their way up the east coast. The 7th Division drove to the Yalu at Hyesanjin (*upper right*) on 21 November.

MacArthur now faced a major decision. The X Corps—its units scattered widely across mountainous terrain at the end of tenuous supply routes—was far in advance of the Eighth Army, and there was no actual contact between those two commands. Guerrilla warfare still raged behind them. The NKA was almost destroyed; the CCF had struck and then retired, but massive CCF armies were known to be concentrating north of the Yalu. If the CCF intended to intervene aggressively, the overextended U.N. forces were in grave danger: to advance would be to risk an overwhelming counterattack; to halt and prepare to defend would allow the enemy to attack at the time and place of his own choosing.

Characteristically, MacArthur chose to renew his offensive, with the double objective of clarifying the situation and destroying all CCF—as well as NKA—units remaining in Korea. The Eighth Army brought its IX Corps forward into line and, after a week's delay because of logistical difficulties, resumed its advance on 24 November. Opposition was slight that day and the next. MacArthur now planned to shift the X Corps' axis of advance farther westward, so that its attack would converge with that of the Eighth Army.

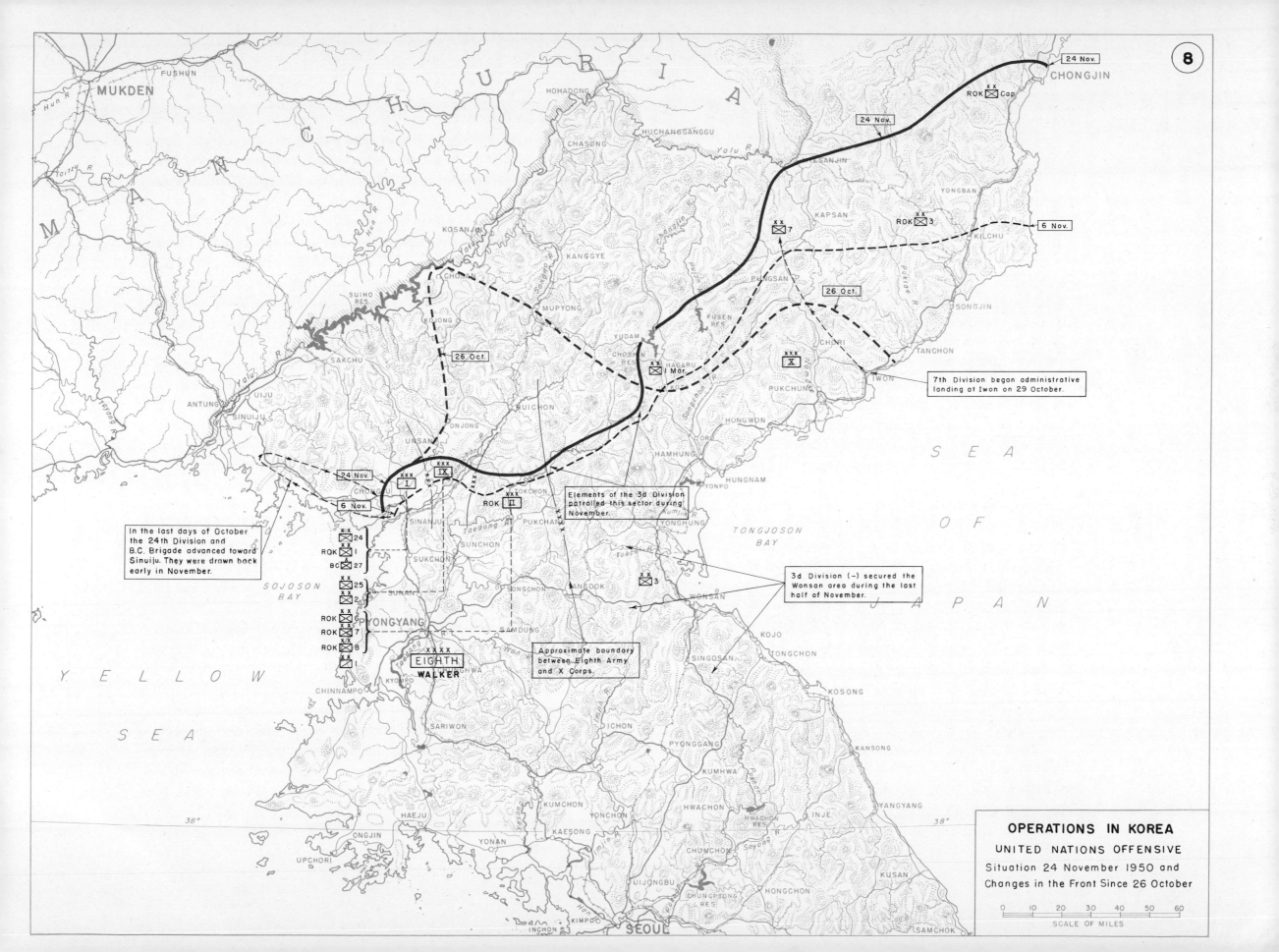

8

In the last days of October the 24th Division and B.C. Brigade advanced toward Sinuiju. They were drawn back early in November.

7th Division began administrative landing at Iwon on 29 October.

Elements of the 3d Division patrolled this sector during November.

3d Division (–) secured the Wonsan area during the last half of November.

Approximate boundary between Eighth Army and X Corps.

OPERATIONS IN KOREA

UNITED NATIONS OFFENSIVE

Situation 24 November 1950 and Changes in the Front Since 26 October

SCALE OF MILES
0   10   20   30   40   50   60

Many aspects of the Chinese Communist intervention in Korea are obscure; the following summation is the best that can be assembled from available sources.

Communist China, with Russian approval, apparently had decided by early October to intervene if U.N. troops, other than ROK units, crossed the 38th Parallel. Shortly after American troops did so (9 October), the CCF Fourth Field Army—Communist China's finest—began entering Korea. On 15 October, MacArthur assured President Truman that Communist China would not intervene; that—if it did—not more than 60,000 CCF troops could get across the Yalu; and that his air force would rapidly destroy them. Actually, by that date, approximately 150,000 of the CCF had crossed or were crossing. By early November, the CCF in Korea numbered some 300,000; 180,000 of these faced the Eighth Army, the remainder confronted the X Corps. They moved mostly by night, and their camouflage discipline was perfect. Friendly Koreans reported their presence, but neither U.N. aerial reconnaissance nor aerial photography could locate them, though some large truck convoys were reported.

The American intelligence failure was general and complete. The United States Central Intelligence Agency had been unable to reach any conclusion as to the probability of Chinese Communist intervention. Lacking such guidance, MacArthur had to depend upon his own intelligence agencies; these naturally operated less efficiently in northern Korea than they had previously. But—in addition—there seems to have been a definite unwillingness to admit that Communist China would dare to intervene. Even after strong CCF units had been encountered, explanations were advanced that these were merely "token" forces with the "defensive" mission of protecting hydroelectric installations along the Yalu.

The CCF plan appears to have been to envelop the inland flanks of both the Eighth Army and the X Corps and pocket their remnants against the coasts for subsequent annihilation, while the main CCF thrust continued southward to sweep the entire peninsula. After nightfall on 25 November, a heavy CCF assault struck the ROK II Corps (the 6th, 7th, and 8th ROK Divisions), sent it streaming southward, and swung in behind the I Corps' right flank. Walker immediately committed his reserve, which slowed this enveloping attack, while the I Corps—simultaneously under powerful attacks all along its front—fought its way back across the Chongchon River. In covering this withdrawal, the 2d Division was badly mauled, losing much of its artillery. The line Pyongyang-Wonsan offered a good defensive position, but a CCF column took Songchon (center) while most of the Eighth Army was still north of Pyongyang. However—thanks to its greater road mobility—the Eighth Army was able to break contact in early December and retire to a position along the 38th Parallel. Logistical difficulties helped to slow the CCF pursuit.

On the east coast, the X Corps shifted westward. Maj. Gen. Oliver Smith—much to Almond's dissatisfaction—had deliberately slowed the advance of his 1st Marine Division to keep it concentrated and improve its communications. On 25 November, Almond ordered the marines to seize Mupyong (upper center) and advance to the Yalu; the 7th Division would advance on their right. On the 27th, the two leading marine regiments advanced through Yudam (upper center); that night, three CCF divisions surrounded them. On the east bank of the Choshin Reservoir, elements of the 7th Division were overrun, and Hagaru was surrounded. Other CCF columns filtered through the mountains toward lightly garrisoned Wonsan.

Seeing that the X Corps was in danger of piecemeal destruction, MacArthur ordered its evacuation. The marines—"attacking in another direction"—doggedly fought their way out of the mountains toward Hungnam, while a relief column battered a path inland to meet them. Aerial support and supply were magnificent; even bridging equipment was air-dropped to replace destroyed spans. Unlike the Eighth Army, the X Corps lost comparatively little heavy equipment. It had been a major defeat, but something of a moral victory. CCF casualties had been staggering.

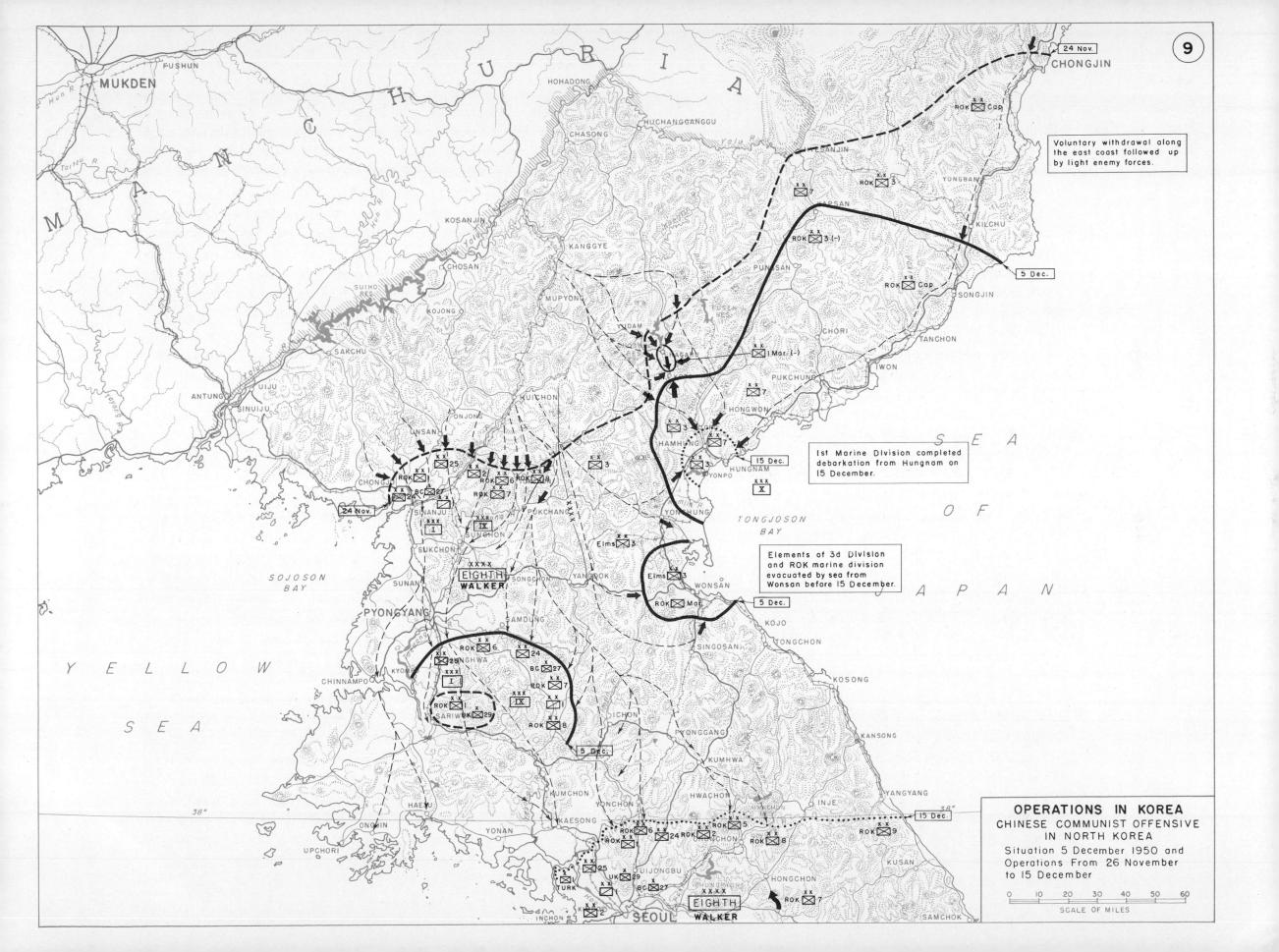

9

Voluntary withdrawal along the east coast followed up by light enemy forces.

1st Marine Division completed debarkation from Hungnam on 15 December.

Elements of 3d Division and ROK marine division evacuated by sea from Wonsan before 15 December.

OPERATIONS IN KOREA
CHINESE COMMUNIST OFFENSIVE IN NORTH KOREA

Situation 5 December 1950 and Operations From 26 November to 15 December

SCALE OF MILES
0   10   20   30   40   50   60

The embarkation of the X Corps at Hungnam (*see map 9*) was a deliberate operation, expertly covered by air and naval forces. All possible supplies and more than 98,000 Korean refugees were evacuated; the harbor installations were wrecked. The process was completed on 24 December; on 27 December, the X Corps finished debarking at Pusan and passed to the control of the Eighth Army (*this map*). On 23 December, Walker had been killed in an automobile accident; his successor was Lt. Gen. Matthew B. Ridgway.

In retrospect, the defeat of the U.N. forces in northern Korea contains several interesting lessons. The U.N. forces—initially, at least—were not greatly outnumbered; they possessed several times the fire power of their opponents and had outstanding superiority in armor and artillery. They were (with the relative exception of ROK units) fully motorized and suffered no major logistical shortages. Finally, they had complete air and naval superiority. Yet they suffered one of the most definite defeats ever inflicted on American forces by a foreign army.

The CCF were largely veterans of years of semi-guerrilla fighting, accustomed to hardship and hunger. After their initial clashes with the Eighth Army in October, they had concluded that—though American fire power was to be feared for its volume, range, and coordination—American troops were highly vulnerable to attacks from the rear and could be demoralized by cutting their communications. Further, they claimed that the Americans had no appetite for night or close-range fighting, and that American infantry were overly dependent on tank, artillery, and air support.

Consequently, the CCF operated basically as light infantry, maneuvering by preference through difficult terrain to establish road blocks in rear of U.N. forces before attacking them from the front or flank. Stories of CCF "human sea" attacks were largely the products of rear-echelon imaginations. Normally, the CCF attacked on a platoon or company front, reinforcing any prospect of success with great determination in an effort to split up the U.N. force under attack and then destroy it in detail. Experts at camouflage, scouting, and cross-country movement, they made habitual use of surprise and night attacks. Such tactics had great psy-chological effect. The road-bound U.N. forces, a modern army in a primitive mountain wilderness, sometimes found themselves as handicapped as Braddock at the Monongahela.

On 30 December, MacArthur warned the JCS that the CCF could, if it wished to make the effort, drive the U.N. forces out of Korea. The JCS replied with an order to defend his position; to retire, if necessary, step by step to the former Pusan perimeter— or even to Japan. He was to keep his units intact and to inflict the greatest possible losses on the enemy. MacArthur passed on these orders to Ridgway, to whom he delegated complete authority to plan and conduct operations in Korea. Ridgway had approximately 365,000 men—including contingents from South Korea, the United States, Great Britain, Australia, Canada, New Zealand, South Africa, France, Greece, the Netherlands, the Philippines, Thailand, Belgium, Turkey, and Luxembourg, as well as medical units from Sweden and India. Later, Ethiopian and Colombian units arrived.

At daybreak on 1 January, 1951, after a night-long mortar and artillery preparation, approximately 500,000 enemy troops (including some rehabilitated NKA units) attacked all along the front, making their main effort against the I and IX Corps on the U.N. left flank and center. The attack achieved no surprise, but developed considerable weight, and the Eighth Army—still discouraged by its recent defeat—appeared unable to halt it. Ridgway therefore traded space for enemy casualties, relying upon the enemy's weak logistical support to eventually slow his advance. Seoul and Inchon were evacuated on 4 January. The retreat was hampered and confused by hordes of refugees, who jammed roads and rail centers, and by increasing guerrilla activity behind the U.N. lines. The CCF did not pursue far below Seoul, but farther east a major CCF-NKA attack drove the 2d Division out of the important road center of Wonju (*upper right*) and penetrated the U.N. position. Ridgway countered this by reinforcing the right flank of the X Corps and bringing the 1st Marine Division forward from its reserve position. Lack of supplies, air interdiction, and heavy casualties finally dragged the enemy advance to a halt along the general line shown (*solid blue line*).

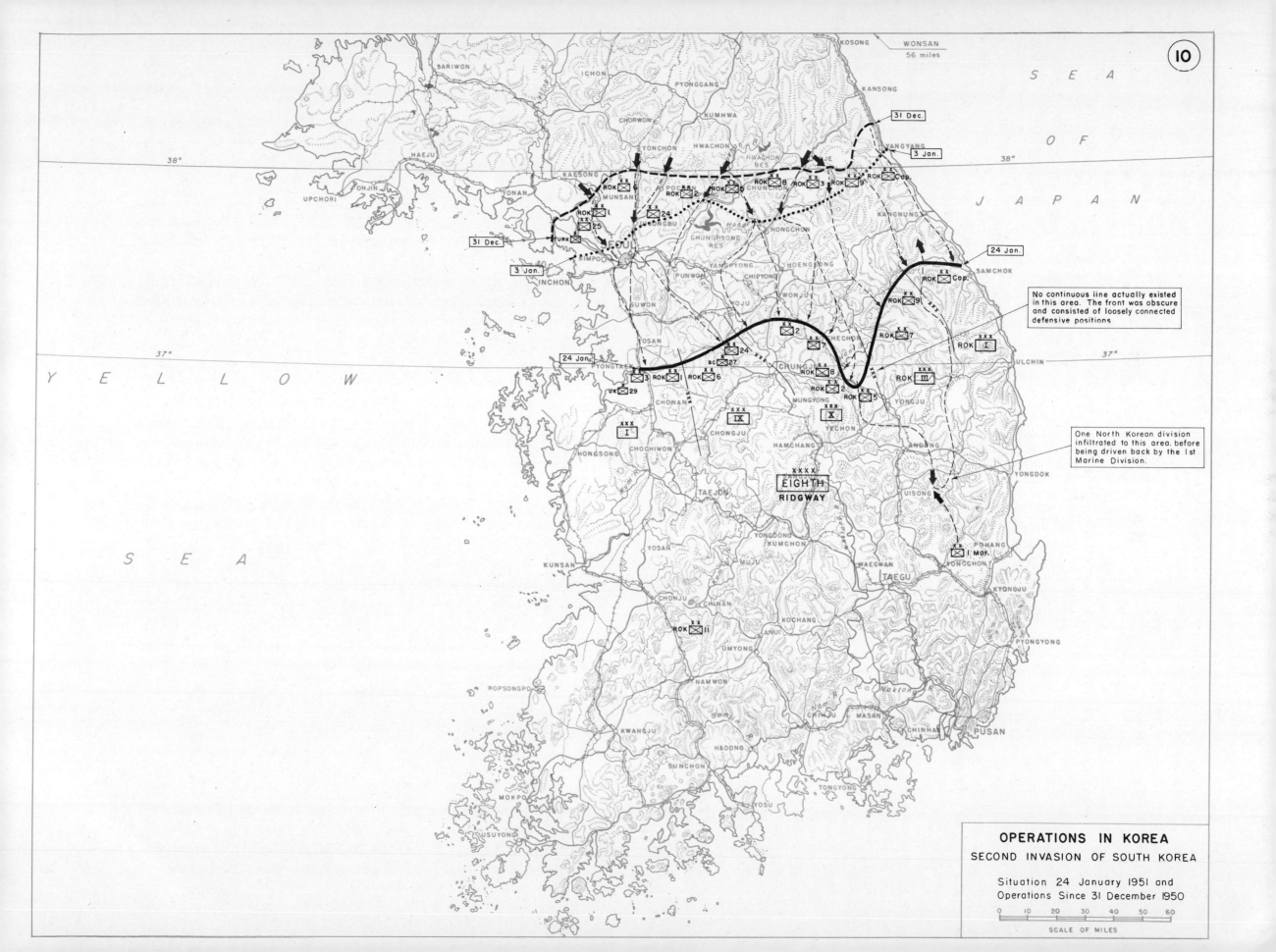

OPERATIONS IN KOREA

SECOND INVASION OF SOUTH KOREA

Situation 24 January 1951 and
Operations Since 31 December 1950

No continuous line actually existed
in this area. The front was obscure
and consisted of loosely connected
defensive positions

One North Korean division
infiltrated to this area, before
being driven back by the 1st
Marine Division.

SCALE OF MILES
0 10 20 30 40 50 60

By late January, it was obvious that the enemy had pulled the bulk of his forces northward for rehabilitation, leaving only light screening forces in contact with the U.N. line. In fact, on 15 January, a reconnaissance in force by the reinforced 27th Infantry Regiment (I Corps) advanced almost to Suwon before finding enemy positions.

Accordingly, Ridgway initiated a war of maneuver, featuring carefully coordinated, limited-objective attacks, which would exploit the U.N. forces' superiority in air power, armor, and artillery. Air and naval action was to be carefully integrated with that of the ground forces. These operations had the primary objectives of killing CCF-NKA troops, and thereby of keeping the enemy forces so off balance that they could not launch another major offensive. Success in these operations would accomplish another Ridgway objective—to restore the morale and initiative of his men, which in many cases were at extremely low ebb. This was especially true of the ROK units, since the Koreans suffered under the psychological handicap of their traditional vassalage to China.

On 25 January, the I and IX Corps began a methodical advance northward, sweeping their entire fronts clean of enemy units as they moved forward. There was little resistance until about 30 January; then the enemy began fighting obstinate delaying actions below Seoul, only to withdraw suddenly on 9 February. Battered Inchon and the Kimpo airfield were recovered on the 10th. On 5 February, the X and ROK III Corps had begun a similar offensive, after a series of preliminary operations in which they had captured Hoengsong (*upper center*). This advance met more resistance; air reconnaissance reported enemy forces concentrating north of Hoengsong. On the night of 11 February, a powerful CCF-NKA force counterattacked, utilizing the usual enveloping tactics. The 3d, 5th, and 8th ROK Divisions were overwhelmed and driven south through Hoengsong; the enemy followed up with a drive toward Wonju. At the road junction of Chipyong, their advance (estimated at three CCF divisions) struck the 23d Infantry Regiment (2d Division) and the French Battalion and was beaten off in three days of hard fighting. Farther east, NKA forces bypassed Wonju and threatened Chechon, but were eventually contained by assembling all immediately available reserves. Meanwhile, the enemy suddenly attacked out of a bridgehead he still held on the south bank of the Han River near Seoul—probably to divert U.N. reserves from the central front. The effort was an expensive failure.

The enemy tried to strengthen his forces on the still fluid central front, but was crippled by a shortage of supplies and the constant pounding of the U.N. air forces. By 18 February, he again began to slip away northward; on 21 February, the U.N. forces resumed their advance in the central sector, slowed more by the spring thaws than by enemy action. On 7 March, Ridgway again attacked on the west coast, bypassing Seoul to the east with the IX and X Corps. The I Corps' patrols found Seoul abandoned on the night of 14 March.

Enemy resistance to the IX and X Corps, at first stubborn, dwindled away. Bad weather and the lack of roads delayed the U.N. forces more than their lightly equipped enemies. An airborne drop at Munsan (*upper center*) trapped only a few enemy troops. Antiguerrilla operations behind the U.N. lines were beginning to take effect, and U.N. naval bombardments and amphibious raids harried both coasts of northern Korea.

At the same time, there were indications that the enemy was massing farther north for a spring offensive. To keep him off balance as long as possible and to secure a strong defensive line from which future limited attacks could be launched, Ridgway decided to cross the 38th Parallel. By 19 April, a satisfactory line had been occupied (*solid red line*). On the 21st, the I and X Corps moved forward toward Chorwon (*top center*) in an effort to dominate the so-called "Iron Triangle"—an open plateau area, containing a number of important road junctions which made it valuable to the enemy as an assembly area and advanced logistical base.

MacArthur, meanwhile, clashed with President Truman over the extension of the war beyond the borders of Korea. To MacArthur, seeking a decisive military victory, the complex of Chinese Communist bases—which, from their Manchurian "sanctuary" just north of the Yalu, supported enemy operations in Korea— were legitimate targets. Truman, fearful of initiating a general war, was determined to limit the conflict to Korea. On 11 April, Truman relieved MacArthur, replacing him with Ridgway.

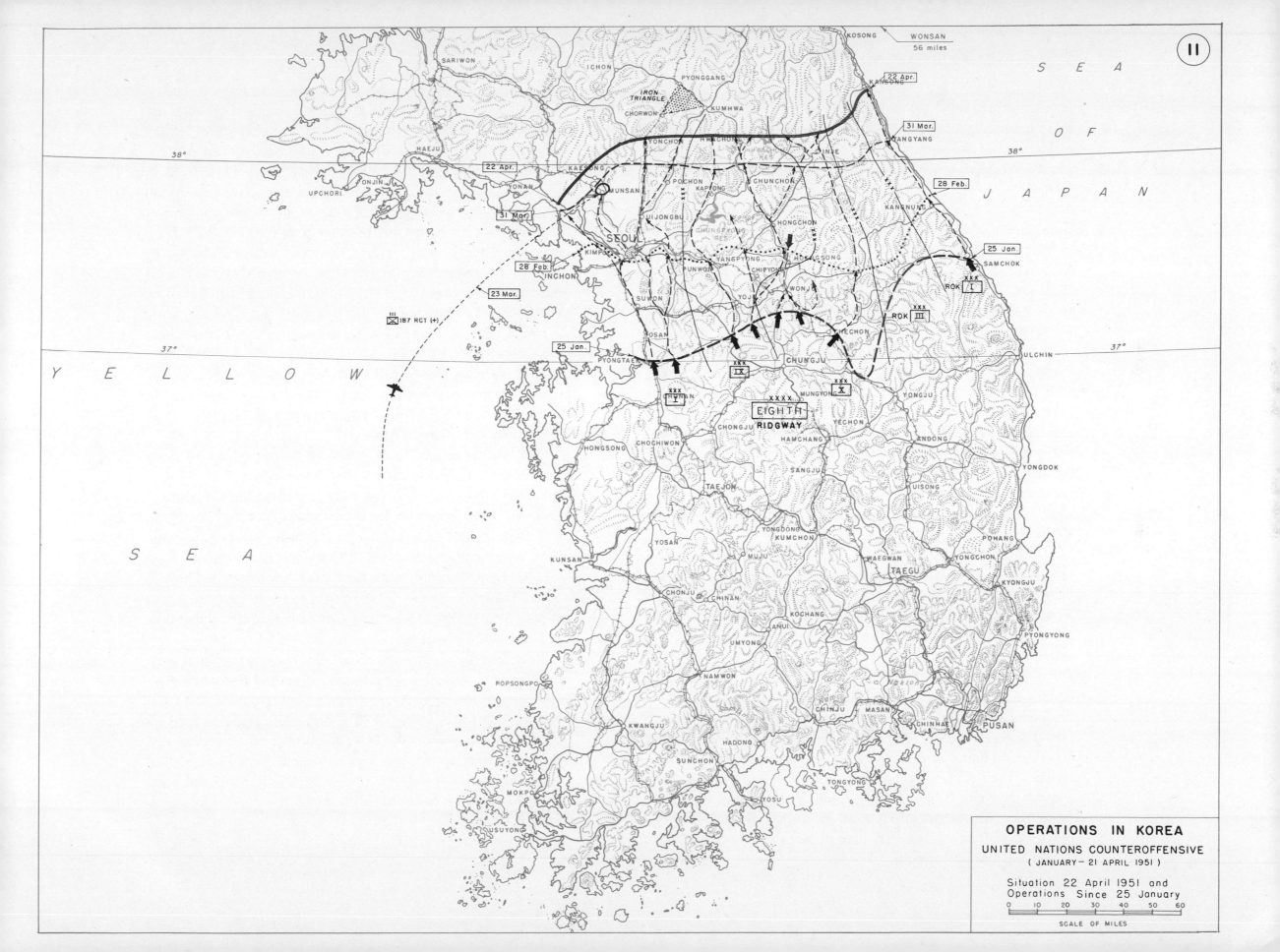

OPERATIONS IN KOREA

UNITED NATIONS COUNTEROFFENSIVE
(JANUARY – 21 APRIL 1951)

Situation 22 April 1951 and
Operations Since 25 January

0 10 20 30 40 50 60

SCALE OF MILES

By early April, aerial reconnaissance had revealed that the enemy was no longer constructing additional defensive positions farther to his rear. At the same time, there were reliable indications that large, fresh CCF-NKA forces had been brought up to the front. Considerable enemy armor had been sighted, and—as a new and acute threat to the U.N. forces—the enemy was making great efforts to construct airfields throughout northern Korea. Enemy propaganda had become increasingly blood-curdling, foretelling an offensive that would either destroy the U.N. forces or drive them out of Korea. Finally, it was obvious that the CCF-NKA forces could not afford to give up the Iron Triangle (*see map 11, top center*).

Lt. Gen. James A. Van Fleet (Ridgway's successor in command of the Eighth Army) had continued his advance on 21 April with full knowledge of these enemy preparations, having previously organized a defensive position along the commanding terrain his troops had occupied on the 19th. If attacked, he was prepared—should it become necessary—to fall back gradually, employing his superior fire power to inflict maximum casualties on the enemy. Once their offensive had been halted, he would counterattack. Meanwhile, U.N. aircraft smothered the new airfields.

During the late afternoon of 22 April, CCF artillery and mortars began a heavy bombardment. Four hours later, aided by the light of a full moon, enemy infantry swarmed to the attack from Yonchon (*this map; center, left*) eastward to the Hwachon Reservoir area. This was actually a diversionary attack; by daybreak, action was general across the whole front, with the enemy making his main effort against the I Corps north of Seoul. Another secondary attack had developed above Inje (*center, right*).

There was no surprise; nor were there innovations in enemy tactics—merely the old routine of freely expended manpower and expert small-unit tactics. Few enemy tanks appeared. Small detachments of CCF infantry attempted to infiltrate the U.N. lines and cut the roads behind them. Assaults were pressed vigorously through the nights, but at daybreak the enemy normally tried to break off contact and conceal himself from the scourging U.N. artillery and tactical aircraft.

During the first hours, the U.N. lines shrugged off these assaults. But the ROK 6th Division (*center*) soon cracked, leaving a major gap through which the CCF troops rushed in an effort to envelop the 1st Marine and 24th Divisions. These divisions cooly refused their exposed flanks and held their ground; British and American troops halted the CCF (*action not shown*) just below the 38th Parallel. Seeing his position compromised, Van Fleet pulled back the I and IX Corps, covering their withdrawal by intensive air and artillery action. The I Corps' left flank came under increasing pressure; on 23 April, a sudden withdrawal by the ROK 1st Division left the 1st Battalion, the Gloucestershire Regiment (British 29th Brigade), isolated on a hill near Choksong (*left center*). Efforts to relieve it were unsuccessful. After a heroic defense, its able-bodied survivors attacked *northward*; approximately forty of them escaped in the ensuing confusion. In eastern Korea, an NKA attack had taken Inje and had then been fought to a standstill by 29 April.

Enemy successes, however, had been dearly bought. By early May, the U.N. forces had contained the enemy drive, reestablished their line (*solid blue line*), and were launching limited counterattacks all along their front. On the extreme left of the U.N. front, the Kumpo Peninsula was cleared; on the extreme right, with strong naval support, the ROK I Corps advanced toward Kansong. Along much of the front, the CCF-NKA forces had broken contact and retired out of U.N. artillery range to reorganize and resupply their troops, leaving only light screening detachments in front of the U.N. positions.

Since the enemy's main effort had been made in the Seoul area, Van Fleet had shifted most of his American and European units to the western end of his line. Now, rapidly regrouping, the CCF shifted strong forces eastward. The movement was observed by U.N. air reconnaissance, and U.N. intelligence officers concluded that a new enemy offensive was imminent. Van Fleet alerted the 3d Division (*not shown*), then in reserve in the Seoul area, to be ready to move eastward on his order.

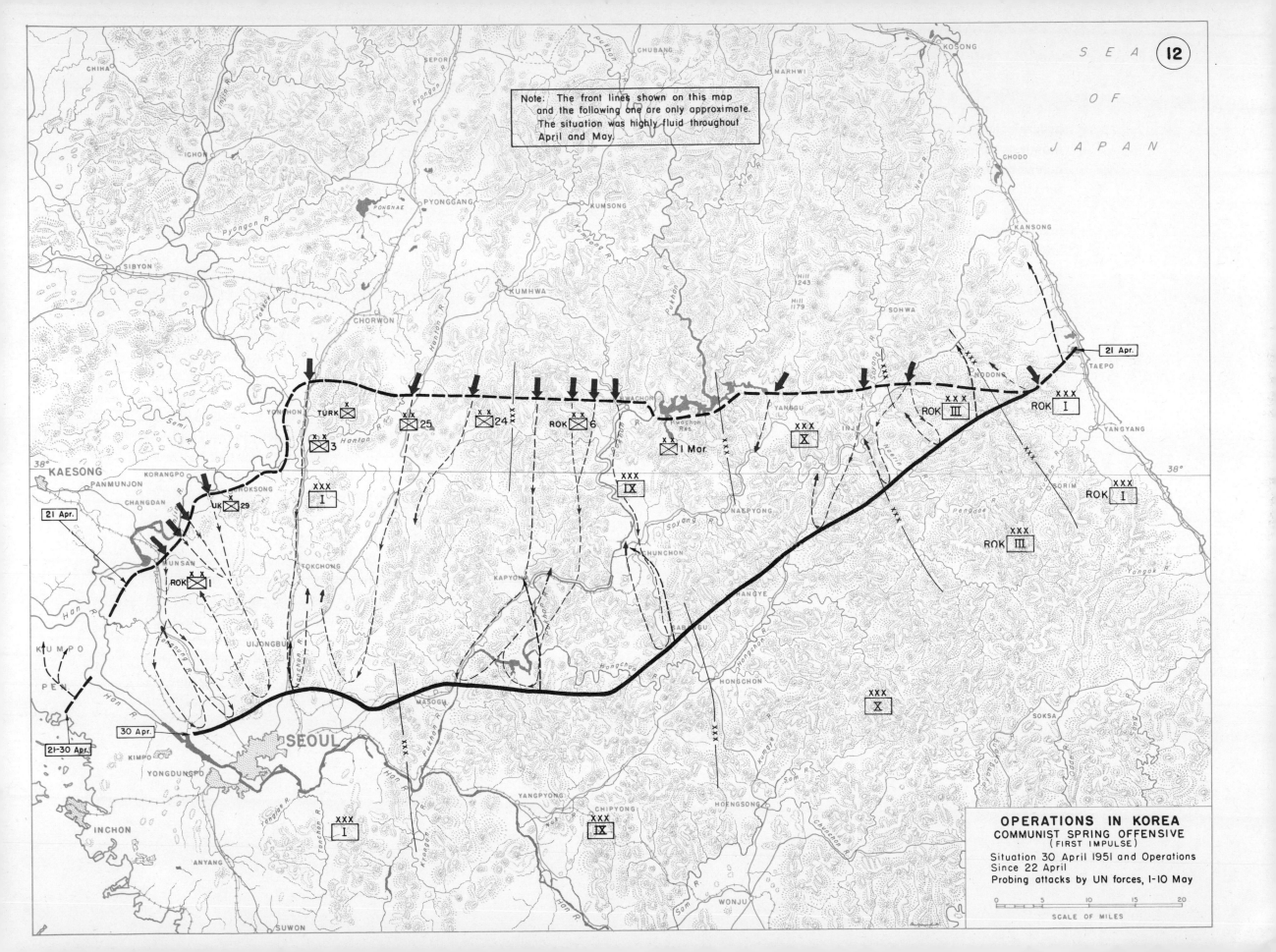

Note: The front lines shown on this map and the following one are only approximate. The situation was highly fluid throughout April and May.

OPERATIONS IN KOREA
COMMUNIST SPRING OFFENSIVE
(FIRST IMPULSE)
Situation 30 April 1951 and Operations Since 22 April
Probing attacks by UN forces, 1-10 May

SCALE OF MILES
0   5   10   15   20

The new enemy concentration appeared to be centered in the general vicinity of Inje (*center, right*). The terrain here was mountainous and extremely rugged, offering a series of strong defensive positions. On the other hand, it was also ideally suited for CCF tactics, and would restrict the effectiveness of U.N. airpower and armor. Much of the U.N. line, by this time, had been greatly strengthened by mine fields, barbed wire entanglements, and napalm fougasses (remotely controlled, buried explosive charges), but it is doubtful if the sectors held by most of the ROK divisions were really well organized. These ROK units had suffered continuous heavy casualties, which had drained away the more experienced junior officers and enlisted men; their replacements were ill trained and unsteady; and too many of their higher unit commanders possessed neither the aptitude nor the training for their assignments. Furthermore, the ROK divisions were relatively weak in artillery and lacked organic armor.

During 15 May, signs of an impending enemy attack multiplied along the fronts of the X and ROK III Corps. Then, with nightfall, came the assault. An estimated twenty-one CCF divisions, with three NKA divisions on their right and six on their left, came surging forward between Naepyong (*center, right*) and Nodong (*right center*). Forty-eight hours later, a strong secondary attack developed along the Pukhan River (*lower center*); a weak NKA force also attacked north of Seoul. The enemy main effort struck the right flank of the X Corps—the ROK 5th and 7th Divisions—in the vicinity of Hangye (*center, right*), sending them pelting to the rear in disorder. Then, swerving westward, strong CCF forces lapped around the right flank and into the rear of the 2d Division, the dispositions of which they appear to have learned through painstaking, covert patrolling.

The 2d Division was not moved; bitter experience had taught it that a CCF attack was like a flash flood, following the lines of least resistance and lacking the ability to sustain itself for more than a few days. Standing firm, the 2d Division—with its attached French and Netherlands Battalions—formed an anvil against which U.N. aircraft and artillery hammered the enemy's canalized advance. On the 18th, the 1st Marine and 2d Divisions attacked to their right (*subsequent action not shown*) to close the gap left by the fleeing ROK divisions. (The IX Corps extended its sector eastward to take over part of the X Corps' original front. At the same time, elements of the 2d Division struck southward to meet the 15th Regimental Combat Team (3d Division) and clear their line of communications.

Worse trouble farther east, however, thwarted the X Corps' efforts to restore the front (*subsequent action shown*). After penetrating the U.N. position, other enemy forces had driven across the rear of the ROK III Corps, cutting its supply line. The ROK III Corps, already withdrawing under considerable frontal pressure, went to pieces. (It was deactivated on 23 May, the X and ROK I Corps taking over the remnants of its forces, wherever they could be rallied.) This debacle forced the ROK I Corps to fall back in turn, refusing its left flank. On the other side of the gap, the X Corps likewise slowly withdrew the 2d Division, while the 1st Marine Division maintained part of its original front. The rest of the 3d Division and the 187th Airborne Regimental Combat Team came into action on the right of the 2d Division. By 20 May, the crisis had passed.

On the U.N. left flank, the attack north of Seoul had been easily crushed. In the center, the attack down the Pukhan River was repulsed by the 25th and ROK 6th Divisions in three days of battle. Caught overextended, their accumulated supplies expended, their communications under merciless air attack, their forces disorganized by tremendous casualties, the CCF-NKA forces were ripe for a counterattack.

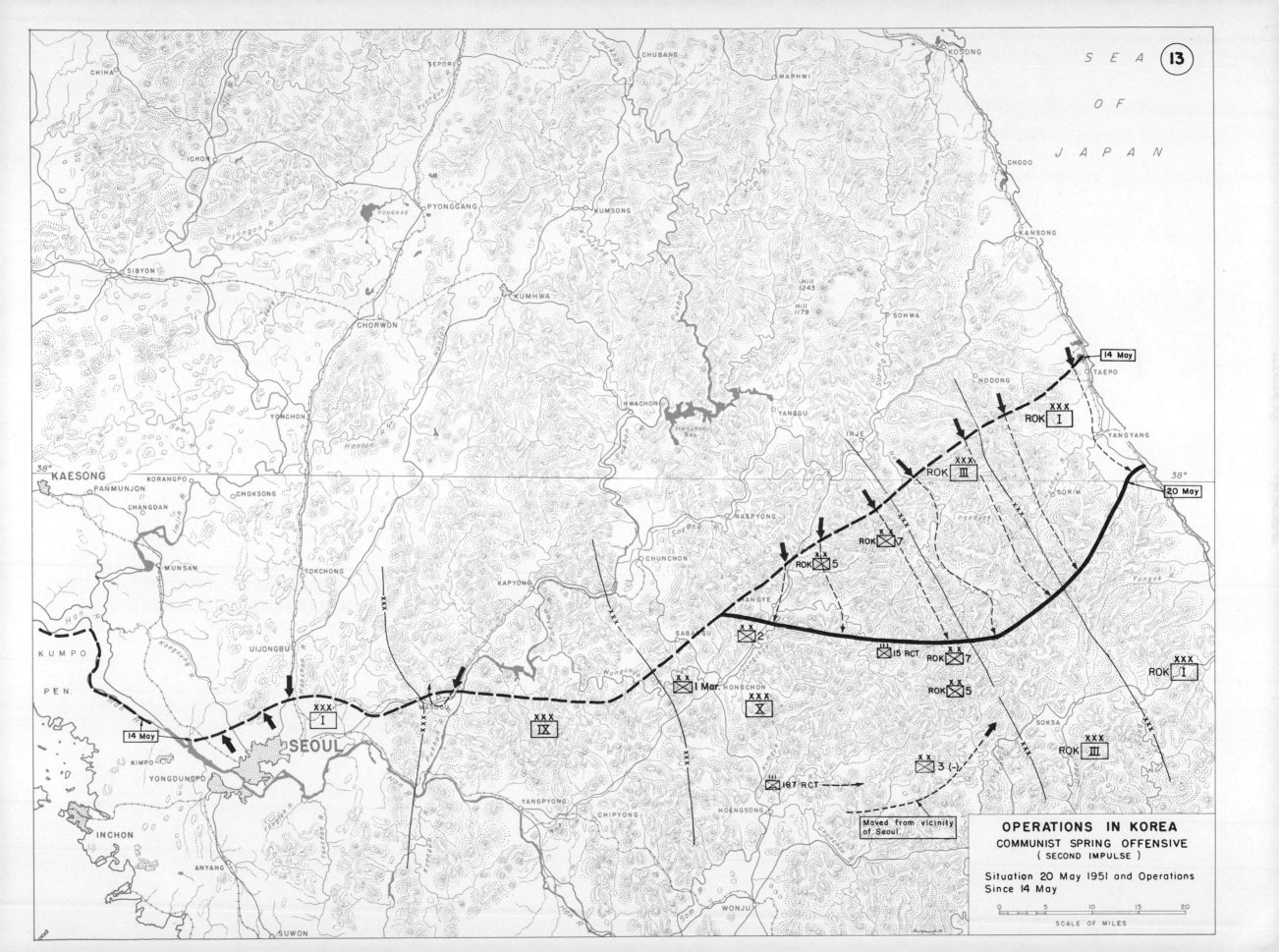

OPERATIONS IN KOREA
COMMUNIST SPRING OFFENSIVE
(SECOND IMPULSE)

Situation 20 May 1951 and Operations
Since 14 May

0   5   10   15   20
SCALE OF MILES

Confident that the enemy offensive would soon run its course, Van Fleet had begun issuing orders on 18 May for a "hot pursuit," which he hoped would destroy the enemy's offensive capability and overrun the Iron Triangle (*upper center*).

The counteroffensive began with limited attacks on the U.N. left flank, which reached the Imjin River north of Munsan (*left center*) on 21 May. By the end of the month, the U.N. forces had recovered most of the territory they had held at the beginning of the enemy's spring offensive. Converging attacks had cut off several enemy units, especially in eastern Korea, but a large part of their personnel had escaped by abandoning their heavy weapons and equipment and infiltrating back northward through the wooded mountains. Regretfully, Van Fleet concluded that he lacked sufficient strength to envelop any significant portion of the enemy's forces, especially as heavy rains were hampering his advance. The JCS—always concerned that Russia might seek to take advantage of the concentration of so large a portion of American ground, naval, and air forces in Korea—was opposed to another drive northward. On 1 June, therefore, Van Fleet decided to establish a strong defensive position across Korea, from which he could conduct local advances to improve his position and keep the enemy off balance. This represented a modification of his original plan, since he now would occupy only the base of the Iron Triangle.

The enemy offered only slight resistance, except below the Iron Triangle. Here, fortifications in depth and bad weather slowed the U.N. offensive, but American, ROK, Turkish, and Philippine troops cleared Chorwon (*center, left*) and Kumhwa (*upper center, overprinted by dotted red line*) on 11 June. Two days later, tank-infantry task forces based on those two towns met at Pyonggang, but withdrew upon finding the enemy strongly entrenched in the commanding hills to the north. (Thereafter—since the Triangle was dominated by the surrounding mountains—neither side made any effort to hold it in strength.) The IX Corps' reconnaissance found the enemy establishing a defensive line south of Kumsong (*upper center*); the X Corps was held to limited gains in the "Punchbowl" area (*upper right*).

The enemy had escaped the U.N. pursuit and was vigorously organizing his own defensive system across Korea. There was no doubt, however, that he had been badly hurt. Estimates of his losses between 22 April and 2 June run as high as 200,000. Enemy personnel had been readier to surrender, and U.N. air forces had thwarted every enemy effort to base his aircraft in North Korea. On 23 June, the Russian delegate to the United Nations proposed cease-fire discussions between the participants in the Korean conflict.

The armistice conference met for the first time on 10 July at Kaesong (*left center*); the enemy initially attempted to turn it into a propaganda farce to prove that the U.N. had been defeated and was suing for peace. This was squelched—if a trifle tardily—and the long wrangling began. Both sides had agreed that hostilities would continue until a truce was signed, but no more large offensives were mounted by either side. Both armies improved their positions behind screens of outposts and patrols. Clashes between these detachments were constant, but the first sizable ones came in July, when U.N. forces cleared the Iron Triangle of CCF units and made gains in the Punchbowl area. Late in August, the truce negotiations broke down. Van Fleet thereupon launched a series of attacks to straighten the U.N. line, clear the Punchbowl, and drive the enemy farther back from the Hwachon Reservoir and the Chorwon-Seoul railroad. These involved extremely difficult operations across intricate ridge lines against a well-entrenched enemy who had vigorous objections to being dispossessed. Much of the U.N. logistical support had to be furnished by air drop or Korean carriers. By late October, however, all objectives had been secured, and the enemy became interested in renewing the armistice discussions. These were shifted to Panmunjon (*left center*). On 12 November, Ridgway ordered Van Fleet to cease offensive operations and begin an active defense.

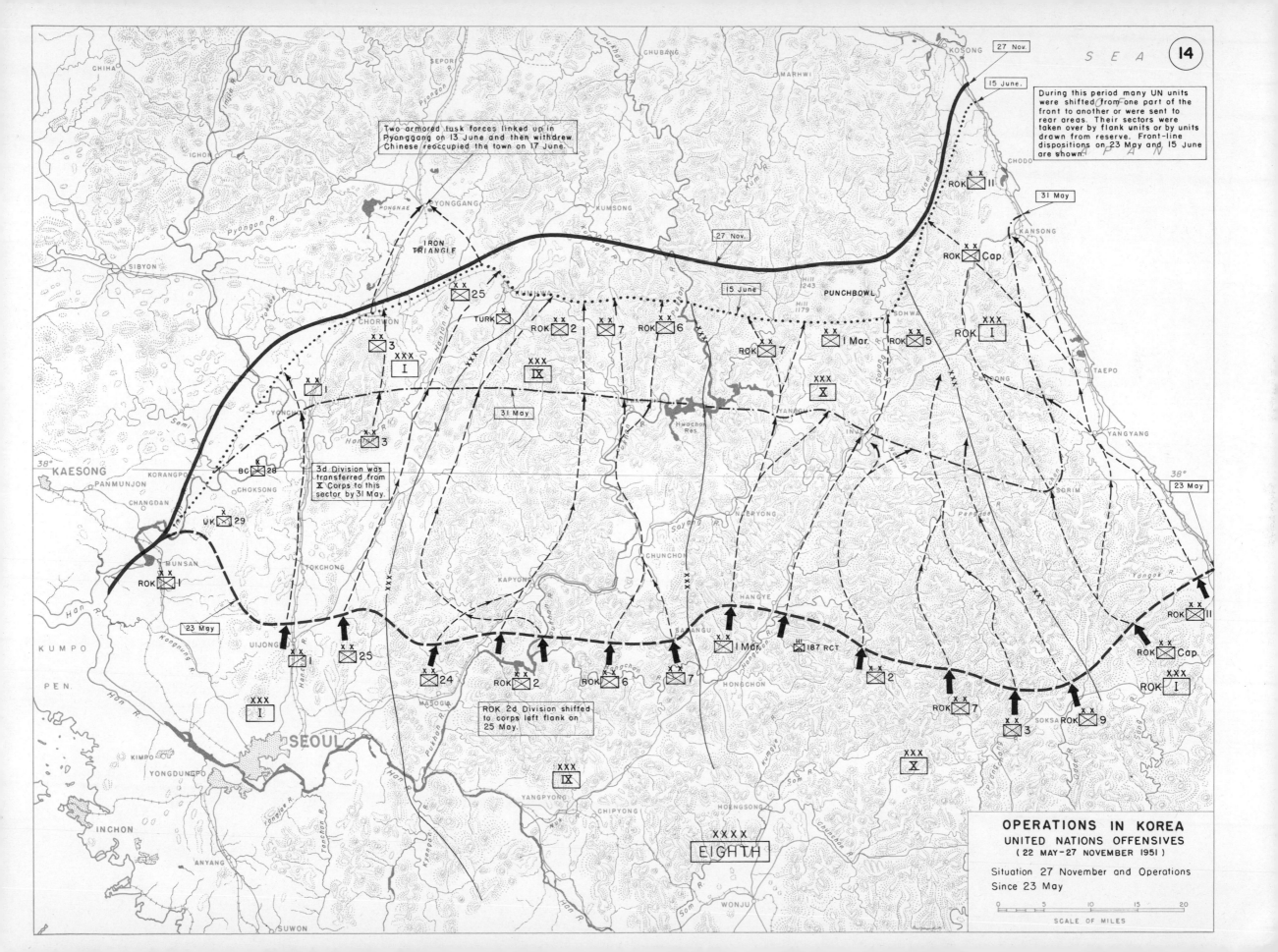

OPERATIONS IN KOREA
UNITED NATIONS OFFENSIVES
(22 MAY – 27 NOVEMBER 1951)

Situation 27 November and Operations
Since 23 May

During the winter, two National Guard divisions, the 40th and the 45th, relieved the 24th and 1st Cavalry Divisions, which were returned to Japan. The enemy reshuffled his troops, concentrating his CCF units at the western end of the front, while the NKA was relegated to the eastern mountains. The usual war of patrol actions, outpost skirmishes, and limited attacks continued. Van Fleet insisted that maximum U.N. fire power be placed on the enemy at every opportunity, in order to inflict maximum casualties. The naval blockade of North Korea was tightened, and ports and coastal roads and railroads kept under constant attack. Heavy air strikes were delivered whenever the weather permitted.

Beginning in August, the U.N. air force had concentrated on a methodical program of interdiction against all of the enemy's logistical operations (Operation STRANGLE). Its actual success cannot be accurately stated, since there is no reliable information from enemy sources. It obviously did, however, increase the enemy's difficulties in supplying and moving his forces.

During 1952, an ominous change took place in the character of these forces. Their numbers steadily increased to an estimated 850,000; modern Russian artillery appeared in large quantities and was employed with increasing skill, partially neutralizing one of the U.N. forces' greatest advantages. Excellent, radar-controlled antiaircraft batteries were brought in to guard important installations, while larger and larger numbers of Russian-built jet planes were based on fields just north of the Yalu River, where they were safe from attack by U.N. forces. These had little effect upon STRANGLE, the U.N. fliers shooting them down in disproportionately large numbers. Finally, to escape U.N. aircraft and artillery, the enemy burrowed like moles, hiding their defenses and rear-echelon installations alike underground.

Action continued to be minor but constant. In early October, a CCF assault with heavy artillery support struck the I-IX Corps boundary northwest of Chorwon; the French Battalion defeated it. The Ethiopian Battalion distinguished itself in several actions. In February, 1953, Lt. Gen. Maxwell D. Taylor replaced Van Fleet. In late May, as negotiations at Panmunjon approached a decisive stage, the CCF began launching a series of powerful attacks. Diversionary operations in the I Corps sector were followed on 10 June by a strong offensive against the ROK II Corps near Kumsong, and on 13 June by a three-division attack on a ROK division holding the right flank of the IX Corps. Both made limited gains at considerable cost. By this time, the negotiators had gradually reached agreement on terms for a truce. Fighting ended at 2200, 27 July.

The Korean conflict was the first United Nations war. As such, it was fought by a heterogeneous command which included (in addition to United States and ROK forces): two British brigades, with supporting artillery and armor; a Canadian brigade, with its own artillery and armor; a Turkish brigade; a Thailand regimental combat team; a Philippine regimental combat team; a New Zealand artillery regiment; two Australian infantry battalions; single battalions from France, Greece, the Netherlands, Colombia, Belgium, and Ethiopia; and an infantry company from Luxembourg. Britain, Canada, Australia, Thailand, France, New Zealand, the Netherlands, and Colombia furnished one or more warships. Canada, Australia, Thailand, Greece, and the Union of South Africa provided air units. In addition, Denmark, Sweden, Norway, Italy, and India furnished medical units.

The problems of feeding, clothing, and coordinating this command were unique. The language difficulty was always a major problem; special dietary requirements taxed the supply system. Yet, with all its inherent difficulties, this command represented the greatest historical mustering of free nations under one flag.

The Korean conflict was a war in which the United States deliberately chose to accept something less than total victory, in the interests of averting a major—and possibly nuclear—war. It is still too early to judge the wisdom of this American course of action; the facts exist, however, that South Korea was saved and Communist aggression exposed and defeated.

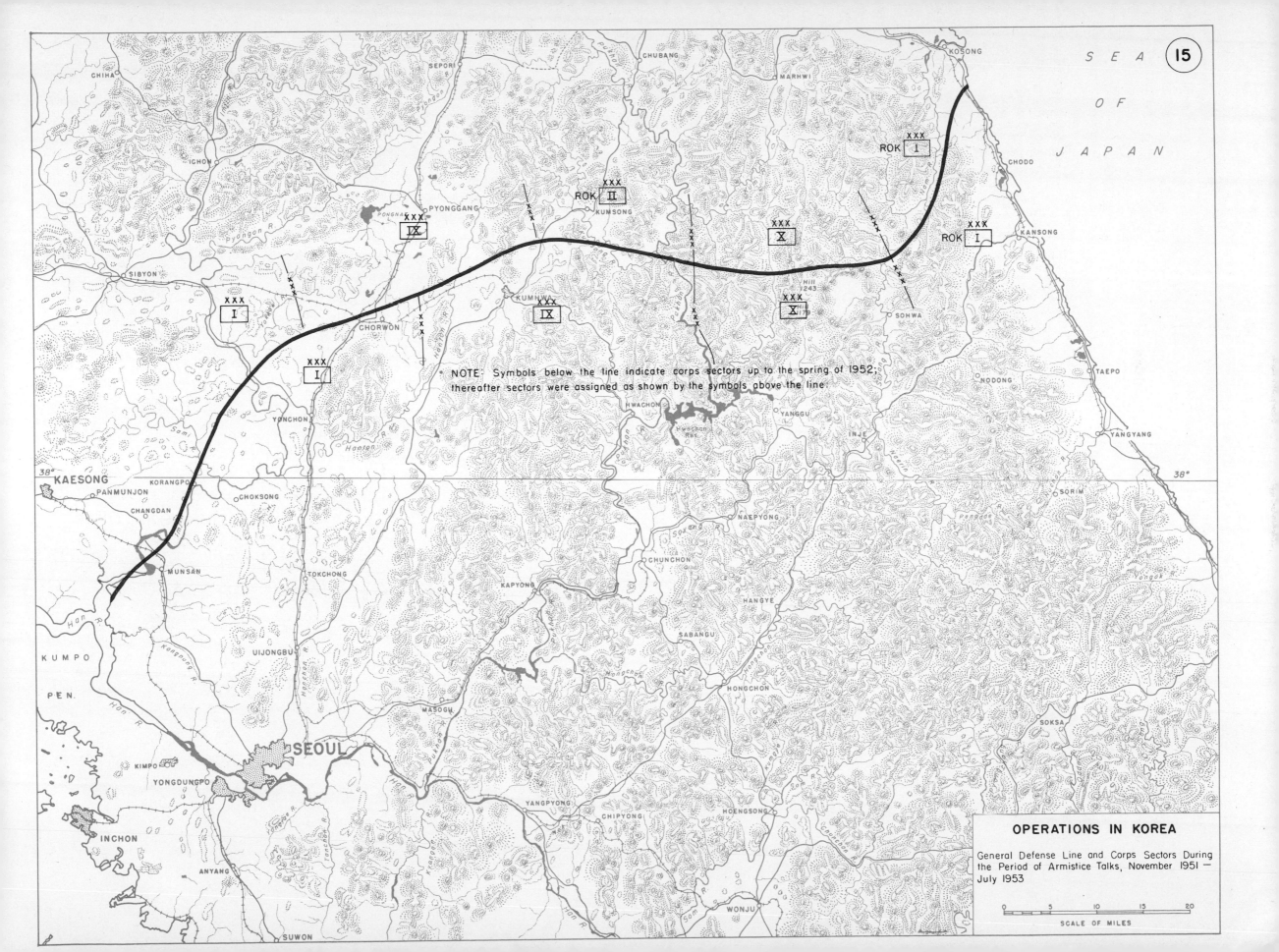

NOTE: Symbols below the line indicate corps sectors up to the spring of 1952; thereafter sectors were assigned as shown by the symbols above the line.

OPERATIONS IN KOREA

General Defense Line and Corps Sectors During the Period of Armistice Talks, November 1951 — July 1953

RECOMMENDED READING LIST

This list does not purport to contain *all* the good books on the military history of the periods covered. However, the selections presented provide the reader with worth-while references for further study in any area he is likely to choose.

WORLD WAR I

BASIC WORKS: MILITARY HISTORY and PHILOSOPHY

BERNHARDI, FRIEDRICH VON. *Germany in the Next War.* London: Edward Arnold, 1912.

Bernhardi believed that Germany's destiny had to be achieved through war, and that Germany must concentrate on preparing for it. However, she must be wily as well as strong—it would be best to lure either France or Russia into attacking first.

——. *On War of Today.* London: Hugh Rees, 1913.

CLAUSEWITZ, KARL VON. *On War.* New York: Random House, 1943.

Clausewitz was one of the major victims of World War I. Most of the errors of both the French and German high commands can be traced to superficial study of his work.

CRAIG, GORDON A. *The Politics of the Prussian Army, 1640-1945.* New York: Oxford University Press, 1956.

This book should be used with Goerlitz's *History of the German General Staff.* Together, they present an excellent, balanced history of one of the world's most famous military institutions. This book is also highly recommended for World War II reference reading.

EARLE, EDWARD M. *Makers of Modern Strategy.* Princeton, N.J.: Princeton University Press, 1943.

From Machiavelli—through Engels and Marx—to Hitler, this book covers the individuals who shaped concepts of strategy up into World War II. The treatment of Clausewitz is particularly good.

FOCH, FERDINAND. *De la Conduite de la Guerre.* Paris: Berger-Levrault, 1904.

——. *Des Principles de la Guerre.* Paris: Berger-Levrault, 1903.

These books were based on Foch's lectures at l'Ecole Superieure de Guerre. The first draws its inspiration from Napoleon, the second from Moltke. Both breathe an aggressive spirit: "In strategy, as in tactics, one attacks."

GOERLITZ, WALTER. *History of the German General Staff, 1657 to 1945.* New York: Frederick A. Praeger, 1952.

A valuable reference work for both World Wars. Use with Craig's *Politics of the Prussian Army.*

GOLTZ, COLMAR, FREIHERR VON DER. *The Conduct of War.* Kansas City, Mo.: The Franklin Hudson Publishing Co., 1896.

The author shared many of his French contemporaries' errors as to the effect of modern weapons on offensive strategy and tactics.

NICKERSON, HOFFMAN. *The Armed Horde, 1793-1939.* New York: G. P. Putnam's Sons, 1940.

An interesting study of the development of mass armies. The author's prediction of their decline during World War II was premature.

PICQ, ARDANT DU. *Battle Studies.* New York: Macmillan Co., 1921.

The author was killed early in the Franco-Prussian war. At once studious and practical, he stressed the importance of the moral factor in war and the need for practical training of officers and men. His ideas, however, became the springboard from which Foch and Grandmaison rose to their delusions that will power could overcome fire power. (Du Picq's ancient history is not too accurate.)

SCHLIEFFEN, ALFRED VON. *Cannae.* Fort Leavenworth: The Command and General Staff School Press, 1936.

Faced with the dreaded prospect of a "two-front" war, Schlieffen sought the secret of quick victory through a "war of annihilation." This book, written after his retirement, exercised great influence on German military thinking. Ironically, it is not accurate history; Schlieffen apparently willfully distorted facts to make them fit his thesis.

OFFICIAL HISTORIES

France

MINISTÈRE DE LA GUERRE, ETAT-MAJOR DE L'ARMÉE, SERVICE HISTORIQUE. *Les Armées Françaises dans la Grand Guerre.* Paris: Imprimerie Nationale, 1922.

Germany

REICHSARCHIV. *Der Weltkrieg, 1914-18.* Berlin: Mittler und Sohn, 1925-39.

This work remains incomplete and untranslated. Much of it, including unpublished material, however, was used in the British official history.

Great Britain

HISTORICAL SECTION, THE COMMITTEE OF IMPERIAL DEFENCE. *History of the Great War.* 45 vols., including maps. London: His Majesty's Stationery Office, 1927-47.

A splendid work, well supplied with good maps.

MINISTRY OF INFORMATION. *Chronology of the War.* 4 vols. London: Constable and Company, 1918.

Italy

SUPREME COMMAND, ROYAL ITALIAN ARMY. *The Battle of the Piave.* London: Hodder and Stoughton, 1919.

United States

AMERICAN BATTLE MONUMENTS COMMISSION. *American Armies and Battlefields in Europe.* Washington, D.C.: U.S. Government Printing Office, 1938.

HISTORICAL DIVISION, DEPARTMENT OF THE ARMY. *United States Army in the World War, 1917-1919.* 17 vols. Washington, D.C.: U.S. Government Printing Office, 1948.

In organization and content, this work is far inferior to the British official history of World War I. It has few and not too satisfactory maps.

HISTORICAL SECTION, ARMY WAR COLLEGE. *Order of Battle of the United States Land Forces in the World War; American Expeditionary Forces, Divisions.* Washington, D.C.: U.S. Government Printing Office, 1931.

——. *Order of Battle of the United States Land Forces in the World War; American Expeditionary Forces; General Headquarters, Armies, Army Corps, Services of Supply, and Separate Forces.* Washington, D.C.: U.S. Government Printing Office, 1937.

——. *Order of Battle of the United States Land Forces in the World War (1917-19), Zone of the Interior.* Washington, D.C.: U.S. Government Printing Office, 1949.

PERSHING, JOHN J. *Final Report of General John J. Pershing, Commander in Chief, American Expeditionary Forces.* Washington, D.C.: U.S. Government Printing Office, 1920.

GENERAL HISTORIES

BUCHAN, JOHN. *A History of the Great War.* 4 vols. Boston: Houghton Mifflin Co., 1922.

This early history of the war contains a number of errors common to works of the period. The author, however, was a man who combined patriotism and integrity to a rare degree; he could see and express the honor as well as the tragedy.

CHURCHILL, WINSTON S. *The World Crisis.* 4 vols. New York: Charles Scribner's Sons, 1932.

A massive book with much information about the workings of the higher levels of government and command.

CRUTTWELL, C. R. M. F. *A History of the Great War.* Oxford: The Clarendon Press, 1934.

A short military history, generally satisfactory except for its account of American operations.

EDMONDS, SIR JAMES E. *A Short History of World War I.* London: Oxford University Press, 1951.

A good, complete, brief history of the war by a noted British historian; the general attitude is somewhat chauvinistic.

FROTHINGHAM, THOMAS C. *The Naval History of the World War.* Cambridge, Mass.: Harvard University Press, 1925.

A good general history of naval operations.

McENTEE, GIRARD L. *Military History of the World War.* New York: Charles Scribner's Sons, 1937.

REINERS, LUDWIG. *The Lamps Went Out in Europe.* New York: Pantheon Books, 1955.

Written from the viewpoint of a self-respecting, fair-minded German, this book covers the background and causes of the war —as well as the war itself—largely in terms of personalities of the men responsible for it. The style is easy and witty.

SARGENT, HERBERT H. *The Strategy on the Western Front.* Chicago: A. C. McClurg and Company, 1920.

A "minority report" by a capable American military historian, written before complete records of World War I were available, but highly interesting for its thesis that both the Germans and the Allies erred in neglecting the Eastern Front.

SEYMOUR, CHARLES. *The Diplomatic Background of the War, 1870-1914.* New Haven, Conn.: Yale University Press, 1916.

A review of the political, economic, and ideological causes of the war.

BATTLES and CAMPAIGNS

ADAMS, JOHN C. *Flight in Winter.* Princeton, N.J.: Princeton University Press, 1942.

A vivid, highly partisan account of Serbia's part in World War I.

BRUSSILOV (or BRUSILOV), ALEXEI A. *A Soldier's Notebook, 1914-1918.* London: Macmillan Co., 1930.

Brussilov was probably the most competent Russian commander; his 1916 offensive definitely was the outstanding Russian operation of the war.

BULLARD, ROBERT LEE. *Personalities and Reminiscences of the War.* Garden City, N.Y.: Doubleday, Page and Co., 1925.

Actually the author's personal experiences during 1917-19.

——, and EARL REEVES. *American Soldiers Also Fought.* New York: Maurice H. Louis, 1939.

An angry, colorful little book, written with the one purpose of telling the world that the United States helped to win the war. It is not great history, but it is interesting.

CALLWELL, SIR C. E. *The Dardanelles.* Boston: Constable & Co., 1924.

CAVALRY SCHOOL. *Cavalry Combat.* Harrisburg, Pa.: The Telegraph Press, 1937.

Descriptions and evaluations of typical cavalry actions during World War I, covering the mounted forces of most of the nations involved.

CHURCHILL, WINSTON S. *The Unknown War.* New York: Charles Scribner's Sons, 1932.

A stirring, impartial account of the Eastern Front in World War I.

RECOMMENDED READING LIST

DUPUY, R. ERNEST. *Perish by the Sword*. Harrisburg, Pa.: Military Service Publishing Co., 1939.
    An excellent history of the Czechoslovakian anabasis out of Russia, and of the Allied detachments in northern Russia and Siberia, 1918-20.

FALKENHAYN, ERICH VON. *The German General Staff and Its Decisions, 1914-1916*. New York: Dodd, Mead & Co., 1920.
    This book, with Ludendorff's, gives the best account of the day-to-day operations of the German high command—possibly tinged with postwar second thoughts.

FRENCH, SIR JOHN. *1914*. Boston: Houghton Mifflin Co., 1919.
    The first year of the war, as remembered by the commander of the British Expeditionary Force.

FROST, HOLLOWAY H. *The Battle of Jutland*. Annapolis, Md.: The United States Naval Institute, 1936.
    An authoritative account.

FULLER, JOHN F. C. *A Military History of the Western World* (Vol. III). New York: Funk & Wagnalls Co., 1954.
    Fuller's experience with the British Tank Corps makes his description of the Battle of Amiens (1918) particularly valuable.

GALET, EMILE J. *Albert, King of the Belgians in the Great War*. Boston: Houghton Mifflin Co., 1931.
    Particularly good for its description of the Liége defenses. Covers 1914 operations only.

GOUGH, SIR HUBERT. *The Fifth Army*. London: Hodder and Stoughton, 1931.
    A well-written account of the Western Front by the aggressive, controversial general whom Lloyd George made the scapegoat for the British defeats in early 1918.

GRAVES, WILLIAM S. *America's Siberian Adventure, 1918-1920*. New York: Cape and Smith, 1931.
    A good account of one of the United States Army's most obscure operations.

HAMILTON, SIR IAN. *Gallipoli Diary*. New York: George H. Doran Co., 1920.
    This book, in large part unconsciously, reveals the reasons for the failure of the Dardanelles campaign. The author, a gallant soldier of the old Imperial school, applied an outmoded method of command to a new type of war.

HARBORD, JAMES G. *The American Army in France*. Boston: Little, Brown & Co., 1936.

HOFFMAN, MAX. *War Diaries and Other Papers*. London: Secker, 1929.

———. *The War of Lost Opportunities*. New York: International Publishers, 1925.
    Hoffman, one of the most gifted soldiers in any army during World War I, appears to have been the actual brains of the Hindenburg-Ludendorff team. Fortunately for the Allies, they left him on the Eastern Front in 1918.

INFANTRY JOURNAL. *Infantry in Battle*. Washington, D.C.: Infantry Journal, 1939.
    Similar to *Cavalry Combat;* covers a wide variety of infantry operations.

IRONSIDE, SIR EDMUND. *Tannenburg*. Edinburgh: William Blackwood and Sons, 1933.

JOFFRE, JOSEPH J. C. *La Préparation de la Guerre et la Conduite des Operations*. Paris: E. Chiron, 1920.
    The war as Joffre remembered it.

JOHNSON, THOMAS M., and FLETCHER PRATT. *The Lost Battalion*. Indianapolis and New York: The Bobbs-Merrill Co., 1938.
    The best existing account of this famous incident—detailed and vivid. Every American officer should read it to learn what leadership can do with green troops against great odds.

KEARSEY, A. *The Battle of Amiens, 1918*. Aldershot, England: Gale & Polden, 1950.
    The best account of this decisive battle.

———. *Strategy and Tactics of the East Prussian Campaign, 1914*. London: Sifton Praed and Co., 1932.

———. *A Study of the Strategy and Tactics of the Mesopotamian Campaign*. Aldershot, England: Gale & Polden.

KENNAN, GEORGE F. *Soviet-American Relations, 1917-1920*. Princeton, N.J.: Princeton University Press, 1956-58.
    Vol. I: *Russia Leaves the War*, 1956.
    Vol. II: *The Decision to Intervene*, 1958.
    Authoritative works by a man who helped to make the history he describes.

KEYES, SIR ROBERT. *The Fight for Gallipoli*. London: Eyre and Spottiswoode, 1941.
    The version of a ranking British naval officer.

KLUCK, ALEXANDER VON. *The March on Paris and the Battle of the Marne*. New York: Longmans, Green & Co., 1920.
    An excellent—though naturally far from impartial—book by the most capable of the German army commanders on the Western Front in 1914.

KNOX, SIR ALFRED. *With the Russian Army, 1914-1917*. London: Hutchinson and Co., 1921.
    Knox was a British military attaché in Russia throughout this period. His book is filled with exact information and unforgettable descriptions of Russia at war.

KUHL, H. VON. *The Marne Campaign, 1914*. Fort Leavenworth, Kansas: The Command and General Staff School Press, 1936.

———, and VON BERGEMANN. *Movements and Supply of the German First Army During August and September, 1914*. Fort Leavenworth, Kansas: The Command and General Staff School Press, 1929.
    Von Kuhl was the capable chief of staff of Von Kluck's German First Army in 1914.

LAWRENCE, THOMAS E. *The Seven Pillars of Wisdom*. New York: Garden City Publishing Co., 1938.
    Lawrence's own account of the British-sponsored Arab revolt against the Turks. Naturally, he somewhat overemphasizes its importance.

LIGGETT, HUNTER. *Commanding an American Army*. Boston: Houghton Mifflin Co., 1925.

LONERGAN, THOMAS C. *It Might Have Been Lost*. New York: G. P. Putnam's Sons, 1929.
    A record of the struggle to form and maintain the American Expeditionary Force as an independent American army.

MARCH, PEYTON C. *The Nation at War*. Garden City, N.Y.: Doubleday, Doran & Co., 1932.
    A frequently caustic book by the United States Army chief of staff, who regarded the commander of the American Expeditionary Force with little affection.

McENTEE, GIRARD L. *Italy's Part in Winning the War*. Princeton, N.J.: Princeton University Press, 1934.
    Probably the most complete available American work on this subject. It is, however, neither balanced nor analytical, and so should be used with caution.

MACINTYRE, DONALD. *Jutland*. New York: W. W. Norton & Co., 1958.
    This recent work points out the great communications handicaps with which the opposing commanders had to contend.

MILES, SHERMAN. *Notes on the Dardanelles Campaign of 1915*. Washington, D.C.: The Coast Artillery Journal, 1955.

MILLIS, WALTER. *Road to War*. Boston: Houghton Mifflin Co., 1935.
    A stimulating account of how the developments of the war gradually drew the United States into it.

MITCHELL, WILLIAM. *Our Air Force*. New York: E. P. Dutton & Co., 1921.

MOOREHEAD, ALAN. *Gallipoli*. New York: Harper & Brothers, 1956.
    An excellent book, written long enough after this campaign to be able to place it in proper, dispassionate perspective.

NEWMANN, GEORG P. *The German Air Force in the Great War*. London: Hodder and Stoughton, 1920.

PERSHING, JOHN J. *My Experiences in the World War*. New York: Frederick A. Stokes Co., 1931.
    A complete, excellent presentation of the experiences of the commander of the American Expeditionary Force.

PÉTAIN, HENRI P. *Verdun*. New York: The Dial Press, 1930.
    This book has considerable value as a description from the French viewpoint of the fighting around Verdun, but is rather lacking in frankness as to the trouble that Pétain's superiors and subordinates had persuading him that Verdun could be held.

PULESTON, W. D. *The Dardanelles Expedition*. Annapolis, Md.: The United States Naval Institute, 1927.

RITTER, GERHARD. *The Schlieffen Plan*. New York: Frederick A. Praeger, 1958.
    A competent, terse review of the various plans developed by Schlieffen as chief of the German General Staff. The author's evaluation of these plans, however, is not distinguished by impartiality.

ROMMEL, ERWIN. *Infantry Attacks*. Washington, D.C.: Combat Forces Press, 1956.
    A series of personal experiences: Belgium and northern France in 1914; trench warfare in the Argonne and Vosges Mountains; the conquest of Rumania; and Caporetto. A classic account of small-unit combat leadership.

SANDERS, LIMAN VON. *My Five Years in Turkey*. Annapolis, Md.: The United States Naval Institute, 1927.
    A fascinating book by the chief of the German military mission to Turkey. His descriptions of the Turkish government and army during World War I are invaluable.

SPEARS, E. L. *Liaison, 1914*. London: William Heinemann, 1930.
    The initial campaigns of World War I, as seen by a British liaison officer with the French General Headquarters.

———. *Prelude to Victory*. London: Jonathan Cape, 1939.
    The Battle of Arras and the Nivelle offensive (1917).

STRAKHOVSKY, LEONID I. *Intervention at Archangel*. Princeton, N.J.: Princeton University Press, 1944.

TOWNSHEND, SIR CHARLES V. F. *My Campaign in Mesopotamia*. London: Thornton Butterworth, 1920.
    The unapologetic account of the brilliant and egotistical British commander, who is now chiefly remembered for his capitulation at Kut in 1916.

TSCHISCHWITZ, VON. *The Army and the Navy During the Conquest of the Baltic Islands in October, 1917*. Fort Leavenworth, Kansas: The Command and General Staff School Press, 1933.
    This comparatively minor action is still worth study as an example of an efficient amphibious operation.

TYNG, SEWELL. *The Campaign of the Marne, 1914*. New York: Longmans, Green & Co., 1935.
    An excellent book which painstakingly recreates this crucial campaign.

VILLARI, LUIGI. *The War on the Italian Front*. London: Cobden-Sanderson, 1932.
    A fervid account of how Italy won World War I for the Allies.

WOLF, LEON. *In Flanders Fields*. New York: The Viking Press, 1959.
    This book deals principally with the British 1917 Flanders offensive. Its coverage is extensive, but not complete, and there is a strong tinge of sensationalism.

RECOMMENDED READING LIST

MEMOIRS, BIOGRAPHIES, and AUTOBIOGRAPHIES

CHARTERIS, JOHN. *Field Marshal Earl Haig.* New York: Charles Scribner's Sons, 1929.

———. *Haig.* New York: Macmillan Co., 1933.

COOPER, DUFF. *Haig.* Garden City, N.Y.: Doubleday, Doran & Co., 1946.

DAVIDSON, SIR JOHN. *Haig: Master of the Field.* London: Peter Nevill, 1953.

FOCH, FERDINAND. *The Memoirs of Marshal Foch.* Garden City, N.Y.: Doubleday, Doran & Co., 1931.

GUEDALLA, PHILIP. *The Two Marshals.* New York: Reynal and Hitchcock, 1943.
Biographies of Bazaine and Pétain, two commanders who were given responsibilities beyond their powers and so led France to defeat.

HAIG, DOUGLAS. *The Private Papers of Douglas Haig,* ed. ROBERT BLAKE. London: Eyre and Spottiswoode, 1952.
Undoubtedly the best available source for information on Haig's personal convictions and reactions.

HINDENBURG, PAUL VON. *Out of My Life.* New York: Harper & Brothers, 1921.

JOFFRE, JOSEPH J. C. *The Personal Memoirs of Joffre.* New York: Harper & Brothers, 1932.

LIDDELL HART, B. H. *Foch, The Man of Orléans.* Boston: Little, Brown & Co., 1932.
A careful, critical biography—undoubtedly one of the author's better books.

LUDENDORFF, ERICH VON. *Ludendorff's Own Story.* New York: Harper & Brothers, 1919.

ROBERTSON, WILLIAM. *From Private to Field-Marshal.* Boston: Houghton Mifflin Co., 1921.
The blunt autobiography of a "ranker."

WAVELL, SIR ARCHIBALD. *Allenby.* New York: Oxford University Press, 1941.
An excellent study in the qualities of leadership.

SOLDIER LIFE, STATISTICAL and TECHNICAL REFERENCES

CHINN, GEORGE M. *The Machine Gun.* 2 vols. Washington, D.C.: U.S. Government Printing Office, 1951.
Prepared for the Bureau of Ordnance, United States Navy, these lavishly illustrated volumes are a complete and authoritative history of this weapon, which had so great an influence on World War I.

GERMAINS, VICTOR W. *The Mechanization of War.* London: Sifton Praed and Co., 1927.
This book is interesting in that it gives the views of an officer who saw things very much as a whole and so was not overly impressed by the performance of the early tank. A good antidote to Fuller's more extreme moods.

HAGOOD, JOHNSON. *The Services of Supply.* Boston: Houghton Mifflin Co., 1927.
The magnitude of the logistical problem confronting the American Expeditionary Forces must be studied to be appreciated.

JOHNSON, DOUGLAS W. *Battlefields of the World War.* New York: Oxford University Press, 1921.

———. *Topography and Strategy in the War.* New York: Henry Holt & Co., 1917.
These two interesting books bring out the great importance of terrain, climate, and weather to a commander.

JONES, RALPH E. *The Fighting Tanks Since 1916.* Washington, D.C.: National Service Publishing Co., 1933.
Probably the best reference book on tanks and tank warfare during the period 1916-33; includes complete photographs, specifications, general information, and combat histories. Especially good for experimental models.

MARTEL, G. LE Q. *In the Wake of the Tank.* London: Sifton Praed and Co., 1931.
A history of the first fifteen years of mechanization in the British Army.

MILLER, HENRY W. *The Paris Gun.* London: George G. Harrup and Co., 1930.
A detailed description of these unusual weapons and their employment, including their relationship to the 1918 German offensives.

SHERMAN, WILLIAM C. *Air Warfare.* New York: The Ronald Press Co., 1926.
Good material on the development of air warfare and individual World War I "aces."

SLESSOR, JOHN C. *Air Power and Armies.* London: Oxford University Press, 1936.
A very complete restudy of air power in World War I by an enthusiastic airman who possibly overstates his case, but has tried to present a thorough picture.

STEWART, OLIVER. *The Strategy and Tactics of Air Fighting.* London: Longmans, Green & Co., 1925.

SWINTON, SIR ERNEST D. *Eyewitness.* Garden City, N.Y.: Doubleday, Doran & Co., 1933.
An account of the origin and development of the tank.

WILGUS, WILLIAM J. *Transporting the A.E.F. in Western Europe.* New York: Columbia University Press, 1931.
An authentic, extremely detailed account by the Deputy Director of Transportation, A.E.F.

WORLD WAR II

BASIC WORKS: MILITARY HISTORY and PHILOSOPHY

BYWATER, HECTOR C. *The Great Pacific War: A History of the American-Japanese Campaign of 1931-33.* Boston: Houghton Mifflin Co., 1932.
Originally published in 1925, this book dealt—rather expertly—with a possible Pacific war between the United States and Japan.

DOUHET, GIULIO. *The Command of the Air.* New York: Coward-McCann, 1942.
A translation of the principal writings of the first prophet of air power, whose books and articles have made a deep impression on military men since 1921. Douhet had little practical knowledge of air power, but—in the larger sense—many of his prophecies have been fulfilled.

FOERTSCH, HERMANN. *The Art of Modern Warfare.* New York: Oskar Piest, 1940.
The author, an officer of the German General Staff, did an excellent job of expressing the theories of warfare held by the German Army at the beginning of World War II.

FULLER, JOHN F. C. *The Army in My Time.* London: Rich and Cowan, 1935.

———. *The Foundations of the Science of War.* London: Hutchinson and Co., 1926.

———. *Generalship: Its Diseases and Their Cure.* London: Faber and Faber, 1933.

———. *Lectures on Field Service Regulations III: Operations Between Mechanized Forces.* London: 1932.

———. *Machine Warfare.* Washington, D.C.: Infantry Journal, 1943.

———. *The Memoirs of an Unconventional Soldier.* London: Nicholson and Watson, 1936.

———. *On Future Warfare.* London: Sifton Praed and Co., 1928.

———. *The Reformation of War.* New York: E. P. Dutton & Co., 1929.
Undoubtedly the most prolific military writer of the 1918-39 period, Fuller argued for more realistic organization and training in preparation for the blitzkrieg warfare which he foresaw. Being an egoist, a fanatic believer in tanks, and something of a mystic, he irritated as much as he inspired—to the detriment of his frequently excellent ideas.

GAULLE, CHARLES DE. *The Army of the Future.* Philadelphia: J. B. Lippincott Co., 1941.
Originally published in 1934, when De Gaulle was a captain, this book called for a long-service, fully equipped, expertly trained professional army capable of waging a blitzkrieg war. The French did not read it.

GERMAINS, VICTOR W. *The Mechanization of War.* London: Sifton Praed and Co., 1927.
Germains, a contemporary of Liddell Hart and Fuller, had a greater ability to see things as they were, if less of a gift for optimism. He was dubious about the theories of both; if his opinions delayed the mechanization of the British Army, he still saw the whole problem of national defense far more clearly than did most.

HAUSHOFER, KARL. *Weltmeere und Weltmächte.* Berlin: Zeitgeschichte-Verlag, 1937.
Haushofer's work in geopolitics appears to have influenced Hitler deeply; it also served to awaken political and military leaders as to the importance of global geography.

HITLER, ADOLF. *Mein Kampf.* New York: Houghton Mifflin Co., 1939.
In this book (first published in 1925), Hitler made plain his goals and his methods. Nobody took it seriously until the shooting started.

ISHIMARU, TŌTA. *Japan Must Fight Britain.* Harrisburg, Pa.: The Telegraph Press, 1936.
The author, a Japanese naval officer, was "deeply interested in preserving peace"; he insisted that this could be done only if England and America gave free rein to Japanese demands for increased immigration, trade, and territorial expansion. In this, he was typical of the jingoist military clique that dominated prewar Japan.

LEVINE, ISAAC D. *Mitchell, Pioneer of Air Power.* New York: Duell, Sloan & Pearce, 1943.

LIDDELL HART, B. H. *The Defense of Britain.* New York: Random House, 1939.
An influential misinterpretation of military history, which preached the doctrine of a strictly defensive strategy, naval blockades, economic warfare, and limited liability on the European continent.

———. *Paris, or The Future of War.* New York: E. P. Dutton & Co., 1925.
Written while Liddell Hart was still much under the influence of Fuller, this is another plea for modern weapons and small "quality" forces.

LEEB, WILHELM VON. *Defense.* Harrisburg, Pa.: Military Service Publishing Co., 1943.
This book (published in Germany in 1938) was obviously influenced by a study of Clausewitz; he recommended that Germany utilize an active defense at the beginning of the next war, while concentrating forces for a decisive counteroffensive. Hitler was not impressed.

LUDENDORFF, ERICH. *Der Totale Krieg.* Munich: Ludendorffs Verlag, 1939.
Ludendorff's writing seems to have been inspired by the theory that his—and, incidentally, Germany's—defeat in World War I was due to lack of popular support. This led him to consider methods of improving Germany's organization for a future, total war; his early association with Hitler ensured wide circulation for his views in pre–World War II Germany.

RECOMMENDED READING LIST

MACKINDER, HALFORD J. *Democratic Ideals and Reality.* New York: Henry Holt & Co., 1919.

The author, an outstanding British geographer, in a series of studies on the geographical bases of land and sea power, carried forward Mahan's studies and—in turn—gave great impetus to Haushofer's geopolitical school.

MAHAN, ALFRED T. *The Influence of Sea Power Upon History, 1660-1783.* Boston: Little, Brown & Co., 1908.

Probably Mahan's most influential work.

MITCHELL, WILLIAM. *Our Air Force.* New York: E. P. Dutton & Co., 1921.

———. *Skyways.* Philadelphia: J. B. Lippincott Co., 1930.

———. *Winged Defense.* New York: G. P. Putnam's Sons, 1925.

Mitchell had a large part in the development of the air power doctrine usually attributed to Douhet. His writing was based on combat aviation service during World War I, but his approach was far more violent and partisan.

PULESTON, WILLIAM D. *The Life and Work of Captain Alfred Thayer Mahan.* New Haven, Conn.: Yale University Press, 1939.

It should be remembered that Mahan's theories had widespread effect in England, continental Europe, and Japan.

SEVERSKY, ALEXANDER DE. *Victory Through Air Power.* New York: Simon and Schuster, 1942.

Seversky was a disciple of Mitchell; he writes from a distinguished background as pilot, inventor, and aircraft designer.

SIGAUD, LOUIS A. *Douhet and Aerial Warfare.* New York: G. P. Putnam's Sons, 1941.

SLESSOR, SIR JOHN C. *Air Power and Armies.* London: Oxford University Press, 1936.

Slessor's thoughtful restudy of air operations in World War I made him a champion of the tank-airplane team and of strategic air power. He also stressed the importance of joint air-ground-naval planning.

TSCHUPPIK, KARL. *Ludendorff: The Tragedy of a Military Mind.* New York: Houghton Mifflin Co., 1932.

VAGTS, ALFRED. *A History of Militarism.* New York: W. W. Norton & Co., 1937.

An able, if at times slightly sensational, work emphasizing the development of European militarism. It probably did not stimulate American preparations for World War II. (A new edition was published in 1959 by Meridian Books, Inc.)

WESTCOTT, ALLAN (ed.). *Mahan on Naval Warfare.* Boston: Little, Brown & Co., 1918.

A collection of Mahan's writings on the importance of sea power.

OFFICIAL HISTORIES

World War II produced an unprecedented outpouring of official and semiofficial histories from the Western nations. All these publications show a high level of accuracy, objectivity, and literary ability. American publications consist principally of the following four series:

1. OFFICE OF THE CHIEF OF MILITARY HISTORY. *The United States Army in World War II.*

This series, not yet complete, is especially noteworthy for its wide coverage and excellent maps and charts. A product of years of careful research, it represents an epoch in American historical writing.

2. OFFICE OF AIR FORCE HISTORY. *The Army Air Force in World War II.* 7 vols.

A terse, comprehensive account of Air Force policies, plans, problems, and operations.

3. HISTORICAL BRANCH, HEADQUARTERS, U.S. MARINE CORPS. *History of the U.S. Marine Corps Operations in World War II.*

This excellent and well-illustrated series is likewise incomplete, but, in the interim, the resulting gap is filled by a group of competent monographs on individual operations.

4. MORISON, SAMUEL ELIOT. *History of United States Naval Operations in World War II.*

Also as yet unfinished, this is a semiofficial history of the Navy's part in World War II. It is well written and deals bluntly with victory and defeat alike.

The most extensive foreign official history is the *History of the Second World War: United Kingdom Military Series.* Canada, Australia, New Zealand, Pakistan, and India are also producing creditable historical works.

A mere listing of these official histories would be extremely long and somewhat pointless, since many of them are extremely specialized works. Instead, we have followed the policy of listing the best and most applicable of them at the head of each subdivision of the following Recommended Reading List, which is organized to parallel the contents of the World War II portion of this ATLAS. (The sponsoring agencies of these histories are listed first rather than the authors, and not necessarily in alphabetical order; however, in instances where a particular series contains several volumes by different authors, these are broken down alphabetically by author [or by title when the author's name is unavailable].)

GENERAL HISTORIES

OFFICE OF THE CHIEF OF MILITARY HISTORY. *The United States Army in World War II: The War Department.* Washington, D.C.: U.S. Government Printing Office.

CLINE, RAY S. *Washington Command Post: The Operations Division,* 1951.

LEIGHTON, RICHARD M., and ROBERT W. COAKLEY. *Global Logistics and Strategy, 1940-1943,* 1955. (A second volume, covering 1943-45, is in preparation.)

MATLOFF, MAURICE, and EDWIN M. SNELL. *Strategic Planning for Coalition Warfare, 1941-1942,* 1953. (A second volume, covering 1943-45, is in preparation.)

An excellent depiction of the problems involved in high-level planning.

SMITH, R. ELBERTON. *The Army and Economic Mobilization,* 1959.

WATSON, MARK S. *Chief of Staff: Prewar Plans and Preparations,* 1950.

OFFICE OF AIR FORCE HISTORY. *The Army Air Forces in World War II,* ed. WESLEY F. CRAVEN and JAMES L. CATE. Chicago: University of Chicago Press.

Vol. I: *Plans and Early Operations,* 1948.

Vol. VII: *Services Around the World,* 1958.

HISTORICAL SECTION, CANADIAN GENERAL STAFF. Ottawa: King's Printer.

STACEY, C. P. *The Canadian Army, 1939-1945,* 1948.

This is a preliminary official historical summary, now gradually being replaced by the more detailed and researched volumes of the *Official History of the Canadian Army in the Second World War.*

DEPARTMENT OF NATIONAL DEFENSE. *Official History of the Canadian Army in the Second World War.* Ottawa: Queen's Printer.

STACEY, C. P. *Six Years of War,* 1955.

The organization and mobilization of the Canadian Army, raiding operations from Britain, and the war against Japan.

UNITED KINGDOM MILITARY SERIES. *History of the Second World War.* London: Her Majesty's Stationery Office.

BUTLER, J. R. M. *Grand Strategy* (Vol. II), 1957.

EHRMAN, JOHN. *Grand Strategy* (Vols. V and VI), 1956.

These outstanding books cover the development of British—and Allied—strategy and policy.

RICHARDS, DENIS, and HILARY ST. G. SAUNDERS. *Royal Air Force, 1939-45,* 3 vols., 1954.

An official history of Royal Air Force operations throughout the world and the policy governing them.

ROSKILL, S. W. *The War at Sea, 1939-1945,* 2 vols., 1956.

Royal Navy operations throughout the war.

ANDERS, WLADYSLAW. *An Army in Exile.* London: Macmillan Co., 1949.

This proud book covers Hitler's invasion of Poland and subsequent Polish-Russian relations, as well as the service of Polish troops in the Middle East and Italy.

ASSMANN, KURT. *Deutsche Schicksalsjahre.* Wiesbaden, Germany: Eberhard Brockhaus, 1951.

A history of Germany's "years of trial."

AUPHAN, PAUL, and JACQUES MORDAL. *The French Navy in World War II.* Annapolis, Md.: The United States Naval Institute, 1959.

BALDWIN, HANSON W. *Great Mistakes of the War.* New York: Harper & Brothers, 1950.

BRYANT, ARTHUR. *The Turn of the Tide.* Garden City, N.Y.: Doubleday & Co., 1957.

The first of two parts of an admiring account of the services of Field Marshal Lord Alanbrooke, Chief of the Imperial General Staff—valuable for its intimate picture of the development of British and Allied policy and strategy.

BUCKLEY, CHRISTOPHER. *Five Ventures.* London: Her Majesty's Stationery Office, 1954.

Spirited accounts of five minor, but critical, campaigns: Iraq (1941), Syria (1941), Persia (1941), Madagascar (1942), and the Dodecanese (1943).

CHURCHILL, WINSTON. *The Second World War.* 6 vols. Boston: Houghton Mifflin Co., 1948-53.

Vol. I: *The Gathering Storm,* 1948.
Vol. II: *Their Finest Hour,* 1949.
Vol. III: *The Grand Alliance,* 1950.
Vol. IV: *The Hinge of Fate,* 1950.
Vol. V: *Closing the Ring,* 1951.
Vol. VI: *Triumph and Tragedy,* 1953.

These six books have the widest scope, greatest detail, and most interesting style of all the various general histories of World War II. You may disagree with the author's opinions and conclusions, but you will also find them stimulating.

CRAIG, GORDON A. *The Politics of the Prussian Army, 1640-1945.* New York: Oxford University Press, 1956.

This book furnishes an excellent review of how Adolf Hitler was able to be the first man to really break the German officers' corps to his will.

FEIS, HERBERT. *Churchill, Roosevelt, Stalin.* Princeton, N.J.: Princeton University Press, 1957.

The story of the British-American-Russian coalition, the ideas and purposes which motivated its members, its moderate successes, and its inevitable collapse.

FREIDIN, SEYMOUR, and WILLIAM RICHARDSON (ed.). *The Fatal Decisions.* New York: William Sloane Associates, 1956.

An analysis of Hitler's strategy and tactics by seven outstanding German commanders.

FREUND, GERALD. *Unholy Alliance.* New York: Harcourt, Brace & Co., 1957.

A record of the post–World War I cooperation between Germany and Russia in developing their respective armed forces.

GALLAND, ADOLF. *The First and the Last.* New York: Henry Holt & Co., 1954.

The rise and decline of the Luftwaffe fighter forces in World War II, including much material on German aircraft development and production.

GAVIN, JAMES M. *Airborne Warfare.* Washington, D.C.: Infantry Journal, 1947.

A terse, informative book which gives good descriptions—backed by small maps—of most of the airborne operations in World War II.

RECOMMENDED READING LIST

GILBERT, FELIX (ed.). *Hitler Directs His War.* New York: Oxford University Press, 1950.

Selected and annotated excerpts from the confidential records of Hitler's daily military conferences.

GOERLITZ, WALTER. *History of the German General Staff, 1657 to 1945.* New York: Frederick A. Praeger, 1952.

GUINGAND, SIR FRANCIS DE. *Operation Victory.* New York: Charles Scribner's Sons, 1947.

The author was Montgomery's chief of staff. He gives an interesting picture of both the British commander and his operations.

HIGGINS, TRUMBULL. *Winston Churchill and the Second Front, 1940-1943.* New York: Oxford University Press, 1957.

KEMP, P. K. *Key to Victory.* Boston: Little, Brown & Co., 1957.

A complete, well-written description of the role of the Royal Navy in World War II.

KENNEDY, SIR JOHN. *The Business of War.* New York: William Morrow & Co., 1958.

A blunt description of the high-level planning of World War II by a former assistant chief of the Imperial General Staff. It provides excellent depictions of Churchill in action; of the effects of politics, personalities, and inter-Allied relations upon strategy; and of the intractability of the American and Royal air forces.

KING, ERNEST J., and WALTER M. WHITEHILL. *Fleet Admiral King: A Naval Record.* New York: W. W. Norton & Co., 1952.

The war as seen from the viewpoint of the American chief of naval operations.

KINGSTON-MCCLOUGHRY, E. J. *The Direction of War.* New York: Frederick A. Praeger, 1955.

A critique of the political direction and high command in war, including valuable information on the organization and operation of SHAEF.

LEE, ASHER. *The German Air Force.* New York: Harper & Brothers, 1946.

LIDDELL HART, B. H. *The Other Side of the Hill.* London: Cassell and Co., 1948.

Comments on various phases of German World War II military operations by different German generals; useful because of the different types of warfare it includes. (Published in America as *The German Generals Talk.*)

MARSHALL, GEORGE C. *Report on the Army: Biennial Reports of General George C. Marshall, Chief of Staff of the United States Army, July 1, 1939, to June 30, 1943, to the Secretary of War.* Washington, D.C.: Infantry Journal, 1943.

————. *The Winning of the War in Europe and the Pacific: Biennial Report of the Chief of Staff of the United States Army, July 1, 1943, to June 30, 1945, to the Secretary of War.* New York: Simon and Schuster, 1945.

These books—actually official publications—give an excellent general background of American participation in World War II. They are especially valuable for their account of the initial American preparations.

MARTIENSSEN, ANTHONY. *Hitler and His Admirals.* New York: E. P. Dutton & Co., 1949.

MORISON, SAMUEL ELIOT. *Strategy and Compromise.* Boston: Little, Brown & Co., 1958.

A tough-minded little book on the development of Allied strategy, furnishing a realistic appraisal of the various conflicting pressures which affected Anglo-American planning, and of the compromises which these pressures made necessary.

PATTON, GEORGE S. *War As I Knew It.* Boston: Houghton Mifflin Co., 1947.

The rapid-paced story of a man who obviously liked to fight; contains some penetrating and forceful observations on leadership and the practical side of fighting a war.

PULESTON, WILLIAM D. *The Influence of Force in Foreign Relations* New York: D. Van Nostrand Co., 1955.

A version of World War II military-political relationships, emphasizing the influence of naval power.

ROSCOE, THEODORE. *United States Submarine Operations in World War II.* Annapolis, Md.: The United States Naval Institute, 1949.

ROSINSKI, HERBERT. *The German Army.* Washington, D.C.: Infantry Journal, 1944.

RUGE, FRIEDRICH. *Der Seekrieg: The German Navy's Story, 1939-1945.* Annapolis, Md.: The United States Naval Institute, 1957.

A general history of the naval side of World War II, showing the interaction of land and sea operations. It is particularly useful for its accounts of the development of the German Navy, the invasion of Norway, and the fighting along the Murmansk route to Russia.

SHULMAN, MILTON. *Defeat in the West.* New York: E. P. Dutton & Co., 1948.

Written by a former Canadian intelligence officer, this book was based on the interrogation of captured German officers and the study of German documents. Though further research has modified some of its conclusions, it remains valuable.

SKORZENY, OTTO. *Skorzeny's Secret Missions.* New York: E. P. Dutton & Co., 1951.

Among the various adventures herein described, the rescue of Mussolini and the Battle of the Bulge are particularly interesting.

TIPPELSKIRCH, KURT VON. *Geschichte das Zweiten Weltkriegs.* Bonn: Athenäum-Verlag, 1951.

A competent over-all German history of World War II.

TRUSCOTT, LUCIAN K. *Command Missions.* New York: E. P. Dutton & Co., 1954.

General Truscott's personal story of his experiences as a commander in North Africa, Italy, and France—a thoughtful book which discusses most of the major problems in troop leading and army administration. Also describes the organization of the Ranger battalions.

WILSON, SIR HENRY MAITLAND. *Eight Years Overseas.* London: Hutchinson and Co., 1948.

EARLY CAMPAIGNS

DEPARTMENT OF THE ARMY. Washington, D.C.: U.S. Government Printing Office.

KENNEDY, ROBERT M. *The German Campaign in Poland (1939),* 1955.

This is the best available history of the conquest of Poland.

BELGIAN MINISTRY OF FOREIGN AFFAIRS. *Belgium: The Official Account of What Happened, 1939-1940.* New York: Didier Publishers.

UNITED KINGDOM MILITARY SERIES. *History of the Second World War.* London: Her Majesty's Stationery Office.

COLLIER, BASIL. *The Defence of the United Kingdom,* 1957.

This book covers the entire war. Its accounts of the German V-1 and V-2 attacks are particularly good. Like all the British official histories, it is very well written and amply provided with maps.

DERRY, T. K. *The Campaign in Norway,* 1952.

ELLIS, L. F. *The War in France and Flanders, 1939-1940,* 1953.

Probably the best Allied account of this campaign.

NETHERLANDS GOVERNMENT INFORMATION BUREAU. London: Allen & Unwin.

DOORMAN, P. L. G. *Military Operations in the Netherlands,* 1944.

This short book covers the fall of the Netherlands in 1940.

BUCKLEY, CHRISTOPHER. *Greece and Crete, 1941.* London: Her Majesty's Stationery Office, 1952.

A sound semiofficial history.

FLEMING, PETER. *Operation Sea Lion.* New York: Simon and Schuster, 1957.

While not as completely documented as Wheatley's book of the same title, this is an excellent popular history, with much worth-while material on the British reaction to the German threat of invasion.

GREINER, HELMUTH. *Die Oberste Wehrmachtführung, 1939-1943.* Wiesbaden, Germany: Limes Verlag, 1951.

HUBATSCH, WALTHER. *Die Deutsche Besetzung von Dänemark und Norwegen, 1940.* Göttingen, Germany: Wissenschaftlicher Verlag, 1952.

LANGDON-DAVIES, JOHN. *Invasion in the Snow.* Boston: Houghton Mifflin Co., 1941.

A good popular account of the Soviet-Finnish War.

PERTINAX. *The Gravediggers of France.* Garden City, N.Y.: Doubleday, Doran & Co., 1944.

A study of the reasons for France's sudden collapse, with character studies of the leading French figures, civil and military, who contributed to it.

ROBERTSON, TERENCE. *Channel Dash.* New York: E. P. Dutton & Co., 1958.

The dash of three German warships through the English Channel from Brest to Germany in February, 1942. It reads like a detective thriller, but is excellent historical writing.

SMYTH, SIR JOHN. *Before the Dawn.* London: Cassell and Co., 1957.

A good personal account of the preliminary operations of the B.E.F. and of the withdrawal through Dunkirk.

SPEARS, SIR EDWARD. *Assignment to Catastrophe.* 2 vols. New York: A. A. Wyn, 1954-55.

The story of Churchill's representative to the French government. General Spears loved France, and he wrote a clear, detailed account of how France fell.

TAYLOR, TELFORD. *The March of Conquest: The German Victories in Western Europe, 1940.* New York: Simon and Schuster, 1958.

A new, carefully researched history of the German victories during 1940. It gives an excellent description of the German armed forces of that period.

WEYGAND, MAXINE. *Recalled to Service.* Garden City, N.Y.: Doubleday & Co., 1952.

WHEATLEY, RONALD. *Operation Sea Lion.* Oxford: Oxford University Press, 1958.

An excellent book, based on original documentary evidence, describing the development of the German plan for the invasion of England, its relationship to Hitler's over-all strategy, and the reasons for its abandonment.

THE WAR IN EASTERN EUROPE

OFFICE OF THE CHIEF OF MILITARY HISTORY. *The United States Army in World War II.* Washington, D.C.: U.S. Government Printing Office.

VAIL MOTTER, T. H. *The Middle East Theater: The Persian Corridor and Aid to Russia,* 1952.

DEPARTMENT OF THE ARMY. *Historical Study: The German Campaign in Russia—Planning and Operations (1940-1942).* Washington, D.C.: U.S. Government Printing Office, 1955.

This pamphlet—prepared, unavoidably, largely from German sources—is very well done and is undoubtedly the most reliable reference work on the Eastern Front.

ANDERS, WLADYSLAW. *Hitler's Defeat in Russia.* Chicago: Henry Regnery Co., 1953.

The author had a bitterly acquired knowledge of Russia, but his sources concerning the actual fighting are all second- or third-hand.

RECOMMENDED READING LIST

BLUMENTRITT, GUENTHER. *Von Rundstedt.* London: Odhams Press, 1952.

DEANE, JOHN R. *The Strange Alliance.* New York: The Viking Press, 1947.
> The author was head of the American military mission to Russia, 1943-45. As such, he was given little opportunity to observe actual operations, but received an extensive education in the problem of doing business with the Russians.

GARTHOFF, RAYMOND L. *Soviet Military Doctrine.* Glencoe, Ill.: The Free Press, 1953.
> An outstanding postwar study of Russian military doctrine, its origins, and its actual application. Based largely on Russian sources, it is an excellent reference for the Russian armed forces of World War II.

GUDERIAN, HEINZ. *Panzer Leader.* New York: E. P. Dutton & Co., 1952.
> Contains a valuable account of Hitler's 1941 invasion of Russia.

GUILLAUME, AUGUSTIN. *Soviet Arms and Soviet Power.* Washington, D.C.: Infantry Journal, 1949.
> An attempt to explain Russian methods of warfare during World War II and to outline the history of that war on the Eastern Front. Most of the author's material was drawn from official Russian sources and is therefore probably exaggerated and possibly false. His own conclusions, however, are shrewd and interesting.

JACKSON. W. G. F. *Seven Roads to Moscow.* New York: Philosophical Library, 1958.
> A historical review of the various invasions of Russia.

LÉDERREY. *La Défaite Allemande a l'Est.* Paris: Charles-Lavanzelle & Co., 1951.

LEE, ASHER. *The Soviet Air Force.* New York: Harper & Brothers, 1950.

LIDDELL HART, B. H. (ed.). *The Red Army.* New York: Harcourt, Brace & Co., 1956.
> A study of the development and characteristics of the Russian Army, drawn from a variety of sources.

MANSTEIN, ERICH VON. *Lost Victories.* Chicago: Henry Regnery Co., 1958.
> The author was probably the ablest German commander in World War II. His book appears highly objective; its analysis of Hitler is excellent.

MELLENTHIN, F. W. VON. *Panzer Battles.* Norman, Okla.: University of Oklahoma Press, 1956.
> This book covers German armored operations in Poland, Flanders and France, the Balkans, North Africa, Russia, and the Bulge. His service on the Eastern Front began with Stalingrad and ended with the stabilization of the Vistula front in late 1944.

SAUNDERS, M. G. *The Soviet Navy.* New York: Frederick A. Praeger, 1958.

SAYRE, JOEL. *Persian Gulf Command.* New York: Random House, 1945.
> A short, popular account of this important link in the chain of Lend-Lease deliveries.

SCHRÖTER, HEINZ. *Stalingrad.* New York: E. P. Dutton & Co., 1958.
> The author was a war correspondent with the German Sixth Army; he claims to have based this book on official German documents.

TOEPKE, GÜNTER. *Stalingrad.* Stade: Kogge Verlag, 1949.

THE WAR IN WESTERN EUROPE

OFFICE OF THE CHIEF OF MILITARY HISTORY. *The United States Army in World War II: The European Theater of Operations.* Washington, D.C.: U.S. Government Printing Office.
Ardennes Campaign (in preparation).
Breakout and Pursuit (in preparation).

COLE, H. M. *The Lorraine Campaign,* 1950.

HARRISON, GORDON A. *Cross-Channel Attack,* 1951.
> This gripping book is a military classic, combining careful organization with imaginative writing.

The Last Offensive (in preparation).

POGUE, FORREST C. *The Supreme Command,* 1954.

RUPPENTHAL, ROLAND G. *Logistical Support of the Armies* (Vol. I), 1953. (Vol. II is in preparation.)

Siegfried Line Campaign (in preparation).

Southern France and Alsace (in preparation).

OFFICE OF AIR FORCE HISTORY. *The Army Air Forces in World War II,* ed. Wesley F. Craven and James L. Cate. Chicago: University of Chicago Press.
Vol. I: *Plans and Early Operations,* 1948.
Vol. II: *Europe: Torch to Pointblank, August 1942 to December 1943,* 1949.
Vol. III: *Argument to V-E Day, January 1944 to May 1945,* 1951.

MORISON, SAMUEL ELIOT. *The Atlantic Battle Won.* Boston: Little, Brown & Co., 1956.

————. *The Battle of the Atlantic.* Boston: Little Brown & Co., 1948.

————. *The Invasion of France and Germany.* Boston: Little, Brown & Co., 1957.

DEPARTMENT OF NATIONAL DEFENSE. *Official History of the Canadian Army in the Second World War.* Ottawa: Queen's Printer.
STACEY, C. P. *Six Years of War,* 1955.
> Has excellent descriptions of Dieppe and other pre-invasion raids launched by Canadian troops from Britain.

BRADLEY, OMAR N. *A Soldier's Story.* New York: Henry Holt & Co., 1951.

EISENHOWER, DWIGHT D. *Crusade in Europe.* Garden City, N.Y.: Doubleday & Co., 1948.
> The invasion of Europe as described by the Allied Supreme Commander; valuable as an account of why and how things were done.

HARRIS, SIR ARTHUR. *Bomber Offensive.* New York: Macmillan Co., 1947.

HECHLER, KEN. *The Bridge at Remagen.* New York: Ballantine Books, 1957.
> An extremely good depiction of this crucial event from both the American and German viewpoints.

HOWARTH, DAVID. *D-Day: The Sixth of June, 1944.* New York: McGraw-Hill Book Co., 1959.
> D-Day, told from the viewpoints of various leaders whose courage and decision went far toward making the difference between success and defeat on Omaha Beach.

JOHNS, GLOVER S., JR. *The Clay Pigeons of St. Lô.* Harrisburg, Pa.: Military Service Publishing Co.
> The story of the American infantry battalion which took—and held—St. Lô.

LATTRE DE TASSIGNY, JEAN DE. *The History of the French First Army.* London: Allen & Unwin, 1952.
> The story of the French contribution to the invasion and liberation of southern France.

LEIGH, RANDOLPH. *48 Million Tons to Eisenhower.* Washington, D.C.: Infantry Journal, 1945.
> An interesting popular history of the Service of Supply.

MARSHALL, S. L. A. *Bastogne: The Story of the First Eight Days.* Washington, D.C.: Infantry Journal, 1946.

MERRIAM, ROBERT L. *Dark December.* New York: Ziff-Davis Publishing Co., 1947.
> A good popular account of the Battle of the Bulge.

MONTGOMERY, BERNARD L. *Normandy to the Baltic.* Boston: Houghton Mifflin Co., 1948.
> Montgomery's version of the campaign in Western Europe.

MORGAN, SIR FREDERICK. *Overture to Overlord.* Garden City, N.Y.: Doubleday & Co., 1950.
> A description of the preliminary planning that was necessary to mount the Anglo-American invasion of Europe.

NORTH, JOHN. *North-West Europe, 1944-5.* London: Her Majesty's Stationery Office, 1953.
> Another of the excellent British semiofficial histories, this one covering the operations of the 21st Army Group.

SPEIDEL, HANS. *Invasion 1944.* Chicago: Henry Regnery Co., 1950.
> An account of the Anglo-American landing in Normandy by Rommel's chief of staff. Includes valuable material on German command problems.

THOMPSON, R. W. *At Whatever Cost.* New York: Coward-McCann, 1957.
> A detailed, well-written report of the Dieppe Raid and of the lessons learned from its failure.

TURNER, JOHN F. *Invasion '44.* New York: G. P. Putnam's Sons, 1959.
> This book is useful for its coverage of the British landings on D-Day.

URQUHART, R. E. *Arnhem.* London: Cassell and Co., 1958.
> A well-written account of a daring operation which almost succeeded.

WESTPHAL, SIEGFRIED. *The German Army in the West.* London: Cassell and Co., 1951.
> The author was chief of staff to Rommel in Africa, to Kesselring in Italy, and to Rundstedt in France.

WILMOT, CHESTER. *The Struggle for Europe.* New York: Harper & Brothers, 1952.
> One of the best histories of operations in Western Europe. Written from the English viewpoint, it nevertheless presents a balanced, generally impartial account.

THE WAR IN NORTH AFRICA

OFFICE OF THE CHIEF OF MILITARY HISTORY. *The United States Army in World War II.* Washington, D.C.: U.S. Government Printing Office.
HOWE, GEORGE F. *The Mediterranean Theater of Operations: Northwest Africa: Seizing the Initiative in the West,* 1957.
> Highly accurate, comprehensive, and really readable.

MORISON, SAMUEL ELIOT. *Operations in North African Waters.* Boston: Little, Brown & Co., 1947.

UNITED KINGDOM MILITARY SERIES. *History of the Second World War.* London: Her Majesty's Stationery Office.
HARRIS, C. R. S. *Allied Military Administration of Italy, 1943-1945,* 1957.
PLAYFAIR, I. S. O. *The Mediterranean and the Middle East* (Vols. I and II), 1954-56.
> These two excellent volumes cover operations in this area (including East Africa) through the middle of 1941. Further volumes of this authoritative series will be forthcoming.

AUSTRALIAN WAR MEMORIAL. Canberra, Australia: The Advertiser Printing Office.
LONG, GAVIN. *To Benghazi,* 1952.
> The first volume of the Australian Army's official World War II history, covering Australian mobilization and preliminary operations in North Africa.

BARCLAY, C. N. *Against Great Odds.* London: Sifton Praed and Co., 1955.
> The story of the first British offensive in Libya, 1940-41.

COWLES, VIRGINIA. *The Phantom Major.* New York: Harper & Brothers, 1958.
> A popular account of the operations of the British Secret Air Service in North Africa.

RECOMMENDED READING LIST

CUNNINGHAM, ANDREW B. *A Sailor's Odyssey.* New York: E. P. Dutton & Co., 1951.
> The autobiography of the Allied naval commander in the Mediterranean.

MONTGOMERY, BERNARD L. *El Alamein to the River Sangro.* New York: E. P. Dutton & Co., 1949.

SCHMIDT, HEINZ W. *With Rommel in the Desert.* London: George G. Harrup and Co., 1951.
> Written by a member of Rommel's staff, this book gives a realistic picture of desert warfare.

CAMPAIGNS IN ITALY and SICILY

OFFICE OF THE CHIEF OF MILITARY HISTORY. *The United States Army in World War II: The Mediterranean Theater.* Washington, D.C.: U.S. Government Printing Office.
The Advance to the Alps (in preparation).
The Drive on Rome (in preparation).
Salerno to Cassino (in preparation).
Sicily: The Surrender of Italy (in preparation).
The Strategic and Logistical History: Mediterranean Theater of Operations (in preparation).

MORISON, SAMUEL ELIOT. *Sicily-Salerno-Anzio.* Boston: Little, Brown & Co., 1954.

DEPARTMENT OF NATIONAL DEFENSE. *Official History of the Canadian Army in the Second World War.* Ottawa: Queen's Printer.
NICHOLSON, C. W. L. *The Canadians in Italy,* 1957.

BADOGLIO, PIETRO. *Italy in the Second World War.* London: Oxford University Press, 1948.

CLARK, MARK W. *Calculated Risk.* New York: Harper & Brothers, 1950.

COCCHIA, ALDO. *The Hunters and the Hunted.* Annapolis, Md.: The United States Naval Institute, 1958.
> A history of the Italian Navy in World War II, interesting for its description of the effective Italian "human torpedoes."

LINKLATER, ERIC. *The Campaign in Italy.* London: Her Majesty's Stationery Office, 1951.
> An excellent semiofficial British military history, one of a series being produced pending the completion of the official histories. At present, this book is probably the best account available of this campaign.

MAJDALANY, FRED. *The Battle of Cassino.* Boston: Houghton Mifflin Co., 1957.
> One of the best books on World War II—the gripping, detailed story of the successive attempts to take a little Italian hill town.

MONTGOMERY, BERNARD L. *El Alamein to the River Sangro.* New York: E. P. Dutton & Co., 1949.

THE WAR WITH JAPAN

OFFICE OF THE CHIEF OF MILITARY HISTORY. *The United States Army in World War II.* Washington, D.C.: U.S. Government Printing Office.

The China-Burma-India Theater:
ROMANUS, CHARLES F., and RILEY SUNDERLAND. *Stilwell's Mission to China,* 1953.
———. *Stilwell's Command Problems,* 1956.
———. *Time Runs Out in the CBI* (in preparation).

The Technical Services:
STAUFFER, ALVIN P. *The Quartermaster Corps: Operations in the War Against Japan,* 1956.

The War in the Pacific:
APPLEMAN, ROY E., JAMES M. BURNS, and RUSSELL A. GUGELER. *Okinawa: The Last Battle,* 1948.
The Campaign in the Marianas (in preparation).

CANNON, M. HAMLIN. *Leyte: The Return to the Philippines,* 1954.
Cartwheel: The Reduction of Rabaul (in preparation).
CROWL, PHILIP A., and EDMUND G. LOVE. *Seizure of the Gilberts and Marshalls,* 1955.
MILLER, JOHN, JR. *Guadalcanal: The First Offensive,* 1949.
MILNER, SAMUEL. *Victory in Papua,* 1957.
MORTON, LOUIS. *The Fall of the Philippines,* 1953.
> One of the best of the official histories so far published; a very outspoken analysis of the reasons for the American defeat.

SMITH, ROBERT R. *The Approach to the Philippines,* 1953.
Strategy and Command (2 vols. in preparation).
Triumph in the Philippines (in preparation).

OFFICE OF AIR FORCE HISTORY. *The Army Air Forces in World War II,* ed. Wesley F. Craven and James L. Cate. Chicago: University of Chicago Press.
Vol. I: *Plans and Early Operations,* 1948.
Vol IV: *The Pacific—Guadalcanal to Saipan, August 1942 to July 1944,* 1950.
Vol. V: *The Pacific—Matterhorn to Nagasaki, June 1944 to August 1945,* 1953.

HISTORICAL BRANCH, HEADQUARTERS, U.S. MARINE CORPS. *History of the U.S. Marine Corps Operations in World War II.* Washington, D.C.: U.S. Government Printing Office.
HOUGH, FRANK O., VERLE E. LUDWIG, and HENRY I. SHAW, JR. *Pearl Harbor to Guadalcanal,* 1958.
> This is Vol. I of the final Marine Corps official history, which is being prepared through the revision and correction of earlier publications such as those listed below:

BARTLEY, WHITMAN S. *Iwo Jima: Amphibious Epic,* 1954.
BOGGS, CHARLES W., JR. *Marine Aviation in the Philippines,* 1951.
HEINL, ROBERT D., JR., and JOHN A. CROWN. *The Marshalls: Increasing the Tempo,* 1954.
HOFFMAN, CARL W. *The Seizure of Tinian,* 1951.
HOUGH, FRANK O., and JOHN A. CROWN. *The Campaign on New Britain,* 1952.
LODGE, O. R. *The Recapture of Guam,* 1954.
NICHOLS, CHARLES S., JR., and HENRY I. SHAW, JR. *Okinawa: Victory in the Pacific,* 1955.
RENTZ, JOHN N. *Marines in the Central Solomons,* 1952.

MORISON, SAMUEL ELIOT. *Aleutians, Gilberts, and Marshalls.* Boston: Little, Brown & Co., 1951.
———. *Breaking the Bismarcks Barrier.* Boston: Little, Brown & Co., 1950.
———. *Coral Sea, Midway, and Submarine Actions.* Boston: Little, Brown & Co., 1949.
———. *Leyte.* Boston: Little, Brown & Co., 1958.
———. *New Guinea and the Marianas.* Boston: Little, Brown & Co., 1953.
———. *The Rising Sun in the Pacific.* Boston: Little, Brown & Co., 1948.
> This volume is especially valuable for its unsparing account of Pearl Harbor.

———. *The Struggle for Guadalcanal.* Boston: Little, Brown & Co., 1950.

DEPARTMENT OF NATIONAL DEFENSE. *Official History of the Canadian Army in the Second World War.* Ottawa: Queen's Printer.
STACEY, C. P. *Six Years of War,* 1955.
> This volume contains fine accounts of Canadian participation in the defense of Hong Kong and in operations in the Aleutian Islands.

UNITED KINGDOM MILITARY SERIES. *History of the Second World War.* London: Her Majesty's Stationery Office.
DONNISON, F. S. V. *British Military Administration in the Far East, 1943-46,* 1956.
KIRBY, S. WOODBURN. *The War Against Japan* (Vols. I and II), 1957-58.
> Vol. I deals with the initial Japanese victories—Hong Kong, Malaya, Singapore, and the Netherlands East Indies. Vol. II covers the loss of Burma and operations in the Pacific through September, 1943.

AUSTRALIAN WAR MEMORIAL. Canberra, Australia: The Advertiser Printing Office.
WIGMORE, LIONEL. *The Japanese Thrust,* 1957.

Official History of New Zealand in the Second World War, 1939-45. Wellington, N.Z.: Government Printer.
GILLESPIE, OLIVER A. *The Pacific,* 1952.

CARTER, WORRALL R., and ELMER E. DUVALL. *Ships, Salvage, and Sinews of War.* Washington, D.C.: U.S. Government Printing Office, 1954.
> The story of fleet logistics in Atlantic and Mediterranean waters.

EICHELBERGER, ROBERT L. *Our Jungle Road to Tokyo.* New York: The Viking Press, 1950.

FIELD, JAMES A., JR. *The Japanese at Leyte Gulf.* Princeton, N.J.: Princeton University Press, 1947.

FEIS, HERBERT. *The China Tangle.* Princeton, N.J.: Princeton University Press, 1953.

FUCHIDA, MITSUO, and MASATAKE OKUMIYA. *Midway: The Battle That Doomed Japan.* Annapolis, Md.: The United States Naval Institute, 1955.
> The Japanese Navy's version of this decisive battle.

HALSEY, WILLIAM F., and J. BRYAN, III. *Admiral Halsey's Story.* New York: McGraw-Hill Book Co., 1947.

INOGUCHI, RIKIHEI, and TADASHI NAKAJIMA. *The Divine Wind.* Annapolis, Md.: The United States Naval Institute, 1958.
> The Japanese history of the Kamikaze Force.

ISELY, JETER A., and PHILIP A. CROWL. *The U.S. Marines and Amphibious War.* Princeton, N.J.: Princeton University Press, 1951.
> This book covers the Marine Corps' prewar experimentation in and development of amphibious tactics, techniques, and equipment.

KENNEY, GEORGE C. *General Kenney Reports: A Personal History of the Pacific War.* New York: Duell, Sloan & Pearce, 1949.

KRUEGER, WALTER. *From Down Under to Nippon.* Washington, D.C.: Combat Forces Press, 1953.
> A good personal account by the commander who led the main attack northward against Japan.

LORD, WALTER. *Day of Infamy.* New York: Henry Holt & Co., 1957.
> A detailed, exciting account of the Japanese attack on Pearl Harbor, with its major emphasis on the reactions of various servicemen and civilians to the sudden crisis.

OGBURN, CHARLTON, JR. *The Marauders.* New York: Harper & Brothers, 1959.
> The history of "Merrill's Marauders"; one of the most gripping World War II books yet written.

OKUMIYA, MASATAKE, and JIRO HORIKOSHI. *Zero.* New York: E. P. Dutton & Co., 1956.
> One of the best general Japanese accounts of World War II, covering Japanese air operations from 1937 through 1945.

PERCIVAL, A. E. *The War in Malaya.* London: Eyre and Spottiswoode, 1949.
> The story of the fall of Malaya and Singapore, written by the defeated British commander.

RECOMMENDED READING LIST

PRATT, FLETCHER. *The Marines' War.* New York: William Sloane Associates, 1948.
   A breezy, popular history in Pratt's best style.

SAKAI, SABURO, and MARTIN CAIDIN. *Samurai!* New York: E. P. Dutton & Co., 1958.
   A vivid description of the Japanese Naval Air Force in World War II by the greatest surviving Japanese fighter pilot.

SHERMAN, FREDERICK C. *Combat Command: The American Aircraft Carriers in the Pacific War.* New York: E. P. Dutton & Co., 1950.

SHERROD, ROBERT. *History of Marine Corps Aviation in World War II.* Washington, D.C.: Combat Forces Press, 1952.

SLIM, SIR WILLIAM. *Defeat into Victory.* London: Cassell and Co., 1956.
   Allied operations in Burma, 1942-45; the best over-all history of the Burmese campaigns yet published. Slim is a thorough soldier, deeply interested in the problems of leadership.

SMITH, HOLLAND M., and PERCY FINCH. *Coral and Brass.* New York: Charles Scribner's Sons, 1949.
   The blunt story of an outspoken Marine general.

SMYTH, SIR JOHN. *Before the Dawn.* London: Cassell and Co., 1957.
   A good account of the first, disastrous days of the war in Burma.

STILWELL, JOSEPH. *The Stilwell Papers.* New York: William Sloane Associates, 1948.
   The graphic, hard-bitten account of a "doughboy general" who never learned to suffer fools, gladly or otherwise.

TAYLOR, THEODORE. *The Magnificent Mitscher.* New York: W. W. Norton & Co., 1954.

TREFOUSSE, HANS L. (ed.). *What Happened at Pearl Harbor.* New York: Twayne Publishers, 1958.
   A collection of basic documents pertaining to the Japanese attack on Pearl Harbor.

WAINWRIGHT, JONATHAN M. *General Wainwright's Story.* Garden City, N.Y.: Doubleday & Co., 1946.

WILLOUGHBY, CHARLES A., and JOHN CHAMBERLAIN. *MacArthur, 1941-1951.* New York: McGraw-Hill Book Co., 1954.
   Written by a staff officer and devoted admirer of General MacArthur, this book is a strictly partisan account of MacArthur's views and operations.

WOODWARD, C. VANN. *The Battle for Leyte Gulf.* New York: Macmillan Co., 1947.

MEMOIRS, BIOGRAPHIES, and AUTOBIOGRAPHIES

ARNOLD, HENRY H. *Global Mission.* New York: Harper & Brothers, 1949.
   The history of the United States Air Force, as reflected in the life of the author.

BRERETON, LEWIS H. *Brereton Diaries.* New York: William Morrow & Co., 1946.
   General Brereton served in the Pacific, Middle East, and Europe during World War II and therefore had an unusually wide variety of experiences.

KESSELRING, ALBERT. *Kesselring: A Soldier's Record.* New York: William Morrow & Co., 1954.

LEAHY, WILLIAM D. *I Was There.* New York: McGraw-Hill Book Co., 1950.
   The memoirs of Roosevelt's personal chief of staff, who was present at all of the major policy-making conferences of the period.

LEE, CLARK, and RICHARD HENSCHEL. *Douglas MacArthur.* New York: Henry Holt & Co., 1952.

LIDDELL HART, B. H. (ed.). *The Rommel Papers.* New York: Harcourt, Brace & Co., 1953.
   Rommel's own account of World War II, plus an interesting biography and a number of sidelights on how Hitler ruled Europe.

MANNERHEIM, CARL G. E. VON. *Memoirs of Marshal Mannerheim.* New York: E. P. Dutton & Co., 1954.

MONTGOMERY, BERNARD L. *The Memoirs of Field-Marshal the Viscount Montgomery of Alamein, K.G.* New York: The World Publishing Co., 1958.
   A cheerfully opinionated book, presenting the uninhibited opinions of an experienced soldier who was usually more or less at odds with his superiors.

RIDGWAY, MATTHEW B. *Soldier.* New York: Harper & Brothers, 1956.
   This book contains valuable accounts of World War II airborne operations.

BLUMENTRITT, GUENTHER. *Von Rundstedt.* London: Odhams Press, 1952.

SALISBURY-JONES, SIR GUY. *So Full a Glory.* New York: Frederick A. Praeger, 1955.
   An admiring biography of Marshal de Lattre de Tassigny, soldier of France.

YOUNG, DESMOND. *Rommel.* London: Collins, 1950.
   The biography of an expert and dedicated German master of armored warfare, as seen by an admiring enemy.

SOLDIER LIFE, STATISTICAL and TECHNICAL REFERENCES

OFFICE OF THE CHIEF OF MILITARY HISTORY. *The United States Army in World War II: The Technical Services.* Washington, D.C.: U.S. Government Printing Office.
   The Chemical Corps (3 vols. in preparation).
   COLL, BLANCHE D., JEAN E. KEITH, and HERBERT H. ROSENTHAL. *The Corps of Engineers: Troops and Equipment,* 1958. (Three more volumes are in preparation.)
   The Medical Department, 1 vol.
   The Ordnance Department, 1 vol. (Two more volumes are in preparation.)
   The Quartermaster Corps, 3 vols. (A fourth volume is in preparation.)
   The Signal Corps, 2 vols. (A third volume is in preparation.)
   The Transportation Corps, 3 vols.

OFFICE OF AIR FORCE HISTORY. *The Army Air Forces in World War II,* ed. Wesley F. Craven and James L. Cate. Chicago: University of Chicago Press.
   Vol. VII: *Men and Planes,* 1958.
   This volume is recommended for its descriptions of the various types of American aircraft.

BARNES, G. M. *Weapons of World War II.* New York: D. Van Nostrand Co., 1947.
   Good pictures and specifications of American weapons and ammunition; the accompanying text is weakened by indiscriminate praise given to all of them.

BAXTER, JAMES P. *Scientists Against Time.* Boston: Little, Brown & Co., 1946.
   A description of the work of the Office of Scientific Research and Development and its contribution to the Allied victory.

DORNBERGER, WALTER. *V-2.* New York: The Viking Press, 1954.
   The author was the commanding officer of the Peenemünde Rocket Research Institute.

GREY, CARL R. *Railroading in Eighteen Countries.* New York: Charles Scribner's Sons, 1955.
   The story of the Military Railway Service.

LAURENCE, WILLIAM L. *Dawn Over Zero: The Story of the Atomic Bomb.* New York: Alfred A. Knopf, 1946.

MACDONALD, CHARLES B. *Company Commander.* Washington, D.C.: Infantry Journal, 1947.
   Written by an infantry company commander on the Western Front, this book captures the atmosphere of battle and the weight of responsibility which the small-unit commander must carry.

NELSON, DONALD M. *Arsenal of Democracy.* New York: Harcourt, Brace & Co., 1946.
   The story of American war production.

THE KOREAN WAR

OFFICE OF THE CHIEF OF MILITARY HISTORY, DEPARTMENT OF THE ARMY. Washington, D.C.: U.S. Government Printing Office, 1952.
   MILLER, JOHN, JR., OWEN J. CARROLL, and MARGARET E. TACKLEY. *Korea: 1951-1953.*
   WARD, ORLANDO. *Korea, 1950.*
   These are preliminary accounts, largely pictorial in nature, which make no pretense of being a final history. They are, however, about the best general histories as yet available.

MONTROSS, LYNN, and NICHOLAS A. CANZONA. *U.S. Marine Operations in Korea, 1950-1953.* 3 vols. Washington, D.C.: U.S. Government Printing Office, 1954-57.
   A detailed, well-documented official account of Marine operations, ending with the Hungnam evacuation.

BARCLAY, C. N. *The First Commonwealth Division.* Aldershot, England: Gale & Polden, 1954.
   A typically well-written British work on the service of Commonwealth troops in Korea.

CAGLE, MALCOLM W., and FRANK A. MANSON. *The Sea War in Korea.* Annapolis, Md.: The United States Naval Institute, 1957.
   A complete and interesting account of Navy operations during the Korean War—everything from single whaleboat raids to major operations.

CLARK, MARK W. *From the Danube to the Yalu.* New York: Harper & Brothers, 1954.

DEAN, WILLIAM F., and WILLIAM L. WORDEN. *General Dean's Story.* New York: The Viking Press, 1954.

GUGELER, RUSSELL A. *Combat Actions in Korea.* Washington, D.C.: Combat Forces Press, 1954.
   A collection of accounts describing interesting and instructive small-unit actions.

KARIG, WALTER, MALCOLM W. CAGLE, and FRANK A. MANSON. *Battle Report: The War in Korea.* New York: Rinehart & Co., 1952.
   An early account, based on official Navy records.

LINKLATER, ERIC. *Our Men in Korea.* London: Her Majesty's Stationery Office, 1952.

MARSHALL, S. L. A. *The River and the Gauntlet.* New York: William Morrow & Co., 1953.
   The well-told story of the defeat of the Eighth Army by the Chinese Communists in November, 1950.

———. *Pork Chop Hill.* New York: William Morrow & Co., 1956.
   Excellent descriptions of the fight for Pork Chop Hill and of six small-unit actions.

MILLIS, WALTER. *Arms and the State.* New York: The Twentieth Century Fund, 1958.
   This book includes a good review of American civil-military relations during the Korean War.

POATS, RUTHERFORD M. *Decision in Korea.* New York: Robert M. McBride Co., 1954.
   An excellent popular history of the Korean War.

RIDGWAY, MATTHEW B. *Soldier.* New York: Harper & Brothers, 1956.

THOMAS, R. C. W. *The War in Korea: 1950-1953.* Aldershot, England: Gale & Polden, 1954.

VATCHER, WILLIAM H., JR. *Panmunjom.* New York: Frederick A. Praeger, 1958.
   A detailed review of the truce negotiations, demonstrating how the Communists apply Clausewitz's teachings in their version of diplomacy.

RECOMMENDED READING LIST

WESTOVER, JOHN G. *Combat Support in Korea.* Washington, D.C.: Combat Forces Press, 1955.
 The missions and functions of the various services in support of the combat troops, taken from actual experiences in the field in Korea.

THE FUTURE OF WARFARE

For those interested in further reading, the following representative books on the future of warfare are offered without comment.

BRODIE, BERNARD. *Air Strategy in a Nuclear Age.* Princeton, N.J.: Princeton University Press, 1958.

BUSH, VANNEVAR. *Modern Arms and Free Men.* New York: Simon and Schuster, 1949.

COX, DONALD, and MICHAEL STOIKO. *Spacepower.* Philadelphia: The John C. Winston Co., 1958.

DAUGHERTY, WILLIAM E., and MORRIS JANOWITZ. *A Psychological Warfare Casebook.* Baltimore: The Johns Hopkins Press, 1958.

DINERSTEIN, H. S. *War and the Soviet Union.* New York: Frederick A. Praeger, 1959.

ELIOT, GEORGE F. *Victory Without War, 1958-1961.* Annapolis, Md.: The United States Naval Institute, 1958.

GARTHOFF, RAYMOND L. *Soviet Strategy in the Nuclear Age.* New York: Frederick A. Praeger, 1958.

GAVIN, JAMES M. *War and Peace in the Space Age.* New York: Harper & Brothers, 1958.

HUNTINGTON, SAMUEL P. *The Soldier and the State.* Cambridge, Mass.: Harvard University Press, 1957.

KAUFMANN, WILLIAM W. *Military Policy and National Security.* Princeton, N.J.: Princeton University Press, 1956.

KINGSTON-MCCLOUGHRY, E. J. *Global Strategy.* New York: Frederick A. Praeger, 1957.

————. *The Direction of War.* New York: Frederick A. Praeger, 1955.

KINTNER, WILLIAM R. *Forging a New Sword.* New York: Harper & Brothers, 1958.

KISSINGER, HENRY A. *Nuclear Weapons and Foreign Policy.* New York: Harper & Brothers, 1957.

LEE, ASHER (ed.). *The Soviet Air and Rocket Forces.* New York: Frederick A. Praeger, 1959.

LEY, WILLY. *Rockets, Missiles, and Space Travel.* New York: The Viking Press, 1958.

LINEBARGER, PAUL M. A. *Psychological Warfare.* Washington, D.C.: Combat Forces Press, 1954.

LOOSBROCK, JOHN F. (ed.). *Space Weapons.* New York: Frederick A. Praeger, 1959.

MARSHALL, S. L. A. *Sinai Victory.* New York: William Morrow & Co., 1958.

————. *Men Against Fire.* New York: William Morrow & Co., 1947.

MATAXIS, THEODORE C., and SEYMOUR L. GOLDBERG. *Nuclear Tactics.* Harrisburg, Pa.: Military Service Publishing Co., 1958.

MIKSCHE, F. O. *Atomic Weapons and Armies.* New York: Frederick A. Praeger, 1955.

————. *The Failure of Atomic Strategy.* New York: Frederick A. Praeger, 1959.

OSGOOD, ROBERT E. *Limited War: The Challenge to American Strategy.* Chicago: University of Chicago Press, 1957.

PARSON, NELS A., JR. *Guided Missiles in War and Peace.* Cambridge, Mass.: Harvard University Press, 1958.

PLATT, WASHINGTON. *Strategic Intelligence Production.* New York: Frederick A. Praeger, 1957.

REINHARDT, GEORGE C. *American Strategy in the Atomic Age.* Norman, Okla.: University of Oklahoma Press, 1955.

————, and W. R. KINTNER. *Atomic Weapons in Land Combat.* Harrisburg, Pa.: Military Service Publishing Co., 1953.

RIGG, ROBERT B. *War—1974.* Harrisburg, Pa.: Military Service Publishing Co., 1958.

SAUNDERS, M. G. (ed.). *The Soviet Navy.* New York: Frederick A. Praeger, 1958.

SLESSOR, SIR JOHN C. *Strategy for the West.* New York: William Morrow & Co., 1954.

————. *The Great Deterrent.* New York: Frederick A. Praeger, 1957.

WORLEY, MARVIN L., JR. *A Digest of New Developments in Army Weapons, Tactics, Organization, and Equipment.* Harrisburg, Pa.: Military Service Publishing Co., 1958.

SELECTED LIST OF RECENT BOOKS (1959–63)

WORLD WAR I

FALLS, CYRIL. *The Great War.* New York: G. P. Putnam's Sons, 1959.

HORNE, ALISTAIR. *The Price of Glory: Verdun 1916.* New York: St Martin's Press, 1963.

O'CONNOR, RICHARD. *Black Jack Pershing.* Garden City, N.Y.: Doubleday & Co., 1961.

PITT, BARRIE. *1918: The Last Act.* New York: W. W. Norton & Co., Inc., 1963.

ROBINSON, DOUGLAS H. *The Zeppelin in Combat.* London: G. T. Foulis & Co., 1962.

STALLINGS, LAWRENCE. *The Doughboys.* New York: Harper & Row, 1963.

TRASK, DAVID F. *The United States in the Supreme War Council.* Middletown, Conn.: Wesleyan University Press, 1961.

WATT, RICHARD M. *Dare Call It Treason.* New York: Simon and Schuster, 1963.

WORLD WAR II

DIVINE, ARTHUR D. *The Nine Days of Dunkirk.* New York: W. W. Norton & Co., 1959.

FALK, STANLEY L. *Bataan: The March of Death.* New York: W. W. Norton & Co., 1962.

HUNTER, CHARLES N. *Galahad.* San Antonio, Tex.: The Naylor Co., 1963.

MORISON, SAMUEL ELIOT. *The Liberation of the Philippines.* Boston: Little, Brown & Co., 1959.

————. *Victory in the Pacific.* Boston: Little, Brown & Co., 1960.

OFFICE OF THE CHIEF OF MILITARY HISTORY. *The United States Army in World War II.* Washington, D.C.: U.S. Government Printing Office.

 SMITH, ROBERT R. *Triumph in the Philippines,* 1963.

 BLUMENSON, MARTIN. *Breakout and Pursuit,* 1960.

 MACDONALD, CHARLES B. *The Siegfried Line Campaign,* 1963.

POND, HUGH. *Salerno.* London: William Kimber, 1961.

SHIRER, WILLIAM L. *The Rise and Fall of the Third Reich.* New York: Simon and Schuster, 1960.

UNITED KINGDOM MILITARY SERIES.

 ELLIS, L. F. *Victory in the West.* Vol. I: *The Battle of Normandy.* London: Her Majesty's Stationery Office, 1962.

VAUGHAN-THOMAS, WYNFORD. *Anzio.* New York: Holt, Rinehart & Winston, 1961.

THE KOREAN WAR

BIDERMAN, ALBERT D. *March to Calumny.* New York: The Macmillan Co., 1963.

FEHRENBACH, T. R. *This Kind of War.* New York: The Macmillan Co., 1963.

OFFICE OF THE CHIEF OF MILITARY HISTORY. *The U.S. Army in the Korean War.* Washington, D.C.: U.S. Government Printing Office.

 APPLEMAN, ROY E. *South to the Naktong, North to the Yalu,* 1961.

WHITING, ALLEN S. *China Crosses the Yalu.* New York: The Macmillan Co., 1960.